ROAD ATLAS
ATLANTE STRADALE
ATLAS DE CARRETERAS
ATLAS ROUTIER
STRASSENATLAS

EUROPE
EUROPA

Contents

II-III Legend
IV-V Central-northern Europe 1: 8 000 000
VI-VII Central-southern Europe 1: 8 000 000
VIII-IX Useful information
2-207 **Road atlas**
208-239 Towns and urban areas
240-280 Index of names

Sommario

II-III Legenda
IV-V Europa centro-settentrionale 1: 8 000 000
VI-VII Europa centro-meridionale 1: 8 000 000
VIII-IX Informazioni utili
2-207 **Atlante stradale**
208-239 Città e aree urbane
240-280 Indice dei nomi

Sumario

II-III Leyenda
IV-V Europa centro-norte 1: 8 000 000
VI-VII Europa centro-sur 1: 8 000 000
VIII-IX Direcciones útiles
2-207 **Atlas de carreteras**
208-239 Ciudades y áreas urbanas
240-280 Índice de topónimos

Sommaire

II-III Légende
IV-V Europe centre-nord 1: 8 000 000
VI-VII Europe centre-sud 1: 8 000 000
VIII-IX Informations utiles
2-207 **Atlas routier**
208-239 Villes et aires urbaines
240-280 Index des noms

Inhaltsverzeichnis

II-III Zeichenerklärung
IV-V Mittelnördliche Europa 1: 8 000 000
VI-VII Mittelsüdliche Europa 1: 8 000 000
VIII-IX Nützliche Auskünfte
2-207 **Straßenatlas**
208-239 Städte und Zufahrten
240-280 Namenverzeichnis

(GB) Legend	(I) Legenda
Toll motorway, dual carriageway	Autostrada a pedaggio a doppia carreggiata
Toll motorway, single carriageway	Autostrada a pedaggio a singola carreggiata
Non-toll motorway, dual carriageway	Autostrada senza pedaggio a doppia carreggiata
Non-toll motorway, single carriageway	Autostrada senza pedaggio a singola carreggiata
Interchange; restricted interchange; service area	Svincolo; svincolo con limitazione; area di servizio
Motorway under construction	Autostrada in costruzione
Motorway in tunnel	Autostrada in galleria
Number of motorway; european road; national road; regional or local road	Numero di autostrada; itinerario europeo; strada nazionale; strada regionale o locale
National road, dual carriageway	Strada nazionale a doppia carreggiata
National road, single carriageway	Strada nazionale a singola carreggiata
Regional road, dual carriageway	Strada regionale a doppia carreggiata
Regional road, single carriageway	Strada regionale a singola carreggiata
Local road, dual carriageway	Strada locale a doppia carreggiata
Local road, single carriageway	Strada locale a singola carreggiata
Secondary road	Strada secondaria
Road under construction	Strada in costruzione
Road in tunnel	Strada in galleria
Motorway distances in kilometres (miles in United Kingdom and Ireland)	Distanze in chilometri (miglia nel Regno Unito e Irlanda) sulle autostrade
Road distances in kilometres (miles in United Kingdom and Ireland)	Distanze in chilometri (miglia nel Regno Unito e Irlanda) sulle strade
Gradient 14% and over; gradient 6%–13%	Pendenza maggiore del 14%; pendenza dal 6% al 13%
Panoramic routes	Percorsi panoramici
Pass with height and winter closure	Passo di montagna, quota e periodo di chiusura invernale
Toll point	Barriera di pedaggio
Railway and tunnel	Ferrovia e tunnel ferroviario
Ferry route (with car transportation) and destination	Linea di traghetto (con trasporto auto) e destinazione
Transport of cars by rail	Trasporto auto per ferrovia
National park, natural reserve	Parco nazionale, riserva naturale
International boundaries	Confini internazionali
Internal boundary	Confine interno
International airport	Aeroporto internazionale
Religious building	Edificio religioso
Castle, fortress	Castello, fortezza
Isolated monument	Monumento isolato
Ruins, archaeological area	Rovine, area archeologica
Cave	Grotta
Natural curiosity	Curiosità naturale
Panoramic view	Punto panoramico
Other curiosities (botanical garden, zoo, amusement park etc.)	Altre curiosità (giardino botanico, zoo, parco divertimenti ecc.)
Town or place of great tourist interest	Città o luogo di grande interesse turistico
Interesting town or place	Città o luogo interessante

	E Leyenda	**F** Légende	**D** Zeichenerklärung
	Autopista de doble vía de peaje	Autoroute à péage et chaussées séparées	Zweibahnige Autobahn mit Gebühr
	Autopista de una vía de peaje	Autoroute à péage et chaussée unique	Einbahnige Autobahn mit Gebühr
	Autopista de doble vía sin peaje	Autoroute sans péage à chaussées séparées	Zweibahnige Autobahn ohne Gebühr
	Autopista de una vía sin peaje	Autoroute sans péage à chaussée unique	Einbahnige Autobahn ohne Gebühr
○—⑫—○—⑬—Ⓢ	Acceso; acceso parcial; estación de servicio	Échangeur; échangeur partiel; aire de service	Anschlussstelle; Autobahnein- und/oder -ausfahrt; Tankstelle
▪▪▪▪▪▪▪▪▪▪▪▪▪	Autopista en construcción	Autoroute en construction	Autobahn in Bau
══╪══════╪══	Túnel en autopista	Tunnel autoroutier	Autobahntunnel
A11 E50 N13 D951	Número de autopista; carretera europea; carretera nacional; carretera regional o local	Numéro d'autoroute; route européenne; route nationale; route régionale ou locale	Straßennummer: Autobahn; Europastraße; Nationalstraße; Regional- oder Lokalstraße
	Carretera nacional de doble vía	Route nationale à chaussées séparées	Zweibahnige Nationalstraße
	Carretera nacional de vía unica	Route nationale à chaussée unique	Einbahnige Nationalstraße
	Carretera regional de doble vía	Route régionale à chaussées séparées	Zweibahnige Regionalstraße
	Carretera regional de vía unica	Route régionale à chaussée unique	Einbahnige Regionalstraße
	Carretera local de doble vía	Route locale à chaussées séparées	Zweibahnige Lokalstraße
	Carretera local de vía unica	Route locale à chaussée unique	Einbahnige Lokalstraße
	Carretera secundaria	Route secondaire	Nebenstraße
═══════════════	Carretera en construcción	Route en construction	Straße in Bau
══╪══════╪══	Túnel en carretera	Tunnel routier	Straßentunnel
▼ 63 ▼	Distancias en kilómetros (millas en Gran Bretaña e Irlanda) en autopista	Distances autoroutières en kilomètres (miles en Royaume-Uni et Irlande)	Autobahnentfernungen in Kilometern (Meilen in Großbritannien und Irland)
▼ 23 ▼	Distancias en kilómetros (millas en Gran Bretaña e Irlanda) en carretera	Distances routières en kilomètres (miles en Royaume-Uni et Irlande)	Straßenentfernungen in Kilometern (Meilen in Großbritannien und Irland)
➤ ➤➤	Pendientes superiores al 14%; pendientes entre 6%–13%	Pente 14% et outre; pente 6%–13%	Steigungen über 14%; Steigungen 6%–13%
	Rutas panorámicas	Routes panoramiques	Aussichtsstraßen
Col d'Izoard ➤‹‹ 2360 10-6 🏠	Puerto de montaña con altura y cierre invernal	Col avec altitude et fermeture en hiver	Pass mit Höhe und Wintersperre
	Peaje	Barrière de péage	Gebührenstelle
═══╪═ ╪═══	Ferrocarril y túnel	Chemin de fer et tunnel	Eisenbahn und Tunnel
Bastia	Línea marítima (con transporte de coches) y destino	Ligne de navigation (bac pour voitures) et destination	Schiffahrtslinie (Autofähre) und Ziel
— — — —	Transporte de coches por ferrocarril	Transport de voitures par chemin de fer	Autoverladung per Bahn
	Parque nacional, reserva natural	Parc national, réserve naturelle	Nationalpark, Naturschutzgebiet
━━━━━━━━━	Límites internacionales	Frontières internationales	Staatsgrenzen
━━━━━━━━━	Límite interno	Frontière intérieure	Verwaltungsgrenze
⊕	Aeropuerto internacional	Aéroport international	Internationaler Flughafen
⋔	Edificio religioso	Édifice religieux	Religiösgebäude
⋈	Castillo, fortaleza	Château, château-fort	Schloss, Festung
⊥	Monumento aislado	Monument isolé	Alleinstehendes Denkmal
∴	Ruinas, zona arqueológica	Ruines, site archéologique	Ruinen, archäologisches Ausgrabungsgebiet
∩	Cueva	Grotte	Höhle
✳	Paraje de interés natural	Curiosité naturelle	Natursehenswürdigkeit
☀	Vista panorámica	Vue panoramique	Rundblick
★	Otras curiosidades (jardín botánico, zoo, parque de atracciones etc.)	Autres curiosités (jardin botanique, zoo, parc d'attractions etc.)	Andere Sehenswürdigkeiten (Botanischer Garten, Zoo, Freizeitpark usw.)
LONDON	Ciudad o lugar de gran interés turístico	Localité ou site de grand intérêt touristique	Ortschaft oder Platz von großem touristischen Interesse
BIRMINGHAM	Ciudad o lugar interesante	Localité ou site remarquable	Sehenswerte Ortschaft oder Platz

EUROPEAN ROAD NETWORK
RETE STRADALE EUROPEA
RED EUROPEA DE CARRETERAS
RÉSEAU ROUTIER EUROPÉEN
EUROPÄISCHES STRASSENNETZ

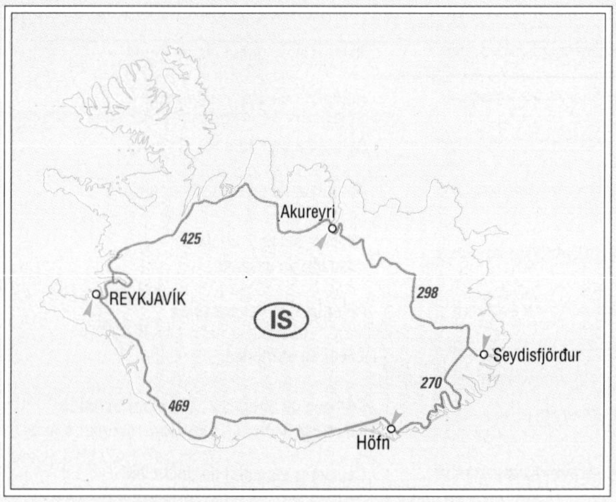

LEGEND - SEGNI CONVENZIONALI - LEYENDA - LÉGENDE - ZEICHENERKLÄRUNG

Motorway and road with motorway characteristics
Autostrada e strada con caratteristiche autostradali
Autopista y autovía con calzadas separadas
Autoroute et route de type autoroutier
Autobahn und Schnellstraße mit getrennten Fahrbahnen

Other roads
Altre strade
Otras carreteras
Autres routes
Sonstige Straßen

E15 M1 — Road number
Numero di strada
Número de carretera
Numéro de route
Straßennummer

169 — Distances in kilometres
Distanze in chilometri
Distancias en kilómetros
Distances en kilomètres
Distanzen in Kilometern

Distances in Great Britain and Ireland are expressed in miles.
Nel Regno Unito e in Irlanda le distanze sono espresse in miglia.
Las distancias en Gran Bretaña e Irlanda son expresas en millas.
Les distances en Grande-Bretagne et Irlande sont exprimées en miles.
Entfernungsangaben in Großbritannien und Irland sind in Meilen wiedergegeben.

Scale - Scala - Escala - Échelle - Maßstab
1 : 8 000 000 (1 cm = 80 km - 1 inch =126,24 miles)

0 100 200 300 400 km
0 50 100 150 200 250 miles

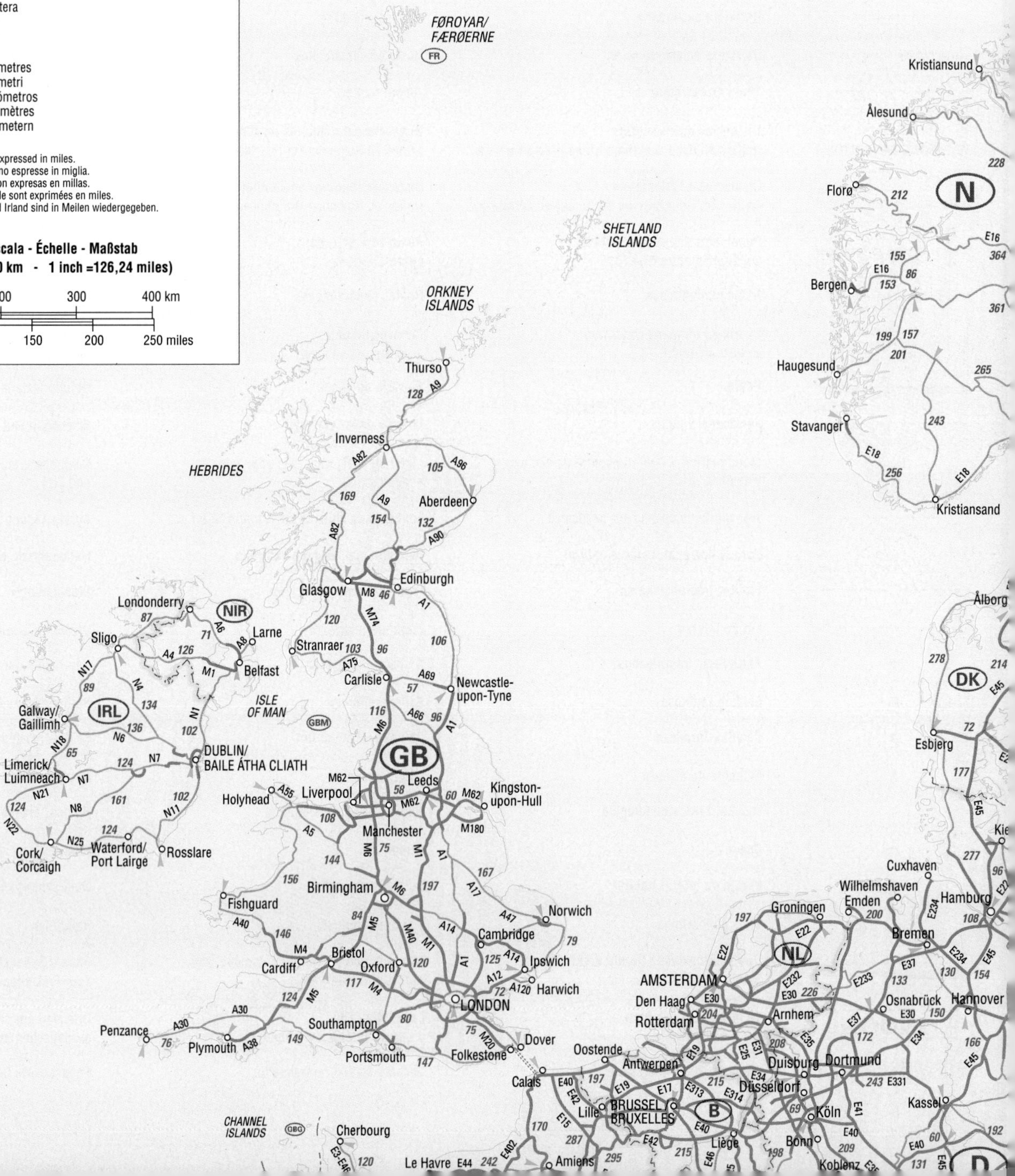

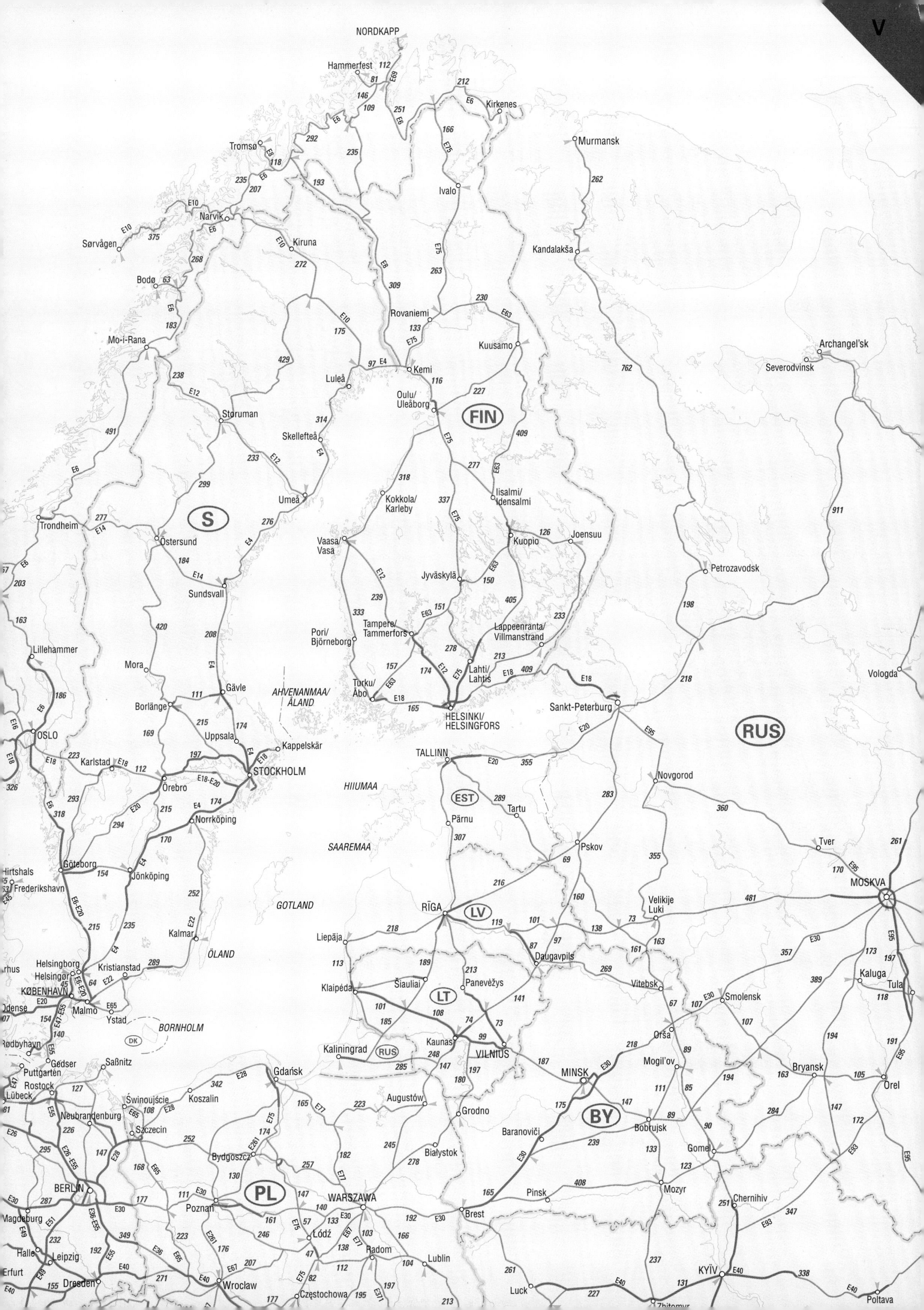
NORDKAPP
Hammerfest
Kirkenes
Murmansk
Tromsø
Ivalo
Narvik
Sørvågen
Kiruna
Kandalakša
Bodø
Rovaniemi
Mo-i-Rana
Kuusamo
Archangel'sk
Severodvinsk
Kemi
Luleå
Oulu/
Uleåborg
FIN
Storuman
Skellefteå
Umeå
Kokkola/
Karleby
Iisalmi/
Idensalmi
Trondheim
S
Östersund
Vaasa/
Vasa
Kuopio
Joensuu
Petrozavodsk
Sundsvall
Jyväskylä
Lillehammer
Pori/
Björneborg
Tampere/
Tammerfors
Lappeenranta/
Villmanstrand
Mora
Lahti/
Lahtis
Vologda
Gävle
Turku/
Åbo
AHVENANMAA/
ÅLAND
Borlänge
HELSINKI/
HELSINGFORS
Sankt-Peterburg
RUS
OSLO
Uppsala
Kappelskär
Karlstad
STOCKHOLM
TALLINN
Örebro
HIIUMAA
Novgorod
EST
Tartu
Norrköping
Pärnu
SAAREMAA
Tver
Pskov
Göteborg
Jönköping
Hirtshals
Frederikshavn
MOSKVA
GOTLAND
RĪGA
LV
Velikije
Luki
Kalmar
Liepāja
ÖLAND
Daugavpils
Helsingborg
Helsingør
Kristianstad
Kaluga
Tula
KØBENHAVN
Šiauliai
Panevėžys
Vitebsk
Odense
Malmö
Ystad
Klaipėda
LT
Smolensk
BORNHOLM
DK
Rødbyhavn
Kaliningrad
RUS
Kaunas
VILNIUS
Orša
Gedser
Saßnitz
Mogil'ov
Bryansk
Orel
Puttgarten
Rostock
Gdańsk
MINSK
Lübeck
Koszalin
Świnoujście
Augustów
Neubrandenburg
Grodno
BY
Szczecin
Baranoviči
Bobrujsk
Gomel
Białystok
Bydgoszcz
BERLIN
PL
WARSZAWA
Pinsk
Mozyr
Chernihiv
Magdeburg
Poznań
Brest
Łódź
Halle
Leipzig
Radom
Lublin
Erfurt
Dresden
Wrocław
Częstochowa
Luck
KYÏV
Zhitomyr
Poltava

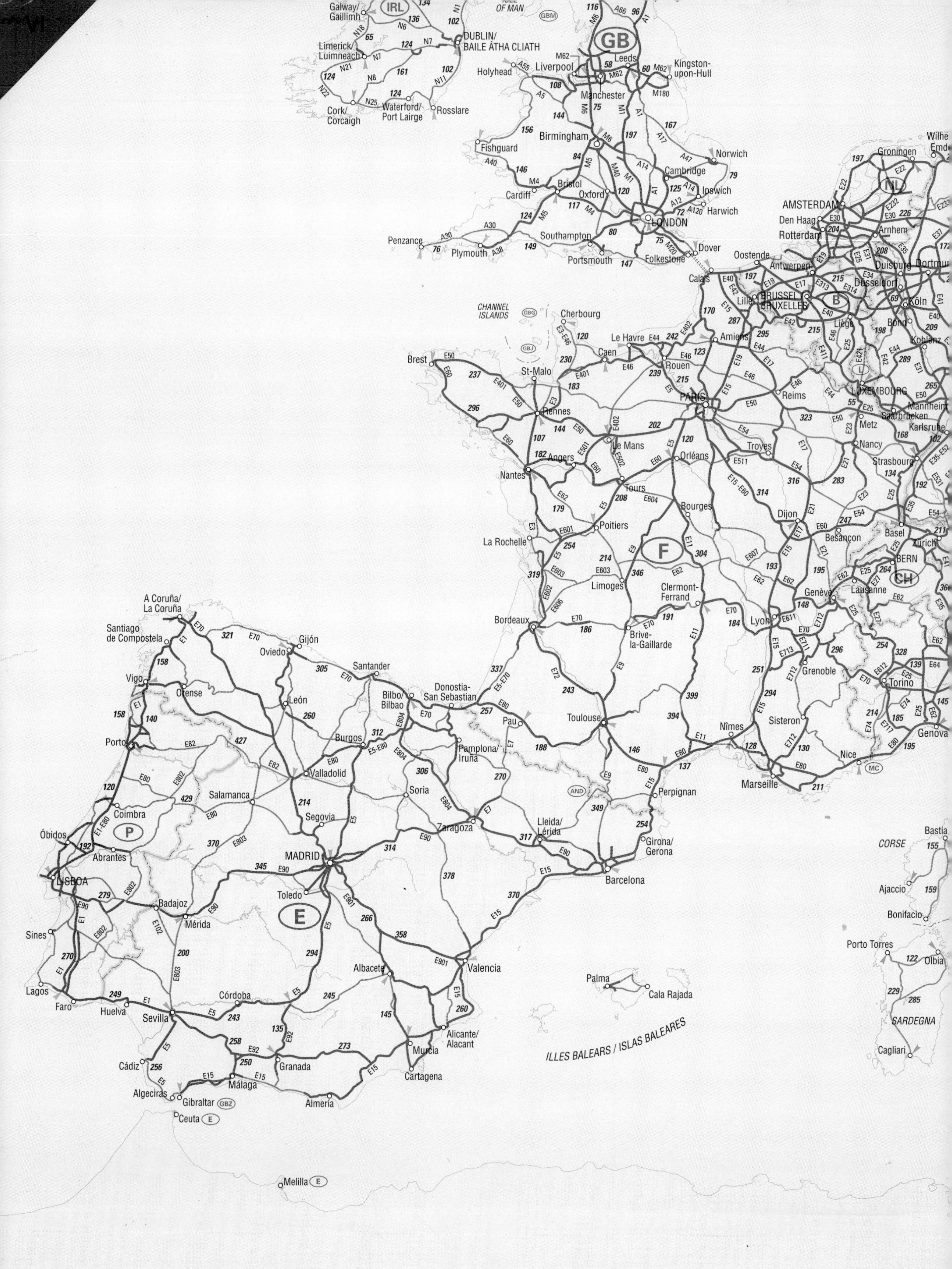

VI
IRL
Galway/
Gaillimh
DUBLIN/
BAILE ÁTHA CLIATH
Limerick/
Luimneach
Cork/
Corcaigh
Waterford/
Port Lairge
Rosslare
GB
Holyhead
Liverpool
Leeds
Kingston-
upon-Hull
Manchester
Birmingham
Fishguard
Norwich
Cambridge
Ipswich
Harwich
Bristol
Oxford
Cardiff
LONDON
Penzance
Plymouth
Southampton
Portsmouth
Folkestone
Dover
NL
Groningen
AMSTERDAM
Den Haag
Rotterdam
Arnhem
Duisburg
Oostende
Antwerpen
Düsseldorf
Calais
Lille
BRUSSEL
BRUXELLES
B
Köln
Liège
Bonn
Koblenz
CHANNEL
ISLANDS
Cherbourg
Le Havre
Amiens
Caen
Rouen
Brest
St-Malo
PARIS
Reims
LUXEMBOURG
Mannheim
Saarbrücken
Karlsruhe
Rennes
Metz
Le Mans
Nancy
Troyes
Strasbourg
Angers
Orléans
Nantes
Tours
Bourges
Dijon
Basel
Zürich
Poitiers
Besançon
La Rochelle
F
BERN
CH
Limoges
Clermont-
Ferrand
Genève
Lausanne
Bordeaux
Lyon
Brive-
la-Gaillarde
Grenoble
Torino
A Coruña/
La Coruña
Santiago
de Compostela
Gijón
Oviedo
Santander
Vigo
Orense
León
Bilbo/
Bilbao
Donostia-
San Sebastian
Pau
Toulouse
Sisteron
Genova
Nîmes
Porto
Burgos
Pamplona/
Iruña
Valladolid
Nice
Marseille
Soria
Perpignan
Coimbra
Salamanca
AND
P
Segovia
Zaragoza
Lleida/
Lérida
Óbidos
Abrantes
MADRID
Girona/
Gerona
Bastia
CORSE
LISBOA
Toledo
Barcelona
Ajaccio
Badajoz
E
Mérida
Bonifacio
Sines
Porto Torres
Olbia
Albacete
Valencia
Palma
Cala Rajada
Lagos
Faro
Huelva
Sevilla
Córdoba
SARDEGNA
Alicante/
Alacant
Murcia
Cagliari
Cartagena
ILLES BALEARS / ISLAS BALEARES
Cádiz
Granada
Málaga
Algeciras
Gibraltar
GBZ
Almería
Ceuta
Melilla

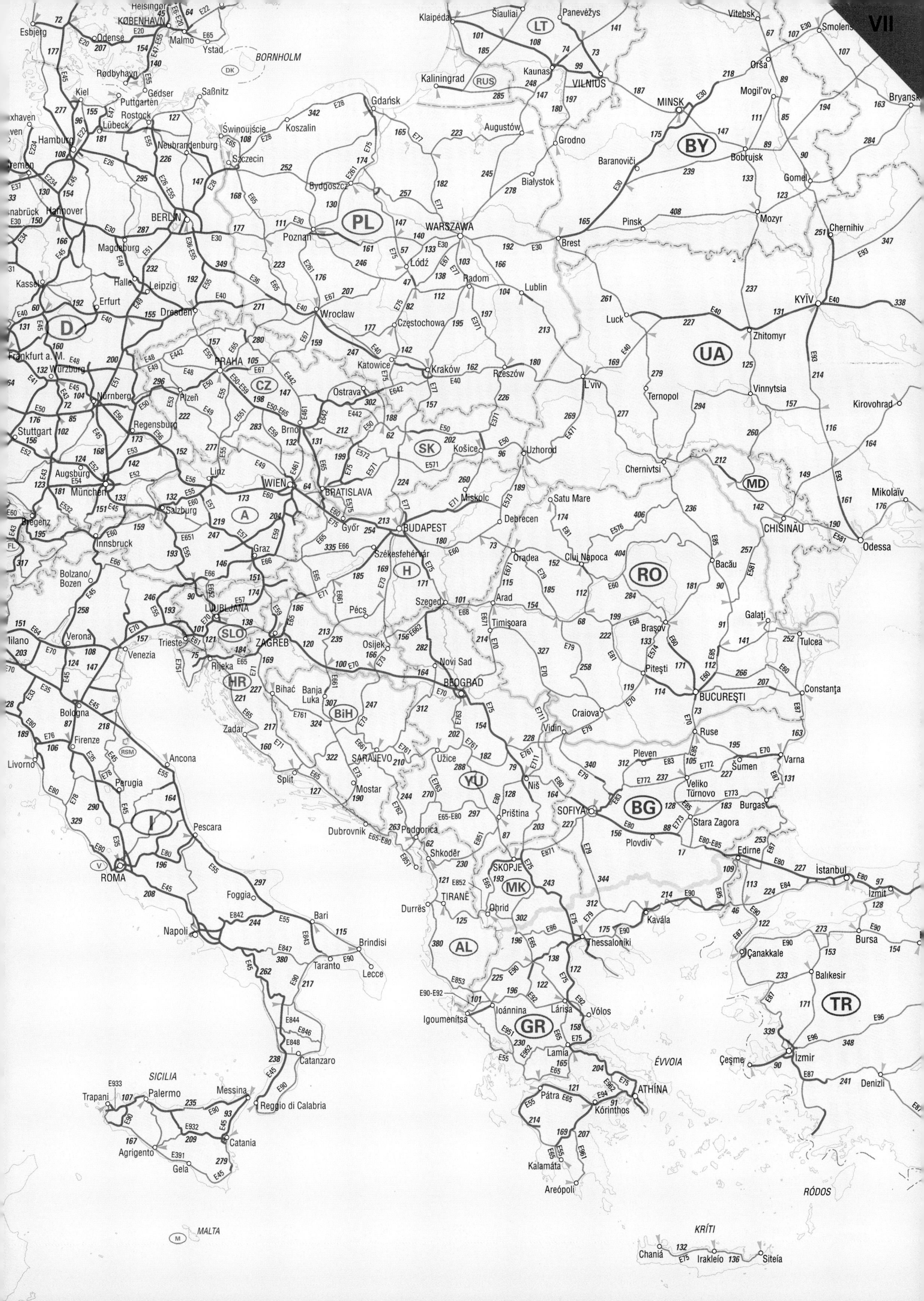
Esbjerg
Odense
KØBENHAVN
Malmö
Ystad
BORNHOLM
DK
Rødbyhavn
Gedser
Kiel
Puttgarten
Saßnitz
Rostock
Lübeck
Hamburg
Świnoujście
Koszalin
Gdańsk
Neubrandenburg
Szczecin
Klaipėda
Šiauliai
Panevėžys
LT
Kaliningrad
RUS
Kaunas
VILNIUS
Vitebsk
Smolensk
Orša
MINSK
Mogil'ov
Bryansk
Augustów
Grodno
BY
Baranoviči
Bobrujsk
Gomel
Białystok
Bydgoszcz
Hannover
BERLIN
PL
Poznań
WARSZAWA
Pinsk
Mozyr
Brest
Chernihiv
Magdeburg
Łódź
Radom
Lublin
Kassel
Halle
Leipzig
Erfurt
Dresden
Wrocław
Częstochowa
Luck
KYÏV
Zhitomyr
D
Frankfurt a. M.
Würzburg
PRAHA
Katowice
Kraków
Rzeszów
L'viv
UA
CZ
Nürnberg
Plzeň
Ostrava
Ternopol
Vinnytsia
Kirovohrad
Stuttgart
Regensburg
Brno
SK
Košice
Uzhorod
Chernivtsi
Augsburg
München
Linz
WIEN
BRATISLAVA
Miskolc
MD
Mikolaïv
Satu Mare
Bregenz
Salzburg
A
Győr
BUDAPEST
Debrecen
CHIŞINĂU
Odessa
FL
Innsbruck
Graz
Székesfehérvár
Oradea
Cluj Napoca
Bacău
Bolzano/Bozen
H
RO
LJUBLJANA
Pécs
Szeged
Arad
Galaţi
Milano
Verona
Venezia
Trieste
SLO
ZAGREB
Timişoara
Braşov
Tulcea
Rijeka
Osijek
Novi Sad
Piteşti
HR
BEOGRAD
BUCUREŞTI
Constanţa
Bologna
Bihać
Banja Luka
BiH
Craiova
Vidin
Ruse
Firenze
RSM
Zadar
Pleven
Šumen
Varna
Livorno
Ancona
SARAJEVO
Užice
Veliko Tŭrnovo
Perugia
Split
Mostar
YU
Niš
BG
Burgas
I
SOFIYA
Stara Zagora
Pescara
Dubrovnik
Podgorica
Priština
Plovdiv
Shkodër
Edirne
V
ROMA
SKOPJE
İstanbul
İzmit
MK
Foggia
TIRANË
Durrës
Ohrid
Kavála
Bari
Napoli
Brindisi
AL
Thessaloníki
Bursa
Çanakkale
Taranto
Lecce
Balıkesir
Igoumenítsa
Ioánnina
Lárisa
Vólos
TR
GR
Catanzaro
Lamía
ÉVVOIA
İzmir
Çeşme
SICILIA
Denizli
Palermo
Messina
Trapani
Reggio di Calabria
ATHÍNA
Pátra
Kórinthos
Catania
Agrigento
Gela
Kalamáta
Areópoli
RÓDOS
MALTA
M
KRÍTI
Chaniá
Irakleío
Siteía

USEFUL INFORMATION - INFORMAZIONI UTILI
DIRECCIONES ÚTILES - INFORMATIONS UTILES
NÜTZLICHE AUSKÜNFTE

		👤	🚗	☎	SOS	130	90	50	‰
A	Österreich	A/C, D	F, G	0043	112	130	100	50	0,5 ‰
AL	Shqiperia	A, E	F, H	00355	[a] 19; 17	-	80	50	0,0 ‰
AND	Andorra, Andorre	A/C, D	F, G	00376	110; 116	-	60-90	30-50	0,5 ‰
B	België, Belgique	A/C, D	F, G	0032	112	120	90	50	0,5 ‰
BG	Bălgarija	A/B, D	F, G	00359	166; 150	120	90	50	0,5 ‰
BiH	Bosna i Hercegovina	A, D	F, G	00387	92; 94	120	80	60	0,5 ‰
BY	Belarus'	B, E	F, H	00375	02; 03	110	90	60	0,0 ‰
CH	Schweiz, Suisse, Svizzera	A/C, D	F, G	0041	117; 144	120	80	50	0,8 ‰
CZ	Česká Republika	A, D	F, G	00420	158; 155	130	90	50	0,0 ‰
D	Deutschland	A/C, D	F, G	0049	112	130	100	50	0,5 ‰
DK	Danmark	A/C, D	F, G	0045	112	110	80	50	0,5 ‰
E	España	A/C, D	F, G	0034	112	120	90-100	50	0,3-0,5 ‰
EST	Eesti	A, D	F, G	00372	110; 112	-	90-110	50	0,0 ‰
F	France	A/C, D	F, G	0033	112	130	90-110	50	0,5 ‰
FIN	Suomi, Finland	A/C, D	F, G	00358	112	100-120	80-100	50	0,5 ‰
FL	Fürstentum Liechtenstein	A/C, D	F, G	0041	117; 144	-	80	50	0,8 ‰
GB	Great Britain and N. Ireland	A/C, D	F, G	0044	999; 112	112 (70 mph)	96 (60 mph)	48 (30 mph)	0,8 ‰
GR	Hellas	A/C, D	F, G	0030	112	120	110	50	0,5 ‰
H	Magyarország	A/C, D	F, G	0036	112	130	90	50	0,0 ‰
HR	Hrvatska	A/C, D	F, G	00385	92; 94	130	80-100	50	0,5 ‰
I	Italia	A/C, D	F, G	0039	112	130	96	50	0,5 ‰
IRL	Ireland	A/C, D	F, G	00353	112	112	80-90	48	0,8 ‰
IS	Ísland	A/C, D	F, G	00354	112	-	90	50	0,5 ‰
L	Lëtzebuerg, Luxembourg	A/C, D	F, G	00352	112	120	90	50	0,8 ‰
LT	Lietuva	A, D	F, H	00370	112	110-130	90-110	60	0,0 ‰
LV	Latvija	A, D	F, G	00371	112	-	64	50	0,5 ‰
M	Malta	A/C, D	F, G	00356	191; 196	-	90	40	0,0 ‰
MC	Principauté de Monaco	A/C, D	F, G	00377	112	-	90	50	0,5 ‰
MD	Moldova	B, E	F, H	00373	902; 903	-	80-100	40	0,0 ‰
MK	Makedonija	A, D	F, G	00389	92; 94	120	80	50-60	0,5 ‰
N	Norge	A/C, D	F, G	0047	112; 113	90	80-100	50	0,2 ‰
NL	Nederland	A/C, D	F, G	0031	112	120	90-100	50	0,5 ‰
P	Portugal	A/C, D	F, G	00351	112	120	90-110	50	0,5 ‰
PL	Polska	A, D	F, G	0048	997; 999	130	90	60	0,2 ‰
RO	România	A, D/E	F, G	0040	955; 961	120	90-110	50	0,0 ‰
RUS	Rossija	B, E	F, H	007	02; 03	-	70-90	60	0,0 ‰
S	Sverige	A/C, D	F, G	0046	112	110	90	50	0,2 ‰
SK	Slovensko	A, D	F, G	00421	158; 155	130	90-100	60	0,0 ‰
SLO	Slovenija	A/C, D	F, G	00386	113; 112	130	90	50	0,5 ‰
TR	Türkiye Cumhuriyeti	A/C, D	F, G	0090	155; 112	130	90-110	50	0,5 ‰
UA	Ukrajina	B, E	F, H	00380	02; 03	130	80-100	60	0,0 ‰
YU	Jugoslavija	B, D	F, H	00381	94; 92	120		60	0,5 ‰

[a] Tiranë

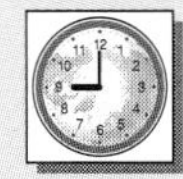

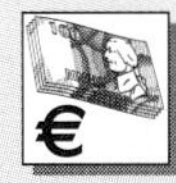

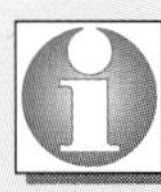

-	+1	*Euro (€)*	(43) 1 21114
-	+1	*Lek*	(355) 4 34185
-	+1	*Euro (€)*	(376) 827117
-	+1	*Euro (€)*	(32) 2 5138940
-	+2	*Lev (BGN)*	(359) 2 9802324
-	+1	*Konvertabilna Marka (KM)*	(387) 33219565
-	+2	*Rubel (Rbl)*	(375) 1 72237360
-	+1	*Schweizer Franken (CHF)*	(41) 31 3281212
-	+1	*Koruna Česká (CZK)*	(420) 2 24482562
-	+1	*Euro (€)*	(49) 30 3247679
✓	+1	*Danske Krone (Dkr)*	(45) 33 111415
-	+1	*Euro (€)*	(34) 915166700
✓	+2	*Kroon (EEK)*	(372) 6990420
-	+1	*Euro (€)*	(33) 1 49525310
✓	+2	*Euro (€)*	(358) 9 41769300
-	+1	*Schweizer Franken (CHF)*	(423) 2396300
-	0	*Pound Sterling (£)*	(44) 1719286221
-	+2	*Euro (€)*	(30) 103271300
✓	+1	*Forint (Ft)*	(36) 1 4728700
-	+1	*Kuna (K)*	(385) 1 4556455
-	+1	*Euro (€)*	(39) 06 49711
-	0	*Euro (€)*	(353) 1 6024000
✓	0	*Íslensk Króna (isk)*	(354) 5 623045
-	+1	*Euro (€)*	(352) 42828210
✓	+2	*Litas*	(370) 2 622610
✓	+2	*Lats (LVL)*	(371) 7044377
-	+1	*Maltese Lira (Lml)*	(356) 224444
-	+1	*Euro (€)*	(377) 92166116
-	+2	*Leu*	(373) 2 540288
-	+1	*Denar*	(389) 91 118498
✓	+1	*Norwegian Krone (NKr)*	(47) 23106200
-	+1	*Euro (€)*	(31) 0 9004004040
-	0	*Euro (€)*	(351) 21 3466307
✓	+1	*Złoty (Zl)*	(48) 22 8260788
-	+2	*Leu (ROL)*	(40) 1 3145164
✓	[b]+3	*Russian Ruble (RUB)*	(7) 95 2482208
✓	+1	*Svensk Krona (SKR)*	(46) 8 7255500
-	+1	*Slovenská Koruna (Sk)*	(421) 2 54433715
✓	+1	*Tolar (SLT)*	(386) 1 5891840
-	+2	*Turkish Liras (TL)*	(90) 312 2315572
-	+2	*Hrivna (UAH)*	(380) 44 4502811
-	+1	*Yugoslav Dinar (YUN)*	(381) 11 635622

[b] *Moskva*

Legend
Legenda
Leyenda
Légende
Zeichenerklärung

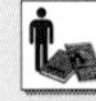

Required personal papers
Documenti personali richiesti
Papeles personales requeridos
Papiers personnels requis
Verlangte Personalpapiere

A Passport
Passaporto
Pasaporte
Passeport
Reisepass

B Passport with visa
Passaporto con visto
Pasaporte con visa
Passeport avec visa
Reisepass mit Visum

C Identity card
Carta d'identità
Carné de identidad
Carte d'identité
Personalausweis

D Driver's licence
Patente di guida
Carné de conducir
Permis de conduire
Führerschein

E International driver's licence
Patente di guida internazionale
Carné de conducir internacional
Permis international de conduire
Internationaler Führerschein

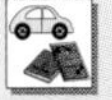

Required motor vehicle papers
Documenti auto richiesti
Documentos auto requeridos
Documents-automobile requis
Verlangte Autopapiere

F Log-book
Carta di circolazione
Carné de circulación
Permis de circulation
Kraftfahrzeugschein

G Green card
Carta verde
Carta verde
Carte verte
Grüne Versicherungskarte

H Special insurance
Assicurazione speciale
Seguro especial
Assurance spéciale
Spezialversicherung

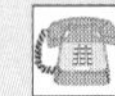

International code
Prefisso internazionale
Prefijo telefónico internacional
Indicatif international
Internationale Vorwahl

Emergency numbers
Numeri d'emergenza
Números de emergencia
Numéros d'urgence
Notrufnummern

 (km/h)

Speed limit on motorway
Limite di velocità in autostrada
Límite de velocidad en autopista
Limite de vitesse sur l'autoroute
Höchstgeschwindigkeit auf der Autobahn

 (km/h)

Speed limit outside the towns
Limite di velocità su strade extraurbane
Límite de velocidad en carreteras extraurbanas
Limite de vitesse sur les routes extra-urbaines
Höchstgeschwindigkeit außerhalb der Städte

 (km/h)

Speed limit in towns
Limite di velocità nei centri abitati
Límite de velocidad en ciudades
Limite de vitesse dans les villes
Höchstgeschwindigkéit innerhalb der Städte

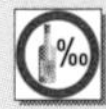

Maximum permitted alcohol level
Tasso alcolemico massimo tollerato
Límite alcohólico màximo consentido
Taux d'alcoolémie maximum admis
Höchsterlaubte Blutalkoholgehalt

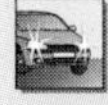

Lights on during the day
Obbligo luci accese di giorno
Encender los faros durante el dia
Feux allumés obligatoires de jour
Licht einschalten während des Tages

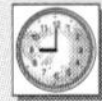

Time zone from Greenwich
Fuso orario da Greenwich
Huso horario de Greenwich
Fuseaux horaires de Greenwich
Zeitzone mit Bezug auf Greenwich

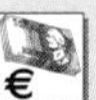

Local currency
Valuta locale
Divisa local
Devise locale
Lokalwährung

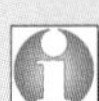

Tourist offices
Uffici turistici
Oficinas de turismo
Bureaux de tourisme
Touristenämter

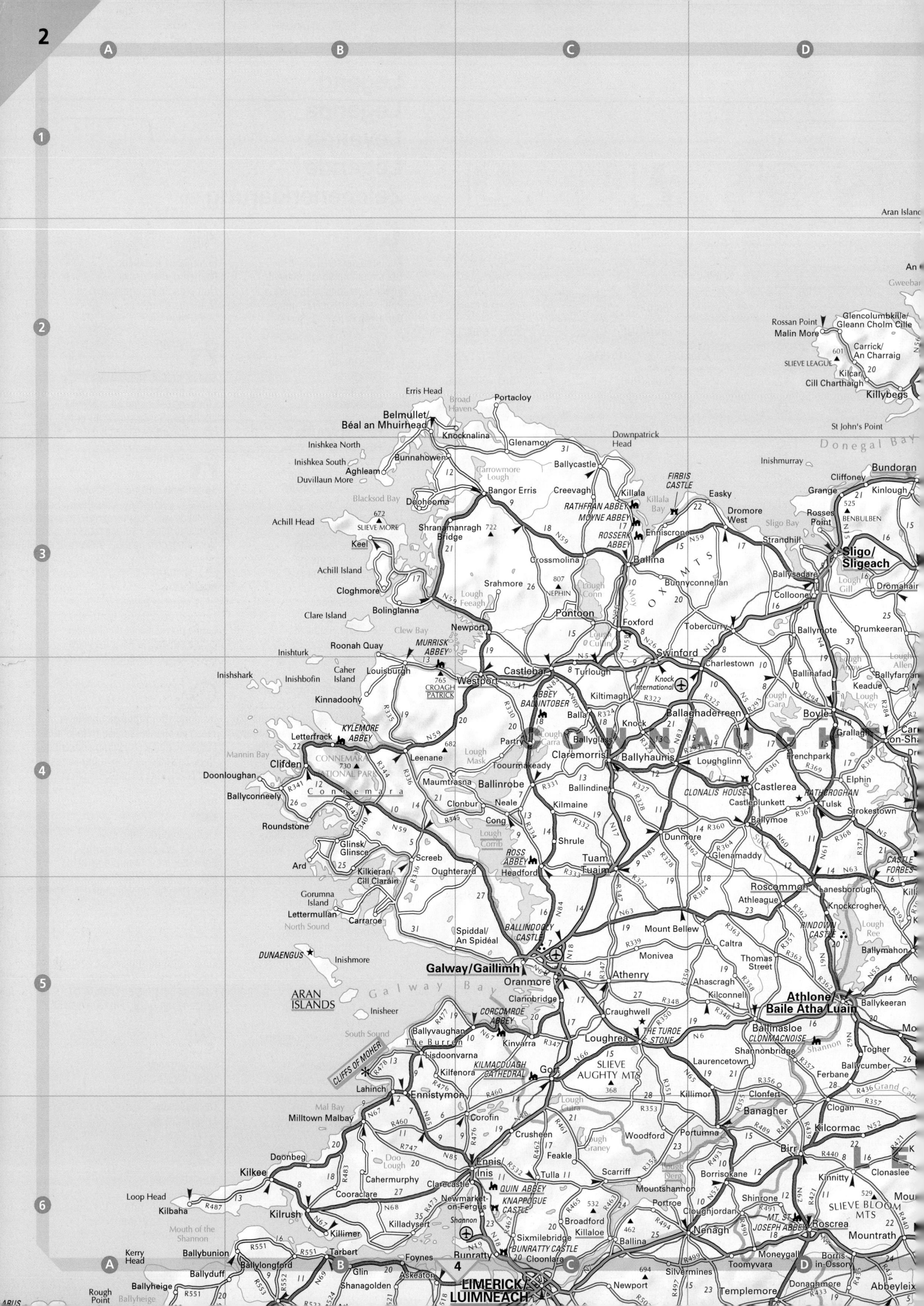
A
B
C
D
1
2
3
4
5
6
Aran Island
Rossan Point
Glencolumbkille/ Gleann Cholm Cille
Malin More
Carrick/ An Charraig
SLIEVE LEAGUE
Kilcar
Cill Charthaigh
Killybegs
St John's Point
Donegal Bay
Erris Head
Broad Haven
Portacloy
Belmullet/ Béal an Mhuirhead
Knocknalina
Glenamoy
Downpatrick Head
Inishkea North
Inishkea South
Bunnahowen
Ballycastle
Aghleam
Duvillaun More
Carrowmore Lough
Bangor Erris
Creevagh
Killala
Killala Bay
FIRBIS CASTLE
Easky
Inishmurray
Bundoran
Cliffoney
Kinlough
Blacksod Bay
Doohooma
RATHFRAN ABBEY
MOYNE ABBEY
Dromore West
Grange
Rosses Point
BENBULBEN
Achill Head
SLIEVE MORE
Shranamanragh Bridge
ROSSERK ABBEY
Enniscrone
Sligo Bay
Strandhill
Keel
Crossmolina
Ballina
OX MTS
Sligo/ Sligeach
Achill Island
NEPHIN
Lough Conn
Bunnyconnellan
Ballysadare
Lough Gill
Dromahair
Cloghmore
Srahmore
Lough Feeagh
Collooney
Clare Island
Bolinglanna
Pontoon
Foxford
Clew Bay
Newport
Lough Cullin
Tobercurry
Ballymote
Drumkeeran
Inishturk
Roonah Quay
MURRISK ABBEY
Swinford
Charlestown
Lough Arrow
Lough Allen
Inishshark
Inishbofin
Caher Island
Louisburgh
Castlebar
Turlough
Knock International
Ballinafad
Ballyfarnan
CROAGH PATRICK
Westport
Keadue
Kinnadoohy
ABBEY BALLINTOBER
Kiltimagh
Lough Gara
Lough Key
Balla
Ballaghaderreen
Boyle
Knock
Grallagh
Carrick-on-Shannon
Letterfrack
KYLEMORE ABBEY
Mannin Bay
Lough Carra
Partry
Ballyglass
Lough Mask
CONNACHT
Claremorris
Ballyhaunis
Loughglinn
Frenchpark
Clifden
CONNEMARA NATIONAL PARK
Leenane
Tourmakeady
Elphin
Doonloughan
Connemara
Maumtrasna
Ballinrobe
Ballindine
Castlerea
CLONALIS HOUSE
RATHCROGHAN
Ballyconneely
Clonbur
Neale
Kilmaine
Castleplunkett
Tulsk
Strokestown
Roundstone
Cong
Dunmore
Ballymoe
Lough Corrib
Shrule
Glenamaddy
Glinsk/ Glinsce
Screeb
ROSS ABBEY
Ard
Kilkieran/ Cill Ciaráin
Oughterard
Headford
Tuam/ Tuaim
CASTLE FORBES
Roscommon
Lanesborough
Gorumna Island
Lettermullan
Athleague
Knockcroghery
Carraroe
North Sound
Spiddal/ An Spidéal
BALLINDOOLY CASTLE
Mount Bellew
RINDOWN CASTLE
Lough Ree
DUNAENGUS
Inishmore
Monivea
Caltra
Thomas Street
Ballymahon
Galway/Gaillimh
Oranmore
Athenry
Ahascragh
ARAN ISLANDS
Galway Bay
Kilconnell
Athlone/ Baile Átha Luain
Clarinbridge
Ballykeeran
Inisheer
CORCOMROE ABBEY
Craughwell
Ballinasloe
South Sound
Ballyvaughan
Kinvarra
THE TUROE STONE
The Burren
Loughrea
CLONMACNOISE
Shannonbridge
Shannon
Togher
CLIFFS OF MOHER
Lisdoonvarna
Kilfenora
KILMACDUAGH CATHEDRAL
Gort
SLIEVE AUGHTY MTS
Laurencetown
Ballycumber
Ferbane
Lahinch
Ennistymon
Killimor
Clonfert
Grand Canal
Mal Bay
Milltown Malbay
Corofin
Lough Cutra
Banagher
Clogan
Crusheen
Woodford
Portumna
Kilcormac
Doonbeg
Doo Lough
Birr
Kilkee
Ennis/ Inis
Feakle
Lough Graney
Scarriff
Lough Derg
Borrisokane
Clonaslee
Cahermurphy
Clarecastle
Tulla
Mountshannon
Kinnitty
Loop Head
Kilbaha
Cooraclare
Newmarket-on-Fergus
QUIN ABBEY
KNAPPOGUE CASTLE
Portroe
Shinrone
SLIEVE BLOOM MTS
Kilrush
Killadysert
Broadford
Killaloe
Cloughjordan
MT. ST. JOSEPH ABBEY
Roscrea
Mouth of the Shannon
Killimer
Shannon
BUNRATTY CASTLE
Ballina
Nenagh
Mountrath
Kerry Head
Ballybunion
Tarbert
Foynes
Bunratty
Cloonlara
Moneygall
Borris-in-Ossory
Ballylongford
Ballyduff
Glin
Askeaton
LIMERICK/ LUIMNEACH
Silvermines
Toomyvara
Ballyheige
Shanagolden
Newport
Templemore
Donaghmore
Abbeyleix
Rough Point
4

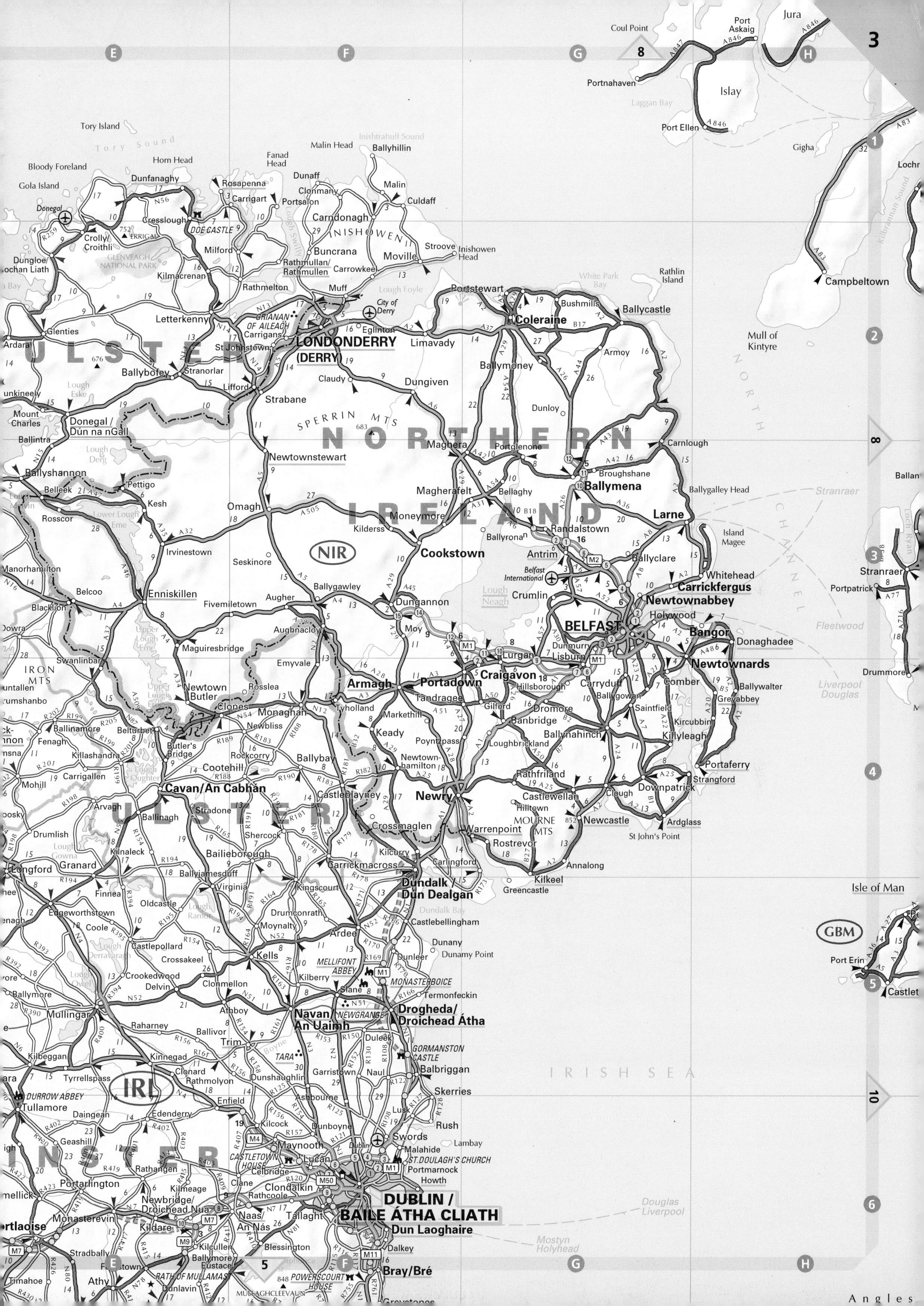
3
Jura
Coul Point
Port Askaig
Portnahaven
Islay
Laggan Bay
Port Ellen
Gigha
Campbeltown
Mull of Kintyre
Rathlin Island
Tory Island
Bloody Foreland
Horn Head
Gola Island
Dunfanaghy
Fanad Head
Malin Head
Inishtrahull Sound
Ballyhillin
Malin
Culdaff
Rosapenna
Carrigart
Portsalon
Clonmany
Carndonagh
Dunaff
Cresslough
Crolly/Croithlí
ERRIGAL
DOE CASTLE
Milford
Buncrana
INISHOWEN
Moville
Stroove
Inishowen Head
GLENVEAGH NATIONAL PARK
Dungloe/Clochan Liath
Kilmacrenan
Rathmullan/Rathmullen
Carrowkeel
Rathmelton
Muff
Lough Foyle
Portstewart
White Park Bay
Bushmills
Ballycastle
Coleraine
Letterkenny
Glenties
GRIANAN OF AILEACH
Carrigans
City of Derry
Eglinton
LONDONDERRY (DERRY)
Limavady
St Johnston
Ardara
ULSTER
Ballybofey
Stranorlar
Lifford
Strabane
Claudy
Dungiven
Ballymoney
Armoy
Dunloy
Lough Eske
Mount Charles
Donegal / Dún na nGall
Ballintra
SPERRIN MTS
NORTHERN IRELAND
Maghera
Portglenone
Carnlough
Newtownstewart
Lough Derg
Ballyshannon
Belleek
Pettigo
Kesh
Lower Lough Erne
Rosscor
Omagh
Magherafelt
Bellaghy
Broughshane
Ballymena
Ballygalley Head
Larne
Moneymore
Kilderss
Ballyronan
Randalstown
Antrim
Island Magee
Irvinestown
Seskinore
NIR
Cookstown
Belfast International
Ballyclare
Whitehead
Carrickfergus
Stranraer
Portpatrick
Manorhamilton
Belcoo
Enniskillen
Fivemiletown
Augher
Ballygawley
Dungannon
Lough Neagh
Crumlin
Newtownabbey
Holywood
Blacklion
Upper Lough Erne
Maguiresbridge
Aughnacloy
Moy
BELFAST
Bangor
Donaghadee
Lurgan
Lisburn
Dunmurry
Hillsborough
Newtownards
IRON MTS
Swanlinbar
Emyvale
Armagh
Portadown
Craigavon
Carryduff
Comber
Ballywalter
Newtown Butler
Rosslea
Tandragee
Gilford
Dromore
Ballygowan
Saintfield
Greyabbey
Kircubbin
Clones
Monaghan
Tyholland
Markethill
Banbridge
Ballynahinch
Killyleagh
Ballinamore
Belturbet
Newbliss
Keady
Poyntzpass
Loughbrickland
Portaferry
Strangford
Fenagh
Butler's Bridge
Rockcorry
Killashandra
Cootehill
Ballybay
Newtownhamilton
Rathfriland
Carrigallen
Mohill
Cavan/An Cabhán
Castleblayney
Newry
Castlewellan
Clough
Downpatrick
Arvagh
Stradone
Ballinagh
Hilltown
MOURNE MTS
Newcastle
Ardglass
St John's Point
Crossmaglen
Warrenpoint
Rostrevor
Shercock
Drumlish
Kilnaleck
Bailieborough
Kilcurry
Carlingford
Annalong
Longford
Granard
Ballyjamesduff
Carrickmacross
Kilkeel
Greencastle
Virginia
Kingscourt
Dundalk / Dún Dealgan
Finnea
Oldcastle
Isle of Man
Edgeworthstown
Lough Ramor
Drumconrath
Dundalk Bay
Castlebellingham
Coole
Moynalty
Ardee
Dunany
Dunany Point
Castlepollard
Crossakeel
Kells
Dunleer
GBM
Port Erin
Castlet
Crookedwood
Delvin
Clonmellon
MELLIFONT ABBEY
Kilberry
MONASTERBOICE
Slane
Termonfeckin
Ballymore
Mullingar
Athboy
NEWGRANGE
Navan/An Uaimh
Drogheda/Droichead Átha
Raharney
Ballivor
Trim
Duleek
GORMANSTON CASTLE
Kilbeggan
Kinnegad
TARA
Clonard
Rathmolyon
Dunshaughlin
Garristown
Naul
Balbriggan
IRISH SEA
Tyrrellspass
IRL
DURROW ABBEY
Tullamore
Daingean
Edenderry
Enfield
Ashbourne
Skerries
Lusk
Rush
Kilcock
Dunboyne
Geashill
Maynooth
Swords
Lambay
Malahide
Lucan
CASTLETOWN HOUSE
ST. DOULAGH'S CHURCH
Rathangan
Celbridge
Portmarnock
Howth
Portarlington
Kilmeage
Clane
Clondalkin
Rathcoole
Monasterevin
Newbridge/Droichead Nua
Naas/An Nás
Tallaght
DUBLIN / BAILE ÁTHA CLIATH
Dun Laoghaire
Douglas Liverpool
Kildare
Kilcullen
Blessington
Dalkey
Mostyn Holyhead
Stradbally
Ballymore Eustace
Bray/Bré
RATH OF MULLAMAST
Dunlavin
POWERSCOURT HOUSE
MULLAGHCLEEVAUN
Athy
Timahoe
Liverpool Douglas
Fleetwood
Stranraer
Drummore
Ballan
Lochr
Kilbrannan Sound
NORTH CHANNEL
Angles

A B C 2 D

1

2

3

4

5

6

Mannin Bay
Letterfrack
KYLEMORE ABBEY
Clifden
Doonloughan
Ballyconneely
CONNEMARA NATIONAL PARK
730
682
Leenane
2
Partry
Knock
Ballaghaderreen
CONNACHT
Maumtrasna
Ballinrobe
Toourmakeady
Claremorris
Ballyhaunis
Connemara
Clonbur
Neale
Kilmaine
Ballindine
Roundstone
Maumturk
Cong
Shrule
Dunmore
Glinsk/Glinsce
Screeb
Oughterard
ROSS ABBEY
Headford
Tuam/Tuaim
Ard
Kilkieran/Cill Ciaráin
Gorumna Island
Lettermullan
Carraroe
Spiddal/An Spidéal
BALLINDOOLY CASTLE
Mount Bellew
Monivea
Galway Bay
Athenry
DUNAENGUS
Inishmore
Galway/Gaillimh
Oranmore
Clarinbridge
Craughwell
ARAN ISLANDS
Inisheer
CORCOMROE ABBEY
THE TUROE STONE
Inishmaan
Ballyvaughan
Kinvarra
Loughrea
N6
South Sound
The Burren
Kilmacduagh Cathedral
Gort
SLIEVE AUGHTY MTS
Killimor
Cliffs of Moher
Lisdoonvarna
Kilfenora
368
Laurencetown
Lahinch
Ennistymon
Corofin
Woodford
Portumna
Mal Bay
Milltown Malbay
Crusheen
Feakle
Doonbeg
Doo Lough
Ennis/Inis
Tulla
Scarriff
Mountshannon
Kilkee
Cahermurphy
Clarecastle
QUIN ABBEY
Loop Head
Kilbaha
Cooraclare
Newmarket-on-Fergus
KNAPPOGUE CASTLE
Broadford
Killaloe
Ballina
Kilrush
Killadysert
Sixmilebridge
Kerry Head
Ballybunion
Ballylongford
Tarbert
Glin
Askeaton
BUNRATTY CASTLE
Cloonlara
Silvermines
Ballyheige
Ballyduff
Shanagolden
Bunratty
Nenagh
Rough Point
Listowel
Athea
Newcastle West
Rathkeale
LIMERICK/LUIMNEACH
Newport
Borriso...
Sybil Point
GALLARUS ORATORY
953
Stradbally
Kilshannig
Ardfert
Abbeydorney
357
Duagh
Ardagh
Adare
Patrickswell
Croom
Cappamore
Inishtooskert
827
BEENOSKEE
Camp
Fenit
Abbeyfeale
West
Ballingarry
DESMOND'S CASTLE
Oola
Great Blaskett Island
852
BAURTREGAUM
Tralee/Trá Lí
Kilinlea
Kilmeedy
Bruff
Hospital
Herbertstown
Slea Head
Dingle/An Daingean
Anascaul
Inch
Castlemaine
Castleisland
Dromcolliher
Kilmallock
Tipperary/Tiobraid Arann
Galbally
Golden
LEACANABUAILE STONE FORT
Killorglin
Milltown
Farranfore
Charleville/Rath Luirc
Kilfinnane
Ballylanders
Doulus Head
Kells
Beaufort
Ballydesmond
Newmarket
Liscarroll
KILCOLMAN CASTLE
Kildorrery
GALTEE MTS
Cahir
Valentia
CARRANTOOHIL 1041
Aghadoe
Killarney/Cill Airne
Kanturk
Buttevant
MITCHELSTOWN CAVES
Knights Town
Caherciveen
GAP OF DUNLOE
774
KILLARNEY NATIONAL PARK
Muckross
Cloonbannin
Mallow
Mitchelstown
Barryporeen
Clogheen
Ardfinnan
Ballinskelligs
Mastergeehy
Boheeshil
MULLAGHANATTIN
MUCKROSS HOUSE
Cloonkeen
Banteer
Castletownroche
Glanworth
KNOCKMEALDOWN MTS
Bolus Head
Waterville
STAIGUE FORT
Sneem
840
MANGERTON MTN
Millstreet
BOGGERAGH MTS 645
Fermoy
Ballyduff
MT MELLERAY MY
Caherdaniel
Parknasilla
Kenmare
Kilgarvan
Carriganimmy
M U N S T E R
Rathcormack
Lismore
Cappoquin
Scariff
Cod's Head
Lauragh
KNOCKBOY 707
Macroom
Glenville
Conna
Tallow
STRANCALLY CASTLE
Firkeel
Allihies
Glengarriff
Adrigole
686
GARNISH GARDENS
Inchigeelagh
Coachford
BLARNEY CASTLE
Blarney
Watergrasshill
Dungourney
Dursey
Castletownbere
DUNBOY CASTLE
Bear
BANTRY HOUSE
Bantry
Dunmanway
Kilmichael
Crookstown
CORK/CORCAIGH
Glanmire
Clashmore
Ballyroon
Durrus
Enniskean
Bandon
Inishannon
Passage West
Cobh
Midleton
Muntervary or Sheep' Head
Ballydehob
Drimoleague
Ballinascarty
Ballinhassig
Carrigaline
Ringaskiddy
Castlemartyr
Cloyne
Ballymacoda
Mizen Head
Goleen
Schull
Leap
Clonakilty
Timoleague
Belgooly
Crosshaven
Inch
Whitegate
Ballycotton
Crookhaven
Skibbereen
Kinsale
Clear Island
Baltimore
Castletownshend
Ross Carbery
Courtmacsherry
Ballinspittle
Youghal Bay
Roaringwater Bay
Toe Head
Galley Head
Clonakilty Bay
Old Head of Kinsale
Swansea

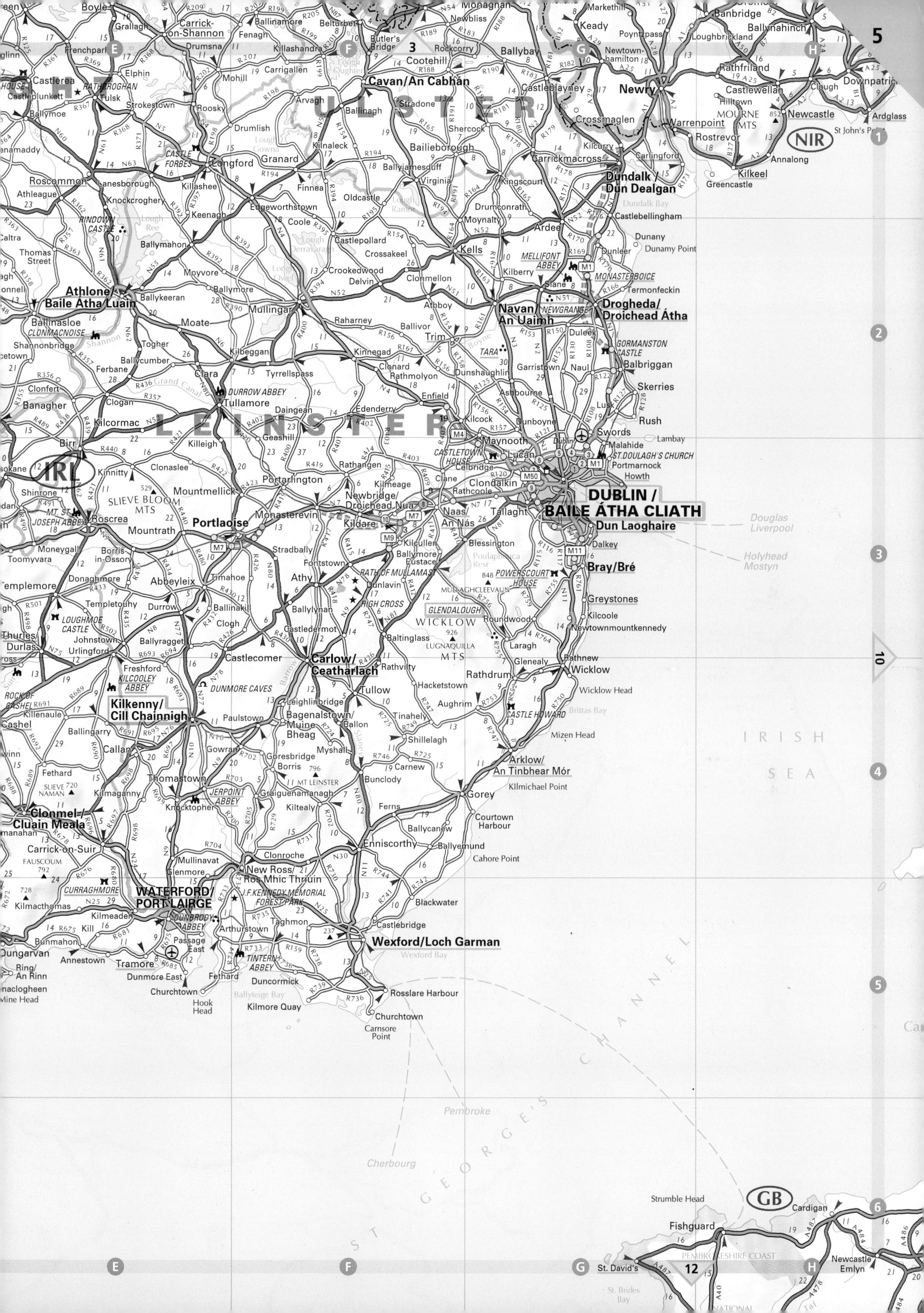
Boyle
Carrick-on-Shannon
Ballinamore
Belturbet
Monaghan
Newbliss
Markethill
Banbridge
Ballynahinch
Keady
Poyntzpass
Loughbrickland
Frenchpark
Grallagh
Drumsna
Fenagh
Killashandra
Butler's Bridge
Cootehill
Rockcorry
Ballybay
Newtown-hamilton
Newry
Rathfriland
Castlewellan
Clough
Downpatrick
Castlerea
Elphin
Rathcroghan
Tulsk
Castleplunkett
Mohill
Carrigallen
Cavan/An Cabhán
Castleblayney
Hilltown
Mourne Mts
Newcastle
Ardglass
Ballymoe
Strokestown
Rooskey
Arvagh
Ballinagh
Stradone
Ulster
Crossmaglen
Warrenpoint
Rostrevor
Drumlish
Kilnaleck
Shercock
Bailieborough
Kilcurry
Carlingford
Annalong
NIR
St John's Point
Castle Forbes
Longford
Granard
Ballyjamesduff
Carrickmacross
Dundalk/Dún Dealgan
Kilkeel
Greencastle
Roscommon
Lanesborough
Killashee
Finnea
Virginia
Kingscourt
Athleague
Knockcroghery
Edgeworthstown
Oldcastle
Drumconrath
Dundalk Bay
Castlebellingham
Rindown Castle
Keenagh
Coole
Moynalty
Ardee
Dunany
Dunany Point
Ballymahon
Castlepollard
Crossakeel
Kells
Dunleer
Thomas Street
Mellifont Abbey
Kilberry
Crookedwood
Delvin
Clonmellon
Monasterboice
Moyvore
Ballymore
Slane
Termonfeckin
Athlone/Baile Átha Luain
Ballykeeran
Mullingar
Athboy
Navan/An Uaimh
Newgrange
Drogheda/Droichead Átha
Ballinasloe
Clonmacnoise
Moate
Raharney
Ballivor
Trim
Duleek
Shannonbridge
Togher
Kilbeggan
Kinnegad
Tara
Gormanston Castle
Ferbane
Clara
Tyrrellspass
Clonard
Rathmolyon
Dunshaughlin
Garristown
Naul
Balbriggan
Clonfert
Durrow Abbey
Enfield
Ashbourne
Skerries
Banagher
Clogan
Tullamore
Daingean
Edenderry
Lusk
Rush
Kilcormac
Leinster
Kilcock
Dunboyne
Swords
Lambay
Birr
Killeigh
Geashill
Maynooth
Malahide
Castletown House
Lucan
St. Doolagh's Church
IRL
Kinnitty
Clonaslee
Rathangen
Celbridge
Portmarnock
Howth
Portarlington
Kilmeage
Clane
Clondalkin
Shinrone
Slieve Bloom Mts
Mountmellick
Newbridge/Droichead Nua
Rathcoole
Dublin/Baile Átha Cliath
Mt. St. Joseph Abbey
Roscrea
Portlaoise
Monasterevin
Kildare
Naas/An Nás
Tallaght
Dun Laoghaire
Douglas
Liverpool
Mountrath
Kilcullen
Blessington
Dalkey
Moneygall
Borris-in-Ossory
Stradbally
Ballymore Eustace
Poulaphouca Resr
Holyhead
Mostyn
Toomyvara
Fontstown
Bray/Bré
Templemore
Donaghmore
Abbeyleix
Timahoe
Athy
Rath of Mullamast
Powerscourt House
Dunlavin
Mullaghcleevaun
Greystones
Templetouhy
Durrow
Ballinakill
Ballylynan
High Cross
Glendalough
Kilcoole
Loughmoe Castle
Wicklow
Roundwood
Newtownmountkennedy
Thurles
Durlas
Johnstown
Urlingford
Ballyragget
Clogh
Castledermot
Baltinglass
Lugnaquilla
Mts
Laraghh
Castlecomer
Carlow/Ceatharlach
Rathvilly
Glenealy
Rathnew
Freshford
Kilcooley Abbey
Dunmore Caves
Tullow
Rathdrum
Wicklow Head
Rock of Cashel
Hacketstown
Brittas Bay
Killenaule
Kilkenny/Cill Chainnigh
Paulstown
Leighlinbridge
Aughrim
Castle Howard
Cashel
Bagenalstown/Muine Bheag
Tinahely
Ballingarry
Callan
Gowran
Ballon
Shillelagh
Mizen Head
Irish Sea
Myshall
Fethard
Goresbridge
Borris
Carnew
Arklow/An Tinbhear Mór
Slieve Naman
Thomastown
Mt Leinster
Bunclody
Kilmichael Point
Kilmaganny
Jerpoint Abbey
Graiguenamanagh
Gorey
Clonmel/Cluain Meala
Knocktopher
Kiltealy
Ferns
Courtown Harbour
Ballycanew
Carrick-on-Suir
Enniscorthy
Ballyedmund
Fauscoum
Mullinavat
Clonroche
Cahore Point
Glenmore
New Ross/Ros Mhic Thriúin
Curraghmore
J.F. Kennedy Memorial Forest Park
Kilmacthomas
Waterford/Port Láirge
Blackwater
Kilmeaden
Dunbrody Abbey
Castlebridge
Kill
Arthurstown
Taghmon
Wexford/Loch Garman
Bunmahon
Passage East
Wexford Bay
Dungarvan
Annestown
Tramore
Tintern Abbey
Ring/An Rinn
Dunmore East
Fethard
Duncormick
Helvick Head
Churchtown
Ballyteige Bay
Rosslare Harbour
Hook Head
Kilmore Quay
Churchtown
Carnsore Point
Pembroke
Cherbourg
St George's Channel
Strumble Head
GB
Cardigan
Fishguard
Pembrokeshire Coast
St. David's
St. Brides Bay
Newcastle Emlyn
10
12
E
F
G
H
1
2
3
4
5
6

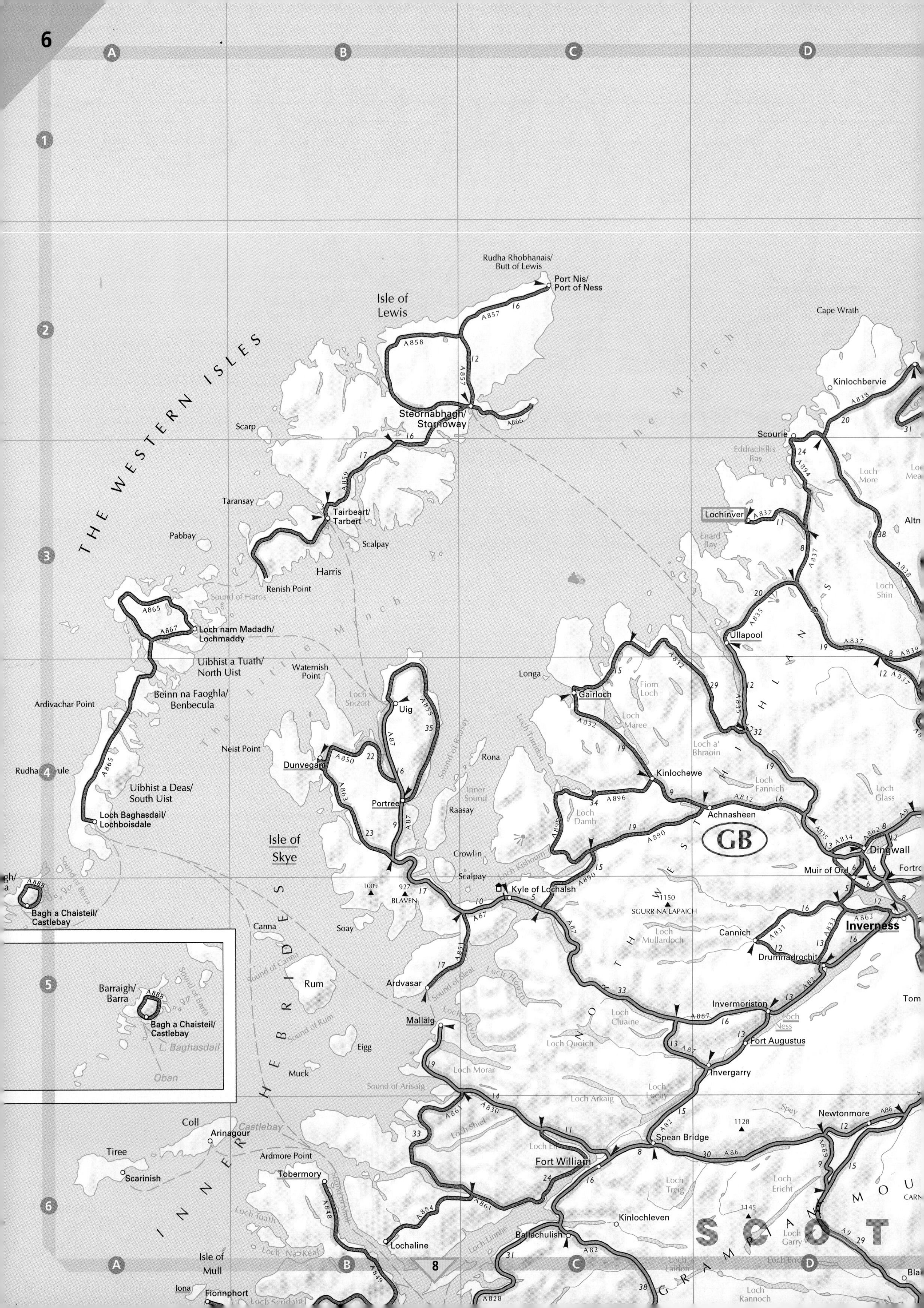

6
A
B
C
D
1
2
3
4
5
6
Rudha Rhobhanais/
Butt of Lewis
Port Nis/
Port of Ness
Isle of
Lewis
A857
16
A858
12
A857
Steornabhagh/
Stornoway
A866
Cape Wrath
Kinlochbervie
A838
20
31
Scourie
Eddrachillis
Bay
24
A894
Loch
More
Altn
38
THE WESTERN ISLES
The Minch
Scarp
16
17
A859
Taransay
Tairbeart/
Tarbert
Scalpay
Pabbay
Harris
Renish Point
Sound of Harris
Lochinver
A837
11
Enard
Bay
8
A837
A838
Loch
Shin
20
A835
A865
A867
Loch nam Madadh/
Lochmaddy
Uibhist a Tuath/
North Uist
Beinn na Faoghla/
Benbecula
Ardivachar Point
The Little Minch
Waternish
Point
Loch
Snizort
Uig
A855
35
A87
Ullapool
19
A837
8
A839
12
A837
Longa
Gairloch
15
A832
29
Fiom
Loch
Loch
Maree
A832
12
A835
32
19
Loch a'
Bhraoin
Neist Point
Dunvegan
A850
22
16
Sound of Raasay
Rona
Loch Torridon
Kinlochewe
9
Loch
Fannich
A832
16
Loch
Glass
Rudha
yule
A865
Uibhist a Deas/
South Uist
Loch Baghasdail/
Lochboisdale
A863
Portree
9
A87
23
Inner
Sound
Raasay
34
A896
Loch
Damh
A896
19
A890
Achnasheen
A835
13
A834
A862
Dingwall
Isle of
Skye
GB
Crowlin
Scalpay
Loch Kishorn
15
A890
Muir of Ord
Fortro
Sound of Barra
A888
Bagh a Chaisteil/
Castlebay
1009
927
BLAVEN
17
Kyle of Lochalsh
5
10
A87
1150
SGURR NA LAPAICH
Loch
Mullardoch
16
A862
Inverness
16
Cannich
A831
A833
13
12
Drumnadrochit
Canna
Soay
Sound of Canna
A851
17
Rum
Ardvasar
Sound of Sleat
Loch Hourn
A87
33
Barraigh/
Barra
A888
Bagh a Chaisteil/
Castlebay
Sound of Barra
L. Baghasdail
Oban
Mallaig
Sound of Rum
Loch Nevis
Eigg
Loch
Cluaine
A887
16
Invermoriston
13
A82
Loch
Ness
13
Fort Augustus
Loch Quoich
13
A87
Invergarry
Tom
Muck
19
Loch Morar
Sound of Arisaig
14
A830
A861
Loch Shiel
Loch Arkaig
Loch
Lochy
15
A82
Spey
Newtonmore
A86
12
1128
INNER HEBRIDES
NORTH WEST HIGHLANDS
Coll
Arinagour
Castlebay
Tiree
Scarinish
Ardmore Point
Tobermory
Sound of Mull
33
11
Loch Eil
Fort William
Spean Bridge
8
30
A86
A889
9
15
A848
Loch Tuath
A884
24
A861
16
Loch
Treig
Loch
Ericht
Kinlochleven
1145
SCOT
MOU
CARN
Lochaline
Loch Linnhe
Ballachulish
A82
A9
29
Loch
Garry
Isle of
Mull
Loch Na Keal
8
Loch
Laidon
Loch Ericht
GRAMPIAN
31
A849
38
Loch
Rannoch
Blai
Iona
Fionnphort
Loch Scridain
A828

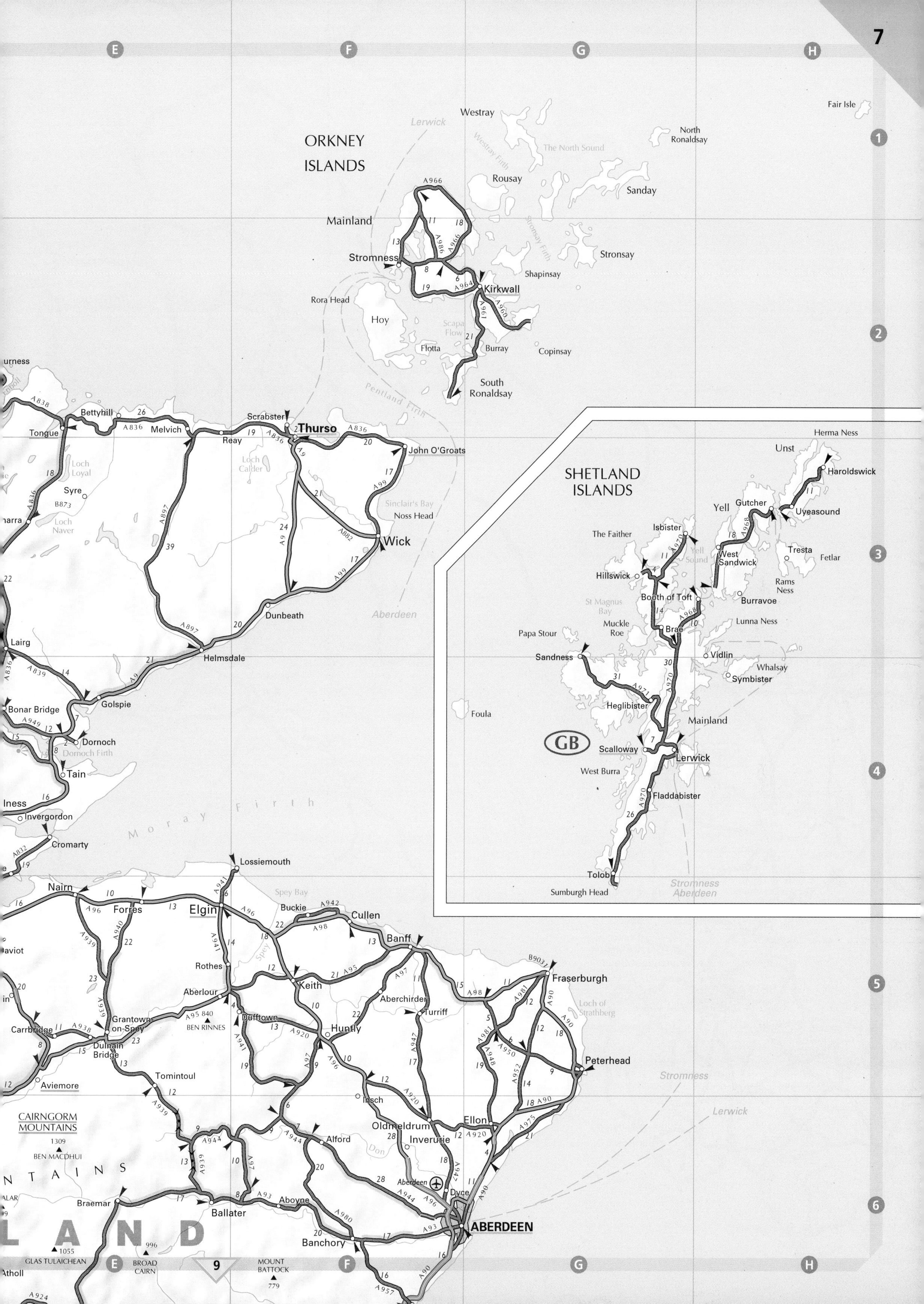

Fair Isle

ORKNEY ISLANDS

Westray

Lerwick

Westray Firth

The North Sound

North Ronaldsay

A966

Rousay

Sanday

Mainland

11   18

13

Stronsay Firth

Stronsay

Stromness

A986   A965

8   6   A964

19   A964   Kirkwall   A960

Shapinsay

Rora Head

A961   A960

Hoy

Scapa Flow

21

Copinsay

Flotta   Burray

South Ronaldsay

Pentland Firth

Aberdeen

Herma Ness

SHETLAND ISLANDS

Unst

Haroldswick

urness

A838

Bettyhill

A836   26

Tongue

A836   Melvich

18   Loch Loyal

Syre   B873

Loch Naver

22

arra

A836

A839

Lairg

A836   14   A839   12

Bonar Bridge   7

A949   12

Dornoch

Dornoch Firth   8

Tain

ness   16

Invergordon

A832   19

Cromarty

Scrabster

Thurso   A836

Reay   A836   A9   19   20

Loch Calder

21   17

A9   A99   24

A882

A99   17

Wick

Sinclair's Bay   Noss Head

Dunbeath

A897   20

Helmsdale

Golspie

39

A9

21

John O'Groats

Yell   Gutcher

Uyeasound

The Faither   Isbister   A920   11   18   A968   Tresta

Hillswick   4   West Sandwick   Fetlar

Booth of Toft   Rams Ness

St Magnus Bay   14   A968   Burravoe

Muckle Roe   Brae   10   Lunna Ness

Papa Stour   A971   A970   30   Vidlin

Sandness   Whalsay

Foula   31   Symbister

Heglibister   Mainland

GB   Scalloway   7   Lerwick

West Burra   Fladdabister

26

Tolob

Sumburgh Head

Stromness   Aberdeen

Moray   Firth

Nairn   10

A96   Forres   13   Elgin   A96   Buckie   A942   Cullen

6   Spey Bay   A98

aviot   A939   22   22   18   13   Banff

A910   Rothes   12   B903

in   20   A95 840   Keith   21   A95   A97   A98   Fraserburgh

23   Aberlour   10   Aberchirder   5   11   A981   A90   Loch of Strathberg

Carrbridge   11   A938   Grantown-on-Spey   A95 840   4   Dufftown   13   A920   Huntly   22   Turriff   A981   12   Peterhead

8   Dulnain Bridge   23   BEN RINNES   A941   19   A96   10   17   A948   A952   9

15   13   Tomintoul   12   Insch   A920   18   A90

Aviemore   12   6   Oldmeldrum   28   Ellon   A920

CAIRNGORM MOUNTAINS   A939   9   A944   Alford   Inverurie   4

1309   BEN MACDHUI   13   10   A97   18   A947

NTAINS   A939   20   28   Aberdeen ✈ Dyce   11

AR   Braemar   17   Ballater   8   A93   Aboyne   A980   A944   A96   ABERDEEN

924   Banchory   20   A93   A90

LAND   996   17   16

GLAS TULAICHEAN   BROAD CAIRN   MOUNT BATTOCK   A957

1055   9   779

Atholl

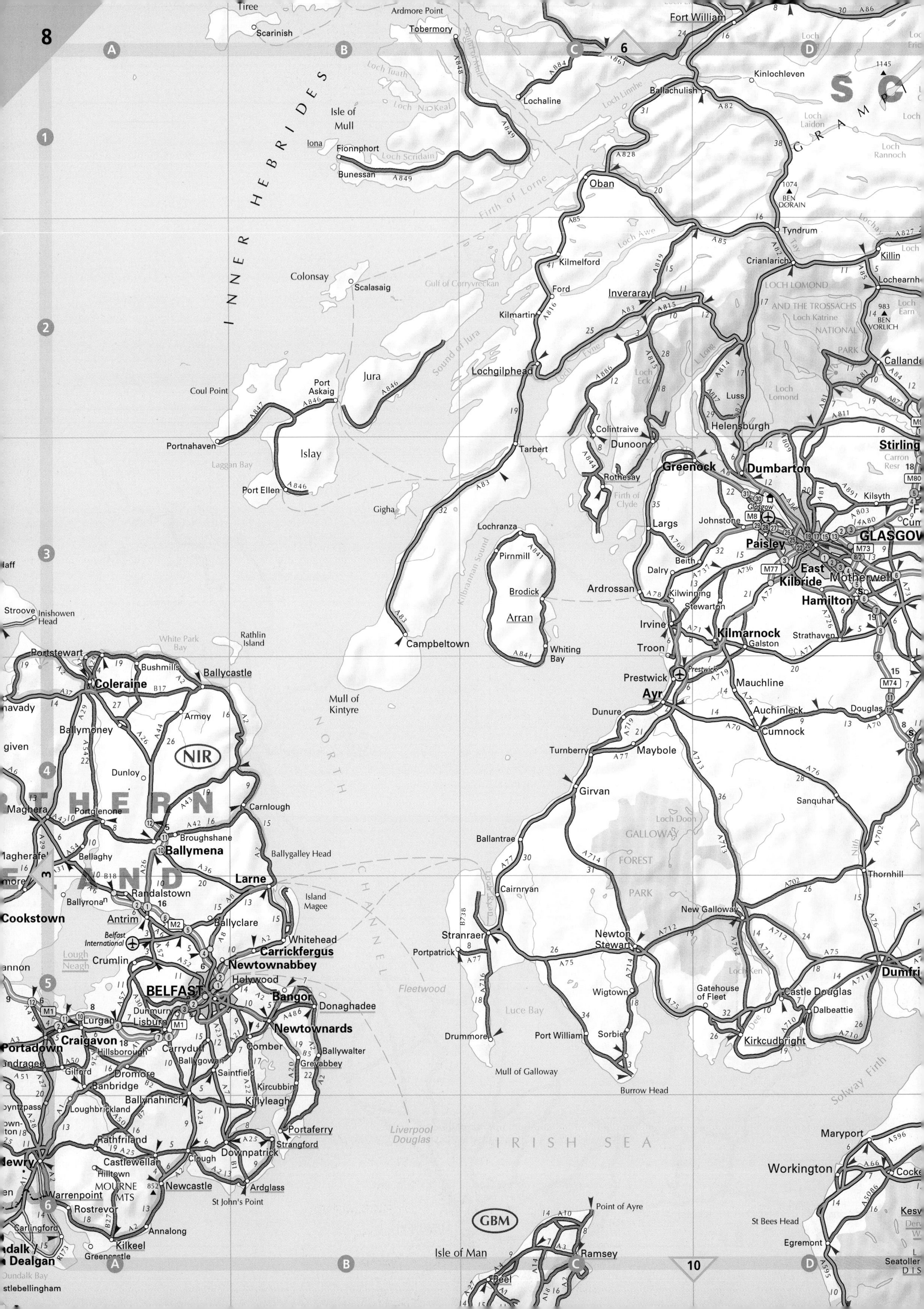

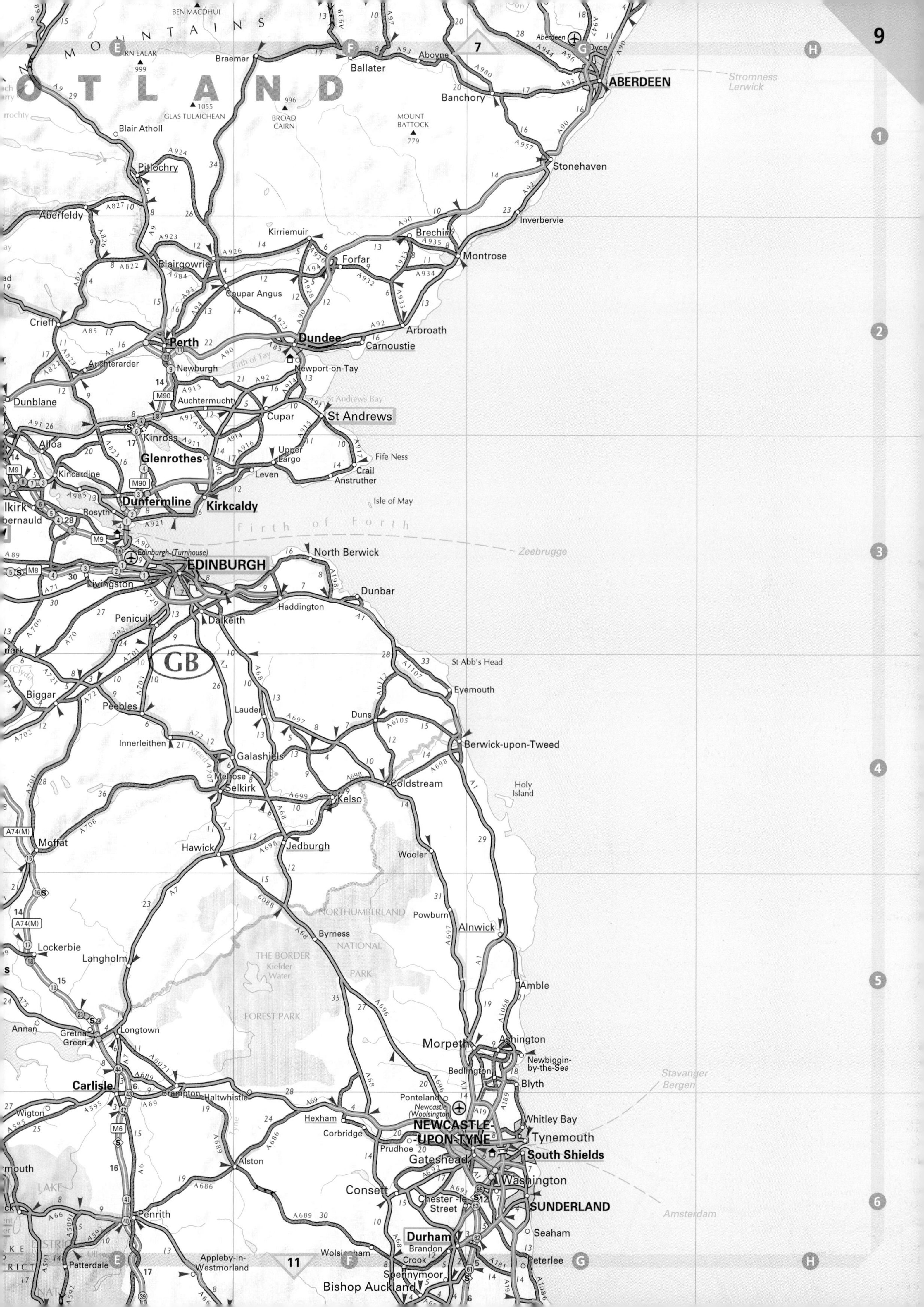
SCOTLAND
GB
ABERDEEN
Stonehaven
Inverbervie
Montrose
Brechin
Forfar
Kirriemuir
Arbroath
Carnoustie
Dundee
Perth
Blairgowrie
Coupar Angus
Pitlochry
Aberfeldy
Blair Atholl
Crieff
Auchterarder
Dunblane
Newburgh
Newport-on-Tay
Auchtermuchty
Cupar
St Andrews
Kinross
Glenrothes
Alloa
Kincardine
Dunfermline
Kirkcaldy
Leven
Upper Largo
Crail
Anstruther
Fife Ness
Isle of May
Rosyth
Firth of Forth
North Berwick
EDINBURGH
Livingston
Haddington
Dunbar
Dalkeith
Penicuik
Biggar
Peebles
Innerleithen
Lauder
Galashiels
Melrose
Selkirk
Duns
Eyemouth
St Abb's Head
Berwick-upon-Tweed
Coldstream
Kelso
Holy Island
Moffat
Hawick
Jedburgh
Wooler
Powburn
Alnwick
Byrness
NORTHUMBERLAND NATIONAL PARK
THE BORDER FOREST PARK
Kielder Water
Lockerbie
Langholm
Amble
Morpeth
Ashington
Newbiggin-by-the-Sea
Bedlington
Blyth
Annan
Gretna Green
Longtown
Carlisle
Brampton
Haltwhistle
Wigton
Hexham
Corbridge
Ponteland
Newcastle (Woolsington)
NEWCASTLE-UPON-TYNE
Whitley Bay
Tynemouth
South Shields
Gateshead
Prudhoe
Alston
Consett
Washington
SUNDERLAND
Chester-le-Street
Durham
Seaham
Peterlee
Brandon
Crook
Spennymoor
Bishop Auckland
Wolsingham
Penrith
Appleby-in-Westmorland
Patterdale
Ballater
Aboyne
Banchory
Braemar
Aberdeen
Dyce
MOUNT BATTOCK
BROAD CAIRN
GLAS TULAICHEAN
BEN MACDHUI
Stromness Lerwick
Zeebrugge
Stavanger Bergen
Amsterdam
7
11

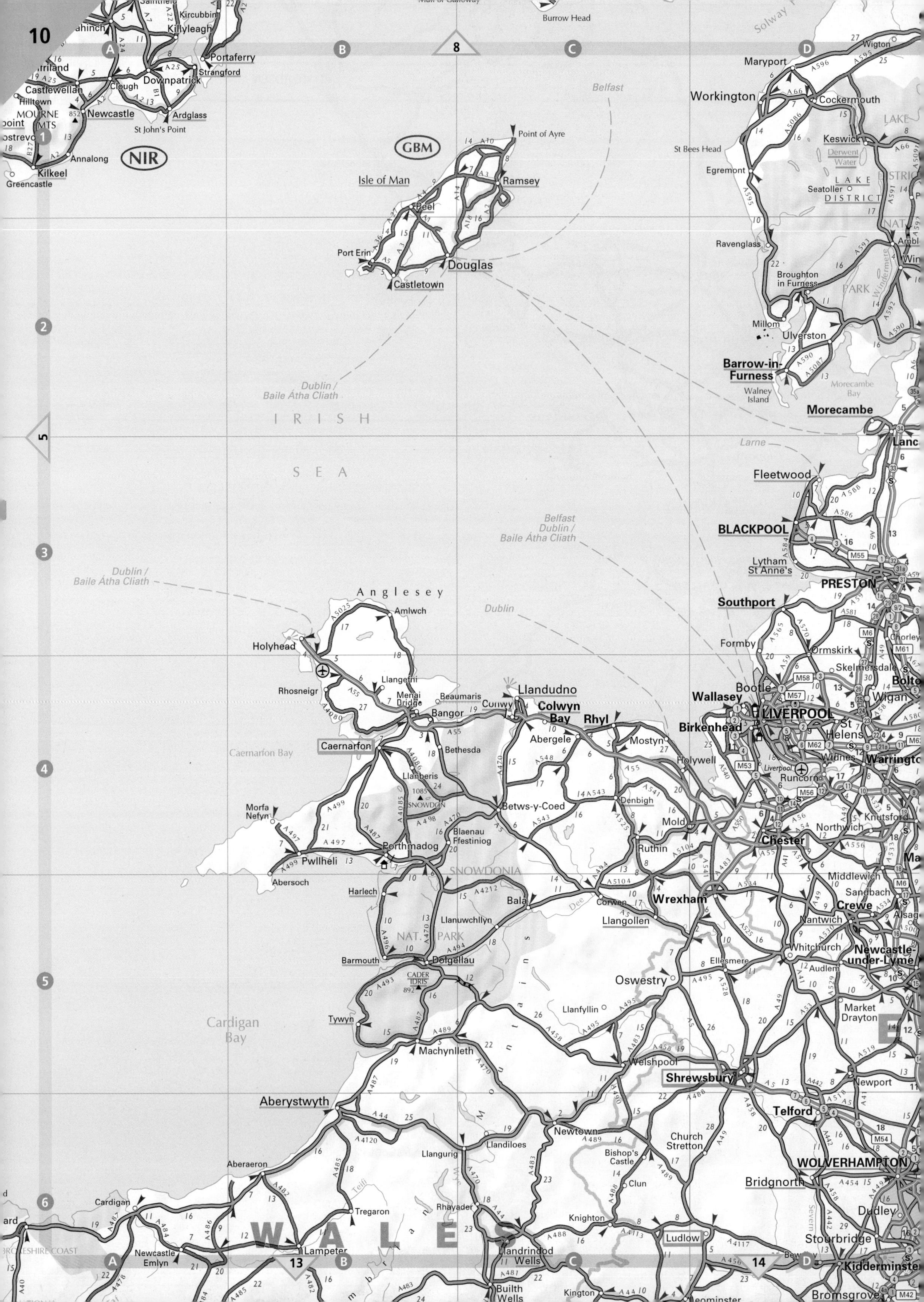
Kircubbin
Killyleagh
Portaferry
Strangford
Downpatrick
Clough
Castlewellan
Hilltown
MOURNE MTS
Newcastle
Ardglass
St John's Point
Annalong
Kilkeel
Greencastle
NIR
Burrow Head
Belfast
GBM
Point of Ayre
Isle of Man
Ramsey
Peel
Port Erin
Douglas
Castletown
Dublin / Baile Átha Cliath
IRISH SEA
Maryport
Workington
Cockermouth
Keswick
Derwent Water
St Bees Head
Egremont
Seatoller
LAKE DISTRICT
Ravenglass
Broughton in Furness
Millom
Ulverston
Barrow-in-Furness
Walney Island
Morecambe Bay
Morecambe
Larne
Fleetwood
BLACKPOOL
Lytham St Anne's
PRESTON
Southport
Formby
Ormskirk
Skelmersdale
Bootle
Wallasey
LIVERPOOL
Birkenhead
St Helens
Widnes
Runcorn
Warrington
Chorley
Wigan
Liverpool
Belfast Dublin / Baile Átha Cliath
Dublin / Baile Átha Cliath
Dublin
Anglesey
Amlwch
Holyhead
Llangefni
Rhosneigr
Menai Bridge
Beaumaris
Bangor
Llandudno
Conwy
Colwyn Bay
Rhyl
Abergele
Mostyn
Holywell
Caernarfon
Caernarfon Bay
Bethesda
Llanberis
SNOWDON
Betws-y-Coed
Denbigh
Mold
Chester
Northwich
Knutsford
Morfa Nefyn
Blaenau Ffestiniog
Porthmadog
Pwllheli
Abersoch
Ruthin
SNOWDONIA
Harlech
Bala
Corwen
Wrexham
Llangollen
Middlewich
Sandbach
Crewe
Nantwich
Llanuwchllyn
NAT. PARK
Whitchurch
Newcastle-under-Lyme
Barmouth
Dolgellau
CADER IDRIS
Ellesmere
Audlem
Oswestry
Tywyn
Llanfyllin
Market Drayton
Cardigan Bay
Machynlleth
Welshpool
Shrewsbury
Newport
Telford
Aberystwyth
Newtown
Church Stretton
Llandiloes
Llangurig
Bishop's Castle
Clun
WOLVERHAMPTON
Bridgnorth
Aberaeron
Cardigan
Tregaron
Rhayader
Knighton
Dudley
Stourbridge
Ludlow
WALES
Newcastle Emlyn
Lampeter
Llandrindod Wells
Bewdley
Kidderminster
Builth Wells
Kington
Leominster
Bromsgrove
Cambrian Mountains

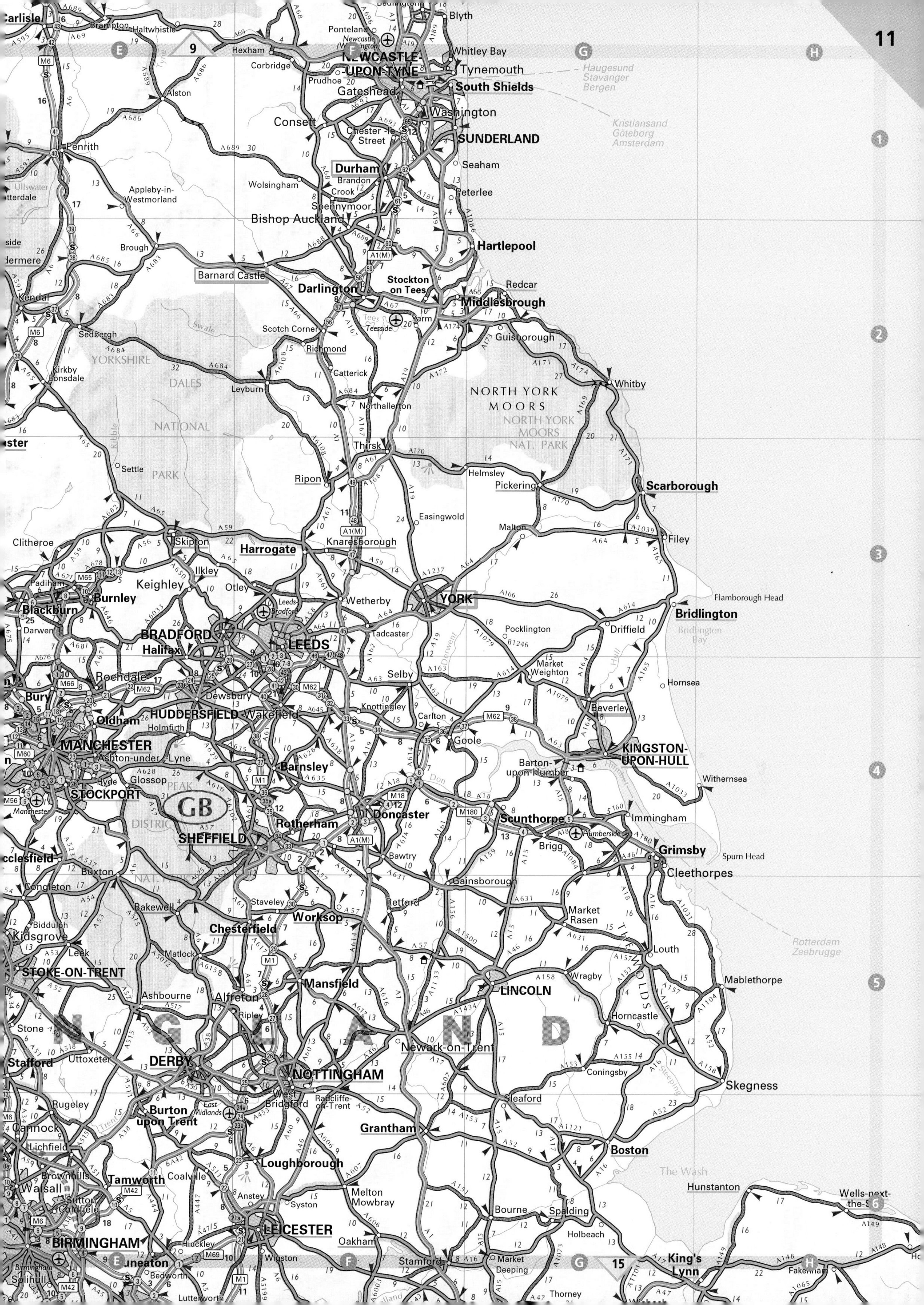
Carlisle
Newcastle (Woolsington)
NEWCASTLE-UPON-TYNE
Tynemouth
South Shields
Gateshead
Washington
SUNDERLAND
Haugesund
Stavanger
Bergen
Kristiansand
Göteborg
Amsterdam
Hexham
Corbridge
Prudhoe
Ponteland
Blyth
Whitley Bay
Haltwhistle
Brampton
Alston
Consett
Chester-le-Street
Durham
Brandon
Crook
Spennymoor
Bishop Auckland
Seaham
Peterlee
Hartlepool
Penrith
Ullswater
Appleby-in-Westmorland
Wolsingham
Brough
Barnard Castle
Darlington
Stockton on Tees
Redcar
Middlesbrough
Teesside
Yarm
Guisborough
Kendal
Sedbergh
Scotch Corner
Richmond
Catterick
YORKSHIRE DALES NATIONAL PARK
Kirkby Lonsdale
Leyburn
Northallerton
Whitby
NORTH YORK MOORS
NORTH YORK MOORS NAT. PARK
Thirsk
Helmsley
Pickering
Settle
Ripon
Scarborough
Easingwold
Malton
Filey
Clitheroe
Skipton
Harrogate
Knaresborough
Ilkley
Keighley
Otley
Burnley
Blackburn
Darwen
Leeds-Bradford
Wetherby
YORK
Bridlington
Flamborough Head
Bridlington Bay
Driffield
Pocklington
Tadcaster
BRADFORD
Halifax
LEEDS
Selby
Market Weighton
Hornsea
Rochdale
Bury
Dewsbury
Oldham
HUDDERSFIELD
Wakefield
Knottingley
Carlton
Goole
Beverley
KINGSTON-UPON-HULL
Holmfirth
MANCHESTER
Ashton-under-Lyne
Barnsley
Barton-upon-Humber
Withernsea
Glossop
Hyde
STOCKPORT
Manchester
PEAK DISTRICT NAT. PARK
GB
Rotherham
Doncaster
Scunthorpe
Immingham
SHEFFIELD
Humberside
Brigg
Grimsby
Spurn Head
Cleethorpes
Macclesfield
Buxton
Bawtry
Gainsborough
Congleton
Bakewell
Staveley
Worksop
Retford
Market Rasen
Biddulph
Kidsgrove
Chesterfield
Leek
Louth
Rotterdam
Zeebrugge
STOKE-ON-TRENT
Matlock
Mansfield
Wragby
LINCOLN
Mablethorpe
Ashbourne
Alfreton
Ripley
Horncastle
Stone
ENGLAND
Newark-on-Trent
Stafford
Uttoxeter
DERBY
NOTTINGHAM
Coningsby
Skegness
Rugeley
Burton upon Trent
East Midlands
West Bridgford
Radcliffe-on-Trent
Sleaford
Cannock
Grantham
Boston
Lichfield
Loughborough
Brownhills
Tamworth
Coalville
The Wash
Hunstanton
Walsall
Sutton Coldfield
Melton Mowbray
Wells-next-the-Sea
Anstey
Syston
Bourne
Spalding
BIRMINGHAM
Hinckley
LEICESTER
Oakham
Holbeach
Nuneaton
Wigston
Stamford
Market Deeping
King's Lynn
Fakenham
Solihull
Bedworth
Lutterworth
Thorney
9
15

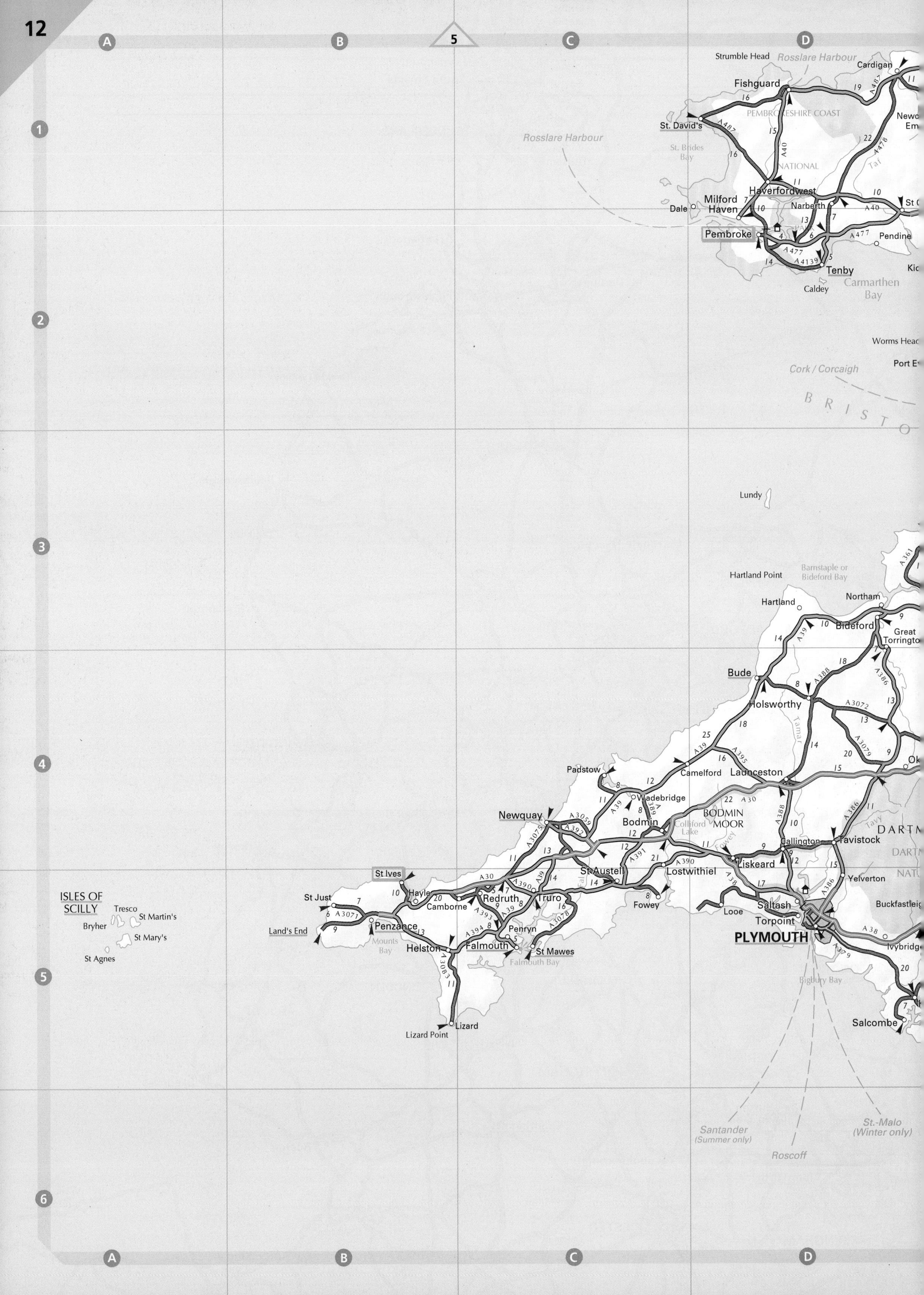

A   B   5   C   D

1

2

3

4

5

6

A   B   C   D

Strumble Head   Rosslare Harbour
Fishguard   Cardigan
16   19   11
PEMBROKESHIRE COAST   A487   A487
St. David's   A40   Newc
A487   15   Em
St. Brides   22   A478
Bay   16   NATIONAL   10
Dale   Milford   7   Haverfordwest   A40   St C
Haven   10   Narberth
Pembroke   4   13   7   A477   Pendine
A477   6
14   A4139   5   Kic
Tenby
Caldey   Carmarthen
Bay

Rosslare Harbour

Worms Head
Cork / Corcaigh   Port E
BRISTO

Lundy

Barnstaple or
Hartland Point   Bideford Bay
A361
Hartland   Northam
Bideford
14   A39   10   Great
Bude   A388   18   Torrington
8   A386   13
Holsworthy   A3072
18   14   A3079   9
25   A395   20   Ok
Padstow   A39   16   Launceston   A386   11
8   12   Camelford   A30   A388   DARTM
Newquay   11   Wadebridge   BODMIN   22   10   DART
A3059   8   MOOR   Colliford   Gallington   Tavistock   NAT.
A392   Bodmin   Lake   9
St Ives   13   12   A391   21   Liskeard   Yelverton
St Just   10   Hayle   A30   14   St Austel   Lostwithiel   1.7   Buckfastleig
7   20   A390   14   8   Looe   Saltash
Land's End   6   A3071   Camborne   Redruth   Truro   Fowey   Torpoint   A38
9   Penzance   Penryn   A3078   PLYMOUTH   Ivybridge
Helston   Falmouth   5   20
Mounts   A3083   St Mawes
Bay   Falmouth Bay   Bigbury Bay   Salcombe

ISLES OF
SCILLY   Tresco   St Martin's
Bryher
St Mary's
St Agnes

Lizard
Lizard Point

Santander   St.-Malo
(Summer only)   (Winter only)
Roscoff

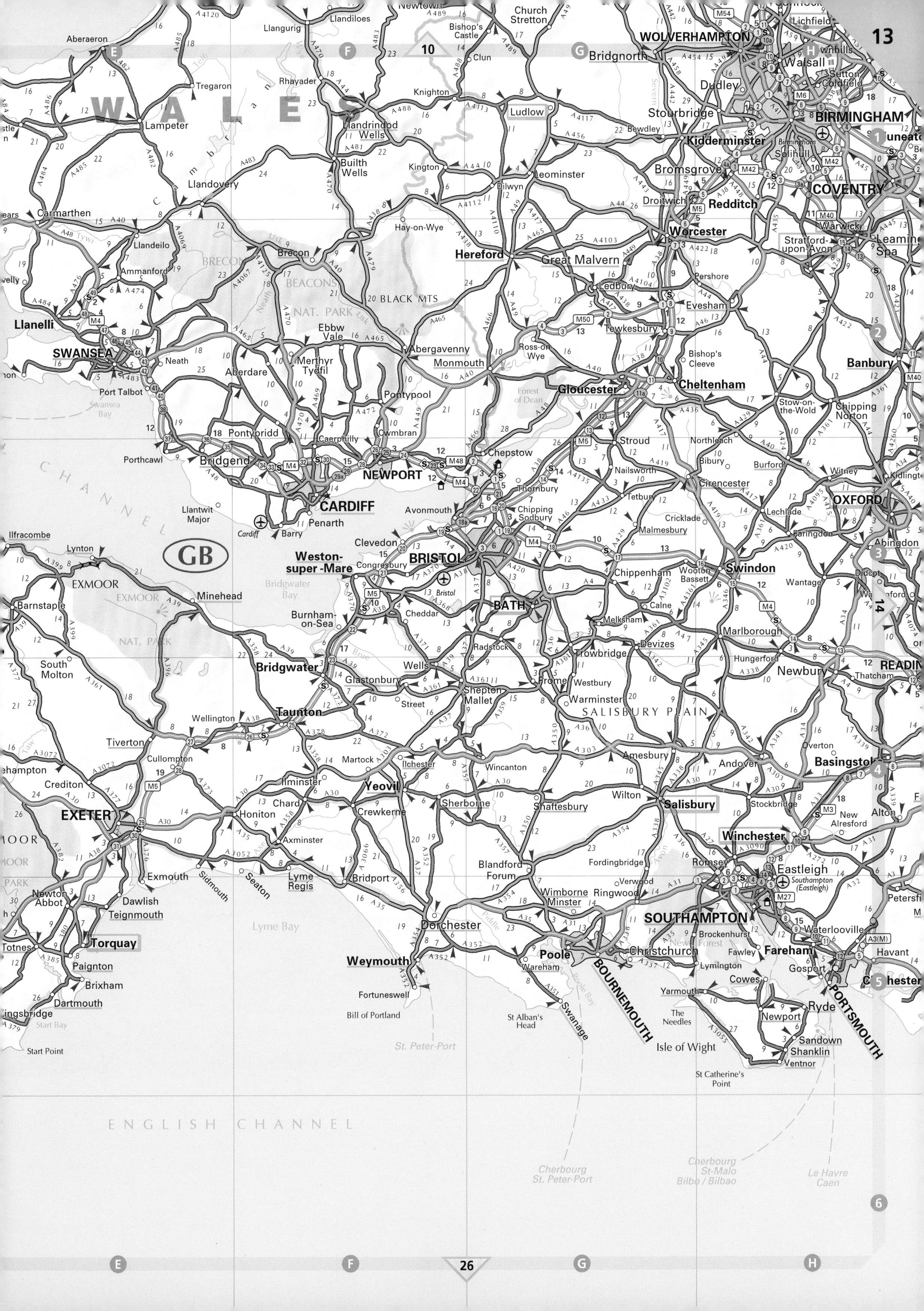
WALES
Cambrian
Aberaeron
Llangurig
Llandiloes
Bishop's Castle
Church Stretton
Clun
Bridgnorth
WOLVERHAMPTON
Lichfield
Walsall
Sutton Coldfield
Dudley
Stourbridge
BIRMINGHAM
Kidderminster
Bewdley
Solihull
Bromsgrove
COVENTRY
Redditch
Droitwich
Worcester
Warwick
Stratford-upon-Avon
Leamington Spa
Tregaron
Rhayader
Knighton
Ludlow
Lampeter
Llandrindod Wells
Builth Wells
Kington
Leominster
Dilwyn
Llandovery
Carmarthen
Llandeilo
Hay-on-Wye
Hereford
Great Malvern
Ledbury
Pershore
Evesham
Tewkesbury
Brecon
BRECON BEACONS NAT. PARK
BLACK MTS
Ammanford
Llanelli
SWANSEA
Neath
Port Talbot
Swansea Bay
Aberdare
Merthyr Tydfil
Ebbw Vale
Abergavenny
Monmouth
Ross-on-Wye
Gloucester
Cheltenham
Bishop's Cleeve
Banbury
Pontypool
Cwmbran
Pontypridd
Caerphilly
Bridgend
Porthcawl
NEWPORT
CARDIFF
Penarth
Barry
Llantwit Major
Chepstow
Forest of Dean
Stroud
Thornbury
Chipping Sodbury
Avonmouth
Nailsworth
Tetbury
Cirencester
Northleach
Bibury
Burford
Stow-on-the-Wold
Chipping Norton
Witney
Kidlington
OXFORD
Lechlade
Faringdon
Abingdon
Didcot
Wallingford
Cricklade
Malmesbury
Swindon
Wootton Bassett
Chippenham
Calne
Wantage
Clevedon
BRISTOL
Weston-super-Mare
Congresbury
BATH
Melksham
Devizes
Marlborough
Hungerford
Newbury
Thatcham
READING
CHANNEL
GB
Ilfracombe
Lynton
EXMOOR
EXMOOR NAT. PARK
Minehead
Barnstaple
South Molton
Bridgwater Bay
Burnham-on-Sea
Cheddar
Radstock
Trowbridge
Wells
Bridgwater
Glastonbury
Street
Shepton Mallet
Frome
Westbury
Warminster
SALISBURY PLAIN
Wellington
Taunton
Tiverton
Cullompton
Crediton
EXETER
Martock
Ilchester
Wincanton
Amesbury
Andover
Overton
Basingstoke
Ilminster
Yeovil
Chard
Crewkerne
Sherborne
Shaftesbury
Wilton
Salisbury
Stockbridge
New Alresford
Alton
Honiton
Axminster
Exmouth
Sidmouth
Seaton
Lyme Regis
Bridport
Blandford Forum
Fordingbridge
Romsey
Winchester
Eastleigh
Southampton (Eastleigh)
Newton Abbot
Dawlish
Teignmouth
Torquay
Paignton
Brixham
Dartmouth
Totnes
Kingsbridge
Start Bay
Start Point
Lyme Bay
Dorchester
Weymouth
Fortuneswell
Bill of Portland
Wimborne Minster
Verwood
Ringwood
Wareham
Poole
BOURNEMOUTH
Christchurch
Lymington
St Alban's Head
Swanage
SOUTHAMPTON
Brockenhurst
New Forest
Fawley
Fareham
Waterlooville
Havant
Gosport
PORTSMOUTH
Chichester
Cowes
Yarmouth
The Needles
Newport
Ryde
Isle of Wight
Sandown
Shanklin
Ventnor
St Catherine's Point
St. Peter-Port
Cherbourg
St. Peter-Port
Cherbourg
St-Malo
Bilbo / Bilbao
Le Havre
Caen
ENGLISH CHANNEL
E
F
G
H
10
14
26

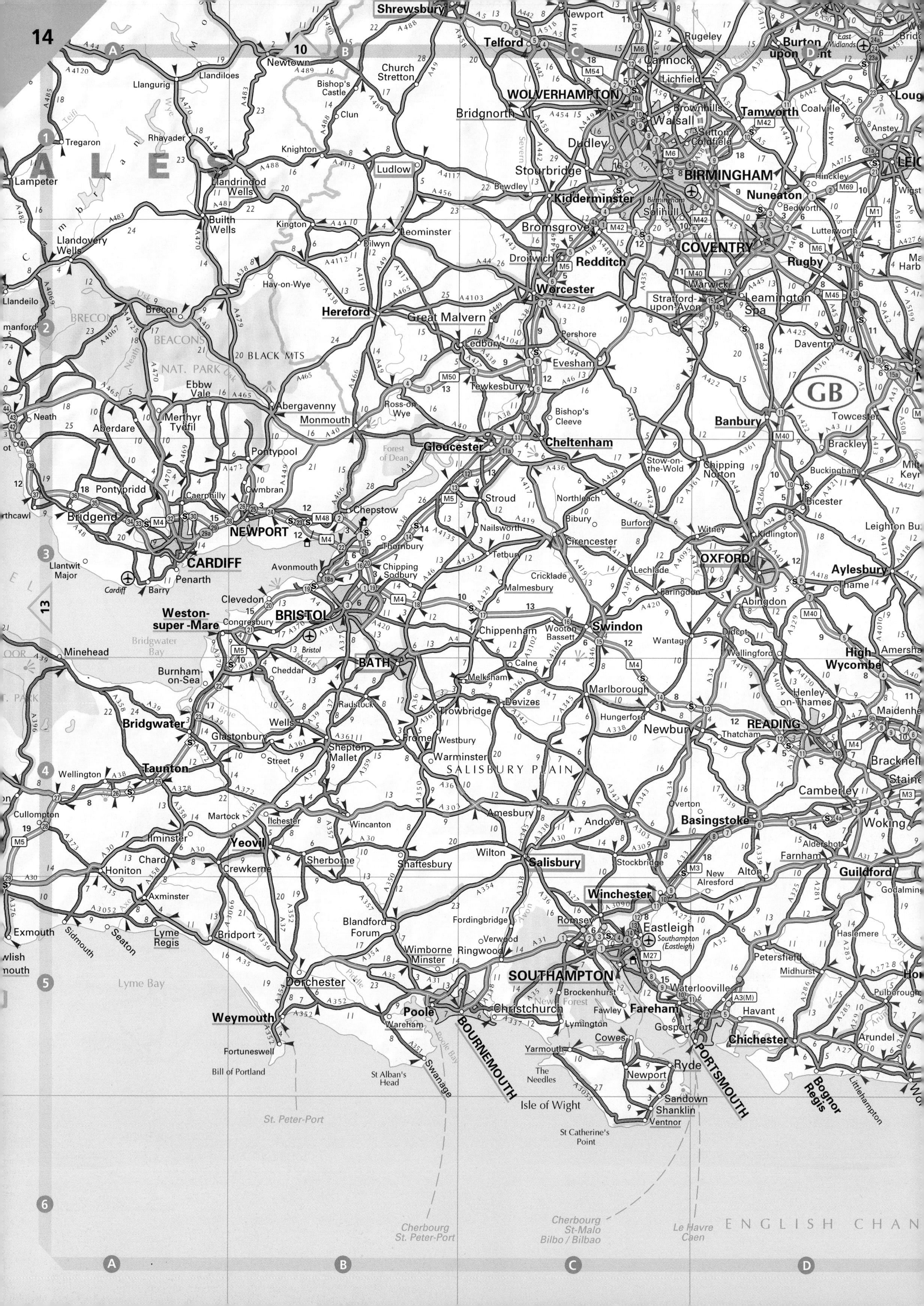
Shrewsbury
Telford
Newport
Rugeley
Burton upon Trent
Newtown
Llanidloes
Llangurig
Church Stretton
Bishop's Castle
Clun
Cannock
Lichfield
WOLVERHAMPTON
Walsall
Tamworth
Coalville
Bridgnorth
Dudley
Sutton Coldfield
Tregaron
Rhayader
Knighton
Ludlow
Stourbridge
BIRMINGHAM
Hinckley
Lampeter
Llandrindod Wells
Bewdley
Kidderminster
Solihull
Nuneaton
Builth Wells
Kington
Leominster
Bromsgrove
Bedworth
Lutterworth
Llandovery Wells
Dilwyn
Droitwich
Redditch
COVENTRY
Rugby
Hay-on-Wye
Worcester
Warwick
Stratford-upon-Avon
Leamington Spa
Llandeilo
Brecon
BRECON BEACONS NAT. PARK
Hereford
Great Malvern
Pershore
Daventry
Ledbury
Evesham
BLACK MTS
Tewkesbury
Ebbw Vale
Abergavenny
Ross-on-Wye
Towcester
Neath
Aberdare
Merthyr Tydfil
Monmouth
Bishop's Cleeve
Banbury
Forest of Dean
Gloucester
Cheltenham
Brackley
Pontypool
Stow-on-the-Wold
Chipping Norton
Buckingham
Pontypridd
Cwmbran
Caerphilly
Chepstow
Stroud
Northleach
Bicester
Bridgend
NEWPORT
Nailsworth
Bibury
Burford
Witney
Kidlington
Thornbury
Cirencester
Tetbury
Llantwit Major
CARDIFF
Penarth
Barry
Cardiff
Avonmouth
Chipping Sodbury
Cricklade
Lechlade
OXFORD
Aylesbury
Malmesbury
Faringdon
Thame
Clevedon
Abingdon
Weston-super-Mare
BRISTOL
Congresbury
Chippenham
Wootton Bassett
Swindon
Bristol
Wantage
Didcot
Minehead
Bridgwater Bay
Burnham-on-Sea
Cheddar
BATH
Calne
Wallingford
High Wycombe
Melksham
Marlborough
Henley-on-Thames
Radstock
Trowbridge
Devizes
Hungerford
Newbury
Thatcham
READING
Maidenhead
Bridgwater
Wells
Glastonbury
Shepton Mallet
Frome
Westbury
Street
Warminster
SALISBURY PLAIN
Bracknell
Taunton
Wellington
Camberley
Martock
Ilchester
Wincanton
Amesbury
Andover
Overton
Basingstoke
Woking
Cullompton
Ilminster
Yeovil
Wilton
Chard
Crewkerne
Sherborne
Shaftesbury
Salisbury
Stockbridge
Alton
Farnham
Guildford
Honiton
New Alresford
Axminster
Winchester
Blandford Forum
Fordingbridge
Romsey
Eastleigh
Southampton (Eastleigh)
Haslemere
Exmouth
Sidmouth
Seaton
Lyme Regis
Bridport
Verwood
Wimborne Minster
Ringwood
Petersfield
Midhurst
Lyme Bay
Dorchester
SOUTHAMPTON
Brockenhurst
New Forest
Waterlooville
Weymouth
Poole
Wareham
Christchurch
Lymington
Fawley
Fareham
Havant
Gosport
BOURNEMOUTH
Cowes
Chichester
Arundel
Fortuneswell
Bill of Portland
St Alban's Head
Swanage
Yarmouth
The Needles
Ryde
PORTSMOUTH
Newport
Bognor Regis
Littlehampton
Sandown
Shanklin
Isle of Wight
Ventnor
St. Peter-Port
St Catherine's Point
Cherbourg St. Peter-Port
Cherbourg St-Malo Bilbo / Bilbao
Le Havre Caen
ENGLISH CHAN
GB
WALES
Cambrian
A
B
C
D
1
2
3
4
5
6
10
13

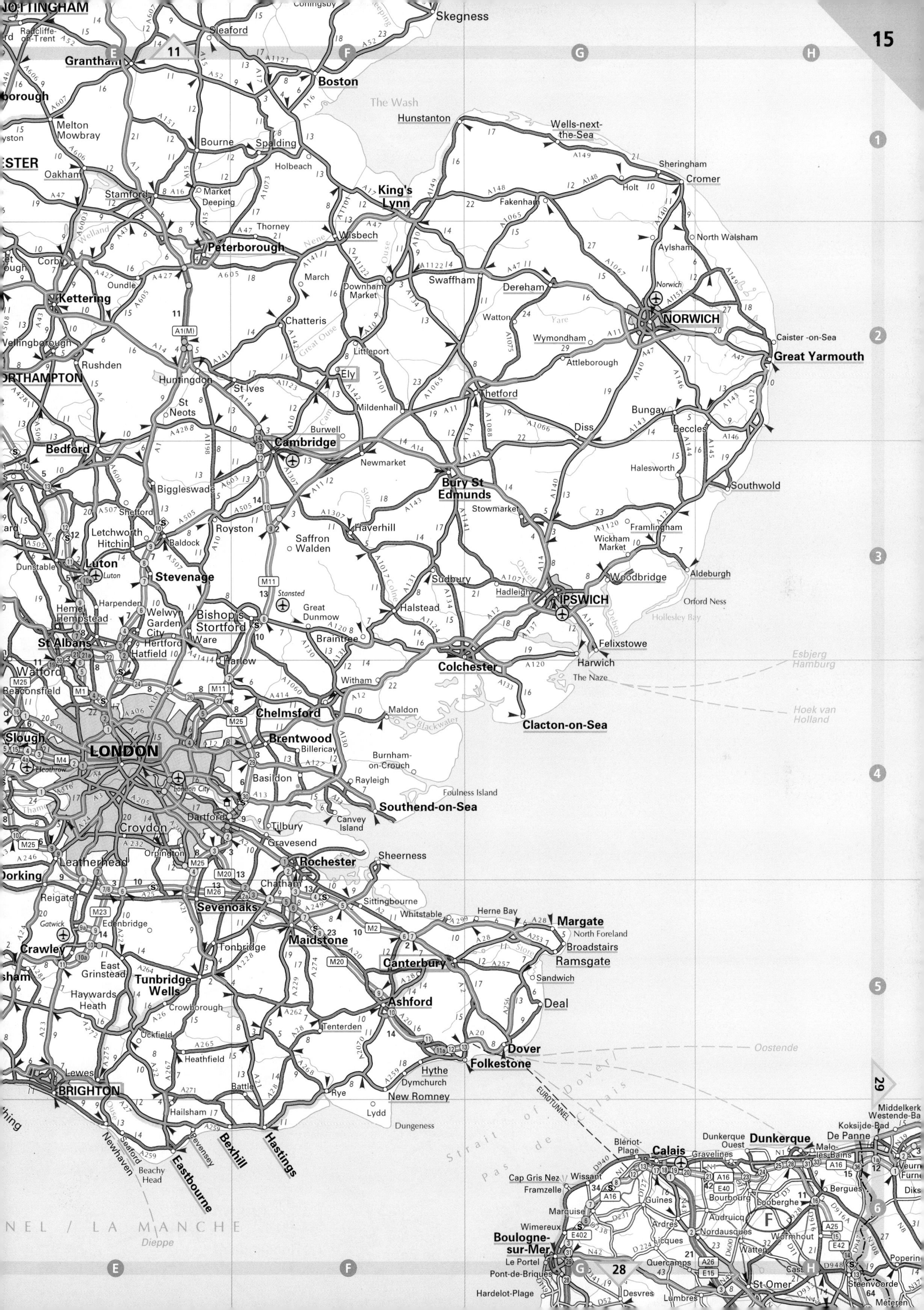

Skegness
Boston
The Wash
Hunstanton
Wells-next-the-Sea
Sheringham
Cromer
King's Lynn
Fakenham
Holt
North Walsham
Aylsham
Swaffham
Dereham
NORWICH
Caister-on-Sea
Great Yarmouth
Wymondham
Attleborough
Thetford
Bungay
Beccles
Diss
Halesworth
Southwold
Bury St Edmunds
Stowmarket
Framlingham
Wickham Market
Aldeburgh
Woodbridge
IPSWICH
Orford Ness
Felixstowe
Harwich
The Naze
Colchester
Clacton-on-Sea
Esbjerg
Hamburg
Hoek van Holland
Cambridge
Newmarket
Ely
Peterborough
Wisbech
Spalding
Grantham
Sleaford
Stamford
Kettering
Huntingdon
St Ives
Bedford
Luton
Stevenage
Royston
Saffron Walden
Haverhill
Sudbury
Halstead
Braintree
Bishop's Stortford
Harlow
Chelmsford
Maldon
Witham
Brentwood
Billericay
Basildon
Burnham-on-Crouch
Rayleigh
Southend-on-Sea
Foulness Island
Canvey Island
LONDON
Slough
Watford
St Albans
Croydon
Dartford
Tilbury
Gravesend
Rochester
Chatham
Sheerness
Sittingbourne
Whitstable
Herne Bay
Margate
North Foreland
Broadstairs
Ramsgate
Sandwich
Deal
Canterbury
Maidstone
Sevenoaks
Tonbridge
Tunbridge Wells
Ashford
Tenterden
Dover
Folkestone
Hythe
Dymchurch
New Romney
Lydd
Dungeness
Rye
Hastings
Bexhill
Eastbourne
Beachy Head
Newhaven
Seaford
BRIGHTON
Lewes
Crawley
Gatwick
Reigate
Leatherhead
Dorking
Hailsham
Crowborough
Heathfield
Battle
Oostende
Strait of Dover
Pas de Calais
EUROTUNNEL
Calais
Dunkerque
Gravelines
Bourbourg
Bergues
Wissant
Cap Gris Nez
Boulogne-sur-Mer
Le Portel
Marquise
Wimereux
Guînes
Ardres
Audruicq
Licques
St-Omer
Desvres
Lumbres
Hardelot-Plage
De Panne
Koksijde-Bad
Middelkerk
Steenvoorde
Poperinge
Meteren
LA MANCHE
Dieppe

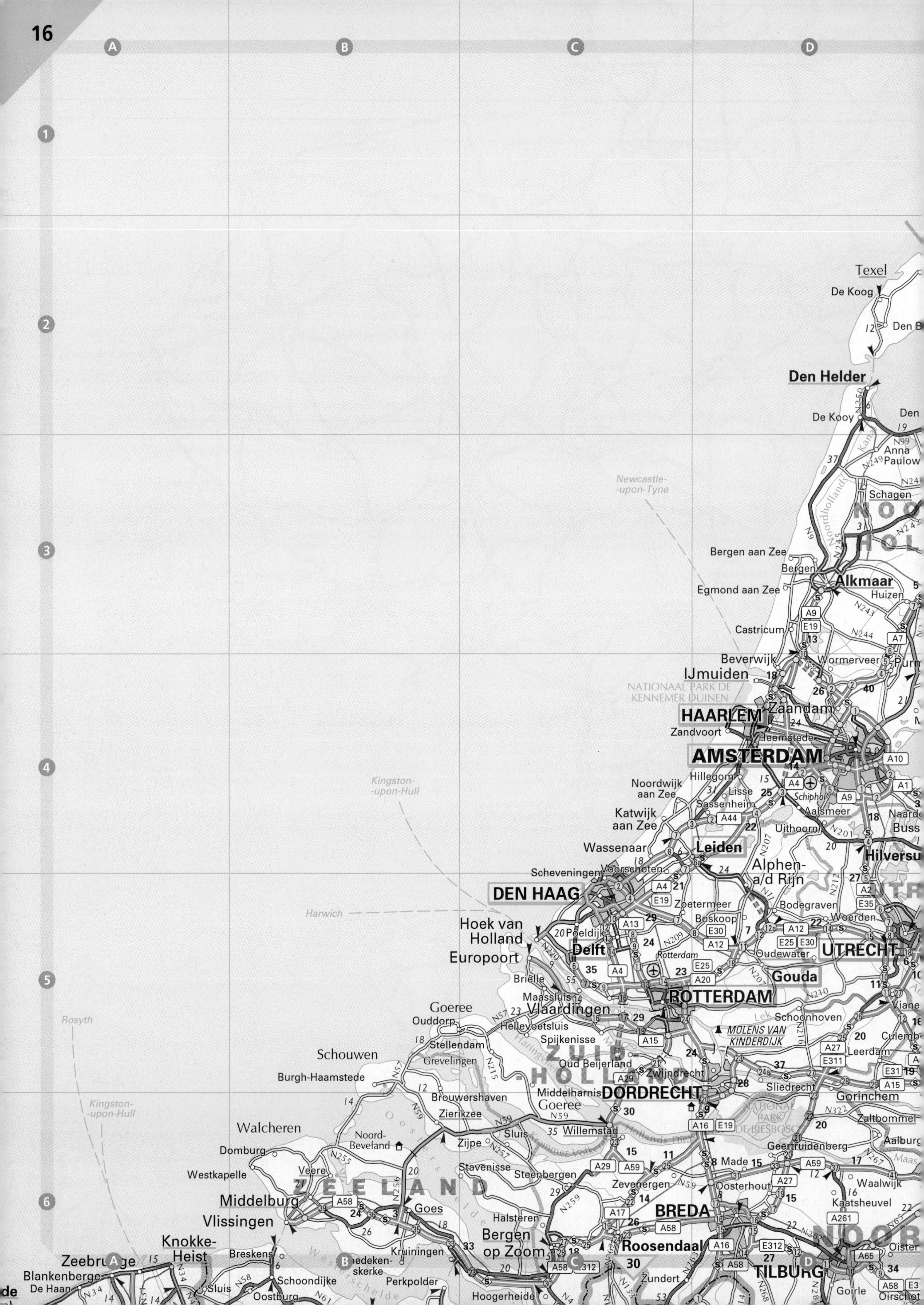
A
B
C
D
1
2
3
4
5
6
Texel
De Koog
Den Helder
De Kooy
Anna Paulowna
Schagen
Newcastle-upon-Tyne
Bergen aan Zee
Bergen
Alkmaar
Egmond aan Zee
Huizen
Castricum
Beverwijk
Wormerveer
IJmuiden
NATIONAAL PARK DE KENNEMER DUINEN
HAARLEM
Zaandam
Zandvoort
Heemstede
AMSTERDAM
Kingston-upon-Hull
Hillegom
Noordwijk aan Zee
Lisse
Schiphol
Sassenheim
Aalsmeer
Katwijk aan Zee
Uithoorn
Wassenaar
Leiden
Alphen-a/d Rijn
Scheveningen
Voorschoten
DEN HAAG
Zoetermeer
Bodegraven
Woerden
Harwich
Hoek van Holland
Poeldijk
Boskoop
Europoort
Delft
Rotterdam
Oudewater
UTRECHT
Gouda
Brielle
Maassluis
ROTTERDAM
Goeree
Ouddorp
Vlaardingen
Hellevoetsluis
Schoonhoven
Rosyth
Spijkenisse
MOLENS VAN KINDERDIJK
Culemborg
Stellendam
Leerdam
Schouwen
Grevelingen
ZUID-HOLLAND
Oud Beijerland
Zwijndrecht
Burgh-Haamstede
Sliedrecht
Gorinchem
Brouwershaven
Middelharnis
DORDRECHT
Kingston-upon-Hull
Zierikzee
Goeree
NATIONAAL PARK DE BIESBOSCH
Zaltbommel
Walcheren
Noord-Beveland
Willemstad
Zijpe
Sluis
Domburg
Geertruidenberg
Aalburg
Veere
Made
Westkapelle
Stavenisse
Steenbergen
Zevenbergen
Oosterhout
Waalwijk
ZEELAND
Middelburg
Goes
Kaatsheuvel
Vlissingen
BREDA
Halsteren
Knokke-Heist
Breskens
Bergen op Zoom
Kruiningen
Roosendaal
Zeebrugge
Yerseke
Blankenberge
Biervliet
Oostburg
Perkpolder
Woensdrecht
Westerschelde
Hoogerheide
Zundert
TILBURG
De Haan
Sluis
Schoondijke
Goirle
Oisterwijk
Oirschot

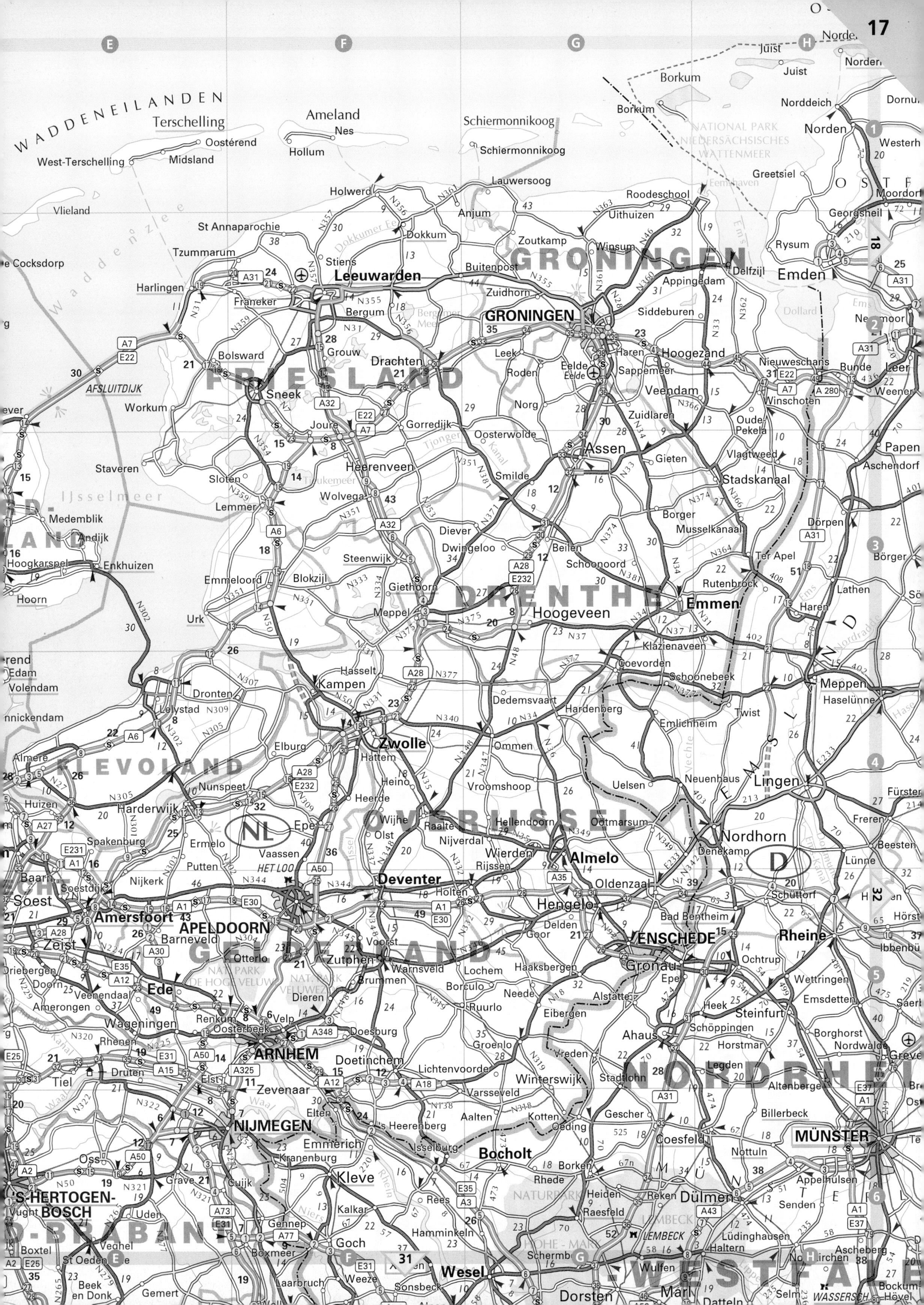

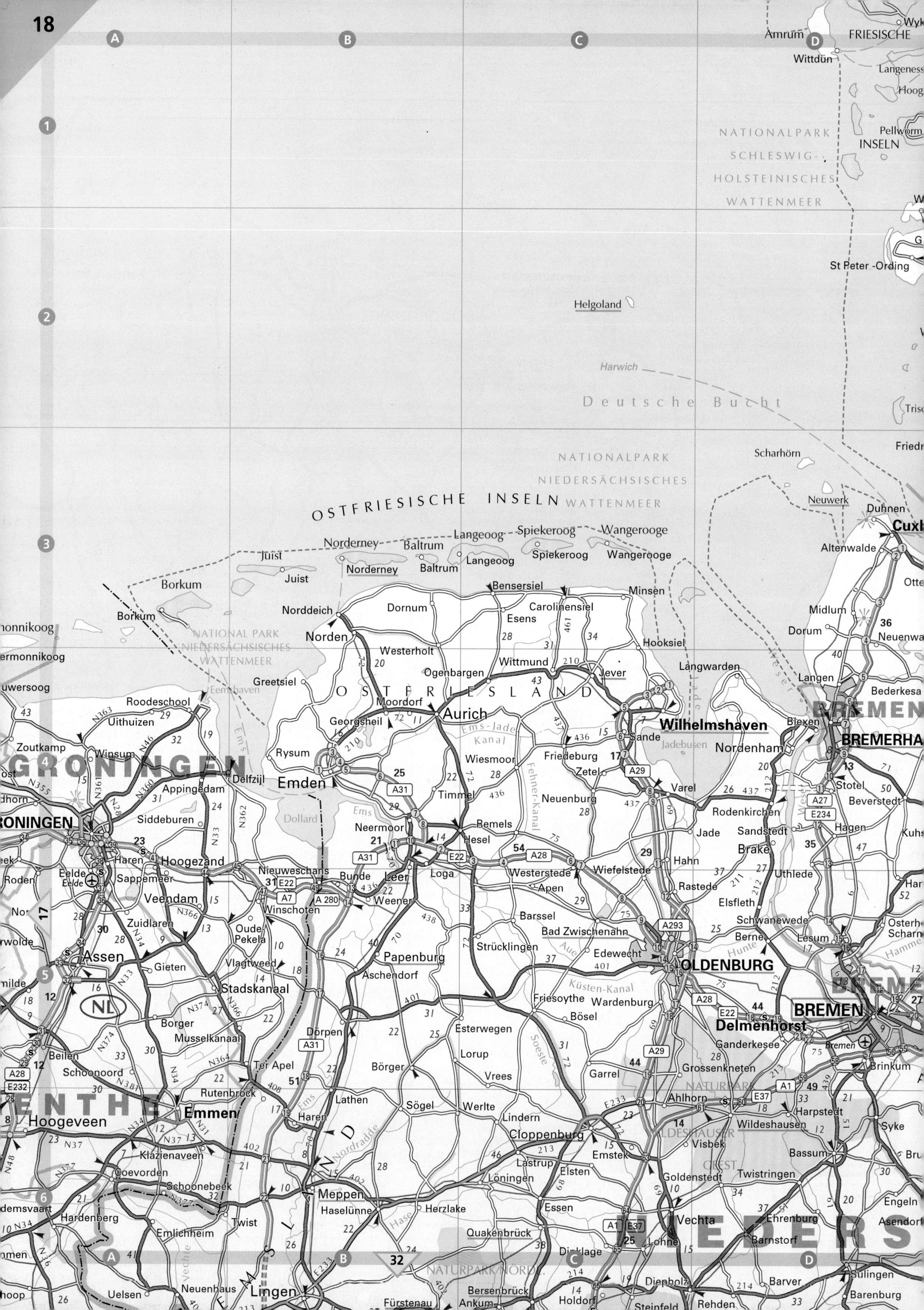
Amrum
Wittdün
FRIESISCHE
Langeness
Hoog
Pellworm
INSELN
NATIONALPARK
SCHLESWIG-
HOLSTEINISCHES
WATTENMEER
St Peter -Ording
Helgoland
Harwich
Deutsche Bucht
Scharhörn
NATIONALPARK
NIEDERSÄCHSISCHES
WATTENMEER
OSTFRIESISCHE INSELN
Neuwerk
Duhnen
Cuxh
Altenwalde
Borkum
Juist
Norderney
Baltrum
Langeoog
Spiekeroog
Wangerooge
Bensersiel
Carolinensiel
Minsen
Dornum
Esens
Norddeich
Norden
NATIONAL PARK
NIEDERSÄCHSISCHES
WATTENMEER
Westerholt
Ogenbargen
Wittmund
Jever
Hooksiel
Langwarden
Midlum
Dorum
Neuenwa
Langen
Bederkesa
Greetsiel
OSTFRIESLAND
Eemshaven
Moordorf
Aurich
Georgsheil
Wilhelmshaven
Blexen
BREMEN
BREMERHA
Roodeschool
Uithuizen
Rysum
Sande
Jadebusen
Nordenham
Zoutkamp
Winsum
GRONINGEN
Wiesmoor
Friedeburg
Zetel
Stotel
Beverstedt
Delfzijl
Emden
Appingedam
Dollard
Timmel
Neuenburg
Varel
Rodenkirchen
Siddeburen
Neermoor
Remels
Hesel
Jade
Sandstedt
Hagen
RONINGEN
Haren
Hoogezand
Sappemeer
Nieuweschans
Bunde
Leer
Loga
Westerstede
Wiefelstede
Hahn
Brake
Uthlede
Roden
Eelde
Weener
Apen
Rastede
Elsfleth
Veendam
Winschoten
Schwanewede
Zuidlaren
Oude Pekela
Barssel
Bad Zwischenahn
Berne
Lesum
Assen
Gieten
Vlagtweed
Papenburg
Strücklingen
Edewecht
OLDENBURG
Aschendorf
Stadskanaal
Küsten-Kanal
Friesoythe
Wardenburg
BREMEN
NL
Borger
Bösel
Delmenhorst
Musselkanaal
Dörpen
Esterwegen
Ganderkesee
Beilen
Lorup
Schoonoord
Ter Apel
Börger
Vrees
Garrel
Grossenkneten
Brinkum
Rutenbrock
Lathen
Sögel
Werlte
Ahlhorn
Harpstedt
Hoogeveen
Emmen
Haren
Lindern
Cloppenburg
Visbek
Wildeshausen
Syke
Klazienaveen
Emstek
Bassum
Coevorden
Lastrup
Elsten
Goldenstedt
Twistringen
Schoonebeek
Löningen
Meppen
Haselünne
Herzlake
Essen
Vechta
Ehrenburg
Engeln
Hardenberg
Twist
Emlichheim
Quakenbrück
Barnstorf
Asendorf
Dinklage
Lohne
NIEDERS
Uelsen
Neuenhaus
Lingen
Fürstenau
Bersenbrück
Ankum
Holdorf
Diepholz
Steinfeld
Rehden
Barver
Sulingen
Barenburg
NATURPARK NÖRD.
32

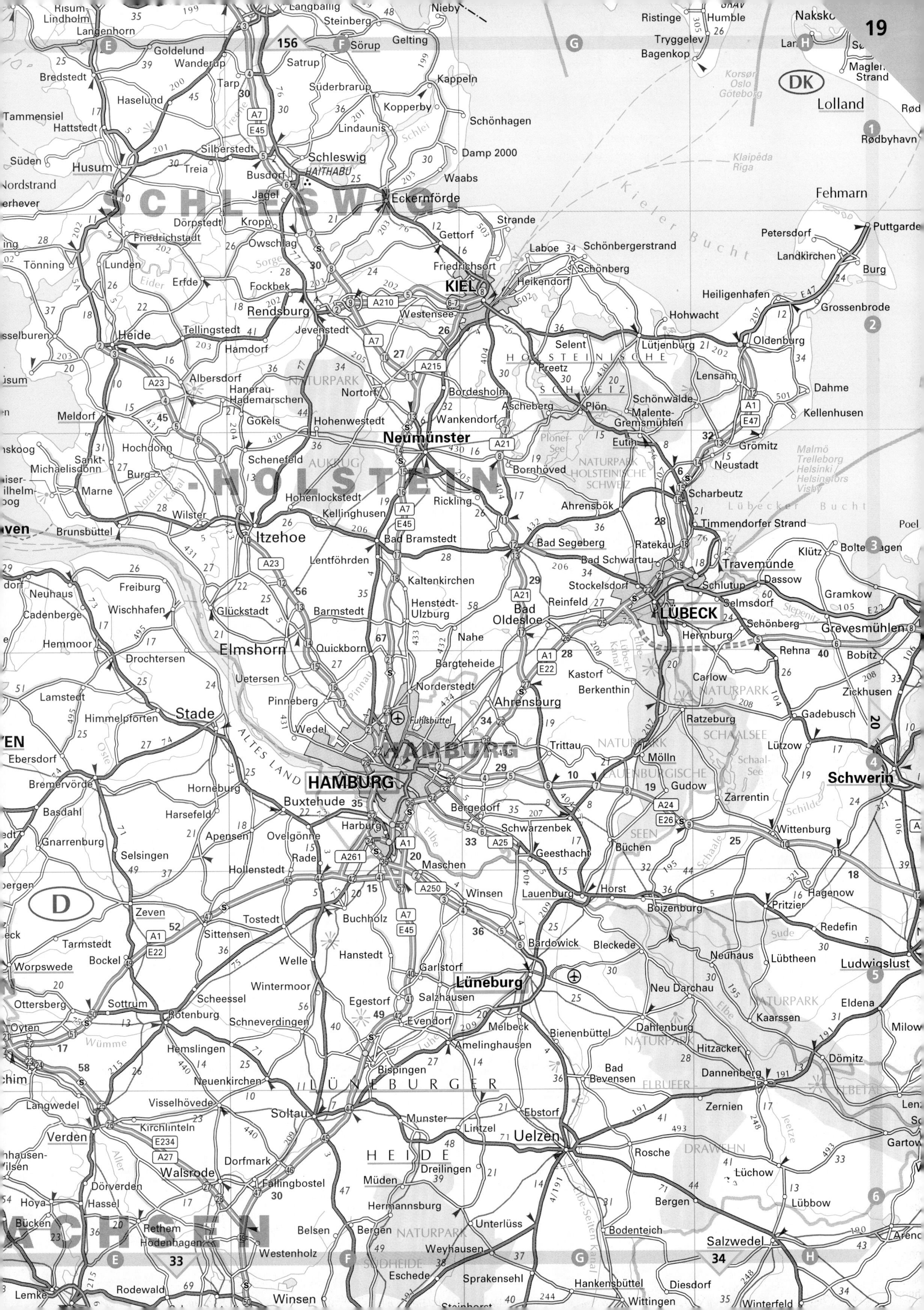
DK
D
Lolland
Fehmarn
Kieler Bucht
Lübecker Bucht
SCHLESWIG-HOLSTEIN
HOLSTEINISCHE SCHWEIZ
NATURPARK AUKRUG
NATURPARK HOLSTEINISCHE SCHWEIZ
NATURPARK LAUENBURGISCHE SEEN
SCHAALSEE
LÜNEBURGER HEIDE
NATURPARK SÜDHEIDE
NATURPARK ELBUFER-DRAWEHN
ALTES LAND
Risum-Lindholm
Langenhorn
Bredstedt
Tammensiel
Hattstedt
Süden
Husum
Nordstrand
Tönning
Heide
Meldorf
Marne
Brunsbüttel
Goldelund
Wanderup
Haselund
Tarp
Langballig
Steinberg
Sörup
Gelting
Nieby
Satrup
Süderbrarup
Kappeln
Kopperby
Schönhagen
Lindaunis
Schleswig
Haithabu
Silberstedt
Treia
Busdorf
Damp 2000
Waabs
Jagel
Eckernförde
Dörpstedt
Kropp
Friedrichstadt
Owschlag
Lunden
Erfde
Fockbek
Rendsburg
Tellingstedt
Hamdorf
Jevenstedt
Westensee
Kiel
Friedrichsort
Gettorf
Strande
Laboe
Schönberg
Schönbergerstrand
Heikendorf
Preetz
Selent
Lütjenburg
Hohwacht
Plön
Eutin
Malente-Gremsmühlen
Schönwalde
Oldenburg
Heiligenhafen
Grossenbrode
Burg
Puttgarden
Petersdorf
Landkirchen
Lensahn
Dahme
Kellenhusen
Grömitz
Neustadt
Scharbeutz
Timmendorfer Strand
Travemünde
Ratekau
Bad Schwartau
Lübeck
Schlutup
Dassow
Klütz
Boltenhagen
Gramkow
Selmsdorf
Schönberg
Herrnburg
Grevesmühlen
Rehna
Bobitz
Carlow
Gadebusch
Zickhusen
Schwerin
Lützow
Ratzeburg
Mölln
Gudow
Zarrentin
Wittenburg
Hagenow
Pritzier
Redefin
Ludwigslust
Lübtheen
Neuhaus
Boizenburg
Eldena
Dömitz
Dannenberg
Hitzacker
Dahlenburg
Neu Darchau
Kaarssen
Lüchow
Lübbow
Zernien
Gartow
Salzwedel
Winterfeld
Diesdorf
Wittingen
Hankensbüttel
Bodenteich
Rosche
Uelzen
Ebstorf
Bad Bevensen
Bienenbüttel
Lüneburg
Bardowick
Bleckede
Lauenburg
Horst
Geesthacht
Schwarzenbek
Büchen
Trittau
Ahrensburg
Bargteheide
Norderstedt
Hamburg
Fuhlsbüttel
Bergedorf
Harburg
Winsen
Maschen
Buchholz
Hanstedt
Garlstorf
Salzhausen
Egestorf
Evendorf
Melbeck
Amelinghausen
Bispingen
Munster
Lintzel
Soltau
Schneverdingen
Neuenkirchen
Visselhövede
Dorfmark
Fallingbostel
Walsrode
Kirchlinteln
Verden
Langwedel
Rotenburg
Sottrum
Ottersberg
Oyten
Hemslingen
Scheessel
Wintermoor
Welle
Tostedt
Sittensen
Zeven
Tarmstedt
Bockel
Worpswede
Selsingen
Hollenstedt
Rade
Ovelgönne
Apensen
Harsefeld
Buxtehude
Horneburg
Stade
Himmelpforten
Bremervörde
Basdahl
Gnarrenburg
Ebersdorf
Lamstedt
Hemmoor
Drochtersen
Cadenberge
Wischhafen
Freiburg
Neuhaus
Glückstadt
Elmshorn
Uetersen
Pinneberg
Wedel
Quickborn
Barmstedt
Henstedt-Ulzburg
Kaltenkirchen
Lentföhrden
Bad Bramstedt
Kellinghusen
Hohenlockstedt
Itzehoe
Wilster
Burg
Hochdonn
Schenefeld
Gokels
Hohenwestedt
Hanerau-Hademarschen
Albersdorf
Nortorf
Bordesholm
Wankendorf
Neumünster
Ascheberg
Bornhöved
Rickling
Bad Segeberg
Ahrensbök
Stockelsdorf
Reinfeld
Bad Oldesloe
Nahe
Kastorf
Berkenthin
Sankt-Michaelisdonn
Müden
Hermannsburg
Dreilingen
Unterlüss
Bergen
Belsen
Weyhausen
Eschede
Sprakensehl
Westenholz
Rethem
Hodenhagen
Hassel
Hoya
Dörverden
Bücken
Rodewald
Lemke
Winsen
Ristinge
Humble
Tryggelev
Bagenkop
Nakskov
Maglehem Strand
Rødbyhavn
Korsør
Oslo
Göteborg
Klaipėda
Riga
Malmö
Trelleborg
Helsinki
Helsingfors
Visby
156
33
34
20

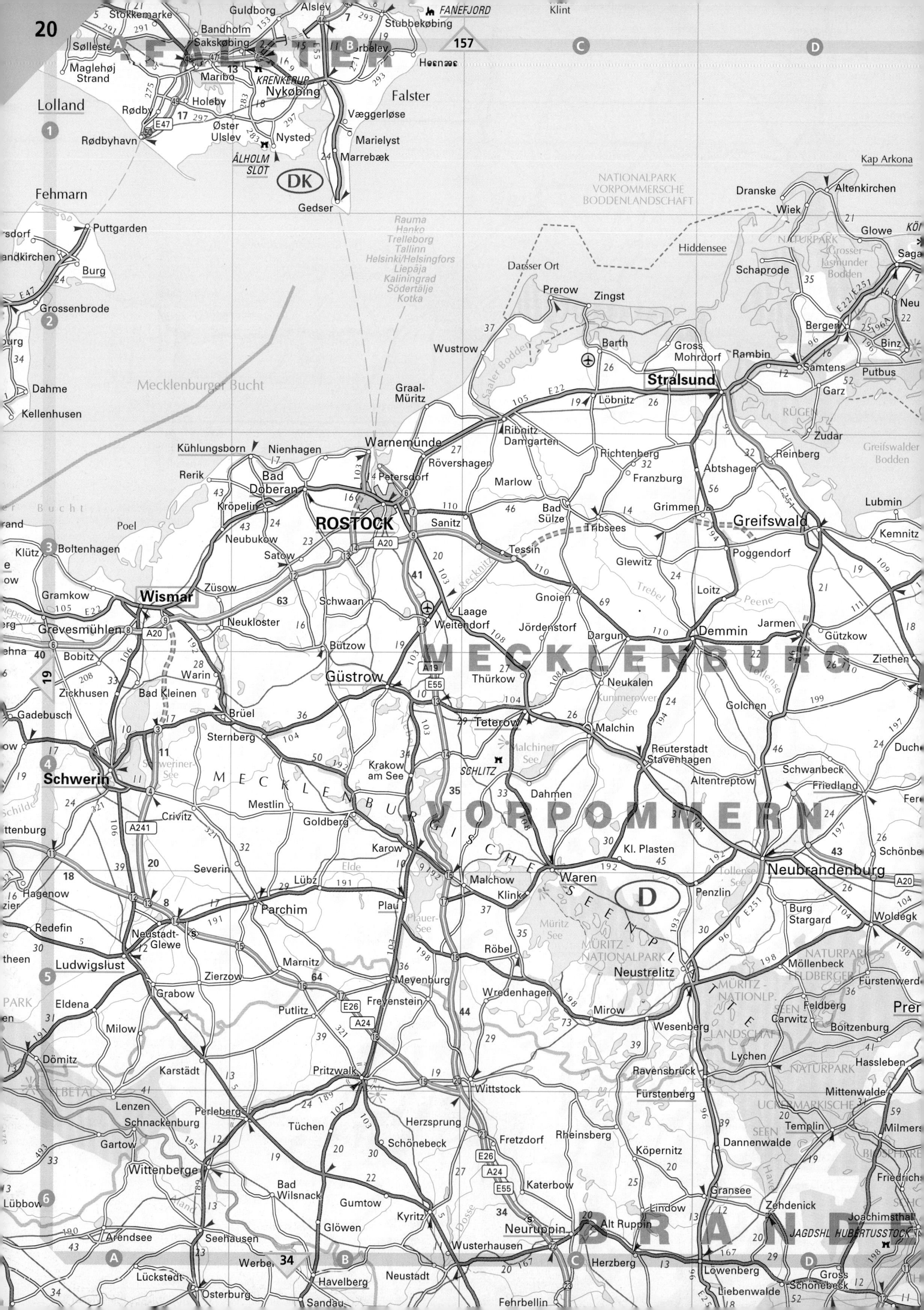
Stokkemarke
Guldborg
Alslev
FANEFJORD
Klint
Bandholm
Stubbekøbing
Sakskøbing
Sølleste
FALSTER
Orbelev
157
Maglehøj
Strand
Maribo
Hesnæs
KRENKERUP
Nykøbing
Lolland
Holeby
Falster
Rødby
Væggerløse
Øster
Ulslev
Rødbyhavn
Nysted
Marielyst
Marrebæk
ÅLHOLM
SLOT
DK
Fehmarn
Gedser
NATIONALPARK
VORPOMMERSCHE
BODDENLANDSCHAFT
Kap Arkona
Dranske
Altenkirchen
Wiek
Rauma
Hanko
Trelleborg
Tallinn
Helsinki/Helsingfors
Liepāja
Kaliningrad
Södertälje
Kotka
Puttgarden
Glowe
Hiddensee
Burg
Darsser Ort
Schaprode
Grossenbrode
Prerow
Zingst
Bergen
Binz
Wustrow
Barth
Gross
Mohrdorf
Rambin
Samtens
Putbus
Dahme
Mecklenburger Bucht
Graal-
Müritz
Stralsund
Garz
Löbnitz
Kellenhusen
RÜGEN
Ribnitz-
Damgarten
Zudar
Kühlungsborn
Nienhagen
Warnemünde
Rövershagen
Richtenberg
Reinberg
Greifswalder
Bodden
Rerik
Bad
Doberan
Petersdorf
Franzburg
Abtshagen
Marlow
Kröpelin
Bad
Sülze
Grimmen
Lubmin
ROSTOCK
Sanitz
Tribsees
Greifswald
Poel
Neubukow
Kemnitz
Boltenhagen
Satow
Tessin
Poggendorf
Klütz
Glewitz
Wismar
Zūsow
Schwaan
Gnoien
Loitz
Gramkow
Trebel
Peene
Laage
Weitendorf
Neukloster
Jarmen
Grevesmühlen
Jördenstorf
Dargun
Demmin
Gützkow
Bobitz
Bützow
Warin
MECKLENBURG
Ziethen
Güstrow
Thürkow
Neukalen
Zickhusen
Bad Kleinen
Kummerower
See
Gadebusch
Brüel
Teterow
Golchen
Sternberg
Malchin
Reuterstadt
Stavenhagen
Schweriner
See
Krakow
am See
Malchiner
See
Duch
Schwerin
SCHLITZ
Schwanbeck
MECKLENBURGISCHE
Altentreptow
Friedland
Mestlin
Dahmen
Crivitz
Goldberg
VORPOMMERN
Karow
Kl. Plasten
Neubrandenburg
Severin
Elde
Waren
Hagenow
Lübz
Malchow
Penzlin
Klink
D
Burg
Stargard
Parchim
Plau
Woldegk
Redefin
Plauer-
See
Müritz
See
SEENPLATTE
Neustadt-
Glewe
Röbel
MÜRITZ-
NATIONALPARK
NATURPARK
FELDBERGER
Möllenbeck
Ludwigslust
Neustrelitz
Marnitz
Zierzow
Fürstenwerder
Meyenburg
Grabow
Eldena
Wredenhagen
Feldberg
Freyenstein
Carwitz
Mirow
Putlitz
Milow
Wesenberg
Boitzenburg
Dömitz
Lychen
Hassleben
Karstädt
Pritzwalk
Ravensbrück
Wittstock
Fürstenberg
Mittenwalde
Lenzen
Schnackenburg
Perleberg
Herzsprung
Tüchen
Templin
Gartow
Fretzdorf
Rheinsberg
Schönebeck
Dannenwalde
Köpernitz
Wittenberge
Katerbow
Bad
Wilsnack
Gransee
Gumtow
Lübbow
Zehdenick
Lindow
Glöwen
Kyritz
Neuruppin
Alt Ruppin
Joachimsthal
Arendsee
Seehausen
JAGDSCHL. HUBERTUSSTOCK
BRANDE
Wusterhausen
Werben
Herzberg
Löwenberg
Lückstedt
Neustadt
Gross
Schönebeck
Havelberg
Liebenwalde
Osterburg
Sandau
Fehrbellin

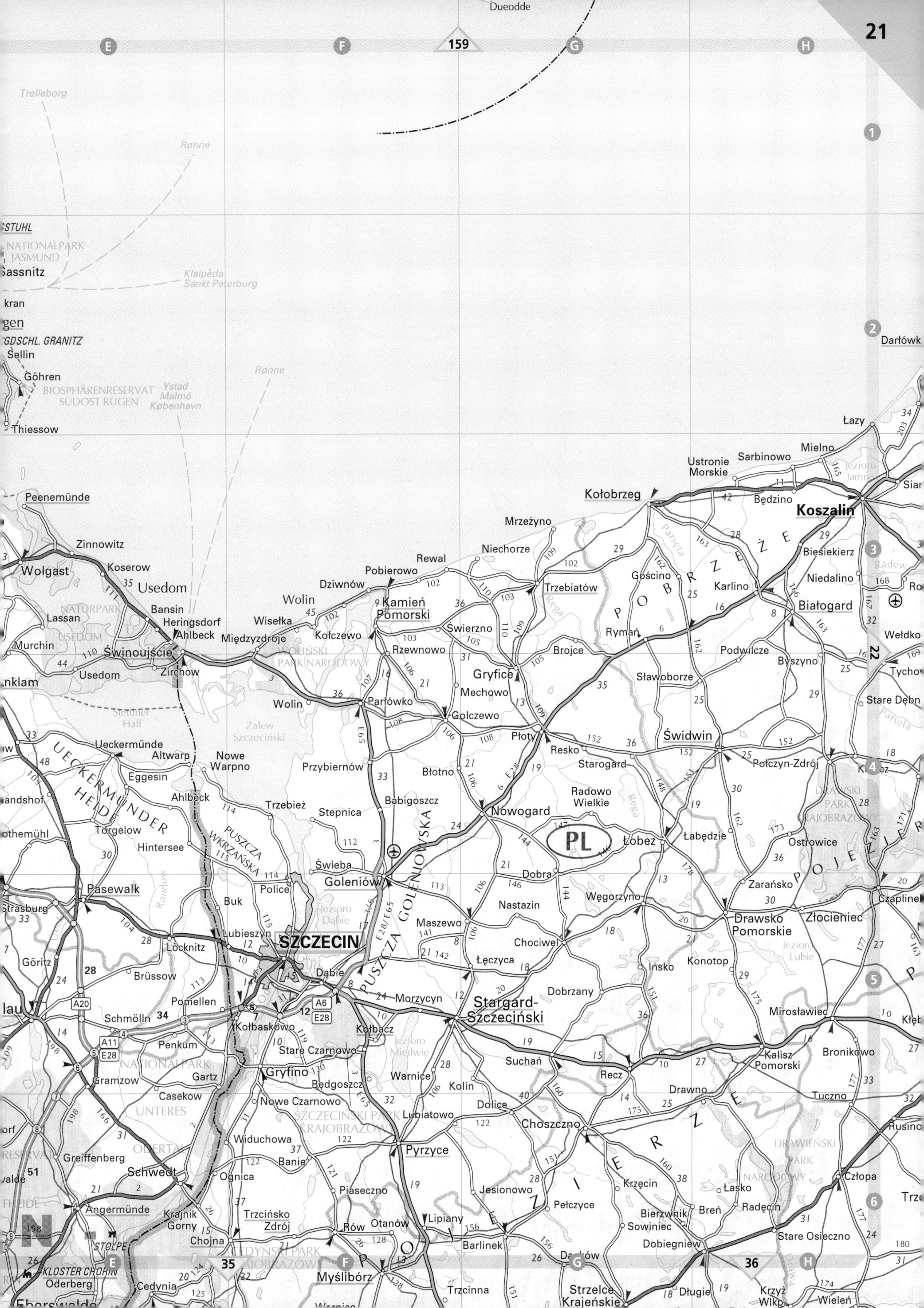
Dueodde
159
Trelleborg
Rønne
NATIONALPARK JASMUND
Sassnitz
Klaipėda
Sankt Peterburg
Sellin
Göhren
BIOSPHÄRENRESERVAT SÜDOST RÜGEN
Ystad
Malmö
København
Rønne
Thiessow
Darłówk
Łazy
Mielno
Sarbinowo
Ustronie Morskie
Kołobrzeg
Będzino
Koszalin
Peenemünde
Zinnowitz
Wolgast
Koserow
Usedom
Bansin
Heringsdorf
Ahlbeck
Lassan
NATURPARK USEDOM
Murchin
Świnoujście
Zirchow
Usedom
Anklam
Międzyzdroje
WOLIŃSKI PARK NARODOWY
Wisełka
Wolin
Dziwnów
Pobierowo
Rewal
Niechorze
Mrzeżyno
Trzebiatów
Kamień Pomorski
Kołczewo
Rzewnowo
Świerzno
Gryfice
Mechowo
Golczewo
Parłówko
Wolin
Stettiner Haff
Zalew Szczeciński
Ueckermünde
UECKERMÜNDER HEIDE
Altwarp
Nowe Warpno
Eggesin
Ahlbeck
Torgelow
Hintersee
PUSZCZA WKRZAŃSKA
Pasewalk
Strasburg
Przybiernów
Trzebież
Stepnica
Babigoszcz
Świeba
Police
Goleniów
PUSZCZA GOLENIOWSKA
Nowogard
Błotno
Płoty
Resko
Starogard
Radowo Wielkie
PL
Łobez
Dobra
Brojce
Rymań
Gościno
POBRZEŻE
Karlino
Białogard
Biesiekierz
Niedalino
Podwilcze
Sławoborze
Byszyno
Świdwin
Połczyn-Zdrój
Stare Dębno
Łabędzie
Ostrowice
Zarańsko
DRAWSKI PARK KRAJOBRAZOWY
Drawsko Pomorskie
Złocieniec
Czaplinek
Węgorzyno
Nastazin
Maszewo
Chociwel
Łęczyca
Ińsko
Konotop
Jezioro Lubie
Buk
Lubieszyn
Löcknitz
SZCZECIN
Dąbie
Jezioro Dąbie
Göritz
Brüssow
Pomellen
Schmölln
Kołbaskowo
Morzyczyn
Stargard-Szczeciński
Dobrzany
Kołbacz
Jezioro Miedwie
Mirosławiec
Kalisz Pomorski
Bronikowo
Penkum
Stare Czarnowo
NATIONALPARK UNTERES ODERTAL
Gartz
Gryfino
Warnice
Suchań
Recz
Gramzow
Casekow
Bedgoszcz
Nowe Czarnowo
SZCZECIŃSKI PARK KRAJOBRAZOWY
Kolin
Dolice
Lubiatowo
Choszczno
Drawno
Tuczno
Greiffenberg
Schwedt
Widuchowa
Banie
Pyrzyce
POJEZIERZE
Krzęcin
Łasko
DRAWIEŃSKI PARK NARODOWY
Człopa
Angermünde
Ognica
Piaseczno
Jesionowo
Pełczyce
Bierzwnik
Breń
Radęcin
Krajnik Górny
Chojna
Trzcińsko Zdrój
Rów
Otanów
Lipiany
Barlinek
Sowiniec
Dobiegniew
Stare Osieczno
STOLPE
KLOSTER CHORIN
Oderberg
Cedynia
Myślibórz
Trzcinna
Dąków
Strzelce Krajeńskie
Długie
Krzyż Wlkp.
Wieleń
35
36
22

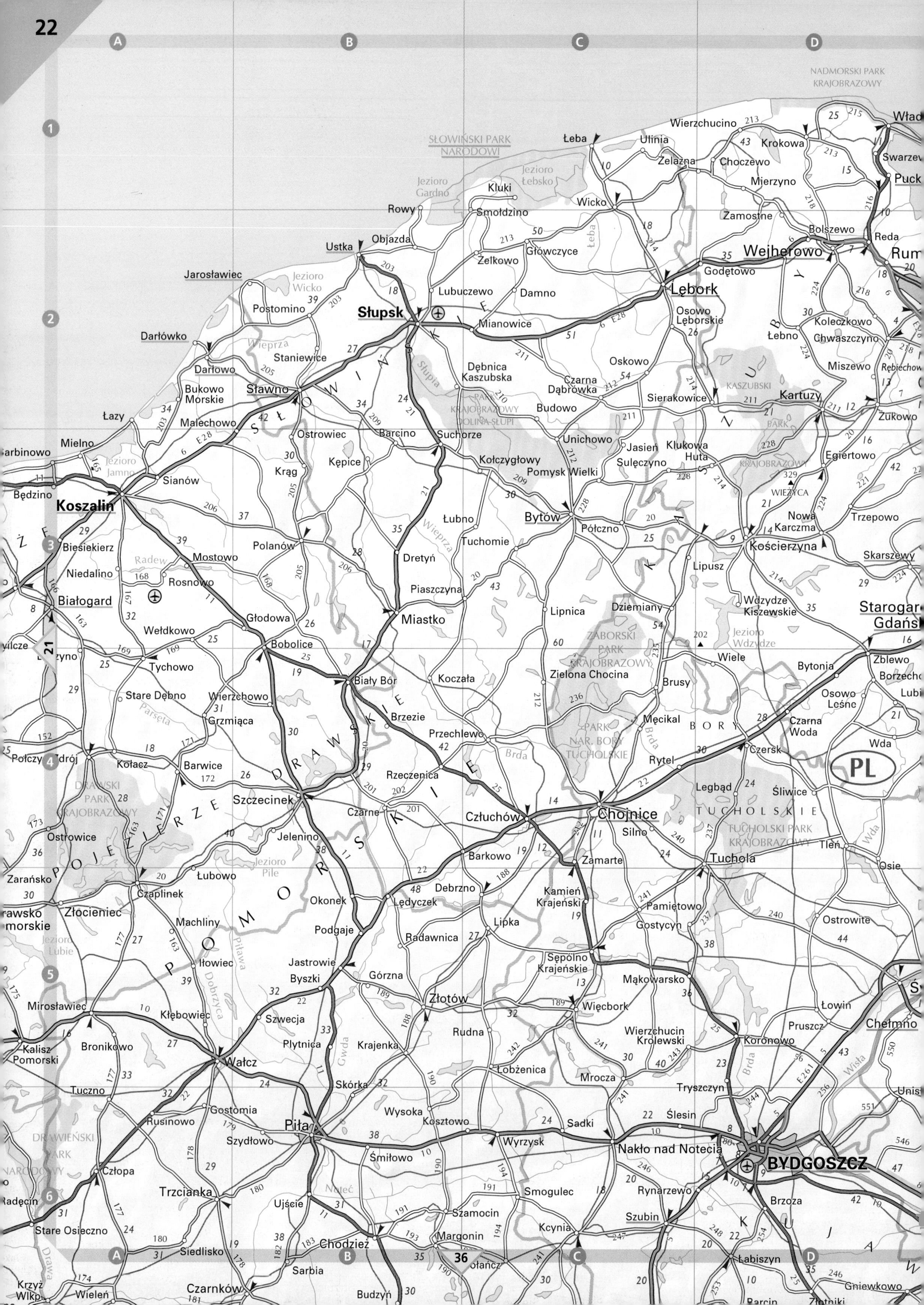

NADMORSKI PARK KRAJOBRAZOWY
SŁOWIŃSKI PARK NARODOWY
Jezioro Gardno
Jezioro Łebsko
Jezioro Wicko
Jezioro Jamno
Wierzchucino
Łeba
Ulinia
Żelazna
Choczewo
Krokowa
Władysławowo
Swarzewo
Puck
Mierzyno
Kluki
Rowy
Smołdzino
Wicko
Zamostne
Bolszewo
Reda
Rumia
Ustka
Objazda
Główczyce
Żelkowo
Wejherowo
Godętowo
Jarosławiec
Postomino
Słupsk
Lubuczewo
Damno
Lębork
Osowo Lęborskie
Koleczkowo
Chwaszczyno
Łebno
Darłówko
Darłowo
Staniewice
Mianowice
Oskowo
Miszewo
Rębiechowo
Dębnica Kaszubska
Czarna Dąbrówka
Sierakowice
Kartuzy
Bukowo Morskie
Sławno
Budowo
Żukowo
Łazy
Malechowo
PARK KRAJOBRAZOWY DOLINA SŁUPI
KASZUBSKI PARK KRAJOBRAZOWY
Ostrowiec
Barcino
Suchorze
Unichowo
Jasień
Klukowa Huta
Mielno
Kępice
Kołczygłowy
Sulęczyno
Egiertowo
Sarbinowo
Krąg
Pomysk Wielki
Będzino
Sianów
WIEŻYCA
Koszalin
Łubno
Bytów
Nowa Karczma
Trzepowo
Półczno
Biesiekierz
Polanów
Tuchomie
Kościerzyna
Skarszewy
Mostowo
Dretyń
Lipusz
Radew
Niedalino
Rosnowo
Piaszczyna
Starogard Gdański
Wdzydze Kiszewskie
Białogard
Miastko
Lipnica
Dziemiany
Głodowa
Jezioro Wdzydze
Wełdkowo
ZABORSKI PARK KRAJOBRAZOWY
Bobolice
Wiele
Bytonia
Zblewo
Borzechowo
Tychowo
Białe Bór
Koczała
Zielona Chocina
Brusy
Stare Dębno
Wierzchowo
Osowo Leśne
Lubichowo
Parsęta
Brzezie
Grzmiąca
Przechlewo
Męcikal
BORY TUCHOLSKIE
Czarna Woda
PARK NAR. BORY TUCHOLSKIE
Połczyn Zdrój
Kołacz
Barwice
Brda
Rytel
Czersk
Wda
DRAWSKI PARK KRAJOBRAZOWY
Rzeczenica
Legbąd
Śliwice
PL
Szczecinek
Czarne
Człuchów
Chojnice
TUCHOLSKI PARK KRAJOBRAZOWY
Ostrowice
Jelenino
Silno
Tleń
Zaraańsko
Lubowo
Jezioro Pile
Barkowo
Zamarte
Tuchola
Osie
Czaplinek
Debrzno
Kamień Krajeński
Drawsko Pomorskie
Złocieniec
Okonek
Lędyczek
Pamiętowo
Ostrowite
Machliny
Podgaje
Lipka
Gostycyn
Jezioro Lubie
Radawnica
Sępólno Krajeńskie
Iłowiec
Jastrowie
Piława
Dobrzyca
Byszki
Górzna
Mąkowarsko
Świecie
Mirosławiec
Złotów
Więcbork
Łowin
Kłębowiec
Szwecja
Rudna
Wierzchucin Królewski
Chełmno
Kalisz Pomorski
Bronikowo
Plytnica
Krajenka
Koronowo
Pruszcz
Wałcz
Łobżenica
Mrocza
Tuczno
Skórka
Tryszczyn
Gwda
Wisła
Gostomia
Wysoka
Kosztowo
Sadki
Ślesin
Unisław
Rusinowo
Piła
DRAWIEŃSKI PARK NARODOWY
Szydłowo
Wyrzysk
Nakło nad Notecią
Śmiłowo
BYDGOSZCZ
Człopa
Trzcianka
Noteć
Smogulec
Rynarzewo
Radęcin
Ujście
Szamocin
Brzoza
Stare Osieczno
Kcynia
Szubin
Margonin
Chodzież
Siedlisko
Łabiszyn
Drawa
Sarbia
Gołańcz
Krzyż Wlkp.
Wieleń
Czarnków
Budzyń
Barcin
Złotniki
Gniewkowo
POJEZIERZE DRAWSKIE
POJEZIERZE POMORSKIE
SŁOWIŃSKIE
KASZUBY
KUJAWY

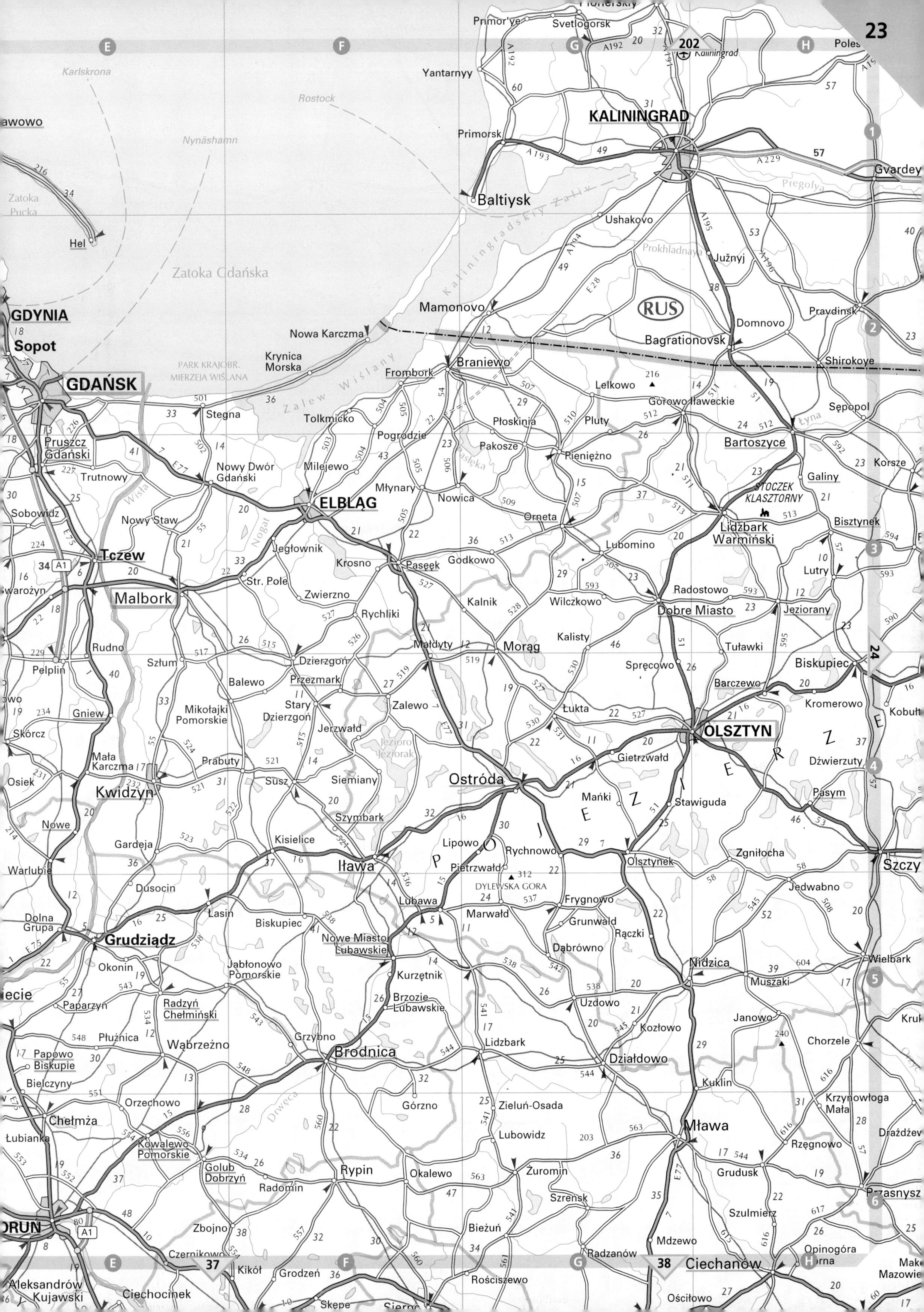
KALININGRAD
GDAŃSK
GDYNIA
Sopot
ELBLĄG
OLSZTYN
RUS
Baltiysk
Svetlogorsk
Primor'ye
Yantarnyy
Primorsk
Mamonovo
Bagrationovsk
Ushakovo
Južnyj
Domnovo
Pravdinsk
Shirokoye
Gvardey
Zatoka Gdańska
Zatoka Pucka
Hel
Nowa Karczma
Krynica Morska
Frombork
Braniewo
Tolkmicko
Pogrodzie
Milejewo
Młynary
Nowica
Orneta
Pieniężno
Płoskinia
Pakosze
Lelkowo
Górowo Iławeckie
Pluty
Bartoszyce
Sępopol
Korsze
Galiny
STOCZEK KLASZTORNY
Lidzbark Warmiński
Bisztynek
Lutry
Jeziorany
Dobre Miasto
Radostowo
Lubomino
Wilczkowo
Kalisty
Tuławki
Biskupiec
Barczewo
Kromerowo
Spręcowo
Łukta
Gietrzwałd
Dźwierzuty
Pasym
Stawiguda
Mańki
Olsztynek
Zgniłocha
Jedwabno
Szczy
Wielbark
Muszaki
Nidzica
Janowo
Chorzele
Krzynowłoga Mała
Rzęgnowo
Przasnysz
Grudusk
Szulmierz
Opinogóra Górna
Ciechanów
Mława
Kuklin
Działdowo
Kozłowo
Uzdowo
Dąbrówno
Rączki
Grunwald
Frygnowo
Marwałd
DYLEWSKA GÓRA
Rychnowo
Pietrzwałd
Lipowo
Ostróda
Morąg
Kalnik
Godkowo
Pasęek
Krosno
Jegłowik
Str. Pole
Zwierzno
Rychliki
Małdyty
Dzierzgoń
Przezmark
Stary Dzierzgoń
Zalewo
Jerzwałd
Jezioro Jeziorak
Siemiany
Susz
Szymbark
Kisielice
Iława
Lubawa
Nowe Miasto Lubawskie
Kurzętnik
Brzozie Lubawskie
Lidzbark
Brodnica
Górzno
Zieluń-Osada
Lubowidz
Żuromin
Szreńsk
Bieżuń
Radzanów
Mdzewo
Rościszewo
Ościłowo
Okalewo
Rypin
Radomin
Golub Dobrzyń
Zbojno
Czernikowo
Kikół
Grodzeń
Skępe
Ciechocinek
Aleksandrów Kujawski
TORUŃ
Kowalewo Pomorskie
Chełmża
Łubianka
Orzechowo
Bielczyny
Papowo Biskupie
Płużnica
Wąbrzeźno
Grzybno
Radzyń Chełmiński
Paparzyn
Jabłonowo Pomorskie
Okonin
Grudziądz
Biskupiec
Lasin
Dusocin
Gardeja
Dolna Grupa
Warlubie
Nowe
Kwidzyn
Mała Karczma
Osiek
Prabuty
Mikołajki Pomorskie
Balewo
Szłum
Skórcz
Gniew
Pelplin
Rudno
Malbork
Tczew
Nowy Staw
Nowy Dwór Gdański
Stegna
Pruszcz Gdański
Trutnowy
Sobowidz
Swarożyn
PARK KRAJOBR. MIERZEJA WIŚLANA
Zalew Wiślany
Kaliningradskiy Zaliv
Pregolya
Prokhladnaya
Łyna
Wisła
Nogat
Drwęca
Karlskrona
Rostock
Nynäshamn
POJEZIERZE
E
F
G
H
202
37
38
24

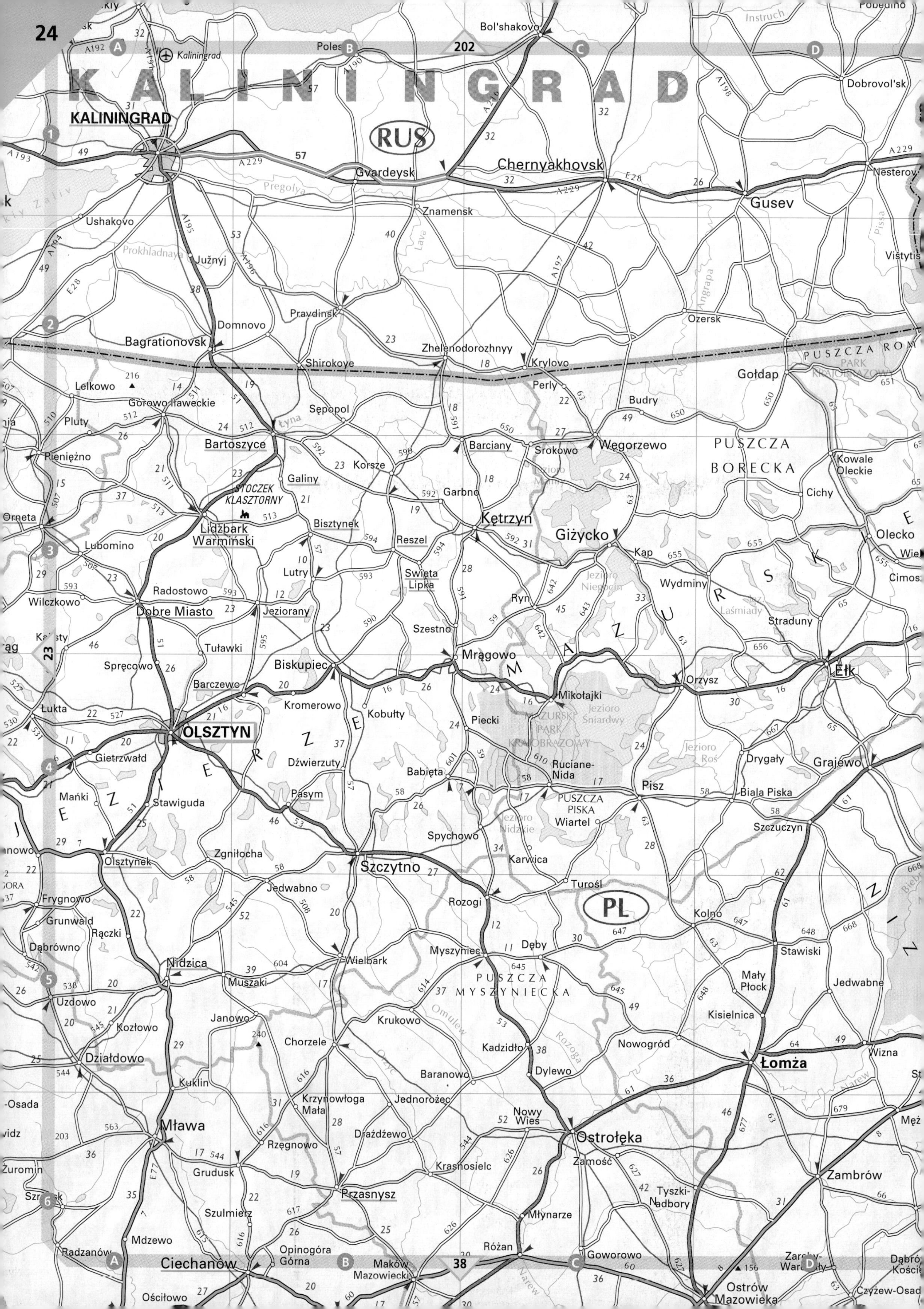
KALININGRAD
RUS
PL
KALININGRAD
Kaliningrad
Bol'shakovo
Polessk
Instruch
Dobrovol'sk
Gvardeysk
Chernyakhovsk
Nesterov
Gusev
Znamensk
Pregolya
Ushakovo
Prokhladnaya
Južnyj
Pravdinsk
Ozersk
Vištytis
Domnovo
Bagrationovsk
Shirokoye
Zhelenodorozhnyy
Krylovo
PUSZCZA ROMINCKA
PARK KRAJOBRAZOWY
Gołdap
Lelkowo
Górowo Iławeckie
Sępopol
Perły
Budry
Pluty
Bartoszyce
Barciany
Srokowo
Węgorzewo
PUSZCZA BORECKA
Pieniężno
Korsze
Galiny
Kowale Oleckie
STOCZEK KLASZTORNY
Garbno
Cichy
Orneta
Lidzbark Warmiński
Bisztynek
Kętrzyn
Giżycko
Olecko
Lubomino
Reszel
Kap
Lutry
Święta Lipka
Wydminy
Radostowo
Jezioro Niegocin
Wilczkowo
Dobre Miasto
Jeziorany
Ryn
Jezioro Łaśmiady
Straduny
Szestno
Tuławki
Mrągowo
MAZURSKIE
Biskupiec
Spręcowo
Orzysz
Ełk
Barczewo
Mikołajki
Kromerowo
Kobułty
Łukta
OLSZTYN
Piecki
MAZURSKI PARK KRAJOBRAZOWY
Jezioro Śniardwy
Gietrzwałd
Jezioro Roś
Drygały
Dźwierzuty
Babięta
Ruciane-Nida
Grajewo
Pasym
Pisz
Biała Piska
Mańki
Stawiguda
PUSZCZA PISKA
Wiartel
Jezioro Nidzkie
Spychowo
Szczuczyn
Zgniłocha
Karwica
Olsztynek
Szczytno
Jedwabno
Turośl
Frygnowo
Rozogi
Grunwald
Kolno
Rączki
Dąbrówno
Myszyniec
Dęby
Stawiski
Nidzica
Wielbark
Muszaki
PUSZCZA MYSZYNIECKA
Mały Płock
Jedwabne
Uzdowo
Kozłowo
Janowo
Kisielnica
Krukowo
Omulew
Działdowo
Chorzele
Kadzidło
Nowogród
Łomża
Wizna
Kuklin
Dylewo
Baranowo
Rozoga
Krzynowłoga Mała
Jednorożec
Narew
Mława
Nowy Wieś
Ostrołęka
Drążdżewo
Rzęgnowo
Żuromin
Grudusk
Krasnosielc
Zamość
Zambrów
Przasnysz
Tyszki-Nadbory
Szulmierz
Młynarze
Mdzewo
Opinogóra Górna
Różan
Radzanów
Ciechanów
Maków Mazowiecki
Goworowo
Ostrów Mazowiecka
Ościsłowo
Czyżew-Osada
202
38
23

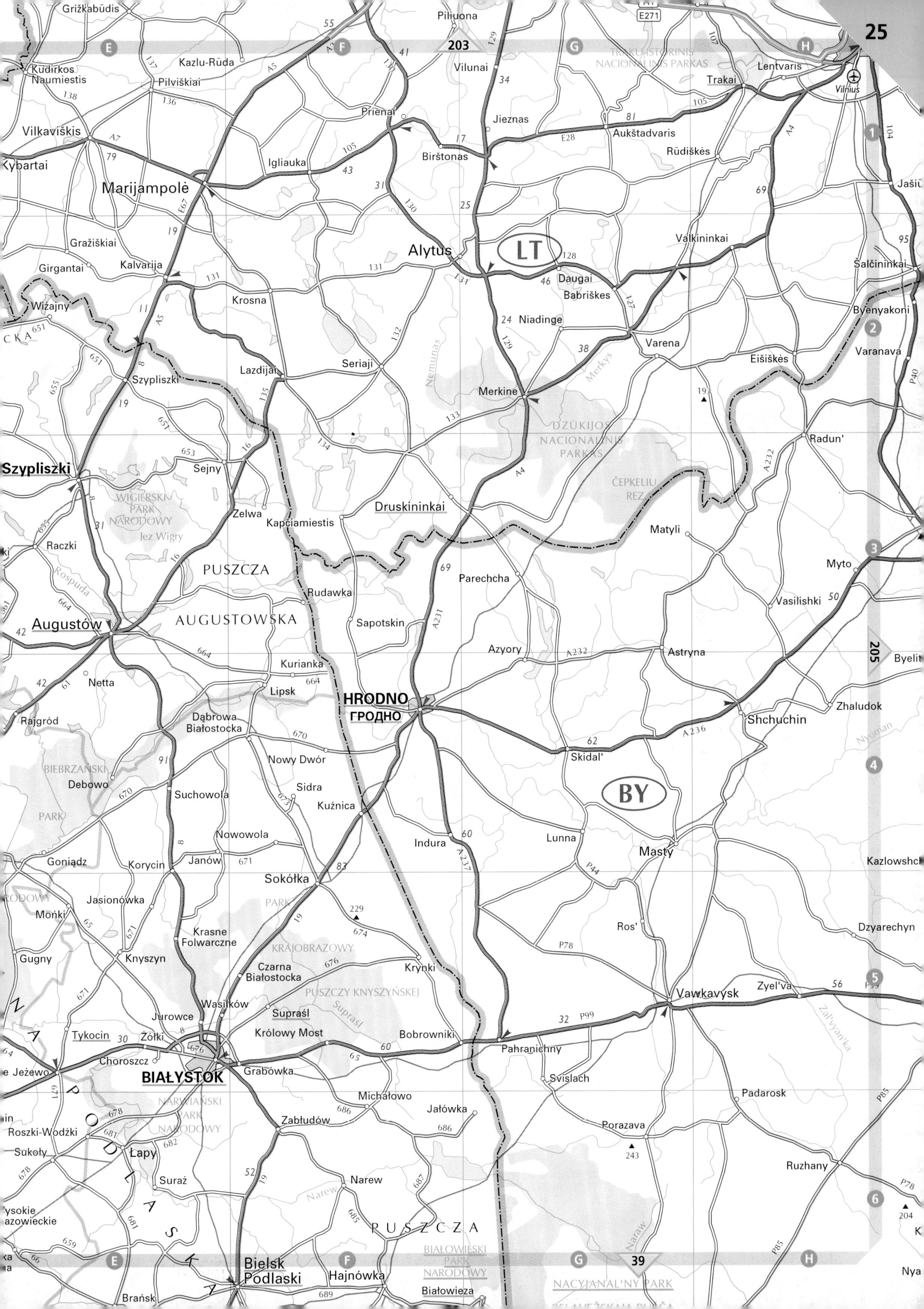
Griżkabūdis
Piliuona
E271
203
Vilunai
Kudirkos Naumiestis
Kazlu-Rūda
Pilviškiai
TRAKU ISTORINIS NACIONALINIS PARKAS
Lentvaris
Trakai
Vilnius
Prienai
Jieznas
Vilkaviškis
Aukštadvaris
Rūdiškės
Kybartai
Igliauka
Birštonas
Marijampolė
Jašiū
Grąžiškiai
Alytus
LT
Valkininkai
Girgantai
Kalvarija
Daugai
Šalčininkai
Babriškes
Wiżajny
Krosna
Niadinge
Byenyakoni
Varena
Eišiškės
Varanava
Lazdijai
Seriaji
Szypliszki
Merkine
Nemunas
Merkys
DZŪKIJOS NACIONALINIS PARKAS
Radun'
Szypliszki
Sejny
WIGIERSKI PARK NARODOWY
Jez Wigry
ČEPKELIU REZ.
Zelwa
Kapčiamiestis
Druskininkai
Matyli
Raczki
PUSZCZA
Myto
Rospuda
Parechcha
Rudawka
AUGUSTOWSKA
Vasilishki
Augustów
Sapotskin
205
Byelit
Azyory
Astryna
Kurianka
Netta
Lipsk
HRODNO
ГРОДНО
Zhaludok
Rajgród
Dąbrowa Białostocka
Shchuchin
Nyoman
Skidal'
Nowy Dwór
BIEBRZAŃSKI PARK
Debowo
BY
Suchowola
Sidra
Kuźnica
Nowowola
Lunna
Indura
Masty
Goniądz
Korycin
Janów
Kazlowshc
Sokółka
Jasionówka
Mońki
Ros'
Dzyarechyn
Krasne Folwarczne
KRAJOBRAZOWY
Gugny
Knyszyn
Czarna Białostocka
Krynki
Vawkavysk
Zyel'va
PUSZCZY KNYSZYŃSKIEJ
Wasilków
Supraśl
Jurowce
Tykocin
Żółki
Królowy Most
Bobrowniki
Pahranichny
Zal'vyanka
Choroszcz
Jeżewo
BIAŁYSTOK
Grabówka
Svislach
NARWIAŃSKI PARK NARODOWY
Michałowo
Padarosk
Jałówka
Zabłudów
Roszki-Wodźki
Porazava
Sukoły
Łapy
Ruzhany
Suraż
Narew
Wysokie Mazowieckie
PUSZCZA
Naraw
BIAŁOWIESKI PARK NARODOWY
Bielsk Podlaski
Hajnówka
39
NACYJANAL'NY PARK
Nya
Brańsk
Białowieza
PODLASKA

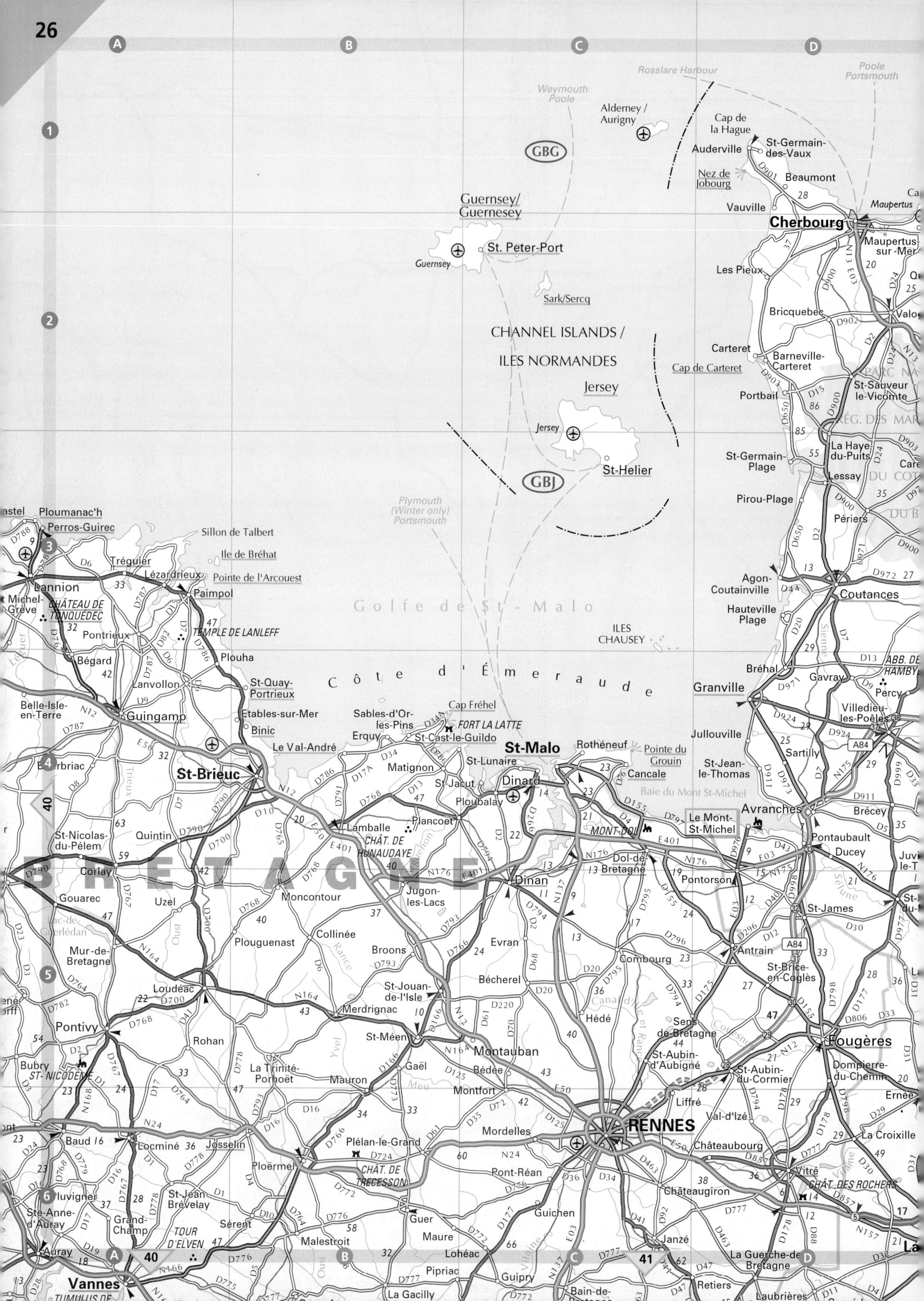
A
B
C
D
1
2
3
4
5
6
40
41
Rosslare Harbour
Poole Portsmouth
Weymouth Poole
Alderney / Aurigny
GBG
Cap de la Hague
Auderville
St-Germain-des-Vaux
Nez de Jobourg
Beaumont
Vauville
Cherbourg
Maupertus
Maupertus-sur-Mer
Guernsey/ Guernesey
St. Peter-Port
Guernsey
Sark/Sercq
CHANNEL ISLANDS / ILES NORMANDES
Jersey
St-Helier
GBJ
Les Pieux
Bricquebec
Valognes
Carteret
Barneville-Carteret
Cap de Carteret
Portbail
St-Sauveur le-Vicomte
La Haye-du-Puits
St-Germain-Plage
Lessay
Pirou-Plage
Périers
Plymouth (Winter only) Portsmouth
Ploumanac'h
Perros-Guirec
Sillon de Talbert
Ile de Bréhat
Tréguier
Lézardrieux
Pointe de l'Arcouest
Lannion
Paimpol
CHÂTEAU DE TONQUÉDEC
TEMPLE DE LANLEFF
Pontrieux
Golfe de St-Malo
Agon-Coutainville
Coutances
Hauteville Plage
ILES CHAUSEY
Bégard
Plouha
St-Quay-Portrieux
Côte d'Émeraude
Bréhal
Gavray
Granville
Percy
ABB. DE HAMBYE
Villedieu-les-Poêles
Belle-Isle-en-Terre
Guingamp
Etables-sur-Mer
Binic
Sables-d'Or-les-Pins
Cap Fréhel
FORT LA LATTE
Erquy
St-Cast-le-Guildo
Le Val-André
St-Malo
Rothéneuf
Pointe du Grouin
Jullouville
Sartilly
St-Brieuc
Matignon
St-Lunaire
Dinard
Cancale
St-Jean-le-Thomas
St-Jacut
Ploubalay
Baie du Mont St-Michel
Avranches
Brécey
Lamballe
CHÂT. DE HUNAUDAYE
Plancoët
MONT-DOL
Le Mont-St-Michel
Pontaubault
Quintin
St-Nicolas-du-Pélem
Corlay
BRETAGNE
Dinan
Dol-de-Bretagne
Pontorson
Ducey
St-James
Gouarec
Uzel
Moncontour
Jugon-les-Lacs
Collinée
Plouguenast
Broons
Evran
Combourg
Antrain
St-Brice-en-Coglès
Mur-de-Bretagne
Loudéac
St-Jouan-de-l'Isle
Bécherel
Hédé
Merdrignac
Sens-de-Bretagne
Pontivy
Rohan
St-Méen
Montauban
Fougères
St-Aubin-d'Aubigné
St-Aubin-du-Cormier
Dompierre-du-Chemin
Bubry
ST-NICODÈME
La Trinité-Porhoët
Gaël
Mauron
Bédée
Montfort
Liffré
Ernée
Val-d'Izé
RENNES
Baud
Locminé
Josselin
Plélan-le-Grand
Mordelles
Châteaubourg
La Croixille
Ploërmel
CHÂT. DE TRECESSON
Pont-Réan
Vitré
CHÂT. DES ROCHERS
Pluvigner
St-Jean-Brévelay
Châteaugiron
Ste-Anne-d'Auray
Grand-Champ
Guer
Guichen
Sérent
TOUR D'ELVEN
Malestroit
Maure
Janzé
Auray
Lohéac
La Guerche-de-Bretagne
Vannes
Pipriac
Guipry
Retiers
La Gacilly
Bain-de-
Laubrières

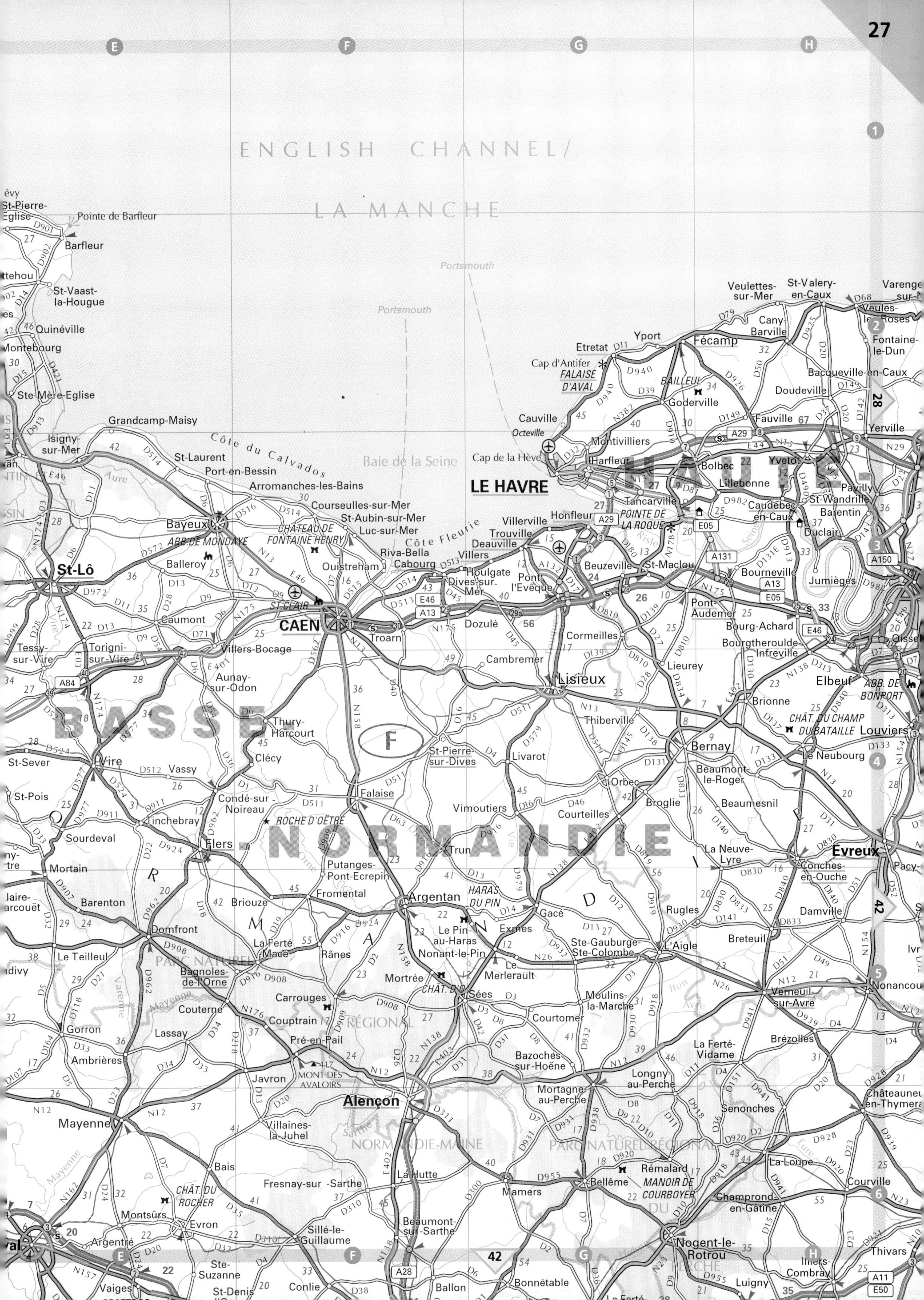

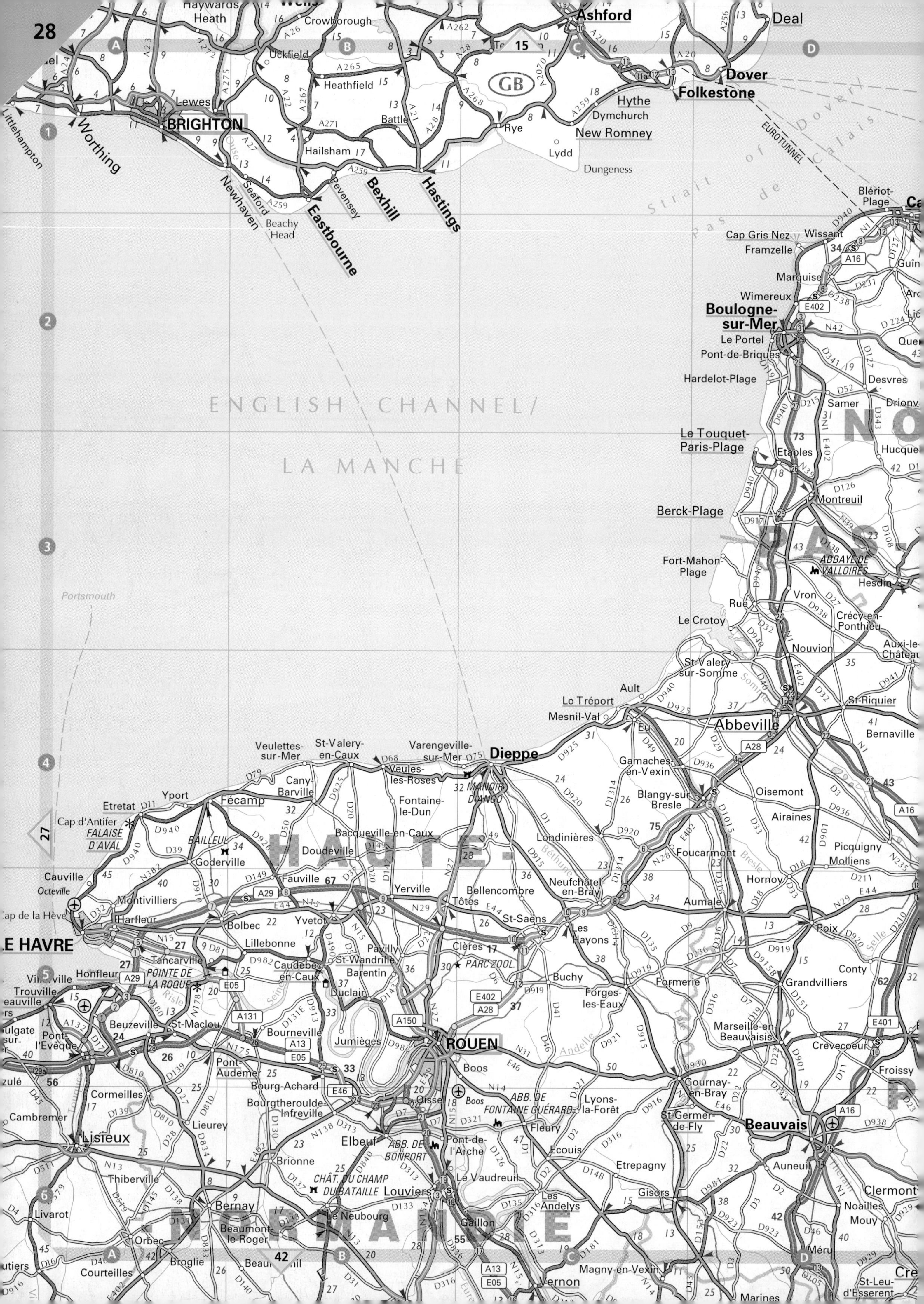
GB
ENGLISH CHANNEL/
LA MANCHE
Strait of Dover/Pas de Calais
EUROTUNNEL
HAUTE-
NORMANDIE
Haywards Heath
Crowborough
Ashford
Deal
Uckfield
Heathfield
Lewes
BRIGHTON
Worthing
Littlehampton
Battle
Rye
Hythe
Dymchurch
New Romney
Lydd
Dungeness
Dover
Folkestone
Hailsham
Bexhill
Hastings
Pevensey
Eastbourne
Newhaven
Seaford
Beachy Head
Portsmouth
Blériot-Plage
Cap Gris Nez
Wissant
Framzelle
Marquise
Wimereux
Boulogne-sur-Mer
Le Portel
Pont-de-Briques
Hardelot-Plage
Desvres
Samer
Le Touquet-Paris-Plage
Etaples
Hucqueliers
Montreuil
Berck-Plage
Fort-Mahon-Plage
ABBAYE DE VALLOIRES
Hesdin
Rue
Vron
Le Crotoy
Crécy-en-Ponthieu
Nouvion
Auxi-le-Château
St-Valery-sur-Somme
Ault
Le Tréport
Mesnil-Val
Eu
Abbeville
St-Riquier
Bernaville
Dieppe
Varengeville-sur-Mer
Veulettes-sur-Mer
St-Valery-en-Caux
Veules-les-Roses
MANOIR D'ANGO
Cany-Barville
Fontaine-le-Dun
Gamaches-en-Vexin
Blangy-sur-Bresle
Oisemont
Airaines
Yport
Fécamp
Etretat
Cap d'Antifer
FALAISE D'AVAL
BAILLEUL
Goderville
Bacqueville-en-Caux
Doudeville
Londinières
Foucarmont
Picquigny
Molliens
Cauville
Octeville
Montivilliers
Fauville
Yerville
Bellencombre
Neufchâtel-en-Bray
Hornoy
Aumale
Cap de la Hève
Harfleur
Bolbec
Yvetot
Tôtes
St-Saëns
Les Hayons
Poix
LE HAVRE
Tancarville
Lillebonne
Pavilly
Clères
POINTE DE LA ROQUE
Caudebec-en-Caux
St-Wandrille
Barentin
PARC ZOOL.
Conty
Honfleur
Trouville
Deauville
Duclair
Buchy
Formerie
Grandvilliers
Forges-les-Eaux
Beuzeville
St-Maclou
Pont-l'Evêque
Bourneville
Jumièges
ROUEN
Marseille-en-Beauvaisis
Crevecoeur
Pont-Audemer
Boos
Froissy
Bourg-Achard
Cormeilles
Bourgtheroulde-Infreville
Oissel
ABB. DE FONTAINE GUÉRARD
Lyons-la-Forêt
Gournay-en-Bray
St-Germer-de-Fly
Beauvais
Cambremer
Lisieux
Lieurey
Elbeuf
ABB. DE BONPORT
Pont-de-l'Arche
Fleury
Ecouis
Etrepagny
Brionne
Auneuil
Thiberville
CHÂT. DU CHAMP DU BATAILLE
Louviers
Le Vaudreuil
Gisors
Clermont
Livarot
Bernay
Les Andelys
Noailles
Mouy
Le Neubourg
Gaillon
Orbec
Beaumont-le-Roger
Méru
Broglie
Courteilles
Magny-en-Vexin
Vernon
St-Leu-d'Esserent
Marines
Beaumesnil

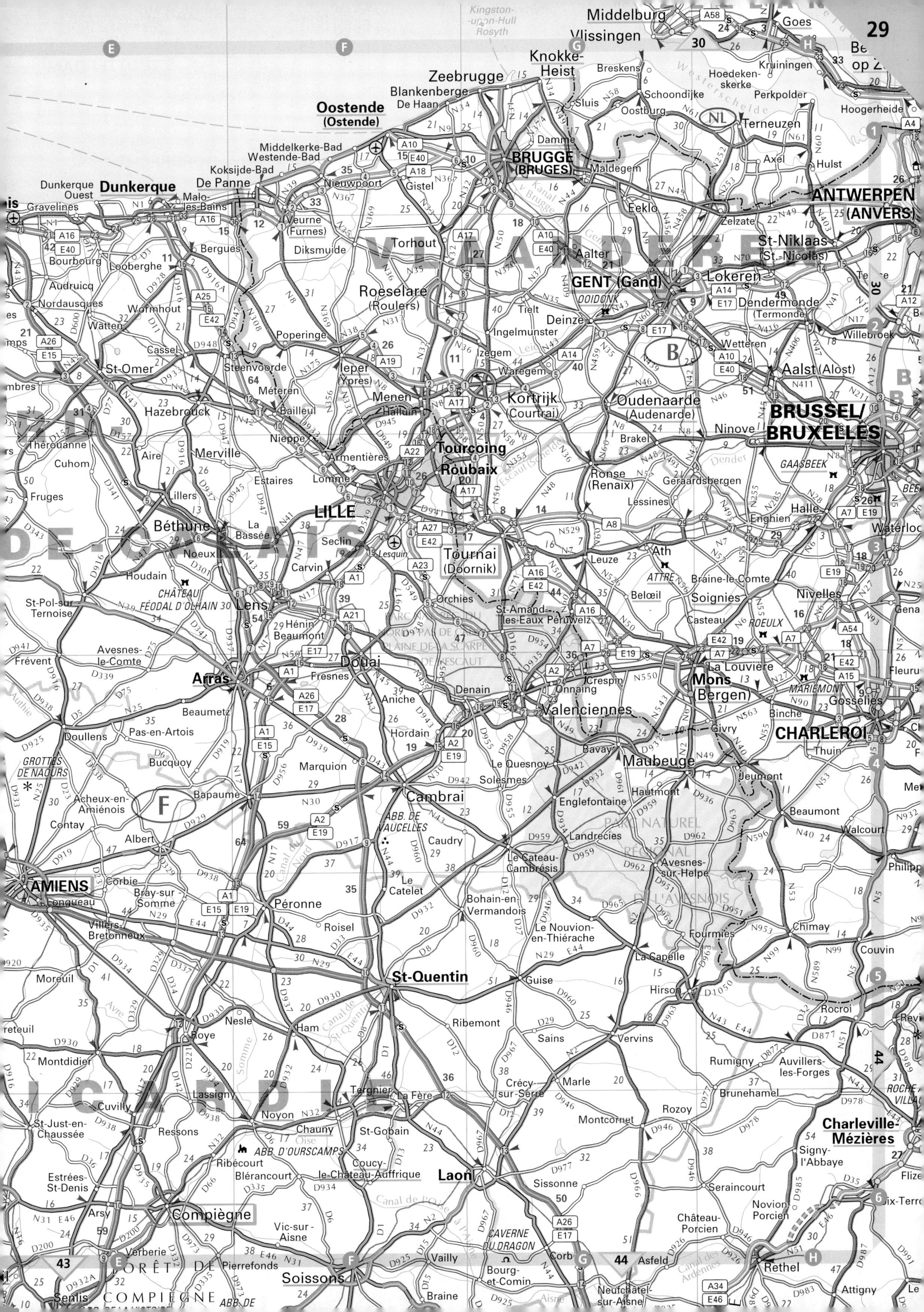
Middelburg
Vlissingen
Goes
Knokke-Heist
Zeebrugge
Blankenberge
De Haan
Oostende
(Ostende)
Breskens
Schoondijke
Oostburg
Sluis
NL
Terneuzen
Hoedekenskerke
Kruiningen
Perkpolder
Hoogerheide
Middelkerke-Bad
Westende-Bad
Koksijde-Bad
De Panne
Nieuwpoort
Gistel
Damme
BRUGGE
(BRUGES)
Maldegem
Axel
Hulst
ANTWERPEN
(ANVERS)
Dunkerque Ouest
Dunkerque
Malo-les-Bains
Gravelines
Veurne
(Furnes)
Eeklo
Zelzate
St-Niklaas
(St-Nicolas)
Bergues
Bourbourg
Looberghe
Diksmuide
Torhout
Aalter
VLAANDEREN
GENT (Gand)
Lokeren
Audruicq
Nordausques
Wormhout
Watten
Roeselare
(Roulers)
Tielt
Deinze
Dendermonde
(Termonde)
Willebroek
Cassel
Poperinge
Ingelmunster
Izegem
Wetteren
St-Omer
Steenvoorde
Ieper
(Ypres)
Waregem
Aalst (Alost)
Meteren
Menen
Kortrijk
(Courtrai)
Oudenaarde
(Audenarde)
Hazebrouck
Bailleul
Halluin
BRUSSEL/
BRUXELLES
Ninove
Thérouanne
Nieppe
Tourcoing
Brakel
Cuhom
Aire
Merville
Armentières
Roubaix
GAASBEEK
Lomme
Estaires
Ronse
(Renaix)
Geraardsbergen
Fruges
Lillers
LILLE
Lessines
Enghien
Halle
Waterloo
Béthune
La Bassée
Seclin
Lesquin
Tournai
(Doornik)
Leuze
Ath
Noeux
Houdain
CHÂTEAU
FÉODAL D'OLHAIN
Carvin
ATTRE
Braine-le-Comte
Nivelles
Beloeil
Soignies
St-Pol-sur-Ternoise
Lens
Orchies
St-Amand-les-Eaux
Péruwelz
Hénin
Beaumont
ROEULX
Casteau
Avesnes-le-Comte
Frévent
Arras
Douai
Fresnes
Crespin
La Louvière
Mons
(Bergen)
MARIEMONT
Gosselies
Denain
Onnaing
Valenciennes
Binche
Beaumetz
Aniche
Doullens
Pas-en-Artois
Hordain
Givry
CHARLEROI
Thuin
Bavay
GROTTES
DE NAOURS
Bucquoy
Marquion
Le Quesnoy
Maubeuge
Jeumont
Solesmes
Acheux-en-Amiénois
Bapaume
Cambrai
Hautmont
Englefontaine
Contay
ABB. DE
VAUCELLES
Beaumont
Albert
Caudry
Landrecies
PARC NATUREL
RÉGIONAL
DE L'AVESNOIS
Walcourt
Le Cateau-Cambrésis
Avesnes-sur-Helpe
AMIENS
Corbie
Le Catelet
Longueau
Bray-sur-Somme
Péronne
Bohain-en-Vermandois
Villers-Bretonneux
Roisel
Le Nouvion-en-Thiérache
Chimay
Fourmies
Couvin
La Capelle
Moreuil
St-Quentin
Guise
Hirson
Rocroi
Nesle
Ham
Ribemont
Sains
Vervins
Roye
Montdidier
Rumigny
Auvillers-les-Forges
Crécy-sur-Serre
Marle
Lassigny
Tergnier
La Fère
Brunehamel
Cuvilly
Noyon
Chauny
St-Gobain
Montcornet
Rozoy
Charleville-Mézières
St-Just-en-Chaussée
Ressons
ABB. D'OURSCAMPS
Coucy-le-Château-Auffrique
Signy-l'Abbaye
Ribécourt
Blérancourt
Laon
Sissonne
Estrées-St-Denis
Seraincourt
Compiègne
Novion-Porcien
Arsy
Vic-sur-Aisne
Château-Porcien
CAVERNE
DU DRAGON
Verberie
FORÊT DE COMPIÈGNE
Pierrefonds
Vailly
Corbény
Asfeld
Rethel
Soissons
Bourg-et-Comin
Senlis
Braine
Neufchâtel-sur-Aisne
Attigny
PICARDIE
NORD-PAS-DE-CALAIS

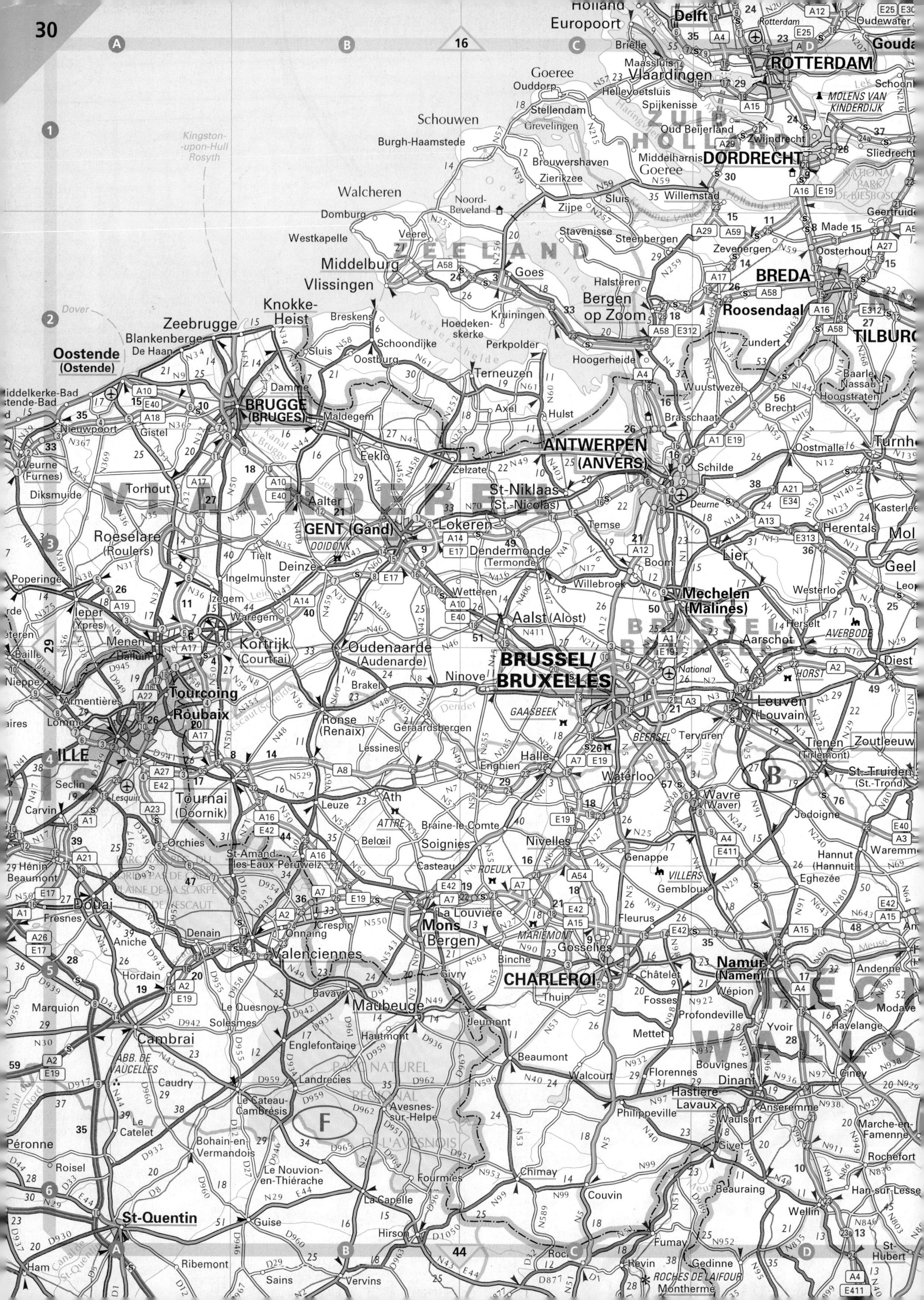

Holland
Europoort
Delft
Rotterdam
Oudewater
Gouda
Brielle
Maassluis
ROTTERDAM
Goeree
Ouddorp
Vlaardingen
Hellevoetsluis
Schoonhoven
Spijkenisse
MOLENS VAN KINDERDIJK
Stellendam
Grevelingen
Schouwen
ZUID-HOLLAND
Oud Beijerland
Zwijndrecht
Burgh-Haamstede
Kingston-upon-Hull Rosyth
Middelharnis
Goeree
DORDRECHT
Sliedrecht
Brouwershaven
Zierikzee
NATIONAAL PARK DE BIESBOSCH
Walcheren
Noord-Beveland
Sluis
Willemstad
Hollands Diep
Zijpe
Geertruidenberg
Domburg
Stavenisse
Steenbergen
Made
Westkapelle
Veere
Zevenbergen
Oosterhout
ZEELAND
Middelburg
Goes
Halsteren
BREDA
Vlissingen
Bergen op Zoom
Roosendaal
Tilburg
Dover
Knokke-Heist
Breskens
Hoedekenskerke
Kruiningen
Zeebrugge
Blankenberge
Westerschelde
Perkpolder
Zundert
Oostende (Ostende)
De Haan
Sluis
Schoondijke
Oostburg
Hoogerheide
Baarle-Nassau
Terneuzen
Hoogstraten
Middelkerke-Bad
Westende-Bad
Damme
Wuustwezel
Brecht
BRUGGE (BRUGES)
Maldegem
Axel
Hulst
Nieuwpoort
Gistel
Brasschaat
Turnhout
ANTWERPEN (ANVERS)
Eeklo
Zelzate
Oostmalle
Veurne (Furnes)
Schilde
Torhout
VLAANDEREN
St-Niklaas (St-Nicolas)
Deurne
Kasterlee
Diksmuide
Aalter
Temse
GENT (Gand)
Lokeren
Herentals
Roeselare (Roulers)
OOIDONK
Dendermonde (Termonde)
Boom
Lier
Mol
Tielt
Deinze
Poperinge
Ingelmunster
Willebroek
Geel
Westerlo
Izegem
Wetteren
Mechelen (Malines)
Ieper (Ypres)
Waregem
Aalst (Alost)
BRUSSEL
Herselt
AVERBODE
Menen
Halluin
Kortrijk (Courtrai)
Oudenaarde (Audenarde)
BRUSSEL/ BRUXELLES
National
Aarschot
Bailleul
Nieppe
Armentières
Tourcoing
Brakel
Ninove
HORST
Diest
Roubaix
GAASBEEK
Leuven (Louvain)
Lomme
Ronse (Renaix)
Geraardsbergen
Tervuren
Lessines
BEERSEL
Tienen (Tirlemont)
Zoutleeuw
LILLE
Halle
Enghien
Waterloo
St-Truiden (St-Trond)
Seclin
Lesquin
Tournai (Doornik)
Wavre (Waver)
Carvin
Leuze
Ath
Jodoigne
ATTRE
Braine-le-Comte
Orchies
Nivelles
Soignies
Genappe
Hannut (Hannuit)
Waremme
Hénin-Beaumont
Beloeil
St-Amand-les-Eaux
Péruwelz
VILLERS
Casteau
ROEULX
Gembloux
Eghezée
Douai
Crespin
La Louvière
Fleurus
Fresnes
Denain
Onnaing
Mons (Bergen)
MARIEMONT
Gosselies
Aniche
Valenciennes
Binche
Namur (Namen)
Andenne
Hordain
CHARLEROI
Châtelet
Thuin
Wépion
Givry
Fosses
Profondeville
Marquion
Bavay
Maubeuge
Le Quesnoy
Jeumont
Solesmes
Mettet
Yvoir
Havelange
Cambrai
Hautmont
Englefontaine
WALLONIE
Beaumont
Florennes
Bouvignes
ABB. DE VAUCELLES
Caudry
PARC NATUREL RÉGIONAL DE L'AVESNOIS
Walcourt
Dinant
Ciney
Landrecies
Le Cateau-Cambrésis
Avesnes-sur-Helpe
Hastière-Lavaux
Anseremme
Philippeville
Waulsort
Marche-en-Famenne
Le Catelet
Péronne
Bohain-en-Vermandois
Givet
Rochefort
Roisel
Le Nouvion-en-Thiérache
Fourmies
Chimay
Beauraing
Han-sur-Lesse
Couvin
La Capelle
Wellin
St-Quentin
Guise
Hirson
Fumay
St-Hubert
Ham
Ribemont
Sains
Vervins
Rocroi
Revin
ROCHES DE LAIFOUR
Gedinne
Monthermé

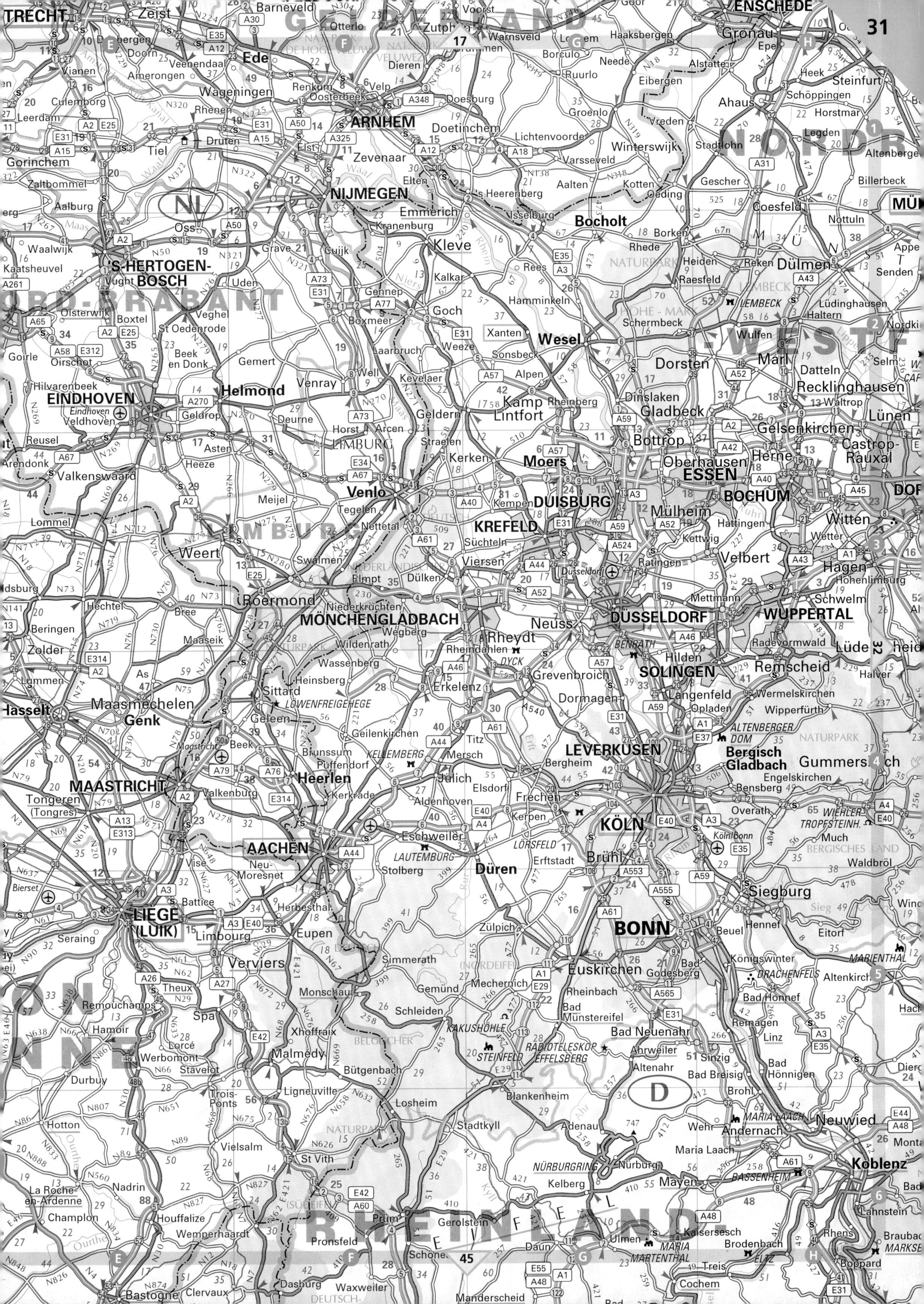

ENSCHEDE
GELDERLAND
NL
NOORD-BRABANT
NORDRHEIN-WESTFALEN
LIMBURG
RHEINLAND-
EIFEL
D
Barneveld
Zeist
Ede
Wageningen
ARNHEM
Zutphen
Doetinchem
Zevenaar
NIJMEGEN
Emmerich
Kleve
Tiel
Gorinchem
Zaltbommel
Oss
Waalwijk
'S-HERTOGEN-
BOSCH
Uden
Veghel
Boxtel
Oisterwijk
EINDHOVEN
Helmond
Venray
Venlo
Weert
Roermond
Geldrop
Valkenswaard
Lommel
Hasselt
Genk
Maasmechelen
MAASTRICHT
Tongeren
(Tongres)
LIEGE
(LUIK)
Verviers
Eupen
Spa
Malmedy
St Vith
Bastogne
Clervaux
Houffalize
La Roche-
en-Ardenne
Sittard
Geleen
Heerlen
Kerkrade
AACHEN
Düren
Stolberg
Monschau
Schleiden
MÖNCHENGLADBACH
Rheydt
Viersen
KREFELD
DUISBURG
Moers
Wesel
Bocholt
Dorsten
Gladbeck
Bottrop
Oberhausen
ESSEN
BOCHUM
Mülheim
Gelsenkirchen
Recklinghausen
Herne
Castrop-
Rauxal
Witten
Hagen
Velbert
DÜSSELDORF
Neuss
WUPPERTAL
SOLINGEN
Remscheid
LEVERKUSEN
Bergisch
Gladbach
KÖLN
Brühl
Siegburg
BONN
Bad
Godesberg
Euskirchen
Königswinter
Bad Honnef
Remagen
Linz
Bad Neuenahr
Ahrweiler
Sinzig
Andernach
Neuwied
Koblenz
Lahnstein
Mayen
Nürburg
Adenau
Daun
Gerolstein
Prüm
Cochem
Boppard
Coesfeld
Dülmen
Ahaus
Gronau
Borken
Lünen
Marl
Haltern
Gummersbach
Kleve
Kalkar
Goch
Geldern
Kempen
Grevenbroich
Dormagen
Erkelenz
Jülich
Frechen
Kerpen
Zülpich
Bad Münstereifel
Rheinbach
Blankenheim

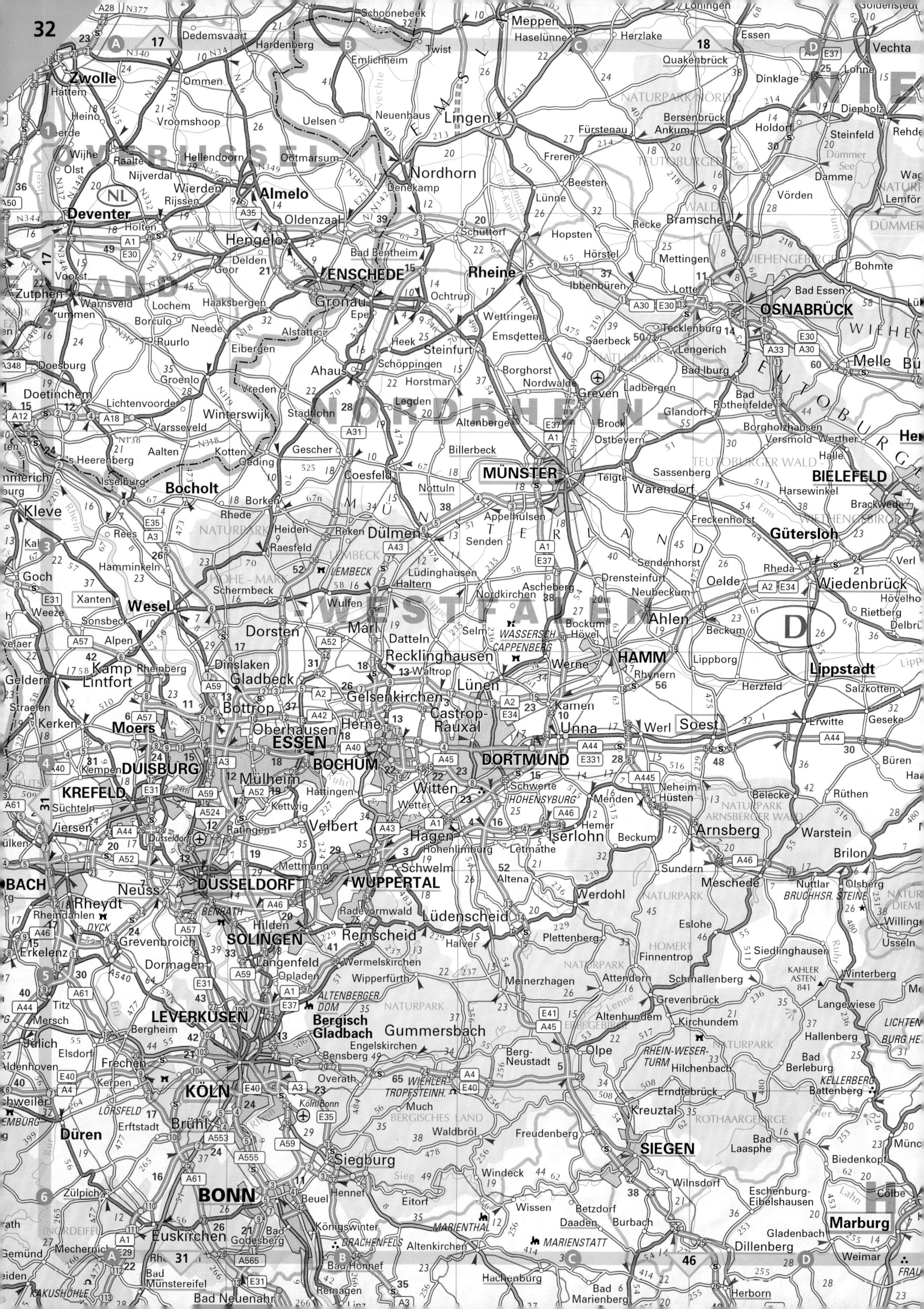
OVERIJSSEL
NORDRHEIN-WESTFALEN
MÜNSTERLAND
TEUTOBURGER WALD
NL
D
Zwolle
Hattem
Heino
Dedemsvaart
Hardenberg
Ommen
Vroomshoop
Raalte
Wijhe
Olst
Nijverdal
Hellendoorn
Wierden
Rijssen
Almelo
Deventer
Holten
Hengelo
Oldenzaal
Delden
Goor
ENSCHEDE
Gronau
Haaksbergen
Lochem
Zutphen
Warnsveld
Borculo
Neede
Ruurlo
Eibergen
Groenlo
Doesburg
Doetinchem
Lichtenvoorde
Winterswijk
Varsseveld
Aalten
's Heerenberg
Emmerich
Kleve
Goch
Xanten
Wesel
Bocholt
Rees
Isselburg
Borken
Rhede
Heiden
Reken
Raesfeld
Dülmen
Coesfeld
Gescher
Stadtlohn
Vreden
Ahaus
Legden
Horstmar
Schöppingen
Heek
Steinfurt
Ochtrup
Epe
Alstätte
Bad Bentheim
Schüttorf
Nordhorn
Denekamp
Neuenhaus
Uelsen
Emlichheim
Schoonebeek
Twist
Meppen
Haselünne
Lingen
Freren
Fürstenau
Beesten
Lünne
Rheine
Hopsten
Recke
Hörstel
Ibbenbüren
Mettingen
Bramsche
Wettringen
Emsdetten
Greven
Borghorst
Nordwalde
Saerbeck
Altenberge
Ladbergen
Lengerich
Tecklenburg
Lotte
OSNABRÜCK
Bad Iburg
Bad Rothenfelde
Glandorf
Melle
Bad Essen
Bohmte
Quakenbrück
Essen
Dinklage
Vechta
Lohne
Holdorf
Bersenbrück
Ankum
Steinfeld
Diepholz
Damme
Vörden
Herzlake
Löningen
MÜNSTER
Telgte
Warendorf
Sassenberg
Versmold
Borgholzhausen
Halle
Werther
BIELEFELD
Harsewinkel
Brackwede
Gütersloh
Freckenhorst
Sendenhorst
Drensteinfurt
Neubeckum
Oelde
Rheda
Wiedenbrück
Verl
Ahlen
Beckum
Lippstadt
Lippborg
Herzfeld
Salzkotten
Geseke
Erwitte
Soest
Werl
HAMM
Rhynern
Werne
Bockum-Hövel
Ascheberg
Nordkirchen
Lüdinghausen
Senden
Appelhülsen
Nottuln
Billerbeck
Haltern
Lembeck
Wulfen
Dorsten
Marl
Datteln
Selm
Recklinghausen
Waltrop
Lünen
Kamen
Unna
Gelsenkirchen
Herne
Castrop-Rauxel
DORTMUND
BOCHUM
ESSEN
Oberhausen
Bottrop
Gladbeck
Dinslaken
Moers
DUISBURG
Kamp Lintfort
Rheinberg
Alpen
Sonsbeck
Geldern
Kerken
Kempen
KREFELD
Süchteln
Viersen
Mülheim
Hattingen
Witten
Wetter
Hagen
Schwerte
Iserlohn
Hemer
Menden
Neheim-Hüsten
Arnsberg
Belecke
Rüthen
Warstein
Brilon
Büren
Velbert
Kettwig
Ratingen
Mettmann
WUPPERTAL
Schwelm
DÜSSELDORF
Neuss
Rheydt
Grevenbroich
Dormagen
Erkelenz
Hilden
SOLINGEN
Remscheid
Radevormwald
Lüdenscheid
Altena
Werdohl
Plettenberg
Sundern
Meschede
Eslohe
Finnentrop
Attendorn
Schmallenberg
Winterberg
Olpe
Meinerzhagen
Gummersbach
Wipperfürth
Wermelskirchen
Langenfeld
Opladen
LEVERKUSEN
Bergisch Gladbach
Bergheim
Jülich
Elsdorf
Frechen
Kerpen
KÖLN
Brühl
Erftstadt
Düren
Zülpich
Euskirchen
BONN
Siegburg
Hennef
Bad Godesberg
Königswinter
Bad Honnef
Remagen
Bad Münstereifel
Bad Neuenahr
Overath
Much
Waldbröl
Eitorf
Windeck
Wissen
Betzdorf
Altenkirchen
Hachenburg
Freudenberg
SIEGEN
Kreuztal
Hilchenbach
Bad Berleburg
Bad Laasphe
Dillenberg
Herborn
Marburg
Weimar
Biedenkopf
Gladenbach
Wilnsdorf
Burbach
Daaden
Olsberg
Siedlinghausen
Langewiese
Hallenberg
Battenberg

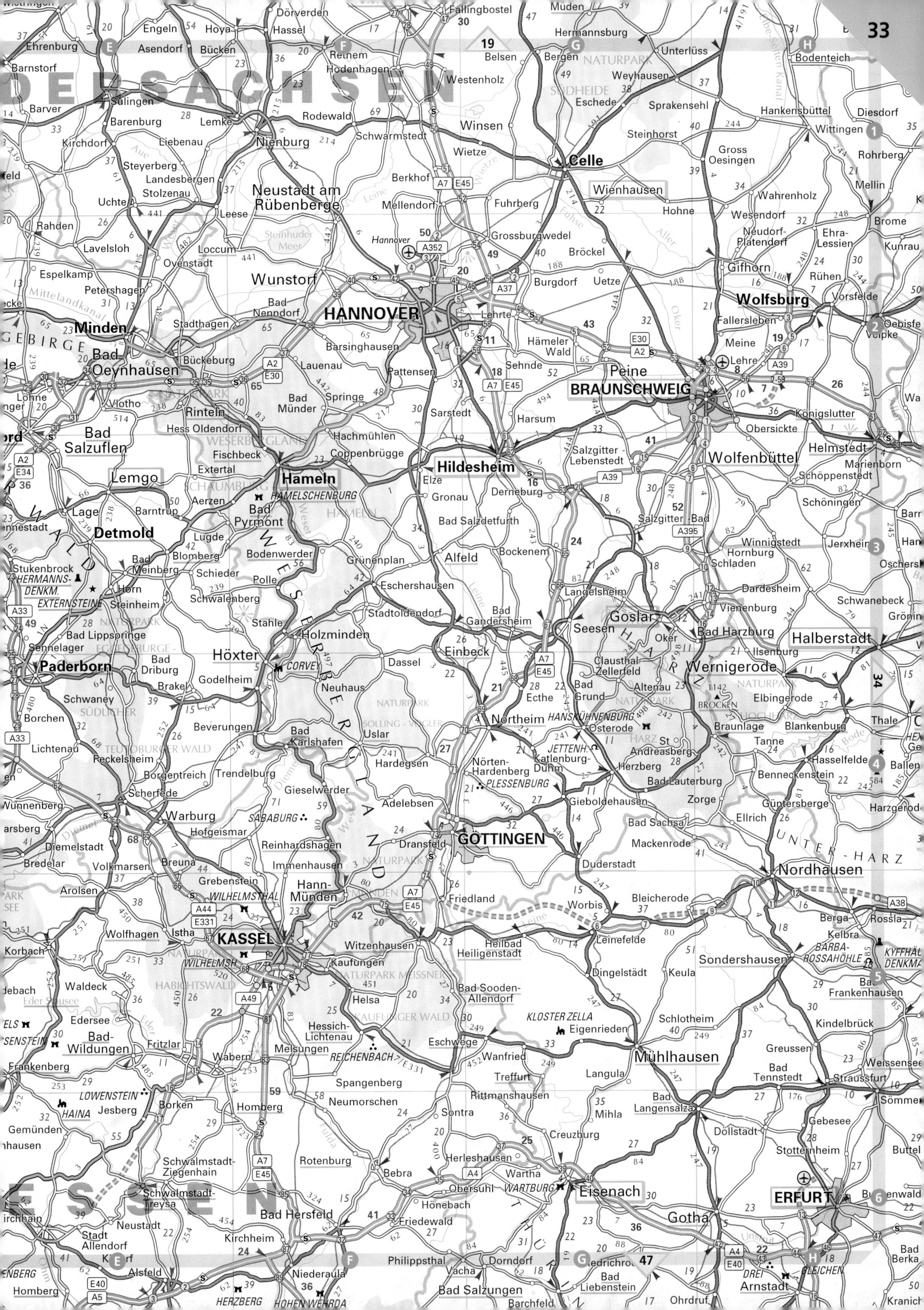

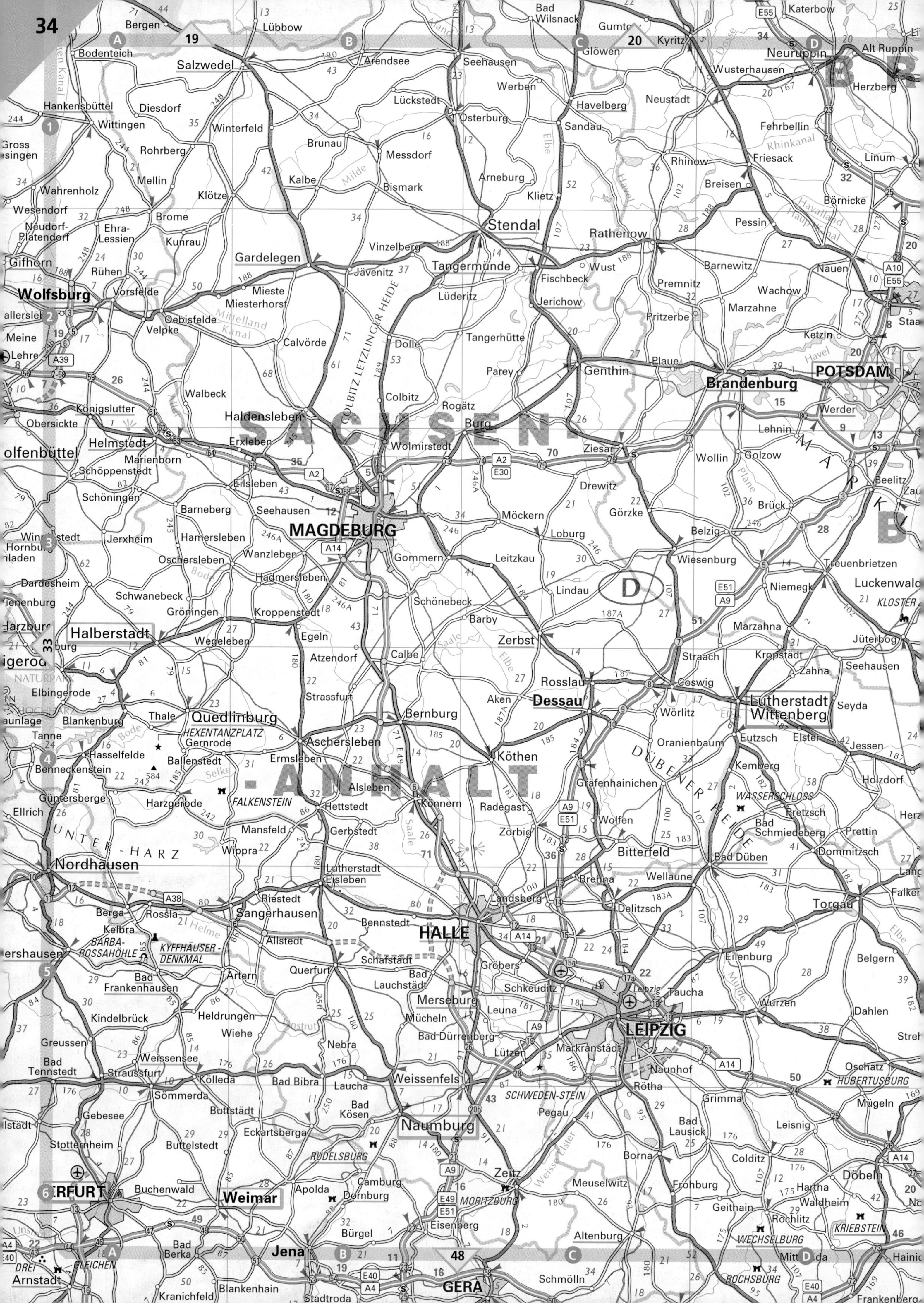
SACHSEN-ANHALT
MAGDEBURG
HALLE
LEIPZIG
POTSDAM
Brandenburg
Stendal
Salzwedel
Wolfsburg
Gifhorn
Helmstedt
Halberstadt
Quedlinburg
Dessau
Lutherstadt Wittenberg
Lutherstadt Eisleben
Nordhausen
Sangerhausen
Merseburg
Weissenfels
Naumburg
Zeitz
Weimar
ERFURT
Jena
GERA
Altenburg
Borna
Grimma
Wurzen
Torgau
Eilenburg
Delitzsch
Bitterfeld
Köthen
Bernburg
Aschersleben
Zerbst
Rosslau
Burg
Genthin
Rathenow
Tangermünde
Gardelegen
Haldensleben
Havelberg
Neuruppin
Nauen
Werder
Belzig
Jüterbog
Luckenwalde
Döbeln
Kyritz
Glöwen
Osterburg
Seehausen
Arendsee
Klötze
Oebisfelde
Schönebeck
Staßfurt
Wernigerode
Thale
Blankenburg
Mansfeld
Hettstedt
Querfurt
Schkeuditz
Markranstädt
Lützen
Apolda
Arnstadt
Sömmerda
Bad Frankenhausen
Artern
Rochlitz
Colditz
Bad Düben
Oranienbaum
Gräfenhainichen
Wörlitz
Coswig
Kemberg
Jessen
Zahna
Treuenbrietzen
Beelitz
Ketzin
Premnitz
Jerichow
Wolmirstedt
Oschersleben
Egeln
Calbe
Barby
Gommern
Möckern
Loburg
Ziesar
Wiesenburg
SCHWEDEN-STEIN
KYFFHÄUSER-DENKMAL
BARBA-ROSSAHÖHLE
FALKENSTEIN
RUDELSBURG
MORITZBURG
WECHSELBURG
ROCHSBURG
KRIEBSTEIN
HUBERTUSBURG
WASSERSCHLOSS
HEXENTANZPLATZ
DRAI GLEICHEN
KLOSTER
COLBITZ LETZLINGER HEIDE
DÜBENER HEIDE
UNTER-HARZ
Mittelland Kanal
Elbe
Saale
Havel
Mulde

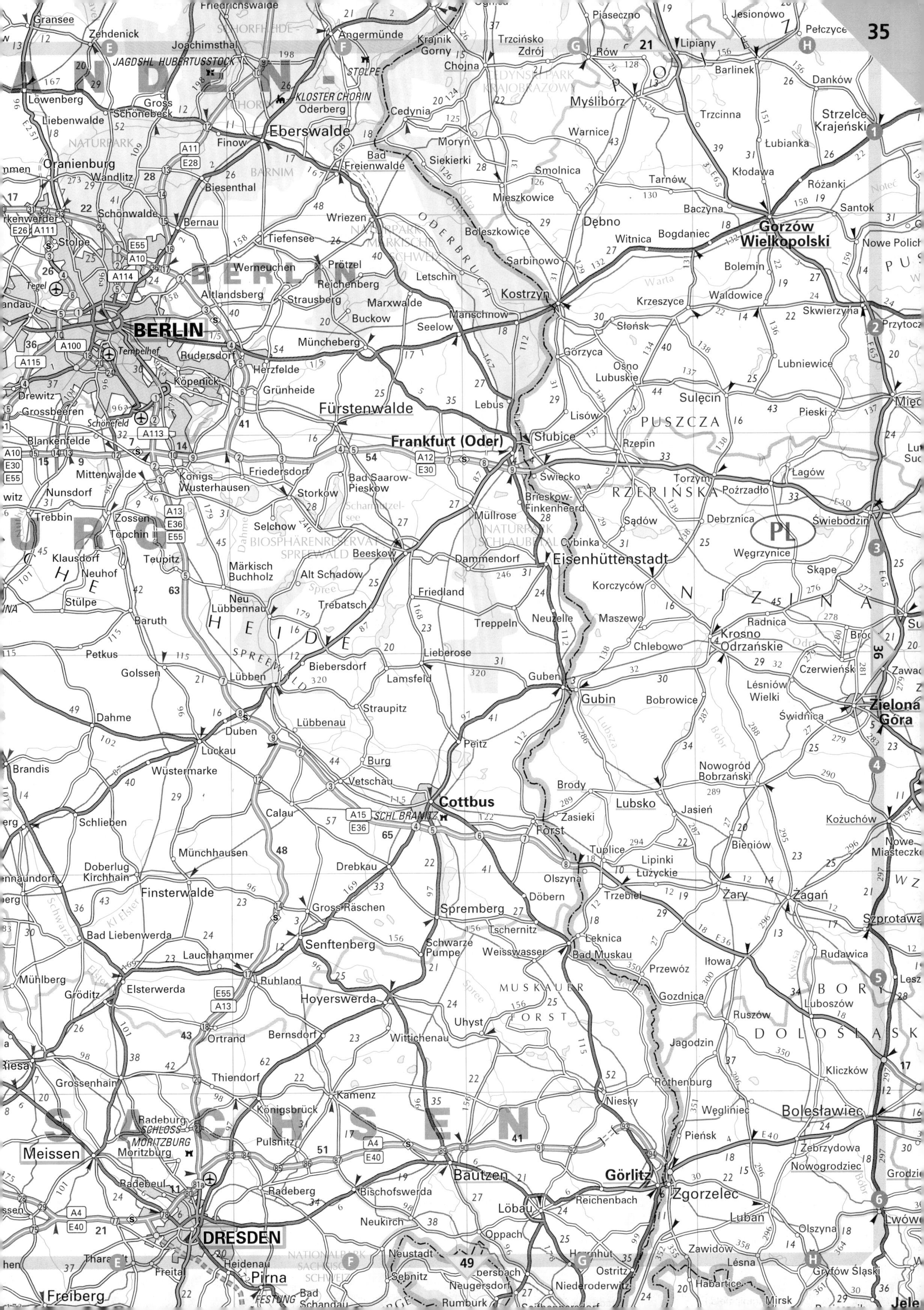
Gransee
Zehdenick
Joachimsthal
JAGDSHL. HUBERTUSSTOCK
Angermünde
STOLPE
KLOSTER CHORIN
Oderberg
Krajnik Gorny
Chojna
Trzcińsko Zdrój
Piaseczno
Jesionowo
Pełczyce
Lipiany
Rów
Barlinek
Danków
Myślibórz
Löwenberg
Gross Schönebeck
Liebenwalde
NATURPARK
Oranienburg
Wandlitz
Finow
Eberswalde
Cedynia
Moryń
Siekierki
Bad Freienwalde
BARNIM
Biesenthal
Warnice
Trzcinna
Strzelce Krajeńskie
Łubianka
Kłodawa
Smolnica
Mieszkowice
Tarnów
Baczyna
Różanki
Santok
Schönwalde
Bernau
Wriezen
ODERBRUCH
Boleszkowice
Dębno
Witnica
Bogdaniec
Gorzów Wielkopolski
Nowe Polichno
Stolpe
Tiefensee
Tegel
Werneuchen
Prötzel
Reichenberg
BERLIN
Letschin
Sarbinowo
Bolemin
Altlandsberg
Strausberg
Marxwalde
Buckow
Kostrzyn
Krzeszyce
Waldowice
Skwierzyna
Przytoczna
Manschnow
Seelow
Słońsk
Müncheberg
Tempelhof
Rudersdorf
Herzfelde
Köpenick
Grünheide
Górzyca
Ośno Lubuskie
Lubniewice
Drewitz
Grossbeeren
Schönefeld
Fürstenwalde
Lebus
Sulęcin
Pieski
Lisów
PUSZCZA
Blankenfelde
Frankfurt (Oder)
Słubice
Rzepin
Mittenwalde
Königs Wusterhausen
Friedersdorf
Bad Saarow-Pieskow
Storkow
Świecko
Torzym
Łagów
Pożrzadło
Nunsdorf
Trebbin
Zossen
Töpchin
Selchow
Scharmützelsee
BIOSPHÄRENRESERVAT SPREEWALD
Müllrose
Brieskow-Finkenheerd
NATURPARK SCHLAUBETAL
RZEPIŃSKA
Sądów
Debrznica
Świebodzin
PL
Klausdorf
Neuhof
Teupitz
Märkisch Buchholz
Beeskow
Dammendorf
Cybinka
Eisenhüttenstadt
Węgrzynice
Skąpe
Stülpe
Baruth
Neu Lübbennau
Alt Schadow
Trebatsch
Friedland
Korczyców
NIZINA
Neuzelle
Maszewo
Radnica
Petkus
HEIDE
SPREEWALD
Treppeln
Krosno Odrzańskie
Chlebowo
Lieberose
Biebersdorf
Golssen
Lübben
Lamsfeld
Guben
Gubin
Bobrowice
Czerwieńsk
Lesniów Wielki
Zielona Góra
Świdnica
Dahme
Duben
Luckau
Lübbenau
Straupitz
Peitz
Brandis
Wüstermarke
Burg
Vetschau
Nowogród Bobrzański
Brody
Lubsko
Jasień
Schlieben
Calau
SCHL.BRANITZ
Cottbus
Zasieki
Forst
Kożuchów
Münchhausen
Doberlug Kirchhain
Drebkau
Tuplice
Lipinki Łużyckie
Bieniów
Nowe Miasteczko
Olszyna
Trzebiel
Żary
Żagań
Finsterwalde
Gross Räschen
Spremberg
Döbern
Bad Liebenwerda
Senftenberg
Schwarze Pumpe
Tschernitz
Łęknica
Bad Muskau
Szprotawa
Lauchhammer
Weisswasser
Przewóz
Iłowa
Rudawica
Mühlberg
Gröditz
Elsterwerda
Ruhland
Hoyerswerda
MUSKAUER FORST
Gozdnica
BORY
Luboszów
Ruszów
DOLNOŚLĄSKIE
Riesa
Ortrand
Bernsdorf
Wittichenau
Uhyst
Jagodzin
Kliczków
Grossenhain
Thiendorf
Kamenz
Rothenburg
Niesky
Radeburg
SCHLOSS MORITZBURG
Königsbrück
Węgliniec
Bolesławiec
SACHSEN
Meissen
Moritzburg
Pulsnitz
Pieńsk
Zebrzydowa
Nowogrodziec
Radebeul
Bautzen
Görlitz
Zgorzelec
Radeberg
Bischofswerda
Löbau
Reichenbach
Lubań
Olszyna
Lwówek
Neukirch
DRESDEN
Oppach
Zawidów
Lesna
Tharandt
Freital
Heidenau
NATIONALPARK SÄCHSISCHE SCHWEIZ
Neustadt
Herrnhut
Ostritz
Gryfów Śląski
Pirna
FESTUNG
Sebnitz
Ebersbach
Neugersdorf
Niederoderwitz
Habartice
Freiberg
Bad Schandau
Rumburk
Mirsk
Jelenia

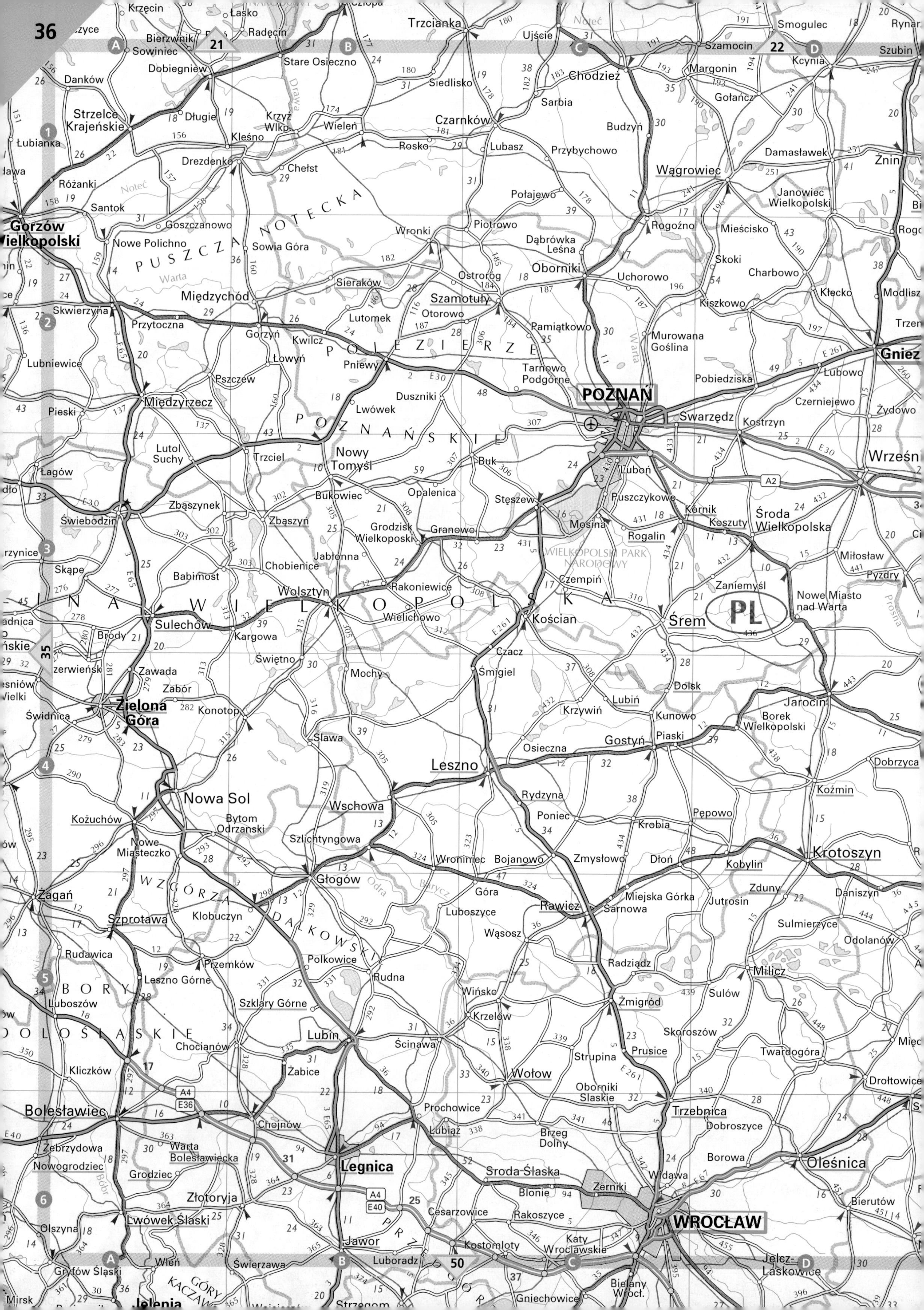
Krzęcin
Łasko
Radęcin
Bierzwnik
Sowiniec
Dobiegniew
Stare Osieczno
Danków
Strzelce Krajeńskie
Długie
Krzyż Wlkp.
Wieleń
Łubianka
Kleśno
Drezdenko
Chełst
Różanki
Noteć
Santok
Gorzów Wielkopolski
Goszczanowo
Nowe Polichno
Sowia Góra
PUSZCZA NOTECKA
Warta
Skwierzyna
Przytoczna
Międzychód
Gorzyń
Kwilcz
Lubniewice
Pszczew
Łowyń
Pniewy
Międzyrzecz
Pieski
Lutol Suchy
Trzciel
Łagów
Świebodzin
Zbąszynek
Zbąszyń
Bukowiec
Nowy Tomyśl
Lwówek
Duszniki
POJEZIERZE POZNAŃSKIE
Trzcianka
Ujście
Chodzież
Siedlisko
Sarbia
Czarnków
Rosko
Lubasz
Budzyń
Przybychowo
Połajewo
Wronki
Piotrowo
Dąbrówka Leśna
Oborniki
Sieraków
Ostroróg
Szamotuły
Lutomek
Otorowo
Pamiątkowo
Tarnowo Podgórne
POZNAŃ
Swarzędz
Luboń
Buk
Opalenica
Stęszew
Puszczykowo
Mosina
Rogalin
Kórnik
Grodzisk Wielkopolski
Granowo
WIELKOPOLSKI PARK NARODOWY
Smogulec
Rynar
Samoczin
Kcynia
Szubin
Margonin
Gołańcz
Damasławek
Żnin
Wągrowiec
Janowiec Wielkopolski
Rogoźno
Mieścisko
Skoki
Charbowo
Kłecko
Uchorowo
Kiszkowo
Murowana Goślina
Pobiedziska
Gniezno
Łubowo
Czerniejewo
Żydowo
Kostrzyn
Września
Środa Wielkopolska
Koszuty
Miłosław
Pyzdry
Zaniemyśl
Nowe Miasto nad Wartą
Śrem
Prosna
PL
Czempiń
Kościan
Rakoniewice
Wielichowo
Jabłonna
Chobienice
Babimost
Wolsztyn
Sulechów
Kargowa
Świętno
Skąpe
Brody
Czerwieńsk
Zawada
Zabór
Zielona Góra
Świdnica
Konotop
Mochy
Śmigiel
Czacz
Sława
Krzywiń
Lubiń
Dolsk
Kunowo
Piaski
Gostyń
Osieczna
Leszno
Jarocin
Borek Wielkopolski
Dobrzyca
Koźmin
Nowa Sól
Bytom Odrzański
Wschowa
Rydzyna
Poniec
Krobia
Pępowo
Kożuchów
Nowe Miasteczko
Szlichtyngowa
Wroniniec
Bojanowo
Zmysłowo
Dłoń
Kobylin
Krotoszyn
Żagań
Szprotawa
Głogów
Góra
Rawicz
Sarnowa
Miejska Górka
Jutrosin
Zduny
Daniszyn
WZGÓRZA DALKOWSKIE
Klobuczyn
Luboszyce
Wąsosz
Sulmierzyce
Odolanów
Rudawica
Przemków
Polkowice
Rudna
Radziądz
Milicz
Leszno Górne
BORY DOLNOŚLĄSKIE
Luboszów
Szklary Górne
Wińsko
Żmigród
Sulów
Krzelów
Lubin
Ścinawa
Skoroszów
Chocianów
Prusice
Twardogóra
Kliczków
Żabice
Strupina
Wołow
Obornik Śląskie
Drołtowice
Bolesławiec
Chojnów
Prochowice
Lubiąż
Brzeg Dolny
Trzebnica
Dobroszyce
Żebrzydowa
Warta Bolesławiecka
Nowogrodziec
Grodziec
Legnica
Środa Śląska
Zerniki
Widawa
Borowa
Oleśnica
Złotoryja
Błonie
Bierutów
Lwówek Śląski
Cesarzowice
Rakoszyce
WROCŁAW
Olszyna
Jawor
Kostomłoty
Katy Wrocławskie
Gryfów Śląski
Wleń
Świerzawa
Luboradz
Jelcz-Laskowice
Mirsk
Jelenia
Strzegom
Gniechowice
Bielany Wrocł.
GÓRY KACZAWSKIE
A
B
C
D
21
22
35
50
1
2
3
4
5
6
A2
A4
E30
E36
E40
E65
E67
E261

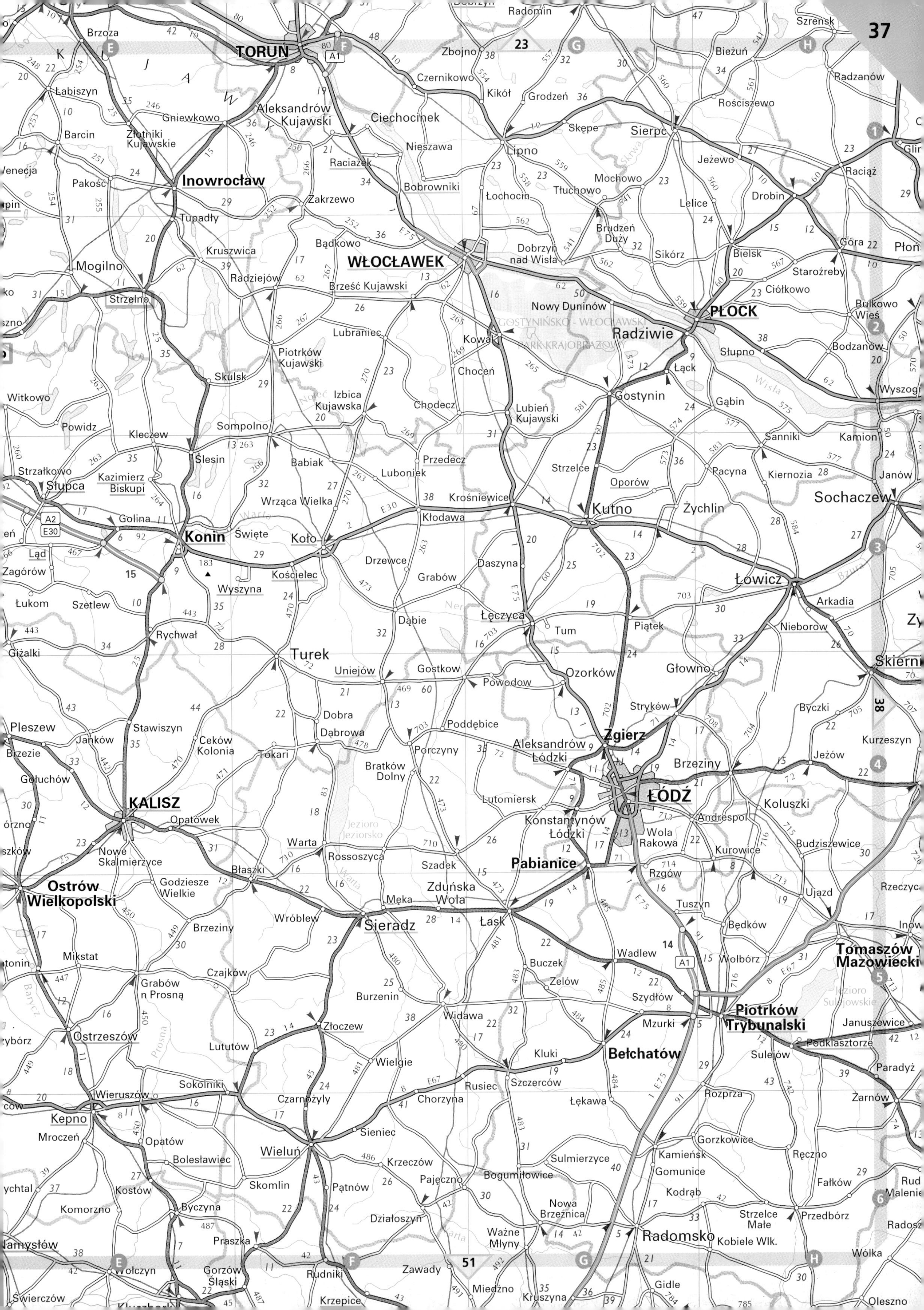
Brzoza
TORUŃ
Radomin
Zbojno
Szreńsk
Bieżuń
Radzanów
Łabiszyn
Czernikowo
Kikół
Grodzeń
Rościszewo
Gniewkowo
Aleksandrów Kujawski
Ciechocinek
Skępe
Sierpc
Barcin
Złotniki Kujawskie
Nieszawa
Lipno
Jeżewo
Raciąż
Pakość
Raciążek
Mochowo
Inowrocław
Bobrowniki
Tłuchowo
Drobin
Zakrzewo
Łochocin
Lelice
Tupadły
Brudzeń Duży
Bielsk
Góra
Płońsk
Kruszwica
Bądkowo
WŁOCŁAWEK
Dobrzyń nad Wisłą
Sikórz
Staroźreby
Mogilno
Radziejów
Brześć Kujawski
Ciółkowo
Strzelno
Nowy Duninów
PŁOCK
Bulkowo Wieś
GOSTYNIŃSKO - WŁOCŁAWSKI PARK KRAJOBRAZOWY
Radziwie
Lubraniec
Kowal
Słupno
Bodzanów
Piotrków Kujawski
Choceń
Łąck
Skulsk
Gostynin
Wyszogród
Witkowo
Izbica Kujawska
Chodecz
Lubień Kujawski
Gąbin
Powidz
Sompolno
Sanniki
Kamion
Kleczew
Ślesin
Babiak
Przedecz
Strzelce
Pacyna
Kiernozia
Janów
Strzałkowo
Kazimierz Biskupi
Luboniek
Oporów
Słupca
Wrząca Wielka
Krośniewice
Kutno
Żychlin
Sochaczew
Golina
Kłodawa
Konin
Święte
Koło
Lądek
Zagórów
Drzewce
Daszyna
Łowicz
Grabów
Wyszyna
Kościelec
Łukom
Szetlew
Arkadia
Dąbie
Łęczyca
Piątek
Nieborów
Rychwał
Tum
Giżalki
Turek
Ozorków
Głowno
Skierniewice
Uniejów
Gostków
Powodów
Stryków
Byczki
Dobra
Pleszew
Janków
Stawiszyn
Ceków Kolonia
Dąbrowa
Poddębice
Zgierz
Jeżów
Kurzeszyn
Brzezie
Tokary
Porczyny
Aleksandrów Łódzki
Brzeziny
Gołuchów
Bratków Dolny
ŁÓDŹ
KALISZ
Lutomiersk
Koluszki
Opatówek
Jezioro Jeziorsko
Konstantynów Łódzki
Andrespol
Nowe Skalmierzyce
Warta
Wola Rakowa
Budziszewice
Rossoszyca
Szadek
Pabianice
Kurowice
Ostrów Wielkopolski
Godziesze Wielkie
Błaszki
Rzgów
Ujazd
Zduńska Wola
Rzeczyca
Męka
Tuszyn
Brzeziny
Wróblew
Sieradz
Łask
Będków
Tomaszów Mazowiecki
Mikstat
Wadlew
Wolbórz
Czajków
Buczek
Zelów
Grabów n Prosną
Burzenin
Szydłów
Piotrków Trybunalski
Widawa
Mzurki
Ostrzeszów
Złoczew
Januszewice
Lututów
Kluki
Bełchatów
Podklasztorze
Sulejów
Wielgie
Paradyż
Sokolniki
Rusiec
Szczerców
Wieruszów
Czarnożyły
Chorzyna
Łękawa
Rozprza
Żarnów
Kępno
Sieniec
Mroczeń
Opatów
Wieluń
Gorzkowice
Bolesławiec
Krzeczów
Sulmierzyce
Kamieńsk
Ręczno
Skomlin
Bogumiłowice
Gomunice
Kostów
Pątnów
Pajęczno
Kodrąb
Fałków
Komorzno
Byczyna
Nowa Brzeźnica
Strzelce Małe
Przedbórz
Działoszyn
Praszka
Ważne Młyny
Radomsko
Kobiele Wlk.
Namysłów
Wołczyn
Gorzów Śląski
Rudniki
Zawady
Wólka
Świerczów
Krzepice
Miedźno
Kruszyna
Gidle
Oleszno

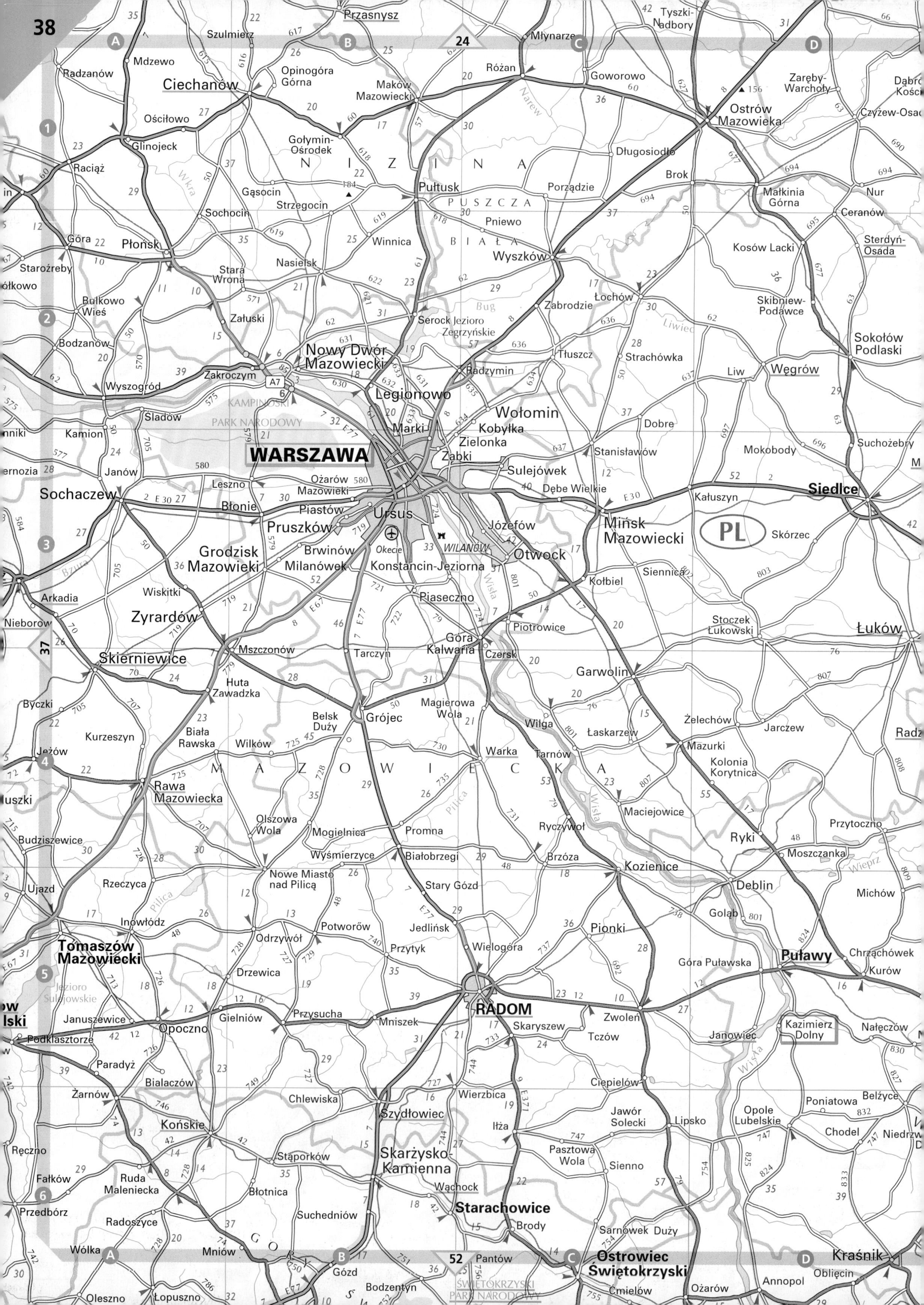
Przasnysz
Tyszki-Nadbory
Szulmierz
Mdzewo
Radzanów
Ciechanów
Opinogóra Górna
Maków Mazowiecki
Różan
Młynarze
Goworowo
Zaręby-Warchoły
Ostrów Mazowiecka
Czyżew-Osada
Ościłowo
Glinojeck
Gołymin-Ośrodek
Raciąż
N I Z I N A
Długosiodło
Brok
Małkinia Górna
Nur
Gąsocin
Pułtusk
Porządzie
Strzegocin
Sochocin
P U S Z C Z A
Pniewo
Ceranów
Góra
Płońsk
Winnica
B I A Ł A
Kosów Lacki
Sterdyń-Osada
Wyszków
Starożreby
Nasielsk
Stara Wrona
Łochów
Bulkowo Wieś
Załuski
Zabrodzie
Skibniew-Podawce
Serock
Jezioro Zegrzyńskie
Bug
Liwiec
Sokołów Podlaski
Bodzanów
Nowy Dwór Mazowiecki
Tłuszcz
Strachówka
Zakroczym
Radzymin
Liw
Węgrów
Wyszogród
Legionowo
Śladów
KAMPINOSKI PARK NARODOWY
Wołomin
Kobyłka
Marki
Zielonka
Dobre
Kamion
WARSZAWA
Ząbki
Stanisławów
Mokobody
Suchożebry
Janów
Sulejówek
Leszno
Ożarów Mazowiecki
Dębe Wielkie
Sochaczew
Błonie
Piastów
Ursus
Pruszków
Kałuszyn
Siedlce
Józefów
Mińsk Mazowiecki
PL
Skórzec
Grodzisk Mazowiecki
Brwinów
Okęcie
Wilanów
Otwock
Milanówek
Konstancin-Jeziorna
Sienica
Kołbiel
Arkadia
Wiskitki
Piaseczno
Bzura
Wisła
Nieborów
Żyrardów
Piotrowice
Stoczek Łukowski
Łuków
Mszczonów
Tarczyn
Góra Kalwaria
Czersk
Skierniewice
Huta Zawadzka
Garwolin
Byczki
Grójec
Belsk Duży
Magierowa Wola
Wilga
Kurzeszyn
Biała Rawska
Wilków
Łaskarzew
Żelechów
Jarczew
Jeżów
Warka
Tarnów
Mazurki
Kolonia Korytnica
M A Z O W I E C K A
Rawa Mazowiecka
Maciejowice
Olszowa Wola
Mogielnica
Promna
Ryczywół
Przytoczno
Ryki
Budziszewice
Białobrzegi
Brzóza
Moszczanka
Wyśmierzyce
Nowe Miasto nad Pilicą
Kozienice
Dęblin
Wieprz
Ujazd
Rzeczyca
Stary Gózd
Michów
Pilica
Inowłódz
Potworów
Jedlińsk
Gołąb
Tomaszów Mazowiecki
Odrzywół
Przytyk
Wielogóra
Pionki
Puławy
Chrząchówek
Kurów
Drzewica
Góra Puławska
Jezioro Sulejowskie
RADOM
Januszewice
Gielniów
Przysucha
Mniszek
Skaryszew
Zwoleń
Tczów
Opoczno
Podklasztorze
Janowiec
Kazimierz Dolny
Nałęczów
Paradyż
Białaczów
Ciepielów
Żarnów
Chlewiska
Wierzbica
Poniatowa
Bełżyce
Szydłowiec
Jawór Solecki
Lipsko
Opole Lubelskie
Końskie
Iłża
Chodel
Niedrzwica
Ręczno
Stąporków
Skarżysko-Kamienna
Pasztowa Wola
Sienno
Fałków
Ruda Maleniecka
Błotnica
Wąchock
Przedbórz
Suchedniów
Starachowice
Radoszyce
Brody
Sarnówek Duży
Wólka
Mniów
G Ó R Y
Pantów
Ostrowiec Świętokrzyski
Kraśnik
Gózd
Bodzentyn
ŚWIĘTOKRZYSKI PARK NARODOWY
Obliecin
Oleszno
Łopuszno
Ćmielów
Ożarów
Annopol
24
37
52
A
B
C
D
1
2
3
4
5
6

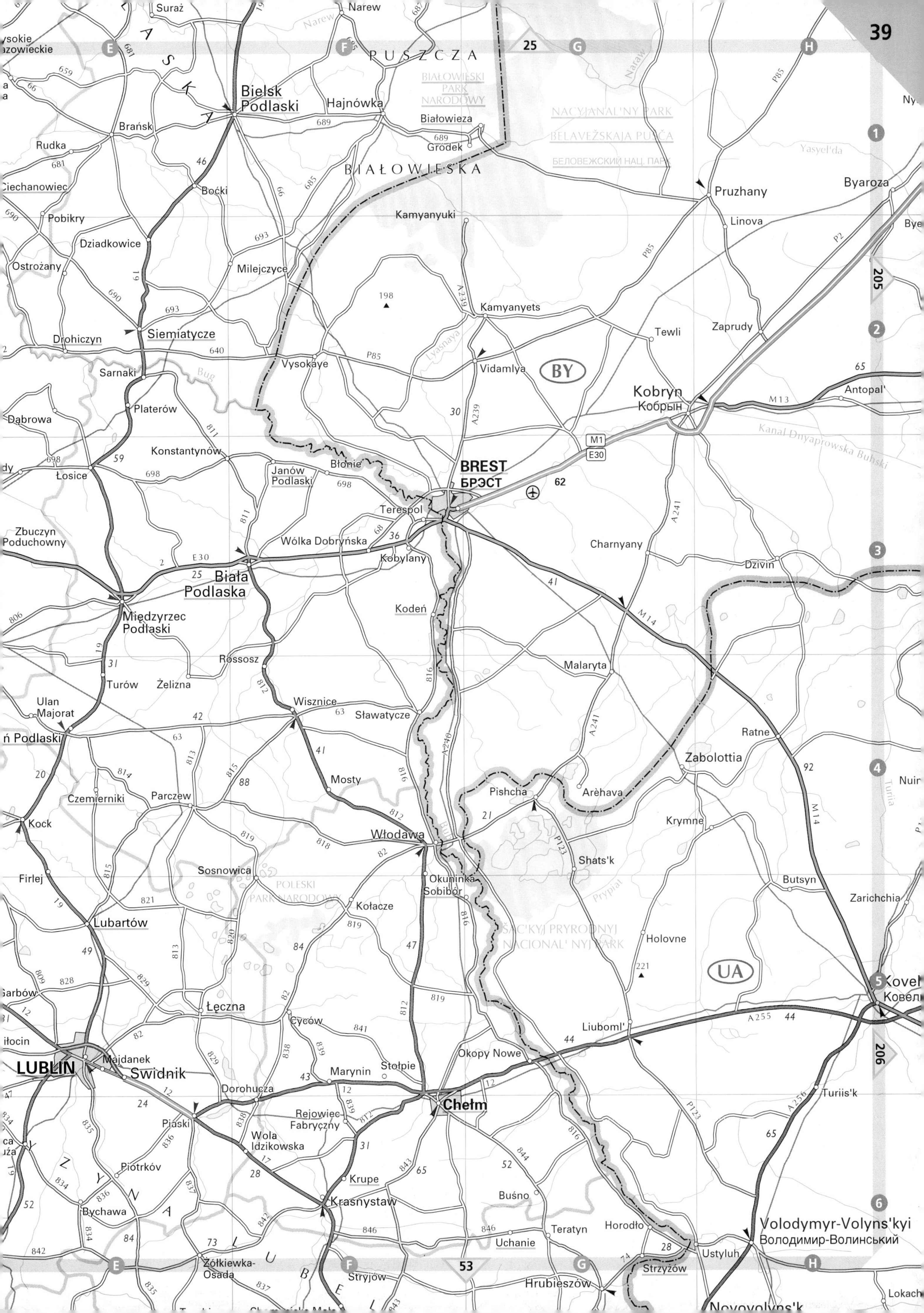
Bielsk Podlaski
Hajnówka
Białowieza
Grodek
PUSZCZA BIAŁOWIESKA
BIAŁOWIESKI PARK NARODOWY
NACYJANAL'NY PARK BELAVEŽSKAJA PUŠČA
БЕЛОВЕЖСКИЙ НАЦ. ПАРК
Pruzhany
Byaroza
Linova
Kamyanyuki
Kamyanyets
Tewli
Zaprudy
Vysokaye
Vidamlya
BY
Kobryn
Кобрын
Antopal'
Siemiatycze
Drohiczyn
Sarnaki
Platerów
Dąbrowa
Konstantynów
Łosice
Janów Podlaski
Błonie
BREST
БРЭСТ
Terespol
Wólka Dobryńska
Kobylany
Biała Podlaska
Międzyrzec Podlaski
Charnyany
Dzivin
Kodeń
Rossosz
Żelizna
Turów
Malaryta
Wisznice
Sławatycze
Ratne
Zabolottia
Mosty
Parczew
Czemierniki
Pishcha
Arèhava
Kock
Włodawa
Krymne
Shats'k
Sosnowica
POLESKI PARK NARODOWY
Okuninka
Sobibór
Kołacze
ŠAC'KYJ PRYRODNYJ NACIONAL'NYJ PARK
Butsyn
Zarichchia
Holovne
Lubartów
UA
Kovel
Ковель
Łęczna
Cyców
Liuboml'
LUBLIN
Majdanek
Swidnik
Marynin
Stołpie
Okopy Nowe
Dorohucza
Chełm
Rejowiec Fabryczny
Piaski
Wola Idzikowska
Turiis'k
Piotrków
Krupe
Krasnystaw
Bychawa
Buśno
Horodło
Teratyn
Uchanie
Volodymyr-Volyns'kyi
Володимир-Волинський
Ustyluh
Żółkiewka-Osada
Stryjów
Strzyżów
Hrubieszów
Novovolyns'k
Lokach
Bug
Narew
Suraż
Brańsk
Rudka
Ciechanowiec
Boćki
Pobikry
Dziadkowice
Milejczyce
Ostrożany
Zbuczyn Poduchowny
Ulan Majorat
Firlej
Garbów
Kanal Dnyaprowska Buhski
Prypiat
Turiia
Yasyel'da
Lyasnaya
Narew
Naraw
Nuir
Byc
Ny
25
53
205
206
E
F
G
H
1
2
3
4
5
6
M1
E30
M13
M14
P85
P2
A239
A241
A240
P123
A255
A256
62
198
221

A B C D

1

Plymouth

Lampaul
Ile d'Ouessant
Ile de Molène
Ile de Beniguet

L'Aber-Wrac'h
Ploudalmézeau
Lampaul-Plouarzel
le Folgoët
Lannilis
Plabennec
St-Renan
Le Conquet
POINTE DE ST-MATHIEU
BREST
Guipavas
Plougastel-Daoulas
Camaret
Pointe de Penhir
Crozon
Morgat
Landévennec

Brignogan Plage
Ile de Batz
Roscoff
St-Pol-de-Léon
Plouescat
Carantec
Lesneven
CHÂTEAU DE KERJEAN
Landivisiau
St-Thégonnec
Landerneau
Guimiliau
Sizun
Daoulas
Le Faou
MONTS
MONTAGNE ST-MICHEL

Trégastel
Ploumanac'h
Trébeurden
Perros-Guirec
Primel-Trégastel
Plougasnou
Locquirec
Lanmeur
Morlaix
Plestin-les-Grèves
St-Michel-en-Grève
Plouaret
Plouïgneau
ROCHE DE KIRIOU
PARC NATUREL RÉGIONAL D'ARRÉE
ROC TRÉVÉZEL
Huelgoat
D'ARMORIC

Tréguier
Lézardrieu
Lannion
Pontrieux
Bégard
Lanvollon
Belle-Isle-en-Terre
Guingamp
Bourbriac
Callac
St-

2

PARC NATUREL RÉGIONAL D'ARMORIQUE

Ile de Sein
Pointe du Van
Pointe du Raz
Audierne
Pont-Croix
Tréboul
Douarnenez
Locronan
Plozévet
CHAPELLE DE LANGUIDOU
Plonéour Lanvern
Pont-l'Abbé
St-Guénolé
POINTE DE PENMARCH
Guilvinec
Loctudy
Bénodet

Baie d'Audierne

MENEZ HOM
Pentrez-Plage
Ste-Anne-la-Palud
Châteaulin
ROCHE DU FEU
Briec
Quimper
VIRE COURT
N.-D. DE KERDEVOT
Fouesnant
Beg-Meil
Concarneau

Pleyben
Châteauneuf-du-Faou
Coray
Scaër
Gourin
Rosporden
Bannalec
Carhaix-Plouguer
MONTAGNES NOIRES
Plouray
Le Faouët
STE-BARBE
ST-FIACRE
Kernascléden
Guémené-sur-Scorff

St-Nicolas-du-Pélem
Corlay
Gouarec
Mur-de-Bretagne
Lac de Guerlédan
Rostrenen

Quintin
Uzel
Loudéac
Pontivy
ST-NICODÈME
Bubry

3

ILES DE GLÉNAN
Pont-Aven
Port-Manech
Quimperlé
Le Pouldu
Lorient
Larmor
Port-Louis
Ile de Groix
Groix

Plouay
Pont-Scorff
Hennebont
Baud
Locminé
Pluvigner
Ste-Anne-d'Auray
Belz
Grand-Champ
Auray
St-Jean-Brévelay
TOUR D'ELVEN

4

MENEC
Carnac
La Trinité
St-Pierre-Quiberon
Quiberon
Locmariaquer
Port-Navalo
Vannes
TUMULUS DE GAVRINIS
Sarzeau
Muzil

5

Pointe des Poulains
Sauzon
GROTTE DE L'APOTHICAIRERIE
Le Palais
Bangor
Belle-Ile
Locmaria
Ile de Houat
Ile de Hoedic
CHÂT. DE SUSCINIO
Piriac-sur-Mer
Penest

6

Guérande
Le Croisic
Pointe du Croisic
Batz-sur-Mer
KORRIGANS
Côte d'Amour

A B C D

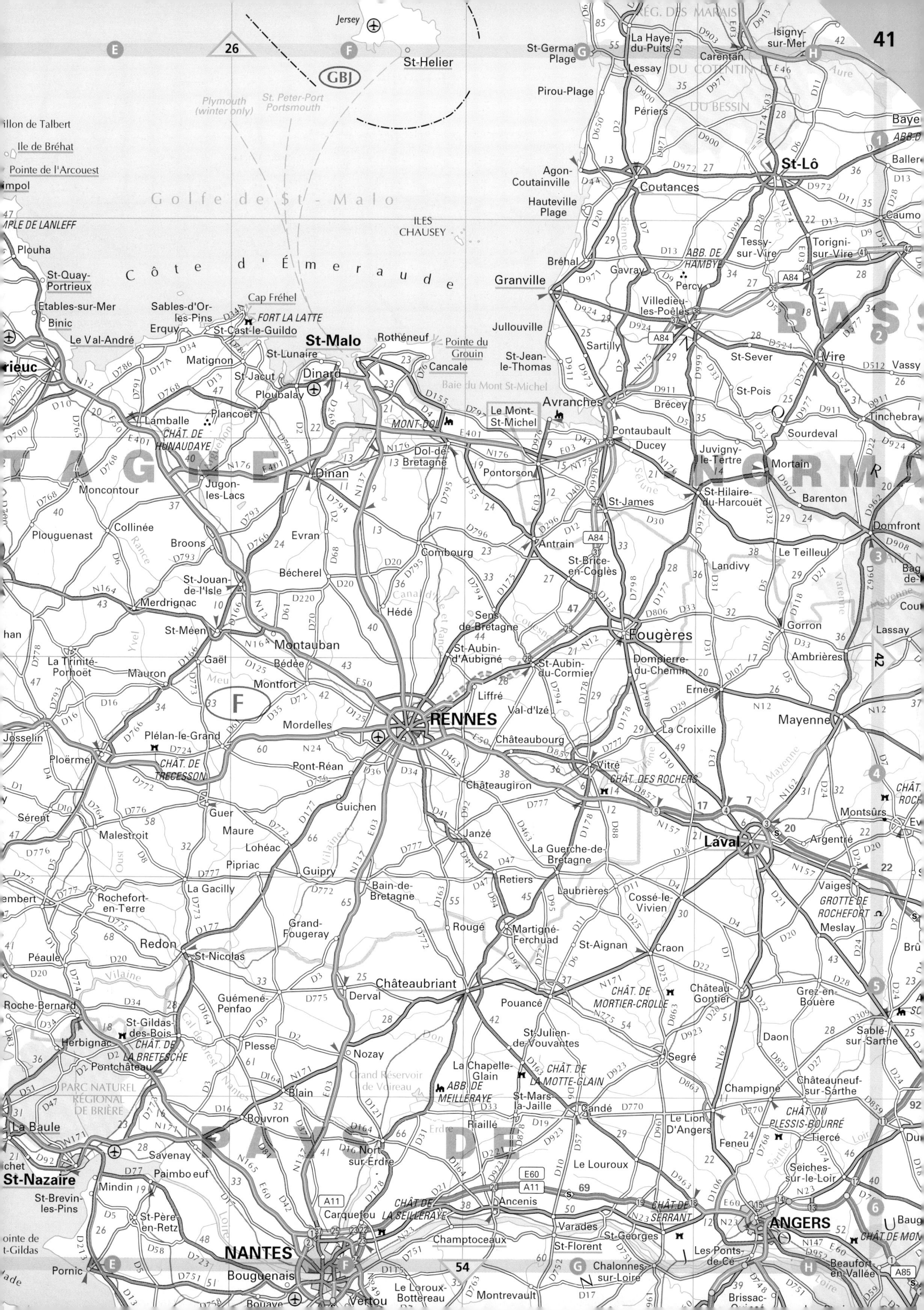
Jersey
St-Helier
GBJ
Plymouth (winter only)
St. Peter Port Portsmouth
Golfe de St-Malo
Côte d'Émeraude
ILES CHAUSEY
Ile de Bréhat
Pointe de l'Arcouest
Plouha
St-Quay-Portrieux
Etables-sur-Mer
Binic
Le Val-André
Cap Fréhel
FORT LA LATTE
Sables-d'Or-les-Pins
Erquy
St-Cast-le-Guildo
St-Malo
Rothéneuf
Pointe du Grouin
Cancale
St-Lunaire
Dinard
Matignon
St-Jacut
Ploubalay
Plancoët
Lamballe
CHÂT. DE HUNAUDAYE
Baie du Mont St-Michel
MONT-DOL
Le Mont-St-Michel
Avranches
Dol-de-Bretagne
Pontorson
Dinan
Jugon-les-Lacs
Moncontour
Collinée
Plouguenast
Broons
Evran
Combourg
Bécherel
St-Jouan-de-l'Isle
Merdrignac
St-Méen
Montauban
Hédé
Sens-de-Bretagne
St-Aubin-d'Aubigné
St-Aubin-du-Cormier
Fougères
Antrain
St-Brice-en-Coglès
St-James
Ducey
Pontaubault
La Trinité-Porhoët
Mauron
Gaël
Bédée
Montfort
Liffré
Val-d'Izé
RENNES
Mordelles
Plélan-le-Grand
CHÂT. DE TRECESSON
Josselin
Ploërmel
Pont-Réan
Châteaubourg
Vitré
CHÂT. DES ROCHERS
Châteaugiron
Guichen
Guer
Maure
Lohéac
Janzé
La Guerche-de-Bretagne
Sérent
Malestroit
Pipriac
La Gacilly
Guipry
Bain-de-Bretagne
Retiers
Rochefort-en-Terre
Redon
St-Nicolas
Grand-Fougeray
Rougé
Martigné-Ferchuad
Laubrières
Cossé-le-Vivien
St-Aignan
Craon
Péaule
Roche-Bernard
Châteaubriant
Derval
Guémené-Penfao
Pouancé
CHÂT. DE MORTIER-CROLLE
Château-Gontier
St-Gildas-des-Bois
CHÂT. DE LA BRETESCHE
Herbignac
Pontchâteau
Plesse
Nozay
St-Julien-de-Vouvantes
Segré
PARC NATUREL RÉGIONAL DE BRIÈRE
Grand Réservoir de Vioreau
La Chapelle-Glain
CHÂT. DE LA MOTTE-GLAIN
ABB. DE MEILLERAYE
St-Mars-la-Jaille
Blain
Bouvron
Candé
Riaillé
Le Lion-D'Angers
Champigné
Châteauneuf-sur-Sarthe
CHÂT. DU PLESSIS-BOURRÉ
La Baule
St-Nazaire
Savenay
Nort-sur-Erdre
Feneu
Tiercé
Paimboeuf
Mindin
St-Brevin-les-Pins
St-Père-en-Retz
Le Louroux
Seiches-sur-le-Loir
Carquefou
CHÂT. DE LA SEILLERAYE
Ancenis
CHÂT. DE SERRANT
ANGERS
Champtoceaux
Varades
St-Florent
St-Georges
NANTES
Bouguenais
Pornic
Vertou
Le Loroux-Bottereau
Montrevault
Chalonnes-sur-Loire
Les Ponts-de-Cé
Beaufort-en-Vallée
CHÂT. DE MON
Brissac
St-Germain-Plage
La Haye-du-Puits
Lessay
Carentan
Isigny-sur-Mer
Pirou-Plage
Périers
St-Lô
Agon-Coutainville
Coutances
Hauteville Plage
Bréhal
Gavray
ABB. DE HAMBYE
Percy
Tessy-sur-Vire
Torigni-sur-Vire
Granville
Villedieu-les-Poêles
Jullouville
Sartilly
St-Jean-le-Thomas
St-Sever
Vire
Vassy
St-Pois
Brécey
Sourdeval
Tinchebray
Juvigny-le-Tertre
Mortain
St-Hilaire-du-Harcouët
Barenton
Domfront
Le Teilleul
Landivy
Gorron
Lassay
Ambrières
Dompierre-du-Chemin
Ernée
Mayenne
La Croixille
Montsûrs
Laval
Argentré
Vaiges
GROTTE DE ROCHEFORT
Meslay
Grez-en-Bouère
Daon
Sablé-sur-Sarthe
RÉG. DES MARAIS DU COTENTIN ET DU BESSIN
BASSE NORMANDIE
BRETAGNE
PAYS DE LA LOIRE
26
42
54

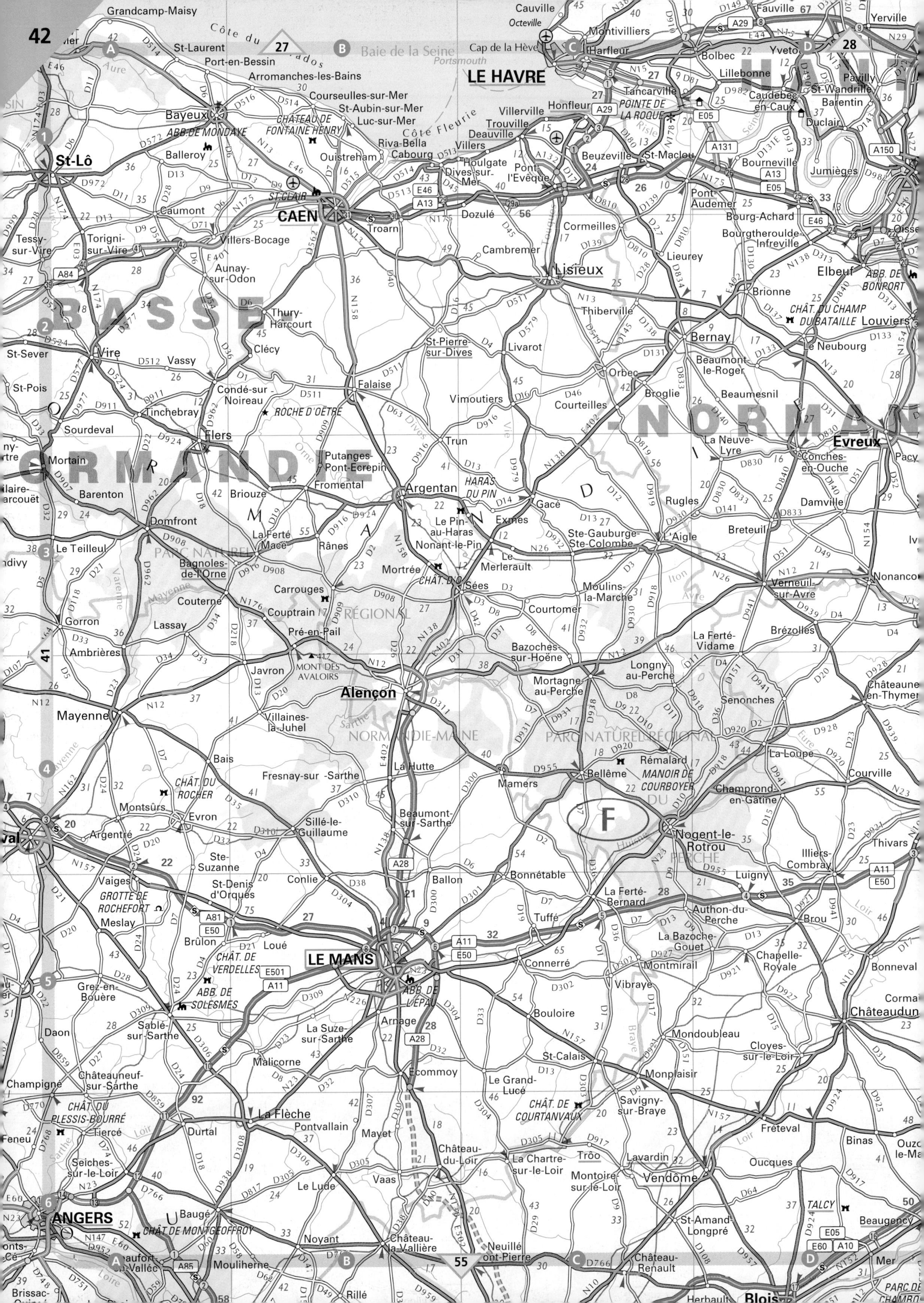

Grandcamp-Maisy
Côte du Bessin
27
Baie de la Seine
Portsmouth
Cauville
Octeville
Montivilliers
Harfleur
Cap de la Hève
LE HAVRE
Fauville
Yerville
Bolbec
Yvetot
28
Lillebonne
Pavilly
St-Wandrille
Tancarville
Caudebec-en-Caux
Barentin
Duclair
Jumièges
POINTE DE LA ROQUE
St-Laurent
Port-en-Bessin
Arromanches-les-Bains
Courseulles-sur-Mer
St-Aubin-sur-Mer
Luc-sur-Mer
CHÂTEAU DE FONTAINE HENRY
Bayeux
ABB. DE MONDAYE
Côte Fleurie
Villerville
Honfleur
Trouville
Deauville
Villers
Riva-Bella
Cabourg
Ouistreham
Houlgate
Dives-sur-Mer
Pont-l'Evêque
Beuzeville
St-Maclou
Bourneville
Pont-Audemer
Bourg-Achard
Bourgtheroulde-Infreville
Oissel
St-Lô
Balleroy
Caumont
ST-CLAIR
CAEN
Troarn
Dozulé
Cormeilles
Cambremer
Lisieux
Lieurey
Elbeuf
ABB. DE BONPORT
Tessy-sur-Vire
Torigni-sur-Vire
Villers-Bocage
Aunay-sur-Odon
Thury-Harcourt
BASSE
Thiberville
Brionne
CHÂT. DU CHAMP DE BATAILLE
Louviers
Bernay
Le Neubourg
St-Sever
Vire
Vassy
Clécy
St-Pierre-sur-Dives
Livarot
Orbec
Beaumont-le-Roger
St-Pois
Condé-sur-Noireau
Falaise
Broglie
Beaumesnil
Tinchebray
ROCHE D'OËTRE
Vimoutiers
Courteilles
Sourdeval
Flers
Trun
NORMANDIE
La Neuve-Lyre
Evreux
Conches-en-Ouche
Pacy
Mortain
Putanges-Pont-Ecrepin
Fromental
Argentan
HARAS DU PIN
Gacé
Barenton
Briouze
Rugles
Damville
Domfront
La Ferté-Macé
Le Pin-au-Haras
Exmes
L'Aigle
Breteuil
Le Teilleul
PARC NATUREL
Rânes
Nonant-le-Pin
Ste-Gauburge-Ste-Colombe
Bagnoles-de-l'Orne
Mortrée
CHÂT. D'O
Le Merlerault
Sées
Verneuil-sur-Avre
Nonancourt
Couterne
Carrouges
Moulins-la-Marche
Couptrain
RÉGIONAL
Courtomer
Gorron
Lassay
Pré-en-Pail
Ambrières
Bazoches-sur-Hoëne
La Ferté-Vidame
Brézolles
MONT DES AVALOIRS
Javron
Longny-au-Perche
Alençon
Mortagne-au-Perche
Senonches
Châteauneuf-en-Thymerais
Mayenne
Villaines-la-Juhel
NORMANDIE-MAINE
PARC NATUREL RÉGIONAL
Bais
La Hutte
Rémalard
La Loupe
MANOIR DE COURBOYER
Fresnay-sur-Sarthe
Mamers
Bellême
Courville
CHÂT. DU ROCHER
Champrond-en-Gâtine
Montsûrs
Evron
Beaumont-sur-Sarthe
Nogent-le-Rotrou
Argentré
Sillé-le-Guillaume
PERCHE
Thivars
Illiers-Combray
Ste-Suzanne
Bonnétable
Luigny
Vaiges
St-Denis-d'Orques
Conlie
Ballon
La Ferté-Bernard
GROTTE DE ROCHEFORT
Meslay
Tuffé
Authon-du-Perche
Brou
Brûlon
Loué
LE MANS
Connerré
La Bazoche-Gouet
Montmirail
Chapelle-Royale
Bonneval
CHÂT. DE VERDELLES
Vibraye
Grez-en-Bouère
ABB. DE SOLESMES
ABB. DE L'EPAU
Bouloire
Châteaudun
Sablé-sur-Sarthe
La Suze-sur-Sarthe
Arnage
Mondoubleau
Daon
Malicorne
St-Calais
Cloyes-sur-le-Loir
Champigné
Châteauneuf-sur-Sarthe
Ecommoy
Le Grand-Lucé
Monplaisir
CHÂT. DU PLESSIS-BOURRÉ
CHÂT. DE COURTANVAUX
Savigny-sur-Braye
La Flèche
Pontvallain
Tiercé
Durtal
Mayet
Fréteval
Binas
Seiches-sur-le-Loir
Château-du-Loir
La Chartre-sur-le-Loir
Trôo
Lavardin
Montoire-sur-le-Loir
Vendôme
Oucques
Le Lude
Vaas
ANGERS
Baugé
CHÂT. DE MONTGEOFFROY
TALCY
Beaugency
St-Amand-Longpré
Noyant
Château-la-Vallière
Neuillé-Pont-Pierre
55
Château-Renault
Mer
Mouliherne
Beaufort-en-Vallée
Brissac
Rillé
Herbault
Blois
PARC DE CHAMBORD

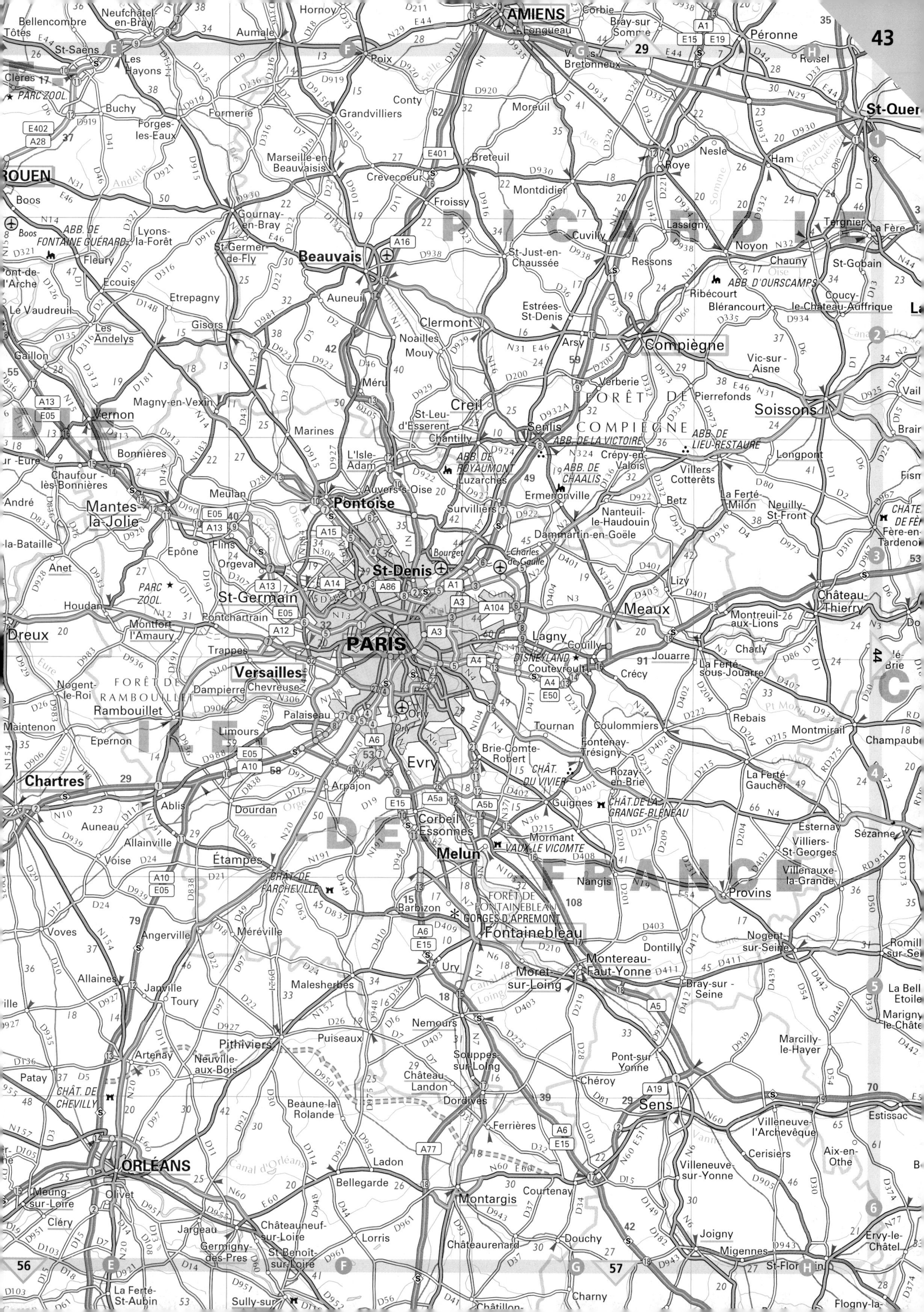
PICARDIE
ÎLE-DE-FRANCE
AMIENS
Longueau
Corbie
Bray-sur-Somme
Péronne
Neufchâtel-en-Bray
Bellencombre
Hornoy
Aumale
Poix
Villers-Bretonneux
St-Saëns
Les Hayons
Clères
PARC ZOOL.
Buchy
Forges-les-Eaux
Formerie
Grandvilliers
Conty
Moreuil
Roisel
St-Quentin
Ham
Nesle
Roye
Breteuil
Marseille-en-Beauvaisis
Crevecoeur
Montdidier
Froissy
ROUEN
Boos
ABB. DE FONTAINE GUÉRARD
Lyons-la-Forêt
Gournay-en-Bray
St-Germer-de-Fly
Beauvais
St-Just-en-Chaussée
Cuvilly
Lassigny
Noyon
Tergnier
La Fère
Chauny
St-Gobain
Ressons
ABB. D'OURSCAMPS
Ribécourt
Blérancourt
Coucy-le-Château-Auffrique
Pont-de-l'Arche
Fleury
Ecouis
Etrepagny
Auneuil
Le Vaudreuil
Les Andelys
Gisors
Clermont
Noailles
Mouy
Estrées-St-Denis
Arsy
Compiègne
Vic-sur-Aisne
Gaillon
Méru
Verberie
FORÊT DE COMPIEGNE
Pierrefonds
Soissons
Magny-en-Vexin
Creil
St-Leu-d'Esserent
Chantilly
Senlis
ABB. DE LA VICTOIRE
ABB. DE LIEU-RESTAURE
Vernon
Marines
Bonnières
L'Isle-Adam
ABB. DE ROYAUMONT
Luzarches
Crépy-en-Valois
ABB. DE CHAALIS
Longpont
Villers-Cotterêts
Chaufour-lès-Bonnières
Meulan
Auvers-s-Oise
Pontoise
Ermenonville
La Ferté-Milon
Neuilly-St-Front
Mantes-la-Jolie
Survilliers
Nanteuil-le-Haudouin
Betz
CHÂTEAU DE FÈRE
Fère-en-Tardenois
Epône
Flins
Orgeval
St-Denis
Bourget
Charles de Gaulle
Dammartin-en-Goële
Anet
PARC ZOOL.
St-Germain
Lizy
Houdan
Montfort-l'Amaury
Pontchartrain
Meaux
Château-Thierry
Dreux
Trappes
PARIS
Lagny
Couilly
DISNEYLAND
Montreuil-aux-Lions
Jouarre
Charly
Versailles
Chevreuse
Coutevroult
Crécy
La Ferté-sous-Jouarre
Nogent-le-Roi
FORÊT DE RAMBOUILLET
Dampierre
Rambouillet
Palaiseau
Orly
Tournan
Coulommiers
Rebais
Montmirail
Maintenon
Limours
Epernon
Evry
Brie-Comte-Robert
Fontenay-Trésigny
Champaubert
Chartres
CHÂT. DU VIVIER
Rozay-en-Brie
La Ferté-Gaucher
Arpajon
Ablis
Dourdan
Corbeil-Essonnes
Guignes
CHÂT. DE LA GRANGE-BLENEAU
Auneau
Allainville
Mormant
Esternay
Sézanne
Villiers-St-Georges
Étampes
Melun
VAUX-LE VICOMTE
Villenauxe-la-Grande
CHÂT. DE FARCHEVILLE
Voise
Nangis
Provins
FORÊT DE FONTAINEBLEAU
Barbizon
GORGES D'APREMONT
Fontainebleau
Voves
Angerville
Méréville
Dontilly
Nogent-sur-Seine
Romilly-sur-Seine
Montereau-Faut-Yonne
Moret-sur-Loing
Ury
Allaines
Janville
Toury
Malesherbes
Bray-sur-Seine
La Belle Etoile
Marigny-le-Châtel
Nemours
Puiseaux
Pithiviers
Artenay
Neuville-aux-Bois
Souppes-sur-Loing
Marcilly-le-Hayer
Pont-sur-Yonne
Patay
CHÂT. DE CHEVILLY
Château-Landon
Chéroy
Beaune-la-Rolande
Dordives
Sens
Estissac
Ferrières
Villeneuve-l'Archevêque
ORLÉANS
Ladon
Cerisiers
Aix-en-Othe
Villeneuve-sur-Yonne
Meung-sur-Loire
Olivet
Bellegarde
Montargis
Courtenay
Cléry
Jargeau
Châteauneuf-sur-Loire
Lorris
Germigny-des-Pres
St-Benoît-sur-Loire
Châteaurenard
Douchy
Joigny
Mignennes
Ervy-le-Châtel
St-Florentin
La Ferté-St-Aubin
Sully-sur-Loire
Charny
Châtillon
Flogny-la-
56
57
44
53
A1
A3
A4
A5
A6
A10
A13
A14
A15
A16
A19
A77
A86
A104
E05
E15
E50
E401
E402

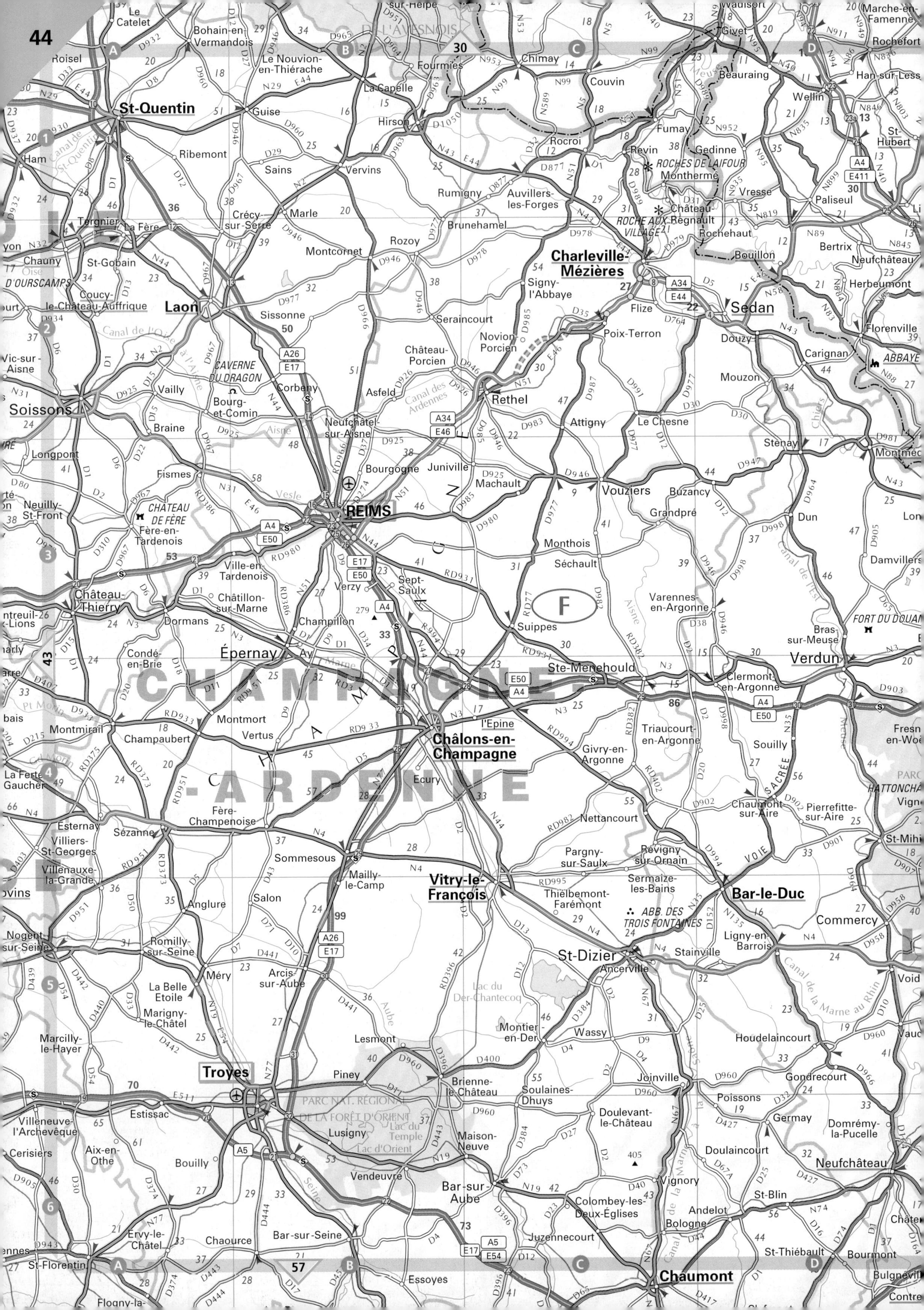
CHAMPAGNE-ARDENNE
F
Le Catelet
Bohain-en-Vermandois
Le Nouvion-en-Thiérache
Fourmies
Chimay
Couvin
Givet
Beauraing
Rochefort
Han-sur-Lesse
Wellin
St-Hubert
Roisel
St-Quentin
Guise
La Capelle
Hirson
Rocroi
Fumay
Revin
Gedinne
ROCHES DE LAIFOUR
Monthermé
Vresse
Paliseul
Château-Regnault
ROCHE AUX VILLAGE
Rochehaut
Bouillon
Bertrix
Neufchâteau
Herbeumont
Ham
Ribemont
Sains
Vervins
Rumigny
Auvillers-les-Forges
Tergnier
La Fère
Crécy-sur-Serre
Marle
Brunehamel
Rozoy
Montcornet
Charleville-Mézières
Chauny
St-Gobain
Coucy-le-Château-Auffrique
Laon
Signy-l'Abbaye
Sedan
Flize
Sissonne
Seraincourt
Novion-Porcien
Poix-Terron
Douzy
Florenville
Carignan
Château-Porcien
Mouzon
Soissons
Vailly
CAVERNE DU DRAGON
Bourg-et-Comin
Corbeny
Asfeld
Rethel
Attigny
Le Chesne
Braine
Neufchâtel-sur-Aisne
Stenay
Longpont
Fismes
Bourgogne
Juniville
Machault
Vouziers
Buzancy
Neuilly-St-Front
CHATEAU DE FÈRE
Fère-en-Tardenois
REIMS
Grandpré
Dun
Monthois
Damvillers
Séchault
Château-Thierry
Ville-en-Tardenois
Châtillon-sur-Marne
Verzy
Sept-Saulx
Varennes-en-Argonne
Dormans
Champillon
Suippes
FORT DU DOUAUMONT
Bras-sur-Meuse
Condé-en-Brie
Épernay
Ay
Ste-Menehould
Verdun
Clermont-en-Argonne
Montmirail
Montmort
Champaubert
Vertus
l'Epine
Châlons-en-Champagne
Triaucourt-en-Argonne
Souilly
Givry-en-Argonne
Ecury
La Ferté-Gaucher
Fère-Champenoise
Nettancourt
Chaumont-sur-Aire
Pierrefitte-sur-Aire
Esternay
Sézanne
Villiers-St-Georges
Villenauxe-la-Grande
Sommesous
Pargny-sur-Saulx
Revigny-sur-Ornain
Mailly-le-Camp
Vitry-le-François
Sermaize-les-Bains
Thiéblemont-Farémont
Bar-le-Duc
Commercy
Salon
Anglure
ABB. DES TROIS FONTAINES
Nogent-sur-Seine
Romilly-sur-Seine
St-Dizier
Ligny-en-Barrois
Stainville
Ancerville
Méry
Arcis-sur-Aube
La Belle Etoile
Lac du Der-Chantecoq
Marigny-le-Châtel
Montier-en-Der
Wassy
Marcilly-le-Hayer
Lesmont
Houdelaincourt
Troyes
Piney
Brienne-le-Château
Soulaines-Dhuys
Joinville
Gondrecourt
PARC NAT. RÉGIONAL DE LA FORÊT D'ORIENT
Lac du Temple
Lac d'Orient
Villeneuve-l'Archevêque
Estissac
Lusigny
Maison-Neuve
Doulevant-le-Château
Poissons
Germay
Domrémy-la-Pucelle
Cerisiers
Aix-en-Othe
Bouilly
Vendeuvre
Doulaincourt
Neufchâteau
Bar-sur-Aube
Vignory
Colombey-les-Deux-Églises
St-Blin
Andelot
Bologne
Ervy-le-Châtel
Chaource
Bar-sur-Seine
Juzennecourt
St-Thiébault
Bourmont
St-Florentin
Essoyes
Chaumont
Bulgnéville
Flogny-la-
Canal des Ardennes
Canal de l'Est
Canal de la Marne au Rhin
Aisne
Vesle
Marne
Aube
Seine
Meuse
VOIE SACRÉE

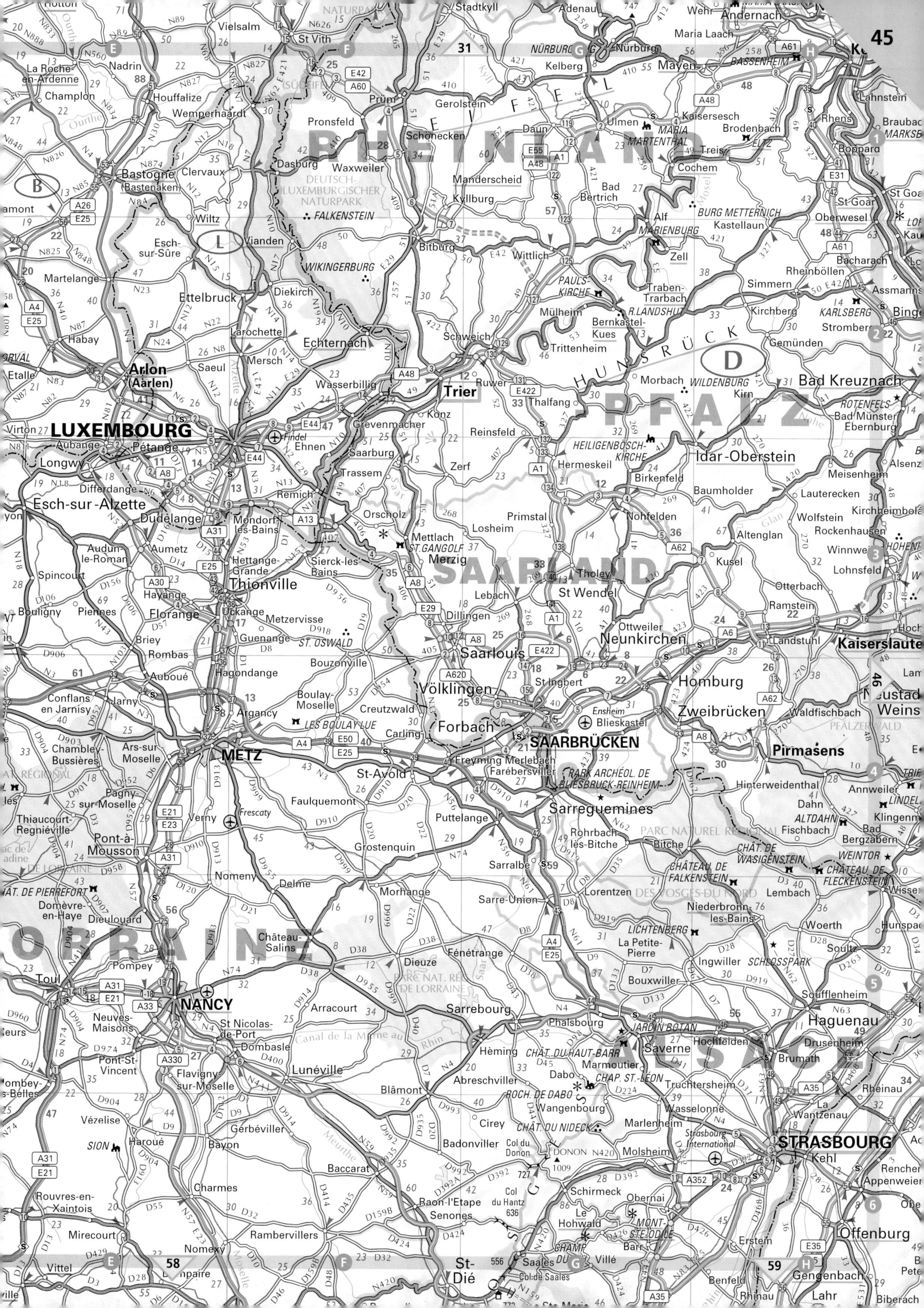

RHEINLAND
PFALZ
SAARLAND
ORRAINE
ALSACE
EIFEL
HUNSRÜCK
Andernach
Maria Laach
Nürburg
Mayen
Kelberg
Adenau
Stadtkyll
St Vith
Vielsalm
La Roche-en-Ardenne
Nadrin
Houffalize
Champlon
Wemperhaardt
Prüm
Gerolstein
Daun
Ulmen
Kaisersesch
Brodenbach
Lahnstein
Rhens
Boppard
Braubach
St Goar
Oberwesel
Bacharach
Kaub
Rheinböllen
Bingen
Cochem
Treis
MARIA MARTENTHAL
ELTZ
BURG METTERNICH
Alf
MARIENBURG
Zell
Kastellaun
Simmern
Kirchberg
KARLSBERG
Stromberg
Gemünden
Bad Kreuznach
Bad Münster
Ebernburg
ROTENFELS
Bad Bertrich
Manderscheid
Kyllburg
Schönecken
Pronsfeld
Dasburg
Waxweiler
DEUTSCH-LUXEMBURGISCHER NATURPARK
FALKENSTEIN
Bastogne (Bastenaken)
Clervaux
Wiltz
Vianden
Esch-sur-Sûre
Bitburg
Wittlich
WIKINGERBURG
Diekirch
Ettelbruck
Martelange
Traben-Trarbach
PAULS-KIRCHE
Mülheim
Bernkastel-Kues
R.LANDSHUT
Trittenheim
Schweich
Echternach
Larochette
Mersch
Saeul
Habay
Arlon (Aarlen)
Etalle
Virton
LUXEMBOURG
Aubange
Pétange
Longwy
Differdange
Esch-sur-Alzette
Dudelange
Mondorf-les-Bains
Wasserbillig
Trier
Ruwer
Konz
Grevenmacher
Ehnen
Findel
Saarburg
Trassem
Remich
Orscholz
Mettlach
ST.GANGOLF
Merzig
Zerf
Reinsfeld
Thalfang
Morbach
WILDENBURG
Kirn
Idar-Oberstein
HEILIGENBOSCH-KIRCHE
Hermeskeil
Birkenfeld
Baumholder
Nohfelden
Primstal
Losheim
Tholey
St Wendel
Lebach
Dillingen
Saarlouis
Völklingen
Ottweiler
Neunkirchen
Homburg
Zweibrücken
Kusel
Altenglan
Lauterecken
Meisenheim
Wolfstein
Rockenhausen
Winnweiler
Lohnsfeld
Otterbach
Ramstein
Landstuhl
Kaiserslautern
Alsenz
Kirchheimbolanden
HOHENECKEN
Neustadt
Weinstr.
Waldfischbach
PFÄLZERWALD
Pirmasens
Hinterweidenthal
Dahn
ALTDAHN
Annweiler
LINDELBRUNN
Klingenmünster
Fischbach
Bad Bergzabern
WEINTOR
CHÂTEAU DE FLECKENSTEIN
Wissembourg
Lembach
Hunspach
Soultz
Woerth
Niederbronn-les-Bains
CHÂTEAU DE FALKENSTEIN
CHÂT. DE WASIGENSTEIN
Bitche
PARC NATUREL REGIONAL DES VOSGES DU NORD
Rohrbach-lès-Bitche
Sarreguemines
PARC ARCHÉOL. DE BLIESBRUCK-REINHEIM
Blieskastel
Ensheim
SAARBRÜCKEN
St Ingbert
Forbach
Freyming Merlebach
Farébersviller
Carling
Creutzwald
Boulay-Moselle
LES BOULAY LUE
Bouzonville
ST. OSWALD
Sierck-les-Bains
Hettange-Grande
Thionville
Audun-le-Roman
Aumetz
Hayange
Florange
Uckange
Metzervisse
Guenange
Spincourt
Bouligny
Piennes
Briey
Rombas
Hagondange
Auboué
Conflans en Jarnisy
Jarny
Argancy
METZ
Ars-sur-Moselle
Chambley-Bussières
St-Avold
Faulquemont
Puttelange
Grostenquin
Sarralbe
Sarre-Union
Lorentzen
Morhange
Delme
Nomeny
Verny
Frescaty
Pagny-sur-Moselle
Thiaucourt-Regniéville
Pont-à-Mousson
CHÂT. DE PIERREFORT
Domèvre-en-Haye
Dieulouard
Château-Salins
Dieuze
Fénétrange
PARC NAT. RÉG. DE LORRAINE
Pompey
Toul
NANCY
Neuves-Maisons
St Nicolas-de-Port
Dombasle
Arracourt
Sarrebourg
Phalsbourg
JARDIN BOTAN.
Saverne
CHÂT. DU HAUT-BARR
Hochfelden
LICHTENBERG
La Petite-Pierre
Ingwiller
Bouxwiller
SCHLOSSPARK
Soufflenheim
Haguenau
Drusenheim
Brumath
Rheinau
La Wantzenau
Marmoutier
Dabo
CHAP. ST.-LÉON
ROCH. DE DABO
Wangenbourg
CHÂT. DU NIDECK
Truchtersheim
Wasselonne
Marlenheim
Strasbourg International
STRASBOURG
Kehl
Molsheim
Obernai
Schirmeck
MONT-STE-ODILE
Le Hohwald
Barr
Erstein
Offenburg
Appenweier
Renchen
Gengenbach
Lahr
Benfeld
Rhinau
Biberach
Villé
Saales
Col de Saales
St-Dié
Senones
Raon-l'Etape
Col du Hantz
Col du Donon
DONON
Badonviller
Cirey
Abreschviller
Hèming
Blâmont
Lunéville
Baccarat
Rambervillers
Gerbéviller
Bayon
Charmes
Flavigny-sur-Moselle
Pont-St-Vincent
Vézelise
Haroué
SION
Mirecourt
Rouvres-en-Xaintois
Vittel
Nomexy
Canal de la Marne au Rhin

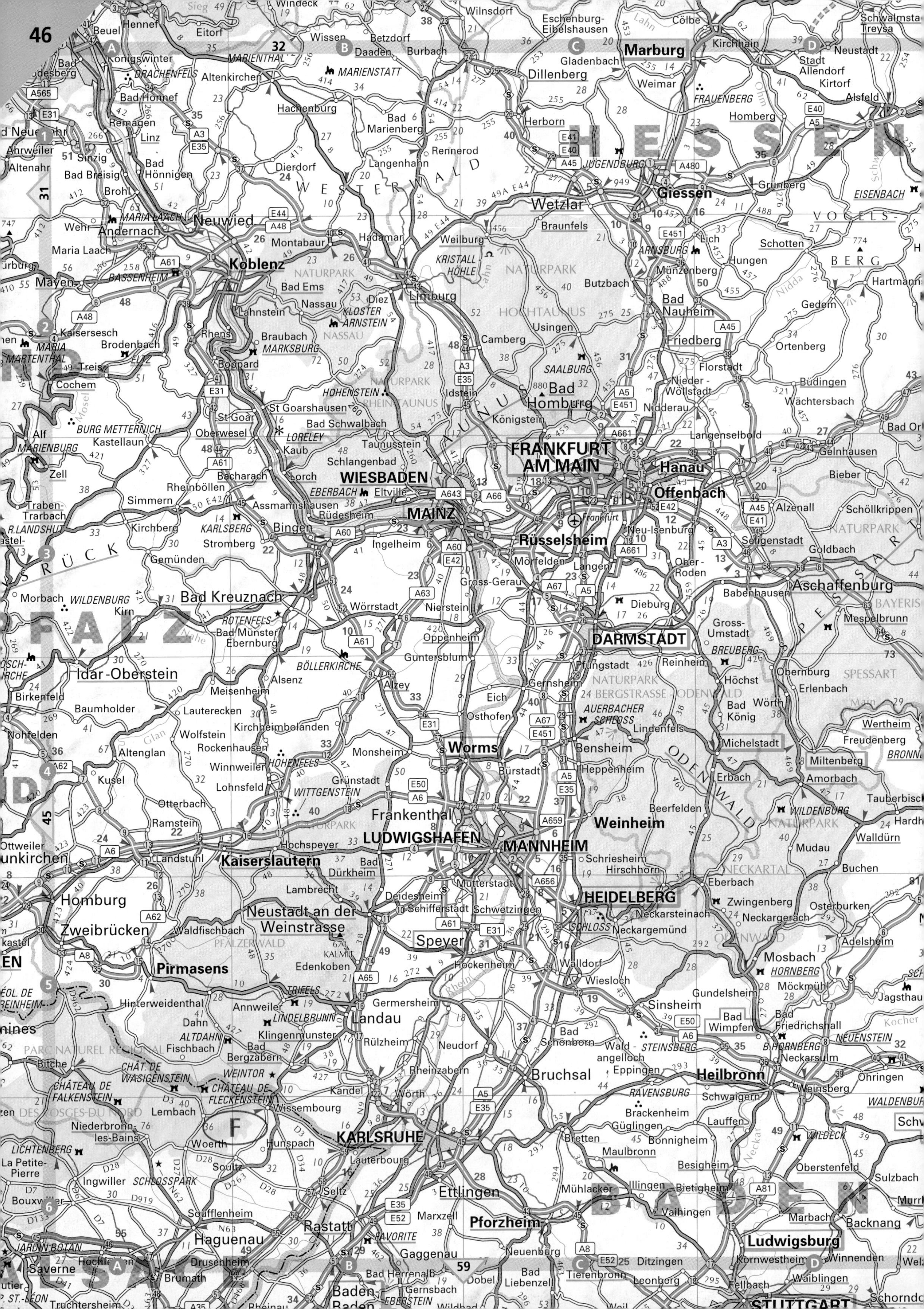
HESSEN
PFALZ
BADEN
ALSACE
WESTERWALD
TAUNUS
ODENWALD
SPESSART
VOGELSBERG
HUNSRÜCK
Beuel
Hennef
Eitorf
Windeck
Sieg
Wissen
Betzdorf
Daaden
Burbach
Wilnsdorf
Eschenburg-Eibelshausen
Cölbe
Schwalmstadt-Treysa
Königswinter
Bad Godesberg
DRACHENFELS
Altenkirchen
MARIENTHAL
MARIENSTATT
Dillenberg
Gladenbach
Marburg
Kirchhain
Stadt Allendorf
Neustadt
Kirtorf
Weimar
FRAUENBERG
Alsfeld
Bad Honnef
Remagen
Hachenburg
Bad Marienberg
Herborn
Homberg
Bad Neuenahr
Ahrweiler
Altenahr
Sinzig
Linz
Bad Breisig
Bad Hönningen
Dierdorf
Rennerod
Langenhahn
JUGENDBURG
Giessen
Grünberg
EISENBACH
Brohl
MARIA LAACH
Neuwied
Wetzlar
Braunfels
Lich
Schotten
Hungen
Andernach
Maria Laach
Wehr
Montabaur
Hadamar
Weilburg
ARNSBURG
Münzenberg
Koblenz
Mayen
BASSENHEIM
Bad Ems
KRISTALLHÖHLE
NATURPARK
Butzbach
Hartmann
Limburg
Diez
Nassau
KLOSTER ARNSTEIN
Lahnstein
HOCHTAUNUS
Bad Nauheim
Gedern
Kaisersesch
Rhens
Braubach
MARKSBURG
NASSAU
Usingen
Camberg
Friedberg
Ortenberg
MARIA MARTENTHAL
Brodenbach
ELTZ
Treis
Boppard
SAALBURG
Florstadt
Cochem
HOHENSTEIN
Idstein
Bad Homburg
Nieder-Wöllstadt
Büdingen
Wächtersbach
St Goarshausen
RHEINTAUNUS
Königstein
Nidderau
BURG METTERNICH
St Goar
Bad Schwalbach
Alf
MARIENBURG
Kastellaun
Oberwesel
LORELEY
Taunusstein
FRANKFURT AM MAIN
Langenselbold
Gelnhausen
Bad Orb
Kaub
Schlangenbad
Zell
Bacharach
Lorch
WIESBADEN
Hanau
Bieber
Rheinböllen
EBERBACH
Eltville
Offenbach
Traben-Trarbach
Simmern
Assmannshausen
Rüdesheim
MAINZ
Alzenau
Schöllkrippen
R. LANDSHUT
Kirchberg
KARLSBERG
Bingen
Frankfurt
Neu-Isenburg
Seligenstadt
Stromberg
Ingelheim
Rüsselsheim
Goldbach
Gemünden
Mörfelden
Langen
Ober-Roden
Morbach
WILDENBURG
Kirn
Bad Kreuznach
Gross-Gerau
Aschaffenburg
Babenhausen
BAYERIS
Wörrstadt
Nierstein
Dieburg
ROTENFELS
Bad Münster
Ebernburg
Oppenheim
Gross-Umstadt
Mespelbrunn
DARMSTADT
BREUBERG
Idar-Oberstein
BÖLLERKIRCHE
Guntersblum
Pfungstadt
Reinheim
Obernburg
Höchst
Erlenbach
Birkenfeld
Alsenz
Alzey
Gernsheim
BERGSTRASSE-ODENWALD
Meisenheim
Eich
Bad König
Wörth
Baumholder
Lauterecken
Osthofen
AUERBACHER SCHLOSS
Lindenfels
Wertheim
Nohfelden
Wolfstein
Kirchheimbolanden
Worms
Bensheim
Michelstadt
Freudenberg
Rockenhausen
Altenglan
Monsheim
Bürstadt
Miltenberg
Winnweiler
HOHENFELS
Heppenheim
Kusel
Grünstadt
Erbach
Amorbach
Lohnsfeld
WITTGENSTEIN
Otterbach
Frankenthal
Beerfelden
Tauberbischofsheim
WILDENBURG
Ramstein
Weinheim
Hardheim
LUDWIGSHAFEN
MANNHEIM
Mudau
Walldürn
Ottweiler
Neunkirchen
Landstuhl
Kaiserslautern
Hochspeyer
Bad Dürkheim
Schriesheim
Hirschhorn
NECKARTAL
Buchen
Lambrecht
Mutterstadt
Eberbach
Homburg
Deidesheim
Schifferstadt
Schwetzingen
HEIDELBERG
Zwingenberg
Osterburken
Neustadt an der Weinstrasse
Neckarsteinach
Neckargerach
Zweibrücken
Waldfischbach
Speyer
SCHLOSS
Neckargemünd
Adelsheim
PFÄLZERWALD
KALMIT
Mosbach
Pirmasens
Edenkoben
Hockenheim
Walldorf
HORNBERG
Wiesloch
Gundelsheim
Möckmühl
Jagsthausen
TRIFELS
Hinterweidenthal
Annweiler
Germersheim
Sinsheim
Bad Wimpfen
Bad Friedrichshall
Dahn
LINDELBRUNN
Landau
ALTDAHN
Klingenmünster
Rülzheim
Neudorf
Bad Schönborn
Wald-angelloch
STEINSBERG
HORNBERG
NEUENSTEIN
Neckarsulm
PARC NATUREL REGIONAL
Fischbach
Bad Bergzabern
Rheinzabern
Bruchsal
Eppingen
Heilbronn
Öhringen
Bitche
CHÂT. DE WASIGENSTEIN
WEINTOR
Weinsberg
CHÂTEAU DE FALKENSTEIN
CHÂTEAU DE FLECKENSTEIN
Kandel
Wörth
RAVENSBURG
Schwaigern
WALDENBURG
DES VOSGES DU NORD
Lembach
Wissembourg
Brackenheim
Niederbronn-les-Bains
KARLSRUHE
Güglingen
Lauffen
WILDECK
Woerth
Hunspach
Bretten
Bonnigheim
LICHTENBERG
Soultz
Lauterbourg
Maulbronn
Besigheim
Oberstenfeld
La Petite-Pierre
Ingwiller
SCHLOSSPARK
Seltz
Ettlingen
Mühlacker
Illingen
Bietigheim
Sulzbach
Bouxwiller
Soufflenheim
Marxzell
Pforzheim
Vaihingen
Marbach
Backnang
Haguenau
Rastatt
FAVORITE
Ludwigsburg
JARDIN BOTAN.
Hochfelden
Drusenheim
Gaggenau
Neuenbürg
Ditzingen
Kornwestheim
Winnenden
Saverne
Brumath
Bad Herrenalb
Dobel
Bad Liebenzell
Tiefenbronn
Leonberg
Waiblingen
Fellbach
ST-LÉON
Truchtersheim
Baden-Baden
Gernsbach
EBERSTEIN
STUTTGART
Schorndorf
Rheinau
Wildbad

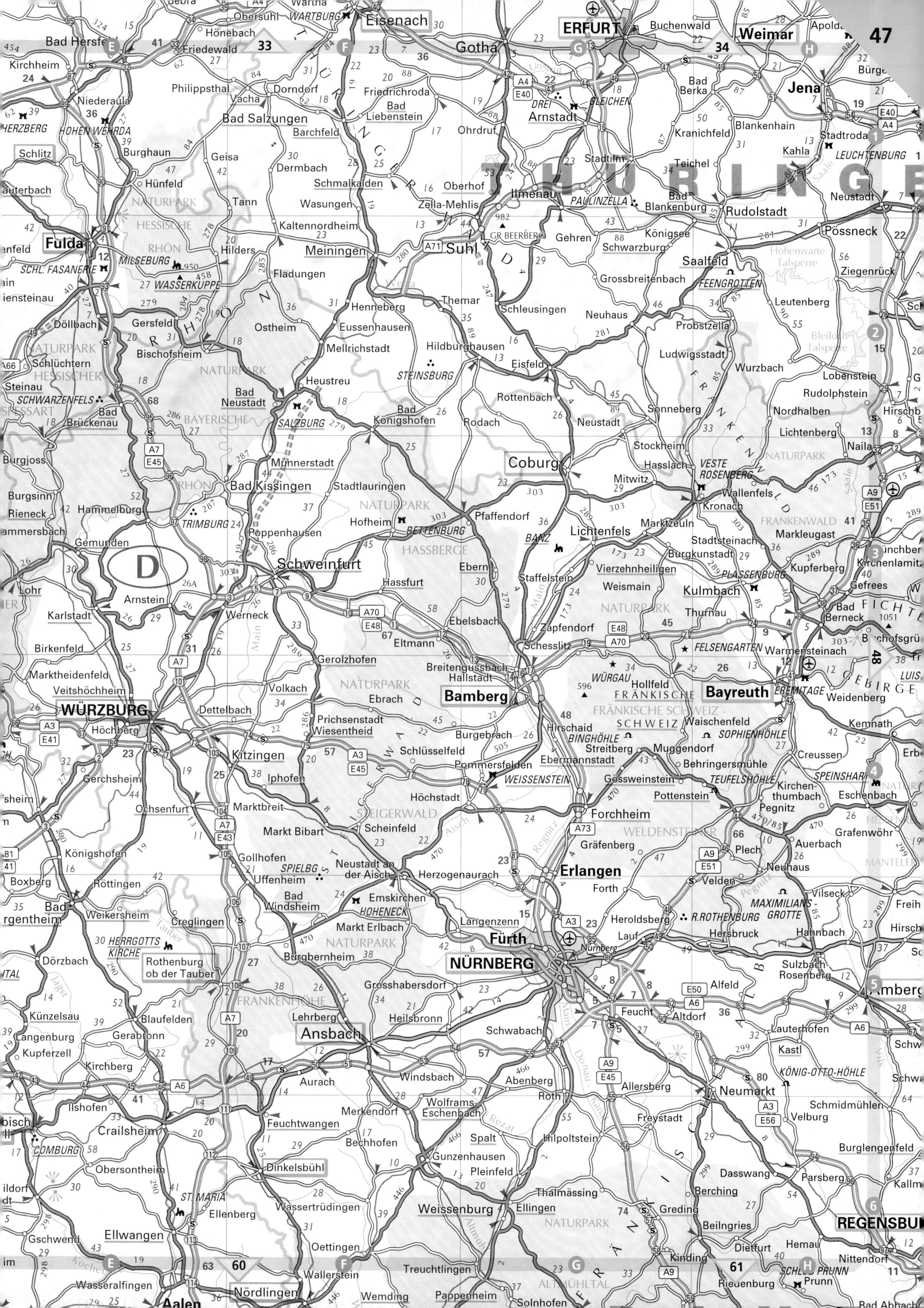

Eisenach
Gotha
ERFURT
Buchenwald
Weimar
Apolda
Bad Hersfeld
Obersuhl
WARTBURG
Hönebach
Friedewald
Kirchheim
Philippsthal
Dorndorf
Friedrichroda
Bad Liebenstein
Arnstadt
DREI GLEICHEN
Bad Berka
Jena
Niederaula
HERZBERG
HOHEN WEHRDA
Vacha
Bad Salzungen
Barchfeld
Ohrdruf
Kranichfeld
Blankenhain
Stadtroda
Schlitz
Burghaun
Geisa
Dermbach
Stadtilm
Teichel
Kahla
LEUCHTENBURG
Hünfeld
Schmalkalden
Oberhof
THÜRINGER WALD
Lauterbach
NATURPARK HESSISCHE RHÖN
Tann
Wasungen
Zella-Mehlis
Ilmenau
PAULINZELLA
Bad Blankenburg
Rudolstadt
Neustadt
Kaltennordheim
GR BEERBERG
Gehren
Königsee
Pössneck
Fulda
Hilders
Meiningen
Suhl
Schwarzburg
Saalfeld
Hohenwarte Talsperre
Ziegenrück
SCHL. FASANERIE
MILSEBURG
WASSERKUPPE
Fladungen
Grossbreitenbach
FEENGROTTEN
Leutenberg
Steinau
Themar
Schleusingen
Neuhaus
Henneberg
Ostheim
Döllbach
Gersfeld
Eussenhausen
Probstzella
Bleiloch Talsperre
Schlüchtern
Bischofsheim
Mellrichstadt
Hildburghausen
Ludwigsstadt
NATURPARK HESSISCHER SPESSART
RHÖN
Heustreu
Eisfeld
STEINSBURG
Wurzbach
Lobenstein
SCHWARZENFELS
Bad Neustadt
Rottenbach
Rudolphstein
Bad Brückenau
BAYERISCHE RHÖN
SALZBURG
Bad Königshofen
Rodach
Sonneberg
Nordhalben
Neustadt
Lichtenberg
Naila
Burgjoss
Münnerstadt
Stockheim
Coburg
Hasslach
VESTE ROSENBERG
Bad Kissingen
Stadtlauringen
Mitwitz
Wallenfels
Burgsinn
Rieneck
Hammelburg
TRIMBURG
NATURPARK HASSBERGE
Hofheim
BETTENBURG
Pfaffendorf
Kronach
FRANKENWALD
Gemünden
Poppenhausen
BANZ
Lichtenfels
Marktzeuln
Stadtsteinach
Markleugast
D
Schweinfurt
Ebern
Staffelstein
Vierzehnheiligen
Burgkunstadt
PLASSENBURG
Kupferberg
Kirchenlamitz
Gefrees
Lohr
Arnstein
Hassfurt
Weismain
Kulmbach
Bad Berneck
Karlstadt
Werneck
Ebelsbach
NATURPARK
Thurnau
FICHTELGEBIRGE
Eltmann
Zapfendorf
Bischofsgrün
Schesslitz
FELSENGARTEN
Warmensteinach
Birkenfeld
Gerolzhofen
Breitengüssbach
Hallstadt
WÜRGAU
Hollfeld
Marktheidenfeld
NATURPARK STEIGERWALD
Volkach
Ebrach
Bamberg
FRÄNKISCHE SCHWEIZ
Bayreuth
EREMITAGE
Weidenberg
Veitshöchheim
WÜRZBURG
Dettelbach
Prichsenstadt
Wiesentheid
Burgebrach
Hirschaid
BINGHÖHLE
Streitberg
Waischenfeld
SOPHIENHÖHLE
Kemnath
Höchberg
Schlüsselfeld
Muggendorf
Creussen
Kitzingen
Pommersfelden
WEISSENSTEIN
Ebermannstadt
Behringersmühle
Gerchsheim
Iphofen
Gössweinstein
TEUFELSHÖHLE
SPEINSHART
Kirchenthumbach
Eschenbach
Ochsenfurt
Marktbreit
Höchstadt
Pottenstein
Pegnitz
Forchheim
Markt Bibart
Scheinfeld
Aisch
WELDENSTEINER FORST
Grafenwöhr
Königshofen
Gollhofen
SPIELBG
Uffenheim
Neustadt an der Aisch
Herzogenaurach
Gräfenberg
Erlangen
Auerbach
Plech
Neuhaus
Boxberg
Röttingen
Bad Windsheim
Emskirchen
HOHENECK
Forth
Velden
Vilseck
Bad Mergentheim
Weikersheim
Creglingen
Markt Erlbach
Langenzenn
Heroldsberg
R.ROTHENBURG
MAXIMILIANS GROTTE
Freihung
HERRGOTTS KIRCHE
Rothenburg ob der Tauber
Fürth
Lauf
Hersbruck
Hahnbach
Dörzbach
Burgbernheim
NATURPARK FRANKENHÖHE
NÜRNBERG
Sulzbach-Rosenberg
Grosshabersdorf
Alfeld
Amberg
Künzelsau
Blaufelden
Lehrberg
Heilsbronn
Feucht
Altdorf
Langenburg
Gerabronn
Ansbach
Schwabach
Lauterhofen
Kupferzell
Kirchberg
Kastl
KÖNIG-OTTO-HÖHLE
Aurach
Windsbach
Abenberg
Allersberg
Neumarkt
Ilshofen
Wolframs-Eschenbach
Roth
Merkendorf
Schmidmühlen
Velburg
Crailsheim
Feuchtwangen
Freystadt
COMBURG
Bechhofen
Spalt
Hilpoltstein
Burglengenfeld
Dinkelsbühl
Gunzenhausen
Obersontheim
Pleinfeld
Dasswang
Parsberg
ST. MARIA
Thalmässing
Berching
Ellenberg
Wassertrüdingen
Weissenburg
Ellingen
Greding
Ellwangen
NATURPARK ALTMÜHLTAL
Beilngries
REGENSBURG
Gschwend
Oettingen
Dietfurt
Hemau
Kinding
Nittendorf
Wallerstein
Treuchtlingen
SCHLOSS PRUNN
Prunn
Wasseralfingen
Riedenburg
Aalen
Nördlingen
Wemding
Pappenheim
Solnhofen
Bad Abbach

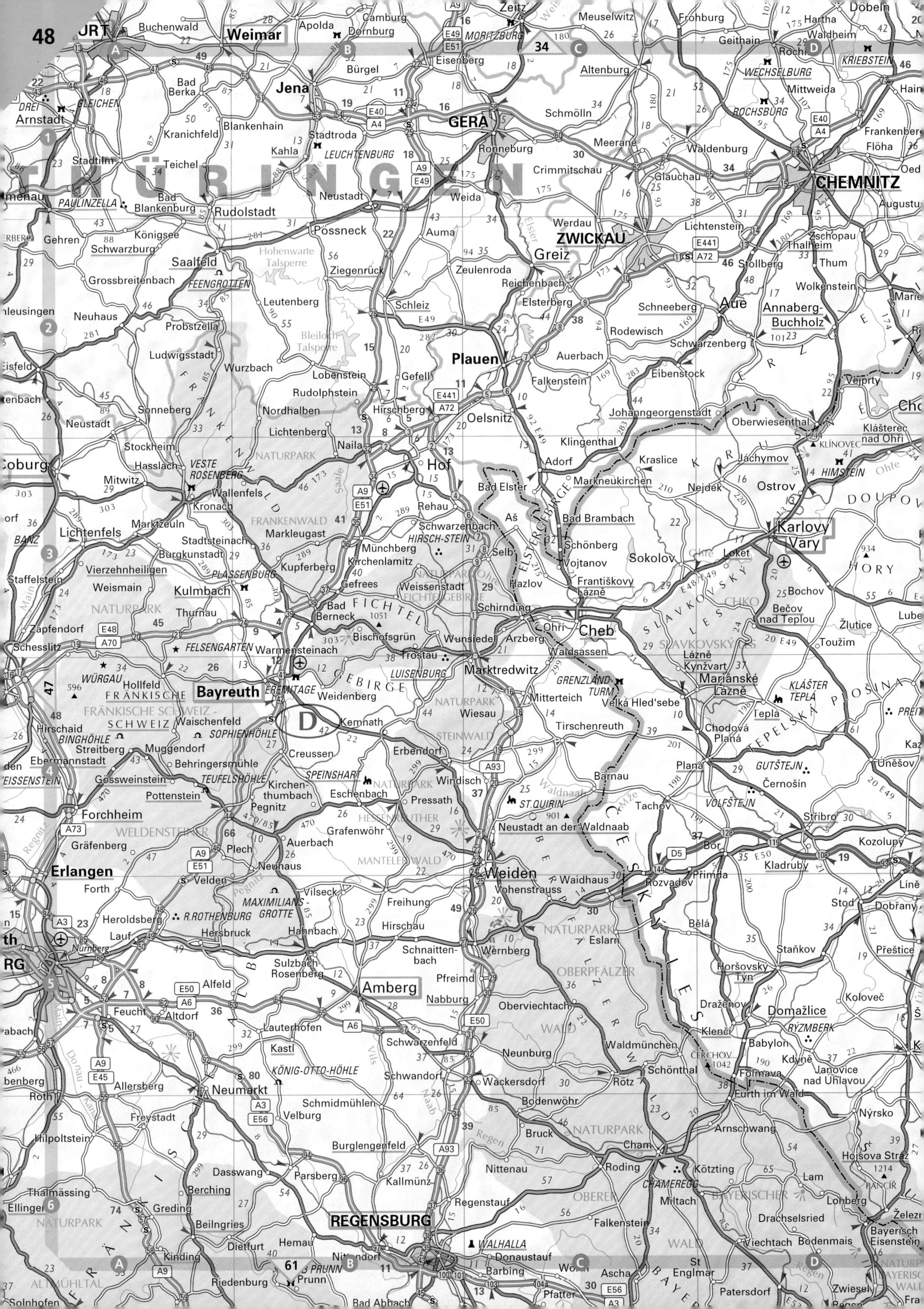
THÜRINGEN
Weimar
Jena
GERA
CHEMNITZ
ZWICKAU
Plauen
Hof
Bayreuth
Kulmbach
Coburg
Erlangen
Amberg
Weiden
REGENSBURG
Cheb
Karlovy Vary
Mariánské Lázně
Domažlice
Neumarkt
Forchheim
Saalfeld
Rudolstadt
Arnstadt
Greiz
Aue
Annaberg-Buchholz
Marktredwitz
FICHTELGEBIRGE
FRANKENWALD
FRÄNKISCHE SCHWEIZ
OBERPFÄLZER WALD
SLAVKOVSKÝ LES
KRUŠNÉ HORY
ČESKÝ LES
BAYERISCHER WALD
TEPELSKÁ PLOŠINA
DOUPOVSKÉ HORY
D

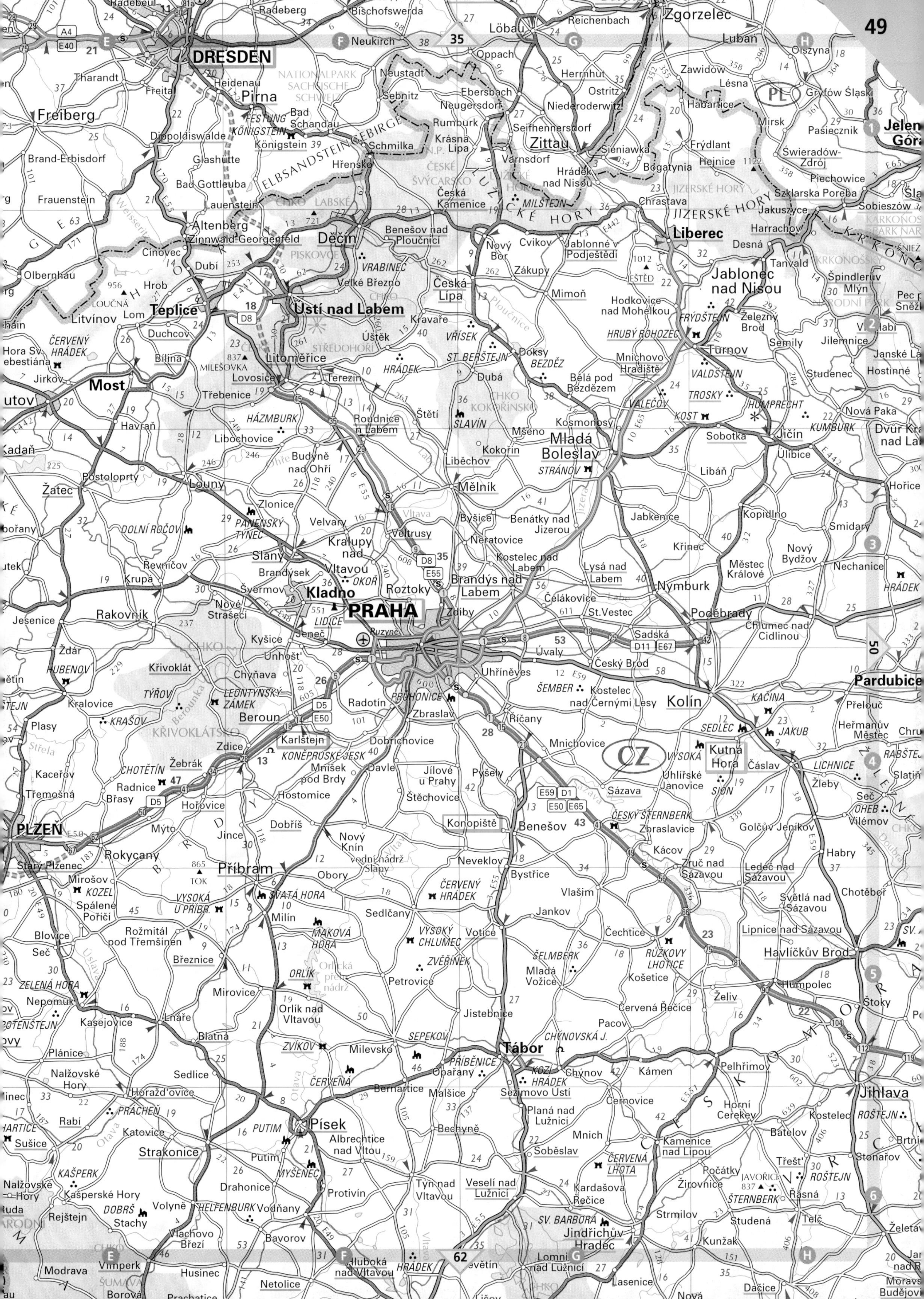
Radebeul
Radeberg
Bischofswerda
Löbau
Reichenbach
Zgorzelec
DRESDEN
Neukirch
Lubań
Olszyna
Tharandt
Heidenau
Freital
NATIONALPARK SÄCHSISCHE SCHWEIZ
Neustadt
Oppach
Herrnhut
Zawidów
Lésna
Pirna
Sebnitz
Ebersbach
Neugersdorf
Ostritz
Niederoderwitz
Habartice
PL
Gryfów Śląski
Freiberg
Bad Schandau
FESTUNG KÖNIGSTEIN
Rumburk
Seifhennersdorf
Mirsk
Pasiecznik
Jelenia Góra
Dippoldiswalde
Königstein
Schmilka
ELBSANDSTEINGEBIRGE
Krásná Lipa
Zittau
Sieniawka
Frýdlant
Brand-Erbisdorf
Glashütte
Hřensko
Varnsdorf
Bogatynia
Hejnice
Świeradów-Zdrój
Bad Gottleuba
ČESKÉ ŠVÝCARSKO
LUŽICKÉ HORY
Hrádek nad Nisou
JIZERSKÉ HORY
Piechowice
Frauenstein
Lauenstein
CHKO LABSKÉ
Česká Kamenice
MILŠTEJN
Chrastava
Szklarska Poręba
Jakuszyce
Sobieszów
Altenberg
Zinnwald-Georgenfeld
Děčín
Benešov nad Ploučnicí
Liberec
Harrachov
KARKONOSKI PARK NARODOWY
Cínovec
Nový Bor
Cvikov
Jablonné v Podještědí
Desná
KRKONOŠE
Olbernhau
Dubí
PISKOVCE
VRABINEC
Ještěd
Tanvald
Jablonec nad Nisou
Špindlerův Mlýn
Hrob
Velké Březno
Česká Lípa
Zákupy
Mimoň
Hodkovice nad Mohelkou
Pec pod Sněžkou
LOUČNÁ
Teplice
Ústí nad Labem
Litvínov
Lom
Kravaře
VRÍSEK
FRÝDŠTEJN
Železný Brod
Vrchlabí
Duchcov
Úštěk
HRUBÝ ROHOZEC
Semily
Jilemnice
ČERVENÝ HRÁDEK
STŘEDOHOŘÍ
ST. BERŠTEJN
Doksy
Turnov
Jánské Lázně
Hora Sv. Šebestiána
Bílina
Litoměřice
Mnichovo Hradiště
Studenec
Hostinné
MILEŠOVKA
Terezín
BEZDĚZ
Jirkov
Lovosice
HRÁDEK
Dubá
Bělá pod Bezdězem
VALDŠTEJN
Most
Třebenice
TROSKY
Chomutov
CHKO KOKOŘÍNSKO
VALEČOV
HUMPRECHT
Nová Paka
HÁZMBURK
Roudnice n Labem
Štětí
SLAVÍN
Kosmonosy
KOST
Havraň
Mšeno
Mladá Boleslav
Sobotka
Jičín
KUMBURK
Dvůr Králové nad Labem
Libochovice
Kadaň
Budyně nad Ohří
Kokořín
STRÁNOV
Úlibice
Postoloprty
Liběchov
Libáň
Žatec
Louny
Mělník
Hořice
Zlonice
PANENSKÝ TÝNEC
Vltava
Byšice
Benátky nad Jizerou
Jabkenice
Kopidlno
DOLNÍ ROČOV
Velvary
Veltrusy
Smidary
Neratovice
Křinec
Nový Bydžov
Kralupy nad Vltavou
Slaný
Řevničov
Kostelec nad Labem
Lysá nad Labem
Městec Králové
Nechanice
Brandýsek
Krupá
OKOŘ
Brandýs nad Labem
Nymburk
HRÁDEK
Švermov
Kladno
Roztoky
Čelákovice
Nové Strašecí
Jesenice
Rakovník
PRAHA
Zdiby
St. Vestec
Poděbrady
LIDICE
Sadská
Chlumec nad Cidlinou
Kyšice
Jeneč
Ruzyně
Úvaly
Ždár
Unhošť
Český Brod
HUBENOV
Křivoklát
Chyňava
Uhříněves
Pardubice
TÝŘOV
LEONTÝNSKÝ ZÁMEK
Radotín
PRŮHONICE
ŠEMBER
Kostelec nad Černými Lesy
Kolín
KAČINA
Přelouč
Kralovice
Beroun
Zbraslav
Říčany
SEDLEC
JAKUB
KRAŠOV
KŘIVOKLÁTSKO
Heřmanův Městec
Plasy
Karlštejn
Dobřichovice
Mnichovice
CZ
VYSOKÁ
Kutná Hora
Zdice
KONĚPRUSKÉ JESK
Čáslav
LICHNICE
RABŠTEJN
Žebrák
Mníšek pod Brdy
Davle
Jílové u Prahy
Pyšely
Uhlířské Janovice
Kaceřov
CHOTĚTÍN
Sázava
SION
Žleby
Třemošná
Radnice
Břasy
Hostomice
Štěchovice
Seč
OHEB
Hořovice
ČESKÝ ŠTERNBERK
Vilémov
PLZEŇ
Konopiště
Benešov
Zbraslavice
Golčův Jeníkov
Mýto
Jince
Dobříš
Nový Knín
Kácov
Habry
Rokycany
Starý Plzenec
Příbram
vodní nádrž Slapy
Neveklov
Zruč nad Sázavou
Ledeč nad Sázavou
TOK
Obory
Bystřice
Vlašim
Chotěboř
Mirošov
KOZEL
Spálené Poříčí
VYSOKÁ U PŘÍBR.
SVATÁ HORA
ČERVENÝ HRÁDEK
Světlá nad Sázavou
Milín
Sedlčany
Jankov
Blovice
Rožmitál pod Třemšínem
MAKOVÁ HORA
VYSOKÝ CHLUMEC
Votice
Čechtice
Lipnice nad Sázavou
Seč
Březnice
ZVĚŘÍNEK
ŠELMBERK
RŮŽKOVY LHOTICE
Havlíčkův Brod
ZELENÁ HORA
ORLÍK
Orlická přehr. nádrž
Petrovice
Mladá Vožice
Košetice
Nepomuk
Mirovice
Humpolec
Orlík nad Vltavou
Želiv
Kasejovice
Lnáře
Jistebnice
Červená Řečice
Štoky
ZELENÁ HORA
Plánice
Blatná
ZVÍKOV
SEPEKOV
CHÝNOVSKÁ J.
Pacov
Milevsko
Tábor
Pelhřimov
Nalžovské Hory
PŘÍBĚNICE
Oparany
KOZÍ HRÁDEK
Chýnov
Kámen
Sedlice
ČERVENÁ
Horažďovice
Bernartice
Malšice
Sezimovo Ústí
Jihlava
PRÁCHEŇ
Planá nad Lužnicí
Černovice
Horní Cerekev
ROŠTEJN
Rabí
Písek
PUTIM
Bechyně
Kostelec
Katovice
Albrechtice nad Vltou
Mnich
Batelov
Sušice
Strakonice
Soběslav
Kamenice nad Lipou
Brtnice
Putim
ČERVENÁ LHOTA
Třešť
Stonařov
KAŠPERK
MYŠENEC
Počátky
JAVOŘICE
Nalžovské Hory
Kašperské Hory
Drahonice
Protivín
Týn nad Vltavou
Veselí nad Lužnicí
Kardašova Řečice
Žirovnice
ROŠTEJN
DOBRŠ
Volyně
HELFENBURK
Vodňany
ŠTERNBERK
Řásná
Rejštejn
Stachy
Strmilov
Studená
Telč
Vlachovo Březí
SV. BARBORA
Jindřichův Hradec
Želetava
Bavorov
Kunžak
Modrava
Vimperk
Hluboká nad Vltavou
HRÁDEK
Lomnice nad Lužnicí
Husinec
Netolice
Lasenice
Dačice
Moravské Budějovice
ŠUMAVA
Borová
Prachatice
Nová
Bystřice

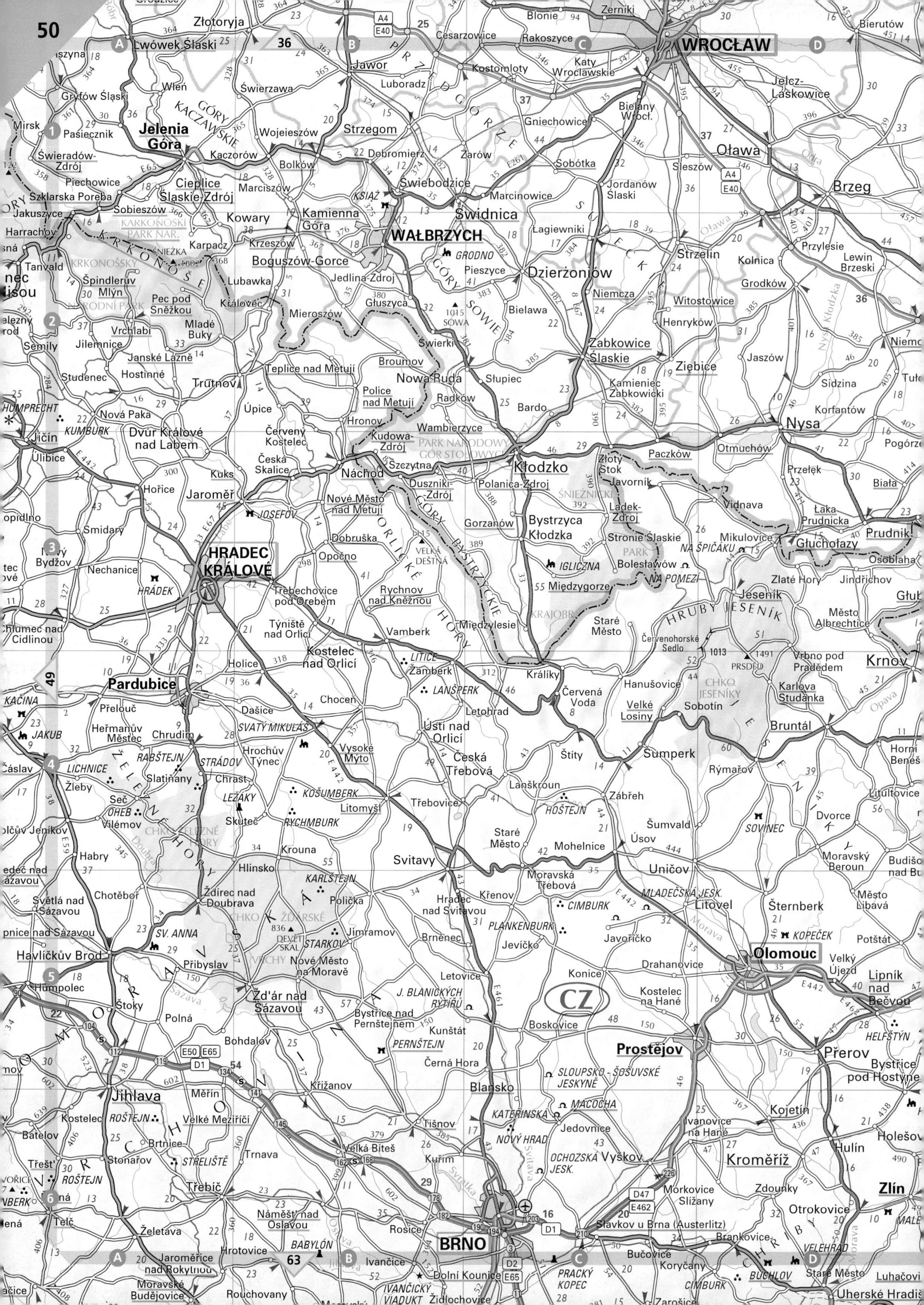
Złotoryja
Lwówek Śląski
Gryfów Śląski
Mirsk
Pasiecznik
Świeradów-Zdrój
Piechowice
Szklarska Poreba
Jakuszyce
Harrachov
Tanvald
Wleń
Jelenia Góra
Kaczorów
Cieplice Śląskie-Zdrój
Sobieszów
Kowary
Karpacz
Śnieżka 1602
Krkonošský Národní Park
Karkonoski Park Nar.
Krkonoše
Góry Kaczawskie
Špindlerův Mlýn
Pec pod Sněžkou
Vrchlabí
Jilemnice
Semily
Janské Lázně
Mladé Buky
Trutnov
Studenec
Hostinné
Nová Paka
Kumburk
Jičín
Úlibice
Dvůr Králové nad Labem
Hořice
Kuks
Jaroměř
Josefov
Smidary
Nový Bydžov
Nechanice
Hrádek
Hradec Králové
Chlumec nad Cidlinou
Pardubice
Kačina
Přelouč
Heřmanův Městec
Chrudim
Jakub
Čáslav
Lichnice
Rabštejn
Slatiňany
Žleby
Seč
Oheb
Vilémov
Habry
Chotěboř
Světlá nad Sázavou
Havlíčkův Brod
Humpolec
Štoky
Polná
Jihlava
Kostelec
Batelov
Roštejn
Třešť
Telč
Stonařov
Brtnice
Střeliště
Třebíč
Želetava
Jaroměřice nad Rokytnou
Moravské Budějovice
Hrotovice
Náměšť nad Oslavou
Babylón
Ivančice
Rosice
Dolní Kounice
Ivančický Viadukt
Židlochovice
Rouchovany
BRNO
Slavkov u Brna (Austerlitz)
Pracký Kopec
Bučovice
Koryčany
Brankovice
Buchlov
Velehrad
Staré Město
Uherské Hradiště
Luhačovice
Zlín
Otrokovice
Zdounky
Kroměříž
Hulín
Holešov
Kojetín
Přerov
Bystřice pod Hostýnem
Helfštýn
Lipník nad Bečvou
Velký Újezd
Olomouc
Prostějov
Kostelec na Hané
Drahanovice
Konice
Boskovice
Javoříčko
Litovel
Šternberk
Kopeček
Uničov
Moravský Beroun
Šumvald
Úsov
Mohelnice
Zábřeh
Šumperk
Velké Losiny
Sobotín
Bruntál
Rýmařov
Sovinec
Dvorce
Karlova Studánka
Vrbno pod Pradědem
Praděd 1491
Krnov
Hrubý Jeseník
Jeseníky
CHKO Jeseníky
Jeseník
Zlaté Hory
Jindřichov
Město Albrechtice
Osoblaha
Głuchołazy
Prudnik
Mikulovice
Vidnava
Javorník
Złoty Stok
Lądek-Zdrój
Stronie Śląskie
Na Špičáku
Bolesławów
Na Pomezí
Międzygorze
Igliczna
Bystrzyca Kłodzka
Gorzanów
Kłodzko
Polanica-Zdrój
Duszniki-Zdrój
Szczytna
Kudowa-Zdrój
Park Narodowy Gór Stołowych
Náchod
Nové Město nad Metují
Dobruška
Opočno
Česká Skalice
Červený Kostelec
Hronov
Police nad Metují
Broumov
Teplice nad Metují
Úpice
Nowa Ruda
Radków
Wambierzyce
Bardo
Słupiec
Świerki
Góry Sowie
Sowa 1015
Głuszyca
Jedlina-Zdrój
Mieroszów
Boguszów-Gorce
Krzeszów
Lubawka
Královec
Kamienna Góra
Wałbrzych
Grodno
Książ
Świebodzice
Świdnica
Marcinowice
Pieszyce
Bielawa
Dzierżoniów
Łagiewniki
Niemcza
Ząbkowice Śląskie
Kamieniec Ząbkowicki
Ziębice
Henryków
Strzelin
Witostowice
Sobótka
Jordanów Śląski
Żarów
Strzegom
Dobromierz
Bolków
Marciszów
Wojcieszów
Świerzawa
Jawor
Luboradz
Kostomłoty
Przedgórze Sudeckie
Gniechowice
Bielany Wrocł.
Katy Wrocławskie
Cesarzowice
Rakoszyce
Błonie
Żerniki
WROCŁAW
Jelcz-Laskowice
Bierutów
Oława
Sleszów
Brzeg
Przylesie
Lewin Brzeski
Kolnica
Grodków
Jaszów
Nysa
Sidzina
Korfantów
Otmuchów
Paczków
Przełęk
Biała
Łąka Prudnicka
Pogórze
Niemo
Tułowice
Orlické Hory
Velká Deštná 1115
Góry Bystrzyckie
Třebechovice pod Orebem
Týniště nad Orlicí
Rychnov nad Kněžnou
Vamberk
Kostelec nad Orlicí
Litice
Žamberk
Lanšperk
Międzylesie
Králíky
Červená Voda
Staré Město
Červenohorské Sedlo
Hanušovice
Štíty
Letohrad
Ústí nad Orlicí
Česká Třebová
Choceň
Holice
Dašice
Svatý Mikuláš
Vysoké Mýto
Hrochův Týnec
Stradov
Chrast
Ležáky
Skuteč
Košumberk
Rychmburk
Litomyšl
Třebovice
Lanškroun
Hoštejn
Staré Město
Moravská Třebová
Svitavy
Hlinsko
Krouna
Karlštejn
Polička
Ždírec nad Doubravou
Sv. Anna
Přibyslav
CHKO Žďárské Vrchy
Devět Skal 836
Starkov
Jimramov
Nové Město na Moravě
Žďár nad Sázavou
Bystřice nad Pernštejnem
J. Blanického Rytířů
Letovice
Kunštát
Pernštejn
Černá Hora
Brněnec
Jevíčko
Hradec nad Svitavou
Křenov
Plankenburk
Cimburk
Mladečská Jesk.
Bohdalov
Měřín
Velké Meziříčí
Křižanov
Trnava
Velká Bíteš
Tišnov
Kuřim
Blansko
Kateřinská
Macocha
Sloupsko-Šošovské Jeskyně
Jedovnice
Nový Hrad
Ochozská Jesk.
Vyškov
Morkovice Slížany
Ivanovice na Hané
Železné Hory
CHKO Železné Hory
Českomoravská Vrchovina
Chřiby
CZ
Humprecht
Sudety

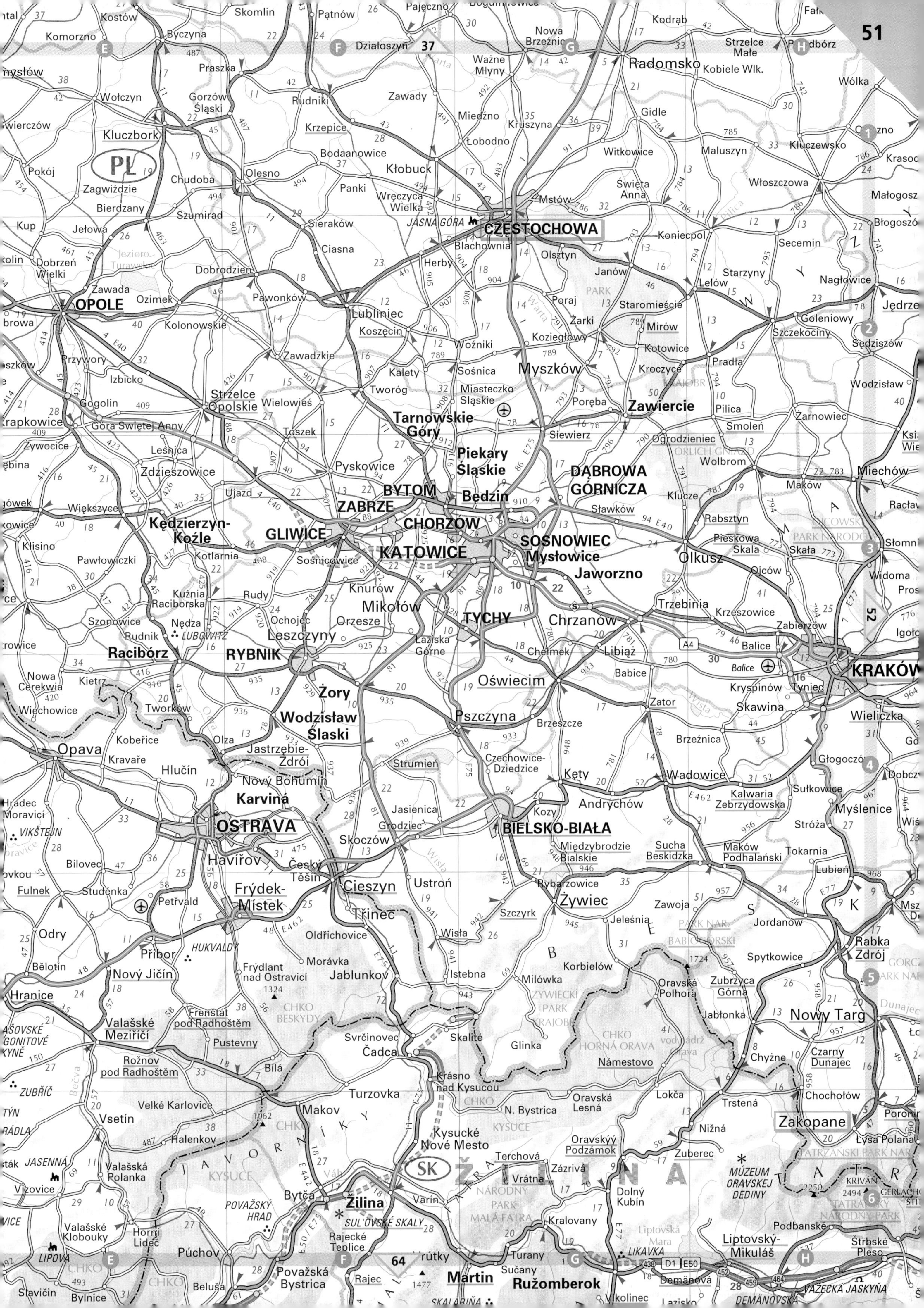
PL
SK
Kluczbork
Olesno
Kłobuck
Radomsko
CZĘSTOCHOWA
JASNA GÓRA
Blachownia
Koniecpol
Włoszczowa
Secemin
Lelów
Szczekociny
Sędziszów
Opole
OPOLE
Ozimek
Dobrodzień
Lubliniec
Koszęcin
Woźniki
Myszków
Zawiercie
Pilica
Wolbrom
Miechów
Strzelce Opolskie
Tarnowskie Góry
Piekary Śląskie
Siewierz
Ogrodzieniec
Kędzierzyn-Koźle
GLIWICE
ZABRZE
BYTOM
CHORZÓW
Będzin
DĄBROWA GÓRNICZA
KATOWICE
SOSNOWIEC
Mysłowice
Jaworzno
Olkusz
Ojców
Skała
Racibórz
RYBNIK
Mikołów
TYCHY
Chrzanów
Trzebinia
Krzeszowice
Libiąż
Oświęcim
Babice
Zator
Skawina
KRAKÓW
Wieliczka
Żory
Wodzisław Śląski
Jastrzębie-Zdrój
Pszczyna
Czechowice-Dziedzice
Kęty
Wadowice
Andrychów
Kalwaria Zebrzydowska
Myślenice
Opava
Hlučín
Nový Bohumín
Karviná
OSTRAVA
Havířov
Český Těšín
Cieszyn
Skoczów
Ustroń
BIELSKO-BIAŁA
Międzybrodzie Bialskie
Sucha Beskidzka
Maków Podhalański
Frýdek-Místek
Třinec
Żywiec
Szczyrk
Wisła
Jordanów
Rabka Zdrój
Nový Jičín
Příbor
Jablunkov
Istebna
Milówka
Korbielów
Oravská Polhora
Zubrzyca Górna
Jabłonka
Nowy Targ
Czarny Dunajec
Hranice
Valašské Meziříčí
Frenštát pod Radhoštěm
Rožnov pod Radhoštěm
Čadca
Skalité
Turzovka
Vsetín
Makov
Kysucké Nové Mesto
Námestovo
Trstená
Chochołów
Zakopane
Žilina
Bytča
Varín
Terchová
Dolný Kubín
Zuberec
MÚZEUM ORAVSKEJ DEDINY
Liptovský Mikuláš
Štrbské Pleso
Púchov
Považská Bystrica
Martin
Ružomberok
Vrútky
JAVORNÍKY
BESKYDY
MALÁ FATRA
TATRY
KRIVÁŇ
2494
SUL'OVSKÉ SKALY
LIKAVKA

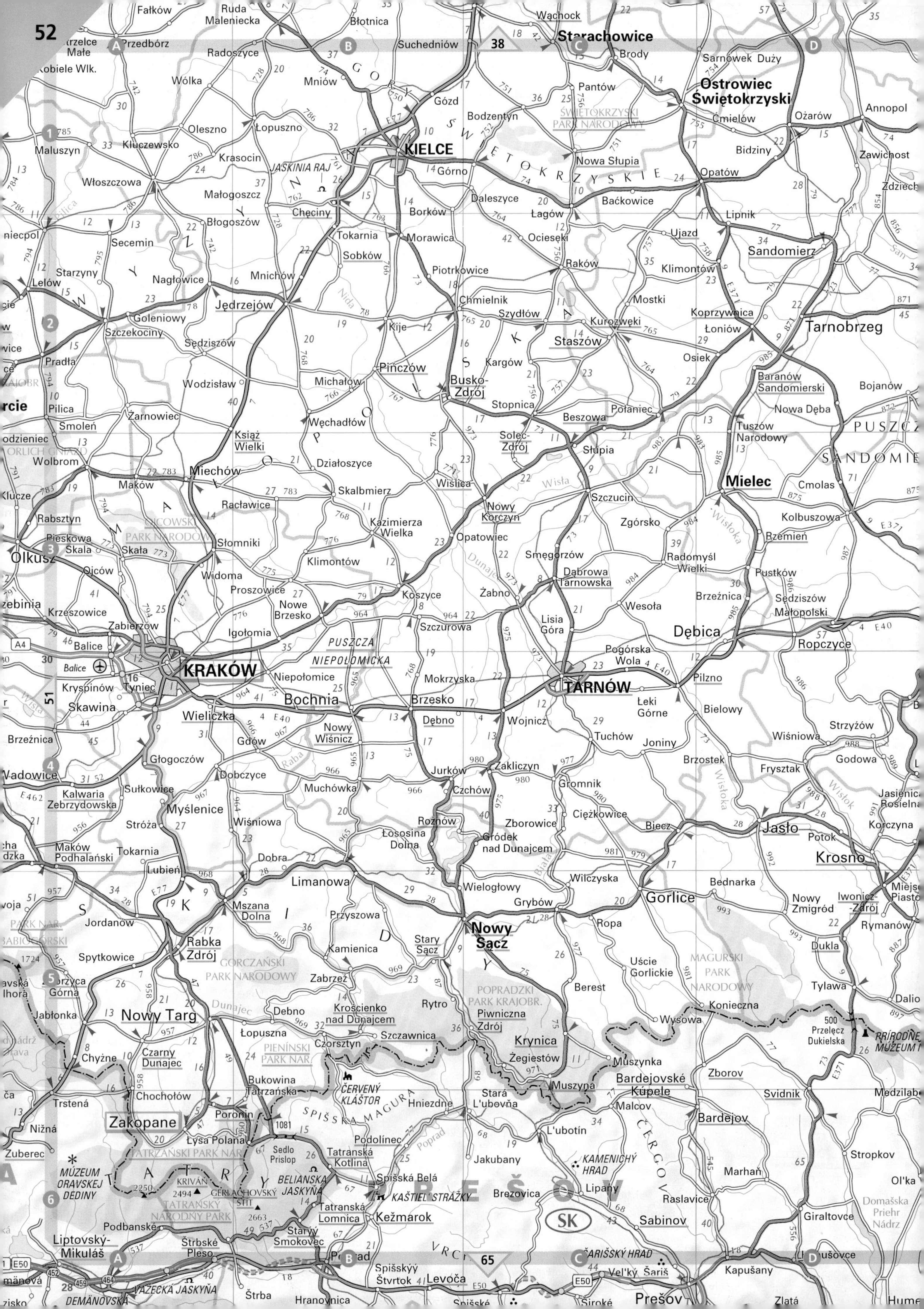

Fałków
Ruda Maleniecka
Błotnica
Wąchock
Starachowice
Przedbórz
Suchedniów
38
Radoszyce
Brody
Sarnówek Duży
Mniów
Ostrowiec Świętokrzyski
Wólka
Pantów
GÓRY
Gózd
Bodzentyn
ŚWIĘTOKRZYSKI PARK NARODOWY
Ożarów
Annopol
Ćmielów
Oleszno
Łopuszno
Maluszyn
Kluczewsko
KIELCE
Nowa Słupia
Bidziny
Zawichost
Krasocin
JASKINIA RAJ
Górno
ŚWIĘTOKRZYSKIE
Opatów
Włoszczowa
Małogoszcz
Daleszyce
Baćkowice
Zdziechów
Chęciny
Borków
Łagów
Lipnik
Błogoszów
Tokarnia
Morawica
Ocieseki
Ujazd
Secemin
Sobków
Sandomierz
Piotrkowice
Raków
Klimontów
Starzyny
Nagłowice
Mnichów
Lelów
Jędrzejów
Chmielnik
Mostki
Szydłów
Kurozwęki
Koprzywnica
Goleniowy
Tarnobrzeg
Szczekociny
Kije
Łoniów
Sędziszów
Staszów
Osiek
Pradła
Pińczów
Kargów
Busko-Zdrój
Wodzisław
Michałów
Baranów Sandomierski
Bojanów
Pilica
Stopnica
Połaniec
Nowa Dęba
Żarnowiec
Węchadłów
Beszowa
Smoleń
Tuszów Narodowy
PUSZCZA SANDOMIERSKA
Książ Wielki
Solec-Zdrój
Słupia
Wolbrom
Działoszyce
Miechów
Mielec
Maków
Wiślica
Cmolas
Klucze
Skalbmierz
Szczucin
Rabsztyn
Racławice
Nowy Korczyn
Kolbuszowa
Kazimierza Wielka
Zgórsko
OJCOWSKI PARK NARODOWY
Rzemień
Pieskowa Skała
Skała
Słomniki
Opatowiec
Olkusz
Smęgorzów
Radomyśl Wielki
Ojców
Klimontów
Pustków
Widoma
Dąbrowa Tarnowska
Proszowice
Koszyce
Żabno
Brzeźnica
Sędziszów Małopolski
Krzeszowice
Nowe Brzesko
Wesoła
Zabierzów
Lisia Góra
Igołomia
Szczurowa
Dębica
Balice
Ropczyce
PUSZCZA NIEPOŁOMICKA
Pogórska Wola
KRAKÓW
Niepołomice
Mokrzyska
Pilzno
Kryspinów
Tyniec
TARNÓW
Skawina
Bochnia
Brzesko
Łęki Górne
Bielowy
Wieliczka
Wojnicz
Dębno
Strzyżów
Brzeźnica
Nowy Wiśnicz
Tuchów
Gdów
Joniny
Wiśniowa
Godowa
Głogoczów
Brzostek
Frysztak
Wadowice
Zakliczyn
Dobczyce
Jurków
Gromnik
Kalwaria Zebrzydowska
Sułkowice
Muchówka
Czchów
Jasienica Rosielna
Myślenice
Ciężkowice
Rożnów
Zborowice
Stróża
Wiśniowa
Łososina Dolna
Biecz
Jasło
Korczyna
Gródek nad Dunajcem
Potok
Maków Podhalański
Tokarnia
Krosno
Dobra
Lubień
Limanowa
Wilczyska
Bednarka
Wielogłowy
Gorlice
Nowy Żmigród
Iwonicz-Zdrój
Jordanów
Mszana Dolna
Grybów
Przyszowa
Ropa
Rymanów
PARK NAR. BABIOGÓRSKI
Rabka Zdrój
Stary Sącz
Nowy Sącz
Spytkowice
Kamienica
Dukla
GORCZAŃSKI PARK NARODOWY
Uście Gorlickie
MAGURSKI PARK NARODOWY
Zabrzeż
Tylawa
Zubrzyca Górna
Rytro
POPRADZKI PARK KRAJOBR.
Berest
Krościenko nad Dunajcem
Piwniczna Zdrój
Konieczna
Nowy Targ
Debno
Jabłonka
Wysowa
500 Przełęcz Dukielska
Łopuszna
Szczawnica
Krynica
Chyżne
Czarny Dunajec
PIENIŃSKI PARK NAR.
Czorsztyn
Żegiestów
Muszynka
Bukowina Tatrzańska
ČERVENÝ KLÁŠTOR
Muszyna
Bardejovské Kúpele
Zborov
Trstená
Chochołów
Svidník
Medzilaborce
Nižná
Zakopane
Poronin
SPIŠSKÁ MAGURA
Hniezdne
Stará Ľubovňa
Malcov
Bardejov
Zuberec
Łysa Polana
Sedlo Prislop
Ľubotín
ČERGOV
TATRZAŃSKI PARK NAR.
Podolínec
Tatranská Kotlina
Jakubany
KAMENICHÝ HRAD
Stropkov
MÚZEUM ORAVSKEJ DEDINY
TATRY
KRIVÁŇ
2494
GERLACHOVSKÝ ŠTÍT
2663
BELIANSKA JASKYŇA
Spišská Belá
KAŠTIEĽ STRÁŽKY
PREŠOV
Brezovica
Lipany
Marhaň
Oľka
TATRANSKÝ NÁRODNÝ PARK
Tatranská Lomnica
Kežmarok
Raslavice
SK
Sabinov
Giraltovce
Domašska Priehr Nádrž
Podbanské
Liptovský-Mikuláš
Štrbské Pleso
Starý Smokovec
Poprad
65
ŠARIŠSKÝ HRAD
Dlhé Kľušovce
Spišskýý Štvrtok
Levoča
Veľký Šariš
Kapušany
VAŽECKÁ JASKYŇA
Štrba
DEMÄNOVSKÁ
Hranovnica
Široké
Prešov
Zlatá

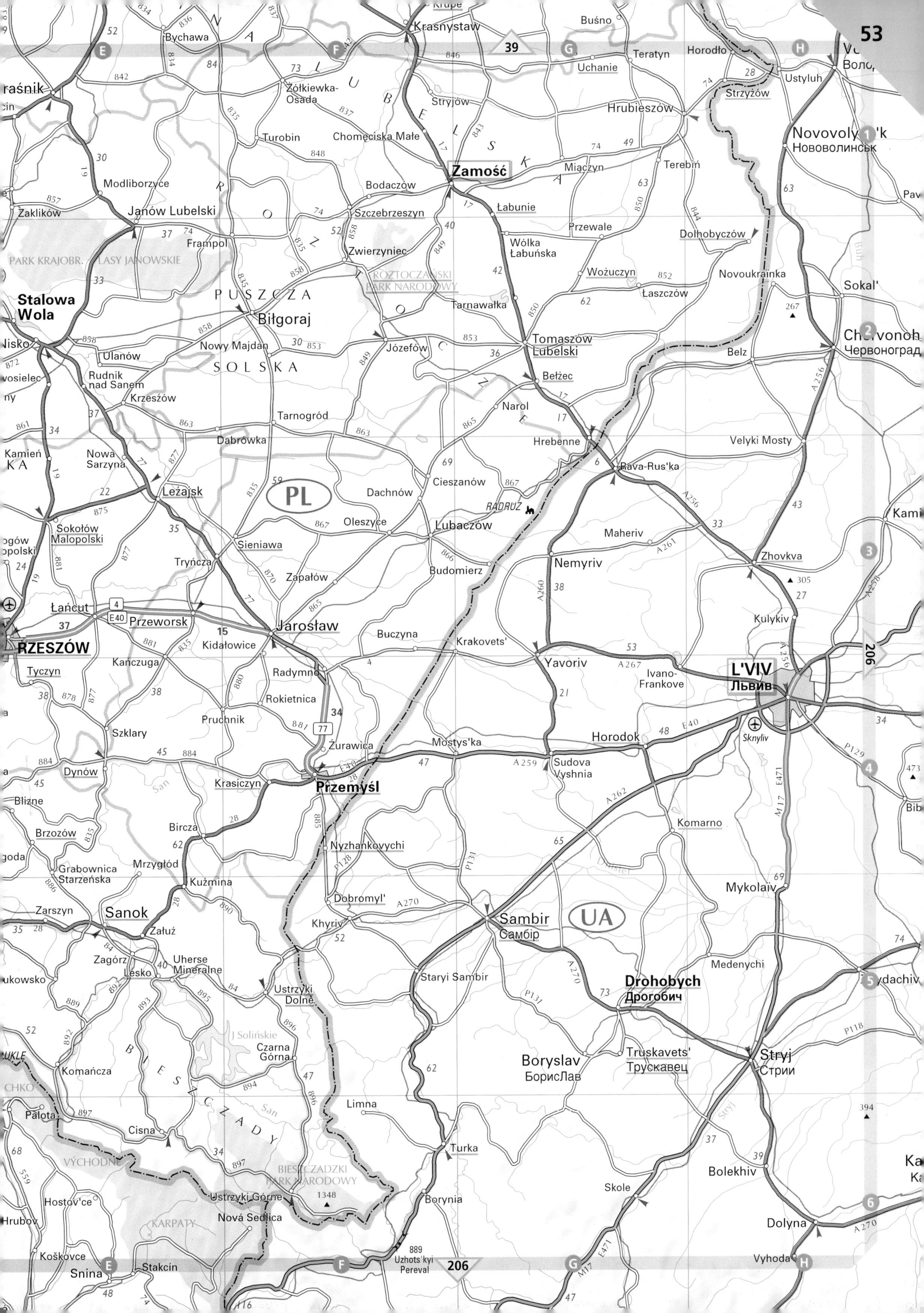
Krasnystaw
Bychawa
Busńo
Teratyn
Horodło
Uchanie
Ustyluh
Strzyżów
Hrubieszów
Kraśnik
Żółkiewka-Osada
Stryjów
Turobin
Chomęciska Małe
Novovolyns'k
Нововолинськ
Zamość
Miączyn
Terebiń
Modliborzyce
Janów Lubelski
Zaklików
Bodaczów
Szczebrzeszyn
Łabunie
Frampol
Przewale
Dołhobyczów
Zwierzyniec
Wólka Łabuńska
PARK KRAJOBR. LASY JANOWSKIE
ROZTOCZAŃSKI PARK NARODOWY
Wożuczyn
Łaszczów
Novoukrainka
Sokal'
Stalowa Wola
PUSZCZA SOLSKA
Biłgoraj
Tarnawatka
Nisko
Ulanów
Nowy Majdan
Józefów
Tomaszów Lubelski
Chervonohrad
Червоноград
Belz
Rudnik nad Sanem
Krzeszów
Bełżec
Narol
Tarnogród
Dabrówka
Hrebenne
Velyki Mosty
Kamień
Nowa Sarzyna
Rava-Rus'ka
Cieszanów
PL
Dachnów
Leżajsk
RADRUŻ
Sokołów Małopolski
Oleszyce
Lubaczów
Maheriv
Sieniawa
Nemyriv
Zhovkva
Tryńcza
Budomierz
Zapałów
Łańcut
Przeworsk
Kulykiv
Jarosław
RZESZÓW
Kidałowice
Buczyna
Krakovets'
Yavoriv
Tyczyn
Kańczuga
Radymno
Ivano-Frankove
L'VIV
Львів
Rokietnica
Pruchnik
Szklary
Żurawica
Mostys'ka
Horodok
Skynliv
Dynów
Krasiczyn
Przemyśl
Sudova Vyshnia
Blizne
Komarno
Brzozów
Bircza
Nyzhankovychi
Grabownica Starzeńska
Mrzygłód
Kuźmina
Mykolaiv
Zarszyn
Sanok
Dobromyl'
Khyriv
Sambir
Самбір
UA
Załuż
Zagórz
Lesko
Uherse Mineralne
Medenychi
Staryi Sambir
Drohobych
Дрогобич
Ustrzyki Dolne
J. Solińskie
Czarna Górna
Komańcza
Boryslav
БорисЛав
Truskavets'
Трускавець
Stryj
Стрий
BIESZCZADY
Limna
Palota
Cisna
Turka
Bolekhiv
Skole
VÝCHODNÉ KARPATY
BIESZCZADZKI PARK NARODOWY
Ustrzyki Górne
Hostov'ce
Nová Sedlica
Borynia
Dolyna
Koškovce
Snina
Stakčín
Uzhots'kyi Pereval
Vyhoda
206

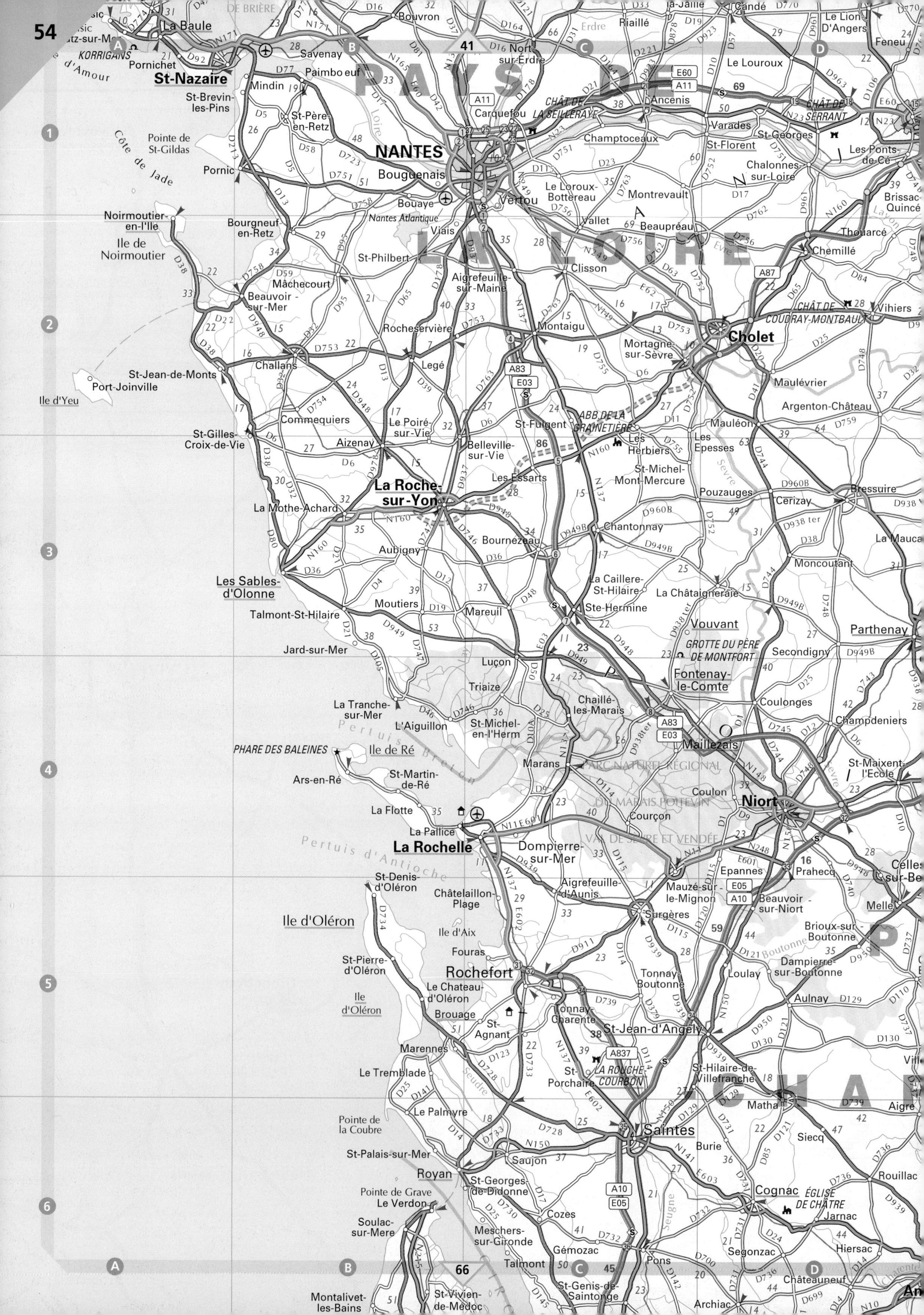

PAYS DE LA LOIRE
La Baule
KORRIGANS
Pornichet
St-Nazaire
Savenay
Bouvron
Nort-sur-Erdre
Riaillé
Candé
Le Lion-d'Angers
Feneu
Paimboeuf
Mindin
St-Brevin-les-Pins
St-Père-en-Retz
Pointe de St-Gildas
Côte de Jade
Pornic
NANTES
Bouguenais
Carquefou
CHÂT. DE LA SEILLERAYE
Ancenis
Le Louroux
Varades
St-Georges
CHÂT. DE SERRANT
Champtoceaux
St-Florent
Les Ponts-de-Cé
Chalonnes-sur-Loire
Le Loroux-Bottereau
Montrevault
Brissac-Quincé
Bouaye
Vertou
Nantes Atlantique
Noirmoutier-en-l'Ile
Ile de Noirmoutier
Bourgneuf-en-Retz
Viais
Vallet
Beaupréau
Thouarcé
Chemillé
St-Philbert
Clisson
Machecourt
Beauvoir-sur-Mer
Aigrefeuille-sur-Maine
CHÂT. DE COUDRAY-MONTBAULT
Vihiers
Cholet
Montaigu
Rocheservière
Mortagne-sur-Sèvre
Challans
Legé
St-Jean-de-Monts
Port-Joinville
Ile d'Yeu
Maulévrier
Argenton-Château
Commequiers
Le Poiré-sur-Vie
St-Fulgent
ABB. DE LA GRAINETIÈRE
Les Herbiers
Mauléon
Les Epesses
St-Gilles-Croix-de-Vie
Aizenay
Belleville-sur-Vie
St-Michel-Mont-Mercure
Les Essarts
La Roche-sur-Yon
Pouzauges
Bressuire
Cerizay
La Mothe-Achard
Chantonnay
Bournezeau
Aubigny
Moncoutant
La Maucat
Les Sables-d'Olonne
La Caillere-St-Hilaire
La Châtaigneraie
Talmont-St-Hilaire
Moutiers
Mareuil
Ste-Hermine
Vouvant
GROTTE DU PÈRE DE MONTFORT
Parthenay
Secondigny
Jard-sur-Mer
Luçon
Fontenay-le-Comte
Triaize
Coulonges
Champdeniers
La Tranche-sur-Mer
L'Aiguillon
St-Michel-en-l'Herm
Chaillé-les-Marais
Maillezais
Pertuis Breton
PHARE DES BALEINES
Ile de Ré
St-Martin-de-Ré
Ars-en-Ré
Marans
PARC NATUREL RÉGIONAL DU MARAIS POITEVIN
VAL DE SÈVRE ET VENDÉE
St-Maixent-l'Ecole
Coulon
Niort
Courçon
La Flotte
La Pallice
La Rochelle
Dompierre-sur-Mer
Pertuis d'Antioche
Prahecq
Celles-sur-Be
St-Denis-d'Oléron
Aigrefeuille-d'Aunis
Châtelaillon-Plage
Mauzé-sur-le-Mignon
Epannes
Beauvoir-sur-Niort
Melle
Ile d'Oléron
Surgères
Ile d'Aix
Fouras
Brioux-sur-Boutonne
St-Pierre-d'Oléron
Rochefort
Tonnay-Boutonne
Loulay
Dampierre-sur-Boutonne
Le Chateau-d'Oléron
Aulnay
Tonnay-Charente
Brouage
St-Agnant
St-Jean-d'Angély
Marennes
LA ROCHE-COURBON
St-Porchaire
St-Hilaire-de-Villefranche
Le Tremblade
Le Palmyre
Matha
Aigre
Pointe de la Coubre
Saintes
Burie
Siecq
St-Palais-sur-Mer
Saujon
Royan
St-Georges-de-Didonne
Cognac
ÉGLISE DE CHÂTRE
Jarnac
Rouillac
Pointe de Grave
Le Verdon
Cozes
Soulac-sur-Mere
Meschers-sur-Gironde
Gémozac
Segonzac
Hiersac
Talmont
Pons
Châteauneuf
St-Genis-de-Saintonge
Montalivet-les-Bains
St-Vivien-de-Médoc
Archiac
41
66

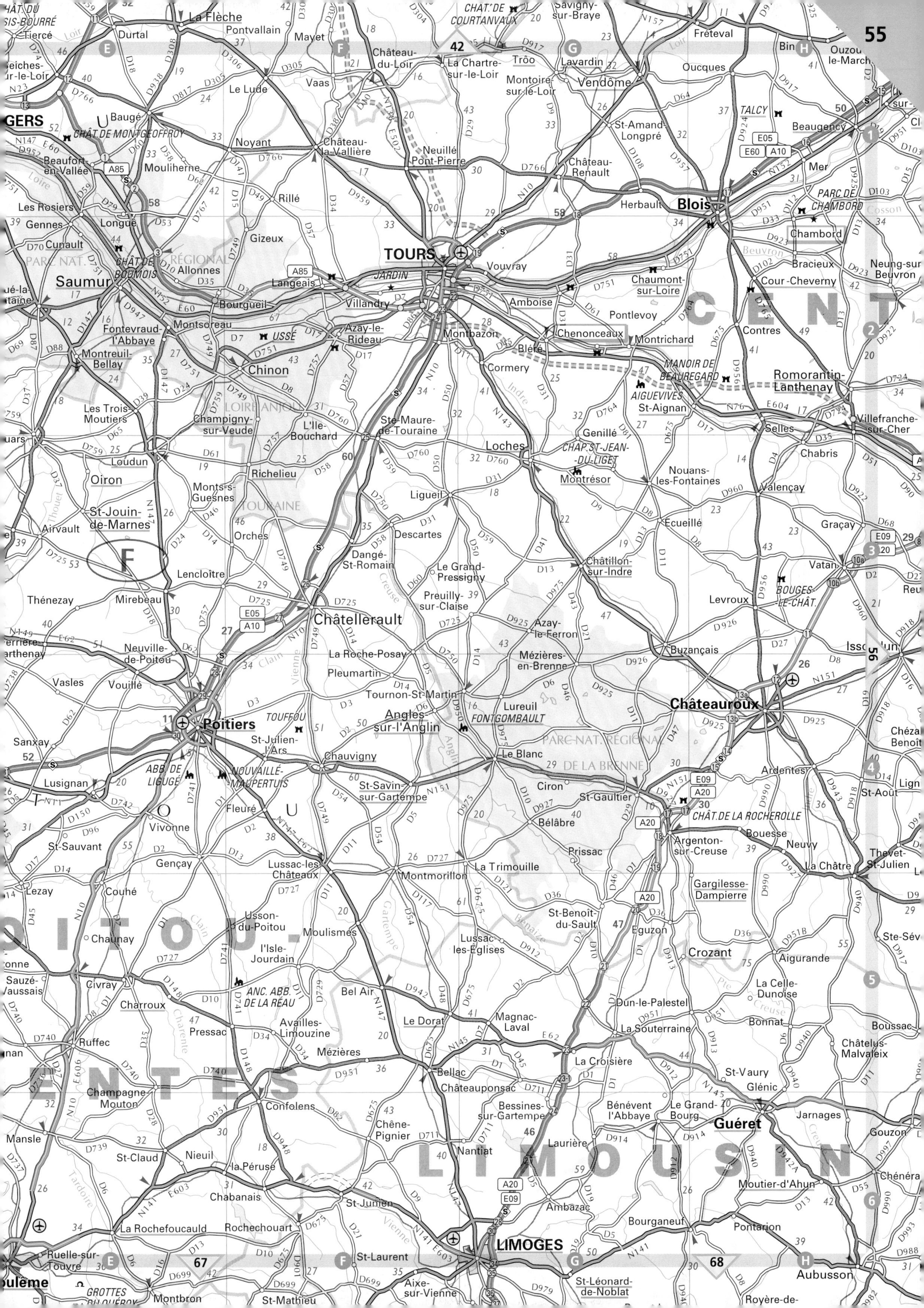

La Flèche
Durtal
Pontvallain
Mayet
CHÂT. DE COURTANVAUX
Savigny-sur-Braye
Fréteval
Château-du-Loir
La Chartre-sur-le-Loir
Trôo
Lavardin
Montoire-sur-le-Loir
Vendôme
Ocques
Bin
Le Lude
Vaas
Baugé
CHÂT. DE MONTGEOFFROY
Noyant
Château-la-Vallière
Neuillé-Pont-Pierre
St-Amand-Longpré
TALCY
Beaugency
Beaufort-en-Vallée
Mouliherne
Château-Renault
Mer
Rillé
Herbault
Blois
PARC DE CHAMBORD
Chambord
Les Rosiers
Gennes
Longué
Cunault
Gizeux
TOURS
Vouvray
Allonnes
Saumur
Langeais
JARDIN
Villandry
Chaumont-sur-Loire
Bracieux
Cour-Cheverny
Neung-sur-Beuvron
Amboise
Bourgueil
Fontevraud-l'Abbaye
Montsoreau
USSÉ
Azay-le-Rideau
Montbazon
Pontlevoy
Montrichard
Chenonceaux
Contres
Bléré
Montreuil-Bellay
Chinon
Cormery
MANOIR DE BEAUREGARD
Romorantin-Lanthenay
AIGUEVIVES
St-Aignan
Les Trois-Moutiers
Champigny-sur-Veude
L'Ile-Bouchard
Ste-Maure-de-Touraine
Genillé
Selles
Villefranche-sur-Cher
Loches
CHAP. ST-JEAN-DU-LIGET
Chabris
Loudun
Oiron
Richelieu
Montrésor
Nouans-les-Fontaines
Valençay
Monts-s-Guesnes
Ligueil
St-Jouin-de-Marnes
Airvault
Orches
Descartes
Ecueillé
Graçay
Dangé-St-Romain
Le Grand-Pressigny
Châtillon-sur-Indre
Vatan
Lencloître
BOUGES-LE-CHÂT.
Thénezay
Mirebeau
Preuilly-sur-Claise
Levroux
Châtellerault
Azay-le-Ferron
Neuville-de-Poitou
La Roche-Posay
Mézières-en-Brenne
Buzançais
Vasles
Vouillé
Pleumartin
Tournon-St-Martin
Lureuil
FONTGOMBAULT
Châteauroux
Poitiers
TOUFFOU
Angles-sur-l'Anglin
Sanxay
St-Julien-l'Ars
Chauvigny
Le Blanc
PARC NAT. RÉGIONAL DE LA BRENNE
Ardentes
Lusignan
ABB. DE LIGUGÉ
NOUVAILLÉ-MAUPERTUIS
St-Savin-sur-Gartempe
Ciron
St-Gaultier
CHÂT. DE LA ROCHEROLLE
Fleuré
Vivonne
Bélâbre
Argenton-sur-Creuse
Bouesse
Neuvy
St-Sauvant
Gençay
Lussac-les-Châteaux
Montmorillon
La Trimouille
Prissac
La Châtre
Thevet-St-Julien
Lezay
Couhé
Gargilesse-Dampierre
St-Benoît-du-Sault
Usson-du-Poitou
Moulismes
Eguzon
Chaunay
Lussac-les-Eglises
Crozant
Aigurande
L'Isle-Jourdain
Sauzé-Vaussais
Civray
ANC. ABB. DE LA RÉAU
Bel Air
La Celle-Dunoise
Charroux
Dun-le-Palestel
Pressac
Availles-Limouzine
Le Dorat
Magnac-Laval
La Souterraine
Bonnat
Boussac
Ruffec
Mézières
La Croisière
Châtelus-Malvaleix
Bellac
Châteauponsac
St-Vaury
Glénic
Champagne-Mouton
Confolens
Bessines-sur-Gartempe
Bénévent-l'Abbaye
Le Grand-Bourg
Jarnages
Guéret
Chêne-Pignier
Mansle
St-Claud
Nieuil
Nantiat
Laurière
Gouzon
La Péruse
Moutier-d'Ahun
Chabanais
St-Junien
Ambazac
Rochechouart
La Rochefoucauld
Bourganeuf
Pontarion
LIMOGES
Ruelle-sur-Touvre
St-Laurent
Aubusson
GROTTES DU QUÉROY
Montbron
St-Mathieu
Aixe-sur-Vienne
St-Léonard-de-Noblat
LIMOUSIN

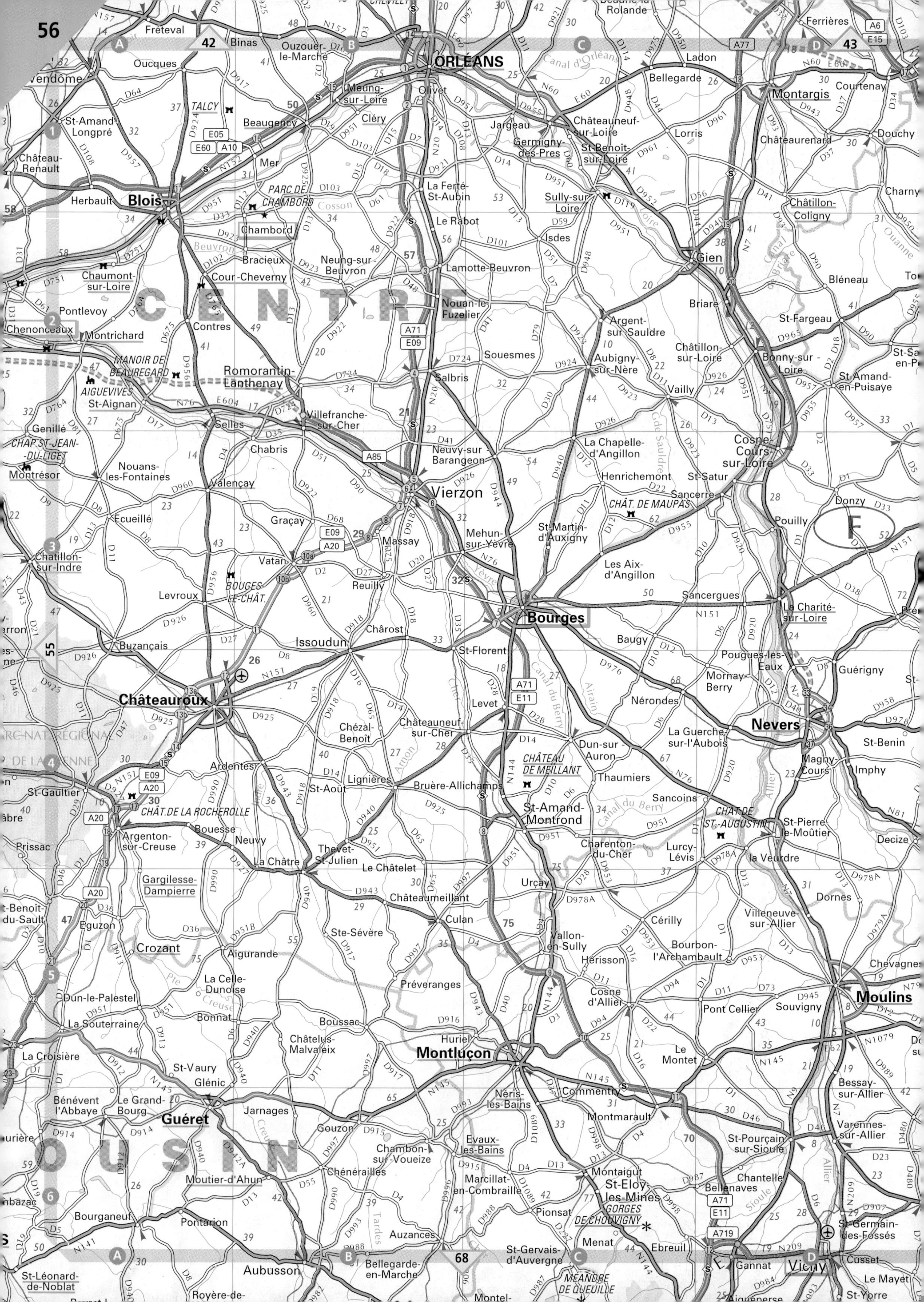

42
43
55
68
A
B
C
D
E
F
1
2
3
4
5
6
CENTRE
OUSIN
Fréteval
Binas
Ouzouer-le-Marché
ORLÉANS
Beaune-la-Rolande
Ferrières
Ladon
Bellegarde
Montargis
Courtenay
Douchy
Châteaurenard
Charny
Châtillon-Coligny
Bléneau
Ouques
Vendôme
St-Amand-Longpré
TALCY
Beaugency
Meung-sur-Loire
Cléry
Olivet
Jargeau
Châteauneuf-sur-Loire
Germigny-des-Prés
St-Benoît-sur-Loire
Lorris
Château-Renault
Mer
Herbault
Blois
PARC DE CHAMBORD
Chambord
La Ferté-St-Aubin
Sully-sur-Loire
Le Rabot
Isdes
Gien
Bracieux
Neung-sur-Beuvron
Lamotte-Beuvron
Chaumont-sur-Loire
Cour-Cheverny
Pontlevoy
Chenonceaux
Montrichard
Contres
Nouan-le-Fuzelier
Argent-sur-Sauldre
Briare
St-Fargeau
Châtillon-sur-Loire
Bonny-sur-Loire
St-Amand-en-Puisaye
MANOIR DE BEAUREGARD
AIGUEVIVES
St-Aignan
Romorantin-Lanthenay
Souesmes
Salbris
Aubigny-sur-Nère
Vailly
Villefranche-sur-Cher
Selles
Genillé
CHAP. ST-JEAN-DU-LIGET
Montrésor
Chabris
Neuvy-sur-Barangeon
La Chapelle-d'Angillon
Henrichemont
Cosne-Cours-sur-Loire
St-Satur
Sancerre
Nouans-les-Fontaines
Valençay
Vierzon
CHÂT. DE MAUPAS
Donzy
Écueillé
Graçay
Massay
Mehun-sur-Yèvre
St-Martin-d'Auxigny
Pouilly
Châtillon-sur-Indre
Vatan
BOUGES-LE-CHÂT.
Reuilly
Les Aix-d'Angillon
Levroux
Bourges
Sancergues
La Charité-sur-Loire
Buzançais
Issoudun
Chârost
St-Florent
Baugy
Pougues-les-Eaux
Guérigny
Châteauroux
Levet
Mornay-Berry
Nérondes
Chézal-Benoît
Châteauneuf-sur-Cher
Dun-sur-Auron
La Guerche-sur-l'Aubois
Nevers
St-Benin
Ardentes
St-Août
Lignières
Bruère-Allichamps
CHÂTEAU DE MEILLANT
Thaumiers
Magny-Cours
Imphy
St-Gaultier
CHÂT. DE LA ROCHEROLLE
St-Amand-Montrond
Sancoins
CHÂT. DE ST.-AUGUSTIN
St-Pierre-le-Moûtier
Decize
Prissac
Argenton-sur-Creuse
Bouesse
Neuvy
La Châtre
Thevet-St-Julien
Le Châtelet
Charenton-du-Cher
Lurcy-Lévis
la Veurdre
Gargilesse-Dampierre
Châteaumeillant
Urçay
Dornes
St-Benoît-du-Sault
Eguzon
Culan
Cérilly
Villeneuve-sur-Allier
Crozant
Aigurande
Ste-Sévère
Vallon-en-Sully
Bourbon-l'Archambault
Hérisson
Chevagnes
La Celle-Dunoise
Préveranges
Dun-le-Palestel
Cosne d'Allier
Moulins
Bonnat
Pont Cellier
Souvigny
La Souterraine
Boussac
Châtelus-Malvaleix
Huriel
Montluçon
La Croisière
St-Vaury
Le Montet
Glénic
Bessay-sur-Allier
Bénévent l'Abbaye
Le Grand-Bourg
Guéret
Jarnages
Néris-les-Bains
Commentry
Montmarault
Gouzon
Varennes-sur-Allier
St-Pourçain-sur-Sioule
Chambon-sur-Voueize
Évaux-les-Bains
Chénérailles
Moutier-d'Ahun
Marcillat-en-Combraille
Montaigut
St-Eloy-les-Mines
Chantelle
Bellenaves
Bourganeuf
Pontarion
Pionsat
GORGES DE CHOUVIGNY
St-Germain-des-Fossés
Auzances
Menat
Ebreuil
St-Léonard-de-Noblat
Aubusson
Bellegarde-en-Marche
St-Gervais-d'Auvergne
Gannat
Vichy
Cusset
MÉANDRE DE QUEUILLE
Royère-de-
Le Mayet
St-Yorre
Canal d'Orléans
Canal de Briare
Canal du Berry
Loire
Cosson
Beuvron
Yèvre
Cher
Allier
Sioule
Creuse
Sauldre
A10
A71
A20
A85
A77
A6
A719
E05
E60
E09
E11
E15
E62
N20
N7
N76
N151
N144
N145
N9
N141

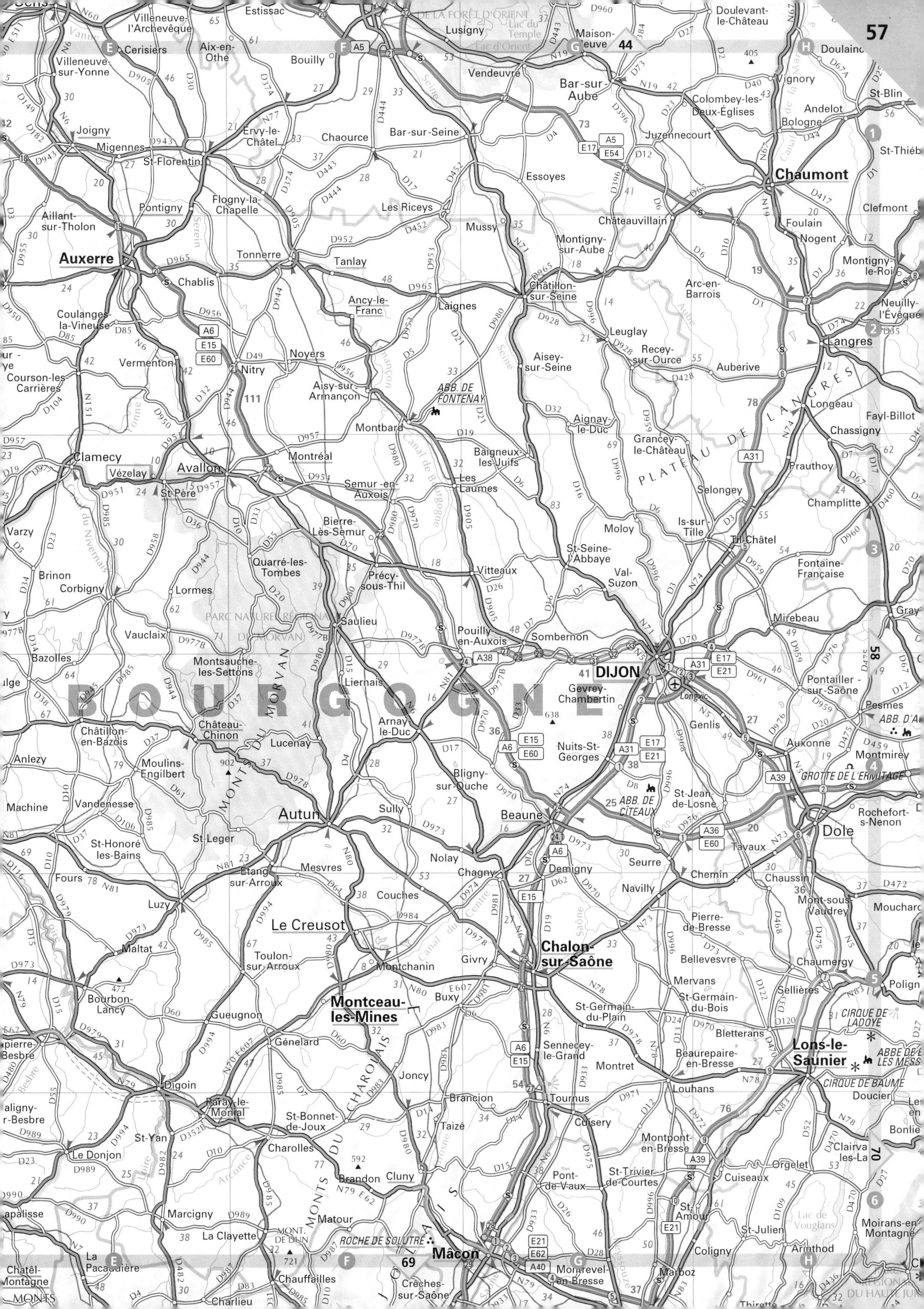
BOURGOGNE
Auxerre
Chaumont
DIJON
Chalon-sur-Saône
Mâcon
Lons-le-Saunier
Dole
Beaune
Autun
Le Creusot
Montceau-les-Mines
Avallon
Tonnerre
Langres
Châtillon-sur-Seine
Bar-sur-Aube
Bar-sur-Seine
Clamecy
Vézelay
Château-Chinon
Saulieu
Montbard
Semur-en-Auxois
Digoin
Paray-le-Monial
Charolles
Cluny
Tournus
Louhans
PARC NATUREL RÉGIONAL DU MORVAN
MONTS DU MORVAN
PLATEAU DE LANGRES
MONTS DU CHAROLAIS
ABB. DE FONTENAY
ABB. DE CÎTEAUX
ROCHE DE SOLUTRÉ
GROTTE DE L'ERMITAGE
CIRQUE DE BAUME
CIRQUE DE LADOYE
44
58
69
70

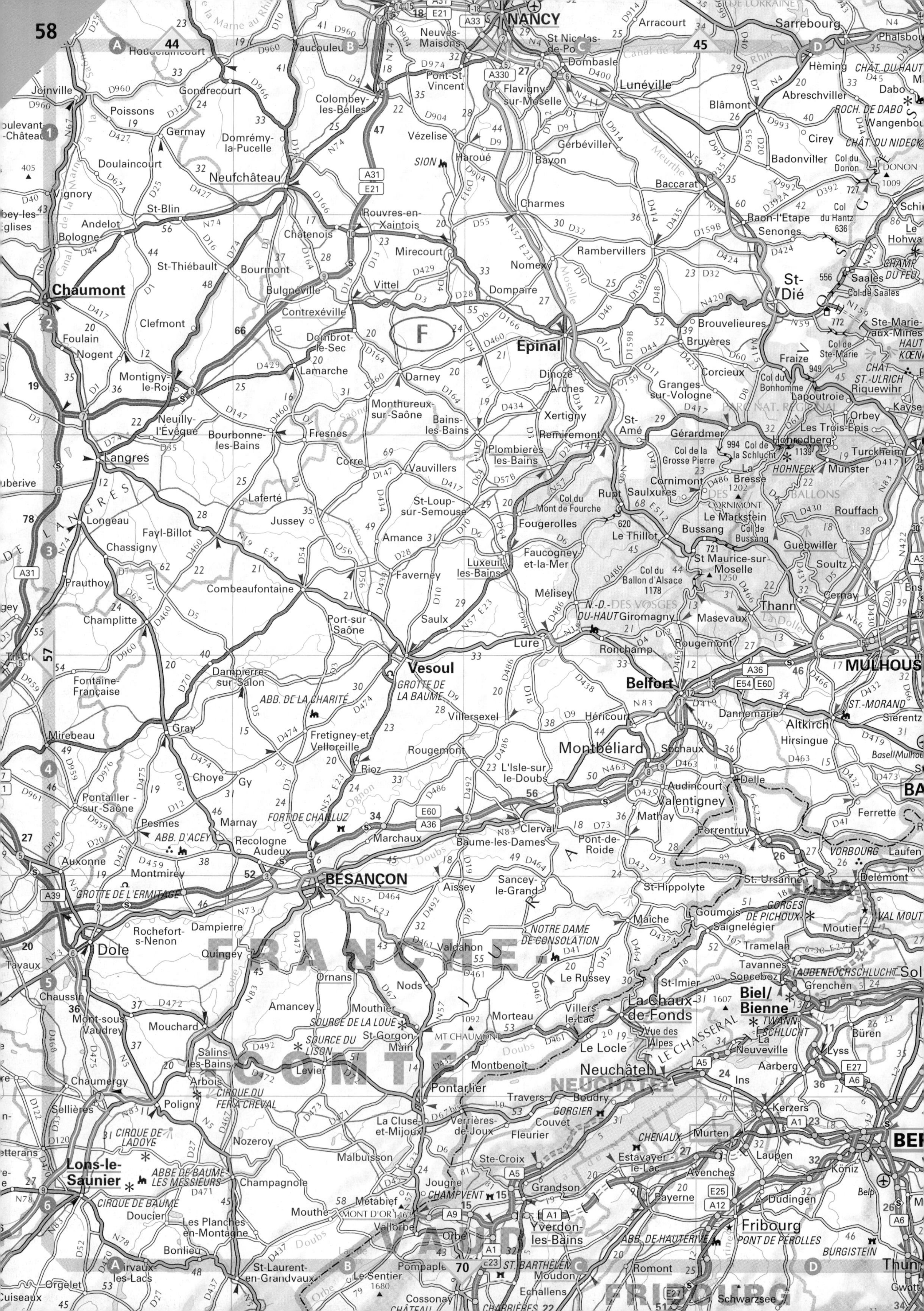
NANCY
Sarrebourg
Lunéville
Neufchâteau
Chaumont
Épinal
St-Dié
Langres
Vesoul
Belfort
MULHOUSE
Montbéliard
BESANÇON
Dole
Lons-le-Saunier
Pontarlier
Neuchâtel
La Chaux-de-Fonds
Biel/Bienne
Fribourg
Yverdon-les-Bains
FRANCHE-COMTÉ
JURA
VAUD
NEUCHÂTEL
FRIBOURG
Mirecourt
Vittel
Contrexéville
Remiremont
Gérardmer
Lure
Gray
Auxonne
Arbois
Poligny
Champagnole
Ornans
Baume-les-Dames
Luxeuil-les-Bains
Plombières-les-Bains
Bains-les-Bains
Rambervillers
Baccarat
Charmes
Toul
Vaucouleurs
Joinville
Gondrecourt
Domrémy-la-Pucelle
Colombey-les-Belles
Bourbonne-les-Bains
Port-sur-Saône
Villersexel
Héricourt
Delle
Porrentruy
Delémont
Saignelégier
Le Locle
Morteau
Maîche
Murten
Avenches
Payerne
Thann
Guebwiller
Cernay
Altkirch
Munster

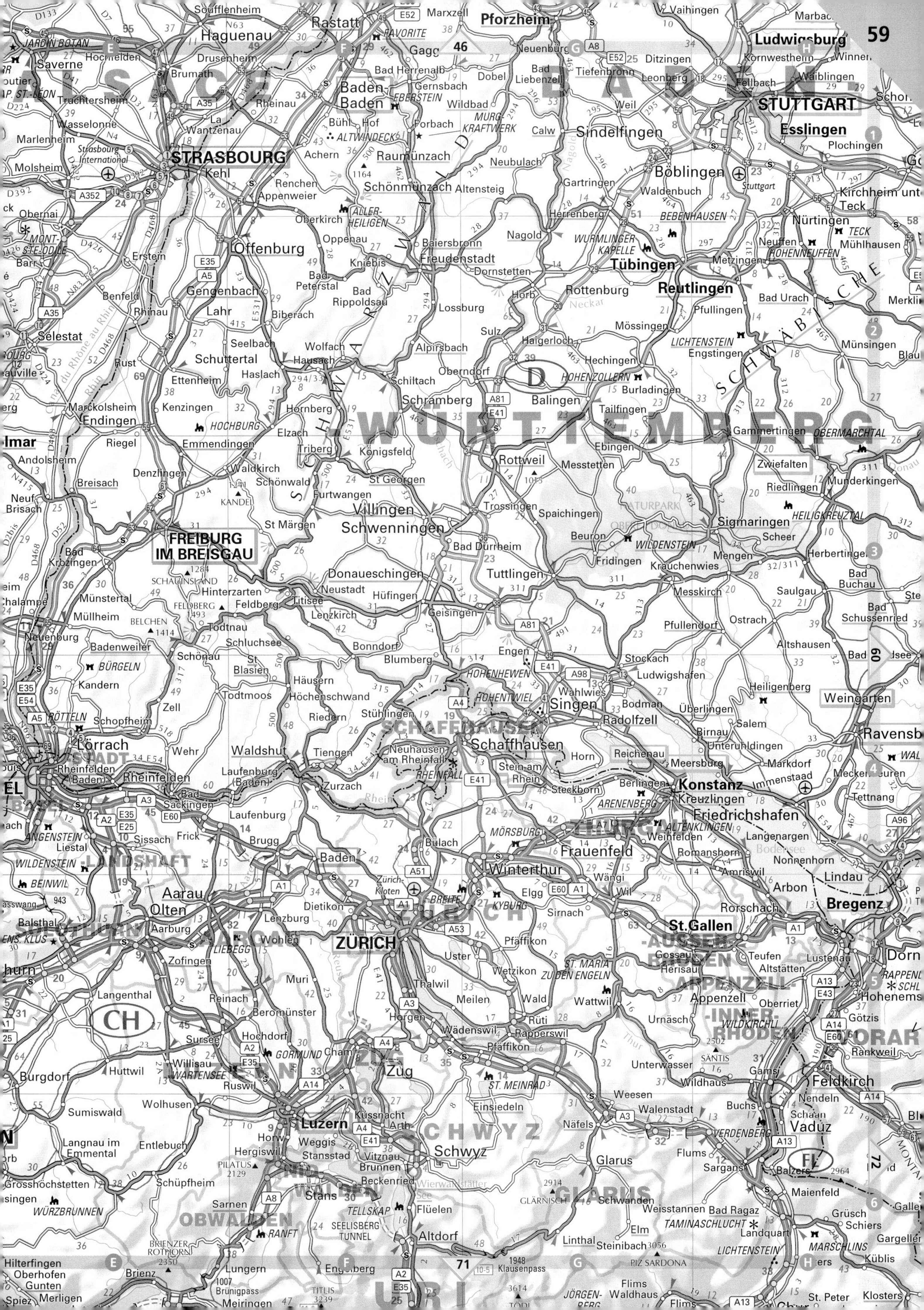

Soufflenheim
Haguenau
Rastatt
Marxzell
Pforzheim
Vaihingen
Marbach
Ludwigsburg
Saverne
Hochfelden
Brumath
Drusenheim
Gaggenau
Bad Herrenalb
Neuenbürg
Bad Liebenzell
Tiefenbronn
Ditzingen
Leonberg
Kornwestheim
Winnenden
Waiblingen
Fellbach
Baden-Baden
Gernsbach
Eberstein
Dobel
Wildbad
Weil
Stuttgart
Esslingen
Plochingen
Truchtersheim
Wasselonne
Rheinau
La Wantzenau
Bühl
Hof
Forbach
Murg-Kraftwerk
Calw
Sindelfingen
Altwindeck
Marlenheim
Strasbourg International
Strasbourg
Kehl
Achern
Raumünzach
Neubulach
Böblingen
Molsheim
Renchen
Appenweier
Schönmünzach
Altensteig
Gärtringen
Waldenbuch
Kirchheim unter Teck
Obernai
Mont-Ste-Odile
Oberkirch
Allerheiligen
Herrenberg
Bebenhausen
Nürtingen
Teck
Oppenau
Baiersbronn
Nagold
Wurmlinger Kapelle
Neuffen
Hohenneuffen
Mühlhausen
Barr
Erstein
Offenburg
Freudenstadt
Kniebis
Dornstetten
Tübingen
Metzingen
Reutlingen
Bad Peterstal
Bad Rippoldsau
Gengenbach
Benfeld
Rhinau
Lahr
Biberach
Lossburg
Horb
Rottenburg
Neckar
Bad Urach
Pfullingen
Sélestat
Seelbach
Schuttertal
Wolfach
Hausach
Alpirsbach
Sulz
Haigerloch
Mössingen
Lichtenstein
Engstingen
Münsingen
Rust
Ettenheim
Haslach
Schiltach
Oberndorf
Hechingen
Hohenzollern
Burladingen
Schramberg
Balingen
Tailfingen
Marckolsheim
Endingen
Kenzingen
Hochburg
Hornberg
Elzach
Gammertingen
Obermarchtal
Riegel
Emmendingen
Triberg
Königsfeld
Rottweil
Ebingen
Messtetten
Zwiefalten
Andolsheim
Breisach
Denzlingen
Waldkirch
Schönwald
St Georgen
Riedlingen
Munderkingen
Neuf Brisach
Kandel
Furtwangen
Villingen
Schwenningen
Trossingen
Spaichingen
Naturpark Obere Donau
Sigmaringen
Heiligkreuztal
St Märgen
Freiburg im Breisgau
Bad Dürrheim
Beuron
Wildenstein
Scheer
Mengen
Herbertingen
Bad Krozingen
Schauinsland
Donaueschingen
Tuttlingen
Fridingen
Krauchenwies
Bad Buchau
Hinterzarten
Neustadt
Titisee
Hüfingen
Messkirch
Saulgau
Münstertal
Feldberg
Lenzkirch
Geisingen
Bad Schussenried
Müllheim
Belchen
Todtnau
Ostrach
Pfullendorf
Neuenburg
Schluchsee
Altshausen
Badenweiler
Schönau
Bonndorf
Blumberg
Engen
Stockach
Bad Waldsee
Bürgeln
St Blasien
Hohenhewen
Ludwigshafen
Kandern
Häusern
Höchenschwand
Hohentwiel
Wahlwies
Singen
Bodman
Heiligenberg
Weingarten
Todtmoos
Zell
Röteln
Schopfheim
Riedern
Stühlingen
Schaffhausen
Radolfzell
Überlingen
Salem
Birnau
Ravensburg
Lörrach
Wehr
Waldshut
Tiengen
Neuhausen am Rheinfall
Horn
Reichenau
Unteruhldingen
Meersburg
Markdorf
Meckenbeuren
Basel-Stadt
Rheinfelden (Baden)
Rheinfelden
Laufenburg (Baden)
Zurzach
Rheinfall
Stein am Rhein
Berlingen
Steckborn
Konstanz
Kreuzlingen
Immenstaad
Tettnang
Bad Säckingen
Arenenberg
Friedrichshafen
Laufenburg
Basel-Landschaft
Angenstein
Liestal
Sissach
Frick
Brugg
Bülach
Mörsburg
Thurgau
Altenklingen
Weinfelden
Langenargen
Bodensee
Romanshorn
Nonnenhorn
Wildenstein
Baden
Winterthur
Frauenfeld
Amriswil
Lindau
Beinwil
Aarau
Olten
Dietikon
Zürich-Kloten
Breite
Kyburg
Elgg
Wängi
Wil
Arbon
Bregenz
Balsthal
Aarburg
Lenzburg
Wohlen
Zürich
Sirnach
Rorschach
St.Gallen
Solothurn
Aargau
Liebegg
Zofingen
Uster
Pfäffikon
Appenzell-Ausser-Rhoden
Gossau
Herisau
Teufen
Lustenau
Dornbirn
Altstätten
Wetzikon
St. Maria zu den Engeln
Muri
Thalwil
Meilen
Wald
Wattwil
Appenzell
Oberriet
Hohenems
Langenthal
Reinach
Beromünster
Rüti
Urnäsch
Appenzell-Inner-Rhoden
Wildkirchli
Götzis
CH
Sursee
Hochdorf
Horgen
Wädenswil
Rapperswil
Pfäffikon
Säntis
Rankweil
Vorarlberg
Gormund
Cham
Willisau
Wartensee
Luzern
Zug
Unterwasser
Wildhaus
Gams
Feldkirch
Burgdorf
Huttwil
Ruswil
St. Meinrad
Weesen
Walenstadt
Buchs
Nendeln
Schaan
Vaduz
Sumiswald
Wolhusen
Küssnacht
Arth
Einsiedeln
Näfels
Verdenberg
Langnau im Emmental
Entlebuch
Horw
Weggis
Stansstad
Schwyz
Vitznau
Brunnen
Glarus
Flums
Sargans
FL
Balzers
Pilatus
Schüpfheim
Beckenried
Vierwaldstätter See
Glärnisch
Schwanden
Maienfeld
Grosshöchstetten
Würzbrunnen
Sarnen
Stans
Obwalden
Nidwalden
Tellskap
Flüelen
Weisstannen
Bad Ragaz
Grüsch
Schiers
Taminaschlucht
Ranft
Seelisberg Tunnel
Altdorf
Elm
Linthal
Steinibach
Landquart
Marschlins
Gargellen
Brienzer Rothorn
Piz Sardona
Lichtenstein
Küblis
Hilterfingen
Oberhofen
Gunten
Brienz
Lungern
Engelberg
Klausenpass
Flims Waldhaus
Brünigpass
Titlis
Tödi
Jörgenberg
St. Peter
Klosters
Spiez
Merligen
Meiringen
Uri
Alsace
Baden-Württemberg
Schwarzwald
Schwäbische
D

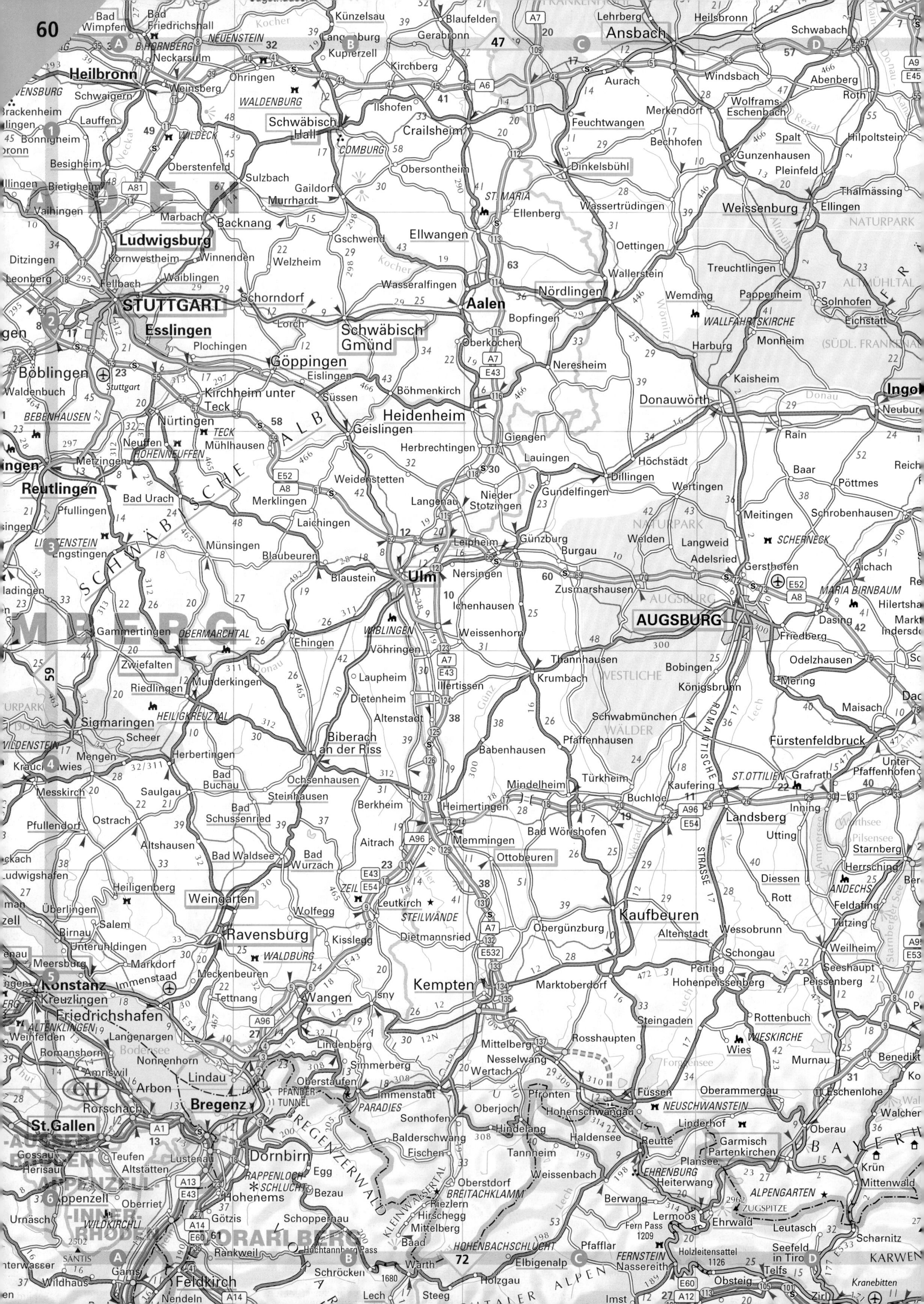

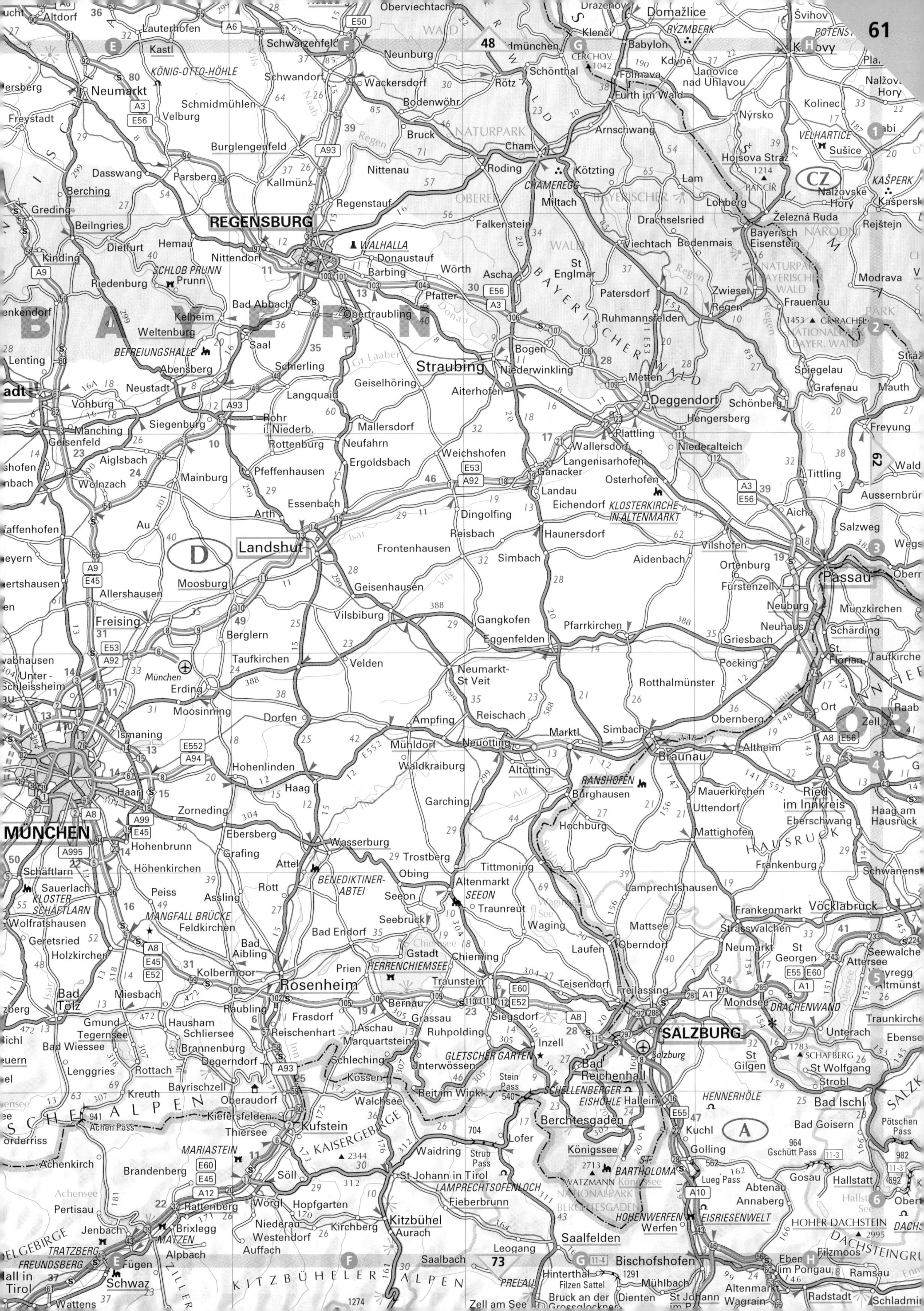

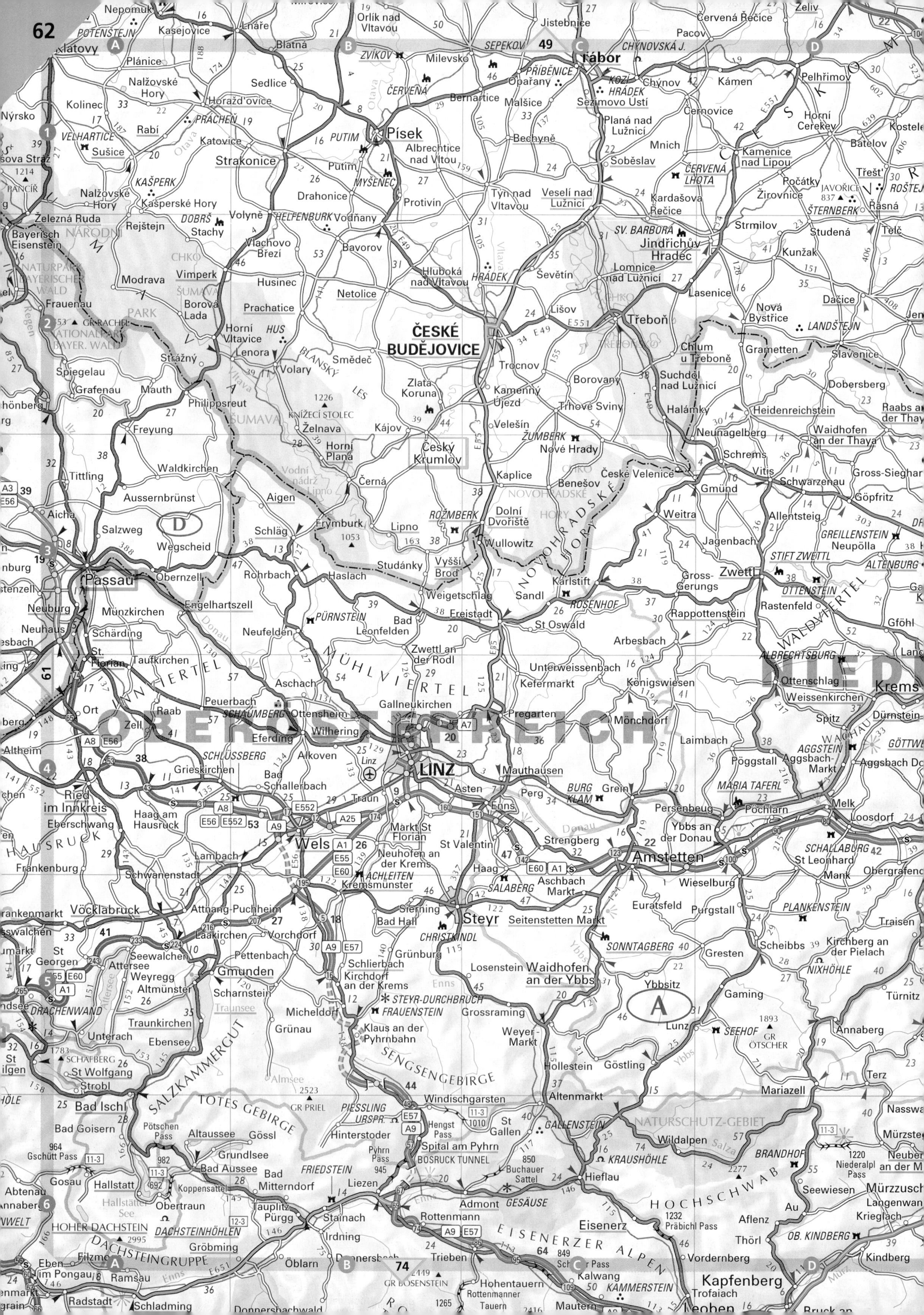
Nepomuk
POTENŠTEJN
Kasejovice
Lnáře
Orlík nad Vltavou
Jistebnice
Červená Řečice
Želiv
Klatovy
Blatná
SEPEKOV
49
CHÝNOVSKÁ J.
Pacov
Plánice
ZVÍKOV
Milevsko
Tábor
Pelhřimov
Nalžovské Hory
Sedlice
ČERVENÁ
PŘÍBĚNICE
Opařany
KOZÍ HRÁDEK
Chýnov
Kámen
Kolinec
Horažďovice
Bernartice
Malšice
Sezimovo Ústí
Nýrsko
PRÁCHEŇ
Cernovice
Horní Cerekev
VELHARTICE
Rabí
Písek
Planá nad Lužnicí
Kostele
Sušice
Katovice
PUTIM
Albrechtice nad Vltou
Bechyně
Mnich
Batelov
Strakonice
Soběslav
Kamenice nad Lipou
Šova Stráž
KAŠPERK
Putim
MYŠENEC
ČERVENÁ LHOTA
Počátky
Třešť
ROŠTEJ
PANCÍŘ
Nalžovské Hory
Drahonice
Protivín
Týn nad Vltavou
Veselí nad Lužnicí
JAVOŘICE
Žirovnice
Kašperské Hory
Kardašova Řečice
Řásná
Železná Ruda
DOBRŠ
Volyně
HELFENBURK
Vodňany
ŠTERNBERK
Rejštejn
Stachy
Strmilov
Bayerisch Eisenstein
NÁRODNÍ
SV. BARBORA
Studená
Telč
Vlachovo Březí
Bavorov
Jindřichův Hradec
Kunžak
CHKO
Hluboká nad Vltavou
HRÁDEK
Ševětín
Lomnice nad Lužnicí
NATURPARK BAYERISCHER WALD
Modrava
Vimperk
Husinec
Dačice
Netolice
Lasenice
ŠUMAVA
Frauenau
Borová Lada
Prachatice
Lišov
Nová Bystřice
Jen
GR. RACHEL
NATIONALPARK BAYER. WALD
Horní Vltavice
HUS
ČESKÉ BUDĚJOVICE
Třeboň
LANDŠTEJN
PARK
Lenora
Chlum u Třeboně
Grametten
Slavonice
Strážný
Volary
Smědeč
Trocnov
BLANSKÝ LES
Suchdol nad Lužnicí
Dobersberg
Spiegelau
Borovany
Grafenau
Mauth
Zlatá Koruna
Philippsreut
Kamenný Újezd
Trhové Sviny
Halámky
Heidenreichstein
Raabs a. der Thaya
Schönberg
KNÍŽECÍ STOLEC
Velešín
Freyung
Želnava
Kájov
ŽUMBERK
Nové Hrady
Neunagelberg
Waidhofen an der Thaya
Horní Planá
Český Krumlov
Schrems
ŠUMAVA
Tittling
Waldkirchen
Kaplice
Benešov
České Velenice
Vitis
Gross-Sieghar
Vodní nádrž Lipno
Černá
NOVOHRADSKÉ HORY
Schwarzenau
Aussernbrünst
Aigen
Gmünd
Göpfritz
Aicha
ROŽMBERK
Dolní Dvořiště
Weitra
Allentsteig
D
Salzweg
Frymburk
Lipno
Schlägl
GREILLENSTEIN
Wegscheid
Wullowitz
Jagenbach
Neupölla
Studánky
Vyšší Brod
STIFT ZWETTL
ALTENBURG
Passau
Obernzell
Rohrbach
Haslach
Gross-Gerungs
Zwettl
Karlstift
Sandl
OTTENSTEIN
Weigetschlag
ROSENHOF
Rastenfeld
Neuburg
Münzkirchen
Engelhartszell
Freistadt
Rappottenstein
Gföhl
PÜRNSTEIN
Bad Leonfelden
St Oswald
Neuhaus
Schärding
Neufelden
Arbesbach
WALDVIERTEL
Zwettl an der Rodl
St. Florian
Taufkirchen
ALBRECHTSBURG
MÜHLVIERTEL
Unterweissenbach
NIED
Kefermarkt
Königswiesen
Ottenschlag
INNVIERTEL
Aschach
Krems
Weissenkirchen
Gallneukirchen
Ort
Peuerbach
SCHAUMBERG
Ottensheim
Pregarten
Mönchdorf
Spitz
Dürnstein
Zell
Raab
OBERÖSTERREICH
Wilhering
Eferding
WACHAU
Laimbach
Altheim
SCHLÜSSBERG
Alkoven
AGGSTEIN
Aggsbach-Markt
GÖTTWE
Grieskirchen
Linz
LINZ
Mauthausen
Pöggstall
Aggsbach Do
Ried im Innkreis
Bad Schallerbach
Traun
Asten
Perg
BURG KLAM
Grein
MARIA TAFERL
Haag am Hausruck
Enns
Persenbeug
Pöchlarn
Melk
Loosdorf
Eberschwang
Wels
Markt St Florian
Donau
Ybbs an der Donau
HAUSRUCK
St Valentin
Strengberg
SCHALLABURG
Amstetten
St Leonhard
Frankenburg
Lambach
Neuhofen an der Krems
Haag
Aschbach Markt
Wieselburg
Mank
Obergrafenc
Schwanenstadt
ACHLEITEN
Kremsmünster
SALABERG
Euratsfeld
Purgstall
PLANKENSTEIN
Frankenmarkt
Vöcklabruck
Attnang-Puchheim
Sierning
Steyr
Seitenstetten Markt
Traisen
Laakirchen
Vorchdorf
Bad Hall
CHRISTKINDL
Scheibbs
Kirchberg an der Pielach
Seewalchen
Pettenbach
Grünburg
SONNTAGBERG
Gresten
St Georgen
Attersee
Weyregg
Schlierbach
NIXHÖHLE
Gmunden
Altmünster
Scharnstein
Kirchdorf an der Krems
Losenstein
Waidhofen an der Ybbs
Ybbsitz
Gaming
Türnitz
DRACHENWAND
Traunsee
Micheldorf
STEYR-DURCHBRUCH
FRAUENSTEIN
Grossraming
A
Traunkirchen
Grünau
Klaus an der Pyhrnbahn
Weyer-Markt
Lunz
SEEHOF
GR ÖTSCHER
Annaberg
Unterach
Ebensee
SALZKAMMERGUT
SCHAFBERG
St Wolfgang
SENGSENGEBIRGE
Hollenstein
Göstling
St Gilgen
Strobl
Almsee
Terz
Bad Ischl
TOTES GEBIRGE
GR PRIEL
PIESSLING URSPR.
Windischgarsten
Altenmarkt
Mariazell
Nasswa
Bad Goisern
Pötschen Pass
Altaussee
Gössl
Hinterstoder
Hengst Pass
St Gallen
GALLENSTEIN
NATURSCHUTZ-GEBIET
Mürzste
Gschütt Pass
Grundlsee
Spital am Pyhrn
Wildalpen
Salza
Neuber an der M
Gosau
Bad Aussee
Pyhrn Pass
BOSRUCK TUNNEL
Buchauer Sattel
KRAUSHÖHLE
BRANDHOF
Niederalpl Pass
Hallstatt
Koppensattel
Bad Mitterndorf
FRIEDSTEIN
Liezen
Hieflau
Mürzzusch
Abtenau
Hallstätter See
Obertraun
Admont
GESÄUSE
HOCHSCHWAB
Seewiesen
Langenwan
Annaberg
Tauplitz
Pürgg
Stainach
Rottenmann
Eisenerz
Präbichl Pass
Aflenz
Au
Krieglach
WELT
HOHER DACHSTEIN
DACHSTEINHÖHLEN
Irdning
EISENERZER ALPEN
Thörl
OB. KINDBERG
DACHSTEINGRUPPE
Gröbming
Filzmoos
Eben im Pongau
Ramsau
Öblarn
Donnersbach
74
Trieben
Schober Pass
Vordernberg
Kindberg
GR BÖSENSTEIN
Hohentauern
Rottenmanner Tauern
Kalwang
KAMMERSTEIN
Kapfenberg
Trofaiach
Radstadt
Schladming
Donnersbachwald
Mautern
Leoben
Bruck an

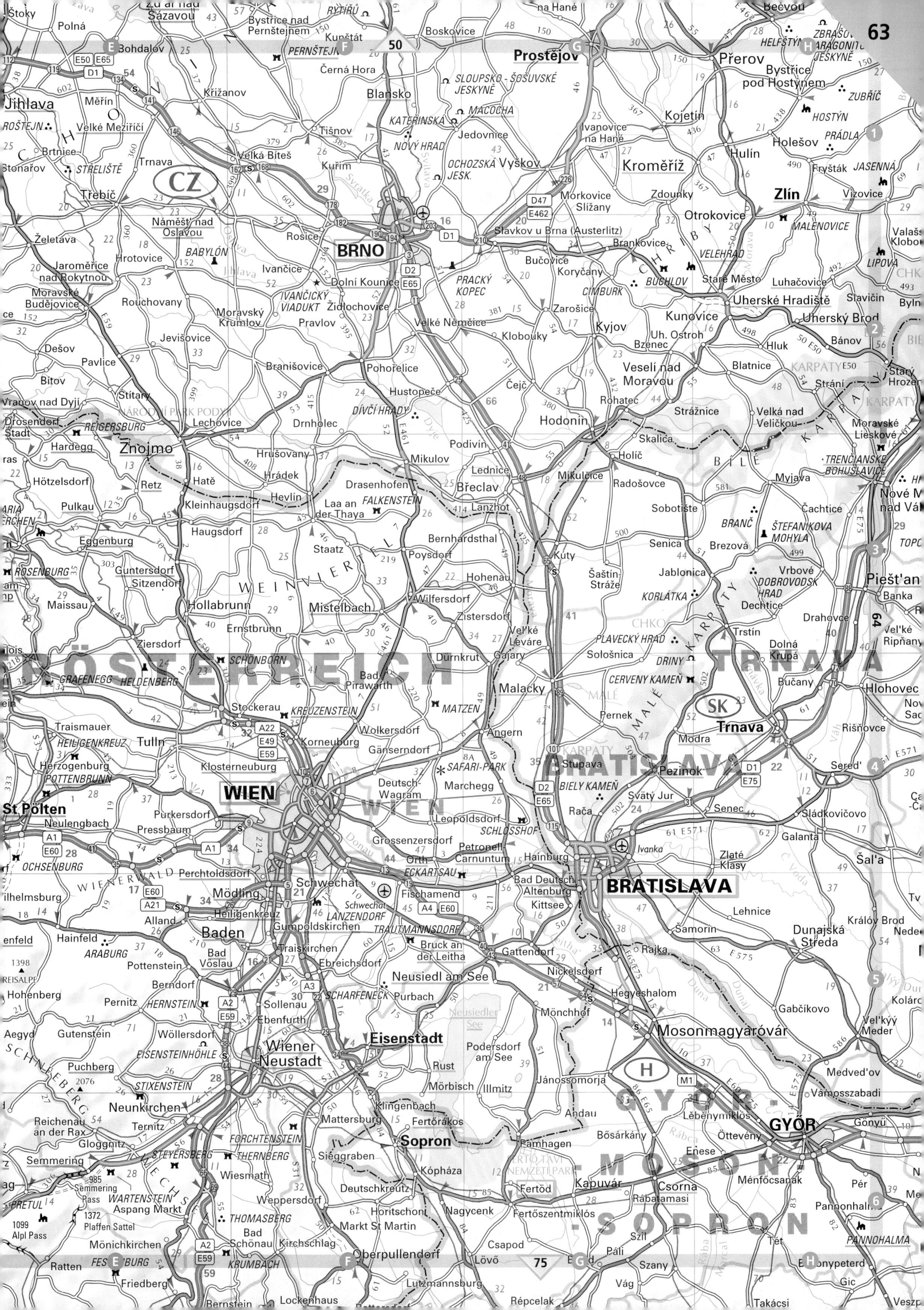

Polná
Bohdalov
Bystřice nad Pernštejnem
Kunštát
Boskovice
Prostějov
Přerov
Bystřice pod Hostýnem
Jihlava
Měřín
Velké Meziříčí
Křižanov
Černá Hora
Blansko
SLOUPSKO - ŠOSUVSKÉ JESKYNĚ
MACOCHA
Kojetín
HOSTÝN
ZUBŘÍČ
Tišnov
KATEŘINSKÁ
NOVÝ HRAD
Jedovnice
Ivanovice na Hané
Holešov
PRÁDLA
Brtnice
Velká Bíteš
Trnava
Kuřim
OCHOZSKÁ JESK.
Vyškov
Kroměříž
Hulín
Fryšták
JASENNÁ
STŘELIŠTĚ
CZ
Třebíč
Morkovice Slížany
Zdounky
Zlín
Vizovice
Náměšť nad Oslavou
Otrokovice
MALENOVICE
Želetava
Rosice
BRNO
Slavkov u Brna (Austerlitz)
Brankovice
Hrotovice
BABYLÓN
VELEHRAD
Jaroměřice nad Rokytnou
Ivančice
Dolní Kounice
Bučovice
Koryčany
BUCHLOV
Staré Město
Luhačovice
LIPOVÁ
Moravské Budějovice
Rouchovany
IVANČICKÝ VIADUKT
Židlochovice
PRACKÝ KOPEC
CIMBURK
Uherské Hradiště
Slavičín
Moravský Krumlov
Pravlov
Velké Němčice
Zarošice
Kunovice
Uherský Brod
Dešov
Jevišovice
Klobouky
Kyjov
Uh. Ostroh
Bzenec
Hluk
Bánov
Pavlice
Branišovice
Pohořelice
Veselí nad Moravou
Blatnice
KARPATY
Bítov
Hustopeče
Čejč
Strání
Stítary
Vranov nad Dyjí
NÁRODNÍ PARK PODYJÍ
DÍVČÍ HRADY
Rohatec
Strážnice
Velká nad Veličkou
Drosendorf Stadt
REIGERSBURG
Lechovice
Drnholec
Hodonín
Moravské Lieskové
Hardegg
Znojmo
Hrušovany
Podivín
Skalica
Holíč
Mikulov
Lednice
TRENČIANSKE BOHUSLAVICE
Hötzelsdorf
Retz
Hatě
Hrádek
Drasenhofen
Břeclav
Mikulčice
Radošovce
Myjava
Nové Mesto nad Váhom
Pulkau
Kleinhaugsdorf
Hevlín
Laa an der Thaya
FALKENSTEIN
Lanžhot
Sobotište
Čachtice
Eggenburg
Haugsdorf
BRANČ
ŠTEFANIKOVA MOHYLA
Bernhardsthal
Senica
Brezová
ROSENBURG
Guntersdorf
Sitzendorf
Staatz
Poysdorf
Kúty
Jablonica
Vrbové
DOBROVODSK HRAD
Piešťany
WEINVIERTEL
Hohenau
Šaštín-Stráže
KORLÁTKA
Dechtice
Banka
Maissau
Hollabrunn
Mistelbach
Wilfersdorf
Zistersdorf
Drahovce
Ernstbrunn
Veľké Leváre
PLAVECKÝ HRAD
Trstín
Dolná Krupá
Veľké Ripňany
Ziersdorf
Sološnica
DRINY
ÖSTERREICH
SCHÖNBORN
Dürnkrut
Gajary
TRNAVA
GRAFENEGG
HELDENBERG
Bad Pirawarth
CERVENY KAMEŇ
Bučany
Hlohovec
Malacky
Stockerau
KREUZENSTEIN
MATZEN
MALÉ KARPATY
SK
Pernek
Modra
Trnava
Rišňovce
Traismauer
Wolkersdorf
Angern
HEILIGENKREUZ
Tulln
Korneuburg
Gänserndorf
Herzogenburg
POTTENBRUNN
Klosterneuburg
SAFARI-PARK
Stupava
BRATISLAVA
Pezinok
Sereď
Deutsch-Wagram
Marchegg
BIELY KAMEŇ
St Pölten
WIEN
Svätý Jur
Purkersdorf
Rača
Senec
Sládkovičovo
Neulengbach
Pressbaum
Leopoldsdorf
SCHLOSSHOF
Galanta
Grossenzersdorf
Petronell Carnuntum
Hainburg
Ivanka
Zlaté Klasy
Šaľa
OCHSENBURG
Orth
ECKARTSAU
Perchtoldsdorf
Schwechat
Bad Deutsch Altenburg
WIENERWALD
Fischamend
Mödling
Wilhelmsburg
Kittsee
Heiligenkreuz
LANZENDORF
Lehnice
Alland
Gumpoldskirchen
TRAUTMANNSDORF
Šamorín
Hainfeld
Baden
Dunajská Streda
Kráľov Brod
ARABURG
Bad Vöslau
Traiskirchen
Bruck an der Leitha
Gattendorf
Rajka
Pottenstein
Ebreichsdorf
Nickelsdorf
Berndorf
Neusiedl am See
Hohenberg
Pernitz
HERNSTEIN
Sollenau
SCHARFENECK
Purbach
Hegyeshalom
Gabčíkovo
Ebenfurth
Mönchhof
Aegyd
Gutenstein
Wöllersdorf
Neusiedler See
Mosonmagyaróvár
Veľký Meder
Wiener Neustadt
Eisenstadt
Podersdorf am See
EISENSTEINHÖHLE
Puchberg
Rust
Jánossomorja
Medveďov
STIXENSTEIN
Mörbisch
Illmitz
Vámosszabadi
Neunkirchen
Klingenbach
Andau
Reichenau an der Rax
Ternitz
Mattersburg
Fertőrákos
Lébényimiklós
GYŐR
Gönyű
FORCHTENSTEIN
Sopron
Bősárkány
Öttevény
Gloggnitz
Pamhagen
Semmering
STEYERSBERG
THERNBERG
Sieggraben
Enese
GYŐR-MOSON-SOPRON
Kópháza
FERTŐ TÁVI NEMZETI PARK
Wiesmath
Deutschkreutz
Fertőd
Kapuvár
Csorna
Ménfőcsanak
Pér
Semmering Pass
WARTENSTEIN
Aspang Markt
Weppersdorf
Rábatamási
Pannonhalma
1372 Plaffen Sattel
THOMASBERG
Horitschon
Nagycenk
Fertőszentmiklós
1099 Alpl Pass
Markt St Martin
Mönichkirchen
Bad Schönau
Kirchschlag
Csapod
Szil
PANNONHALMA
FESTENBURG
KRUMBACH
Oberpullendorf
Lövő
Páli
Szany
Ratten
Friedberg
Lutzmannsburg
Vág
Gic
Lockenhaus
Répcelak
Takácsi
Bernstein
Veszprém

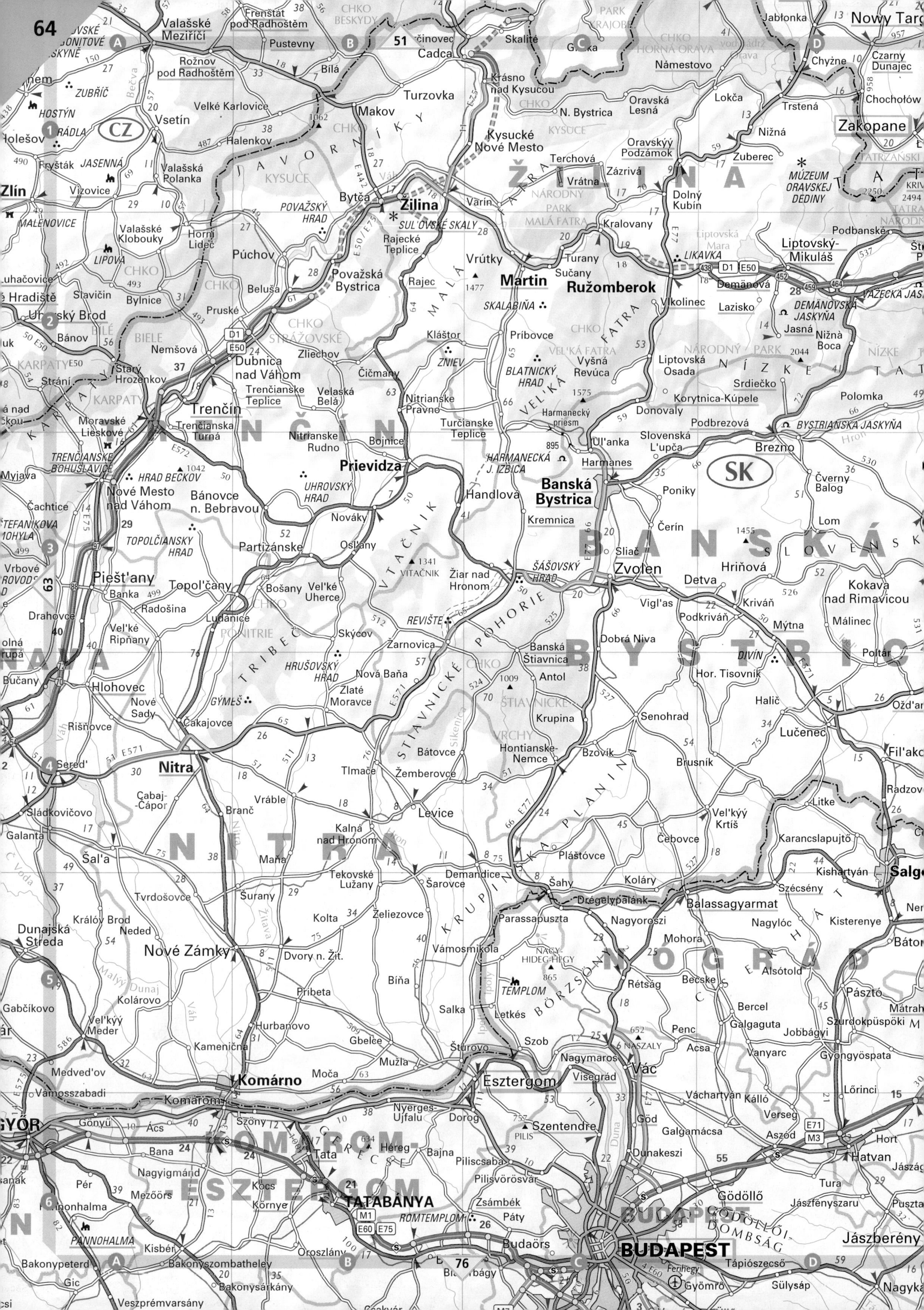
Valašské Meziříčí
Frenštát pod Radhoštěm
CHKO BESKYDY
Pustevny
Rožnov pod Radhoštěm
Bílá
Čadca
Skalité
Krásno nad Kysucou
Turzovka
Makov
Velké Karlovice
Vsetín
CZ
Halenkov
Zlín
Fryšták
JASENNÁ
Valašská Polanka
Vizovice
JAVORNÍKY
KYSUCE
Bytča
Žilina
POVAŽSKÝ HRAD
SUL'OVSKÉ SKALY
Rajecké Teplice
Valašské Klobouky
Horní Lideč
Púchov
LIPOVÁ
Luhačovice
Uherské Hradiště
Slavičín
Bylnice
Považská Bystrica
Rajec
Vrútky
Martin
Ružomberok
Uherský Brod
Bánov
Beluša
Pruské
BIELE KARPATY
Nemšová
CHKO STRÁŽOVSKÉ
Dubnica nad Váhom
Zliechov
Čičmany
Kláštor
ZNIEV
Príbovce
BLATNICKÝ HRAD
Vyšná Revúca
Liptovská Osada
Strání
Starý Hrozenkov
Trenčianske Teplice
Velaská Belá
Trenčín
Trenčianska Turná
Nitrianske Pravno
Turčianske Teplice
Moravské Lieskové
TRENČÍN
Nitrianske Rudno
Bojnice
Prievidza
TRENČIANSKE BOHUSLAVICE
HRAD BECKOV
Myjava
Nové Mesto nad Váhom
Bánovce n. Bebravou
UHROVSKÝ HRAD
Handlová
Čachtice
Nováky
VTÁČNIK
TOPOL'ČIANSKY HRAD
Partizánske
Oslany
Piešťany
Topol'čany
Bošany
Vel'ké Uherce
Žiar nad Hronom
ŠÁŠOVSKÝ HRAD
Zvolen
Detva
Banka
Radošina
Ludanice
PONITRIE
Skýcov
REVIŠTE
Vigl'aš
Podkriváň
Kriváň
Vel'ké Ripňany
TRIBEČ
Žarnovica
ŠTIAVNICKÉ POHORIE
Banská Štiavnica
Dobrá Niva
Mýtna
HRUŠOVSKÝ HRAD
Nová Baňa
Antol
DIVÍN
Hlohovec
GÝMEŠ
Zlaté Moravce
Hor. Tisovník
Nové Sady
ŠTIAVNICKÉ VRCHY
Krupina
Senohrad
Lučenec
Čakajovce
Rišňovce
Bátovce
Hontianske-Nemce
Bzovík
Brusník
Sereď
Nitra
Tlmače
Žemberovce
Sládkovičovo
Cabaj-Čápor
Vráble
Branč
Levice
KRUPINSKÁ PLANINA
Vel'ký Krtíš
Galanta
NITRA
Kalná nad Hronom
Čebovce
Šal'a
Maňa
Tekovské Lužany
Demandice
Šarovce
Pláštovce
Šahy
Kolláry
Tvrdošovce
Šurany
Drégelypalánk
Balassagyarmat
Král'ov Brod
Neded
Kolta
Želiezovce
Parassapuszta
Nagyoroszi
Dunajská Streda
Nové Zámky
Dvory n. Žit.
Vámosmikola
Mohora
NÓGRÁD
Kolárovo
Bíňa
TEMPLOM
Rétság
Becske
Gabčíkovo
Pribeta
BÖRZSÖNY
Vel'ký Meder
Hurbanovo
Salka
Letkés
Bercel
Galgaguta
Jobbágyi
Kameničná
Gbelce
Štúrovo
Szob
Penc
Acsa
Vanyarc
Medved'ov
Mužla
Moča
Komárno
Esztergom
Nagymaros
Vác
Visegrád
Vámosszabadi
Komárom
Nyergesújfalu
Dorog
Szentendre
Vácharytán
Kálló
GYŐR
Gönyű
Ács
Szőny
KOMÁROM-ESZTERGOM
Hereg
Bajna
Piliscsaba
Göd
Galgamácsa
Verseg
Aszód
Hatvan
Bana
Tata
Dunakeszi
Nagyigmánd
Pér
Kocs
Pilisvörösvár
Gödöllő
Tura
Mezőörs
Kisbér
TATABÁNYA
Zsámbék
Páty
Jászfényszaru
Pannonhalma
PANNONHALMA
Környe
ROMTEMPLOM
BUDAPEST
Budaörs
GÖDÖLLŐI-DOMBSÁG
Jászberény
Bakonypéterd
Bakonyszombathely
Oroszlány
Biatorbágy
Ferihegy
Tápiószecső
Gic
Bakonysárkány
Veszprémvarsány
Gyömrő
Sülysap
Nagykáta
Jabłonka
Nowy Targ
Chyżne
Czarny Dunajec
Námestovo
Oravská Lesná
N. Bystrica
Lokča
Trstená
Chochołów
Zakopane
Nižná
Kysucké Nové Mesto
Oravský Podzámok
Zuberec
MÚZEUM ORAVSKEJ DEDINY
Terchová
Zázrivá
ŽILINA
Vrátna
NÁRODNÝ PARK MALÁ FATRA
Dolný Kubín
Varín
Kralovany
Podbanské
Liptovský Mikuláš
LIKAVKA
Turany
Sučany
Demänová
Vlkolínec
Lazisko
DEMÄNOVSKÁ JASKYŇA
Jasná
SKALABIŇA
Nižná Boca
CHKO VEL'KÁ FATRA
NÁRODNÝ PARK NÍZKE TATRY
Srdiečko
Korytnica-Kúpele
Polomka
Donovaly
Harmanecký priesm
Podbrezová
BYSTRIANSKA JASKYŇA
Ul'anka
Slovenská L'upča
Brezno
HARMANECKÁ J. IZBICA
Harmanec
Banská Bystrica
SK
Poniky
Čierny Balog
Kremnica
Čerín
Lom
BANSKÁ BYSTRICA
Sliač
Hriňová
Kokava nad Rimavicou
Málinec
Poltár
Halič
Ožďany
Fil'akovo
Radzovce
Litke
Karancslapujtő
Kishartyán
Salgótarján
Szécsény
Nagylóc
Kisterenye
Bátonyterenye
Alsótold
Pásztó
Mátraháza
Szurdokpüspöki
Gyöngyöspata
Lőrinci
Hort
Jászág
Pusztamonostor

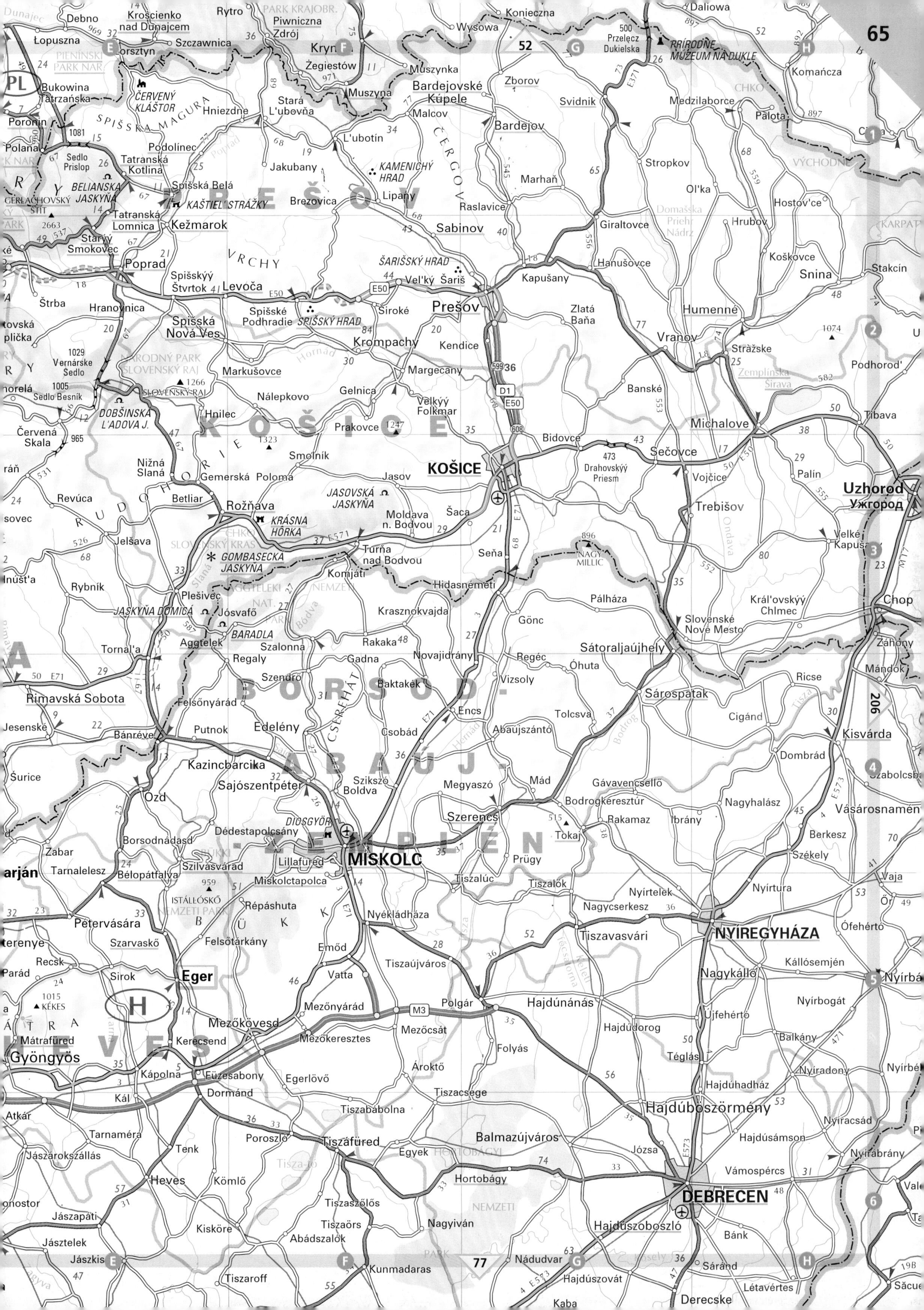
Debno
Łopuszna
Krościenko nad Dunajcem
Szczawnica
Czorsztyn
Rytro
PARK KRAJOBR.
Piwniczna Zdrój
Krynica
Żegiestów
Muszyna
Muszynka
Konieczna
Wysowa
52
500 Przełęcz Dukielska
PRÍRODNÉ MÚZEUM NA DUKLE
Daliowa
Komańcza
PIENIŃSKI PARK NAR.
Bukowina Tatrzańska
ČERVENÝ KLÁŠTOR
SPIŠSKÁ MAGURA
Hniezdne
Stará Ľubovňa
Bardejovské Kúpele
Zborov
Svidník
Medzilaborce
Palota
Poronin
Polana
Sedlo Prislop
Tatranská Kotlina
Podolínec
Malcov
Bardejov
Ľubotín
ČERGOV
Jakubany
KAMENICHÝ HRAD
Stropkov
Marhaň
BELIANSKA JASKYŇA
GERLACHOVSKÝ ŠTÍT
Spišská Belá
KAŠTIEĽ STRÁŽKY
PREŠOV
Brezovica
Lipany
Raslavice
Oľka
Hostov'ce
Tatranská Lomnica
Kežmarok
Sabinov
Giraltovce
Domašska Prieh. Nádrž
Hrubov
Starý Smokovec
VRCHY
ŠARIŠSKÝ HRAD
Hanušovce
Koškovce
Snina
Stakčín
Poprad
Spišskýý Štvrtok
Levoča
Veľký Šariš
Kapušany
Štrba
Hranovnica
Spišské Podhradie
SPIŠSKÝ HRAD
Široké
Prešov
Zlatá Baňa
Humenné
Spišská Nová Ves
Krompachy
Kendice
Vranov
Strážske
Podhorod'
Vernárske Sedlo
NÁRODNÝ PARK SLOVENSKÝ RAJ
Markušovce
Margecany
Banské
Zemplínska Šírava
Sedlo Besník
SLOVENSKÝ RAJ
Nálepkovo
Gelnica
Veľkýý Folkmar
Hnilec
DOBŠINSKÁ ĽADOVÁ J.
KOŠICE
Prakovce
Bidovce
Michalove
Tibava
Červená Skala
Nižná Slaná
Smolník
KOŠICE
Drahovský Priesm
Sečovce
Vojčice
Palín
Uzhorod
Ужгород
Gemerská Poloma
Jasov
JASOVSKÁ JASKYŇA
Revúca
Betliar
Rožňava
KRÁSNA HÔRKA
Moldava n. Bodvou
Šaca
Trebišov
Jelšava
SLOVENSKÝ KRAS
GOMBASECKÁ JASKYŇA
Turňa nad Bodvou
Seňa
NAGY MILLIC
Veľké Kapušany
Komjáti
Hidasnémeti
Rybník
Plešivec
AGGTELEKI NAT. PARK
Jósvafő
BARADLA
JASKYŇA DOMICA
Krasznokvajda
Pálháza
Kráľovskýý Chlmec
Chop
Gönc
Slovenské Nové Mesto
Tornaľa
Aggtelek
Szalonna
Rakaka
Novajidrány
Sátoraljaújhely
Záhony
Regéc
Óhuta
Regaly
Gadna
Szendrő
Baktakék
Vizsoly
Mándok
Rimavská Sobota
BORSOD-
CSERHÁT
Sárospatak
Ricse
Felsőnyárád
Encs
Tolcsva
Cigánd
Jesenské
Bánréve
Putnok
Edelény
Csobád
Abaújszántó
Kisvárda
ABAÚJ-
Kazincbarcika
Dombrád
Šurice
Sajószentpéter
Szikszó
Boldva
Megyaszó
Mád
Gávavencsellő
Ózd
Bodrogkeresztúr
Nagyhalász
Vásárosnamén
DIOSGYŐR
Szerencs
Rakamaz
Ibrány
Dédestapolcsány
ZEMPLÉN
Tokaj
Berkesz
Borsodnádasd
Zabar
MISKOLC
Prügy
Székely
Tarnalelesz
Bélapátfalva
Szilvásvárad
Lillafüred
Miskolctapolca
Tiszalúc
Tiszalök
Nyírtelek
Nyírtura
Vaja
ISTÁLLÓSKŐ NEMZETI PARK
Répáshuta
BÜKK
Nagycserkesz
Pétervására
Nyékládháza
Tiszavasvári
NYÍREGYHÁZA
Ófehértó
Szarvaskő
Felsőtárkány
Emőd
Recsk
Kállósemjén
Parád
Sirok
Eger
Vatta
Tiszaújváros
Nagykálló
Nyírbátor
KÉKES
MÁTRA
H
Mezőnyárád
Polgár
Hajdúnánás
Nyírbogát
Mezőkövesd
Mezőkeresztes
Mezőcsát
Újfehértó
Mátrafüred
HEVES
Kerecsend
Hajdúdorog
Balkány
Gyöngyös
Kápolna
Folyás
Téglás
Nyírbéltek
Füzesabony
Aroktő
Egerlövő
Nyíradony
Kál
Dormánd
Hajdúhadház
Tiszacsege
Atkár
Tiszababolna
Hajdúböszörmény
Nyíracsád
Tarnaméra
Tenk
Poroszló
Tiszafüred
Balmazújváros
Hajdúsámson
Jászárokszállás
Egyek
HORTOBÁGYI
Józsa
Nyírábrány
Heves
Kömlő
Hortobágy
Vámospércs
Jászapáti
Tiszaszőlős
NEMZETI
DEBRECEN
Tiszaörs
Nagyiván
Hajdúszoboszló
Jásztelek
Kisköre
Abádszalók
Bánk
Jászkisér
Kunmadaras
Nádudvar
Sáránd
Tiszaroff
Hajdúszovát
Létavértes
Kaba
Derecske
Sácuieni
77

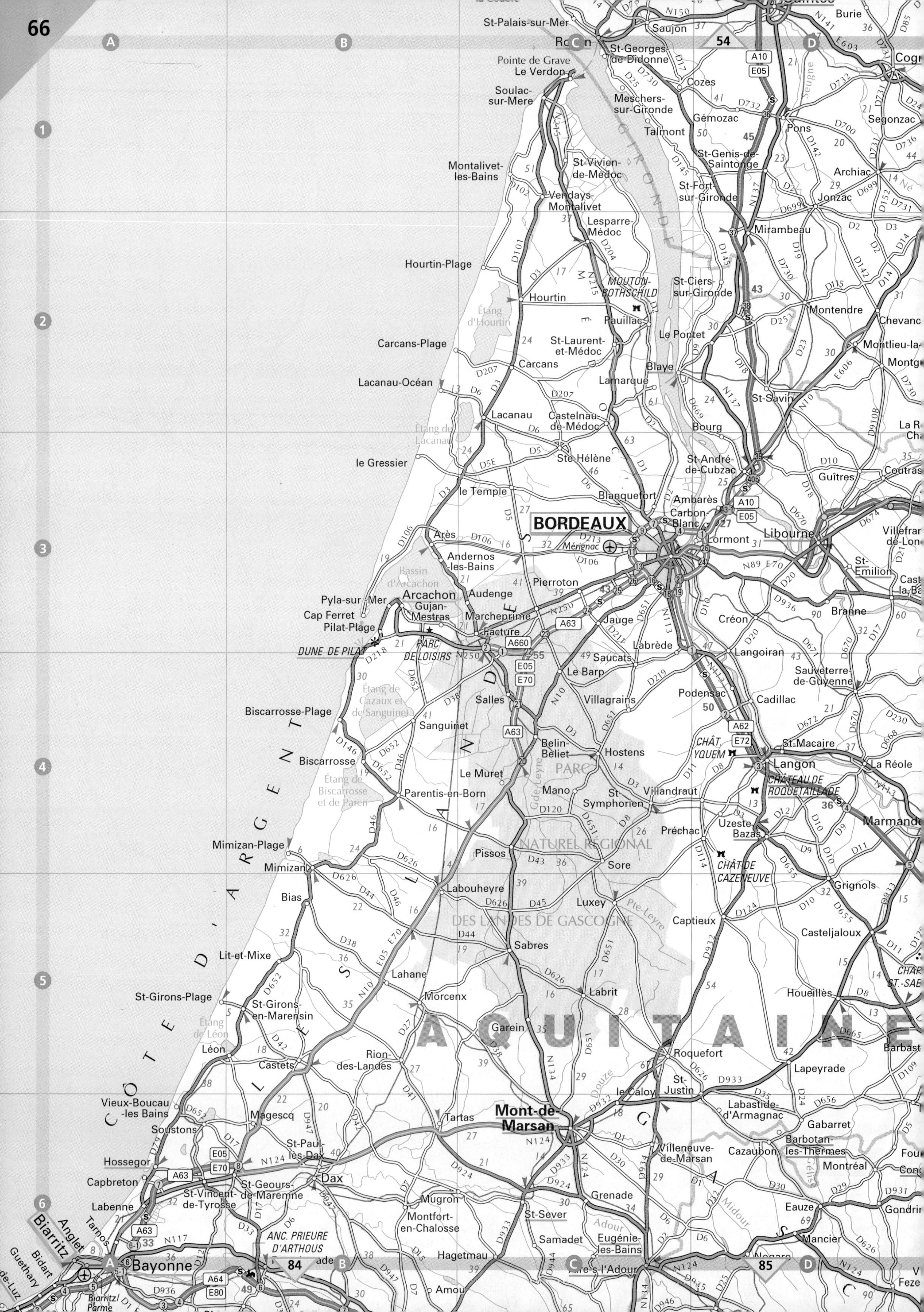
St-Palais-sur-Mer
Saujon
St-Georges-de-Didonne
Pointe de Grave
Le Verdon
Soulac-sur-Mere
Meschers-sur-Gironde
Cozes
Gémozac
Talmont
Pons
Segonzac
St-Genis-de-Saintonge
Archiac
Montalivet-les-Bains
St-Vivien-de-Médoc
St-Fort-sur-Gironde
Jonzac
Vendays-Montalivet
Lesparre-Médoc
Mirambeau
GIRONDE
Hourtin-Plage
MOUTON-ROTHSCHILD
St-Ciers-sur-Gironde
Hourtin
Montendre
Étang d'Hourtin
Pauillac
Le Pontet
Chevanceaux
Carcans-Plage
St-Laurent-et-Médoc
Montlieu-la-Garde
Carcans
Blaye
Lacanau-Océan
Lamarque
St-Savin
Lacanau
Castelnau-de-Médoc
Bourg
Étang de Lacanau
le Gressier
Ste-Hélène
St-André-de-Cubzac
Guîtres
Coutras
le Temple
Blanquefort
Ambarès
Carbon-Blanc
Libourne
BORDEAUX
Arès
Mérignac
Lormont
Andernos-les-Bains
St-Emilion
Bassin d'Arcachon
Arcachon
Pierroton
Pyla-sur-Mer
Gujan-Mestras
Audenge
Cap Ferret
Pilat-Plage
Marcheprime
Créon
Branne
Facture
Jauge
DUNE DE PILAT
PARC DE LOISIRS
Labrède
Langoiran
Saucats
Sauveterre-de-Guyenne
Le Barp
Étang de Cazaux et de Sanguinet
Salles
Podensac
Cadillac
Biscarrosse-Plage
Villagrains
Sanguinet
CHÂT. YQUEM
St-Macaire
Belin-Béliet
Hostens
Langon
La Réole
Biscarrosse
Le Muret
PARC
CHÂTEAU DE ROQUETAILLADE
Étang de Biscarrosse et de Parentis
Parentis-en-Born
Mano
St-Symphorien
Villandraut
Marmande
Uzeste
Préchac
Bazas
NATUREL RÉGIONAL
Mimizan-Plage
Pissos
Sore
CHÂT. DE CAZENEUVE
Mimizan
Labouheyre
Grignols
Bias
Luxey
Captieux
DES LANDES DE GASCOGNE
Casteljaloux
Sabres
Lit-et-Mixe
Lahane
Labrit
Houeillès
St-Girons-Plage
Morcenx
St-Girons-en-Marensin
Étang de Léon
Garein
AQUITAINE
Léon
Rion-des-Landes
Roquefort
Barbaste
Castets
Lapeyrade
St-Justin
Vieux-Boucau-les-Bains
Le Caloy
Magescq
Labastide-d'Armagnac
Tartas
Mont-de-Marsan
Gabarret
Soustons
Barbotan-les-Thermes
St-Paul-lès-Dax
Villeneuve-de-Marsan
Cazaubon
Hossegor
Capbreton
Dax
Montréal
St-Geours-de-Maremne
St-Vincent-de-Tyrosse
Grenade
Labenne
Mugron
Eauze
Gondrin
Montfort-en-Chalosse
St-Sever
Biarritz
Anglet
Tarnos
ANC. PRIEURE D'ARTHOUS
Samadet
Eugénie-les-Bains
Mancier
Bayonne
Hagetmau
Aire-s-l'Adour
Nogaro
Bidart
Guethary
Amou
CÔTE D'ARGENT
LANDES
MÉDOC
GASCOGNE
Adour
Midour
Douze
54
84
85

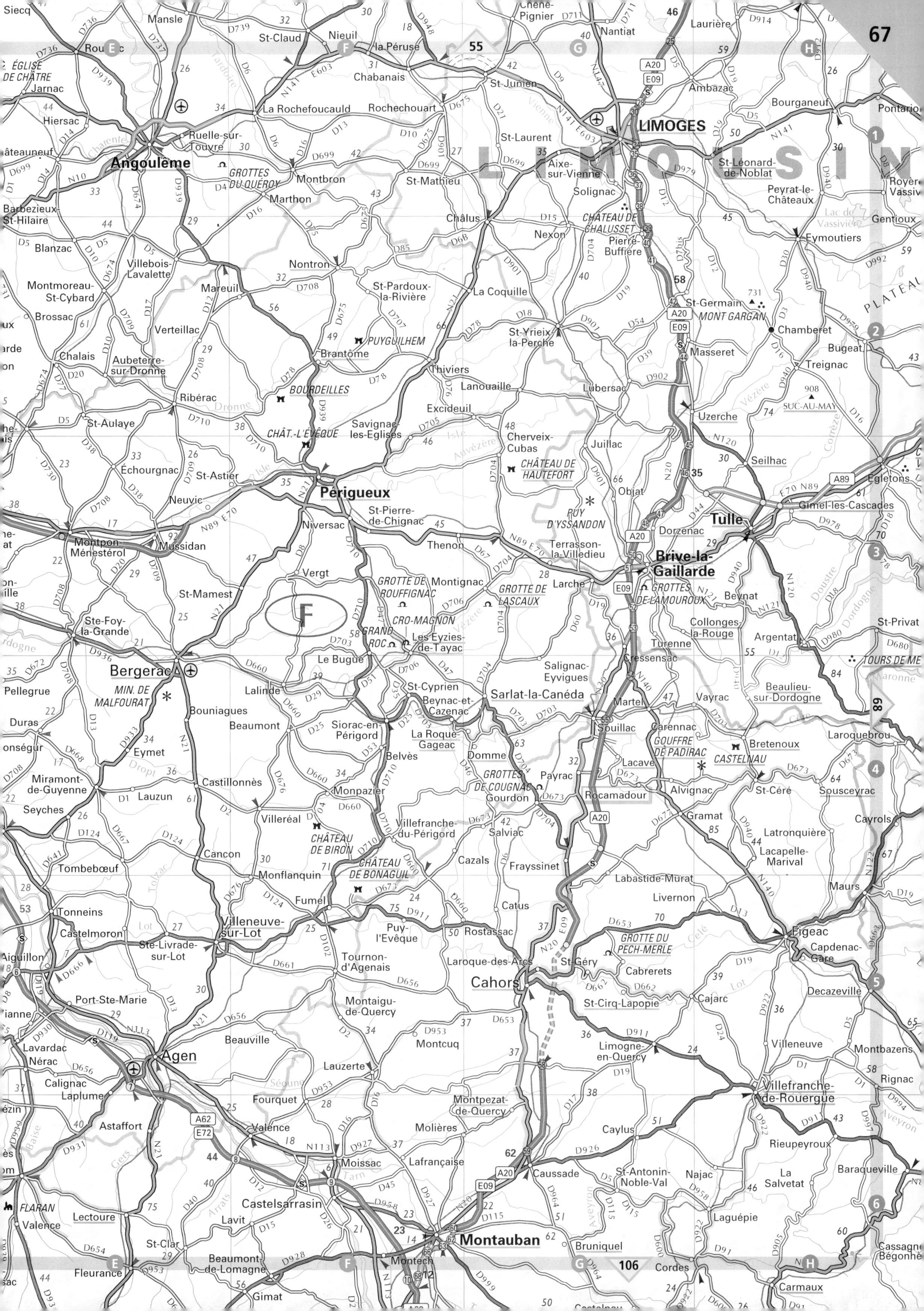

LIMOUSIN
Siecq
Mansle
St-Claud
Nieuil
la Péruse
Chêne-Pignier
Nantiat
Laurière
Rouillac
ÉGLISE DE CHÂTRE
Jarnac
Chabanais
St-Junien
Ambazac
Bourganeuf
Pontarion
Hiersac
La Rochefoucauld
Rochechouart
LIMOGES
Ruelle-sur-Touvre
St-Laurent
Châteauneuf
Angoulême
GROTTES DU QUÉROY
Montbron
St-Mathieu
Aixe-sur-Vienne
St-Léonard-de-Noblat
Royère
Vassivière
Barbezieux-St-Hilaire
Marthon
Solignac
Peyrat-le-Château
Lac de Vassivière
Gentioux
Châlus
CHÂTEAU DE CHALUSSET
Nexon
Pierre-Buffière
Eymoutiers
Blanzac
Villebois-Lavalette
Nontron
La Coquille
Montmoreau-St-Cybard
Mareuil
St-Pardoux-la-Rivière
St-Germain
MONT GARGAN
Chamberet
PLATEAU
Brossac
Verteillac
PUYGUILHEM
St-Yrieix-la-Perche
Masseret
Bugeat
Chalais
Aubeterre-sur-Dronne
Brantôme
Thiviers
Treignac
Lanouaille
Lubersac
SUC-AU-MAY
Ribérac
BOURDEILLES
Excideuil
Uzerche
St-Aulaye
CHÂT.-L'ÉVÊQUE
Savignac-les-Églises
Cherveix-Cubas
Juillac
Échourgnac
St-Astier
CHÂTEAU DE HAUTEFORT
Seilhac
Egletons
Neuvic
Périgueux
Objat
Gimel-les-Cascades
St-Pierre-de-Chignac
PUY D'YSSANDON
Tulle
Niversac
Dorzenac
Montpon-Ménestérol
Mussidan
Thenon
Terrasson-la-Villedieu
Brive-la-Gaillarde
Vergt
GROTTE DE ROUFFIGNAC
Montignac
GROTTE DE LASCAUX
Larche
GROTTES DE LAMOUROUX
Beynat
St-Mamest
CRO-MAGNON
Ste-Foy-la-Grande
GRAND ROC
Les Eyzies-de-Tayac
Collonges-la-Rouge
Argentat
St-Privat
Turenne
Le Bugue
Salignac-Eyvigues
Cressensac
TOURS DE MERLE
Bergerac
MIN. DE MALFOURAT
Lalinde
St-Cyprien
Beynac-et-Cazenac
Sarlat-la-Canéda
Martel
Vayrac
Beaulieu-sur-Dordogne
Pellegrue
Bouniagues
Beaumont
Siorac-en-Périgord
La Roque-Gageac
Souillac
Carennac
GOUFFRE DE PADIRAC
Bretenoux
CASTELNAU
Laroquebrou
Duras
Eymet
Belvès
Domme
Lacave
Monségur
GROTTES DE COUGNAC
Payrac
Gourdon
Rocamadour
Alvignac
St-Céré
Sousceyrac
Miramont-de-Guyenne
Castillonnès
Lauzun
Monpazier
Gramat
Seyches
Villeréal
CHÂTEAU DE BIRON
Villefranche-du-Périgord
Salviac
Latronquière
Lacapelle-Marival
Cayrols
Cancon
CHÂTEAU DE BONAGUIL
Cazals
Frayssinet
Tombebœuf
Monflanquin
Labastide-Murat
Livernon
Maurs
Fumel
Catus
Tonneins
Puy-l'Evêque
Villeneuve-sur-Lot
Rostassac
Castelmoron
Ste-Livrade-sur-Lot
Tournon-d'Agenais
Laroque-des-Arcs
St-Géry
GROTTE DU PECH-MERLE
Figeac
Capdenac-Gare
Aiguillon
Cahors
Cabrerets
Decazeville
Port-Ste-Marie
Montaigu-de-Quercy
St-Cirq-Lapopie
Cajarc
Beauville
Montcuq
Limogne-en-Quercy
Villeneuve
Montbazens
Lavardac
Nérac
Agen
Lauzerte
Calignac
Laplume
Fourquet
Montpezat-de-Quercy
Villefranche-de-Rouergue
Rignac
Astaffort
Valence
Molières
Caylus
Rieupeyroux
Moissac
Lafrançaise
Caussade
St-Antonin-Noble-Val
Najac
La Salvetat
Baraqueville
FLARAN
Lectoure
Castelsarrasin
Lavit
Laguépie
Montauban
Bruniquel
Cassagnes-Bégonhès
St-Clar
Beaumont-de-Lomagne
Montech
Cordes
Carmaux
Fleurance
Gimat
Castelnau
Charente
Vienne
Isle
Dronne
Vézère
Corrèze
Dordogne
Lot
Célé
Tarn
Aveyron
Garonne
Gers
Baïse
Dropt

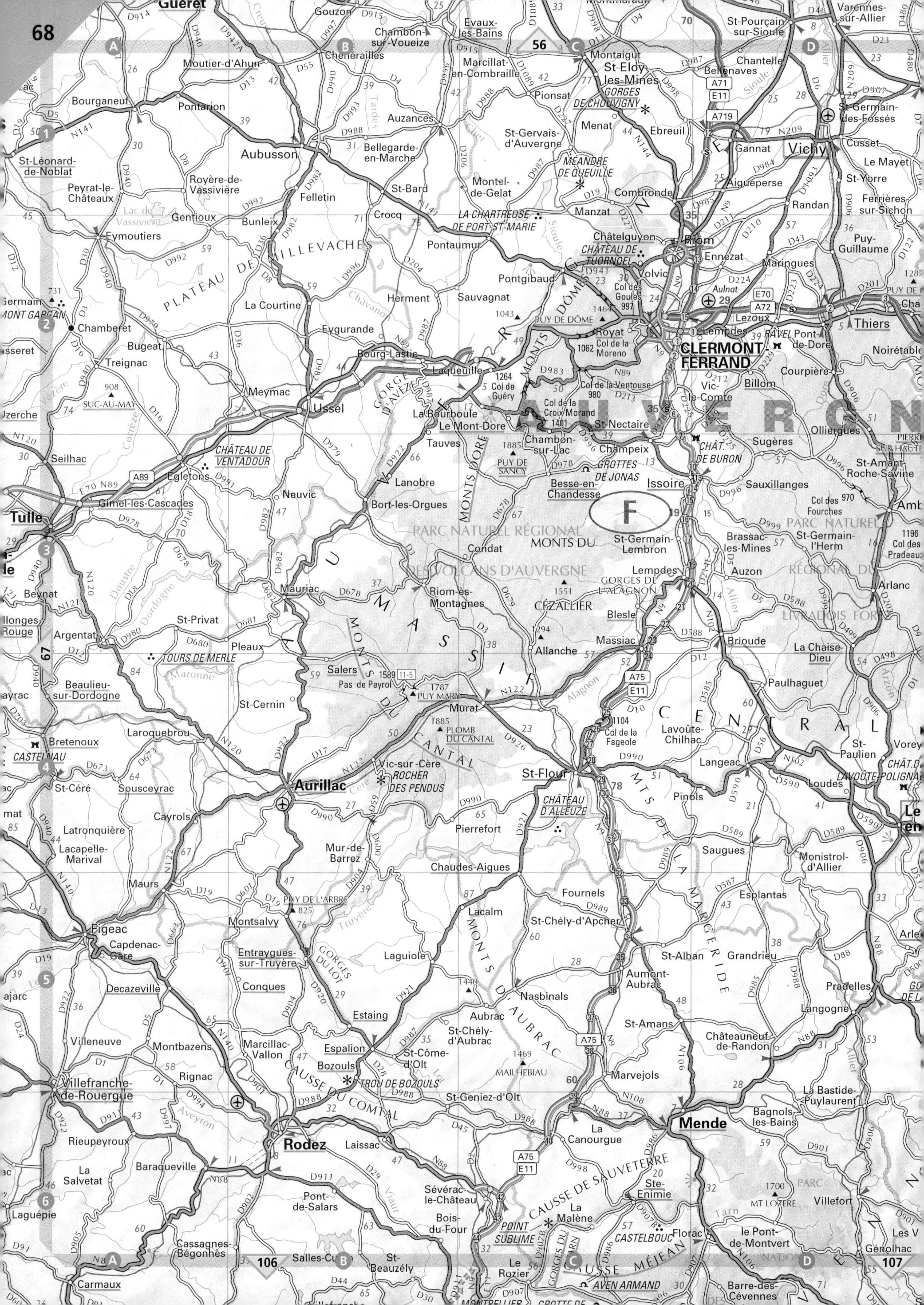

Guéret
Gouzon
Chambon-sur-Voueize
Evaux-les-Bains
56
Montaigut
St-Pourçain-sur-Sioule
Varennes-sur-Allier
Moutier-d'Ahun
Chénérailles
Marcillat-en-Combraille
St-Eloy-les-Mines
GORGES DE CHOUVIGNY
Bellenaves
Chantelle
Bourganeuf
Pontarion
Auzances
Pionsat
Menat
Ebreuil
St-Germain-des-Fossés
St-Léonard-de-Noblat
Aubusson
Bellegarde-en-Marche
St-Gervais-d'Auvergne
Gannat
Vichy
Cusset
Peyrat-le-Château
Royère-de-Vassivière
Felletin
St-Bard
Montel-de-Gelat
MEANDRE DE QUEUILLE
Combronde
Aigueperse
Le Mayet
St-Yorre
Lac de Vassivière
Gentioux
Bunleix
Crocq
LA CHARTREUSE DE PORT-ST-MARIE
Manzat
Randan
Ferrières-sur-Sichon
Eymoutiers
Pontaumur
Châtelguyon
Riom
CHÂTEAU DE TUORNOEL
Ennezat
Puy-Guillaume
Maringues
PLATEAU DE MILLEVACHES
Pontgibaud
Volvic
Col des Goules 997
Aulnat
St-Germain
MONT GARGAN
Chamberet
La Courtine
Herment
Sauvagnat
PUY DE DÔME
Royat
Lezoux
Lempdes
Thiers
Pont-de-Dore
RAVEL
Bugeat
Eygurande
Col de la Moreno
CLERMONT-FERRAND
Noirétable
Treignac
Bourg-Lastic
Laqueuille
MONTS DÔME
Col de la Ventouse
Billom
Courpière
Col de Guéry
Meymac
908 SUC-AU-MAY
Ussel
GORGE D'AVÈZE
La Bourboule
Le Mont-Dore
Col de la Croix Morand
Vic-le-Comte
AUVERGNE
Uzerche
Tauves
Chambon-sur-Lac
St-Nectaire
Champeix
CHÂT. DE BURON
Sugères
Olliergues
Seilhac
CHÂTEAU DE VENTADOUR
PUY DE SANCY
GROTTES DE JONAS
St-Amant-Roche-Savine
Egletons
Besse-en-Chandesse
Issoire
Sauxillanges
Tulle
Gimel-les-Cascades
Neuvic
Lanobre
Bort-les-Orgues
MONTS DORE
F
Col des Fourches
PARC NATUREL RÉGIONAL DES VOLCANS D'AUVERGNE
MONTS DU CÉZALLIER
St-Germain-Lembron
Brassac-les-Mines
St-Germain-l'Herm
PARC NATUREL RÉGIONAL DU LIVRADOIS FOREZ
Condat
Lempdes
Auzon
GORGES DE L'ALAGNON
Arlanc
Beynat
Mauriac
Riom-ès-Montagnes
Blesle
MASSIF CENTRAL
St-Privat
Argentat
Massiac
Brioude
La Chaise-Dieu
Pleaux
TOURS DE MERLE
Allanche
MONTS DU CANTAL
Salers
Pas de Peyrol
PUY MARY
Paulhaguet
Beaulieu-sur-Dordogne
St-Cernin
Murat
Laroquebrou
PLOMB DU CANTAL
Col de la Fageole
Lavoûte-Chilhac
St-Paulien
Bretenoux
CASTELNAU
Vic-sur-Cère
ROCHER DES PENDUS
St-Flour
Langeac
CHÂT. DE LAVOÛTE-POLIGNAC
St-Céré
Sousceyrac
Aurillac
CHÂTEAU D'ALLEUZE
Pinols
Loudes
MTS DE LA MARGERIDE
Cayrols
Latronquière
Lacapelle-Marival
Pierrefort
Mur-de-Barrez
Saugues
Monistrol-d'Allier
Chaudes-Aigues
Maurs
PUY DE L'ARBRE
Fournels
Esplantas
Lacalm
St-Chély-d'Apcher
Figeac
Montsalvy
Capdenac-Gare
Entraygues-sur-Truyère
GORGES DU LOT
Laguiole
MONTS D'AUBRAC
St-Alban
Grandrieu
Aumont-Aubrac
Decazeville
Conques
Nasbinals
Pradelles
Langogne
Estaing
Aubrac
St-Amans
Villeneuve
Montbazens
Marcillac-Vallon
Espalion
St-Chély-d'Aubrac
St-Côme-d'Olt
Châteauneuf-de-Randon
Rignac
Bozouls
TROU DE BOZOULS
MAILHEBIAU
Marvejols
Villefranche-de-Rouergue
CAUSSE DU COMTAL
St-Geniez-d'Olt
La Bastide-Puylaurent
Rieupeyroux
Rodez
Laissac
La Canourgue
Mende
Bagnols-les-Bains
Baraqueville
La Salvetat
CAUSSE DE SAUVETERRE
Ste-Enimie
Pont-de-Salars
Sévérac-le-Château
MT LOZÈRE
Villefort
Laguépie
POINT SUBLIME
La Malène
CASTELBOUC
Florac
Bois-du-Four
le Pont-de-Montvert
Cassagnes-Bégonhès
GORGES DU TARN
CAUSSE MÉJEAN
Génolhac
106
Salles-Curan
St-Beauzély
Le Rozier
107
Carmaux
AVEN ARMAND
Barre-des-Cévennes
67

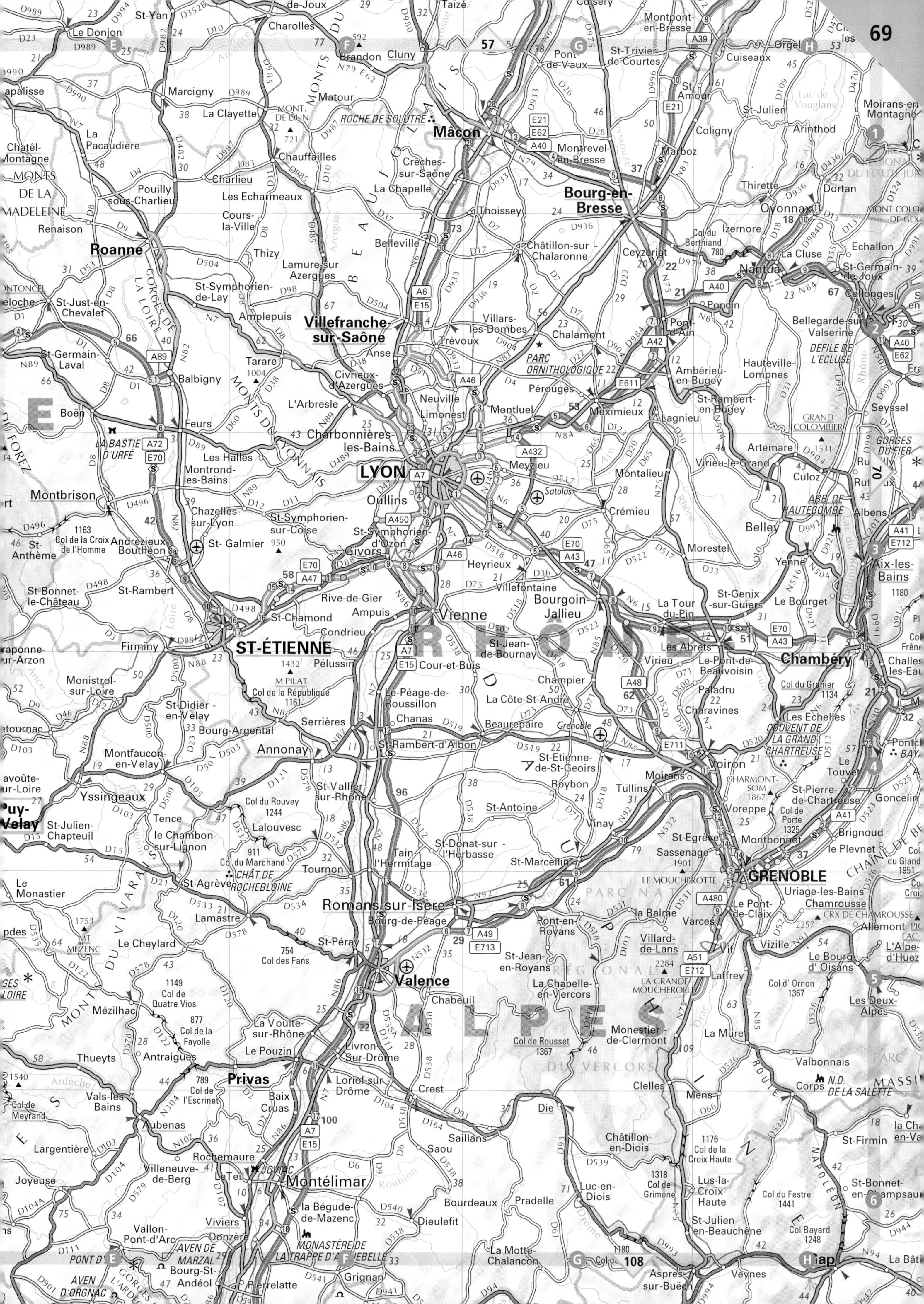
Le Donjon
St-Yan
Charolles
Brandon
Cluny
Taizé
Montpont-en-Bresse
Pont-de-Vaux
St-Trivier-de-Courtes
Cuiseaux
Orgelet
Marcigny
La Clayette
Matour
ROCHE DE SOLUTRÉ
Mâcon
St-Amour
St-Julien
Moirans-en-Montagne
Arinthod
Coligny
La Pacaudière
Chauffailles
Crêches-sur-Saône
Montrevel-en-Bresse
Marboz
MONTS DE LA MADELEINE
Charlieu
Pouilly-sous-Charlieu
Les Echarmeaux
La Chapelle
Bourg-en-Bresse
Thirette
Dortan
Oyonnax
Renaison
Cours-la-Ville
Thoissey
Izernore
Col du Berthiand 780
Echallon
Roanne
Thizy
Belleville
Châtillon-sur-Chalaronne
Ceyzériat
Nantua
La Cluse
St-Germain-de-Joux
Lamure-sur-Azergues
Collonges
St-Symphorien-de-Lay
GORGES DE LA LOIRE
St-Just-en-Chevalet
Amplepuis
Villefranche-sur-Saône
Villars-les-Dombes
Chalamont
Poncin
Pont-d'Ain
Bellegarde-sur-Valserine
DEFILÉ DE L'ECLUSE
Trévoux
Anse
St-Germain-Laval
Tarare
PARC ORNITHOLOGIQUE
Ambérieu-en-Bugey
Hauteville-Lompnes
Balbigny
Civrieux-d'Azergues
Pérouges
Boën
L'Arbresle
Neuville
Montluel
Meximieux
St-Rambert-en-Bugey
Seyssel
Feurs
MONTS DU LYONNAIS
Limonest
Lagnieu
GRAND COLOMBIER
LA BASTIE D'URFÉ
Charbonnières-les-Bains
Artemare
GORGES DU FIER
Les Halles
Montrond-les-Bains
LYON
Meyzieu
Montalieu
Virieu-le-Grand
Culoz
Montbrison
Oullins
Satolas
Chazelles-sur-Lyon
St-Symphorien-sur-Coise
Crémieu
ABB. DE HAUTECOMBE
Albens
Col de la Croix de l'Homme
Andrézieux-Bouthéon
St-Galmier
St-Symphorien-d'Ozon
Givors
Belley
St-Anthème
Heyrieux
Morestel
Yenne
Aix-les-Bains
Villefontaine
St-Genix-sur-Guiers
St-Bonnet-le-Château
St-Rambert
Rive-de-Gier
Ampuis
Bourgoin-Jallieu
La Tour-du-Pin
Le Bourget
St-Chamond
Vienne
Condrieu
Firminy
ST-ÉTIENNE
St-Jean-de-Bournay
Les Abrets
Chambéry
Craponne-sur-Arzon
Pélussin
RHÔNE
Virieu
Le-Pont-de-Beauvoisin
Challes-les-Eaux
M PILAT
Col de la République 1161
Cour-et-Buis
Champier
Monistrol-sur-Loire
Col du Granier 1134
Paladru
St-Didier-en-Velay
Le-Péage-de-Roussillon
La Côte-St-André
Charavines
Bourg-Argental
Serrières
Chanas
Beaurepaire
Les Echelles
COUVENT DE LA GRANDE CHARTREUSE
Annonay
St-Rambert-d'Albon
Grenoble
St-Etienne-de-St-Geoirs
Voiron
Montfaucon-en-Velay
Moirans
CHARMONT-SOM 1867
Le Touvet
Yssingeaux
St-Vallier-sur-Rhône
Roybon
Tullins
St-Pierre-de-Chartreuse
Goncelin
Puy-en-Velay
Tence
Col du Rouvey 1244
Lalouvesc
St-Antoine
Voreppe
Col de Porte 1325
St-Julien-Chapteuil
le Chambon-sur-Lignon
Vinay
Brignoud
Col du Marchand
CHÂT. DE ROCHEBLOINE
Tain-l'Hermitage
St-Donat-sur-l'Herbasse
St-Egrève
Montbonnot
Le Monastier
St-Agrève
Tournon
St-Marcellin
Sassenage
le Plevnet
LE MOUCHEROTTE
GRENOBLE
Uriage-les-Bains
Chamrousse
Lamastre
Romans-sur-Isère
Bourg-de-Péage
PARC NATUREL RÉGIONAL DU VERCORS
la Balme
Le Pont-de-Claix
Varces
CRX DE CHAMROUSSE
Allemont
MT MÉZENC
Le Cheylard
Col des Fans
St-Péray
Pont-en-Royans
Villard-de-Lans
Vif
Vizille
L'Alpe-d'Huez
Le Bourg d'Oisans
St-Jean-en-Royans
Valence
Laffrey
LA GRANDE MOUCHEROLLE
Col d'Ornon 1367
Col de Quatre Vios
Mézilhac
Col de la Fayolle
Chabeuil
La Chapelle-en-Vercors
Les Deux-Alpes
ALPES
La Voulte-sur-Rhône
Monestier-de-Clermont
Col de Rousset 1367
La Mure
Thueyts
Antraigues
Le Pouzin
Livron-Sur-Drôme
Valbonnais
Privas
Col de l'Escrinet
Loriol-sur-Drôme
Crest
Clelles
Corps
N.D. DE LA SALETTE
Vals-les-Bains
Baix
Cruas
Die
Mens
Col de Meyrand
Aubenas
Saillans
Châtillon-en-Diois
Col de la Croix Haute
St-Firmin
Largentière
Saou
Rochemaure
Joyeuse
Villeneuve-de-Berg
Le Teil
JOVIAC
Montélimar
Col de Grimone
Lus-la-Croix-Haute
Col du Festre
St-Bonnet-en-Champsaur
Luc-en-Diois
Bourdeaux
Pradelle
la Bégude-de-Mazenc
Dieulefit
Vallon-Pont-d'Arc
Viviers
Donzère
St-Julien-en-Beauchêne
Col Bayard
MONASTÈRE DE LA TRAPPE D'AIGUEBELLE
AVEN DE MARZAL
Bourg-St-Andéol
La Motte-Chalancon
Aspres-sur-Buëch
Veynes
Gap
AVEN D'ORGNAC
Pierrelatte
Grignan
ROUTE NAPOLÉON
70

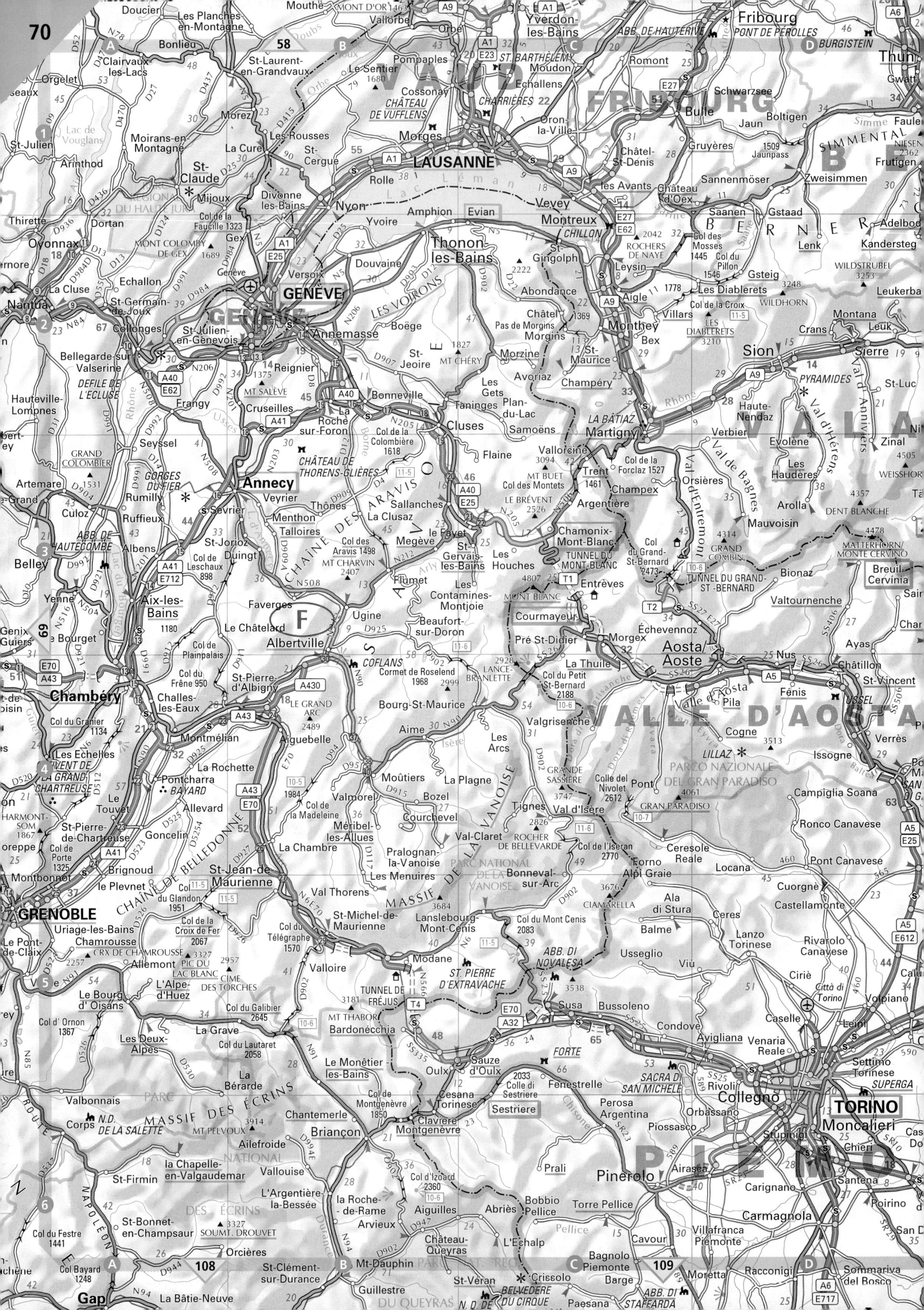

58
55
69
108
109
F
VAUD
FRIBOURG
BERNE
VALAIS
SAVOIE
VALLE D'AOSTA
PIEMONTE
Lac Léman
LAUSANNE
GENÈVE
Annecy
Chambéry
GRENOBLE
TORINO
Aosta/ Aoste
Fribourg
Thun
Sion
Sierre
Martigny
Montreux
Vevey
Thonon-les-Bains
Evian
Annemasse
Nyon
Morges
Yverdon-les-Bains
Bulle
Gruyères
Château d'Oex
Gstaad
Saanen
Zweisimmen
Frutigen
Adelboden
Lenk
Kandersteg
Leukerbad
Crans
Montana
Aigle
Monthey
Villars
Leysin
Verbier
Champex
Chamonix-Mont-Blanc
TUNNEL DU MONT-BLANC
TUNNEL DU GRAND-ST-BERNARD
Courmayeur
Pré St-Didier
La Thuile
Cogne
Breuil-Cervinia
Valtournenche
MATTERHORN/ MONTE CERVINO
4478
DENT BLANCHE
4357
WEISSHORN
4505
GRAND COMBIN
4314
MONT BLANC
4807
GRAN PARADISO
4061
PARCO NAZIONALE DEL GRAN PARADISO
Megève
Sallanches
Cluses
Bonneville
Morzine
Avoriaz
Les Gets
Samoëns
Flaine
Thônes
Albertville
Ugine
Faverges
Aix-les-Bains
Bourg-St-Maurice
Les Arcs
La Plagne
Moûtiers
Courchevel
Méribel-les-Allues
Val Thorens
Les Menuires
Val-Claret
Tignes
Val d'Isère
Col de l'Iseran 2770
Bonneval-sur-Arc
Lanslebourg-Mont-Cenis
Col du Mont Cenis 2083
Modane
TUNNEL DE FRÉJUS
St-Michel-de-Maurienne
St-Jean-de-Maurienne
Col du Galibier 2645
Col du Lautaret 2058
Col du Télégraphe 1570
Valloire
Bardonècchia
Oulx
Sauze d'Oulx
Sestriere
Cesana Torinese
Claviere
Montgenèvre
Col de Montgenèvre 1850
Briançon
Col d'Izoard 2360
MASSIF DES ÉCRINS
PARC NATIONAL DES ÉCRINS
PARC NATIONAL DE LA VANOISE
MASSIF DE LA VANOISE
CHAÎNE DES ARAVIS
CHAÎNE DE BELLEDONNE
Les Deux-Alpes
L'Alpe-d'Huez
Le Bourg-d'Oisans
La Grave
Chamrousse
Uriage-les-Bains
Susa
Pinerolo
Collegno
Moncalieri
Rivoli
Gap
Guillestre
Mt-Dauphin
St-Clément-sur-Durance
St-Véran
Château-Queyras
Abriès
Nantua
Oyonnax
St-Claude
Morez
Les Rousses
Gex
Divonne-les-Bains
St-Julien-en-Genevois
Bellegarde-sur-Valserine
Seyssel
Rumilly
Belley
Culoz
Montmélian
Pontcharra
Allevard
Les Echelles
A1
A5
A6
A9
A32
A40
A41
A43
A430
E25
E27
E62
E70
E612
E712
E717
T1
T2
T4

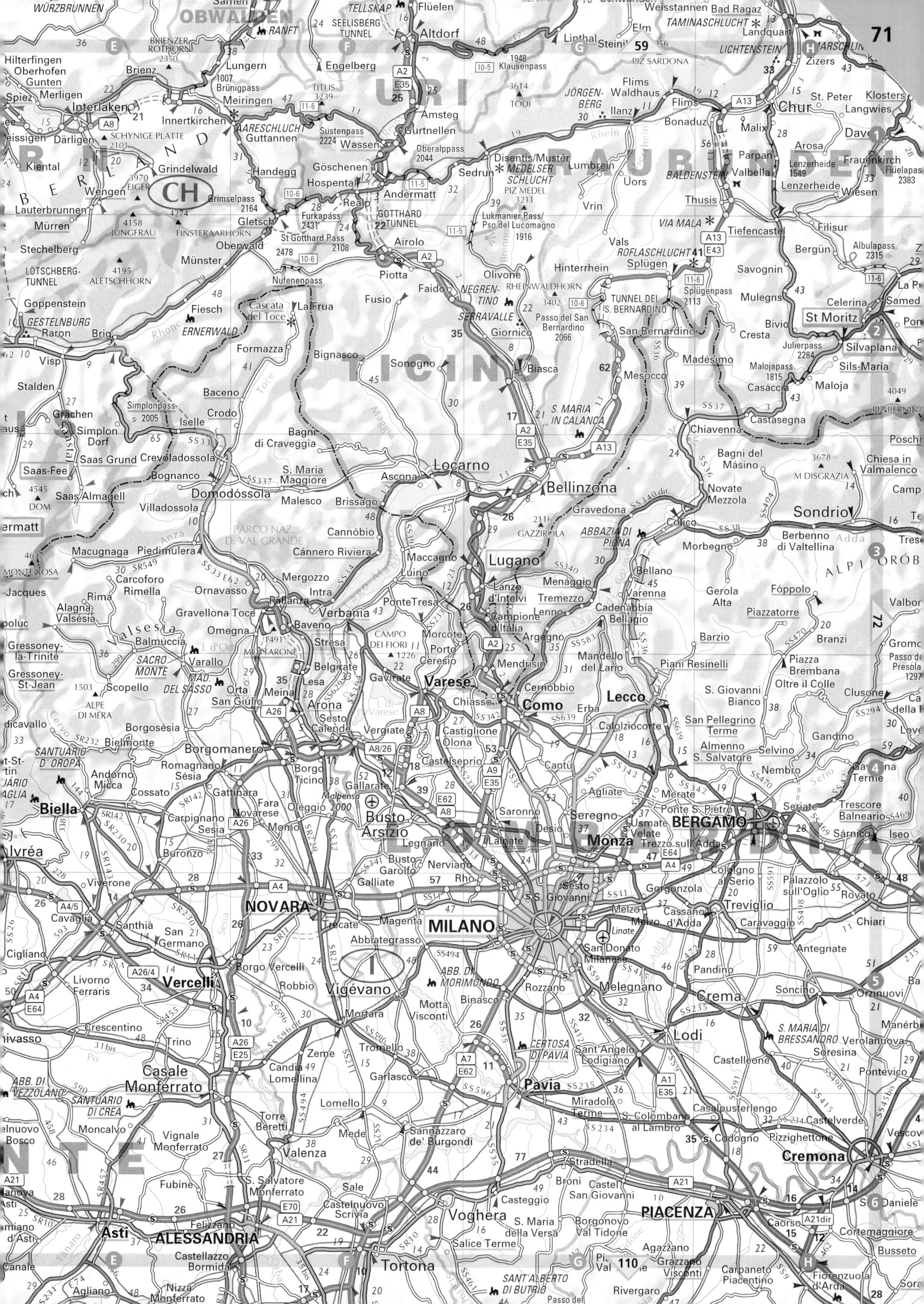
OBWALDEN
URI
GRAUBÜNDEN
TICINO
LOMBARDIA
BERNER OBERLAND
CH
I
Würzbrunnen
Ranft
Tellskap
Flüelen
Altdorf
Seelisberg Tunnel
Weisstannen
Bad Ragaz
Taminaschlucht
Landquart
Elm
Linthal
Klausenpass
Brienzer Rothorn
Lungern
Hilterfingen
Oberhofen
Gunten
Spiez
Merligen
Brienz
Brünigpass
Meiringen
Engelberg
Titlis
Interlaken
Innertkirchen
Aareschlucht
Guttannen
Sustenpass
Wassen
Gurtnellen
Amsteg
Schynige Platte
Därligen
Kiental
Grindelwald
Handegg
Göschenen
Hospental
Andermatt
Oberalppass
Disentis/Mustér
Sedrun
Medelser Schlucht
Piz Medel
Lukmanier Pass/Pso del Lucomagno
Eiger
Wengen
Lauterbrunnen
Mürren
Jungfrau
Finsteraarhorn
Grimselpass
Gletsch
Furkapass
Realp
Gotthard Tunnel
St Gotthard Pass
Airolo
Oberwald
Münster
Stechelberg
Lötschberg-Tunnel
Aletschhorn
Nufenenpass
Piotta
Faido
Fusio
Goppenstein
Fiesch
Ernerwald
Cascata del Toce
La Frua
Gestelnburg
Raron
Brig
Visp
Formazza
Bignasco
Sonogno
Stalden
Grächen
Simplonpass
Simplon Dorf
Saas Grund
Saas-Fee
Saas Almagell
Dom
Baceno
Crodo
Iselle
Crevoladossola
Bognanco
Domodóssola
Villadossola
Bagni di Craveggia
S. Maria Maggiore
Malesco
Locarno
Ascona
Brissago
Cannóbio
Cánnero Riviera
Parco Naz. d. Val Grande
Macugnaga
Piedimulera
Monte Rosa
Carcoforo
Rimella
Rima
Alagna Valsésia
Ornavasso
Mergozzo
Intra
Pallanza
Verbania
Gravellona Toce
Omegna
Baveno
Stresa
Mottarone
Belgirate
Lesa
Meina
Arona
Orta San Giulio
Varallo
Sacro Monte
Balmúccia
Valsesia
Gressoney-la-Trinité
Gressoney-St-Jean
Scopello
Alpe di Mera
Borgosésia
Bielmonte
Santuario d'Oropa
Andorno Micca
Biella
Cossato
Romagnano Sésia
Gattinara
Borgomanero
Borgo Ticino
Sesto Calende
Vergiate
Gallarate
Malpensa 2000
Busto Arsizio
Legnano
Oleggio
Fara Novarese
Momo
Carpignano Sesia
Buronzo
Ivrea
Viverone
Cavaglià
Santhià
San Germano
Cigliano
Vercelli
Livorno Ferraris
Borgo Vercelli
Novara
Trecate
Magenta
Abbiategrasso
Robbio
Vigévano
Mortara
Crescentino
Trino
Casale Monferrato
Santuario di Crea
Abb. di Vezzolano
Moncalvo
Vignale Monferrato
Candia Lomellina
Zeme
Tromello
Garlasco
Lomello
Torre Beretti
Valenza
Mede
Sannazzaro de' Burgondi
Fubine
S. Salvatore Monferrato
Felizzano
Asti
Alessandria
Castellazzo Bormida
Nizza Monferrato
Agliano
Canale
Sale
Castelnuovo Scrivia
Tortona
Voghera
Salice Terme
Casteggio
S. Maria della Versa
Stradella
Broni
Castel San Giovanni
Borgonovo Val Tidone
Piacenza
Agazzano
Grazzano Visconti
Rivergaro
Carpaneto Piacentino
Fiorenzuola d'Arda
Cortemaggiore
Busseto
Caorso
San Daniele
Cremona
Pizzighettone
Codogno
Castelverde
Casalpusterlengo
S. Colombano al Lambro
Miradolo Terme
Pavia
Certosa di Pavia
Sant'Alberto di Butrio
Binasco
Motta Visconti
Abb. di Morimondo
Rozzano
Melegnano
Sant'Angelo Lodigiano
Lodi
Castelleone
Crema
Soncino
S. Maria di Bressanoro
Soresina
Verolanuova
Pontevico
Orzinuovi
Antegnate
Pandino
Caravaggio
Treviglio
Chiari
Rovato
Palazzolo sull'Oglio
Cologno al Serio
Cassano d'Adda
Melzo
Gorgonzola
San Donato Milanese
Linate
Milano
Sesto S. Giovanni
Monza
Rho
Nerviano
Busto Garolfo
Galliate
Lainate
Saronno
Desio
Seregno
Agliate
Cantù
Castelseprio
Castiglione Olona
Varese
Gavirate
Campo dei Fiori
Como
Chiasso
Cernobbio
Mendrisio
Porto Ceresio
Morcote
Campione d'Italia
Lanzo d'Intelvi
Ponte Tresa
Luino
Maccagno
Lugano
Argegno
Tremezzo
Lenno
Menaggio
Cadenabbia
Bellagio
Varenna
Bellano
Mandello del Lario
Lecco
Erba
Calolziocorte
Merate
Ponte S. Pietro
Usmate Velate
Trezzo sull'Adda
Bergamo
Seriate
Sárnico
Trescore Balneario
Iseo
Almenno S. Salvatore
San Pellegrino Terme
Selvino
Nembro
Gandino
Clusone
S. Giovanni Bianco
Oltre il Colle
Piazza Brembana
Piani Resinelli
Barzio
Branzi
Piazzatorre
Fóppolo
Gerola Alta
Morbegno
Berbenno di Valtellina
Sondrio
Alpi Orobie
Colico
Abbazia di Piona
Gravedona
Novate Mezzola
Bagni del Másino
Chiesa in Valmalenco
M. Disgrazia
Chiavenna
Castasegna
Maloja
Casáccia
Malojapass
Madésimo
Sils-Maria
Silvaplana
Julierpass
St Moritz
Celerina
Samedan
Bivio
Cresta
Mulegns
Savognin
Bergün
Albulapass
Filisur
Tiefencastel
Splügen
Splügenpass
Roflaschlucht
Via Mala
Thusis
Baldenstein
Hinterrhein
Rheinwaldhorn
Tunnel del S. Bernardino
Passo del San Bernardino
San Bernardino
Mesocco
S. Maria in Calanca
Vals
Vrin
Uors
Lumbrein
Ilanz
Jörgen-Berg
Flims Waldhaus
Flims
Bonaduz
Chur
Malix
Parpan
Valbella
Lenzerheide
Arosa
Wiesen
Davos
Frauenkirch
Flüelapass
Klosters
Langwies
St. Peter
Zizers
Marschlins
Lichtenstein
Piz Sardona
Tödi
Olivone
Negrentino
Serravalle
Giornico
Biasca
Bellinzona
Gazzirola
Piz Bernina
Poschiavo
Valbondione
Lovere
Gromo
Passo di Presolana
Manerbio
Piz Sardona
A2
A4
A8
A9
A13
A21
A26
A7
A1
E25
E35
E62
E64
E70
59
72
110

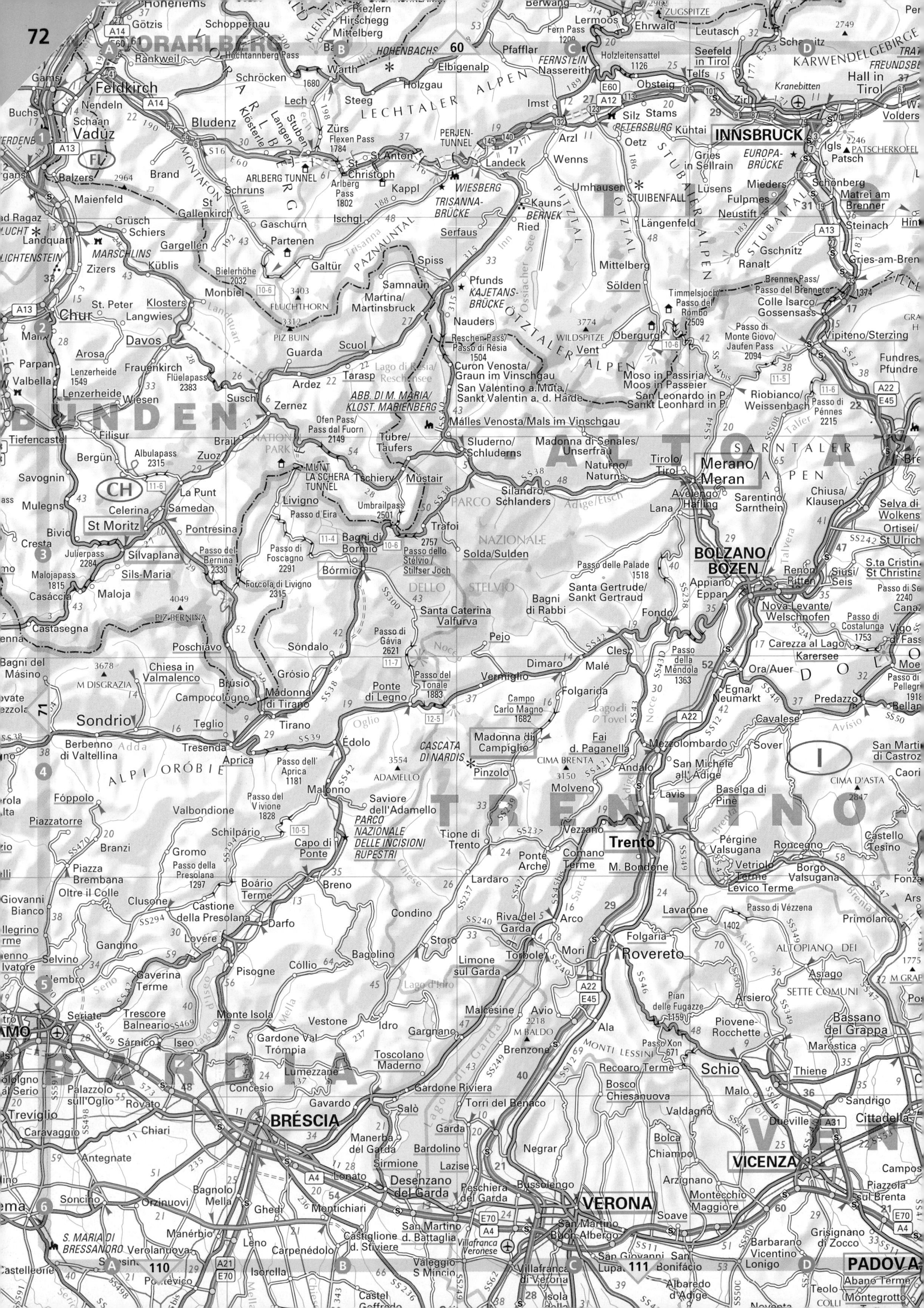
VORARLBERG
Hohenems
Götzis
Rankweil
Feldkirch
Nendeln
Buchs
Schaan
Vaduz
FL
Balzers
Maienfeld
Bad Ragaz
Landquart
LICHTENSTEIN
Grüsch
Schiers
MARSCHLINS
Zizers
Küblis
Chur
St. Peter
Langwies
Klosters
Arosa
Davos
Parpan
Valbella
Lenzerheide
Frauenkirch
Flüelapass 2383
Wiesen
Filisur
Tiefencastel
Bergün
Albulapass 2315
Savognin
Mulegns
Celerina
Samedan
La Punt
Zuoz
CH
St Moritz
Pontresina
Bivio
Cresta
Julierpass 2284
Silvaplana
Sils-Maria
Malojapass 1815
Maloja
Casáccia
Castasegna
Passo del Bernina 2330
PIZ BERNINA
Poschiavo
Brusio
Campocologno
Madonna di Tirano
Tirano
Grósio
Sóndalo
Bórmio
Bagni di Bormio
Livigno
Passo d'Eira
Passo di Foscagno 2291
Forcola di Livigno 2315
Schoppernau
Hochtannberg Pass
Schröcken
Warth
Lech
Zürs
Flexen Pass 1784
Stuben
Klösterle
Bludenz
Brand
MONTAFON
Schruns
St Gallenkirch
Gaschurn
Gargellen
Partenen
Bielerhöhe 2032
Galtür
Monbiel
FLUCHTHORN
PIZ BUIN
Riezlern
Hirschegg
Mittelberg
HOHENBACHS
Elbigenalp
Holzgau
Steeg
LECHTALER ALPEN
St Anton
St Christoph
Arlberg Pass 1802
ARLBERG TUNNEL
Kappl
Ischgl
WIESBERG
TRISANNA-BRÜCKE
PERJEN-TUNNEL
Landeck
Serfaus
Spiss
PAZNAUNTAL
Samnaun
Martina/Martinsbruck
Pfunds
KAJETANS-BRÜCKE
Nauders
Reschen Pass/Passo di Résia 1504
Scuol
Guarda
Ardez
Tarasp
Susch
Zernez
Brail
NATIONAL PARK
Ofen Pass/Pass dal Fuorn 2149
Lago di Résia/Reschensee
Curon Venosta/Graun im Vinschgau
San Valentino a.Muta/Sankt Valentin a. d. Haide
ABB. DI M. MARIA/KLOST. MARIENBERG
Málles Venosta/Mals im Vinschgau
Túbre/Taufers
Müstair
MUNT LA SCHERA TUNNEL
Tschierv
Umbrailpass 2501
Sluderno/Schluderns
Trafoi
Passo dello Stélvio/Stilfser Joch 2757
PARCO NAZIONALE DELLO STELVIO
Solda/Sulden
Santa Caterina Valfurva
Passo di Gávia 2621
Pejo
Passo del Tonale 1883
Ponte di Legno
Vermiglio
Dimaro
Malé
Cles
Berwang
Lermoos
Ehrwald
ZUGSPITZE
Fern Pass 1209
FERNSTEIN
Nassereith
Pfafflar
Holzleitensattel 1126
Obsteig
Imst
Silz
Stams
Telfs
Seefeld in Tirol
Leutasch
Scharnitz
KARWENDELGEBIRGE
Zirl
Kranebitten
Hall in Tirol
Volders
INNSBRUCK
Igls
Patsch
PATSCHERKOFEL
EUROPA-BRÜCKE
Kühtai
PETERSBURG
Arzl
Wenns
Oetz
Gries in Sellrain
Umhausen
STUIBENFALL
Lüsens
Mieders
Schönberg
Fulpmes
Neustift
Matrei am Brenner
Steinach
Gschnitz
Ranalt
Gries-am-Brenner
Kauns
BERNEK
Ried
PITZTAL
ÖTZTAL
STUBAIER ALPEN
Längenfeld
Mittelberg
Sölden
Brenner Pass/Passo del Brennero 1374
Timmelsjoch/Passo del Rombo 2509
Colle Isarco/Gossensass
Passo di Monte Giovo/Jaufen Pass 2094
Vipiteno/Sterzing
WILDSPITZE 3774
Vent
Obergurgl
ÖTZTALER ALPEN
Moso in Passiria/Moos in Passeier
San Leonardo in Passiria/Sankt Leonhard in Passeier
Riobianco/Weissenbach
Passo di Pénnes 2215
Fundres/Pfunder
Madonna di Senales/Unserfrau
Naturno/Naturns
Tirolo/Tirol
Merano/Meran
Avelengo/Hafling
Lana
Silandro/Schlanders
SARNTALER ALPEN
Sarentino/Sarnthein
Chiusa/Klausen
Selva di Val Gardena/Wolkenstein
Ortisei/St Ulrich
BOLZANO/BOZEN
Renon/Ritten
Siusi/Seis
S.ta Cristina/St Christina
Passo delle Palade 1518
Santa Gertrude/Sankt Gertraud
Bagni di Rabbi
Appiano/Eppan
Nova Levante/Welschnofen
Fondo
Passo della Mendola 1363
Carezza al Lago/Karersee
Passo di Costalunga 1753
Ora/Auer
Egna/Neumarkt
Predazzo
Cavalese
Folgarida
Campo Carlo Magno 1682
Lago di Tovel
Madonna di Campiglio
Fai d. Paganella
Mezzolombardo
Sover
San Michele all'Adige
CIMA BRENTA 3150
Andalo
Molveno
Lavis
Baselga di Piné
I
CIMA D'ASTA 2847
TRENTINO
Sondrio
Teglio
Chiesa in Valmalenco
M DISGRAZIA 3678
Berbenno di Valtellina
Tresenda
Aprica
Passo dell'Aprica 1181
ALPI ORÓBIE
Édolo
ADAMELLO 3554
CASCATA DI NARDIS
Pinzolo
Malonno
Saviore dell'Adamello
Fóppolo
Valbondione
Passo del Vivione 1828
Schilpário
Capo di Ponte
PARCO NAZIONALE DELLE INCISIONI RUPESTRI
Tione di Trento
Vezzano
Trento
Pérgine Valsugana
Roncegno
Castello Tesino
Piazzatorre
Branzi
Gromo
Passo della Presolana 1297
Piazza Brembana
Oltre il Colle
Boário Terme
Breno
Lardaro
Ponte Arche
Comano Terme
M. Bondone
Vetriolo Terme
Levico Terme
Borgo Valsugana
Clusone
Castione della Presolana
Darfo
Lovére
Condino
Riva del Garda
Arco
Lavarone
Passo di Vézzena 1402
Primolano
Gandino
Storo
Torbole
Mori
Folgaria
Rovereto
ALTOPIANO DEI SETTE COMUNI
Asiago
Selvino
Gaverina Terme
Pisogne
Bagolino
Cóllio
Limone sul Garda
Lago d'Idro
Pian delle Fugazze 1159
Arsiero
Seriate
Trescore Balneario
Monte Isola
Vestone
Idro
Malcesine
Avio
M BALDO 2218
Piovene-Rocchette
Bassano del Grappa
Sárnico
Iseo
Gardone Val Trómpia
Gargnano
Ala
Brenzone
Passo Xon 671
MONTI LESSINI
Schio
Thiene
Maróstica
Toscolano Maderno
Lumezzane
Recoaro Terme
Bosco Chiesanuova
Palazzolo sull'Oglio
Rovato
Concesio
Gardone Riviera
Lago di Garda
Torri del Benaco
Malo
Sandrigo
Cittadella
Treviglio
Chiari
BRÉSCIA
Gavardo
Salò
Garda
Valdagno
Dueville
Caravaggio
Manerba del Garda
Bardolino
Negrar
Bolca
Chiampo
VICENZA
Antegnate
Sirmione
Lazise
Lonato
Desenzano del Garda
Peschiera del Garda
Bussolengo
Arzignano
Montecchio Maggiore
Piazzola sul Brenta
Soncino
Orzinuovi
Bagnolo Mella
Ghedi
Montichiari
VERONA
Soave
S. MARIA DI BRESSANORO
Manérbio
Verolanuova
Leno
Carpenédolo
Castiglione d. Stiviere
San Martino d. Battaglia
Villafranca Veronese
San Martino Buon Albergo
Barbarano Vicentino
Grisignano di Zocco
Valeggio S Mincio
Villafranca di Verona
San Giovanni Lupatoto
San Bonifácio
Lonigo
PADOVA
Pontevico
Isorella
Castel Goffredo
Albaredo d'Adige
Isola
Abano Terme
Montegrotto
Teolo
110
111
71
60
A
B
C
D
1
2
3
4
5
6

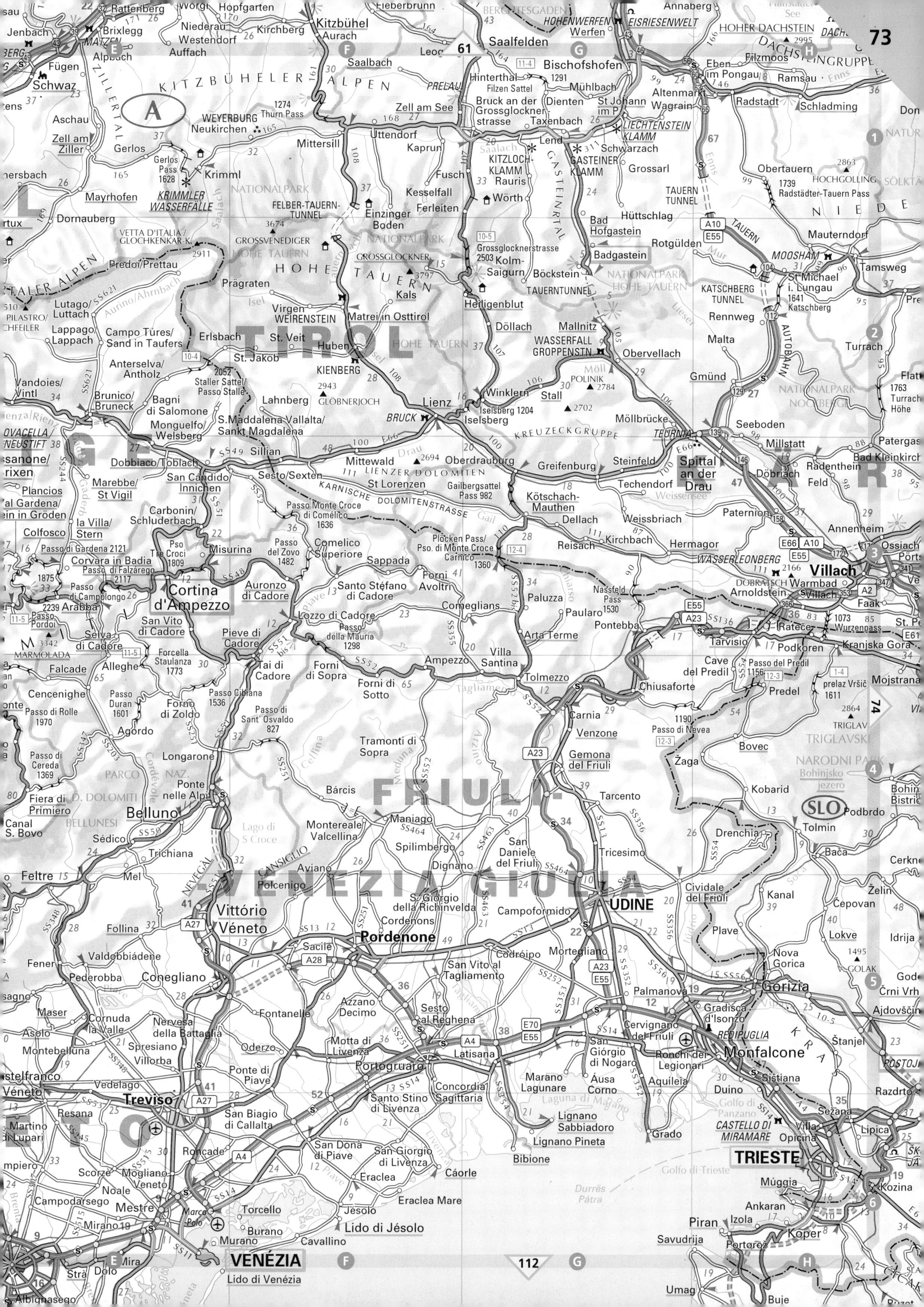
Rattenberg
Wörgl
Hopfgarten
Fieberbrunn
BERCHTESGADEN
Annaberg
Jenbach
Brixlegg
Niederau
Westendorf
Kirchberg
Kitzbühel
Aurach
HOHENWERFEN
Werfen
EISRIESENWELT
HOHER DACHSTEIN
DACHSTEINGRUPPE
MATZEN
Alpbach
Auffach
Leogang
61
Saalfelden
Filzmoos
Fügen
Saalbach
Bischofshofen
Eben im Pongau
Ramsau
Schwaz
ZILLERTAL
KITZBÜHELER ALPEN
PRELAU
Hinterthal
Filzen Sattel
Mühlbach
Altenmarkt
Radstadt
Schladming
A
Aschau
1274 Thurn Pass
WEYERBURG
Zell am See
Bruck an der Grossglockner strasse
Dienten
St Johann im P.
Wagrain
Neukirchen
Taxenbach
LIECHTENSTEIN KLAMM
Zell am Ziller
Gerlos
Mittersill
Uttendorf
Lend
Kaprun
Schwarzach
Gerlos Pass 1628
Krimml
KRIMMLER WASSERFÄLLE
Mayrhofen
NATIONALPARK
Fusch
KITZLOCH-KLAMM
Rauris
GASTEINER KLAMM
Grossarl
Obertauern
Radstädter-Tauern Pass
HOCHGOLLING
Kesselfall
Ferleiten
Wörth
GASTEINERTAL
TAUERN TUNNEL
Hüttschlag
NIEDERE TAUERN
Dornauberg
FELBER-TAUERN-TUNNEL
Einzinger Boden
Bad Hofgastein
Mauterndorf
VETTA D'ITALIA / GLOCHKENKAR-K.
3674
GROSSVENEDIGER
HOHE TAUERN
GROSSGLOCKNER
3797
Grossglocknerstrasse
2503
Kolm-Saigurn
Rotgülden
Badgastein
MOOSHAM
Tamsweg
Predoi/Prettau
Prägraten
Böckstein
TAUERNTUNNEL
St Michael i. Lungau
KATSCHBERG TUNNEL
Katschberg
Virgen
Kals
WEIRENSTEIN
Matrei in Osttirol
Heiligenblut
Rennweg
Lutago/Luttach
Lappago/Lappach
Campo Tures/Sand in Taufers
Döllach
Mallnitz
Malta
Turrach
TIROL
Erlsbach
St. Veit
Huben
St. Jakob
WASSERFALL GROPPENSTN.
Obervellach
KIENBERG
Anterselva/Antholz
Staller Sattel/Passo Stalle
POLINIK
2784
Gmünd
NATIONALPARK NOCKBERGE
Flattnitz
1763 Turracher Höhe
Vandoies/Vintl
Brunico/Bruneck
Bagni di Salomone
2943
GLÖBNERJOCH
Lahnberg
Lienz
Winklern
Stall
Iselsberg 1204
2702
Möllbrücke
Seeboden
BRUCK
S.Maddalena Vallalta/Sankt Magdalena
Monguelfo/Welsberg
KREUZECKGRUPPE
TEURNIA
Millstatt
Patergassen
Bad Kleinkirchheim
NOVACELLA/NEUSTIFT
Bressanone/Brixen
Sillian
Dobbiaco/Toblach
Mittewald
2694
Oberdrauburg
Greifenburg
Steinfeld
Spittal an der Drau
Radenthein
Döbriach
Marebbe/St Vigil
San Candido/Innichen
Sesto/Sexten
LIENZER DOLOMITEN
St Lorenzen
Gailbergsattel Pass 982
Techendorf
Feld
Plancios
Val Gardena/Stein in Gröden
KARNISCHE DOLOMITENSTRASSE
Kötschach-Mauthen
Weissensee
Carbonin/Schluderbach
Passo Monte Croce di Comélico 1636
Dellach
Weissbriach
Paternion
la Villa/Stern
Annenheim
Colfosco
Passo di Gardena 2121
Pso Tre Croci 1809
Misurina
Passo del Zovo 1482
Comelico Superiore
Plöcken Pass/Pso. di Monte Croce Carnico 1360
Reisach
Kirchbach
Hermagor
Ossiach
Corvara in Badia
Passo di Falzarego 2117
1875
Sappada
WASSERLEONBERG
2166
DOBRATSCH
Villach
Warmbad
Cortina d'Ampezzo
Auronzo di Cadore
Santo Stéfano di Cadore
Forni Avoltri
Paluzza
Nassfeld Pass 1530
Arnoldstein
Faak
Passo di Campolongo
2239
Arabba
Passo Pordoi
Lozzo di Cadore
Comeglians
Paularo
Pontebba
1073 Wurzenpass
St. Paul
San Vito di Cadore
Passo della Mauria 1298
Arta Terme
Tarvisio
Ratece
Podkoren
Kranjska Gora
3342
MARMOLADA
Selva di Cadore
Pieve di Cadore
Forcella Staulanza 1773
Villa Santina
Ampezzo
Cave del Predil
Passo del Predil 1156
Falcade
Alleghe
Tai di Cadore
Forni di Sopra
Forni di Sotto
Tolmezzo
Chiusaforte
Mojstrana
Cencenighe
Passo Duran 1601
Passo Cibiana 1536
Tagliamento
Predel
prelaz Vršič 1611
Passo di Rolle 1970
Forno di Zoldo
Passo di Sant' Osvaldo 827
Carnia
2864
TRIGLAV
74
Agordo
Venzone
1190 Passo di Nevea
Passo di Cereda 1369
Tramonti di Sopra
Gemona del Friuli
Bovec
Longarone
Žaga
TRIGLAVSKI NARODNI PARK
Bohinjsko jezero
PARCO NAZ. D. DOLOMITI BELLUNESI
Ponte nelle Alpi
Fiera di Primiero
Bárcis
FRIULI-VENEZIA GIULIA
Tarcento
Kobarid
Bohinjska Bistrica
Belluno
Lago di S Croce
Montereale Valcellina
Maniago
San Daniele del Friuli
SLO
Podbrdo
Canal S. Bovo
Tolmin
Drenchia
Sédico
Spilimbergo
Tricesimo
Bača
Trichiana
CANSIGLIO
Dignano
Feltre
Mel
Aviano
Polcenigo
Cividale del Friuli
Cerkno
Kanal
Želin
S. Giorgio della Richinvelda
NEVEGAL
Vittório Véneto
Campoformido
UDINE
Čepovan
Cordenons
Follina
Pordenone
Sacile
Codróipo
Mortegliano
Plave
Lokve
Idrija
Valdobbiádene
Nova Gorica
1495 V. GOLAK
Fener
Pederobba
Conegliano
San Vito al Tagliamento
Palmanova
Gorizia
Godovič
Črni Vrh
Possagno
Azzano Decimo
Maser
Cornuda
Nervesa della Battaglia
Fontanelle
Sesto al Reghena
Gradisca d'Isonzo
REDIPUGLIA
Ajdovščina
Asolo
la Valle
Spresiano
Oderzo
Motta di Livenza
Latisana
Cervignano del Friuli
Monfalcone
KRAS
Štanjel
Montebelluna
Villorba
San Giórgio di Nogaro
Ronchi dei Legionari
POSTOJNA
Castelfranco Véneto
Vedelago
Ponte di Piave
Portogruaro
Concordia Sagittaria
Marano Lagunare
Áusa Corno
Aquileia
Sistiana
Duino
Razdrto
Treviso
Santo Stino di Livenza
Laguna di Marano
Golfo di Panzano
Sežana
Resana
San Biagio di Callalta
Lignano Sabbiadoro
Grado
CASTELLO DI MIRAMARE
Villa Opicina
Lipica
San Martino di Lupari
Lignano Pineta
Roncade
San Donà di Piave
San Giorgio di Livenza
Bibione
TRIESTE
Golfo di Trieste
Kozina
Campiero
Scorzè
Mogliano Veneto
Eraclea
Cáorle
Noale
Múggia
Campodarsego
Mestre
Torcello
Jésolo
Eraclea Mare
Durrës Pátra
Ankaran
Mirano
Marco Polo
Burano
Lido di Jésolo
Piran
Izola
Koper
Murano
Cavallino
Savudrija
Portorož
Mira
VENÉZIA
112
Strà
Dolo
Lido di Venézia
Umag
Buje
Albignasego

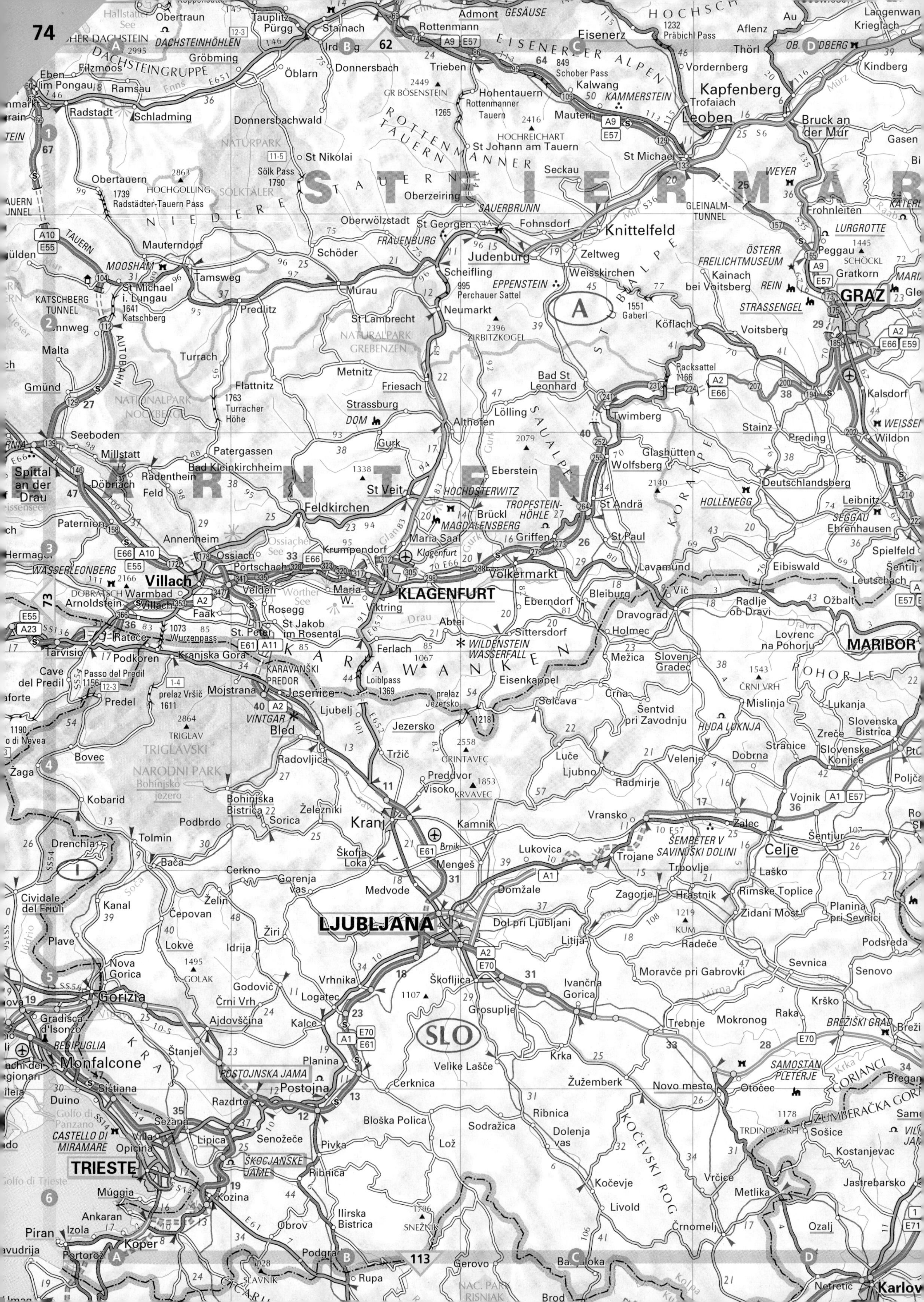

DACHSTEINGRUPPE
Radstadt
Schladming
Gröbming
Stainach
Rottenmann
Admont
GESÄUSE
EISENERZER ALPEN
Eisenerz
Präbichl Pass
Trieben
Hohentauern
ROTTENMANNER TAUERN
St Johann am Tauern
Kapfenberg
Trofaiach
Leoben
Bruck an der Mur
St Michael
Seckau
NIEDERE TAUERN
Obertauern
Radstädter-Tauern Pass
Sölk Pass
St Nikolai
Oberzeiring
Oberwölzstadt
Mauterndorf
Tamsweg
St Michael i. Lungau
KATSCHBERG TUNNEL
Katschberg
Murau
Judenburg
Knittelfeld
Zeltweg
Weisskirchen
Fohnsdorf
STEIERMARK
GLEINALM-TUNNEL
Frohnleiten
Peggau
Gratkorn
GRAZ
Köflach
Voitsberg
Kalsdorf
Wildon
Predlitz
Turrach
St Lambrecht
Neumarkt
Perchauer Sattel
ZIRBITZKOGEL
Metnitz
Friesach
Bad St Leonhard
Packsattel
Twimberg
Stainz
Preding
Deutschlandsberg
Leibnitz
Ehrenhausen
Spielfeld
Eibiswald
Malta
Gmünd
Flattnitz
Turracher Höhe
Strassburg
Althofen
Lölling
SAUALPE
Wolfsberg
St Andrä
St Paul
KORALPE
Seeboden
Millstatt
Spittal an der Drau
Radenthein
Bad Kleinkirchheim
Patergassen
KÄRNTEN
St Veit
Eberstein
HOCHOSTERWITZ
Brückl
Griffen
Feldkirchen
Annenheim
Ossiach
Villach
Pörtschach
Krumpendorf
Maria Saal
KLAGENFURT
Völkermarkt
Lavamünd
Velden
Maria W.
Viktring
Rosegg
St Jakob im Rosental
Arnoldstein
Warmbad Villach
Faak
Wurzenpass
Tarvisio
Ferlach
Eberndorf
Bleiburg
Sittersdorf
Eisenkappel
KARAWANKEN
Loiblpass
Dravograd
Vič
Radlje ob Dravi
Ožbalt
MARIBOR
Lovrenc na Pohorju
Kranjska Gora
Podkoren
Rateče
Passo del Predil
prelaz Vršič
Mojstrana
Jesenice
Bled
Ljubelj
Jezersko
Solčava
Mežica
Slovenj Gradec
Črna
Šentvid pri Zavodnju
Mislinja
POHORJE
Lukanja
Slovenska Bistrica
Zreče
Slovenske Konjice
TRIGLAV
TRIGLAVSKI NARODNI PARK
Bohinjsko jezero
Bovec
Žaga
Kobarid
Radovljica
Tržič
GRINTAVEC
Preddvor
Visoko
Luče
Ljubno
Velenje
Dobrna
Stranice
Radmirje
Bohinjska Bistrica
Sorica
Železniki
Podbrdo
Tolmin
Kranj
Kamnik
Vransko
Žalec
Vojnik
Celje
Šentjur
Škofja Loka
Menges
Lukovica
Trojane
ŠEMPETER V SAVINJSKI DOLINI
Trbovlje
Laško
Rimske Toplice
Zidani Most
Hrastnik
Zagorje
Cerkno
Baca
Medvode
Domžale
Cividale del Friuli
Kanal
Čepovan
Žiri
LJUBLJANA
Dol pri Ljubljani
Litija
Radeče
Planina pri Sevnici
Plave
Lokve
Idrija
Nova Gorica
Gorizia
Godovič
Črni Vrh
Vrhnika
Škofljica
Ivančna Gorica
Moravče pri Gabrovki
Sevnica
Senovo
Krško
Ajdovščina
Logatec
Kalce
Grosuplje
SLO
Trebnje
Mokronog
Raka
BREŽIŠKI GRAD
Monfalcone
Gradisca d'Isonzo
REDIPUGLIA
Štanjel
Planina
POSTOJNSKA JAMA
Postojna
Cerknica
Velike Lašče
Krka
Žužemberk
Novo mesto
Otočec
GORJANCI
Duino
Sistiana
Razdrto
Sežana
Lipica
Senožeče
Bloška Polica
Sodražica
Ribnica
Dolenja vas
KOČEVSKI ROG
ŽUMBERAČKA GORA
TRIESTE
CASTELLO DI MIRAMARE
Opicina
Villa
ŠKOCJANSKE JAME
Pivka
Lož
Kočevje
Vrčice
Metlika
Kostanjevac
Jastrebarsko
Múggia
Kozina
Ilirska Bistrica
SNEŽNIK
Livold
Črnomelj
Ozalj
Piran
Izola
Ankaran
Koper
Portorož
Podgrad
Obrov
Rupa
Gerovo
Babno Polje
Brod
Netretić
Golfo di Trieste
Golfo di Panzano

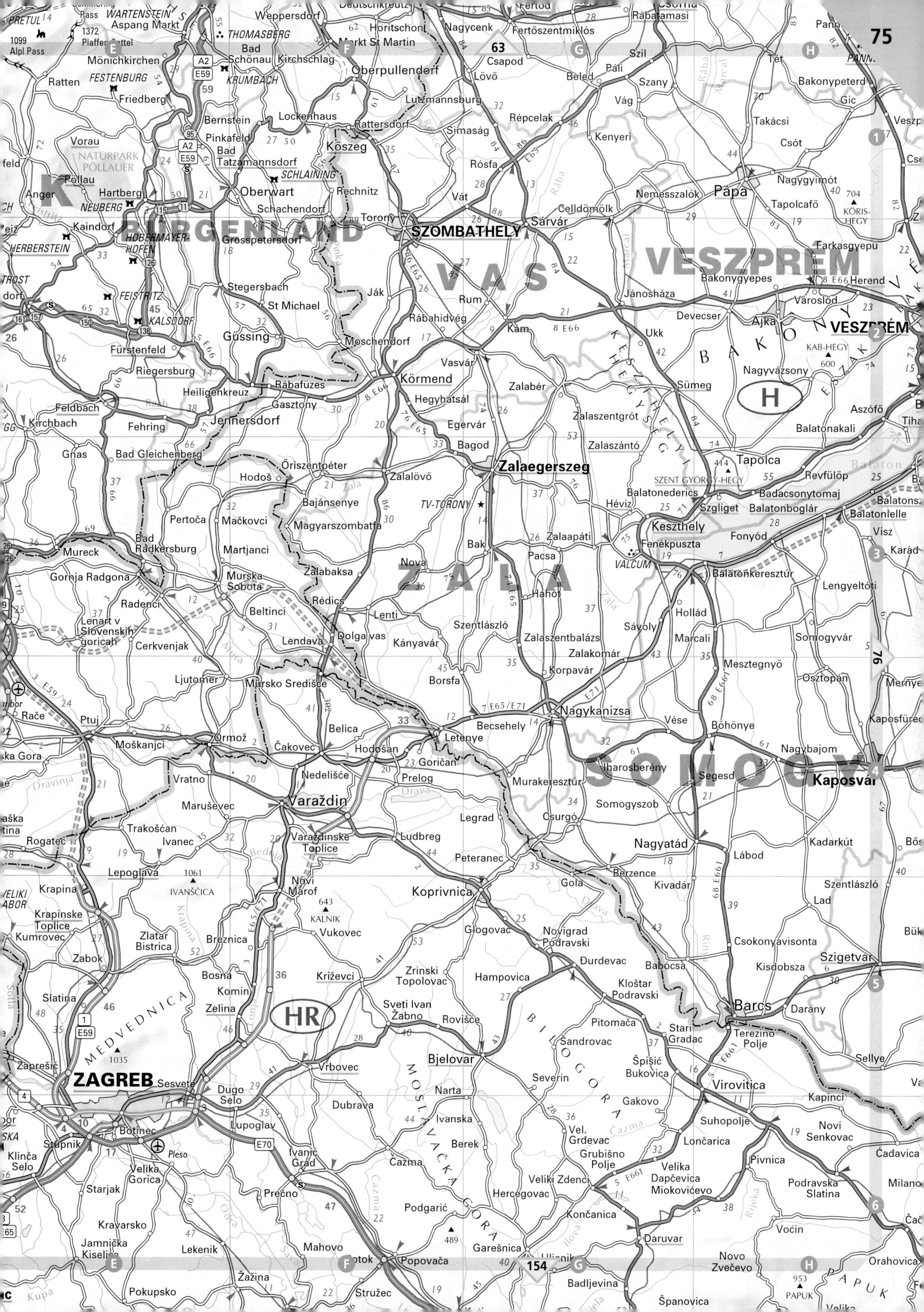
Wartenstein
Aspang Markt
Weppersdorf
Horitschon
Nagycenk
Fertőszentmiklós
Rábatamási
Thomasberg
Mönichkirchen
Bad Schönau
Kirchschlag
Markt St Martin
Csapod
Szil
Tét
Ratten
Festenburg
Krumbach
Oberpullendorf
Lövő
Beled
Páli
Szany
Bakonypeterd
Friedberg
Lutzmannsburg
Vág
Gic
Bernstein
Lockenhaus
Rattersdorf
Répcelak
Takácsi
Vorau
Pinkafeld
Simaság
Kenyeri
Csót
Naturpark Pöllauer
Bad Tatzmannsdorf
Kőszeg
Rósfa
Schlaining
Pöllau
Anger
Hartberg
Oberwart
Rechnitz
Nemesszalók
Pápa
Nagygyimót
Neuberg
Schachendorf
Vát
Celldömölk
Tapolcafő
Kőris-hegy
Kaindorf
Torony
Szombathely
Sárvár
Burgenland
Hobermayer-hofen
Grosspetersdorf
Herberstein
Farkasgyepű
Vas
Veszprém
Stegersbach
Ják
Bakonygyepes
Herend
Feistritz
St Michael
Rum
Jánosháza
Városlőd
Kalsdorf
Rábahidvég
Devecser
Ajka
Güssing
Moschendorf
Kám
Ukk
Fürstenfeld
Vasvár
Bakony
Kab-hegy
Riegersburg
Körmend
Zalabér
Keszthelyi-hegység
Sümeg
Nagyvázsony
Heiligenkreuz
Rábafüzes
Hegyhátsál
H
Feldbach
Gasztony
Aszófő
Kirchbach
Fehring
Jennersdorf
Egervár
Zalaszentgrót
Balatonakali
Bagod
Zalaszántó
Gnas
Bad Gleichenberg
Őriszentpéter
Zalaegerszeg
Tapolca
Hodoš
Zalalövő
Szent György-hegy
Révfülöp
Balaton
Balatonederics
Badacsonytomaj
Bajánsenye
TV-torony
Hévíz
Szigliget
Balatonboglár
Pertoča
Mačkovci
Magyarszombatfa
Keszthely
Balatonlelle
Bad Radkersburg
Zalaapáti
Fonyód
Mureck
Martjanci
Bak
Fenékpuszta
Visz
Gornja Radgona
Murska Sobota
Nova
Pacsa
Valcum
Karád
Zalabaksa
Zala
Balatonkeresztúr
Radenci
Rédics
Hahót
Lengyeltóti
Beltinci
Lenti
Holládi
Lenart v Slovenskih goricah
Szentlászló
Sávoly
Cerkvenjak
Lendava
Dolga vas
Kányavár
Zalaszentbalázs
Marcali
Somogyvár
Zalakomár
Mesztegnyő
Ljutomer
Mursko Središće
Borsfa
Korpavár
Osztopán
Maribor
Rače
Ptuj
Belica
Nagykanizsa
Letenye
Becsehely
Vése
Böhönye
Kaposfüred
Moškanjci
Ormož
Čakovec
Hodošan
Goričan
Nagybajom
Somogy
Iharosberény
Segesd
Kaposvár
Vratno
Nedelišće
Prelog
Murakeresztúr
Somogyszob
Marušavec
Varaždin
Legrad
Csurgó
Trakošćan
Varaždinske Toplice
Nagyatád
Kadarkút
Rogatec
Ivanec
Ludbreg
Lábod
Peteranec
Berzence
Lepoglava
Ivanščica
Novi Marof
Koprivnica
Gola
Kivadár
Szentlászló
Krapina
Kalnik
Lad
Krapinske Toplice
Vukovec
Glogovac
Novigrad Podravski
Kumrovec
Zlatar Bistrica
Breznica
Csokonyavisonta
Đurđevac
Babócsa
Szigetvár
Zabok
Križevci
Zrinski Topolovac
Hampovica
Kisdobsza
Bosna
Komin
Kloštar Podravski
Slatina
Medvednica
Zelina
HR
Sveti Ivan Žabno
Barcs
Darány
Rovišće
Bilogora
Pitomača
Stari Gradac
Terezino Polje
Šandrovac
Bjelovar
Špišić Bukovica
Sellye
Zaprešić
Zagreb
Sesvete
Vrbovec
Severin
Virovitica
Dugo Selo
Narta
Gakovo
Kapinci
Dubrava
Ivanska
Suhopolje
Novi Senkovac
Botinec
Lupoglav
Vel. Grdevac
Lončarica
Stupnik
Pleso
Berek
Grubišno Polje
Klinča Selo
Velika Gorica
Ivanić Grad
Čazma
Pivnica
Čađavica
Moslavačka Gora
Veliki Zdenci
Velika Dapčevica
Miokovićevo
Podravska Slatina
Starjak
Prečno
Hercegovac
Podgarić
Končanica
Voćin
Kravarsko
Daruvar
Jamnička Kiselica
Lekenik
Mahovo
Garešnica
Popovača
Novo Zvečevo
Orahovica
Žažina
Papuk
Pokupsko
Stružec
Badljevina
Špancovica
Kupa
Sava
Drava
Mura
Rába
Marcal
A2
E59
E65
E66
E71
E70
E661
63
154

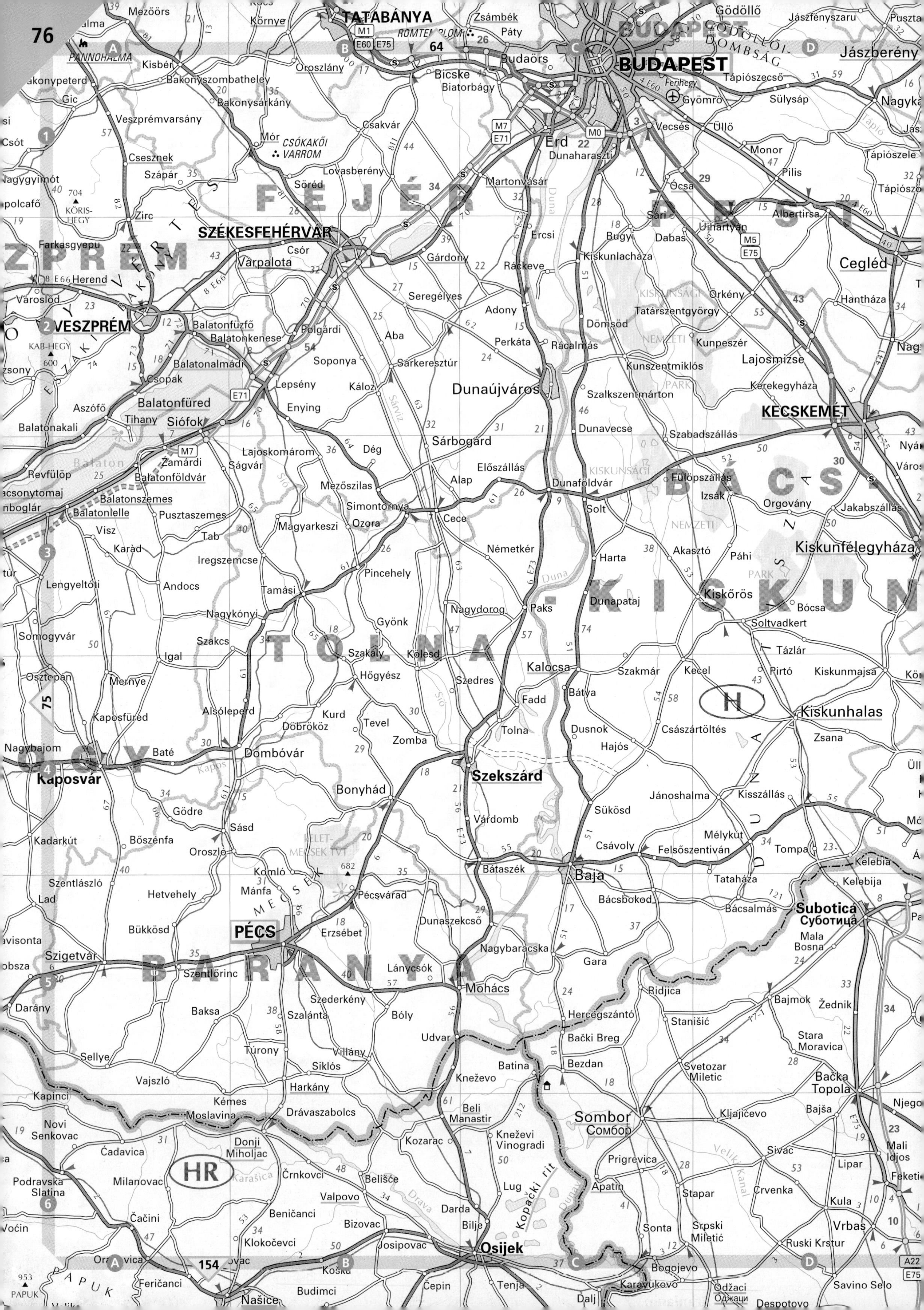
Mezőörs
Kőrnye
TATABÁNYA
M1
E60
E75
ROMTEMPLOM
64
Zsámbék
Páty
26
Gödöllő
GÖDÖLLŐI-DOMBSÁG
Jászfényszaru
Jászberény
BUDAPEST
PANNONHALMA
Kisbér
Bakonyszombathely
Oroszlány
Bicske
Biatorbágy
Budaörs
Ferihegy
Tápiószecső
Gyömrő
Sülysáp
Nagykáta
Bakonypeterd
Gic
Bakonysárkány
Veszprémvarsány
Csákvár
M7
E71
Érd
M0
Vecsés
Üllő
Mór
CSÓKAKŐI VARROM
Dunaharaszti
Monor
Tápiószele
Csót
Csesznek
Lovasberény
Szápár
Martonvásár
Pilis
Tápiószőlős
Nagygyimót
704
KŐRIS-HEGY
Söréd
FEJÉR
PEST
Ócsa
Polcafő
Zirc
Albertirsa
Sári
Újhartyán
Bugyi
Dabas
Ercsi
SZÉKESFEHÉRVÁR
M5
E75
Farkasgyepű
VESZPRÉM
Csór
Várpalota
Gárdony
Ráckeve
Kiskunlacháza
Cegléd
Herend
Városlőd
Seregélyes
Örkény
Hantháza
Tatárszentgyörgy
Adony
VESZPRÉM
Balatonfűzfő
Balatonkenese
Polgárdi
Dömsöd
KAB-HEGY
600
Perkáta
Ráckalmás
Kunpeszér
Lajosmizse
Aba
Soponya
Sárkeresztúr
Kunszentmiklós
Balatonalmádi
Csopak
Lepsény
Káloz
Dunaújváros
Kerekegyháza
Szalkszentmárton
PARK
E71
Balatonfüred
Enying
Aszófő
Tihany
Siófok
KECSKEMÉT
Balatonakali
Dunavecse
Sárbogárd
Szabadszállás
Balaton
M7
Zamárdi
Lajoskomárom
Dég
Előszállás
KISKUNSÁGI
Fülöpszállás
BÁCS-
Révfülöp
Ságvár
Balatonföldvár
Alap
Dunaföldvár
Balatonszemes
Mezőszilas
Simontornya
Cece
Solt
Izsák
Orgovány
Jakabszállás
Balatonlelle
Pusztaszemes
Magyarkeszi
Ozora
NEMZETI
Visz
Tab
Karád
Németkér
Harta
Akasztó
Páhi
Kiskunfélegyháza
Iregszemcse
Pincehely
Lengyeltóti
Andocs
Tamási
Dunapataj
Kiskőrös
KISKUN
Nagykónyi
Nagydorog
Paks
Bócsa
Gyönk
Soltvadkert
Somogyvár
Szakcs
TOLNA
Tázlár
Igal
Szakály
Kölesd
Kalocsa
Szakmár
Kecel
Pirtó
Kiskunmajsa
Osztopán
Mernye
Hőgyész
Szedres
Fadd
Bátya
H
75
Kaposfüred
Alsóleperd
Kurd
Tevel
Dusnok
Császártöltés
Kiskunhalas
Döbrököz
Zomba
Tolna
Zsana
Nagybajom
Baté
Dombóvár
Hajós
Kaposvár
Szekszárd
Bonyhád
Jánoshalma
Kisszállás
Gödre
Sásd
Várdomb
Süküsd
Kadarkút
Bőszénfa
Oroszló
Mélykút
KELET-MECSEK TVT
Csávoly
Felsőszentiván
Tompa
682
Bátaszék
Baja
Kelebia
Szentlászló
Komló
Mánfa
Tataháza
Lad
Hetvehely
Pécsvárad
Bácsbokod
Bácsalmás
Subotica
Суботица
Bükkösd
PÉCS
MECSEK
Erzsébet
Dunaszekcső
Mala Bosna
Szigetvár
Nagybaracska
Gara
BARANYA
Szentlőrinc
Lánycsók
Mohács
Ridjica
Bajmok
Darány
Szederkény
Baksa
Szalánta
Bóly
Hercegszántó
Stanišić
Žednik
Udvar
Bački Breg
Stara Moravica
Sellye
Túrony
Villány
Siklós
Batina
Bezdan
Svetozar Miletić
Vajszló
Kneževo
Bačka Topola
Harkány
Kapinci
Kémes
Moslavina
Drávaszabolcs
Beli Manastir
Sombor
Сомбор
Kljajićevo
Bajša
Njegoš
Novi Senkovac
Čađavica
Donji Miholjac
Kozarac
Kneževi Vinogradi
Mali Idjos
Sivac
Lipar
Prigrevica
HR
Karašica
Podravska Slatina
Milanovac
Črnkovci
Belišće
Lug
Kopački rit
Apatin
Stapar
Crvenka
Feketić
Veliki Kanal
Valpovo
Drava
Dunav
Kula
Čačini
Beničanci
Darda
Bizovac
Bilje
Sonta
Srpski Miletić
Vrbas
Voćin
Klokočevci
Josipovac
Osijek
Ruski Krstur
Orahovica
154
Koška
Bogojevo
A22
E75
953
PAPUK
Feričanci
Budimci
Čepin
Tenja
Karavukovo
Odžaci
Оџаци
Savino Selo
Našice
Dalj
Despotovo

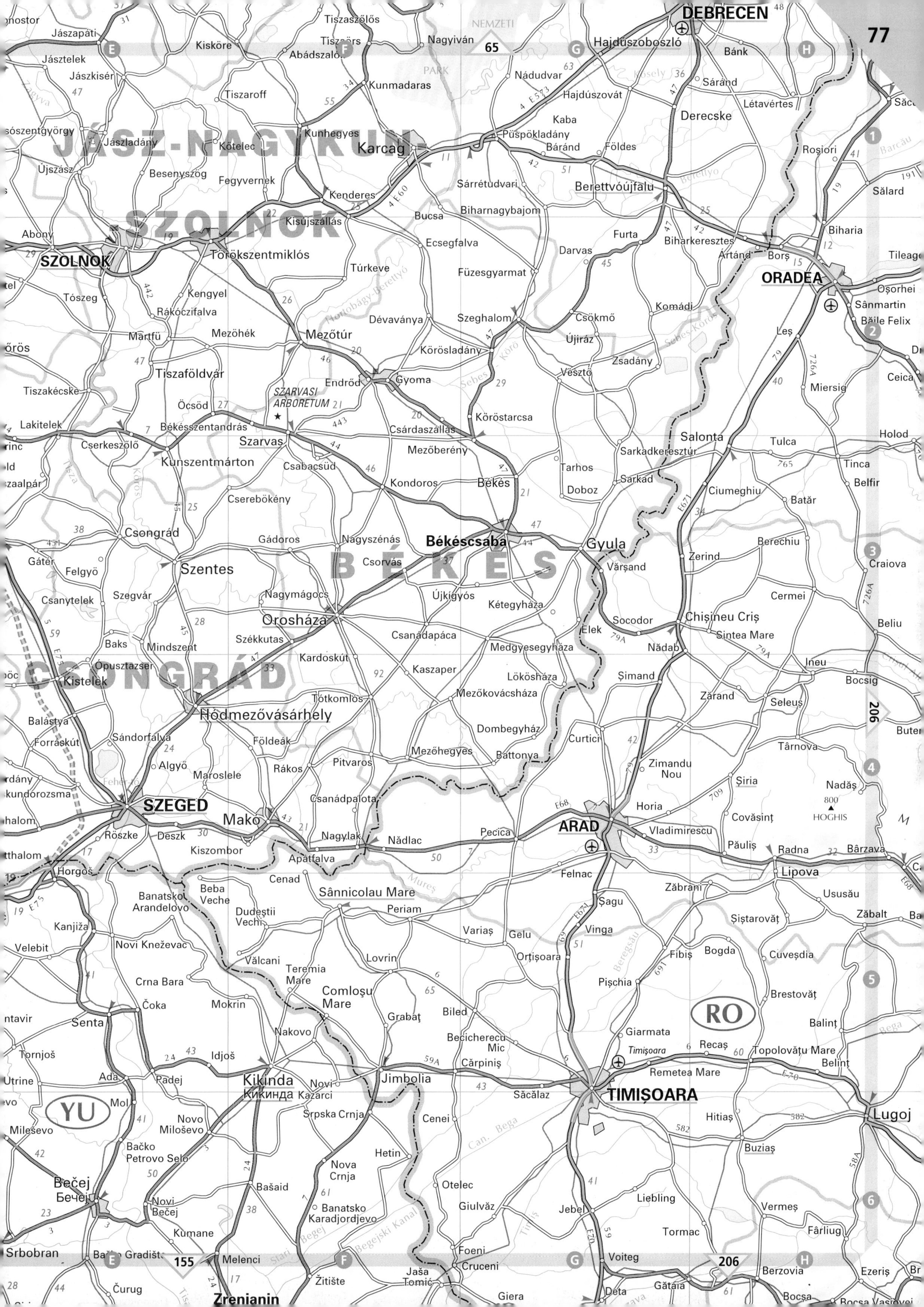
DEBRECEN
Hajdúszoboszló
Karcag
SZOLNOK
Törökszentmiklós
Mezőtúr
Gyoma
Szarvas
Békés
Békéscsaba
Gyula
Orosháza
Hódmezővásárhely
SZEGED
Makó
ORADEA
Salonta
ARAD
TIMIȘOARA
Kikinda
Кикинда
Senta
Bečej
Бечеј
Zrenjanin
Lugoj
Lipova
JÁSZ-NAGYKUN-SZOLNOK
BÉKÉS
CSONGRÁD
RO
YU
155
206

A B C D

1

Punta Candelaria
Cedeira
Cabo Prior
Valdoviño
Mé de Boi
CASTILLO DE MOECHE
Illas Sisargas
Cabo San Adrián
Malpica de Bergantiños
Punta del Roncudo
Cabo Prioriño
Ferrol
Xubia
Neda
San Sadurniño
CAST. DE NARAIO
Cabo Vilán
Laxe
Ponteceso
A CORUÑA / LA CORUÑA
Murgados
Ares
Cabañas
Pontedeume
CAST. DE ANDRADE
Embalse de la Ribeira

2

Camariñas
CEREIXO
Baio
San Roque
Arteixo
El Real
Cambre
As Pontes de García Rodrig
Puentes de García Rodrig
Monfero
Embalse de Eume
Muxía
CASTRO DE BORNEIRO
Carballo
Laracha
Guísamo
Betanzos
Cabo Touriñán
Vimianzo
Zás
Silva
Cerceda
Mesón do Vento
Carral
Coirós
Irixoa
Pedre
C552
Brandomil
Santa Comba
Bembirre
Ordes
Lanzá
Lourdes
Guitiriz
Cee
Corcubión
Ponte Oliveras
Trazo
Portomouro
Oroso
Ru
Teixeiro
Baamonde
STA. MARIA DE MEZONZO

Fisterra / Finisterre
Cabo Fisterra
Pino do Val
A Baña
Negreira
Sigüeiro
Pastor
SOBRADO DOS MONXES
Sobrado
Carnota
Embalse Barrié de la Mera
Santiago de Compostela
STA. MARIA DE CONXO
Santiago
El Pino
Arzúa
Friol
Rabad

3

Muros
Punta Carreiros
Ría de Muros
Noia / Noya
Padrón
Enfesta / Pontecesures
Teo
Ramallosa
A53
Ponte Ulla
Fontedias
Melide
Palas de Rei
El Picato 660
Porto do Son
Cimadevilla
Catoira
PAZO DE OCA
Cruces
Guntín
Pobra do Caramiñal / Puebla del Caramiñal
Vilagarcía de Arousa
Cuntis
A Estrada
Silleda
Agolada
Monterroso
Narón
Portoma

Cabo Corrubedo
Oleiros
Santa Eugènia
Illa de Arousa
Vilanova de Arousa
Caldas de Reis
A Lagoa / Campo Lameiro
Forcarei
Lalín
Rodeiro
Taboada
Punta de Couso
O Grove
Cambados
A Toxa
O Convento Poio
Cerdedo
SouteLo
Alto de Santo Domingo
Dozón
Castro
STA. MARIA DA REAL
Chantada
Escairón
Bóv

4

Illa de Sálvora
Sanxenxo
Marín
Pontevedra
Ponte-Caldelas
1012
Beariz
Piñor
Cea
La Barrela
Pantón
Illa de Ons
Hío
Moaña
CAST. DE SOUTOMAIOR
Avión
O Carballiño
Maside
Cambeo
Embalse dos Peares
Monforte de Lemos
Illas Cíes
Cangas
Redondela
VIGO
Leiro
Punxin
Sober

5

Panxón
Nigrán
Mondariz-Balneario
Mondariz
Ribadavia
Cartelle
OURENSE / ORENSE
Parada del Sil
Cabo Silleiro
Baiona
Ramallosa
Ponteareas
O Porriño
A Cañiza
Cortegada
Ramirás
A Merca
Esgos
Castro Caldelas
Puerto de Cerde 890
Arrabal / Oia
Valença do Minho
Tui
Salvaterra de Miño
Melgaço
Padrenda
Celanova
Maceda
A Guarda / La Guardia
Moncão
São Gregório
Allariz
Xunqueira de Ambía
Puerto de Alto do Rodicio 950
Paredes
A Pobra Trive
MTE. DE STA. TEGRA
Caminha
Vila Nova de Cerveira
Extremo
Verea
Sandiás
Vilar de Barrio
Embalse de Chandrexa
1778 MANZANEL
SERRA DE Q

6

Moledo
Vila Praia de Âncora
Afife
Lanhelas
Paredes
SERRA DA PENEDA
1416
Arcos de Valdevez
Soajo
Bande
Xinzo de Limia / Ginzo de Limia
Trasmiras
Laza
Villarí de Cons
Campobecerros
VIANA DO CASTELO
STA. LUZIA
Ponte de Lima
Lindoso
Muíños
Entrimo
Verín
Ríos
Viana do Castelo
Darque
Deão
Balugães
Ponte da Barca
Portela do Home
PARQUE NACIONAL DA PENEDA
Randín
Baltar
Cualedro 849
A Gudiñ
Castelo do Neiva
SERRA DO GERÊS
Barragem de Paradela
Montalegre
Oimbra
Vilardevós
Esposende
Feitos
Vila Verde
N. S. D'ABADIA
Gerês
Paradela
Gralhos
Vila Verde da Baia
Barcelos
TIBÃES
BOM JESUS DO MONTE
Louredo
Barragem do Alto Rabagão
N. SENHORA DA AZINHEIRA
Estela
Braga

GALICIA
RIAS GALLEGAS
SIERRA DO FARO
SERRA DO SUÍDO
SERRA DA PENEDA

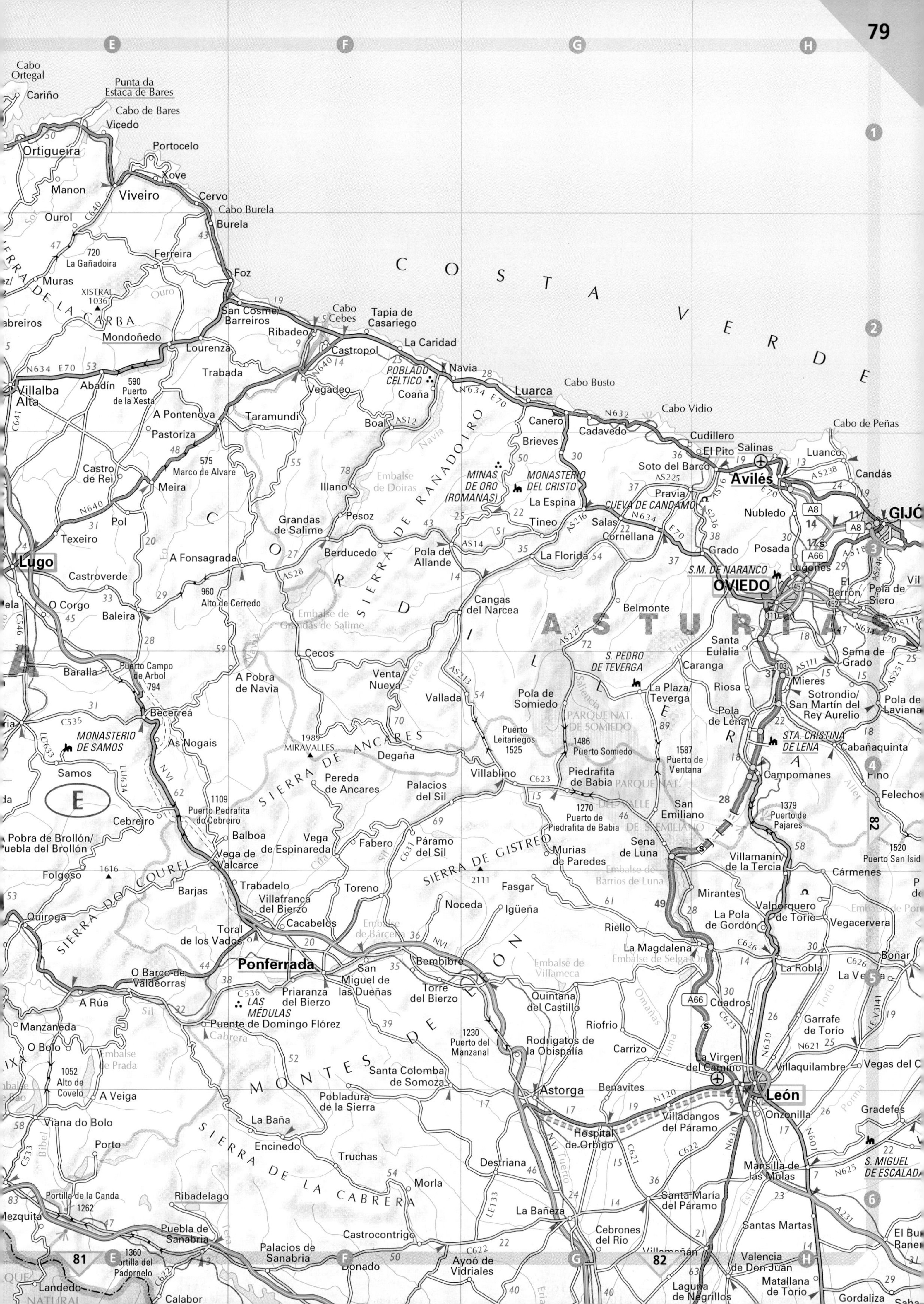

COSTA VERDE
ASTURIAS
CORDILLERA
SIERRA DE RAÑADOIRO
SIERRA DE ANCARES
SIERRA DE GISTREO
SIERRA DO COUREL
MONTES DE LEÓN
SIERRA DE LA CABRERA
SIERRA DE LA CARBA
Cabo Ortegal
Cariño
Punta da Estaca de Bares
Cabo de Bares
Vicedo
Ortigueira
Portocelo
Xove
Manon
Viveiro
Cervo
Cabo Burela
Burela
Ourol
720 La Gañadoira
Ferreira
Foz
Muras
XISTRAL 1036
San Cosme/Barreiros
Mondoñedo
Cabo Cebes
Tapia de Casariego
Ribadeo
Castropol
La Caridad
Lourenzá
Trabada
Navia
POBLADO CELTICO
Coaña
Vegadeo
Luarca
Cabo Busto
Villalba Alta
Abadín
590 Puerto de la Xesta
A Pontenova
Taramundi
Boal
Canero
Cabo Vidio
Cadavedo
Cudillero
El Pito
Salinas
Luanco
Cabo de Peñas
Pastoriza
Brieves
Soto del Barco
Avilés
Candás
575 Marco de Alvare
Castro de Rei
Meira
Embalse de Doiras
Illano
MINAS DE ORO (ROMANAS)
MONASTERIO DEL CRISTO
La Espina
Pravia
CUEVA DE CANDAMO
Nubledo
GIJÓN
Pol
Texeiro
Grandas de Salime
Pesoz
Tineo
Salas
Cornellana
Grado
Posada
Lugo
A Fonsagrada
Berducedo
Pola de Allande
La Florida
S.M. DE NARANCO
Lugones
OVIEDO
Pola de Siero
El Berrón
Castroverde
960 Alto de Cerredo
O Corgo
Baleira
Embalse de Grandas de Salime
Cangas del Narcea
Belmonte
Santa Eulalia
Sama de Grado
Cecos
S. PEDRO DE TEVERGA
Caranga
Baralla
Puerto Campo de Arbol 794
A Pobra de Navia
Venta Nueva
Vallada
Pola de Somiedo
La Plaza/Teverga
Riosa
Mieres
Sotrondio/San Martín del Rey Aurelio
Pola de Laviana
Becerreá
MONASTERIO DE SAMOS
As Nogais
PARQUE NAT. DE SOMIEDO
Pola de Lena
STA. CRISTINA DE LENA
Cabañaquinta
Samos
1989 MIRAVALLES
Degaña
Puerto Leitariegos 1525
1486 Puerto Somiedo
1587 Puerto de Ventana
Campomanes
Pino
Felechosa
E
Pereda de Ancares
Villablino
Piedrafita de Babia
PARQUE NAT. DEL VALLE DE S. EMILIANO
1109 Puerto Pedrafita do Cebreiro
Palacios del Sil
Cebreiro
1270 Puerto de Piedrafita de Babia
San Emiliano
1379 Puerto de Pajares
A Pobra de Brollón/Puebla del Brollón
Balboa
Vega de Espinareda
Fabero
Páramo del Sil
Murias de Paredes
Sena de Luna
Villamanín/de la Tercia
1520 Puerto San Isidro
Folgoso
1616
Vega de Valcarce
2111
Embalse de Barrios de Luna
Cármenes
Barjas
Trabadelo
Toreno
Fasgar
Mirantes
Villafranca del Bierzo
Noceda
Igüeña
La Pola de Gordón
Valporquero de Torío
Vegacervera
Quiroga
Cacabelos
Embalse de Bárcena
Riello
Toral de los Vados
La Magdalena
Embalse de Selga de Ordás
Ponferrada
San Miguel de las Dueñas
Bembibre
Embalse de Villameca
La Robla
Boñar
O Barco de Valdeorras
Torre del Bierzo
La Vecilla
A Rúa
LAS MÉDULAS
Priaranza del Bierzo
Quintana del Castillo
Cuadros
Garrafe de Torío
Manzaneda
Puente de Domingo Flórez
Ríofrio
O Bolo
Embalse de Prada
1230 Puerto del Manzanal
Rodrigatos de la Obispalía
Carrizo
1052 Alto de Covelo
A Veiga
Santa Colomba de Somoza
La Virgen del Camino
Villaquilambre
Vegas del Condado
Pobladura de la Sierra
Astorga
Benavites
León
Viana do Bolo
La Baña
Hospital de Órbigo
Villadangos del Páramo
Onzonilla
Gradefes
Porto
Encinedo
Truchas
Destriana
Mansilla de las Mulas
S. MIGUEL DE ESCALADA
Portilla de la Canda 1262
Ribadelago
Morla
La Bañeza
Santa María del Páramo
Mezquita
Puebla de Sanabria
Castrocontrigo
Cebrones del Rio
Santas Martas
1360 Portilla del Padornelo
Palacios de Sanabria
Ayoó de Vidriales
Villamañán
Valencia de Don Juan
Donado
Landedo
Calabor
Laguna de Negrillos
Matallana de Torío
Gordaliza
81
82

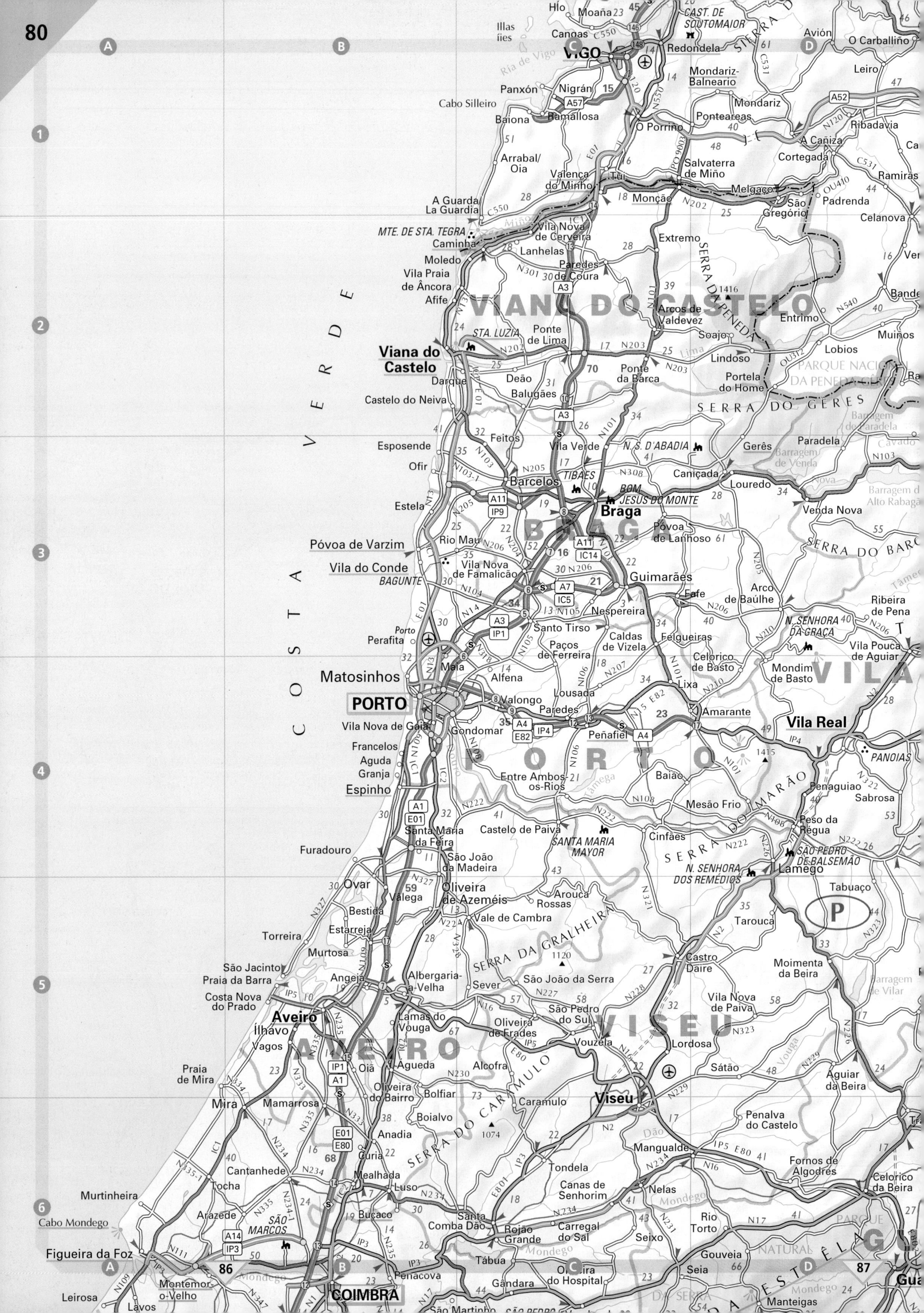
COSTA VERDE
VIANA DO CASTELO
BRAGA
PORTO
AVEIRO
VISEU
VIGO
Cangas
Moaña
Illas Cíes
CAST. DE SOUTOMAIOR
Redondela
Avión
O Carballiño
Mondariz-Balneario
Mondariz
Leiro
Panxón
Nigrán
Cabo Silleiro
Baiona
Ramallosa
O Porriño
Ponteareas
Ribadavia
A Cañiza
Cortegada
Arrabal/Oia
Valença do Minho
Tui
Salvaterra de Miño
Melgaço
Ramirás
A Guarda La Guardia
Monção
São Gregório
Padrenda
Celanova
MTE. DE STA. TEGRA
Vila Nova de Cerveira
Caminha
Lanhelas
Extremo
Moledo
Vila Praia de Âncora
Afife
Paredes de Coura
SERRA DA PENEDA
Arcos de Valdevez
Soajo
Entrimo
Lobios
Bande
Muiños
STA. LUZIA
Ponte de Lima
Viana do Castelo
Ponte da Barca
Lindoso
Portela do Home
PARQUE NACIONAL DA PENEDA-GERÊS
Darque
Deão
Balugães
Castelo do Neiva
SERRA DO GERÊS
Barragem de Paradela
Esposende
Feitos
Vila Verde
N. S. D'ABADIA
Gerês
Paradela
Barragem de Venda Nova
Ofir
Barcelos
TIBÃES
Caniçada
Loureda
BOM JESUS DO MONTE
Braga
Estela
Venda Nova
Barragem do Alto Rabagão
Rio Mau
Póvoa de Lanhoso
Póvoa de Varzim
Vila do Conde
BAGUNTE
Vila Nova de Famalicão
Guimarães
Fafe
Arco de Baúlhe
Ribeira de Pena
Nespereira
N. SENHORA DA GRAÇA
Porto
Perafita
Santo Tirso
Caldas de Vizela
Felgueiras
Vila Pouca de Aguiar
Paços de Ferreira
Celorico de Basto
Mondim de Basto
Matosinhos
Maia
Alfena
Lixa
PORTO
Valongo
Lousada
Paredes
Amarante
Vila Real
Vila Nova de Gaia
Gondomar
Penafiel
PANOIAS
Francelos
Aguda
Granja
Espinho
Entre Ambos-os-Rios
Baião
SERRA DO MARÃO
Penaguião
Sabrosa
Mesão Frio
Peso da Régua
Santa Maria da Feira
Castelo de Paiva
SANTA MARIA MAYOR
Cinfães
SÃO PEDRO DE BALSEMÃO
Furadouro
São João da Madeira
N. SENHORA DOS REMÉDIOS
Lamego
Ovar
Válega
Oliveira de Azeméis
Arouca
Rossas
Tabuaço
Bestida
Vale de Cambra
Tarouca
Estarreja
Torreira
SERRA DA GRALHEIRA
Murtosa
Castro Daire
Moimenta da Beira
São Jacinto
Praia da Barra
Angeja
Albergaria-a-Velha
Sever
São João da Serra
Barragem de Vilar
Costa Nova do Prado
São Pedro do Sul
Vila Nova de Paiva
Aveiro
Lamas do Vouga
Oliveira de Frades
Ílhavo
Vagos
Vouzela
Lordosa
Praia de Mira
Oiã
Águeda
Alcofra
Sátão
Aguiar da Beira
Oliveira do Bairro
Bolfiar
SERRA DO CARAMULO
Mira
Mamarrosa
Caramulo
Viseu
Boialvo
Penalva do Castelo
Anadia
Curia
Mangualde
Fornos de Algodres
Cantanhede
Tocha
Mealhada
Luso
Tondela
Canas de Senhorim
Nelas
Celorico da Beira
Murtinheira
Arazede
SÃO MARCOS
Buçaco
Santa Comba Dão
Rojão Grande
Carregal do Sal
Rio Torto
Seixo
Cabo Mondego
Figueira da Foz
Tábua
Oliveira do Hospital
Gouveia
Seia
PARQUE NATURAL DA SERRA DA ESTRELA
Montemor-o-Velho
Penacova
Gândara
Leirosa
Lavos
COIMBRA
Manteigas
São Martinho
86
87
A
B
C
D
1
2
3
4
5
6

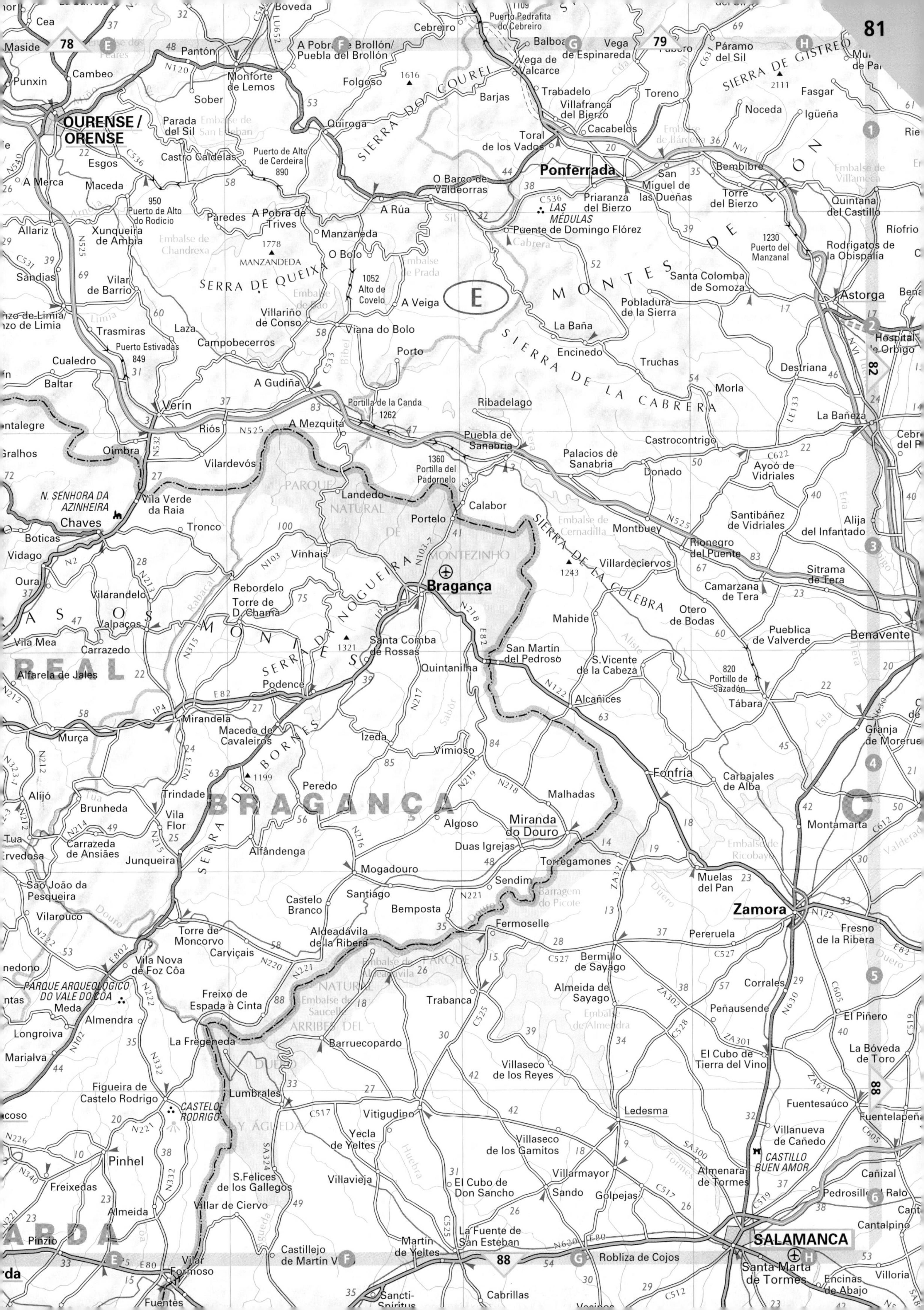
Cea
Maside
78
Boveda
Cebreiro
Puerto Pedrafita do Cebreiro
Balboa
Vega de Espinareda
79
Páramo del Sil
SIERRA DE GISTREO
Pantón
A Pobra de Brollón/ Puebla del Brollón
Monforte de Lemos
Vega de Valcarce
Punxin
Cambeo
Folgoso
1616
SIERRA DO COUREL
Trabadelo
Toreno
2111
Fasgar
Sober
Barjas
Villafranca del Bierzo
Noceda
Igüeña
OURENSE / ORENSE
Parada del Sil
Embalse de San Esteban
Quiroga
Cacabelos
Embalse de Bárcena
Toral de los Vados
Esgos
Castro Caldelas
Puerto de Alto de Cerdeira 890
Ponferrada
San Miguel de las Dueñas
Bembibre
Embalse de Villameca
A Merca
Maceda
O Barco de Valdeorras
Torre del Bierzo
950 Puerto de Alto do Rodicio
Paredes
A Pobra de Trives
A Rúa
Priaranza del Bierzo
LAS MÉDULAS
Quintana del Castillo
Allariz
Xunqueira de Ambia
Embalse de Chandrexa
Manzaneda
1778 MANZANDEDA
Puente de Domingo Flórez
Cabrera
1230 Puerto del Manzanal
Riófrio
Rodrigatos de la Obispalía
O Bolo
Embalse de Prada
SERRA DE QUEIXA
MONTES DE LEÓN
Sandias
Vilar de Barrio
1052 Alto de Covelo
Santa Colomba de Somoza
A Veiga
E
Embalse de Bao
Astorga
Pobladura de la Sierra
Villariño de Conso
Viana do Bolo
La Baña
Hospital de Órbigo
Xinzo de Limia
Trasmiras
Laza
Campobecerros
Puerto Estivadas 849
Porto
SIERRA DE LA CABRERA
Encinedo
Truchas
Destriana
82
Cualedro
Baltar
A Gudiña
Morla
Portilla de la Canda 1262
Ribadelago
La Bañeza
Verín
Ríos
A Mezquita
Puebla de Sanabria
Castrocontrigo
Montalegre
Oimbra
Vilardevós
1360 Portilla del Padornelo
Palacios de Sanabria
Ayoó de Vidriales
Donado
Cebrones del Río
Gralhos
N. SENHORA DA AZINHEIRA
Vila Verde da Raia
PARQUE NATURAL DE MONTEZINHO
Landedo
Calabor
Santibáñez de Vidriales
Chaves
Tronco
Portelo
Embalse de Cernadilla
Montbuey
Alija del Infantado
Boticas
Vidago
Vinhais
Rionegro del Puente
SIERRA DE LA CULEBRA
Villardeciervos
1243
Sitrama de Tera
Oura
Rebordelo
Bragança
Camarzana de Tera
Vilarandelo
Torre de D. Chama
SERRA DA NOGUEIRA
Otero de Bodas
Mahide
BARROSO
Valpaços
Santa Comba de Rossas
1321
Pueblica de Valverde
Benavente
Vila Mea
Carrazedo
MONTES
San Martín del Pedroso
S. Vicente de la Cabeza
820 Portillo de Sazadón
REAL
Alfarela de Jales
Quintanilha
Podence
Alcañices
Tábara
Mirandela
Macedo de Cavaleiros
Granja de Moreruela
Murça
Izeda
Vimioso
Fonfría
SERRA DE BORNES
Peredo
1199
Carbajales de Alba
Alijó
Trindade
Malhadas
Brunheda
Vila Flor
BRAGANÇA
Miranda do Douro
C
Algoso
Montamarta
Tua
Carrazeda de Ansiães
Duas Igrejas
Embalse de Ricobayo
Alfândenga
Torregamones
Junqueira
Mogadouro
Muelas del Pan
Sendim
São João da Pesqueira
Santiago
Castelo Branco
Barragem do Picote
Zamora
Bemposta
Vilarouco
Fermoselle
Fresno de la Ribera
Torre de Moncorvo
Aldeadávila de la Ribera
Pereruela
Carviçais
Bermillo de Sayago
Vila Nova de Foz Côa
Embalse de Aldeadávila
PARQUE NATURAL ARRIBES DEL DUERO
Corrales
PARQUE ARQUEOLÓGICO DO VALE DO CÔA
Freixo de Espada à Cinta
Almeida de Sayago
Meda
Embalse de Saucelle
Trabanca
Peñausende
Almendra
Embalse de Almendra
El Piñero
Longroiva
La Fregeneda
Barruecopardo
Marialva
El Cubo de Tierra del Vino
La Bóveda de Toro
Villaseco de los Reyes
Figueira de Castelo Rodrigo
CASTELO RODRIGO
Lumbrales
Vitigudino
Ledesma
Fuentesaúco
88
Fuentelapeña
Yecla de Yeltes
Villaseco de los Gamitos
Villanueva de Cañedo
CASTILLO BUEN AMOR
Pinhel
Freixedas
S. Felices de los Gallegos
Villavieja
El Cubo de Don Sancho
Villarmayor
Almenara de Tormes
Cañizal
Almeida
Sando
Golpejas
Pedrosillo el Ralo
Villar de Ciervo
La Fuente de San Esteban
Cantalpino
GUARDA
Pinzio
Castillejo de Martín Viejo
Martín de Yeltes
SALAMANCA
Vilar Formoso
Robliza de Cojos
Santa Marta de Tormes
Encinas de Abajo
Villoria
Guarda
Fuentes
Sancti-Spíritus
Cabrillas

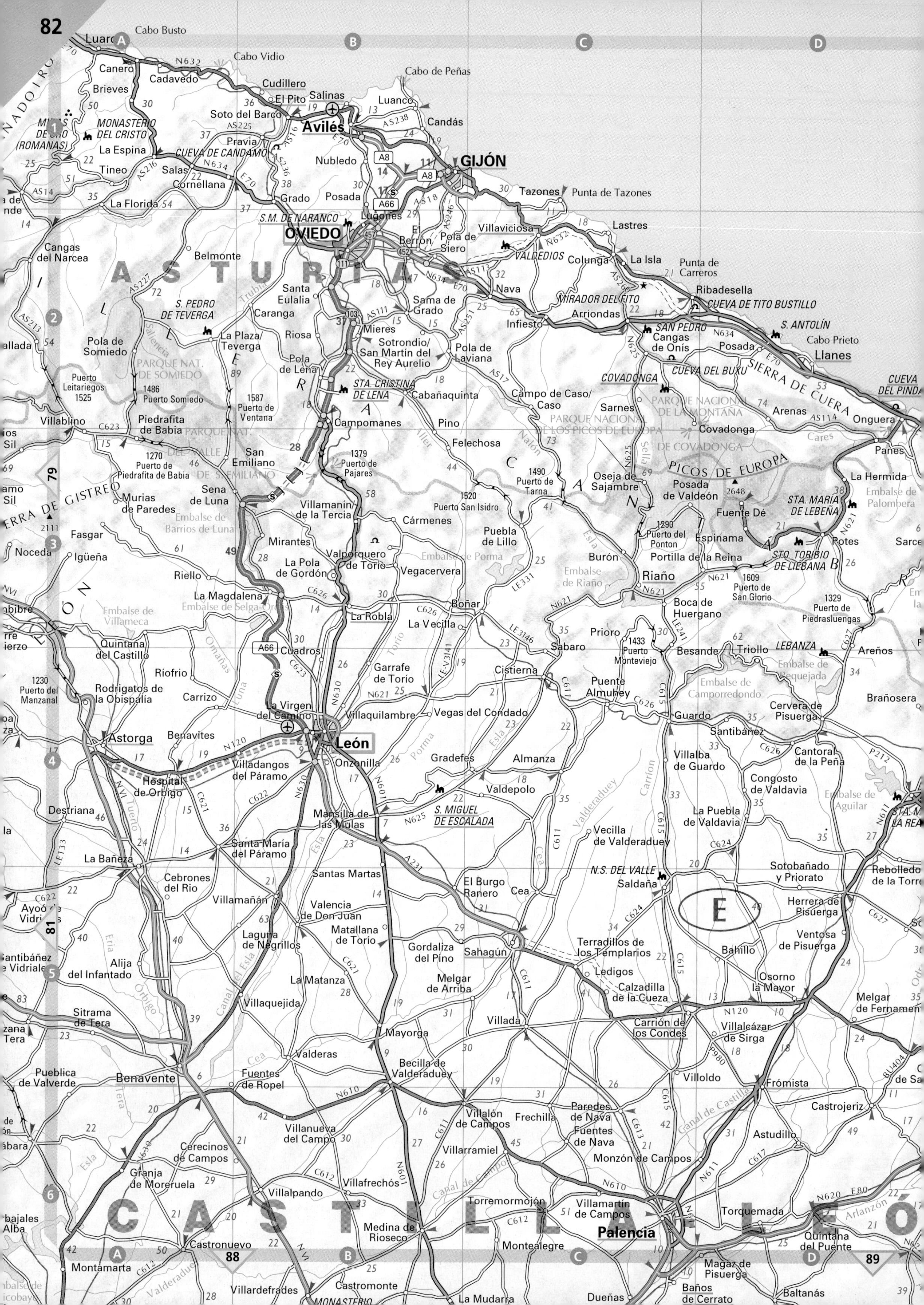
ASTURIAS
CANTABRIA
CASTILLA Y LEÓN
LEÓN
Oviedo
Gijón
Avilés
León
Palencia
Astorga
Benavente
Cabo Busto
Cabo Vidio
Cabo de Peñas
Luarca
Cudillero
Salinas
Luanco
Candás
Pravia
Grado
Tineo
Salas
Cornellana
Villaviciosa
Tazones
Punta de Tazones
Lastres
Colunga
La Isla
Ribadesella
Cueva de Tito Bustillo
Llanes
Cabo Prieto
Arriondas
Cangas de Onís
Covadonga
Infiesto
Nava
Pola de Siero
Mieres
Pola de Lena
Pola de Laviana
Cangas del Narcea
Belmonte
Pola de Somiedo
Villablino
Parque Nacional de los Picos de Europa
Picos de Europa
Potes
Riaño
Boñar
La Robla
Cistierna
Guardo
Cervera de Pisuerga
Saldaña
Sahagún
Mansilla de las Mulas
La Bañeza
Carrión de los Condes
Frómista
Osorno la Mayor
Villalón de Campos
Medina de Rioseco
Villalpando
Mayorga
Dueñas
Torquemada
Castrojeriz
Astudillo
Baltanás
Castronuevo
Montamarta
Villardefrades
La Mudarra
Castromonte
Magaz de Pisuerga
Baños de Cerrato
79
81
88
89

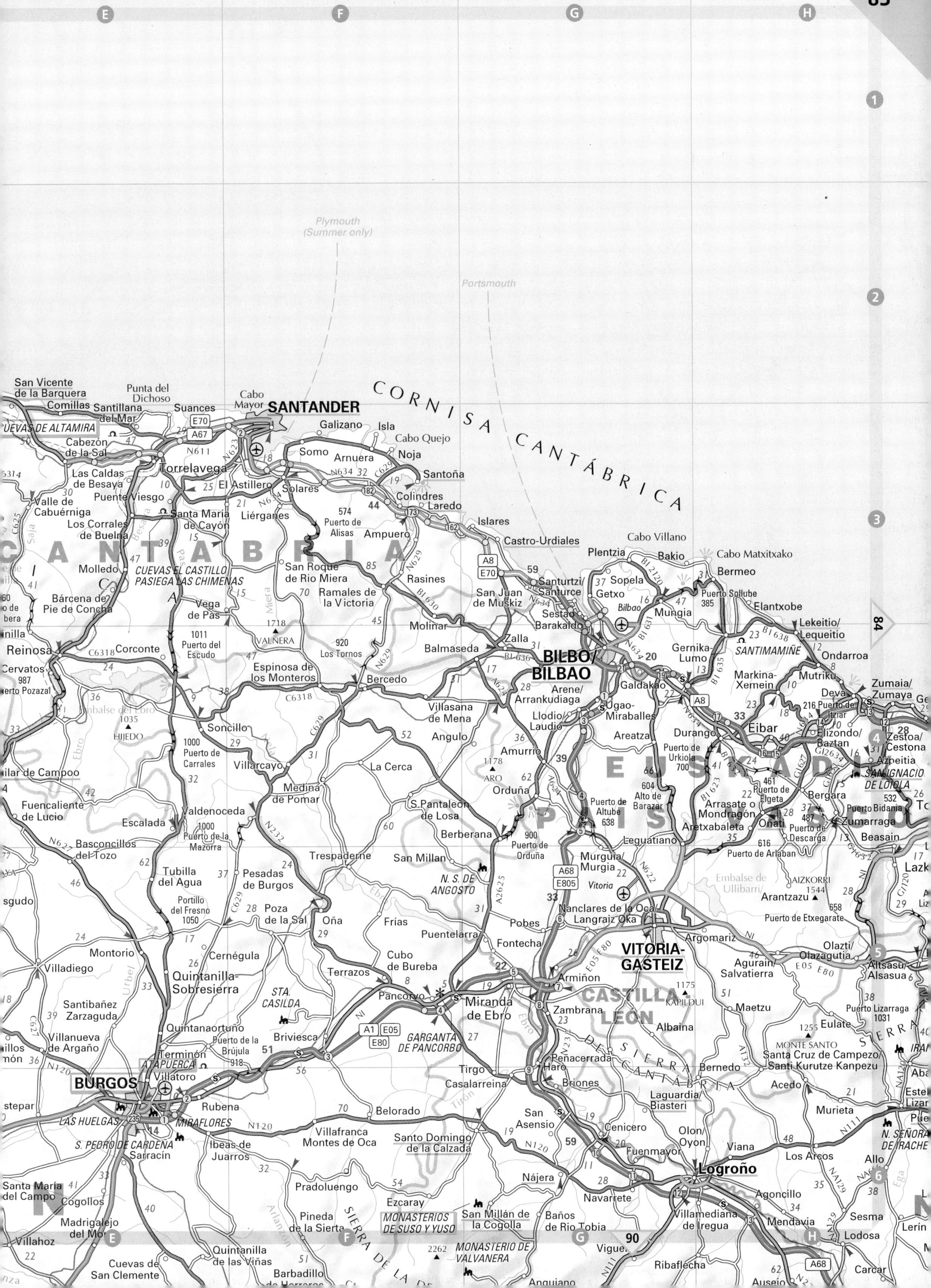

E F G H

1

2

Plymouth
(Summer only)

Portsmouth

CORNISA CANTÁBRICA

3

84

EUSKADI

PAIS

4

CASTILLA
LEÓN

5

90

6

San Vicente
de la Barquera
Comillas Santillana
del Mar
CUEVAS DE ALTAMIRA
Cabezón
de la Sal
Las Caldas
de Besaya
Valle de
Cabuérniga
Los Corrales
de Buelna
Molledo
Bárcena de
Pie de Concha
Reinosa
Cervatos
987
Puerto Pozazal
Suances
Torrelavega
Puente Viesgo
Santa María
de Cayón
Liérganes
El Astillero
Solares
SANTANDER
Cabo
Mayor
Galizano Isla
Cabo Quejo
Somo Arnuera Noja
Santoña
Colindres
Laredo
Islares
Castro-Urdiales
Puerto de
Alisas
574
Ampuero
San Roque
de Río Miera
Rasines
Ramales de
la Victoria
Molinar
Balmaseda
Zalla
Plentzia Bakio
Cabo Villano
Cabo Matxitxako
Bermeo
Puerto Sollube
Elantxobe
Lekeitio/
Lequeitio
Ondarroa
Mutriku
Deva
Zumaia/
Zumaya
Zestoa/
Cestona
Azpeitia
SAN IGNACIO
DE LOIOLA
Zumarraga
Beasain
Lazk
CANTABRIA
CUEVAS EL CASTILLO
PASIEGA LAS CHIMENAS
Vega
de Pas
VALNERA
1718
Espinosa de
los Monteros
Corconte
Puerto del
Escudo
Los Tornos
920
Bercedo
Villasana
de Mena
Angulo
Amurrio
Orduña
ARO
1178
Santurtzi/
Santurce
Sestao
Barakaldo
San Juan
de Muskiz
BILBO/
BILBAO
Arene/
Arrankudiaga
Llodio/
Laudio
Areatza
Getxo
Sopela
Mungia
Gernika-
Lumo
SANTIMAMIÑE
Galdakao
Ugao-
Miraballes
Durango
Eibar
Markina-
Xemein
Puerto de
Urkiola
700
Puerto de
Izkiar
Elizondo/
Baztan
Bergara
Oñati
Arrasate o
Mondragón
Aretxabaleta
Leguatiano
Puerto de
Elgeta
Puerto de
Descarga
Puerto Bidania
AIZKORRI
1544
Arantzazu
Soncillo
Puerto de
Carrales
1000
Villarcayo
La Cerca
Medina
de Pomar
S. Pantaleón
de Losa
Berberana
Puerto de
Orduña
Puerto de
Altube
Alto de
Barazar
Murguia/
Murgia
Vitoria
Nanclares de la Oca
Langraiz Oka
Argomariz
Puerto de Etxegarate
Puerto de Arlabán
Olazti/
Olazagutia
Altsasu/
Alsasua
Fuencaliente
de Lucio
Escalada
Valdenoceda
Puerto de la
Mazorra
Trespaderne
San Millán
N. S. DE
ANGOSTO
Murieta
Basconcillos
del Tozo
Tubilla
del Agua
Pesadas
de Burgos
Portillo
del Fresno
1050
Poza
de la Sal
Oña
Frías
Cubo
de Bureba
Puentelarra
Pobes
Fontecha
Armiñón
Zambrana
Albaina
Peñacerrada
Bernedo
Acedo
Aguráin/
Salvatierra
Maeztu
Santa Cruz de Campezo/
Santi Kurutze Kanpezu
Eulate
Montorio
Villadiego
Santibañez
Zarzaguda
Villanueva
de Argaño
Quintanaortuño
Cernégula
Quintanilla-
Sobresierra
Terrazos
Pancorbo
Miranda
de Ebro
Briviesca
STA.
CASILDA
Puerto de la
Brújula
918
Haro
Casalarreina
Tirgo
Briones
Laguardia/
Biasteri
VITORIA-
GASTEIZ
KAPILDUI
1175
MONTE SANTO
SIERRA DE CANTABRIA
Puerto Lizarraga
1031
BURGOS
LAS HUELGAS
MIRAFLORES
S. PEDRO DE CARDEÑA
Villatoro
Rubena
Ibeas de
Juarros
Villafranca
Montes de Oca
Belorado
Pradoluengo
Ezcaray
San Asensio
Santo Domingo
de la Calzada
San Millán de
la Cogolla
Cenicero
Fuenmayor
Olon
Oyon
Viana
Los Arcos
Allo
Lerín
Nájera
Navarrete
Logroño
Villamediana
de Iregua
Agoncillo
Mendavia
Sesma
Lodosa
Santa María
del Campo
Cogollos
Madrigalejo
del Mo
Villahoz
Cuevas de
San Clemente
Quintanilla
de las Viñas
MONASTERIOS
DE SUSO Y YUSO
MONASTERIO DE
VALVANERA
2262
Baños
de Río Tobia
Barbadillo
Anguiano
Viguo
Ribaflecha
Carcar
N. SEÑORA
DE IRACHE

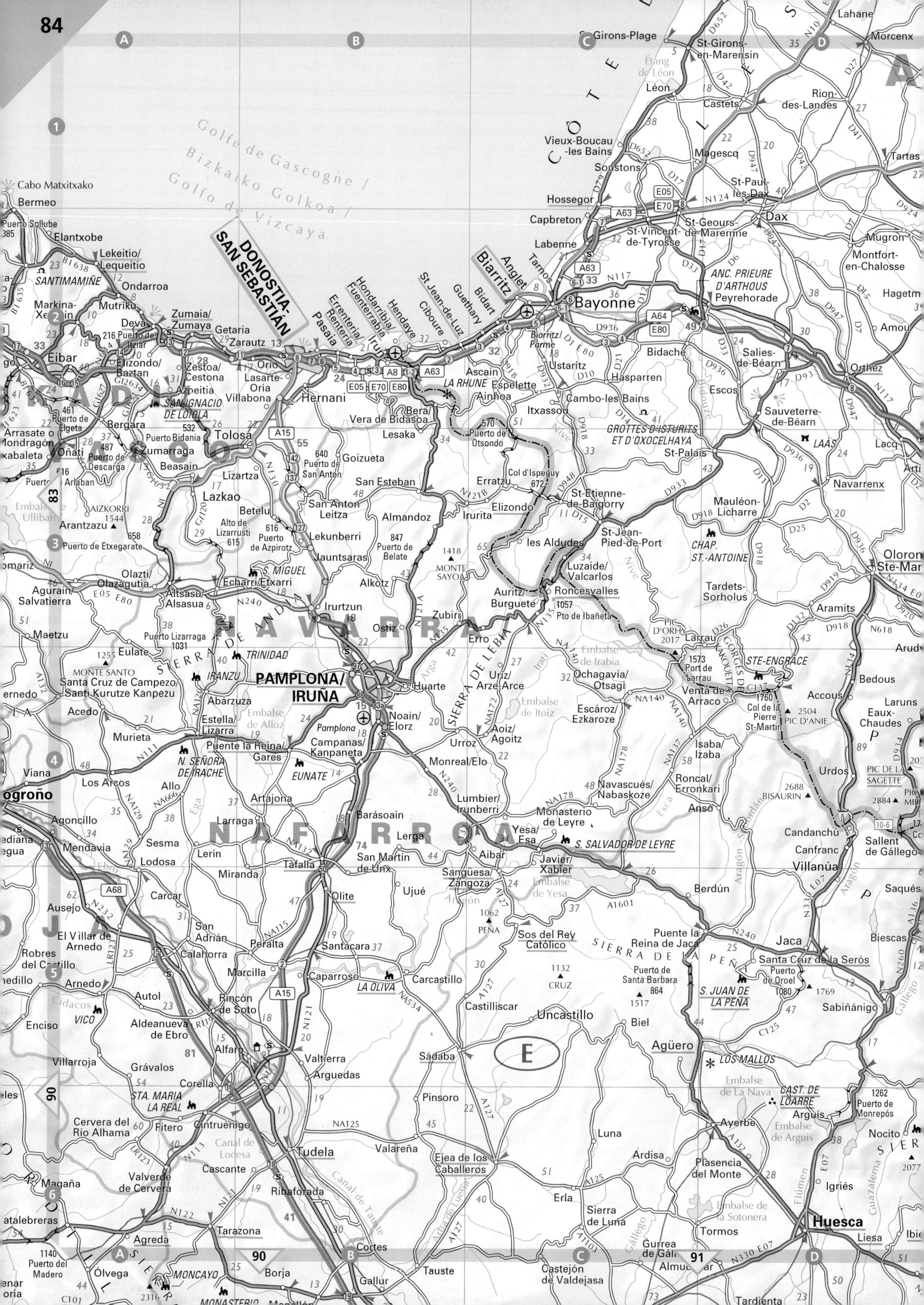

Golfe de Gascogne /
Bizkaiko Golkoa /
Golfo de Vizcaya
CÔTE
DONOSTIA-
SAN SEBASTIÁN
Biarritz
Anglet
Bayonne
PAMPLONA/
IRUÑA
NAVARRA
NAFARROA
SIERRA DE ANDIA
SIERRA DE LEIRE
SIERRA DE LA PEÑA
Cabo Matxitxako
Bermeo
Elantxobe
Lekeitio/
Lequeitio
SANTIMAMIÑE
Ondarroa
Markina-
Xemein
Mutriku
Deva
Zumaia/
Zumaya
Getaria
Zarautz
Eibar
Elizondo/
Baztan
Zestoa/
Cestona
Azpeitia
SAN IGNACIO
DE LOIOLA
Bergara
Puerto de Elgeta
Arrasate o
Mondragón
Oñati
Puerto Bidania
Tolosa
Zumarraga
Beasain
Puerto de Descarga
Arlaban
Lizartza
Lazkao
AIZKORRI
1544
Arantzazu
Puerto de Etxegarate
Embalse de Ullibarri
Olazti/
Olazagutia
Agurain/
Salvatierra
Altsasu/
Alsasua
Echarri/Etxarri
S. MIGUEL
Maetzu
Puerto Lizarraga
1031
Eulate
TRINIDAD
IRANZU
MONTE SANTO
Santa Cruz de Campezo/
Santi Kurutze Kanpezu
Acedo
Abárzuza
Estella/
Lizarra
Embalse de Alloz
Murieta
Puente la Reina/
Gares
N. SEÑORA
DE IRACHE
EUNATE
Viana
Los Arcos
Logroño
Allo
Artajona
Agoncillo
Mendavia
Larraga
Sesma
Lerín
Lodosa
Miranda
Tafalla
Olite
Carcar
Ausejo
El Villar de
Arnedo
San
Adrián
Calahorra
Peralta
Robres
del Castillo
Arnedo
Marcilla
Autol
Rincón
de Soto
VICO
Enciso
Aldeanueva
de Ebro
Alfaro
Villarroja
Grávalos
Corella
STA. MARIA
LA REAL
Cervera del
Río Alhama
Fitero
Cintruénigo
Canal de Lodosa
Tudela
Cascante
Magaña
Valverde
de Cervera
Ribaforada
Tarazona
Agreda
1140
Puerto del
Madero
Ólvega
MONCAYO
2316
Borja
Cortes
Gallur
Mallén
Orio
Lasarte-
Oria
Villabona
Hernani
Pasaia
Errenteria/
Rentería
Hondarribia/
Fuenterrabia
Irun
Hendaye
Ciboure
St Jean-de-Luz
Guethary
Bidart
LA RHUNE
Ascain
Espelette
Ainhoa
Vera de Bidasoa
Bera/
Lesaka
Puerto de Otsondo
Goizueta
Puerto de
San Anton
San Esteban
San Anton
Leitza
Almandoz
Betelu
Alto de
Lizarrusti
Puerto
de Azpirotz
Lekunberri
Jauntsaras
Puerto de
Belate
Alkotz
Irurtzun
Ostiz
Zubiri
Erro
Auritz/
Burguete
Roncesvalles
Pto de Ibañeta
MONTE
SAYOA
Irurita
Elizondo
Erratzu
Col d'Ispeguy
Huarte
Noain/
Elorz
Pamplona
Campanas/
Kanpaneta
Uriz/
Arze-Arce
Embalse de Irabia
Embalse de Itoiz
Aoiz/
Agoitz
Urroz
Monreal/Elo
Lumbier/
Irunberri
Barásoain
Lerga
San Martin
de Unx
Ujué
Aibar
Sangüesa/
Zangoza
Yesa/
Esa
Monasterio
de Leyre
S. SALVADOR DE LEYRE
Javier/
Xabier
Embalse de Yesa
Sos del Rey
Católico
PEÑA
Santacara
Caparroso
LA OLIVA
Carcastillo
Castilliscar
Uncastillo
Valtierra
Arguedas
Sádaba
Pinsoro
Valareña
Ejea de los
Caballeros
Tauste
Castejón
de Valdejasa
Luna
Ardisa
Erla
Sierra
de Luna
Biel
CRUZ
Puerto de
Santa Barbara
Ochagavía/
Otsagi
Escároz/
Ezkaroze
Navascués/
Nabaskoze
Isaba/
Izaba
Roncal/
Erronkari
Ansó
Venta de
Arraco
Col de la
Pierre
St-Martin
PIC D'ANIE
BISAURIN
PIC
D'ORHY
Larrau
Port de
Larrau
STE-ENGRÂCE
GORGES DE KAKOUETA
Berdún
Puente la
Reina de Jaca
Jaca
Santa Cruz de la Serós
Puerto
de Oroel
S. JUAN DE
LA PEÑA
Sabiñánigo
Agüero
LOS MALLOS
Embalse
de La Nava
CAST. DE
LOARRE
Ayerbe
Embalse
de Arguis
Arguis
Puerto de
Monrepós
Nocito
Plasencia
del Monte
Embalse de
la Sotonera
Tormos
Gurrea
de Gállego
Almudévar
Huesca
Igriés
Liesa
Tardienta
Canfranc
Villanúa
Candanchú
Sallent
de Gállego
Saqués
Biescas
Urdos
PIC DE LA
SAGETTE
Bedous
Accous
Laruns
Eaux-
Chaudes
Aramits
Oloron
Ste-Marie
Tardets-
Sorholus
CHAP.
ST.-ANTOINE
Mauléon-
Licharre
Navarrenx
Lacq
Sauveterre-
de-Béarn
LAÀS
Escos
Salies-
de-Béarn
Orthez
St-Palais
GROTTES D'ISTURITS
ET D'OXOCELHAYA
St-Etienne-
de-Baigorry
St-Jean-
Pied-de-Port
les Aldudes
Luzaide/
Valcarlos
Itxassou
Cambo-les-Bains
Hasparren
Bidache
Ustaritz
Biarritz/
Parme
Bayonne
Tarnos
Labenne
Capbreton
Hossegor
Soustons
Vieux-Boucau
-les Bains
St-Vincent-
de-Tyrosse
St-Geours-
de-Maremne
ANC. PRIEURE
D'ARTHOUS
Peyrehorade
Dax
St-Paul-
lès-Dax
Magescq
Castets
Léon
Étang
de Léon
St-Girons-
en-Marensin
St-Girons-Plage
Lahane
Morcenx
Rion-
des-Landes
Tartas
Mugron
Montfort-
en-Chalosse
Hagetmau
Amou
Arthez
Arudy
E

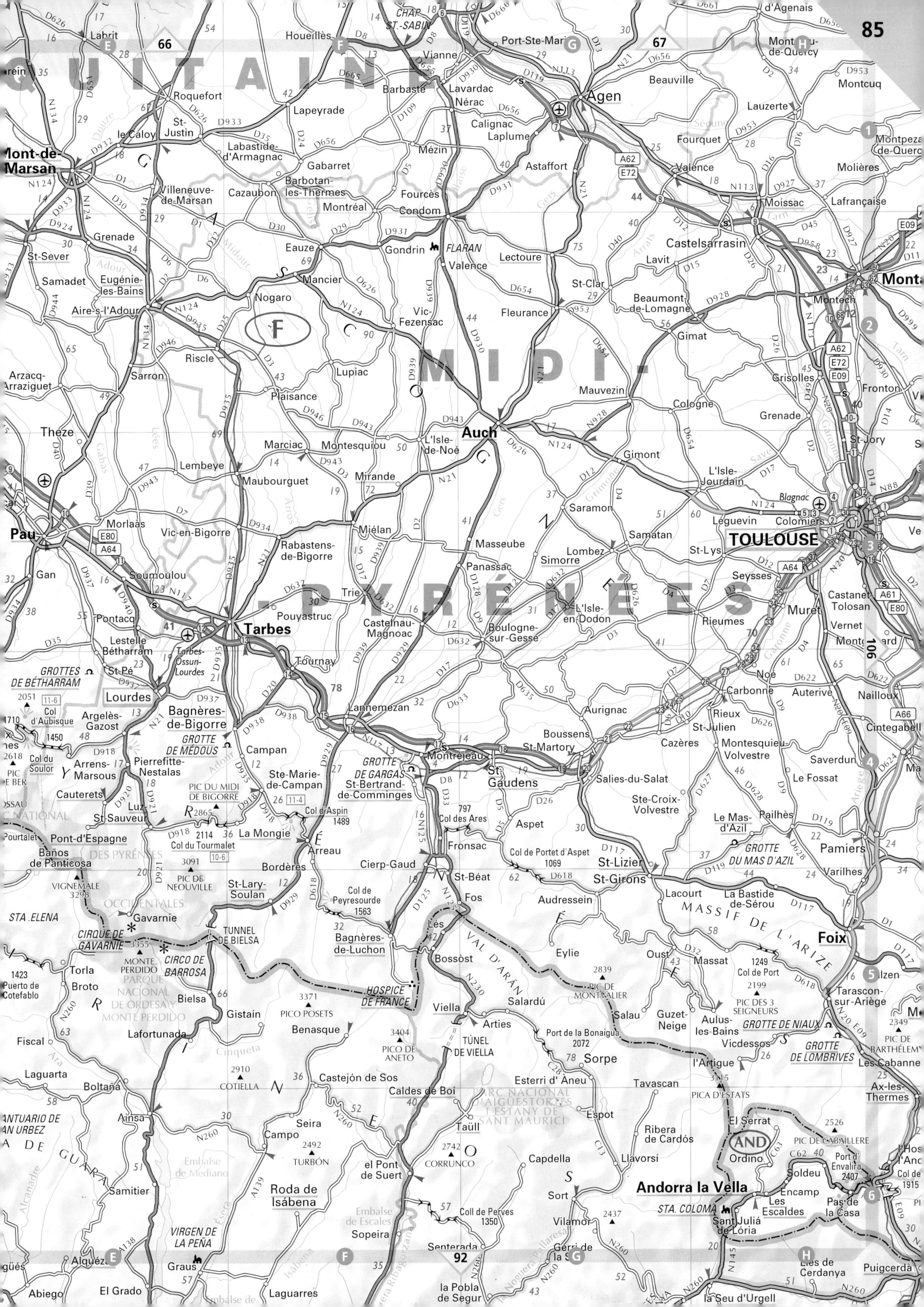

QUITAINE
MIDI-PYRÉNÉES
GASCOGNE
PYRÉNÉES
Labrit
Houeillès
CHAP. ST.-SABIN
Port-Ste-Marie
Mont-de-Marsan
Roquefort
St-Justin
le Caloy
Labastide-d'Armagnac
Lapeyrade
Barbaste
Lavardac
Nérac
Vianne
Calignac
Laplume
Agen
Beauville
Montcuq
Lauzerte
Fourquet
Montpezat-de-Quercy
Valence
Molières
Moissac
Lafrançaise
Castelsarrasin
Lavit
Montauban
Montech
Beaumont-de-Lomagne
Gimat
Grisolles
Fronton
Grenade
Cologne
Mauvezin
St-Jory
L'Isle-Jourdain
Blagnac
Colomiers
Léguevin
TOULOUSE
St-Lys
Seysses
Castanet-Tolosan
Muret
Vernet
Rieumes
Gimont
Samatan
Lombez
Simorre
Saramon
L'Isle-en-Dodon
Boulogne-sur-Gesse
Masseube
Panassac
Auch
Fleurance
Lectoure
St-Clar
Astaffort
Mézin
Gabarret
Barbotan-les-Thermes
Montréal
Fources
Condom
Gondrin
FLARAN
Valence
Eauze
Cazaubon
Villeneuve-de-Marsan
Grenade
St-Sever
Samadet
Eugénie-les-Bains
Aire-s-l'Adour
Mancier
Nogaro
Vic-Fezensac
Riscle
Sarron
Lupiac
Plaisance
Marciac
Montesquiou
L'Isle-de-Noé
Mirande
Miélan
Arzacq-Arraziguet
Theze
Lembeye
Maubourguet
Pau
Morlaàs
Vic-en-Bigorre
Rabastens-de-Bigorre
Gan
Soumoulou
Pontacq
Tarbes
Trie
Pouyastruc
Castelnau-Magnoac
Lestelle-Bétharram
Tarbes-Ossun-Lourdes
St-Pé
GROTTES DE BÉTHARRAM
Lourdes
Tournay
Bagnères-de-Bigorre
Lannemezan
GROTTE DE MÉDOUS
Argelès-Gazost
Col d'Aubisque
Col du Soulor
Arrens-Marsous
Pierrefitte-Nestalas
Campan
Ste-Marie-de-Campan
GROTTE DE GARGAS
St-Bertrand-de-Comminges
Montréjeau
St-Gaudens
St-Martory
Boussens
Aurignac
Carbonne
Noé
Auterive
Nailloux
Cintegabelle
Rieux
St-Julien
Cazères
Montesquieu-Volvestre
Saverdun
Le Fossat
Salies-du-Salat
Ste-Croix-Volvestre
Le Mas-d'Azil
Pailhès
GROTTE DU MAS D'AZIL
Pamiers
Varilhes
Cauterets
Luz
St-Sauveur
PIC DU MIDI DE BIGORRE
Col d'Aspin
La Mongie
Col du Tourmalet
Pont-d'Espagne
Baños de Panticosa
Arreau
Bordères
Cierp-Gaud
Fronsac
Col des Ares
Aspet
Col de Portet d'Aspet
St-Lizier
St-Girons
Lacourt
La Bastide-de-Sérou
MASSIF DE L'ARIZE
Foix
PIC DE NEOUVILLE
VIGNEMALE
St-Lary-Soulan
Col de Peyresourde
St-Béat
Fos
Audressein
Gavarnie
STA. ELENA
CIRQUE DE GAVARNIE
TUNNEL DE BIELSA
CIRCO DE BARROSA
MONTE PERDIDO
PARQUE NACIONAL DE ORDESA Y MONTE PERDIDO
Les
Bagnères-de-Luchon
Bossòst
VAL D'ARAN
Eylie
Oust
Massat
Col de Port
Tarascon-sur-Ariège
Torla
Broto
Bielsa
HOSPICE DE FRANCE
PIC DE MONTVALIER
PIC DES 3 SEIGNEURS
Puerto de Cotefablo
Gistaín
PICO POSETS
Viella
Salardú
Salau
Guzet-Neige
Aulus-les-Bains
GROTTE DE NIAUX
Fiscal
Lafortunada
Benasque
Arties
Port de la Bonaigua
Vicdessos
GROTTE DE LOMBRIVES
PICO DE ANETO
TÚNEL DE VIELLA
Sorpe
l'Artigue
Les Cabannes
Ax-les-Thermes
Laguarta
COTIELLA
Castejón de Sos
Esterri d'Àneu
Tavascan
PICA D'ESTATS
Boltaña
Caldes de Boí
PARC NACIONAL D'AIGÜESTORTES I ESTANY DE SANT MAURICI
Espot
SANTUARIO DE SAN URBEZ
SIERRA DE GUARA
Ainsa
Seira
Campo
Taüll
Ribera de Cardós
El Serrat
AND
Ordino
PIC DE CABAILLERE
Port d'Envalira
TURBÓN
CORRUNCO
Embalse de Mediano
Capdella
Llavorsí
Soldeu
Samitier
el Pont de Suert
Andorra la Vella
Encamp
Les Escaldes
Pas de la Casa
Roda de Isábena
Sort
STA. COLOMA
Sant Julià de Lòria
Embalse de Escales
Coll de Perves
Vilamor
VIRGEN DE LA PEÑA
Sopeira
Senterada
Gerri de la Sal
Alquézar
Graus
Les de Cerdanya
Puigcerdà
Abiego
El Grado
Laguarres
la Pobla de Segur
la Seu d'Urgell
Embalse de

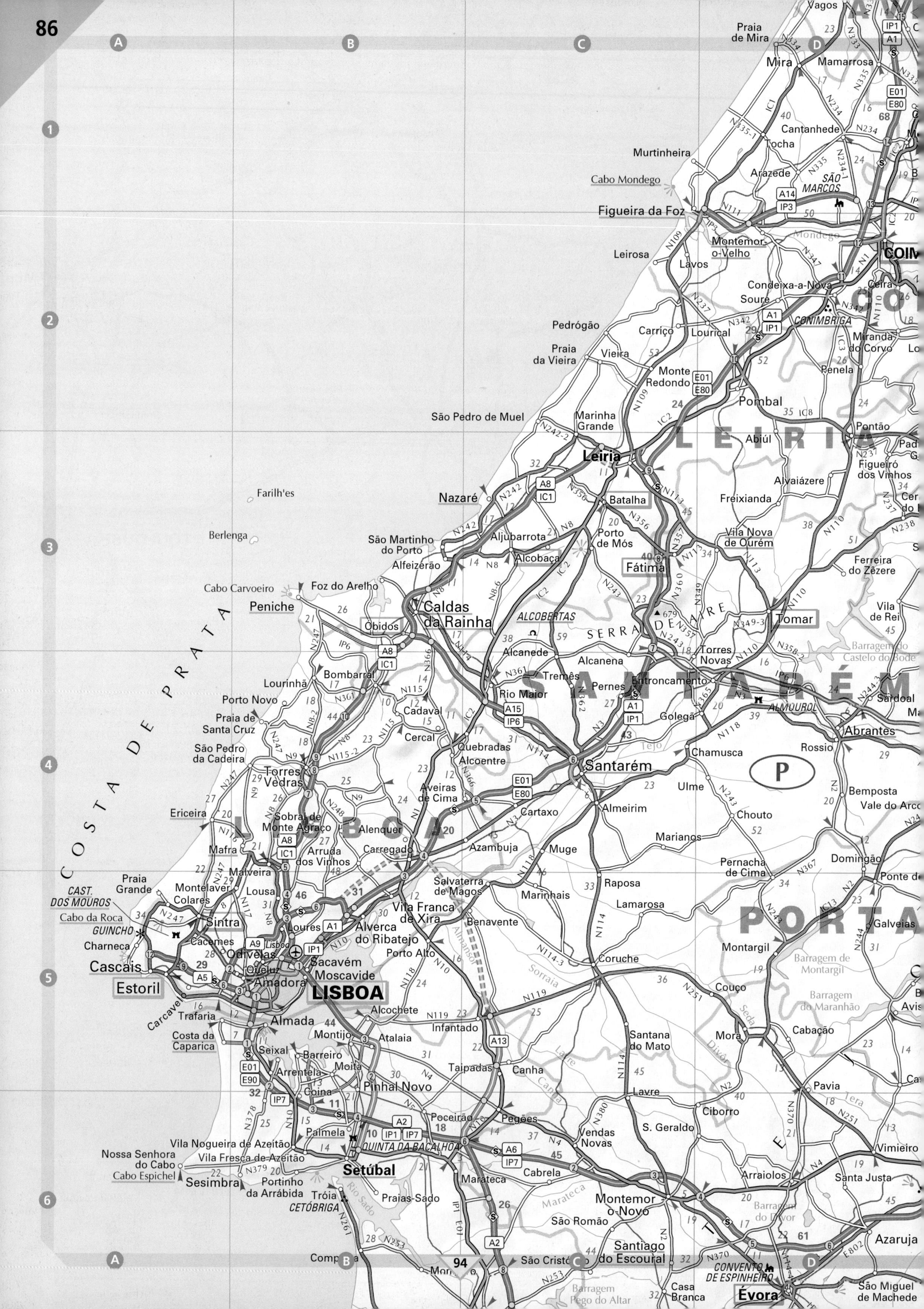

Mira
Figueira da Foz
Cabo Mondego
Montemor-o-Velho
Coimbra
Condeixa-a-Nova
Soure
Pombal
Leiria
Marinha Grande
São Pedro de Muel
Nazaré
Batalha
Alcobaça
Fátima
Tomar
Caldas da Rainha
Óbidos
Peniche
Cabo Carvoeiro
Berlenga
Farilhões
COSTA DE PRATA
Torres Vedras
Ericeira
Mafra
Sintra
Cascais
Estoril
Cabo da Roca
LISBOA
Amadora
Almada
Barreiro
Setúbal
Sesimbra
Cabo Espichel
Santarém
Entroncamento
Abrantes
Almeirim
Coruche
Montemor-o-Novo
Évora
LEIRIA
LISBOA
SANTARÉM
PORTALEGRE
SERRA DE AIRE
94

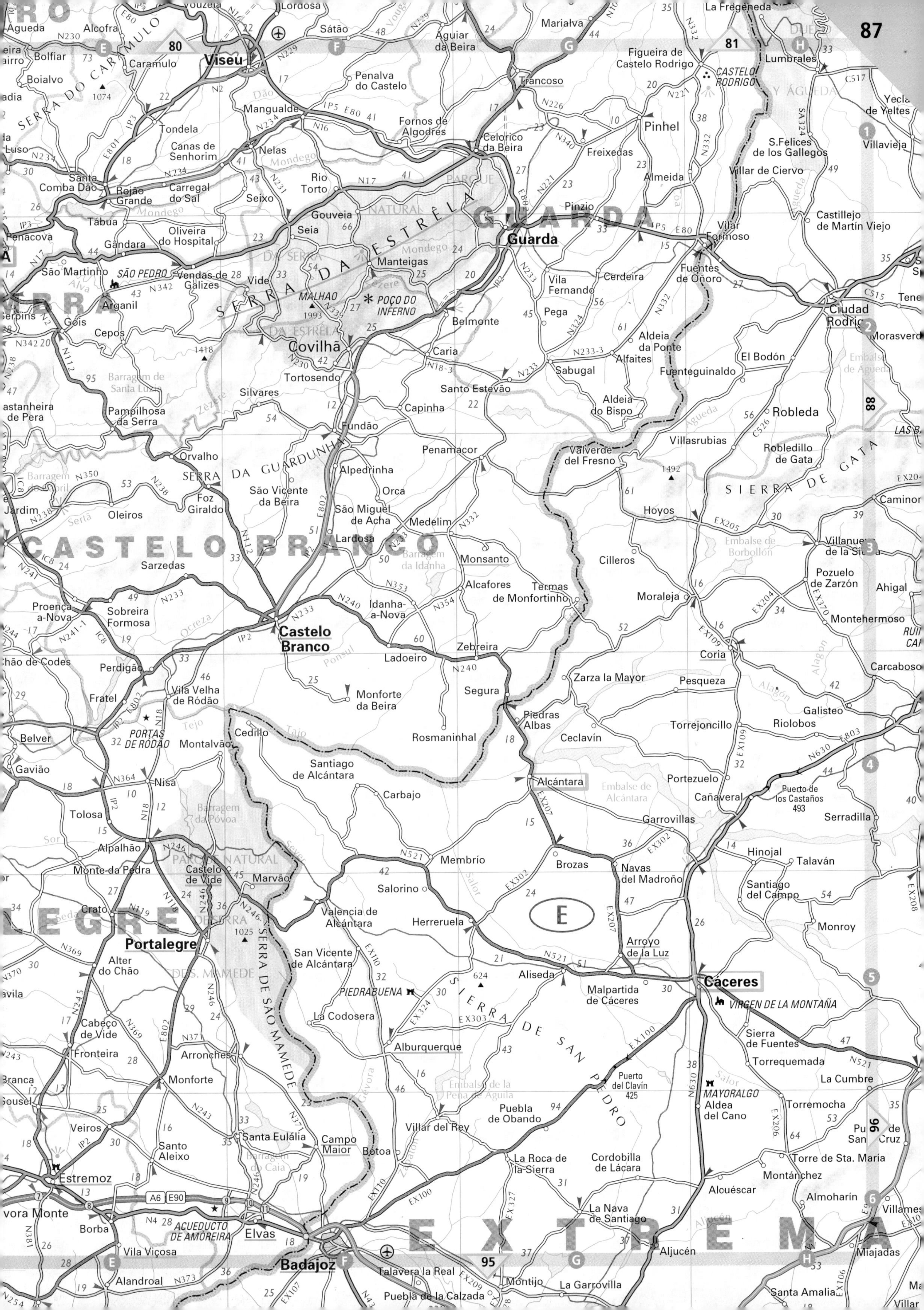

Viseu
Guarda
Covilhã
Castelo Branco
Portalegre
Cáceres
Badajoz
Elvas
Estremoz
Ciudad Rodrigo
SERRA DA ESTRÊLA
SERRA DA GUARDUNHA
SIERRA DE GATA
SIERRA DE SAN PEDRO
SERRA DE SÃO MAMEDE
SERRA DO CARAMULO
CASTELO BRANCO
GUARDA
EXTREMA
LEGRE
Mangualde
Nelas
Seia
Gouveia
Manteigas
Belmonte
Fundão
Trancoso
Celorico da Beira
Pinhel
Almeida
Vilar Formoso
Fuentes de Oñoro
Sabugal
Penamacor
Idanha-a-Nova
Monsanto
Alcántara
Coria
Moraleja
Nisa
Marvão
Castelo de Vide
Valencia de Alcántara
Alburquerque
Campo Maior
Arronches
Monforte
Borba
Vila Viçosa
Miajadas
Montánchez
Talavera la Real
Montijo
La Garrovilla
Puebla de la Calzada
Aljucén
Arroyo de la Luz
Brozas
Garrovillas
Cañaveral
Robleda
Hoyos
Sátão
Tondela
Santa Comba Dão
Arganil
Góis
Oleiros
Sertã
Proença-a-Nova
Vila Velha de Ródão
Alpalhão
Crato
Fronteira
Sousel
Alter do Chão
Aguiar da Beira
Fornos de Algodres
Penalva do Castelo
Figueira de Castelo Rodrigo
Lumbrales
Puerto de los Castaños 493
Puerto del Clavín 425
PORTAS DE RÓDÃO
POÇO DO INFERNO
MALHAO 1993
VIRGEN DE LA MONTAÑA
MAYORALGO
PIEDRABUENA
ACUEDUCTO DE AMOREIRA
CASTELO RODRIGO
SÃO PEDRO
80
81
88
95
96
E
F
G
H

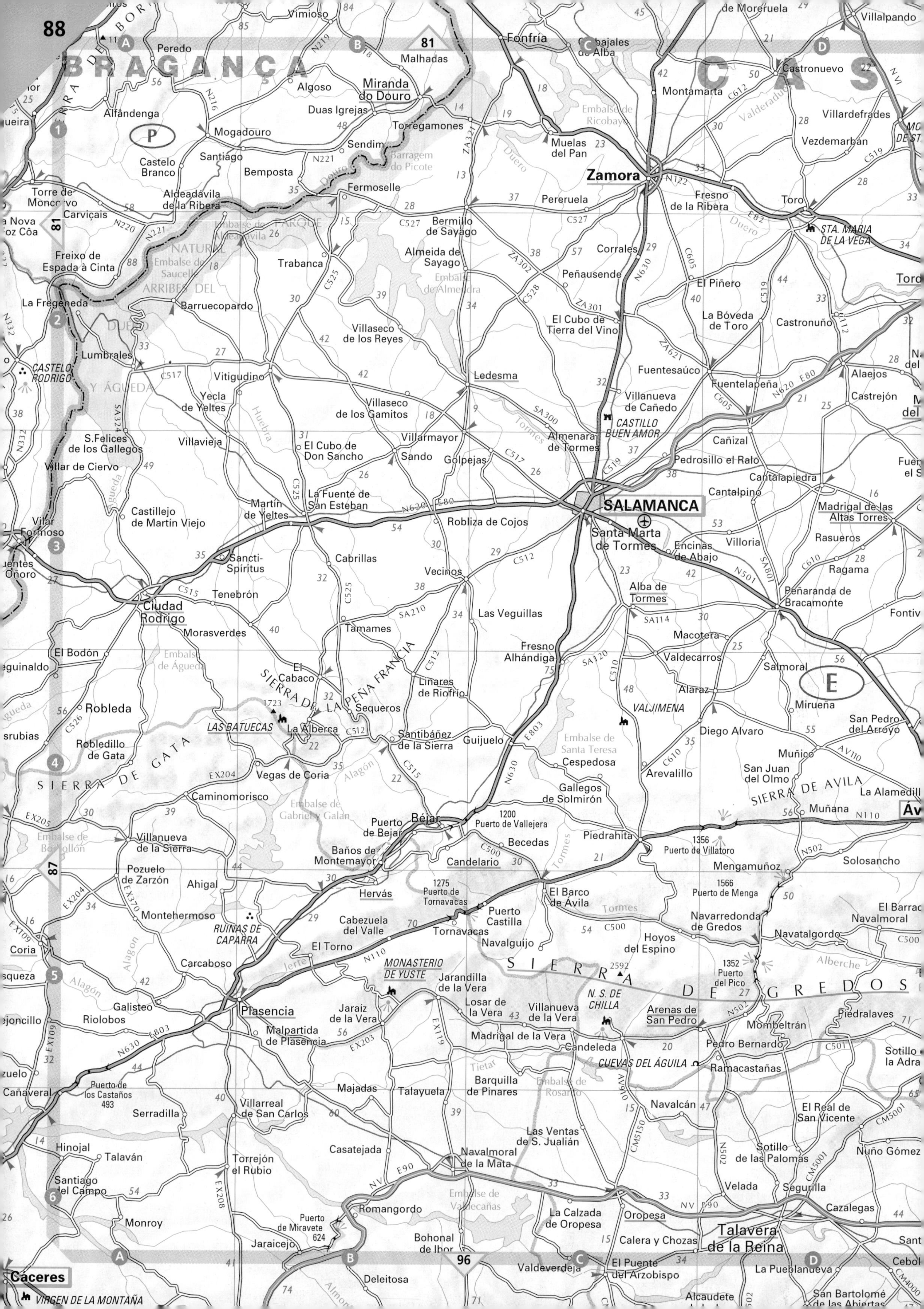

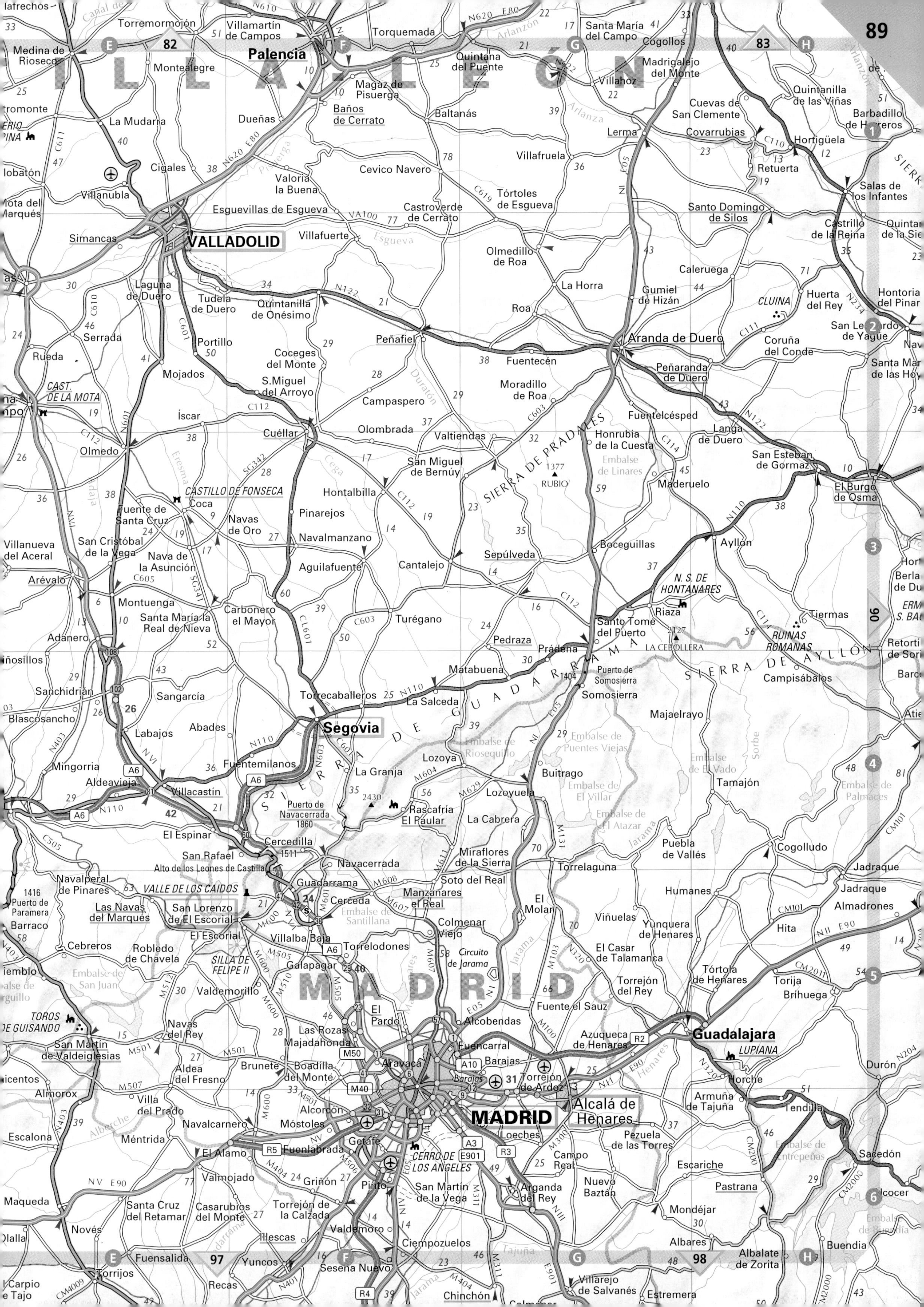
82
83
90
97
98
Palencia
Torremormojón
Villamartín de Campos
Torquemada
Santa María del Campo
Cogollos
Medina de Rioseco
Montealegre
Quintana del Puente
Madrigalejo del Monte
Villahoz
Magaz de Pisuerga
Baños de Cerrato
Dueñas
La Mudarra
Baltanás
Cuevas de San Clemente
Quintanilla de las Viñas
Barbadillo de Herreros
Lerma
Covarrubias
Hortigüela
Villafruela
Retuerta
Cigales
Valoria la Buena
Cevico Navero
Villanubla
Esguevillas de Esgueva
Castroverde de Cerrato
Tórtoles de Esgueva
Santo Domingo de Silos
Salas de los Infantes
Castrillo de la Reina
Simancas
VALLADOLID
Villafuerte
Olmedillo de Roa
Caleruega
Laguna de Duero
Tudela de Duero
Quintanilla de Onésimo
La Horra
Gumiel de Hizán
Huerta del Rey
Hontoria del Pinar
Roa
CLUINA
San Leonardo de Yagüe
Serrada
Portillo
Coceges del Monte
Peñafiel
Aranda de Duero
Coruña del Conde
Rueda
Fuentecén
Peñaranda de Duero
Santa María de las Hoyas
CAST. DE LA MOTA
Mojados
S.Miguel del Arroyo
Campaspero
Moradillo de Roa
Fuentelcésped
Langa de Duero
Íscar
Cuéllar
Olombrada
Valtiendas
Honrubia de la Cuesta
Olmedo
San Miguel de Bernúy
SIERRA DE PRADALES
1377 RUBIO
Embalse de Linares
Maderuelo
San Esteban de Gormaz
El Burgo de Osma
CASTILLO DE FONSECA
Coca
Hontalbilla
Fuente de Santa Cruz
Pinarejos
Navas de Oro
Villanueva del Aceral
San Cristóbal de la Vega
Navalmanzano
Nava de la Asunción
Aguilafuente
Cantalejo
Sepúlveda
Boceguillas
Ayllón
Arévalo
Montuenga
N. S. DE HONTANARES
Riaza
Tiermas
RUINAS ROMANAS
Santa María la Real de Nieva
Carbonero el Mayor
Turégano
Santo Tomé del Puerto
Adanero
Pedraza
Prádena
LA CEBOLLERA
SIERRA DE AYLLÓN
Campisábalos
Sanchidrián
Matabuena
Puerto de Somosierra
Somosierra
Blascosancho
Sangarcía
Torrecaballeros
La Salceda
Majaelrayo
Labajos
Abades
Segovia
SIERRA DE GUADARRAMA
Embalse de Riosequillo
Embalse de Puentes Viejas
Embalse de El Vado
Mingorria
Fuentemilanos
La Granja
Lozoya
Buitrago
Tamajón
Aldeavieja
Villacastín
Lozoyuela
Embalse de El Villar
Embalse de Palmaces
Puerto de Navacerrada 1860
Rascafría
El Paular
La Cabrera
Embalse de El Atazar
El Espinar
Cercedilla
Puebla de Vallés
Cogolludo
San Rafael
Navacerrada
Miraflores de la Sierra
Torrelaguna
Jadraque
Alto de los Leones de Castilla
Navalperal de Pinares
VALLE DE LOS CAIDOS
Guadarrama
Soto del Real
Humanes
Almadrones
1416 Puerto de Paramera
Las Navas del Marqués
San Lorenzo de El Escorial
Cerceda
Manzanares el Real
El Molar
Barraco
Embalse de Santillana
Colmenar Viejo
Viñuelas
Yunquera de Henares
Hita
El Escorial
Villalba Baja
Torrelodones
Circuito de Jarama
El Casar de Talamanca
Cebreros
Robledo de Chavela
SILLA DE FELIPE II
Galapagar
Tórtola de Henares
Torija
Embalse de San Juan
Valdemorillo
MADRID
Torrejón del Rey
Brihuega
TOROS DE GUISANDO
Navas del Rey
El Pardo
Fuente el Sauz
San Martín de Valdeiglesias
Las Rozas
Majadahonda
Alcobendas
Azuqueca de Henares
Guadalajara
Fuencarral
LUPIANA
Aldea del Fresno
Brunete
Boadilla del Monte
Aravaca
Barajas
Torrejón de Ardoz
Durón
Almorox
Villa del Prado
Alcorcón
Alcalá de Henares
Horche
Armuña de Tajuña
Tendilla
Navalcarnero
Móstoles
Pezuela de las Torres
Escalona
Méntrida
Getafe
Loeches
El Álamo
Fuenlabrada
CERRO DE LOS ANGELES
Campo Real
Escariche
Embalse de Entrepeñas
Sacedón
Valmojado
Griñón
Pinto
San Martín de la Vega
Arganda del Rey
Nuevo Baztán
Pastrana
Maqueda
Santa Cruz del Retamar
Casarubios del Monte
Torrejón de la Calzada
Mondéjar
Novés
Valdemoro
Illescas
Ciempozuelos
Albares
Buendía
Fuensalida
Yuncos
Seseña Nuevo
Albalate de Zorita
Torrijos
Recas
Villarejo de Salvanés
Estremera
Chinchón
Alcocer

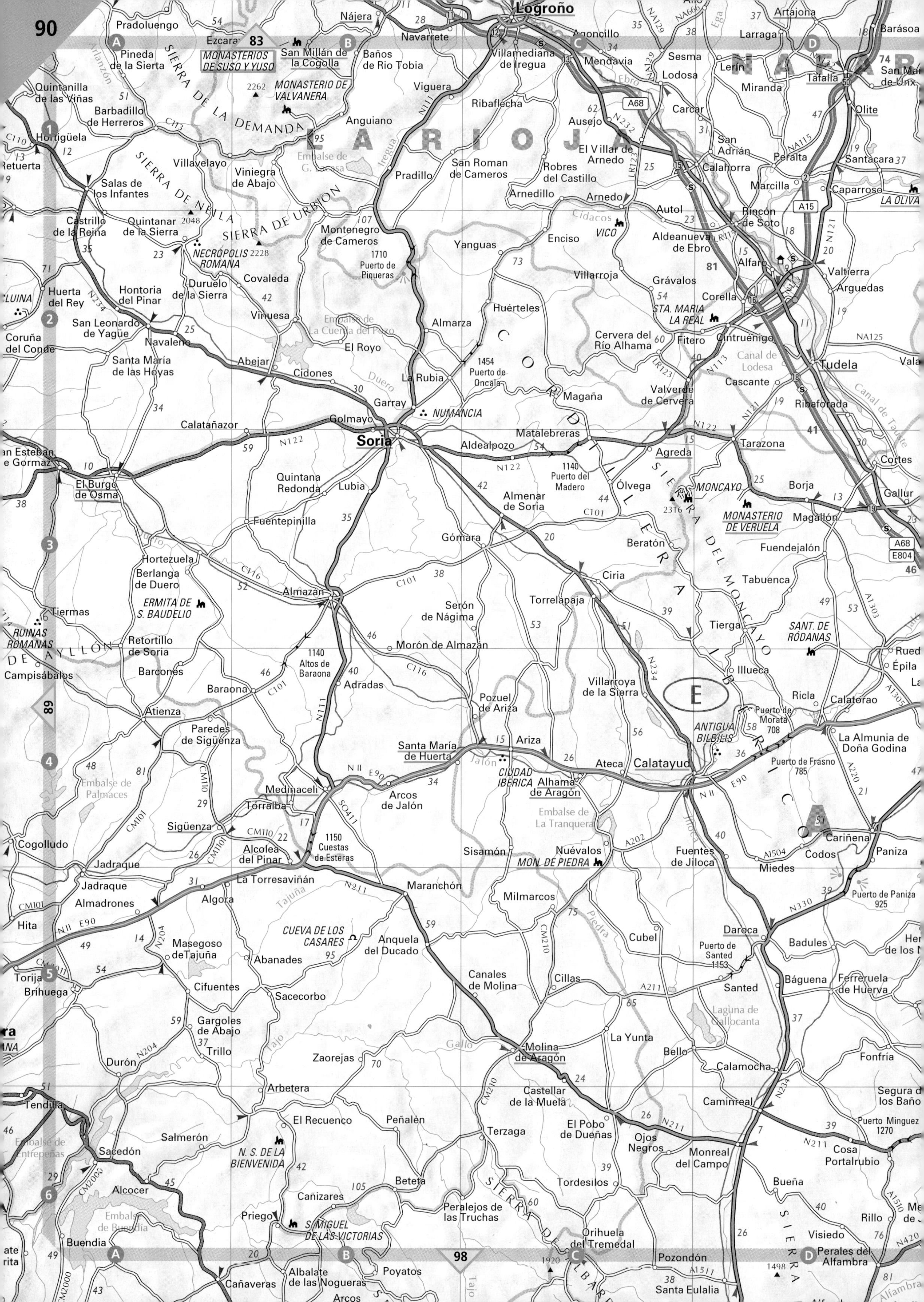

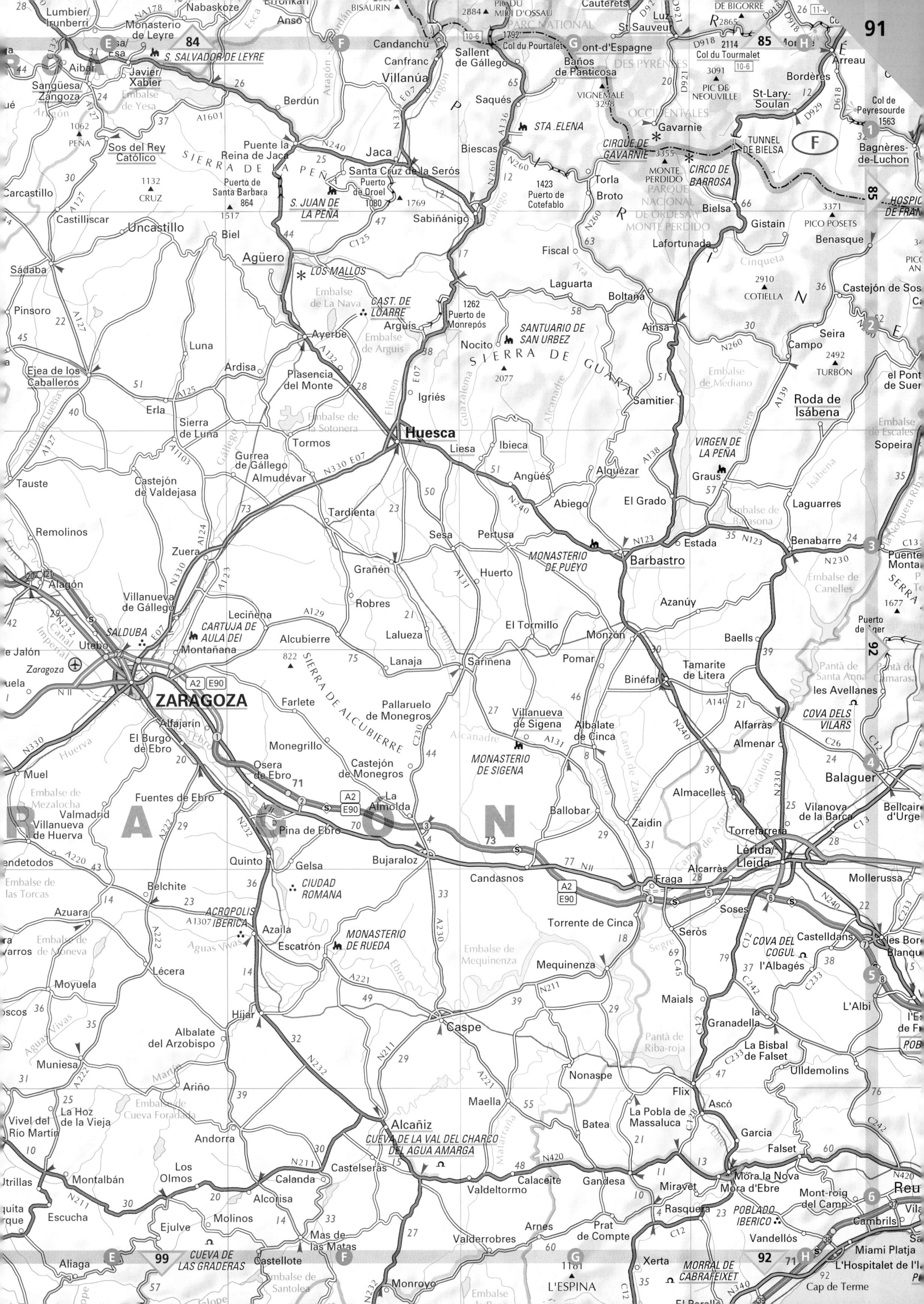

Lumbier/ Irunberri
Monasterio de Leyre
Nabaskoze
Ansó
BISAURIN
PIC DU MIDI D'OSSAU
PARC NATIONAL
Cauterets
Luz
St-Sauveur
DE BIGORRE
84
S. SALVADOR DE LEYRE
Candanchú
Canfranc
Villanúa
Sallent de Gállego
Col du Pourtalet
Pont-d'Espagne
Baños de Panticosa
DES PYRÉNÉES
Col du Tourmalet
85
Arreau
Bordères
Aibar
Javier/ Xabier
Sangüesa/ Zangoza
Embalse de Yesa
Berdún
Saqués
VIGNEMALE 3298
PIC DE NEOUVILLE
St-Lary-Soulan
Col de Peyresourde 1563
OCCIDENTALES
Gavarnie
STA. ELENA
PEÑA
Sos del Rey Católico
Puente la Reina de Jaca
Jaca
Biescas
CIRQUE DE GAVARNIE
MONTE PERDIDO 3355
CIRCO DE BARROSA
TUNNEL DE BIELSA
F
Bagnères-de-Luchon
SIERRA DE LA PEÑA
Santa Cruz de la Serós
Puerto de Oroel
Puerto de Santa Barbara 864
CRUZ
Carcastillo
S. JUAN DE LA PEÑA
Sabiñánigo
1423 Puerto de Cotefablo
Torla
Broto
PARQUE NACIONAL DE ORDESA Y MONTE PERDIDO
Bielsa
Gistaín
PICO POSETS
HOSPICE DE FRANCE
Castilliscar
Uncastillo
Biel
Agüero
LOS MALLOS
Fiscal
Lafortunada
Benasque
Sádaba
Embalse de La Nava
CAST. DE LOARRE
Puerto de Monrepós
Laguarta
Boltaña
COTIELLA
Castejón de Sos
Pinsoro
Ayerbe
Arguis
Embalse de Arguis
Nocito
SANTUARIO DE SAN URBEZ
Aínsa
Campo
Seira
TURBÓN
Luna
SIERRA DE GUARA
Embalse de Mediano
el Pont de Suert
Ejea de los Caballeros
Ardisa
Plasencia del Monte
Igriés
Samitier
Roda de Isábena
Erla
Sierra de Luna
Embalse de la Sotonera
Huesca
Tormos
Liesa
Ibieca
VIRGEN DE LA PEÑA
Embalse de Escales
Sopeira
Gurrea de Gállego
Almudévar
Angüés
Alquézar
Graus
Tauste
Castejón de Valdejasa
Tardienta
Abiego
El Grado
Laguarres
Embalse de Barasona
Remolinos
Zuera
Sesa
Pertusa
MONASTERIO DE PUEYO
Barbastro
Estada
Benabarre
Alagón
Grañén
Huerto
Embalse de Canelles
Puerto de Monte
Villanueva de Gállego
Leciñena
Robres
Azanúy
SALDUBA
CARTUJA DE AULA DEI
Montañana
Alcubierre
Lalueza
El Tormillo
Monzón
Baells
Utebo
Jalón
Zaragoza
Lanaja
Sariñena
Pomar
Tamarite de Litera
SIERRA DE ALCUBIERRE
Binéfar
Pantà de Santa Anna
les Avellanes
ZARAGOZA
Farlete
Pallaruelo de Monegros
Villanueva de Sigena
Albalate de Cinca
COVA DELS VILARS
Alfajarín
El Burgo de Ebro
Monegrillo
Alfarràs
Almenar
Muel
Osera de Ebro
Castejón de Monegros
MONASTERIO DE SIGENA
Balaguer
Embalse de Mezalocha
Fuentes de Ebro
La Almolda
Ballobar
Almacelles
Valmadrid
Villanueva de Huerva
ARAGÓN
Pina de Ebro
Zaidín
Vilanova de la Barca
Bellcaire d'Urgell
Torrefarrera
Quinto
Gelsa
Bujaraloz
Candasnos
Fraga
Lérida/ Lleida
Alcarràs
Mollerussa
Embalse de las Torcas
Belchite
CIUDAD ROMANA
Soses
Azuara
ACROPOLIS IBERICA
Azaila
Escatrón
MONASTERIO DE RUEDA
Torrente de Cinca
Seròs
COVA DEL COGUL
Castelldans
les Borges Blanques
Embalse de Moneva
Aguas Vivas
Embalse de Mequinenza
Mequinenza
l'Albagés
Lécera
Moyuela
Híjar
Caspe
Maials
L'Albi
Albalate del Arzobispo
Pantà de Riba-roja
la Granadella
La Bisbal de Falset
Muniesa
Nonaspe
Ulldemolins
Ariño
Flix
Ascó
Maella
La Hoz de la Vieja
Embalse de Cueva Foradada
Vivel del Río Martín
Batea
La Pobla de Massaluca
Alcañiz
Garcia
Andorra
CUEVA DE LA VAL DEL CHARCO DEL AGUA AMARGA
Falset
Castelserás
Móra la Nova
Montalbán
Los Olmos
Calanda
Calaceite
Gandesa
Miravet
Móra d'Ebre
Mont-roig del Camp
Reus
Utrillas
Valdeltormo
Alcorisa
Escucha
Molinos
Rasquera
POBLADO IBERICO
Cambrils
Ejulve
Arnes
Prat de Compte
Vandellòs
Mas de las Matas
Valderrobres
CUEVA DE LAS GRADERAS
99
Aliaga
Castellote
Embalse de Santolea
Xerta
MORRAL DE CABRAFEIXET
92
Miami Platja
L'Hospitalet de l'Infant
L'ESPINA
Monroyo
Cap de Terme

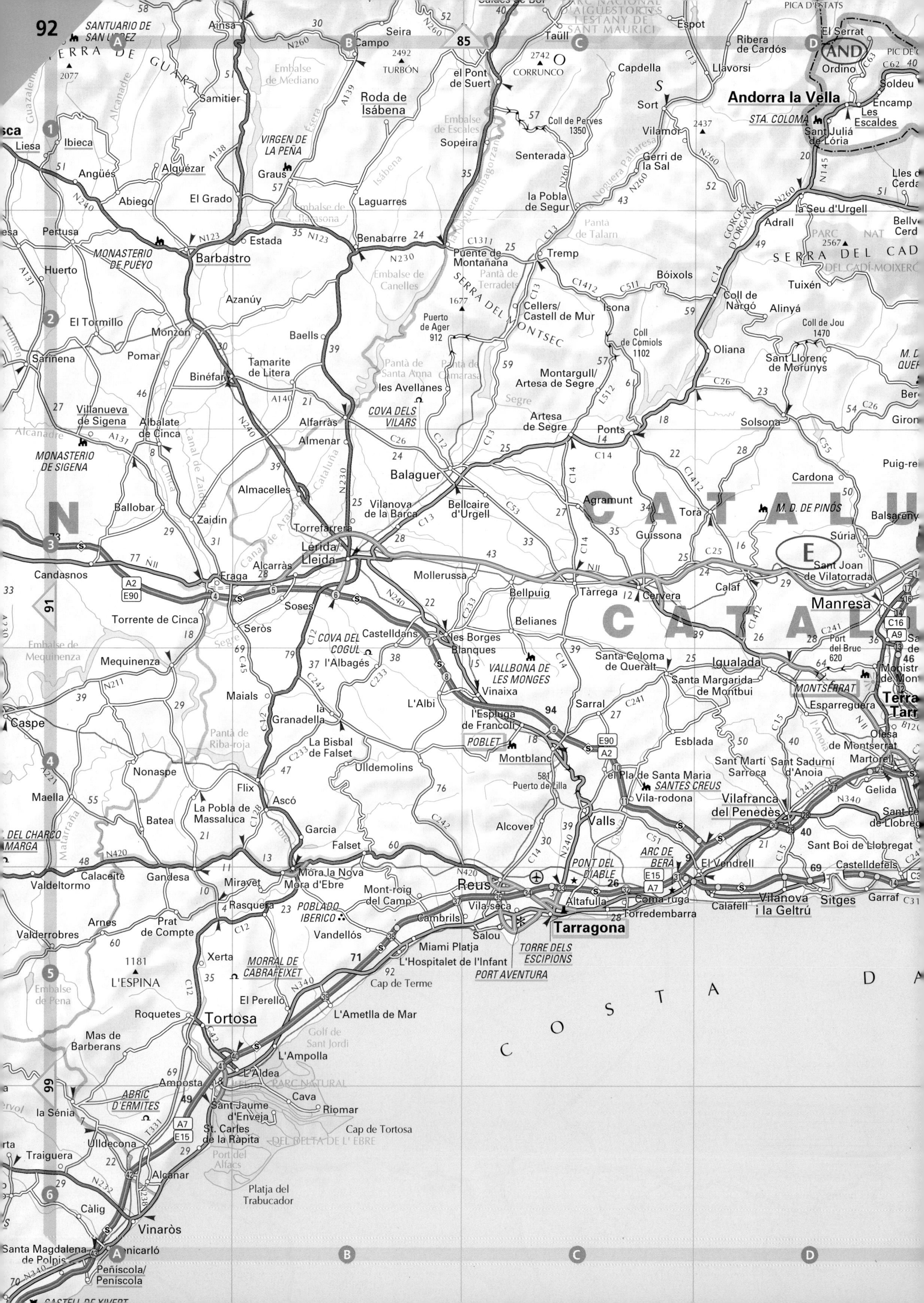

SANTUARIO DE SAN URBEZ
SIERRA DE GUARA
Aínsa
Campo
Seira
Roda de Isábena
TURBÓN
el Pont de Suert
CORRUNCO
PARC NACIONAL D'AIGÜESTORTES I ESTANY DE SANT MAURICI
Taüll
Espot
Capdella
Ribera de Cardós
Llavorsí
PICA D'ESTATS
El Serrat
AND
Ordino
Andorra la Vella
Soldeu
Encamp
Les Escaldes
STA. COLOMA
Sant Julià de Lòria
Sort
Vilamor
Gerri de la Sal
Coll de Perves 1350
Senterada
Sopeira
Embalse de Escales
Samitier
Liesa
Ibieca
Angüés
Alquézar
VIRGEN DE LA PEÑA
Graus
Embalse de Mediano
Abiego
El Grado
Laguarres
Embalse de Barasona
la Pobla de Segur
Pantà de Talarn
la Seu d'Urgell
Adrall
GORGES D'ORGANYÀ
PARC NAT
SERRA DEL CADÍ
DEL CADÍ-MOIXERÓ
Lles de Cerdanya
Bellver de Cerdanya
Pertusa
Huerto
MONASTERIO DE PUEYO
Barbastro
Estada
Benabarre
Puente de Montañana
Tremp
Pantà de Terradets
Embalse de Canelles
SERRA DEL MONTSEC
Cellers/Castell de Mur
Isona
Bóixols
Coll de Nargó
Alinyà
Tuixén
Azanúy
El Tormillo
Monzón
Sariñena
Pomar
Baells
Puerto de Ager 912
Coll de Comiols 1102
Oliana
Coll de Jou 1470
Sant Llorenç de Morunys
Tamarite de Litera
Binéfar
Pantà de Santa Anna
Pantà de Camarasa
les Avellanes
Montargull/Artesa de Segre
Villanueva de Sigena
Albalate de Cinca
MONASTERIO DE SIGENA
Alfarràs
COVA DELS VILARS
Artesa de Segre
Ponts
Solsona
Almenar
Balaguer
Cardona
Puig-reig
Almacelles
Vilanova de la Barca
Bellcaire d'Urgell
Agramunt
Torà
M. D. DE PINÓS
Ballobar
Zaidín
Torrefarrera
Guissona
Balsareny
Súria
CATALUÑA
CATALUNYA
Candasnos
Fraga
Alcarràs
Lérida/Lleida
Mollerussa
Cervera
Calaf
Sant Joan de Vilatorrada
Manresa
Tàrrega
Bellpuig
Torrente de Cinca
Soses
Serós
Belianes
COVA DEL COGUL
Castelldans
les Borges Blanques
l'Albagés
Embalse de Mequinenza
Mequinenza
VALLBONA DE LES MONGES
Santa Coloma de Queralt
Igualada
Santa Margarida de Montbui
MONTSERRAT
Port del Bruc 620
Maials
Vinaixa
L'Albi
Sarral
Esparreguera
Caspe
la Granadella
l'Espluga de Francolí
POBLET
Montblanc
Esblada
Olesa de Montserrat
Martorell
Pantà de Riba-roja
La Bisbal de Falset
Ulldemolins
Puerto de Lilla 581
el Pla de Santa Maria
SANTES CREUS
Vila-rodona
Sant Martí Sarroca
Sant Sadurní d'Anoia
Nonaspe
Flix
Maella
Ascó
La Pobla de Massaluca
Batea
Garcia
Falset
Valls
Alcover
Vilafranca del Penedès
Gelida
Sant Feliu de Llobregat
Sant Boi de Llobregat
Castelldefels
DEL CHARCO MARGA
Calaceite
Gandesa
Miravet
Móra la Nova
Móra d'Ebre
Mont-roig del Camp
Reus
PONT DEL DIABLE
ARC DE BERÀ
El Vendrell
Valdeltormo
Rasquera
POBLADO IBERICO
Cambrils
Vila-seca
Altafulla
Coma-ruga
Torredembarra
Calafell
Vilanova i la Geltrú
Sitges
Garraf
Arnes
Prat de Compte
Vandellós
Salou
Tarragona
Valderrobres
Xerta
Miami Platja
L'Hospitalet de l'Infant
TORRE DELS ESCIPIONS
PORT AVENTURA
1181
L'ESPINA
MORRAL DE CABRAFEIXET
Cap de Terme
Embalse de Pena
El Perelló
L'Ametlla de Mar
COSTA DA
Roquetes
Tortosa
Mas de Barberans
Golf de Sant Jordi
L'Ampolla
Amposta
L'Aldea
PARC NATURAL DEL DELTA DE L'EBRE
ABRIC D'ERMITES
Cava
Riomar
la Sénia
Sant Jaume d'Enveja
Cap de Tortosa
Ulldecona
St. Carles de la Ràpita
Traiguera
Port del Alfacs
Alcanar
Platja del Trabucador
Càlig
Vinaròs
Santa Magdalena de Polpis
Benicarló
Peñíscola/Peníscola
CASTELL DE XIVERT

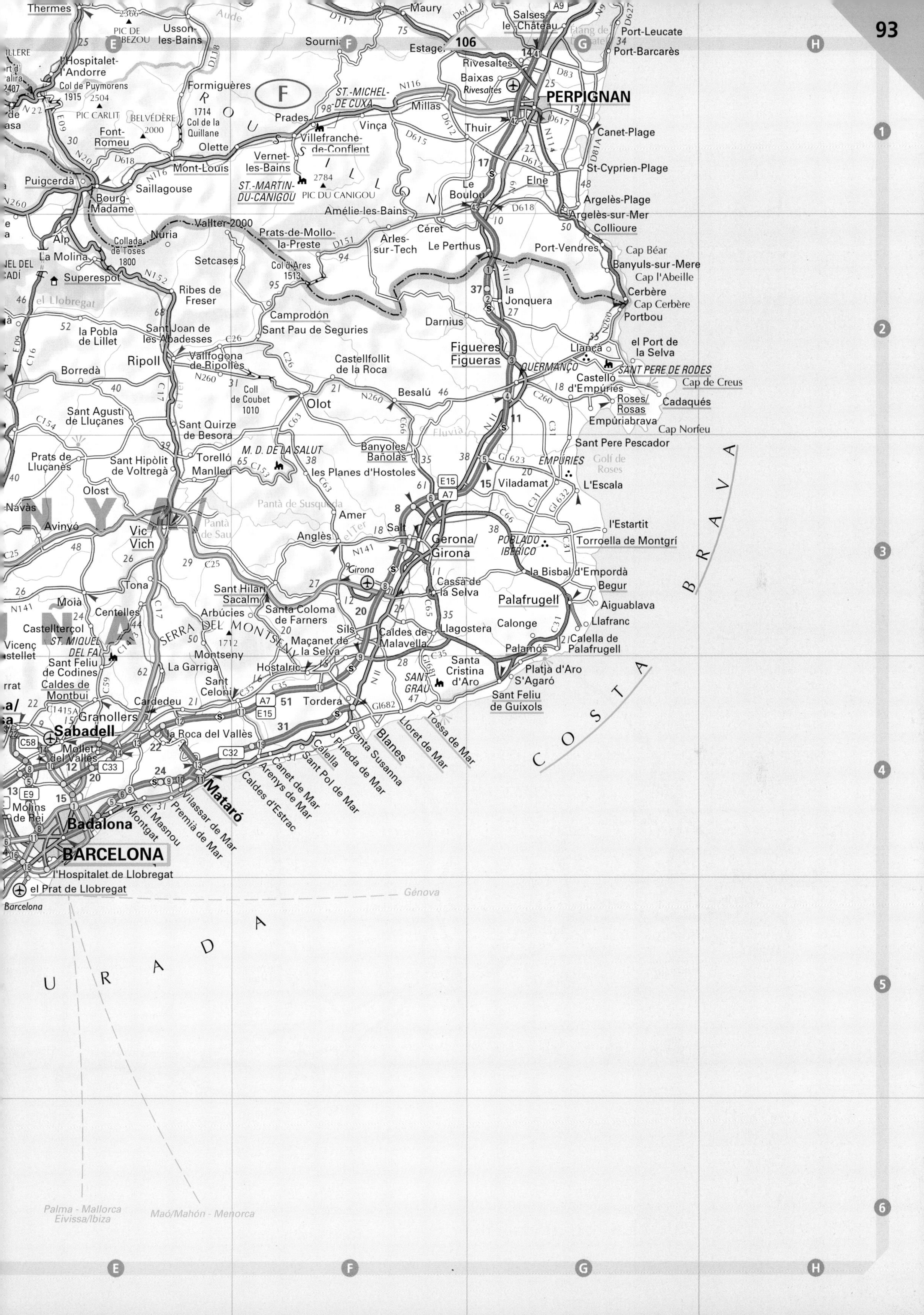
PERPIGNAN
Port-Leucate
Port-Barcarès
Salses-le-Château
Rivesaltes
Estagel
Maury
Sournia
Usson-les-Bains
Thermes
Formiguères
l'Hospitalet-près-l'Andorre
Col de Puymorens
Prades
Millas
Thuir
Canet-Plage
St-Cyprien-Plage
Elne
Argelès-Plage
Argelès-sur-Mer
Collioure
Port-Vendres
Banyuls-sur-Mere
Cerbère
Portbou
Le Boulou
Le Perthus
Céret
Arles-sur-Tech
Amélie-les-Bains
Prats-de-Mollo-la-Preste
Vernet-les-Bains
Villefranche-de-Conflent
Vinça
Olette
Mont-Louis
Font-Romeu
Saillagouse
Puigcerdà
Bourg-Madame
ROUSSILLON
ST.-MICHEL-DE CUXA
ST.-MARTIN-DU-CANIGOU
PIC DU CANIGOU
Núria
La Molina
Alp
Superespot
Setcases
Camprodón
Sant Pau de Seguries
Ribes de Freser
Sant Joan de les Abadesses
la Pobla de Lillet
Ripoll
Borredà
Vallfogona de Ripollès
Olot
Castellfollit de la Roca
Besalú
Darnius
la Jonquera
Figueres/Figueras
Llançà
el Port de la Selva
SANT PERE DE RODES
Cap de Creus
Cadaqués
Castelló d'Empúries
Roses/Rosas
Empúriabrava
Sant Pere Pescador
EMPÚRIES
L'Escala
Viladamat
Banyoles/Bañolas
les Planes d'Hostoles
M. D. DE LA SALUT
Sant Quirze de Besora
Sant Agustí de Lluçanes
Prats de Lluçanès
Sant Hipòlit de Voltregà
Torelló
Manlleu
Olost
Vic/Vich
Tona
Amer
Anglès
Salt
Gerona/Girona
l'Estartit
Torroella de Montgrí
la Bisbal d'Empordà
Begur
Aiguablava
Llafranc
Calella de Palafrugell
Palafrugell
Calonge
Palamós
Platja d'Aro
S'Agaró
Sant Feliu de Guíxols
Santa Cristina d'Aro
Llagostera
Cassà de la Selva
Caldes de Malavella
Sils
Maçanet de la Selva
Hostalric
Tordera
Blanes
Lloret de Mar
Tossa de Mar
Santa Coloma de Farners
Sant Hilari Sacalm
Arbúcies
Montseny
SERRA DEL MONTSENY
La Garriga
Sant Celoni
Cardedeu
Granollers
Sabadell
Mollet del Vallès
la Roca del Vallès
Centelles
Moià
Castellterçol
ST. MIQUEL DEL FAI
Sant Feliu de Codines
Caldes de Montbui
Mataró
Santa Susanna
Pineda de Mar
Calella
Sant Pol de Mar
Canet de Mar
Arenys de Mar
Caldes d'Estrac
Vilassar de Mar
Premià de Mar
El Masnou
Montgat
Badalona
BARCELONA
l'Hospitalet de Llobregat
el Prat de Llobregat
Molins de Rei
COSTA BRAVA
Gènova
Palma - Mallorca
Eivissa/Ibiza
Maó/Mahón - Menorca

A   B   C   D

COSTA AZUL

SETÚBAL

BEJA

FARO

Nossa Senhora do Cabo
Cabo Espichel
Vila Nogue... de Azeitão
Vila Fresca de Azeitão
Sesimbra
Portinho da Arrábida
Tróia
CETÓBRIGA
Setúbal
Palme...
Quinta da Bacalhó
Poceirão
Pegões
Vendas Novas
S. Geraldo
Ciborro
Arraiolos
Marateca
Cabrela
Montemor o-Novo
Convento de Espinheiro
Praias-Sado
São Romão
Santiago do Escoural
Évora
Comporta
Montalvo
São Cristóvão
Casa Branca
Alcácer do Sal
Alcáçovas
Viana do Alentejo
São M...
Casa Branca
Melides
Grândola
São Romão
Torrão
Santo André
Lagoa de Santo André
São Francisco da Serra
Barragem de Vale de Gaio
Alvito
SERRA
Cabo de Sines
Sines
Santiago do Cacém
Azinheira dos Barros
Santa Margarida do Sado
Odivelas
Barragem de Odivelas
Cuba
Vidig...
Porto Covo
Abela
Ferreira do Alentejo
Matos
Pedrõg...
São Domingos
Alvalade
Beringel
Ermidas-Aldeia
Cercal
Bicos
Ervidel
Santa Vitória
Beja
Baleizão
Vila Nova de Milfontes
Derreada
Aljustrel
Carregueiro
Trindade
Salvada
São Luis
Torre Vã
Albernoa
Serp...
Almograve
Santa Luzia
Garvão
Entradas
Vale de Açor
Odemira
Telheiro
São Martinho das Amoreiras
Ourique
Castro Verde
Zambujeira do Mar
Barragem do Monte da Rocha
CASTRO DA COLA
São Marcos da Ataboeira
Alcaria Ruiva
Mértola
São Teotónio
Barragem de Santa Clara
Santana da Serra
São João dos Caldeireiros
Odeceixe
Santa Clara a-Velha
Gomes Aires
Semblana
Vale do P...
Praia de Monte Clérigo
Rogil
Nave Redonda
Almodôvar
São Miguel do Pinheiro
Santa An... de Camba...
Arrifana
Aljezur
SERRA DE MONCHIQUE
São Marcos da Serra
São Pedro de Solis
Alfambras
TÓIA
Monchique
Dogueno
Espírito Santo
Marmelete
Barragem da Bravura
São Barnabé
Ameixial
Carrapateira
Bordeira
Barragem do Funcho
Martim Longo
Bensafrim
Barragem de Arade
São Bartolomeu de Messines
Pereiro
Cachopo
Castelejo
Vila do Bispo
Silves
Messines de Baixo
S. Sil... de Gu...
Cabo São Vicente
Salema
Mexilhoeira Grande
Salir
Barranco do Velho
Odeleite
Ponta de Sagres
Burgau
Lagos
Alvor
Lagoa
Portimão
Paderne
Querença
Portos dos Fusos
Sagres
Vau
Carvoeiro
Loulé
São Brás de Alportel
PONTA DA PIEDADE
PONTAL
Armação de Pera
Albufeira
Vilamoura
Quarteira
Vale de Lobos
Estoi
MILREU
Moncarapacho
Tavira
Monte Gordo
Vila Real de Santo António
Ayamo...
Faro
Olhão
Fuzeta
Cabo de Santa Maria
Castro-Marim

SERRA DO CALDEIRÃO

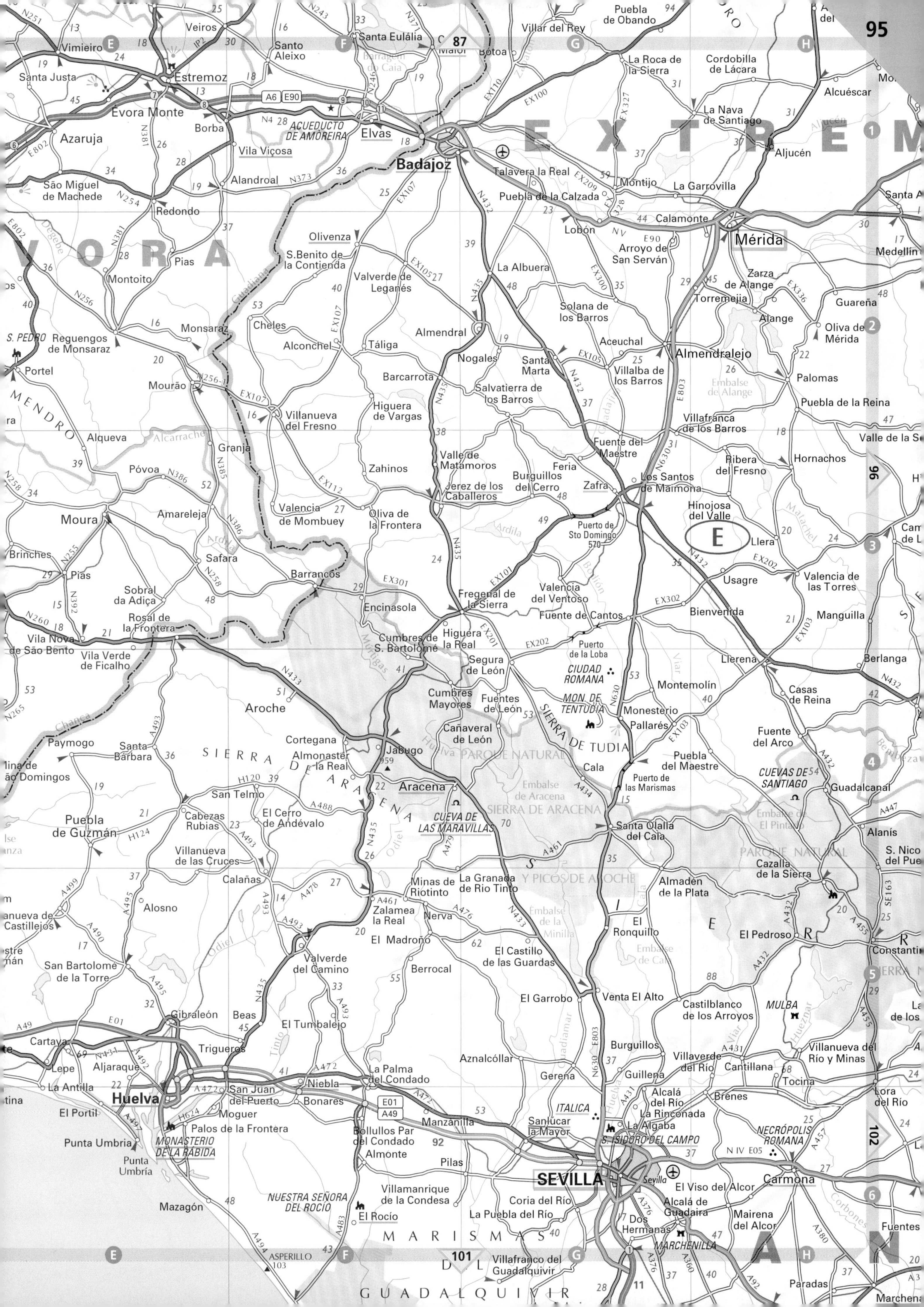
Vimieiro
Veiros
Santa Justa
Estremoz
Evora Monte
Borba
Azaruja
Santo Aleixo
Santa Eulália
Barragem do Caia
Botoa
Villar del Rey
Puebla de Obando
La Roca de la Sierra
Cordobilla de Lácara
Alcuéscar
La Nava de Santiago
Aljucén
ACUEDUCTO DE AMOREIRA
Elvas
Badajoz
Vila Viçosa
Alandroal
São Miguel de Machede
Redondo
Talavera la Real
Montijo
La Garrovilla
Puebla de la Calzada
Lobón
Calamonte
Mérida
Arroyo de San Serván
Medellín
EXTREM
ÉVORA
Pias
Montoito
Olivenza
S.Benito de la Contienda
Valverde de Leganés
La Albuera
Zarza de Alange
Torremejía
Alange
Guareña
Oliva de Mérida
Solana de los Barros
Aceuchal
Almendralejo
Reguengos de Monsaraz
Monsaraz
S. PEDRO
Portel
Cheles
Alconchel
Táliga
Almendral
Nogales
Santa Marta
Villalba de los Barros
Palomas
Embalse de Alange
Puebla de la Reina
Mourão
Barcarrota
Salvatierra de los Barros
Villanueva del Fresno
Higuera de Vargas
Villafranca de los Barros
Valle de la S
ALMENDRO
Alqueva
Alcarrache
Granja
Fuente del Maestre
Ribera del Fresno
Hornachos
Póvoa
Zahinos
Valle de Matamoros
Feria
Burguillos del Cerro
Zafra
Los Santos de Maimona
Jerez de los Caballeros
Moura
Amareleja
Valencia de Mombuey
Oliva de la Frontera
Hinojosa del Valle
Puerto de Sto Domingo 570
Llera
Brinches
Safara
Ardila
Pias
Barrancos
Sobral da Adiça
Rosal de la Frontera
Encinasola
Fregenal de la Sierra
Valencia del Ventoso
Usagre
Valencia de las Torres
Fuente de Cantos
Bienvenida
Manguilla
Vila Nova de São Bento
Vila Verde de Ficalho
Cumbres de S. Bartolomé
Higuera la Real
Segura de León
Puerto de la Loba
CIUDAD ROMANA
Llerena
Berlanga
Aroche
Cumbres Mayores
Fuentes de León
MON. DE TENTUDÍA
SIERRA DE TUDIA
Montemolín
Monesterio
Pallarés
Casas de Reina
Fuente del Arco
Paymogo
Santa Bárbara
Cortegana
Jabugo
Almonaster la Real
Cañaveral de León
Cala
Puebla del Maestre
CUEVAS DE SANTIAGO
Guadalcanal
Mina de São Domingos
SIERRA DE ARACENA
PARQUE NATURAL
San Telmo
Aracena
Embalse de Aracena
Puerto de las Marismas
Puebla de Guzmán
Cabezas Rubias
El Cerro de Andévalo
CUEVA DE LAS MARAVILLAS
Santa Olalla del Cala
Alanís
Villanueva de las Cruces
Calañas
Minas de Riotinto
La Granada de Rio Tinto
Y PICOS DE AROCHE
Almadén de la Plata
Cazalla de la Sierra
S. Nico del Pue
Alosno
Zalamea la Real
Nerva
El Ronquillo
El Pedroso
Constantina
Villanueva de Castillejos
El Madroño
Embalse de la Minilla
El Castillo de las Guardas
Valverde del Camino
Berrocal
San Bartolomé de la Torre
Embalse de Cala
El Garrobo
Venta El Alto
Castilblanco de los Arroyos
MULBA
Gibraleón
Beas
El Tumbalejo
Cartaya
Lepe
Aljaraque
Trigueros
Aznalcóllar
Burguillos
Villaverde del Río
Cantillana
Villanueva del Río y Minas
La Antilla
Huelva
San Juan del Puerto
Niebla
La Palma del Condado
Gerena
Guillena
Tocina
Lora del Río
El Portil
Moguer
Bonares
ITALICA
Alcalá del Río
Brenes
La Rinconada
La Algaba
Punta Umbría
Palos de la Frontera
MONASTERIO DE LA RÁBIDA
Bollullos Par del Condado
Manzanilla
Sanlúcar la Mayor
S. ISIDORO DEL CAMPO
NECRÓPOLIS ROMANA
Almonte
Pilas
SEVILLA
El Viso del Alcor
Carmona
Mazagón
NUESTRA SEÑORA DEL ROCÍO
El Rocío
Villamanrique de la Condesa
Coria del Río
La Puebla del Río
Alcalá de Guadaira
Mairena del Alcor
Dos Hermanas
MARCHENILLA
Fuentes
MARISMAS
ASPERILLO 103
Villafranco del Guadalquivir
GUADALQUIVIR
Paradas
Marchena
ANDALUCÍA
87
96
101
102

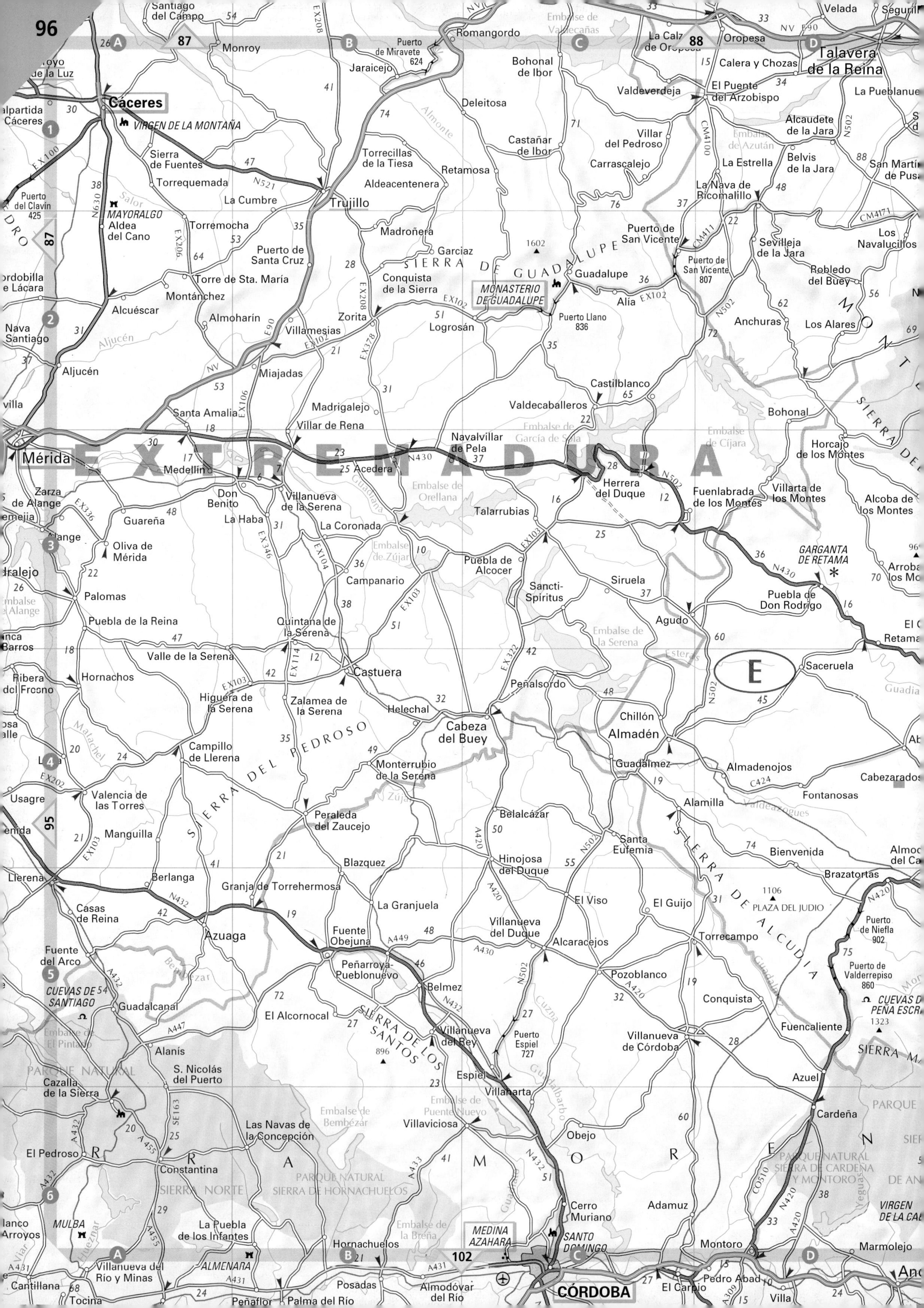
Santiago del Campo
87
Monroy
Puerto de Miravete 624
Jaraicejo
Romangordo
Embalse de Valdecañas
La Calzada de Oropesa
88
Oropesa
Velada
Segurilla
Talavera de la Reina
Arroyo de la Luz
Cáceres
Malpartida de Cáceres
VIRGEN DE LA MONTAÑA
Bohonal de Ibor
Valdeverdeja
El Puente del Arzobispo
Calera y Chozas
La Pueblanueva
Deleitosa
Almonte
Castañar de Ibor
Villar del Pedroso
Carrascalejo
Alcaudete de la Jara
Embalse de Azután
Belvis de la Jara
San Martín de Pusa
La Estrella
Sierra de Fuentes
Torrecillas de la Tiesa
Retamosa
Torrequemada
Aldeacentenera
La Nava de Ricomalillo
Puerto del Clavín 425
La Cumbre
Trujillo
Salor
MAYORALGO
Aldea del Cano
Torremocha
Madroñera
Puerto de San Vicente
Sevilleja de la Jara
Los Navalucillos
Puerto de Santa Cruz
Garciaz
SIERRA DE GUADALUPE
1602
Puerto de San Vicente 807
Robledo del Buey
Cordobilla de Lácara
Torre de Sta. María
Montánchez
Conquista de la Sierra
MONASTERIO DE GUADALUPE
Guadalupe
Alía
Alcuéscar
Zorita
Logrosán
Puerto Llano 836
Anchuras
Los Alares
Nava de Santiago
Almoharín
Villamesías
Aljucén
Miajadas
Castilblanco
Valdecaballeros
Madrigalejo
Santa Amalia
Villar de Rena
Bohonal
Embalse de García de Sola
Embalse de Cíjara
Horcajo de los Montes
Mérida
EXTREMADURA
Medellín
Acedera
Navalvillar de Pela
Herrera del Duque
Fuenlabrada de los Montes
Villarta de los Montes
Alcoba de los Montes
Zarza de Alange
Don Benito
Villanueva de la Serena
Embalse de Orellana
Talarrubias
Guadiana
Guareña
La Haba
La Coronada
Alange
Oliva de Mérida
Embalse de Zújar
Puebla de Alcocer
Siruela
GARGANTA DE RETAMA
Almendralejo
Campanario
Sancti-Spiritus
Puebla de Don Rodrigo
Arroba de los Montes
Palomas
Embalse de Alange
Agudo
Puebla de la Reina
Quintana de la Serena
Embalse de la Serena
Villafranca de los Barros
Valle de la Serena
Castuera
E
Esteras
Saceruela
Ribera del Fresno
Hornachos
Higuera de la Serena
Zalamea de la Serena
Peñalsordo
Guadiana
Helechal
Chillón
Cabeza del Buey
Almadén
Malachel
Campillo de Llerena
SIERRA DEL PEDROSO
Monterrubio de la Serena
Guadalmez
Almadenojos
Cabezarados
Usagre
Valencia de las Torres
Zújar
Fontanosas
95
Alamilla
Valdeazogues
Peraleda del Zaucejo
Belalcázar
Manguilla
Santa Eufemia
SIERRA DE ALCUDIA
Bienvenida
Llerena
Berlanga
Blazquez
Hinojosa del Duque
Brazatortas
Granja de Torrehermosa
1106
PLAZA DEL JUDIO
El Viso
Casas de Reina
La Granjuela
El Guijo
Puerto de Niefla 902
Azuaga
Fuente Obejuna
Villanueva del Duque
Alcaracejos
Torrecampo
Fuente del Arco
Peñarroya-Pueblonuevo
Puerto de Valderrepiso 860
Bembézar
Pozoblanco
CUEVAS DE SANTIAGO
Belmez
Guadalcanal
El Alcornocal
SIERRA DE LOS SANTOS
Conquista
CUEVAS DE PEÑA ESCRITA
Embalse de El Pintado
Villanueva del Rey
Fuencaliente
1323
Alanís
896
Puerto Espiel 727
Villanueva de Córdoba
PARQUE NATURAL
SIERRA MADRONA
S. Nicolás del Puerto
Cazalla de la Sierra
Espiel
Azuel
Villaharta
Embalse de Puente Nuevo
Embalse de Bembézar
Cardeña
Las Navas de la Concepción
Villaviciosa
Obejo
Guadalbarbo
El Pedroso
SIERRA MORENA
Constantina
PARQUE NATURAL SIERRA DE HORNACHUELOS
SIERRA NORTE
PARQUE NATURAL SIERRA DE CARDEÑA Y MONTORO
Cerro Muriano
Adamuz
VIRGEN DE LA CABEZA
Blanco Arroyos
MULBA
La Puebla de los Infantes
Embalse de la Breña
MEDINA AZAHARA
SANTO DOMINGO
Hornachuelos
Montoro
Marmolejo
102
ALMENARA
Villanueva del Río y Minas
Cantillana
Tocina
Posadas
Almodóvar del Río
Peñaflor
Palma del Río
CÓRDOBA
El Carpio
Pedro Abad
Villa del Río
Andújar

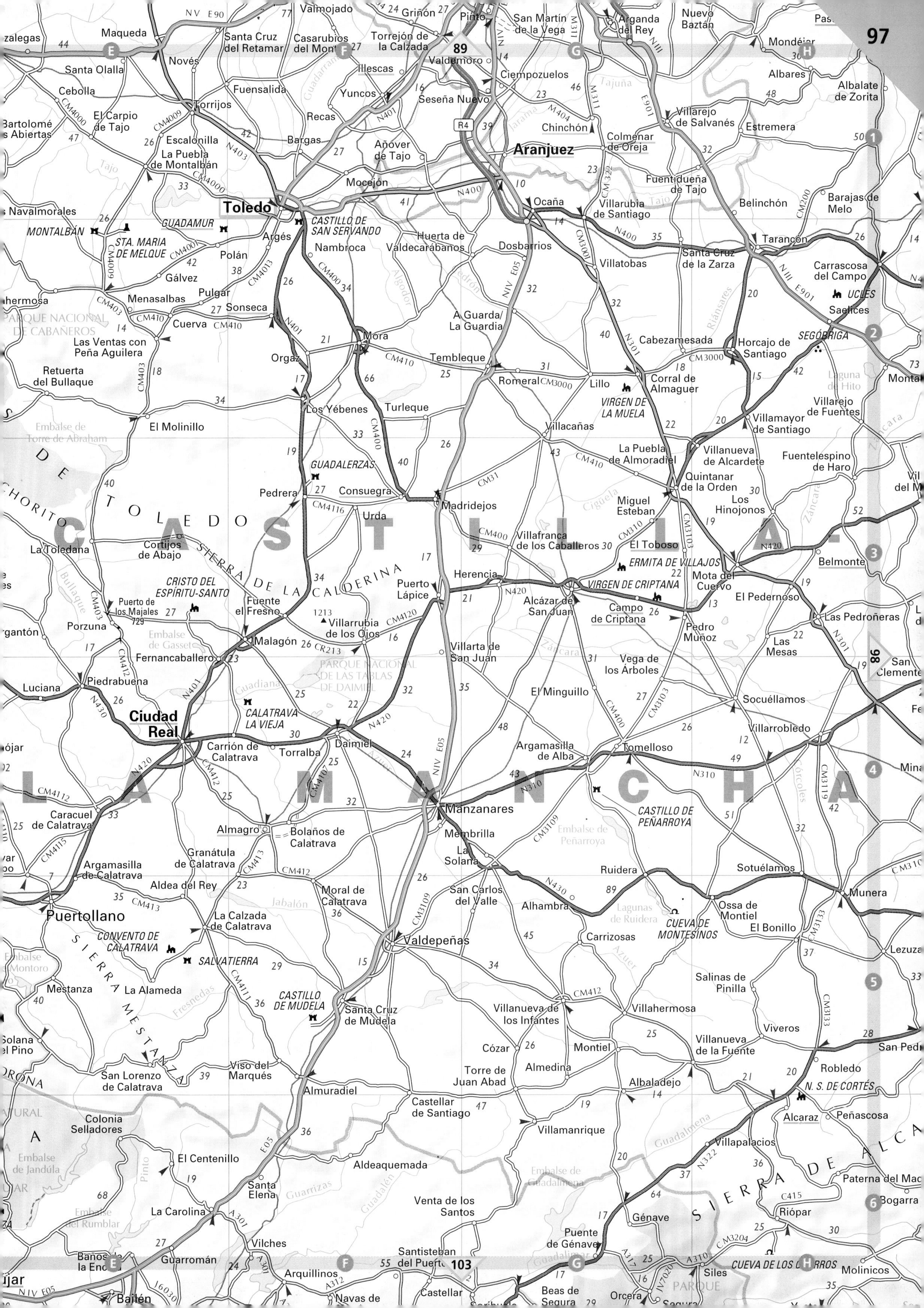
Maqueda
Valmojado
Griñón
Pinto
San Martín de la Vega
Arganda del Rey
Nuevo Baztán
Mondéjar
Santa Cruz del Retamar
Casarubios del Monte
Torrejón de la Calzada
89
Valdemoro
Novés
Santa Olalla
Illescas
Ciempozuelos
Albares
Albalate de Zorita
Cebolla
Fuensalida
Yuncos
Seseña Nuevo
Torrijos
El Carpio de Tajo
Recas
Villarejo de Salvanés
Chinchón
Estremera
Escalonilla
Bargas
Añover de Tajo
Aranjuez
Colmenar de Oreja
La Puebla de Montalbán
Fuentidueña de Tajo
Mocejón
Toledo
Ocaña
Villarubia de Santiago
Belinchón
Barajas de Melo
Navalmorales
GUADAMUR
CASTILLO DE SAN SERVANDO
MONTALBÁN
STA. MARIA DE MELQUE
Argés
Nambroca
Huerta de Valdecarábanos
Dosbarrios
Tarancón
Polán
Santa Cruz de la Zarza
Villatobas
Carrascosa del Campo
Gálvez
UCLES
Menasalbas
Pulgar
Saelices
Sonseca
PARQUE NACIONAL DE CABAÑEROS
Cuerva
A Guarda/ La Guardia
Mora
Las Ventas con Peña Aguilera
Orgaz
Cabezamesada
Horcajo de Santiago
SEGÓBRIGA
Tembleque
Retuerta del Bullaque
Romeral
Lillo
Corral de Almaguer
Villarejo de Fuentes
Los Yébenes
Turleque
VIRGEN DE LA MUELA
El Molinillo
Embalse de Torre de Abraham
Villacañas
Villamayor de Santiago
La Puebla de Almoradiel
Villanueva de Alcardete
Fuentelespino de Haro
GUADALERZAS
Pedrera
Consuegra
Madridejos
Quintanar de la Orden
Miguel Esteban
Los Hinojonos
Urda
MONTES DE TOLEDO
Cortijos de Abajo
La Toledana
CASTILLA-LA MANCHA
Villafranca de los Caballeros
El Toboso
Belmonte
ERMITA DE VILLAJOS
SIERRA DE LA CALDERINA
CRISTO DEL ESPÍRITU-SANTO
Puerto Lápice
Herencia
Mota del Cuervo
VIRGEN DE CRIPTANA
El Pedernoso
Alcázar de San Juan
Puerto de los Majales
Fuente el Fresno
Porzuna
1213
Villarrubia de los Ojos
Campo de Criptana
Las Pedroñeras
Pedro Muñoz
Embalse de Gasset
Malagón
Las Mesas
Fernancaballero
Villarta de San Juan
Vega de los Árboles
San Clemente
PARQUE NACIONAL DE LAS TABLAS DE DAIMIEL
Piedrabuena
Luciana
El Minguillo
Socuéllamos
CALATRAVA LA VIEJA
Ciudad Real
Villarrobledo
Daimiel
Carrión de Calatrava
Torralba
Argamasilla de Alba
Tomelloso
CASTILLO DE PEÑARROYA
Caracuel de Calatrava
Manzanares
Almagro
Bolaños de Calatrava
Membrilla
Embalse de Peñarroya
Granátula de Calatrava
Argamasilla de Calatrava
La Solana
Ruidera
Sotuélamos
Munera
Aldea del Rey
Moral de Calatrava
San Carlos del Valle
Ossa de Montiel
Puertollano
Alhambra
Lagunas de Ruidera
El Bonillo
La Calzada de Calatrava
CUEVA DE MONTESINOS
CONVENTO DE CALATRAVA
Carrizosas
SIERRA MESTANZA
Valdepeñas
Lezuza
SALVATIERRA
Salinas de Pinilla
Mestanza
La Alameda
CASTILLO DE MUDELA
Santa Cruz de Mudela
Villanueva de los Infantes
Villahermosa
Viveros
Cózar
Montiel
Villanueva de la Fuente
San Pedro
Solana del Pino
Torre de Juan Abad
Almedina
Robledo
San Lorenzo de Calatrava
Viso del Marqués
Albaladejo
N. S. DE CORTÉS
Almuradiel
Castellar de Santiago
Alcaraz
Peñascosa
Colonia Selladores
Villamanrique
Villapalacios
Embalse de Jándula
El Centenillo
Aldeaquemada
SIERRA DE ALCARAZ
Paterna del Madera
Santa Elena
Embalse de Guadalmena
Bogarra
La Carolina
Venta de los Santos
Génave
Riópar
Embalse del Rumblar
Vilches
Puente de Génave
Baños de la Encina
Guarromán
Santisteban del Puerto
103
CUEVA DE LOS CHORROS
Arquillinos
Siles
Molinicos
Andújar
Castellar
Beas de Segura
Orcera
Bailén
Navas de

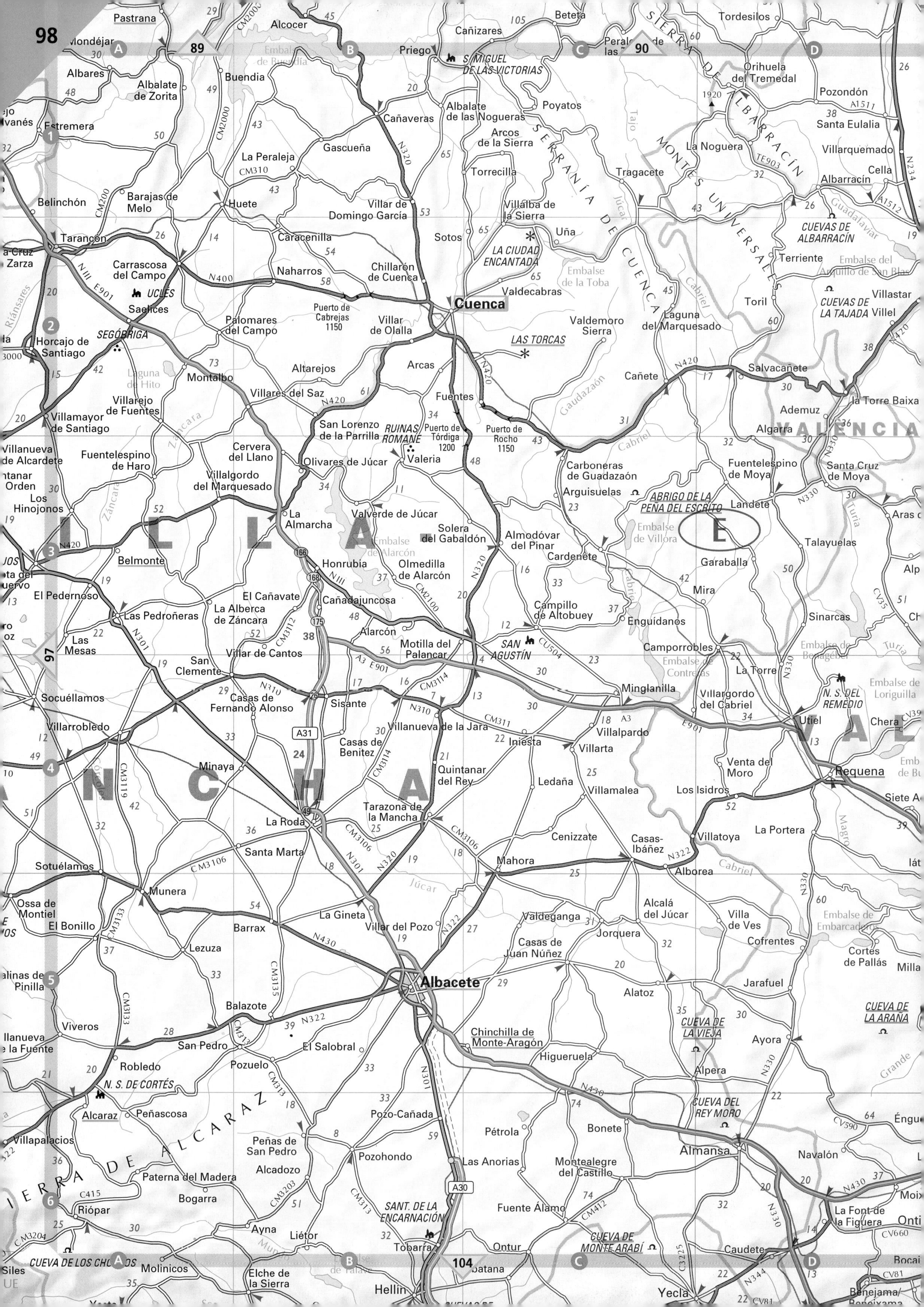
89
90
97
104
Pastrana
Alcocer
Beteta
Tordesilos
Mondéjar
Priego
Cañizares
S. MIGUEL DE LAS VICTORIAS
SIERRA DE ALBARRACÍN
Orihuela del Tremedal
Albares
Albalate de Zorita
Buendia
Albalate de las Nogueras
Poyatos
Pozondón
Estremera
Cañaveras
Arcos de la Sierra
SERRANÍA DE CUENCA
MONTES UNIVERSALES
Santa Eulalia
Gascueña
La Noguera
Villarquemado
La Peraleja
Torrecilla
Tragacete
Albarracín
Cella
Belinchón
Barajas de Melo
Huete
Villar de Domingo García
Villalba de la Sierra
CUEVAS DE ALBARRACÍN
Tarancón
Caracenilla
Sotos
Uña
LA CIUDAD ENCANTADA
Terriente
Zarza
Carrascosa del Campo
Naharros
Chillarón de Cuenca
Embalse de la Toba
UCLÉS
Saelices
Valdecabras
Cuenca
CUEVAS DE LA TAJADA
Villastar
Villel
Toril
SEGÓBRIGA
Horcajo de Santiago
Palomares del Campo
Puerto de Cabrejas 1150
Villar de Olalla
Valdemoro Sierra
Laguna del Marquesado
LAS TORCAS
Laguna del Hito
Montalbo
Altarejos
Arcas
Cañete
Salvacañete
Villarejo de Fuentes
Villares del Saz
Fuentes
Ademuz
La Torre Baixa
Villamayor de Santiago
San Lorenzo de la Parrilla
RUINAS ROMANE
Puerto de Tórdiga 1200
Puerto de Rocho 1150
Algarra
VALENCIA
Villanueva de Alcardete
Fuentelespino de Haro
Cervera del Llano
Olivares de Júcar
Valeria
Carboneras de Guadazaón
Fuentelespino de Moya
Santa Cruz de Moya
Orden
Los Hinojosos
Villalgordo del Marquesado
Arguisuelas
ABRIGO DE LA PEÑA DEL ESCRITO
Landete
La Almarcha
Valverde de Júcar
Solera del Gabaldón
Almodóvar del Pinar
Embalse de Villora
Aras
Embalse de Alarcón
Cardenete
Talayuelas
Belmonte
Honrubia
Olmedilla de Alarcón
Garaballa
El Pedernoso
El Cañavate
Cañadajuncosa
Campillo de Altobuey
Mira
Las Pedroñeras
La Alberca de Záncara
Enguídanos
Sinarcas
Las Mesas
Alarcón
Motilla del Palancar
SAN AGUSTÍN
Camporrobles
Embalse de Contreras
Embalse de Benagéber
San Clemente
Villar de Cantos
La Torre
Embalse de Loriguilla
Socuéllamos
Casas de Fernando Alonso
Sisante
Minglanilla
Villargordo del Cabriel
N. S. DEL REMEDIO
Villarrobledo
Villanueva de la Jara
Villalpardo
Utiel
Chera
Casas de Benitez
Iniesta
Villarta
Minaya
Quintanar del Rey
Ledaña
Venta del Moro
Requena
Villamalea
Los Isidros
Siete A
La Roda
Tarazona de la Mancha
Cenizzate
Casas-Ibáñez
Villatoya
La Portera
Santa Marta
Sotuélamos
Munera
Mahora
Alborea
Ossa de Montiel
Alcalá del Júcar
Villa de Ves
El Bonillo
Barrax
La Gineta
Villar del Pozo
Valdeganga
Jorquera
Cofrentes
Embalse de Embarcaderos
Lezuza
Casas de Juan Núñez
Cortes de Pallás
Pinilla
Albacete
Jarafuel
Balazote
Alatoz
CUEVA DE LA ARAÑA
Viveros
El Salobral
Chinchilla de Monte-Aragón
CUEVA DE LA VIEJA
Ayora
San Pedro
Pozuelo
Higueruela
Robledo
Alpera
N. S. DE CORTÉS
CUEVA DEL REY MORO
Alcaraz
Peñascosa
SIERRA DE ALCARAZ
Pozo-Cañada
Pétrola
Bonete
Villapalacios
Peñas de San Pedro
Pozohondo
Las Anorias
Montealegre del Castillo
Almansa
Navalón
Paterna del Madera
Alcadozo
Bogarra
Riópar
Ayna
SANT. DE LA ENCARNACIÓN
Fuente Álamo
La Font de la Figuera
Liétor
CUEVA DE MONTE ARABÍ
Tobarra
Ontur
Caudete
CUEVA DE LOS CHORROS
Siles
Molinicos
Elche de la Sierra
Hellín
Yecla
Benejama/Beneixama
A3
A30
A31
N320
N400
N420
N301
N310
N322
N330
N430
N344
E901
N III
Cabriel
Júcar
Záncara
Guadazaón
Turia
Magro
Riánsares

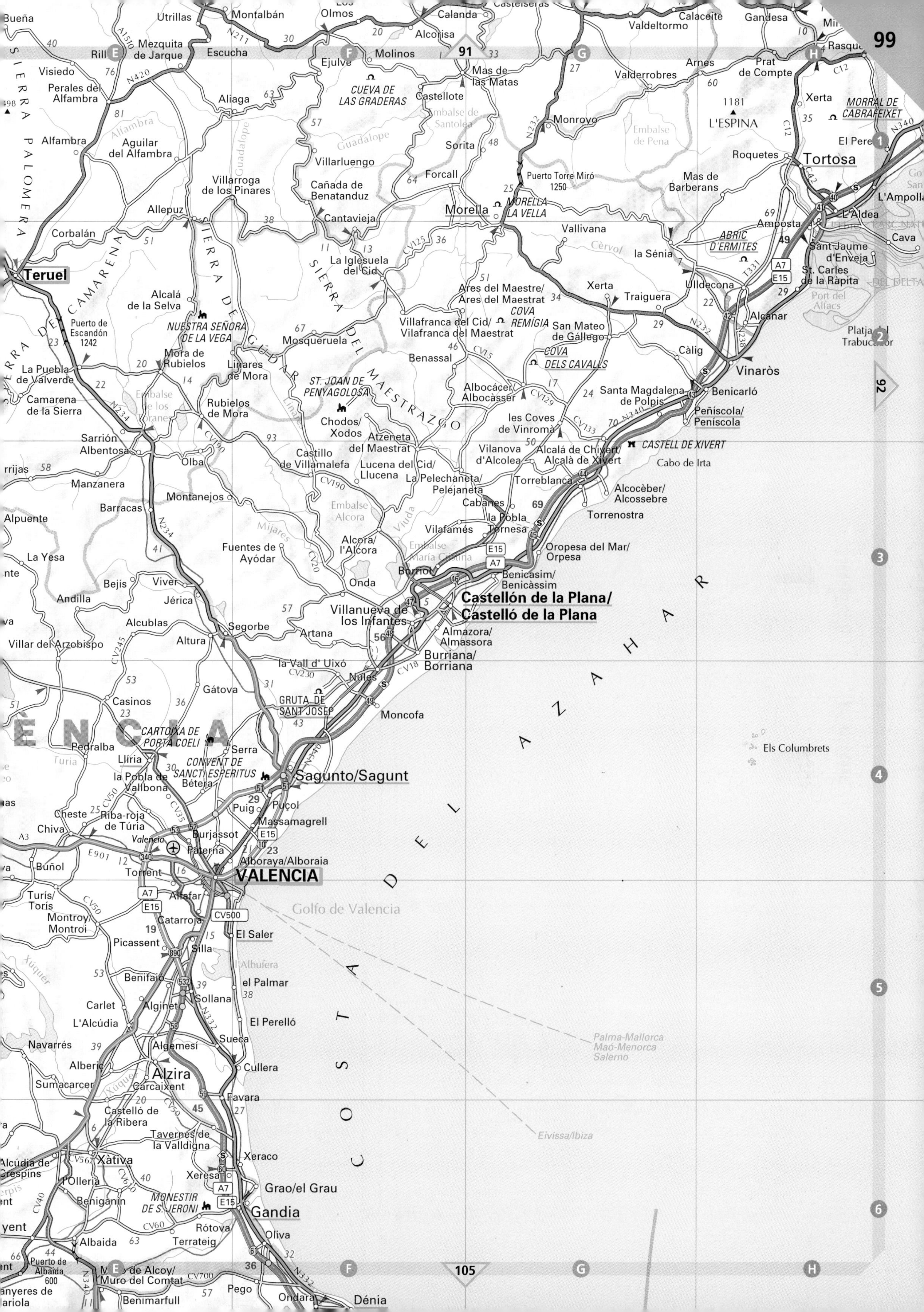
Teruel
Tortosa
Morella
Vinaròs
Benicarló
Peñíscola/ Peníscola
Castellón de la Plana/ Castelló de la Plana
Sagunto/Sagunt
VALENCIA
Golfo de Valencia
Alzira
Xàtiva
Gandia
Dénia
COSTA DEL AZAHAR
SIERRA DE GÚDAR
SIERRA DEL MAESTRAZGO
SIERRA PALOMERA
SIERRA DE CAMARENA
Els Columbrets
Cabo de Irta
Palma-Mallorca
Maó-Menorca
Salerno
Eivissa/Ibiza
Amposta
L'Ampolla
Sant Jaume d'Enveja
St. Carles de la Ràpita
Alcanar
Ulldecona
Vilafamés
Onda
Burriana/ Borriana
Nules
Moncofa
Segorbe
Llíria
Cullera
Sueca
Oliva
91
105
92

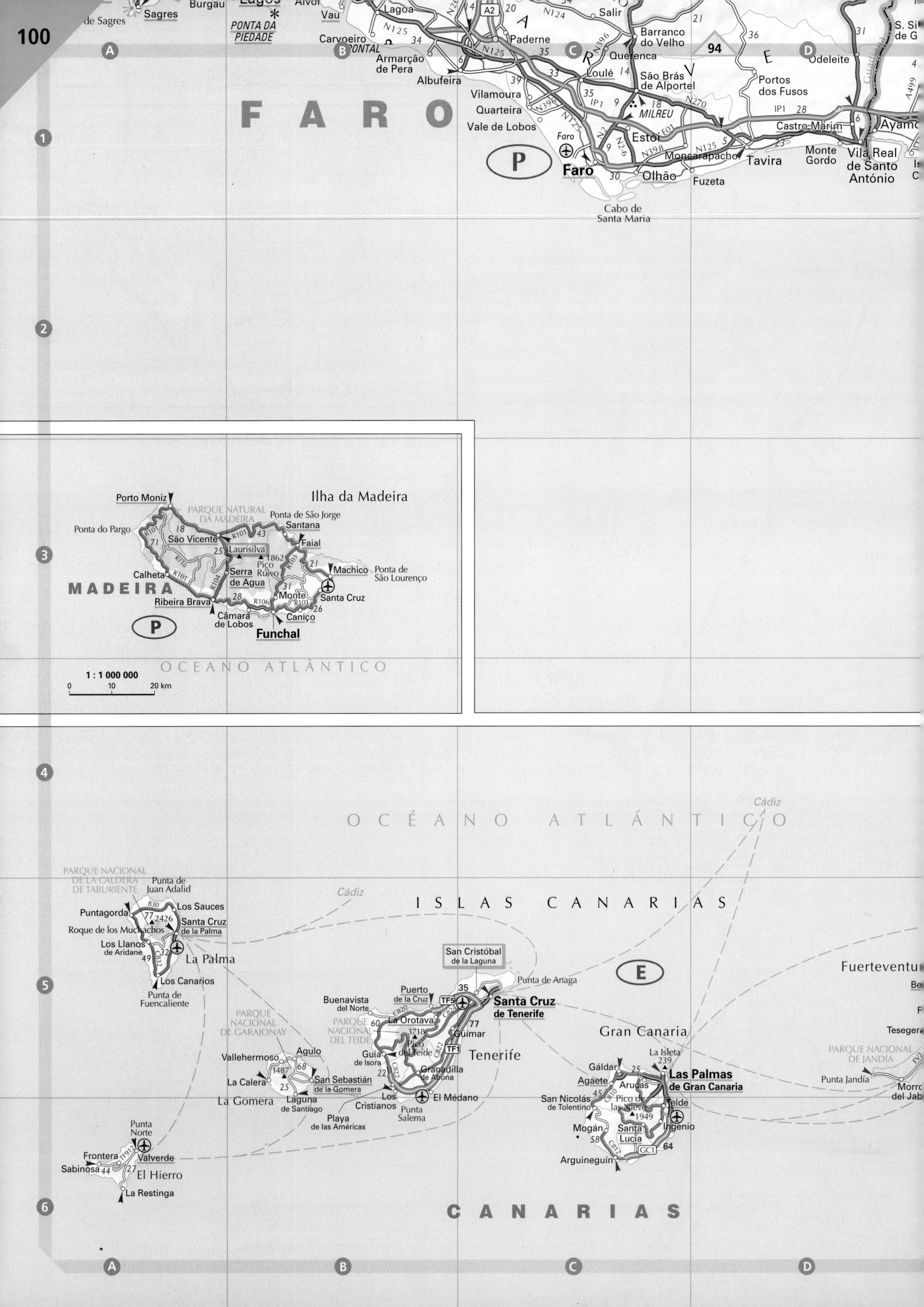

FARO
Sagres
Lagoa
Carvoeiro
Armação de Pera
Albufeira
Paderne
Salir
Barranco do Velho
Querença
Loulé
São Brás de Alportel
Portos dos Fusos
Odeleite
Vilamoura
Quarteira
Vale de Lobos
MILREU
Estoi
Castro Marim
Faro
Olhão
Moncarapacho
Tavira
Fuzeta
Monte Gordo
Vila Real de Santo António
Cabo de Santa Maria
PONTA DA PIEDADE
94
MADEIRA
Ilha da Madeira
Porto Moniz
PARQUE NATURAL DA MADEIRA
Ponta de São Jorge
Santana
Ponta do Pargo
São Vicente
Laurisilva
Faial
Pico Ruivo
Machico
Ponta de São Lourenço
Calheta
Serra de Agua
Monte
Santa Cruz
Ribeira Brava
Câmara de Lobos
Caniço
Funchal
OCEANO ATLÂNTICO
1 : 1 000 000
OCÉANO ATLÁNTICO
Cádiz
ISLAS CANARIAS
PARQUE NACIONAL DE LA CALDERA DE TABURIENTE
Punta de Juan Adalid
Puntagorda
Los Sauces
Santa Cruz de la Palma
Roque de los Muchachos
Los Llanos de Aridane
La Palma
Los Canarios
Punta de Fuencaliente
San Cristóbal de la Laguna
Punta de Anaga
Santa Cruz de Tenerife
Buenavista del Norte
Puerto de la Cruz
La Orotava
PARQUE NACIONAL DEL TEIDE
Pico del Teide
Güimar
Tenerife
Guía de Isora
Granadilla de Abona
El Médano
Los Cristianos
Punta Salema
Playa de las Américas
PARQUE NACIONAL DE GARAJONAY
Vallehermoso
Agulo
La Calera
San Sebastián de la Gomera
La Gomera
Laguna de Santiago
Gran Canaria
La Isleta
Gáldar
Agaete
Arucas
Las Palmas de Gran Canaria
San Nicolás de Tolentino
Pico de las Nieves
Telde
Ingenio
Mogán
Santa Lucía
Arguineguín
Fuerteventura
PARQUE NACIONAL DE JANDÍA
Punta Jandía
Punta Norte
Frontera
Valverde
Sabinosa
El Hierro
La Restinga
CANARIAS

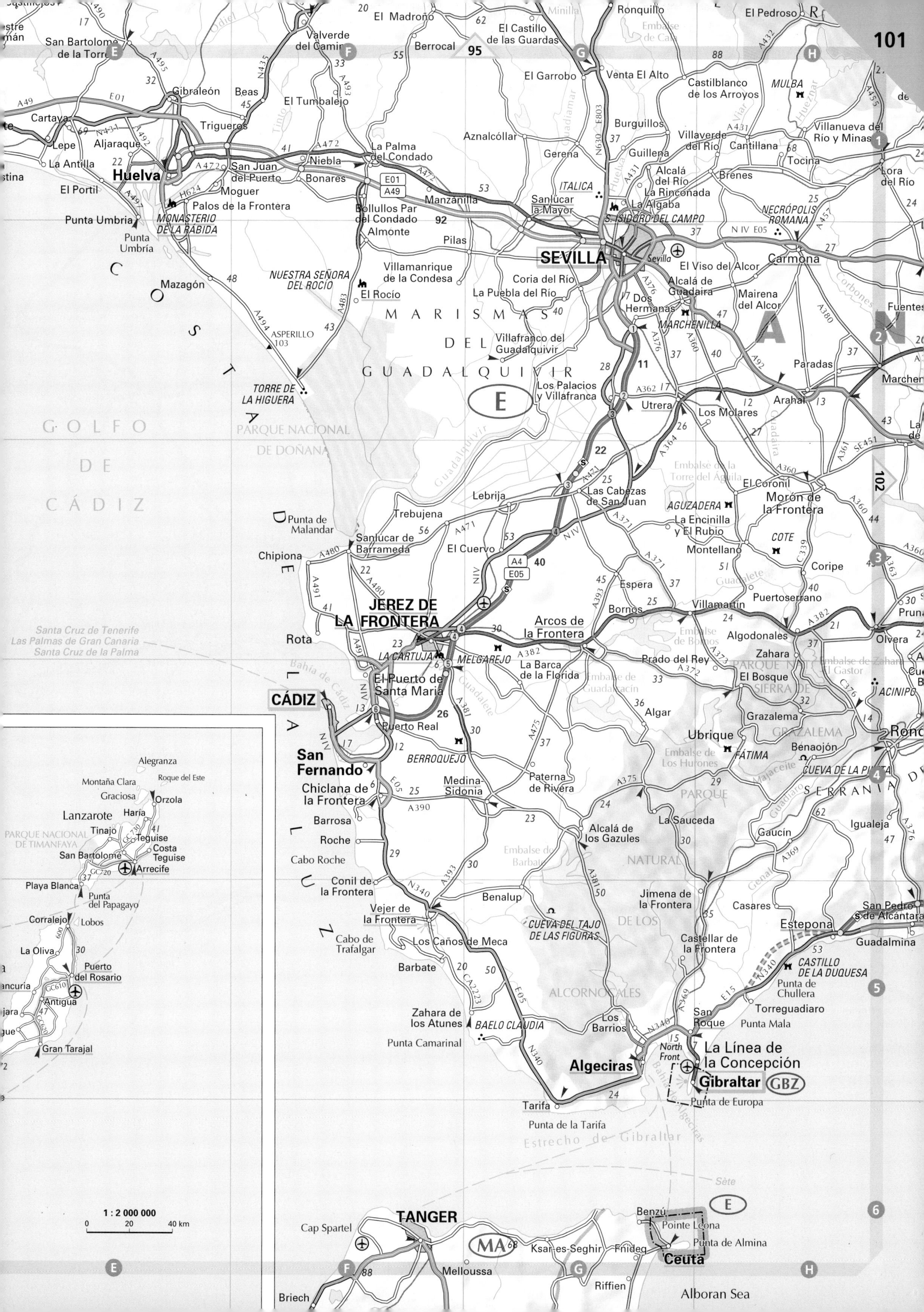
Huelva
SEVILLA
JEREZ DE
LA FRONTERA
CÁDIZ
San Fernando
Algeciras
Gibraltar
La Línea de
la Concepción
TANGER
Ceuta
GOLFO
DE
CÁDIZ
COSTA DE LA LUZ
MARISMAS DEL GUADALQUIVIR
PARQUE NACIONAL
DE DOÑANA
Estrecho de Gibraltar
Alboran Sea
Gibraleón
Trigueros
Moguer
Palos de la Frontera
Punta Umbria
Mazagón
Niebla
La Palma del Condado
Bollullos Par del Condado
Almonte
El Rocío
Carmona
Dos Hermanas
Utrera
Lebrija
Sanlúcar de Barrameda
Chipiona
Rota
El Puerto de Santa María
Puerto Real
Chiclana de la Frontera
Conil de la Frontera
Vejer de la Frontera
Barbate
Tarifa
Medina-Sidonia
Arcos de la Frontera
Ubrique
Morón de la Frontera
Olvera
Jimena de la Frontera
San Roque
Estepona
Lanzarote
Arrecife
Puerto del Rosario
1 : 2 000 000
0 20 40 km

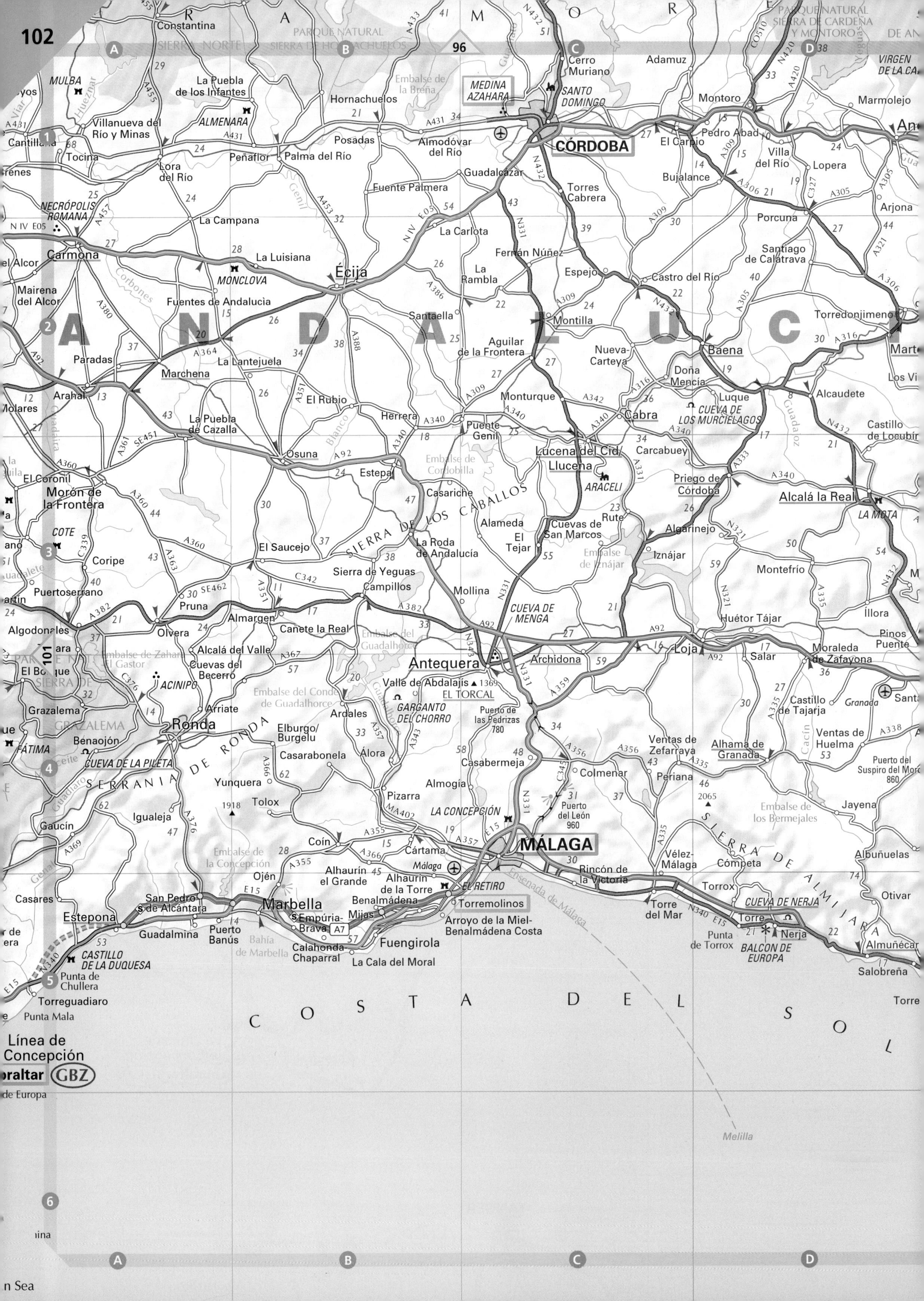

Constantina
PARQUE NATURAL SIERRA NORTE
PARQUE NATURAL SIERRA DE HORNACHUELOS
96
PARQUE NATURAL SIERRA DE CARDEÑA Y MONTORO
MULBA
La Puebla de los Infantes
Hornachuelos
Embalse de la Breña
MEDINA AZAHARA
SANTO DOMINGO
Cerro Muriano
Adamuz
Montoro
Marmolejo
VIRGEN DE LA CA
Villanueva del Río y Minas
ALMENARA
Cantillana
Tocina
Peñaflor
Palma del Río
Posadas
Almodóvar del Río
CÓRDOBA
El Carpio
Pedro Abad
Villa del Río
Lopera
Lora del Río
Guadalcázar
Fuente Palmera
Torres Cabrera
Bujalance
Porcuna
Arjona
NECRÓPOLIS ROMANA
La Campana
La Carlota
Santiago de Calatrava
Carmona
La Luisiana
Fernán Núñez
Écija
La Rambla
Espejo
Castro del Río
Mairena del Alcor
MONCLOVA
Fuentes de Andalucía
Santaella
Montilla
Torredonjimeno
ANDALUCIA
Paradas
Marchena
La Lantejuela
Aguilar de la Frontera
Nueva-Carteya
Baena
Arahal
El Rubio
Monturque
Doña Mencía
Luque
Alcaudete
La Puebla de Cazalla
Herrera
Puente Genil
Cabra
CUEVA DE LOS MURCIÉLAGOS
Castillo de Locubín
Osuna
Estepa
Embalse de Cordobilla
Lucena del Cid/Llucena
Carcabuey
El Coronil
Morón de la Frontera
Casariche
ARACELI
Priego de Córdoba
Alcalá la Real
LA MOTA
SIERRA DE LOS CABALLOS
COTE
El Saucejo
La Roda de Andalucía
Alameda
El Tejar
Cuevas de San Marcos
Rute
Algarinejo
Iznájar
Embalse de Iznájar
Montefrío
Coripe
Sierra de Yeguas
Campillos
Mollina
CUEVA DE MENGA
Puertoserrano
Pruna
Almargen
Olvera
Cañete la Real
Embalse del Guadalhorce
Huétor Tájar
Íllora
Algodonales
Alcalá del Valle
Cuevas del Becerro
Antequera
Archidona
Loja
Salar
Moraleda de Zafayona
Pinos Puente
El Bosque
SIERRA DE GRAZALEMA
ACINIPO
Valle de Abdalajís
EL TORCAL
Castillo de Tajarja
Grazalema
Arriate
Embalse del Conde de Guadalhorce
GARGANTO DEL CHORRO
Puerto de las Pedrizas 780
Ardales
Ventas de Huelma
FÁTIMA
Benaoján
Ronda
Elburgo/Burgelu
Ventas de Zafarraya
Alhama de Granada
CUEVA DE LA PILETA
SERRANIA DE RONDA
Casarabonela
Álora
Casabermeja
Colmenar
Periana
Puerto del Suspiro del Moro 860
Yunquera
Almogía
Tolox
Pizarra
Puerto del León 960
Jayena
Gaucín
Igualeja
LA CONCEPCIÓN
Embalse de los Bermejales
SIERRA DE ALMIJARA
Coín
Cártama
MÁLAGA
Embalse de la Concepción
Ojén
Alhaurín el Grande
Alhaurín de la Torre
Rincón de la Victoria
Vélez-Málaga
Cómpeta
Albuñuelas
Casares
EL RETIRO
Torrox
Otívar
San Pedro de Alcántara
Marbella
Benalmádena
Torremolinos
Ensenada de Málaga
Torre del Mar
CUEVA DE NERJA
Estepona
Empúria-Brava
Mijas
Arroyo de la Miel-Benalmádena Costa
Torre
Nerja
Guadalmina
Puerto Banús
Bahía de Marbella
Calahonda-Chaparral
Fuengirola
Punta de Torrox
BALCON DE EUROPA
Almuñécar
CASTILLO DE LA DUQUESA
La Cala del Moral
Salobreña
Punta de Chullera
Torreguadiaro
Punta Mala
COSTA DEL SOL
Línea de Concepción
GBZ
Melilla

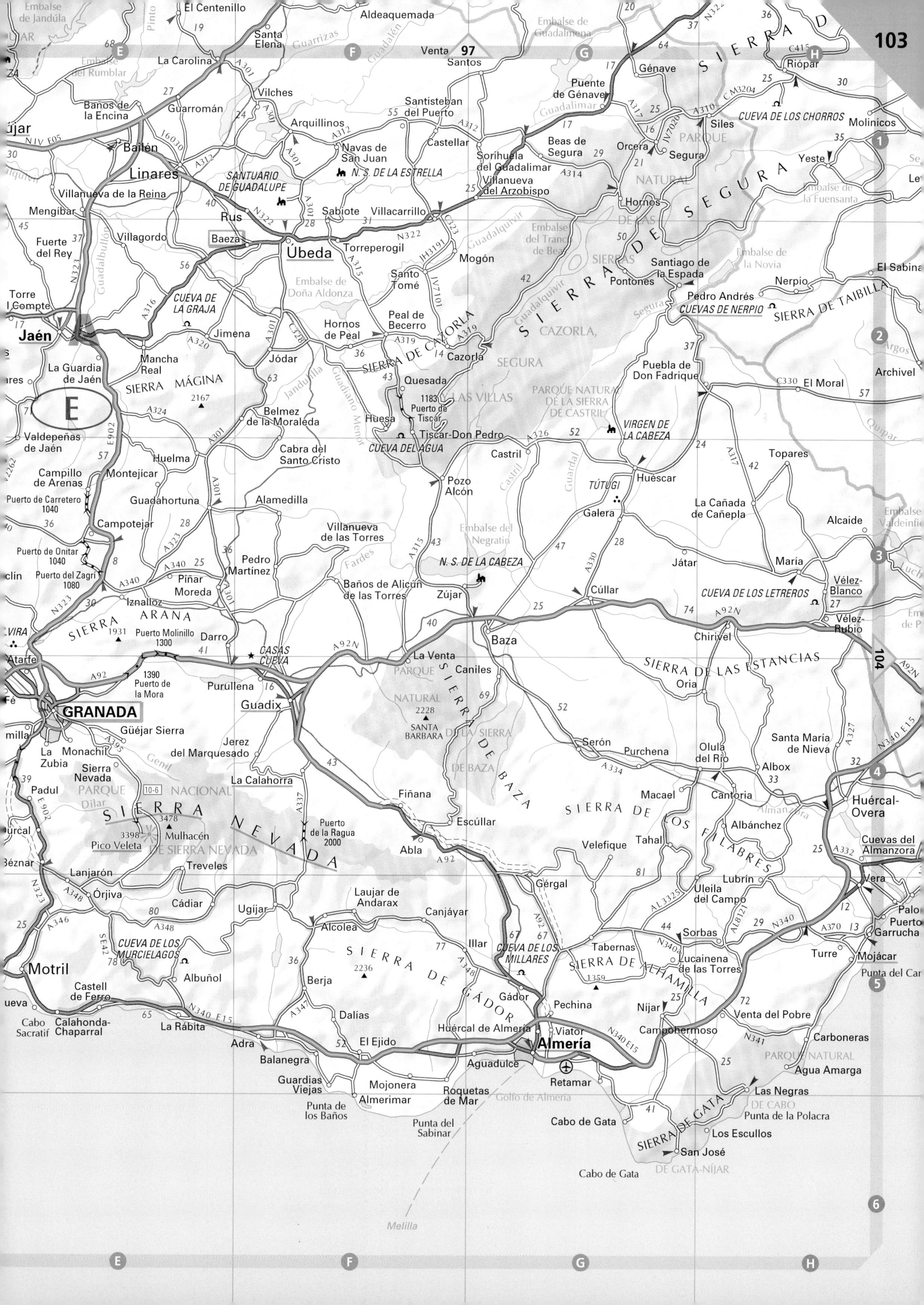
El Centenillo
Aldeaquemada
Santa Elena
La Carolina
Venta de los Santos
97
Génave
Puente de Génave
Riópar
Vilches
Guarromán
Baños de la Encina
Santisteban del Puerto
Arquillinos
Castellar
Navas de San Juan
Bailén
Linares
Siles
Molinicos
Orcera
Segura
Beas de Segura
Sorihuela del Guadalimar
Villanueva del Arzobispo
Yeste
SANTUARIO DE GUADALUPE
N. S. DE LA ESTRELLA
Villanueva de la Reina
Mengíbar
Rus
Sabiote
Villacarrillo
Hornos
Fuerte del Rey
Villagordo
Baeza
Úbeda
Torreperogil
Mogón
Santiago de la Espada
Pontones
Santo Tomé
Nerpio
El Sabinar
Torre del Compte
CUEVA DE LA GRAJA
Hornos de Peal
Peal de Becerro
Pedro Andrés
CUEVAS DE NERPIO
SIERRA DE TAIBILLA
Jaén
Jimena
Jódar
Cazorla
SIERRA DE CAZORLA
SIERRA DE SEGURA
CUEVA DE LOS CHORROS
PARQUE NATURAL DE LAS SIERRAS DE CAZORLA, SEGURA Y LAS VILLAS
La Guardia de Jaén
Mancha Real
SIERRA MÁGINA
Quesada
Puebla de Don Fadrique
Archivel
El Moral
1183 Puerto de Tíscar
Belmez de la Moraleda
Huesa
Tíscar-Don Pedro
PARQUE NATURAL DE LA SIERRA DE CASTRIL
VIRGEN DE LA CABEZA
Valdepeñas de Jaén
CUEVA DEL AGUA
Cabra del Santo Cristo
Castril
Huelma
Topares
Campillo de Arenas
Montejícar
Pozo Alcón
Huéscar
Puerto de Carretero 1040
Guadahortuna
TÚTUGI
Alamedilla
La Cañada de Cañepla
Galera
Campotejar
Villanueva de las Torres
Alcaide
Puerto de Onitar 1040
Embalse del Negratín
Pedro Martínez
Játar
María
Puerto del Zagrí 1080
Píñar
Moreda
N. S. DE LA CABEZA
Baños de Alicún de las Torres
Zújar
Cúllar
CUEVA DE LOS LETREROS
Vélez-Blanco
Iznalloz
SIERRA ARANA
Vélez-Rubio
1931
Puerto Molinillo 1300
Darro
CASAS CUEVA
Baza
Chirivel
Atarfe
1390 Puerto de la Mora
La Venta
Caniles
SIERRA DE LAS ESTANCIAS
104
Purullena
Guadix
Oria
GRANADA
Güéjar Sierra
2228 SANTA BARBARA
PARQUE NATURAL DE LA SIERRA DE BAZA
SIERRA DE BAZA
Jerez del Marquesado
Serón
Purchena
Olula del Río
Santa María de Nieva
La Zubia
Monachil
Sierra Nevada
Albox
La Calahorra
Padul
PARQUE NACIONAL DE SIERRA NEVADA
SIERRA NEVADA
Macael
Cantoria
Huércal-Overa
Fiñana
3478 Mulhacén
3398 Pico Veleta
Puerto de la Ragua 2000
SIERRA DE LOS FILABRES
Escúllar
Albánchez
Tahal
Cuevas del Almanzora
Abla
Velefique
Lanjarón
Treveles
Lubrín
Vera
Órjiva
Gérgal
Uleila del Campo
Cádiar
Laujar de Andarax
Canjáyar
Ugíjar
Alcolea
Sorbas
Palomares
Puerto de Garrucha
CUEVA DE LOS MURCIELAGOS
Illar
CUEVA DE LOS MILLARES
Tabernas
SIERRA DE ALHAMILLA
Lucainena de las Torres
Turre
Mojácar
Motril
SIERRA DE GÁDOR
2236
1359
Punta del Cargo
Berja
Albuñol
Gádor
Pechina
Níjar
Castell de Ferro
Dalías
Venta del Pobre
Cabo Sacratif
Calahonda-Chaparral
La Rábita
Huércal de Almería
Viator
Campohermoso
Carboneras
Adra
El Ejido
Almería
Balanegra
Aguadulce
Retamar
PARQUE NATURAL DE CABO DE GATA-NÍJAR
Agua Amarga
Guardias Viejas
Mojonera
Roquetas de Mar
Golfo de Almería
Las Negras
Almerimar
Punta de la Polacra
Punta de los Baños
Punta del Sabinar
Cabo de Gata
SIERRA DE GATA
Los Escullos
San José
Melilla
E
F
G
H
1
2
3
4
5
6

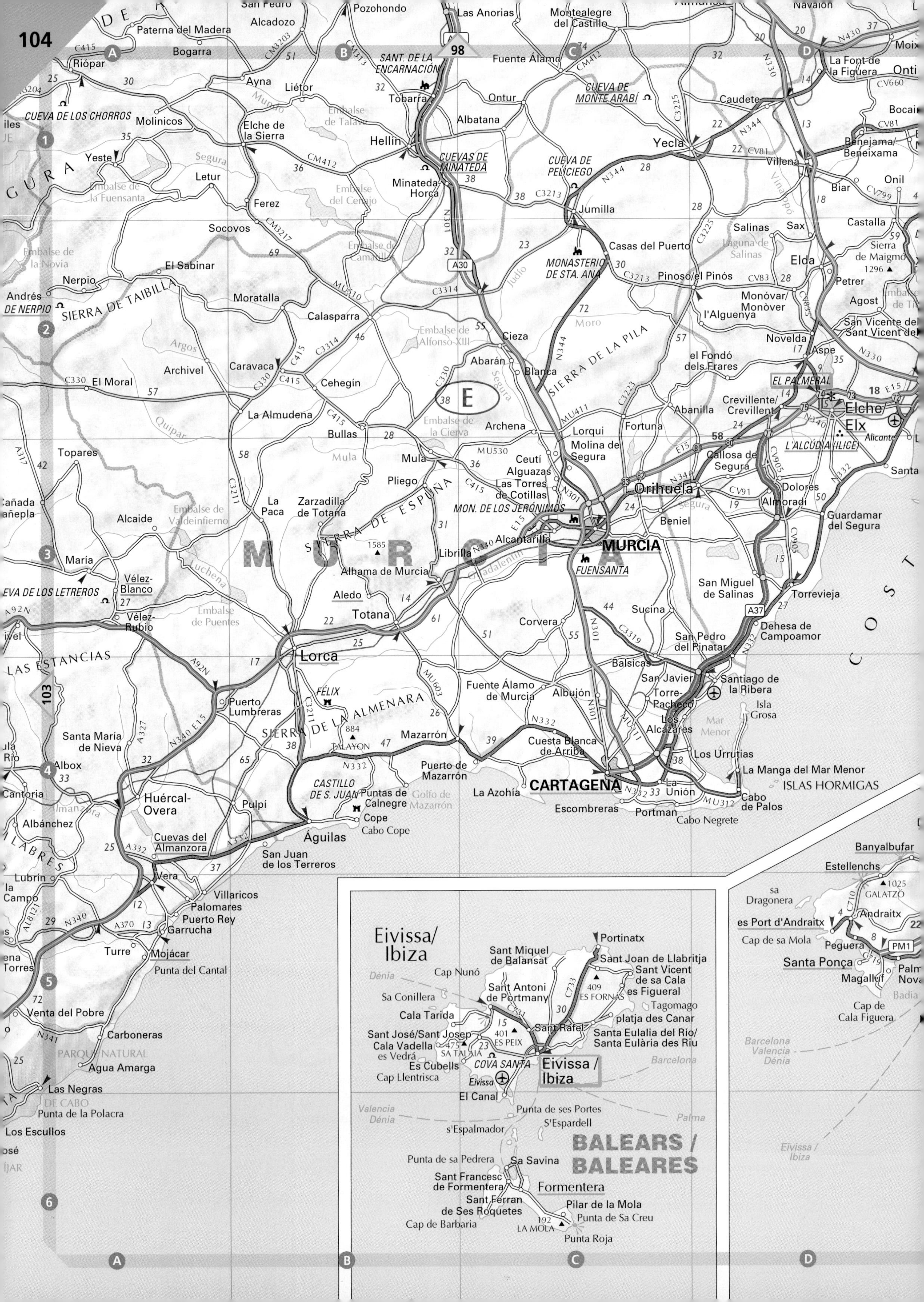
Paterna del Madera
San Pedro
Alcadozo
Pozohondo
Las Anorias
Montealegre del Castillo
Navalón
Riópar
Bogarra
98
SANT. DE LA ENCARNACIÓN
Fuente Álamo
La Font de la Figuera
Ontinyent
Moixent
CUEVA DE LOS CHORROS
Ayna
Liétor
Tobarra
Ontur
CUEVA DE MONTE ARABÍ
Caudete
Bocairent
Molinicos
Elche de la Sierra
Embalse de Talave
Albatana
Hellín
Yecla
Villena
Benejama/ Beneixama
Yeste
CUEVAS DE MINATEDA
CUEVA DE PELICIEGO
Letur
Embalse de la Fuensanta
Embalse del Cenajo
Minateda-Horca
Biar
Onil
Ferez
Jumilla
Castalla
Socovos
Salinas
Sax
Embalse de la Novia
Embalse de Camarillas
Casas del Puerto
Laguna de Salinas
Sierra de Maigmó
1296
El Sabinar
MONASTERIO DE STA. ANA
Pinoso/el Pinós
Elda
Petrer
Nerpio
Monóvar/ Monòver
Agost
Andrés DE NERPIO
SIERRA DE TAIBILLA
Moratalla
Calasparra
l'Alguenya
San Vicente del Raspeig/ Sant Vicent del Raspeig
Embalse de Alfonso XIII
Cieza
Moro
Novelda
Aspe
Argos
Abarán
SIERRA DE LA PILA
el Fondó dels Frares
Archivel
Caravaca
Blanca
EL PALMERAL
El Moral
Cehegín
E
Crevillente/ Crevillent
Elche/ Elx
La Almudena
Archena
Abanilla
Embalse de la Cierva
Lorquí
Fortuna
Alicante
Bullas
Molina de Segura
L'ALCÚDIA (ILICE)
Topares
Mula
Ceutí
Callosa de Segura
Alguazas
Santa Pola
Pliego
Las Torres de Cotillas
Orihuela
Dolores
Cañada
MON. DE LOS JERONIMOS
Almoradí
La Paca
Zarzadilla de Totana
SIERRA DE ESPUÑA
Guardamar del Segura
Alcaide
Embalse de Valdeinfierno
Beniel
Alcantarilla
MURCIA
1585
MURCIA
FUENSANTA
María
Librilla
Alhama de Murcia
Guadalentín
Luchena
Vélez-Blanco
Aledo
San Miguel de Salinas
Torrevieja
CUEVA DE LOS LETREROS
Totana
Sucina
Vélez-Rubio
Embalse de Puentes
Corvera
Dehesa de Campoamor
San Pedro del Pinatar
LAS ESTANCIAS
Lorca
COSTA
Balsicas
103
FÉLIX
San Javier
Santiago de la Ribera
Puerto Lumbreras
Fuente Álamo de Murcia
Albujón
Torre-Pacheco
Isla Grosa
SIERRA DE LA ALMENARA
884
Mar Menor
Santa María de Nieva
TALAYÓN
Mazarrón
Los Alcázares
Cuesta Blanca de Arriba
Albox
Puerto de Mazarrón
Los Urrutias
CASTILLO DE S. JUAN
La Manga del Mar Menor
Cantoria
Huércal-Overa
Puntas de Calnegre
Golfo de Mazarrón
La Azohía
CARTAGENA
La Unión
ISLAS HORMIGAS
Cabo de Palos
Pulpí
Escombreras
Portman
Cabo Negrete
Albánchez
Cope
Cabo Cope
Almanzora
Águilas
Cuevas del Almanzora
Banyalbufar
San Juan de los Terreros
Estellenchs
Lubrín
Vera
1025 GALATZÓ
Villaricos
sa Dragonera
Palomares
Andraitx
Puerto Rey
es Port d'Andraitx
Garrucha
Cap de sa Mola
Turre
Peguera
PM1
Mojácar
Santa Ponça
Palma Nova
Punta del Cantal
Magalluf
Eivissa/ Ibiza
Portinatx
Sant Miquel de Balansat
Sant Joan de Llabritja
Badia
Venta del Pobre
Dénia
Cap Nunó
Sant Vicent de sa Cala
Cap de Cala Figuera
409 ES FORNÁS
es Figueral
Sant Antoni de Portmany
Tagomago
Sa Conillera
Carboneras
Cala Tarida
platja des Canar
Sant Rafel
PARQUE NATURAL
401 ES PEIX
Sant José/Sant Josep
Santa Eulalia del Río/ Santa Eulària des Riu
Barcelona Valencia Dénia
Agua Amarga
Cala Vadella
475 SA TALAIA
es Vedrá
Barcelona
COVA SANTA
Es Cubells
Eivissa / Ibiza
Cap Llentrisca
Las Negras
El Canal
DE CABO
Punta de la Polacra
Valencia Dénia
Punta de ses Portes
Palma
S'Espardell
Los Escullos
s'Espalmador
BALEARS / BALEARES
Eivissa / Ibiza
Punta de sa Pedrera
Sa Savina
Sant Francesc de Formentera
Formentera
Sant Ferran de Ses Roquetes
Pilar de la Mola
Punta de Sa Creu
Cap de Barbaria
192 LA MOLA
Punta Roja
A
B
C
D
1
2
3
4
5
6

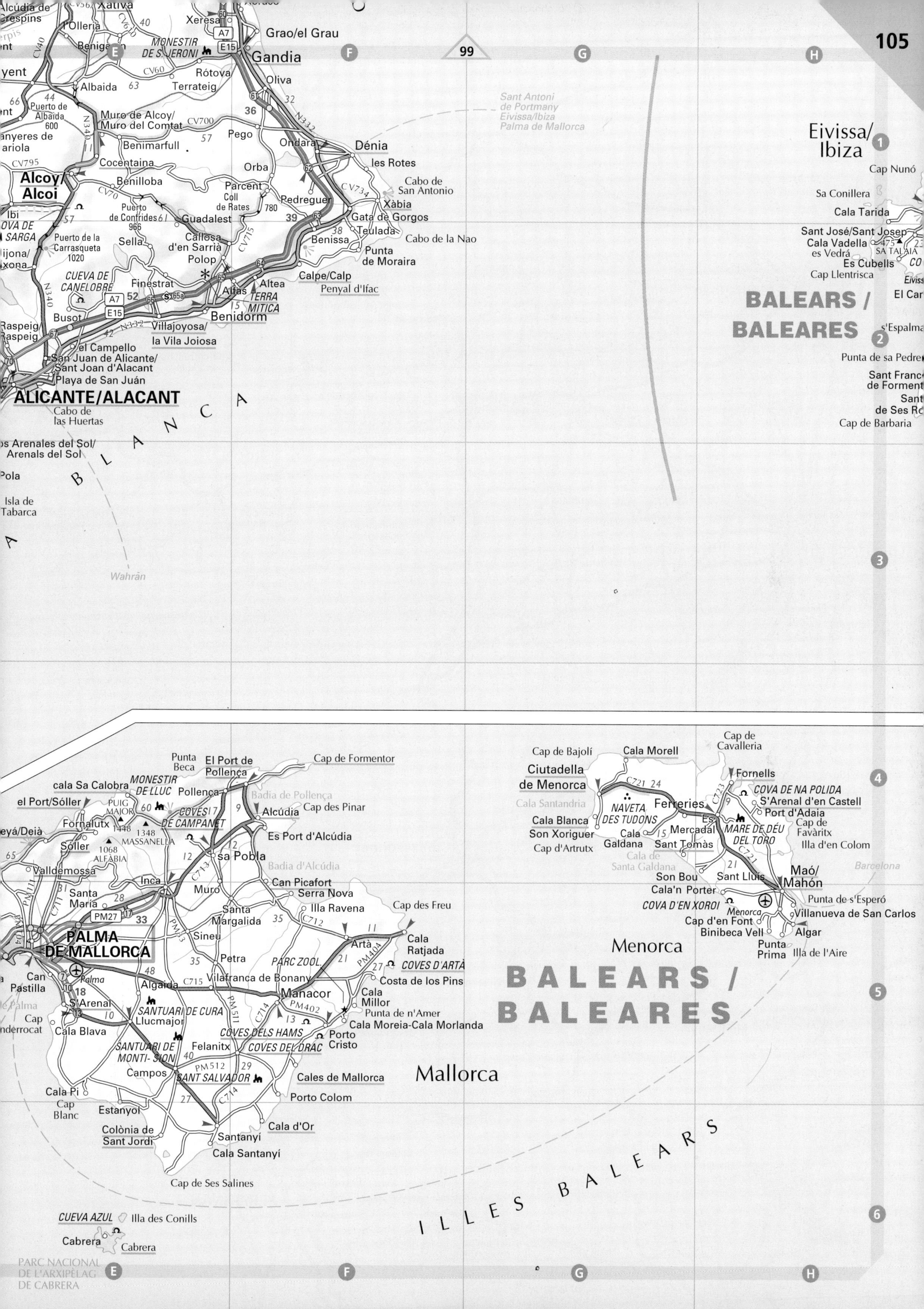

BALEARS / BALEARES

Eivissa/Ibiza

Cap Nunó
Sa Conillera
Cala Tarida
Sant José/Sant Josep
Cala Vadella
es Vedrà
Es Cubells
Cap Llentrisca
El Car
s'Espalma
Punta de sa Pedre
Sant Franc
de Forment
Sant
de Ses Rd
Cap de Barbaria
Sant Antoni
de Portmany
Eivissa/Ibiza
Palma de Mallorca

Menorca

Cap de Bajolí
Cala Morell
Cap de Cavalleria
Ciutadella
de Menorca
Fornells
COVA DE NA POLIDA
Cala Santandria
Ferreries
S'Arenal d'en Castell
Port d'Adaia
Cala Blanca
NAVETA
DES TUDONS
Mercadal
Es
MARE DE DÉU
DEL TORO
Cap de
Favàritx
Son Xoriguer
Cala
Galdana
Sant Tomàs
Illa d'en Colom
Cap d'Artrutx
Cala de
Santa Galdana
Maó/
Mahón
Barcelona
Son Bou
Sant Lluís
Cala'n Porter
COVA D'EN XOROI
Punta de s'Esperó
Villanueva de San Carlos
Cap d'en Font
Binibeca Vell
Algar
Punta
Prima
Illa de l'Aire

Mallorca

Punta Beca
El Port de Pollença
Cap de Formentor
cala Sa Calobra
MONESTIR DE LLUC
Pollença
Badia de Pollença
Fornalutx
el Port/Sóller
PUIG MAJOR
1448
COVES DE CAMPANET
Alcúdia
Cap des Pinar
eyá/Deià
Sóller
1348
MASSANELLA
Es Port d'Alcúdia
Valldemossa
1068
ALFÀBIA
sa Pobla
Badia d'Alcúdia
Santa Maria
Inca
Muro
Can Picafort
Serra Nova
Illa Ravena
Cap des Freu
PM27
Santa Margalida
Petra
Sineu
Artà
Cala Ratjada
COVES D'ARTÀ
Costa de los Pins
PALMA DE MALLORCA
Vilafranca de Bonany
PARC ZOOL.
Manacor
Can Pastilla
Palma
Algaida
Cala Millor
Punta de n'Amer
Cala Moreia-Cala Morlanda
s'Arenal
SANTUARI DE CURA
Llucmajor
COVES DELS HAMS
Porto Cristo
Cala Blava
SANTUARI DE MONTI-SION
Felanitx
COVES DEL DRAC
Cala Pi
Campos
SANT SALVADOR
Cales de Mallorca
Cap Blanc
Estanyol
Porto Colom
Colònia de Sant Jordi
Cala d'Or
Santanyí
Cala Santanyí
Cap de Ses Salines

CUEVA AZUL
Illa des Conills
Cabrera
Cabrera
PARC NACIONAL DE L'ARXIPÈLAG DE CABRERA

BALEARS / BALEARES

ILLES BALEARS

(mainland)

l'Olleria
Benigànim
MONESTIR DE S. JERONI
Grao/el Grau
Albaida
Rótova
Terrateig
Gandia
Muro de Alcoy/
Muro del Comtat
Pego
Oliva
Benimarfull
Cocentaina
Ondara
Dénia
les Rotes
Alcoy/
Alcoi
Benilloba
Parcent
Coll de Rates
Orba
Cabo de San Antonio
Ibi
Puerto de Confrides
Guadalest
Pedreguer
Xàbia
Callosa d'en Sarrià
Gata de Gorgos
Sella
Polop
Benissa
Teulada
Cabo de la Nao
Finestrat
Altea
Punta de Moraira
Busot
Alfàs
TERRA MÍTICA
Calpe/Calp
Penyal d'Ifac
Benidorm
Villajoyosa/
la Vila Joiosa
el Campello
San Juan de Alicante/
Sant Joan d'Alacant
Playa de San Juán
ALICANTE/ALACANT
Cabo de las Huertas
Arenales del Sol/
Arenals del Sol
Pola
Isla de Tabarca
Wahrän

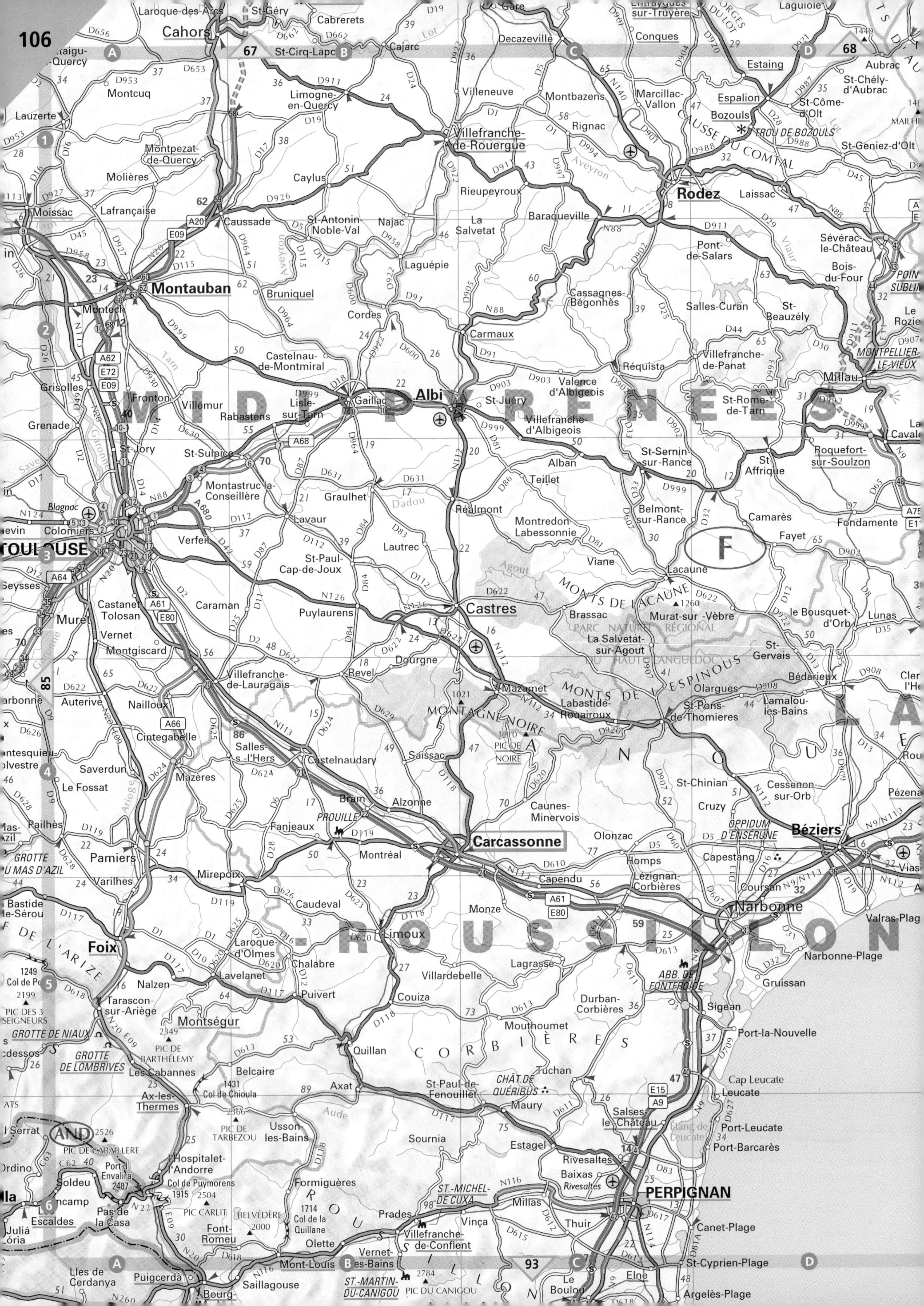

Laroque-des-Arcs
St-Géry
Cahors
Cabrerets
Cajarc
Decazeville
Conques
Laguiole
67
St-Cirq-Lapc
68
Estaing
Aubrac
St-Chély-d'Aubrac
St-Côme-d'Olt
Espalion
Bozouls
TROU DE BOZOULS
CAUSSE DU COMTAL
St-Geniez-d'Olt
Montcuq
Limogne-en-Quercy
Villeneuve
Montbazens
Marcillac-Vallon
Rignac
Lauzerte
Villefranche-de-Rouergue
Montpezat-de-Quercy
Molières
Caylus
Rieupeyroux
Rodez
Laissac
Moissac
Lafrançaise
Caussade
St-Antonin-Noble-Val
Najac
La Salvetat
Baraqueville
Sévérac-le-Château
Pont-de-Salars
Laguépie
Bois-du-Four
Montauban
Bruniquel
Cordes
Cassagnes-Bégonhès
Salles-Curan
St-Beauzély
Montech
Carmaux
Requista
Villefranche-de-Panat
MONTPELLIER-LE-VIEUX
Millau
Castelnau-de-Montmiral
Valence d'Albigeois
Grisolles
Fronton
Villemur
Rabastens
Lisle-sur-Tarn
Gaillac
Albi
St-Juéry
Villefranche-d'Albigeois
St-Rome-de-Tarn
MIDI-PYRÉNÉES
Grenade
St-Jory
St-Sulpice
Alban
St-Sernin-sur-Rance
St-Affrique
Roquefort-sur-Soulzon
Montastruc-la-Conseillère
Graulhet
Teillet
Blagnac
Colomiers
TOULOUSE
Lavaur
Réalmont
Montredon-Labessonnie
Belmont-sur-Rance
Camarès
Fondamente
Verfeil
Lautrec
St-Paul-Cap-de-Joux
Viane
Fayet
F
Lacaune
Seysses
Muret
Castanet-Tolosan
Caraman
Puylaurens
Castres
MONTS DE LACAUNE
Brassac
Murat-sur-Vèbre
le Bousquet-d'Orb
Lunas
PARC NATUREL RÉGIONAL DU HAUT LANGUEDOC
La Salvetat-sur-Agout
Vernet
Montgiscard
St-Gervais
Villefranche-de-Lauragais
Revel
Dourgne
Mazamet
MONTS DE L'ESPINOUS
Bédarieux
Olargues
Lamalou-les-Bains
Auterive
Nailloux
MONTAGNE NOIRE
Labastide-Rouairoux
St-Pons-de-Thomières
Cintegabelle
Salles-s.-l'Hers
Castelnaudary
Saissac
PIC DE NOIRE
LANGUEDOC
Saverdun
Le Fossat
Mazères
St-Chinian
Cessenon-sur-Orb
Bram
Alzonne
Cruzy
Pailhès
Fanjeaux
PROUILLE
Caunes-Minervois
OPPIDUM D'ENSERUNE
Béziers
GROTTE DU MAS D'AZIL
Pamiers
Montréal
Carcassonne
Olonzac
Capestang
Homps
Mirepoix
Varilhes
Capendu
Lézignan-Corbières
Coursan
Narbonne
Bastide-de-Sérou
Caudeval
Monze
Valras-Plage
Foix
Laroque-d'Olmes
Limoux
ROUSSILLON
Chalabre
Lagrasse
Narbonne-Plage
Nalzen
Lavelanet
Villardebelle
ABB. DE FONTFROIDE
Gruissan
Tarascon-sur-Ariège
Puivert
Couiza
Durban-Corbières
PIC DES 3 SEIGNEURS
Montségur
Mouthoumet
Sigean
GROTTE DE NIAUX
GROTTE DE LOMBRIVES
PIC DE BARTHÉLEMY
Quillan
CORBIÈRES
Port-la-Nouvelle
Les Cabannes
Belcaire
Tuchan
Col de Chioula
Axat
St-Paul-de-Fenouillet
CHÂT. DE QUÉRIBUS
Cap Leucate
Leucate
Ax-les-Thermes
Maury
Salses-le-Château
AND
PIC DE CABAILLERE
PIC DE TARBEZOU
Usson-les-Bains
Sournia
Estagel
Port-Leucate
Port-Barcarès
l'Hospitalet-l'Andorre
Port d'Envalira
Soldeu
Col de Puymorens
Formiguères
Rivesaltes
Baixas
ST.-MICHEL-DE-CUXA
PERPIGNAN
Pas de la Casa
PIC CARLIT
BELVÉDÈRE
Col de la Quillane
Prades
Millas
Thuir
Canet-Plage
Escaldes
Font-Romeu
Olette
Villefranche-de-Conflent
Vinça
Lles de Cerdanya
Puigcerdà
Mont-Louis
Vernet-les-Bains
93
St-Cyprien-Plage
Saillagouse
ST-MARTIN-DU-CANIGOU
PIC DU CANIGOU
Elne
Le Boulou
Argelès-Plage
Bourg-Madame
A
B
C
D
1
2
3
4
5
6

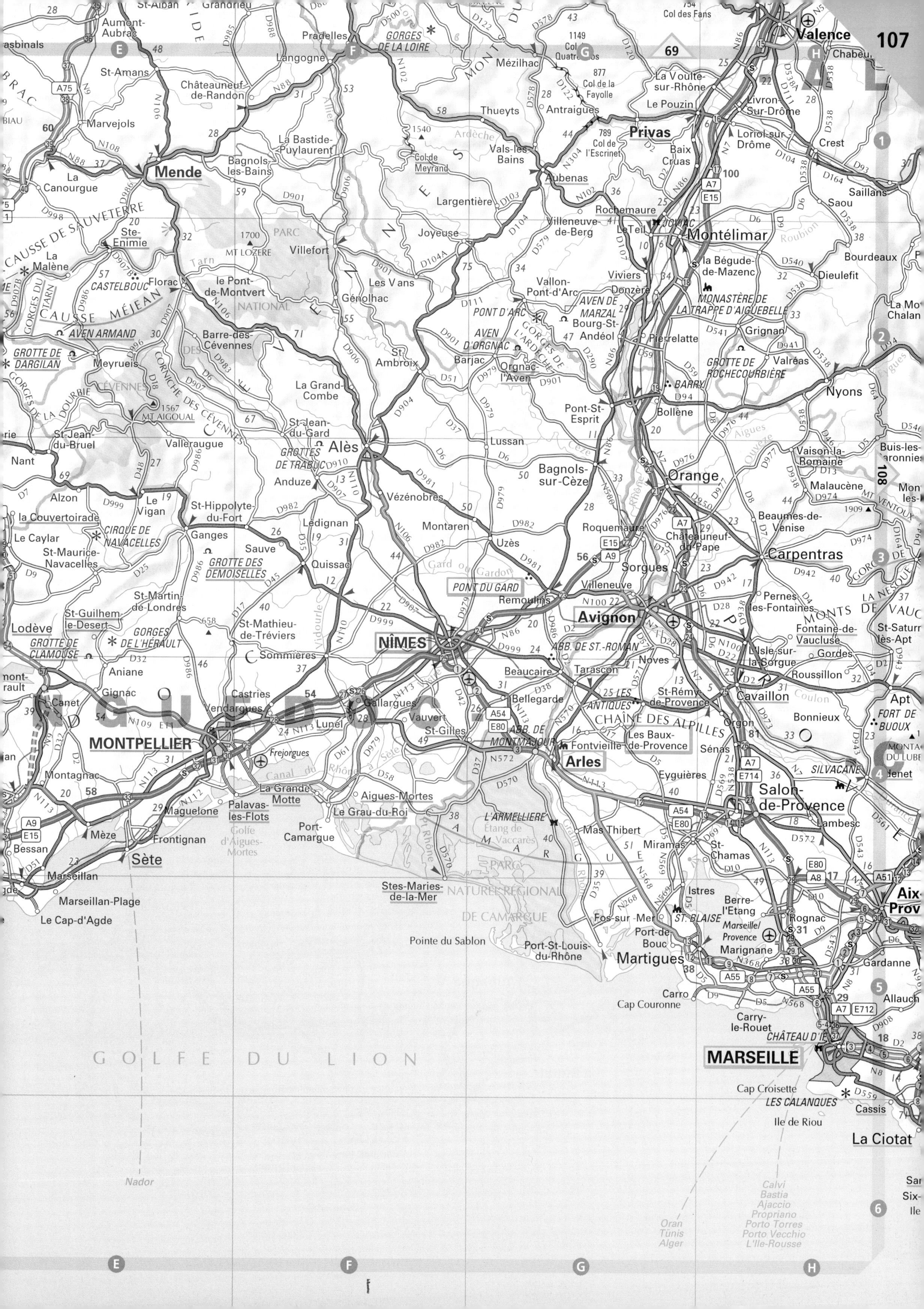

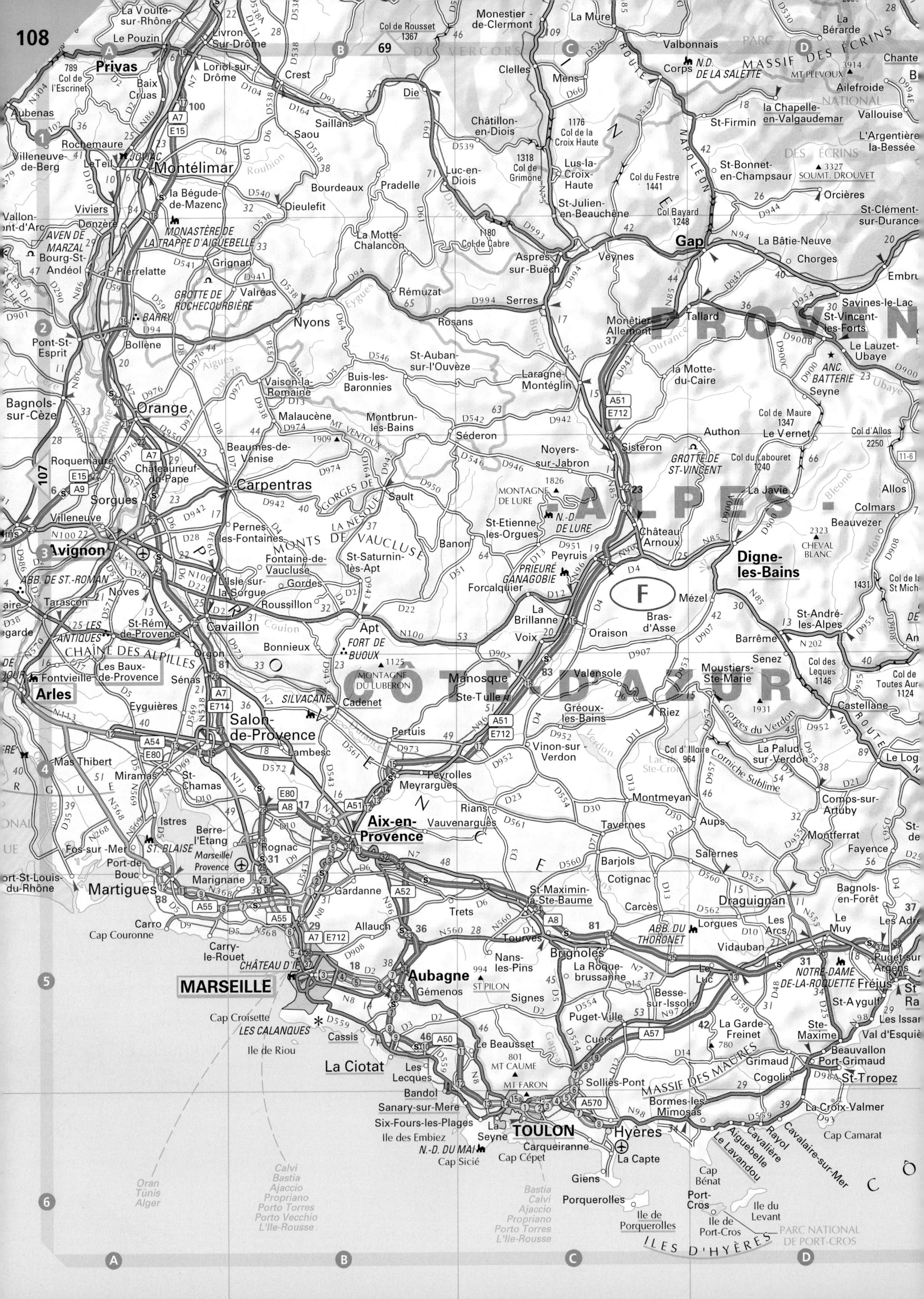
Privas
Montélimar
Orange
Avignon
Arles
Carpentras
Cavaillon
Salon-de-Provence
Aix-en-Provence
MARSEILLE
Aubagne
La Ciotat
TOULON
Hyères
Gap
Sisteron
Digne-les-Bains
Manosque
Draguignan
St-Tropez
Fréjus
Nyons
Die
Apt
PROVENCE-ALPES-CÔTE-D'AZUR
MASSIF DES ÉCRINS
MONTS DE VAUCLUSE
CHAÎNE DES ALPILLES
MASSIF DES MAURES
ILES D'HYÈRES
PARC NATIONAL DE PORT-CROS

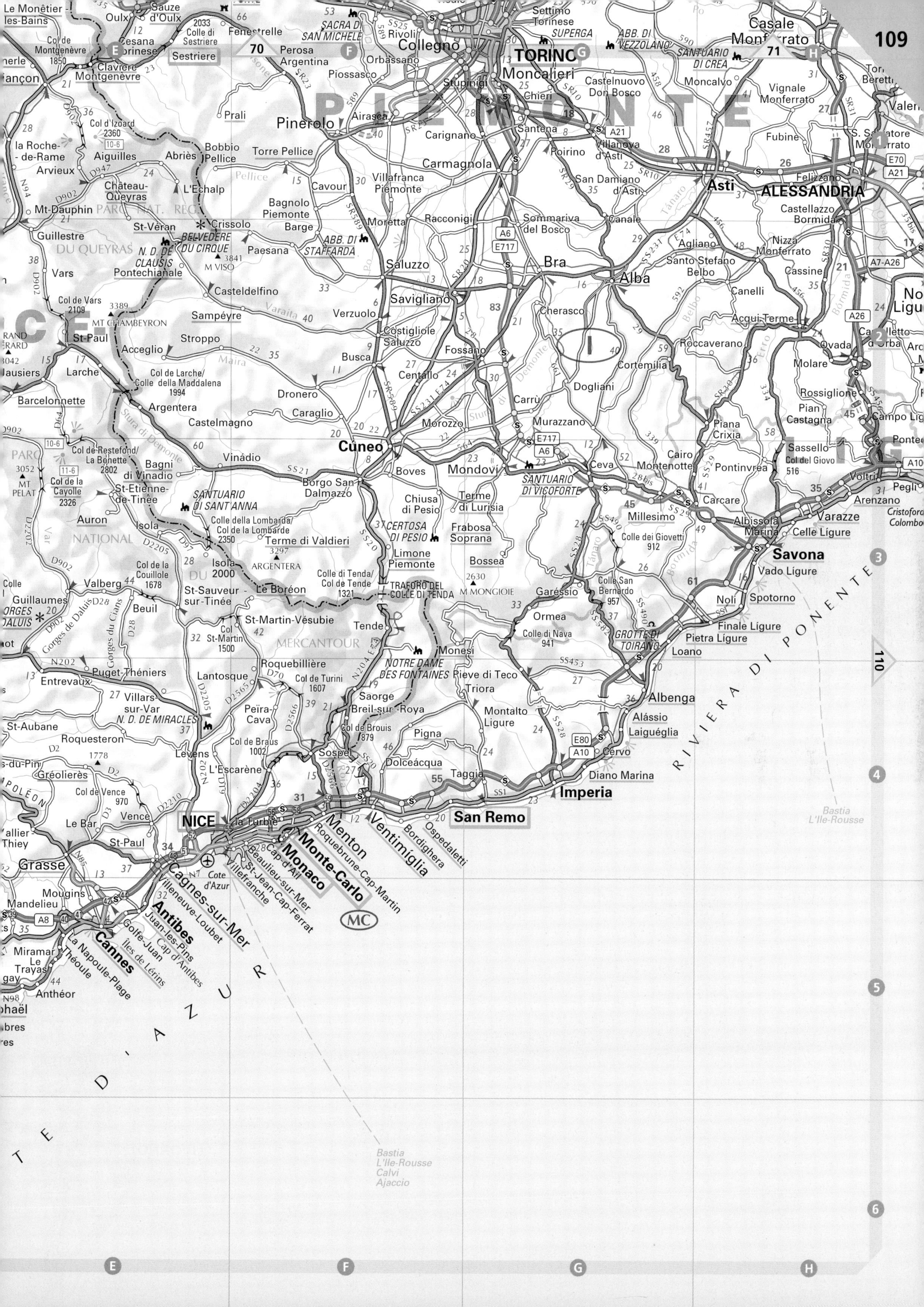

PIEMONTE
TORINO
Moncalieri
Collegno
Pinerolo
Carmagnola
Asti
ALESSANDRIA
Casale Monferrato
Alba
Bra
Saluzzo
Savigliano
Fossano
Cúneo
Mondovì
Ceva
Savona
Albenga
Imperia
San Remo
Ventimíglia
Menton
Monte-Carlo
Monaco
NICE
Cagnes-sur-Mer
Antibes
Cannes
Grasse
Barcelonnette
Briançon
RIVIERA DI PONENTE
COTE D'AZUR

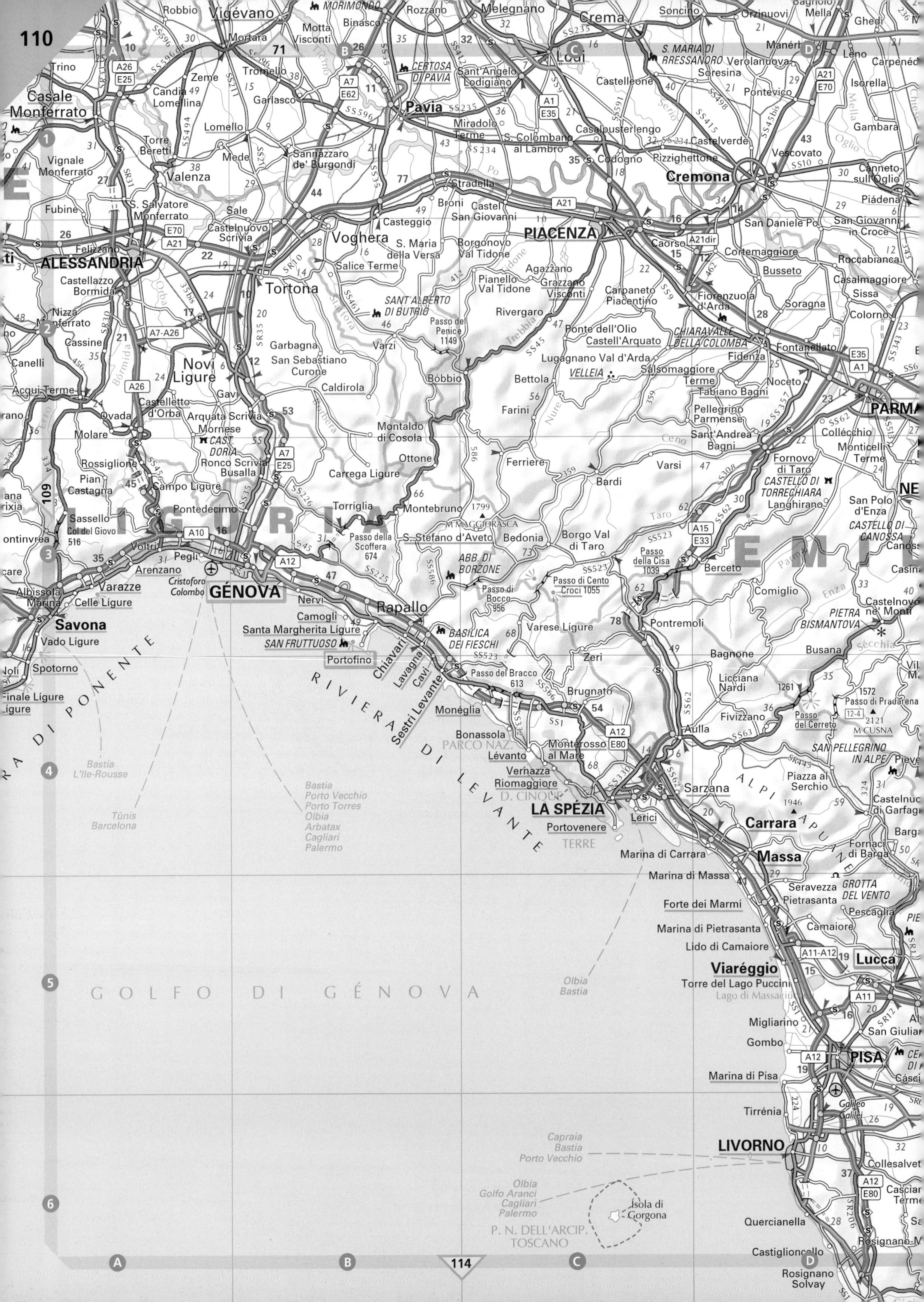
Robbio
Vigévano
MORIMONDO
Rozzano
Melegnano
Crema
Soncino
Orzinuovi
Mella
Ghedi
Mortara
71
Motta Visconti
Binasco
Lodi
S. MARIA DI BRESSANORO
Verolanuova
Manerbio
Leno
Carpenedolo
Trino
Zeme
Tromello
CERTOSA DI PAVIA
Sant'Angelo Lodigiano
Castelleone
Soresina
Pontevico
Isorella
Casale Monferrato
Candia Lomellina
Garlasco
Pavia
Miradolo Terme
Castelpusterlengo
Gambara
Lomello
Torre Beretti
Mede
Sannazzaro de' Burgondi
S. Colombano al Lambro
Codogno
Pizzighettone
Castelverde
Vescovato
Vignale Monferrato
Valenza
Stradella
Cremona
Canneto sull'Oglio
Fubine
S. Salvatore Monferrato
Sale
Broni
Castel San Giovanni
Piadena
Castelnuovo Scrivia
Casteggio
PIACENZA
San Daniele Po
San Giovanni in Croce
Felizzano
ALESSANDRIA
Voghera
S. Maria della Versa
Borgonovo Val Tidone
Caorso
Cortemaggiore
Roccabianca
Salice Terme
Agazzano
Busseto
Castellazzo Bormida
Tortona
Pianello Val Tidone
Grazzano Visconti
Carpaneto Piacentino
Casalmaggiore
Sissa
SANT'ALBERTO DI BUTRIO
Fiorenzuola d'Arda
Soragna
Nizza Monferrato
Rivergaro
Colorno
Passo del Penice 1149
Ponte dell'Olio
Castell'Arquato
CHIARAVALLE DELLA COLOMBA
Cassine
Garbagna
Varzi
Fidenza
Fontanellato
Canelli
Novi Ligure
San Sebastiano Curone
Lugagnano Val d'Arda
VELLEIA
Salsomaggiore Terme
Noceto
Acqui Terme
Gavi
Caldirola
Bobbio
Bettola
Tabiano Bagni
PARMA
Castelletto d'Orba
Arquata Scrivia
Farini
Pellegrino Parmense
Ovada
Mornese
CAST. DORIA
Montaldo di Cosola
Sant'Andrea Bagni
Collecchio
Molare
Monticelli Terme
Rossiglione
Ronco Scrivia
Busalla
Ottone
Ferriere
Fornovo di Taro
Varsi
Pian Castagna
Campo Ligure
Carrega Ligure
Bardi
CASTELLO DI TORRECHIARA
Langhirano
Pontedecimo
Torriglia
Montebruno
1799
San Polo d'Enza
Sassello
Col del Giovo 516
LIGURIA
M. MAGGIORASCA
CASTELLO DI CANOSSA
Voltri
Pegli
Passo della Scoffera 674
S. Stefano d'Aveto
Bedonia
Borgo Val di Taro
Passo della Cisa 1039
Berceto
EMILIA
Arenzano
Cristoforo Colombo
GÉNOVA
ABB. DI BORZONE
Passo di Cento Croci 1055
Albissola Marina
Varazze
Celle Ligure
Nervi
Camogli
Rapallo
Passo di Bocco 956
Comiglio
Castelnovo ne' Monti
Savona
Santa Margherita Ligure
BASILICA DEI FIESCHI
Varese Ligure
Pontremoli
PIETRA BISMANTOVA
Vado Ligure
SAN FRUTTUOSO
Portofino
Chiavari
Lavagna
Cavi
Zeri
Bagnone
Busana
Noli
Spotorno
Passo del Bracco 613
Licciana Nardi
Finale Ligure
RIVIERA DI PONENTE
Sestri Levante
Brugnato
Passo di Pradarena 1572
Moneglia
Fivizzano
Passo del Cerreto
2121 M. CUSNA
Aulla
Bonassola
PARCO NAZ.
Monterosso al Mare
SAN PELLEGRINO IN ALPE
Bastia
L'Ile-Rousse
Lévanto
Vernazza
Riomaggiore
Sarzana
Piazza al Serchio
RIVIERA DI LEVANTE
D. CINQUE
Bastia
Porto Vecchio
Porto Torres
Olbia
Arbatax
Cagliari
Palermo
LA SPÉZIA
Lerici
1946
ALPI APUANE
Castelnuovo di Garfagnana
Túnis
Barcelona
Portovenere
TERRE
Carrara
Marina di Carrara
Massa
Fornaci di Barga
Marina di Massa
Seravezza
Pietrasanta
GROTTA DEL VENTO
Forte dei Marmi
Pescaglia
Marina di Pietrasanta
Camaiore
Lido di Camaiore
Viaréggio
Lucca
Torre del Lago Puccini
Lago di Massaciuccoli
GOLFO DI GÉNOVA
Olbia
Bastia
Migliarino
San Giuliano
Gombo
PISA
Marina di Pisa
Galileo Galilei
Tirrénia
Capraia
Bastia
Porto Vecchio
LIVORNO
Collesalvetti
Olbia
Golfo Aranci
Cagliari
Palermo
Ísola di Gorgona
Quercianella
Casciana Terme
P. N. DELL'ARCIP. TOSCANO
Castiglioncello
Rosignano Marittimo
Rosignano Solvay
A
B
C
D
1
2
3
4
5
6
109
114

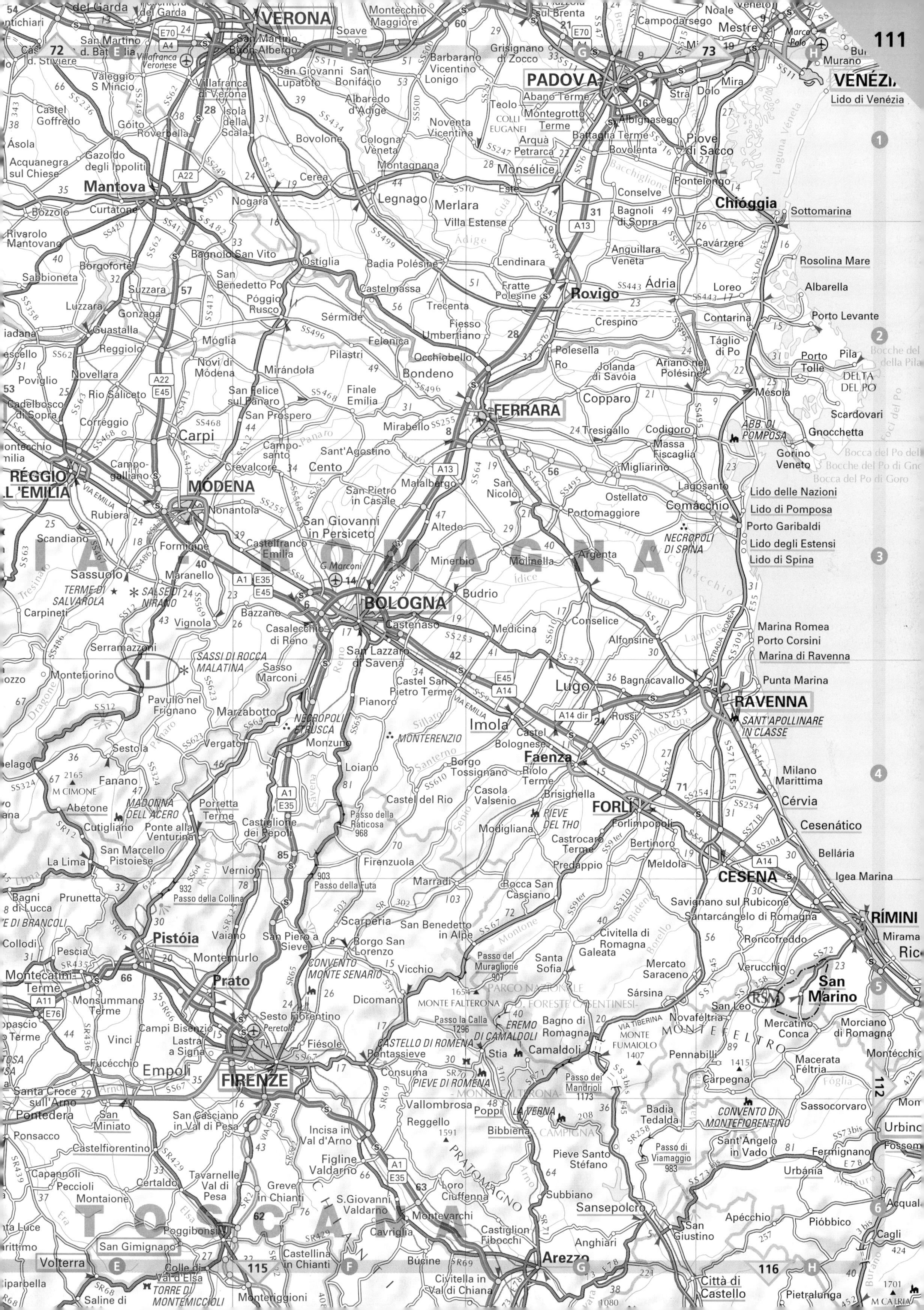

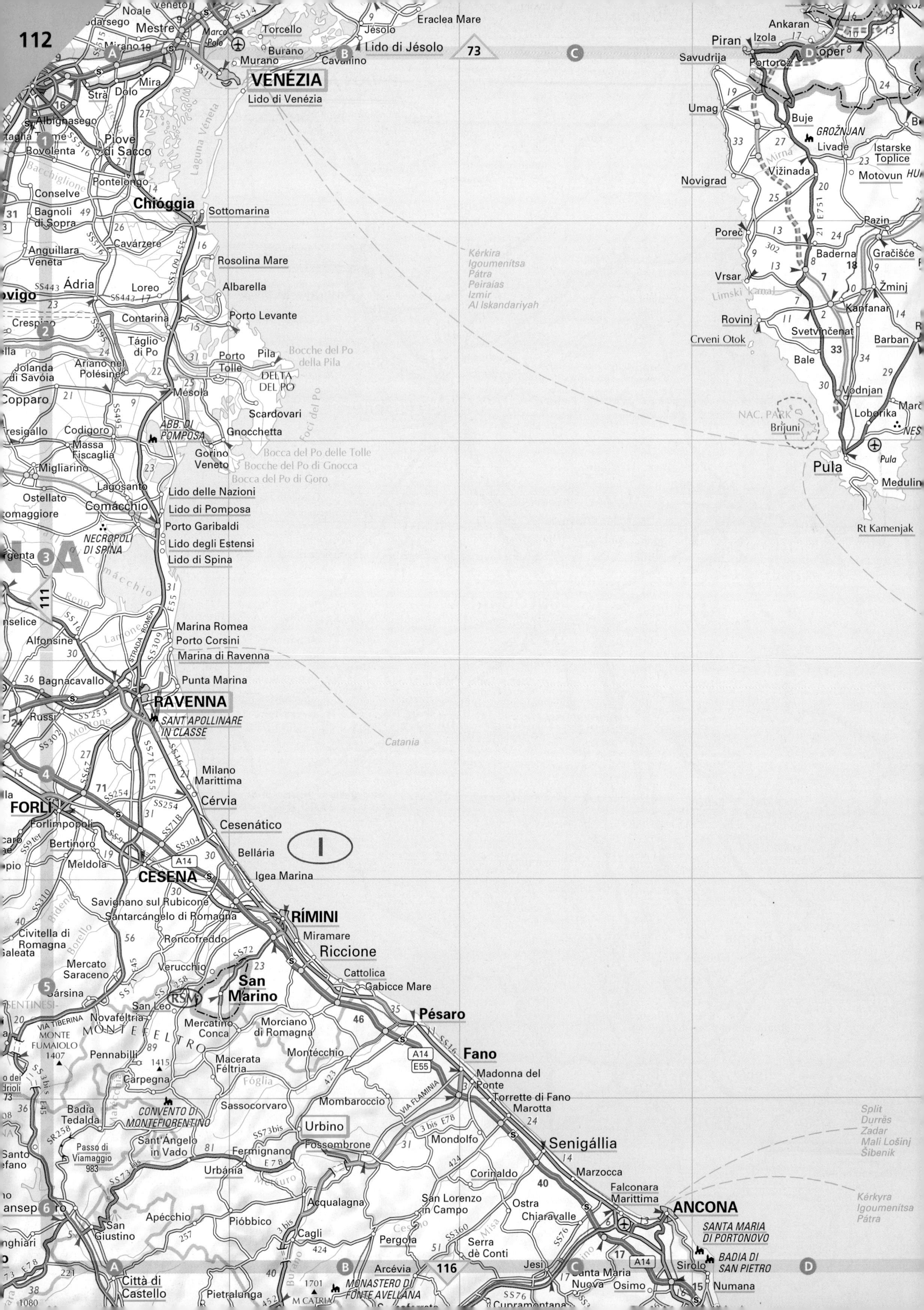

Noale
Veneto
SS14
Mestre
Marco Polo
Mirano 19
Torcello
Jésolo
Eracléa Mare
Ankaran
Piran
Izola
oper 8
Murano
Burano
Lido di Jésolo
73
Savudrija
Portorož
Cavallino
VENÉZIA
Lido di Venézia
Umag
GROŽNJAN
HU
Strà Dolo
Mira
Albignasego
Piove di Sacco
Buje
Livade
Istarske Toplice
Bovolenta
Pontelongo
Novigrad
Vižinada
Motovun
Conselve
Bagnoli di Sopra
Chióggia
Sottomarina
E751
31
49
Cavárzere
Porec
Baderna
Gračišće
Anguillara Veneta
Ádria
Loreo
Rosolina Mare
Vrsar
Žminj
ovigo
Crespino
Albarella
Kamfanar
Contarina
Porto Levante
Rovinj
Svetvinčenat
Barban
Táglio di Po
Porto Tolle
Pila
Crveni Otok
33
Ariano nel Polésine
DELTA DEL PO
Bale
Vódnjan
Jolanda di Savóia
Mésola
Scardovari
Loberika
Copparo
ABB. DI POMPOSA
Gnocchetta
NAC. PARK
Brijuni
Pula
resigallo
Codigoro
Massa Fiscaglia
Gorino Veneto
Migliarino
Lagosanto
Lido delle Nazioni
Pula
Medulin
Ostellato
Comácchio
Lido di Pomposa
Porto Garibaldi
Rt Kamenjak
rgenta
NECROPOLI DI SPINA
Lido degli Estensi
Lido di Spina
111
Alfonsine
Marina Romea
Porto Corsini
Marina di Ravenna
Bagnacavallo
Punta Marina
Russi
RAVENNA
SANT'APOLLINARE IN CLASSE
Catania
FORLÍ
Milano Maríttima
71
Cérvia
Forlimpopoli
Cesenático
Bertinoro
Bellária
Meldola
CESENA
Igea Marina
Savignano sul Rubicone
Santarcángelo di Romagna
RÍMINI
Civitella di Romagna Galeata
Roncofreddo
Miramare
Riccione
Mercato Saraceno
Verucchio
Cattolica
Gabicce Mare
Bársina
San Leo
San Marino
ENTINESI
Novafeltria
Mercatino Conca
Morciano di Romagna
Pésaro
VIA TIBERINA
MONTE FUMAIOLO 1407
Pennabilli
Montécchio
Fano
Madonna del Ponte
Carpegna
CONVENTO DI MONTEFIORENTINO
Macerata Féltria
Sassocorvaro
Mombaroccio
VIA FLAMINIA
Torrette di Fano
Marotta
Badia Tedalda
Sant'Angelo in Vado
Urbino
Fossombrone
Mondolfo
Senigállia
Passo di Viamaggio 983
Fermignano
Marzocca
Urbánia
Corinaldo
Santo
Acqualagna
San Lorenzo in Campo
Ostra
Chiaravalle
Falconara Maríttima
ANCONA
Apécchio
Pióbbico
Cagli
Pergola
Serra dè Conti
SANTA MARIA DI PORTONOVO
Città di Castello
Pietralunga
116
Arcévia
Jesi
Santa Maria Nuova
Osimo
Numana
Sirolo
BADIA DI SAN PIETRO

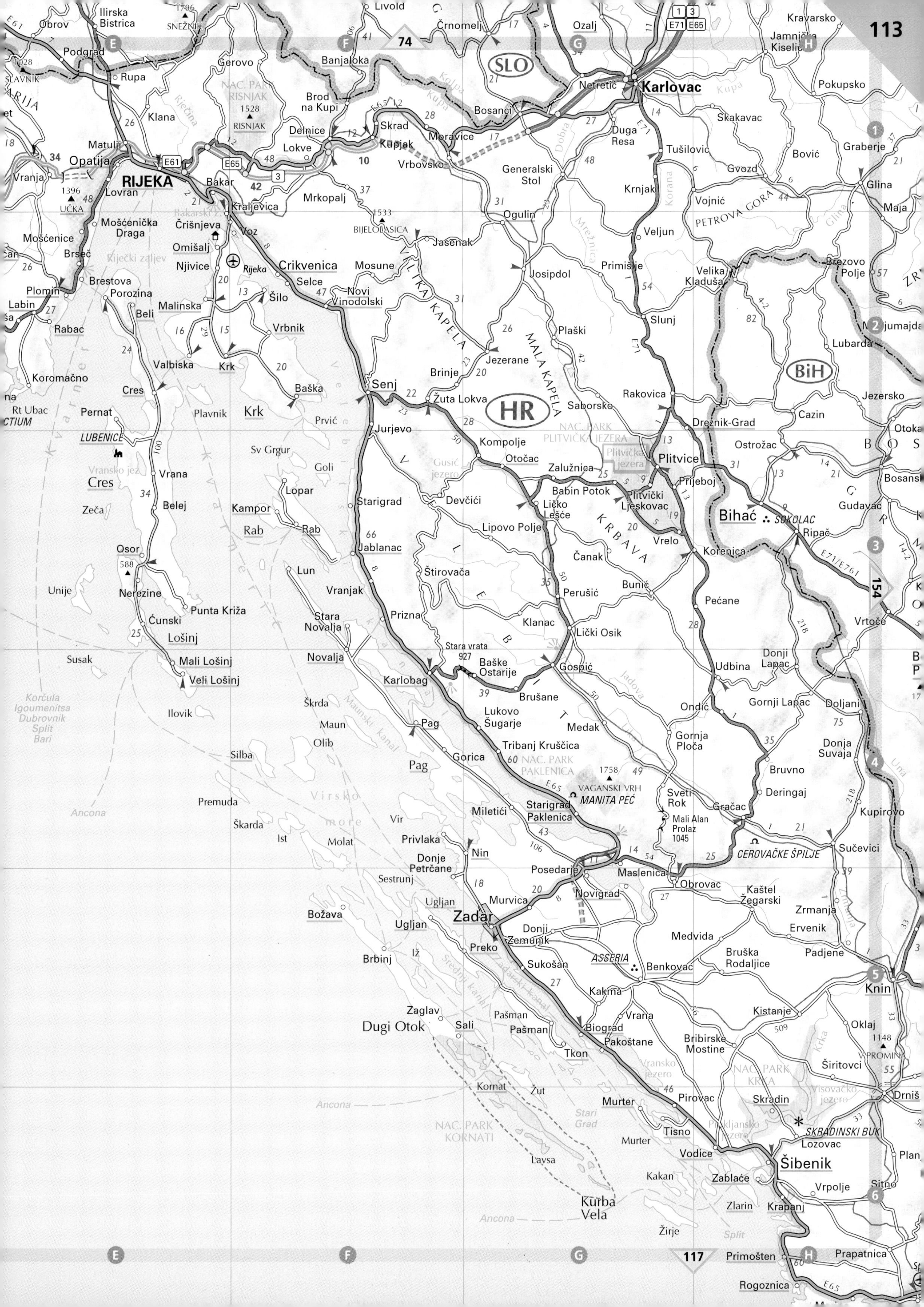

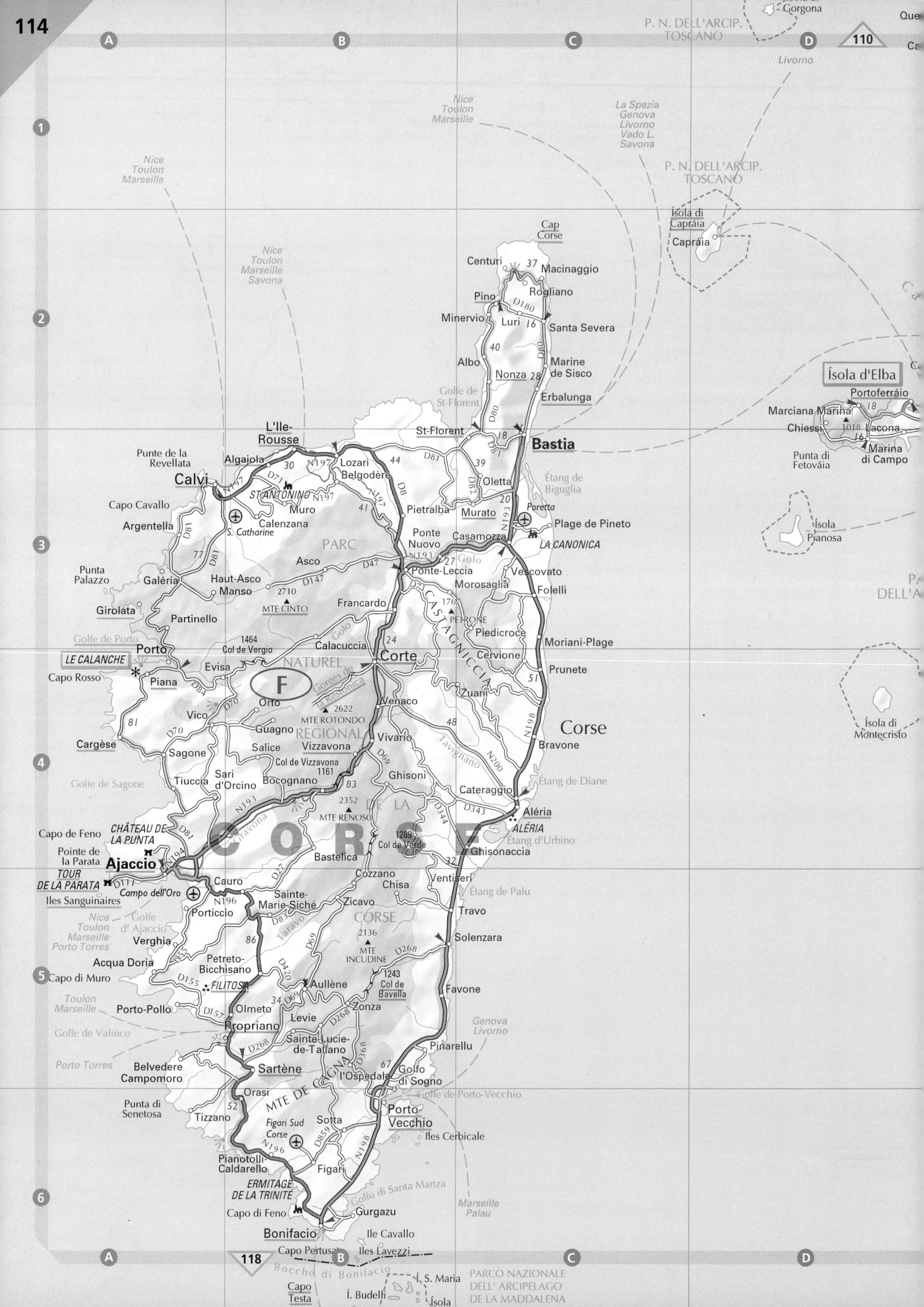

110

Gorgona

Livorno

Nice
Toulon
Marseille

La Spezia
Genova
Livorno
Vado L.
Savona

Nice
Toulon
Marseille
Savona

P. N. DELL'ARCIP.
TOSCANO

Ísola di
Capráia

Capráia

Nice
Toulon
Marseille

Cap
Corse

Centuri   37   Macinaggio
Pino   Rogliano
Minervio   Luri   16
                        Santa Severa
Albo   40
Nonza   28   Marine
                        de Sisco
Erbalunga

Golfe de
St-Florent

St-Florent   18

Bastia

Ísola d'Elba

Portoferráio   18
Marciana Marina   Lacona
Chiessi   1018   16
Punta di   Marina
Fetováia   di Campo

L'Ile-
Rousse
Punte de la
Revellata   Algajola   Lozari
Calvi   30   N197   Belgodère   44
ST-ANTONINO   D71   41
Capo Cavallo   Muro   Pietralba
Argentella   Calenzana   Ponte
          S. Catharine   Nuovo
              77   PARC   N193
Punta   Galéria   Haut-Asco   Ponte-Leccia
Palazzo   Manso   Morosaglia
          2710   Vescovato
Girolata   MTE CINTO   Folelli
Partinello   Francardo
Golfe de Porto   1464   PETRONE
Porto   Col de Vergio   Piedicroce
LE CALANCHE   Calacuccia   **Corte**   Cervione
Capo Rosso   Evisa   NATUREL   Morani-Plage
          Piana   F   Prunete
              Orto   Gorges de   51
          Vico   la Restonica   Venaco   Zuani
Cargèse   Guagno   2622   Bravone
          Salice   MTE ROTONDO
Sagone   Vizzavona   Vivario
          Col de Vizzavona
Tiuccia   Sari   1161   Ghisoni
Golfe de Sagone   d'Orcino   Bocognano   83
Capo de Feno   CHÂTEAU DE   MTE RENOSO   Cateraggio
          LA PUNTA   2352
Pointe de   N194   1289   Aléria
la Parata   **Ajaccio**   Col de Verde   ALÉRIA
TOUR   Campo dell'Oro   Bastelica   Ghisonaccia
DE LA PARATA   Cozzano
Iles Sanguinaires   N196   Sainte-   Chisa   Ventiseri
          Porticcio   Marie-Siché
          Zicavo   Travo
Verghia   CORSE
Acqua Doria   MTE   Solenzara
          Petreto-   INCUDINE
Capo di Muro   Bicchisano   2136
          FILITOSA   1243   Favone
Toulon   Porto-Pollo   Aullène   Col de
Marseille   D157   Olmeto   Bavella
Golfe de Valinco   Propriano   Levie   Zonza
          Sainte-Lucie-   Pinarellu
Porto Torres   Belvedere   de-Tallano
          Campomoro   Sartène   67   Golfo
Punta di   l'Ospedale   di Sogno
Senetosa   Orasi   MTE DE   Golfe de Porto-Vecchio
          Tizzano   52   **Porto-**
              Figari Sud   **Vecchio**
          Pianotolli-   Corse   Sotta   Iles Cerbicale
          Caldarello   Figari   Golfu di Santa Manza
          ERMITAGE
          DE LA TRINITÉ   Marseille
              Palau
          Capo di Feno   Gurgazu
          Bonifacio   Ile Cavallo
          Capo Pertusato   Iles Lavezzi

C O R S E

Corse

Étang de Diane

Étang d'Urbino

Étang de Palu

Ísola
Pianosa

Ísola di
Montecristo

PARCO NAZIONALE
DELL'ARCIPELAGO
DE LA MADDALENA

Bocche di Bonifacio

f. S. Maria

Capo
Testa   f. Budelli   Ísola

118

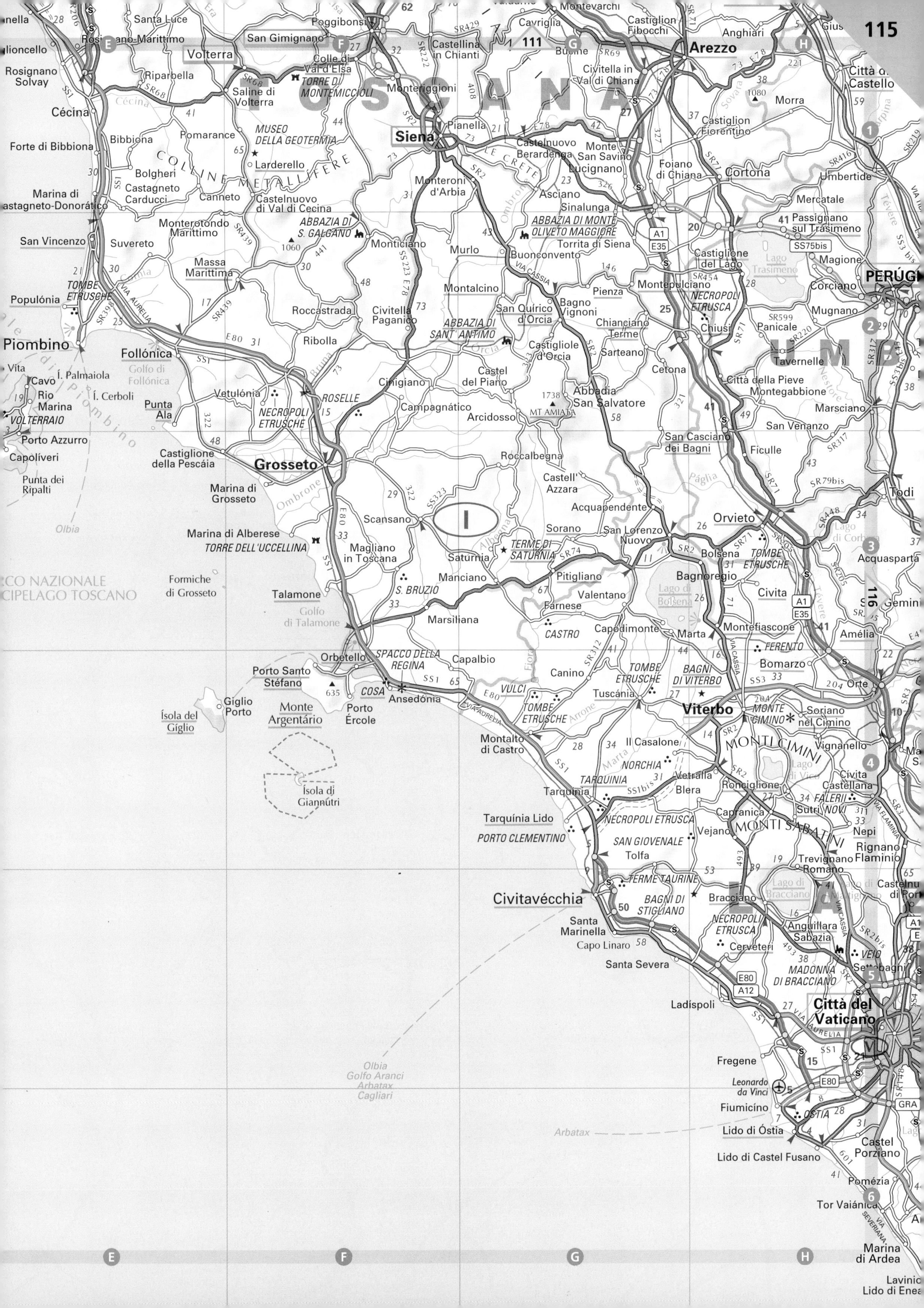
TOSCANA
UMBRIA
COLLINE METALLIFERE
Volterra
San Gimignano
Poggibonsi
Colle di Val d'Elsa
Castellina in Chianti
Cavriglia
Montevarchi
Castiglion Fibocchi
Anghiari
Arezzo
Città di Castello
Rosignano Marittimo
Rosignano Solvay
Riparbella
Saline di Volterra
TORRE DI MONTEMICCIOLI
Monteriggioni
Civitella in Val di Chiana
Morra
Cécina
Pianella
Siena
Castiglion Fiorentino
Forte di Bibbiona
Bibbiona
Pomarance
MUSEO DELLA GEOTERMIA
Castelnuovo Berardenga
Monte San Savino
Lucignano
Foiano di Chiana
Cortona
Umbertide
Larderello
Bolgheri
Castagneto Carducci
Canneto
Castelnuovo di Val di Cecina
Monteroni d'Arbia
Asciano
Sinalunga
Marina di Castagneto-Donorático
Mercatale
Passignano sul Trasimeno
Monterotondo Marittimo
ABBAZIA DI S. GALGANO
ABBAZIA DI MONTE OLIVETO MAGGIORE
Torrita di Siena
San Vincenzo
Suvereto
Monticiano
Murlo
Buonconvento
Castiglione del Lago
Lago Trasimeno
Magione
Massa Marittima
Montalcino
Pienza
Montepulciano
PERÚGIA
Corciano
TOMBE ETRUSCHE
Populónia
VIA AURELIA
Roccastrada
Civitella Paganico
Bagno Vignoni
San Quirico d'Orcia
ABBAZIA DI SANT'ANTIMO
Chianciano Terme
NECROPOLI ETRUSCA
Chiusi
Mugnano
Panicale
Piombino
Follónica
Golfo di Follónica
Ribolla
Castiglione d'Orcia
Sarteano
Cetona
Tavernelle
Vita
Cavo
Rio Marina
Í. Palmaiola
Í. Cerboli
Cinigiano
Castel del Piano
Città della Pieve
Montegabbione
Vetulónia
ROSELLE
Punta Ala
NECROPOLI ETRUSCHE
Campagnático
Arcidosso
MT AMIATA
Abbadia San Salvatore
Marsciano
VOLTERRAIO
Porto Azzurro
Capolíveri
Punta dei Ripalti
Castiglione della Pescáia
Grosseto
San Casciano dei Bagni
San Venanzo
Roccalbegna
Ficulle
Marina di Grosseto
Ombrone
Castell' Azzara
Acquapendente
Todi
Olbia
Scansano
Marina di Alberese
TORRE DELL'UCCELLINA
Sorano
San Lorenzo Nuovo
Orvieto
Magliano in Toscana
TERME DI SATURNIA
Saturnia
Bolsena
TOMBE ETRUSCHE
Acquasparta
PARCO NAZIONALE ARCIPELAGO TOSCANO
Formiche di Grosseto
Manciano
S. BRUZIO
Pitigliano
Bagnoregio
Lago di Bolsena
Civita
Talamone
Golfo di Talamone
Valentano
Farnese
Marsiliana
CASTRO
Capodimonte
Marta
Montefiascone
Amélia
FERENTO
Orbetello
SPACCO DELLA REGINA
Capalbio
Bomarzo
Porto Santo Stéfano
Canino
TOMBE ETRUSCHE
BAGNI DI VITERBO
Orte
COSA
Ansedónia
VULCI
Tuscánia
Viterbo
MONTE CIMINO
Soriano nel Cimino
Ísola del Gíglio
Giglio Porto
Monte Argentário
Porto Ércole
VIA AURELIA
Montalto di Castro
Il Casalone
MONTI CIMINI
Vignanello
NORCHIA
Civita Castellana
Ísola di Giannútri
TARQUINIA
Vetralla
Tarquínia
Blera
Ronciglione
Lago di Vico
FALERII NOVI
Sutri
Capranica
Tarquínia Lido
NECROPOLI ETRUSCA
Vejano
MONTI SABATINI
Nepi
PORTO CLEMENTINO
SAN GIOVENALE
Tolfa
Rignano Flaminio
Trevignano Romano
VIA FLAMINIA
TERME TAURINE
Civitavécchia
BAGNI DI STIGLIANO
Bracciano
Lago di Bracciano
Castelnuovo di Porto
Santa Marinella
NECROPOLI ETRUSCA
Anguillara Sabazia
Capo Linaro
Cerveteri
VEIO
Santa Severa
MADONNA DI BRACCIANO
Settebagni
VIA CASSIA
Ladíspoli
Città del Vaticano
Fregene
Leonardo da Vinci
Fiumicino
OSTIA
Lido di Óstia
Lido di Castel Fusano
Castel Porziano
Arbatax
Olbia
Golfo Aranci
Arbatax
Cagliari
Pomézia
Tor Vaiánica
VIA SEVERIANA
Marina di Ardea
Lavinio
Lido di Enea
A1
E35
E78
E80
A12
GRA
SS75bis
111
116
62
E
F
G
H
1
2
3
4
5
6

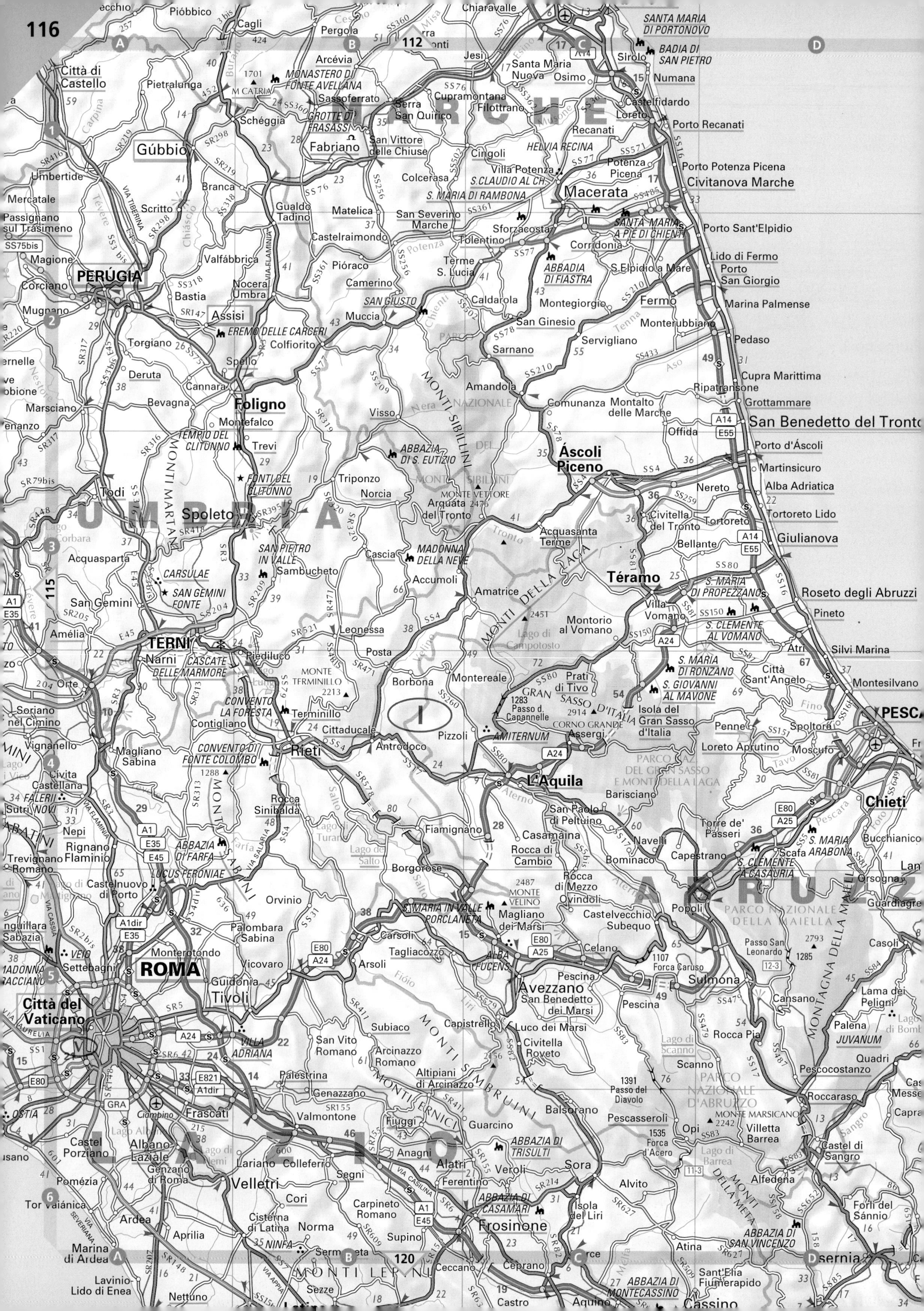

112
115
120
MARCHE
UMBRIA
LAZIO
ABRUZZO
Cagli
Piòbbico
Pergola
Chiaravalle
SANTA MARIA DI PORTONOVO
BADIA DI SAN PIETRO
Sirolo
Numana
Jesi
Santa Maria Nuova
Osimo
Arcévia
MONASTERO DI FONTE AVELLANA
M. CATRIA
Città di Castello
Pietralunga
Sassoferrato
Cupramontana
Filottrano
Castelfidardo
Loreto
Porto Recanati
Recanati
Serra San Quirico
Schéggia
GROTTE DI FRASASSI
Fabriano
San Vittore delle Chiuse
Gúbbio
Cingoli
HELVIA RECINA
Umbertide
Villa Potenza
S. CLAUDIO AL CH.
Potenza Picena
Porto Potenza Picena
Civitanova Marche
Colcerasa
Macerata
Mercatale
Branca
Scritto
Gualdo Tadino
Matelica
S. MARIA DI RAMBONA
San Severino Marche
Passignano sul Trasimeno
Sforzacosta
SANTA MARIA A PIÈ DI CHIENTI
Porto Sant'Elpidio
Castelraimondo
Tolentino
Corridonia
Magione
Valfábbrica
Terme S. Lucia
ABBADIA DI FIASTRA
S. Elpidio a Mare
Lido di Fermo
Porto San Giorgio
PERÚGIA
Pióraco
Camerino
Corciano
Bastia
Nocera Umbra
Caldarola
Montegiorgio
Fermo
Marina Palmense
Mugnano
Assisi
SAN GIUSTO
Muccia
San Ginesio
Monterubbiano
EREMO DELLE CARCERI
Colfiorito
Torgiano
Sarnano
Servigliano
Pedaso
Spello
Deruta
Cannara
Amandola
Cupra Marittima
Ripatransone
Bevagna
Foligno
Visso
Comunanza
Montalto delle Marche
Grottammare
Marsciano
Montefalco
San Benedetto del Tronto
Offida
TEMPIO DEL CLITUNNO
Trevi
ABBAZIA DI S. EUTIZIO
MONTI SIBILLINI
Áscoli Piceno
Porto d'Áscoli
Martinsicuro
FONTI DEL CLITUNNO
Triponzo
Norcia
MONTE VETTORE 2476
Nereto
Alba Adriatica
Todi
Arquata del Tronto
Civitella del Tronto
Tortoreto Lido
Tortoreto
MONTI MARTANI
Spoleto
Acquasanta Terme
Giulianova
Bellante
Acquasparta
SAN PIETRO IN VALLE
Cascia
MADONNA DELLA NEVE
Téramo
CARSULAE
Sambucheto
SAN GEMINI FONTE
Accumoli
S. MARIA DI PROPEZZANO
Roseto degli Abruzzi
San Gemini
Amatrice
MONTI DELLA LAGA
Villa Vomano
Pineto
Montorio al Vomano
S. CLEMENTE AL VOMANO
Amélia
Leonessa
Lago di Campotosto
TERNI
Narni
CASCATE DELLE MARMORE
Piediluco
Posta
Atri
Silvi Marina
Orte
MONTE TERMINILLO 2213
Borbona
Montereale
S. MARIA DI RONZANO
Città Sant'Angelo
Montesilvano
Prati di Tivo
S. GIOVANNI AL MAVONE
Soriano nel Cimino
CONVENTO LA FORESTA
Terminillo
GRAN SASSO D'ITALIA
Passo d. Capannelle
CORNO GRANDE 2914
Isola del Gran Sasso d'Italia
PESCARA
Contigliano
Cittaducale
Pizzoli
AMITERNUM
Assergi
Penne
Spoltore
Vignanello
Magliano Sabina
CONVENTO DI FONTE COLOMBO
Rieti
Antrodoco
Loreto Aprutino
Moscufo
Civita Castellana
MONTI SABINI
PARCO NAZ. DEL GRAN SASSO E MONTI DELLA LAGA
L'Aquila
Barisciano
FALERII NOVI
Sutri
Rocca Sinibalda
Chieti
Nepi
San Paolo di Peltuino
Torre de' Passeri
Rignano Flaminio
ABBAZIA DI FARFA
Fiamignano
Lago del Turano
Casamaina
Navelli
Trevignano Romano
Lago del Salto
Rocca di Cambio
Bominaco
Capestrano
S. MARIA ARABONA
Bucchianico
LUCUS FERONIAE
Castelnuovo di Porto
Borgorose
S. CLEMENTE A CASAURIA
Scafa
Orsogna
Rocca di Mezzo
MONTE VELINO 2487
Ovindoli
Orvinio
S. MARIA IN VALLE PORCLANETA
Magliano dei Marsi
Castelvecchio Subequo
Popoli
PARCO NAZIONALE DELLA MAIELLA
Guardiagrele
Sabazia
Palombara Sabina
Carsoli
VEIO
Settebagni
Monterotondo
Tagliacozzo
ALBA FUCENS
Celano
Passo San Leonardo
MONTAGNA DELLA MAIELLA
Casoli
ROMA
Vicovaro
Arsoli
Forca Caruso
Sulmona
Avezzano
Pescina
Guidonia
Tivoli
San Benedetto dei Marsi
Città del Vaticano
Cansano
Lama dei Peligni
Capistrello
Luco dei Marsi
Palena
JUVANUM
VILLA ADRIANA
Subiaco
Civitella Roveto
Rocca Pia
OSTIA
San Vito Romano
Arcinazzo Romano
MONTI SIMBRUINI
Lago di Scanno
Scanno
Quadri
Pescocostanzo
Altipiani di Arcinazzo
Palestrina
Passo del Diavolo
PARCO NAZIONALE D'ABRUZZO
Roccaraso
Genazzano
Balsorano
Ciampino
Frascati
Valmontone
MONTI ERNICI
Pescasseroli
MONTE MARSICANO 2242
Guarcino
Fiuggi
Villetta Barrea
Castel Porziano
Albano Laziale
ABBAZIA DI TRISULTI
Forca d'Acero
Opi
Castel di Sangro
Lago di Barrea
Lariano
Colleferro
Anagni
Alatri
Sora
Genzano di Roma
Segni
Veroli
Ferentino
Alvito
MONTI DELLA META
Alfedena
Pomézia
Velletri
Cori
ABBAZIA DI CASAMARI
Isola del Liri
Tor Vaiánica
Carpineto Romano
Ardea
Forlì del Sánnio
Cisterna di Latina
Norma
Frosinone
Aprilia
NINFA
Supino
ABBAZIA DI SAN VINCENZO
Marina di Ardea
Sermoneta
Atina
Isernia
MONTI LEPINI
Ceccano
Ceprano
Lavinio-Lido di Enea
Sezze
Sant'Elia Fiumerapido
Nettuno
ABBAZIA DI MONTECASSINO
Castro
Aquino
Cassino

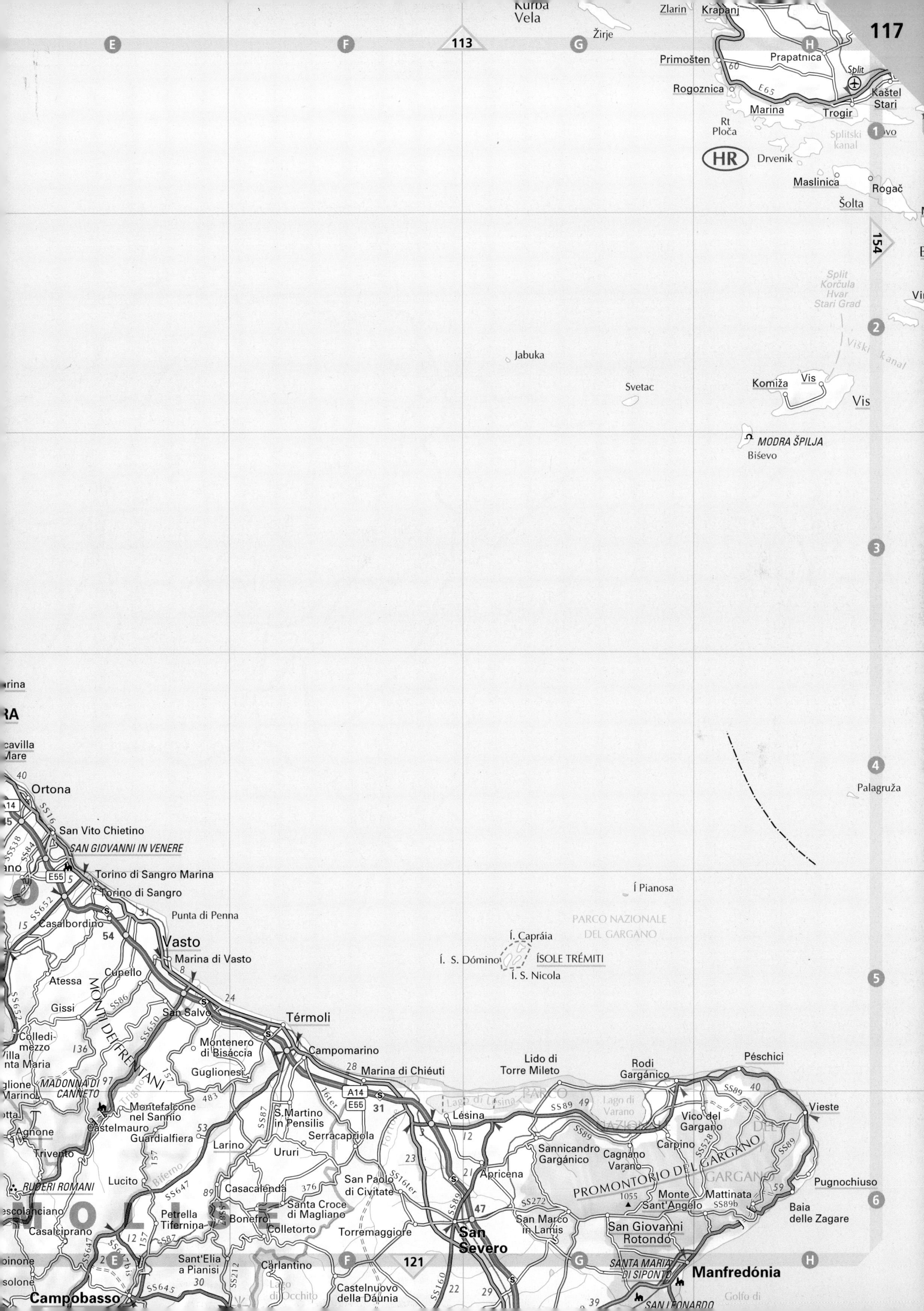

Kurba Vela

Zlarin   Krapanj

Žirje

Primošten

Prapatnica

Rogoznica

Split

E65

Kaštel Stari

Marina

Rt Ploča

Trogir

HR   Drvenik

Maslinica

Rogač

Šolta

154

Split
Korčula
Hvar
Stari Grad

Viški kanal

Jabuka

Svetac

Komiža   Vis

Vis

MODRA ŠPILJA

Biševo

Palagruža

Ortona

San Vito Chietino

SAN GIOVANNI IN VENERE

Torino di Sangro Marina

Torino di Sangro

Punta di Penna

Casalbordino

Vasto

Marina di Vasto

Cupello

Atessa

Í Pianosa

PARCO NAZIONALE
DEL GARGANO

Í. Capráia

Í. S. Dómino   ÍSOLE TRÉMITI

Í. S. Nicola

Gissi

San Salvo

Térmoli

Colledi-
mezzo

Villa
nta Maria

Montenero
di Bisáccia

Campomarino

Lido di
Torre Mileto

Rodi
Gargánico

Péschici

Guglionesi

Marina di Chiéuti

PARCO

SS89

gione
Marinc

MADONNA DI
CANNETO

Montefalcone
nel Sannio

A14

E55

Lésina

Lago di Lésina

Lago di
Varano

Vieste

Castelmauro

Guardialfiera

S. Martino
in Pensilis

Serracapriola

SS89

Vico del
Gargano

Agnone

Larino

Ururi

Sannicandro
Gargánico

Cagnano
Varano

Carpino

Trivento

RUDERI ROMANI

Lucito

Casacalenda

San Paolo
di Civitate

Apricena

PROMONTORIO DEL GARGANO

GARGANO

Pugnochiuso

oinone

Petrella
Tifernina

Bonefro

Santa Croce
di Magliano

Torremaggiore

San
Severo

San Marco
in Lamis

Monte
Sant'Angelo

Mattinata

San Giovanni
Rotondo

Baia
delle Zagare

Casalciprano

MOLISE

Sant'Elia
a Pianisi

Cárlantino

121

SANTA MARIA
DI SIPONTO

Manfredónia

Campobasso

Castelnuovo
della Dáunia

Lago
dell'Occhito

Golfo di

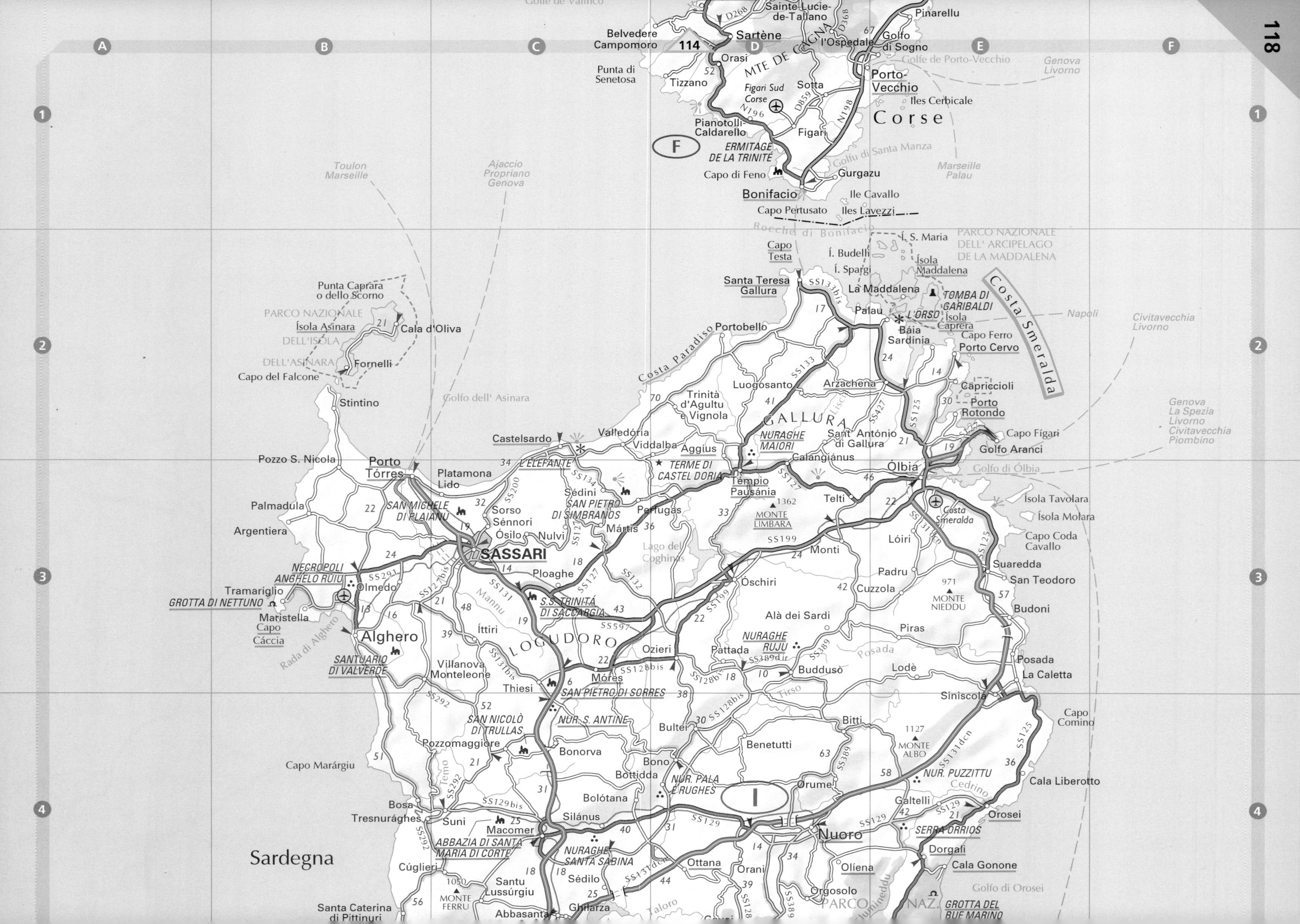

Corse

Porto-Vecchio

Sardegna

SASSARI

Costa Smeralda

Olbia

Nuoro

Alghero

Porto Tórres

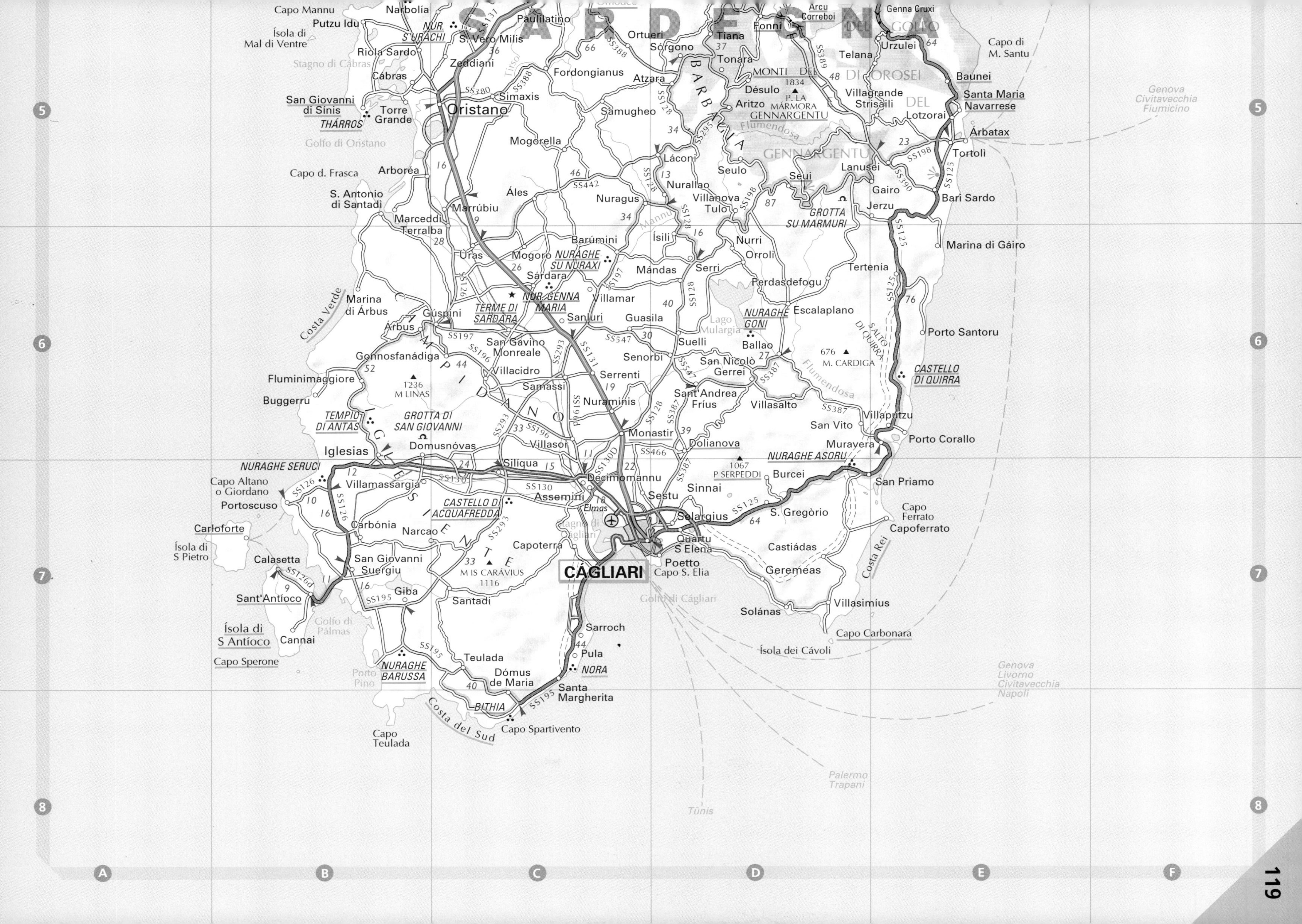
SARDEGNA
CÁGLIARI
Oristano
Iglesias
Carbónia
Golfo di Cágliari
Golfo di Oristano
Golfo di Pálmas
Costa Verde
Costa Rei
Costa del Sud
Capo Teulada
Capo Spartivento
Capo Carbonara
Capo Ferrato
Capoferrato
Capo Sperone
Capo Mannu
Capo S. Elia
Capo d. Frasca
Capo di M. Santu
Capo Altano o Giordano
Ísola di S Pietro
Ísola di S Antíoco
Ísola dei Cávoli
Ísola di Mal di Ventre
Carloforte
Calasetta
Sant'Antíoco
Cannai
Portoscuso
Tortolì
Árbatax
Lanusei
Bari Sardo
Baunei
Santa Maria Navarrese
Muravera
Villaputzu
Porto Corallo
San Vito
Villasimíus
Pula
Sarroch
Quartu S Elena
Poetto
Sínnai
Selargius
Sestu
Monastir
Decimomannu
Assemini
Elmas
Capoterra
Villacidro
San Gavino Monreale
Sanluri
Gúspini
Árbus
Terralba
Marrúbiu
Uras
Mogoro
Áles
Barúmini
Ísili
Láconi
Sórgono
Fonni
Aritzo
Désulo
Tonara
Seui
Seulo
Jerzu
Gairo
Perdasdefogu
Escalaplano
Ballao
Dolianova
Senorbì
Mándas
Nurri
Orroli
Serri
Teulada
Santadi
Narcao
Giba
Domusnóvas
Villamassargia
Siliqua
Fluminimaggiore
Buggerru
Gonnosfanádiga
Cábras
Riola Sardo
Narbolía
Simaxis
Samugheo
Fordongianus
Paulilatino
BARBAGIA
GENNARGENTU
MONTI DEL GENNARGENTU
1834 P. LA MÁRMORA
1236 M LINAS
1116 M IS CARÁVIUS
1067 P SERPEDDI
676 M. CARDIGA
Lago Mulargia
Flumendosa
Tirso
NURAGHE SU NURAXI
NURAGHE ASORU
NURAGHE BARUSSA
NURAGHE SERUCI
NURAGHE GONI
THÁRROS
NORA
BITHIA
CASTELLO DI QUIRRA
CASTELLO DI ACQUAFREDDA
GROTTA SU MARMURI
GROTTA DI SAN GIOVANNI
TEMPIO DI ANTAS
TERME DI SARDARA
SS125
SS131
SS128
SS126
SS195
SS130
SS387
Genova Civitavecchia Fiumicino
Genova Livorno Civitavecchia Napoli
Palermo Trapani
Tunis
A
B
C
D
E
F
5
6
7
8

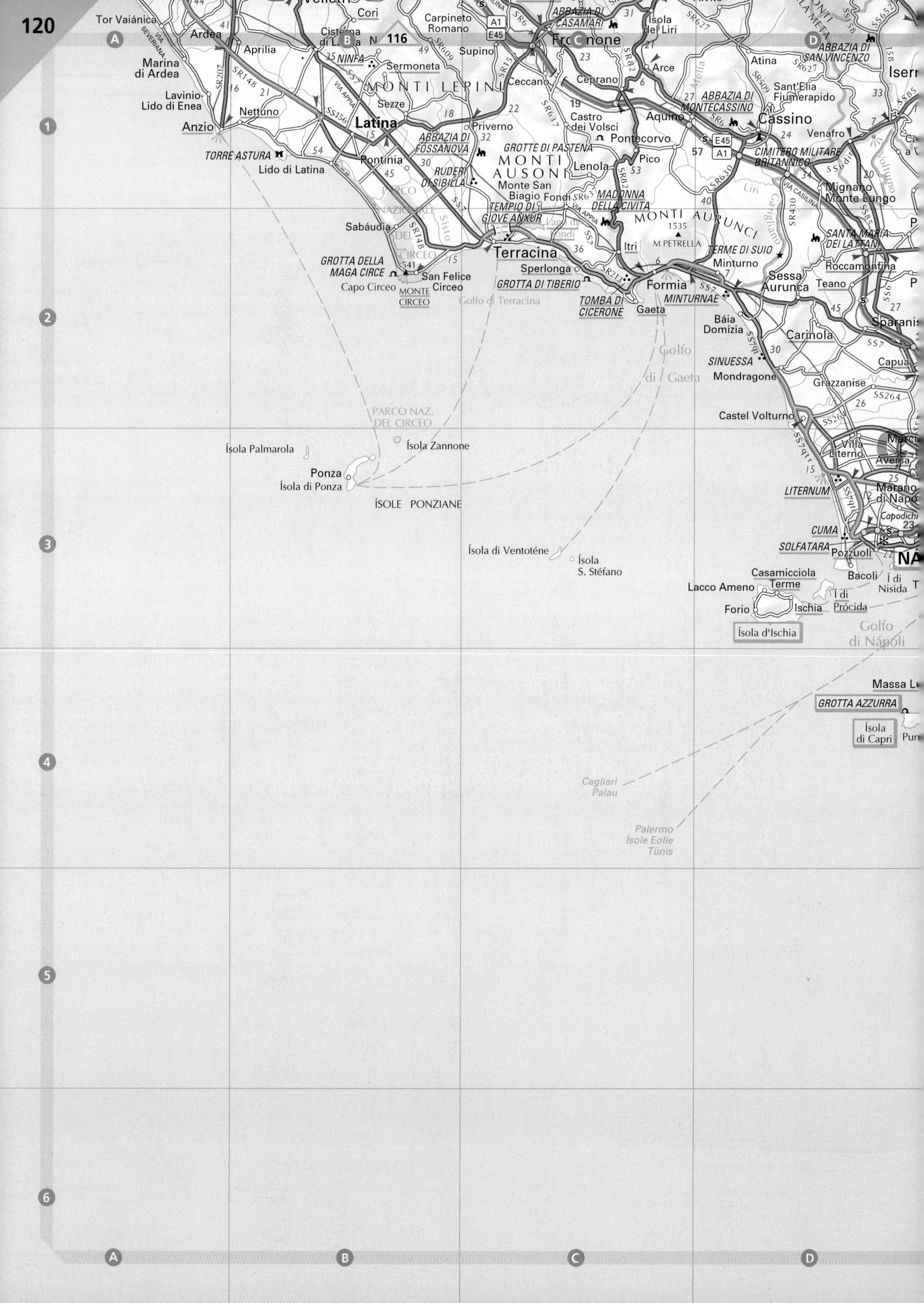

Tor Vaiánica
Ardea
Aprilia
Marina di Ardea
Lavinio-Lido di Enea
Anzio
Nettúno
Latina
TORRE ASTURA
Lido di Latina
Pontinia
Sabáudia
GROTTA DELLA MAGA CIRCE
Capo Circeo
San Felice Circeo
MONTE CIRCEO
Cori
Cisterna di L.
NINFA
Sermoneta
Sezze
Priverno
ABBAZIA DI FOSSANOVA
RUDERI DI SIBILLA
Terracina
Sperlonga
GROTTA DI TIBERIO
Golfo di Terracina
Carpineto Romano
Supino
MONTI LEPINI
Ceccano
Castro dei Volsci
Pontecorvo
Pico
Lenola
MONTE AUSONI
Monte San Biagio Fondi
TEMPIO DI GIOVE ANXUR
Itri
M PETRELLA
MADONNA DELLA CIVITA
TOMBA DI CICERONE
Gaeta
ABBAZIA DI CASAMARI
Isola del Liri
Frosinone
Ceprano
Aquino
ABBAZIA DI MONTECASSINO
Arce
Alvito
Atina
Sant'Elia Fiumerapido
Cassino
CIMITERO MILITARE BRITANNICO
Venafro
ABBAZIA DI SAN VINCENZO
Iser
MONTI AURUNCI
Terme di Suio
Minturno
MINTURNAE
Formia
Sessa Aurunca
Teano
Roccamonfina
Báia Domízia
Carinola
SINUESSA
Mondragone
Grazzanise
Castel Volturno
Villa Literno
LITERNUM
CUMA
SOLFATARA
Pozzuoli
Casamicciola Terme
Lacco Ameno
Forio
Ischia
Ísola d'Ischia
Bacoli
Í di Nisida
Í di Prócida
Golfo di Nápoli
Capua
Sparanis
Marci
Avesa
Marano di Napo
Capodichi
NÁ
T
Massa L
GROTTA AZZURRA
Ísola di Capri
Pun
Golfo di Gaeta

Ísola Palmarola
Ísola Zannone
Ponza
Ísola di Ponza
ÍSOLE PONZIANE
Ísola di Ventoténe
Ísola S. Stéfano
PARCO NAZ. DEL CIRCEO

Cagliari Palau
Palermo Ísole Eolie Tùnis

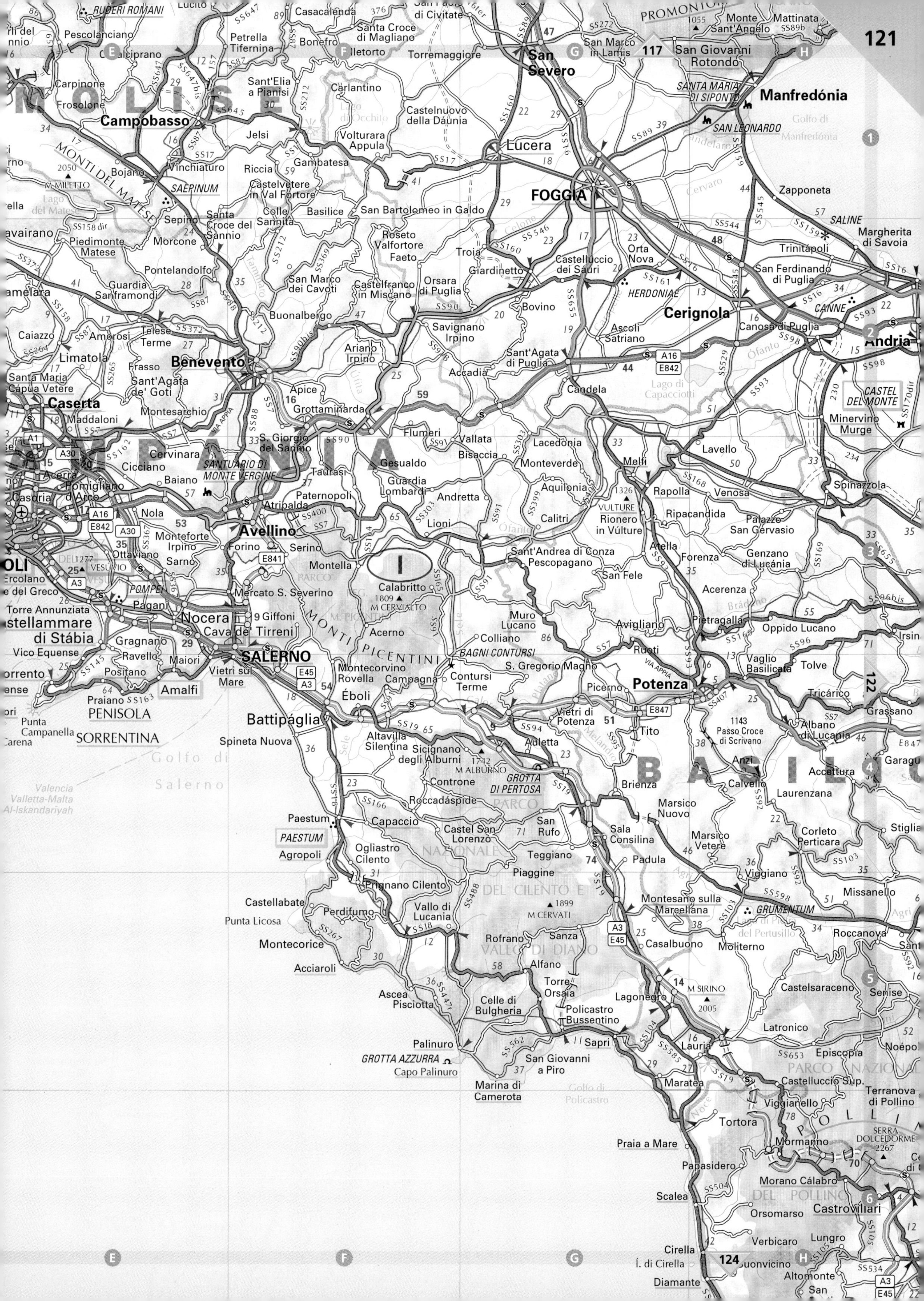
MOLISE
Campobasso
Carpinone
Frosolone
Pescolanciano
Petrella Tifernina
Casacalenda
Santa Croce di Magliano
Bonefro
Torremaggiore
San Severo
San Marco in Lamis
San Giovanni Rotondo
Monte Sant'Angelo
Mattinata
PROMONTORIO
Sant'Elia a Pianisi
Carlantino
Castelnuovo della Dáunia
Volturara Appula
Jelsi
Gambatesa
Riccia
Vinchiaturo
Bojano
MONTI DEL MATESE
M. MILETTO
Lago del Matese
SAEPINUM
Sepino
Castelvetere in Val Fortore
Colle Sannita
Basilice
San Bartolomeo in Galdo
Lucera
FOGGIA
SANTA MARIA DI SIPONTO
Manfredónia
SAN LEONARDO
Golfo di Manfredónia
Zapponeta
SALINE
Margherita di Savoia
Trinitápoli
San Ferdinando di Puglia
Ortа Nova
Castelluccio dei Sauri
HERDONIAE
Cerignola
CANNE
Canosa di Puglia
Andria
Troia
Giardinetto
Roseto Valfortore
Faeto
Santa Croce del Sannio
Morcone
Piedimonte Matese
Pontelandolfo
Guardia Sanframondi
San Marco dei Cavoti
Castelfranco in Miscano
Orsara di Puglia
Bovino
Ascoli Satriano
Buonalbergo
Savignano Irpino
Ariano Irpino
Sant'Agata di Puglia
Accadia
Candela
Lago di Capacciotti
CASTEL DEL MONTE
Minervino Murge
Caiazzo
Amorosi
Telese Terme
Benevento
Limatola
Frasso
Sant'Agata de' Goti
Santa Maria Cápua Vetere
Caserta
Maddaloni
Montesarchio
Apice
Grottaminarda
Flumeri
Vallata
Bisaccia
Lacedónia
Monteverde
Melfi
Lavello
Spinazzola
CAMPANIA
Cervinara
Cicciano
S. Giorgio del Sannio
SANTUARIO DI MONTE VERGINE
Gesualdo
Taurasi
Guardia Lombardi
Andretta
Aquilonia
VULTURE
Rapolla
Venosa
Acerra
Pomigliano d'Arco
Casoria
Baiano
Nola
Atripalda
Paternopoli
Avellino
Monteforte Irpino
Lioni
Calitri
Rionero in Vúlture
Ripacandida
Palazzo San Gervasio
Ottaviano
VESUVIO
Sarno
Forino
Serino
Montella
Sant'Andrea di Conza
Pescopagano
Atella
Forenza
Genzano di Lucánia
Ercolano
Torre del Greco
POMPEI
Pagani
Mercato S. Severino
Calabritto
M. CERVIALTO
San Fele
Acerenza
Torre Annunziata
Castellammare di Stábia
Nocera
Giffoni
Cava de' Tirreni
MONTI PICENTINI
Acerno
Muro Lucano
Colliano
Avigliano
Pietragalla
Oppido Lucano
Vico Equense
Gragnano
Ravello
Maiori
Positano
Sorrento
Amalfi
Praiano
Vietri sul Mare
SALERNO
BAGNI CONTURSI
S. Gregorio Magno
Ruoti
Potenza
Vaglio Basilicata
Tolve
Tricárico
Grassano
PENISOLA SORRENTINA
Punta Campanella
Montecorvino Rovella
Campagna
Contursi Terme
Éboli
Battipáglia
Picerno
Vietri di Potenza
Tito
Passo Croce di Scrivano
Albano di Lucania
Spineta Nuova
Altavilla Silentina
Sicignano degli Alburni
M. ALBURNO
Auletta
GROTTA DI PERTOSA
Golfo di Salerno
BASILICATA
Anzi
Calvello
Accettura
Laurenzana
Valencia
Valletta-Malta
Al-Iskandariyah
Controne
Roccadáspide
Brienza
Marsico Nuovo
Paestum
PAESTUM
Capaccio
Agropoli
Castel San Lorenzo
San Rufo
Sala Consilina
Marsico Vetere
Corleto Perticara
Stigliano
Ogliastro Cilento
Teggiano
Padula
Viggiano
Missanello
Prignano Cilento
Piaggine
PARCO NAZIONALE DEL CILENTO E VALLO DI DIANO
Castellabate
Punta Licosa
Perdifumo
Vallo di Lucania
M. CERVATI
Montesano sulla Marcellana
GRUMENTUM
Lago di Pietra del Pertusillo
Roccanova
Montecorice
Acciaroli
Rofrano
Sanza
Casalbuono
Moliterno
Alfano
Torre Orsaia
Lagonegro
M. SIRINO
Castelsaraceno
Senise
Ascea
Pisciotta
Celle di Bulgheria
Policastro Bussentino
Latronico
Palinuro
GROTTA AZZURRA
Capo Palinuro
Sapri
San Giovanni a Piro
Lauria
Episcopia
Noépoli
Marina di Camerota
Golfo di Policastro
Maratea
Castelluccio Sup.
Terranova di Pollino
Viggianello
Tortora
Praia a Mare
Mormanno
SERRA DOLCEDORME
Papasidero
Morano Cálabro
PARCO NAZIONALE DEL POLLINO
Scalea
Castrovillari
Orsomarso
Verbicaro
Lungro
Cirella
Í. di Cirella
Diamante
Buonvicino
Altomonte
E
F
G
H
122
124
117

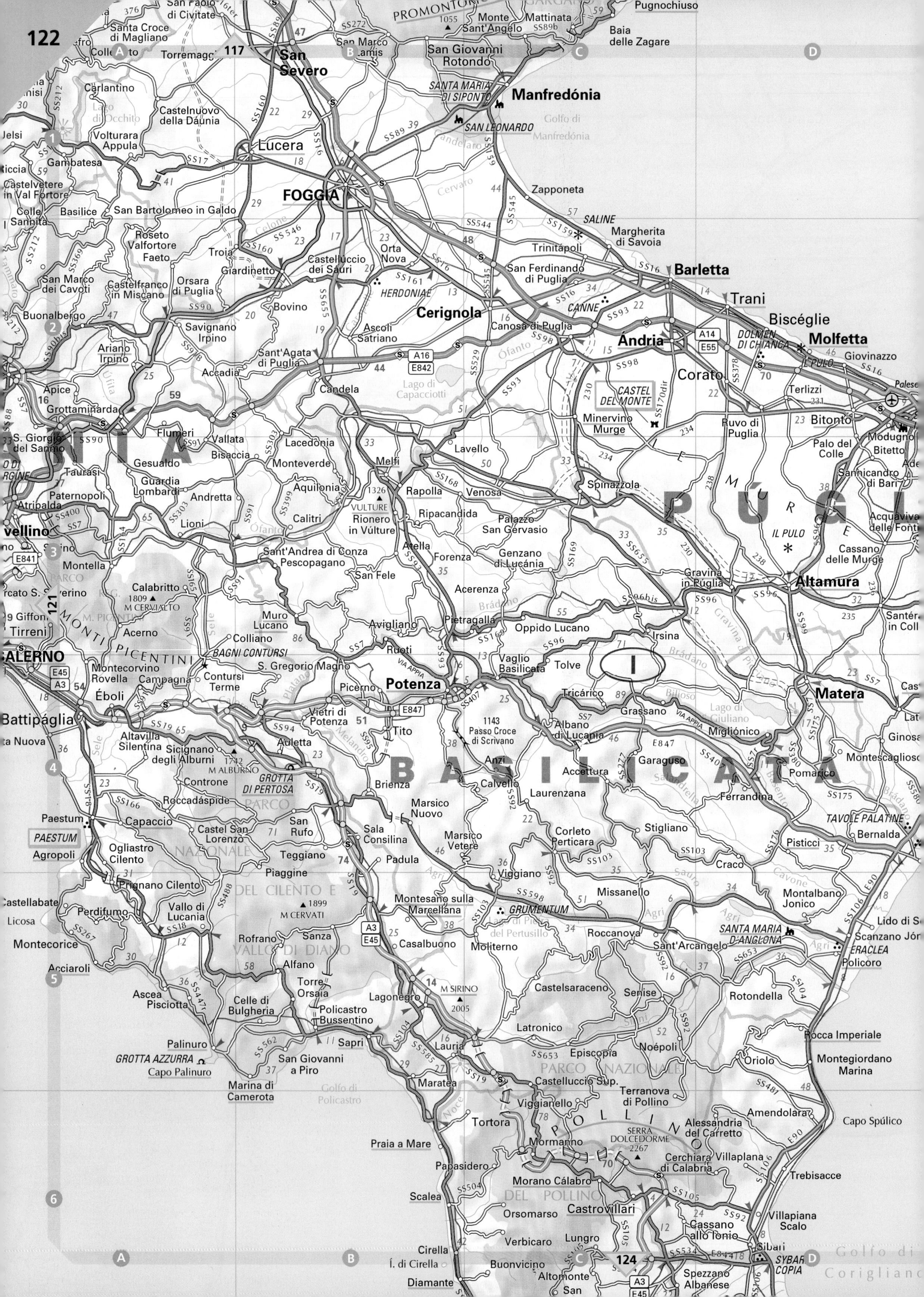

A
B
C
D
1
2
3
4
5
6
117
121
124
San Severo
Santa Croce di Magliano
Torremaggiore
San Marco in Lamis
Monte Sant'Angelo
Mattinata
Pugnochiuso
Baia delle Zagare
San Giovanni Rotondo
Santa Maria di Siponto
Manfredónia
Golfo di Manfredónia
San Leonardo
Carlantino
Lago di Occhito
Castelnuovo della Dáunia
Volturara Appula
Lucera
Gambatesa
Castelvetere in Val Fortore
FOGGIA
Zapponeta
Colle Sannita
Basilice
San Bartolomeo in Galdo
Saline
Margherita di Savoia
Roseto Valfortore
Faeto
Troia
Giardinetto
Castelluccio dei Sauri
Orta Nova
Trinitápoli
San Ferdinando di Puglia
Barletta
Trani
Bisceglie
Molfetta
Giovinazzo
San Marco dei Cavoti
Castelfranco in Miscano
Orsara di Puglia
Herdoniae
Cerignola
Canne
Buonalbergo
Bovino
Savignano Irpino
Ascoli Satriano
Canosa di Puglia
Ándria
Dolmen di Chianca
Il Pulo
Ariano Irpino
Sant'Agata di Puglia
Accadia
Lago di Capacciotti
Castel del Monte
Corato
Terlizzi
Palese
Apice
Grottaminarda
Candela
Minervino Murge
Ruvo di Puglia
Bitonto
Modugno
S. Giorgio del Sannio
Flumeri
Vallata
Lacedónia
Lavello
Bisaccia
Palo del Colle
Bitetto
Gesualdo
Monteverde
Melfi
Venosa
Spinazzola
Sannicandro di Bari
Taurasi
Guardia Lombardi
Aquilonia
Rapolla
Paternopoli
Andretta
Vulture
Rionero in Vúlture
Ripacandida
Palazzo San Gervasio
Murge
Atripalda
Lioni
Calitri
Acquaviva delle Fonti
Avellino
Montella
Sant'Andrea di Conza
Pescopagano
Atella
Forenza
Genzano di Lucánia
Cassano delle Murge
San Fele
Gravina in Púglia
Altamura
Calabritto
M. Cervialto
Acerenza
Monti Picentini
Giffoni
Muro Lucano
Avigliano
Pietragalla
Oppido Lucano
Irsina
Santéramo in Colle
Acerno
Colliano
Bagni Contursi
Ruoti
Vaglio Basilicata
Tolve
Salerno
Montecorvino Rovella
Campagna
Contursi Terme
S. Gregorio Magno
Picerno
Potenza
Via Appia
Matera
Éboli
Battipáglia
Vietri di Potenza
Tito
Passo Croce di Scrivano
Tricárico
Grassano
Lago di S. Giuliano
Albano di Lucania
Migliónico
Altavilla Silentina
Sicignano degli Alburni
Auletta
M. Alburno
Grotta di Pertosa
Anzi
Garaguso
Ginosa
Montescaglioso
Basilicata
Controne
Brienza
Calvello
Accettura
Pomarico
Roccadáspide
Laurenzana
Ferrandina
Paestum
Capaccio
Castel San Lorenzo
San Rufo
Marsico Nuovo
Sala Consilina
Tavole Palatine
Bernalda
Agropoli
Ogliastro Cilento
Teggiano
Padula
Marsico Vetere
Corleto Perticara
Stigliano
Pisticci
Piaggine
Viggiano
Craco
Prignano Cilento
Parco Nazionale del Cilento e Vallo di Diano
M. Cervati
Missanello
Montalbano Jonico
Castellabate
Perdifumo
Vallo di Lucania
Montesano sulla Marcellana
Grumentum
Lago di Pietra del Pertusillo
Licosa
Rofrano
Sanza
Roccanova
Santa Maria d'Anglona
Lido di Scanzano
Scanzano Jónico
Montecorice
Casalbuono
Moliterno
Sant'Arcangelo
Eraclea
Policoro
Acciaroli
Alfano
Torre Orsaia
M. Sirino
Lagonegro
Castelsaraceno
Senise
Rotondella
Ascea
Pisciotta
Celle di Bulgheria
Policastro Bussentino
Latronico
Rocca Imperiale
Palinuro
Sapri
Lauria
Episcopia
Noépoli
Oriolo
Montegiordano Marina
Grotta Azzurra
Capo Palinuro
San Giovanni a Piro
Parco Nazionale del Pollino
Castelluccio Sup.
Marina di Camerota
Golfo di Policastro
Maratea
Terranova di Pollino
Viggianello
Amendolara
Tortora
Serra Dolcedorme
Alessandria del Carretto
Capo Spúlico
Praia a Mare
Mormanno
Cerchiara di Calabria
Villaplana
Papasidero
Trebisacce
Morano Cálabro
Scalea
Castrovillari
Villapiana Scalo
Orsomarso
Cassano allo Ionio
Verbicaro
Lungro
Sibari
Sybaris Copia
Cirella
Í. di Cirella
Buonvicino
Altomonte
Spezzano Albanese
Diamante
Golfo di Corigliano

E   F   G   H

1

Kérkyra
Igoumenitsa
Pátra
Durrës
Bar
Rijeka
Split
Dubrovnik
Korčula

2

BARI
FÉNICE
ILSIGNANO
Mola
di Bari
Capurso
Rutigliano
Polignano a Mare
Casamássima
Conversano
Monópoli
Turi
Castellana
Grotte
GROTTE DI
CASTELLANA
Savelletri
Putignano
Torre Canne
GROTTA DI
PUTIGNANO
Fasano
Rosa Marina
Gióia
del Colle
Alberobello
Villanova
Noci
Torre S. Sabina
ZONA
DEI TRULLI
Cisternino
Ostuni
Locorotondo
Martina Franca
San Vito
dei Normanni
Céglie
Messápica
Brindisi - Casale
Kérkyra
Igoumenitsa
Pátra
Vlorë
Móttola
San Michele
Salentino
GROTTA
S. GIOVANNI
Brindisi
Palagianello
Villa
Castelli
Massafra
Crispiano
Mesagne
Palagiano
Grottaglie
Francavilla
Fontana
Latiano
San Pietro
Vernotico
Statte
Oria
Casalabate
TÁRANTO
San Giorgio
Iónico
Carosino
Torre
Santa Susanna
San
Dónaci
Squinzano
Marina
di Ginosa
Sava
San Pancrazio
Salentino
Campi
Salentina
San Cataldo
METAPONTIUM
Capo
San Vito
Lizzano
Manduria
Veglie
LECCE
Torricella
Rocca Vecchia
lido di
Metaponto
Lido
Silvana
Avetrana
Monteroni
di Lecce
Cavallino
Campomarino
Copertino
Calimera
Porto
Cesareo
Martano
Galatina
Nardò
Galatone
Otranto
Capo d'Ótranto
Durrës
Vlorë
G O L F O   D I
Gallípoli
Máglie
Minervino di Lecce
Parábita
Santa Cesarea
Terme
T Á R A N T O
Casarano
Ruffano
GROTTA ZINZULUSA
Taviano
Tricase
Ugento
Taurisano
Corsano
Presicce
AUSENTUM
Gagliano
del Capo
Marina di
Léuca
Capo S Maria
di Léuca

3

4

5

6

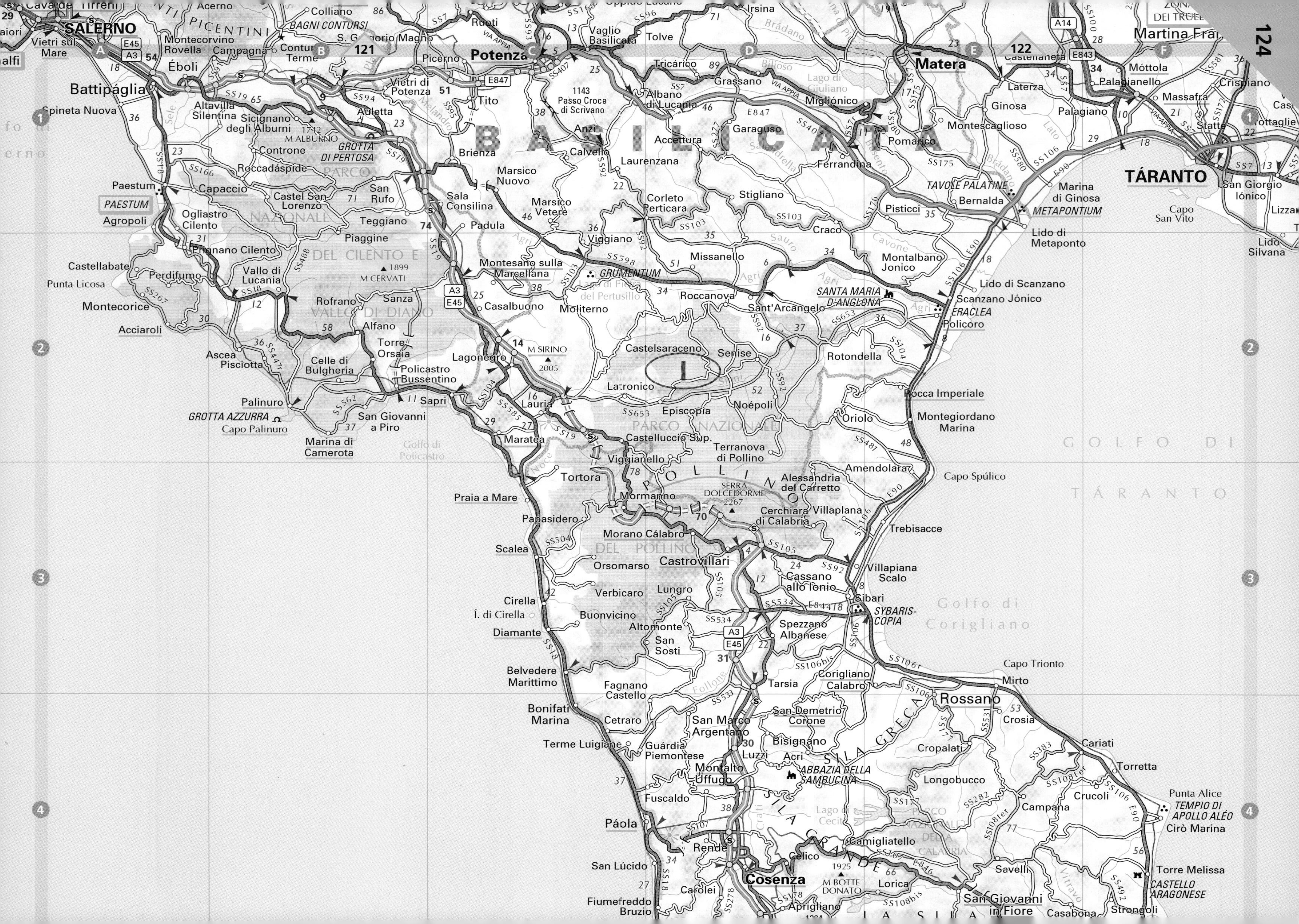
SALERNO
Vietri sul Mare
Battipáglia
Spineta Nuova
Éboli
Montecorvino Rovella
Campagna
Contursi Terme
BAGNI CONTURSI
Colliano
Acerno
PICENTINI
Altavilla Silentina
Sicignano degli Alburni
M ALBURNO 1742
Controne
GROTTA DI PERTOSA
Auletta
Roccadáspide
Paestum
PAESTUM
Agropoli
Capaccio
Castel San Lorenzo
Ogliastro Cilento
Prignano Cilento
Castellabate
Punta Licosa
Perdifumo
Montecorice
Acciaroli
Vallo di Lucania
Ascea
Pisciotta
Palinuro
GROTTA AZZURRA
Capo Palinuro
Celle di Bulgheria
Rofrano
Marina di Camerota
San Giovanni a Piro
Sapri
Policastro Bussentino
Golfo di Policastro
Torre Orsaia
Alfano
Sanza
VALLO DI DIANO
DEL CILENTO E
PARCO NAZIONALE
M CERVATI 1899
Piaggine
Teggiano
San Rufo
Sala Consilina
Padula
Polla
Brienza
Marsico Nuovo
Marsico Vetere
Montesano sulla Marcellana
Casalbuono
Lagonegro
M SIRINO 2005
Lauria
Maratea
Moliterno
Lago di Pietra del Pertusillo
GRUMENTUM
Viggiano
Tito
Picerno
Vietri di Potenza
Potenza
Ruoti
Vaglio Basilicata
Tolve
Irsina
1143 Passo Croce di Scrivano
Anzi
Calvello
Laurenzana
Corleto Perticara
Albano di Lucania
Tricárico
Grassano
Accettura
Garaguso
Miglionico
Lago di San Giuliano
BASILICATA
Matera
Pomarico
Ferrandina
Montescaglioso
Stigliano
Missanello
Roccanova
Craco
Pisticci
Bernalda
TAVOLE PALATINE
METAPONTIUM
Lido di Metaponto
Marina di Ginosa
Montalbano Jonico
Sant'Arcangelo
SANTA MARIA D'ANGLONA
Lido di Scanzano
Scanzano Jónico
ERACLEA
Policoro
Castelsaraceno
Senise
Latronico
Episcopia
Noépoli
Rotondella
Rocca Imperiale
Montegiordano Marina
Oriolo
Castelluccio Sup.
Terranova di Pollino
Viggianello
PARCO NAZIONALE DEL POLLINO
POLLINO
SERRA DOLCEDORME 2267
Alessandria del Carretto
Amendolara
Capo Spúlico
Cerchiara di Calabria
Villaplana
Trebisacce
Tortora
Praia a Mare
Mormanno
Papasidero
Morano Cálabro
Scalea
Orsomarso
Castrovillari
Villapiana Scalo
Cassano allo Ionio
Sibari
SYBARIS-COPIA
Golfo di Corigliano
GOLFO DI TÁRANTO
Cirella
Í. di Cirella
Verbicaro
Lungro
Buonvicino
Altomonte
San Sosti
Diamante
Spezzano Albanese
Belvedere Marittimo
Fagnano Castello
Tarsia
Corigliano Calabro
Capo Trionto
Mirto
Rossano
Crosia
Bonifati Marina
Cetraro
San Marco Argentano
San Demetrio Corone
Terme Luigiane
Guárdia Piemontese
Bisignano
Luzzi
Acri
SILA GRECA
ABBAZIA DELLA SAMBUCINA
Cropalati
Cariati
Torretta
Montalto Uffugo
Longobucco
Crucoli
Punta Alice
TEMPIO DI APOLLO ALÉO
Cirò Marina
Fuscaldo
Páola
Campana
Camigliatello
SILA GRANDE
Celico
Rende
San Lúcido
Cosenza
M BOTTE DONATO 1925
Lorica
Savelli
Torre Melissa
CASTELLO ARAGONESE
Fiumefreddo Bruzio
Carolei
Aprigliano
San Giovanni in Fiore
Casabona
Strongoli
Laterza
Castellaneta
Ginosa
Palagiano
Palagianello
Móttola
Massafra
Crispiano
Statte
Martina Franca
TÁRANTO
San Giorgio Iónico
Capo San Vito
Lido Silvana
A3
E45
E847
E90
A14
E843

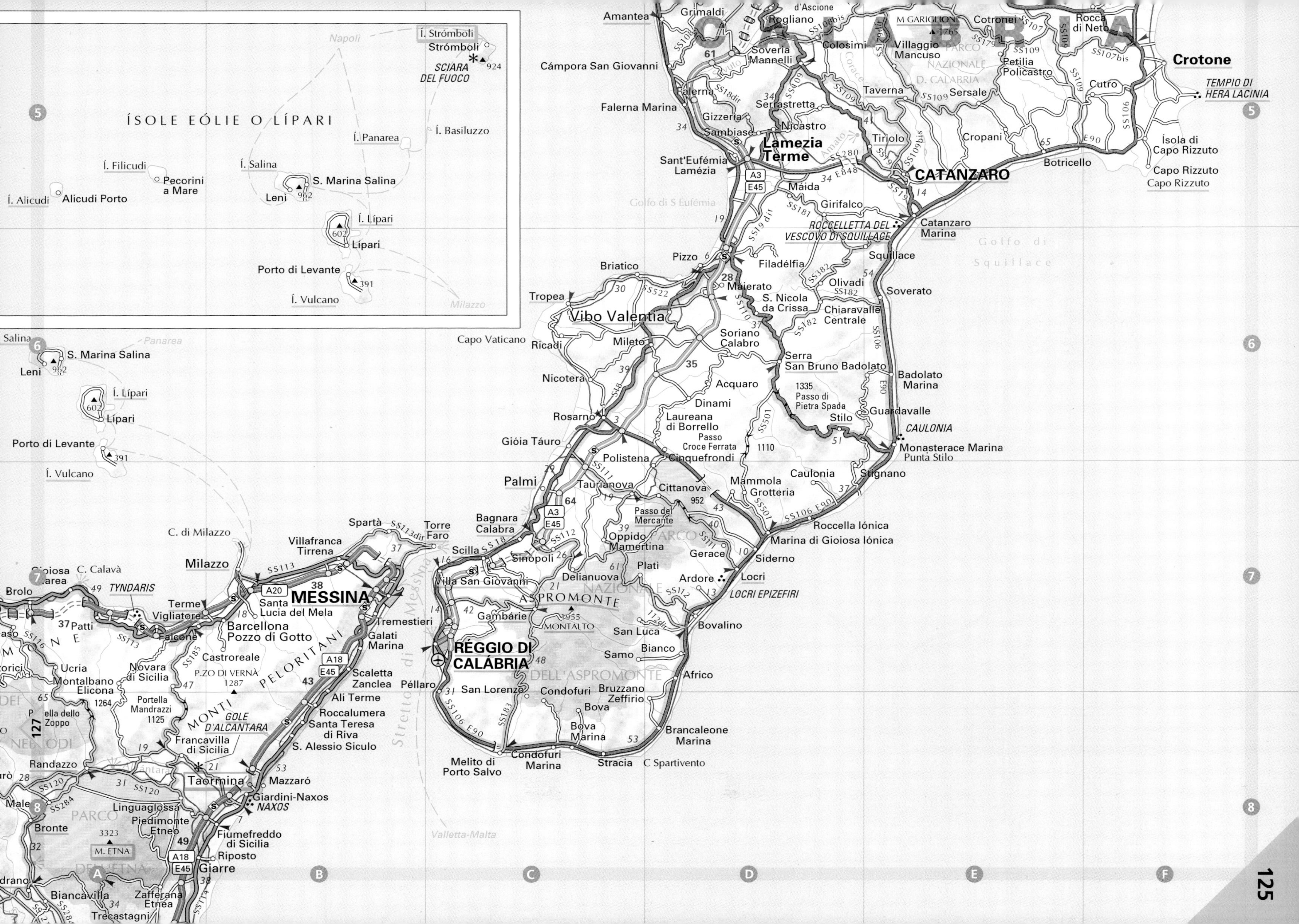

Crotone

TEMPIO DI HERA LACINIA

Isola di Capo Rizzuto
Capo Rizzuto
Capo Rizzuto

Rocca di Neto
SS106

SS107bis
SS107
SS109
Cotronei
Petilia Policastro
Cutro
Botricello

M GARIGLIONE
Villaggio Mancuso
PARCO NAZIONALE D. CALABRIA
SS109 Sersale
Cropani

CATANZARO

Colosimi
Taverna
Tiriolo
Sorbo
Catanzaro Marina

Golfo di Squillace

d'Ascione
Rogliano
Soveria Mannelli
Nicastro
Sersastretta
Maida
Girifalco
Squillace
Soverato

Lamezia Terme

A3 E45
Gizzeria
Sambiase
Sant'Eufémia Lamézia
Filadélfia
Olivadi
Chiaravalle Centrale
Badolato
Badolato Marina
CAULONIA
Monasterace Marina
Punta Stilo

Amantea
Câmpora San Giovanni
Falerna Marina
Pizzo
Maierato
Soriano Calabro
Serra San Bruno
Passo di Pietra Spada
Stilo
Guardavalle
Stignano

Golfo di S Eufémia

Briatico
Mileto
Acquaro
Dinami
Mammola
Grotteria
Caúlonia
Roccella Iónica
Marina di Gioiosa Iónica
Siderno

Vibo Valentia
Tropea
Ricadi
Nicotera
Laureana di Borrello
Croce Ferrata
Cinquefrondi
Cittanova
Passo del Mercante
Gerace
Ardore
Locri
LOCRI EPIZEFIRI

Capo Vaticano
Rosarno
Polistena
Taurianova
Oppido Mamertina
Plati
San Luca
Bianco
Bovalino
Africo
Brancaleone Marina

Gióia Táuro
Palmi
A3 E45
Sinopoli
Delianuova
Samo
Bova
Bova Marina
Condofuri
Condofuri Marina
Stracia
C Spartivento

Bagnara Calabra
Scilla
Villa San Giovanni
Gambárie
PARCO NAZIONALE DELL'ASPROMONTE
MONTALTO
San Lorenzo
Condofuri
Melito di Porto Salvo

Torre Faro
RÉGGIO DI CALABRIA
Péllaro

Stretto di Messina

Spartà
Tremestieri
Galati Marina
Scaletta Zanclea
Ali Terme
Roccalumera
Santa Teresa di Riva
S. Alessio Siculo
Mazzaró

Villafranca Tirrena
MESSINA
A18 E45

Giardini-Naxos
NAXOS
Fiumefreddo di Sicilia
Riposto
Giarre

Santa Lucia del Mela
Barcellona Pozzo di Gotto
Castroreale
Francavilla di Sicilia
Taormina
A18 E45

A20
Milazzo
Terme
Vigliatore
Novara di Sicilia
Portella Mandrazzi
Linguaglossa
Piedimonte Etneo
Zafferana Etnea

C. di Milazzo
Novara di Sicilia
Francavilla di Sicilia
GOLE D'ALCANTARA
M. ETNA
Biancavilla
Randazzo
Bronte
Male

MONTI PELORITANI

ÍSOLE EÓLIE O LÍPARI

Í. Strómboli
SCIARA DEL FUOCO
Strómboli
Í. Basiluzzo

Í. Filicudi
Í. Panarea

Í. Alicudi
Alicudi Porto
Pecorini a Mare
S. Marina Salina
Leni
Í. Salina
Í. Lípari
Lípari

Porto di Levante
Í. Vulcano

Napoli
Milazzo
Panarea

Í. Salina
S. Marina Salina
Í. Lípari
Lípari
Leni
Porto di Levante
Í. Vulcano

TYNDARIS
Gioiosa
C. Calavà
Patti
Brolo
Naso
Ucria
Montalbano Elicona
Giarre
PARCO

A B C D

1

Cágliari
Ústica
Cágliari
Génova
Livorno
Nápoli

Capo S. Vito
San Vito lo Capo
Ísola delle Fémmine
Capo Gallo
Mondello
P Ráisi
Ísola delle Femmine
600 Golfo di Palermo
Punta Ráisi
Cínisi
MONTE PELLEGRINO
Capaci
SS113
San Martino delle Scale
PALERMO
E90
A29
Monreale
C. Zafferano
SOLUNTO
Balestrate
Bagheria
Castelluzzo
Castellammare del Golfo
Partinico
SS186
SS113
39
Custonaci
20
SS187
San Giuseppe Jato
Misilmeri
Términi Imerese
Erice
Valderice
38
Álcamo
SS113
Piana degli Albanesi
A19
Trápani
SS113 32
SS187
Marineo
E90
Trabia
Paceco
Buseto Palizzolo
A29dir
SS113 17
San Cipirello
23
Cáccamo
13
E933
12
19
SEGESTA
Calátafimi
MADONNA DEL ROSARIO
SS121
58
Buonfornello
Birgi
31
Camporeale
Villafrati
Cerda
MOZIA
SS115
31
SS188a
A29
E90
41
1613
Mezzojuso
Roccapalumba
Alia
Calta
Í. dello Stagnone
Gibellina
Corleone
R BUSAMBRA
Campofelice di Fitalia
6
Marsala
SS188
Salemi
Santa Ninfa
RUDERI DI GIBELLINA
44
Campofiorito
24
Lercara Friddi
68
Petrosino
22
Partanna
22
Bisacquino
Prizzi
17
VALLE
Lago della Trinità
SS188
Santa Margherita di Bélice
Sambuca di Sicília
Palazzo Adriano
Cammarata
Castelvetrano
35
SS188b
18
Lago Aráncio
34
Chiusa Scláfani
Bivona
Santo Stéfano Quisquina
Mussomeli
Mazara del Vallo
E90 E931 31
SS115
35
Menfi
43
Búrgio
Casteltérmini
A29
Campobello di Mazara
Marinella
Caltabellotta
Alessándria della Rocca
85
San Biágio Plátani
Serradifalc
ROCCHE DI CUSA
SELINUNTE
SAN CALOGERO
16
Ribera
Cianciana
Milena
Granitola Torretta
C. Granítola
C. S. Marco
Sciacca
ERACLEA MINOA
61
Montallegro
Raffadali
Cattolica Eraclea
Aragona
Racalmuto
Sicilia
Siculiana
Agrigento
VALLE DEI TEMPLI
Favara
Naro
SS640
35
Porto Empedocle
SS410
Campobe di Licata
CASTELLO DI MONTECHIARO
44
Palma di Montechiaro

Trápani
Pantelleria
Tracino
836 M.GNA GRANDE
Ísola di Pantelleria
I

Porto Empedocle
Ísola di Linosa
Linosa
Gozo
Salerno
Réggio di Calabria
Catánia
Siracusa
Victoria
M
Mgarr
ÍSOLE PELÁGIE
I
Mellieha
21
Mosta
Sliema
Ísola di Lampione
Rabat
Valletta
Dingli
Luqa
Vittoriosa
Zurrieq
Malta
Birzebbuga
Lampedusa
Ísola di Lampedusa

Í. Maréttimo
686
Maréttimo
Í. di Lévanzo
Levanzo
ÍSOLE ÉGADI
Favignana
Í. Favignana

Pantelleria
Túnis

A B C D

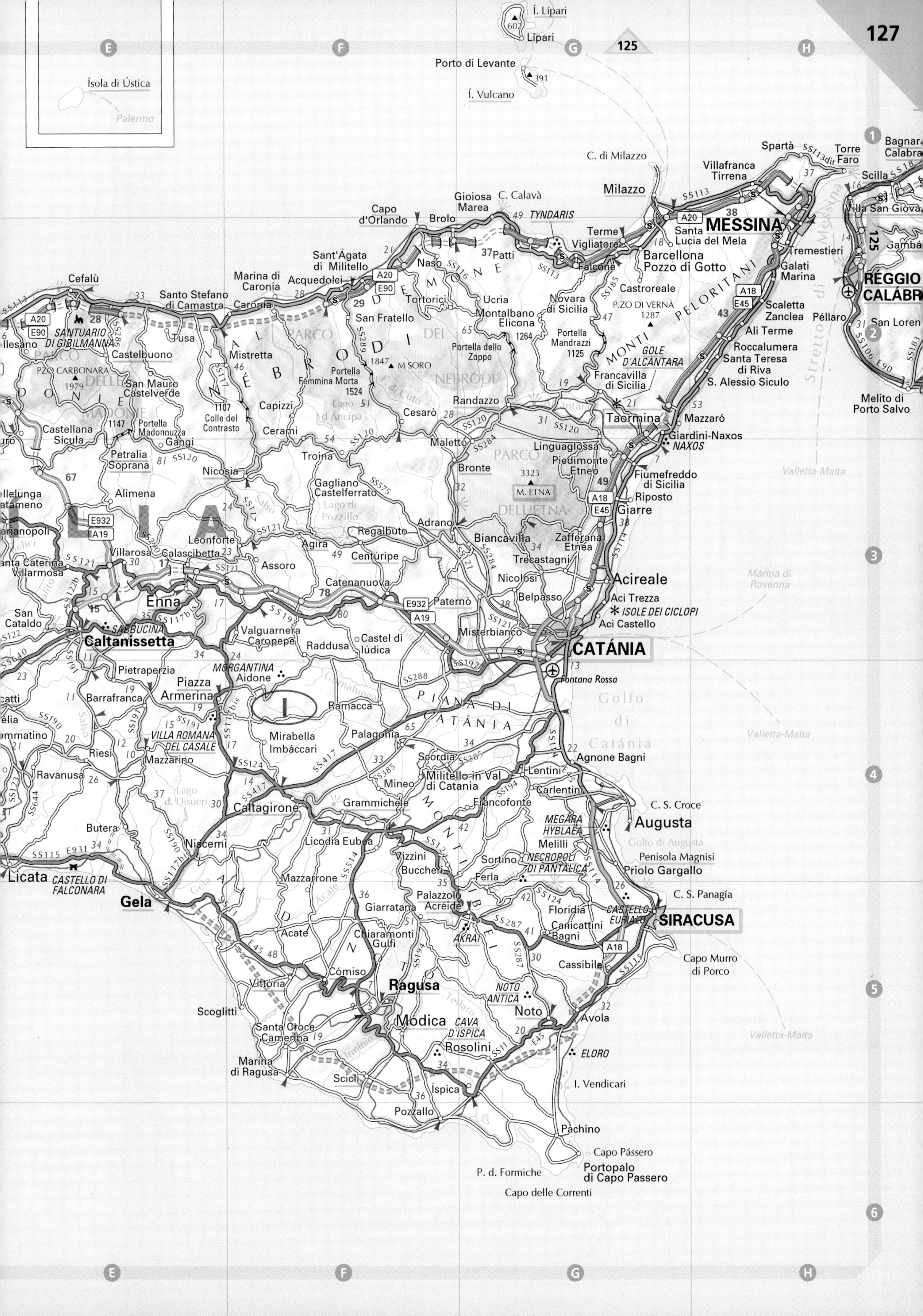
E
F
G
H
125
Í. Lípari
Lípari
Porto di Levante
Í. Vulcano
Ísola di Ústica
Palermo
C. di Milazzo
Milazzo
Spartà
Villafranca Tirrena
Torre Faro
Scilla
Bagnara Calabra
Gioiosa Marea
C. Calavà
Capo d'Orlando
Brolo
TYNDARIS
Patti
Terme Vigliatore
Santa Lucia del Mela
MESSINA
Barcellona Pozzo di Gotto
Falcone
Tremestieri
Galati Marina
RÉGGIO CALÁBRIA
Villa San Giovanni
Gambarie
Sant'Ágata di Militello
Naso
Marina di Caronía
Acquedolci
Caronia
Santo Stefano di Camastra
Cefalù
SANTUARIO DI GIBILMANNA
Tortorici
Ucria
Montalbano Elicona
Novara di Sicilia
Castroreale
P.ZO DI VERNÀ 1287
MONTI PELORITANI
Scaletta Zanclea
Péllaro
San Lorenzo
Ali Terme
Roccalumera
Santa Teresa di Riva
S. Alessio Siculo
Melito di Porto Salvo
Stretto di Messina
San Fratello
Tusa
Castelbuono
Mistretta
PARCO DEI NEBRODI
NÉBRODI
1847 M SORO
Portella dello Zoppo
Portella Mandrazzi 1125
GOLE D'ALCANTARA
Francavilla di Sicilia
Taormina
Mazzaró
Giardini-Naxos
NAXOS
PZO CARBONARA 1979
PARCO DELLE MADONIE
San Mauro Castelverde
Portella Fémmina Morta 1524
Capizzi
Lago d'Áncipa
Cesarò
Randazzo
Castellana Sicula
Portella Madonnuzza
Gangi
Colle del Contrasto
Cerami
Maletto
Linguaglossa
Piedimonte Etneo
Fiumefreddo di Sicilia
Riposto
Giarre
Petralia Soprana
Troina
Bronte
PARCO DELL'ETNA
3323 M. ETNA
Nicosia
Gagliano Castelferrato
Lago di Pozzillo
Alimena
Regalbuto
Adrano
Biancavilla
Zafferana Etnea
Trecastagni
Nicolosi
Belpasso
Acireale
Aci Trezza
ISOLE DEI CICLOPI
Aci Castello
Leonforte
Agira
Centúripe
Villarosa
Calascibetta
Assoro
Catenanuova
Santa Caterina Villarmosa
Enna
Paternò
Misterbianco
CATÁNIA
Fontana Rossa
San Cataldo
SABBUCINA
Caltanissetta
Valguarnera Caropepe
Raddusa
Castel di Iúdica
Pietraperzia
MORGANTINA
Aidone
Piazza Armerina
Barrafranca
Ramacca
PIANA DI CATÁNIA
Golfo di Catánia
VILLA ROMANA DEL CASALE
Mirabella Imbáccari
Palagonia
Riesi
Mazzarino
Scordia
Agnone Bagni
Lentini
Ravanusa
Mineo
Militello in Val di Catania
Carlentini
Francofonte
Lago d. Disueri
Caltagirone
Grammichele
C. S. Croce
Augusta
MEGARA HYBLAEA
Melilli
Golfo di Augusta
Butera
Niscemi
Licodia Eubea
Vizzini
Buccheri
Sortino
NECROPOLI DI PANTALICA
Penisola Magnisi
Priolo Gargallo
Licata
CASTELLO DI FALCONARA
Mazzarrone
Ferla
Gela
Palazzolo Acréide
Giarratana
C. S. Panagía
Floridia
CASTELLO EURIALO
SIRACUSA
AKRAI
Canicattini Bagni
Acate
Chiaramonti Gulfi
MONTI IBLEI
Cassibile
Capo Murro di Porco
Cómiso
Vittoria
Ragusa
NOTO ANTICA
Noto
Scoglitti
Santa Croce Camerina
Modica
CAVA D'ISPICA
Avola
Rosolini
Marina di Ragusa
ELORO
Scicli
Íspica
I. Vendicari
Pozzallo
Pachino
Capo Pássero
Portopalo di Capo Passero
P. d. Formiche
Capo delle Correnti
Valletta-Malta
Marina di Ravenna
A20
A18
A19
E90
E45
E932
E931
SS113
SS120
SS121
SS124
SS115
SS114
SS417
1
2
3
4
5
6

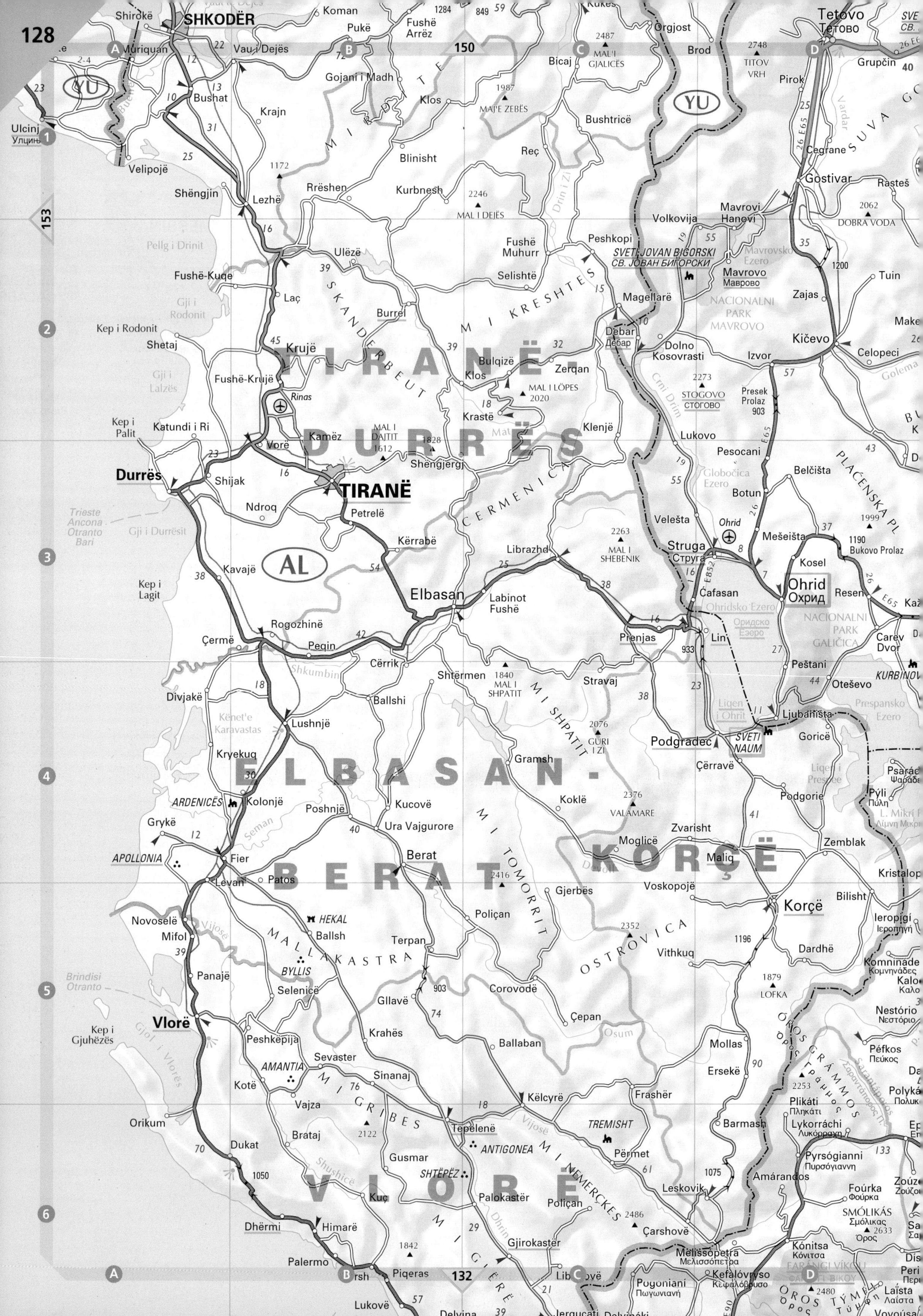

SHKODËR
Shirokë
Koman
Pukë
Fushë Arrëz
Kukës
Orgjost
Tetovo
Тетово
Muriquan
Vau i Dejës
150
Bicaj
MAL'I GJALICËS
2487
Brod
TITOV VRH
2748
Grupčin
Gojani i Madh
Pirok
Bushat
Klos
1987
MAJ'E ZEBËS
YU
Krajn
Bushtricë
Ulcinj
Улцињ
Velipojë
Blinisht
Reç
Cegrane
SUVA
Gostivar
Rasteš
Shëngjin
Lezhë
Rrëshen
Kurbnesh
2246
MAL I DEJËS
Mavrovi Hanovi
Volkovija
2062
DOBRA VODA
153
Pellg i Drinit
Fushë Muhurr
Peshkopi
SVETI JOVAN BIGORSKI
СВ. ЈОВАН БИГОРСКИ
Mavrovo
Маврово
Ulëzë
Selishtë
Tuin
Fushë-Kuqe
Zajas
Laç
Gji i Rodonit
SKANDERBEUT
Burrel
MI KRESHTES
Magellarë
NACIONALNI PARK MAVROVO
Kep i Rodonit
Debar
Дебар
Dolno Kosovrasti
Kičevo
Shetaj
Krujë
Bulqizë
Zerqan
Izvor
Celopeci
TIRANË-
Klos
MAL I LÕPES
2020
2273
STOGOVO
СТОГОВО
Presek Prolaz
903
Fushë-Krujë
Gji i Lalzës
Rinas
Krastë
Kep i Palit
Katundi i Ri
MAL I DAJTIT
1612
Klenjë
Lukovo
DURRËS
Vorë
Kamëz
1828
Shëngjergj
Pesocani
Durrës
Shijak
TIRANË
Globočica Ezero
Botun
Belčišta
PLAĆENSKA PL
Trieste
Ancona
Otranto
Bari
Gji i Durrësit
Ndroq
Petrelë
CERMENICA
Veleška
Ohrid
Mešeišta
1999
Kërrabë
2263
MAL I SHEBENIK
Struga
Струга
1190
Bukovo Prolaz
Kavajë
AL
Librazhd
Kosel
Kep i Lagit
Elbasan
Labinot Fushë
Cafasan
Ohrid
Охрид
Resen
Ohridsko Ezero
Оридско Езеро
NACIONALNI PARK GALIČICA
Rogozhinë
Çermë
Peqin
Prenjas
Lin
933
Carev Dvor
Cërrik
Shtërmen
1840
MAL I SHPATIT
Stravaj
Pestani
Otesevo
KURBINOV
Shkumbin
Divjakë
Ballshi
MI SHPATIT
Ligen i Ohrit
Ljubaništa
Prespansko Ezero
Kënet'e Karavastas
Lushnjë
2076
GURI I ZI
Podgradec
SVETI NAUM
Goricë
Kryekuq
Gramsh
ELBASAN-
Çërravë
Liqeni i Presëe
Psarádes
Ψαράδες
ARDENICËS
Kolonjë
Kucovë
Koklë
2376
VALAMARE
Podgorie
Pýli
Πύλη
Poshnjë
L. Mikrí Préspa
Grykë
Ura Vajgurore
MI TOMORRIT
Moglicë
Zvarisht
Zemblak
APOLLONIA
Fier
Berat
KORÇË
Maliq
Seman
Levan
Patos
BERAT
2416
Devoll
Voskopojë
Kristalopigí
Gjerbës
Korçë
Novoselë
HEKAL
Poliçan
Bilisht
Mifol
Ballsh
2352
Ieropigí
Ιεροπηγή
Vjosë
MALLAKASTRA
Terpan
OSTROVICA
1196
Vithkuq
Dardhë
BYLLIS
Komninádes
Κομνηνάδες
Brindisi
Otranto
Panajë
Selenicë
903
Corovodë
1879
LOFKA
Kalo
Gllavë
Nestório
Νεστόριο
Kep i Gjuhëzës
Vlorë
Gjol i Vlorës
Peshkëpija
Krahës
Çepan
Osum
Ballaban
OROS GRAMMOS
Mollas
Pefkos
Πεύκος
Sevaster
AMANTIA
Sinanaj
Ersekë
Kotë
MI GRIBES
Frashër
Polykárpi
2253
Orikum
Vajza
Këlcyrë
TREMISHT
Plikáti
Πληκάτι
Brataj
2122
Tepelenë
Barmash
Lykorráchi
Λυκόρραχη
Dukat
ANTIGONEA
MI NEMERÇKES
Përmet
Pyrsógianni
Πυρσόγιαννη
1050
Gusmar
SHTËPËZ
Shushicë
VLORË
Amárandos
Leskovik
1075
Kuç
Palokastër
Poliçan
Foúrka
Φούρκα
SMÓLIKÁS
Σμόλικας
Όρος
2633
Dhërmi
Himarë
2486
Çarshovë
Dhrin
Gjirokastër
Kónitsa
Κόνιτσα
1842
Melissópetra
Μελισσόπετρα
Palermo
Piqeras
132
Libohovë
Pogoniani
Πωγωνιανή
Kefalóvryso
Κεφαλόβρυσο
Laista
Λαΐστα
Lukovë
MI GJERË
2480
OROS TÝMFI
Delvina
Jergucati
Delvináki
Vovousa

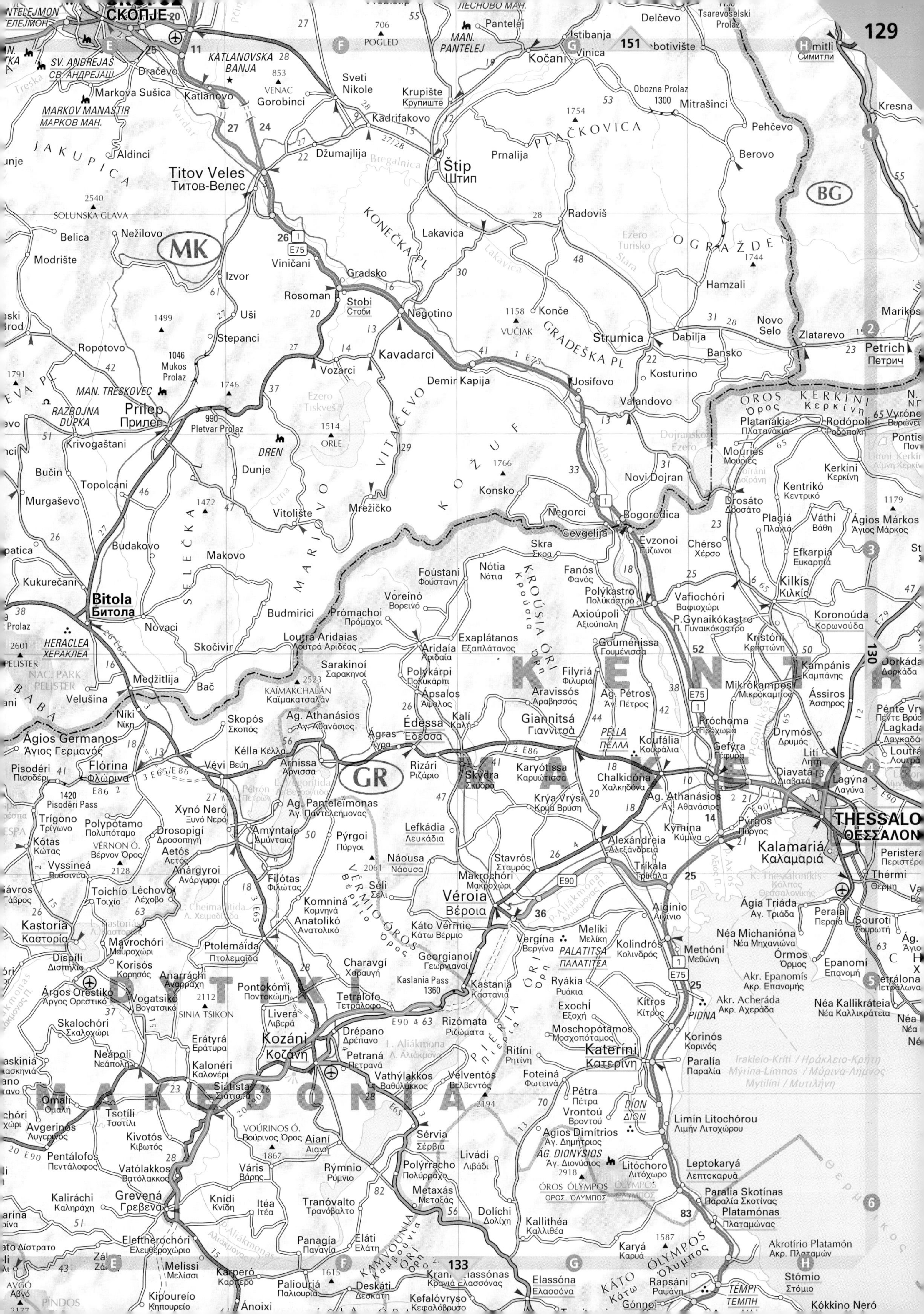

СКОПЈЕ
KATLANOVSKA BANJA
SV. ANDREJAŠ
СВ. АНДРЕЈАШ
Dračevo
Markova Sušica
MARKOV MANASTIR
МАРКОВ МАН.
Katlanovo
VENAC
Gorobinci
Sveti Nikole
POGLED
MAN. PANTELEJ
Pantelej
Krupište
Крупиште
Kadrifakovo
Kočani
Vinica
Istibanja
Delčevo
Tsarevoselski Prolaz
Obozna Prolaz
Mitrašinci
PLAČKOVICA
Pehčevo
Berovo
Kresna
JAKUPICA
Aldinci
Titov Veles
Титов-Велес
Džumajlija
Bregalnica
Štip
Штип
Prnalija
SOLUNSKA GLAVA
Belica
Nežilovo
MK
Modrište
Izvor
Viničani
E75
KONEČKA PL
Lakavica
Radoviš
OGRAŽDEN
Ezero Turisko
BG
Gradsko
Rosoman
Stobi
Стоби
Negotino
VUČJAK
Konče
Hamzali
GRADEŠKA PL
Strumica
Dabilja
Novo Selo
Zlatarevo
Marikos
Petrich
Петрич
Bansko
Kosturino
Uši
Stepanci
Ropotovo
Mukos Prolaz
Kavadarci
Vozarci
Demir Kapija
Josifovo
Valandovo
MAN. TRESKOVEC
RAZBOJNA DUPKA
Prilep
Прилеп
Pletvar Prolaz
Ezero Tikveš
ORLE
VITAČEVO
KOŽUF
Óros Kerkíni
Όρος Κερκίνη
Platanákia
Πλατανάκια
Rodópoli
Ροδόπολη
Vyróneia
Dojransko Ezero
Krivogaštani
DREN
Dunje
Mouriés
Μουριές
Kerkíni
Κερκίνη
Bučin
Topolcani
Novi Dojran
Kentrikó
Κεντρικό
Murgaševo
Konsko
Drosáto
Δροσάτο
SELEČKA PL
MARIOVO
Crna
Vitolište
Mrežičko
Negorci
Bogorodica
Gevgelija
Plagiá
Πλαγιά
Váthi
Βάθη
Ágios Márkos
Άγιος Μάρκος
Budakovo
Skra
Σκρα
Évzonoi
Εύζωνοι
Chérso
Χέρσο
Efkarpía
Ευκαρπία
Kukurečani
Makovo
Foústani
Φούστανη
Nótia
Νότια
KROÚSIA ÓRI
Fanós
Φανός
Bitola
Битола
Polýkastro
Πολύκαστρο
Vafiochóri
Βαφιοχώρι
Kilkís
Κιλκίς
Voreinó
Βορεινό
Budmirici
Prómachoi
Πρόμαχοι
Axioúpoli
Αξιούπολη
P. Gynaikókastro
Π. Γυναικόκαστρο
Koronoúda
Κορωνούδα
HERACLEA
ХЕРАКЛЕА
Novaci
Loutrá Aridaías
Λουτρά Αριδαίας
Exaplátanos
Εξαπλάτανος
Gouménissa
Γουμένισσα
Kristóni
Κρηστώνη
PELISTER
NAC. PARK PELISTER
Skočivir
Aridaía
Αριδαία
KENTRIKI
Dorkáda
Δορκάδα
Sarakinoí
Σαρακηνοί
Polykárpi
Πολυκάρπι
Filyriá
Φιλυριά
Kampánis
Καμπάνης
Medžitlija
Bač
KAÏMAKCHALÁN
Καϊμακτσαλάν
Ápsalos
Άψαλος
Aravissós
Αραβησσός
Ag. Pétros
Άγ. Πέτρος
Mikrókampos
Μικρόκαμπος
Ássiros
Άσσηρος
BABA
Velušina
Níki
Νίκη
Skopós
Σκοπός
Ag. Athanásios
Άγ. Αθανάσιος
Édessa
Έδεσσα
Kalí
Καλή
Giannitsá
Γιαννιτσά
Próchoma
Πρόχωμα
Pénte Vrýses
Lagkadás
Λαγκαδάς
Ágios Germanós
Άγιος Γερμανός
Ágras
Άγρα
PELLA
ΠΕΛΛΑ
Koufália
Κουφάλια
Drymós
Δρυμός
Kélla
Κέλλα
Gefýra
Γέφυρα
Lití
Λητή
Loutrá
Pisodéri
Πισοδέρι
Flórina
Φλώρινα
Vévi
Βεύη
Arnissa
Άρνισσα
GR
Rizári
Ριζάριο
Skýdra
Σκύδρα
MAKEDONIA
Karyótissa
Καρυώτισσα
Chalkidóna
Χαλκηδόνα
Diavatá
Διαβατά
Lagýna
Λαγυνά
E86
Pisodéri Pass
L. Petron
L. Vegoritida
Ag. Panteleímonas
Άγ. Παντελεήμονας
Krya Vrysi
Κρύα Βρύση
Ag. Athanásios
Άγ. Αθανάσιος
THESSALONÍKI
ΘΕΣΣΑΛΟΝΙΚΗ
Trígono
Τρίγωνο
Polypótamo
Πολυπόταμο
Xynó Neró
Ξυνό Νερό
Lefkádia
Λευκάδια
Pýrgoi
Πύργοι
Kýmina
Κύμινα
Pýrgos
Πύργος
Kótas
Κώτας
VÉRNON Ó.
Βέρνον Όρος
Drosopigí
Δροσοπηγή
Amýntaio
Αμύνταιο
Alexándreia
Αλεξάνδρεια
Kalamariá
Καλαμαριά
Peristerá
Περιστερά
Vyssineá
Βυσσινέα
Aetós
Αετός
Anárgyroi
Ανάργυροι
Náousa
Νάουσα
Stavrós
Σταυρός
Tríkala
Τρίκαλα
K. Thessalonikis
Thérmi
Θέρμη
Kastoriá
Καστοριά
Toichio
Τοιχιό
Léchovo
Λέχοβο
Filótas
Φιλώτας
VÉRMIO ÓROS
Βέρμιο Όρος
Séli
Σέλι
Makrochóri
Μακροχώρι
Véroia
Βέροια
Aigínio
Αιγίνιο
Ágia Triáda
Αγ. Τριάδα
Peraia
Περαία
Souroti
Σουρωτή
L. Kastorias
Mavrochóri
Μαυροχώρι
L. Cheimaditida
Λ. Χειμαδίτιδα
Komniná
Κομνηνά
Anatolikó
Ανατολικό
Káto Vérmio
Κάτω Βέρμιο
Vergína
Βεργίνα
Melíki
Μελίκη
Kolindrós
Κολινδρός
Néa Michanióna
Νέα Μηχανιώνα
Dispilió
Διστηλιό
Ptolemaída
Πτολεμαΐδα
Korisós
Κορησός
Georgianoí
Γεωργιανοί
PALATITSA
ΠΑΛΑΤΙΤΣΑ
Methóni
Μεθώνη
Órmos
Όρμος
Epanomí
Επανομή
Árgos Orestikó
Άργος Ορεστικό
DYTIKI
Anarráchi
Ανάρραχη
Charavgí
Χαραυγή
Kaslania Pass
Kastaniá
Καστανιά
Ryákia
Ρυάκια
Akr. Epanomís
Ακρ. Επανομής
Vogatsikó
Βογατσικό
SINIA TSIKON
Pontokómi
Ποντοκώμη
Tetrálofo
Τετράλοφο
PIERIA
Exochí
Εξοχή
Kítros
Κίτρος
Akr. Acherada
Ακρ. Αχεράδα
PIDNA
Néa Kallikráteia
Νέα Καλλικράτεια
Skalochóri
Σκαλοχώρι
Erátyra
Εράτυρα
Liverá
Λιβερά
Rizómata
Ριζώματα
L. Aliákmona
Λ. Αλιάκμονα
Moschopótamos
Μοσχοπόταμος
Korinós
Κορινός
Neápoli
Νεάπολη
Kozáni
Κοζάνη
Drépano
Δρέπανο
Petraná
Πετρανά
Ritíni
Ρητίνη
Kateríni
Κατερίνη
Paralía
Παραλία
Iraklείο-Kríti / Ηράκλειο-Κρήτη
Mýrina-Límnos / Μύρινα-Λήμνος
Mytilíni / Μυτιλήνη
Kaloneri
Καλονέρι
Siátista
Σιάτιστα
Vathýlakkos
Βαθύλακκος
Velventós
Βελβεντός
Foteiná
Φωτεινά
Omalí
Ομαλή
Tsotíli
Τσοτύλι
Pétra
Πέτρα
DÍON
ΔΙΟΝ
Vrontoú
Βροντού
Limín Litochórou
Λιμήν Λιτοχώρου
Avgerinós
Αυγερινός
VOÚRINOS Ó.
Βούρινος Όρος
Kivotós
Κιβωτός
Aianí
Αιανή
Sérvia
Σέρβια
Agios Dimítrios
Άγ. Δημήτριος
ÁG. DIONÝSIOS
Άγ. Διονύσιος
Pentálofos
Πεντάλοφος
Vatólakkos
Βατόλακκος
Váris
Βάρης
Rýmnio
Ρύμνιο
Polýrracho
Πολύρραχο
Livádi
Λιβάδι
Litóchoro
Λιτόχωρο
Leptokaryá
Λεπτοκαρυά
ÓROS ÓLYMPOS
ΟΡΟΣ ΟΛΥΜΠΟΣ
Kalirráchi
Καληράχη
Grevená
Γρεβενά
Knidi
Κνίδη
Itéa
Ιτέα
Tranóvalto
Τρανόβαλτο
Metaxás
Μεταξάς
Dolíchi
Δολίχη
Paralía Skotínas
Παραλία Σκοτίνας
Platamónas
Πλαταμώνας
Kallithéa
Καλλιθέα
Eleftherochóri
Ελευθεροχώρι
Eláti
Ελάτη
Panagia
Παναγιά
KAMVOÚNIA
Καμβούνια
Karyá
Καρυά
ÓLYMPOS
Όλυμπος
Akrotírio Platamón
Ακρ. Πλαταμών
Melíssi
Μελίσσι
Karperó
Καρπερό
Paliouriá
Παλιουριά
Deskáti
Δεσκάτη
Kraniá Elassónas
Κρανιά Ελασσόνας
Elassóna
Ελασσόνα
KÁTO
Κάτω
Rapsáni
Ραψάνη
Stómio
Στόμιο
AVGÓ
Αβγό
PÍNDOS
Kipoureío
Κηπουρείο
Ánoixi
Kefalóvryso
Κεφαλόβρυσο
Gónnoi
TEMPI
ΤΕΜΠΗ
Kókkino Neró

151
130
133

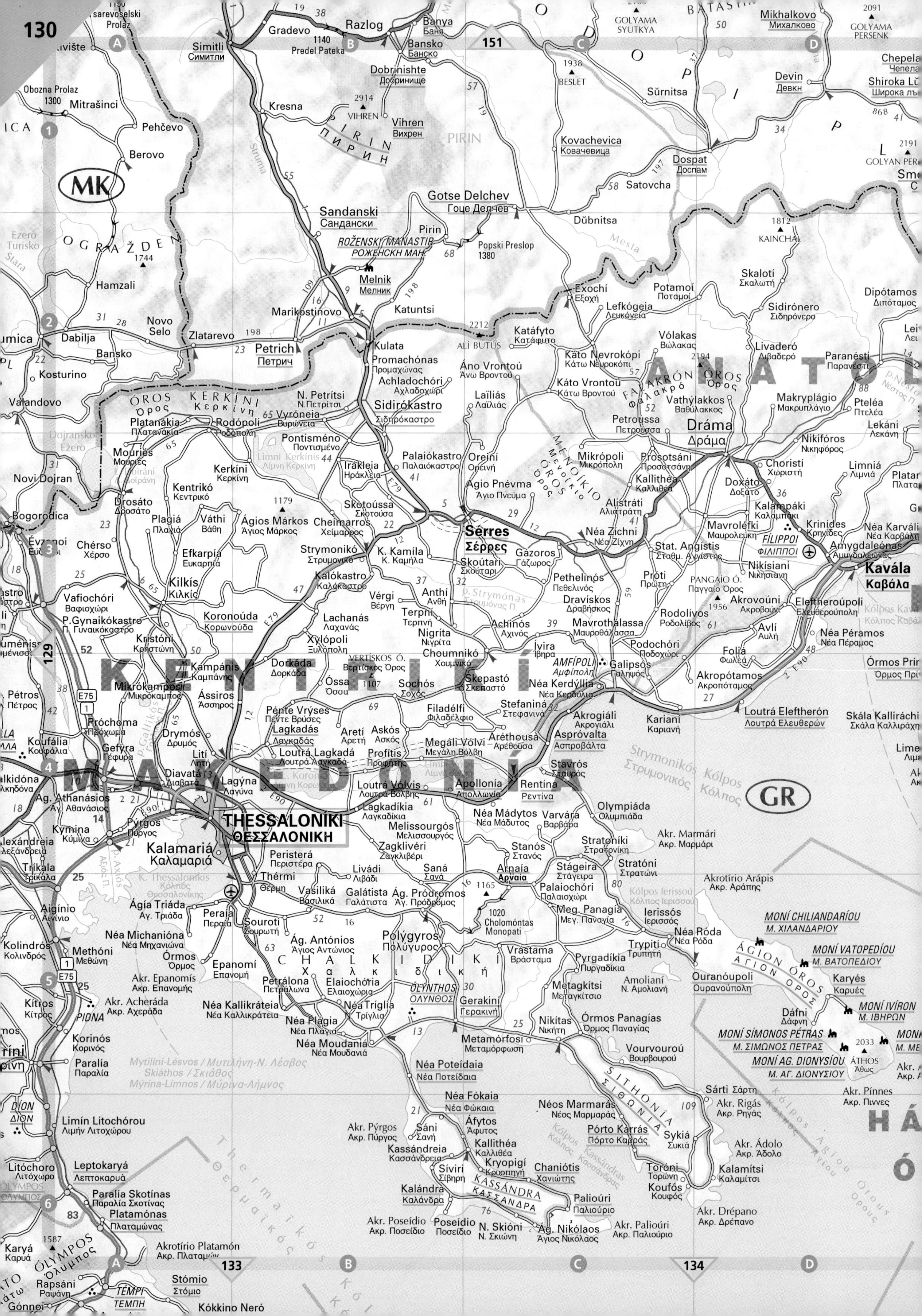

151
133
134
129
MK
GR
KENTRIKÍ MAKEDONÍA
ANATOL
PIRIN
ПИРИН
OGRAŽDEN
ÓROS KERKÍNI
Όρος Κερκίνη
MENOÍKIO ÓROS
Μενοίκιο Όρος
FALAKRÓN ÓROS
Φαλακρό Όρος
CHALKIDIKÍ
Χαλκιδική
SITHONÍA
ΣΙΘΩΝΙΑ
KASSÁNDRA
ΚΑΣΣΑΝΔΡΑ
ÁGION ÓROS
ΑΓΙΟΝ ΟΡΟΣ
ÓLYMPOS
Όλυμπος
Strymonikós Kólpos
Στρυμονικός Κόλπος
Thermaïkós Kólpos
Θερμαϊκός Κόλπος
Kólpos Kassándras
Κόλπος Κασσάνδρας
Kólpos Agíou Órous
Κόλπος Αγίου Όρους
Kólpos Ierissoú
Κόλπος Ιερισσού
K. Thessalonikis
Κόλπος Θεσσαλονίκης
Limni Kerkinis
Λίμνη Κερκίνη
Limni Volvi
Λίμνη Βόλβη
Dojransko Ezero
Ezero Turisko
Mesta
Struma
Simitli
Симитли
Gradevo
Razlog
Banya
Баня
Bansko
Банско
1140
Predel Pateka
Dobrinishte
Добринище
2914
VIHREN
Vihren
Вихрен
Kresna
Mikhalkovo
Михалково
GOLYAMA SYUTKYA
GOLYAMA PERSENK
1938
BESLET
Devin
Девин
Shiroka Lŭ
Chepela
Sŭrnitsa
Kovachevica
Ковачевица
Dospat
Доспат
Satovcha
Gotse Delchev
Гоце Делчев
Dŭbnitsa
1812
KAINCHAL
Sandanski
Сандански
Pirin
ROŽENSKI MANASTIR
РОЖЕНСКИ МАН.
Popski Preslop
1380
Melnik
Мелник
Katuntsi
Marikostinovo
Obozna Prolaz
1300
Mitrašinci
Pehčevo
Berovo
1744
Hamzali
Novo Selo
Dabilja
Bansko
Kosturino
Valandovo
Zlatarevo
Petrich
Петрич
2212
ALÍ BUTÚS
Kulata
Promachónas
Προμαχώνας
Achladochóri
Αχλαδοχώρι
Sidirókastro
Σιδηρόκαστρο
N. Petrítsi
Ν.Πετρίτσι
Vyróneia
Βυρώνεια
Rodópoli
Ροδόπολη
Platanákia
Πλατανάκια
Mouriés
Μουριές
Novi Dojran
Bogorodica
Évzonoi
Exochí
Εξοχή
Lefkógeia
Λευκόγεια
Potamoí
Ποταμοί
Skalotí
Σκαλωτή
Dipótamos
Διπόταμος
Sidirónero
Σιδηρόνερο
Katáfyto
Κατάφυτο
Vólakas
Βώλακας
Livaderó
Λιβαδερό
Káto Nevrokópi
Κάτω Νευροκόπι
2194
Áno Vrontoú
Άνω Βροντού
Káto Vrontoú
Κάτω Βροντού
Paranésti
Παρανέστι
Laïliás
Λαϊλιάς
Vathýlakkos
Βαθύλακκος
Makryplágio
Μακρυπλάγιο
Ptéléa
Πτελέα
Lekáni
Λεκάνη
Petroussa
Πετρούσα
Dráma
Δράμα
Nikifóros
Νικηφόρος
Pontisméno
Ποντισμένο
Palaiókastro
Παλαιόκαστρο
Oreiní
Ορεινή
Mikrópoli
Μικρόπολη
Prosotsáni
Προσοτσάνη
Choristí
Χωριστή
Limniá
Λιμνιά
Irákleia
Ηράκλεια
Kerkíni
Κερκίνη
Kentrikó
Κεντρικό
Agio Pnévma
Άγιο Πνεύμα
Kallithéa
Καλλιθέα
Doxáto
Δοξάτο
Drosáto
Δροσάτο
1179
Skotoússa
Σκοτούσα
Alistráti
Αλιστράτη
Kalampáki
Καλαμπάκι
Plagiá
Πλαγιά
Váthi
Βάθη
Ágios Márkos
Άγιος Μάρκος
Cheimarros
Χείμαρρος
Sérres
Σέρρες
Néa Zíchni
Νέα Ζίχνη
Mavrolefki
Μαυρολεύκη
Krinídes
Κρηνίδες
Néa Karváli
Chérso
Χέρσο
Efkarpía
Ευκαρπία
Strymonikó
Στρυμονικό
K. Kamíla
Κ. Καμήλα
Skoútari
Σκούταρι
Gázoros
Γάζωρος
Stat. Angístis
Σταθ. Αγγίστης
FILIPPOI
ΦΙΛΙΠΠΟΙ
Amygdaleónas
Αμυγδαλεώνας
Kavála
Καβάλα
Kalókastro
Καλόκαστρο
Pethelinós
Πεθελινός
Próti
Πρώτη
PANGAÍO Ó.
Παγγαίο Όρος
Nikísiani
Νικήσιανη
Vafiochóri
Βαφιοχώρι
Kilkís
Κιλκίς
Vérgi
Βέργη
Anthí
Ανθή
Terpni
Τερπνή
p. Strymónas
Dravískos
Δραβήσκος
1956
Akrovoúni
Ακροβούνι
Eleftheroúpoli
Ελευθερούπολη
Kólpos Kavála
P.Gynaikókastro
Π. Γυναικόκαστρο
Koronoúda
Κορωνούδα
Lachanás
Λαχανάς
Nigríta
Νιγρίτα
Achinós
Αχινός
Mavrothálassa
Μαυροθάλασσα
Rodolívos
Ροδολίβος
Avlí
Αυλή
Néa Péramos
Νέα Πέραμος
Kristóni
Κριστώνη
Xylópoli
Ξυλόπολη
Chouмnikó
Χουμνικό
Ívira
Ίβηρα
Podochóri
Ποδοχώρι
Foliá
Φωλεά
Órmos Prínou
Kampánis
Καμπάνης
Dorkáda
Δορκάδα
VERTÍSKOS Ó.
Βερτίσκος Όρος
AMFÍPOLI
Αμφίπολη
Galipsós
Γαληψός
Akropótamos
Ακροπόταμος
Mikrókampos
Μικρόκαμπος
Óssa
Όσσα
1107
Sochós
Σοχός
Skepastó
Σκεπαστό
Néa Kerdýllia
Νέα Κερδύλλια
Ássiros
Άσσηρος
Pétros
Πέτρος
Stefaniná
Στεφανινά
Pénte Vrýses
Πέντε Βρύσες
Filadélfi
Φιλαδέλφιο
Akrogiáli
Ακρογιάλι
Kariani
Καριανή
Loutrá Eleftherón
Λουτρά Ελευθερών
Skála Kallirachi
Σκάλα Καλλιράχη
Próchoma
Πρόχωμα
Lagkadás
Λαγκαδάς
Aretí
Αρετή
Askós
Ασκός
Megáli Vólvi
Μεγάλη Βόλβη
Aréthousa
Αρέθουσα
Asprovalta
Ασπρόβαλτα
Koufália
Κουφάλια
Gefýra
Γέφυρα
Drymós
Δρυμός
Lití
Λητή
Loutrá Lagkadá
Λουτρά Λαγκαδά
Profítis
Προφήτης
Stavrós
Σταυρός
Chalkidóna
Diavatá
Διαβατά
Lagýna
Λαγύνα
Loutrá Vólvis
Λουτρά Βόλβης
Apollonía
Απολλωνία
Rentína
Ρεντίνα
Ag. Athanásios
Άγ. Αθανάσιος
Pýrgos
Πύργος
THESSALONÍKI
ΘΕΣΣΑΛΟΝΙΚΗ
Lagkadíkia
Λαγκαδίκια
Néa Mádytos
Νέα Μάδυτος
Varvára
Βαρβάρα
Olympiáda
Ολυμπιάδα
Kýmina
Κύμινα
Aléxándreia
Melissourgós
Μελισσουργός
Akr. Marmári
Ακρ. Μαρμάρι
Kalamariá
Καλαμαριά
Peristerá
Περιστέρα
Zagklivéri
Ζαγκλιβέρι
Stanós
Στανός
Stratoníki
Στρατονίκη
Tríkala
Τρίκαλα
Thérmi
Θέρμη
Livádi
Λιβάδι
Saná
Σανά
Arnaía
Αρναία
Stágeira
Στάγειρα
Stratóni
Στρατώνι
Akrotírio Arápis
Ακρ. Αράπης
Vasiliká
Βασιλικά
Galátista
Γαλάτιστα
Ág. Pródromos
Άγ. Πρόδρομος
1165
Palaiochóri
Παλαιοχώρι
Aigínio
Ágia Triáda
Αγ. Τριάδα
Peraía
Περαία
1020
Cholomóntas
Monopati
Meg. Panagía
Μεγ. Παναγία
Ierissós
Ιερισσός
MONÍ CHILIANDARÍOU
Μ. ΧΙΛΙΑΝΔΑΡΙΟΥ
Souroti
Σουρωτή
Polýgyros
Πολύγυρος
Néa Róda
Νέα Ρόδα
Trypití
Τρυπητή
MONÍ VATOPEDÍOU
Μ. ΒΑΤΟΠΕΔΙΟΥ
Kolindrós
Κολινδρός
Methóni
Μεθώνη
Néa Michanióna
Νέα Μηχανιώνα
Órmos
Όρμος
Epanomí
Επανομή
Ág. Antónios
Άγιος Αντώνιος
Vrastama
Βράσταμα
Pyrgadíkia
Πυργαδίκια
Ouranoúpoli
Ουρανούπολη
Karyés
Καρυές
Akr. Epanomís
Ακρ. Επανομής
Petrálona
Πετράλωνα
Elaiochória
Ελαιοχώρια
ÓLYNTHOS
ΟΛΥΝΘΟΣ
Metagkítsi
Μεταγκίτσιο
Amolianí
Ν. Αμολιανή
Kítros
Κίτρος
Akr. Acheráda
Ακρ. Αχεράδα
PIDNA
Néa Kallikráteia
Νέα Καλλικράτεια
Néa Triglia
Ν. Τρίγλια
Gerakiní
Γερακινή
Nikítas
Νικήτη
Órmos Panagías
Όρμος Παναγίας
MONÍ IVÍRON
Μ. ΙΒΗΡΩΝ
Dáfni
Δάφνη
Korinós
Κορινός
Néa Plagia
Νέα Πλάγια
Néa Moudaniá
Νέα Μουδανιά
Metamórfosi
Μεταμόρφωση
Vourvouroú
Βουρβουρού
MONÍ SÍMONOS PÉTRAS
Μ. ΣΙΜΩΝΟΣ ΠΕΤΡΑΣ
2033
ÁTHOS
Άθως
MONÍ AG. DIONYSÍOU
Μ. ΑΓ. ΔΙΟΝΥΣΙΟΥ
Paralía
Παραλία
Mytilíni-Lésvos / Μυτιλήνη-Ν. Λέσβος
Skíathos / Σκιάθος
Mýrina-Límnos / Μύρινα-Λήμνος
Néa Poteídaia
Νέα Ποτείδαια
Sárti
Σάρτη
Akr. Rigás
Ακρ. Ρηγάς
Akr. Pínnes
Ακρ. Πιννες
DÍON
ΔΙΟΝ
Limín Litochórou
Λιμήν Λιτοχώρου
Néa Fókaia
Νέα Φώκαια
Áfytos
Άφυτος
Néos Marmarás
Νέος Μαρμαράς
Akr. Pýrgos
Ακρ. Πύργος
Sáni
Σανή
Kassándreia
Κασσάνδρεια
Kallithéa
Καλλιθέα
Pórto Karrás
Πόρτο Καρράς
Sykiá
Συκιά
Akr. Ádolo
Ακρ. Άδολο
Litóchoro
Λιτόχωρο
Leptokaryá
Λεπτοκαρυά
Siviri
Σίβηρη
Kryopigí
Κρυοπηγή
Chaniótis
Χανιώτης
Toróni
Τορώνη
Kalamítsi
Καλαμίτσι
Paralía Skotínas
Παραλία Σκοτίνας
Kalándra
Καλάνδρα
Palioúri
Παλιούρι
Koufós
Κουφός
Akr. Drépano
Ακρ. Δρέπανο
Platamónas
Πλαταμώνας
Akr. Poseídio
Ακρ. Ποσείδιο
Poseídio
Ποσείδιο
N. Skióni
Ν. Σκιώνη
Ag. Nikólaos
Άγιος Νικόλαος
Akr. Palioúri
Ακρ. Παλιούρι
1587
Karyá
Καρυά
Akrotírio Platamón
Ακρ. Πλαταμών
Rapsáni
Ραψάνη
Stómio
Στόμιο
TEMPI
ΤΕΜΠΗ
Gónnoi
Kókkino Neró
E75
E79
E90

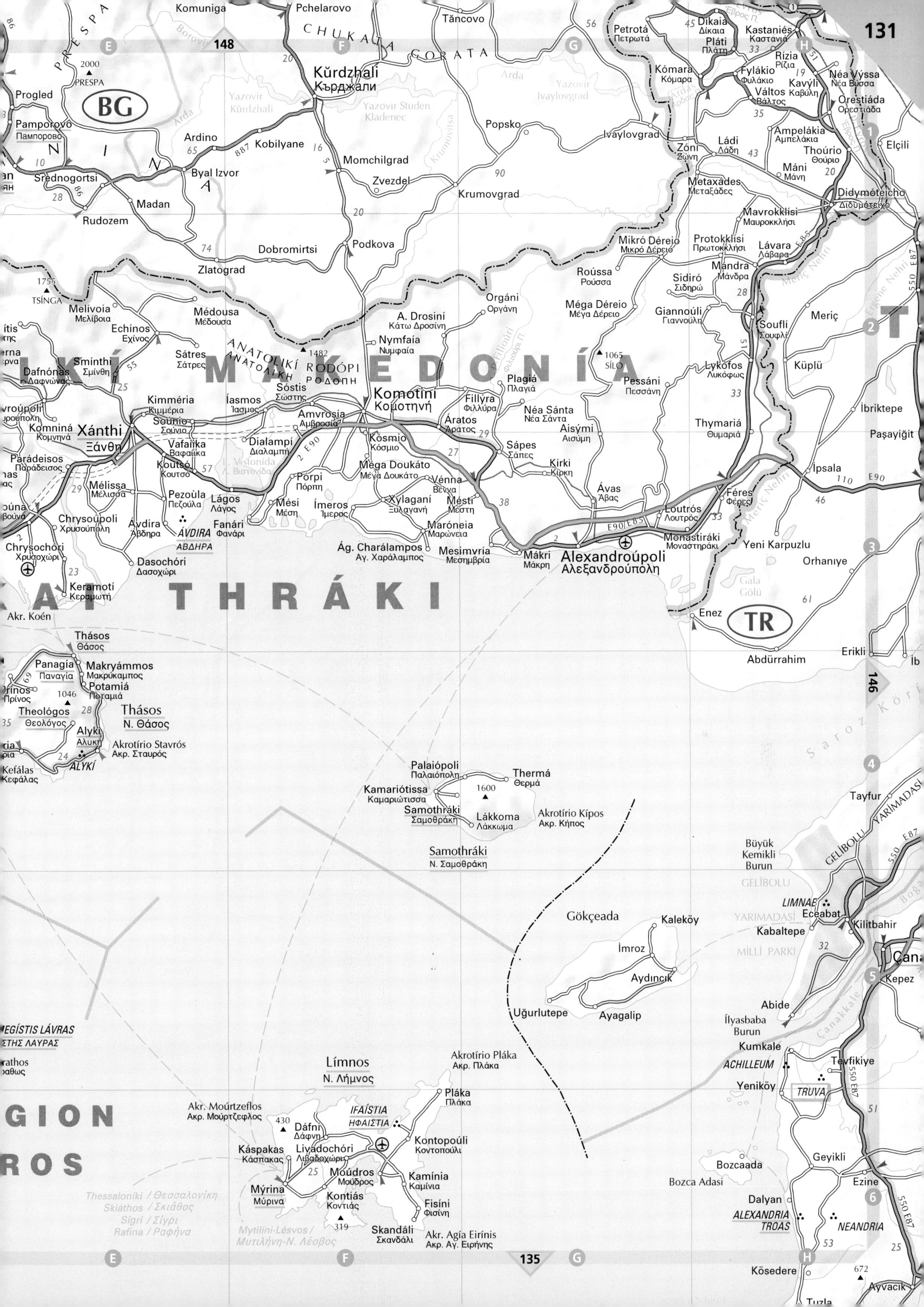

BG
TR
MAKEDONÍA
ANATOLIKÍ RODÓPI
ΑΝΑΤΟΛΙΚΗ ΡΟΔΟΠΗ
THRÁKI
Kŭrdzhali
Къpджaли
Komotiní
Κομοτηνή
Xánthi
Ξάνθη
Alexandroúpoli
Αλεξανδρούπολη
Didymóteicho
Διδυμότειχο
Orestiáda
Ορεστιάδα
Soufli
Σουφλί
Thásos
Ν. Θάσος
Samothráki
Ν. Σαμοθράκη
Límnos
Ν. Λήμνος
Gökçeada
Bozca Adasi
Mýrina
Μύρινα
Moúdros
Μούδρος
Keramotí
Κεραμωτή
Ívaylovgrad
Krumovgrad
Momchilgrad
Zlatograd
Madan
Rudozem
Enez
Ipsala
Eceabat
Kilitbahir
Kumkale
Ezine
Ayvacik
Thessaloníki / Θεσσαλονίκη
Skiáthos / Σκιάθος
Sígri / Σίγρι
Rafína / Ραφήνα
Mytilíni-Lésvos / Μυτιλήνη-Ν. Λέσβος
148
135
146

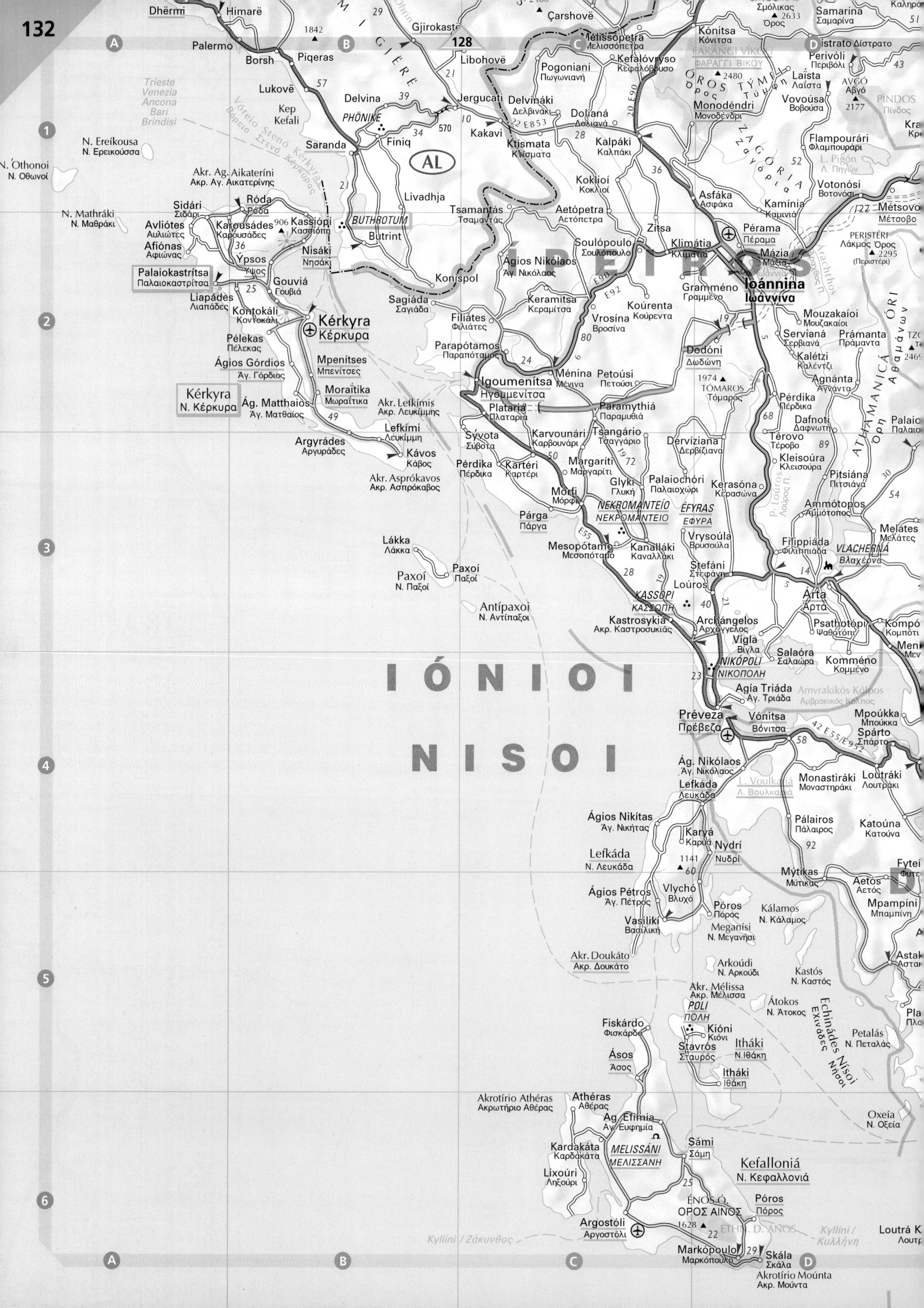
Dhërmi
Himarë
Palermo
Borsh
Piqeras
Lukovë
Gjirokastër
128
Libohovë
Delvina
Jergucati
Saranda
Finiq
Kakavi
AL
Livadhja
Butrint
Konispol
Çarshovë
Mélissopetra
Kónitsa
Kefalóvryso
Pogonianí
Delvináki
Doliana
Kalpáki
Monodéndri
Samarína
Dístrato
Perivóli
Laista
Vovoúsa
Flampourári
Votonósi
Mètsovo
Kamíniа
Asfáka
Pérama
Zítsa
Klimatia
Mázia
Ioánnina
Ιωάννινα
ÍPEIROS
ZAGORIA
Tsamantás
Aetópetra
Soulópoulo
Ágios Nikólaos
Keramitsa
Koúrenta
Vrosína
Dodóni
Sagiáda
Filiátes
Parapótamos
Igoumenítsa
Ηγουμενίτσα
Ménina
Petoúsi
Paramythiá
Plataria
Sývota
Karvounári
Tsangário
Margaríti
Pérdika
Kartéri
Morfí
Glykí
Palaiochóri
Derviziana
Kerasóna
Párga
NEKROMANTEÍO
ÉFYRAS
Mesopótamo
Kanalláki
Vrysoúla
Stefáni
Loúros
KASSOPI
Kastrosykiá
Archángelos
Vigla
NIKÓPOLI
Agía Triáda
Préveza
Vónitsa
Árta
Filippiáda
VLACHERNÁ
Ammótopos
Psathotópi
Salaóra
Komméno
Amvrakikós Kólpos
Mpoúkka
Spárto
Loutráki
Monastiráki
Ág. Nikólaos
Lefkáda
Ágios Nikítas
Karyá
Nydrí
Vlychó
Ágios Pétros
Vasilikí
Póros
Meganísi
Pálairos
Katoúna
Mýtikas
Kálamos
Aetós
Mpampíni
Akr. Doukáto
Arkoúdi
Kastós
Átokos
Echinádes Nísoi
Akr. Mélissa
POLI
Kióni
Stavrós
Itháki
Fiskárdo
Ásos
Athéras
Akrotírio Athéras
Ag. Efimía
Sámi
MELISSÁNI
Kardakáta
Lixoúri
Kefalloniá
Argostóli
ÉNOS Ó.
Póros
Markópoulo
Skála
Akrotírio Moúnta
Kyllíni / Zákynthos
Kyllíni
Oxeía
Petalás
N. Ereíkousa
N. Óthonoi
N. Mathráki
Akr. Ag. Aikateríni
Sidári
Róda
Avliótes
Karousádes
Kassiópi
Afiónas
Palaiokastrítsa
Ýpsos
Nisáki
Gouviá
Liapádes
Kontokáli
Kérkyra
Κέρκυρα
Pélekas
Ágios Górdios
Mpenítses
Moraïtika
Ág. Matthaios
Kérkyra
N. Κέρκυρα
Akr. Lefkímis
Lefkími
Argyrádes
Kávos
Akr. Asprókavos
Lákka
Paxoí
Antípaxoi
Trieste
Venezia
Ancona
Bari
Brindisi
IÓNIOI NISOI

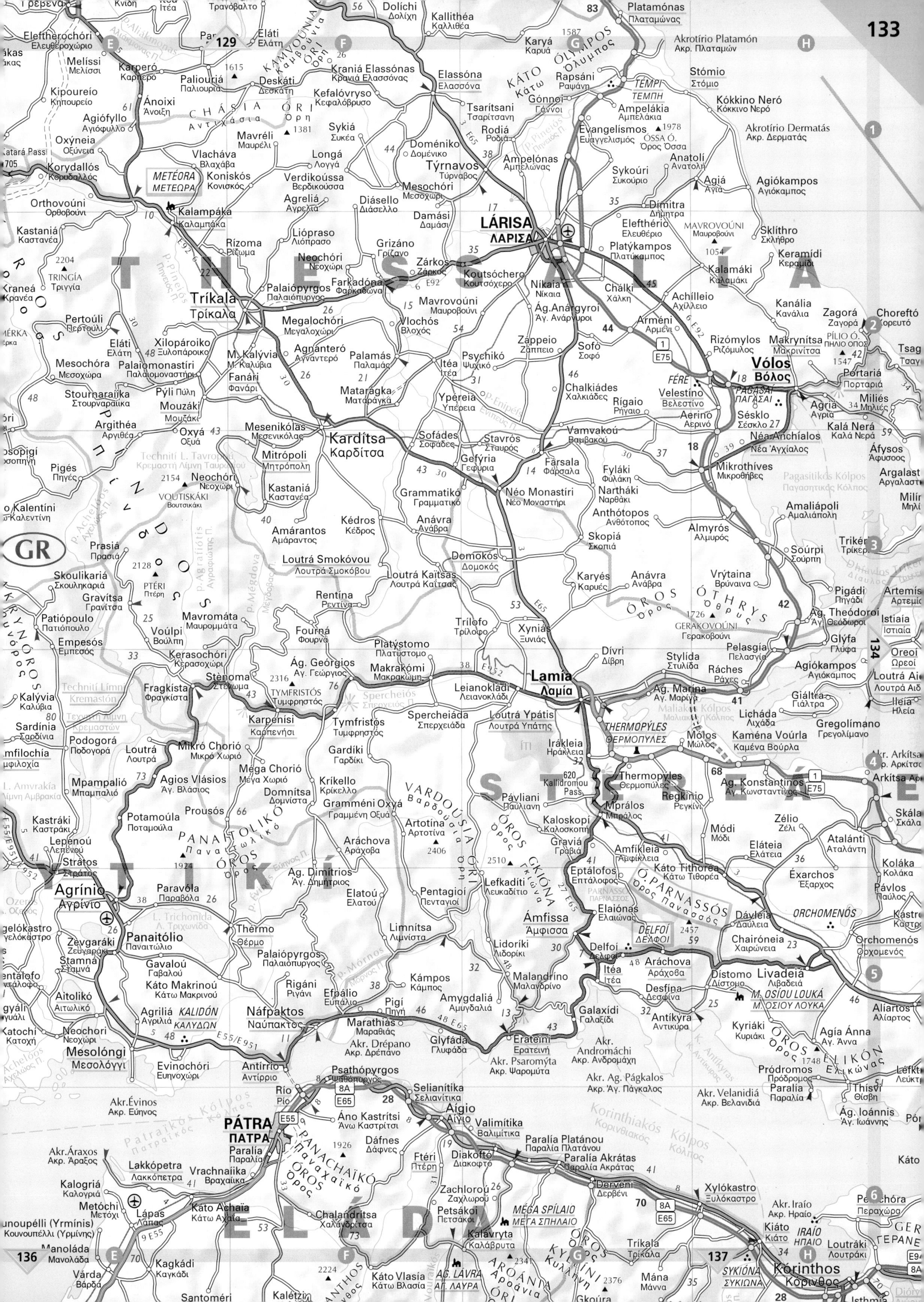
THESSALÍA
STEREÁ ELLÁDA
GR
Platamónas Πλαταμώνας
Akrotírio Platamón Ακρ. Πλαταμών
Dolíchi Δολίχη
Kallithéa Καλλιθέα
Karyá Καρυά
KÁTO ÓLYMPOS Κάτω Όλυμπος
Eleftherochóri Ελευθεροχώρι
Melíssi Μελίσσι
Karperó Καρπερό
Paliouriá Παλιουριά
Deskáti Δεσκάτη
Kraniá Elassónas Κρανιά Ελασσόνας
Elassóna Ελασσόνα
Rapsáni Ραψάνη
Stómio Στόμιο
TÉMPI ΤΕΜΠΗ
Kipoureío Κηπουρείο
Ánoixi Άνοιξη
CHÁSIA ÓRI Αντιχάσια Όρη
Kefalóvryso Κεφαλόβρυσο
Tsarítsani Τσαρίτσανη
Gónnoi Γόννοι
Ampelákia Αμπελάκια
Kókkino Neró Κόκκινο Νερό
Agiófyllo Αγιόφυλλο
Oxýneia Οξύνεια
Mavréli Μαυρέλι
Sykiá Συκέα
Rodiá Ροδιά
Evangelismós Ευαγγελισμός
ÓSSA Ó. Όρος Όσσα
Akrotírio Dermatás Ακρ. Δερματάς
Doméniko Δομένικο
Vlacháva Βλαχάβα
Longá Λογγά
Týrnavos Τύρναβος
Ampelónas Αμπελώνας
Anatolí Ανατολή
Korydallós Κορυδαλλός
METÉORA ΜΕΤΕΩΡΑ
Koniskós Κονισκός
Verdikoússa Βερδικούσσα
Mesochóri Μεσοχώρι
Sykoúri Συκούριο
Agiá Αγιά
Agiókampos Αγιόκαμπος
Orthovoúni Ορθοβούνι
Kalampáka Καλαμπάκα
Agreliá Αγρελιά
Diásello Διάσελλο
Damási Δαμάσι
LÁRISA ΛΑΡΙΣΑ
Dímitra Δήμητρα
Eleftherío Ελευθέριο
MAVROVOÚNI Μαυροβούνι
Sklíthro Σκλήθρο
Kastaniá Καστανέα
Lióprasο Λιόπρασο
Rízoma Ρίζωμα
Grizáno Γριζάνο
Platýkampos Πλατύκαμπος
Keramídi Κεραμίδι
TRINGÍA Τριγγία
Neochóri Νεοχώρι
Zárkos Ζάρκος
Koutsóchero Κουτσόχερο
Kalamáki Καλαμάκι
Kraneá Κρανέα
Tríkala Τρίκαλα
Palaiópyrgos Παλαιόπυργος
Farkadóna Φαρκαδόνα
Níkaia Νίκαια
Chálki Χάλκη
Achílleio Αχίλλειο
Kanália Κανάλια
Zagorá Ζαγορά
Choreftó Χορευτό
Pertoúli Περτούλι
Megalochóri Μεγαλοχώρι
Mavrovoúni Μαυροβούνι
Vlochós Βλοχός
Ág. Anárgyroi Άγ. Ανάργυροι
Arméni Αρμένι
Rizómylos Ριζόμυλος
Makrynítsa Μακρινίτσα
PÍLIO Ó. ΠΗΛΙΟ ΟΡΟΣ
Eláti Ελάτη
Xilopároiko Ξυλοπάροικο
Agnanteró Αγναντερό
Zappeio Ζάππειο
Sofó Σοφό
Mesochóra Μεσοχώρα
Palaiomonastíri Παλαιομοναστήρι
M. Kalývia Μ. Καλύβια
Palamás Παλαμάς
Itéa Ιτέα
Psychikó Ψυχικό
Vólos Βόλος
Portariá Πορταριά
Fanári Φανάρι
FÉRE
Stournaraíika Στουρναραίικα
Pýli Πύλη
Matarágka Ματαράγκα
Ypéreia Υπέρεια
Chalkiádes Χαλκιάδες
Velestíno Βελεστίνο
PAGASAÍ ΠΑΓΑΣΑΙ
Agriá Αγριά
Miliés Μηλιές
Mouzáki Μουζάκι
Rígaio Ρήγαιο
Aerinó Αερινό
Sésklo Σέσκλο
Argithéa Αργιθέα
Oxyá Οξυά
Mesenikólas Μεσενικόλας
Kardítsa Καρδίτσα
Sofádes Σοφάδες
Stavrós Σταυρός
Vamvakoú Βαμβακού
Néa Anchíalos Νέα Αγχίαλος
Kalá Nerá Καλά Νερά
Áfysos Άφυσσος
Technití L. Tavropoú Κρεμαστή Λίμνη Ταυρωπού
Mitrópoli Μητρόπολη
Gefýria Γεφύρια
Fársala Φάρσαλα
Fyláki Φυλάκη
Mikrothíves Μικροθήβες
Pagasitikós Kólpos Παγασητικός Κόλπος
Argalastí Αργαλαστή
Pigés Πηγές
Neochóri Νεοχώρι
VOUTISKÁKI Βουτσικάκι
Kastaniá Καστανέα
Grammatikó Γραμματικό
Néo Monastíri Νέο Μοναστήρι
Nartháki Ναρθάκι
Kalentíni Καλεντίνη
Anthótopos Ανθότοπος
Amaliápoli Αμαλιάπολη
PÍNDOS
Amárantos Αμάραντος
Kédros Κέδρος
Anávra Ανάβρα
Skopiá Σκοπιά
Almyrós Αλμυρός
Prasiá Πρασιά
Loutrá Smokóvou Λουτρά Σμοκόβου
Domokós Δομοκός
Soúrpi Σούρπη
PTÉRI Πτέρη
Skoulikariá Σκουληκαριά
Loutrá Kaïtsas Λουτρά Καΐτσας
Karyés Καρυές
Anávra Ανάβρα
Vrýtaina Βρύναινα
Pigádi Πηγάδι
Gravítsa Γραβίτσα
Rentína Ρεντίνα
ÓROS ÓTHRYS Όρος Όθρυς
GERAKOVOÚNI Γερακοβούνι
Ag. Theódoroi Άγ. Θεόδωροι
Istiaia Ιστιαία
Artemísio Αρτεμίσιο
Patiópoulo Πατιόπουλο
Mavromáta Μαυρομμάτα
Fourná Φουρνά
Trílofo Τρίλοφο
Xyniás Ξυνιάς
Glýfa Γλύφα
Voúlpi Βούλπη
Empesós Εμπεσός
Platýstomo Πλατύστομο
Dívri Δίβρη
Stylída Στυλίδα
Pelasgía Πελασγία
Oreoí Ωρεοί
Kerasochóri Κερασοχώρι
Ág. Geórgios Άγ. Γεώργιος
Makrakómi Μακρακώμη
Ráches Ράχες
Agiókampos Αγιόκαμπος
Loutrá Aidipsoú Λουτρά Αιδ.
Technití Límni Kremastón Τεχνητή Λίμνη Κρεμαστών
Stènoma Στένωμα
TYMFRISTÓS Τυμφρηστός
Spercheiós Σπερχειός Π.
Leianokládi Λειανοκλάδι
Lamía Λαμία
Ag. Marína Αγ. Μαρίνα
Giáltra Γιάλτρα
Ilieia Ηλεία
Fragkísta Φραγκίστα
Kalývia Καλύβια
Karpenísi Καρπενήσι
Tymfristós Τυμφρηστός
Spercheiáda Σπερχειάδα
Loutrá Ypátis Λουτρά Υπάτης
Maliakós Kólpos Μαλιακός Κόλπος
Lichάda Λιχάδα
Gregolímano Γρεγολίμανο
Sardínia Σαρδίνια
THERMOPÝLES ΘΕΡΜΟΠΥΛΕΣ
Mólos Μώλος
Kaména Voúrla Καμένα Βούρλα
Amfilochía Αμφιλοχία
Podogorá Ποδογορά
Loutrá Λουτρά
Mikró Chorió Μικρό Χωριό
Gardíki Γαρδίκι
Irákleia Ηράκλεια
ÍTI
Ak. Arkítsa Ακρ. Αρκίτσα
Arkítsa Αρκίτσα
Mpampalió Μπαμπαλιό
Agios Vlásios Άγ. Βλάσιος
Mega Chorió Μέγα Χωριό
Kríkello Κρίκελλο
Kallidromou Pass
Thermopyles Θερμοπύλες
Ag. Konstantínos Αγ. Κωνσταντίνος
L. Amvrakía Λίμνη Αμβρακία
Domnítsa Δομνίτσα
Gramméni Oxyá Γραμμένη Οξυά
VARDOÚSIA ÓRI Βαρδούσια Όρη
Pávliani Παύλιανη
Regkínio Ρεγκίνι
Kastráki Καστράκι
Prousós
Potamoúla Ποταμούλα
PANAITOLIKÓ ÓROS Παναιτωλικό Όρος
Artotína Αρτοτίνα
Kaloskopí Καλοσκοπή
Mprálos Μπράλος
Zélio Ζέλι
Skála Σκάλα
Lepenoú Λεπενού
Gravia Γραβιά
Módi Μόδι
Atalánti Αταλάντη
Stratos Στράτος
Arάchova Αράχωβα
Amfíkleia Αμφίκλεια
Eláteia Ελάτεια
Kolάka Κολάκα
AITOLÍKÍ
Ag. Dimítrios Άγ. Δημήτριος
ÓROS GKIÓNA Γκιώνα
Eptálofos Επτάλοφος
Káto Tithoréa Κάτω Τιθορέα
Éxarchos Έξαρχος
Agrínio Αγρίνιο
Paravóla Παραβόλα
Lefkadíti Λευκαδίτιο
Elatoú Ελατού
Pentagioí Πενταγιοί
PARNASSÓS
Ó. PARNASSÓS Όρος Παρνασσός
Pávlos Παύλος
Ozerós
L. Trichonída Λ. Τριχωνίδα
Elaiónas Ελαιώνας
ORCHOMENÓS
Kástro
Aggelókastro Αγγελόκαστρο
Zevgaráki Ζευγαράκι
Panaitólio Παναιτώλιο
Thérmo Θέρμο
Limnítsa Λιμνίτσα
Ámfissa Άμφισσα
DELFOÍ ΔΕΛΦΟΙ
Dávleia Δαύλεια
Chairóneia Χαιρώνεια
Orchomenós Ορχομενός
Stamná Σταμνά
Palaiópyrgos Παλαιόπυργος
Lidoríki Λιδορίκι
Delfoí Δελφοί
Arάchova Αράχωβα
Gavaloú Γαβαλού
p. Mórnos Μόρνος Π.
Itéa Ιτέα
Dístomo Δίστομο
Livadeia Λιβαδειά
Angelókastro
Káto Makrinoú Κάτω Μακρινού
Rigáni Ριγάνι
Kámpos Κάμπος
Malandríno Μαλανδρίνο
Desfína Δεσφίνα
M. OSÍOU LOUKÁ Μ. ΟΣΙΟΥ ΛΟΥΚΑ
Aitolikó Αιτωλικό
Efpálio Ευπάλιο
Pigí Πηγή
Amygdaliá Αμυγδαλιά
Galaxídi Γαλαξίδι
Antíkyra Αντίκυρα
Aliartos Αλίαρτος
Agriliá Αγριλιά
KALIDÓN ΚΑΛΥΔΩΝ
Náfpaktos Ναύπακτος
Marathiás Μαραθιάς
Kyriáki Κυριάκι
Agía Ánna Αγ. Άννα
Katochí Κατοχή
Neochori Νεοχώρι
Akr. Drépano Ακρ. Δρέπανο
Glyfáda Γλυφάδα
Erateiní Ερατεινή
Akr. Andromáchi Ακρ. Ανδρομάχη
ÓROS ELIKÓN Ελικών
Mesolóngi Μεσολόγγι
Akr. Psaromýta Ακρ. Ψαρομύτα
Evinochóri Ευηνοχώρι
Antírrio Αντίρριο
Akr. Ag. Pángalos Ακρ. Άγ. Πάγκαλος
Pródromos Πρόδρομος
Lefktra Λεύκτρα
Psathópyrgos Ψαθόπυργος
Paralía Παραλία
Thísvi Θίσβη
Río Ρίο
Selianítika Σελιανίτικα
Akr. Velanidiá Ακρ. Βελανιδιά
Akr. Évinos Ακρ. Εύηνος
Patraïkós Kólpos Πατραϊκός Κόλπος
Aígio Αίγιο
Ág. Ioánnis Άγ. Ιωάννης
Áno Kastrítsi Άνω Καστρίτσι
Korinthiakós Kólpos Κορινθιακός Κόλπος
PÁTRA ΠΑΤΡΑ
Valimítika Βαλιμίτικα
Paralía Παραλία
PANACHAÏKÓ ÓROS Παναχαϊκό Όρος
Dáfnes Δάφνες
Paralía Platánou Παραλία Πλατάνου
Akr. Áraxos Ακρ. Άραξος
Ftéri Πτέρη
Diakoftó Διακοφτό
Paralía Akrátas Παραλία Ακράτας
Káto
Lakkópetra Λακκόπετρα
Vrachnaiika Βραχναίικα
Kalogriá Καλογριά
Zachlorou Ζαχλωρού
Derveni Δερβένι
Xylókastro Ξυλόκαστρο
Metóchi Μετόχι
Lápas Λάπας
Káto Achaïa Κάτω Αχαΐα
Petsákoi Πετσάκοι
MÉGA SPÍLAIO ΜΕΓΑ ΣΠΗΛΑΙΟ
Akr. Iraío Ακρ. Ηραίο
Perachóra Περαχώρα
GERANEIA
Kounoupélli (Yrmínis) Κουνουπέλλι (Υρμίνης)
Chalándritsa Χαλάνδριτσα
Kalávryta Καλάβρυτα
ÓROS KYLÍNI Κυλλήνη
Kiáto Κιάτο
IRAÍO ΗΡΑΙΟ
Loutráki Λουτράκι
Manoláda Μανολάδα
Kagkádi Καγκάδι
Tríkala Τρίκαλα
AROÁNIA
SYKIÓNA ΣΥΚΙΩΝΑ
Kórinthos Κόρινθος
Várda Βάρδα
Káto Vlasía Κάτω Βλασία
AG. LAVRA ΑΓ. ΛΑΥΡΑ
Mána Μάννα
Santoméri
Kalétzi
Isthmia
E65
E75
E92
E55
E952
E951
8A
E
F
G
H
1
2
3
4
5
6
129
134
136
137

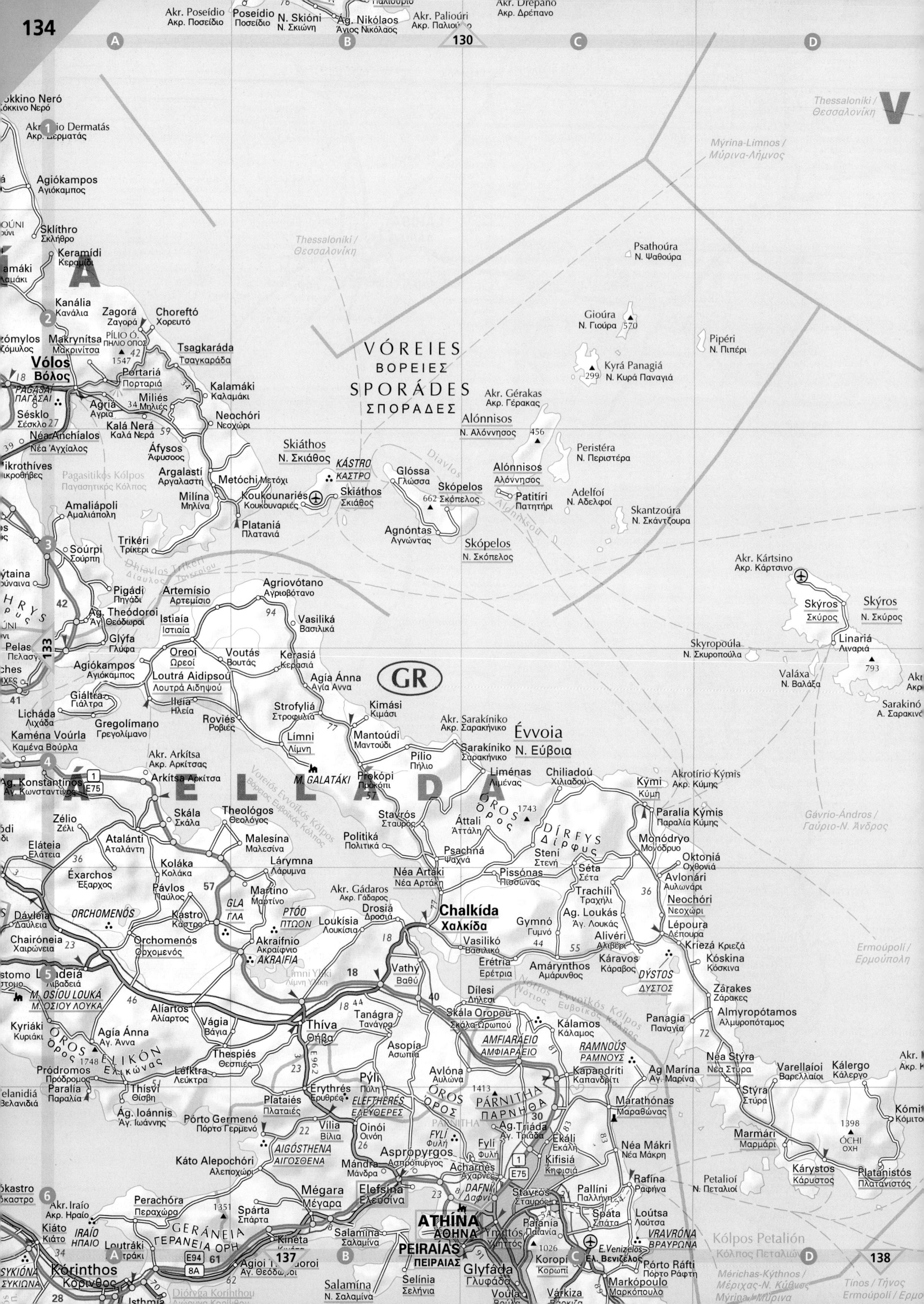

Akr. Poseídio
Ακρ. Ποσείδιο
Poseídio
Ποσείδιο
N. Skióni
Ν. Σκιώνη
Ag. Nikólaos
Άγιος Νικόλαος
Akr. Palioúri
Akr. Drépano
Ακρ. Δρέπανο
130
Thessaloníki /
Θεσσαλονίκη
Mýrina-Límnos /
Μύρινα-Λήμνος
Agiókampos
Αγιόκαμπος
Sklíthro
Σκλήθρο
Keramídi
Kanália
Κανάλια
Zagorá
Ζαγορά
Choreftó
Χορευτό
Makrynitsa
Μακρινίτσα
PÍLIO Ó.
ΠΗΛΙΟ ΟΡΟΣ
1547
Vólos
Βόλος
Portariá
Πορταριά
Tsagkaráda
Τσαγκαράδα
Kalamáki
Καλαμάκι
PAGASAÍ
ΠΑΓΑΣΑΙ
Sésklo
Σέσκλο
Agriá
Αγριά
Miliés
Μηλιές
Neochóri
Νεοχώρι
Kalá Nerá
Καλά Νερά
Néa Anchíalos
Νέα Αγχίαλος
Áfysos
Άφυσος
Pagasitikós Kólpos
Παγασητικός Κόλπος
Argalastí
Αργαλαστή
Metóchi
Μετόχι
Milína
Μηλίνα
Koukounariés
Κουκουναριές
Platania
Πλατανιά
Amaliápoli
Αμαλιάπολη
Trikéri
Τρίκερι
Soúrpi
Σούρπη
VÓREIES
ΒΟΡΕΙΕΣ
SPORÁDES
ΣΠΟΡΑΔΕΣ
Skiáthos
Ν. Σκιάθος
KÁSTRO
ΚΑΣΤΡΟ
Skiáthos
Σκιάθος
Glóssa
Γλώσσα
Skópelos
Σκόπελος
662
Agnóntas
Αγνώντας
Skópelos
Ν. Σκόπελος
Alónnisos
Ν. Αλόννησος
Akr. Gérakas
Ακρ. Γέρακας
456
Alónnisos
Αλόννησος
Patitíri
Πατητήρι
Peristéra
Ν. Περιστέρα
Adelfoí
Ν. Αδελφοί
Skantzoúra
Ν. Σκάντζουρα
Psathoúra
Ν. Ψαθούρα
Gioúra
Ν. Γιούρα
570
Kyrá Panagiá
Ν. Κυρά Παναγιά
299
Pipéri
Ν. Πιπέρι
Akr. Kártsino
Ακρ. Κάρτσινο
Skýros
Σκύρος
Skýros
Ν. Σκύρος
Linariá
Λιναριά
Skyropoúla
Ν. Σκυροπούλα
Valáxa
Ν. Βαλάξα
793
Sarakinó
Pigádi
Πηγάδι
Artemísio
Αρτεμίσιο
Agriovótano
Αγριοβότανο
Ag. Theódoroi
Istiaía
Ιστιαία
Vasiliká
Βασιλικά
Glýfa
Γλύφα
Oreoí
Ωρεοί
Voutás
Βουτάς
Kerasiá
Κερασιά
Agiókampos
Αγιόκαμπος
Loutrá Aidipsoú
Λουτρά Αιδηψού
Agía Ánna
Αγία Άννα
GR
Giáltra
Γιάλτρα
Ileia
Ηλεία
Strofyliá
Στροφυλιά
Kimási
Κιμάσι
Lichάda
Λιχάδα
Gregolímano
Γρεγολίμανο
Roviés
Ροβιές
Kaména Voúrla
Καμένα Βούρλα
Límni
Λίμνη
Mantoúdi
Μαντούδι
Akr. Sarakíniko
Ακρ. Σαρακήνικο
Sarakíniko
Σαρακήνικο
Évvoia
Ν. Εύβοια
Akr. Arkítsa
Ακρ. Αρκίτσας
Arkítsa
Αρκίτσα
Ag. Konstantínos
Αγ. Κωνσταντίνος
M. GALATÁKI
Pílio
Πήλιο
Liménas
Λιμένας
Chiliadoú
Χιλιαδού
Kými
Κύμη
Akrotírio Kýmis
Ακρ. Κύμης
Prokópi
Προκόπι
ELLÁDA
Paralía Kýmis
Παραλία Κύμης
Zélio
Ζέλι
Skála
Σκάλα
Theológos
Θεολόγος
Vóreios Evvoikós Kólpos
Stavrós
Σταυρός
1743
Gávrio-Ándros /
Γαύριο-Ν. Άνδρος
Eláteia
Ελάτεια
Atalánti
Αταλάντη
Malesína
Μαλεσίνα
Politiká
Πολιτικά
Áttali
Άτταλη
DÍRFYS
Δίρφυς
Monódryo
Μονόδρυο
Psachná
Ψαχνά
Stení
Στενή
Oktoniá
Οχθονιά
Koláka
Κολάκα
Lárymna
Λάρυμνα
Néa Artáki
Νέα Αρτάκη
Pissónas
Πισσώνας
Séta
Σέτα
Avlonári
Αυλωνάρι
Éxarchos
Έξαρχος
Pávlos
Παύλος
Martíno
Μαρτίνο
Akr. Gádaros
Ακρ. Γάδαρος
Trachíli
Τραχήλι
Neochóri
Νεοχώρι
ORCHOMENÓS
GLA
ΓΛΑ
PTÓO
ΠΤΩΟΝ
Drosiá
Δροσιά
Chalkída
Χαλκίδα
Ag. Loukás
Άγ. Λουκάς
Lépoura
Λέπουρα
Dávleia
Δαύλεια
Kástro
Κάστρο
Loukísia
Λουκίσια
Gymnó
Γυμνό
Alivéri
Αλιβέρι
Kriezá
Κριεζά
Chairóneia
Χαιρώνεια
Orchomenós
Ορχομενός
Akraífnio
Ακραίφνιο
AKRAIFIA
Vasilikó
Βασιλικό
Eretria
Ερέτρια
Amárynthos
Αμάρυνθος
Káravos
Κάραβος
Kóskina
Κόσκινα
Ermoúpoli /
Ερμούπολη
Livadeia
Λιβαδειά
Límni Ylíki
Λίμνη Υλίκη
Vathý
Βαθύ
DÝSTOS
ΔΥΣΤΟΣ
Zárakes
Ζάρακες
M. OSÍOU LOUKÁ
Μ. ΟΣΙΟΥ ΛΟΥΚΑ
Dílesi
Δήλεσι
Nótios Evvoikós Kólpos
Aliartos
Αλίαρτος
Tanágra
Τανάγρα
Skála Oropoú
Σκάλα Ωρωπού
Almyropótamos
Αλμυροπόταμος
Kyriáki
Κυριάκι
Agía Ánna
Αγ. Άννα
Vágia
Βάγια
Thíva
Θήβα
Panagía
Παναγία
AMFIARÁEIO
ΑΜΦΙΑΡΑΕΙΟ
Kálamos
Κάλαμος
ÓROS ELIKÓN
1748
Thespiés
Θεσπιές
Asopía
Ασωπία
RAMNOÚS
ΡΑΜΝΟΥΣ
Néa Stýra
Νέα Στύρα
Varellaíoi
Βαρελλαίοι
Kálergo
Κάλεργο
Próдromos
Πρόδρομος
Léfktra
Λεύκτρα
Avlóna
Αυλώνα
Kapandríti
Καπανδρίτι
Ag. Marína
Αγ. Μαρίνα
Paralía
Παραλία
Thisví
Θίσβη
Erythrés
Ερυθρές
Pýli
Πύλη
1413
ELEFTHERÉS
ΕΛΕΥΘΕΡΕΣ
ÓROS PÁRNITHA
ΠΑΡΝΗΘΑ
Stýra
Στύρα
Plataiés
Πλαταιές
Marathónas
Μαραθώνας
1398
ÓCHI
ΟΧΗ
Ág. Ioánnis
Άγ. Ιωάννης
Pórto Germenó
Πόρτο Γερμενό
Vília
Βίλια
Oinói
Οινόη
FYLÍ
ΦΥΛΗ
Ag. Triáda
Αγ. Τριάδα
Ekáli
Εκάλη
Kifisiá
Κηφισιά
Néa Mákri
Νέα Μάκρη
Marmári
Μαρμάρι
AIGÓSTHENA
ΑΙΓΟΣΘΕΝΑ
Fylí
Φυλή
Aspropyrgos
Ασπρόπυργος
Káto Alepochóri
Αλεποχώρι
Mándra
Μάνδρα
Acharnés
Αχαρνές
E75
Rafína
Ραφήνα
Petalioí
Ν. Πεταλιοί
Kárystos
Κάρυστος
Platanistós
Πλατανιστός
Akr. Iraío
Ακρ. Ηραίο
Perachóra
Περαχώρα
Mégara
Μέγαρα
Elefsína
Ελευσίνα
DAFNÍ
Stavrós
Σταυρός
Pallíni
Παλλήνη
Spáta
Σπάτα
Loútsa
Λούτσα
Kiáto
Κιάτο
IRAÍO
ΗΡΑΙΟ
1351
Spárta
Σπάρτα
GERÁNEIA
ΓΕΡΑΝΕΙΑ ΟΡΗ
Salamína
Σαλαμίνα
ATHÍNA
ΑΘΗΝΑ
PEIRAIÁS
ΠΕΙΡΑΙΑΣ
Paianía
Ymittós
1026
E. Venizelos
Ελ. Βενιζέλος
VRAVRÓNA
ΒΡΑΥΡΩΝΑ
Kólpos Petalión
Κόλπος Πεταλιών
Loutráki
E94
Agioi Theódoroi
Αγ. Θεόδωροι
137
Koropí
Κορωπί
Pórto Ráfti
Πόρτο Ράφτη
138
SIKYÓNA
ΣΙΚΥΩΝΑ
Kórinthos
Κόρινθος
8A
Salamína
Ν. Σαλαμίνα
Selínia
Σελήνια
Glyfáda
Γλυφάδα
Voúla
Várkiza
Markópoulo
Μαρκόπουλο
Mérichas-Kýthnos /
Μέριχας-Ν. Κύθνος
Tínos / Τήνος
Ermoúpoli / Ερμούπολη
Díorvga Korinthou
Isthmia

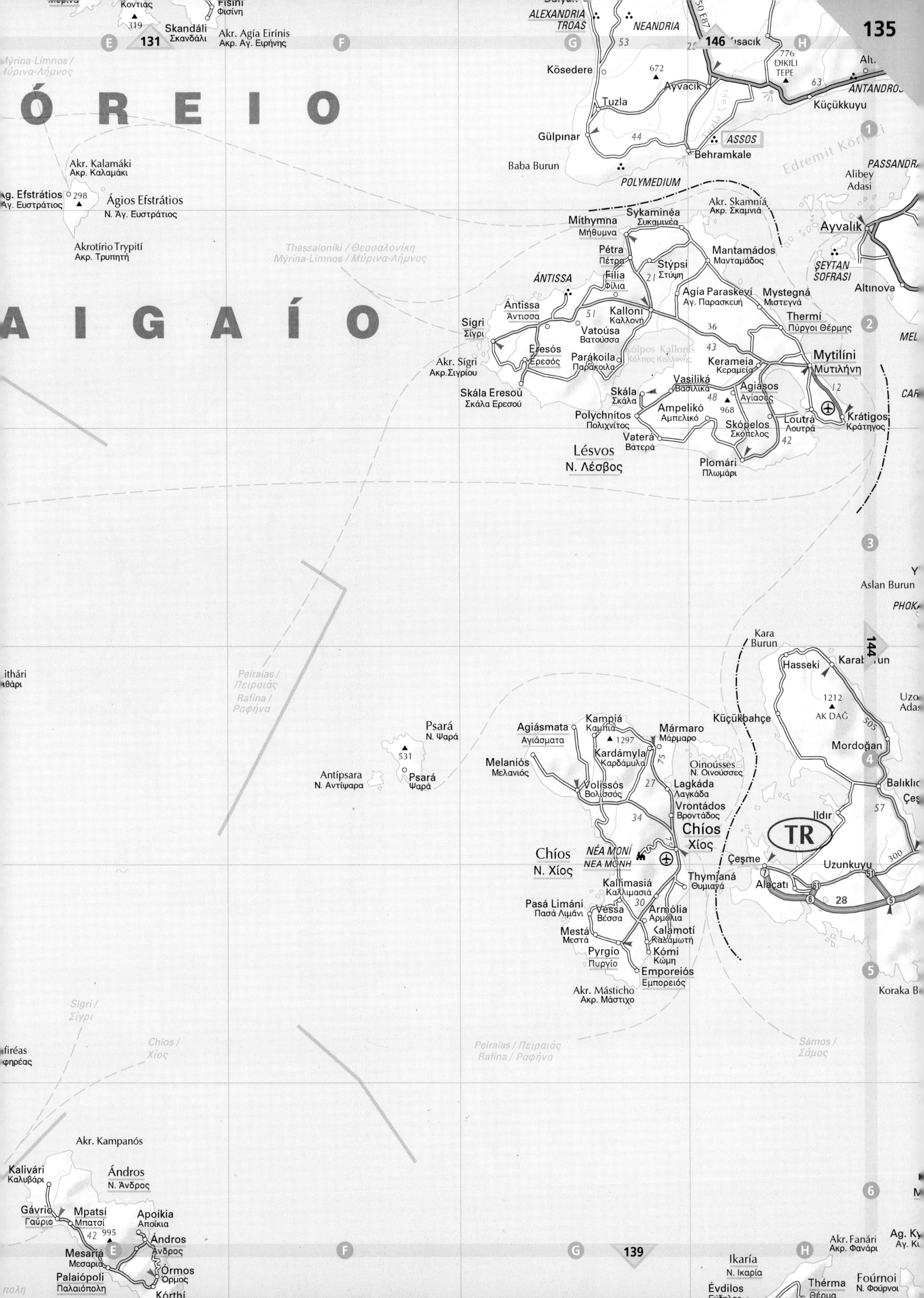

Skandáli
Σκανδάλι
Akr. Agía Eirínis
Ακρ. Αγ. Ειρήνης
ALEXANDRIA TROAS
NEANDRIA
Kösedere
Ayvacık
Tuzla
Gülpınar
ASSOS
Behramkale
Baba Burun
POLYMEDIUM
Küçükkuyu
ANTANDROS
Edremit Körfezi
Alibey Adasi
Ayvalık
ŞEYTAN SOFRASI
Altınova
ÓREIO
AIGAÍO
Akr. Kalamáki
Ακρ. Καλαμάκι
Ágios Efstrátios
Ν. Άγ. Ευστράτιος
Akrotírio Trypití
Ακρ. Τρυπητή
Thessaloníki / Θεσσαλονίκη
Mýrina-Límnos / Μύρινα-Λήμνος
Míthymna
Μήθυμνα
Sykaminéa
Συκαμινέα
Akr. Skamniá
Ακρ. Σκαμνιά
Pétra
Πέτρα
Mantamádos
Μανταμάδος
Stýpsi
Στύψη
ÁNTISSA
Fília
Φίλια
Ántissa
Άντισσα
Agía Paraskeví
Αγ. Παρασκευή
Mystegná
Μιστεγνά
Kalloní
Καλλονή
Thermí
Πύργοι Θέρμης
Sígri
Σίγρι
Vatoúsa
Βατούσα
Eresós
Ερεσός
Akr. Sígri
Ακρ.Σιγρίου
Parákoila
Παράκοιλα
Kólpos Kallonís
Κόλπος Καλλονής
Kerameía
Κεραμεία
Mytilíni
Μυτιλήνη
Skála Eresoú
Σκάλα Ερεσού
Vasiliká
Βασιλικά
Skála
Σκάλα
Agiásos
Αγιάσος
Polychnítos
Πολιχνίτος
Ampelikó
Αμπελικό
Loutrá
Λουτρά
Krátigos
Κράτηγος
Skópelos
Σκόπελος
Vaterá
Βατερά
Lésvos
Ν. Λέσβος
Plomári
Πλωμάρι
Aslan Burun
Kara Burun
Hasseki
AK DAĞ
Küçükbahçe
Mordoğan
Peiraías / Πειραιάς
Rafína / Ραφήνα
Psará
Ν. Ψαρά
Antípsara
Ν. Αντίψαρα
Agiásmata
Αγιάσματα
Kampiá
Καμπιά
Mármaro
Μάρμαρο
Melaniós
Μελανιός
Kardámyla
Καρδάμυλα
Oinoússes
Ν. Οινούσσες
Volissós
Βολισσός
Lagkáda
Λαγκάδα
Vrontádos
Βροντάδος
Chíos
Χίος
Ildır
TR
NÉA MONÍ
ΝΕΑ ΜΟΝΗ
Çeşme
Uzunkuyu
Alaçatı
Thymianá
Θυμιανά
Kallimasiá
Καλλιμασιά
Pasá Limáni
Πασά Λιμάνι
Véssa
Βέσσα
Armólia
Αρμόλια
Mestá
Μεστά
Kalamotí
Καλαμωτή
Pyrgío
Πυργίο
Kómi
Κώμη
Emporeiós
Εμπορειός
Akr. Mástícho
Ακρ. Μάστιχο
Koraka Burun
Sígri / Σίγρι
Chíos / Χίος
Sámos / Σάμος
Akr. Kampanós
Kalivári
Καλυβάρι
Ándros
Ν. Άνδρος
Gávrio
Γαύριο
Mpatsí
Μπατσί
Apoíkia
Αποίκια
Mesariá
Μεσαριά
Órmos
Όρμος
Palaiópoli
Παλαιόπολη
Kórthi
Akr. Fanári
Ακρ. Φανάρι
Ikaría
Ν. Ικαρία
Évdilos
Thérma
Θέρμα
Foúrnoi
Ν. Φούρνοι

131 146 144 139

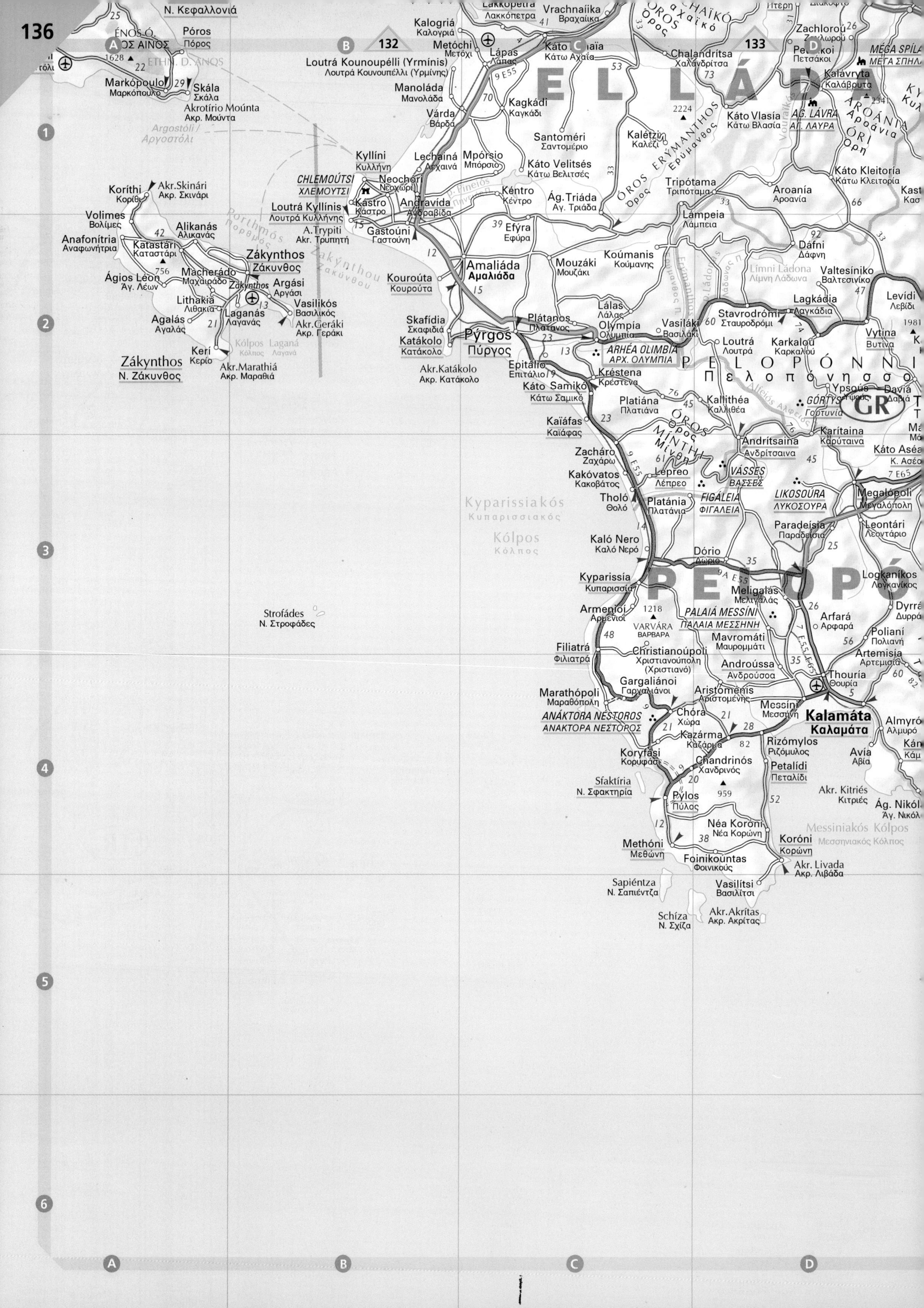
N. Κεφαλλονιά
Póros
Πόρος
Markópoulo
Μαρκόπουλο
Skála
Σκάλα
Akrotírio Moúnta
Ακρ. Μούντα
Argostóli /
Αργοστόλι
132
133
Kalogriá
Καλογριά
Metóchi
Μετόχι
Loutrá Kounoupélli (Yrmínis)
Λουτρά Κουνουπέλλι (Υρμίνης)
Manoláda
Μανολάδα
Várda
Βάρδα
Lápas
Λάπας
Vrachnaíika
Βραχναίικα
Lakkópetra
Λακκόπετρα
Káto Achaïa
Κάτω Αχαΐα
Chalandrítsa
Χαλανδρίτσα
Zachloroú
Petsákoi
Πετσάκοι
MÉGA SPÍLAIO
ΜΕΓΑ ΣΠΗΛΑΙΟ
Kalávryta
Καλάβρυτα
AG. LÁVRA
ΑΓ. ΛΑΥΡΑ
E L L Á D A
Kagkádi
Καγκάδι
Santoméri
Σαντoμέριo
Kalétzi
Καλέτζι
Káto Vlasía
Κάτω Βλασία
AROÁNIA ÓRI
Αροάνια Όρη
ÓROS ERÝMANTHOS
Όρος Ερύμανθος
Kyllíni
Κυλλήνη
Lechainá
Λεχαινά
Mpórsio
Μπόρσιο
Káto Velitsés
Κάτω Βελιτσές
CHLEMOÚTSI
ΧΛΕΜΟΥΤΣΙ
Neochóri
Νεοχώρι
Kástro
Κάστρο
Andravída
Ανδραβίδα
Kéntro
Κέντρο
Ág. Triáda
Αγ. Τριάδα
Tripótama
Τριπόταμα
Aroanía
Αροανία
Káto Kleitoría
Κάτω Κλειτορία
Loutrá Kyllínis
Λουτρά Κυλλήνης
A. Trypiti
Ακρ. Τρυπητή
Gastoúni
Γαστούνη
Efýra
Εφύρα
Lámpeia
Λάμπεια
Dáfni
Δάφνη
Koríthi
Κορίθι
Akr. Skinári
Ακρ. Σκινάρι
Volimes
Βολίμες
Anafonítria
Αναφωνήτρια
Alikanás
Αλικανάς
Katastári
Καταστάρι
Zákynthos
Ζάκυνθος
Porthmós Zakýnthou
Πορθμός Ζακύνθου
Ágios Léon
Άγ. Λέων
Macherádo
Μαχαιράδο
Argási
Αργάσι
Lithakiá
Λιθακιά
Vasilikós
Βασιλικός
Agalás
Αγαλάς
Laganás
Λαγανάς
Akr. Geráki
Ακρ. Γεράκι
Kolpos Laganá
Κόλπος Λαγανά
Kerí
Κερίο
Zákynthos
Ν. Ζάκυνθος
Akr. Marathiá
Ακρ. Μαραθιά
Amaliáda
Αμαλιάδα
Kouroúta
Κουρούτα
Mouzáki
Μουζάκι
Koúmanis
Κούμανης
Límni Ládona
Λίμνη Λάδωνα
Valtesiniko
Βαλτεσινίκο
Skafídia
Σκαφιδιά
Katákolo
Κατάκολο
Pýrgos
Πύργος
Plátanos
Πλάτανος
Lálas
Λάλας
Olympía
Ολυμπία
Vasiláki
Βασιλάκι
Stavrodrómi
Σταυροδρόμι
Lagkádia
Λαγκάδια
Levídi
Λεβίδι
ARHÉA OLIMBÍA
ΑΡΧ. ΟΛΥΜΠΙΑ
Loutrá
Λουτρά
Karkaloú
Καρκαλού
Vytina
Βυτίνα
Akr. Katákolo
Ακρ. Κατάκολο
Epitálio
Επιτάλιο
Kréstena
Κρέστενα
P E L O P Ó N N I
Π ε λ ο π ό ν ν η σ ο
Káto Samikó
Κάτω Σαμικό
Platiána
Πλατιάνα
Kallithéa
Καλλιθέα
GÓRTYS
ΓΟΡΤΥΝΑ
Ypsoús
Davía
Δαβιά
GR
Kaïáfas
Καϊάφας
ÓROS MÍNTHI
Όρος Μίνθη
Karítaina
Καρύταινα
Andrítsaina
Ανδρίτσαινα
Zacháro
Ζαχάρω
Káto Aséa
Κ. Ασέα
Kakóvatos
Κακόβατος
Lépreo
Λέπρεο
VÁSSES
ΒΑΣΣΕΣ
LIKOSOURA
ΛΥΚΟΣΟΥΡΑ
Megalópoli
Μεγαλόπολη
Tholó
Θολό
Platánia
Πλατάνια
FIGÁLEIA
ΦΙΓΑΛΕΙΑ
Kyparissiakós Kólpos
Κυπαρισσιακός Κόλπος
Paradeísia
Παραδείσια
Leontári
Λεοντάριο
Kaló Nero
Καλό Νερό
Dório
Δώριο
Kyparissía
Κυπαρισσία
P E L O P Ó
Logkanikos
Λογκανίκος
Meligalás
Μελιγαλάς
Armenioí
Αρμενιοί
VARVÁRA
ΒΑΡΒΑΡΑ
PALAIÁ MESSÍNI
ΠΑΛΑΙΑ ΜΕΣΣΗΝΗ
Arfará
Αρφαρά
Dyrrá
Δυρρά
Strofádes
Ν. Στροφάδες
Filiatrá
Φιλιατρά
Christianoúpoli
Χριστιανούπολη
(Χριστιανό)
Mavromáti
Μαυρομμάτι
Polianí
Πολιανή
Artemisía
Αρτεμισία
Androúsa
Ανδρούσα
Thouría
Θουρία
Marathópoli
Μαραθόπολη
Gargaliánoi
Γαργαλιάνοι
Aristoménis
Αριστομένης
ANÁKTORA NÉSTOROS
ΑΝΑΚΤΟΡΑ ΝΕΣΤΟΡΟΣ
Chóra
Χώρα
Messíni
Μεσσήνη
Kalamáta
Καλαμάτα
Almyrós
Αλμυρό
Kazárma
Καζάρμα
Rizómylos
Ριζόμυλος
Koryfási
Κορυφάσι
Chandrinós
Χανδρινός
Petalídi
Πεταλίδι
Avía
Αβία
Sfaktíria
Ν. Σφακτηρία
Pylos
Πύλος
Akr. Kitriés
Κιτριές
Ág. Nikólaos
Άγ. Νικόλ
Messiniakós Kólpos
Μεσσηνιακός Κόλπος
Néa Koróni
Νέα Κορώνη
Methóni
Μεθώνη
Koróni
Κορώνη
Foinikoúntas
Φοινικούς
Akr. Livada
Ακρ. Λιβάδα
Sapiéntza
Ν. Σαπιέντζα
Vasilítsi
Βασιλίτσι
Schíza
Ν. Σχίζα
Akr. Akrítas
Ακρ. Ακρίτας
A
B
C
D
1
2
3
4
5
6

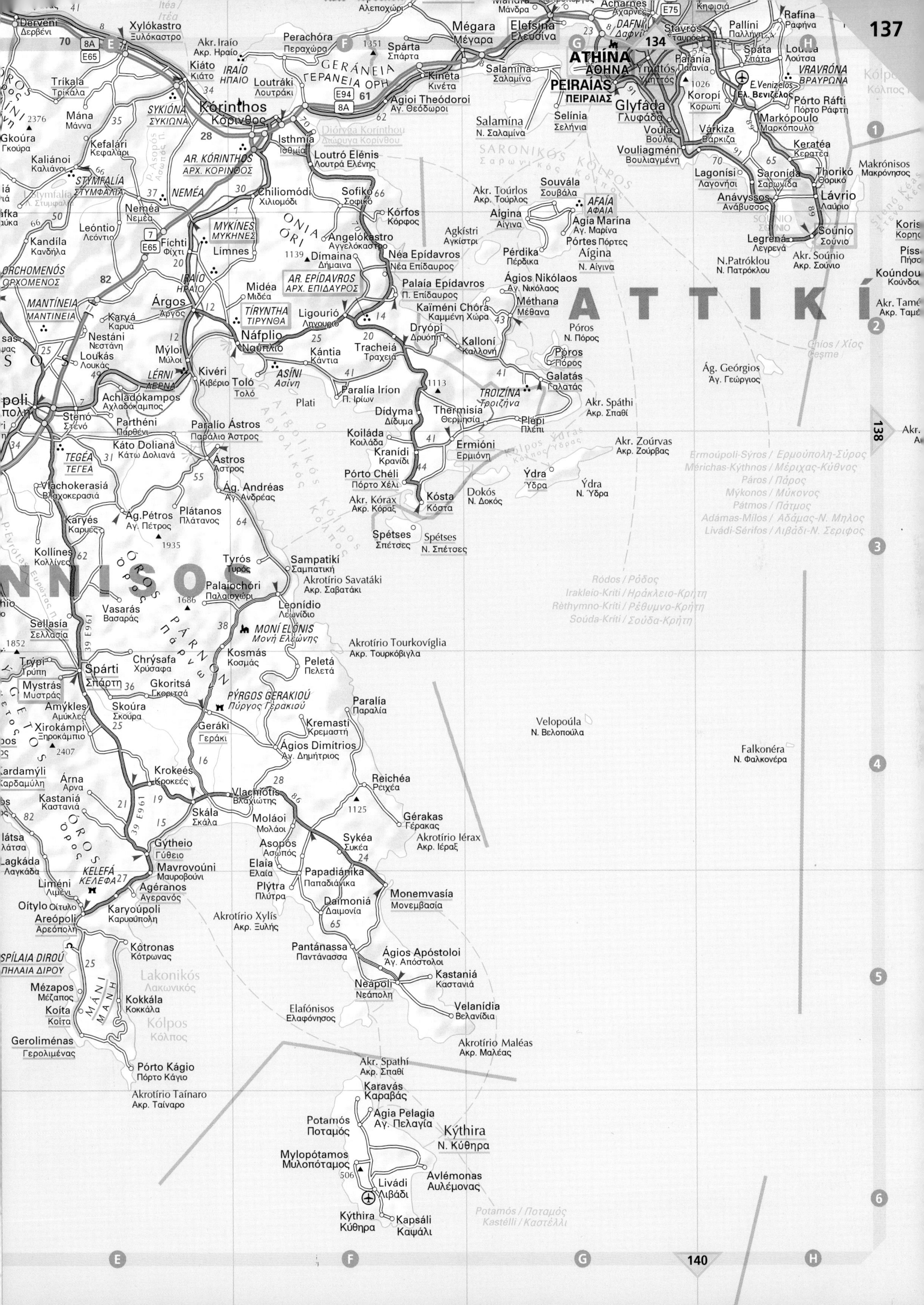
Derveni
Δερβένι
Xylókastro
Ξυλόκαστρο
Akr. Iraío
Ακρ. Ηραίο
Perachóra
Περαχώρα
Spárta
Σπάρτη
Mégara
Μέγαρα
Elefsína
Ελευσίνα
Acharnes
Αχαρνές
Kifisiá
Κηφισιά
Rafína
Ραφήνα
Pallíni
Παλλήνη
Stavrós
DAFNÍ
Δαφνί
ATHÍNA
ΑΘΗΝΑ
PEIRAIÁS
ΠΕΙΡΑΙΑΣ
Ymittós
Υμηττός
Paianía
Παιανία
Spáta
Σπάτα
Loútsa
Λούτσα
VRAVRÓNA
ΒΡΑΥΡΩΝΑ
E.Venizélos
Ελ. Βενιζέλος
Pórto Ráfti
Πόρτο Ράφτη
Markópoulo
Μαρκόπουλο
Koropí
Κορωπί
Glyfáda
Γλυφάδα
Voúla
Βούλα
Várkiza
Βάρκιζα
Vouliagméni
Βουλιαγμένη
Keratéa
Κερατέα
Salamína
Σαλαμίνα
N. Σαλαμίνα
Selínia
Σελήνια
Kiáto
Κιάτο
IRAÍO
ΗΡΑΙΟ
Loutráki
Λουτράκι
GERÁNEIA
ΓΕΡΑΝΕΙΑ ΟΡΗ
Kinéta
Κινέτα
Agioi Theódoroi
Αγ. Θεόδωροι
Tríkala
Τρίκαλα
Mána
Μάννα
SYKIÓNA
ΣΙΚΥΩΝΑ
Kórinthos
Κόρινθος
Isthmía
Ισθμία
Diórvga Korínthou
Διώρυγα Κορίνθου
Loutró Elénis
Λουτρά Ελένης
Gkoúra
Γκούρα
Kefalári
Κεφαλάρι
Kaliánoi
Καλιάνοι
STYMFALÍA
ΣΤΥΜΦΑΛΙΑ
AR. KÓRINTHOS
ΑΡΧ. ΚΟΡΙΝΘΟΣ
NEMÉA
Neméa
Νεμέα
Chiliomódi
Χιλιομόδι
Sofikó
Σοφικό
Kórfos
Κόρφος
ONIA ÓRI
Angelókastro
Αγγελόκαστρο
Dímaina
Δήμαινα
Néa Epídavros
Νέα Επίδαυρος
AR. EPÍDAVROS
ΑΡΧ. ΕΠΙΔΑΥΡΟΣ
Palaiá Epídavros
Π. Επίδαυρος
MYKÍNES
ΜΥΚΗΝΕΣ
Léontio
Λεόντιο
Kandíla
Κανδήλα
Fíchti
Φίχτι
Límnes
Λίμνες
ORCHOMENÓS
ΟΡΧΟΜΕΝΟΣ
IRAÍO
ΗΡΑΙΟ
Midéa
Μιδέα
Árgos
Άργος
MANTÍNEIA
ΜΑΝΤΙΝΕΙΑ
Karyá
Καρυά
TÍRYNTHA
ΤΙΡΥΝΘΑ
Ligourió
Λυγουριό
Náfplio
Ναύπλιο
Nestáni
Νεστάνη
Mýloi
Μύλοι
Loukás
Λουκάς
Kántia
Κάντια
Tracheiá
Τραχειά
Dryópi
Δρυόπη
Kalloní
Καλλονή
LÉRNI
ΛΕΡΝΑ
Kivéri
Κιβέριο
Toló
Τολό
ASÍNI
Ασίνη
Paralía Iríon
Π. Ιρίων
Plati
Achladókampos
Αχλαδόκαμπος
Stenó
Στενό
Parthéni
Παρθένι
Paralío Ástros
Παράλιο Άστρος
Kato Doliana
Κάτω Δολιανά
TEGÉA
ΤΕΓΕΑ
Ástros
Άστρος
Vlachokerasiá
Βλαχοκερασιά
Ág. Andréas
Αγ. Ανδρέας
Ag.Pétros
Αγ. Πέτρος
Plátanos
Πλάτανος
Karyés
Καρυές
Kollínes
Κολλίνες
Tyrós
Τυρός
Sampatikí
Σαμπατική
Akrotírio Savatáki
Ακρ. Σαβατάκι
Palaiochóri
Παλαιοχώρι
Leonídio
Λεωνίδιο
Vasarás
Βασαράς
ÓROS PÁRNON
Πάρνων
MONÍ ELÓNIS
Μονή Ελώνης
Sellasía
Σελλασία
Kosmás
Κοσμάς
Peletá
Πελετά
Akrotírio Tourkovíglia
Ακρ. Τουρκόβιγλια
Trýpi
Τρύπη
Spárti
Σπάρτη
Chrýsafa
Χρύσαφα
Mystrás
Μυστράς
Gkoritsá
Γκοριτσά
PÝRGOS GERAKIOÚ
Πύργος Γερακιού
Amýkles
Αμύκλες
Skoúra
Σκούρα
Xirokámpi
Ξηροκάμπι
Geráki
Γεράκι
Paralía
Παραλία
Kremastí
Κρεμαστή
Ágios Dimítrios
Αγ. Δημήτριος
Kardamýli
Καρδαμύλη
Árna
Άρνα
Kastaniá
Καστανιά
Krokeés
Κροκεές
Vlachiótis
Βλαχιώτης
Reichéa
Ρειχέα
Skála
Σκάλα
Moláoi
Μολάοι
Gérakas
Γέρακας
Akrotírio Iérax
Ακρ. Ιέραξ
Gýtheio
Γύθειο
Asopós
Ασωπός
Sykéa
Συκέα
Lagkáda
Λαγκάδα
Mavrovoúni
Μαυροβούνι
Elaía
Ελαία
Papadiánika
Παπαδιάνικα
KELEFÁ
ΚΕΛΕΦΑ
Liméni
Λιμένι
Agéranos
Αγερανός
Plýtra
Πλύτρα
Monemvasía
Μονεμβασία
Oítylo
Οίτυλο
Karyoúpoli
Καρυούπολη
Daimoniá
Δαιμονιά
Areópoli
Αρεόπολη
Akrotírio Xylís
Ακρ. Ξυλής
Kótronas
Κότρωνας
SPÍLAIA DIROÚ
ΣΠΗΛΑΙΑ ΔΙΡΟΥ
Pantánassa
Παντάνασσα
Ágios Apóstoloi
Άγ. Απόστολοι
Lakonikós
Λακωνικός
Mézapos
Μέζαπος
Neápoli
Νεάπολη
Kastaniá
Καστανιά
Kokkála
Κοκκάλα
Koíta
Κοίτα
MÁNI
ΜΑΝΗ
Elafónisos
Ελαφόνησος
Velanídia
Βελανίδια
Kólpos
Κόλπος
Geroliménas
Γερολιμένας
Akrotírio Maléas
Ακρ. Μαλέας
Pórto Kágio
Πόρτο Κάγιο
Akr. Spathí
Ακρ. Σπαθί
Akrotírio Taínaro
Ακρ. Ταίναρο
Karavás
Καραβάς
Agia Pelagía
Αγ. Πελαγία
Potamós
Ποταμός
Kýthira
N. Κύθηρα
Mylopótamos
Μυλοπόταμος
Avlémonas
Αυλέμονας
Livádi
Λιβάδι
Kýthira
Κύθηρα
Kapsáli
Καψάλι
Potamós / Ποταμός
Kastélli / Καστέλλι
SARONIKÓS KÓLPOS
Σαρωνικός Κόλπος
Akr. Toúrlos
Ακρ. Τούρλος
Souvála
Σουβάλα
AFAÍA
ΑΦΑΙΑ
Aígina
Αίγινα
Agía Marína
Αγ. Μαρίνα
Agkístri
Αγκίστρι
Pórtes
Πόρτες
Pérdika
Πέρδικα
Aígina
N. Αίγινα
Ágios Nikólaos
Αγ. Νικόλαος
Méthana
Μέθανα
Kaïméni Chóra
Καμμένη Χώρα
ATTIKÍ
Póros
N. Πόρος
Póros
Πόρος
Galatás
Γαλατάς
TROIZÍNA
Τροιζήνα
Thermisía
Θερμησία
Plépi
Πλέπι
Akr. Spáthi
Ακρ. Σπαθί
Dídyma
Δίδυμα
Koiláda
Κοιλάδα
Kranídi
Κρανίδι
Ermióni
Ερμιόνη
Akr. Zoúrvas
Ακρ. Ζούρβας
Pórto Chéli
Πόρτο Χέλι
Ýdra
Ύδρα
N. Ύδρα
Kósta
Κόστα
Dokós
N. Δοκός
Akr. Kórax
Ακρ. Κόραξ
Spétses
Σπέτσες
N. Σπέτσες
Lagonísi
Λαγονήσι
Saronída
Σαρωνίδα
Thorikó
Θορικό
Makrónisos
Μακρόνησος
Anávyssos
Ανάβυσσος
Lávrio
Λαύριο
Legrená
Λεγρενά
Soúnio
Σούνιο
Akr. Soúnio
Ακρ. Σούνιο
N.Pátroklou
Ν. Πατρόκλου
Koúndouros
Akr. Tamé
Chíos / Χίος
Çeşme
Ág. Geórgios
Άγ. Γεώργιος
Ermoúpoli-Sýros / Ερμούπολη-Σύρος
Mérichas-Kýthnos / Μέριχας-Κύθνος
Páros / Πάρος
Mýkonos / Μύκονος
Pátmos / Πάτμος
Adámas-Mílos / Αδάμας-Ν. Μηλος
Livádi-Sérifos / Λιβάδι-Ν. Σεριφος
Ródos / Ρόδος
Irakleio-Kríti / Ηράκλειο-Κρήτη
Réthymno-Kríti / Ρέθυμνο-Κρήτη
Soúda-Kríti / Σούδα-Κρήτη
Velopoúla
N. Βελοπούλα
Falkonéra
N. Φαλκονέρα
NNISOS
ÓROS TAÝGETOS
134
138
140

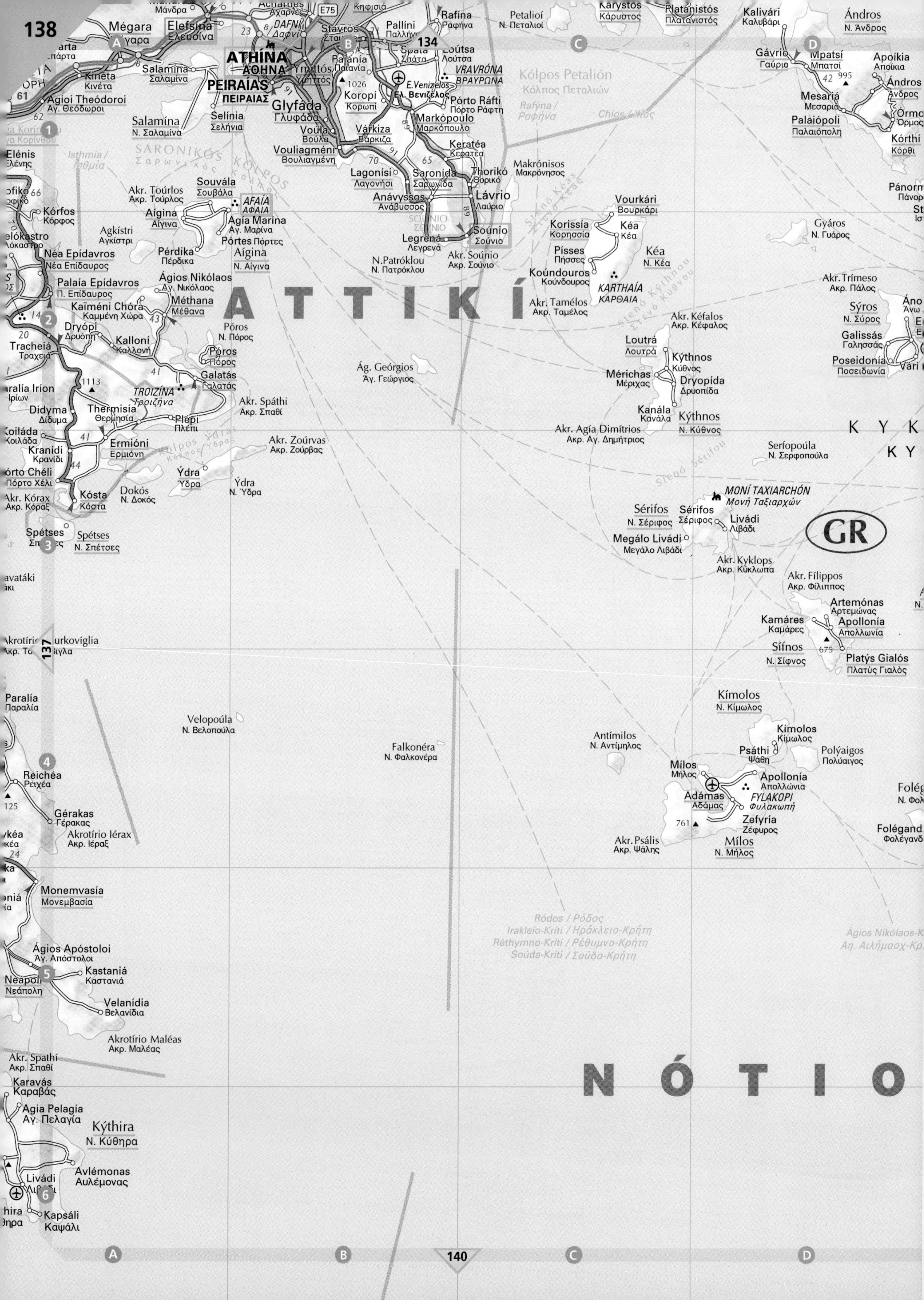
ATTIKÍ
NÓTIO
ATHÍNA
ΑΘΗΝΑ
PEIRAIÁS
ΠΕΙΡΑΙΑΣ
Glyfáda
Γλυφάδα
Mégara
Elefsína
Ελευσίνα
Salamína
Σαλαμίνα
Kinéta
Κινέτα
Agioi Theódoroi
Αγ. Θεόδωροι
Salamína
Ν. Σαλαμίνα
Selínia
Σελήνια
Stavrós
Pallíni
Rafína
Ραφήνα
Petalioí
Ν. Πεταλιοί
Kárystos
Κάρυστος
Platanistós
Πλατανιστός
Kalivári
Καλυβάρι
Ándros
Ν. Άνδρος
Gávrio
Γαύριο
Mpatsí
Μπατσί
Apoíkia
Αποίκια
Ándros
Άνδρος
Mesariá
Μεσαριά
Palaiópoli
Παλαιόπολη
Kórthi
Κόρθι
Loútsa
Λούτσα
Spáta
Σπάτα
Paianía
Παιανία
Ymittós
VRAVRÓNA
ΒΡΑΥΡΩΝΑ
Kólpos Petalión
Κόλπος Πεταλιών
Rafýna / Ραφήνα
Chíos / Χίος
E.Venizelos
Ελ. Βενιζέλος
Koropí
Κορωπί
Pórto Ráfti
Πόρτο Ράφτη
Markópoulo
Μαρκόπουλο
Várkiza
Βάρκιζα
Voúla
Βούλα
Vouliagméni
Βουλιαγμένη
Keratéa
Κερατέα
Lagonísi
Λαγονήσι
Saronída
Σαρωνίδα
Thorikó
Θορικό
Makrónisos
Μακρόνησος
Lávrio
Λαύριο
Anávyssos
Ανάβυσσος
Legrená
Λεγρενά
Soúnio
Σούνιο
Akr. Soúnio
Ακρ. Σούνιο
N.Patróklou
Ν. Πατρόκλου
SARONIKÓS KÓLPOS
Σαρωνικός Κόλπος
Isthmía / Ισθμία
Eléniks
Kórfos
Κόρφος
Akr. Toúrlos
Ακρ. Τούρλος
Souvála
Σουβάλα
AFAÍA
ΑΦΑΙΑ
Aígina
Αίγινα
Agía Marina
Αγ. Μαρίνα
Pórtes
Πόρτες
Agkístri
Αγκίστρι
Pérdika
Πέρδικα
Aígina
Ν. Αίγινα
Néa Epídavros
Νέα Επίδαυρος
Palaía Epídavros
Π. Επίδαυρος
Ágios Nikólaos
Αγ. Νικόλαος
Méthana
Μέθανα
Kaiméni Chóra
Καμμένη Χώρα
Dryópi
Δρυόπη
Kalloní
Καλλονή
Póros
Ν. Πόρος
Póros
Πόρος
Galatás
Γαλατάς
Tracheiá
Τραχειά
Didyma
Δίδυμα
TROIZÍNA
Τροιζήνα
Thermisía
Θερμησία
Plépi
Πλέπι
Akr. Spáthi
Ακρ. Σπαθί
Koiláda
Κοιλάδα
Kranídi
Κρανίδι
Ermióni
Ερμιόνη
Kólpos Ýdras
Akr. Zoúrvas
Ακρ. Ζούρβας
Pórto Chéli
Πόρτο Χέλι
Kósta
Κόστα
Dokós
Ν. Δοκός
Ýdra
Ύδρα
Ýdra
Ν. Ύδρα
Akr. Kórax
Ακρ. Κόραξ
Spétses
Ν. Σπέτσες
Ág. Geórgios
Άγ. Γεώργιος
Vourkári
Βουρκάρι
Korissía
Κορησσία
Kéa
Κέα
Písses
Πήσσες
Kéa
Ν. Κέα
Koúndouros
Κούνδουρος
KARTHAÍA
ΚΑΡΘΑΙΑ
Akr. Tamélos
Ακρ. Ταμέλος
Stenó Kéas
Stenó Kýthnou
Akr. Kéfalos
Ακρ. Κέφαλος
Loutrá
Λουτρά
Kýthnos
Κύθνος
Mérichas
Μέριχας
Dryopída
Δρυοπίδα
Kanála
Κανάλα
Kýthnos
Ν. Κύθνος
Akr. Agía Dimítrios
Ακρ. Αγ. Δημήτριος
Gyáros
Ν. Γυάρος
Akr. Trímeso
Ακρ. Πάλος
Sýros
Ν. Σύρος
Galissás
Γαλησσάς
Poseidonía
Ποσειδωνία
Vári
Serfopoúla
Ν. Σερφοπούλα
Stenó Sérifou
MONÍ TAXIARCHÓN
Μονή Ταξιαρχών
Sérifos
Ν. Σέριφος
Sérifos
Σέριφος
Livádi
Λιβάδι
Megálo Livádi
Μεγάλο Λιβάδι
GR
Akr. Kyklops
Ακρ. Κύκλωπα
Akr. Fílippos
Ακρ. Φίλιππος
Artemónas
Αρτεμώνας
Kamáres
Καμάρες
Apollonía
Απολλωνία
Sífnos
Ν. Σίφνος
Platýs Gialós
Πλατύς Γιαλός
Kímolos
Ν. Κίμωλος
Kímolos
Κίμωλος
Velopoúla
Ν. Βελοπούλα
Antímilos
Ν. Αντίμηλος
Falkonéra
Ν. Φαλκονέρα
Psáthi
Ψάθη
Polýaigos
Πολύαιγος
Mílos
Μήλος
Apollonía
Απολλώνια
Adámas
Αδάμας
FYLAKOPI
Φυλακωπή
Zefyría
Ζέφυρος
Akr. Psális
Ακρ. Ψάλης
Mílos
Ν. Μήλος
Foléganδ
Ródos / Ρόδος
Irakleío-Kríti / Ηράκλειο-Κρήτη
Réthymno-Kríti / Ρέθυμνο-Κρήτη
Soúda-Kríti / Σούδα-Κρήτη
Ágios Nikólaos-K
Paralía
Παραλία
Reichéa
Ρειχέα
Gérakas
Γέρακας
Akrotírio Iérax
Ακρ. Ιέραξ
Monemvasía
Μονεμβασία
Ágios Apóstoloi
Άγ. Απόστολοι
Kastaniá
Καστανιά
Neápoli
Νεάπολη
Velanídia
Βελανίδια
Akrotírio Maléas
Ακρ. Μαλέας
Akr. Spathí
Ακρ. Σπαθί
Karavás
Καραβάς
Agia Pelagía
Αγ. Πελαγία
Kýthira
Ν. Κύθηρα
Avlémonas
Αυλέμονας
Livádi
Kapsáli
Καψάλι
134
137
140

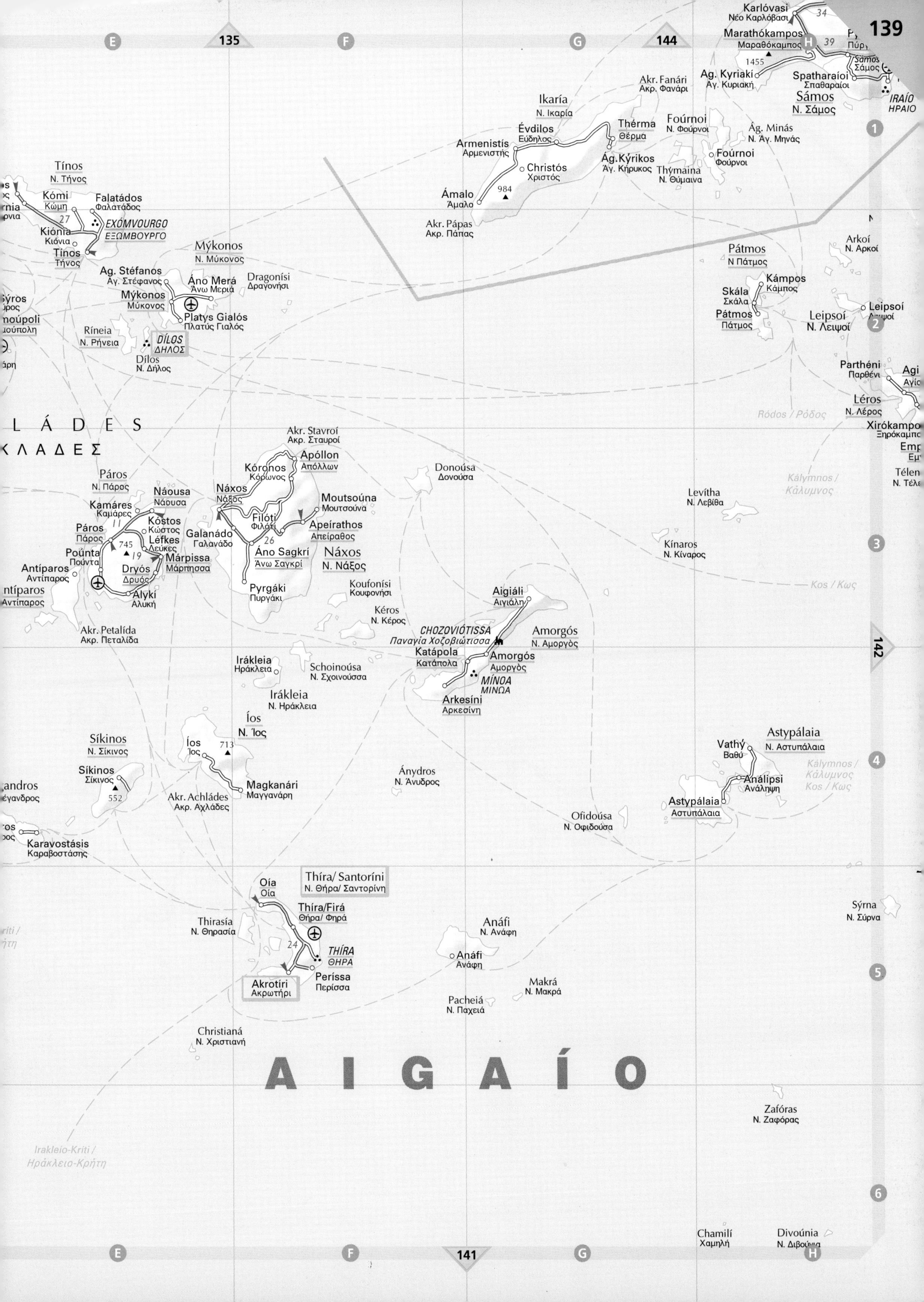
135
144
Karlóvasi
Νέο Καρλόβασι
Marathókampos
Μαραθόκαμπος
Ag. Kyriakí
Αγ. Κυριακή
Spatharaíoi
Σπαθαραίοι
Sámos
Ν. Σάμος
IRAÍO
ΗΡΑΙΟ
Akr. Fanári
Ακρ. Φανάρι
Ikaría
Ν. Ικαρία
Évdilos
Εύδηλος
Thérma
Θέρμα
Foúrnoi
Ν. Φούρνοι
Ág. Minás
Ν. Άγ. Μηνάς
Armenistís
Αρμενιστής
Christós
Χριστός
Ág. Kýrikos
Άγ. Κήρυκος
Thýmaina
Ν. Θύμαινα
Foúrnoi
Φούρνοι
Ámalo
Άμαλο
Akr. Pápas
Ακρ. Πάπας
Tínos
Ν. Τήνος
Kómi
Κώμη
Falatádos
Φαλατάδος
EXÓMVOURGO
ΕΞΩΜΒΟΥΡΓΟ
Kióni
Κιόνια
Tínos
Τήνος
Mýkonos
Ν. Μύκονος
Ag. Stéfanos
Αγ. Στέφανος
Áno Merá
Άνω Μεριά
Dragonísi
Δραγονήσι
Mýkonos
Μύκονος
Platys Gialós
Πλατύς Γιαλός
Ríneia
Ν. Ρήνεια
DÍLOS
ΔΗΛΟΣ
Dílos
Ν. Δήλος
Arkoí
Ν. Αρκοί
Pátmos
Ν Πάτμος
Kámpos
Κάμπος
Skála
Σκάλα
Pátmos
Πάτμος
Leipsoí
Ν. Λειψοί
Parthéni
Léros
Ν. Λέρος
Xirókampo
Ródos / Ρόδος
Akr. Stavroí
Ακρ. Σταυροί
Apóllon
Απόλλων
Kóronos
Κόρωνος
Donoúsa
Δονούσα
Páros
Ν. Πάρος
Náousa
Νάουσα
Náxos
Νάξος
Moutsoúna
Μουτσούνα
Kamáres
Καμάρες
Kóstos
Κώστος
Filóti
Φιλότι
Apeírathos
Απείραθος
Páros
Πάρος
Léfkes
Λεύκες
Galanádo
Γαλανάδο
Levítha
Ν. Λεβίθα
Kálymnos / Κάλυμνος
Poúnta
Πούντα
Márpissa
Μάρπησσα
Áno Sagkrí
Άνω Σαγκρί
Náxos
Ν. Νάξος
Kínaros
Ν. Κίναρος
Antíparos
Αντίπαρος
Drýos
Δρυός
Alykí
Αλυκή
Pyrgáki
Πυργάκι
Koufonísi
Κουφονήσι
Aigiáli
Αιγιάλη
Kos / Κως
Kéros
Ν. Κέρος
Akr. Petalída
Ακρ. Πεταλίδα
CHOZOVIÓTISSA
Παναγία Χοζοβιώτισσα
Amorgós
Ν. Αμοργός
Katápola
Κατάπολα
Amorgós
Αμοργός
Irákleia
Ηράκλεια
Schoinoúsa
Ν. Σχοινούσα
MÍNOA
ΜΙΝΩΑ
Irákleia
Ν. Ηράκλεια
Arkesíni
Αρκεσίνη
Íos
Ν. Ίος
Astypálaia
Ν. Αστυπάλαια
Síkinos
Ν. Σίκινος
Íos
Ίος
Vathý
Βαθύ
Síkinos
Σίκινος
Ánydros
Ν. Άνυδρος
Análipsi
Ανάληψη
Magkanári
Μαγγανάρι
Akr. Achládes
Ακρ. Αχλάδες
Astypálaia
Αστυπάλαια
Ofidoúsa
Ν. Οφιδούσα
Karavostásis
Καραβοστάσης
Thíra/ Santoríni
Ν. Θήρα/ Σαντορίνη
Oía
Οία
Thíra/Firá
Θήρα/ Φηρά
Sýrna
Ν. Σύρνα
Thirasía
Ν. Θηρασία
Anáfi
Ν. Ανάφη
THÍRA
ΘΗΡΑ
Anáfi
Ανάφη
Akrotíri
Ακρωτήρι
Perissa
Περίσσα
Makrá
Ν. Μακρά
Pacheiá
Ν. Παχειά
Christianá
Ν. Χριστιανή
AIGAÍO
Zafóras
Ν. Ζαφόρας
Irakleio-Kriti /
Ηράκλειο-Κρήτη
Chamilí
Χαμηλή
Divoúnia
Ν. Διβούνια
142
141

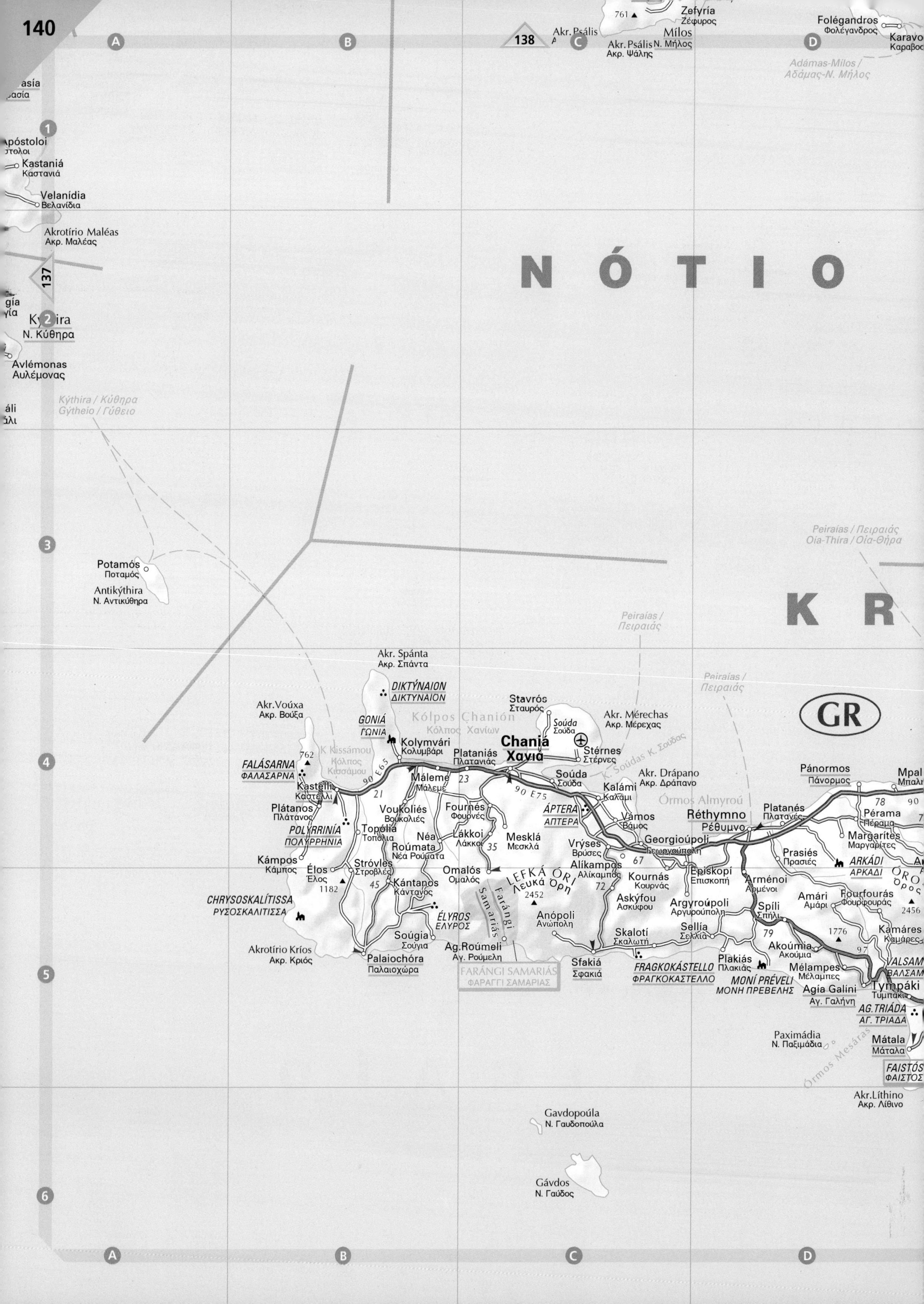

Zefyría
Ζέφυρος
761 ▲
Akr. Psális
Mílos
138
Akr. Psális Ν. Μήλος
Akr. Ψάλης
Folégandros
Φολέγανδρος
Karavo
Καράβος

Adámas-Milos /
Αδάμας-Ν. Μήλος

asía
ρασία

apóstoloi
στολοι

Kastaniá
Καστανιά

Velanídia
Βελανίδια

Akrotírio Maléas
Ακρ. Μαλέας

137

gía
γία

Ky ira
Ν. Κύθηρα

Avlémonas
Αυλέμονας

áli

N Ó T I O

Kýthira / Κύθηρα
Gýtheio / Γύθειο

Peiraías / Πειραιάς
Oía-Thíra / Οία-Θήρα

Potamós
Ποταμός

Antikýthira
Ν. Αντικύθηρα

Peiraías /
Πειραιάς

K R

Peiraías /
Πειραιάς

Akr. Spánta
Ακρ. Σπάντα

DIKTÝNAION
ΔΙΚΤΥΝΑΙΟΝ

Stavrós
Σταυρός

Akr. Mérechas
Ακρ. Μέρεχας

GR

Akr. Voúxa
Ακρ. Βούξα

GONIÁ
ΓΩΝΙΑ

Kólpos Chanión
Κόλπος Χανίων

Soúda
Σούδα

Chaniá
Χανιά

Kolymvári
Κολυμβάρι

Plataniás
Πλατανιάς

Stérnes
Στέρνες

FALÁSARNA
ΦΑΛΑΣΑΡΝΑ

762 ▲

K. Kissámou
Κόλπος Κισσάμου

Máleme
Μάλεμε

23

Soúda
Σούδα

K. Soúdas Κ. Σούδας

Akr. Drápano
Ακρ. Δράπανο

Ór mos Almyroú

Pánormos
Πάνορμος

Mpal
Μπαλ

Kastélli
Καστέλλι

90 E65

21

90 E75

Kalámi
Καλάμι

Platanés
Πλατανές

78
90

Plátanos
Πλάτανος

Voukoliés
Βουκολιές

Fournés
Φουρνές

Vámos
Βάμος

Réthymno
Ρέθυμνο

Pérama
Πέραμα

POLYRRINÍA
ΠΟΛΥΡΡΗΝΙΑ

Topólia
Τοπόλια

Néa
Roúmata
Νέα Ρούματα

Lákkoi
Λάκκοι

Mesklá
Μεσκλά

ÁPTERA
ΑΠΤΕΡΑ

Vrýses
Βρύσες

Georgioúpoli
Γεωργιούπολη

Platanés
Πλατανές

Margarites
Μαργαρίτες

35

67

Prasiés
Πρασιές

ARKÁDI
ΑΡΚΑΔΙ

Á

Kámpos
Κάμπος

Élos
Έλος

Stróvles
Στροβλές

Omalós
Ομαλός

Alíkampos
Αλίκαμπο

Kournás
Κουρνάς

Episkopí
Επισκοπή

ΟΡΟΣ

ÓRO

CHRYSOSKALÍTISSA
ΡΥΣΟΣΚΑΛΙΤΙΣΣΑ

1182

45

Kántanos
Κάντανος

LEFKÁ ÓRI
Λευκά Όρη

72

Askýfou
Ασκύφου

Armέnoi
Αρμένοι

Argyroúpoli
Αργυρούπολη

Amári
Αμάρι

Fourfourás
Φουρφουράς

2456

2452

Farángi Samariás

Anópoli
Ανώπολη

Spíli
Σπήλι

1776

Kamáres
Καμάρες

Akrotírio Kríos
Ακρ. Κριός

ÉLYROS
ΕΛΥΡΟΣ

Skalotí
Σκαλωτή

Sellía
Σελλία

79

Akoúmia
Ακούμια

97

VALSAM
ΒΑΛΣΑΜ

Soúgia
Σούγια

Ag. Roúmeli
Αγ. Ρούμελη

Sfakiá
Σφακιά

Plakiás
Πλακιάς

Mélampes
Μέλαμπες

Palaiochóra
Παλαιοχώρα

FARÁNGI SAMARIÁS
ΦΑΡΑΓΓΙ ΣΑΜΑΡΙΑΣ

FRAGKOKÁSTELLO
ΦΡΑΓΚΟΚΑΣΤΕΛΛΟ

MONÍ PRÉVELI
ΜΟΝΗ ΠΡΕΒΕΛΗΣ

Agia Galíni
Αγ. Γαλήνη

Tympáki
Τυμπάκι

AG. TRIÁDA
ΑΓ. ΤΡΙΑΔΑ

Paximádia
Ν. Παξιμάδια

Mátala
Μάταλα

Órmos Mesarás

FAISTÓS
ΦΑΙΣΤΟΣ

Akr. Líthino
Ακρ. Λίθινο

Gavdopoúla
Ν. Γαυδοπούλα

Gávdos
Ν. Γαύδος

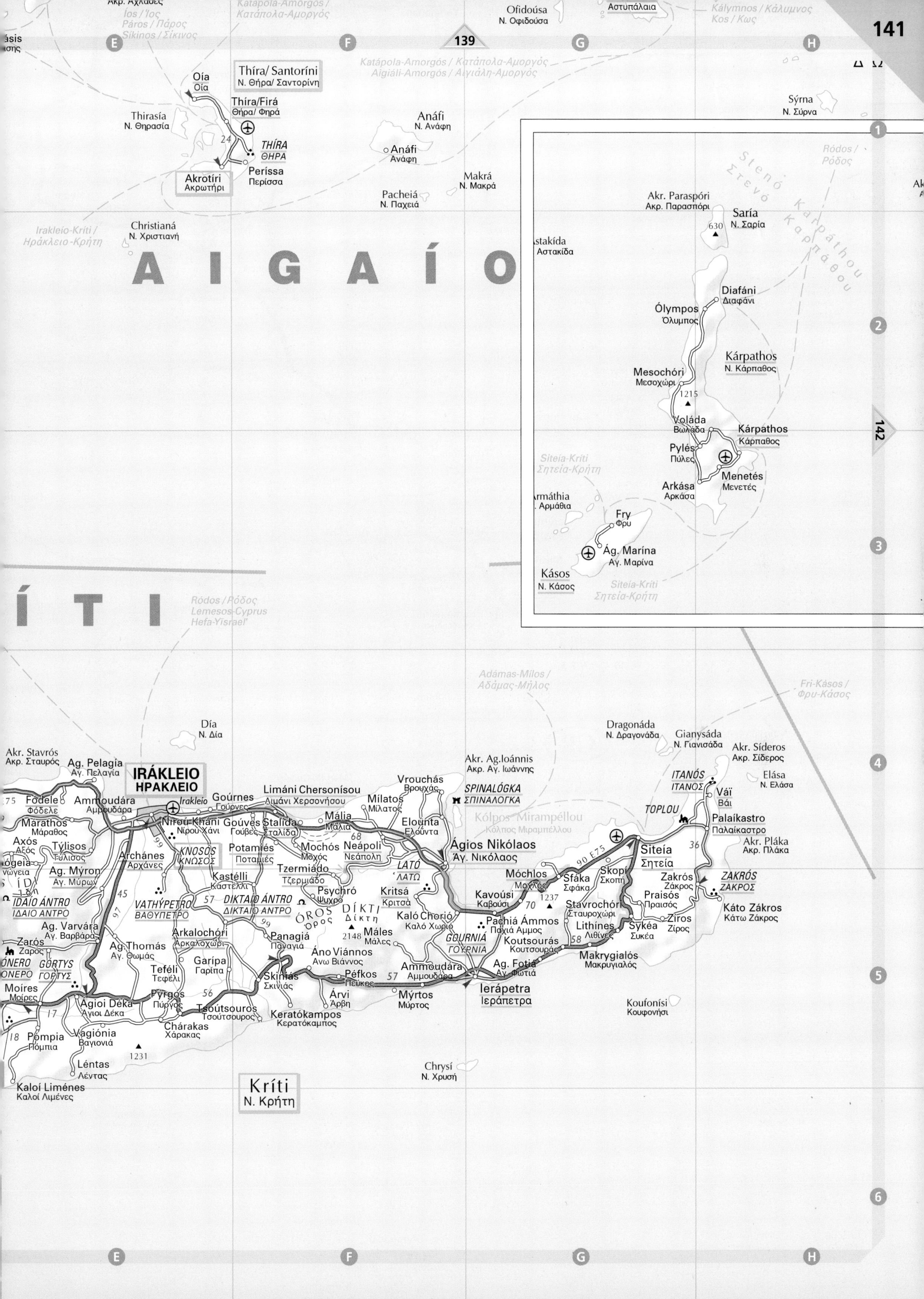

Ofidoúsa
N. Οφιδούσα

Astypálaia
Αστυπάλαια

Kálymnos / Κάλυμνος
Kos / Κως

asis
Akr. Achládes
Ios / Ίος
Páros / Πάρος
Sikinos / Σίκινος

Katápola-Amorgós /
Κατάπολα-Αμοργός

Katápola-Amorgós / Κατάπολα-Αμοργός
Aigiáli-Amorgós / Αιγιάλη-Αμοργός

Sýrna
N. Σύρνα

Oía
Οία

Thíra/ Santoríni
Ν. Θήρα/ Σαντορίνη

139

Ródos /
Ρόδος

Thirasía
Ν. Θηρασία

Thíra/Firá
Θήρα/ Φηρά

1

24

THÍRA
ΘΗΡΑ

Akr. Paraspóri
Ακρ. Παρασπόρι

Stenó Kárpathou
Στενό Καρπάθου

Akrotíri
Ακρωτήρι

Períssa
Περίσσα

Anáfi
Ν. Ανάφη

Saría
Ν. Σαρία
630

Irakleio-Kríti /
Ηράκλειο-Κρήτη

Christianá
Ν. Χριστιανή

Anáfi
Ανάφη

Makrá
Ν. Μακρά

Diafáni
Διαφάνι

2

A I G A Í O

Pacheiá
Ν. Παχειά

Ólympos
Όλυμπος

Astakída
Αστακίδα

Mesochóri
Μεσοχώρι

Kárpathos
Ν. Κάρπαθος

1215

Voláda
Βωλάδα

Kárpathos
Κάρπαθος

142

Í T I

Ródos / Ρόδος
Lemesos-Cyprus
Hefa-Yisrael'

Siteía-Kríti
Σητεία-Κρήτη

Pylés
Πύλες

Arkása
Αρκάσα

Menetés
Μενετές

Armáthia
Ι. Αρμάθια

Fry
Φρυ

3

Ág. Marína
Αγ. Μαρίνα

Kásos
Ν. Κάσος

Siteía-Kríti
Σητεία-Κρήτη

Adámas-Mílos /
Αδάμας-Μήλος

Fri-Kásos /
Φρυ-Κάσος

Akr. Stavrós
Ακρ. Σταυρός

Día
Ν. Δία

Dragonáda
Ν. Δραγονάδα

Gianysáda
Ν. Γιανισάδα

Akr. Síderos
Ακρ. Σίδερος

4

Ag. Pelagía
Αγ. Πελαγία

Vrouchás
Βρουχάς

Akr. Ag.Ioánnis
Ακρ. Αγ. Ιωάννης

Elása
Ν. Ελάσα

IRÁKLEIO
ΗΡΑΚΛΕΙΟ

Limáni Chersonísou
Λιμάνι Χερσονήσου

Milatos
Μίλατος

SPINALÓGKA
ΣΠΙΝΑΛΟΓΚΑ

ITANÓS
ΙΤΑΝΟΣ

Váï
Βάι

75
Fódele
Φόδελε

Ammoudára
Αμμουδάρα

Irakleio

Goúrnes
Γούρνες

Mália
Μάλια

Eloúnta
Ελούντα

Kólpos Mirampéllou
Κόλπος Μιραμπέλλου

TOPLOU

Palaíkastro
Παλαίκαστρο

Marathos
Μάραθος

Nírou Kháni
Νίρου Χάνι

Goúves
Γούβες

Mochós
Μοχός

Neápoli
Νεάπολη

Ágios Nikólaos
Αγ. Νικόλαος

Akr. Pláka
Ακρ. Πλάκα

Axós
Αξός

Tylisos
Τύλισος

Archánes
Αρχάνες

Stalída
Σταλίδα

68

LATÓ
ΛΑΤΩ

Siteía
Σητεία

36

Ag. Myron
Αγ. Μύρων

KNOSÓS
ΚΝΩΣΟΣ

Potamiés
Ποταμιές

Mochlos
Μοχλός

Sfáka
Σφάκα

Skopí
Σκοπή

90 E75

Zakrós
Ζακρός

ZAKRÓS
ΖΑΚΡΟΣ

ogeia

IDAÍO ÁNTRO
ΙΔΑΙΟ ΑΝΤΡΟ

45

Kastélli
Καστέλλι

Tzermiádo
Τζερμιάδο

DIKTAÍO ÁNTRO
ΔΙΚΤΑΙΟ ΑΝΤΡΟ

Psychró
Ψυχρό

Kritsá
Κριτσά

Kavoúsi
Καβούσι

1237

Stavrochóri
Σταυροχώρι

Praisós
Πραισός

Káto Zákros
Κάτω Ζάκρος

ÍD

97

57

ÓROS DÍKTI
ΟΡΟΣ ΔΙΚΤΗ

99

Kaló Chorió
Καλό Χωριό

Pachiá Ámmos
Παχιά Άμμος

Lithínes
Λιθίνες

58

Sýkea
Συκέα

Zíros
Ζίρος

Ag. Varvára
Αγ. Βαρβάρα

VATHYPETRO
ΒΑΘΥΠΕΤΡΟ

Arkalochóri
Αρκαλοχώρι

2148

Máles
Μάλες

GOURNIÁ
ΓΟΥΡΝΙΑ

Koutsourás
Κουτσουράς

Zarós

Ag. Thomás
Αγ. Θωμάς

Panagiá
Παναγιά

Áno Viánnos
Άνω Βιάννος

Ammoudára
Αμμουδάρα

Ag. Fotiá
Αγ. Φωτιά

Makrygialós
Μακρυγιαλός

5

ONERO
ΟΝΕΡΟ

GÓRTYS
ΓΟΡΤΥΣ

Teféli
Τεφέλι

Garípa
Γαρίπα

Péfkos
Πεύκος

57

Ierápetra
Ιεράπετρα

Moíres
Μοίρες

Pýrgos
Πύργος

Skiniás
Σκινιάς

Árvi
Άρβη

Mýrtos
Μύρτος

Koufonísi
Κουφονήσι

Agioi Déka
Αγιοι Δέκα

56

Tsoútsouros
Τσούτσουρος

Keratókampos
Κερατόκαμπος

17

18

Pómpia
Πόμπια

Vagiónia
Βαγιονιά

Chárakas
Χάρακας

1231

Chrysí
Ν. Χρυσή

Léntas
Λέντας

Kaloí Liménes
Καλοί Λιμένες

Kríti
Ν. Κρήτη

E   F   G   H

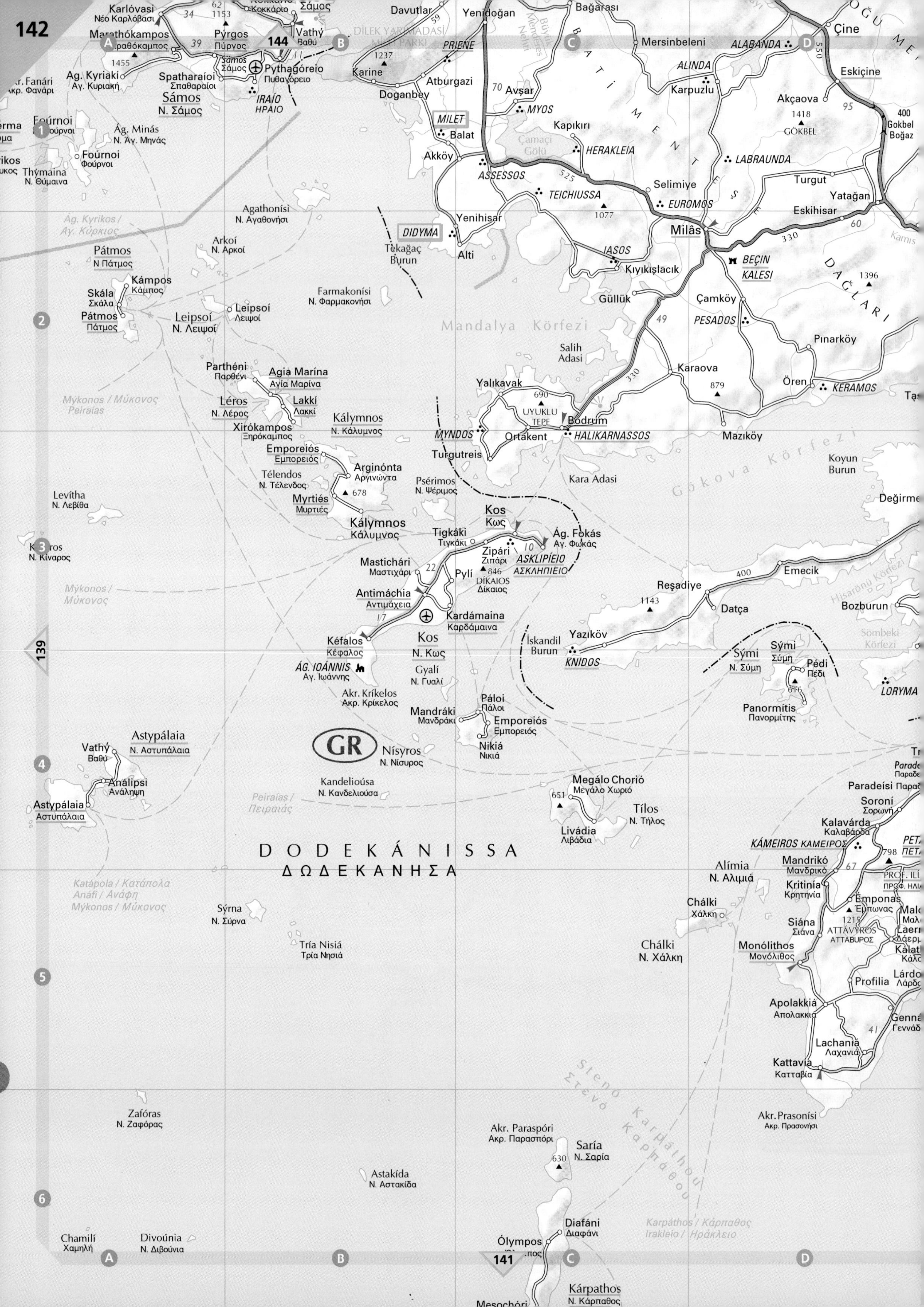
Karlóvasi
Néo Karlóvasi
Marathókampos
Pýrgos
Vathý
Sámos
Pythagóreio
Ag. Kyriakí
Spatharaioi
Sámos
N. Sámos
IRAÍO
Fúrnoi
Ág. Minás
Fúrnoi
Thýmaina
Agathonísi
Arkoí
Pátmos
Kámpos
Skála
Pátmos
Leipsoí
Farmakonísi
DIDYMA
Tekağaç Burun
Davutlar
DİLEK YARIMADASI MİLLİ PARKI
PRIENE
Karine
Doganbey
Atburgazi
MİLET
Balat
Akköy
ASSESSOS
Yenihisar
Altı
Yenidoğan
Avşar
MYOS
Kapıkırı
HERAKLEIA
Çamaçi Gölü
TEICHIUSSA
Bağarası
Mersinbeleni
ALABANDA
ALINDA
Karpuzlu
LABRAUNDA
Selimiye
EUROMOS
Milâs
IASOS
Kıyıkışlacık
Güllük
BEÇİN KALESİ
Çamköy
PESADOS
Çine
Eskiçine
Akçaova
Gökbel
Gokbel Boğaz
Turgut
Yatağan
Eskihisar
Mandalya Körfezi
Salih Adasi
Karaova
Pınarköy
Ören
KERAMOS
Yalıkavak
UYUKLU TEPE
Bodrum
HALIKARNASSOS
MYNDOS
Ortakent
Turgutreis
Mazıköy
Kara Adasi
Gökova Körfezi
Koyun Burun
Değirme
Parthéni
Agia Marína
Léros
Lakkí
Xirókampos
Kálymnos
Emporeiós
Arginónta
Télendos
Myrtiés
Kálymnos
Psérimos
Levítha
Kínaros
Kos
Tigkáki
Ág. Fokás
Zipári
ASKLIPÍEIO
DÍKAIOS
Mastichári
Pylí
Antimáchia
Kardámaina
Kéfalos
Kos
ÁG. IOÁNNIS
Gyalí
Akr. Kríkelos
Reşadiye
Emecik
Datça
Bozburun
Yazıköv
İskandil Burun
KNIDOS
Sými
Pédi
Panormítis
LORYMA
Mandráki
Páloi
Emporeiós
Nikiá
GR
Nísyros
Kandelioúsa
Astypálaia
Vathý
Análipsi
Astypálaia
Megálo Chorió
Tílos
Livádia
DODEKÁNISSA
ΔΩΔΕΚΑΝΗΣΑ
Alímia
Chálki
Chálki
Paradeísi
Soroní
Kalavárda
KÁMEIROS
Mandrikó
Kritinía
Émponas
Siána
ATTÁVYROS
Monólithos
Profilia
Apolakkiá
Lachaniá
Kattavía
Akr. Prasonísi
Sýrna
Tría Nisiá
Zafóras
Akr. Paraspóri
Sariá
Astakída
Chamilí
Divoúnia
Diafáni
Ólympos
Kárpathos
Mesochóri
Stenó Karpáthou
Mykonos / Peiraías
Peiraías
Katápola / Anáfi / Mykonos
Karpáthos / Irakleio

144
139
141

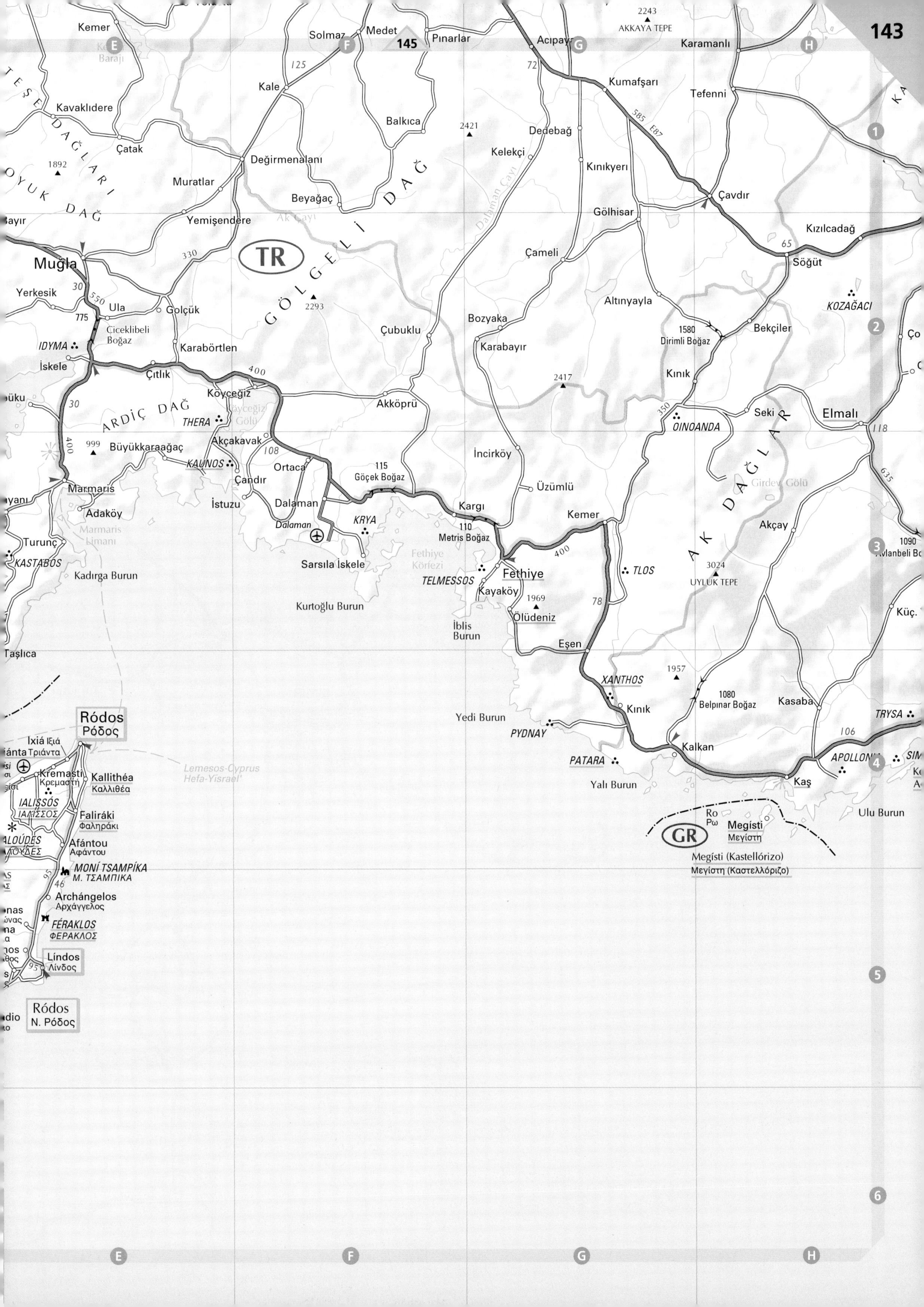
145
TR
GR
Muğla
Marmaris
Köyceğiz
Dalaman
Fethiye
Kemer
Elmalı
Kaş
Kalkan
Ölüdeniz
Ortaca
Acıpayam
Tefenni
Çavdır
Gölhisar
Kızılcadağ
Söğüt
Kınık
Eşen
Kemer
Solmaz
Medet
Pınarlar
Kale
Balkıca
Değirmenalanı
Beyağaç
Kavaklıdere
Çatak
Muratlar
Yemişendere
Yerkesik
Ula
Golçük
Karabörtlen
Çıtlık
İskele
Akçakavak
Büyükkaraağaç
Çandır
İstuzu
Adaköy
Turunç
Kadırga Burun
Kurtoğlu Burun
Sarsıla İskele
Akköprü
Çubuklu
Göçek Boğaz
Kargı
Metris Boğaz
Üzümlü
İncirköy
Bozyaka
Karabayır
Çameli
Altınyayla
Kelekçi
Dedebağ
Kınıkyeri
Kumafşarı
Karamanlı
Dirimli Boğaz
Bekçiler
Seki
Kayaköy
İblis Burun
Yedi Burun
Yalı Burun
Ulu Burun
Kasaba
Belpınar Boğaz
Akçay
Uylık Tepe
Akkaya Tepe
Gölgeli Dağ
Ak Dağlar
Ardiç Dağ
Ciceklibeli Boğaz
Idyma
Thera
Kaunos
Krya
Telmessos
Tlos
Xanthos
Pydnay
Patara
Oinoanda
Kozağacı
Trysa
Apollonia
Kastabos
Megísti
Μεγίστη
Megísti (Kastellórizo)
Μεγίστη (Καστελλόριζο)
Ródos
Ρόδος
Ixiá Ιξιά
Kremastí
Κρεμαστή
Kallithéa
Καλλιθέα
Ialissós
Ιαλυσσός
Faliráki
Φαληράκι
Afántou
Αφάντου
Moní Tsampíka
Μ. Τσαμπίκα
Archángelos
Αρχάγγελος
Féraklos
Φεράκλος
Lindos
Λίνδος
Ródos
N. Ρόδος
Lemesos-Cyprus
Hefa-Yisrael'
Marmaris Limanı
Fethiye Körfezi
Köyceğiz Gölü
Girdev Gölü
Dalaman Çayı
Ak Çayı
E
F
G
H
1
2
3
4
5
6

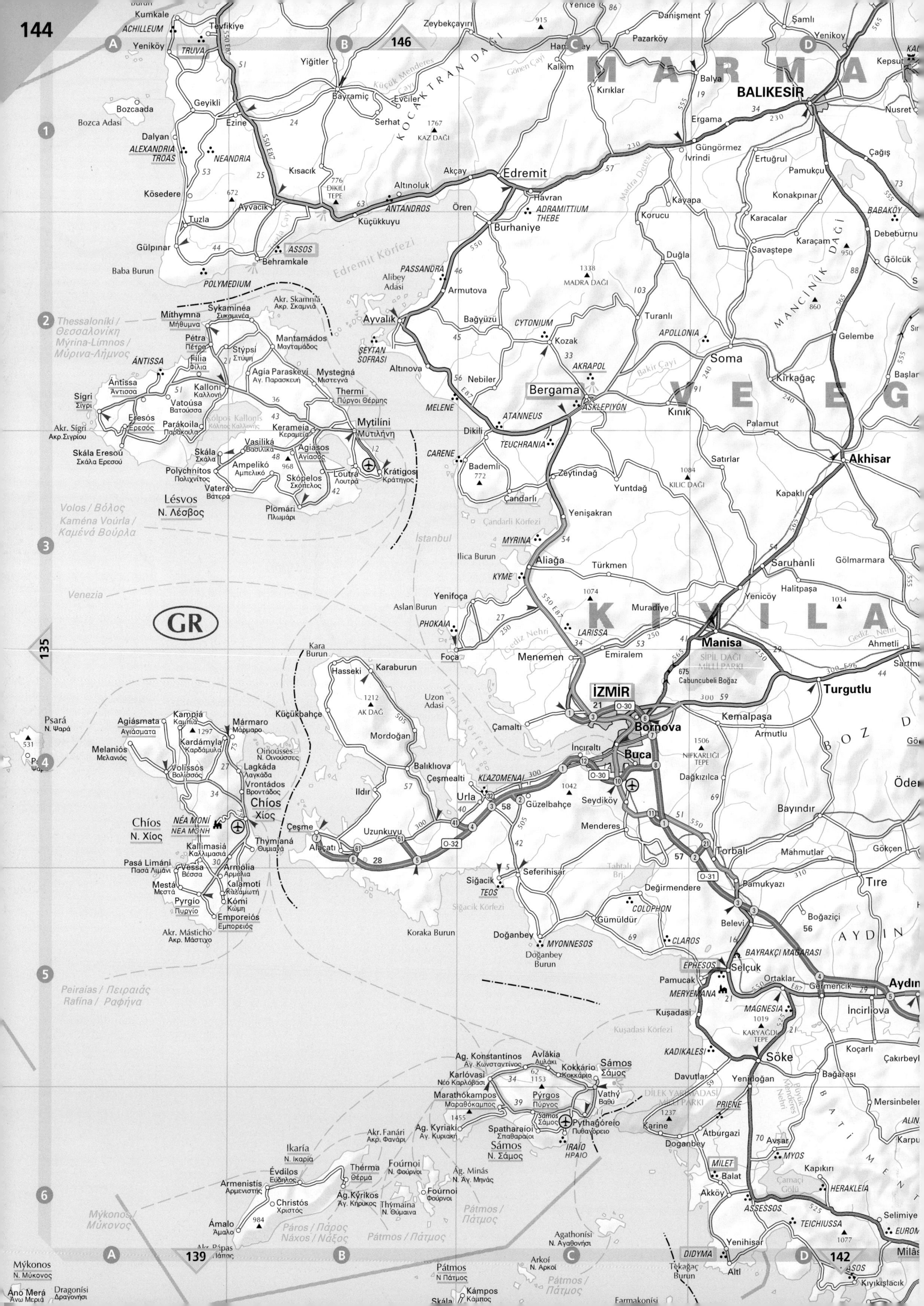

146
Balıkesir
Edremit
Ayvalık
Bergama
Soma
Akhisar
Manisa
İzmir
Bornova
Buca
Turgutlu
Kemalpaşa
Torbalı
Selçuk
Kuşadasi
Söke
Aydın
Tire
Çeşme
Urla
Foça
Aliağa
Menemen
Dikili
Çandarlı
Lésvos
N. Λέσβος
Mytilíni
Μυτιλήνη
Chíos
Χίος
Sámos
Σάμος
Ikaría
N. Ικαρία
Fóurnoi
Pátmos
GR
Edremit Körfezi
Çandarli Körfezi
Kuşadasi Körfezi
Sığacik Körfezi
135
139
142

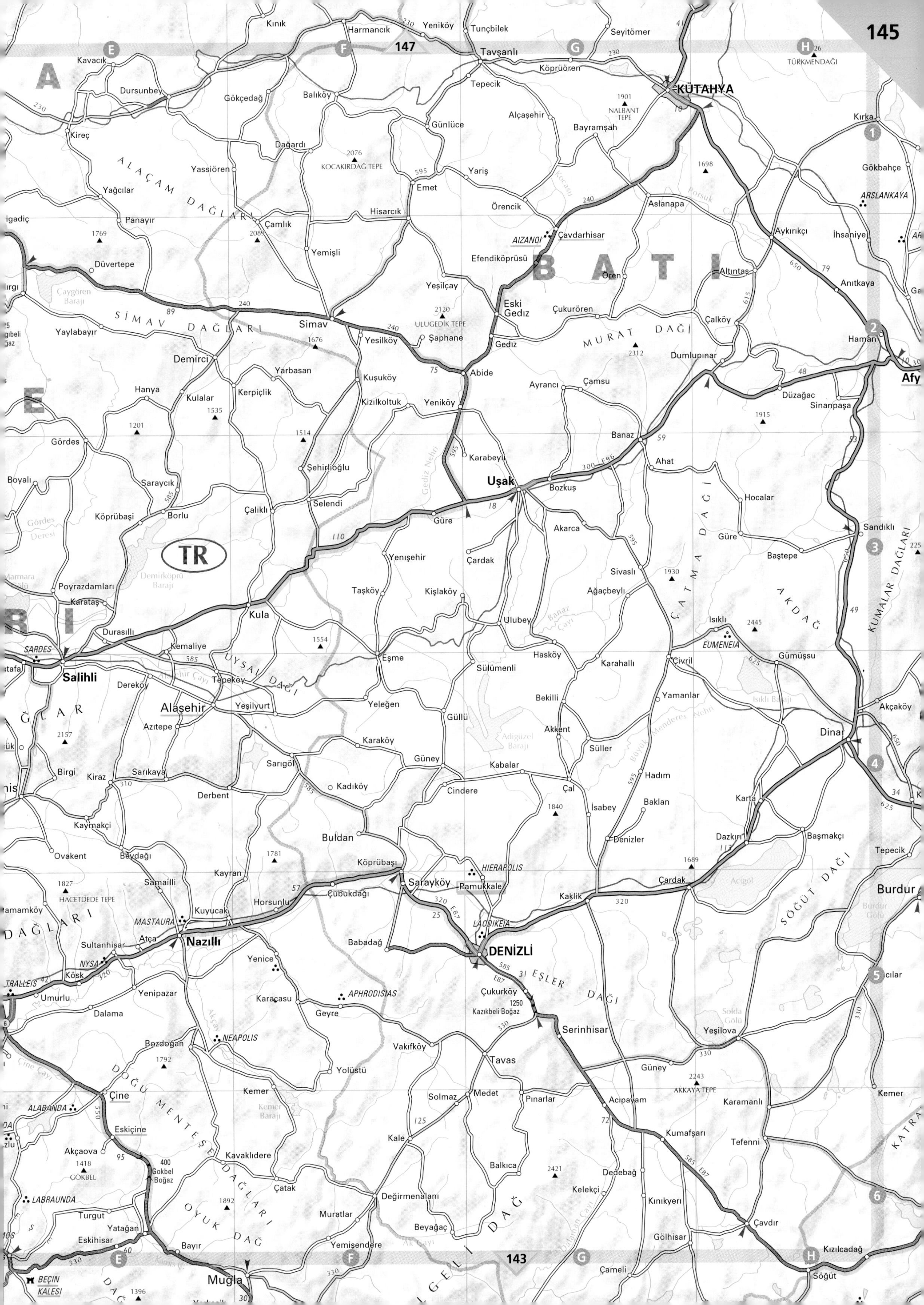
KÜTAHYA
Uşak
DENİZLİ
Salihli
Nazilli
Muğla
Burdur
Dinar
Alaşehir
Simav
Kula
Gediz
Tavşanlı
Sandıklı
BATI
AKDAĞ
MURAT DAĞI
ÇATMA DAĞI
SİMAV DAĞLARI
ALAÇAM DAĞLARI
SÖĞÜT DAĞI
EŞLER DAĞI
KUMALAR DAĞLARI
DOĞU MENTEŞE DAĞLARI
OYUK DAĞ
TR
SARDES
HIERAPOLIS
LAODIKEIA
APHRODISIAS
AIZANOI
EUMENEIA
NEAPOLIS
MASTAURA
NYSA
TRALLEIS
ALABANDA
LABRAUNDA
ARSLANKAYA
147
143

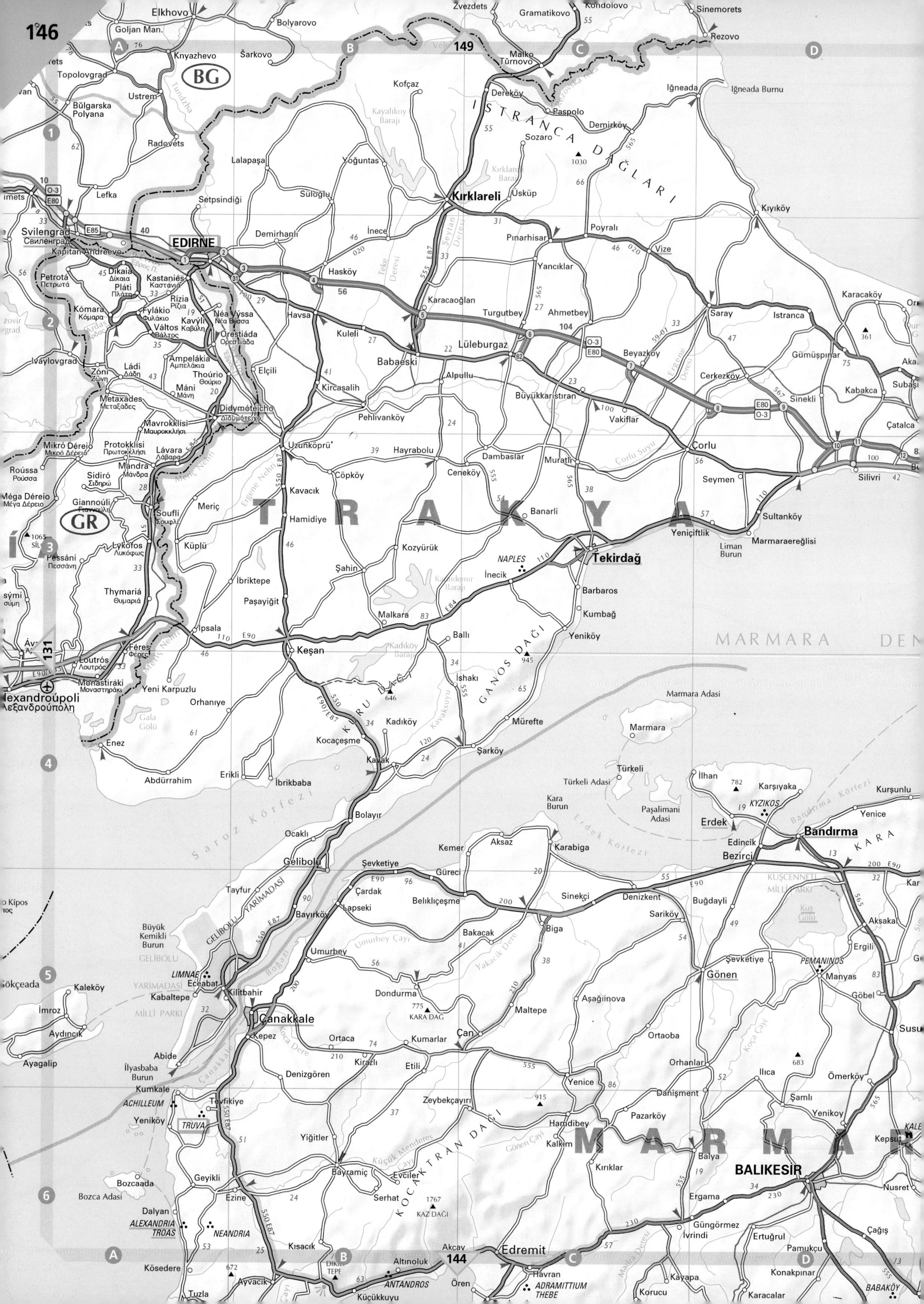
Elkhovo
Zvezdets
Gramatikovo
Kondolovo
Sinemorets
Goljan Man.
Bolyarovo
Rezovo
149
Knyazhevo
Šarkovo
Malko Tŭrnovo
BG
Topolovgrad
Ustrem
Kofçaz
Dereköy
Iğneada
Iğneada Burnu
Bŭlgarska Polyana
Kayalıköy Barajı
Paspolo
Radovets
İSTRANCA DAĞLARI
Demirköy
Sozaro
1030
Lalapaşa
Yoğuntas
Kırklareli Barajı
Lefka
Süloğlu
Kırklareli
Üsküp
Svilengrad
Свиленград
Setpsindiği
Kıyıköy
EDIRNE
Demirhanlı
İnece
Pınarhisar
Poyralı
Vize
Kapitan Andreevo
Petrotá
Πετρωτά
Dikaia
Δίκαια
Kastaniés
Καστανιές
Pláti
Πλάτη
Rízia
Ρίζια
Hasköy
Yancıklar
Kómara
Κόμαρα
Fylákio
Φυλάκιο
Néa Vyssa
Νέα Βύσσα
Karacaoğlan
Karacaköy
Kavýli
Καβύλη
Váltos
Βάλτος
Havsa
Turgutbey
Ahmetbey
Saray
Istranca
Orestiáda
Ορεστιάδα
Kuleli
Lüleburgaz
Beyazköy
Gümüşpınar
Ivaylovgrad
Babaeski
Ampelákia
Αμπελάκια
Zóni
Ζώνη
Ládi
Λάδη
Thoúrio
Θούριο
Elçili
Alpullu
Çerkezköy
Kabakca
Subaşi
Máni
Μάνη
Kırcasalih
Metaxádes
Μεταξάδες
Büyükkarıştıran
Sinekli
Didymóteicho
Διδυμότειχο
Pehlivanköy
Vakiflar
Çatalca
Mavrokklísi
Μαυροκκλήσι
Mikró Déreio
Μικρό Δέρειο
Protokklísi
Πρωτοκκλήσι
Lávara
Λάβαρα
Uzunköprü
Hayrabolu
Dambaslar
Muratlı
Çorlu
Çorlu Suyu
Mandra
Μάνδρα
Roússa
Ρούσσα
Sidiró
Σιδηρώ
Çöpköy
Ceneköy
Seymen
Silivri
Méga Dereio
Μέγα Δέρειο
Kavacık
Giannoúli
Γιαννούλη
Soufli
Σουφλί
Meriç
TRAKYA
Banarli
Sultanköy
GR
Hamidiye
Yeniçiftlik
Marmaraereğlisi
Liman Burun
Lykofos
Λυκόφως
Küplü
Kozyürük
Tekirdağ
Pessáni
Πεσσάνη
NAPLES
Şahin
İnecik
İbriktepe
Kumdemir Barajı
Thymariá
Θυμαριά
Barbaros
Paşayiğit
Kumbağ
Malkara
İpsala
Ballı
Yeniköy
MARMARA DENİZİ
131
Féres
Φέρες
Keşan
Kadıköy Barajı
Loutrós
Λουτρός
GANOS DAĞI
945
Monastiráki
Μοναστηράκι
İshakı
Alexandroúpoli
Αλεξανδρούπολη
Yeni Karpuzlu
KURU DAĞI
646
Marmara Adasi
Orhanıye
Gala Gölü
Kadıköy
Mürefte
Marmara
Kocaçeşme
Kavaksuyu
Enez
Şarköy
Kavak
Abdürrahim
Erikli
İbrikbaba
Türkeli
Türkeli Adasi
İlhan
782
Karşıyaka
Kurşunlu
Kara Burun
KYZIKOS
Paşalimani Adasi
Saroz Körfezi
Bolayır
Erdek
Bandırma Körfezi
Yenice
Erdek Körfezi
Bandırma
Ocaklı
Kemer
Aksaz
Karabiga
Edincik
Bezirci
KARA
Gelibolu
Şevketiye
Güreci
Çardak
Belıklıçeşme
Sinekçi
Denizkent
KUŞCENNETİ MİLLİ PARKI
Kuş Gölü
Tayfur
GELİBOLU YARIMADASI
Lapseki
Buğdayli
Bayırköy
Sariköy
Aksakal
Büyük Kemikli Burun
Bakacak
Biga
Umurbey
Umurbey Çayı
Yakacık Dere
Şevketiye
Ergili
Gönen
PEMANINOS
Manyas
Gökçeada
LIMNAE
Eceabat
Kaleköy
Kabaltepe
MİLLİ PARKI
Kilitbahir
Dondurma
Aşağiinova
Göbel
775
KARA DAĞ
Maltepe
İmroz
Çanakkale
Boğazı
Aydıncık
Kepez
Ortaca
Kumarlar
Çan
Ortaoba
Susurluk
683
Abide
Kirazlı
Etili
Orhanlar
Ayagalip
İlyasbaba Burun
Denizgören
Yenice
Ilıca
Ömerköy
Kumkale
ACHILLEUM
Tevfikiye
Zeybekçayırı
915
Danişment
Şamlı
Yeniköy
Pazarköy
Yenikoy
TRUVA
Hamdibey
KOCA KTRAN DAĞI
Kalkım
MARMARA
Kepsut
Yiğitler
Gönen Çayı
Küçük Menderes
Balya
Kırıklar
BALIKESİR
Bayramiç
Evciler
Geyikli
Bozcaada
Serhat
Nusret
Bozca Adasi
Ezine
1767
KAZ DAĞI
Dalyan
Ergama
ALEXANDRIA TROAS
NEANDRIA
Güngörmez
İvrindi
Ertuğrul
Çağış
Kısacık
Akcay
144
Edremit
Pamukçu
Kösedere
672
DİKİLİ TEPE
Altınoluk
Havran
Konakpınar
Ayvacık
ANTANDROS
Ören
ADRAMITTIUM THEBE
Kayapa
Korucu
Karacalar
BABAKÖY
Tuzla
Küçükkuyu
Mahra Deresi

E   F   G   H

Zonguldak

Pazarbaşı Burun
Akçako
Karaburun
Terkoz   Kumköy   Çayağzi   Sahilköy   Şile   Ağva/Yeşilçay   Kefken   Karaağaç   Karasu   010   Kocaali
Ağaçlı   Rumelifeneri   Alacalı   Kandira   17   Kaynarca   Darıçayırı   Ortaköy
Yassıören   Sarıyer   Beykoz   Teke   74   Akçaova   Kocakaymaz   605   Süğütlü   Soğuksu   FINDIKLI T   Cılım
Arnavutköy   Kemerburgaz   Yeniköy   70   020   Türas   Kaymaz   37   990   Cumaova
Boyalık   46   İSTANBUL   Alemdağ   Mahmutşevketpaşa   Ömerli   Akmeşe   Beşevlet   650   52   Hendek   Gölyaka
E80   Cemke   Barajı   Sapakpınar   Kazımpaşa   ADAPAZARI   E80   Karadere
E80 O-3   15   16   17   Samandıra   Karayakuplu   Akçova   41.02   54   100   140   15   O-4   Karadere
Esenyurt   Küçükçekmece   Üsküdar   E80 O-4   Mollafeneri   Tepecik   İZMİT   Uzuntarla   13   Ekinli   Akyazı   ELMACIK
kçekmece   Gürpınar   Bakırköy Yeşilköy   Maltepe   Kartal   89   E80 O-4   Yarımca   11   Kurtköy   Sapanca   Karapürçek   Kuzuluk   140   Dokurcun
Avcılar   Atatürk   Pendik   Tuzla   Gebze   Hereke   Körfez   Gölcük   Suadiye   12   30   Geyve   Kapıorman   Dağlar
Kızıl Adalar   Darıca   Tavşancıl   Değirmendere   39   Yeniköy   1314   Pamukova   25   150   Kazkıran Geçit 800   Göynük   Hacıa
İzmit Körfez   Altınova   Karamürsel   Sarısu   Bahçecik   30   Beşevler   650   160   Taraklı   150   1140 Meyitler Geçit
Yalova   Yalakdere   Osmaneli   Gölpazarı   Yenipazar
İzmir   Çınarcık   Termal   20   Yeniköy   Bayındır   150   İznik   150   44   Lâç
TR   921   Orhangazi   18   Boyalıca   NIKAIA   Vezirhan   160   Sarıcakaya   Mihalgazi
İmralı Ad   Armutlu   Kapaklı   Sölöz   Narlıca   595   Köprühisar   160   Bilecik   Küplü   Çalti   İnhisar   Dağküplü
Zeytinbağı   Mudanya   Umurbey   Yenişehir   Koyunhis   50   665   Söğüt   SÜNDİKEN   1534
Bayramdere   HISARTEPE DASCYLIUM   Esence   APAMEA   Ericek   51   Boğazköy   595   Demirköy   Çalti
MILETOPOLIS   APOLLONIA   Hasanağa   Gürsu   Turan   22   200 E90   Hasanpaşa   Pazaryeri   Bozüyük   Poyra   200 E90   ESKİŞEHİR
Uluabat   Gölyazı   Çalı   Uludağ   29   İnegöl   Çayyaka   1004   Demirköy   55   İnönü   40 E90   Muttalip
Mustafa Kemalpaşa   Söğütalan   2543 ULUDAĞ   ULUDAĞ MILLI PARKI   Tahtaköprü   Kozpınar   Kümbet   35   Akpınar
Yürücekler   Orhaneli   Keles   Safa   Cihangazi   650   Sobran   230
Devecikonağı   Yeşiller   2052 TEPEL TEPE   Domaniç   Gümüşyeni   Porsuk Barajı
Kansız   Demirci   Böcen   1826 TÜRKMENDAĞI
Alacat   Büyükorhan   595   Yeniköy   Tunçbilek   Seyitömer   41
Kavacık   Kınık   Harmancık   Tavşanlı   230   Köprüören   KÜTAHYA   Kırk
Dursunbey   Gökçedağ   Balıköy   Tepecik   Alçaşehir   1901 NALBANT TEPE   10
Kireç   230   Dağardı   2076 KOCAKIRDAĞ TEPE   Günlüce   Bayramşah   1698   Gökbahçe
Bigadiç   Panayır   Çamlık   Emet   145   Yariş   Örencik   Aslanapa   ARSLANKAYA

A

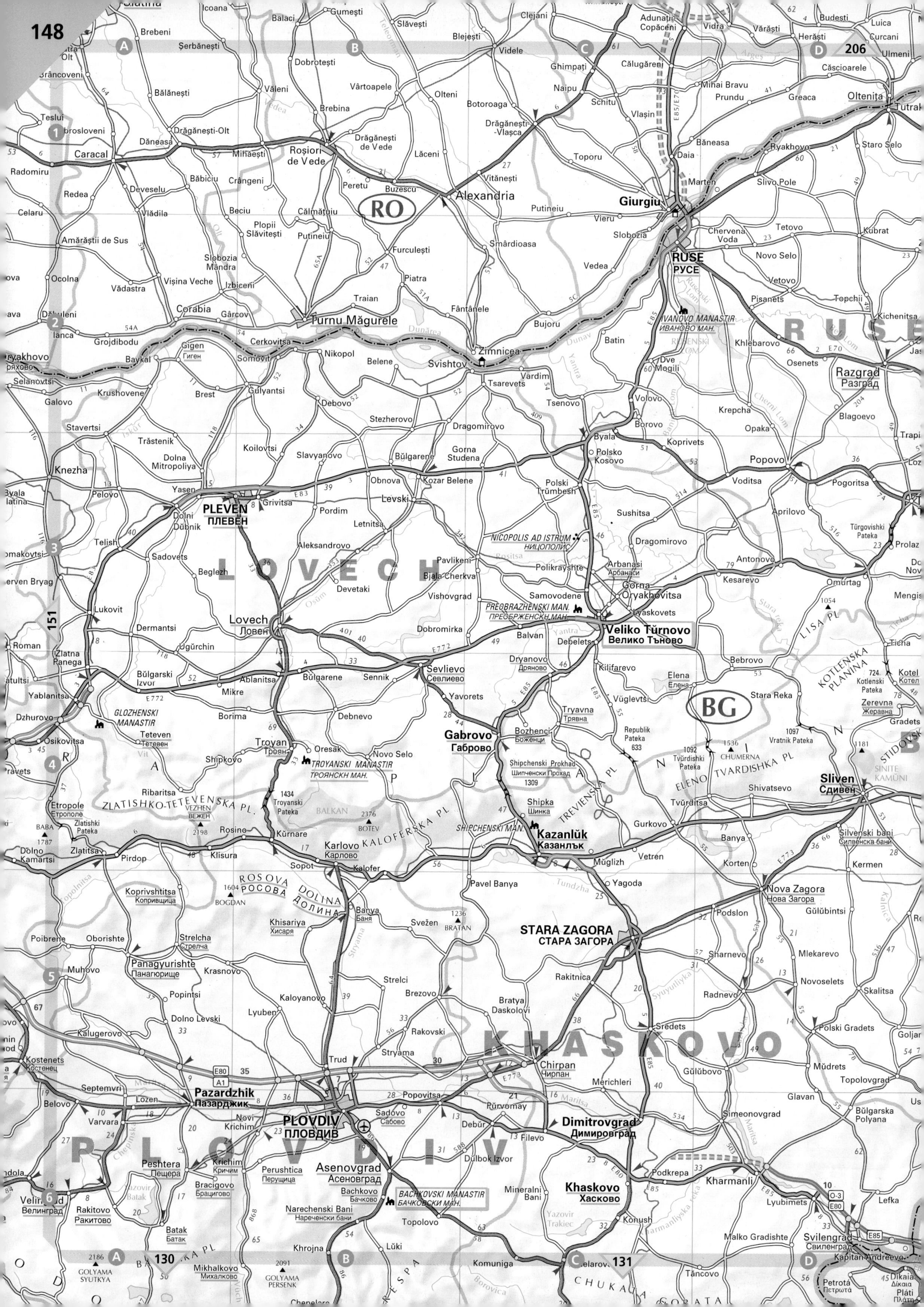

206
RO
Caracal
Roșiori de Vede
Alexandria
Giurgiu
Turnu Măgurele
Zimnicea
Oltenița
Drăgănești-Olt
Drăgănești-Vlașca
Corabia
Videle
Ghimpați
Călugăreni
Mihai Bravu
Prundu
Greaca
Vedea
Putineiu
Vitănești
Smârdioasa
Furculești
Piatra
Traian
Fântânele
Bujoru
Slobozia
RUSE
РУСЕ
IVANOVO MANASTIR
ИВАНОВО МАН.
RUSE
Svishtov
Nikopol
Belene
Gigen
Гиген
Somovit
Baykal
Oryakhovo
Selanovtsi
Gulyantsi
Razgrad
Разград
Tsarevets
Tsenovo
Byala
Popovo
Dve Mogili
Batin
Khlebarovo
Pleven
ПЛЕВЕН
LOVECH
Lovech
Ловеч
Levski
Knezha
NICOPOLIS AD ISTRUM
НИКОПОЛИС
PREOBRAZHENSKI MAN.
ПРЕОБРАЖЕНСКИ МАН.
Gorna Oryakhovitsa
Veliko Tŭrnovo
Велико Търново
Lyaskovets
Polski Trŭmbesh
Sevlievo
Севлиево
Dryanovo
Дряново
Elena
Елена
BG
Gabrovo
Габрово
Tryavna
Трявна
Troyan
Троян
TROYANSKI MANASTIR
ТРОЯНСКИ МАН.
GLOZHENSKI MANASTIR
Teteven
Тетевен
Etropole
Етрополе
Shipchenski Prokhad
Шипченски Проход
Shipka
Шипка
SHIPCHENSKI MAN.
Kazanlŭk
Казанлък
Karlovo
Карлово
BALKAN
ZLATISHKO-TETEVENSKA PL.
KALOFERSKA PL.
ELENO TVARDISHKA PL.
KOTLENSKA PLANINA
LISA PL.
Kotel
Котел
Omurtag
Sliven
Сливен
Nova Zagora
Нова Загора
STARA ZAGORA
СТАРА ЗАГОРА
ROSOVA DOLINA
РОСОВА ДОЛИНА
Koprivshtitsa
Копривщица
Panagyurishte
Панагюрище
Strelcha
Стрелча
Khisariya
Хисаря
Banya
Баня
KHASKOVO
Chirpan
Чирпан
Pazardzhik
Пазарджик
PLOVDIV
ПЛОВДИВ
Asenovgrad
Асеновград
Dimitrovgrad
Димитровград
Khaskovo
Хасково
Kharmanli
Svilengrad
Свиленград
Peshtera
Пещера
Velingrad
Велинград
Batak
Батак
BACHKOVSKI MANASTIR
БАЧКОВСКИ МАН.
Kostenets
Костенец
Rakitovo
Ракитово
Perushtica
Перущица
Bachkovo
Бачково
Narechenski Bani
Нареченски бани
Mineralni Bani
Lyubimets
Simeonovgrad
PLOVDIV
130
131
CHUKATA
E80
E85
E70
E772
E83
A1

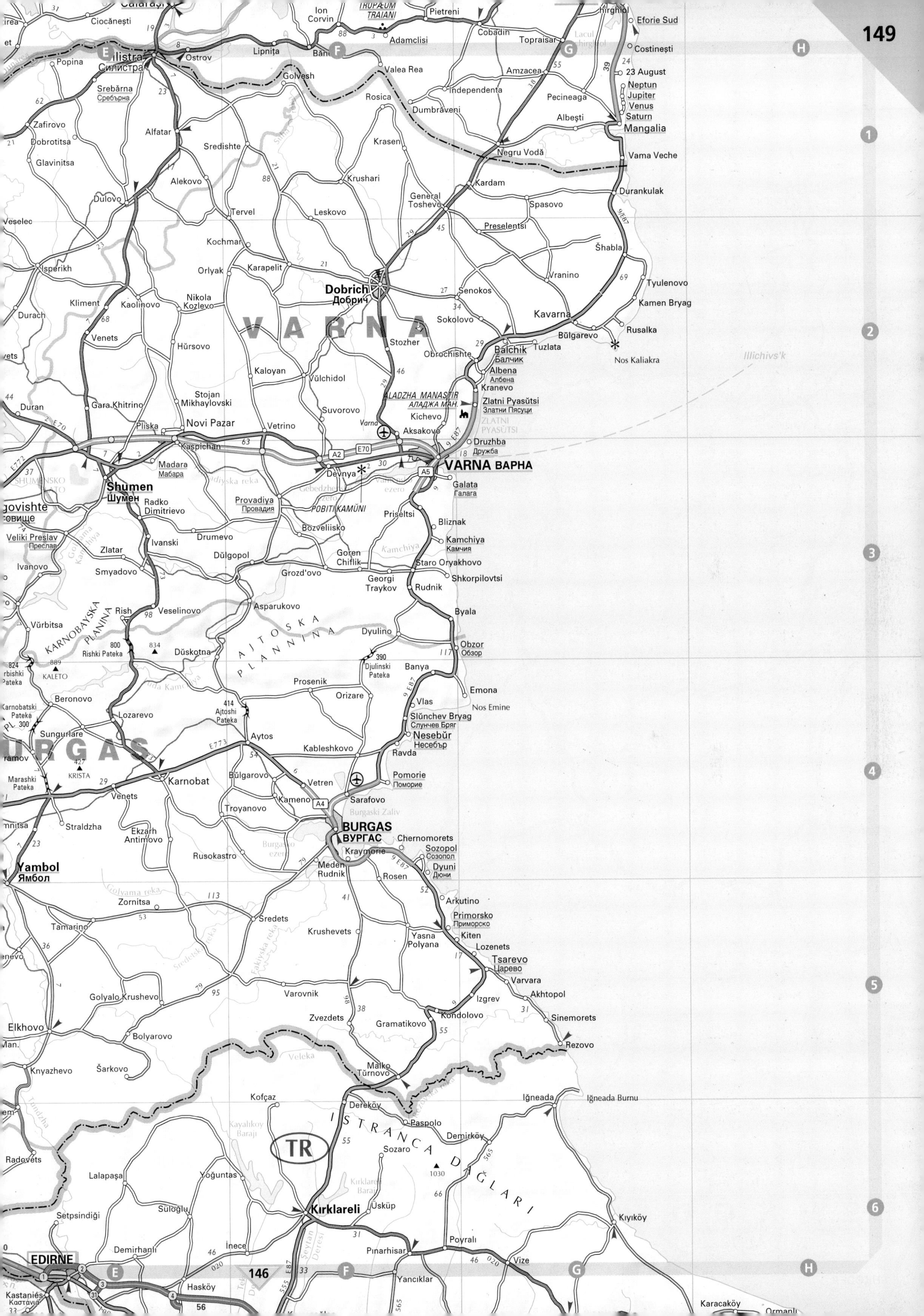
Ciocănești
Ion Corvin
TROPÆUM TRAIANI
Pietreni
Adamclisi
Cobadin
Topraisar
Eforie Sud
Costinești
Ostrov
Lipnița
Băneasa
Popina
Silistra
Силистра
Golvesh
Valea Rea
Amzacea
23 August
Neptun
Jupiter
Venus
Saturn
Mangalia
Srebărna
Сребърна
Independenta
Rosica
Dumbrăveni
Pecineaga
Albești
Zafirovo
Dobrotitsa
Glavinitsa
Alfatar
Sredishte
Krasen
Negru Vodă
Vama Veche
Alekovo
Krushari
Kardam
Durankulak
Dulovo
Tervel
Leskovo
General Toshevo
Spasovo
Veselec
Preselentsi
Kochmar
Šhabla
Isperikh
Orlyak
Karapelit
Vranino
Tyulenovo
Dobrich
Добрич
Kliment
Kaolinovo
Nikola Kozlevo
Senokos
Kamen Bryag
Durach
Sokolovo
Kavarna
Rusalka
VARNA
Venets
Hŭrsovo
Stozher
Obrochishte
Bŭlgarevo
Balchik
Балчик
Tuzlata
Nos Kaliakra
Illichivs'k
Kaloyan
Vŭlchidol
Albena
Албена
Kranevo
Duran
Stojan Mikhaylovski
Gara Khitrino
ALADZHA MANASTIR
АЛАДЖА МАН.
Zlatni Pyasŭtsi
Златни Пясъци
ZLATNI PYASŬTSI
Suvorovo
Kichevo
Pliska
Novi Pazar
Vetrino
Aksakovo
Kaspichan
Druzhba
Дружба
Madara
Мадара
Devnya
VARNA ВАРНА
SHUMENSKO PLATO
Shumen
Шумен
Radko Dimitrievo
Provadiya
Провадия
POBITI KAMŬNI
Galata
Галата
Targovishte
Търговище
Priseltsi
Bliznak
Bozveliisko
Veliki Preslav
Преслав
Drumevo
Ivanski
Kamchiya
Камчия
Zlatar
Dŭlgopol
Goren Chiflik
Staro Oryakhovo
Ivanovo
Smyadovo
Grozd'ovo
Georgi Traykov
Rudnik
Shkorpilovtsi
Rish
Veselinovo
Asparukovo
Vŭrbitsa
KARNOBAYSKA PLANINA
Byala
AJTOSKA PLANNINA
Dyulino
Rishki Pateka
Dŭskotna
Obzor
Обзор
KALETO
Djulinski Pateka
Banya
Emona
Nos Emine
Prosenik
Orizare
Vlas
Beronovo
Ajtoshi Pateka
Karnobatski Pateka
Lozarevo
Slŭnchev Bryag
Слънчев Бряг
Nesebŭr
Несебър
Sungurlare
Aytos
Ravda
BURGAS
Kableshkovo
KRISTA
Karnobat
Bŭlgarovo
Vetren
Pomorie
Поморие
Marashki Pateka
Venets
Kameno
Sarafovo
Troyanovo
Burgaski Zaliv
Straldzha
Ekzarh Antimovo
BURGAS
БУРГАС
Chernomorets
Sozopol
Созопол
Kraymorie
Rusokastro
Burgasko ezero
Yambol
Ямбол
Meden Rudnik
Dyuni
Дюни
Rosen
Arkutino
Zornitsa
Golyama reka
Primorsko
Приморско
Sredets
Tamarino
Krushevets
Kiten
Yasna Polyana
Lozenets
Tsarevo
Царево
Varvara
Akhtopol
Golyalo Krushevo
Varovnik
Izgrev
Zvezdets
Kondolovo
Sinemorets
Elkhovo
Gramatikovo
Bolyarovo
Rezovo
Veleka
Malko Tŭrnovo
Knyazhevo
Šarkovo
Kofçaz
Iğneada
Iğneada Burnu
Dereköy
ISTRANCA DAĞLARI
Kayalıkoy Barajı
Paspolo
Demirköy
TR
Sozaro
Radovets
Lalapaşa
Yoğuntaş
Kırklareli Barajı
Kırklareli
Üsküp
Kıyıköy
Setpsindiği
Süloğlu
Demirhanlı
İnece
Pınarhisar
Poyralı
EDIRNE
Vize
Yancıklar
Hasköy
Kastaniés
Καστανιές
Karacaköy
Ormanlı
146

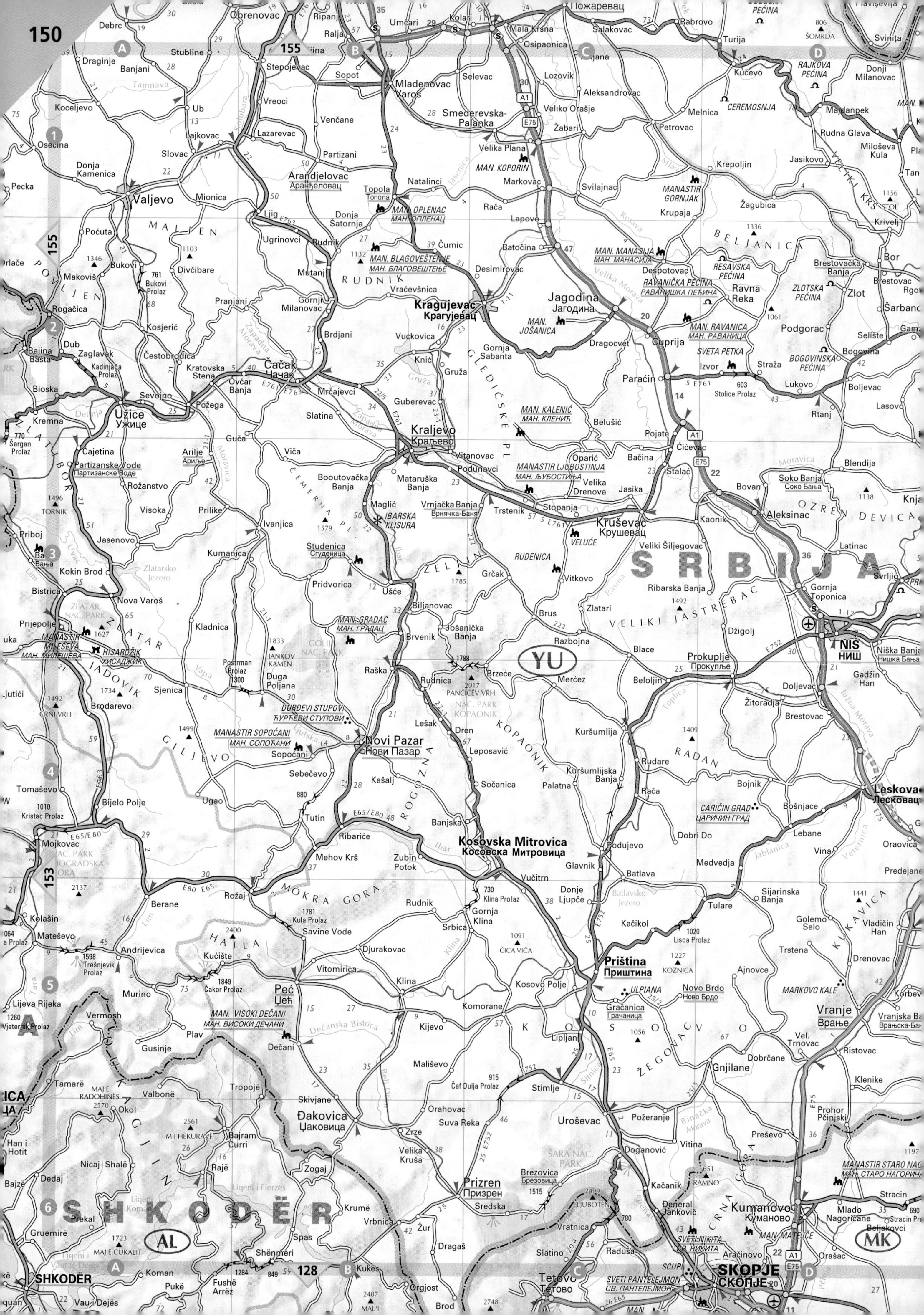
SRBIJA
YU
AL
MK
SHKODËR
Obrenovac
Požarevac
Požarevac
Smederevska-Palanka
Mladenovac Varoš
Valjevo
Arandjelovac
Aranđelovac
Topola
Kragujevac
Крагујевац
Jagodina
Јагодина
Ćuprija
Paraćin
Čačak
Чачак
Užice
Ужице
Kraljevo
Краљево
Kruševac
Крушевац
Niš
НИШ
Novi Pazar
Нови Пазар
Kosovska Mitrovica
Косовска Митровица
Priština
Приштина
Peć
Пећ
Đakovica
Ђаковица
Prizren
Призрен
Uroševac
Gnjilane
Vranje
Врање
Leskovac
Prokuplje
Прокупље
Kumanovo
Куманово
SKOPJE
СКОПЈЕ
Tetovo
Тетово
Shkodër
Aleksinac
Soko Banja
Соко Бања
Bor
Zlot
Kučevo
Majdanpek
Kolašin
Mojkovac
Bijelo Polje
Berane
Rožaj
Sjenica
Prijepolje
Priboj
Nova Varoš
Ivanjica
Požega
Kosjerić
Bajina Bašta
Ub
Lajkovac
Mionica
Ljig
Gornji Milanovac
Dečani
Plav
Gusinje
Andrijevica
Podujevo
Vučitrn
Lipljan
Kosovo Polje
Kačanik
Preševo
Bujanovac
MAN. STUDENICA
Studenica
Студеница
MAN. SOPOĆANI
МАН. СОПОЋАНИ
MAN. VISOKI DEČANI
МАН. ВИСОКИ ДЕЧАНИ
MAN. MANASIJA
МАН. МАНАСИЈА
MAN. RAVANICA
МАН. РАВАНИЦА
MAN. ŽIČA
MAN. GRADAC
МАН. ГРАДАЦ
MAN. OPLENAC
МАН. ОПЛЕНАЦ
MAN. KALENIĆ
МАН. КЛЕНИЋ
MANASTIR LJUBOSTINJA
МАН. ЉУБОСТИЊА
MANASTIR MILEŠEVA
МАН. МИЛЕШЕВА
ĐURĐEVI STUPOVI
ЂУРЂЕВИ СТУПОВИ
CARIČIN GRAD
ЦАРИЧИН ГРАД
Gračanica
Грачаница
ULPIANA
Novo Brdo
Ново Брдо
RUDNIK
KOPAONIK
GOLIJA NAC. PARK
ZLATIBOR
ZLATAR
JADOVIK
GILJEVO
MOKRA GORA
HAJLA
ROGOZNA
ŽEGOVAC
RADAN
VELIKI JASTREBAC
BELJANICA
OZREN DEVICA
KUKAVICA
ČEMERNA PL.
GLEDIĆSKE PL.
MALJEN
POVLJEN
ŽELJIN
ŠARA NAC. PARK
E75
E761
E763
E65
E80
E752
A1
155
153
128

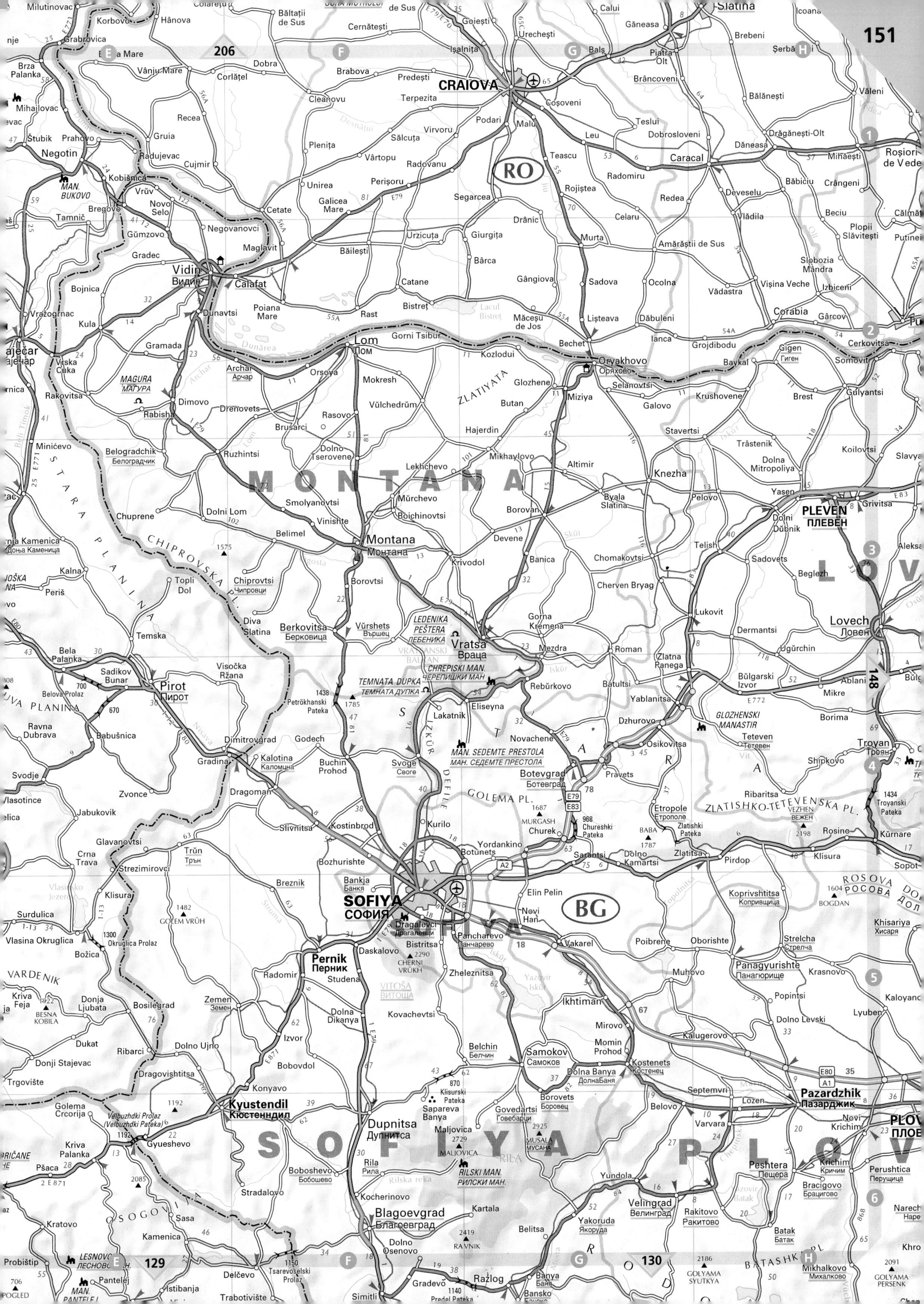

206
CRAIOVA
RO
Slatina
Balş
Piatra-Olt
Caracal
Roşiori de Vede
Corabia
Calafat
Vidin
Видин
Negotin
Lom
Лом
Oryakhovo
Оряхово
MONTANA
Montana
Монтана
ZLATIYATA
Knezha
PLEVEN
ПЛЕВЕН
Lovech
Ловеч
Vratsa
Враца
Berkovitsa
Берковица
Belogradchik
Белоградчик
Chiprovtsi
Чипровци
STARA PLANINA
CHIPROVSKA PL.
Pirot
Пирот
Dimitrovgrad
Kalotina
Калотина
Godech
Svoge
Своге
Botevgrad
Ботевград
Etropole
Етрополе
Teteven
Тетевен
Troyan
Троян
ZLATISHKO-TETEVENSKA PL.
GOLEMA PL.
IZKŬR DEFILE
SOFIYA
СОФИЯ
BG
Pernik
Перник
Dragoman
Slivnitsa
Kostinbrod
Elin Pelin
Ikhtiman
Samokov
Самоков
Kostenets
Костенец
Pazardzhik
Пазарджик
Panagyurishte
Панагюрище
Koprivshtitsa
Копривщица
Pirdop
Zlatitsa
Kyustendil
Кюстендил
Dupnitsa
Дупница
Rila
Рила
RILSKI MAN.
РИЛСКИ МАН.
Blagoevgrad
Благоевград
Velingrad
Велинград
Peshtera
Пещера
Batak
Батак
Yakoruda
Якоруда
Razlog
Bansko
Банско
SOFIYA
PLOV
Trŭn
Трън
Bosilegrad
Kratovo
Delčevo
OSOGOVIJA
VITOŠA
ВИТОША
MUSALA
МУСАЛА
2925
MALJOVICA
2729
RILA
129
130
148

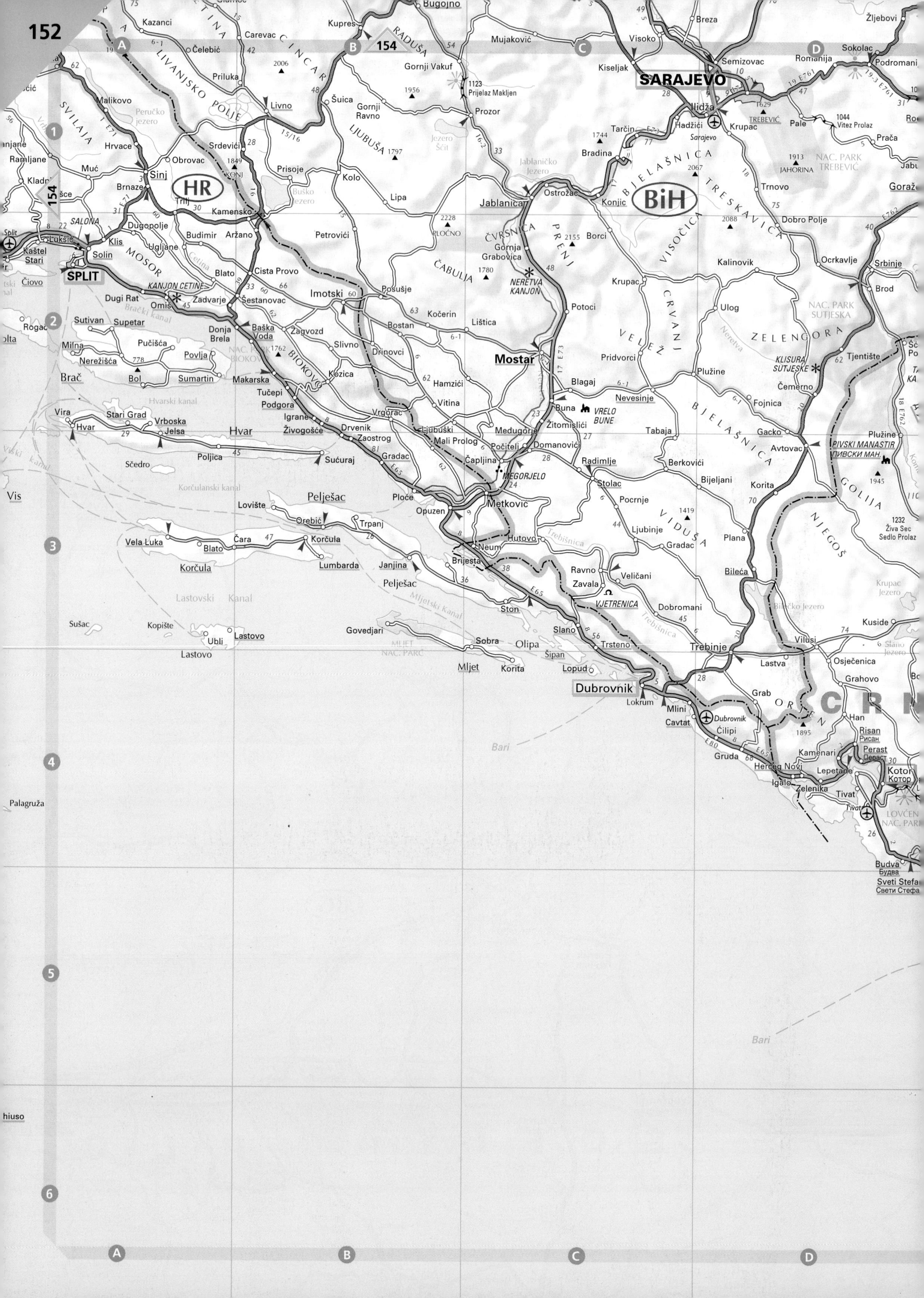

SARAJEVO
Mostar
SPLIT
Dubrovnik
HR
BiH
Sinj
Livno
Imotski
Makarska
Omiš
Solin
Kaštel Stari
Brač
Hvar
Vis
Korčula
Lastovo
Pelješac
Mljet
Metković
Ploče
Neum
Čapljina
Međugorje
Ljubuški
Široki Brijeg
Posušje
Jablanica
Konjic
Ilidža
Hadžići
Pale
Foča
Nevesinje
Stolac
Gacko
Bileća
Trebinje
Cavtat
Herceg Novi
Kotor
Tivat
Budva
Sveti Stefan
Bugojno
Kupres
Prozor
Gornji Vakuf
Kiseljak
Visoko
Breza
Tjentište
Plužine
Avtovac
Vrgorac
Ston
Slano
Risan
Perast
Igalo
Palagruža

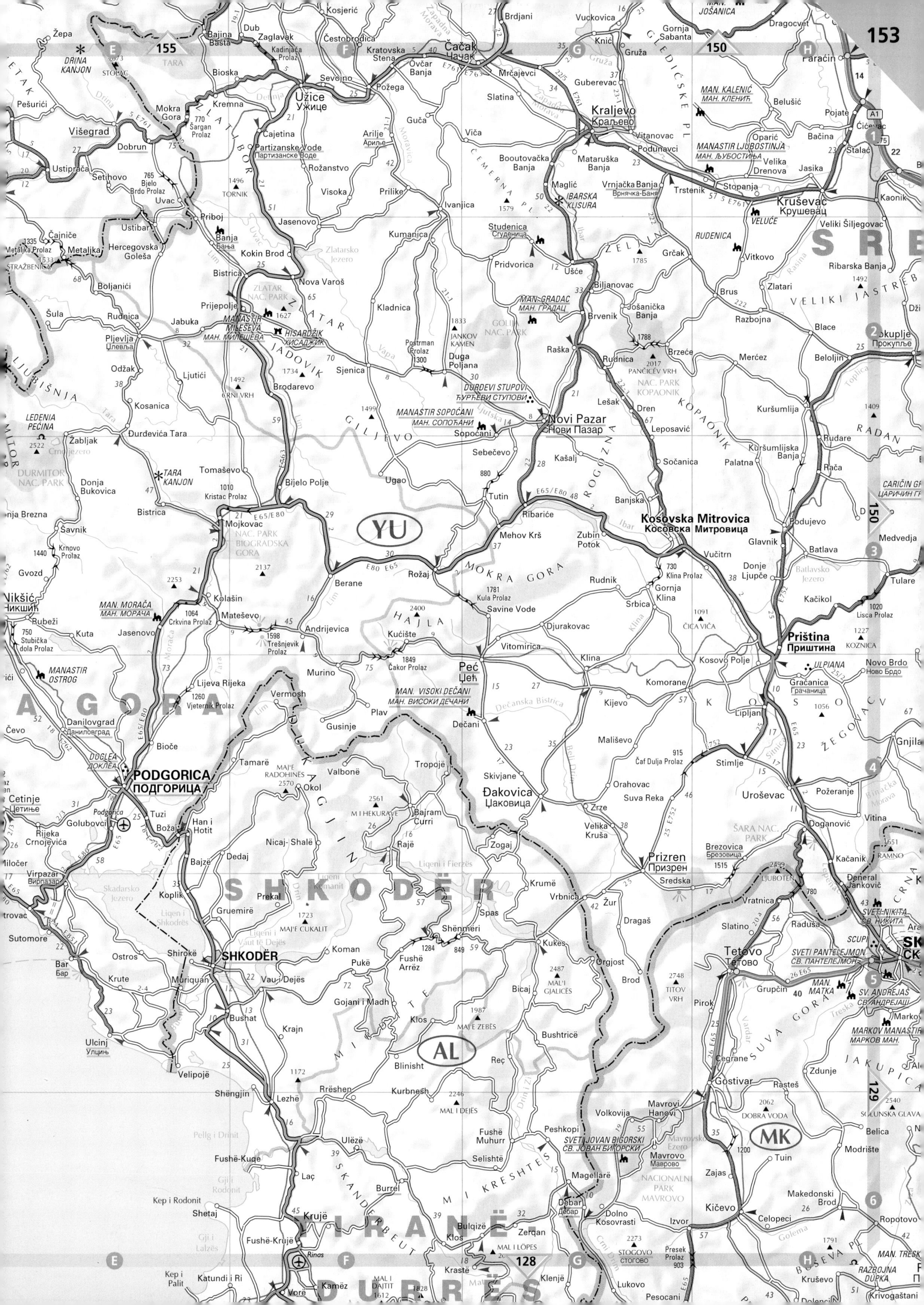
YU
AL
MK
SHKODËR
TIRANË
DURRËS
155
150
128
129
E
F
G
H
1
2
3
4
5
6
Užice
Ужице
Čačak
Чачак
Kraljevo
Краљево
Kruševac
Крушевац
Novi Pazar
Нови Пазар
Kosovska Mitrovica
Косовска Митровица
Priština
Приштина
Peć
Пећ
Đakovica
Ђаковица
Prizren
Призрен
Uroševac
PODGORICA
ПОДГОРИЦА
Cetinje
Цетиње
Nikšić
Никшић
Bar
Бар
Ulcinj
Улцињ
SHKODËR
Lezhë
Krujë
Tetovo
Тетово
Gostivar
Kičevo
Debar
Дебар
Mavrovo
Маврово
Pljevlja
Пљевља
Višegrad
Prijepolje
Priboj
Bijelo Polje
Mojkovac
Kolašin
Berane
Rožaj
Sjenica
Tutin
Ivanjica
Raška
Vrnjačka Banja
Врњачка Бања
Brus
Kuršumlija
Podujevo
Gnjilane
Vitina
Kačanik
Danilovgrad
Даниловград
Žabljak
Plav
Gusinje
Dečani
Rinas
DRINA KANJON
TARA KANJON
IBARSKA KLISURA
MANASTIR SOPOĆANI
МАН. СОПОЋАНИ
MANASTIR MILEŠEVA
МАН. МИЛЕШЕВА
MAN. VISOKI DEČANI
МАН. ВИСОКИ ДЕЧАНИ
MAN. MORAČA
МАН. МОРАЧА
MANASTIR OSTROG
DURMITOR NAC. PARK
NAC. PARK BIOGRADSKA GORA
ZLATAR NAC. PARK
NAC. PARK KOPAONIK
ŠARA NAC. PARK
NACIONALNI PARK MAVROVO
SVETI JOVAN BIGORSKI
СВ. ЈОВАН БИГОРСКИ
ĐURĐEVI STUPOVI
ЂУРЂЕВИ СТУПОВИ
MAN. GRADAC
МАН. ГРАДАЦ
MANASTIR LJUBOSTINJA
МАН. ЉУБОСТИЊА
Skadarsko Jezero
Liqeni i Shkodrës
KOPAONIK
ROGOZNA
MOKRA GORA
HAJLA
GILJEVO
JADOVIK
ZLATAR
ZLATIBOR
ČEMERNA PL.
ŽELIN
KOSOVO
SUVA GORA
MI KRESHTES
SKANDERBEUT
MIRDITE
DUKAGJIN

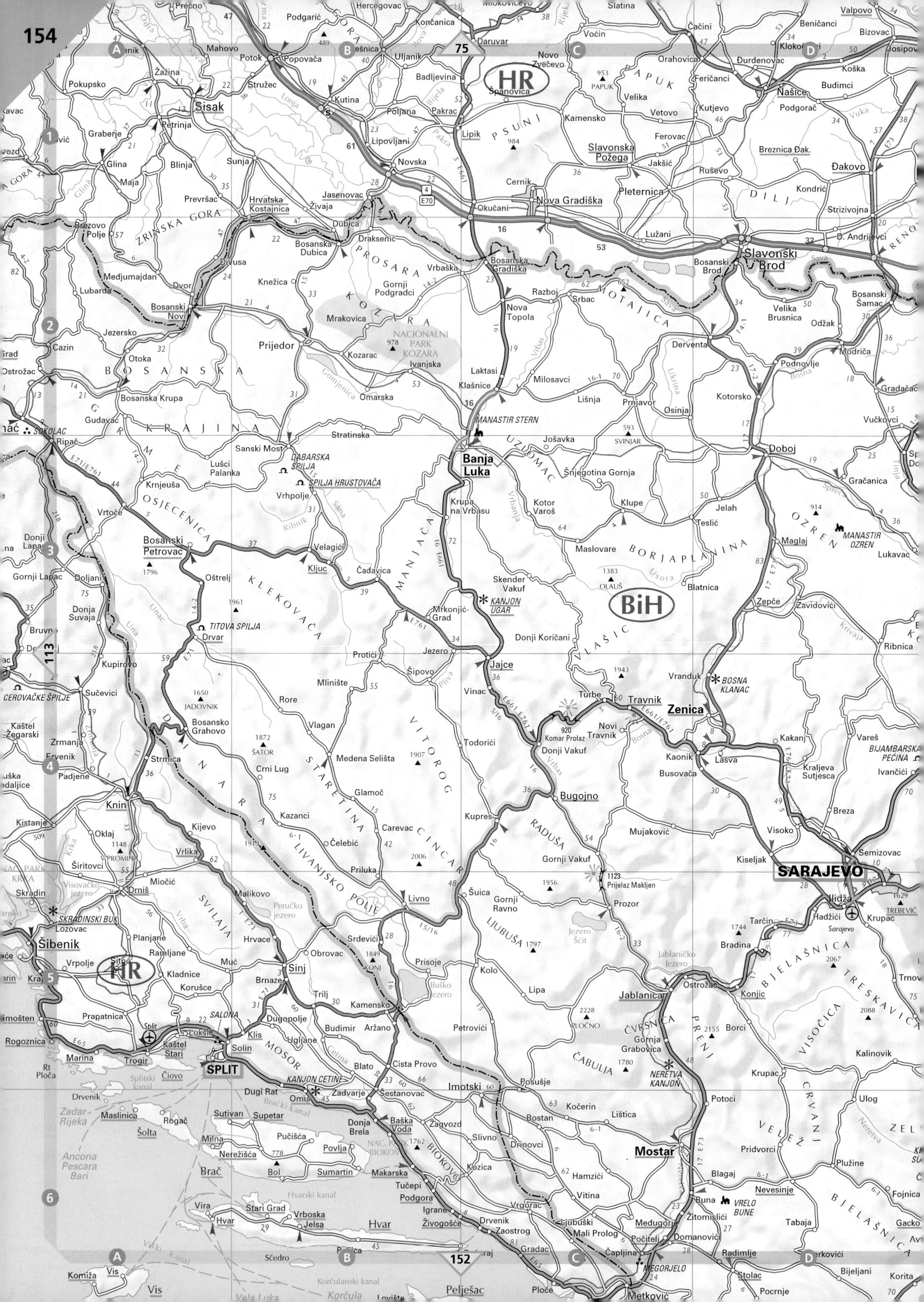

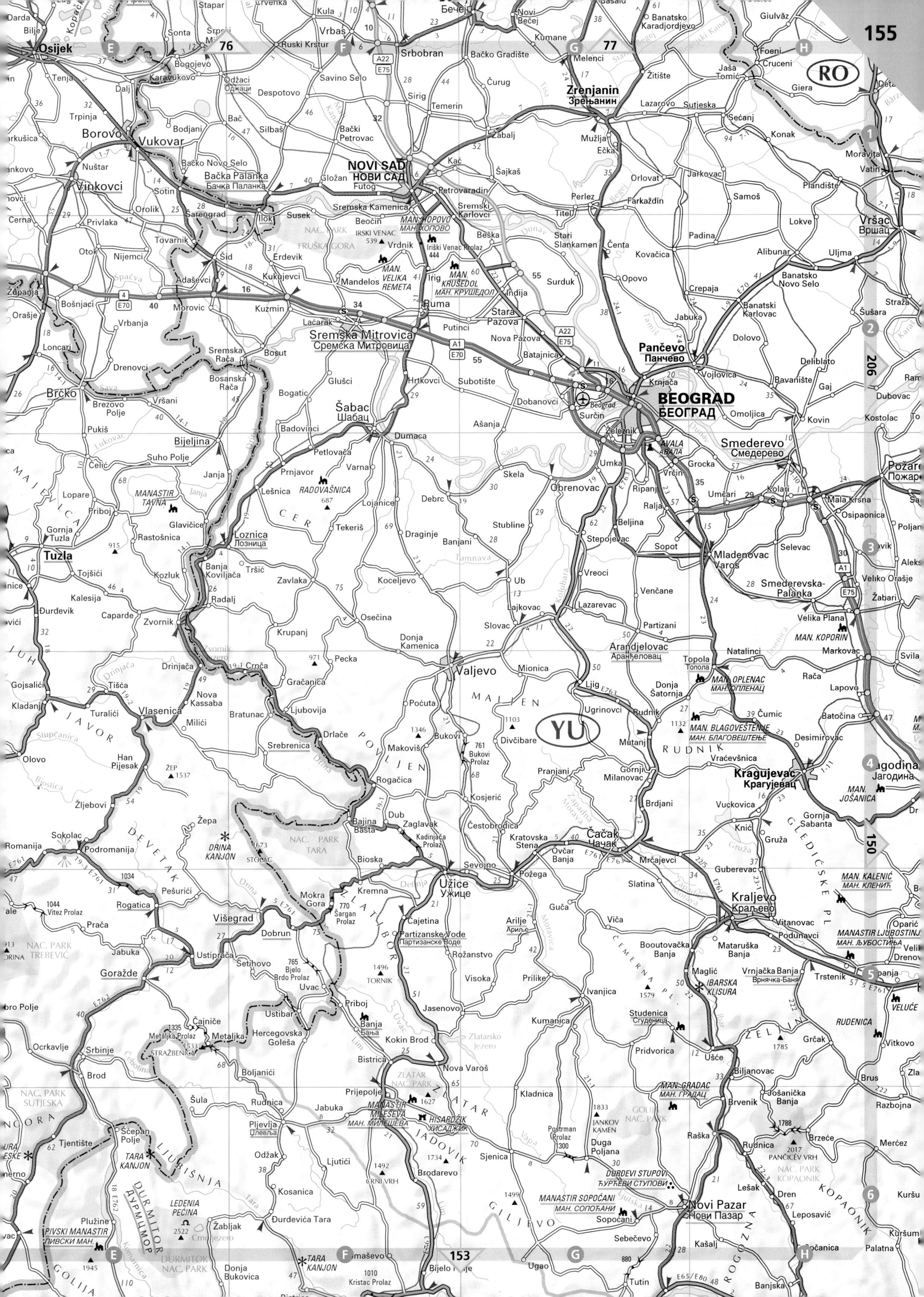

76
77
153
206
150
RO
YU
Osijek
Vukovar
Borovo
Vinkovci
Županja
Brčko
Tuzla
Zvornik
Bijeljina
Loznica
Лозница
Šabac
Шабац
Sremska Mitrovica
Сремска Митровица
Ruma
NOVI SAD
НОВИ САД
Bačka Palanka
Бачка Паланка
Srbobran
Bečej
Zrenjanin
Зрењанин
Pančevo
Панчево
BEOGRAD
БЕОГРАД
Smederevo
Смедерево
Vršac
Вршац
Valjevo
Arandjelovac
Аранђеловац
Topola
Топола
Kragujevac
Крагујевац
Jagodina
Јагодина
Čačak
Чачак
Kraljevo
Краљево
Užice
Ужице
Višegrad
Goražde
Rogatica
Vlasenica
Srebrenica
Ljubovija
Priboj
Prijepolje
Nova Varoš
Pljevlja
Пљевља
Sjenica
Novi Pazar
Нови Пазар
Raška
Ivanjica
Arilje
Arиље
Požega
Mladenovac
Smederevska Palanka
Velika Plana
Požarevac
Пожаревац
Vrnjačka Banja
Врњачка Баня
Ušće
Kladanj
Olovo
Sokolac
Foča
Srbinje
Žabljak
Plužine
Ilok
Šid
Morović
Sremski Karlovci
Inđija
Stara Pazova
Kovin
Kovačica
Opovo
Alibunar
Plandište
Obrenovac
Lazarevac
Ljig
Mionica
Kosjerić
Bajina Bašta
Zlatibor
Kopaonik
Golija
NAC. PARK FRUŠKA GORA
NAC. PARK TARA
NAC. PARK SUTJESKA
NAC. PARK TREBEVIĆ
ZLATAR NAC. PARK
NAC. PARK KOPAONIK
DURMITOR NAC. PARK
MAN. KRUŠEDOL
МАН. КРУШЕДОЛ
MAN. HOPOVO
МАН. ХОПОВО
MAN. OPLENAC
МАН. ОПЛЕНАЦ
MAN. BLAGOVEŠTENJE
МАН. БЛАГОВЕШТЕЊЕ
MAN. KALENIĆ
МАН. КЛЕНИЋ
MANASTIR LJUBOSTINJA
МАН. ЉУБОСТИЊА
MAN. GRADAC
МАН. ГРАДАЦ
MANASTIR MILEŠEVA
МАН. МИЛЕШЕВА
MANASTIR SOPOĆANI
МАН. СОПОЋАНИ
ĐURĐEVI STUPOVI
ЂУРЂЕВИ СТУПОВИ
PIVSKI MANASTIR
ПИВСКИ МАН.
DRINA KANJON
TARA KANJON
IBARSKA KLISURA
E70
E75
A1
E761
E763
E762
E65/E80

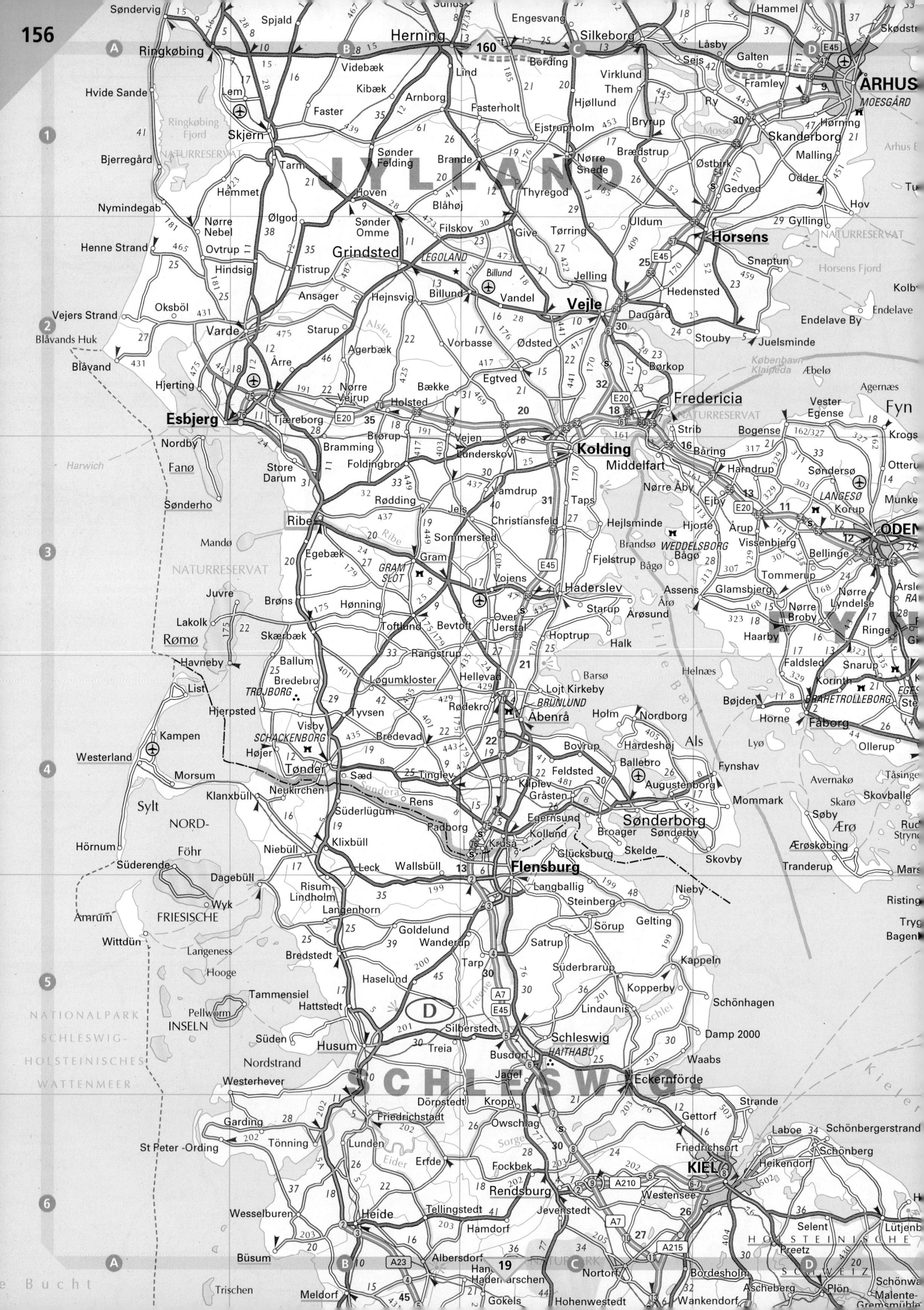
JYLLAND
SCHLESWIG
Fyn
FYN
Søndervig
Spjald
Herning
Engesvang
Silkeborg
Hammel
Skødstrup
Ringkøbing
Videbæk
Lind
Bording
Låsby
Galten
Sejs
ÅRHUS
MOESGÅRD
Hvide Sande
Lem
Kibæk
Arnborg
Fasterholt
Virklund
Them
Framley
Ry
Hjøllund
Ringkøbing Fjord
Faster
Ejstrupholm
Bryrup
Mossø
Hørning
Skanderborg
Århus Bugt
Skjern
Bjerregård
NATURRESERVAT
Tarm
Sønder Felding
Brande
Nørre Snede
Brædstrup
Østbirk
Malling
Odder
Hemmet
Hoven
Blåhøj
Thyregod
Gedved
Nymindegab
Nørre Nebel
Ølgod
Sønder Omme
Filskov
Give
Uldum
Hov
Gylling
Horsens
Tørring
Henne Strand
Ovtrup
Grindsted
LEGOLAND
Billund
Jelling
Snaptun
Horsens Fjord
Hindsig
Tistrup
Hedensted
Ansager
Hejnsvig
Vandel
Vejle
Oksböl
Daugård
Endelave By
Endelave
Vejers Strand
Blåvands Huk
Blåvand
Varde
Starup
Alslev
Vorbasse
Ødsted
Stouby
Juelsminde
Agerbæk
Årre
Børkop
København Klaipeda
Æbelø
Agernæs
Hjerting
Nørre Vejrup
Bække
Egtved
Fredericia
Vester Egense
Esbjerg
Tjæreborg
Holsted
Strib
Bogense
Krogsbølle
Nordby
Brørup
Vejen
Kolding
Bramming
Lunderskov
Middelfart
Båring
Harwich
Fanø
Store Darum
Foldingbro
Harndrup
Søndersø
Otterup
Nørre Aby
Ejby
LANGESØ
Munkebo
Sønderho
Rødding
Vamdrup
Taps
Jels
Korup
Ribe
Christiansfeld
Hejlsminde
Hjorte
Årup
ODENSE
Sommersted
Brandsø
WEDDELSBORG
Bågø
Vissenbjerg
Mandø
Egebæk
Gram
Fjelstrup
Bellinge
GRAM SLOT
Vojens
Tommerup
Juvre
Haderslev
Assens
Glamsbjerg
Årslev
Brøns
Hønning
Starup
Årø
Nørre Lyndelse
Årøsund
Nørre Broby
Lakolk
Toftlund
Bevtoft
Over Jerstal
Rømø
Skærbæk
Hoptrup
Haarby
Ringe
Halk
Havneby
Ballum
Rangstrup
Faldsled
Snarup
Bredebro
Hellevad
Helnæs
Barsø
List
TRØJBORG
Løgumkloster
Lojt Kirkeby
Korinth
Rødekro
BRUNLUND
BRAHETROLLEBORG
Bøjden
Hjerpsted
Tyvsen
Holm
Nordborg
Aabenraa
Horne
Fåborg
Kampen
Visby
Hardeshøj
Als
SCHACKENBORG
Bredevad
Lyø
Ollerup
Westerland
Højer
Bovrup
Ballebro
Fynshav
Tønder
Feldsted
Augustenborg
Avernakø
Tåsinge
Morsum
Sæd
Tinglev
Kliplev
Mommark
Skovballe
Klanxbüll
Neukirchen
Søndera
Gråsten
Skarø
Rens
Søby
Sylt
NORD-
Süderlügum
Egernsund
Sønderborg
Ærø
Padborg
Broager
Sønderby
Kollund
Hörnum
Klixbüll
Kruså
Ærøskøbing
Föhr
Niebüll
Glücksburg
Skelde
Skovby
Süderende
Leck
Wallsbüll
Flensburg
Tranderup
Dagebüll
Risum-Lindholm
Langballig
Nieby
Risting
Wyk
Steinberg
Langenhorn
Amrum
FRIESISCHE
Sörup
Gelting
Goldelund
Wanderup
Satrup
Wittdün
Langeness
Bredstedt
Tarp
Kappeln
Hooge
Haselund
Süderbrarup
Tammensiel
Kopperby
Hattstedt
Lindaunis
Schönhagen
NATIONALPARK SCHLESWIG-HOLSTEINISCHES WATTENMEER
Pellworm
INSELN
Treene
Schlei
D
Silberstedt
Schleswig
Damp 2000
Süden
Husum
Treia
Busdorf
HAITHABU
Waabs
Nordstrand
Jagel
Eckernförde
Westerhever
Dörpstedt
Kropp
Strande
Friedrichstadt
Owschlag
Gettorf
Laboe
Schönbergerstrand
Garding
Sorge
Friedrichsort
Schönberg
St Peter -Ording
Tönning
Lunden
Eider
Erfde
Fockbek
KIEL
Heikendorf
Rendsburg
Westensee
Wesselburen
Heide
Tellingstedt
Jevenstedt
Hamdorf
Selent
Lütjenburg
HOLSTEINISCHE SCHWEIZ
Preetz
Büsum
Albersdorf
Hanerau-Hademarschen
NATURPARK
Nortorf
Bordesholm
Trischen
Meldorf
Gokels
Hohenwestedt
Wankendorf
Ascheberg
Plön
Schönwalde
Malente-Gremsmühlen
Bucht

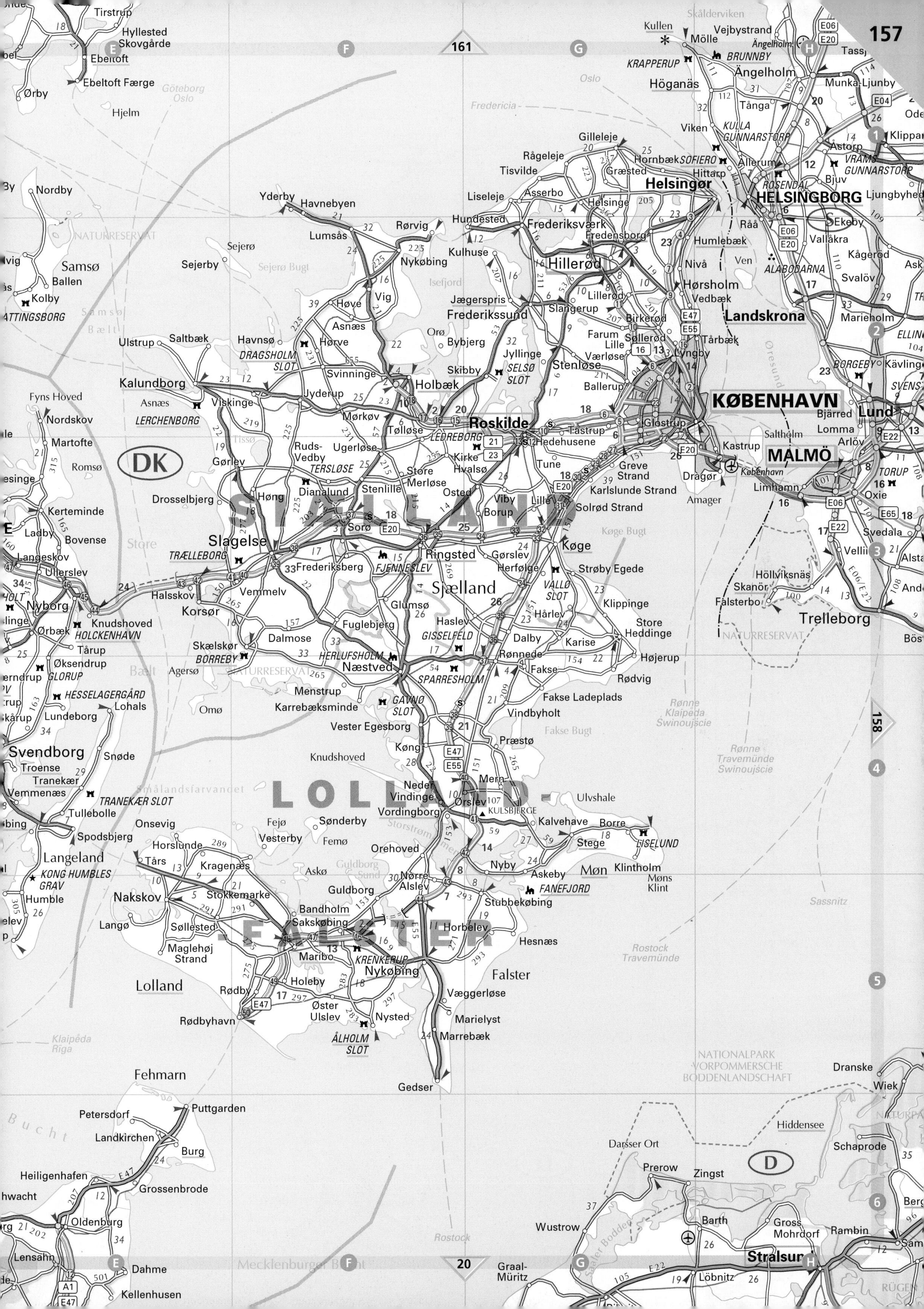
161
Tirstrup
Hyllested
Skovgårde
Ebeltoft
Ebeltoft Færge
Ørby
Hjelm
Kullen
Mölle
Vejbystrand
Ängelholm
Skälderviken
KRAPPERUP
BRUNNBY
Höganäs
Munka-Ljunby
Tånga
Viken
KULLA GUNNARSTORP
Klippan
Åstorp
VRAMS GUNNARSTORP
Gilleleje
Rågeleje
Tisvilde
Hornbæk
SOFIERO
Hittarp
Græsted
Allerum
Bjuv
Helsingør
ROSENDAL
HELSINGBORG
Ljungbyhed
Nordby
Yderby
Havnebyen
Liseleje
Asserbo
Helsinge
Hundested
Frederiksværk
Råå
Ekeby
Rørvig
Lumsås
Fredensborg
Humlebæk
Vallåkra
Kågeröd
Sejerø
Sejerby
Sejerø Bugt
Nykøbing
Kulhuse
Hillerød
Nivå
Ven
ALABODARNA
Svalöv
Samsø
Ballen
Kolby
Hørsholm
Vedbæk
Vig
Isefjord
Lillerød
Høve
Jægerspris
Frederikssund
Slangerup
Birkerød
Landskrona
Marieholm
VISBORG
ATTINGSBORG
Asnæs
Orø
Bybjerg
Farum
Søllerød
Tårbæk
Ulstrup
Saltbæk
Havnsø
Hørve
Lille Værløse
Lyngby
DRAGSHOLM SLOT
Svinninge
Skibby
Jyllinge
SELSØ SLOT
Stenløse
Ballerup
Kalundborg
Holbæk
BORGEBY
Kävlinge
Fyns Hoved
Asnæs
Viskinge
Jyderup
Mørkøv
KØBENHAVN
Bjärred
Lund
Nordskov
LERCHENBORG
Tølløse
Roskilde
Tåstrup
Glostrup
Lomma
Saltholm
Martofte
LEDREBORG
Hedehusene
Kastrup
Arlöv
Romsø
DK
Tissø
Ruds-Vedby
Ugerløse
Kirke Hvalsø
Tune
Greve Strand
Dragør
MALMÖ
TORUP
Gørlev
TERSLØSE
Store Merløse
Osted
Karlslunde Strand
København
Limhamn
Oxie
Kerteminde
Drosselbjerg
Høng
Dianalund
Stenlille
Viby
Lille
Solrød Strand
Amager
Ladby
SJÆLLAND
Borup
Svedala
Bovense
Slagelse
Sorø
Køge Bugt
Store
Langeskov
TRÆLLEBORG
Ringsted
Gørslev
Køge
Vellinge
Ullerslev
Frederiksberg
FJENNESLEV
Herfølge
Strøby Egede
Höllviksnäs
Nyborg
Halsskov
Korsør
Vemmelv
Sjælland
VALLØ SLOT
Skanör
Falsterbo
Klippinge
Knudshoved
HOLCKENHAVN
Glumsø
Hårlev
Trelleborg
Ørbæk
Fuglebjerg
Haslev
Store Heddinge
Tårup
Dalmose
GISSELFELD
Dalby
Karise
NATURRESERVAT
Skælskør
BORREBY
HERLUFSHOLM
Rønnede
Højerup
Øksendrup
Agersø
Næstved
Fakse
GLORUP
SPARRESHOLM
Rødvig
HESSELAGERGÅRD
Menstrup
Lohals
Karrebæksminde
GAVNØ SLOT
Fakse Ladeplads
Rønne
Klaipeda
Swinoujscie
Omø
Vindbyholt
Lundeborg
Vester Egesborg
Fakse Bugt
Præstø
Kong
Svendborg
Knudshoved
Travemünde
Troense
Snøde
Tranekær
Smålandsfarvandet
Neder Vindinge
LOLLAND-
Mern
Ulvshale
Vemmenæs
TRANEKÆR SLOT
KULSBJERGE
Tullebolle
Vordingborg
Ørslev
Onsevig
Fejø
Sønderby
Kalvehave
Borre
Spodsbjerg
Vesterby
Femø
Storstrøm
Stege
LISELUND
Horslunde
Langeland
Orehoved
Tårs
Kragenæs
Guldborg Sund
Nyby
Klintholm
KONG HUMBLES GRAV
Askø
Nørre Alslev
Askeby
Møn
Møns Klint
Humble
Nakskov
Stokkemarke
Guldborg
FANEFJORD
Stubbekøbing
Sassnitz
Bandholm
Sakskøbing
Horbelev
Langø
Søllested
FALSTER
Hesnæs
Maglehøj Strand
Maribo
KRENKERUP
Nykøbing
Rostock
Lolland
Falster
Holeby
Rødby
Vaeggerløse
Øster Ulslev
Nysted
Marielyst
Rødbyhavn
ÅLHOLM SLOT
Marrebæk
Klaipėda
Riga
NATIONALPARK VORPOMMERSCHE BODDENLANDSCHAFT
Dranske
Wiek
Fehmarn
Gedser
Puttgarden
Petersdorf
Hiddensee
Landkirchen
Burg
Darsser Ort
Schaprode
D
Heiligenhafen
Grossenbrode
Prerow
Zingst
Oldenburg
Wustrow
Barth
Gross Mohrdorf
Rambin
Lensahn
Rostock
Mecklenburger Bucht
Dahme
Graal-Müritz
Stralsund
Löbnitz
Kellenhusen
RÜGEN
158
20

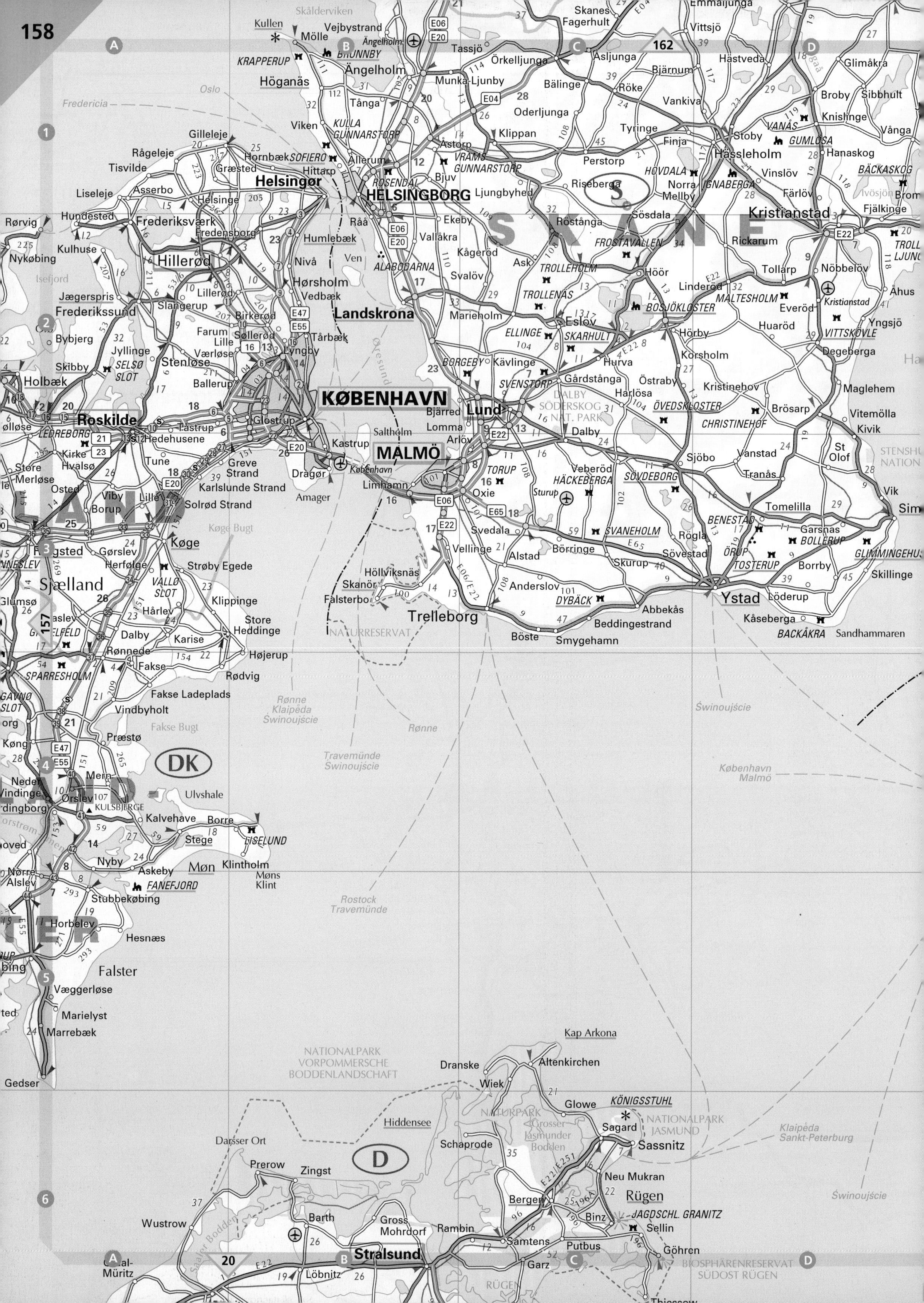
Kullen
Mölle
Ängelholm
Höganäs
Helsingør
HELSINGBORG
Hillerød
Landskrona
KØBENHAVN
Lund
MALMÖ
Roskilde
Køge
Sjælland
Trelleborg
Ystad
Kristianstad
Hässleholm
Eslöv
Höör
Skanör
Falsterbo
Stralsund
Rügen
Sassnitz
Bergen
Binz
Prerow
Zingst
Barth
Falster
Møn
Stege
Gedser
SKÅNE
DK
D
162
157
20

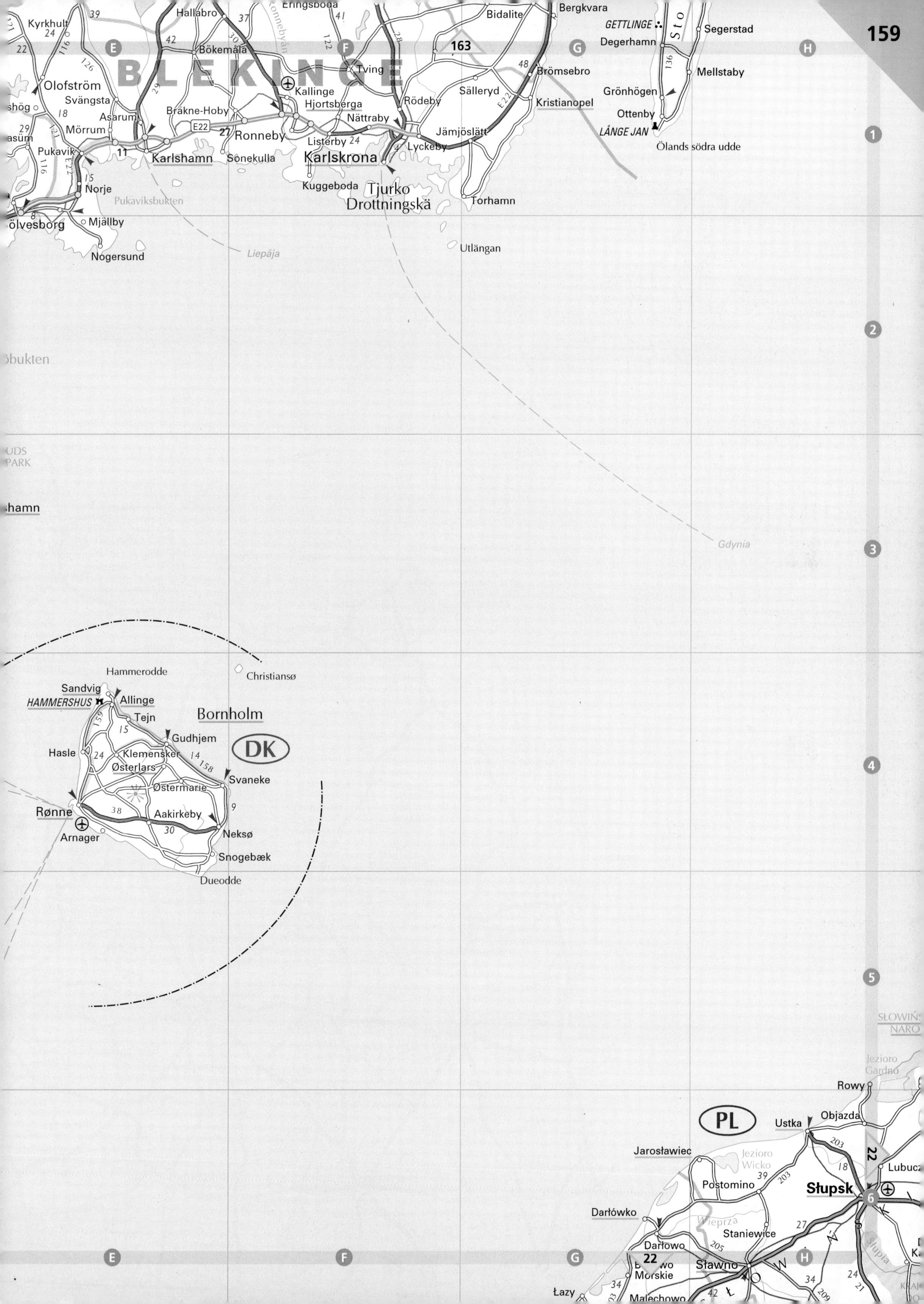
BLEKINGE
Kyrkhult
Hallabro
Eringsboda
Bidalite
Bergkvara
GETTLINGE
Degerhamn
Segerstad
Mellstaby
Grönhögen
Ottenby
LÅNGE JAN
Ölands södra udde
Bökemåla
Tving
Kallinge
Olofström
Svängsta
Asarum
Mörrum
Pukavik
Bräkne-Hoby
Ronneby
Hjortsberga
Nättraby
Rödeby
Sälleryd
Brömsebro
Kristianopel
Jämjöslätt
Listerby
Lyckeby
Karlshamn
Sonekulla
Karlskrona
Norje
Kuggeboda
Tjurko
Drottningskä
Torhamn
Pukaviksbukten
Mjällby
Nogersund
Liepāja
Utlängan
Gdynia
Hammerodde
Christiansø
Sandvig
HAMMERSHUS
Allinge
Tejn
Bornholm
Gudhjem
DK
Hasle
Klemensker
Østerlars
Svaneke
Østermarie
Rønne
Aakirkeby
Arnager
Neksø
Snogebæk
Dueodde
PL
Rowy
Objazda
Ustka
Jarosławiec
Jezioro Wicko
Postomino
Słupsk
Lubuc
Darłówko
Wieprza
Staniewice
Darłowo
Sławno
Morskie
Łazy
Malechowo
Jezioro Gardno
SŁOWIŃ NARO

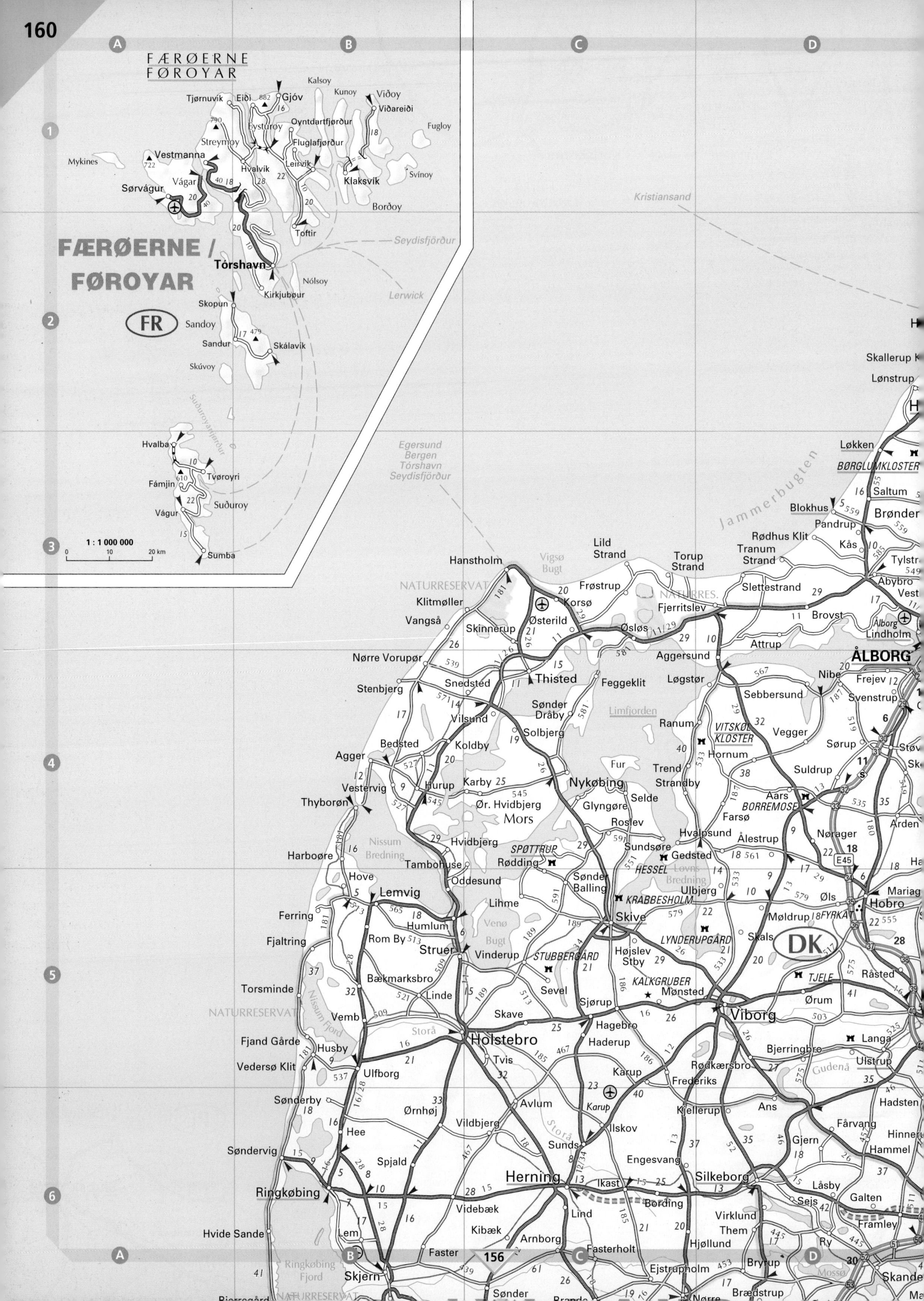

FÆRØERNE
FØROYAR
FÆRØERNE / FØROYAR
FR
1 : 1 000 000
Kalsoy
Kunoy
Viðoy
Viðareiði
Tjørnuvík
Eiði
Gjóv
Eysturoy
Oyntdartfjørður
Fugloy
Streymoy
Fuglafjørður
Mykines
Vestmanna
Leirvík
Svínoy
Hvalvík
Klaksvík
Sørvágur
Vágar
Borðoy
Toftir
Tórshavn
Nólsoy
Kirkjubøur
Skopun
Sandoy
Sandur
Skálavík
Skúvoy
Hvalba
Tvøroyri
Fámjin
Suðuroy
Vágur
Sumba
Seydisfjörður
Lerwick
Kristiansand
Egersund
Bergen
Tórshavn
Seydisfjörður
Jammerbugten
Skallerup
Lønstrup
Løkken
BØRGLUMKLOSTER
Saltum
Blokhus
Brønder
Pandrup
Rødhus Klit
Kås
Tranum Strand
Torup Strand
Lild Strand
Tylstr
Hanstholm
Vigsø Bugt
NATURRESERVAT
Frøstrup
Slettestrand
Abybro
Vest
Klitmøller
Korsø
NATURRES.
Fjerritslev
Brovst
Vangså
Østerild
Ålborg
Skinnerup
Øsløs
Lindholm
Attrup
ÅLBORG
Nørre Vorupør
Aggersund
Thisted
Feggeklit
Løgstør
Nibe
Frejev
Stenbjerg
Snedsted
Sebbersund
Svenstrup
Sønder Dråby
Limfjorden
Vilsund
Ranum
VITSKØL KLOSTER
Vegger
Solbjerg
Bedsted
Sørup
Koldby
Hornum
Agger
Fur
Suldrup
Trend
Hurup
Karby
Nykøbing
Strandby
Vestervig
Aars
Ør. Hvidbjerg
Selde
BORREMOSE
Thyborøn
Mors
Glyngøre
Farsø
Arden
Roslev
Nørager
Hvalpsund
Hvidbjerg
Nissum Bredning
Sundsøre
Ålestrup
Harboøre
SPØTTRUP
Gedsted
Rødding
Tambohuse
HESSEL
Lovns Bredning
Hove
Sønder Balling
Ulbjerg
Mariag
Oddesund
Lemvig
Øls
Hobro
KRABBESHOLM
Lihme
Ferring
Humlum
Skive
Møldrup
FYRKAT
Venø Bugt
Fjaltring
Rom By
LYNDERUPGÅRD
Skals
DK
Struer
Vinderup
STUBBERGÅRD
Højslev Stby
Bækmarksbro
TJELE
Råsted
Torsminde
Sevel
KALKGRUBER
Linde
Mønsted
Ørum
Vemb
Sjørup
Viborg
Skave
Hagebro
Langa
Fjand Gårde
Holstebro
Haderup
Bjerringbro
Husby
Tvis
Vedersø Klit
Ulfborg
Rødkærsbro
Ulstrup
Karup
Gudenå
Frederiks
Sønderby
Avlum
Hadsten
Ørnhøj
Kjellerup
Ans
Hee
Vildbjerg
Ilskov
Fårvang
Sunds
Gjern
Hinneru
Søndervig
Spjald
Engesvang
Hammel
Herning
Silkeborg
Ringkøbing
Ikast
Låsby
Videbæk
Bording
Sejs
Galten
Lind
Virklund
Framley
Kibæk
Them
Hvide Sande
Lem
Arnborg
Hjøllund
Ry
Faster
Fasterholt
156
Ringkøbing Fjord
Skjern
Ejstrupholm
Bryrup
Mossø
Skande
Sønder
Nørre
Brædstrup
Storå
Nissum Fjord
A
B
C
D
1
2
3
4
5
6

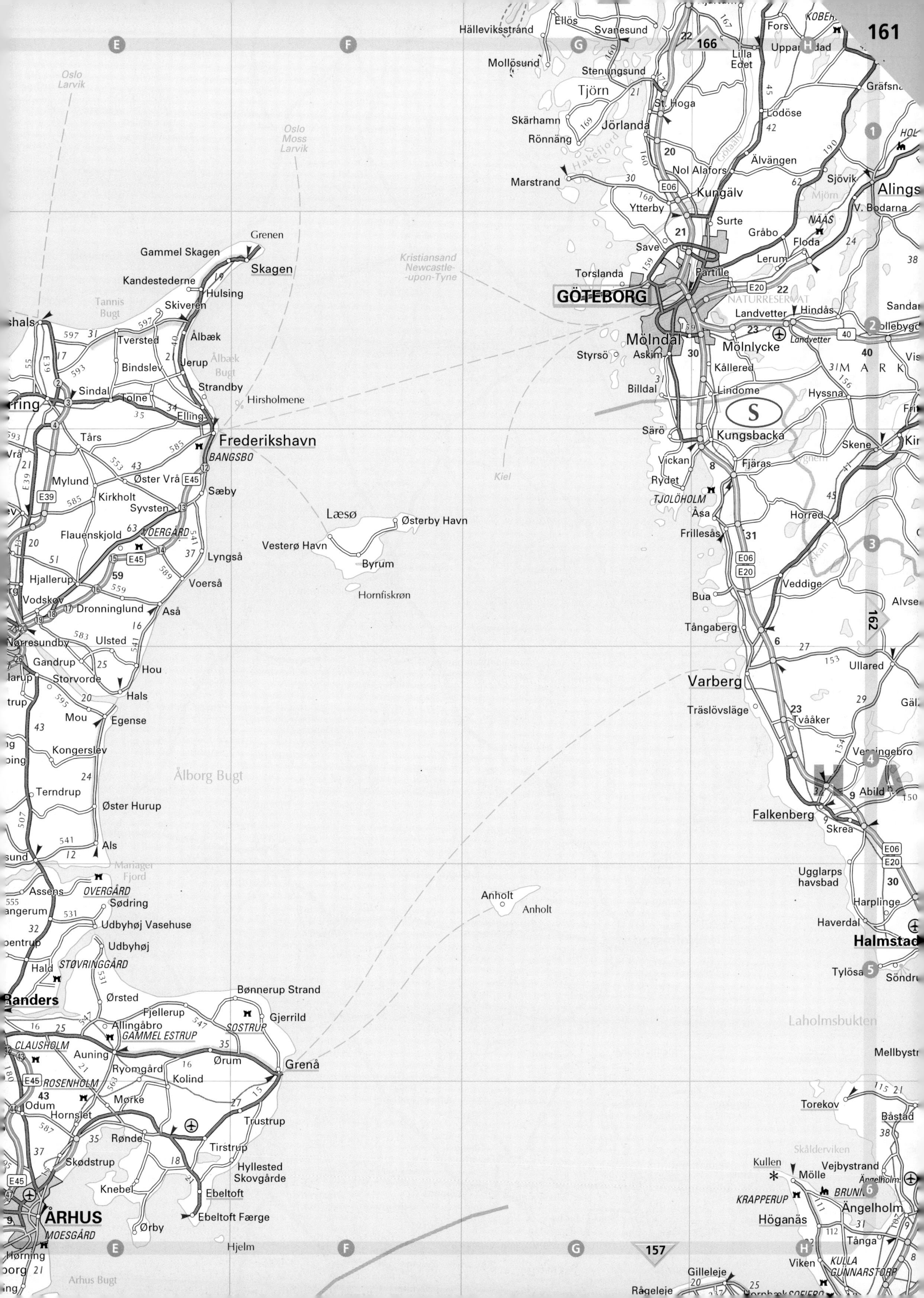

Skagen
Grenen
Gammel Skagen
Kandestederne
Hulsing
Skiveren
Tannis Bugt
Tversted
Ålbæk
Bindslev
Jerup
Ålbæk Bugt
Strandby
Hirsholmene
Sindal
Tolne
Elling
Tårs
Frederikshavn
BANGSBO
Mylund
Øster Vrå
Kirkholt
Sæby
Syvsten
Flauenskjold
VOERGÅRD
Lyngså
Hjallerup
Voerså
Vodskov
Dronninglund
Aså
Nørresundby
Ulsted
Gandrup
Hou
Storvorde
Hals
Mou
Egense
Kongerslev
Terndrup
Øster Hurup
Als
Mariager Fjord
Assens
OVERGÅRD
Sødring
Udbyhøj Vasehuse
Udbyhøj
Hald
STØVRINGGÅRD
Randers
Ørsted
Fjellerup
Bønnerup Strand
Gjerrild
Allingåbro
GAMMEL ESTRUP
SOSTRUP
CLAUSHOLM
Auning
Ørum
Grenå
Ryomgård
Kolind
ROSENHOLM
Odum
Mørke
Hornslet
Trustrup
Rønde
Tirstrup
Skødstrup
Hyllested Skovgårde
Knebel
Ebeltoft
ÅRHUS
MOESGÅRD
Ebeltoft Færge
Ørby
Hørning
Hjelm
Århus Bugt
Ålborg Bugt
Læsø
Østerby Havn
Vesterø Havn
Byrum
Hornfiskrøn
Anholt
Oslo Larvik
Oslo Moss Larvik
Kristiansand Newcastle-upon-Tyne
Kiel
Hälleviksstrand
Ellös
Svanesund
Mollösund
Stenungsund
Tjörn
St. Hoga
Skärhamn
Jörlanda
Rönnäng
Hakefjord
Marstrand
Nol Alafors
Kungälv
Ytterby
Surte
Save
Torslanda
GÖTEBORG
Partille
Lerum
Gråbo
Floda
Lilla Edet
Uppsala
Fors
Lödöse
Älvängen
Sjövik
Alings
V. Bodarna
NÄÄS
Mjörn
Gräfsnäs
NATURRESERVAT
Landvetter
Hindås
Mölndal
Mölnlycke
Styrsö
Askim
Kållered
Billdal
Lindome
Hyssna
MARK
Särö
Kungsbacka
Skene
Vickan
Fjärås
Rydet
TJOLÖHOLM
Åsa
Horred
Frillesås
Veddige
Bua
Tångaberg
Ullared
Varberg
Träslövsläge
Tvååker
Vessigebro
Abild
Falkenberg
Skrea
Ugglarps havsbad
Harplinge
Haverdal
Halmstad
Tylösa
Laholmsbukten
Mellbystr
Torekov
Båstad
Skälderviken
Kullen
Mölle
Vejbystrand
Ängelholm
KRAPPERUP
Höganäs
Tånga
Viken
KULLA GUNNARSTORP
Gilleleje
Rågeleje
166
162
157
E
F
G
H

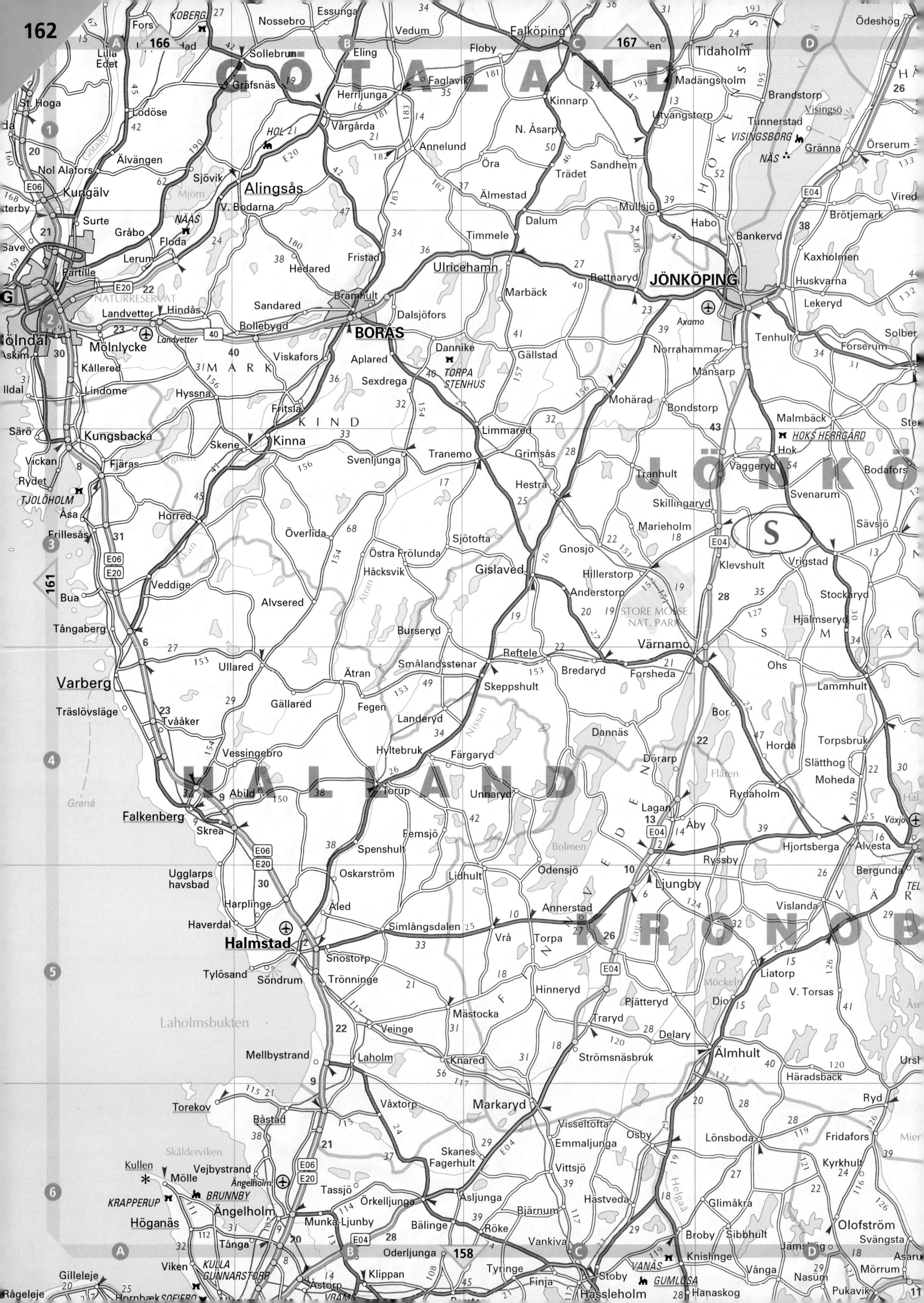
GÖTALAND
HALLAND
JÖNKÖ
KRONOB
Alingsås
Kungälv
Borås
Jönköping
Ulricehamn
Varberg
Falkenberg
Halmstad
Värnamo
Ljungby
Älmhult
Markaryd
Ängelholm
Höganäs
Hässleholm
Gislaved
Kungsbacka
Mölnlycke
Laholmsbukten
Bolmen
STORE MOSSE NAT. PARK
166
167
161
158

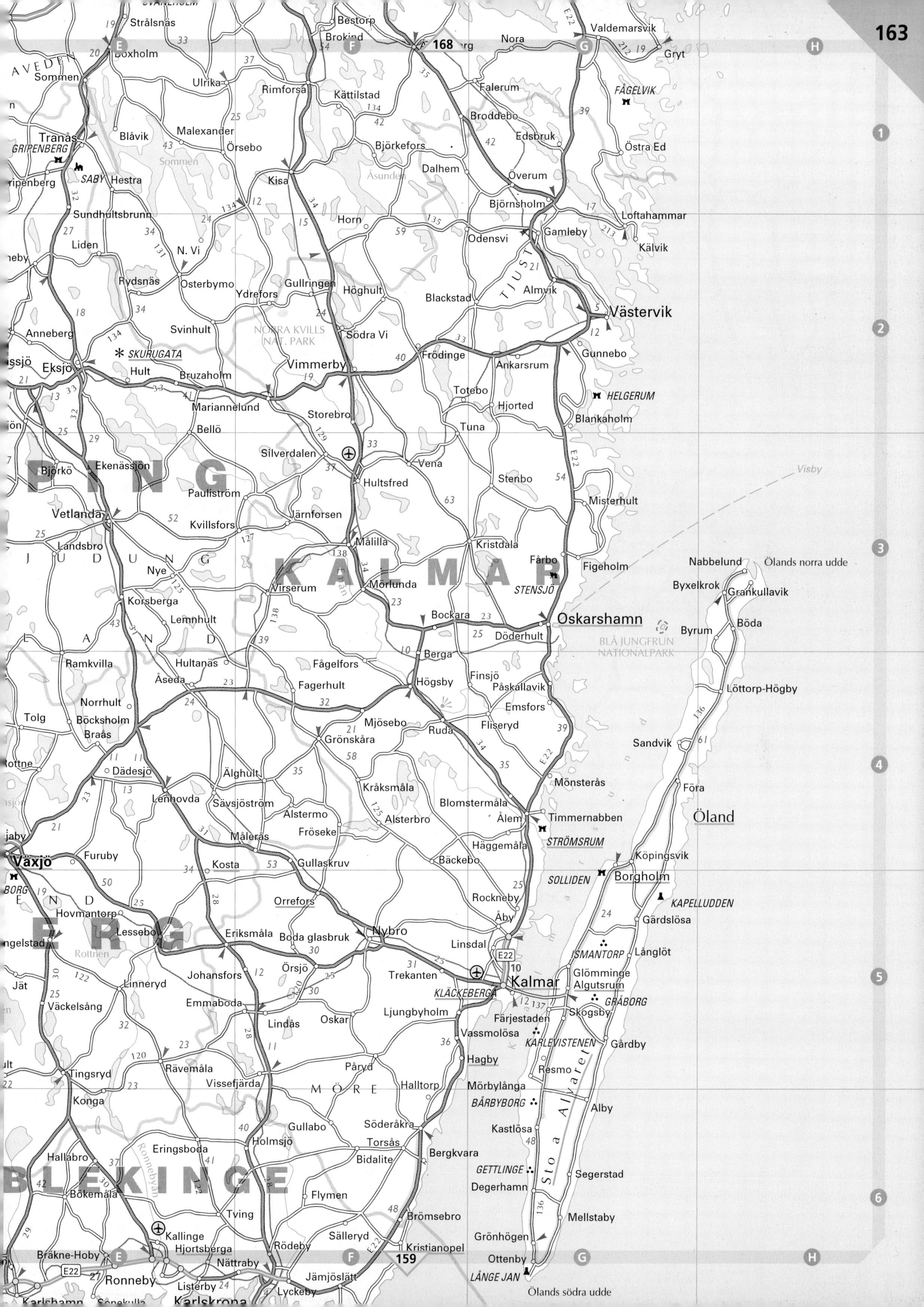

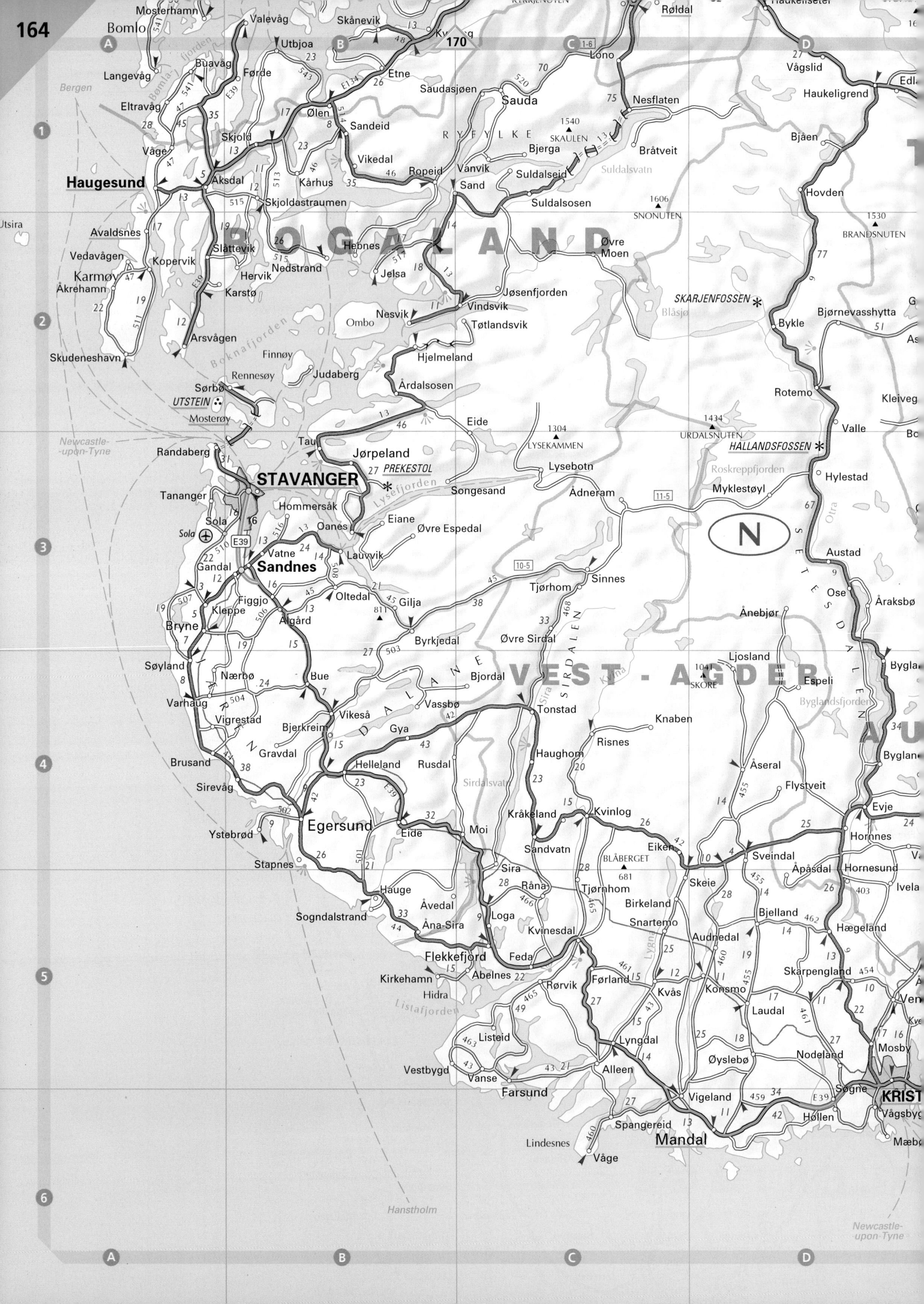
170
BOGALAND
VEST - AGDER
RYFYLKE
SETESDALEN
SIRDALEN
DALANE
JÆREN
N
Bømlafjorden
Boknafjorden
Lysefjorden
Listafjorden
Suldalsvatn
Bergen
Newcastle-upon-Tyne
Hanstholm
Mosterhamn
Bomlo
Valevåg
Skånevik
Røldal
Utbjoa
Langevåg
Buavåg
Førde
Etne
Lono
Vågslid
Haukeligrend
Saudasjøen
Sauda
Nesflaten
Eltravåg
Ølen
Sandeid
SKAULEN
Bjåen
Skjold
Bjerga
Bråtveit
Våge
Vikedal
Ropeid
Vanvik
Suldalseid
Haugesund
Aksdal
Kårhus
Sand
Hovden
Skjoldastraumen
Suldalsosen
SNONUTEN
Utsira
Avaldsnes
BRANDSNUTEN
Vedavågen
Slåttevik
Hebnes
Øvre Moen
Kopervik
Nedstrand
Karmøy
Hervik
Jelsa
Åkrehamn
Karstø
Josenfjorden
SKARJENFOSSEN
Vindsvik
Blåsjø
Ombo
Nesvik
Bjørnevasshytta
Bykle
Arsvågen
Tøtlandsvik
Finnøy
Skudeneshavn
Hjelmeland
Rennesøy
Judaberg
Sørbø
Rotemo
Årdalsosen
UTSTEIN
Mosterøy
Kleiveg
Eide
URDALSNUTEN
Valle
LYSEKAMMEN
HALLANDSFOSSEN
Randaberg
Tau
Jørpeland
PREKESTOL
Lysebotn
Roskreppfjorden
STAVANGER
Hylestad
Tananger
Songesand
Ådneram
Myklestøyl
Hommersåk
Sola
Eiane
Oanes
Øvre Espedal
Vatne
Lauvvik
Austad
Gandal
Sandnes
Sinnes
Tjørhom
Ose
Figgjo
Oltedal
Gilja
Åraksbø
Kleppe
Ålgård
Ånebjør
Bryne
Byrkjedal
Øvre Sirdal
Ljosland
Bygland
Søyland
Nærbø
Bue
Bjordal
SKORE
Espeli
Varhaug
Vassbø
Tonstad
Byglandsfjorden
Vigrestad
Vikeså
Knaben
Bjerkreim
Gya
Risnes
Gravdal
Haughom
Åseral
Brusand
Helleland
Rusdal
Byglandsfjord
Sirevåg
Sirdalsvatn
Flystveit
Kråkeland
Kvinlog
Evje
Egersund
Eide
Moi
Hornnes
Ystebrød
Sandvatn
Eiken
Sveindal
Stapnes
Sira
BLÅBERGET
Åpåsdal
Hornesund
Råna
Skeie
Ivela
Hauge
Tjørnhom
Åvedal
Loga
Birkeland
Bjelland
Sogndalstrand
Åna-Sira
Snartemo
Hægeland
Kvinesdal
Audnedal
Flekkefjord
Feda
Skarpengland
Kirkehamn
Abelnes
Rørvik
Førland
Kvås
Konsmo
Hidra
Laudal
Listeid
Lyngdal
Nodeland
Mosby
Vestbygd
Vanse
Alleen
Øyslebø
Farsund
Vigeland
Søgne
Spangereid
Høllen
Vågsbygd
Lindesnes
Mandal
Våge

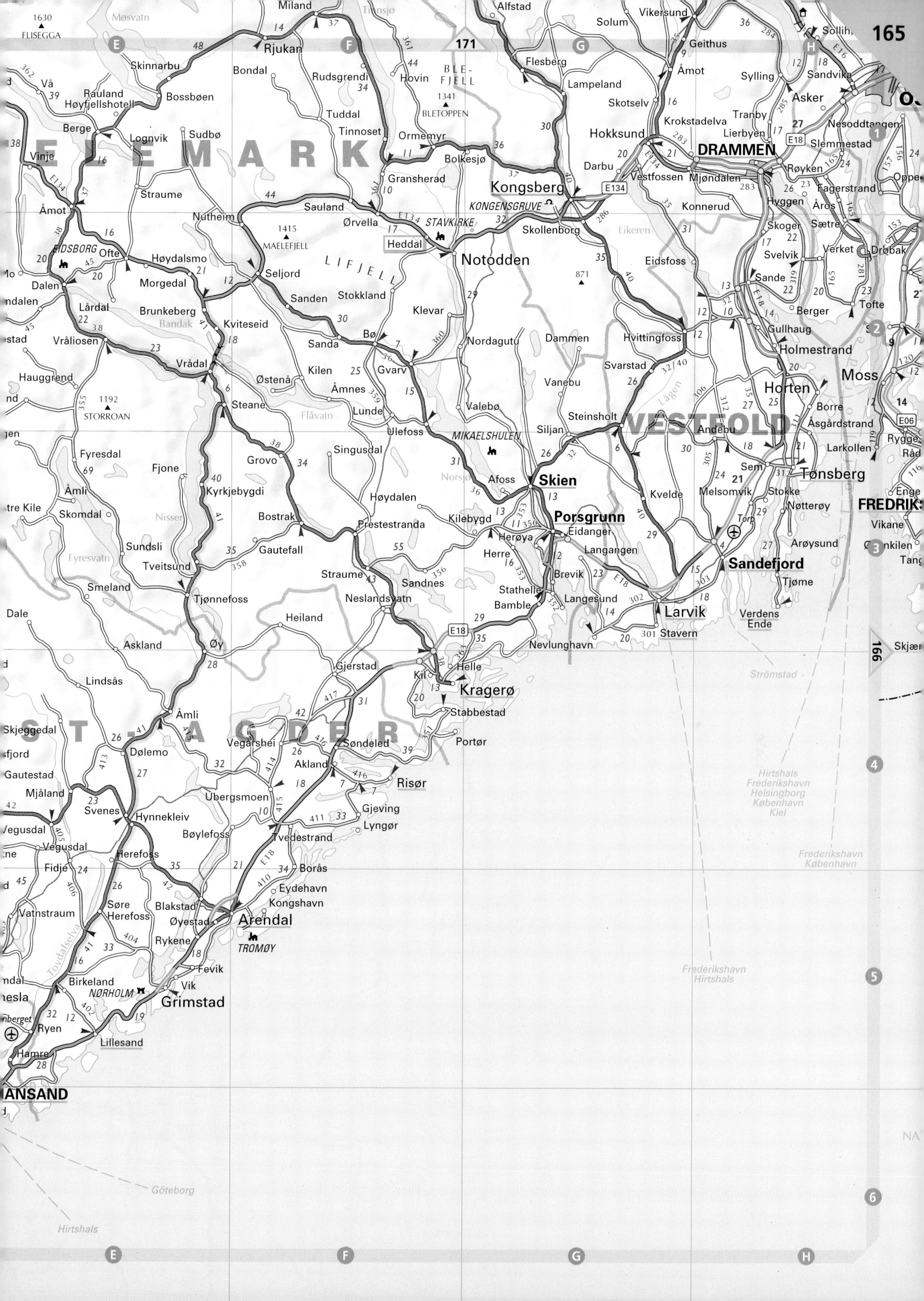
171
166
TELEMARK
VESTFOLD
AUST-AGDER
Møsvatn
FLISEGGA
Miland
Tinnsjø
Alfstad
Solum
Vikersund
Geithus
Sollihøgda
Rjukan
Skinnarbu
Bondal
Rudsgrendi
Hovin
BLEFJELL
BLETOPPEN
Flesberg
Åmot
Sylling
Sandvika
Asker
Vå
Rauland Høyfjellshotell
Bossbøen
Tuddal
Lampeland
Skotselv
Krokstadelva
Tranby
Nesoddtangen
Berge
Lognvik
Sudbø
Tinnoset
Ormemyr
Hokksund
Lierbyen
DRAMMEN
Slemmestad
Vinje
Bolkesjø
Darbu
Vestfossen
Mjøndalen
Røyken
Oppegård
Straume
Gransherad
Kongsberg
Fagerstrand
KONGENSGRUVE
Hyggen
Åros
Åmot
Nutheim
Sauland
Ørvella
STAVKIRKE
Skollenborg
Konnerud
Skoger
Sætre
MAELEFJELL
Heddal
Eikeren
Svelvik
Verket
Drøbak
EIDSBORG
Ofte
Høydalsmo
Notodden
LIFJELL
Seljord
Eidsfoss
Sande
Dalen
Morgedal
Sanden
Stokkland
Berger
Tofte
Lårdal
Brunkeberg
Kviteseid
Klevar
Bandak
Gullhaug
Vråliosen
Sanda
Bø
Nordagutu
Dammen
Hvittingfoss
Holmestrand
Vrådal
Kilen
Gvarv
Svarstad
Moss
Hauggrend
Østenå
Åmnes
Vanebu
Horten
STORROAN
Steane
Flåvatn
Lunde
Valebø
Lågen
Borre
Steinsholt
Åsgårdstrand
Ulefoss
MIKAELSHULEN
Siljan
Andebu
Rygge
Fyresdal
Singusdal
Larkollen
Fjone
Grovo
Norsjø
Afoss
Skien
Sem
Tønsberg
Kyrkjebygdi
Åmli
Høydalen
Kvelde
Melsomvik
Stokke
Skomdal
Nissen
Bostrak
Kilebygd
Porsgrunn
Nøtterøy
FREDRIKSTAD
Prestestranda
Herøya
Eidanger
Torp
Vikane
Sundsli
Gautefall
Herre
Langangen
Arøysund
Fyresvatn
Tveitsund
Brevik
Sandefjord
Straume
Sandnes
Tjøme
Smeland
Neslandsvatn
Stathelle
Langesund
Tjønnefoss
Bamble
Larvik
Verdens Ende
Dale
Heiland
Stavern
Askland
Øy
Nevlunghavn
Skjærhalden
Gjerstad
Helle
Strömstad
Lindsås
Kil
Kragerø
Stabbestad
Åmli
Skjeggedal
Vegårshei
Søndeled
Portør
Dølemo
Akland
Gautestad
Risør
Mjåland
Ubergsmoen
Svenes
Hynnekleiv
Gjeving
Lyngør
Vegusdal
Bøylefoss
Tvedestrand
Hirtshals
Frederikshavn
Helsingborg
København
Kiel
Herefoss
Fidje
Borås
Eydehavn
Kongshavn
Søre Herefoss
Blakstad
Øyestad
Arendal
Vatnstraum
TROMØY
Rykene
Tovdalselva
Fevik
Birkeland
NØRHOLM
Vik
Grimstad
Ryen
Lillesand
Hamre
Göteborg

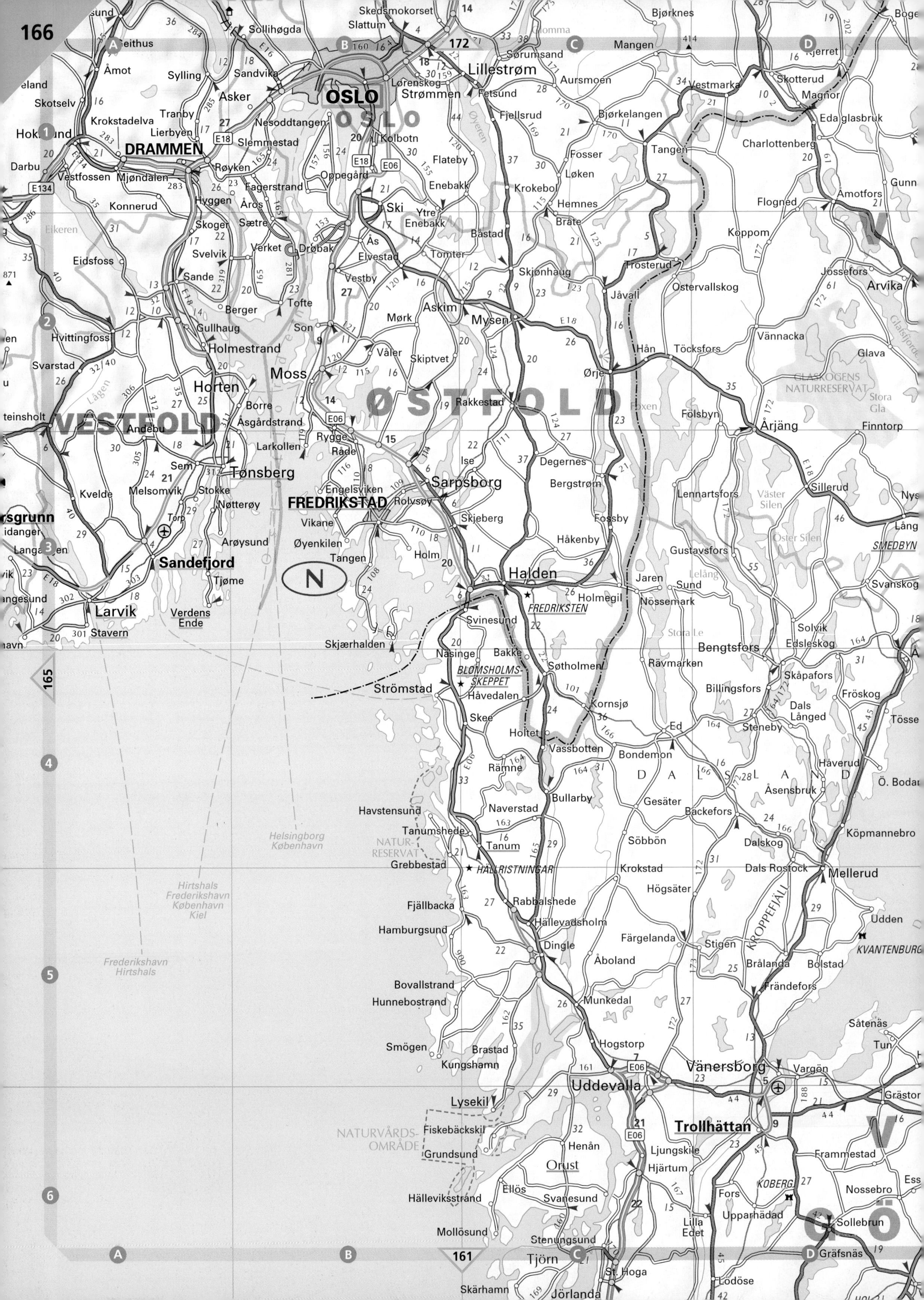
Geithus
Åmot
Sollihøgda
Skedsmokorset
Slattum
Bjørknes
Sørumsand
Mangen
Lillestrøm
Skotterud
Magnor
Sylling
Sandvika
Asker
OSLO
Lørenskog
Strømmen
Fetsund
Aursmoen
Vestmarka
Eda glasbruk
Skotselv
Krokstadelva
Tranby
Lierbyen
Nesoddtangen
Kolbotn
Fjellsrud
Bjørkelangen
Charlottenberg
Hokksund
DRAMMEN
Slemmestad
Tangen
Darbu
Vestfossen
Mjøndalen
Røyken
Oppegård
Flateby
Fosser
Løken
Fagerstrand
Enebakk
Krokebol
Hemnes
Åmotfors
Konnerud
Hyggen
Åros
Ski
Ytre Enebakk
Flogned
Eikeren
Skoger
Sætre
Båstad
Bråte
Koppom
Svelvik
Verket
Drøbak
Ås
Elvestad
Tomter
Frosterud
Eidsfoss
Sande
Vestby
Skjønhaug
Josseforsen
Arvika
Ostervallskog
Berger
Tofte
Askim
Mysen
Jåvall
Hvittingfoss
Gullhaug
Son
Mørk
Holmestrand
Våler
Skiptvet
Hån
Töcksfors
Vännacka
Glava
Svarstad
Moss
Ørje
Horten
ØSTFOLD
Rakkestad
GLASKOGENS NATURRESERVAT
Stora Gla
Foxen
Borre
Åsgårdstrand
Fölsbyn
Årjäng
Finntorp
VESTFOLD
Andebu
Rygge
Råde
Larkollen
Degernes
Ise
Sem
Tønsberg
Kvelde
Melsomvik
Stokke
Sarpsborg
Bergstrøm
Lennartsfors
Väster Silen
Sillerud
Nøtterøy
Engelsviken
FREDRIKSTAD
Rolvsøy
Skjeberg
Fossby
Torp
Vikane
Østra Silen
Åmål
Arøysund
Øyenkilen
Holm
Håkenby
Gustavsfors
SMEDBYN
Sandefjord
Tangen
Halden
Jaren
Sund
Lelång
Svanskog
Tjøme
FREDRIKSTEN
Holmegil
Nössemark
Larvik
Verdens Ende
Svinesund
Stavern
Stora Le
Solvik
Skjærhalden
Bengtsfors
Edsleskog
Näsinge
Bakke
Rävmarken
BLOMSHOLMS-SKEPPET
Søtholmen
Skåpafors
Strömstad
Håvedalen
Billingsfors
Fröskog
Kornsjø
Dals Långed
Skee
Ed
Steneby
Tösse
Holtet
Vassbotten
Bondemon
DALSLAND
Rämne
Håverud
Ö. Bodane
Åsensbruk
Bullarby
Gesäter
Bäckefors
Naverstad
Havstensund
Tanumshede
Söbbön
Dalskog
Köpmannebro
Tanum
NATURRESERVAT
Grebbestad
HÄLLRISTNINGAR
Krokstad
Dals Rostock
Mellerud
Högsäter
KROPPEFJÄLL
Fjällbacka
Rabbalshede
Hällevadsholm
Udden
Hamburgsund
Färgelanda
Stigen
KVANTENBURG
Dingle
Åboland
Brålanda
Bolstad
Bovallstrand
Frändefors
Hunnebostrand
Munkedal
Såtenäs
Smögen
Brastad
Hogstorp
Tun
Kungshamn
Vänersborg
Vargön
Uddevalla
Grästorp
Lysekil
Trollhättan
Fiskebäckskil
NATURVÅRDSOMRÅDE
Henån
Grundsund
Ljungskile
Frammestad
Orust
Hjärtum
Ellös
KOBERG
Nossebro
Svanesund
Fors
Hälleviksstrand
Upparhädad
Lilla Edet
Sollebrunn
Mollösund
Stenungsund
Tjörn
Gräfsnäs
St. Hoga
Skärhamn
Lödöse
Jörlanda
Helsingborg København
Hirtshals Frederikshavn København Kiel
Frederikshavn Hirtshals
165
161
172

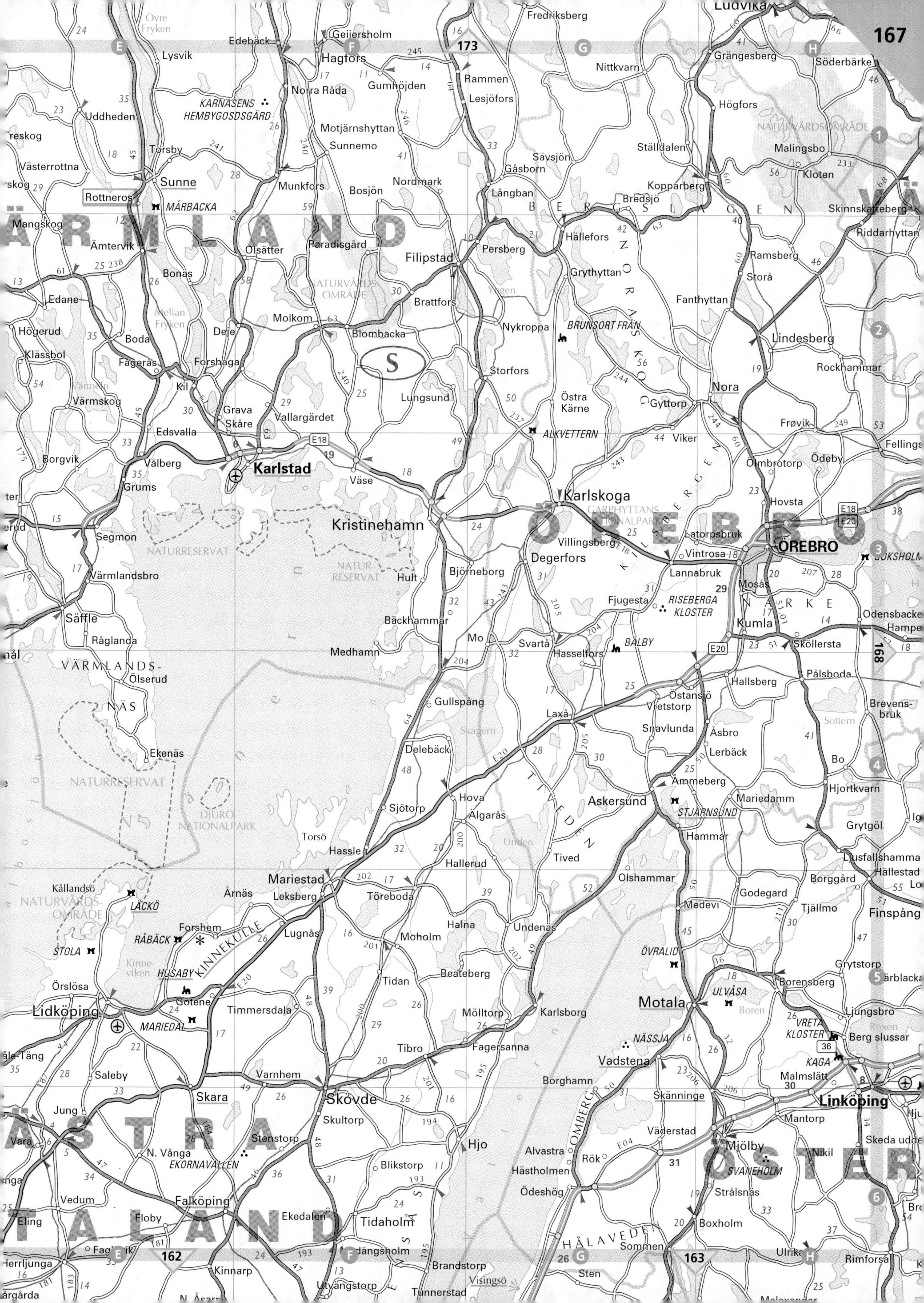

VÄRMLAND
BERGSLAGEN
NORA SKOG
KILSBERGEN
ÖREBRO
NÄRKE
TIVEDEN
VÄSTRA
ÖSTER
TALAND
Ludvika
Fredriksberg
Edebäck
Geijersholm
Hagfors
Rammen
Lesjöfors
Gumhöjden
Norra Råda
Lysvik
Övre Fryken
KARNÄSENS HEMBYGOSDSGÅRD
Uddheden
Motjärnshyttan
Sunnemo
Torsby
Västerrottna
Sunne
Rottneros
MÅRBACKA
Munkfors
Bosjön
Nordmark
Gåsborn
Sävsjön
Långban
Nittkvarn
Grängesberg
Söderbärke
Högfors
NATURVÅRDSOMRÅDE
Ställdalen
Malingsbo
Kloten
Kopparberg
Bredsjö
Skinnskatteberg
Riddarhyttan
Mangskog
Ämtervik
Olsätter
Paradisgård
Filipstad
Persberg
Hällefors
Grythyttan
Ramsberg
Storå
Fanthyttan
Edane
Bonäs
Mellan Fryken
Molkom
Blombacka
Brattfors
Nykroppa
BRUNSORT FRÅN
Lindesberg
Högerud
Boda
Deje
Klässbol
Fagerås
Forshaga
Kil
Storfors
Rockhammar
Värmskog
Grava
Skåre
Vallargärdet
Lungsund
Östra Kärne
Gyttorp
Nora
Frøvik
Edsvalla
ALKVETTERN
Viker
Fellingsbro
Borgvik
Vålberg
Karlstad
Väse
Ölmbrotorp
Ödeby
Grums
Karlskoga
GARPHYTTANS NATIONALPARK
Hovsta
Segmon
NATURRESERVAT
Kristinehamn
Latorpsbruk
Villingsberg
Vintrosa
Degerfors
ÖREBRO
Björneborg
Lannabruk
SOKSHOLM
Värmlandsbro
Hult
Mosås
Säffle
Fjugesta
RISEBERGA KLOSTER
Kumla
Odensbacken
Hampetorp
Rågland
Bäckhammar
Mo
Svartå
Hasselfors
BÅLBY
Sköllersta
Medhamn
VÄRMLANDS-NÄS
Ölserud
Hallsberg
Pålsboda
Gullspång
Östansjö
Vretstorp
Brevens-bruk
Skagern
Laxå
Snavlunda
Åsbro
Sottern
Ekenäs
Delebäck
Lerbäck
Bo
Ämmeberg
Hova
Askersund
Mariedamm
Hjortkvarn
DJURÖ NATIONALPARK
Sjötorp
Älgarås
STJÄRNSUND
Hammar
Grytgöl
Torsö
Unden
Hassle
Tived
Hallerud
Ljusfallshammar
Hällestad
Kållandsö
LÄCKÖ
Mariestad
Årnäs
Leksberg
Töreboda
Olshammar
Godegard
Borggård
Medevi
Tjällmo
Finspång
Forshem
RÅBÄCK
KINNEKULLE
Lugnås
Halna
Moholm
Undenäs
STOLA
ÖVRALID
HUSABY
Kinne-viken
Tidan
Beateberg
Grytstorp
Borensberg
Örslösa
Götene
Timmersdala
Motala
ULVÅSA
Boren
Lidköping
MARIEDAL
Mölltorp
Karlsborg
VRETA KLOSTER
Berg slussar
Ljungsbro
Roxen
Fagersanna
NÄSSJA
Tibro
Vadstena
KAGA
Malmslätt
Saleby
Varnhem
Borghamn
Skara
Skövde
Skänninge
Linköping
Jung
Skultorp
OMBERG
Mantorp
Väderstad
Vara
N. Vånga
Stenstorp
Hjo
Alvastra
Rök
Mjölby
Skeda udde
EKORNAVALLEN
Blikstorp
Hästholmen
Nikil
SVANEHÖLM
Vedum
Falköping
Ödeshög
Strålsnäs
Eling
Floby
Ekedalen
Tidaholm
Boxholm
HÅLAVEDEN
Sommen
Ulrika
Rimforsa
Herrljunga
Kinnarp
Brandstorp
Sten
Visingsö
Utvängstorp
Tunnerstad
E18
E20
E04
173
162
163
168

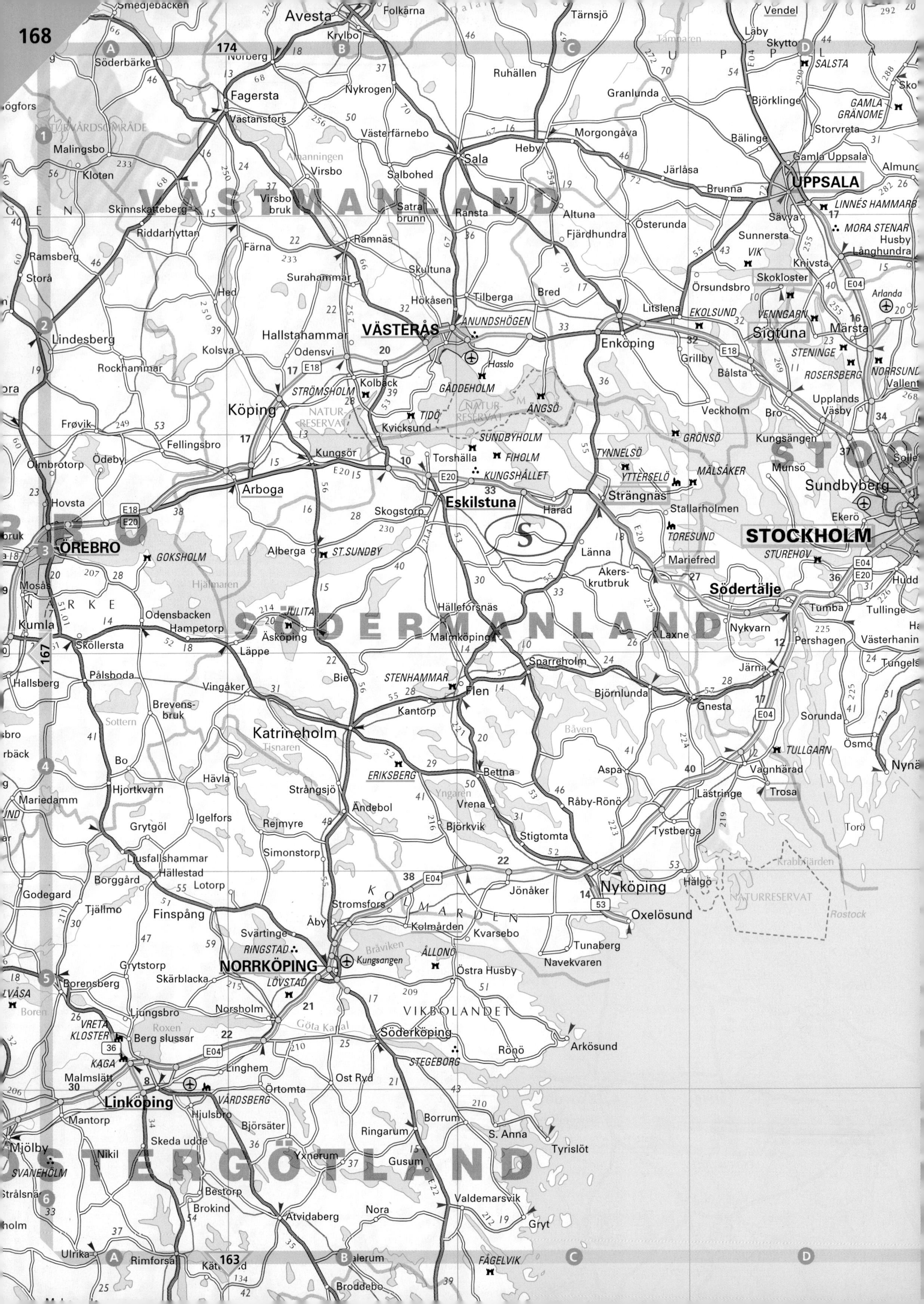
VÄSTMANLAND
UPPSALA
SÖDERMANLAND
STOCKHOLM
ÖSTERGÖTLAND
ÖREBRO
NÄRKE
KOLMÅRDEN
VIKBOLANDET
174
167
163
Smedjebacken
Avesta
Krylbo
Folkärna
Tärnsjö
Vendel
Läby
Skyttorp
SALSTA
Söderbärke
Norberg
Fagersta
Västanfors
Nykrogen
Ruhällen
Granlunda
Björklinge
GAMLA GRÄNOME
Storvreta
Bälinge
Gamla Uppsala
UPPSALA
Malingsbo
Kloten
Västerfärnebo
Sala
Heby
Morgongåva
Järlåsa
Brunna
Virsbo
Salbohed
Skinnskatteberg
Virsbo bruk
Satra brunn
Ransta
Altuna
Österunda
Sävja
LINNÉS HAMMARBY
MORA STENAR
Husby
Långhundra
Riddarhyttan
Ramnäs
Fjärdhundra
Sunnersta
VIK
Knivsta
Ramsberg
Färna
Skultuna
Skokloster
Örsundsbro
Surahammar
Hed
Hökåsen
Tilberga
Bred
Litslena
EKOLSUND
VENNGARN
Märsta
Arlanda
Lindesberg
Hallstahammar
VÄSTERÅS
ANUNDSHÖGEN
Enköping
Sigtuna
Kolsva
Odensvi
Hasslo
Grillby
STENINGE
Bålsta
ROSERSBERG
NORRSUNDA
Rockhammar
Kolbäck
STRÖMSHOLM
GÄDDEHOLM
ÄNGSÖ
Upplands Väsby
Köping
TIDÖ
NATURRESERVAT
Kvicksund
Veckholm
Bro
Frövik
Fellingsbro
SUNDBYHOLM
GRÖNSÖ
Kungsängen
Ölmbrotorp
Ödeby
Kungsör
Torshälla
FIHOLM
TYNNELSÖ
YTTERSELÖ
MÄLSÅKER
Munsö
KUNGSHÅLLET
Sundbyberg
Arboga
Eskilstuna
Strängnäs
Hovsta
Skogstorp
Härad
Stallarholmen
Ekerö
ÖREBRO
GOKSHOLM
Alberga
ST.SUNDBY
TORESUND
STOCKHOLM
Länna
Mariefred
STUREHOV
Hjälmaren
Åkers-krutbruk
Södertälje
Mosås
Odensbacken
Hälleforsnäs
Kumla
JULITA
Hampetorp
Äsköping
Malmköping
Laxne
Nykvarn
Tumba
Tullinge
Sköllersta
Läppe
Pershagen
Västerhaninge
Sparreholm
Järna
Hallsberg
Pålsboda
Bie
STENHAMMAR
Flen
Björnlunda
Gnesta
Vingåker
Kantorp
Brevens-bruk
Sorunda
Sottern
Katrineholm
Tisnaren
Båven
TULLGARN
Ösmo
Bo
ERIKSBERG
Bettna
Aspa
Vagnhärad
Hävla
Strångsjö
Yngaren
Råby-Rönö
Trosa
Mariedamm
Hjortkvarn
Ändebol
Vrena
Lästringe
Igelfors
Rejmyre
Björkvik
Grytgöl
Stigtomta
Tystberga
Torö
Simonstorp
Ljusfallshammar
Hällestad
Jönåker
Nyköping
Hälgö
Krabbfjärden
Borggård
Lotorp
Godegard
Tjällmo
Finspång
Stromsfors
NATURRESERVAT
Oxelösund
Rostock
Åby
Kolmården
Kvarsebo
Svärtinge
RINGSTAD
Bråviken
Tunaberg
ÅLLONÖ
Navekvaren
Grytstorp
NORRKÖPING
Kungsangen
Borensberg
Skärblacka
LÖVSTAD
Östra Husby
Boren
Ljungsbro
Norsholm
VRETA KLOSTER
Roxen
Göta Kanal
Söderköping
Berg slussar
Arkösund
KAGA
Linghem
STEGEBORG
Rönö
Malmslätt
Ost Ryd
Linköping
VÅRDSBERG
Örtomta
Mantorp
Hjulsbro
Borrum
Björsäter
Ringarum
S. Anna
Tyrislöt
Mjölby
Skeda udde
Nikil
Yxnerum
Gusum
SVANEHÖLM
Stråslnäs
Bestorp
Brokind
Valdemarsvik
Atvidaberg
Nora
Gryt
Ulrika
Rimforsa
Kättilstad
Bälerum
FÅGELVIK
Broddebo
E18
E20
E04
E22
A
B
C
D
1
2
3
4
5
6

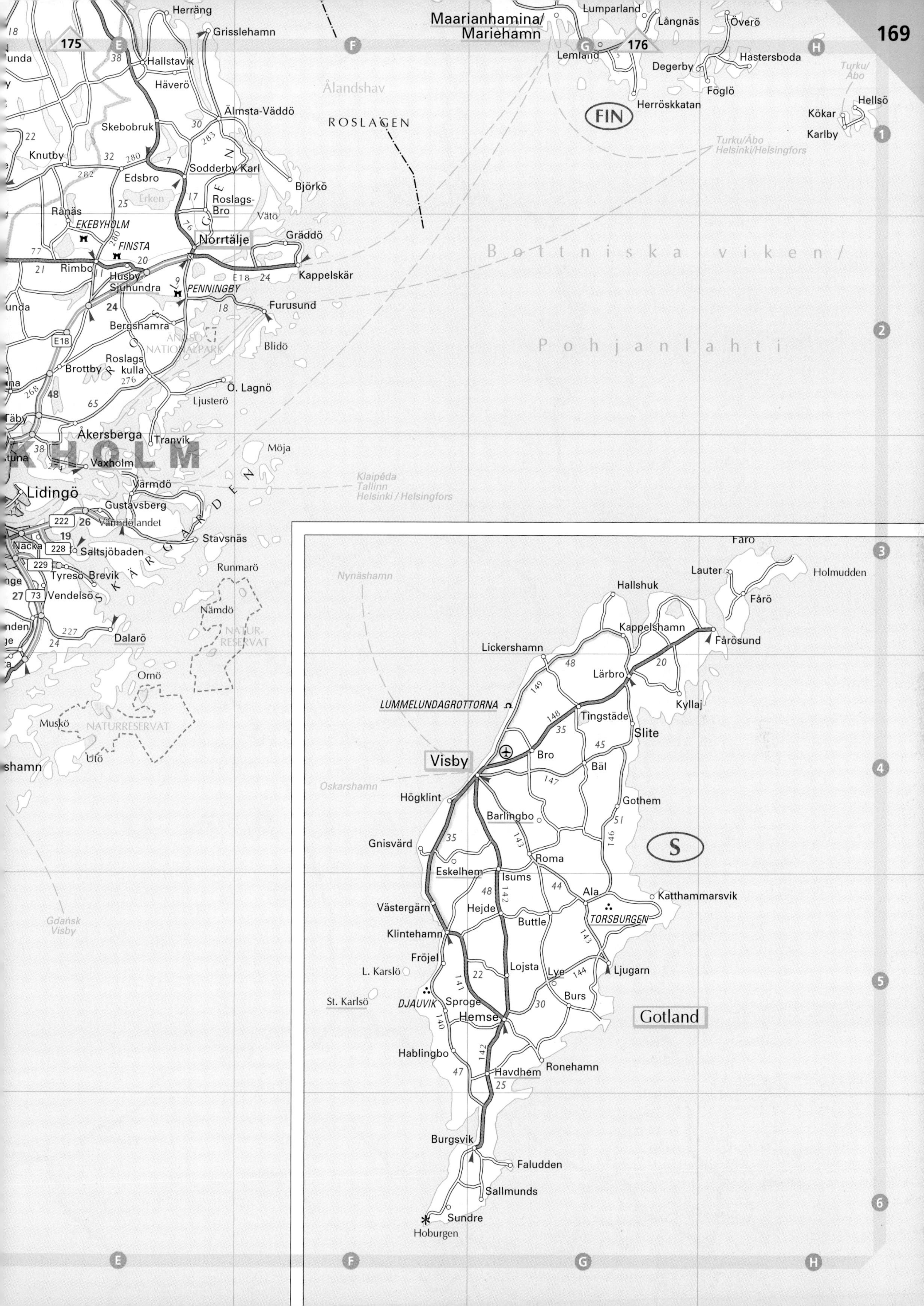

Herräng
Grisslehamn
175
Hallstavik
Häverö
Ålandshav
Älmsta-Väddö
ROSLAGEN
Skebobruk
Knutby
Edsbro
Sodderby Karl
Björkö
Roslags-Bro
Rånäs
EKEBYHOLM
FINSTA
Norrtälje
Gräddö
Rimbo
Husby-Sjuhundra
PENNINGBY
Kappelskär
Furusund
Bergshamra
ÄNGSÖ NATIONALPARK
Blidö
Roslags kulla
Brottby
Ö. Lagnö
Ljusterö
Täby
Åkersberga
Tranvik
Möja
Vaxholm
Lidingö
Värmdö
Gustavsberg
Värmdölandet
Nacka
Saltsjöbaden
Stavsnäs
Runmarö
Tyresö Brevik
Vendelsö
Nämdö
NATURRESERVAT
Dalarö
Ornö
Muskö
NATURRESERVAT
Utö
SKÄRGÅRDEN
Klaipėda
Tallinn
Helsinki / Helsingfors
Gdańsk
Visby
Maarianhamina/ Mariehamn
Lumparland
Långnäs
Överö
176
Lemland
Degerby
Hastersboda
Föglö
Herröskkatan
FIN
Turku/Åbo
Hellsö
Kökar
Karlby
Turku/Åbo
Helsinki/Helsingfors
Bottniska viken/
Pohjanlahti
Nynäshamn
Fårö
Lauter
Holmudden
Hallshuk
Fårö
Kappelshamn
Fårösund
Lickershamn
Lärbro
LUMMELUNDAGROTTORNA
Kyllaj
Tingstäde
Slite
Visby
Bro
Bäl
Oskarshamn
Högklint
Gothem
Barlingbo
S
Gnisvärd
Roma
Eskelhem
Isums
Ala
Katthammarsvik
Västergärn
Hejde
Buttle
TORSBURGEN
Klintehamn
Fröjel
Lojsta
Ljugarn
L. Karlsö
Lye
St. Karlsö
DJAUVIK
Sproge
Burs
Hemse
Gotland
Hablingbo
Havdhem
Ronehamn
Burgsvik
Faludden
Sallmunds
Sundre
Hoburgen

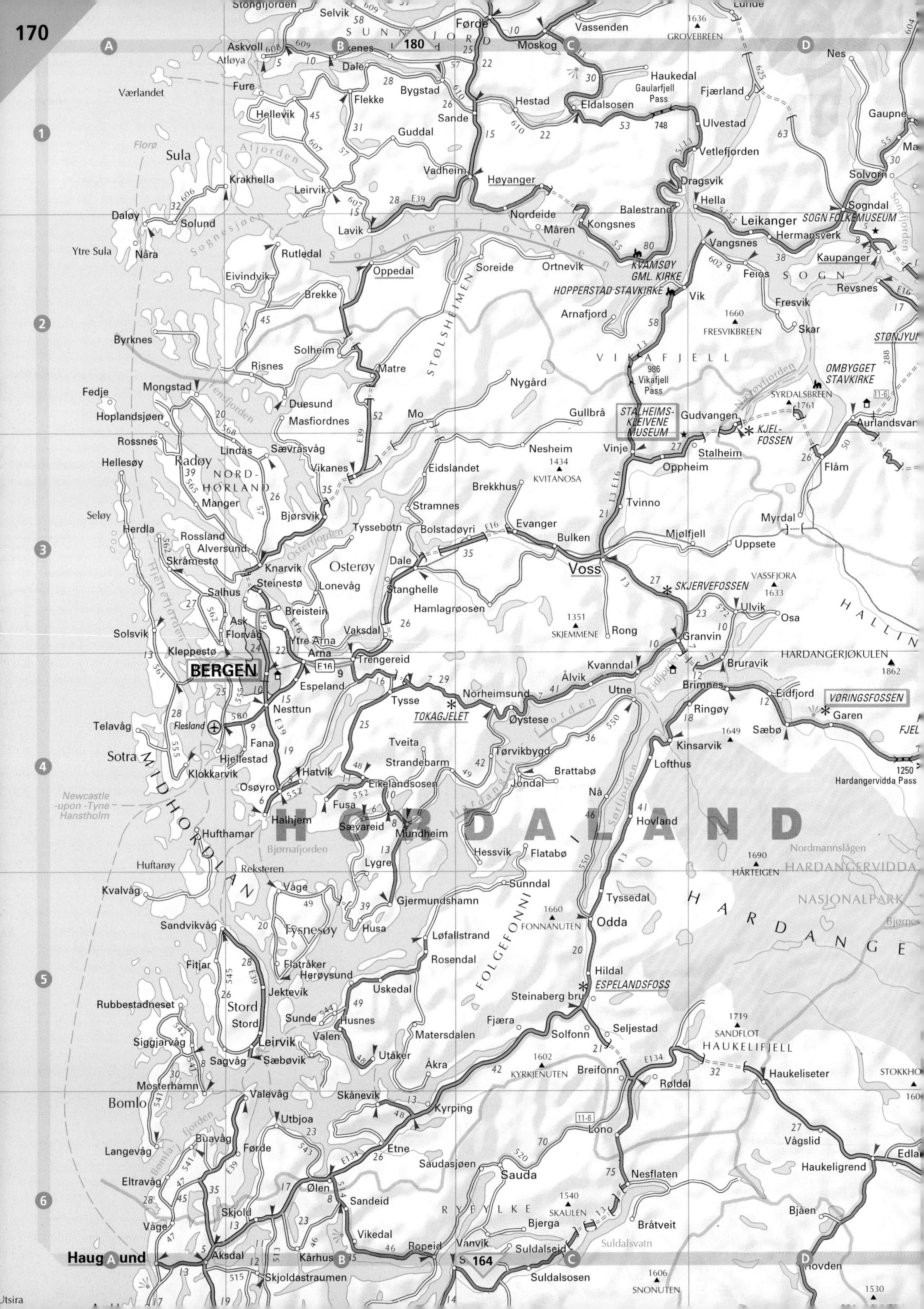
Stongfjorden
Selvik
SUNNFJORD
Førde
Vassenden
GROVEBREEN
Askvoll
Atløya
Skenes
180
Moskog
Nes
Dale
Haukedal
Gaularfjell Pass
Fjærland
Værlandet
Fure
Bygstad
Flekke
Hestad
Eldalsoyen
Hellevik
Sande
Gaupne
Ulvestad
Guddal
Florø
Sula
Afjorden
Vetlefjorden
Vadheim
Høyanger
Solvorn
Krakhella
Leirvik
Dragsvik
Hella
Balestrand
Sogndal
Daløy
Solund
Nordeide
Leikanger
SOGN FOLKEMUSEUM
Kongsnes
Hermansverk
Mâren
Lavik
Sognesjøen
Sognefjorden
Vangsnes
Kaupanger
Ytre Sula
Nåra
Rutledal
KVAMSØY GML. KIRKE
Soreide
Ortnevik
Feios
SOGN
Revsnes
Oppedal
HOPPERSTAD STAVKIRKE
Vik
Eivindvik
Fresvik
Brekke
Arnafjord
FRESVIKBREEN
Skar
Byrknes
STØLSHEIMEN
STØNJYUI
VIKAFJELL
Vikafjell Pass
Solheim
Matre
OMBYGGET STAVKIRKE
Nærøyfjorden
SYRDALSBREEN
Fedje
Mongstad
Nygård
Risnes
Hoplandsjøen
Fensfjorden
Duesund
Masfiordnes
Mo
Gullbrå
STALHEIMS-KLEIVENE MUSEUM
Gudvangen
KJEL-FOSSEN
Aurlandsvan
Rossnes
Sævråsvåg
Lindås
Nesheim
Vinje
Stalheim
Flåm
Hellesøy
Radøy
KVITANOSA
Oppheim
NORDHORLAND
Vikanes
Eidslandet
Brekkhus
Tvinno
Manger
Stramnes
Seløy
Bjørsvik
Myrdal
Herdla
Tyssebotn
Bolstadøyri
Evanger
Mjølfjell
Rossland
Osterfjorden
Bulken
Alversund
Uppsete
Skråmestø
Dale
Voss
Osterøy
Knarvik
VASSFJORA
SKJERVEFOSSEN
Steinestø
Lonevåg
Salhus
Stanghelle
Ulvik
Osa
Breistein
Hamlagrøosen
Hjeltefjorden
Ask
SKJEMMENE
Rong
Solsvik
Florvåg
Vaksdal
Granvin
Ytre Arna
HALLIN
Kleppestø
Arna
HARDANGERJØKULEN
BERGEN
Trengereid
Kvanndal
Bruravik
Espeland
Ålvik
Brimnes
Utne
Eidfjord
Nesttun
Tysse
Norheimsund
VØRINGSFOSSEN
Ringøy
Telavåg
Flesland
TOKAGJELET
Øystese
Garen
Fana
Sæbø
Tveita
Kinsarvik
FJEL
Sotra
Hjellestad
Tørvikbygd
Strandebarm
Lofthus
Klokkarvik
Hatvik
Brattabø
Hardangervidda Pass
Eikelandsosen
Jondal
Newcastle -upon -Tyne Hanstholm
Osøyro
Nå
Fusa
HORDALAND
Halhjem
Sævareid
Hovland
Hufthamar
Mundheim
Sørfjorden
Bjørnafjorden
Nordmannslågen
Hessvik
Flatabø
HÅRTEIGEN
HARDANGERVIDDA
Huftarøy
Lygre
Reksteren
MIDHORDLAND
Kvalvåg
Våge
Sunndal
Tyssedal
NASJONALPARK
Gjermundshamn
FONNANUTEN
Odda
HARDANGE
Sandvikvåg
Tysnesøy
Husa
Bjørnes
Løfallstrand
Rosendal
FOLGEFONNI
Fitjar
Flatråker
Herøysund
Hildal
ESPELANDSFOSS
Jektevik
Uskedal
Steinaberg bru
Rubbestadneset
Stord
Sunde
Husnes
SANDFLOT
Fjæra
Seljestad
Solfonn
HAUKELIFJELL
Siggjarvåg
Leirvik
Valen
Matersdalen
Sagvåg
Sæbøvik
Utåker
KYRKJENUTEN
Breifonn
Røldal
Haukeliseter
STOKKHO
Åkra
Mosterhamn
Valevåg
Skånevik
Bomlo
Kyrping
Utbjoa
Lono
Vågslid
Langevåg
Buavåg
Førde
Etne
Haukeligrend
Edla
Saudasjøen
Sauda
Eltravåg
Nesflaten
Ølen
Sandeid
RYFYLKE
SKAULEN
Skjold
Bjerga
Bråtveit
Bjåen
Våge
Vikedal
Suldalsvatn
Ropeid
Vanvik
Haugesund
Aksdal
Kårhus
Suldalseid
164
Hovden
Skjoldastraumen
Suldalsosen
SNONUTEN
Utsira

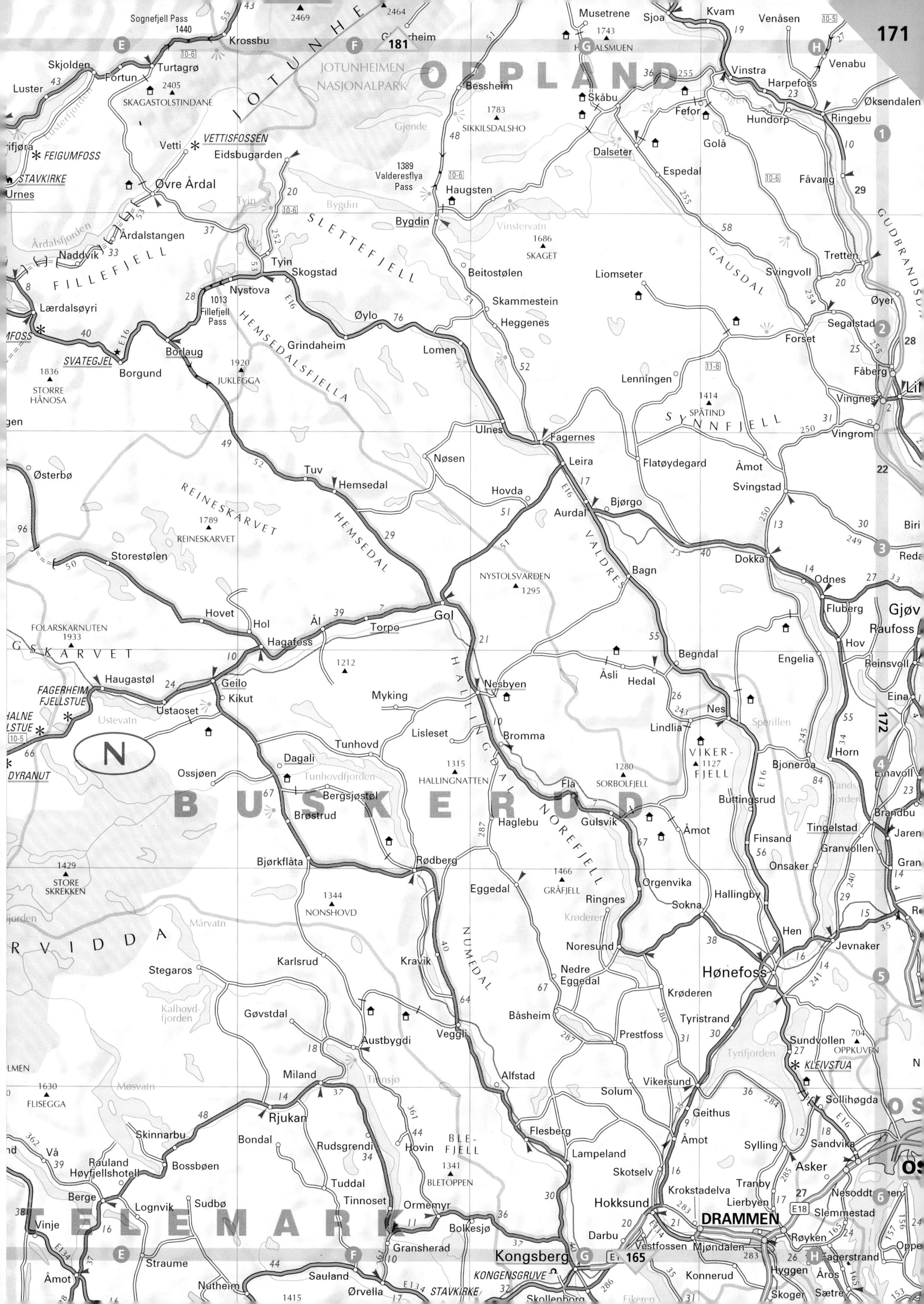
OPPLAND
BUSKERUD
TELEMARK
JOTUNHEIMEN NASJONALPARK
JOTUNHEIMEN
Sognefjell Pass 1440
Krossbu
Skjolden
Turtagrø
Fortun
Luster
2405 SKAGASTOLSTINDANE
Vetti
VETTISFOSSEN
Eidsbugarden
FEIGUMFOSS
STAVKIRKE
Urnes
Øvre Årdal
Årdalstangen
Naddvik
FILLEFJELL
Lærdalsøyri
SVATEGJEL
Borgund
1836 STORRE HÅNOSA
Tyin
Skogstad
Nystova
1013 Fillefjell Pass
Borlaug
1920 JUKLEGGA
HEMSEDALSFJELLA
Grindaheim
Øylo
Lomen
SLETTEFJELL
Bygdin
1389 Valderesflya Pass
Haugsten
Bessheim
1783 SIKKILSDALSHO
Gjende
Vinstervatn
1686 SKAGET
Beitostølen
Skammestein
Heggenes
Musetrene
1743 HALSMUEN
Sjoa
Kvam
Venåsen
Vinstra
Harpefoss
Venabu
Skåbu
Fefor
Hundorp
Ringebu
Øksendalen
Dalseter
Golå
Espedal
Fåvang
GAUSDAL
Tretten
Svingvoll
Liomseter
Øyer
Segalstad
Forset
Fåberg
Lenningen
1414 SPÅTIND
SYNNFJELL
Vingnes
Vingrom
Ulnes
Fagernes
Nøsen
Leira
Flatøydegard
Åmot
Svingstad
Hovda
Aurdal
Bjørgo
Tuv
Hemsedal
HEMSEDAL
REINESKARVET
1789 REINESKARVET
Østerbø
Storestølen
VALDRES
Dokka
Bagn
Odnes
Fluberg
Gjøv
Raufoss
Hov
NYSTOLSVARDEN 1295
Gol
Hovet
Hol
Ål
Torpo
Hagafoss
FOLARSKARNUTEN 1933
SKARVET
1212
HALLINGDAL
Nesbyen
Begndal
Åsli
Hedal
Engelia
Reinsvoll
Eina
Haugastøl
Geilo
Kikut
FAGERHEIM FJELLSTUE
Ustaoset
Ustevatn
Myking
Lisleset
Bromma
Nes
Lindlia
Sperillen
VIKERFJELL 1127
Horn
Bjoneroa
DYRANUT
Dagali
Tunhovd
Tunhovdfjorden
1315 HALLINGNATTEN
1280 SORBOLFJELL
Ossjøen
Bergsjøstøl
Brøstrud
Flå
NOREFJELL
Haglebu
Gulsvik
Buttingsrud
Brandbu
Tingelstad
Jaren
Granvollen
Gran
Finsand
Onsaker
1429 STORE SKREKKEN
Bjørkflåta
Rødberg
1466 GRÅFJELL
Eggedal
Orgenvika
Ringnes
Krøderen
Hallingby
Sokna
1344 NONSHOVD
Mårvatn
VIDDA
Stegaros
Karlsrud
Kravik
NUMEDAL
Noresund
Hen
Jevnaker
Hønefoss
Nedre Eggedal
Krøderen
Kalhovdfjorden
Gøvstdal
Austbygdi
Veggli
Båsheim
Prestfoss
Tyristrand
Sundvollen
704 OPPKUVEN
KLEIVSTUA
Tyrifjorden
Miland
Tinnsjø
Alfstad
Vikersund
Solum
Geithus
Sollihøgda
1630 FLISEGGA
Møsvatn
Rjukan
Skinnarbu
Bondal
Rudsgrendi
Hovin
BLEFJELL
Flesberg
Åmot
Sylling
Sandvika
Vå
Rauland Høyfjellshotell
Bossbøen
1341 BLETOPPEN
Lampeland
Skotselv
Asker
Tuddal
Tinnoset
Krokstadelva
Tranby
Lierbyen
Nesoddtangen
Berge
Lognvik
Sudbø
Ormemyr
Hokksund
DRAMMEN
Slemmestad
Vinje
Bolkesjø
Darbu
Vestfossen
Mjøndalen
Røyken
Gransherad
Kongsberg
Hyggen
Åros
Straume
KONGENSGRUVE
Konnerud
Fagerstrand
Oppegård
Åmot
Nutheim
Sauland
Ørvella
STAVKIRKE
Skollenborg
Fiskum
Skoger
Sætre
1415
165
181
172

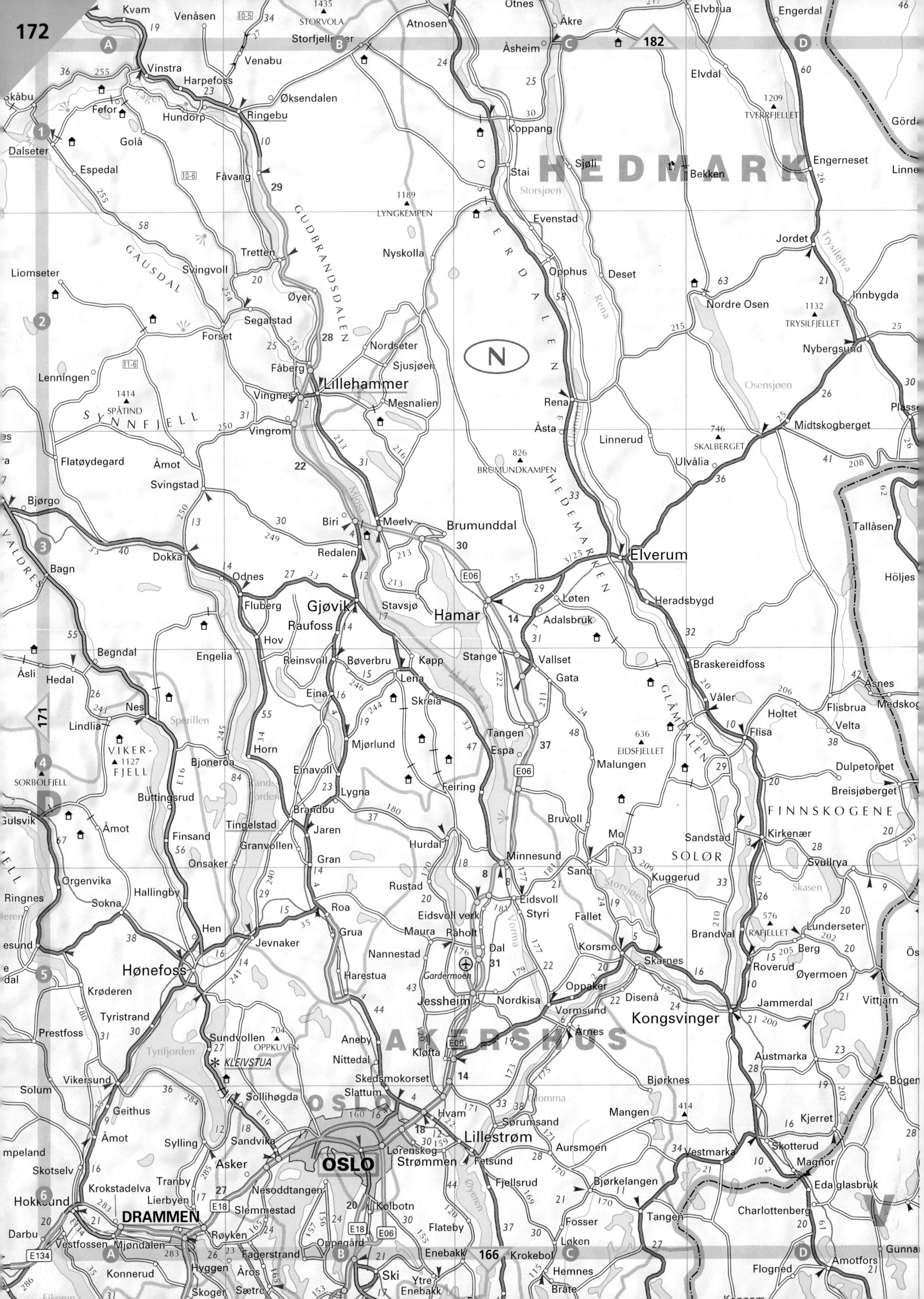
HEDMARK
AKERSHUS
OSLO
GUDBRANDSDALEN
ØSTERDALEN
HEDEMARKEN
GAUSDAL
SYNNFJELL
VALDRES
SOLØR
FINNSKOGENE
GLÅMDALEN
VIKER-FJELL
Kvam
Venåsen
STORVOLA
Storfjellseter
Atnosen
Otnes
Åkre
Åsheim
Elvbrua
Engerdal
Vinstra
Harpefoss
Skåbu
Fefor
Hundorp
Øksendalen
Ringebu
Elvdal
TVERRFJELLET
Gördalen
Golå
Dalseter
Espedal
Fåvang
Koppang
Stai
Sjøli
Bekken
Engerneset
Linnes
Storsjøen
LYNGKEMPEN
Evenstad
Tretten
Nyskolla
Jordet
Trysilelva
Liomseter
Svingvoll
Opphus
Deset
Rena
Øyer
Nordre Osen
Innbygda
Segalstad
TRYSILFJELLET
Forset
Nordseter
Nybergsund
Fåberg
Sjusjøen
Lenningen
Lillehammer
Osensjøen
SPÅTIND
Vingnes
Mesnalien
Rena
Plassen
Vingrom
Åsta
Linnerud
SKALBERGET
Midtskogberget
Flatøydegard
Åmot
Svingstad
BRUMUNDKAMPEN
Ulvålia
Bjørgo
Biri
Moelv
Brumunddal
Tallåsen
Redalen
Dokka
Elverum
Bagn
Odnes
Höljes
Fluberg
Gjøvik
Stavsjø
Hamar
Løten
Heradsbygd
Raufoss
Adalsbruk
Hov
Begndal
Engelia
Reinsvoll
Bøverbru
Kapp
Stange
Vallset
Braskereidfoss
Åsli
Hedal
Lena
Gata
Åsnes
Eina
Skreia
Våler
Flisbruа
Medskogen
Nes
Holtet
Velta
Lindlia
Sperillen
Mjørlund
Tangen
Flisa
Espa
EIDSFJELLET
SORBOLFJELL
Horn
Bjoneroa
Malungen
Dulpetorpet
Einavoll
Feiring
Breisjøberget
Buttingsrud
Lygna
Randsfjorden
Brandbu
Gulsvik
Åmot
Tingelstad
Jaren
Bruvoll
Mo
Sandstad
Kirkenær
Finsand
Granvollen
Hurdal
Gran
Minnesund
Sand
Kuggerud
Svullrya
Onsaker
Orgenvika
Rustad
Skasen
Ringnes
Hallingby
Eidsvoll
Sokna
Roa
Eidsvoll verk
Styri
Fallet
Lunderseter
RAFJELLET
Grua
Maura
Råholt
Brandval
Hen
Jevnaker
Korsmo
Berg
Nannestad
Dal
Skarnes
Hønefoss
Gardermoen
Roverud
Øyermoen
Harestua
Kroderen
Oppaker
Jessheim
Nordkisa
Disenå
Jammerdal
Vittjärn
Tyristrand
Vormsund
Kongsvinger
Prestfoss
Sundvollen
OPPKUVEN
Årnes
Aneby
Tyrifjorden
KLEIVSTUA
Nittedal
Kløfta
Austmarka
Vikersund
Skedsmokorset
Bjørknes
Bogen
Solum
Sollihøgda
Slattum
Glomma
Geithus
Hvam
Mangen
Kjerret
Sørumsand
Åmot
Sylling
Sandvika
Lillestrøm
Skotterud
Asker
Lørenskog
Aursmoen
Vestmarka
Skotselv
Strømmen
Fetsund
Magnor
Tranby
Nesoddtangen
Fjellsrud
Bjørkelangen
Eda glasbruk
Krokstadelva
Lierbyen
Hokksund
DRAMMEN
Slemmestad
Kolbotn
Tangen
Charlottenberg
Darbu
Røyken
Flateby
Fosser
Vestfossen
Mjøndalen
Oppegård
Løken
Fagerstrand
Enebakk
Krokebol
Gunnarskog
Konnerud
Hyggen
Åros
Ski
Hemnes
Flogned
Amotfors
Skoger
Sætre
Ytre Enebakk
Bråte
Øyeren
Mjøsa
Vorma
Glomma
Lågen
Rena
E06
E16
E18
E134
182
171
166

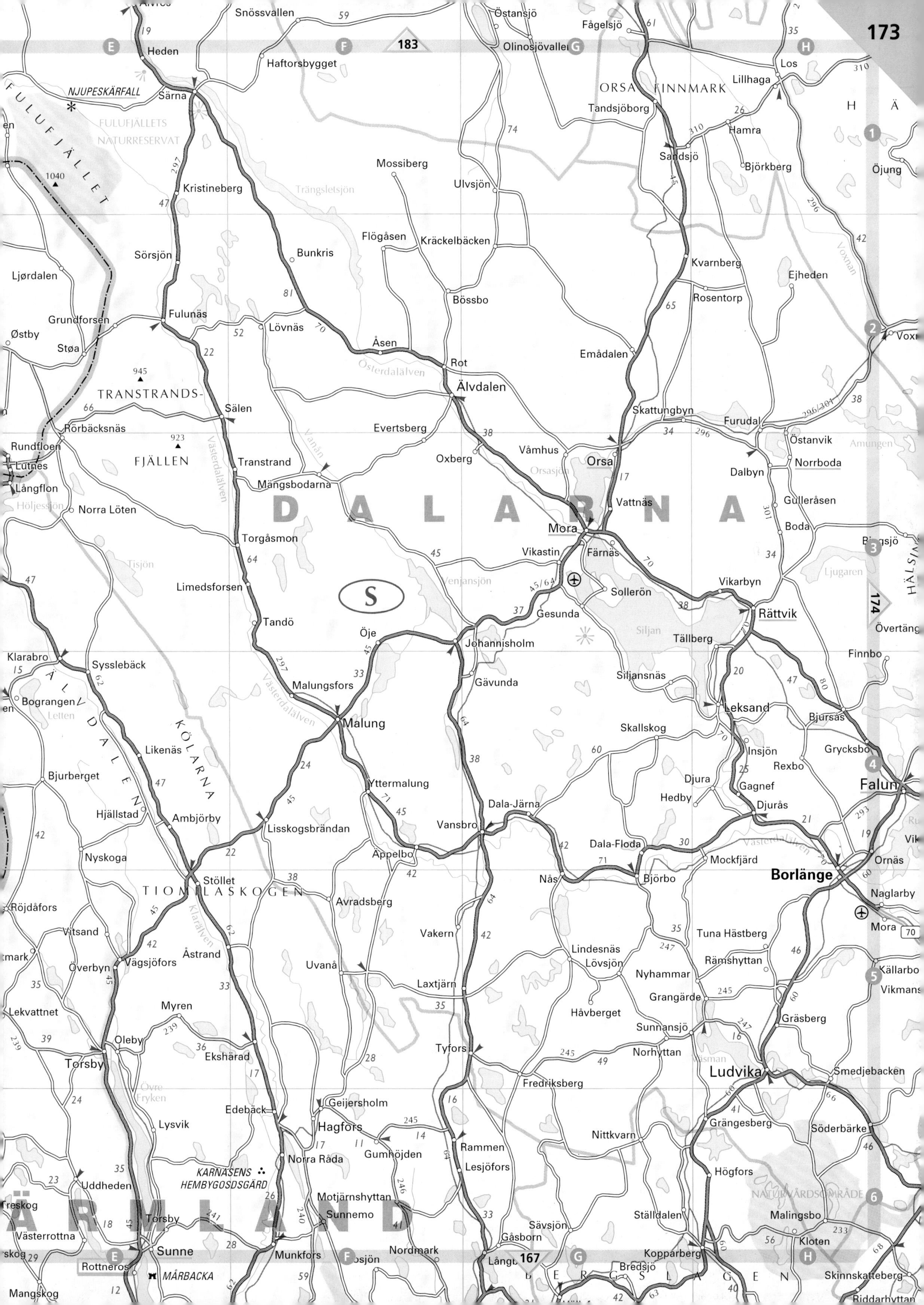

183
167
174
DALARNA
VÄRMLAND
BERGSLAGEN
ORSA FINNMARK
FULUFJÄLLET
FULUFJÄLLETS NATURRESERVAT
NJUPESKÄRFALL
TRANSTRANDS-FJÄLLEN
KÖLARNA
ÄLVDALEN
TIOMILASKOGEN
KARNÄSENS HEMBYGOSDSGÅRD
MÅRBACKA
NATURVÅRDSOMRÅDE
Snössvallen
Östansjö
Fågelsjö
Heden
Haftorsbygget
Olinosjövallen
Los
Lillhaga
Särna
Tandsjöborg
Hamra
Sandsjö
Björkberg
Öjung
Mossiberg
Ulvsjön
Kristineberg
Trängsletsjön
Flögåsen
Kräckelbäcken
Kvarnberg
Ejheden
Sörsjön
Bunkris
Ljørdalen
Bössbo
Rosentorp
Voxnan
Grundforsen
Fulunäs
Lövnäs
Åsen
Rot
Emådalen
Østby
Støa
Voxna
Österdalälven
Älvdalen
Sälen
Rörbäcksnäs
Skattungbyn
Furudal
Evertsberg
Östanvik
Amungen
Rundfloen
Lutnes
Transtrand
Oxberg
Våmhus
Orsa
Norrboda
Långflon
Mångsbodarna
Vanån
Västerdalälven
Orsasjön
Dalbyn
Höljessjön
Norra Löten
Vattnäs
Gulleråsen
Torgåsmon
Mora
Boda
Vikastin
Färnäs
Bingsjö
Tisjön
Venjansjön
Ljugaren
Limedsforsen
Sollerön
Vikarbyn
Tandö
Gesunda
Rättvik
Siljan
Övertång
Öje
Johannisholm
Tällberg
Klarabro
Sysslebäck
Finnbo
Gävunda
Siljansnäs
Bograngen
Letten
Malungsfors
Malung
Leksand
Bjursås
Skallskog
Insjön
Grycksbo
Likenäs
Rexbo
Bjurberget
Yttermalung
Djura
Gagnef
Falun
Hedby
Hjällstad
Djurås
Ambjörby
Dala-Järna
Vansbro
Lisskogsbrändan
Dala-Floda
Ornäs
Nyskoga
Äppelbo
Mockfjärd
Stöllet
Nås
Björbo
Borlänge
Naglarby
Röjdåfors
Avradsberg
Klarälven
Vakern
Tuna Hästberg
Vitsand
Lindesnäs
Åstrand
Lövsjön
Rämshyttan
Källarbo
Överbyn
Vägsjöfors
Uvanå
Nyhammar
Vikmanshyttan
Laxtjärn
Grangärde
Lekvattnet
Myren
Håvberget
Gräsberg
Oleby
Sunnansjö
Ekshärad
Tyfors
Norhyttan
Torsby
Väsman
Ludvika
Smedjebacken
Övre Fryken
Fredriksberg
Geijersholm
Edebäck
Grängesberg
Lysvik
Hagfors
Gumhöjden
Nittkvarn
Rammen
Söderbärke
Norra Råda
Lesjöfors
Högfors
Uddheden
Motjärnshyttan
Sunnemo
Ställdalen
Malingsbo
Västerrottna
Sävsjön
Gåsborn
Kloten
Sunne
Munkfors
Nordmark
Kopparberg
Rottneros
Bredsjö
Skinnskatteberg
Mangskog
Riddarhyttan

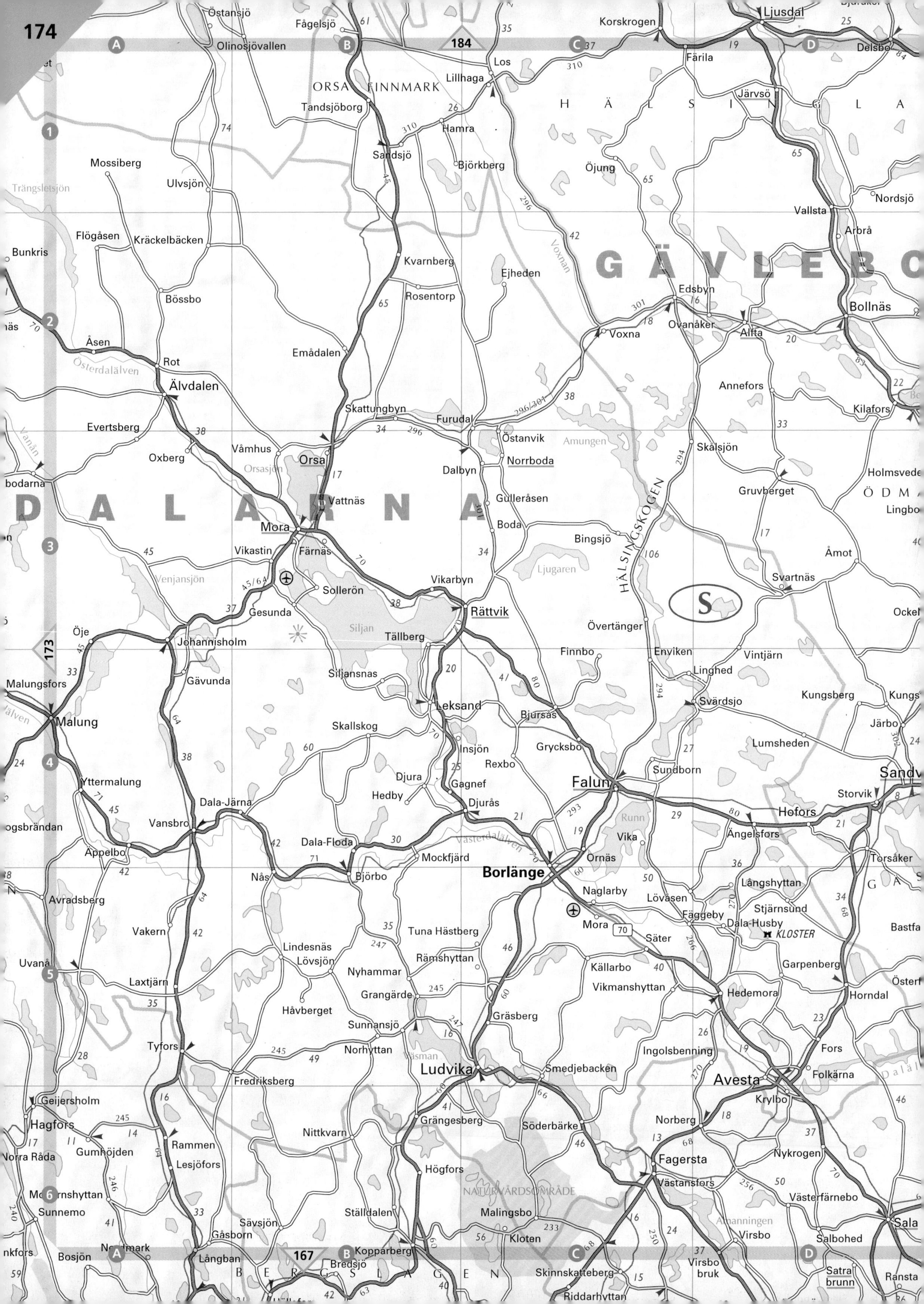

184
173
167
ORSA FINNMARK
H Ä L S I N G L A
G Ä V L E B
D A L A R N A
HÄLSINGSKOGEN
B E R G S L A G E N
NATURVÅRDSOMRÅDE
Östansjö
Fågelsjö
Olinosjövallen
Korskrogen
Ljusdal
Delsbo
Los
Lillhaga
Färila
Järvsö
Tandsjöborg
Hamra
Sandsjö
Björkberg
Öjung
Mossiberg
Ulvsjön
Trängsletsjön
Nordsjö
Vallsta
Arbrå
Flögåsen
Kräckelbäcken
Bunkris
Kvarnberg
Ejheden
Voxnan
Rosentorp
Bössbo
Edsbyn
Bollnäs
Voxna
Ovanåker
Alfta
Åsen
Rot
Emådalen
Österdalälven
Älvdalen
Annefors
Kilafors
Skattungbyn
Furudal
Evertsberg
Östanvik
Amungen
Våmhus
Oxberg
Orsa
Orsasjön
Norrboda
Skålsjön
Dalbyn
Holmsveden
bodarna
Vanån
Vattnäs
Gulleråsen
Gruvberget
Lingbo
Mora
Boda
Bingsjö
Vikastin
Färnäs
Åmot
Venjansjön
Ljugaren
Sollerön
Vikarbyn
Svartnäs
Gesunda
Rättvik
Ockelbo
Öje
Siljan
Övertänger
Johannisholm
Tällberg
Finnbo
Enviken
Vintjärn
Malungsfors
Linghed
Gävunda
Siljansnäs
Kungsberg
Svärdsjö
Malung
Leksand
Bjursås
Järbo
Skallskog
Insjön
Gryckbo
Lumsheden
Rexbo
Sundborn
Sandviken
Djura
Gagnef
Falun
Yttermalung
Storvik
Hedby
Djurås
Dala-Järna
Hofors
Vansbro
Runn
ogsbrändan
Ängelsfors
Vika
Dala-Floda
Appelbo
Mockfjärd
Västerdalälven
Ornäs
Torsåker
Nås
Björbo
Borlänge
Långshyttan
Avradsberg
Naglarby
Lövåsen
Stjärnsund
Fäggeby
Dala-Husby
Vakern
Tuna Hästberg
Mora
KLOSTER
Bastfallet
Säter
Lindesnäs
Lövsjön
Uvanå
Rämshyttan
Garpenberg
Källarbo
Nyhammar
Laxtjärn
Vikmanshyttan
Österfärnebo
Grangärde
Hedemora
Horndal
Håvberget
Gräsberg
Sunnansjö
Tyfors
Norhyttan
Väsman
Ingolsbenning
Fors
Ludvika
Smedjebacken
Fredriksberg
Avesta
Folkärna
Krylbo
Geijersholm
Grängesberg
Hagfors
Söderbärke
Norberg
Nittkvarn
Rammen
Norra Råda
Gumhöjden
Fagersta
Nykrogen
Lesjöfors
Högfors
Västanfors
Mo rnshyttan
Sunnemo
Västerfärnebo
Ställdalen
Malingsbo
Sävsjön
Åmänningen
Sala
Gåsborn
Kloten
Virsbo
Salbohed
Nordmark
Bosjön
Långban
Kopparberg
Bredsjö
Skinnskatteberg
Virsbo bruk
Satrabrunn
Ransta
Riddarhyttan

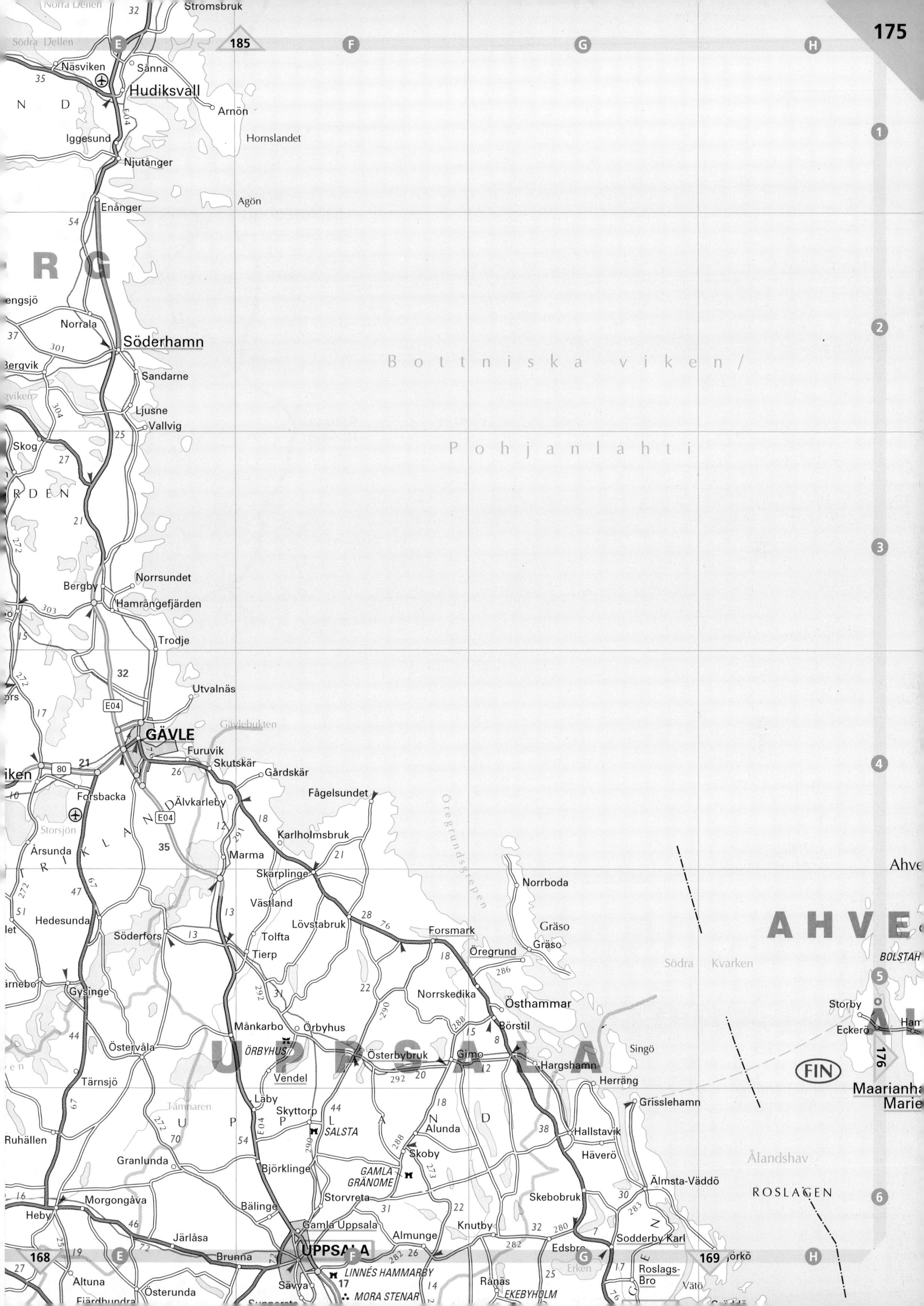
185
E
F
G
H
1
2
3
4
5
6
Hudiksvall
Näsviken
Sånna
Arnön
Iggesund
Hornslandet
Njutånger
Enånger
Agön
Norrala
Söderhamn
Sandarne
Ljusne
Vallvig
Skog
Bottniska viken/
Pohjanlahti
Bergby
Norrsundet
Hamrångefjärden
Trodje
Utvalnäs
GÄVLE
Gävlebukten
Furuvik
Skutskär
Gårdskär
Fågelsundet
Forsbacka
Storsjön
Älvkarleby
Årsunda
Marma
Karlholmsbruk
Skarplinge
Västland
Hedesunda
Söderfors
Lövstabruk
Tolfta
Tierp
Norrboda
Gräso
Forsmark
Öregrund
Södra Kvarken
Gysinge
Norrskedika
Östhammar
Månkarbo
Örbyhus
Börstil
Österbybruk
Gimo
Hargshamn
Singö
Herräng
Grisslehamn
Östervåla
Tärnsjö
ÖRBYHUS
Vendel
UPPSALA
Läby
Skyttorp
SALSTA
Alunda
Hallstavik
Häverö
Tämnaren
Ruhällen
Granlunda
Björklinge
Skoby
GAMLA GRÄNOME
Ålandshav
Storvreta
Älmsta-Väddö
ROSLAGEN
Morgongåva
Bälinge
Skebobruk
Heby
Gamla Uppsala
Knutby
Järlåsa
Almunge
Edsbro
Sodderby Karl
Brunna
168
169
Altuna
LINNÉS HAMMARBY
Roslags-Bro
Sävja
Rånäs
EKEBYHOLM
Österunda
MORA STENAR
Erken
Vätö
Ahve
AHVE
BOLSTAH
Storby
Eckerö
FIN
176
Maarianha
Marie

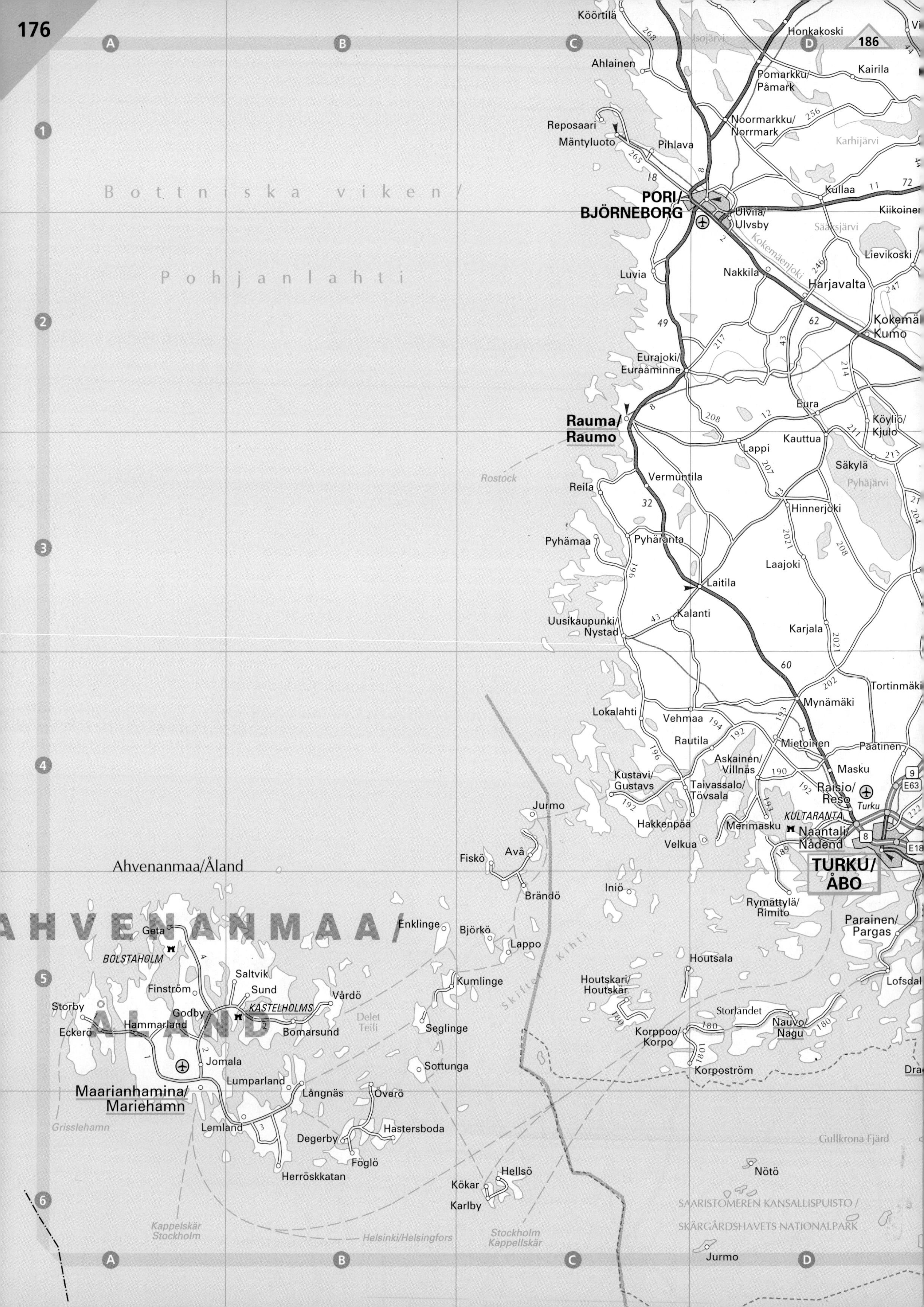

Köörtilä
Honkakoski
Isojärvi
V
Ahlainen
Pomarkku/ Påmark
Kairila
Noormarkku/ Norrmark
Karhijärvi
Reposaari
Mäntyluoto
Pihlava
PORI/ BJÖRNEBORG
Ulvila/ Ulvsby
Kullaa
Kiikoiner
Säaksjärvi
Luvia
Nakkila
Lievikoski
Harjavalta
Eurajoki/ Euraåminne
Kokemä Kumo
Rauma/ Raumo
Eura
Köyliö/ Kjulo
Rostock
Vermuntila
Kauttua
Lappi
Säkylä
Reila
Pyhäjärvi
Pyhämaa
Pyhäranta
Hinnerjöki
Laajoki
Laitila
Uusikaupunki/ Nystad
Kalanti
Karjala
Tortinmäki
Mynämäki
Lokalahti
Vehmaa
Rautila
Mietoinen
Paatinen
Masku
Kustavi/ Gustavs
Askainen/ Villnäs
Taivassalo/ Tövsala
Raisio/ Reso
Turku
E63
Jurmo
KULTARANTA
Hakkenpää
Merimasku
Naantali/ Nådend
TURKU/ ÅBO
Velkua
Fiskö
Avå
Ahvenanmaa/Åland
Brändö
Iniö
Rymättylä/ Rimito
Parainen/ Pargas
AHVENANMAA/
Enklinge
Björkö
Lappo
Houtsala
Geta
Houtskari/ Houtskär
Lofsdal
BOLSTAHOLM
Saltvik
Kumlinge
Storlandet
Nauvo
Nagu
Storby
Finström
Sund
Vårdö
KASTELHOLMS
Korppoo/ Korpo
ÅLAND
Hammarland
Godby
Bomarsund
Delet Teili
Seglinge
Eckerö
Jomala
Sottunga
Korpoström
Dra
Lumparland
Maarianhamina/ Mariehamn
Långnäs
Överö
Lemland
Hastersboda
Nötö
Degerby
Herröskkatan
Föglö
Hellsö
Grislehamn
Kökar
SAARISTOMEREN KANSALLISPUISTO / SKÄRGÅRDSHAVETS NATIONALPARK
Karlby
Kappelskär Stockholm
Helsinki/Helsingfors
Stockholm Kappellskär
Gullkrona Fjärd
Jurmo

Bottniska viken/
Pohjanlahti

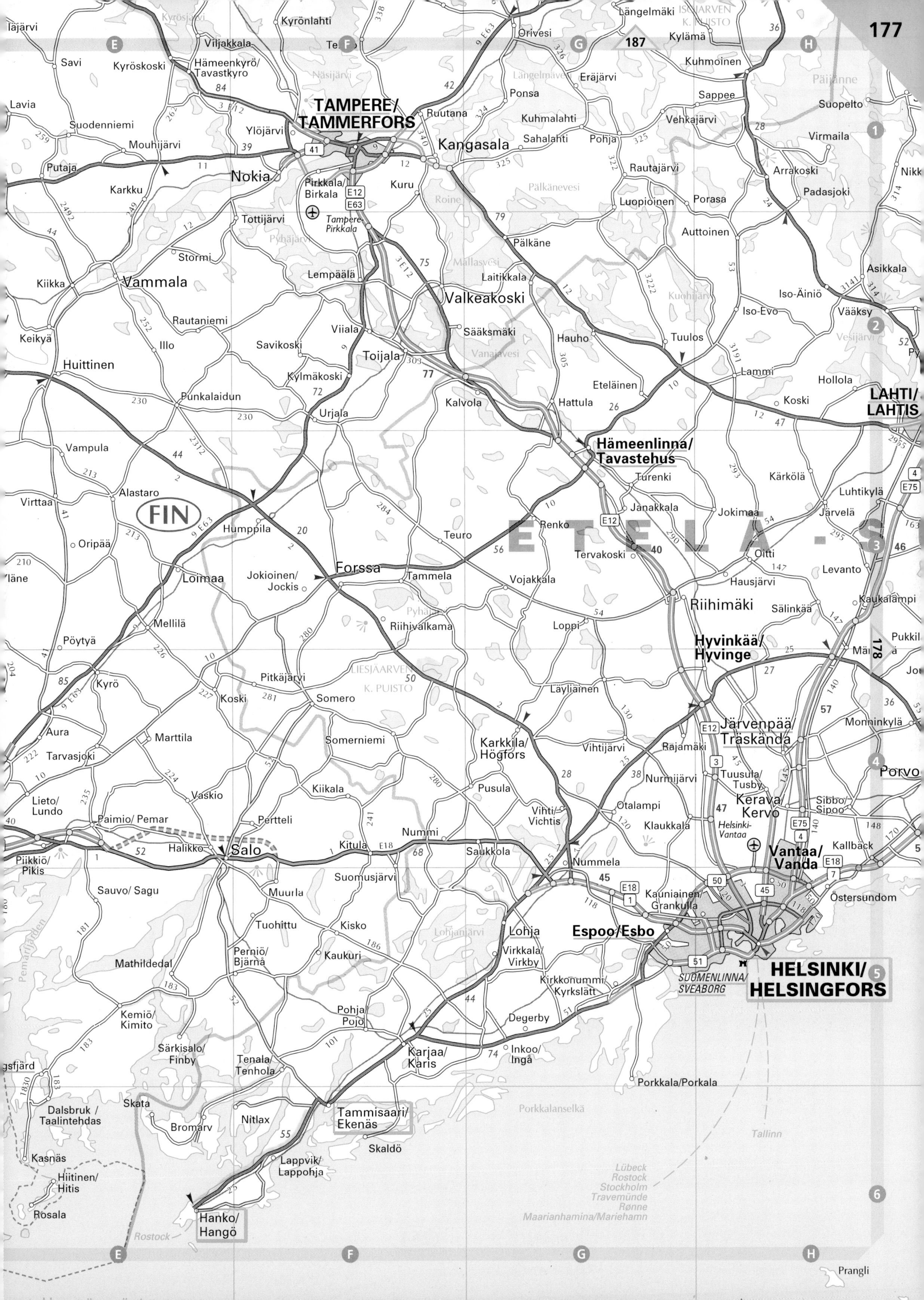
TAMPERE/
TAMMERFORS
Nokia
Kangasala
Valkeakoski
Toijala
Vammala
Huittinen
Forssa
Loimaa
Riihimäki
Hyvinkää/
Hyvinge
Hämeenlinna/
Tavastehus
LAHTI/
LAHTIS
Järvenpää/
Träskända
Kerava/
Kervo
Vantaa/
Vanda
Espoo/Esbo
HELSINKI/
HELSINGFORS
Porvoo
Salo
Lohja
Karkkila/
Högfors
Karjaa/
Karis
Tammisaari/
Ekenäs
Hanko/
Hangö
FIN
ETELÄ-S
SUOMENLINNA/
SVEABORG
Tallinn
Lübeck
Rostock
Stockholm
Travemünde
Rønne
Maarianhamina/Mariehamn
Porkkalanselkä
Porkkala/Porkkala
Prangli
187
178

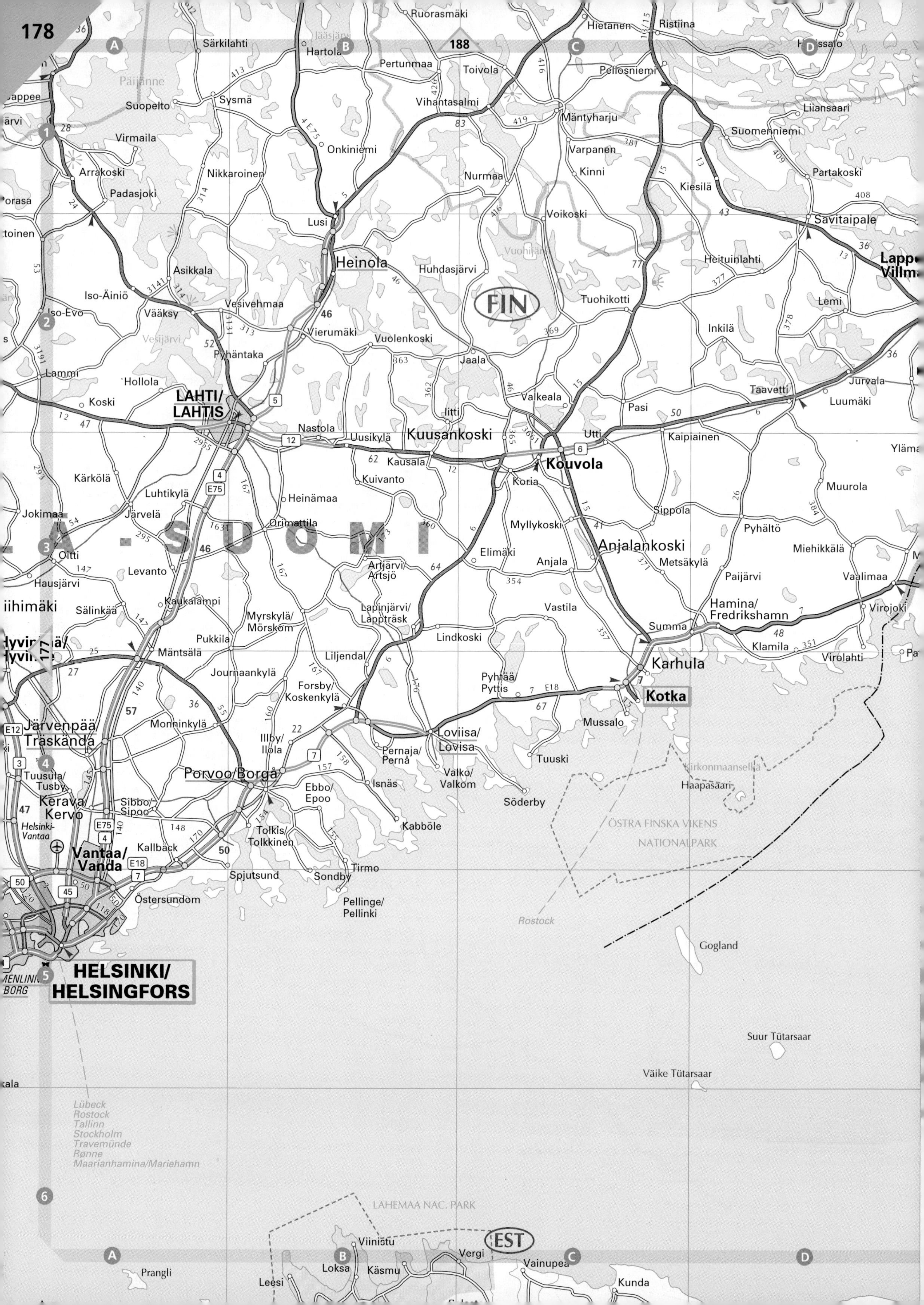
188
177
FIN
EST
HELSINKI/
HELSINGFORS
LAHTI/
LAHTIS
Heinola
Kouvola
Kuusankoski
Kotka
Karhula
Hamina/
Fredrikshamn
Anjalankoski
Porvoo/Borgå
Loviisa/
Lovisa
Järvenpää/
Träskända
Kerava/
Kervo
Vantaa/
Vanda
Savitaipale
Ruorasmäki
Hietanen
Ristiina
Särkilahti
Hartola
Pertunmaa
Toivola
Pellosniemi
Sysmä
Suopelto
Vihantasalmi
Mäntyharju
Liiansaari
Virmaila
Onkiniemi
Suomenniemi
Varpanen
Arrakoski
Padasjoki
Nikkaroinen
Kinni
Nurmaa
Kiesilä
Partakoski
Voikoski
Lusi
Heituinlahti
Huhdasjärvi
Asikkala
Iso-Äiniö
Vesivehmaa
Vääksy
Iso-Evo
Tuohikotti
Lemi
Vierumäki
Vuolenkoski
Inkilä
Pyhäntaka
Jaala
Lammi
Hollola
Valkeala
Jurvala
Taavetti
Koski
Luumäki
Pasi
Iitti
Nastola
Uusikylä
Utti
Kaipiainen
Kausala
Kärkölä
Kuivanto
Koria
Muurola
Luhtikylä
Heinämaa
Jokimaa
Järvelä
Orimattila
Sippola
Myllykoski
Pyhältö
SUOMI
Oitti
Elimäki
Anjala
Miehikkälä
Metsäkylä
Artjärvi/
Artsjö
Hausjärvi
Levanto
Paijärvi
Vaalimaa
Hyvinkää
Sälinkää
Kaukalampi
Vastila
Virojoki
Myrskylä/
Mörskom
Lapinjärvi/
Lappträsk
Summa
Pukkila
Lindkoski
Klamila
Mäntsälä
Liljendal
Virolahti
Journaankylä
Pyhtää/
Pyttis
Forsby/
Koskenkylä
Monninkylä
Mussalo
Illby/
Ilola
Pernaja/
Pernå
Tuuski
Kirkonmaanselkä
Haapasaari
Tuusula/
Tusby
Valko/
Valkom
Isnäs
Ebbo/
Epoo
Söderby
Sibbo/
Sipoo
Helsinki-
Vantaa
Kabböle
ÖSTRA FINSKA VIKENS
NATIONALPARK
Kallbäck
Tolkis/
Tolkkinen
Tirmo
Spjutsund
Sondby
Östersundom
Pellinge/
Pellinki
Rostock
Gogland
Suur Tütarsaar
Väike Tütarsaar
Lübeck
Rostock
Tallinn
Stockholm
Travemünde
Rønne
Maarianhamina/Mariehamn
LAHEMAA NAC. PARK
Viinistu
Vergi
Prangli
Loksa
Käsmu
Vainupea
Leesi
Kunda

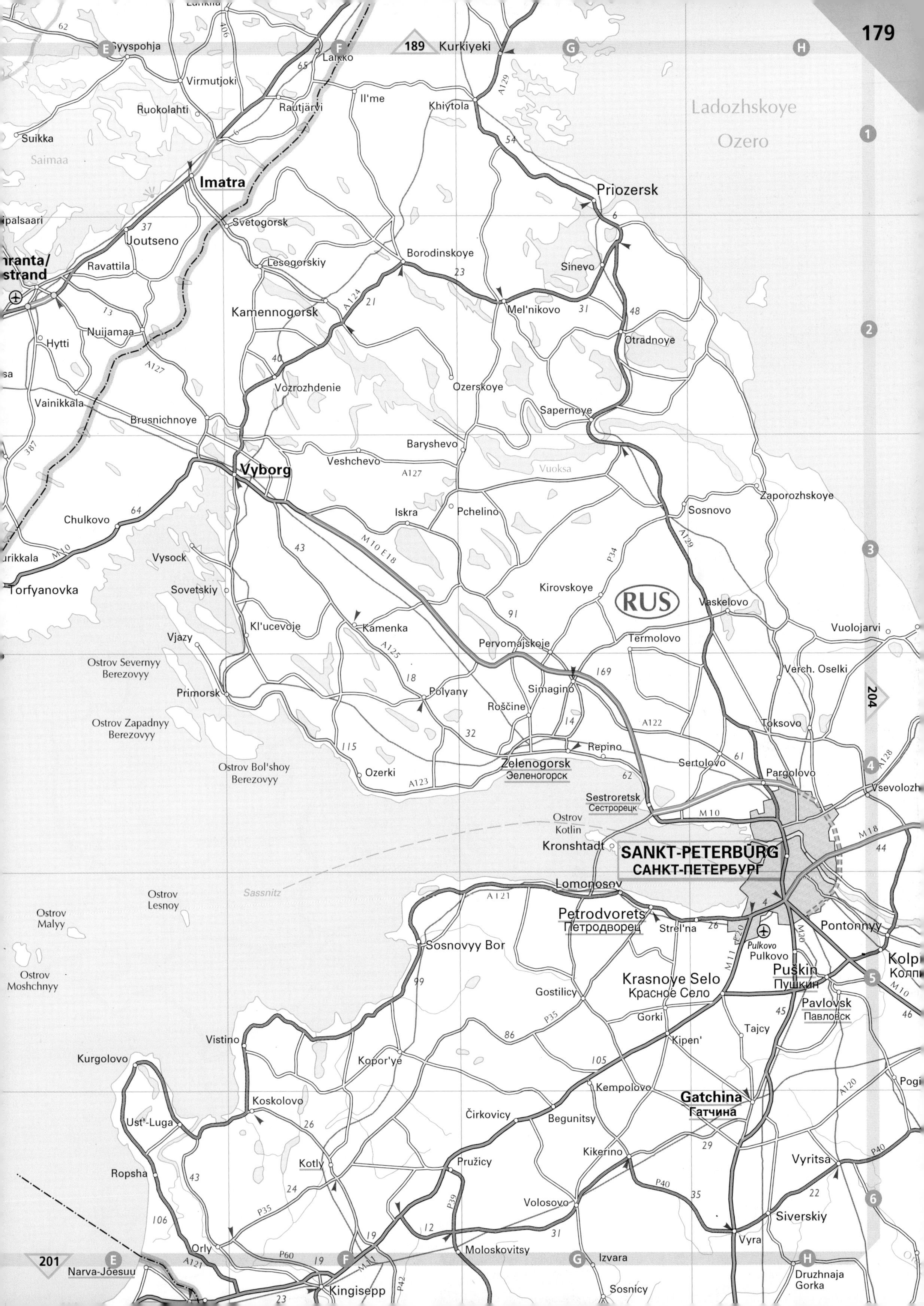
189
Kurkiyeki
Imatra
Svetogorsk
Joutseno
Priozersk
Sinevo
Borodinskoye
Lesogorskiy
Mel'nikovo
Otradnoye
Kamennogorsk
Vozrozhdenie
Ozerskoye
Sapernoye
Vainikkala
Brusnichnoye
Baryshevo
Veshchevo
Vyborg
Vuoksa
Zaporozhskoye
Sosnovo
Iskra
Pchelino
Chulkovo
Vysock
Torfyanovka
Sovetskiy
Kirovskoye
RUS
Vaskelovo
Vuolojarvi
Vjazy
Kl'ucevoje
Kamenka
Termolovo
Pervomajskoje
Verch. Oselki
Ostrov Severnyy Berezovyy
Primorsk
Polyany
Simagino
Roščine
204
Ostrov Zapadnyy Berezovyy
Toksovo
Repino
Sertolovo
Ostrov Bol'shoy Berezovyy
Zelenogorsk
Зеленогорск
Ozerki
Pargolovo
Vsevolozh
Sestroretsk
Сестрорецк
Ostrov Kotlin
Kronshtadt
SANKT-PETERBURG
САНКТ-ПЕТЕРБУРГ
Sassnitz
Lomonosov
Ostrov Lesnoy
Ostrov Malyy
Petrodvorets
Петродворец
Strel'na
Pontonnyy
Pulkovo
Kolp
Колпі
Sosnovyy Bor
Ostrov Moshchnyy
Krasnoye Selo
Красное Село
Puškin
Пушкин
Pavlovsk
Павловск
Gostilicy
Gorki
Vistino
Kipen'
Tajcy
Kurgolovo
Kopor'ye
Kempolovo
Gatchina
Гатчина
Pogi
Koskolovo
Čirkovicy
Begunitsy
Ust'-Luga
Kikerino
Vyritsa
Ropsha
Kotly
Pružicy
Volosovo
Siverskiy
Vyra
201
Narva-Joesuu
Orly
Moloskovitsy
Izvara
Druzhnaja Gorka
Kingisepp
Sosnicy
Gyyspohja
Laikko
Virmutjoki
Ruokolahti
Rautjärvi
Il'me
Khiytola
Suikka
Saimaa
Ladozhskoye Ozero
ipalsaari
nranta/ strand
Ravattila
Nuijamaa
Hytti
urikkala

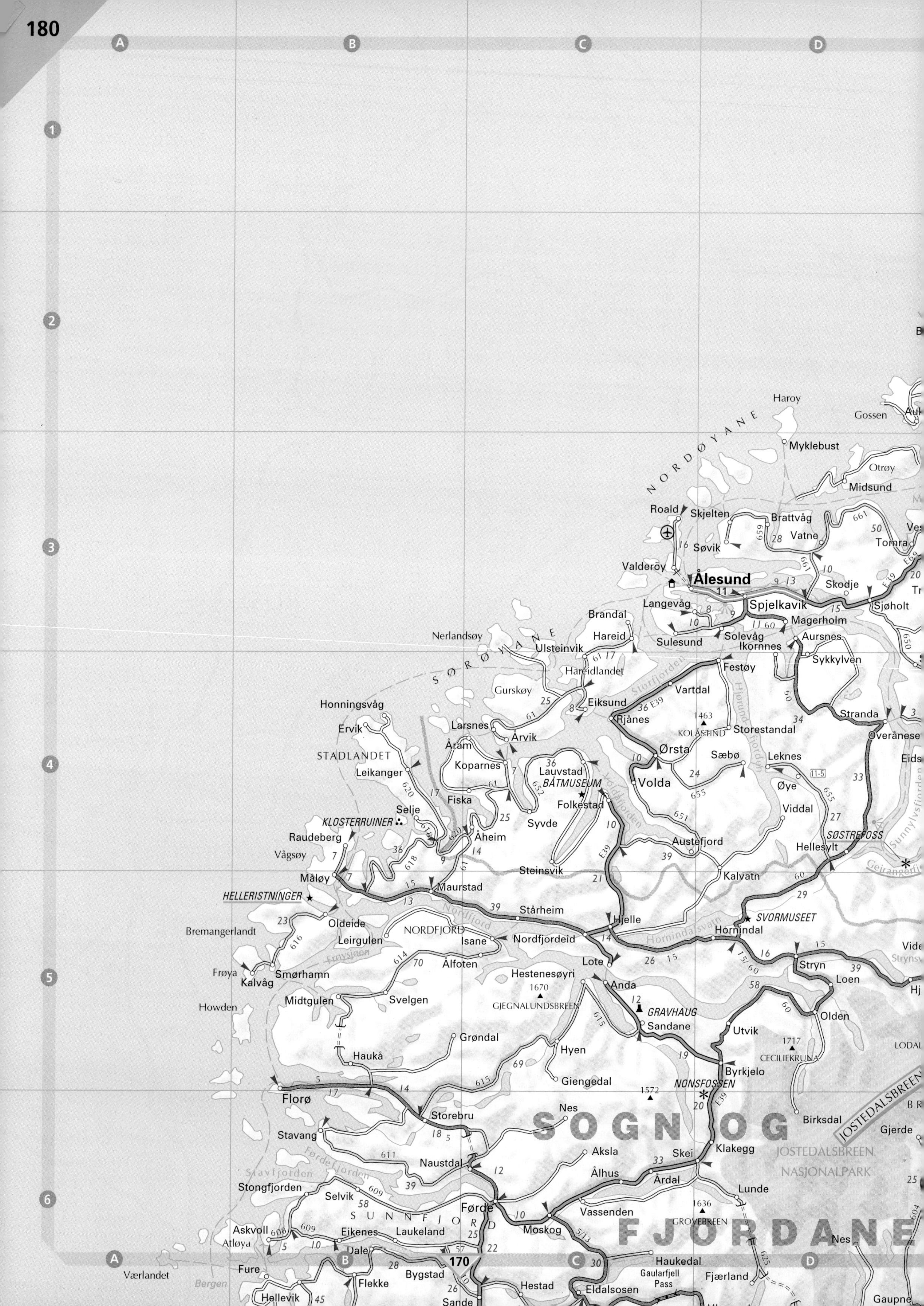

A
B
C
D
1
2
3
4
5
6
Haroy
Gossen
NORDØYANE
Myklebust
Otrøy
Midsund
Roald
Skjelten
Brattvåg
Vatne
Søvik
Tomra
Valderöy
Ålesund
Skodje
Spjelkavik
Sjøholt
Langevåg
Magerholm
Brandal
Hareid
Sulesund
Solevåg
Ikornnes
Aursnes
Nerlandsøy
SØRØYANE
Ulsteinvik
Hareidlandet
Festøy
Sykkylven
Storfjorden
Gurskøy
Eiksund
Vartdal
Hjørundfjorden
Honningsvåg
Larsnes
Rjånes
1463
KOLÅSTIND
Storestandal
Stranda
Ervik
Årvik
Åram
Ørsta
Overånese
STADLANDET
Koparnes
Lauvstad
Sæbø
Leknes
Eids
Leikanger
BÅTMUSEUM
Volda
Øye
Fiska
Folkestad
Voldafjorden
Selje
Syvde
Viddal
KLOSTERRUINER
Åheim
SØSTREFOSS
Raudeberg
Austefjord
Hellesylt
Vågsøy
Sunnylvsfjorden
Geirangerfj
Måløy
Steinsvik
Kalvatn
Maurstad
HELLERISTNINGER
Stårheim
Nordfjord
SVORMUSEET
Bremangerlandt
Oldeide
Hjelle
Hornindal
NORDFJORD
Leirgulen
Isane
Nordfjordeid
Hornindalsvatn
Frøysjøen
Lote
Stryn
Frøya
Smørhamn
Ålfoten
Loen
Kalvåg
Hestenesøyri
Anda
1670
GJEGNALUNDSBREEN
Howden
Midtgulen
Svelgen
GRAVHAUG
Olden
Sandane
Utvik
Grøndal
1717
CECILIEKRUNA
LODAL
Haukå
Hyen
Byrkjelo
Giengedal
NONSFOSSEN
Florø
1572
JOSTEDALSBREEN
Storebru
Nes
SOGN OG
Birksdal
Stavang
Gjerde
Førdefjorden
Aksla
Klakegg
JOSTEDALSBREEN
NASJONALPARK
Naustdal
Skei
Staviforden
Ålhus
Årdal
Stongfjorden
Lunde
Selvik
SUNNFJORD
Førde
1636
Vassenden
GROVEBREEN
Askvoll
Moskog
FJORDANE
Atløya
Eikenes
Laukeland
Nes
Dale
170
Haukedal
Værlandet
Fure
Bygstad
Gaularfjell Pass
Fjærland
Bergen
Flekke
Hestad
Hellevik
Sande
Eldalsoson
Gaupne

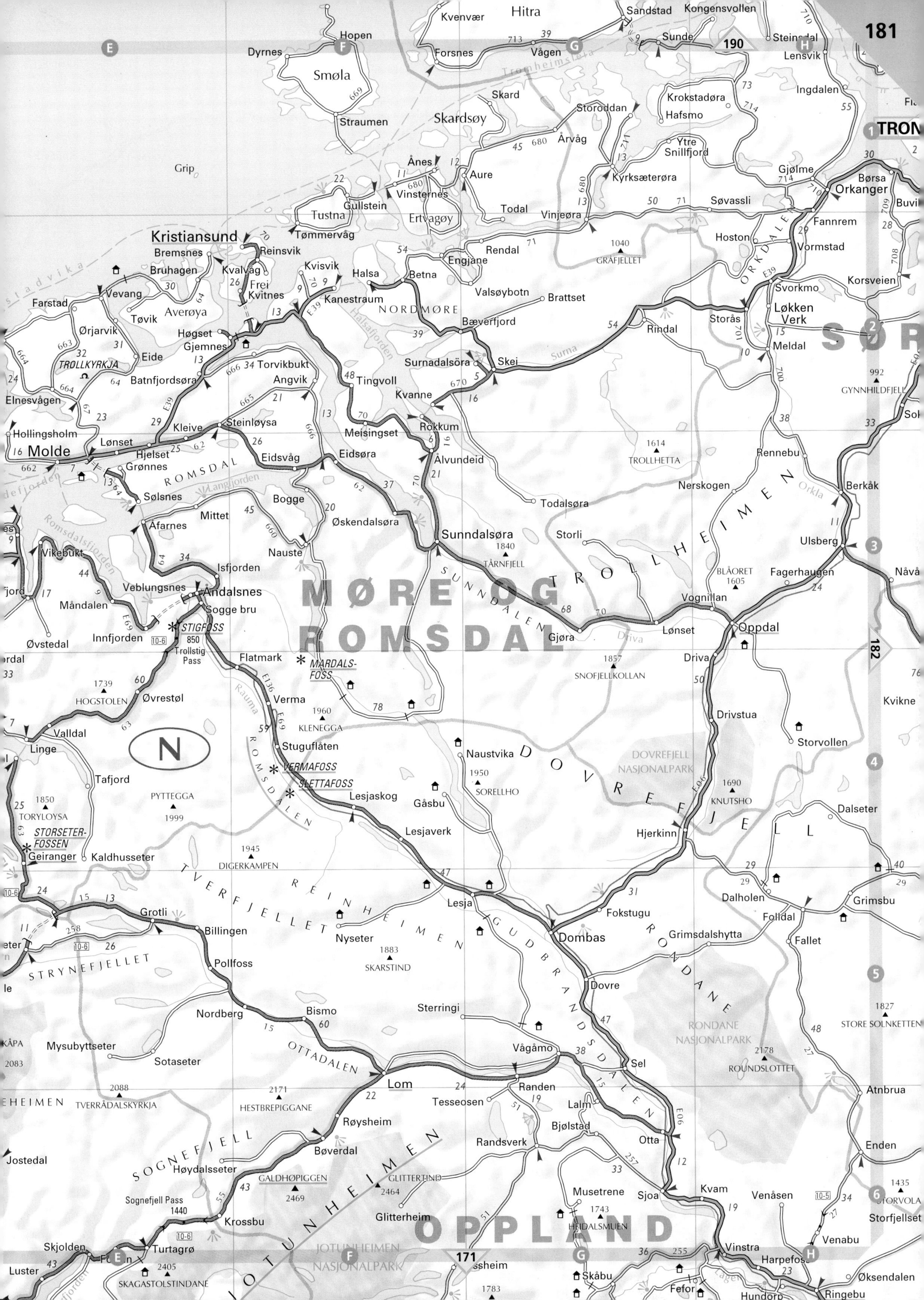
Hitra
Kvenvær
Sandstad
Kongensvollen
Hopen
Dyrnes
Smøla
Forsnes
Vågen
Sunde
Steinsdal
Lensvik
190
Tromheimsleia
Straumen
Skard
Storoddan
Krokstadøra
Hafsmo
Ingdalen
Skardsøy
Årvåg
Ytre Snillfjord
TRON
Grip
Ånes
Aure
Kyrksæterøra
Gjølme
Børsa
Orkanger
Buvi
Tustna
Gullstein
Vinsternes
Ertvågøy
Todal
Vinjeøra
Søvassli
Fannrem
Tømmervåg
Kristiansund
Reinsvik
Bremsnes
Rendal
1040
GRÅFJELLET
Hoston
Vormstad
ORKDALEN
Engjane
Kvisvik
Kvalvåg
Bruhagen
Halsa
Betna
Frei
Kvitnes
Vevang
Averøya
Farstad
Tøvik
Kanestraum
NORDMØRE
Valsøybotn
Brattset
Svorkmo
Korsveien
Løkken Verk
Rindal
Storås
Høgset
Gjemnes
Bæverfjord
Ørjarvik
Eide
TROLLKYRKJA
Torvikbukt
Surnadalsöra
Skei
Surna
Meldal
Batnfjordsøra
Angvik
Tingvoll
Kvanne
992
GYNNHILDFJELL
Elnesvågen
Hollingsholm
Kleive
Steinløysa
Meisingset
Rokkum
Molde
Lønset
Hjelset
Grønnes
Eidsvåg
Eidsøra
Ålvundeid
1614
TROLLHETTA
Rennebu
ROMSDAL
Langfjorden
Sølsnes
Bogge
Todalsøra
Nerskogen
Berkåk
Mittet
Åfarnes
Øskendalsøra
Sunndalsøra
Storli
Romsdalsfjorden
Vikebukt
Nauste
1840
TÅRNFJELL
Ulsberg
Isfjorden
Veblungsnes
Åndalsnes
SUNNDALEN
TROLLHEIMEN
BLÅORET
1605
Fagerhaugen
Nåvå
Måndalen
Sogge bru
MØRE OG ROMSDAL
Vognillan
STIGFOSS
850
Trollstig Pass
Øvstedal
Innfjorden
Gjøra
Lønset
Oppdal
182
Flatmark
MARDALSFOSS
1857
SNOFJELLKOLLAN
Driva
1739
HOGSTOLEN
Øvrestøl
Verma
Kvikne
1960
KLENEGGA
Drivstua
Valldal
Linge
Rauma
Stugufläten
Naustvika
Storvollen
DOVREFJELL NASJONALPARK
Tafjord
VERMAFOSS
SLETTAFOSS
1950
SORELLHO
DOVREFJELL
1690
KNUTSHO
PYTTEGGA
1999
1850
TORYLOYSA
ROMSDALEN
Lesjaskog
Gåsbu
Dalseter
STORSETER-FOSSEN
Geiranger
Kaldhusseter
Lesjaverk
Hjerkinn
1945
DIGERKAMPEN
TVERFJELLET
REINHEIMEN
Lesja
Dalholen
Grimsbu
Grotli
Nyseter
Fokstugu
Folldal
Billingen
1883
SKARSTIND
Dombås
Grimsdalshytta
Fallet
STRYNEFJELLET
Pollfoss
GUDBRANDSDALEN
RONDANE
Dovre
Nordberg
Bismo
Sterringi
1827
STORE SOLNKETTEN
Mysubyttseter
Sotaseter
OTTADALEN
Vågåmo
RONDANE NASJONALPARK
2178
ROUNDSLOTTET
2083
Sel
Lom
Randen
Atnbrua
2088
TVERRÅDALSKYRKJA
2171
HESTBREPIGGANE
Tesseosen
Lalm
Røysheim
Bjølstad
SOGNEFJELL
Otta
Jostedal
Bøverdal
Randsverk
Enden
Høydalsseter
GALDHØPIGGEN
2469
2464
GLITTERTIND
Musetrene
Sjoa
Kvam
Venåsen
1435
STORVOLA
Sognefjell Pass
1440
Krossbu
Glitterheim
1743
HEIDALSMUEN
OPPLAND
Storfjellseter
Venabu
JOTUNHEIMEN
JOTUNHEIMEN NASJONALPARK
Skjolden
Turtagrø
Vinstra
Harpefoss
Luster
2405
SKAGASTOLSTINDANE
171
Skåbu
Fefor
Hundorp
Ringebu
Øksendalen
1783

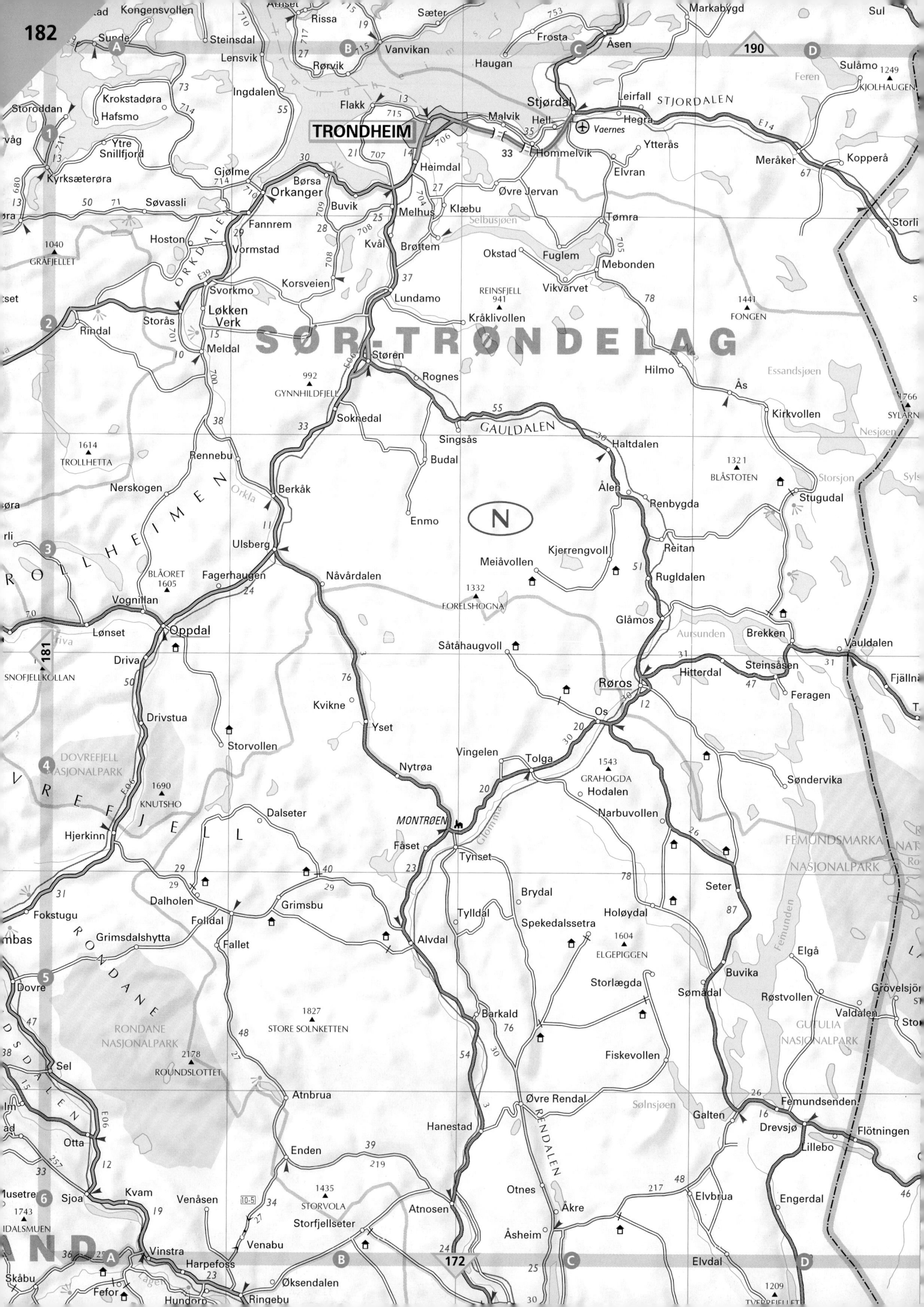
TRONDHEIM
SØR-TRØNDELAG
Orkanger
Løkken Verk
Oppdal
Røros
Stjørdal
Kongensvollen
Sunde
Steinsdal
Lensvik
Rissa
Rørvik
Vanvikan
Sæter
Frosta
Åsen
Markabygd
Sul
Haugan
Sulåmo
KJOLHAUGEN
STJORDALEN
Leirfall
Hegra
Vaernes
Malvik
Hell
Hommelvik
Ytterås
Meråker
Kopperå
Elvran
Storli
Krokstadøra
Hafsmo
Storoddan
Ingdalen
Flakk
Ytre Snillfjord
Kyrksæterøra
Gjølme
Børsa
Heimdal
Øvre Jervan
Søvassli
Buvik
Melhus
Klæbu
Selbusjøen
Tømra
Fannrem
Hoston
GRÅFJELLET
Vormstad
Kvål
Brøttem
Okstad
Fuglem
Mebonden
ORKDALEN
Korsveien
Svorkmo
Lundamo
REINSFJELL
Kråklivollen
Vikvarvet
FONGEN
Storås
Rindal
Meldal
Støren
Rognes
Hilmo
Essandsjøen
Ås
GYNNHILDFJELL
Soknedal
GAULDALEN
Singsås
Haltdalen
Kirkvollen
SYLARNA
Nesjøen
TROLLHETTA
Rennebu
Budal
BLÅSTOTEN
Storsjon
Nerskogen
Berkåk
Orkla
Ålen
Renbygda
Stugudal
Enmo
Ulsberg
Reitan
Kjerrengvoll
Meiåvollen
Rugldalen
TROLLHEIMEN
BLÅORET
Fagerhaugen
Nåvårdalen
FORELSHOGNA
Vognillan
Glåmos
Aursunden
Brekken
Lønset
Vauldalen
Såtåhaugvoll
Driva
SNOFJELLKOLLAN
Hitterdal
Steinsåsen
Fjällnäs
Feragen
Os
Kvikne
Yset
Drivstua
Storvollen
Vingelen
Tolga
GRAHOGDA
Hodalen
Søndervika
DOVREFJELL NASJONALPARK
KNUTSHO
Nytrøa
DOVREFJELL
Dalseter
MONTRØEN
Narbuvollen
Hjerkinn
Fåset
Tynset
FEMUNDSMARKA NASJONALPARK
Glomma
Seter
Dalholen
Grimsbu
Brydal
Fokstugu
Folldal
Tylldal
Holøydal
Spekedalssetra
Grimsdalshytta
Fallet
Alvdal
ELGEPIGGEN
Femunden
Elgå
Storlægda
Buvika
Dovre
Sømådal
Røstvollen
Grövelsjön
RONDANE
Barkald
Valdalen
STORE SOLNKETTEN
GUTULIA NASJONALPARK
RONDANE NASJONALPARK
ROUNDSLOTTET
Fiskevollen
Sel
Atnbrua
Øvre Rendal
Sølnsjøen
Femundsenden
Galten
Hanestad
Drevsjø
Flötningen
Otta
RENDALEN
Lillebo
Enden
Kvam
Otnes
Elvbrua
Engerdal
Sjoa
Venåsen
STORVOLA
Atnosen
Åkre
Musetrø
IDALSMUEN
Storfjellseter
Venabu
Åsheim
Vinstra
Harpefoss
Elvdal
Skåbu
Øksendalen
Fefor
Hundorp
Ringebu
TVERRFJELLET
190
181
172
E6
E14
E39

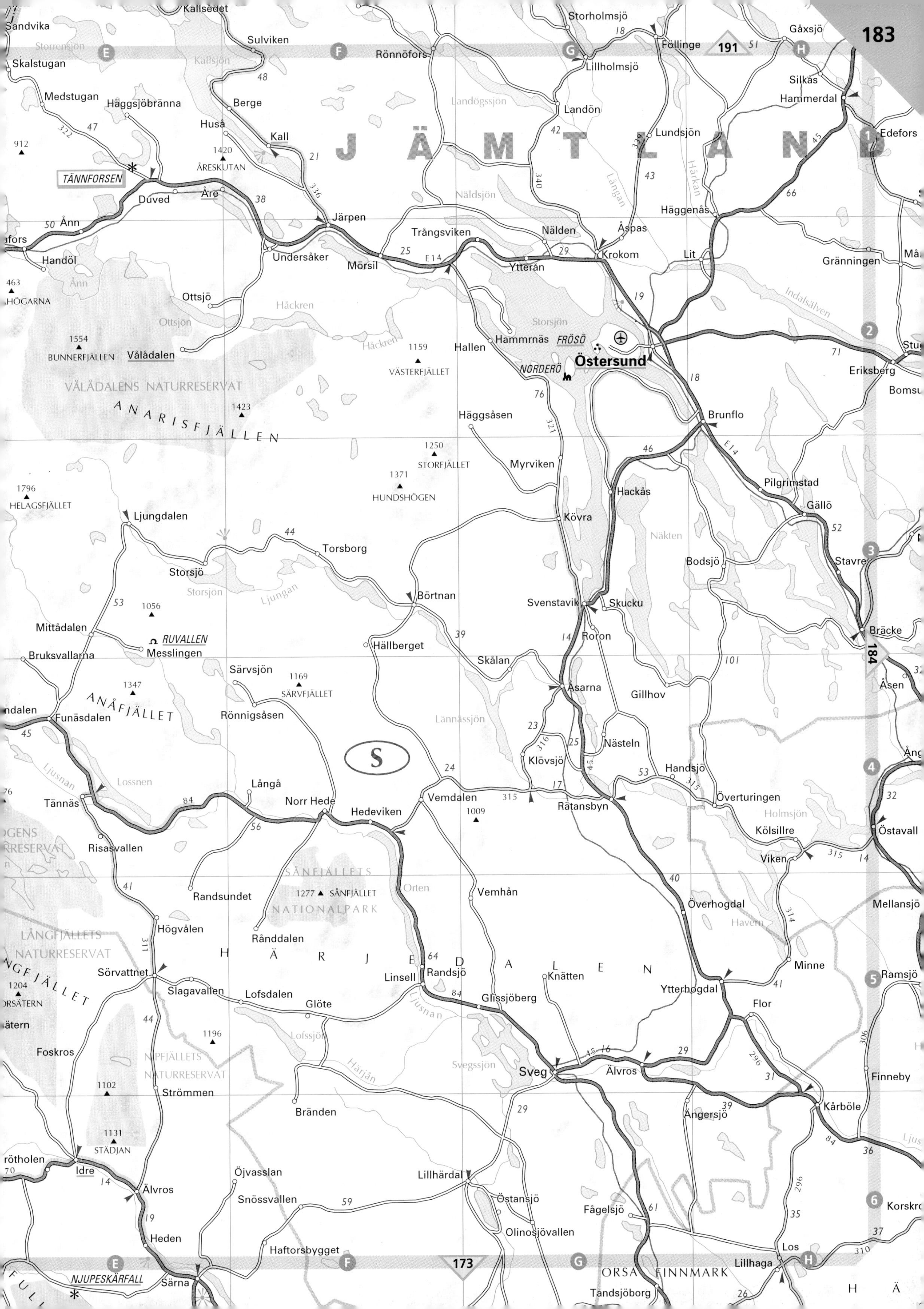
JÄMTLAND
HÄRJEDALEN
Östersund
Frösö
Norderö
Kallsedet
Sandvika
Skalstugan
Sulviken
Rönnöfors
Storholmsjö
Föllinge
Lillholmsjö
Gåxsjö
Silkås
Hammerdal
Edefors
Medstugan
Häggsjöbränna
Berge
Landön
Lundsjön
Huså
Kall
Åreskutan
Tännforsen
Duved
Åre
Ånn
Järpen
Undersåker
Mörsil
Trångsviken
Ytterån
Nälden
Åspas
Krokom
Häggenås
Lit
Gränningen
Handöl
Högarna
Ottsjö
Håckren
Storsjön
Hammrnäs
Hallen
Västerfjället
Bunnerfjällen
Vålådalen
Vålådalens naturreservat
Anarisfjällen
Eriksberg
Bomsu
Brunflo
Häggsåsen
Storfjället
Hundshögen
Myrviken
Helagsfjället
Pilgrimstad
Gällö
Hackås
Kövra
Ljungdalen
Torsborg
Storsjö
Bodsjö
Stavre
Börtnan
Svenstavik
Skucku
Roron
Bräcke
Mittådalen
Ruvallen
Messlingen
Hällberget
Bruksvallarna
Särvsjön
Särvfjället
Skålan
Åsarna
Gillhov
Åsen
Anåfjället
Funäsdalen
Rönnigsåsen
Lännässjön
Nästeln
Klövsjö
Handsjö
Lossnen
Ljusnan
Tännäs
Långå
Norr Hede
Hedeviken
Vemdalen
Rätansbyn
Överturingen
Holmsjön
Kölsillre
Östavall
Risasvallen
Viken
Sånfjällets nationalpark
Sånfjället
Orten
Randsundet
Vemhån
Överhogdal
Havern
Mellansjö
Högvålen
Långfjällets naturreservat
Rånddalen
Minne
Sörvattnet
Linsell
Randsjö
Knätten
Ytterhogdal
Ramsjö
Slagavallen
Lofsdalen
Glissjöberg
Glöte
Flor
Lofssjön
Nipfjällets naturreservat
Foskros
Svegssjön
Sveg
Älvros
Härjån
Finneby
Strömmen
Bränden
Ångersjö
Kårböle
Städjan
Idre
Öjvasslan
Lillhärdal
Älvros
Snössvallen
Östansjö
Fågelsjö
Korskro
Heden
Olinosjövallen
Haftorsbygget
Los
Lillhaga
Njupeskärfall
Särna
Orsa Finnmark
Tandsjöborg
191
173
184

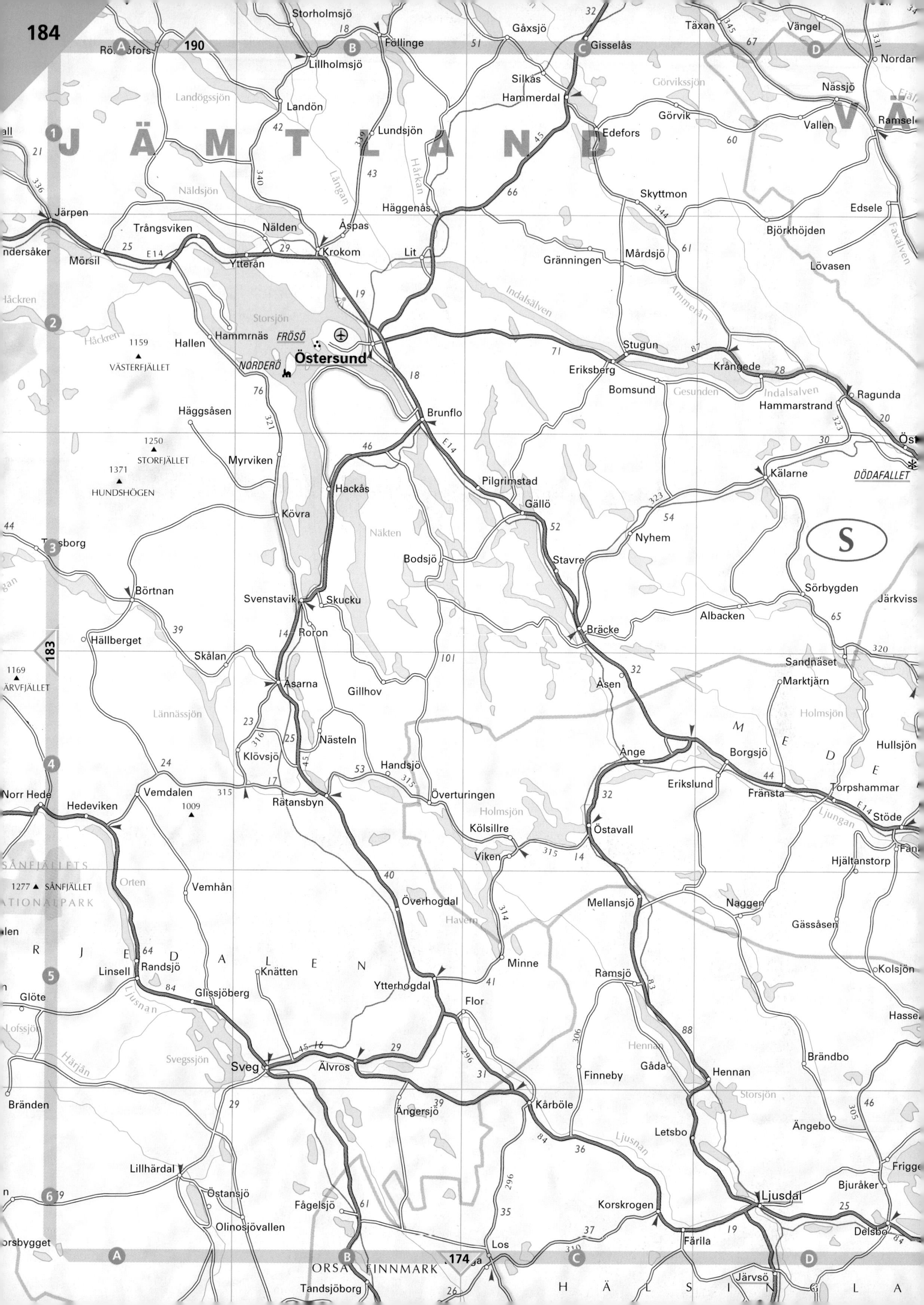
190
Storholmsjö
Föllinge
Gåxsjö
Gisselås
Täxan
Vängel
Nordan
Lillholmsjö
Landögssjön
Landön
Silkås
Hammerdal
Görviksjön
Nässjö
Görvik
Vallen
Ramsele
Edefors
Lundsjön
J Ä M T L A N D
Näldsjön
Långan
Hårkan
Häggenås
Skyttmon
Edsele
Järpen
Trångsviken
Nälden
Åspas
Björkhöjden
Mörsil
Ytterån
Krokom
Lit
Gränningen
Mårdsjö
Lövasen
Indalsälven
Ammerån
Faxälven
Storsjön
Håckren
1159
VÄSTERFJÄLLET
Hallen
Hammrnäs
FRÖSÖ
NORDERÖ
Östersund
Stugun
Eriksberg
Krångede
Bomsund
Gesunden
Ragunda
Hammarstrand
Häggsåsen
Brunflo
1250
STORFJÄLLET
1371
HUNDSHÖGEN
Myrviken
Hackås
Pilgrimstad
Kälarne
DÖDAFALLET
Gällö
Kövra
Nyhem
Näkten
Bodsjö
Stavre
S
Sörbygden
Järkvissle
Börtnan
Svenstavik
Skucku
Albacken
Bräcke
Hällberget
Roron
183
Skålan
Sandnäset
1169
ÄRVFJÄLLET
Åsarna
Gillhov
Åsen
Marktjärn
Lännässjön
Holmsjön
M E D E
Nästeln
Klövsjö
Ånge
Borgsjö
Hullsjön
Handsjö
Erikslund
Fränsta
Torpshammar
Norr Hede
Vemdalen
Rätansbyn
Överturingen
Hedeviken
1009
Stöde
Ljungan
Kölsillre
Östavall
Viken
Hjältanstorp
SÅNFJÄLLETS NATIONALPARK
1277
SÅNFJÄLLET
Orten
Vemhån
Överhogdal
Havern
Mellansjö
Naggen
Gässåsen
H J Ä R J E D A L E N
Linsell
Randsjö
Knätten
Minne
Ramsjö
Kolsjön
Ytterhogdal
Glöte
Glissjöberg
Ljusnan
Flor
Lofssjön
Hasse
Härjån
Svegssjön
Sveg
Älvros
Hennan
Gåda
Hennan
Brändbo
Finneby
Bränden
Kårböle
Ångersjö
Storsjön
Ängebo
Letsbo
Lillhärdal
Frigge
Östansjö
Fågelsjö
Korskrogen
Ljusdal
Bjuråker
Olinosjövallen
Delsbo
Los
Färlla
orsbygget
174
ORSA FINNMARK
Järvsö
Tandsjöborg
H Ä L S I N G L A

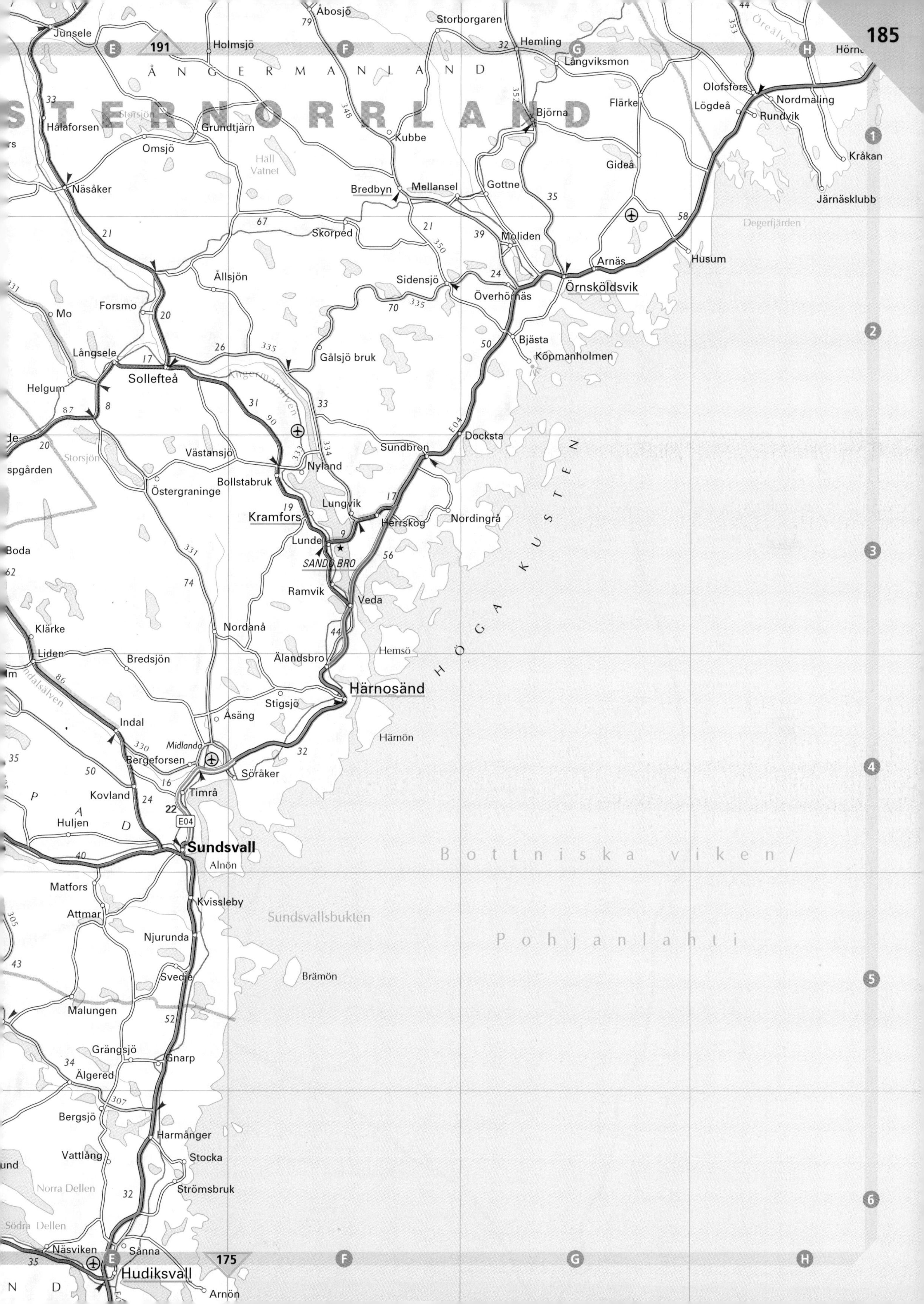

Åbosjö
Storborgaren
Hemling
Långviksmon
Junsele
Holmsjö
191
Å N G E R M A N L A N D
STERNORRLAND
Olofsfors
Nordmaling
Lögdeå
Rundvik
Flärke
Björna
Hålaforsen
Storsjön
Grundtjärn
Kubbe
Omsjö
Häll Vatnet
Gideå
Kråkan
Näsåker
Bredbyn
Mellansel
Gottne
Järnäsklubb
Degerfjärden
Skorped
Moliden
Husum
Arnäs
Örnsköldsvik
Ållsjön
Sidensjö
Överhörnäs
Mo
Forsmo
Bjästa
Köpmanholmen
Gålsjö bruk
Långsele
Sollefteå
Ångermanälven
Helgum
Dockstа
Västansjö
Sundbron
Storsjön
Nyland
spgården
Bollstabruk
Östergraninge
Lungvik
Nordingrå
Kramfors
Herrskog
Lunde
SANDÖ BRO
Boda
Ramvik
Veda
H Ö G A K U S T E N
Nordanå
Klärke
Hemsö
Liden
Bredsjön
Älandsbro
Indalsälven
Härnosänd
Stigsjö
Åsäng
Indal
Härnön
Midlanda
Bergeforsen
Söråker
Timrå
Kovland
Huljen
Sundsvall
Alnön
Bottniska viken/
Matfors
Kvissleby
Attmar
Sundsvallsbukten
Pohjanlahti
Njurunda
Svedje
Brämön
Malungen
Gnarp
Grängsjö
Älgered
Bergsjö
Harmånger
Vattlång
Stocka
Norra Dellen
Strömsbruk
Södra Dellen
Näsviken
Sanna
Hudiksvall
Arnön
175

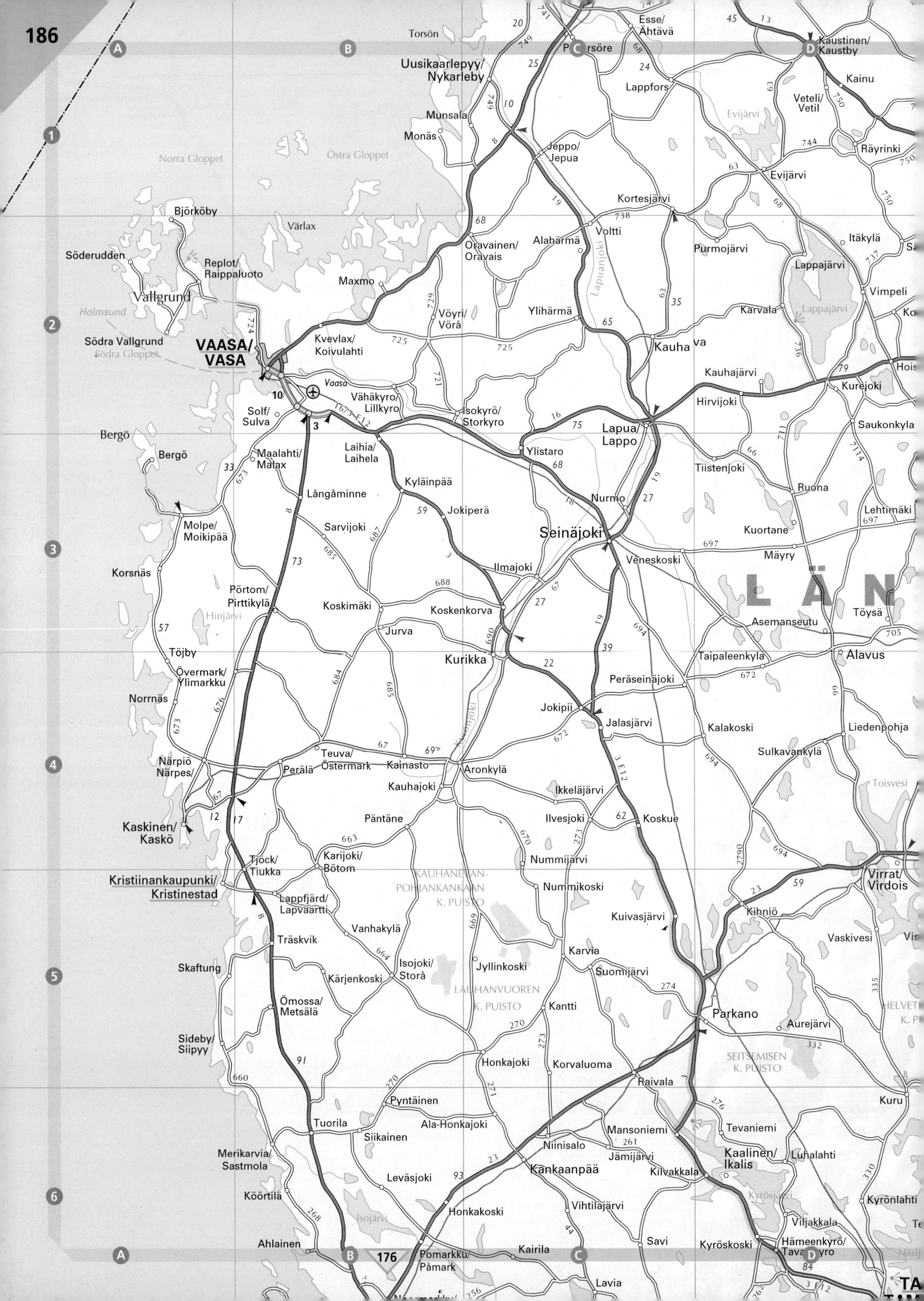

VAASA/
VASA
Uusikaarlepyy/
Nykarleby
Seinäjoki
Lapua/
Lappo
Kauhava
Kurikka
Kaskinen/
Kaskö
Kristiinankaupunki/
Kristinestad
Närpiö
Närpes
Parkano
Kankaanpää
Alavus
Virrat/
Virdois
Lappajärvi
Kaustinen/
Kaustby
Esse/
Ähtävä
Jeppo/
Jepua
Oravainen/
Oravais
Vöyri/
Vörå
Maxmo
Replot/
Raippaluoto
Björköby
Vallgrund
Söderudden
Södra Vallgrund
Norra Gloppet
Östra Gloppet
Värlax
Munsala
Monäs
Kevlax/
Koivulahti
Vähäkyro/
Lillkyro
Isokyrö/
Storkyro
Laihia/
Laihela
Solf/
Sulva
Bergö
Maalahti/
Malax
Molpe/
Moikipää
Korsnäs
Pörtom/
Pirttikylä
Övermark/
Ylimarkku
Töjby
Norrnäs
Teuva/
Östermark
Kauhajoki
Tjöck/
Tiukka
Lappfjärd/
Lapväärtti
Träskvik
Skaftung
Ömossa/
Metsälä
Sideby/
Siipyy
Merikarvia/
Sastmola
Köörtilä
Ahlainen
Pomarkku/
Påmark
Isojoki/
Storå
Honkajoki
Ilmajoki
Koskenkorva
Jalasjärvi
Kuortane
Kortesjärvi
Evijärvi
Alahärmä
Ylihärmä
Ylistaro
Nurmo
Lappfors
Purmojärvi
Vimpeli
Kauhajärvi
Hirvijoki
Kurejoki
Saukonkyla
Kankaanpää
Kaalinen/
Ikalis
Hämeenkyrö/
Tavastkyro
Kyröskoski
Lavia
Kairila
Honkakoski
Niinisalo
Jämijärvi
Karvia
Kantti
Raivala
LÄN
176

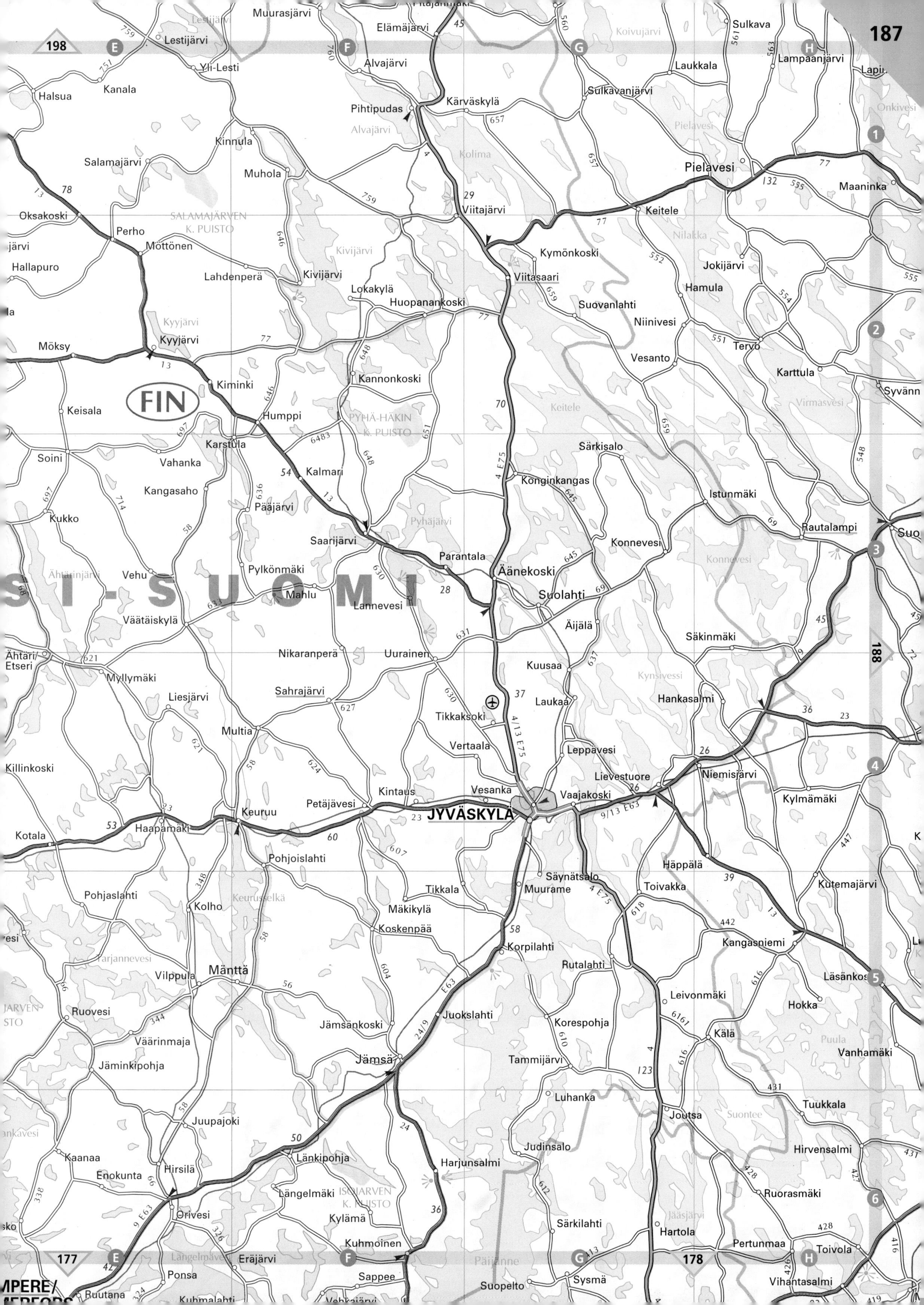
198
177
178
188
FIN
Jyväskylä
Pihtipudas
Viitasaari
Pielavesi
Keitele
Kyyjärvi
Karstula
Saarijärvi
Äänekoski
Suolahti
Konnevesi
Laukaa
Vaajakoski
Keuruu
Haapamäki
Petäjävesi
Muurame
Säynätsalo
Korpilahti
Jämsä
Jämsänkoski
Mänttä
Vilppula
Ruovesi
Orivesi
Kuhmoinen
Joutsa
Hartola
Sysmä
Luhanka
Toivakka
Hankasalmi
Rautalampi
Tervo
Vesanto
Kangasniemi
Multia
Uurainen
Kinnula
Kivijärvi
Perho
Halsua
Lestijärvi
Soini
Pertunmaa
Hirvensalmi
Kuhmalahti
Eräjärvi
Längelmäki
Kannonkoski
Karttula
Maaninka
Pylkönmäki
Sumiainen
Leppävesi
Lievestuore

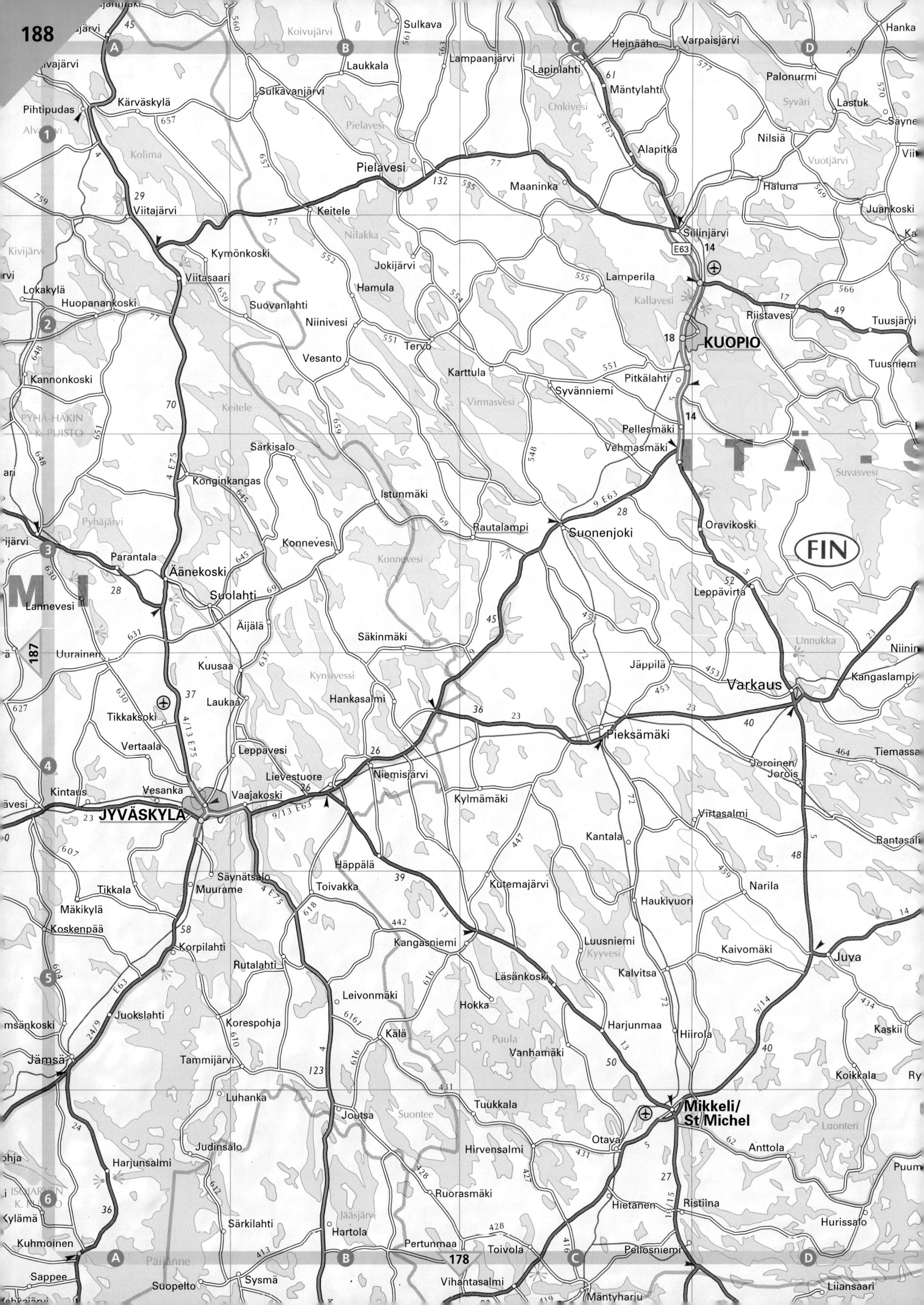
Pihtipudas
Kärväskylä
Sulkava
Laukkala
Sulkavanjärvi
Lampaanjärvi
Lapinlahti
Heinäaho
Varpaisjärvi
Palonurmi
Mäntylahti
Lastuk
Nilsiä
Alapitkä
Pielavesi
Maaninka
Haluna
Juankoski
Viitajärvi
Keitele
Siilinjärvi
Kymönkoski
Jokijärvi
Viitasaari
Lokakylä
Huopanankoski
Hamula
Lamperila
Suovanlahti
Niinivesi
Riistavesi
Tuusjärvi
Tervo
KUOPIO
Kannonkoski
Vesanto
Karttula
Pitkälahti
Syvänniemi
PYHÄ-HÄKIN K. PUISTO
Pellesmäki
Vehmasmäki
Särkisalo
ITÄ-S
Konginkangas
Istunmäki
Rautalampi
Suonenjoki
Oravikoski
Konnevesi
FIN
Parantala
Äänekoski
Leppävirta
Suolahti
Lannevesi
Äijälä
Säkinmäki
Uurainen
Kuusaa
Jäppilä
Varkaus
Kangaslampi
Laukaa
Hankasalmi
Tikkakoski
Pieksämäki
Vertaala
Leppävesi
Joroinen/ Jorois
Tiemassa
Lievestuore
Niemisjärvi
Kintaus
Vesanka
Vaajakoski
Kylmämäki
JYVÄSKYLÄ
Virtasalmi
Kantala
Häppälä
Säynätsalo
Toivakka
Tikkala
Muurame
Kutemajärvi
Narila
Haukivuori
Mäkikylä
Koskenpää
Kangasniemi
Luusniemi
Kaivomäki
Juva
Korpilahti
Rutalahti
Kalvitsa
Läsänkoski
Leivonmäki
Hokka
Juokslahti
Korespohja
Harjunmaa
Kaskii
Kälä
Hiirola
Vanhamäki
Jämsä
Tammijärvi
Koikkala
Luhanka
Tuukkala
Joutsa
Mikkeli/ St Michel
Judinsalo
Hirvensalmi
Otava
Anttola
Harjunsalmi
Ruorasmäki
Hietanen
Ristiina
Särkilahti
Hurissalo
Hartola
Kuhmoinen
Pertunmaa
Toivola
Pellosniemi
Sappee
Suopelto
Sysmä
Vihantasalmi
Mäntyharju
Liiansaari
187
178

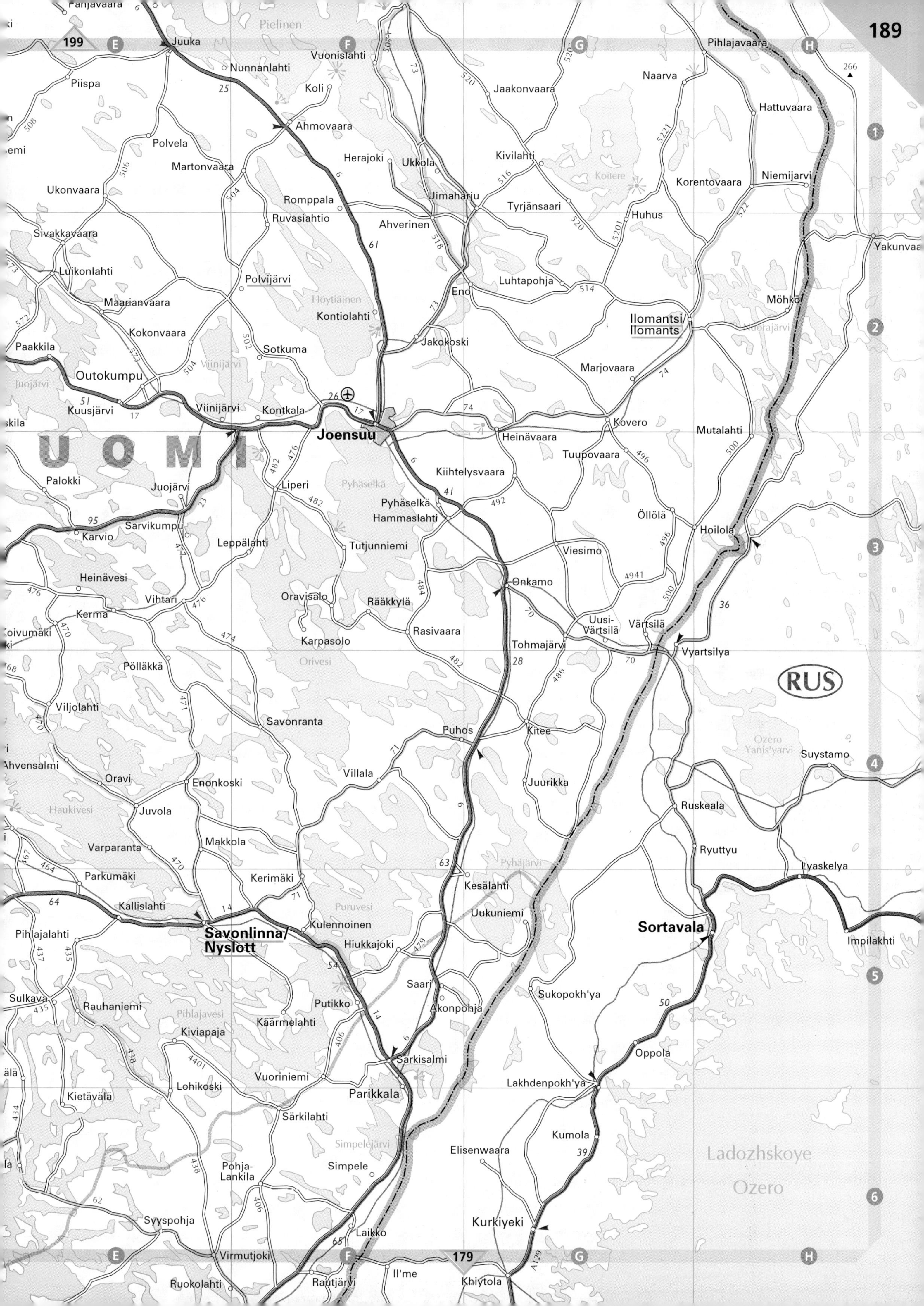

199
179
RUS
UOMI
Joensuu
Savonlinna/
Nyslott
Sortavala
Ilomantsi/
Ilomants
Outokumpu
Juuka
Nunnanlahti
Vuonislahti
Koli
Piispa
Ahmovaara
Polvela
Martonvaara
Ukonvaara
Herajoki
Ukkola
Kivilahti
Jaakonvaara
Naarva
Pihlajavaara
Hattuvaara
Korentovaara
Niemijärvi
Uimaharju
Tyrjänsaari
Huhus
Romppala
Ruvasiahtio
Ahverinen
Sivakkavaara
Luikonlahti
Polvijärvi
Luhtapohja
Eno
Maarianvaara
Kontiolahti
Kokonvaara
Jakokoski
Paakkila
Sotkuma
Marjovaara
Mutalahti
Kuusjärvi
Viinijärvi
Kontkala
Heinävaara
Kovero
Tuupovaara
Palokki
Juojärvi
Liperi
Kiihtelysvaara
Pyhäselkä
Hammaslahti
Öllölä
Hoilola
Karvio
Sarvikumpu
Leppälahti
Tutjunniemi
Viesimo
Heinävesi
Onkamo
Vihtari
Kerma
Oravisalo
Rääkkylä
Rasivaara
Uusi-
Värtsilä
Värtsilä
Vyartsilya
Karpasolo
Tohmajärvi
Pölläkkä
Viljolahti
Savonranta
Puhos
Kitee
Ahvensalmi
Oravi
Enonkoski
Villala
Juurikka
Suystamo
Juvola
Ruskeala
Varparanta
Makkola
Ryuttyu
Parkumäki
Kerimäki
Kesälahti
Lyaskelya
Kallislahti
Uukuniemi
Pihlajalahti
Kulennoinen
Hiukkajoki
Impilakhti
Saari
Sukopokh'ya
Sulkava
Rauhaniemi
Putikko
Akonpohja
Kiviapaja
Käärmelahti
Oppola
Särkisalmi
Lohikoski
Vuoriniemi
Lakhdenpokh'ya
Kietävälä
Parikkala
Särkilahti
Kumola
Elisenwaara
Simpele
Pohja-
Lankila
Syyspohja
Kurkiyeki
Laikko
Virmutjoki
Ruokolahti
Rautjärvi
Il'me
Khiytola
Yakunvaa
Möhkö
Pielinen
Koitere
Höytiäinen
Viinijärvi
Juojärvi
Pyhäselkä
Orivesi
Haukivesi
Puruvesi
Pihlajavesi
Simpelejärvi
Pyhäjärvi
Ozero
Yanis'yarvi
Ladozhskoye
Ozero

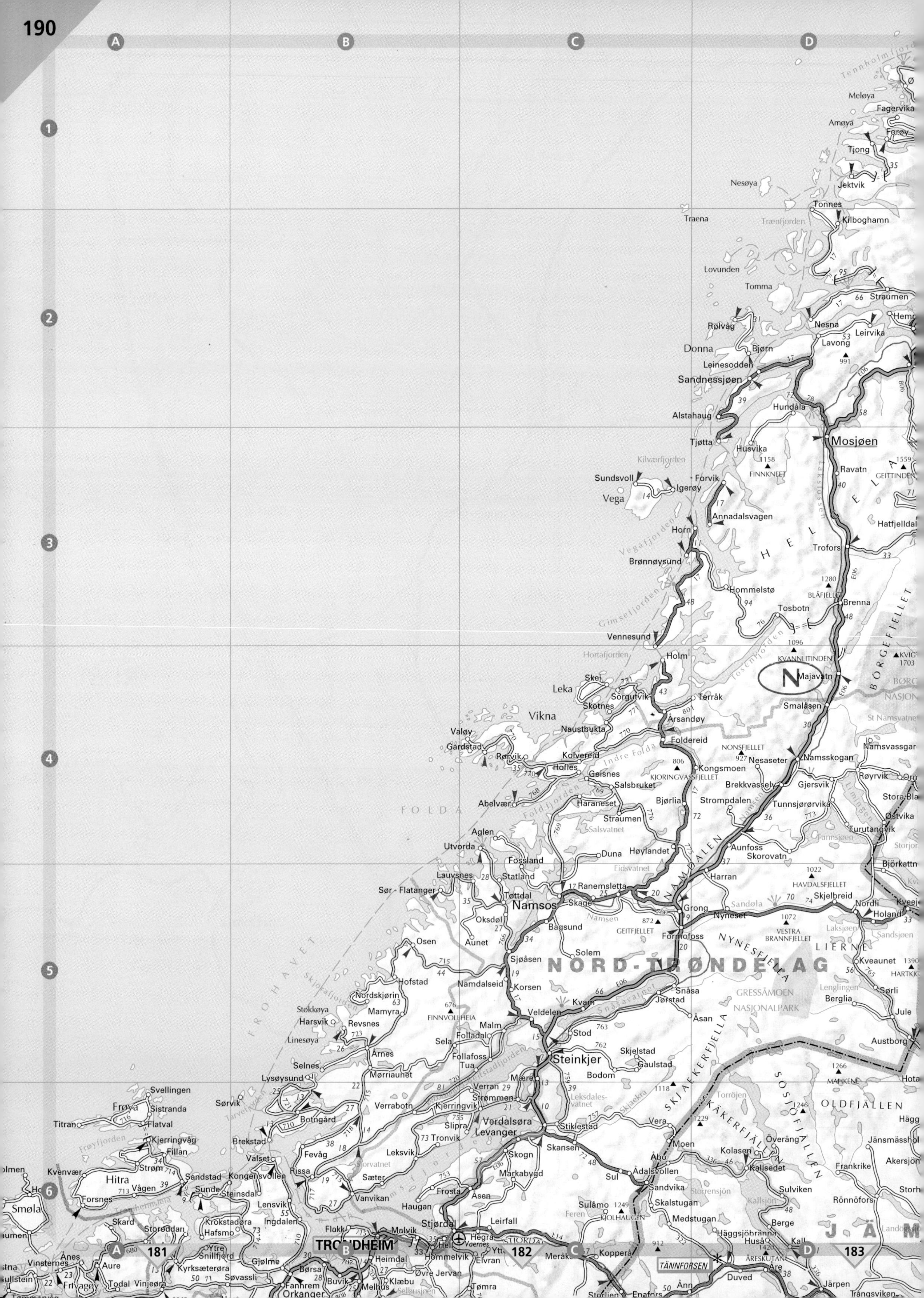
A
B
C
D
1
2
3
4
5
6
Tennholmfjorden
Meløya
Fagervika
Amøya
Forøy
Tjong
Jektvik
Nesøya
Tonnes
Kilboghamn
Træna
Trænfjorden
Lovunden
Tomma
Straumen
Nesna
Leirvika
Rølvåg
Donna
Bjørn
Lavong
Leinesodden
Sandnessjøen
Hundåla
Alstahaug
Mosjøen
Tjøtta
Husvika
FINNKNEET
Kilværfjorden
Forvik
Ravatn
GEITTINDEN
Sundsvoll
Igerøy
Vega
Annadalsvagen
Hatfjelldal
Vegafjorden
Horn
HELGELAND
Trofors
Brønnøysund
Hommelstø
BLÅFJELLET
Brenna
Tosbotn
Gimsefjorden
Vennesund
Toscnfjorden
KVANNLITINDEN
Hortafjorden
Holm
BØRGEFJELLET
KVIGTIND
Majavatn
BØRGEFJELL NASJONALPARK
Skei
Leka
Sørgutvik
Terråk
Skotnes
Vikna
Smalåsen
Naustbukta
Årsandøy
St Namsvatnet
Valøy
Foldereid
Gardstad
NONSFJELLET
Rørvik
Kolvereid
Indre Folda
Namsvassgard
Nesaseter
Namsskogan
Hofles
Kongsmoen
Geisnes
Salsbruket
KJORINGVASSFJELLET
Røyrvik
Brekkvasselv
Gjersvik
Abelvær
Foldfjorden
Haraneset
Bjørlia
Strompdalen
Tunnsjørørvika
Stora Blåsjön
FOLDA
Straumen
Limingen
Østvika
Salsvatnet
Furutangvik
Aglen
Aunfoss
Skorovatn
Utvorda
Duna
Høylandet
Tunnsjøen
Fossland
Eidsvatnet
NAMDALEN
Lauvsnes
Statland
HAVDALSFJELLET
Bjørkattn
Harran
Ranemsletta
Sør-Flatanger
Tøttdal
Skjelbreid
Namsos
Skage
Grong
Sandøla
Nordli
Oksdøl
Namsen
Nyneset
VESTRA BRANNFJELLET
Holand
Kveeje
Bangsund
GEITFJELLET
Formofoss
Aunet
Laksjøen
Sandsjøen
Osen
Solem
NYNESFJELLA
LIERNE
Sjøåsen
NORD-TRØNDELAG
Kveaunet
HARTKJØLEN
FROHAVET
Skjørafjorden
Hofstad
Namdalseid
Korsen
Snåsa
GRESSÅMOEN NASJONALPARK
Lenglingen
Sørli
Nordskjørin
Jørstad
Berglia
Mamyra
Stokkøya
Veldelen
Kvam
Snåsavatnet
Jule
FINNVOLLHEIA
Harsvik
Revsnes
Malm
Åsan
Linesøya
Sela
Folladal
Stod
Austborg
SKJÆKERFJELLA
Årnes
Steinkjer
Skjelstad
Follafoss
Tua
Gaulstad
Selnes
Beitstadfjorden
Mørriaunet
Bodom
Lysøysund
Mære
MAHKENE
Hota
Svellingen
Verran
Leksdalsvatnet
SØSJØFJÄLLEN
Frøya
Sistranda
Sørvik
Strømmen
Torröjen
OLDFJÄLLEN
Titran
Flatval
Tarvafjorden
Verrabotn
Kjerringvik
Skjækra
Hägg
Botngård
Slipra
Verdalsøra
Stiklestad
Vera
KÄKERFJÄLLEN
Frøyfjorden
Kjerringvåg
Brekstad
Tronvik
Levanger
Överäng
Jänsmässholmen
Fillan
Fevåg
Leksvik
Skansen
Moen
Valset
Skogn
Kolasen
Akersjön
Kvenvær
Strøm
Sandstad
Kongensvollen
Rissa
Storvatnet
Sæter
Markabygd
Sul
Åbo
Kallsedet
Frankrike
Hitra
Vågen
Sunde
Trondheimsfjorden
Ådalsvollen
Smøla
Forsnes
Steinsdal
Frosta
Sandvika
Storrensjön
Sulviken
Storhögen
Trondheimsleia
Lensvik
Vanvikan
Åsen
Skalstugan
Rönnöfors
Skard
Krokstadøra
Ingdalen
Haugan
Sulåmo
KJOLHAUGEN
Kallsjön
Feren
Medstugan
Berge
Storoddan
Hafsmo
Stjørdal
Leirfall
Hegra
Værnes
Håggsjöbränna
Kall
Landösjön
JÄMTLAND
Ånes
Mølvik
Stjørdalselva
Husa
Vinsternes
Aure
Snillfjord
TRONDHEIM
Hell
Ytteren
ÅRESKUTAN
Heimdal
Meråker
Kopperå
TÄNNFORSEN
Åre
Kyrksæterøra
Gjølme
Hommelvik
Elvran
Sullstein
Frvagøy
Todal
Vinjeøra
Søvassli
Børsa
Buvik
Øvre Jervan
Duved
Järpen
Melhus
Klæbu
Fannrem
Orkanger
Selbusjøen
Tømra
Storlien
Enafors
Ånn
Trångsviken
181
182
183

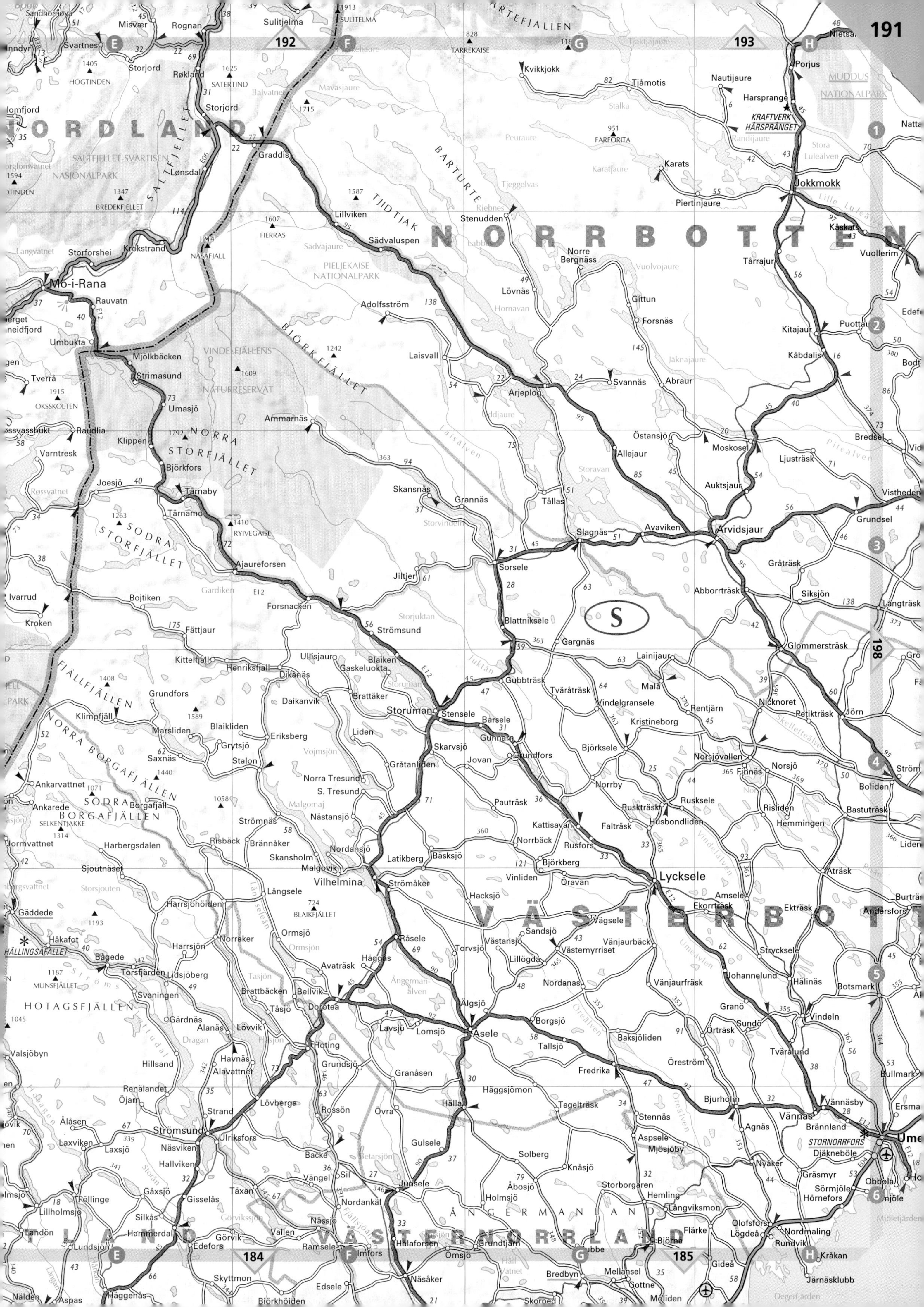
192
193
198
184
185
NORDLAND
NORRBOTTEN
VÄSTERBOTTEN
VÄSTERNORRLAND
ÅNGERMANLAND
SALTFJELLET-SVARTISEN NASJONALPARK
SALTFJELLET
PIELJEKAISE NATIONALPARK
MUDDUS NATIONALPARK
KRAFTVERK HÄRSPRÅNGET
VINDELFJÄLLENS NATURRESERVAT
BARTURTE
TJIDTJAK
BJÖRKFJÄLLET
NORRA STORFJÄLLET
SÖDRA STORFJÄLLET
FJÄLLFJÄLLEN
NORRA BORGAFJÄLLEN
SÖDRA BORGAFJÄLLEN
HOTAGSFJÄLLEN
HÄLLINGSÅFALLET
STORNORRFORS
SULITELMA
TARREKAISE
HOGTINDEN
SATERTIND
FARFORITA
BREDEKFJELLET
FIERRAS
NASAFJALL
OKSSKOLTEN
RYIVEGAISE
SELKENTJAKKE
BLAIKFJÄLLET
MUNSFJÄLLET
Sandhornøya
Misvær
Rognan
Sulitjelma
Svartnes
Storjord
Røkland
Kvikkjokk
Tjåmotis
Nautijaure
Porjus
Harsprånget
Karats
Jokkmokk
Piertinjaure
Kåskats
Vuollerim
Tårrajur
Graddis
Lønsdal
Storjord
Lillviken
Sädvaluspen
Stenudden
Norre Bergnäss
Lövnäs
Gittun
Forsnäs
Kitajaur
Puottaure
Kåbdalis
Mo-i-Rana
Storforshei
Krokstrand
Rauvatn
Umbukta
Mjölkbäcken
Strimasund
Umasjö
Tverrå
Raudlia
Klippen
Björkfors
Joesjö
Tärnaby
Tärnamo
Varntresk
Adolfsström
Laisvall
Arjeplog
Svannäs
Abraur
Ammarnäs
Östansjö
Moskosel
Allejaur
Auktsjaur
Ljusträsk
Skansnäs
Grannäs
Tållas
Slagnäs
Avaviken
Arvidsjaur
Grundsel
Vistheden
Sorsele
Jiltjer
Ajaureforsen
Forsnacken
Strömsund
Bojtiken
Fättjaur
Ivarrud
Kroken
Blattniksele
Gargnäs
Abborrträsk
Gråträsk
Siksjön
Långträsk
Glommersträsk
Lainijaur
Malå
Kittelfjäll
Henriksfjäll
Dikanäs
Ullisjaur
Gaskeluokta
Blaiken
Gubbträsk
Tvärträsk
Vindelgranele
Rentjärn
Nicknoret
Petikträsk
Jörn
Grundfors
Klimpfjäll
Daikanvik
Brattåker
Storuman
Stensele
Barsele
Kristineborg
Marsliden
Blaikliden
Eriksberg
Grytsjö
Liden
Skarvsjö
Gunnarn
Björksele
Norsjövallen
Finnäs
Norsjö
Boliden
Saxnäs
Stalon
Gråtanliden
Jovan
Grundfors
Norrby
Ankarvattnet
Norra Tresund
S. Tresund
Ankarede
Borgafjäll
Pauträsk
Ruskträsk
Rusksele
Risliden
Bastuträsk
Strömnäs
Nästansjö
Kattisavan
Husbondliden
Falträsk
Hemmingen
Risbäck
Brännåker
Nordansjö
Norrbäck
Rusfors
Harbergsdalen
Skansholm
Malgovik
Latikberg
Bäsksjö
Björkberg
Sjoutnäset
Vilhelmina
Strömåker
Vinliden
Öravan
Lycksele
Åträsk
Långsele
Hacksjö
Amsele
Ekorrträsk
Ekträsk
Burträsk
Andersfors
Gäddede
Harrsjöhöiden
Ormsjö
Sandsjö
Vägsele
Håkafot
Harrsjön
Norraker
Råsele
Västansjö
Vänjaurbäck
Västemyrriset
Bågede
Torsfjärden
Lidsjöberg
Häggås
Torvsjö
Lillögda
Stryckséle
Avaträsk
Johannelund
Hälinäs
Botsmark
Svaningen
Brattbäcken
Bellvik
Dorotea
Tåsjö
Nordanås
Vänjaurfräsk
Gärdnäs
Alanäs
Lövvik
Lavsjö
Lomsjö
Älgsjö
Åsele
Borgsjö
Granö
Sundö
Vindeln
Valsjöbyn
Hoting
Grundsjö
Tallsjö
Baksjöliden
Örträsk
Tväralund
Hillsand
Havnäs
Alavattnet
Granåsen
Fredrika
Öreström
Bullmark
Renålandet
Öjarn
Lövberga
Rossön
Häggsjömon
Hälla
Tegelträsk
Bjurholm
Vännäsby
Ersmark
Strand
Ålåsen
Strömsund
Ulriksfors
Övra
Stennäs
Vännäs
Agnäs
Brännland
Umeå
Laxviken
Laxsjö
Näsviken
Gulsele
Aspsele
Mjösjöby
Djäkneböle
Backe
Betarsjön
Solberg
Nyåker
Hallviken
Vängel
Sil
Knåsjö
Gräsmyr
Obbola
Gäxsjö
Täxan
Junsele
Åbosjö
Storborgaren
Sörmjöle
Hörnefors
Föllinge
Gisselås
Nordankal
Holmsjö
Hemling
Lillholmsjö
Silkås
Nässjö
Långviksmon
Olofsfors
Nordmaling
Landön
Hammerdal
Görvik
Vallen
Flärke
Lögdeå
Rundvik
Lundsjön
Edefors
Ramsele
Halaforsen
Grundtjärn
Björna
Kråkan
Omsjö
Gubbe
Imfors
Gideå
Skyttmon
Mellansel
Bredbyn
Nälden
Aspas
Häggenås
Edsele
Näsåker
Gottne
Järnäsklubb
Björkhöiden
Skorped
Moliden
Degerfjärden
Mjölefjärden
Kvikkjokk
Stora Luleälven
Lille Luleälven
Piteälven
Skellefteälven
Vindelälven
Umeälven
Ångermanälven
Laisälven
Juktån
Storavan
Storjuktan
Storuman
Malgomaj
Vojmsjön
Ormsjön
Tåsjön
Flåsjön
Vuolvojaure
Jäknajaure
Hornavan
Uddjaure
Peuraure
Sädvajaure
Riebnes
Tjeggelvas
Stalka
Karatjaure
Randijaure
Mavasjaure
Kårtejaure
Balvatnet
Langvatnet
Røssvatnet
Gardiken
Storsjouten
Tjaktjajaure
E6
E12
E4
E

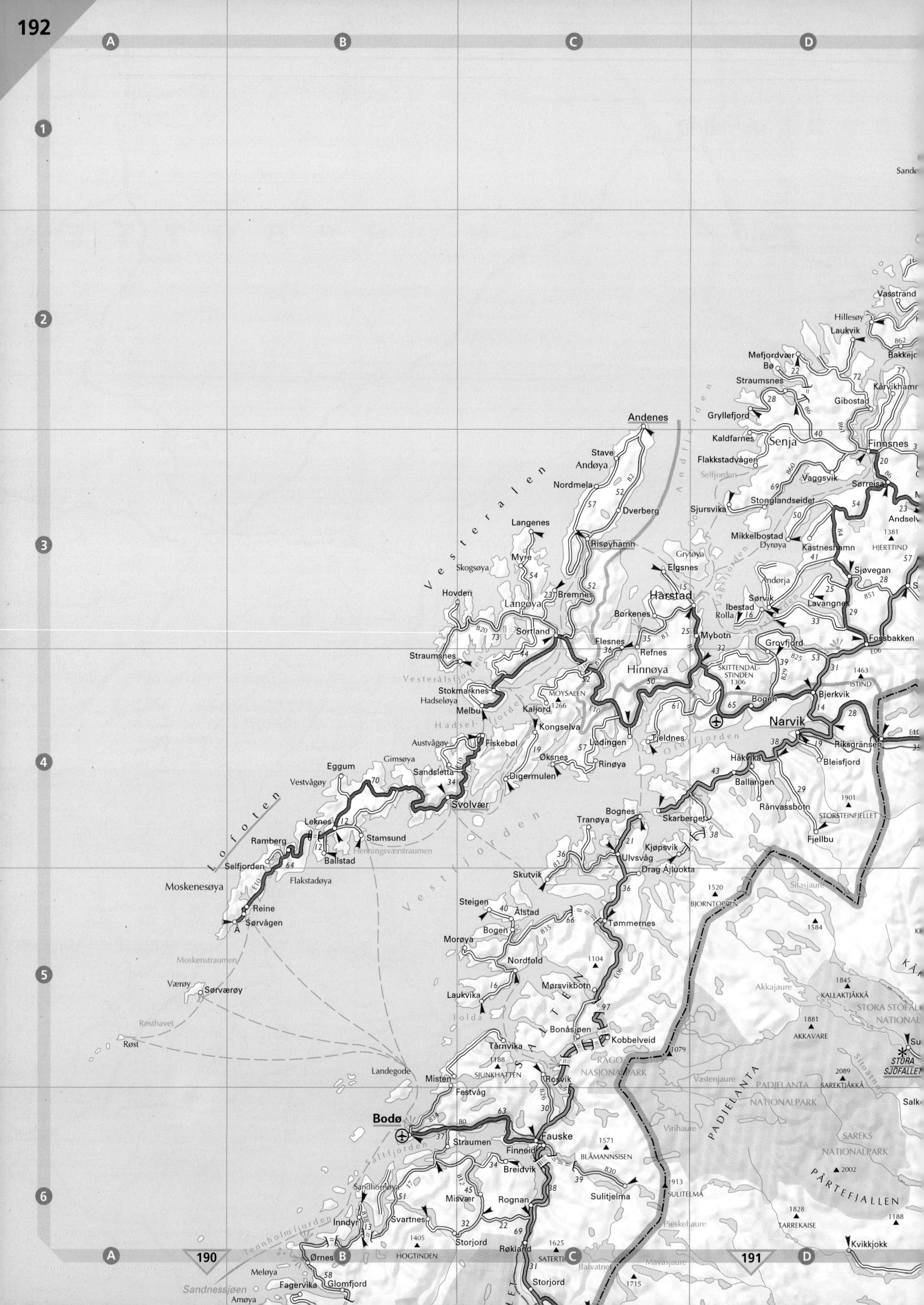
A
B
C
D
1
2
3
4
5
6
Andenes
Stave
Andøya
Nordmela
Dverberg
Risøyhamn
Vesteralen
Langenes
Myre
Skogsøya
Hovden
Langøya
Bremnes
Sortland
Straumsnes
Vesterålsfjorden
Stokmarknes
Hadseløya
Melbu
Hadselfjorden
Harstad
Borkenes
Flesnes
Refnes
Mybotn
Hinnøya
MOYSALEN
Kaljord
Kongselva
Lødingen
Tjeldnes
Øksnes
Rinøya
Digermulen
Fiskebøl
Austvågøy
Sandsletta
Svolvær
Gimsøya
Eggum
Vestvågøy
Leknes
Stamsund
Ballstad
Lofoten
Ramberg
Selfjorden
Flakstadøya
Moskenesøya
Reine
Sørvågen
Å
Moskenstraumen
Værøy
Sørværøy
Røsthavet
Røst
Landegode
Vestfjorden
Henningsværstraumen
Tranøya
Bognes
Skarberget
Kjøpsvik
Ulvsvåg
Drag Ájluokta
Skutvik
Steigen
Ålstad
Bogen
Tømmernes
Morøya
Nordfold
Mørsvikbotn
Laukvika
Folda
Bonåsjøen
Kobbelveid
Tårnvika
SJUNKHATTEN
RAGO NASJONALPARK
Misten
Rosvik
Festvåg
Bodø
Straumen
Fauske
Finneid
Saltfjorden
Breidvik
BLÅMANNSISEN
Sulitjelma
SULITELMA
Misvær
Rognan
Sandhornøya
Inndyr
Svartnes
Storjord
HOGTINDEN
SATERTIND
Røkland
Balvatnet
Ørnes
Meløya
Fagervika
Glomfjord
Sandnessjøen
Amøya
Tennholmfjorden
190
191
Senja
Andfjorden
Mefjordvær
Bø
Straumsnes
Gryllefjord
Kaldfarnes
Flakkstadvågen
Selfjorden
Sjursvika
Stonglandseidet
Vaggsvik
Gibostad
Finnsnes
Sørreisa
Mikkelbostad
Dyrøya
Kastneshamn
Gryøya
Elgsnes
Andørja
Sørvik
Ibestad
Rolla
Lavangnes
Sjøvegan
Fossbakken
Grovfjord
SKITTENDALSTINDEN
ISTIND
HJERTTIND
Bjerkvik
Bogen
Narvik
Ofotfjorden
Håkvika
Ballangen
Bleisfjord
Riksgränsen
Rånvassbotn
STORSTEINFJELLET
Fjellbu
BJORNTOPPEN
Sitasjaure
Akkajaure
KALLAKTJÅKKÅ
STORA SJÖFALLETS NATIONAL
AKKAVARE
STORA SJÖFALLET
Vastenjaure
PADJELANTA
PADJELANTA NATIONALPARK
SAREKTJÅKKÅ
Virihaure
SAREKS NATIONALPARK
PÄRTEFJALLEN
TARREKAISE
Pieskehaure
Mavasjaure
Kvikkjokk
Vasstrand
Hillesøy
Laukvik
Bakkejord
Kårvikhamn
Andselv
Sande

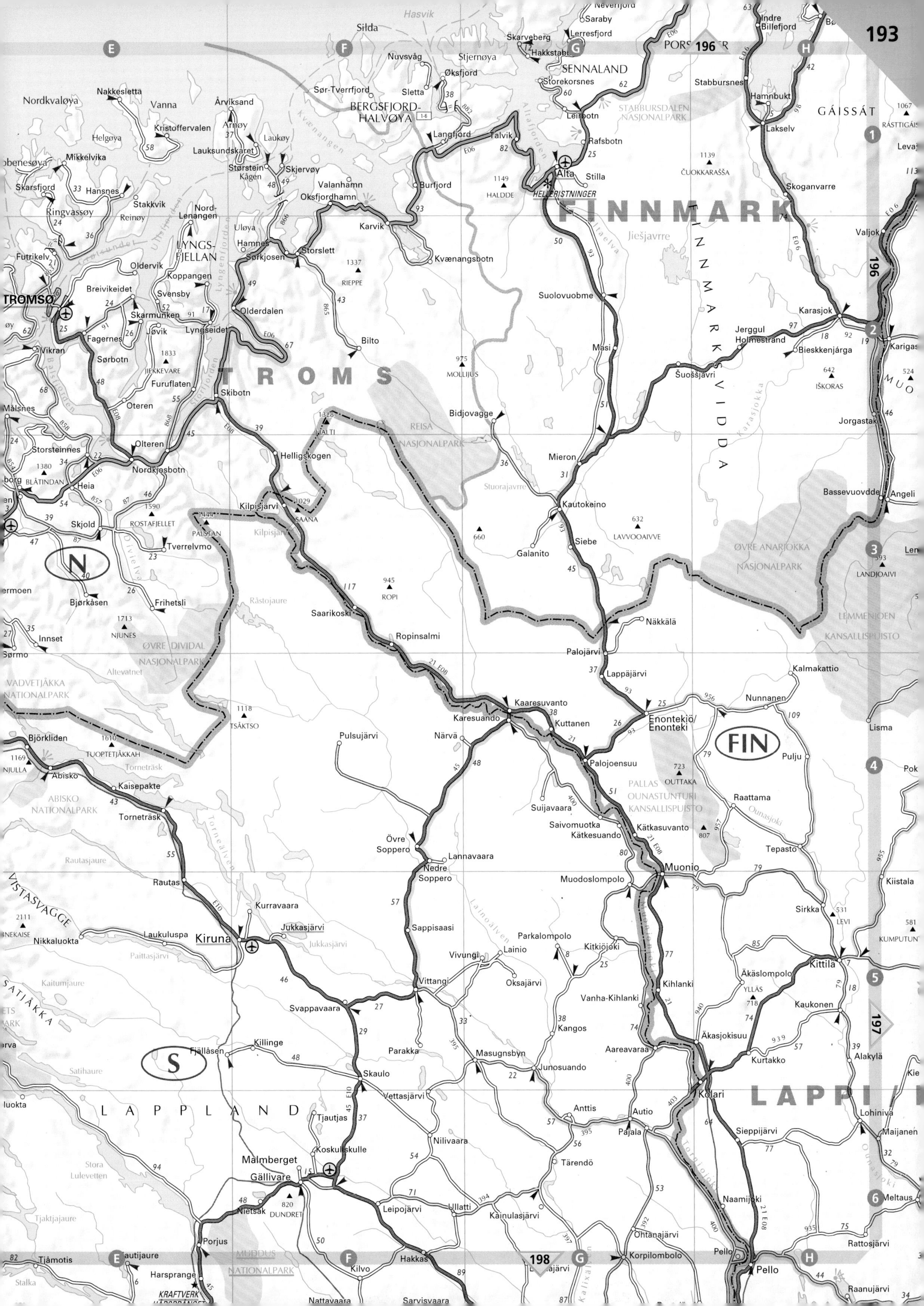
FINNMARK
TROMS
FINNMARKSVIDDA
LAPPLAND
LAPPI
N
S
FIN
Tromsø
Alta
Karasjok
Lakselv
Kautokeino
Masi
Kilpisjärvi
Karesuando
Kaaresuvanto
Enontekiö/Enonteki
Muonio
Kittilä
Kolari
Pello
Kiruna
Gällivare
Malmberget
Abisko
Björkliden
Skibotn
Olderdalen
Lyngseidet
Nordkjosbotn
Storslett
Burfjord
Langfjord
Talvik
Leirbotn
Skoganvarre
Sennaland
Stabbursnes
Hamnbukt
Skaulo
Svappavaara
Vittangi
Pajala
Junosuando
Porjus
Hasvik
Silda
Nuvsvåg
Stjernøya
Øksfjord
Bergsfjord-halvøya
Arnøy
Skjervøy
Lyngsfjellan
Reisa Nasjonalpark
Øvre Dividal Nasjonalpark
Abisko Nationalpark
Stabbursdalen Nasjonalpark
Øvre Anarjokka Nasjonalpark
Lemmenjoen Kansallispuisto
Pallas Ounastunturi Kansallispuisto
Muddus Nationalpark
Helleristninger
196
197
198
E
F
G
H
1
2
3
4
5
6

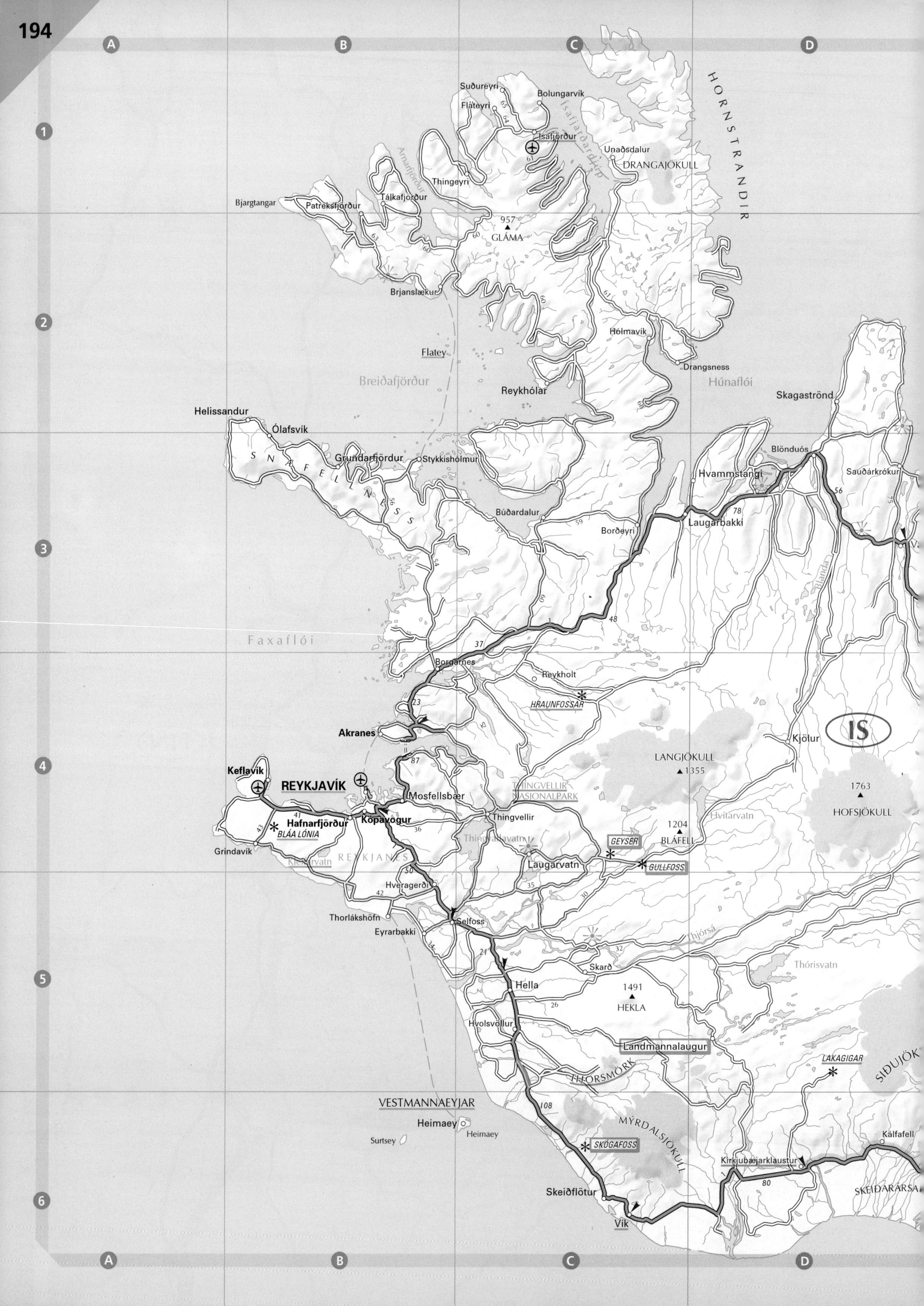

A
B
C
D
1
2
3
4
5
6
HORNSTRANDIR
Suðureyri
Bolungarvík
Flateyri
Ísafjörður
Ísafjarðardjúp
Unaðsdalur
DRANGAJÖKULL
Arnarfjörður
Thingeyri
Bjargtangar
Patreksfjörður
Tálkafjörður
957
GLÁMA
Brjanslækur
Hólmavík
Drangsness
Flatey
Breiðafjörður
Reykhólar
Húnaflói
Skagaströnd
Helissandur
Ólafsvík
SNÆFELLNESS
Grundarfjörður
Stykkishólmur
Blönduós
Hvammstangi
Sauðárkrókur
Búðardalur
Laugarbakki
Borðeyri
Blanda
Faxaflói
Borgarnes
Reykholt
HRAUNFOSSAR
Akranes
Kjölur
IS
LANGJÖKULL
1355
1763
HOFSJÖKULL
Keflavík
REYKJAVÍK
THINGVELLIR NASJONALPARK
Mosfellsbær
Hafnarfjörður
Kópavogur
Thingvellir
BLÁA LÓNIA
1204
BLÁFELL
Hvítarvatn
Grindavík
Thingvallavatn
GEYSER
Kleifarvatn
REYKJANES
Laugarvatn
GULLFOSS
Hveragerði
Thorlákshöfn
Selfoss
Eyrarbakki
Thjórsá
Thórisvatn
Skarð
Hella
1491
HEKLA
Hvolsvöllur
Landmannalaugur
LAKAGIGAR
THORSMÖRK
SIÐUJÖK
VESTMANNAEYJAR
Heimaey
Surtsey
MÝRDALSJÖKULL
SKÓGAFOSS
Kálfafell
Kirkjubæjarklaustur
Skeiðflötur
SKEIÐARÁRSA
Vík

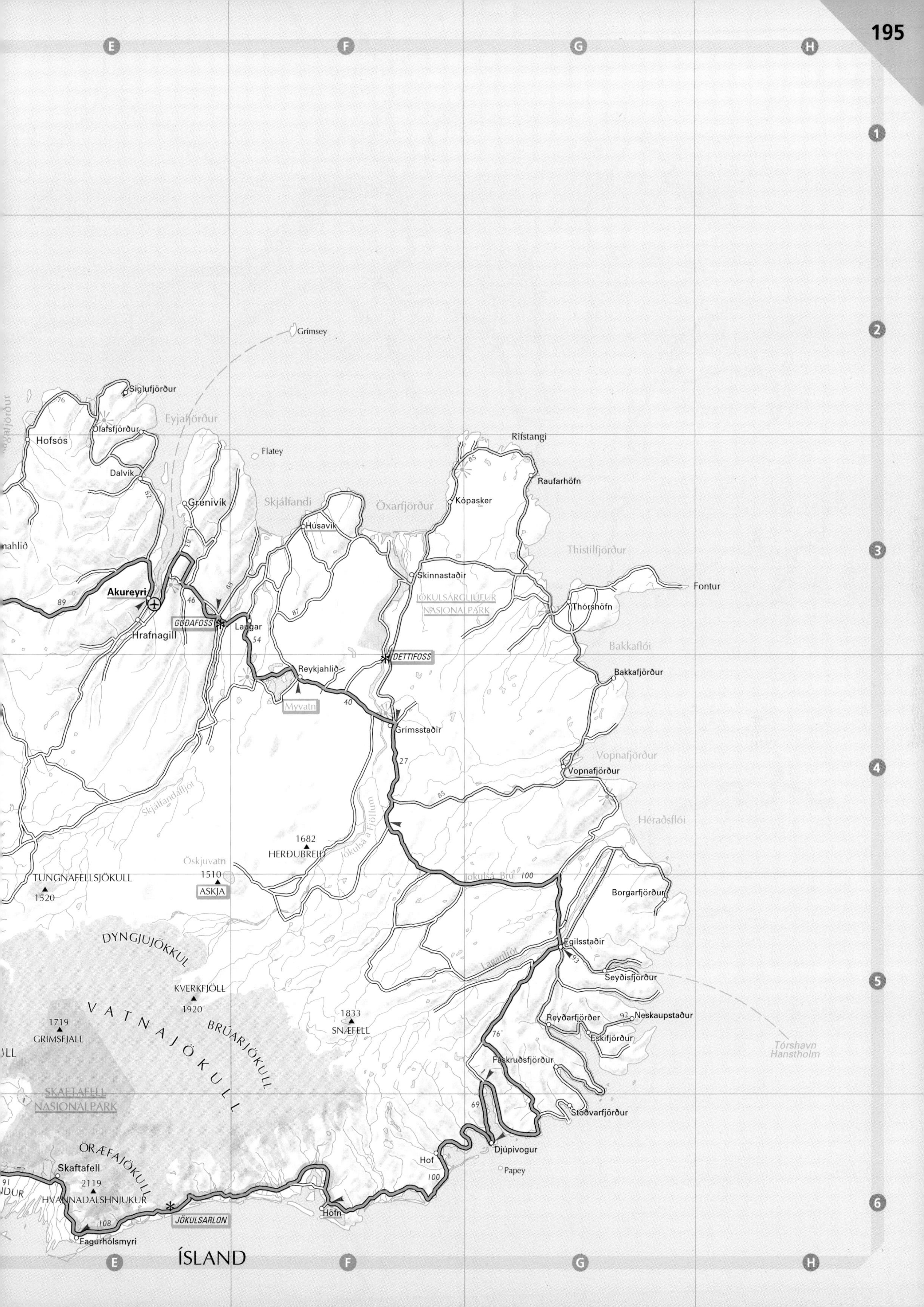
E
F
G
H
1
2
3
4
5
6
Grímsey
Siglufjörður
Eyjafjörður
Ólafsfjörður
Hofsós
Flatey
Dalvík
Rifstangi
Raufarhöfn
Grenivík
Skjálfandi
Öxarfjörður
Kópasker
Húsavík
Thistilfjörður
Skinnastaðir
Fontur
Akureyri
JÖKULSÁRGLJÚFUR NASJONALPARK
Thórshöfn
GOÐAFOSS
Laugar
Hrafnagill
Bakkaflói
DETTIFOSS
Reykjahlíð
Bakkafjörður
Mývatn
Grímsstaðir
Vopnafjörður
Vopnafjörður
Skjálfandafljót
Héraðsflói
1682
HERÐUBREIÐ
Jökulsá á Fjöllum
Öskjuvatn
1510
ASKJA
TUNGNAFELLSJÖKULL
1520
Jökulsá Brú
Borgarfjörður
DYNGJUJÖKULL
Egilsstaðir
Lagarfljót
Seyðisfjörður
KVERKFJÖLL
1920
VATNAJÖKULL
1833
SNÆFELL
Reyðarfjörður
Neskaupstaður
1719
GRIMSFJALL
BRÚARJÖKULL
Eskifjörður
Tórshavn
Hanstholm
Fáskrúðsfjörður
SKAFTAFELL NASJONALPARK
Stöðvarfjörður
ÖRÆFAJÖKULL
Djúpivogur
Hof
Papey
Skaftafell
2119
HVANNADALSHNJUKUR
JÖKULSARLON
Höfn
Fagurhólsmyri
ÍSLAND

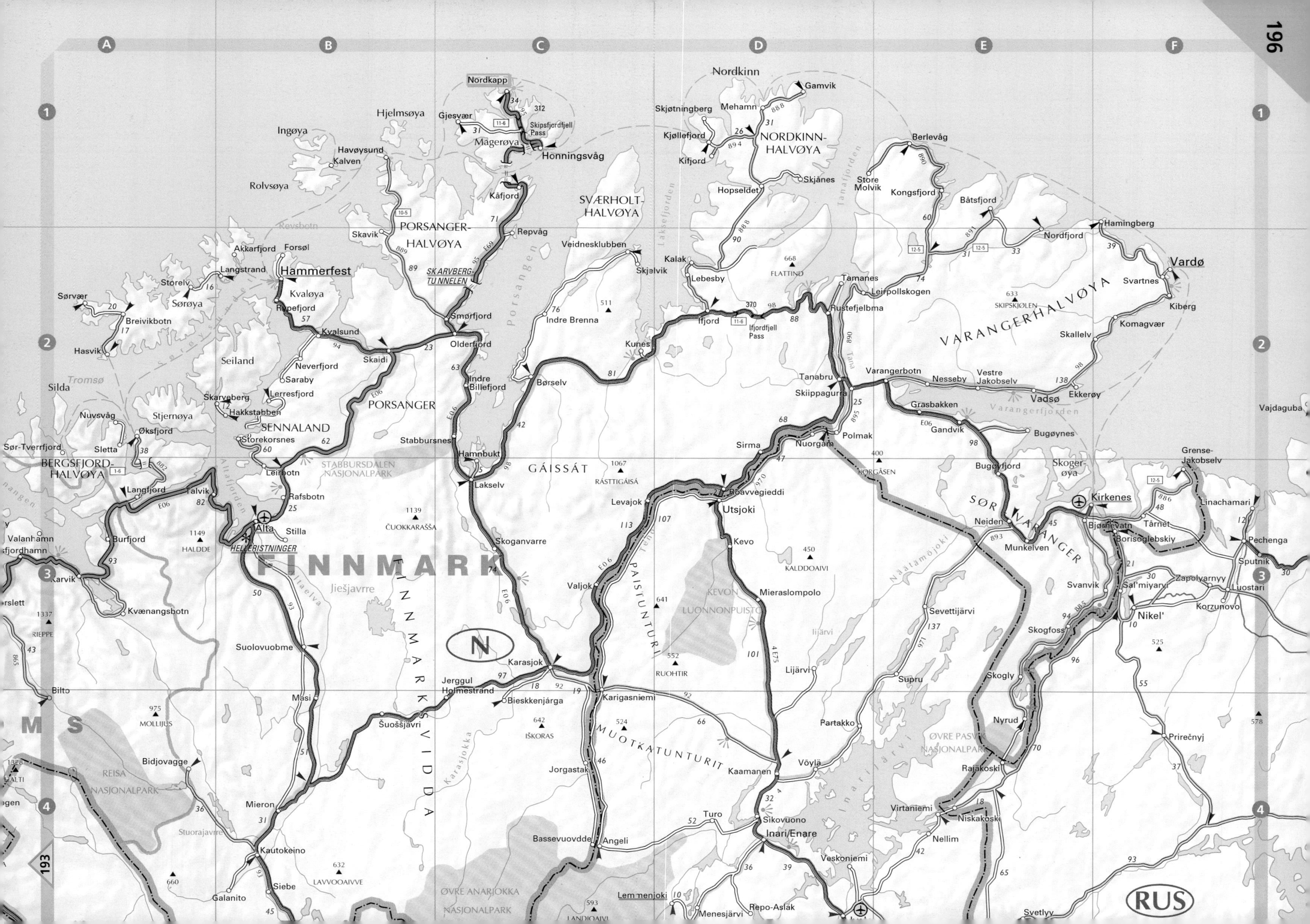
Nordkapp
Gjesvær
Skipsfjordfjell Pass
Magerøya
Honningsvåg
Hjelmsøya
Ingøya
Havøysund
Kalven
Rolvsøya
Kåfjord
Repvåg
PORSANGER-HALVØYA
Skavik
SKARVBERG-TUNNELEN
SVÆRHOLT-HALVØYA
Veidnesklubben
Skjelvik
Nordkinn
Gamvik
Mehamn
Skjøtningberg
Kjøllefjord
Kifjord
NORDKINN-HALVØYA
Skjånes
Hopseidet
Kalak
Lebesby
Berlevåg
Store Molvik
Kongsfjord
Båtsfjord
Nordfjord
Hamningberg
Vardø
Svartnes
Kiberg
Komagvær
VARANGERHALVØYA
Akkarfjord
Forsøl
Hammerfest
Langstrand
Storelv
Sørøya
Sørvær
Breivikbotn
Hasvik
Kvaløya
Repefjord
Kvalsund
Smørfjord
Olderfjord
Indre Brenna
Ifjord
Ifjordfjell Pass
Tamanes
Leirpollskogen
Rustefjelbma
Skallelv
Seiland
Neverfjord
Saraby
Lerresfjord
Skaidi
Kunes
Børselv
Indre Billefjord
Tanabru
Skiippagurra
Varangerbotn
Nesseby
Vestre Jakobselv
Vadsø
Ekkerøy
Vajdaguba
Silda
Tromsø
Nuvsvåg
Stjernøya
Skarveberg
Hakkstabben
SENNALAND
PORSANGER
Stabbursnes
Grasbakken
Gandvik
Bugøynes
Varangerfjorden
Øksfjord
Sletta
Sør-Tverrfjord
BERGSFJORD-HALVØYA
Storekorsnes
Leirbotn
STABBURSDALEN NASJONALPARK
Hamnbukt
Lakselv
GÁISSÁT
RÁSTTIGÁISÁ
Sirma
Nuorgam
Polmak
KORGÅSEN
Bugøyfjord
Skogerøya
Grense-Jakobselv
Langfjord
Talvik
Altafjorden
Rafsbotn
Alta
Stilla
HELLERISTNINGER
Burfjord
HALDDE
Valanhamn
ČUOKKARAŠŠA
Levajok
Roavvegieddi
Utsjoki
Kevo
KALDDOAIVI
SØR-VARANGER
Kirkenes
Neiden
Munkelven
Bjørnevatn
Borisoglebskiy
Tårnet
Linachamari
Pechenga
Sputnik
Luostari
FINNMARK
Karvik
Kvænangsbotn
Jiešjavrre
Skoganvarre
Valjok
PAISTUNTURI
KEVON LUONNONPUISTO
Mieraslompolo
Sevettijärvi
Svanvik
Sal'miyarvi
Zapolyarnyy
Korzunovo
Nikel'
RIEPPE
Suolovuobme
Karasjok
RUOHTIR
Lijärvi
Skogfoss
Bilto
Masi
Jerggul
Holmestrand
Bieskkenjárga
Karigasniemi
Supru
Skogly
Šuoššjávri
MOLLIJUS
FINNMARKSVIDDA
IŠKORAS
MUOTKATUNTURIT
Partakko
Nyrud
Prirečnyj
Bidjovagge
REISA NASJONALPARK
HALTI
Jorgastak
Kaamanen
Vövjä
ØVRE PASVIK NASJONALPARK
Rajakoski
Mieron
Stuorajavre
Turo
Sikovuono
Virtaniemi
Niskakoski
Inari/Enare
Nellim
Bassevuovdde
Angeli
Kautokeino
LAVVOOAIVVE
Veskoniemi
Siebe
Galanito
ØVRE ANARJOKKA NASJONALPARK
Lem menjoki
Repo-Aslak
Menesjärvi
LANDIOAIVI
Svetlyy
RUS
193

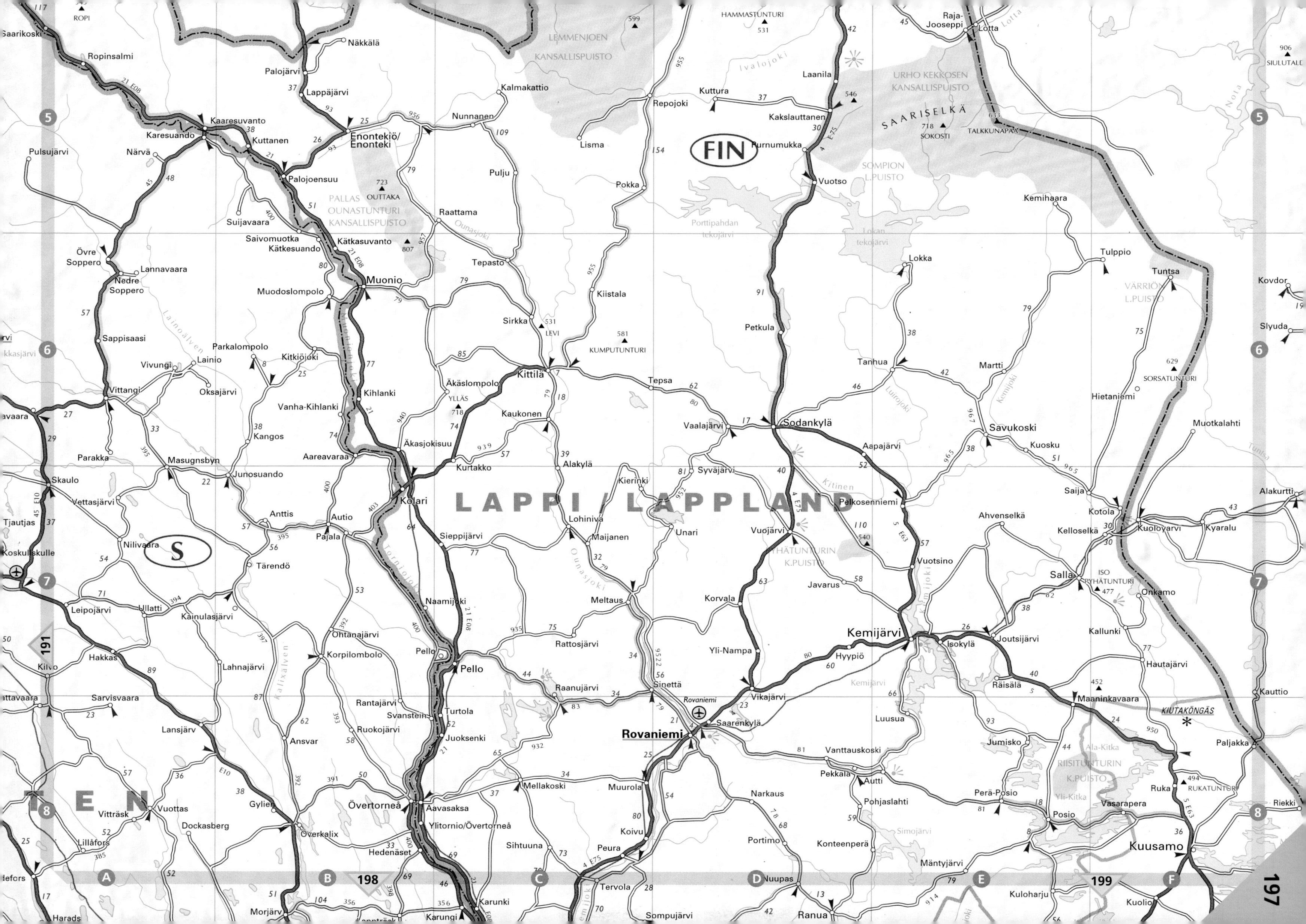
FIN
S
LAPPI / LAPPLAND
Rovaniemi
Kemijärvi
Sodankylä
Kittilä
Muonio
Enontekiö/
Enonteki
Kuusamo
Salla
Savukoski
Pello
Kolari
Övertorneå
Ylitornio/Övertorneå
Pajala
Karesuando
Kaaresuvanto
Vittangi
Ranua
Posio
Pelkosenniemi
Vuotso
Saariselkä
Lokka
Tanhua
Vaalajärvi
Tepsa
Levi
Äkäslompolo
Ylläs
Sirkka
Kaukonen
Muodoslompolo
Junosuando
Masugnsbyn
Tärendö
Korpilombolo
Överkalix
Lansjärv
Kilvo
URHO KEKKOSEN KANSALLISPUISTO
LEMMENJOEN KANSALLISPUISTO
PALLAS OUNASTUNTURI KANSALLISPUISTO
PYHÄTUNTURIN K.PUISTO
RIISITUNTURIN K.PUISTO
VÄRRIÖN L.PUISTO
SOMPION L.PUISTO
Kemijoki
Ounasjoki
Tornionjoki
Kalixälven
Lainioälven
Lokan tekojärvi
Porttipahdan tekojärvi
KIUTAKÖNGÄS
Ruka
RUKATUNTURI
Kovdor
Alakurtti
Tuntsa
Hietaniemi
Kelloselkä
Joutsijärvi
Isokylä
Vikajärvi
Saarenkylä
Sinettä
Meltaus
Raanujärvi
Muurola
Tervola
Mellakoski
Aavasaksa
Hedenäset
Karunki
Raja-
Jooseppi
Lotta
Pulsujärvi
Saarikoski
191
198
199
E75
E63
E08
E10

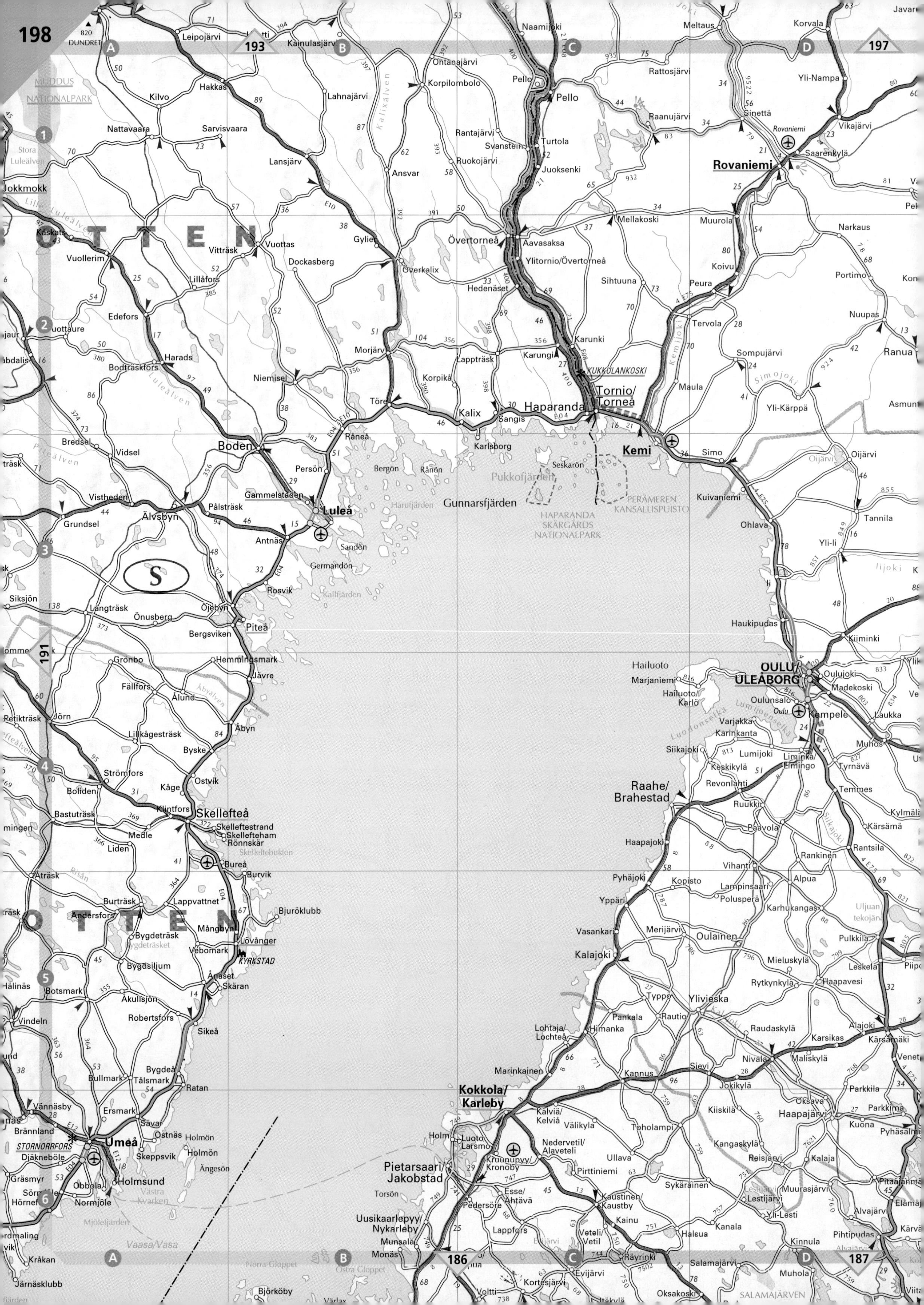
193
197
191
186
187
A
B
C
D
1
2
3
4
5
6
DUNDRET
MUDDUS NATIONALPARK
Leipojärvi
Kainulasjärvi
Naamijoki
Meltaus
Korvala
Javarus
Ohtanajärvi
Rattosjärvi
Yli-Nampa
Hakkas
Kilvo
Lahnajärvi
Korpilombolo
Pello
Nattavaara
Sarvisvaara
Raanujärvi
Sinettä
Vikajärvi
Rovaniemi
Saarenkylä
Stora Luleälven
Rantajärvi
Svanstein
Turtola
Lansjärv
Ansvar
Ruokojärvi
Juoksenki
Jokkmokk
Lille Luleälven
Mellakoski
Muurola
Narkaus
Kåskats
Vuollerim
Vitträsk
Vuottas
Gylien
Övertorneå
Aavasaksa
Ylitornio/Övertorneå
Koivu
Portimo
Dockasberg
Överkalix
Lillåfors
Hedenäset
Sihtuuna
Peura
Edefors
Tervola
Nuupas
Karunki
Karungi
Sompujärvi
Ranua
Harads
Bodträskfors
Luleälven
Morjärv
Lappträsk
KUKKOLANKOSKI
Niemisel
Korpikå
Tornio/ Torneå
Maula
Töre
Kalix
Sangis
Haparanda
Yli-Kärppä
Asmunti
Bredsel
Vidsel
Boden
Råneå
Karlsborg
Kemi
Simo
Oijärvi
Piteälven
Persön
Bergön
Rånön
Seskarön
Pukkofjärden
Vistheden
Gammelstaden
Luleå
Harufjärden
Gunnarsfjärden
HAPARANDA SKÄRGÅRDS NATIONALPARK
PERÄMEREN KANSALLISPUISTO
Kuivaniemi
Tannila
Grundsel
Älvsbyn
Pålsträsk
Antnäs
Sandön
Germandön
Ohlava
Yli-Ii
Iijoki
Siksjön
Rosvik
Kallfjärden
Långträsk
Önusberg
Öjebyn
Piteå
Bergsviken
Haukipudas
Kiiminki
Grönbo
Hemmingsmark
Jävre
Hailuoto
Marjaniemi
OULU/ ULEÅBORG
Oulujoki
Madekoski
Fällfors
Ålund
Åbyälven
Hailuoto/ Karlö
Oulunsalo
Oulu
Kempele
Laukka
Petikträsk
Jörn
Åbyn
Varjakka
Karinkanta
Luodonselkä
Lumijoenselkä
Lillkågeträsk
Byske
Siikajoki
Lumijoki
Liminka/ Limingo
Muhos
Tyrnävä
Keskikylä
Strömfors
Boliden
Kåge
Ostvik
Revonlahti
Raahe/ Brahestad
Temmes
Bastuträsk
Klintfors
Skellefteå
Skelleftestrand
Skelleftehamn
Rönnskär
Skelleftebukten
Ruukki
Paavola
Kylmälä
Kärsämä
Medle
Liden
Haapajoki
Rantsila
Siikajoki
Bureå
Burvik
Rankinen
Åträsk
Pyhäjoki
Vihanti
Alpua
Kopisto
Lampinsaari
Poluspera
Burträsk
Lappvattnet
Bjuröklubb
Yppäri
Karhukangas
Uljuan tekojärvi
Andersfors
Mångbyn
Vasankari
Merijärvi
Oulainen
Pulkkila
Bygdeträsk
Lövånger
Vebomark
KYRKSTAD
Kalajoki
Mieluskylä
Leskelä
Piippola
Bygdsiljum
Åbyn
Åsmark
Rytkynkylä
Haapavesi
Hälinäs
Botsmark
Ånäset
Skäran
Akullsjön
Typpö
Ylivieska
Robertsfors
Pankala
Rautio
Vindeln
Sikeå
Lohtaja/ Lochteå
Himanka
Raudaskylä
Alajoki
Karsikas
Kärsämäki
Bygdeå
Marinkainen
Kannus
Sievi
Nivala
Maliskylä
Venetpalo
Bullmark
Tålsmark
Ratan
Kokkola/ Karleby
Jokikylä
Parkkila
Vännäsby
Ersmark
Kälviä/ Kelviä
Välikylä
Kiiskilä
Oksava
Haapajärvi
Parkkima
Kuona
Pyhäsalmi
Brännland
STORNORRFORS
Umeå
Sävar
Östnäs
Holmön
Holm
Luoto/ Larsmo
Toholampi
Djäkneböle
Skeppsvik
Nedervetil/ Alaveteli
Kangaskylä
Reisjärvi
Kalaja
Holmsund
Ängesön
Pietarsaari/ Jakobstad
Kruunupyy/ Kronoby
Ullava
Pirttiniemi
Gräsmyr
Obbola
Västra Kvarken
Sörmjöle
Hörnefors
Normjöle
Torsön
Esse/ Ähtävä
Sykäräinen
Lestijärvi
Muurasjärvi
Pitkäjärvi
Pedersöre
Kaustinen/ Kaustby
Alvajärvi
Elämäjärvi
Mjölefjärden
Uusikaarlepyy/ Nykarleby
Lappfors
Kainu
Kanala
Yli-Lesti
Pihtipudas
Kärväskylä
Vaasa/Vasa
Munsala
Veteli/ Vetil
Halsua
Kinnula
Kråkan
Monäs
Norra Gloppet
Östra Gloppet
Räyrinki
Salamajärvi
Muhola
Järnäsklubb
Evijärvi
Kortesjärvi
SALAMAJÄRVEN
Oksakoski
Björköby
Voltti

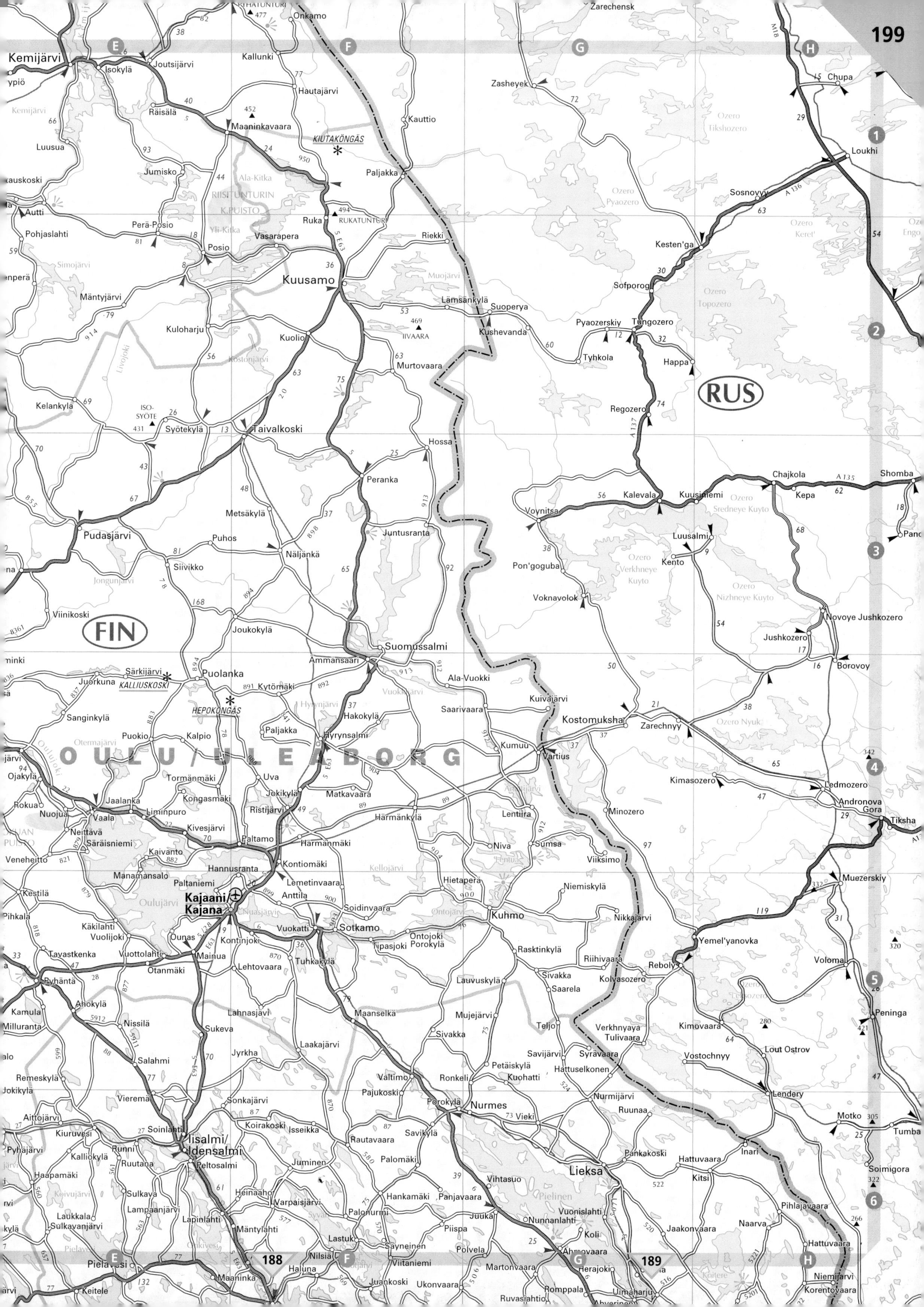
FIN
RUS
OULU/ULEÅBORG
Kemijärvi
Kuusamo
Taivalkoski
Pudasjärvi
Suomussalmi
Puolanka
Kajaani/Kajana
Kuhmo
Sotkamo
Nurmes
Lieksa
Iisalmi/Idensalmi
Kostomuksha
Kalevala
Loukhi
Chupa
Zasheyek
Tungozero
Sofporog
Kesten'ga
Regozero
Voynitsa
Vartius
Muezerskiy
Lendery
Paltamo
Vaala
Pielavesi
Juuka
Hossa
Ruka
Posio
Kiutaköngäs
Kalliuskoski
Hepokongäs
Riisitunturin K.Puisto
Lemetinvaara
Hyrynsalmi
188
189

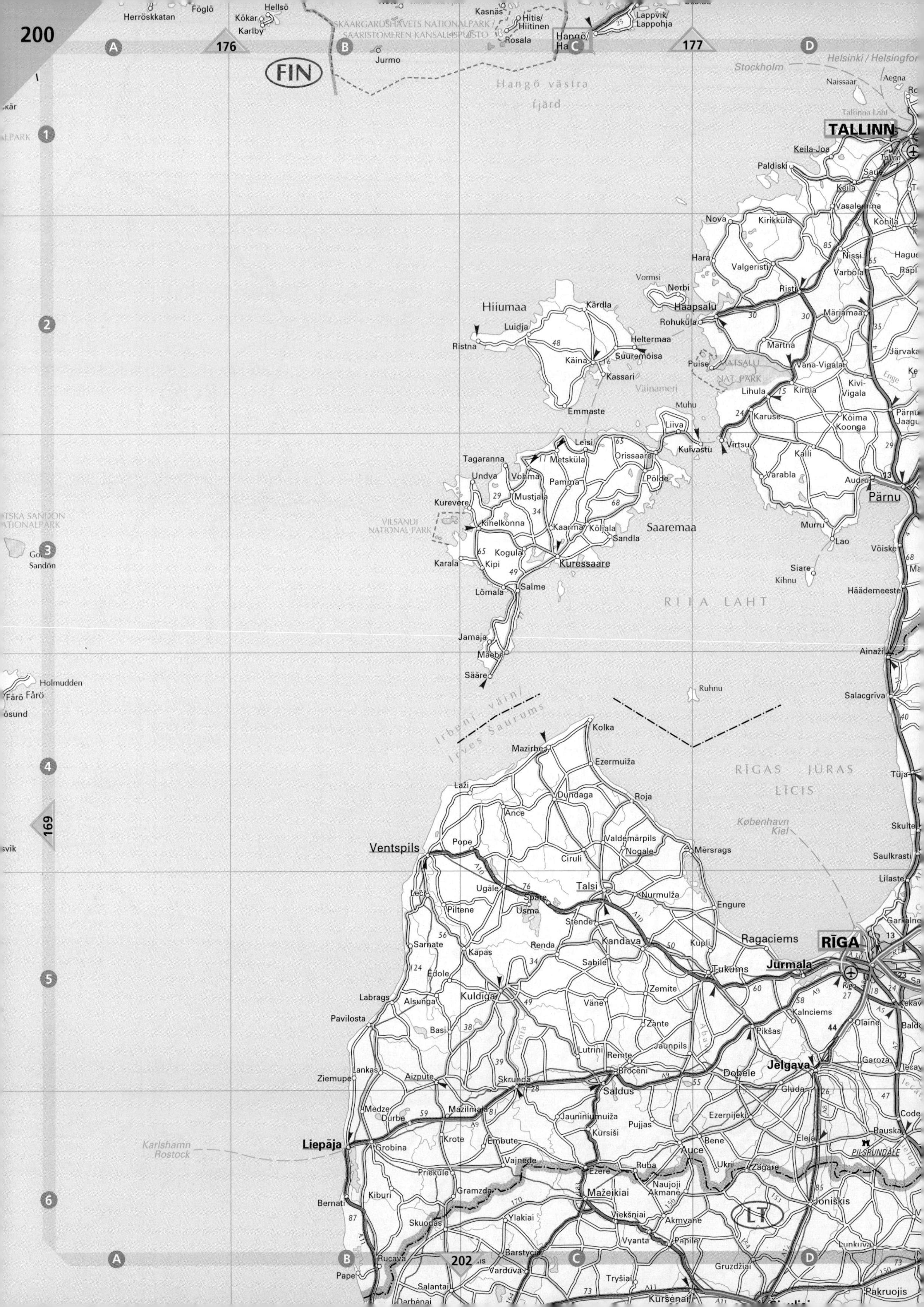

FIN
LT
TALLINN
RĪGA
Hiiumaa
Saaremaa
RIIA LAHT
RĪGAS JŪRAS LĪCIS
Irbeni väin / Irves šaurums
Hangö västra fjärd
Väinameri
VILSANDI NATIONAL PARK
Kärdla
Käina
Haapsalu
Kuressaare
Pärnu
Ventspils
Talsi
Kuldīga
Liepāja
Jūrmala
Jelgava
Tukums
Saldus
Dobele
Mažeikiai
Joniškis
Stockholm
Helsinki / Helsingfors
København Kiel
Karlshamn Rostock
176
177
169
202

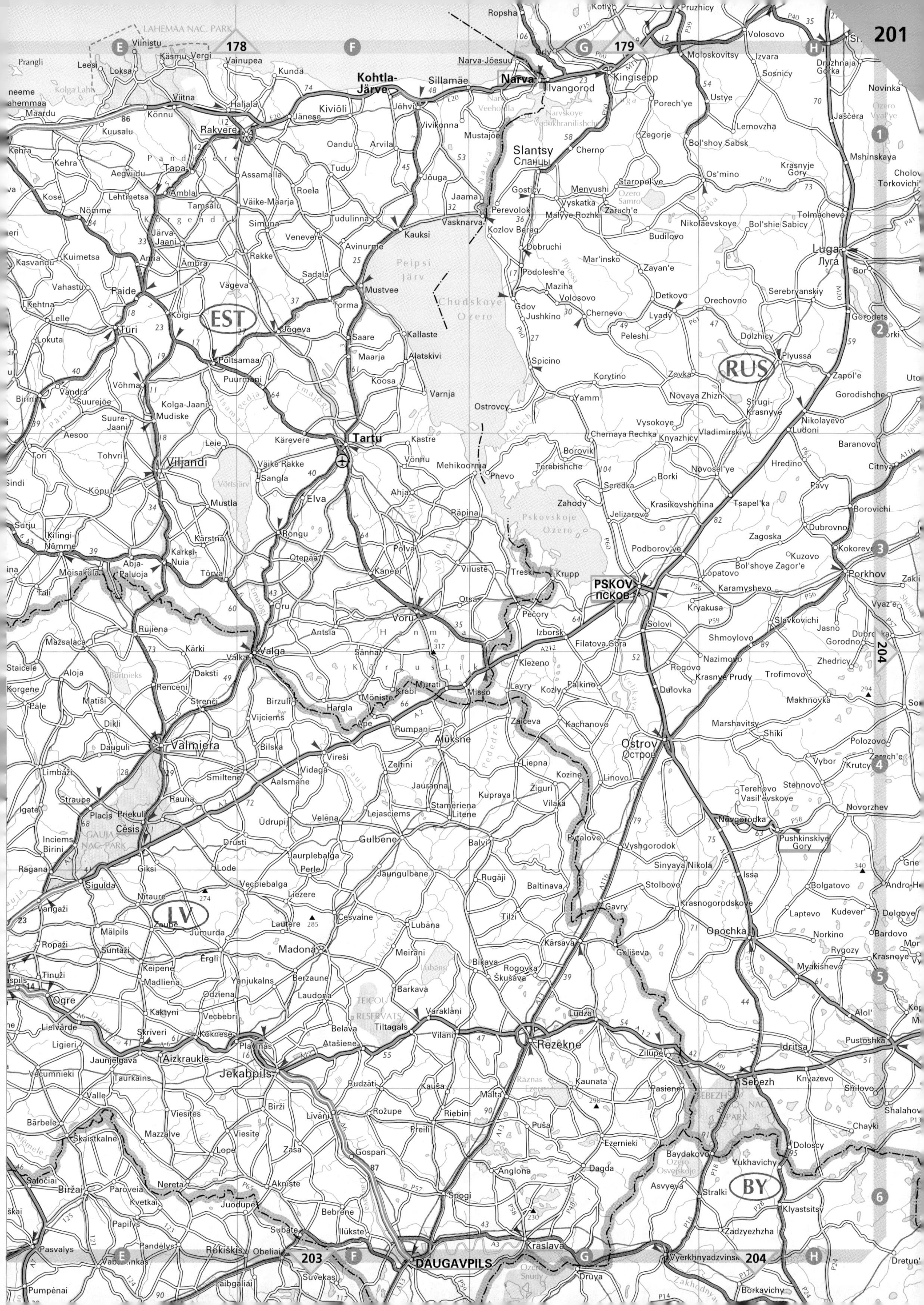
LAHEMAA NAC. PARK
178
179
E
F
G
H
Prangli
Viinistu
Leesi
Loksa
Käsmu
Vergi
Vainupea
Kunda
Kohtla-Järve
Sillamäe
Narva-Jõesuu
Narva
Ivangorod
Kingisepp
Ropsha
Kotly
Pruzhicy
Volosovo
Moloskovitsy
Izvara
Sosnicy
Druzhnaja Gorka
Novinka
Kolga Laht
Maardu
Viitna
Haljala
Kiviõli
Jõhvi
Jänese
Könnu
Kuusalu
Rakvere
Vivikonna
Mustajõe
Narvskoye Vodokhranilishche
Porech'ye
Ustye
Lemovzha
Jaščera
Kehra
Pandivere
Tapa
Aegviidu
Ambla
Assamalla
Oandu
Arvila
Tudu
Jõuga
Slantsy
Сланцы
Cherno
Zegorje
Bol'shoy Sabsk
Mshinskaya
Kose
Lehtmetsa
Nõmme
Tamsalu
Väike-Maarja
Roela
Jaama
Narva
Gosticy
Menyushi
Staropol'ye
Os'mino
Krasnyje Gory
Cholov
Torkovichi
Kõrgendik
Simuna
Tudulinna
Kauksi
Vasknarva
Perevolok
Vyskatka
Malyye Rozhki
Zaruch'e
Ozero Samro
Nikolaevskoye
Bol'shie Sabicy
Tolmachevo
Järva-Jaani
Venevere
Avinurme
Kozlov Bereg
Dobruchi
Mar'insko
Budilovo
Luga
Луга
Kasvandu
Kuimetsa
Amla
Ämbra
Rakke
Peipsi Järv
Podolesh'e
Zayan'e
Bor
Vahastu
Paide
Vägeva
Sadala
Mustvee
Maziha
Volosovo
Detkovo
Orechovno
Serebryanskiy
Kehtna
Lelle
Türi
Koigi
EST
Jõgeva
Torma
Chudskoye Ozero
Gdov
Jushkino
Chernevo
Lyady
Gorodets
Lokuta
Põltsamaa
Saare
Kallaste
Peleshi
Dolzhicy
Spicino
Alatskivi
Maarja
Plyussa
RUS
Zapol'e
Vändra
Suurejõe
Võhma
Puurmani
Koosa
Varnja
Korytino
Zovka
Novaya Zhizn'
Strugi-Krasnyye
Gorodishche
Birini
Kolga-Jaani
Mudiske
Suure-Jaani
Ostrovcy
Yamm
Nikolayevo
Ludoni
Aesoo
Leie
Kärevere
Tartu
Kastre
Vysokoye
Chernaya Rechka
Knyazhicy
Vladimirskiy
Baranovo
Tori
Tohvri
Viljandi
Väike Rakke
Sangla
Võnnu
Mehikoorma
Pnevo
Terebishche
Borovik
Novosel'ye
Hredino
Citnya
Sindi
Võrtsjärv
Köpu
Mustla
Elva
Ahja
Seredka
Borki
Pavy
Zahody
Krasikovshchina
Tsapel'ka
Borovichi
Surju
Räpina
Pskovskoje Ozero
Jelizarovo
Dubrovno
Kilingi-Nõmme
Kärstna
Rõngu
Zagoska
Kuzovo
Kokorevo
Podborov'ye
Bol'shoye Zagor'e
Mõisaküla
Abja-Paluoja
Karksi-Nuia
Tõrva
Otepää
Põlva
Kanepi
Viluste
Treski
Krupp
Lopatovo
PSKOV
ПСКОВ
Karamyshevo
Porkhov
Zakli
Tali
Oru
Võru
Otsa
Pečory
Kryakusa
Vyaz'e
Rūjiena
Antsla
Haanja
Izborsk
Solovi
Slavkovichi
Jasno
Mazsalaca
Kärki
Valga
Valka
317
Filatova Gora
Shmoylovo
Dubrovka
Gorodno
Staicele
Aloja
Burtnieks
Daksti
Rencēni
Sänna
Kõrgustik
Murati
Klezeno
Nazimovo
Zhedricy
Korgene
Matiši
Strenči
Birzuli
Mõniste
Krabi
Misso
Lavry
Kozly
Palkino
Rogovo
Krasnye Prudy
Trofimovo
204
Pāle
Dikli
Vijciems
Hargla
Ape
Rumpani
Zaiceva
Kachanovo
Dulovka
Makhnovka
Dauguli
Valmiera
Bilska
Vireši
Alūksne
Ostrov
Остров
Marshavitsy
Shiki
Polozovo
Limbaži
Smiltene
Vidaga
Aalsmane
Zeltiņi
Liepna
Kozine
Linovo
Vybor
Krutcy
Zarech'e
Straupe
Placis
Priekuļi
Rauna
Jaunanna
Kuprava
Žīguri
Vilaka
Stehnovo
Igate
Cēsis
GAUJA NAC. PARK
Ūdrupij
Velēna
Lejasciems
Stameriena
Litene
Terehovo
Vasil'evskoye
Novgorodka
Novorzhev
Inciems
Birini
Drusti
Gulbene
Balvi
Pytalovo
Vyshgorodok
Pushkinskiye Gory
Ragana
Jaurplebalga
Lode
Perle
Jaungulbene
Sinyaya Nikola
Issa
Sigulda
Giksi
Vecpiebalga
Nitaure
Rugāji
Baltinava
Stolbovo
Bolgatovo
Andro-He
Vangaži
274
LV
Zaube
Liezere
Krasnogorodskoye
Tilži
Gavry
Laptevo
Kudever'
Dolgoye
Mālpils
Jumurda
Lautere
285
Cesvaine
Lubāna
Opochka
Norkino
Bardovo
Ropaži
Suntaži
Ērgli
Madona
Meirani
Kārsava
Goliševa
Rygozy
Krasnoye
Tinuži
Keipene
Madliena
Yanjukalns
Berzaune
Lubāns
Bikava
Rogovka
Škušava
Myakishevo
Ogre
Odziena
Laudona
Barkava
Kaktyni
Vecbebri
TEICOU RESERVATS
Varakļāni
Ludza
Alol'
Lielvārde
Skriveri
Koknese
Belava
Tiltagals
Viļāni
Rēzekne
Zilupe
Idritsa
Pustoshka
Ligieri
Jaunjelgava
Aizkraukle
Pļaviņas
Atašiene
Vecumnieki
Taurkains
Jēkabpils
Rudzāti
Kauša
Malta
Kaunata
Pasiene
Sebezh
Knyazevo
Valle
Birži
Rāznas Ezers
290
SEBEZHSKY NAC. PARK
Shilovo
Viesites
Līvāni
Rožupe
Riebini
Preiļi
Puša
Shalahov
Bārbele
Skaistkalne
Mazzalve
Viesīte
Lope
Zasa
Ezernieki
Chayki
Memele
Gospari
Baydakovo
Ozero Osvejskoje
Yukhavichy
Doloscy
Saločiai
Biržai
Paroveia
Nereta
Akniste
Spogi
Anglona
Dagda
Asvyeya
Stralki
BY
Kvetkai
Juodupė
Bebrene
230
Klyastsitsy
Papilys
Zadzyezhzha
Pasvalys
Pandėlys
Rokiškis
Obeliai
Subate
Ilūkste
203
DAUGAVPILS
Krāslava
Vyerkhnyadzvinsk
Dretun'
Vabalninkas
Suvekas
Ozero Snudy
Drūya
Borkavichy
Pumpėnai
Laibgaliai
Zakhodnyaya Dzvina
1
2
3
4
5
6

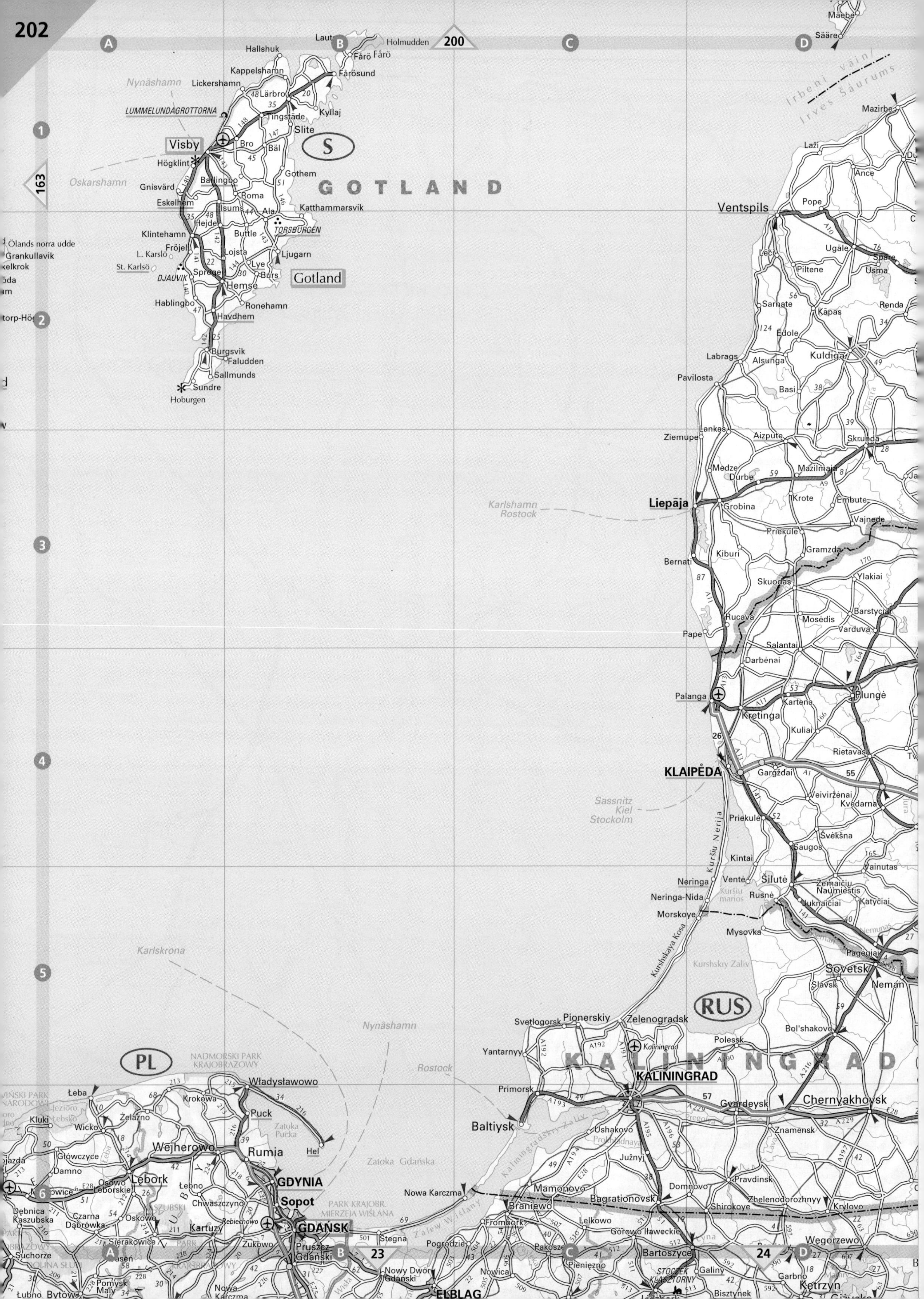
200
163
23
24
A
B
C
D
1
2
3
4
5
6
GOTLAND
Gotland
S
Visby
Hallshuk
Kappelshamn
Lickershamn
Lärbro
Fårö
Fårösund
Holmudden
Kyllaj
Tingstäde
Slite
LUMMELUNDAGROTTORNA
Bro
Bäl
Högklint
Gothem
Gnisvärd
Barlingbo
Roma
Eskelhem
Katthammarsvik
Klintehamn
Hejde
Buttle
TORSBURGEN
Fröjel
L. Karlsö
Ljugarn
St. Karlsö
Lojsta
Lye
DJAUVIK
Sproge
Burs
Hemse
Hablingbo
Ronehamn
Havdhem
Burgsvik
Faludden
Sallmunds
Sundre
Hoburgen
Nynäshamn
Oskarshamn
Ölands norra udde
Grankullavik
Irbeni väin
Irves Šaurums
Mazirbe
Laži
Ance
Ventspils
Pope
Ugāle
Spare
Usma
Leči
Piltene
Sarnate
Kapas
Renda
Edole
Labrags
Alsunga
Kuldiga
Pavilosta
Basi
Ziemupe
Lankas
Aizpute
Skrunda
Medze
Durbe
Mazilmaja
Liepāja
Grobina
Krote
Embute
Vajnede
Karlshamn
Rostock
Priekule
Gramzda
Kiburi
Bernati
Skuodas
Ylakiai
Rucava
Mosėdis
Barstyčiai
Varduva
Pape
Salantai
Darbėnai
Palanga
Kartena
Plungė
Kretinga
Kuliai
Rietavas
KLAIPĖDA
Gargždai
Veiviržėnai
Kvedarna
Sassnitz
Kiel
Stockolm
Priekulė
Švėkšna
Saugos
Kintai
Vainutas
Kuršiu Nerija
Neringa
Ventė
Šilutė
Žemaičiu Naumiestis
Neringa-Nida
Rusnė
Kuršiu marios
Katyčiai
Juknaičiai
Morskoye
Mysovka
Kurshskaya Kosa
Kurshskiy Zaliv
Pagegiai
Sovetsk
Slavsk
Neman
RUS
Karlskrona
Svetlogorsk
Pionerskiy
Zelenogradsk
Bol'shakovo
Polessk
Yantarnyy
Kaliningrad
KALININGRAD
Primorsk
Gvardeysk
Chernyakhovsk
Baltiysk
Ushakovo
Znamensk
Kaliningradskiy Zaliv
Južnyj
Pravdinsk
Mamonovo
Domnovo
Bagrationovsk
Zhelenodorozhnyy
Krylovo
Shirokoye
Nowa Karczma
Braniewo
Frombork
Lelkowo
Górowo Iławeckie
Pieniężno
Bartoszyce
Węgorzewo
Galiny
Kętrzyn
Pogrodzie
Nowica
ELBLĄG
Nowy Dwór Gdański
Stegna
Zalew Wiślany
PARK KRAJOBR. MIERZEJA WIŚLANA
Zatoka Gdańska
Nynäshamn
Rostock
PL
NADMORSKI PARK KRAJOBRAZOWY
Łeba
Władysławowo
Krokowa
Żelazno
Puck
Zatoka Pucka
Hel
Kluki
Wicko
Wejherowo
Rumia
Główczyce
Damno
Lębork
GDYNIA
Sopot
Łebno
Chwaszczyno
Rebiechowo
Dębnica Kaszubska
Czarna Dąbrówka
Oskowo
Kartuzy
GDAŃSK
Sierakowice
Żukowo
Pruszcz Gdański
Suchorze
Pomysk Mały
Bytów
Łubno

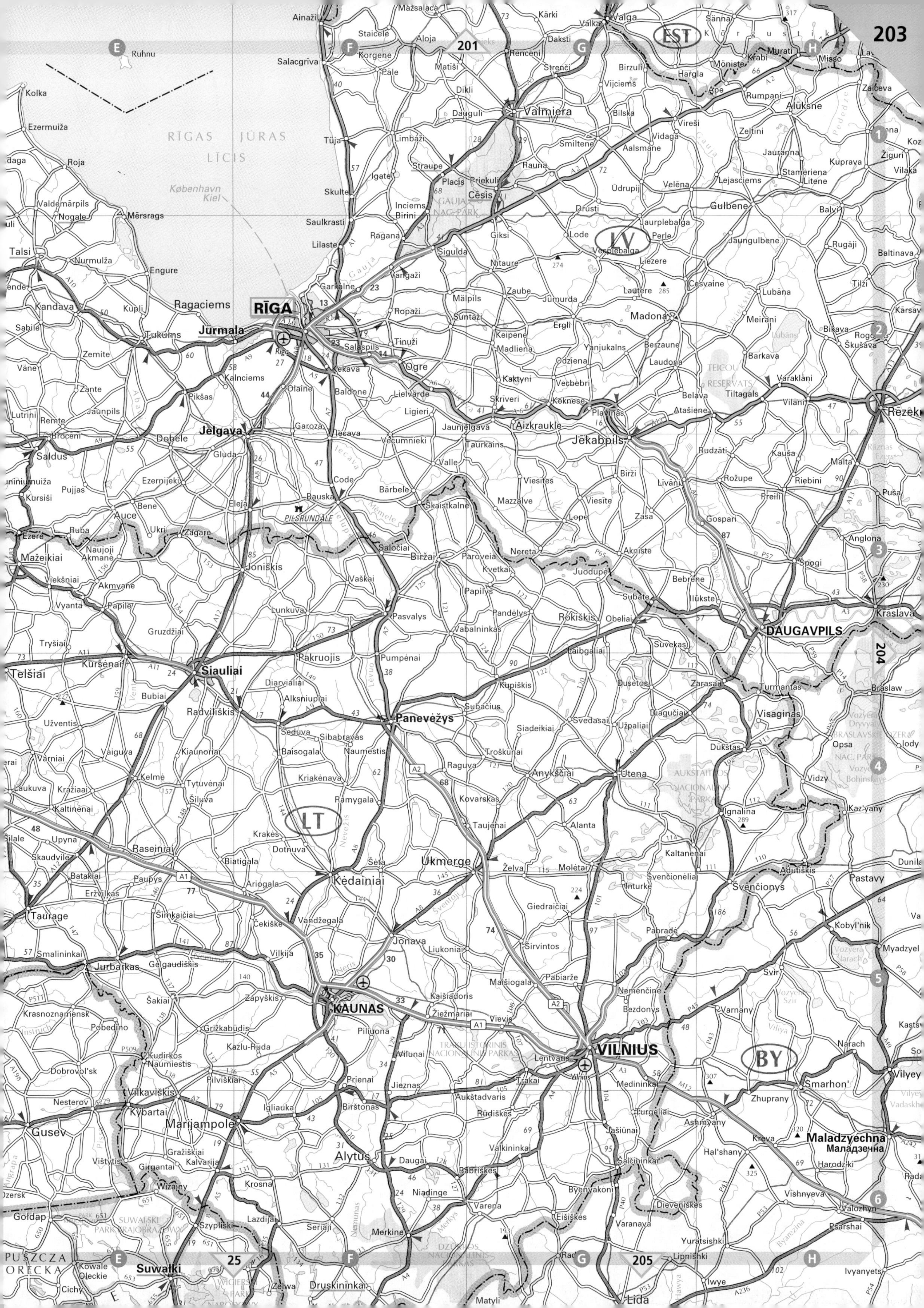
Mazsalaca
Ainaži
Kārki
Valga
Valka
Sänna
EST
Staicele
Aloja
201
Dakšti
Ruhnu
Salacgrīva
Korgene
Renceni
Strenči
Birzuli
Hargla
Mõniste
Krabi
Murati
Misso
Pāle
Matiši
Vijciems
Ape
Rumpani
Alūksne
Zaiceva
Kolka
Dikli
Valmiera
Bilska
Vireši
Ezermuiža
Dauguli
RĪGAS JŪRAS LĪCIS
Tūja
Limbaži
Smiltene
Vidaga
Zeltiņi
Jauranna
Žīguri
Vilaka
Roja
Straupe
Rauna
Aalsmane
Kuprava
Stameriena
Litene
Igate
Priekuļi
Lejasciems
København
Kiel
Placis
Skulte
Cēsis
Ūdrupij
Velēna
Valdemārpils
Inciems
GAUJA NAC. PARK
Gulbene
Nogale
Mērsrags
Birini
Saulkrasti
Drusti
Jaurplebalga
Balvi
Lode
Perle
Ragana
Giksi
LV
Vecpiebalga
Rugāji
Lilaste
Jaungulbene
Talsi
Sigulda
Nurmulža
Nītaure
Liezere
Baltinava
Engure
Vangaži
Cesvaine
Tilži
Lautere
Garkalne
Zaube
Kandava
Lubāna
Ragaciems
RĪGA
Mālpils
Jumurda
Madona
Meirāni
Sabile
Kupli
Ropaži
Suntaži
Ērgļi
Kārsava
Jūrmala
Tukums
Keipene
Bikava
Rogovka
Šķaunas
Salaspils
Berzaune
Zemite
Tinūži
Madliena
Jaunjelgava
Barkava
Vāne
Rīga
Ogre
Odziena
Laudona
Kalnciems
Ķekava
Kaktyni
TEIČU RESERVĀTS
Varakļāni
Zante
Olaine
Baldone
Lielvārde
Vecbebri
Belava
Tiltagals
Piksas
Skrīveri
Koknese
Pļaviņas
Viļāni
Rēzekne
Lutrini
Jaunpils
Ligieri
Aizkraukle
Atašiene
Remte
Jelgava
Garoza
Iecava
Vecumnieki
Taurkains
Jēkabpils
Broceni
Dobele
Gluda
Saldus
Rudzāti
Kauša
Malta
Valle
Birži
Ezernieki
Code
Viesītes
Livani
Rožupe
Riebini
Pujjas
Bārbele
Kursīši
Bene
Bauska
Skaistkalne
Mazzalve
Viesite
Preili
Puša
Eleja
Auce
PILSRUNDĀLE
Zasa
Gospari
Ukri
Lope
Ruba
Žagare
Ezere
Saločiai
Anglona
Naujoji Akmenė
Nereta
Aknīste
Mažeikiai
Biržai
Paroveja
Joniškis
Kvetkai
Juodupė
Spogi
Vaškai
Viekšniai
Akmyane
Papilys
Bebrene
Ilūkste
Vyanta
Papile
Pandėlys
Subate
Lunkuva
Pasvalys
Rokiškis
Obeliai
Krāslava
DAUGAVPILS
Gruzdžiai
Vabalninkas
Tryšiai
Laibgaliai
Suvekas
Telšiai
Kuršėnai
Siauliai
Pakruojis
Pumpėnai
204
Kupiškis
Dusetos
Zarasai
Diarvialiai
Turmantas
Braslaw
Bubiai
Alksniupiai
Radviliškis
Subačius
Diagučiai
Visaginas
Uzventis
Panevėžys
Siadeikiai
Svedasai
Užpaliai
BRASLAVSKIE OZERA
Šeduva
Sibabravas
Dūkštas
Opsa
Vaiguva
Kiaunoriai
Baisogala
Naumestis
NAC. PARK
Varniai
Troškūnai
Raguva
Anykščiai
Utena
Kelmė
AUKŠTAITIJOS NACIONALINIS PARKAS
Vidzy
Laukuva
Kražiai
Tytuvėnai
Kriakėnava
Kovarskas
Kaltinėnai
Šiluva
Ramygala
LT
Ignalina
Kaz'yany
Taujenai
Alanta
Upyna
Krakės
Šilalė
Skaudvilė
Dotnuva
Kaltanėnai
Raseiniai
Biatigala
Šėta
Ukmergė
Želva
Molėtai
Adutiškis
Dunilav
Batakiai
Švenčionėliai
Paupys
Kėdainiai
Inturkė
Švenčionys
Pastavy
Erzvilkas
Ariogala
Giedraičiai
Tauragė
Šimkaičiai
Čekiškė
Vandžegala
Jonava
Pabradė
Kobyl'nik
Širvintos
Liukoniai
Smalininkai
Vilkija
Myadzyel
Jurbarkas
Gelgaudiškis
Maišiogala
Pabiarže
Svir
Kaišiadoris
Nemenčinė
Šakiai
Zapyškis
KAUNAS
Žiežmariai
Bezdonys
Varnany
Krasnoznamensk
Pobedino
Griškabūdis
Piliuona
Vievis
Kazlu-Rūda
Kudirkos Naumiestis
Vilūnai
TRAKŲ ISTORINIS NACIONALINIS PARKAS
Lentvaris
VILNIUS
BY
Narach
Dobrovol'sk
Pilviškiai
Jieznas
Prienai
Trakai
Medininkai
Vilkaviškis
Aukštadvaris
Smarhon'
Vilyey
Nesterov
Kybartai
Igliauka
Birštonas
Rūdiškės
Turgeliai
Zhuprany
Marijampolė
Ashmyany
Gusev
Jašiūnai
Graziškiai
Kalvarija
Alytus
Valkininkai
Kreva
Maladzyechna
Маладзечна
Vištytis
Daugai
Šalčininkai
Hal'shany
Girgantai
Babriškes
Harodz'ki
Wiżajny
Krosna
Niadinge
Byenyakoni
Ozersk
Dieveniškes
Vishnyeva
Gołdap
Varėna
Valozhyn
Szypliski
Lazdijai
Eišiškės
SUWALSKI PARK KRAJOBRAZOWY
Seriaji
Varanava
Merkinė
Psarshai
DZŪKIJOS NACIONALINIS PARKAS
Yuratsishki
PUSZCZA ROMINCKA
Kowale Oleckie
Suwałki
25
Rad
205
Lipnishki
Ivyanyets
Cichy
Zelwa
Druskininkai
Iwye
Matyli
Lida

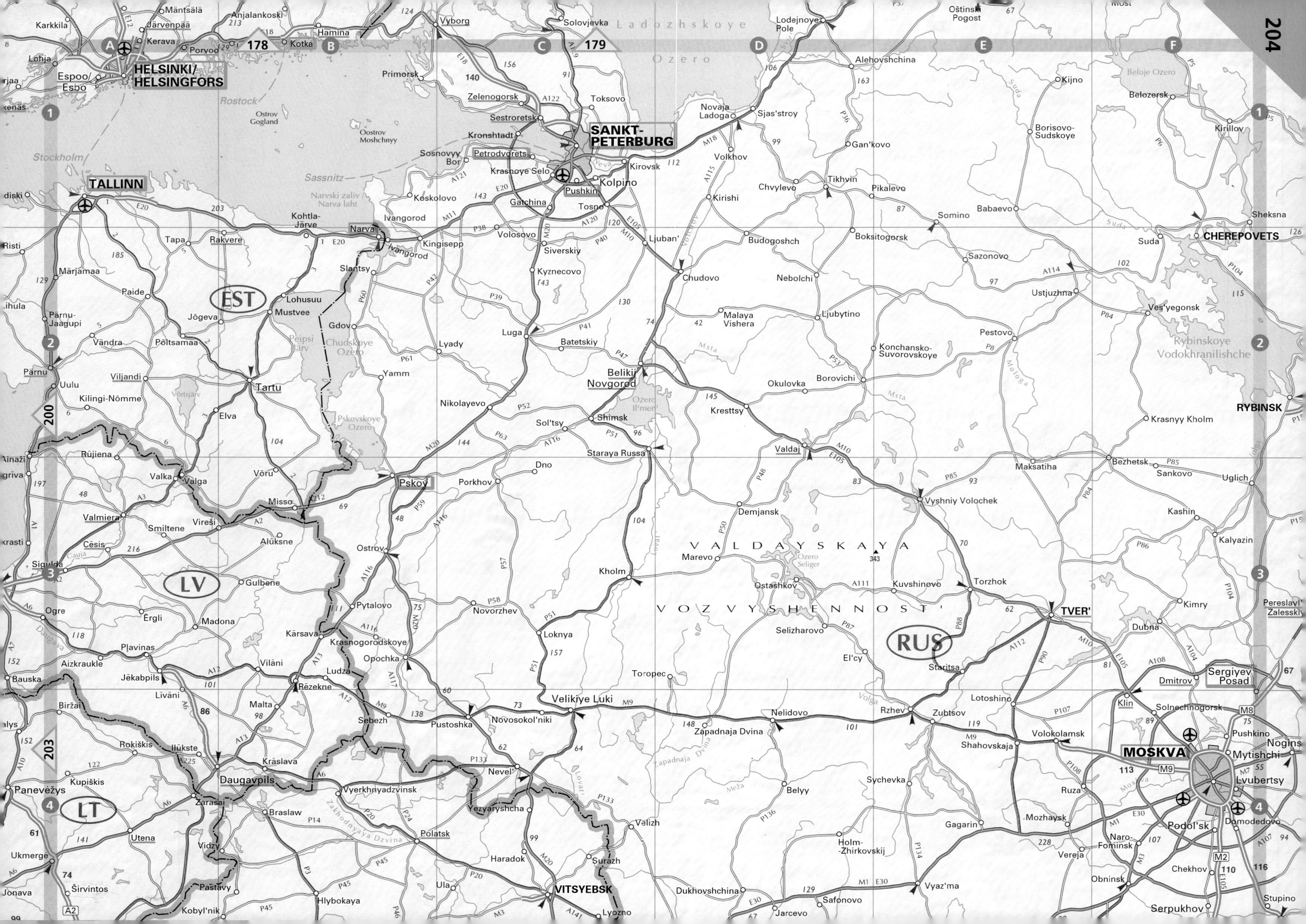

MOSKVA
SANKT-PETERBURG
TALLINN
HELSINKI/HELSINGFORS
RUS
EST
LV
LT
VALDAYSKAYA
VOZVYSHENNOST'
Ladozhskoye Ozero
Rybinskoye Vodokhranilishche
Chudskoye Ozero
Peipsi järv
Pskovskoye Ozero
Ozero Il'men'
Ozero Seliger
Beloje Ozero
Narvski zaliv / Narva laht
CHEREPOVETS
RYBINSK
TVER'
Belikij Novgorod
Pskov
Narva
Tartu
Daugavpils
VITSYEBSK
Vyborg
Kirishi
Tikhvin
Volkhov
Chudovo
Luga
Kingisepp
Gatchina
Pushkin
Kolpino
Tosno
Valdaj
Vyshniy Volochek
Torzhok
Rzhev
Velikiye Luki
Staraya Russa
Kholm
Ostashkov
Toropec
Nelidovo
Zapadnaja Dvina
Nevel'
Porkhov
Ostrov
Opochka
Sebezh
Polatsk
Kirillov
Belozersk
Ves'yegonsk
Uglich
Kalyazin
Kashin
Kimry
Dubna
Dmitrov
Sergiyev Posad
Klin
Volokolamsk
Ruza
Mozhaysk
Podol'sk
Serpukhov
Obninsk
Chekhov
Vyaz'ma
Gagarin
Zubtsov
Staritsa
Sychevka
Belyy
Safonovo
Jarcevo
Dukhovshchina
Velizh
Surazh
Haradok
Rakvere
Jõgeva
Viljandi
Valga
Valka
Võru
Pärnu
Paide
Kohtla-Järve
Valmiera
Cēsis
Sigulda
Madona
Gulbene
Alūksne
Rēzekne
Ludza
Kārsava
Krāslava
Jēkabpils
Aizkraukle
Bauska
Panevėžys
Utena
Kotka
Hamina
Porvoo
Espoo/Esbo
Lohja

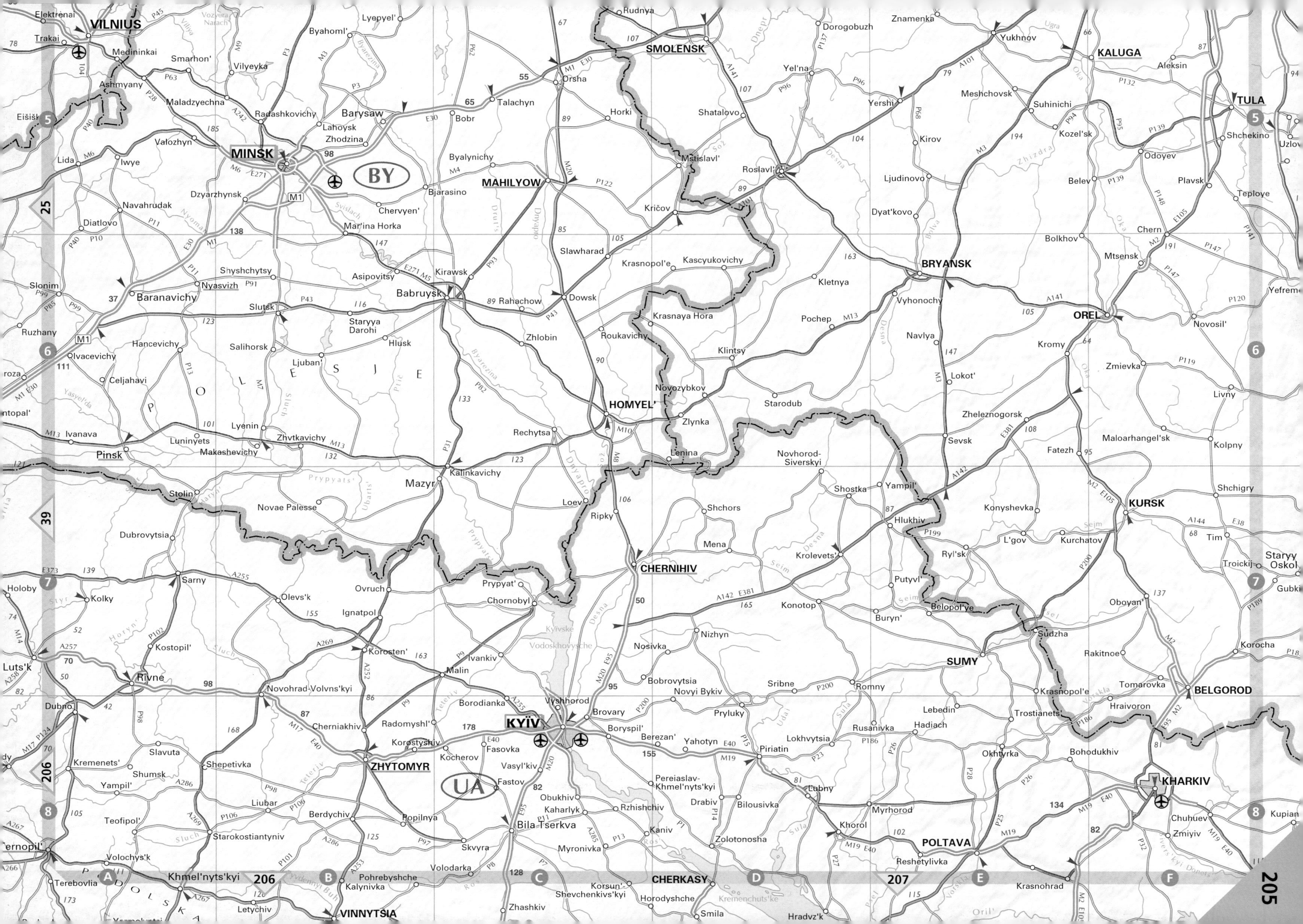

VILNIUS
MINSK
BY
MAHILYOW
SMOLENSK
KALUGA
TULA
BRYANSK
OREL
HOMYEL'
KURSK
CHERNIHIV
SUMY
BELGOROD
KHARKIV
KYÏV
ZHYTOMYR
UA
POLTAVA
CHERKASY
VINNYTSIA
Babruysk
Mazyr
Pinsk
Rivne
Luts'k
Baranavichy
Barysaw
Orsha
Roslavl'
Konotop
Bila Tserkva
Khmel'nyts'kyi
Novohrad-Volyns'kyi
Sarny
Korosten'
Chornobyl
Prypyat'
Kyïvske Vodoskhovyshche
P O L E S J E
25
39
206
207
205

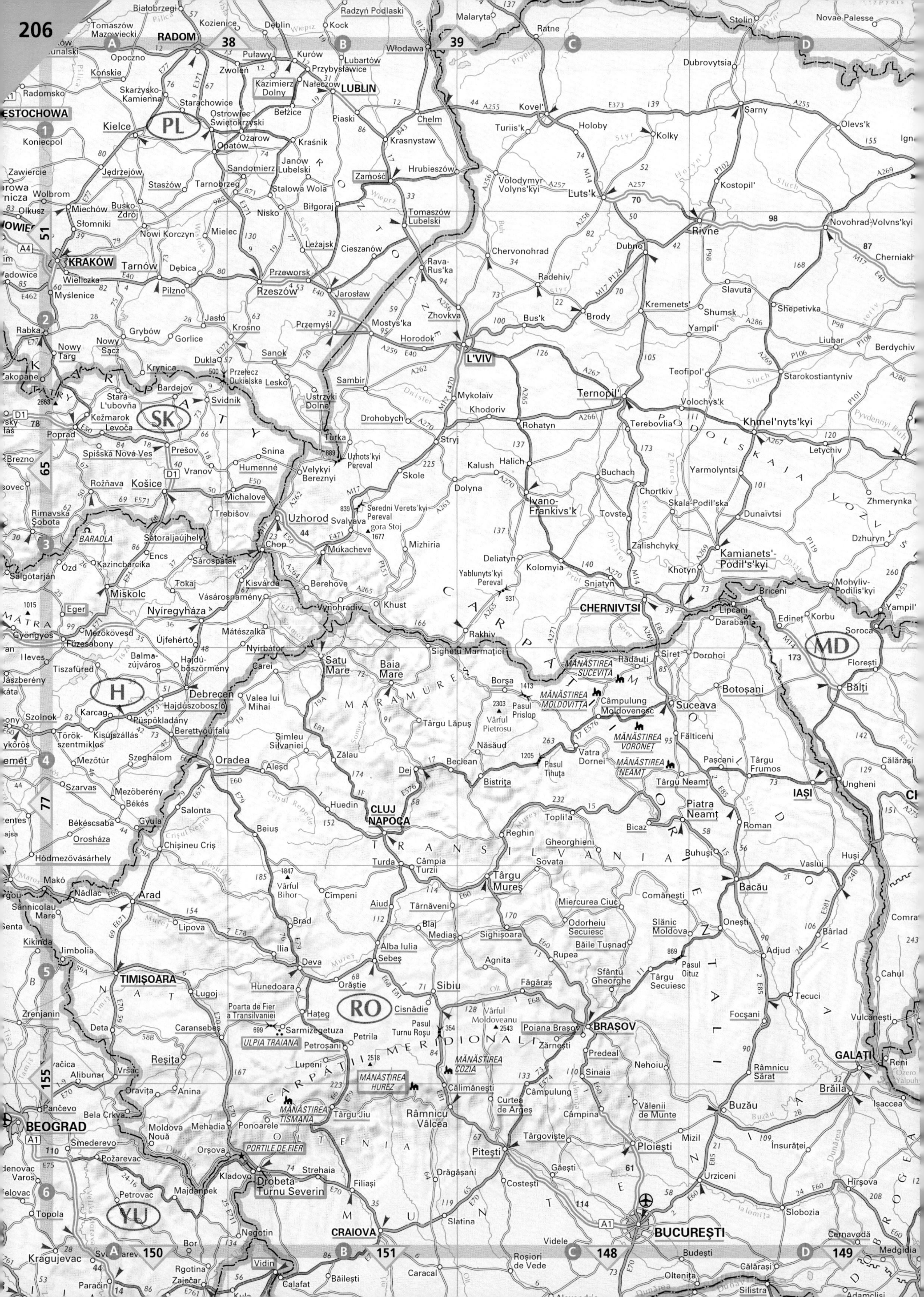

Białobrzegi
Tomaszów Mazowiecki
RADOM
38
Kozienice
Dęblin
Radzyń Podlaski
Kock
Malaryta
Ratne
Stolin
Novae Palesse
Opoczno
Końskie
Puławy
Kurów
Lubartów
Włodawa
39
Dubrovytsia
Zwoleń
Przybysławice
Kazimierz Dolny
Nałęczów
LUBLIN
Radomsko
Skarżysko-Kamienna
Starachowice
Bełżice
ESTOCHOWA
Kielce
PL
Ostrowiec Świętokrzyski
Piaski
Chełm
Kovel'
Turiis'k
Holoby
Sarny
Olevs'k
Koniecpol
Ożarow
Opatów
Kraśnik
Krasnystaw
Kolky
Janów Lubelski
Sandomierz
Jędrzejów
Zawiercie
Staszów
Tarnobrzeg
Stalowa Wola
Zamość
Hrubieszów
Volodymyr-Volyns'kyi
Luts'k
Kostopil'
Wolbrom
Olkusz
Miechów
Busko-Zdrój
Nisko
Biłgoraj
Tomaszów Lubelski
Słomniki
Nowi Korczyn
Mielec
Rivne
Novohrad-Volyns'kyi
Leżajsk
Cieszanów
Chervonohrad
Dubno
Cherniakh
KRAKÓW
Tarnów
Dębica
Przeworsk
Rava-Rus'ka
Radehiv
Slavuta
Wadowice
Wieliczka
Myślenice
Pilzno
Rzeszów
Jarosław
Zhovkva
Brody
Kremenets'
Shumsk
Shepetivka
Rabka
Grybów
Jasło
Przemyśl
Mostys'ka
Bus'k
Yampil'
Nowy Targ
Nowy Sącz
Gorlice
Krosno
Horodok
Liubar
Berdychiv
Zakopane
Krynica
Dukla
Przełęcz Dukielska
Sanok
Lesko
L'VIV
Teofipol'
Starokostiantyniv
TATRY
Stará L'ubovňa
Bardejov
Svidník
Ustrzyki Dolne
Sambir
Mykolaïv
Ternopil'
Volochys'k
Kežmarok
Levoča
SK
Khodoriv
Rohatyn
Terebovlia
Khmel'nyts'kyi
Poprad
Drohobych
Brezno
Spišská Nová Ves
Prešov
Turka
Stryj
Letychiv
Snina
Uzhots'kyi Pereval
Vranov
Humenné
Velykyi Bereznyi
Skole
Kalush
Halich
Buchach
Yarmolyntsi
Rožňava
Košice
Dolyna
Chortkiv
Zhmerynka
Michalove
Soredni Verets'kyi Pereval
Ivano-Frankivs'k
Skala-Podil'ska
Rimavská Sobota
Trebišov
Uzhorod
Svalyava
Tovste
Dunaïvtsi
BARADLA
Sátoraljaújhely
gora Stoj
Dzhuryn
Encs
Chop
Mukacheve
Mizhiria
Zalishchyky
Kazincbarcika
Sárospatak
Deliatyn
Kolomyia
Kamianets'-Podil's'kyi
Ózd
Salgótarján
Tokaj
Kisvárda
Berehove
Yablunyts'kyi Pereval
Snjatyn
Khotyn
Mohyliv-Podilis'kyi
Miskolc
Vásárosnamény
Khust
Briceni
MÁTRA
Eger
Nyíregyháza
Vynohradiv
CHERNIVTSI
Lipcani
Edineț
Korbu
Yampil'
Gyöngyös
Mezőkövesd
Füzesabony
Mátészalka
Újfehértó
Nyírbátor
Rakhiv
Darabani
Soroca
Balmazújváros
Hajdúböszörmény
Satu Mare
Sighetu Marmației
MD
Heves
Tiszafüred
Carei
Baia Mare
MĂNĂSTIREA SUCEVIȚA
Rădăuți
Siret
Dorohoi
Florești
Jászberény
H
Debrecen
Borşa
MĂNĂSTIREA MOLDOVIȚA
Câmpulung Moldovenesc
Botoșani
Bălți
Szolnok
Karcag
Hajdúszoboszló
Valea lui Mihai
MARAMUREȘ
Pasul Prislop
Vârful Pietrosu
Suceava
Püspökladány
Târgu Lăpuș
Törökszentmiklós
Kisújszállás
Berettyóújfalu
Şimleu Silvaniei
MĂNĂSTIREA VORONEȚ
Fălticeni
Năsăud
Vatra Dornei
Mezőtúr
Szeghalom
Oradea
Zălau
Aleşd
Dej
Beclean
Pasul Tihuța
MĂNĂSTIREA NEAMȚ
Pașcani
Târgu Frumos
Călărași
Szarvas
Mezőberény
Békés
Bistrița
Târgu Neamț
IAȘI
Ungheni
Salonta
Huedin
Piatra Neamț
Békéscsaba
Gyula
CLUJ NAPOCA
Toplița
Bicaz
Roman
Orosháza
Beiuș
Reghin
Gheorghieni
Chișineu Criș
TRANSILVANIA
Hódmezővásárhely
Turda
Câmpia Turzii
Sovata
Buhuși
Huși
Vârful Bihor
Târgu Mureș
Bacău
Vaslui
Makó
Nădlac
Arad
Cîmpeni
Aiud
Târnăveni
Miercurea Ciuc
Comănești
Sânnicolau Mare
Lipova
Brad
Blaj
Mediaș
Sighișoara
Odorheiu Secuiesc
Slănic Moldova
Onești
Bârlad
Comra
Kikinda
Jimbolia
Ilia
Alba Iulia
Băile Tușnad
Adjud
Deva
Sebeș
Agnita
Rupea
Pasul Oituz
Cahul
TIMIȘOARA
Hunedoara
Orăștie
Sibiu
Făgăraș
Sfântu Gheorghe
Târgu Secuiesc
Lugoj
RO
Cisnădie
Tecuci
Zrenjanin
Poarta de Fier a Transilvaniei
Hațeg
Vârful Moldoveanu
Vulcanești
Deta
Caransebeș
Sarmizegetuza
Pasul Turnu Roșu
Poiana Brașov
BRAȘOV
Focșani
ULPIA TRAIANA
Petroșani
Petrila
CARPAȚII MERIDIONALI
Zărnești
Reșița
Lupeni
MĂNĂSTIREA COZIA
Predeal
Nehoiu
GALAȚI
Reni
Vršac
Alibunar
MĂNĂSTIREA HUREZ
Sinaia
Râmnicu Sărat
Brăila
Oravița
Anina
Călimănești
Câmpulung
Pančevo
MĂNĂSTIREA TISMANA
Târgu Jiu
Curtea de Argeș
Vălenii de Munte
Buzău
Isaccea
Bela Crkva
Râmnicu Vâlcea
Câmpina
BEOGRAD
Moldova Nouă
Mehadia
Ponoarele
OLTENIA
Târgoviște
Smederevo
Orșova
PORTILE DE FIER
Mizil
Însurăței
Pitești
Ploiești
Požarevac
Kladovo
Drobeta-Turnu Severin
Strehaia
Găești
Urziceni
Hîrșova
Petrovac
Majdanpek
Filiași
Drăgășani
Costești
Slobozia
Topola
YU
Negotin
CRAIOVA
Slatina
BUCUREȘTI
Cernavodă
Kragujevac
Bor
Videle
Medgidia
150
151
148
149
Rgotina
Zaječar
Vidin
Băilești
Caracal
Roșiori de Vede
Budești
Călărași
Paraćin
Calafat
Oltenița
Silistra

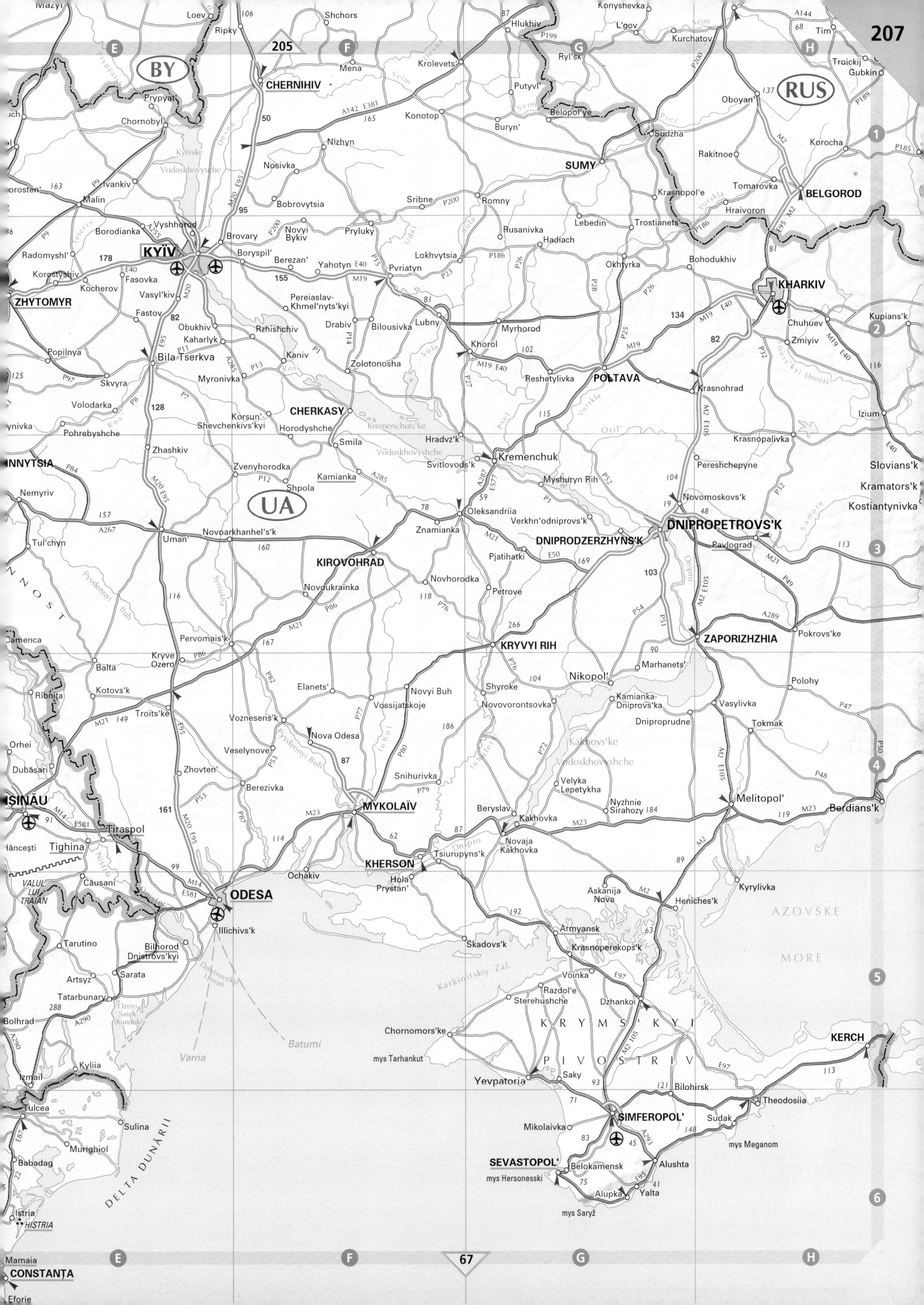
Mazyr
Loev
Ripky
Shchors
Hlukhiv
Konyshevka
L'gov
Kurchatov
Tim
205
E
F
G
H
BY
Mena
CHERNIHIV
Krolevets'
Ryl'sk
Putyvl'
Troickij
Gubkin
RUS
Oboyan'
Prypyat'
Chornobyl'
Konotop
Buryn'
Belopol'ye
Sudzha
Nizhyn
SUMY
Rakitnoe
Korocha
Kyïvske Vodoskhovyshche
Nosivka
Tomarovka
BELGOROD
Ivankiv
Malin
Bobrovytsia
Sribne
Romny
Krasnopol'e
Hraivoron
Korosten'
Lebedin
Trostianets'
Borodianka
Vyshhorod
Brovary
Novyi Bykiv
Pryluky
Rusanivka
Hadiach
Radomyshl'
KYÏV
Boryspil'
Berezan'
Yahotyn
Pvriatyn
Lokhvytsia
Okhtyrka
Bohodukhiv
Korostyshiv
Fasovka
Kocherov
Vasyl'kiv
KHARKIV
ZHYTOMYR
Pereiaslav-Khmel'nyts'kyi
Drabiv
Bilousivka
Lubny
Myrhorod
Fastov
Obukhiv
Rzhishchiv
Kaharlyk
Kupians'k
Chuhuev
Zmiyiv
Popilnya
Bila Tserkva
Kaniv
Khorol
Zolotonosha
Myronivka
Reshetylivka
POLTAVA
Krasnohrad
Skvyra
Volodarka
CHERKASY
Korsun'-Shevchenkivs'kyi
Horodyshche
Kremenchuts'ke Vodoskhovyshche
Izium
Pohrebyshche
Smila
Hradvz'k
Krasnopalivka
Zhashkiv
Kremenchuk
Svitlovods'k
Pereshchepyne
INNYTSIA
Zvenyhorodka
Kamianka
Myshuryn Rih
Slovians'k
Kramators'k
Kostiantynivka
Shpola
Nemyriv
UA
Novomoskovs'k
Oleksandriia
Znamianka
Verkhn'odniprovs'k
DNIPROPETROVS'K
DNIPRODZERZHYNS'K
Uman'
Novoarkhanhel's'k
Tul'chyn
Pjatihatki
Pavlograd
KIROVOHRAD
Novhorodka
Novoukraïnka
Petrove
Pyvdennyi Buh
Pervomais'k
KRYVYI RIH
ZAPORIZHZHIA
Pokrovs'ke
Camenca
Balta
Kryve Ozero
Marhanets'
Nikopol'
Polohy
Ribnita
Kotovs'k
Elanets'
Novyi Buh
Shyroke
Troïts'ke
Voznesens'k
Vossijatskoje
Novovorontsovka
Kamianka-Dniprovs'ka
Vasylivka
Dniproprudne
Tokmak
Orhei
Nova Odesa
Veselynove
Kakhovs'ke Vodoskhovyshche
Dubăsari
Zhovten'
Snihurivka
Velyka Lepetykha
Berezivka
Nyzhnie Sirahozy
Melitopol'
Berdians'k
SINĂU
MYKOLAÏV
Beryslav
Kakhovka
Tiraspol
Tighina
Hânceşti
Novaja Kakhovka
KHERSON
Tsiurupyns'k
Ochakiv
Hola Prystan'
Căuşani
VALUL LUI TRAIAN
ODESA
Askanija Nova
Heniches'k
Kyrylivka
Illichivs'k
AZOVSKE MORE
Tarutino
Bilhorod Dnistrovs'kyi
Skadovs'k
Armyansk
Krasnoperekops'k
Sarata
Artsyz
Karkinitskiy Zal.
Voinka
Tatarbunary
Razdol'e
Sterehushche
Dzhankoi
Bolhrad
Ozero Sasyk (Kunduk)
Batumi
Chornomors'ke
KRYMS'KYI PIVOSTRIV
Varna
KERCH
Kyliia
mys Tarhankut
Saky
Yevpatoria
Izmail
Bilohirsk
Tulcea
Theodosiia
SIMFEROPOL'
Sudak
Sulina
Mikolaivka
Murighiol
mys Meganom
SEVASTOPOL'
Alushta
Babadag
Belokamensk
mys Hersonesski
DELTA DUNĂRII
Alupka
Yalta
Istria
HISTRIA
mys Saryč
Mamaia
CONSTANŢA
Eforie
67

TOWNS AND URBAN AREAS
CITTÀ E AREE URBANE
CIUDADES Y ÁREAS URBANAS
VILLES ET AIRES URBAINES
STÄDTE UND ZUFAHRTEN

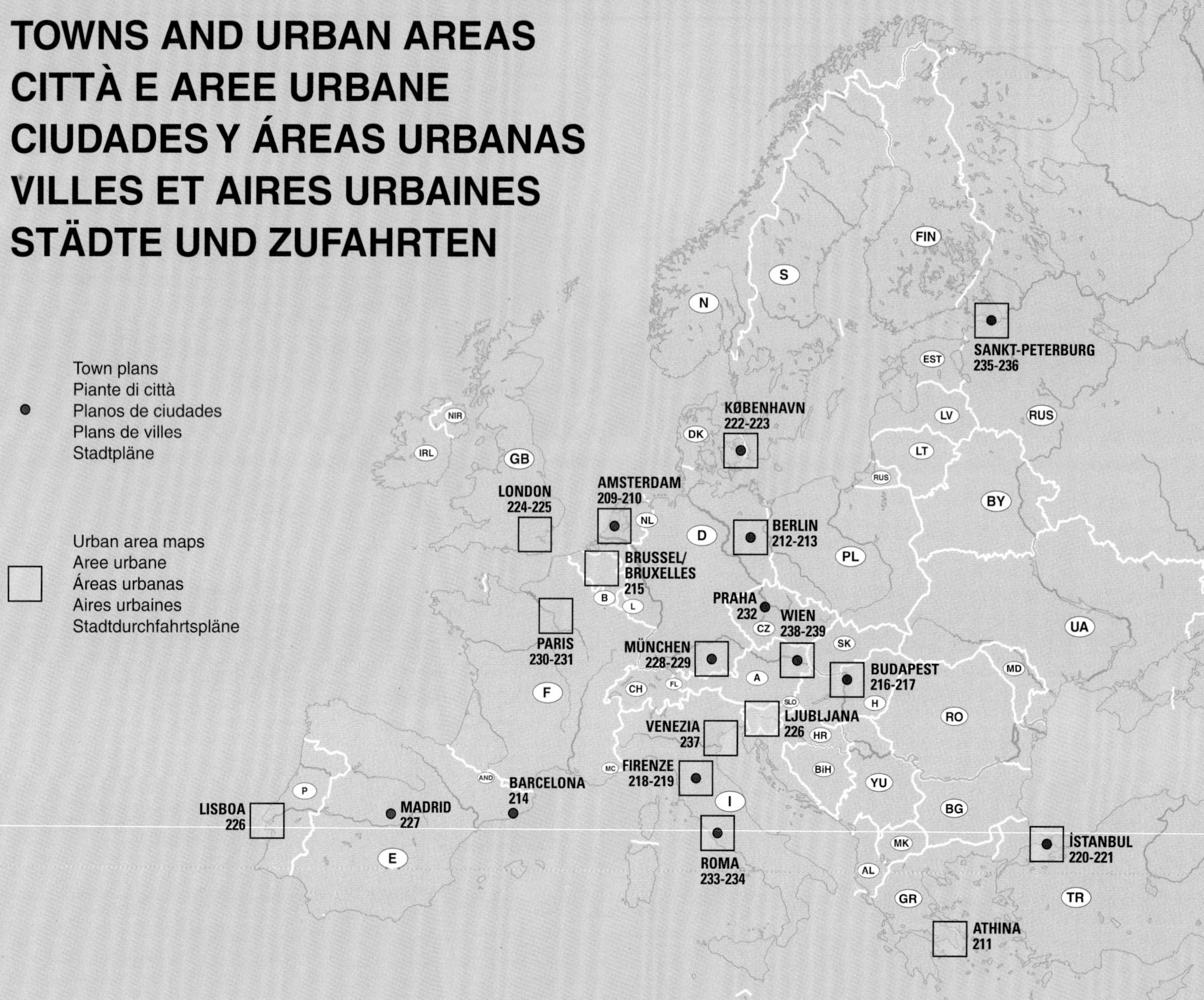

Town plans
Piante di città
Planos de ciudades
Plans de villes
Stadtpläne

Urban area maps
Aree urbane
Áreas urbanas
Aires urbaines
Stadtdurchfahrtspläne

SANKT-PETERBURG
235-236

KØBENHAVN
222-223

AMSTERDAM
209-210

LONDON
224-225

BERLIN
212-213

BRUSSEL/
BRUXELLES
215

PRAHA
232

WIEN
238-239

PARIS
230-231

MÜNCHEN
228-229

BUDAPEST
216-217

LJUBLJANA
226

VENEZIA
237

FIRENZE
218-219

BARCELONA
214

LISBOA
226

MADRID
227

ROMA
233-234

İSTANBUL
220-221

ATHINA
211

GB Legend	I Legenda	E Leyenda	F Légende	D Zeichenerklärung
Buildings	Caseggiati	Edificios	Immeubles	Gebäude
Monuments	Monumenti	Monumentos	Monuments	Denkmäler
Motorways, access points, service areas	Autostrade, caselli, stazioni di servizio	Autopista, accesos, stazioni di servizio	Autoroutes, accès, aires de service	Autobahnen, Anschlüsse, Tankstellen
Roads with motorway characteristics	Superstrade	Autovías	Routes-express	Autobahnähnliche Schnellstraßen
Through roads	Strade di attraversamento	Travesías	Routes de traversée	Hauptdurchfahrtsstraßen
Other roads	Altre strade	Otras carreteras	Autres routes	Sonstige Straßen
A9 N202 Numbering of motorway and national road	Numeri di autostrada e strada nazionale	Números de autopista y carretera nacional	Numéros d'autoroute et route nationale	Autobahnnummer, Staatsstraßennummer
Road in tunnel	Gallerie stradali	Túneles en carretera	Tunnels routiers	Straßentunnels
Utrecht Directions	Direzioni	Direcciones	Directions	Richtungen
Railways and stations	Ferrovie e stazioni	Ferrocarriles y estaciones	Chemins de fer et gares	Eisenbahnen und Bahnhöfe
Gardens and parks; cemeteries	Giardini e parchi; cimiteri	Jardines y parques; cementerios	Jardins et parcs; cimetières	Gärten und Parks; Friedhöfe
Hospital	Ospedale	Hospital	Hôpital	Krankenhaus
Camping	Campeggio	Cámping	Camping	Campingplatz
Ferry route with car transportation	Trasporto auto su traghetto	Transbordador de automóviles	Bac pour autos	Autofähre
Panoramic view	Punto panoramico	Vista panorámica	Vue panoramique	Aussichtspunkt
P Parking	Parcheggio	Aparcamiento	Parking	Parkplatz
M Underground railway stations	Fermate della metropolitana	Estaciones del metro	Stations de métro	U-Bahnhöfe
i Tourist information	Ufficio informazioni	Información turística	Informations touristiques	Touristische Auskünfte
Pedestrian areas	Aree pedonali	Áreas peatonales	Zones réservées aux piétons	Fußgängerzone

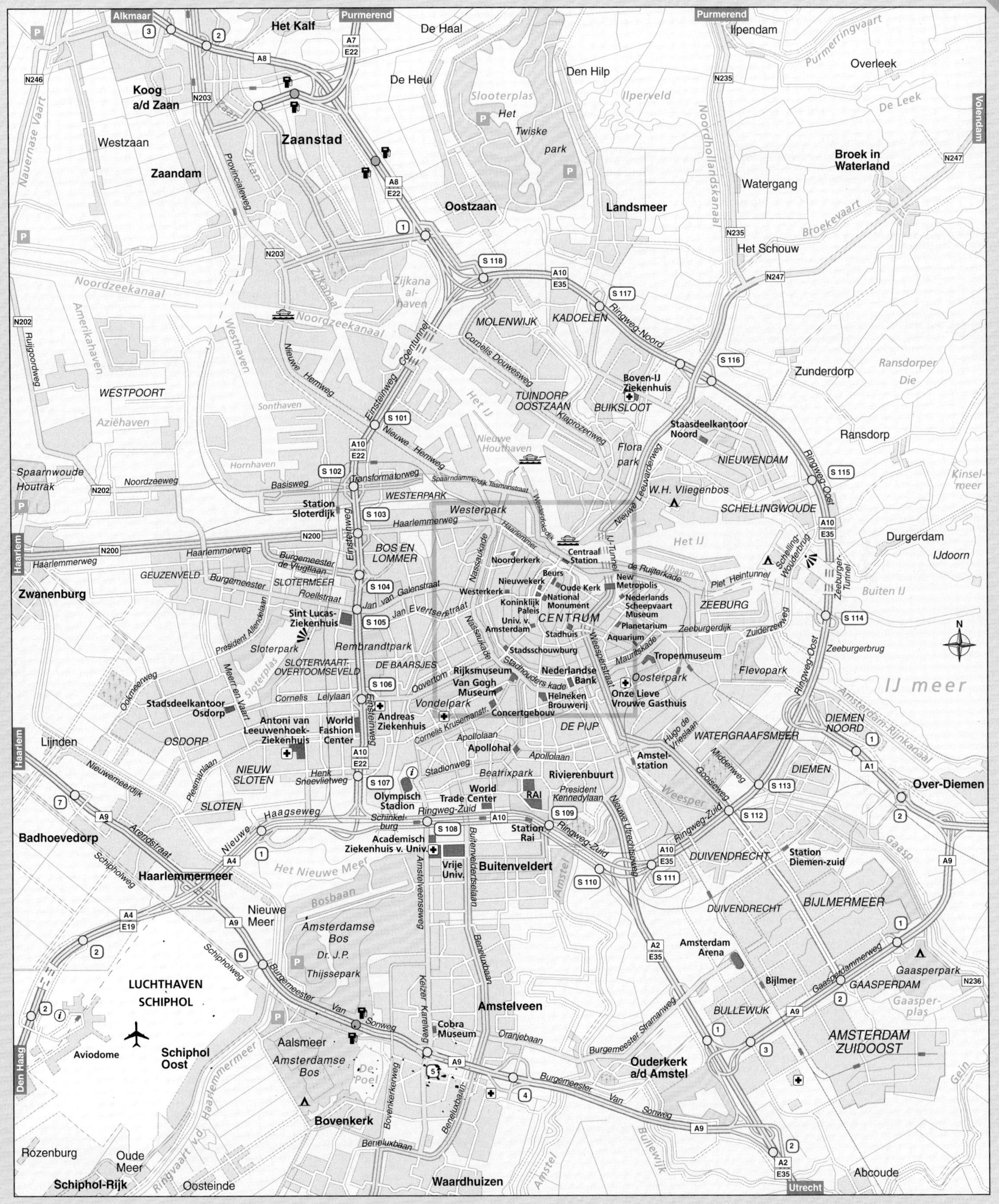
Alkmaar
Purmerend
Het Kalf
De Haal
Ilpendam
Overleek
Koog a/d Zaan
De Heul
Den Hilp
Westzaan
Zaanstad
Slooterplas
Het Twiske park
Ilperveld
De Leek
Volendam
Zaandam
Broek in Waterland
Watergang
Oostzaan
Landsmeer
Het Schouw
Noordzeekanaal
Zijkanaal
Noordhollandskanaal
Purmerringvaart
Broekervaart
Provincialeweg
Nauernase Vaart
Amerikahaven
Westhaven
Ruigoordweg
WESTPOORT
Aziëhaven
Sonthaven
Hornhaven
Spaarnwoude Houtrak
Noordzeeweg
Basisweg
Station Sloterdijk
MOLENWIJK
KADOELEN
Ringweg-Noord
Cornelis Douwesweg
TUINDORP OOSTZAAN
BUIKSLOOT
Boven-IJ Ziekenhuis
Zunderdorp
Ransdorper Die
Ransdorp
Staasdeelkantoor Noord
NIEUWENDAM
Flora park
Kinselmeer
W.H. Vliegenbos
SCHELLINGWOUDE
Het IJ
Nieuwe Houthaven
Coentunnel
Einsteinweg
Nieuwe Hemweg
Transformatorweg
WESTERPARK
Westerpark
Haarlemmerweg
Haarlemmerweg
Durgerdam
IJdoorn
Buiten IJ
Zwanenburg
GEUZENVELD
SLOTERMEER
BOS EN LOMMER
Burgemeester de Vlugtlaan
Roelfsstraat
Jan van Galenstraat
Jan Evertsenstraat
Sint Lucas-Ziekenhuis
Noorderkerk
Centraal Station
Nieuwekerk
Beurs
Oude Kerk
New Metropolis
Westerkerk
Koninklijk Paleis
National Monument
Nederlands Scheepvaart Museum
Univ. v. Amsterdam
CENTRUM
Planetarium
Stadhuis
Aquarium
Zeeburgerdijk
ZEEBURG
Piet Heintunnel
Schellingwouderbrug
Zeeburgertunnel
Zeeburgerbrug
Ringweg-Oost
IJ meer
Flevopark
Tropenmuseum
Mauritskade
President Allendelaan
Sloterpark
Sloterplas
Rembrandtpark
SLOTERVAART-OVERTOOMSEVELD
DE BAARSJES
Stadsschouwburg
Rijksmuseum
Van Gogh Museum
Nederlandse Bank
Oosterpark
Onze Lieve Vrouwe Gasthuis
Heineken Brouwerij
Concertgebouw
Vondelpark
Overtoom
Stadhouderskade
Wibautstraat
Ookmeerweg
Stadsdeelkantoor Osdorp
Meer en Vaart
Cornelis Lelylaan
Antoni van Leeuwenhoek-Ziekenhuis
World Fashion Center
Andreas Ziekenhuis
Cornelis Krusemanstr.
Apollolaan
Apollohal
DE PIJP
Hugo de Vrieslaan
WATERGRAAFSMEER
DIEMEN NOORD
Amsterdam-Rijnkanaal
Lijnden
OSDORP
NIEUW SLOTEN
Henk Sneevlietweg
Stadionweg
Beatrixpark
Rivierenbuurt
Amstel-station
Middenweg
Gooiseweg
DIEMEN
Over-Diemen
Badhoevedorp
Nieuwemeerdijk
Pieterrnanlaan
SLOTEN
Haagseweg
Olympisch Stadion
World Trade Center
RAI
President Kennedylaan
Weesper
Schinkel-burg
Ringweg-Zuid
Station Rai
Nieuwe Utrechtseweg
Academisch Ziekenhuis v. Univ.
Buitenveldertselaan
Vrije Univ.
Buitenveldert
Amstel
DUIVENDRECHT
Station Diemen-zuid
Gaasp
Arendstraat
Schipholweg
Haarlemmermeer
Het Nieuwe Meer
Bosbaan
Nieuwe Meer
Amstelveenseweg
Beneluxbaan
BIJLMERMEER
Amsterdamse Bos
Dr. J.P. Thijssepark
Amsterdam Arena
Gaasperpark
GAASPERDAM
Gaasperplas
LUCHTHAVEN SCHIPHOL
Burgemeester Van Sonweg
Gaasperdammerweg
Bijlmer
BULLEWIJK
Keizer Karelweg
Amstelveen
Burgemeester Stramanweg
AMSTERDAM ZUIDOOST
Cobra Museum
Oranjebaan
Aviodome
Schiphol Oost
Aalsmeer
Amsterdamse Bos
De Poel
Ouderkerk a/d Amstel
Bovenkerkerweg
Ringvaart v.d. Haarlemmermeer
Bovenkerk
Bullewijk
Gein
Rozenburg
Oude Meer
Beneluxbaan
Abcoude
Schiphol-Rijk
Oosteinde
Waardhuizen
Utrecht
Den Haag
Haarlem
N246
N203
N202
N200
N235
N247
N236
A7
A8
A10
A4
A9
A1
A2
E22
E35
E19
S 101
S 102
S 103
S 104
S 105
S 106
S 107
S 108
S 109
S 110
S 111
S 112
S 113
S 114
S 115
S 116
S 117
S 118
N
0 1 2
km

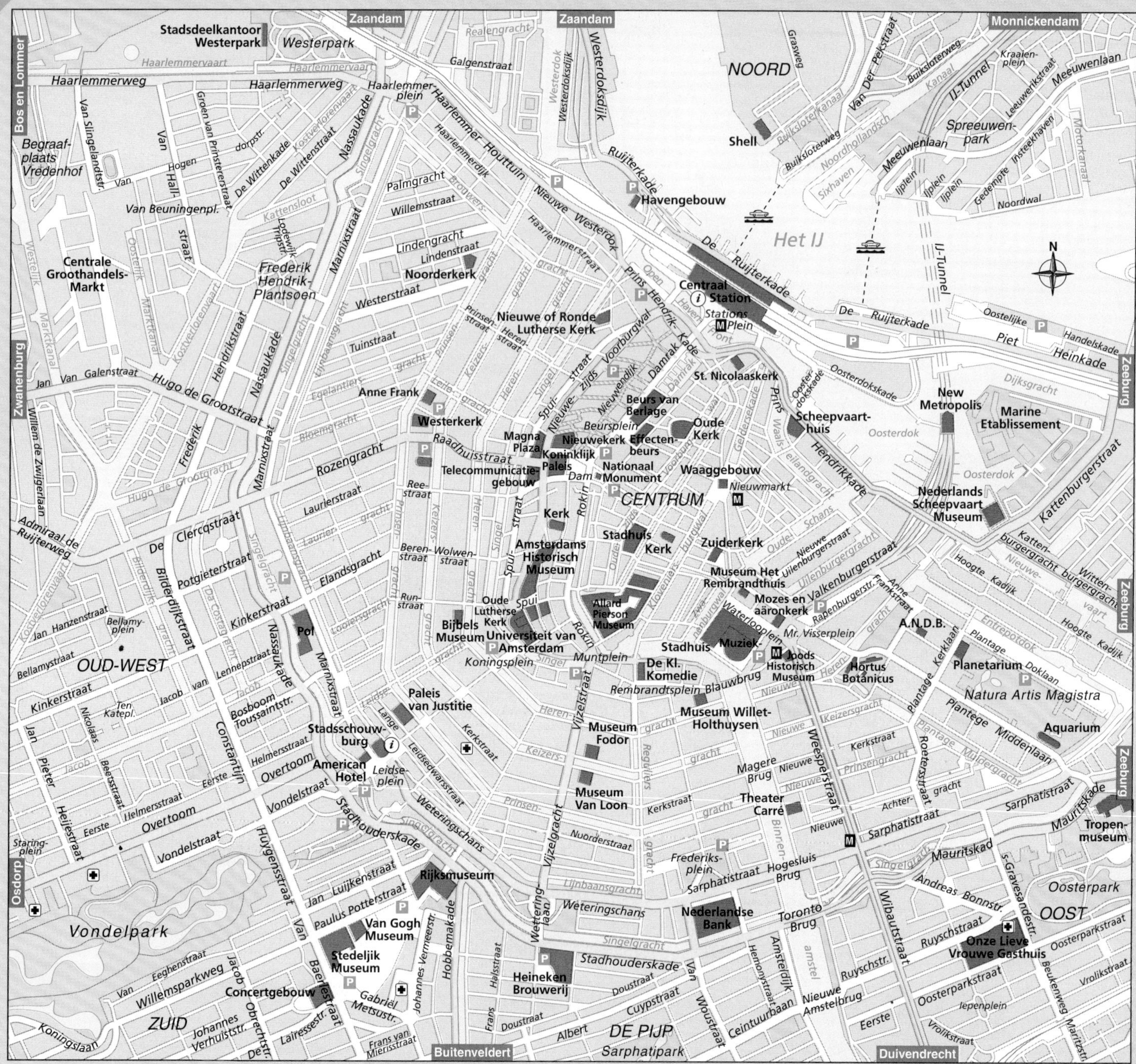

Zaandam
Zaandam
Monnickendam
Bos en Lommer
Zwanenburg
Osdorp
Zeeburg
Zeeburg
Zeeburg
Buitenveldert
Duivendrecht
Stadsdeelkantoor Westerpark
Westerpark
Haarlemmervaart
Haarlemmerweg
Haarlemmerweg
Haarlemmer-plein
Galgenstraat
Realengracht
Westerdok
Westerdoksdijk
NOORD
Grasweg
Shell
Van Der Pekstraat
Buiksloterweg
IJ-Tunnel
Kraaien-plein
Meeuwenlaan
Spreeuwen-park
Noordhollandsch Kanaal
Sixhaven
Gedempte Insteekhaven
Noordwal
Motorkanaal
Begraaf-plaats Vredenhof
Van Slingelandtstr.
Van Hall-straat
Van Beuningenpl.
Hogen
De Wittenkade
De Wittenstraat
Nassaukade
Singelgracht
Marnixstraat
Palmgracht
Willemsstraat
Brouwersgracht
Haarlemmer Houttuinen
Ruijterkade
Havengebouw
Nieuwe Westerdok
Haarlemmerstraat
Het IJ
De Ruijterkade
IJ-Tunnel
N
Centrale Groothandels-Markt
Frederik Hendrik-Plantsoen
Lindengracht
Lindenstraat
Noorderkerk
Westerstraat
Prins Hendrik-kade
Centraal Station
Stations Plein
De Ruijterkade
Oostelijke Handelskade
Piet Heinkade
Nieuwe of Ronde Lutherse Kerk
Tuinstraat
Jan Van Galenstraat
Hugo de Grootstraat
Hendrikstraat
Nassaukade
Anne Frank
Westerkerk
Raadhuisstraat
Damrak
St. Nicolaaskerk
Oosterdokskade
New Metropolis
Marine Etablissement
Dijksgracht
Willem de Zwijgerlaan
Frederik
Rozengracht
Magna Plaza
Nieuwekerk
Koninklijk Paleis
Beurs van Berlage
Beursplein
Effecten-beurs
Oude Kerk
Scheepvaart-huis
Oosterdok
Hendrikkade
Telecommunicatie-gebouw
Dam
Nationaal Monument
Waaggebouw
Nieuwmarkt
CENTRUM
Nederlands Scheepvaart Museum
Kattenburgerstraat
Lauriergracht
Admiraal de Ruijterweg
De Clercqstraat
Kerk
Rokin
Stadhuis
Kerk
Zuiderkerk
Amsterdams Historisch Museum
Kattenburgergracht
Wittenburgergracht
Potgieterstraat
Elandsgracht
Bilderdijkstraat
Museum Het Rembrandthuis
Mozes en Aäronkerk
Valkenburgerstraat
Uilenburgergracht
Oude Lutherse Kerk
Spui
Allard Pierson Museum
Bijbels Museum
Universiteit van Amsterdam
Kinkerstraat
Pof
Stadhuis
Muziek-
Waterlooplein
Mr. Visserplein
Joods Historisch Museum
Hortus Botanicus
A.N.D.B.
Planetarium
Plantage Kerklaan
Jan Hanzenstraat
Bellamy-plein
Bellamystraat
OUD-WEST
Koningsplein
Muntplein
De Kl. Komedie
Rembrandtsplein
Blauwbrug
Natura Artis Magistra
Plantage Middenlaan
Aquarium
Kinkerstraat
Ten Katepl.
Jacob van Lennepstraat
Bosboom Toussaintstr.
Paleis van Justitie
Vijzelstraat
Museum Willet-Holthuysen
Jan Pieter Heijestraat
Constantijn
Stadsschouw-burg
Leidseplein
American Hotel
Kerkstraat
Museum Fodor
Magere Brug
Roetersstraat
Overtoom
Vondelstraat
Overtoom
Eerste
Museum Van Loon
Theater Carré
Weesperstraat
Sarphatistraat
Tropen-museum
Mauritskade
Staring-plein
Vondelstraat
Stadhouderskade
Weteringschans
Nuorderstraat
Frederiks-plein
Sarphatistraat
Hogesluis Brug
Wibautstraat
Mauritskad
Andreas Bonnstr.
Oosterpark
OOST
Vondelpark
Jan Luijkenstraat
Paulus Potterstraat
Rijksmuseum
Van Gogh Museum
Weteringschans
Nederlandse Bank
Toronto Brug
Ruyschstraat
Onze Lieve Vrouwe Gasthuis
Oosterparkstraat
Stedelijk Museum
Hobbemakade
Johannes Vermeerstr.
Heineken Brouwerij
Stadhouderskade
Van Woustraat
Amsteldijk
amstel
Willemsparkweg
Jacob Obrechtstr.
Concertgebouw
Gabriël Metsustr.
Cuyptstraat
Doustraat
Ceintuurbaan
Nieuwe Amstelbrug
Eerste
Iepenplein
Vrolikstraat
Beukenweg
Maritsstr.
Koningslaan
ZUID
Johannes Verhulststr.
De Lairessestraat
Frans van Mierisstraat
Albert Cuypstraat
DE PIJP
Sarphatipark

0 200 400

m

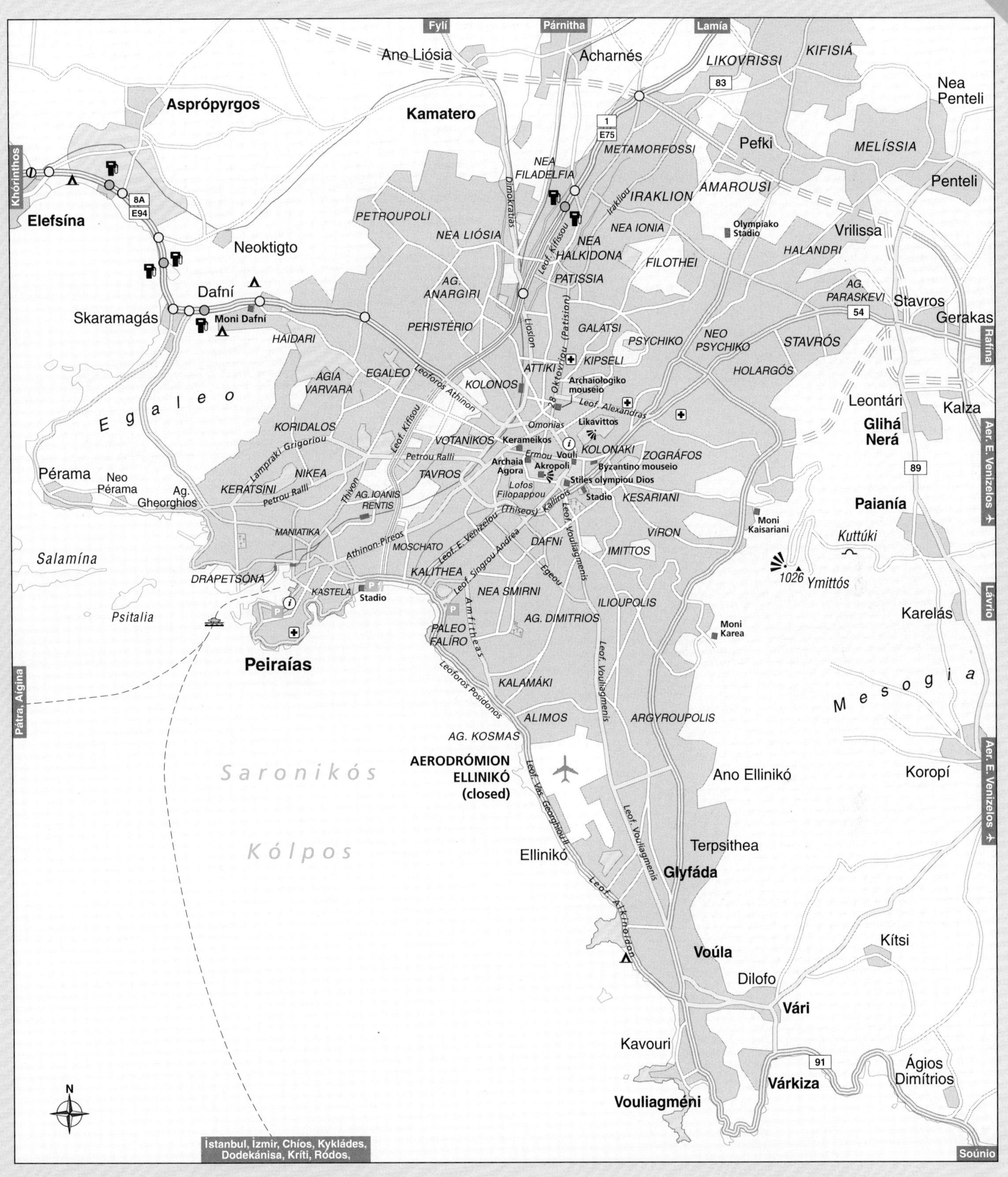

Fylí
Párnitha
Lamía

Ano Liósia
Acharnés
LIKOVRISSI
KIFISIÁ
Nea
Penteli

Asprópyrgos
Kamatero
83

1
E75

METAMORFOSSI
Pefki
MELÍSSIA

*NEA
FILADELFIA*
IRAKLION
AMAROUSI
Penteli

PETROUPOLI
NEA LIÓSIA
NEA IONIA
Olympiako
Stadio
Vrilissa

Elefsína
Neoktigto
*NEA
HALKIDONA*
FILOTHEI
HALANDRI

*AG.
ANARGIRI*
PATISSIA
*AG.
PARASKEVI*
Stavros
54

Dafní
GALÁTSI
Gerakas

Skaramagás
Moni Dafní
PERISTÉRIO
PSYCHIKO
*NEO
PSYCHIKO*
STAVRÓS

HAÍDARI
ATTIKI
KIPSELI
HOLARGÓS

E g a l e o
*AGÍA
VARVARA*
EGALEO
KOLONOS
Archaiologiko
mouseio
Leof. Alexandras
Leontári
Kalza

KORIDALOS
Omonias
Likavittos
**Glihá
Nerá**

Pérama
Neo
Pérama
NIKEA
VOTANIKOS
Kerameïkos
Ermou Vouli
KOLONÁKI
ZOGRÁFOS
89

Ag.
Gheorghios
KERATSINI
Petrou Ralli
Archaía
Agora
Akropoli
Byzantino mouseio
Stiles olympíou Dios
Paianía

MANIATIKA
TAVROS
Lofos
Filopappou
Stadio
KESARIANI

Salamína
DRAPETSÓNA
Athinon-Pireas
MOSCHATO
DAFNÍ
IMITTOS
VÍRON
Moni
Kaisariani
Kuttúki

KASTELA
Stadio
NEA SMIRNI
1026 Ymittós

Psitalia
Peiraías
KALITHEA
AG. DIMITRIOS
ILIOUPOLIS
Moni
Karea
Karelás

*PALEO
FALÍRO*
KALAMÁKI
ARGYROUPOLIS
M e s o g i a

S a r o n i k ó s
ALIMOS
Koropí

AG. KOSMAS

K ó l p o s
**AERODRÓMION
ELLINIKÓ
(closed)**
Ano Ellinikó

Ellinikó
Terpsithea

Glyfáda

Voúla
Kítsi

Dilofo

Vári

Kavouri

Várkiza
91
**Ágios
Dimítrios**

Vouliagméni

N

Soúnio

İstanbul, İzmir, Chíos, Kykládes,
Dodekánisa, Kríti, Ródos,

0   2   4
km

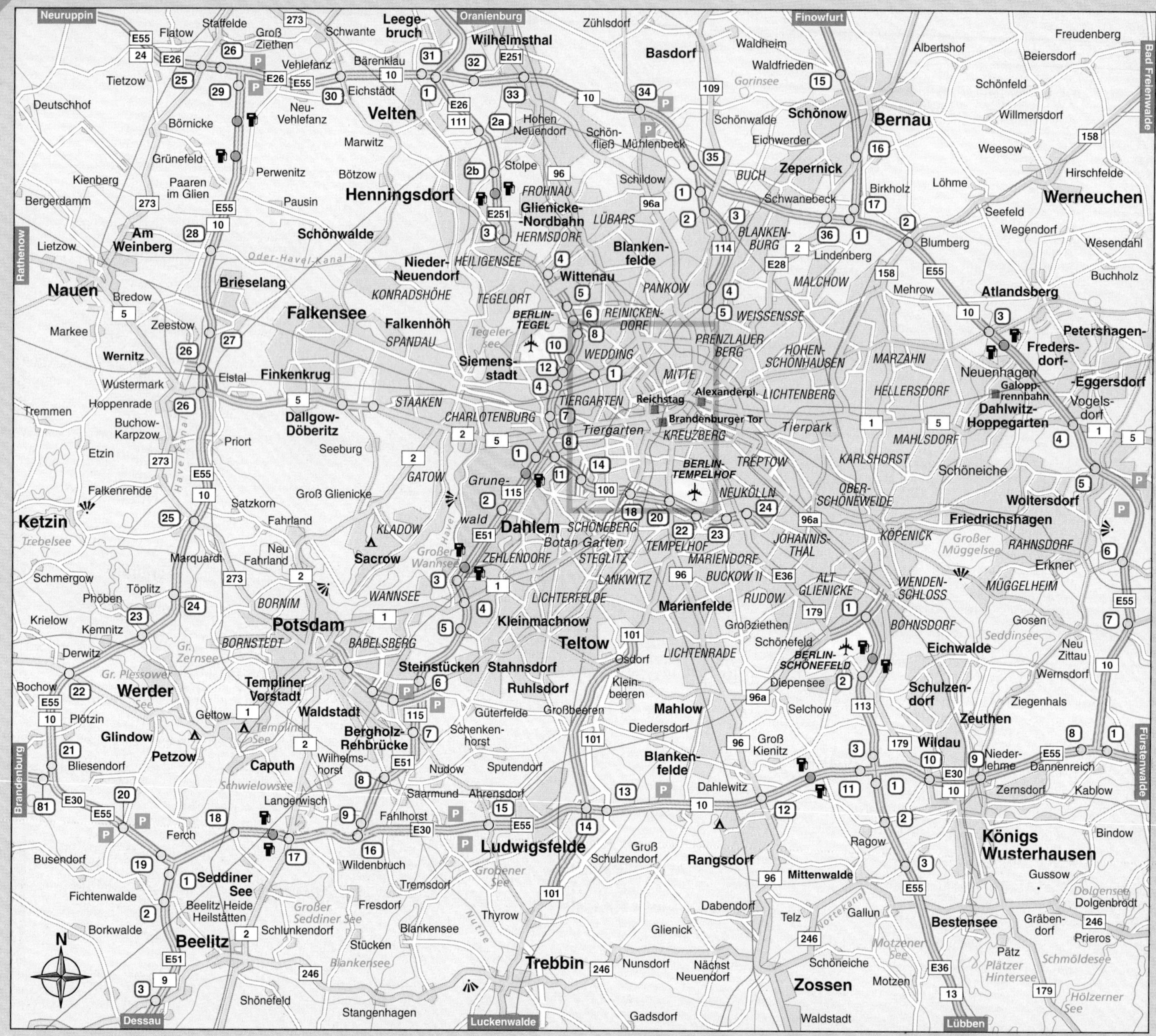
Neuruppin
Oranienburg
Finowfurt
Bad Freienwalde
Rathenow
Brandenburg
Fürstenwalde
Dessau
Luckenwalde
Lübben
Flatow
Staffelde
Groß Ziethen
Schwante
Leegebruch
Wilhelmsthal
Zühlsdorf
Basdorf
Waldheim
Waldfrieden
Gorinsee
Albertshof
Freudenberg
Beiersdorf
Schönfeld
Tietzow
Vehlefanz
Bärenklau
Eichstädt
Neu-Vehlefanz
Velten
Hohen Neuendorf
Schönfließ
Mühlenbeck
Schönwalde
Schönow
Bernau
Willmersdorf
Deutschhof
Börnicke
Marwitz
Eichwerder
Weesow
Grünefeld
Stolpe
Zepernick
Kienberg
Paaren im Glien
Perwenitz
Bötzow
Frohnau
Schildow
Buch
Birkholz
Löhme
Hirschfelde
Bergerdamm
Pausin
Henningsdorf
Glienicke-Nordbahn
Schwanebeck
Werneuchen
Lübars
Seefeld
Am Weinberg
Schönwalde
Hermsdorf
Blankenburg
Wegendorf
Lietzow
Oder-Havel-Kanal
Nieder-Neuendorf
Heiligensee
Blankenfelde
Lindenberg
Blumberg
Wesendahl
Nauen
Brieselang
Wittenau
Malchow
Buchholz
Bredow
Konradshöhe
Tegelort
Pankow
Mehrow
Atlandsberg
Falkensee
Berlin-Tegel
Reinickendorf
Weissensee
Markee
Zeestow
Falkenhöh
Spandau
Tegeler See
Prenzlauer Berg
Hohenschönhausen
Marzahn
Petershagen-Fredersdorf
Wernitz
Siemensstadt
Wedding
Neuenhagen
Wustermark
Elstal
Finkenkrug
Mitte
Lichtenberg
Hellersdorf
Galopprennbahn
Eggersdorf
Tremmen
Hoppenrade
Staaken
Tiergarten
Reichstag
Alexanderpl.
Dahlwitz-Hoppegarten
Vogelsdorf
Buchow-Karpzow
Dallgow-Döberitz
Charlottenburg
Brandenburger Tor
Tierpark
Priort
Seeburg
Kreuzberg
Mahlsdorf
Etzin
Havelkanal
Berlin-Tempelhof
Treptow
Karlshorst
Schöneiche
Gatow
Grunewald
Falkenrehde
Groß Glienicke
Neukölln
Oberschöneweide
Woltersdorf
Satzkorn
Ketzin
Fahrland
Kladow
Dahlem
Schöneberg
Köpenick
Friedrichshagen
Trebelsee
Botan Garten
Tempelhof
Johannisthal
Großer Müggelsee
Rahnsdorf
Marquardt
Neu Fahrland
Sacrow
Großer Wannsee
Zehlendorf
Steglitz
Mariendorf
Erkner
Schmergow
Töplitz
Lankwitz
Buckow II
Alt Glienicke
Wendenschloss
Müggelheim
Phöben
Bornim
Wannsee
Lichterfelde
Rudow
Marienfelde
Krielow
Kemnitz
Potsdam
Kleinmachnow
Großziethen
Gosen
Bornstedt
Babelsberg
Teltow
Bohnsdorf
Seddinsee
Derwitz
Gr. Zernsee
Schönefeld
Berlin-Schönefeld
Eichwalde
Neu Zittau
Gr. Plessower See
Osdorf
Lichtenrade
Steinstücken
Stahnsdorf
Wernsdorf
Bochow
Werder
Templiner Vorstadt
Ruhlsdorf
Kleinbeeren
Diepensee
Schulzendorf
Waldstadt
Mahlow
Selchow
Ziegenhals
Plötzin
Geltow
Templiner See
Güterfelde
Großbeeren
Zeuthen
Glindow
Bergholz-Rehbrücke
Schenkenhorst
Diedersdorf
Groß Kienitz
Wildau
Niederlehme
Petzow
Caputh
Wilhelmshorst
Blankenfelde
Bliesendorf
Nudow
Sputendorf
Dannenreich
Schwielowsee
Dahlewitz
Zernsdorf
Kablow
Saarmund
Ahrensdorf
Langerwisch
Fahlhorst
Ferch
Bindow
Königs Wusterhausen
Ragow
Ludwigsfelde
Busendorf
Wildenbruch
Groß Schulzendorf
Rangsdorf
Seddiner See
Tremsdorf
Großer Seddiner See
Gussow
Mittenwalde
Fichtenwalde
Beelitz Heide
Beelitz Heilstätten
Fresdorf
Dolgensee
Dolgenbrodt
Dabendorf
Borkwalde
Schlunkendorf
Blankensee
Thyrow
Nuthe
Glienick
Telz
Gallun
Nottekanal
Bestensee
Gräbendorf
Prieros
Beelitz
Stücken
Motzener See
Blankensee
Trebbin
Nunsdorf
Nächst Neuendorf
Schöneiche
Pätz
Plätzer Hintersee
Schmöldesee
Zossen
Motzen
Shönefeld
Stangenhagen
Gadsdorf
Waldstadt
Hölzerner See
N

0 3 6 9
km

0 400 800 1200
m

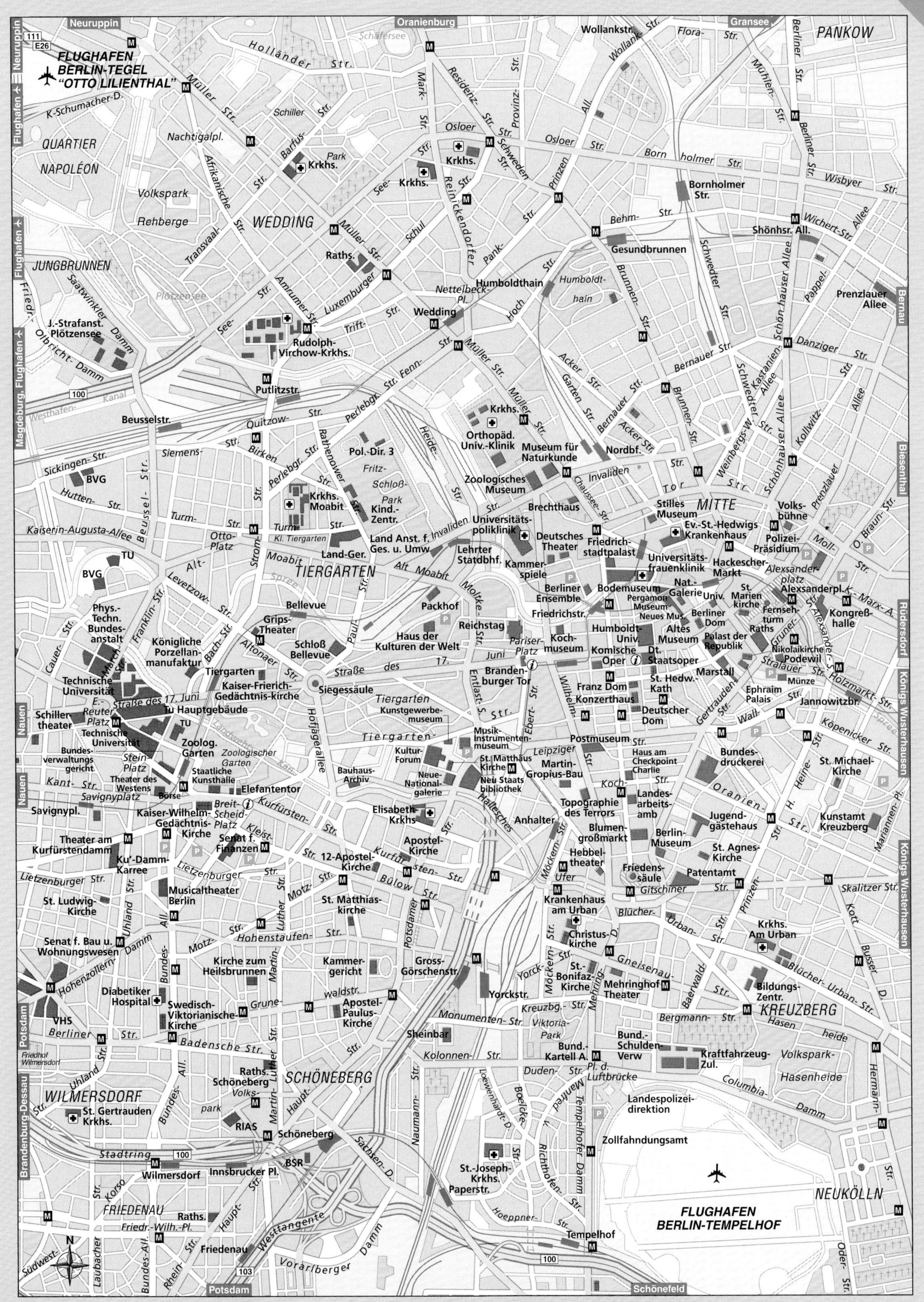

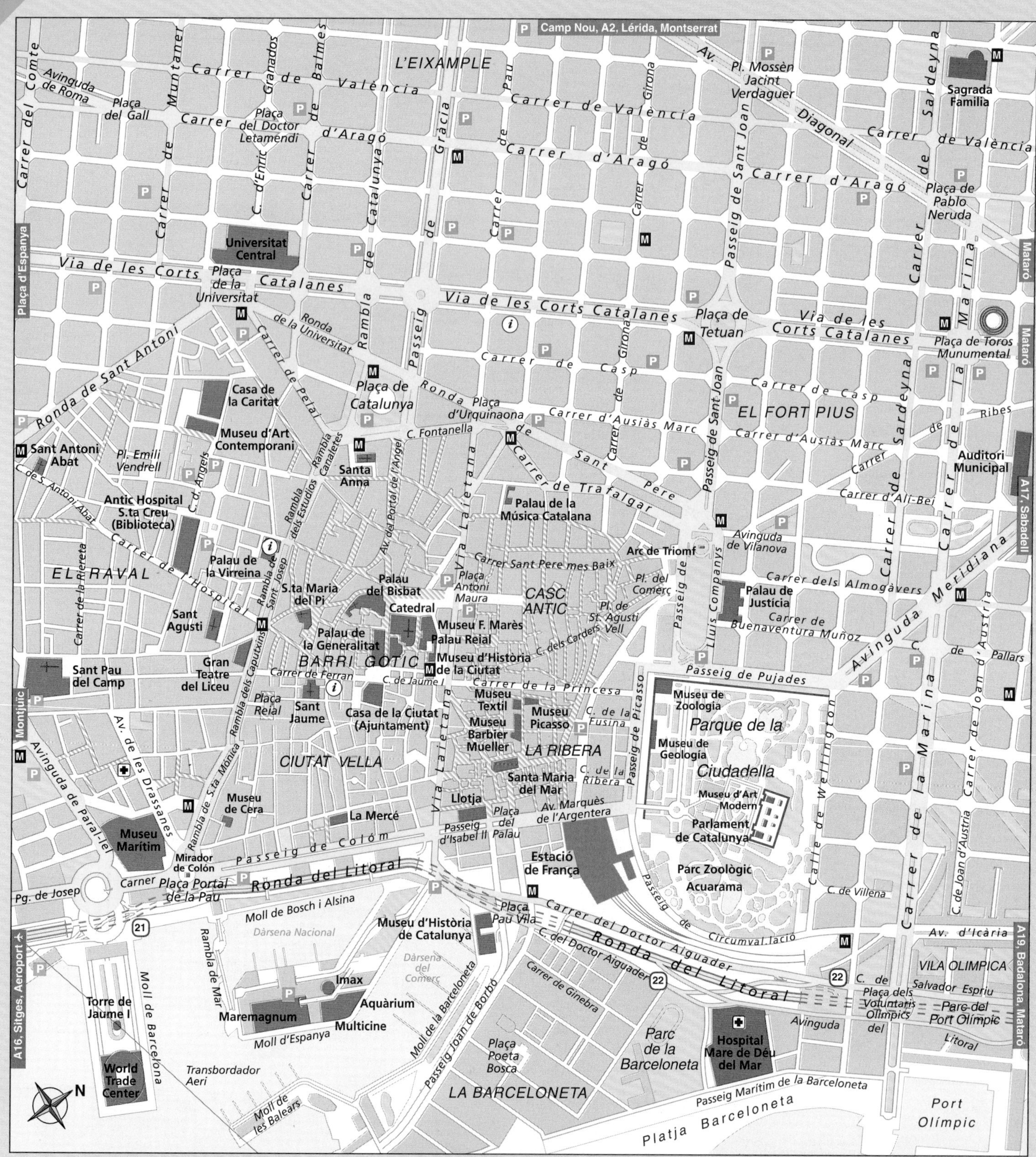

Camp Nou, A2, Lérida, Montserrat

L'EIXAMPLE

Avinguda de Roma

Carrer del Comte

Carrer de Muntaner

Carrer de Granados

Carrer de Balmes

Carrer de València

Pl. Mossèn Jacint Verdaguer

Carrer de València

Carrer de Girona

Av.

Diagonal

Carrer de Sardeyna

Sagrada Familia

Plaça del Gall

Plaça del Doctor Letamendi

d'Aragó

Carrer de

Carrer d'Aragó

Gràcia

Carrer d'Aragó

de

Passeig de Sant Joan

Carrer de València

Plaça de Pablo Neruda

Carrer de la Marina

Mataró

Universitat Central

Plaça d'Espanya

Via de les Corts

Plaça de la Universitat

Catalanes

Via de les Corts Catalanes

Plaça de Tetuan

Via de les Corts Catalanes

Plaça de Toros Munumental

Ronda de Sant Antoni

Carrer de Pelai

Ronda de la Universitat

Rambla de Catalunya

Passeig de Gràcia

Carrer de Casp

Carrer de Girona

EL FORT PIUS

Carrer de Casp

Mataró

Plaça de Catalunya

Plaça d'Urquinaona

Ronda de Sant

Pere

Carrer d'Ausiàs Marc

Passeig de Sant Joan

Carrer de Casp

Carrer de Sardeyna

de Ribes

A17, Sabadell

Casa de la Caritat

Museu d'Art Contemporani

C. Fontanella

Carrer d'Ausiàs Marc

Carrer de la

Auditori Municipal

Sant Antoni Abat

Pl. Emili Vendrell

Santa Anna

Carrer de Trafalgar

Palau de la Música Catalana

Avinguda de Vilanova

Carrer de Ali-Bei

EL RAVAL

Antic Hospital S.ta Creu (Biblioteca)

Carrer de l'Hospital

Palau de la Virreina

S.ta Maria del Pi

Rambla dels Estudios

Rambla Canaletes

Palau del Bisbat

Carrer Sant Pere mes Baix

Plaça Antoni Maura

CASC ANTIC

Arc de Triomf

Pl. del Comerç

Carrer dels Almogàvers

Avinguda Meridiana

Palau de Justícia

Carrer de Buenaventura Muñoz

Carrer de Joan d'Àustria

Pallars

Carrer de la Riereta

Sant Agusti

Catedral

Museu F. Marès

Palau Reial

Pl. de St. Agustí Vell

C. dels Carders

Passeig de Pujades

Museu de Zoologia

Parque de la Ciudadella

Sant Pau del Camp

Gran Teatre del Liceu

Palau de la Generalitat

BARRI GOTIC

Carrer de Ferran

C. de Jaume I

Museu d'Història de la Ciutat

Carrer de la Princesa

Museu Textil

Museu Barbier Mueller

Museu Picasso

C. de la Fusina

Passeig de Picasso

Museu de Geologia

Museu d'Art Modern

Carrer de Wellington

Montjuïc

Plaça Reial

Sant Jaume

Casa de la Ciutat (Ajuntament)

LA RIBERA

LA RIBERA

Santa Maria del Mar

C. de la Ribera

Parlament de Catalunya

Avinguda de Paral·lel

Museu de Cera

Rambla de S.ta Mònica

Llotja

Plaça del Palau

Av. Marquès de l'Argentera

Parc Zoològic Acuarama

C. de Villena

Museu Marítim

La Mercé

CIUTAT VELLA

Passeig de Colóm

Estació de França

Carrer de Joan d'Àustria

Mirador de Colón

Carner Plaça Portal de la Pau

Ronda del Litoral

Plaça Pau Vila

Carrer del Doctor Aiguader

Ronda del Litoral

Pg. de Josep

21

Dàrsena Nacional

Moll de Bosch i Alsina

Museu d'Història de Catalunya

C. del Doctor Aiguader

22

Av. d'Icària

A19, Badalona, Mataró

A16, Sitges, Aeroport ✈

Torre de Jaume I

Moll de Barcelona

Rambla de Mar

Dàrsena del Comerç

Imax

Aquàrium

Carrer de Ginebra

VILA OLIMPICA

Salvador Espriu

Plaça dels Voluntaris Olímpics

Parc del Port Olímpic

Maremagnum

Multicine

Moll d'Espanya

Plaça Poeta Bosca

Parc de la Barceloneta

Hospital Mare de Déu del Mar

Avinguda del

Litoral

World Trade Center

N

Transbordador Aeri

Moll de les Balears

Moll de la Barceloneta

Passeig Joan de Borbó

LA BARCELONETA

Passeig Marítim de la Barceloneta

Platja Barceloneta

Port Olímpic

0 100 200 300 400

m

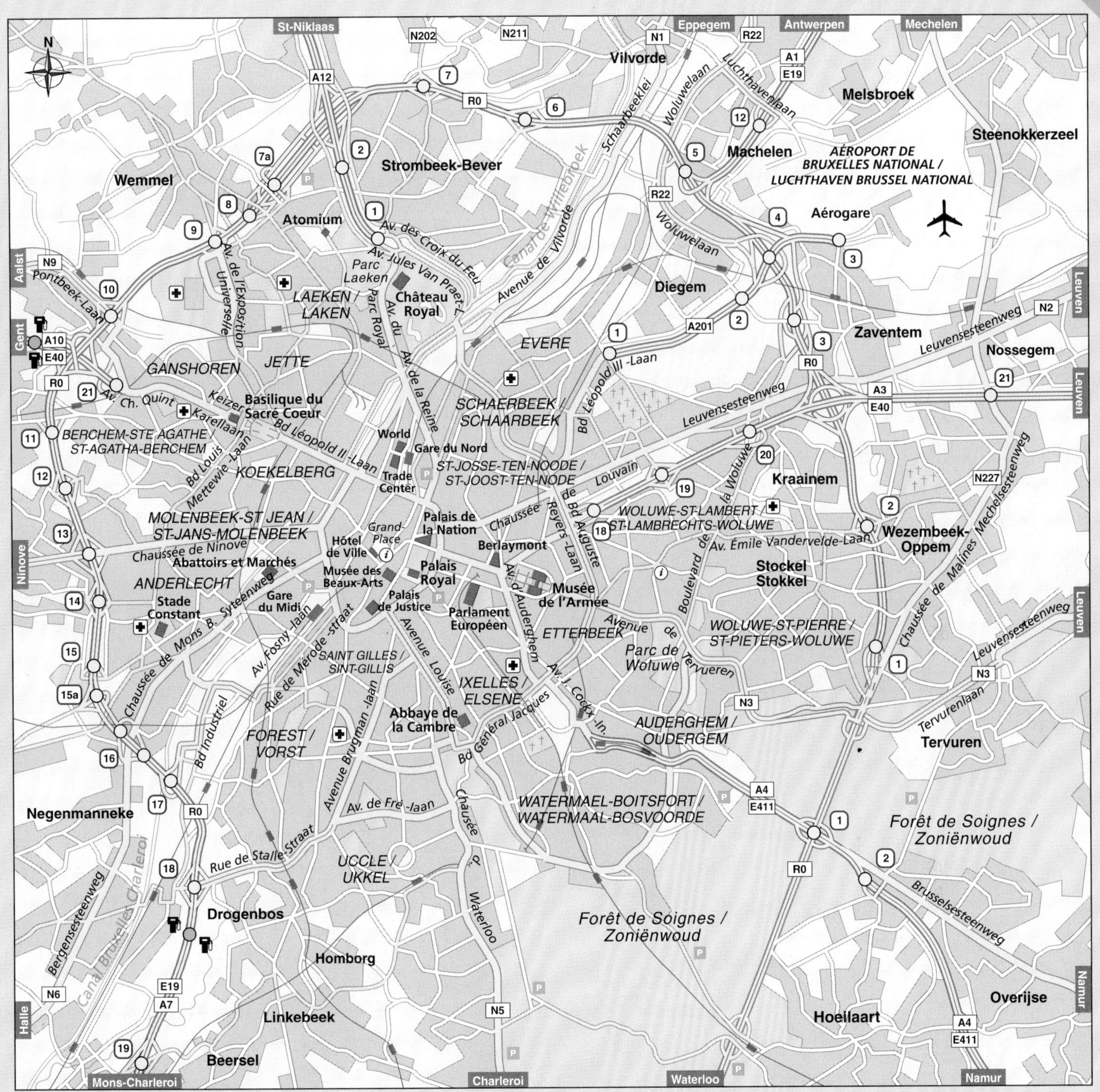
St-Niklaas
Eppegem
Antwerpen
Mechelen
Vilvorde
Melsbroek
Steenokkerzeel
Strombeek-Bever
Wemmel
Machelen
AÉROPORT DE BRUXELLES NATIONAL / LUCHTHAVEN BRUSSEL NATIONAL
Atomium
Aérogare
Parc Laeken
Château Royal
LAEKEN / LAKEN
Diegem
Zaventem
Nossegem
EVERE
GANSHOREN
JETTE
Basilique du Sacré Coeur
SCHAERBEEK / SCHAARBEEK
BERCHEM-STE AGATHE / ST-AGATHA-BERCHEM
World Trade Center
Gare du Nord
ST-JOSSE-TEN-NOODE / ST-JOOST-TEN-NODE
KOEKELBERG
Kraainem
MOLENBEEK-ST JEAN / ST-JANS-MOLENBEEK
Grand-Place
Hôtel de Ville
Palais de la Nation
Berlaymont
WOLUWE-ST-LAMBERT / ST-LAMBRECHTS-WOLUWE
Wezembeek-Oppem
Abattoirs et Marchés
Musée des Beaux-Arts
Palais Royal
Musée de l'Armée
Stockel Stokkel
ANDERLECHT
Stade Constant
Gare du Midi
Palais de Justice
Parlament Européen
ETTERBEEK
WOLUWE-ST-PIERRE / ST-PIETERS-WOLUWE
SAINT GILLES / SINT-GILLIS
Parc de Woluwe
IXELLES / ELSENE
Abbaye de la Cambre
FOREST / VORST
AUDERGHEM / OUDERGEM
Tervuren
Negenmanneke
WATERMAEL-BOITSFORT / WATERMAAL-BOSVOORDE
Forêt de Soignes / Zoniënwoud
UCCLE / UKKEL
Drogenbos
Homborg
Linkebeek
Hoeilaart
Overijse
Beersel
Mons-Charleroi
Charleroi
Waterloo
Namur
Halle
Ninove
Gent
Aalst
Leuven
0 1 2 km

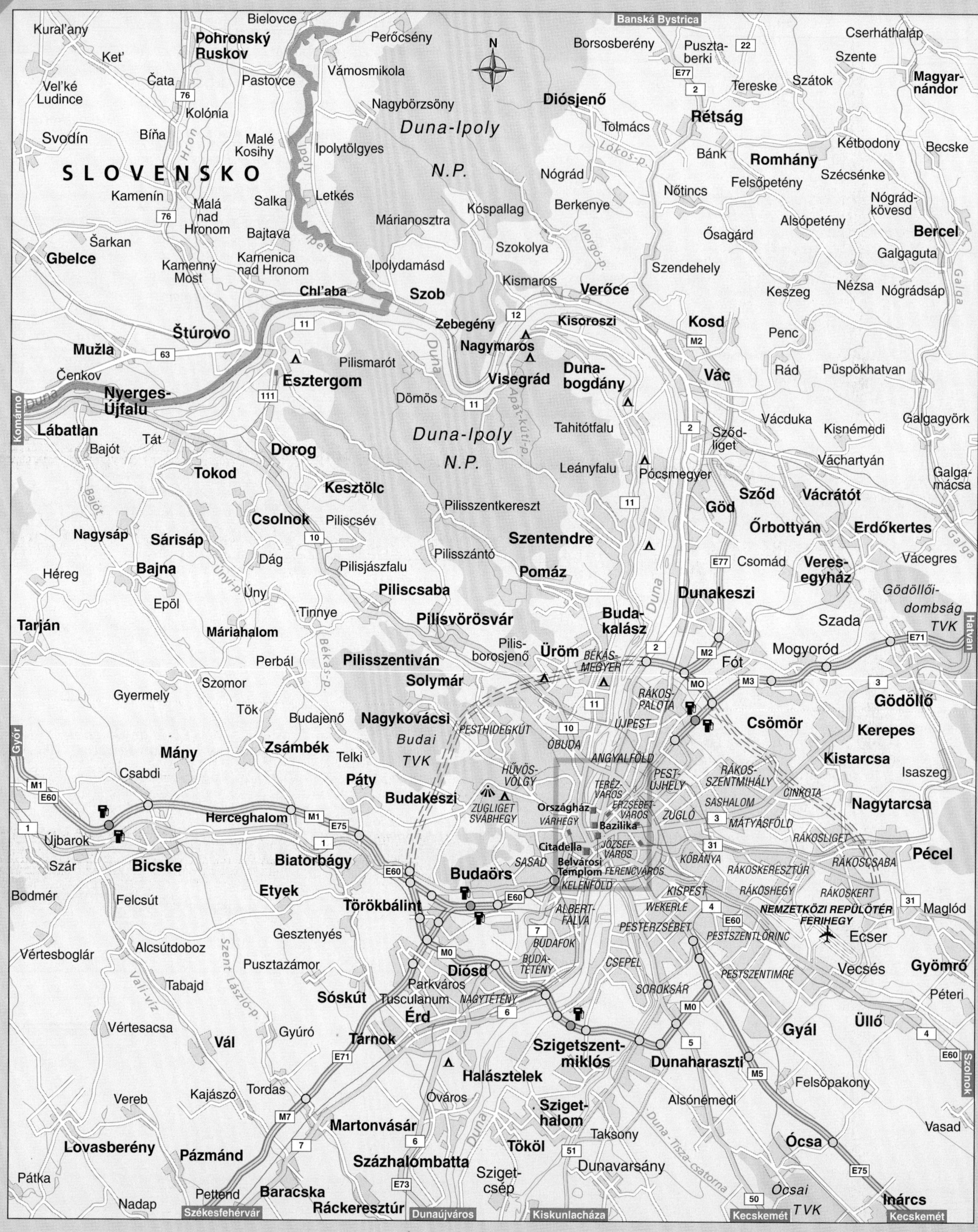

Kuraľany
Ket'
Veľké Ludince
Svodín
Čata
Bíňa
Pohronský Ruskov
Kolónia
Pastovce
Bielovce
Perőcsény
Vámosmikola
Nagybörzsöny
Ipolytölgyes
Diósjenő
Borsosberény
Pusztaberki
Tereske
Szátok
22
E77
2
Cserháthaláp
Szente
Magyarnándor

SLOVENSKO
Kamenín
Malá nad Hronom
Salka
Letkés
Gbelce
Kamenný Most
Kamenica nad Hronom
Bajtava
Chľaba
76
76
Šarkan
Malé Kosihy
Ipolydamásd
Szob
Máriaosztra
Kóspallag
Szokolya
Verőce
12
Nógrád
Berkenye
Tolmács
Bánk
Rétság
Felsőpetény
Nőtincs
Alsópetény
Ősagárd
Szendehely
Szécsénke
Romhány
Kétbodony
Nógrádkövesd
Becske
Bercel
Galgaguta

Mužla
63
Čenkov
Nyerges-Újfalu
Štúrovo
11
Esztergom
111
Pilismarót
Dömös
11
Visegrád
Zebegény
Nagymaros
Kismaros
Kisoroszi
Duna-bogdány
Tahitótfalu
Leányfalu
Pócsmegyer
11
Kosd
M2
Vác
Rád
Sződliget
Vácduka
Kisnémedi
Váchartyán
Keszeg
Nézsa
Nógrádsáp
Penc
Püspökhatvan
Galgagyörk
Galgamácsa

Duna-Ipoly N.P.

Lábatlan
Bajót
Tát
Tokod
Dorog
Kesztölc
Pilisszentkereszt
Pilisszántó
Szentendre
Pomáz
Sződ
Göd
Vácrátót
Őrbottyán
Erdőkertes
Vácegres

Nagysáp
Héreg
Sárisáp
Dág
Bajna
Epöl
Úny
Piliscsév
10
Pilisjászfalu
Piliscsaba
Csomád
E77
Dunakeszi
Veresegyház
Szada
Gödöllői-dombság TVK

Tarján
Máriahalom
Perbál
Tinnye
Pilisvörösvár
Pilisborosjenő
Pilisszentiván
Üröm
Buda-kalász
BÉKÁS-MEGYER
2
M2
Fót
Mogyoród
E71

Gyermely
Szomor
Tök
Pilisszentiván
Solymár
RÁKOS-PALOTA
MO
M3
3
Gödöllő

Mány
Csabdi
Zsámbék
Telki
Budajenő
Nagykovácsi
Budai TVK
PESTHIDEGKÚT
ÓBUDA
11
ÚJPEST
10
ANGYALFÖLD
PEST-ÚJHELY
RÁKOS-SZENTMIHÁLY
CINKOTA
SASHALOM
Csömör
Kerepes
Kistarcsa
Isaszeg
Nagytarcsa

Páty
Herceghalom
M1
E75
Budakeszi
HŰVÖS-VÖLGY
ZUGLIGET
SVÁBHEGY
TERÉZ-VÁROS
ZUGLÓ
3
MÁTYÁSFÖLD
RÁKOSLIGET
Pécel

M1
E60
1
Bicske
Szár
Újbarok
Bodmér
Felcsút
Biatorbágy
1
Etyek
E60
Gesztenyés
Törökbálint
Budaörs
E60
ZUGLIGET
Országház
VÁRHEGY
Bazilika
ERZSÉBET-VÁROS
JÓZSEF-VÁROS
KŐBÁNYA
4
RÁKOSKERESZTÚR
RÁKOSHEGY
RÁKOSCSABA
RÁKOSKERT
31
Maglód

Vértesboglár
Alcsútdoboz
Pusztazámor
MO
Diósd
Citadella
SASAD
Belvárosi Templom
KELENFÖLD
FERENCVÁROS
7
ALBERT-FALVA
BUDAFOK
WEKERLE
KISPEST
NEMZETKÖZI REPÜLŐTÉR FERIHEGY
E60
Ecser
Gyömrő

Tabajd
Sóskút
Parkváros
Tusculanum
Érd
BUDA-TÉTÉNY
NAGYTÉTÉNY
6
PESTERZSÉBET
PESTSZENTLŐRINC
PESTSZENTIMRE
Vecsés
Péteri

Vértesacsa
Vál
Gyúró
Tárnok
SOROKSÁR
MO
Üllő
5
4
E60

Vereb
Kajászó
Tordas
Halásztelek
Óváros
Szigetszent-miklós
Dunaharaszti
M5
Gyál
Felsőpakony
Szolnok

Lovasberény
Pázmánd
M7
7
Martonvásár
6
Százhalombatta
E73
Baracska
Ráckeresztúr
Sziget-halom
Tököl
51
Alsónémedi
Taksony
Dunavarsány
50
Ócsai TVK
E75
Ócsa
Inárcs

Pátka
Nadap
Pettend
Székesfehérvár
Dunaújváros
Kiskunlacháza
Kecskemét
Kecskemét

0 4 8 12
km

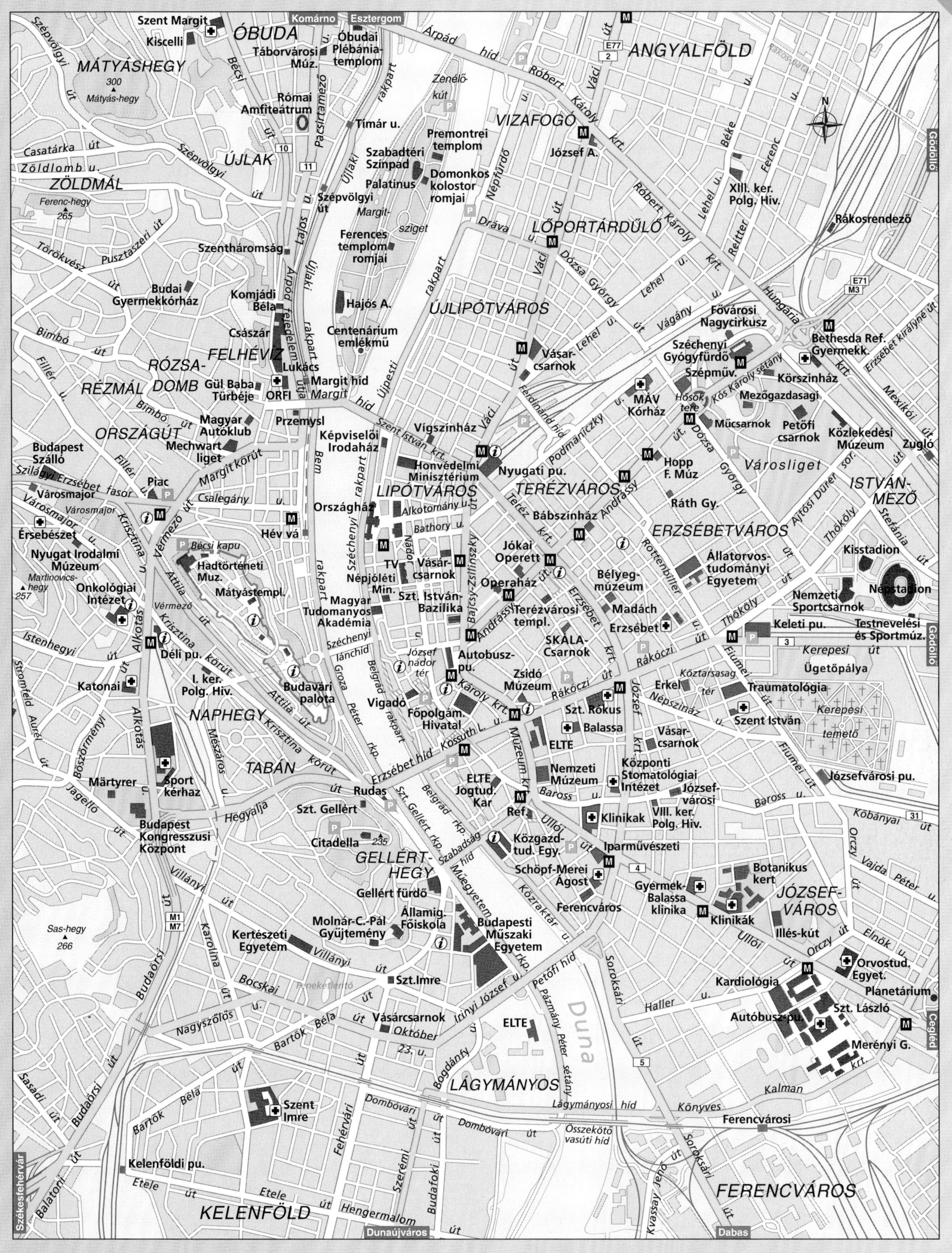

ÓBUDA
Szent Margit
Kiscelli
MÁTYÁSHEGY
300
Mátyás-hegy
Casatárka út
Zöldlomb u.
ZÖLDMÁL
Ferenc-hegy
265
Szépvölgyi
Bécsi
Törökvész
Pusztaszeri út
Bimbó
Budai
Gyermekkórház
Komjádi
Béla
Császár
Szentháromság
FELHÉVIZ
RÓZSA-
DOMB
RÉZMÁL
Gül Baba
Türbéje
ORFI
Lukács
ORSZÁGÚT
Magyar
Autóklub
Mechwart
liget
Budapest
Szálló
Szilágyi Erzsébet fasor
Piac
Városmajor
Városmajor
Érsebészet
Nyugat Irodalmi
Múzeum
Martinovics-
hegy
257
Onkológiai
Intézet
Déli pu.
Katonai
I. ker.
Polg. Hiv.
NAPHEGY
Istenhegyi
Stromfeld
Alkotás
Boszörmenyi
Jagelló
Márterer
Sport
kórház
TABÁN
Budapest
Kongresszusi
Központ
Sas-hegy
266
Kertészeti
Egyetem
GELLÉRT-
HEGY
KELENFÖLD
Kelenföldi pu.
Szent
Imre
LÁGYMÁNYOS
FERENCVÁROS

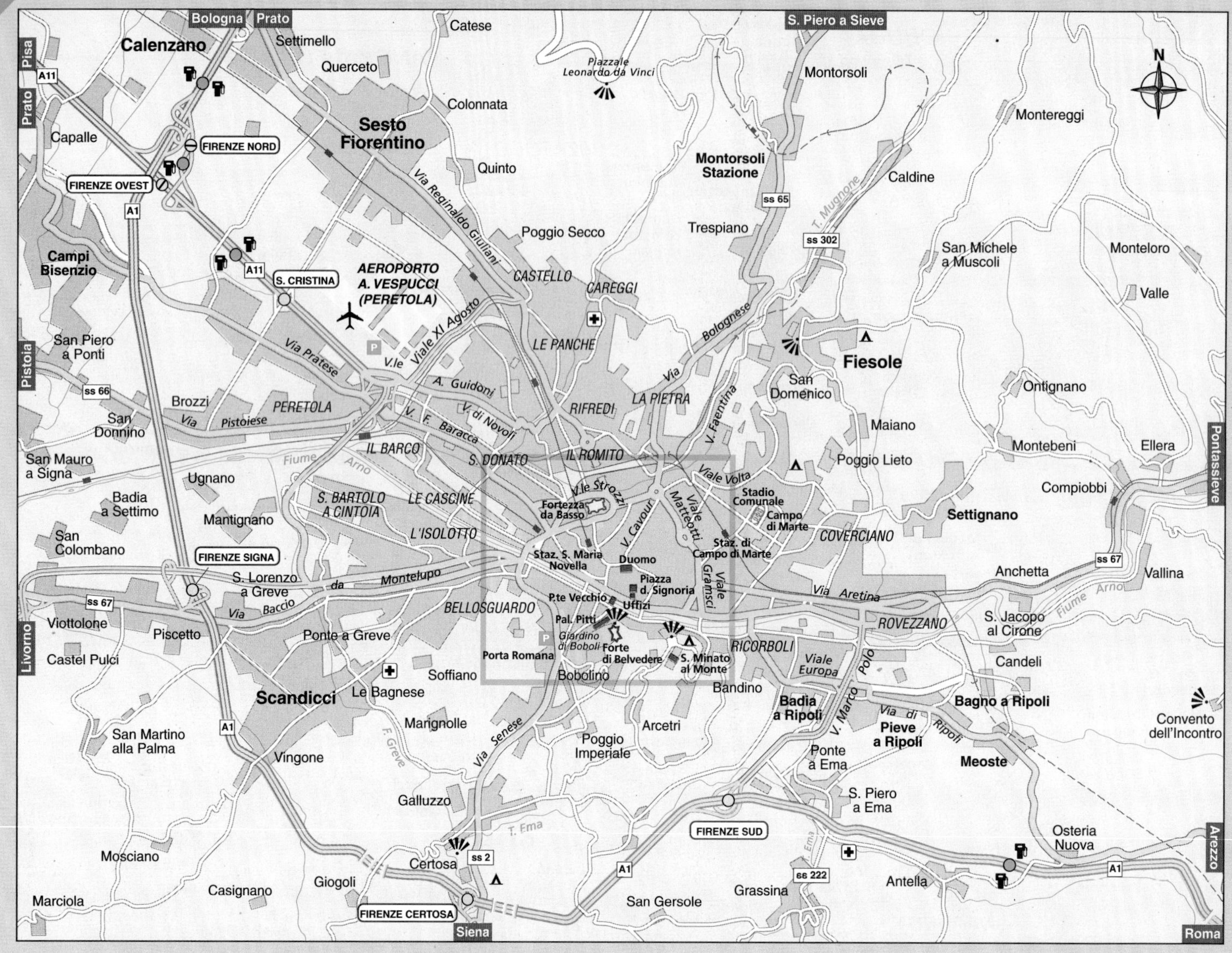

Pisa
Prato
A11
Bologna | Prato
Calenzano
Capalle
Settimello
Querceto
Catese
Colonnata
Sesto Fiorentino
FIRENZE NORD
Firenze Ovest
A1
Campi Bisenzio
S. CRISTINA
A11
Quinto
Poggio Secco
CASTELLO
CAREGGI
S. Piero a Ponti
AEROPORTO A. VESPUCCI (PERETOLA)
Via Reginaldo Giuliani
LE PANCHE
Pistoia
ss 66
San Donnino
Brozzi
Via Pistoiese
PERETOLA
Via Pratese
V.le
Viale XI Agosto
A. Guidoni
V. di Novoli
RIFREDI
LA PIETRA
San Domenico
San Mauro a Signa
Ugnano
IL BARCO
V. F. Baracca
S. DONATO
IL ROMITO
Via
Via Faentina
S. PIERO A SIEVE
Montorsoli
Montorsoli Stazione
ss 65
T. Mugnone
Caldine
ss 302
Trespiano
San Michele a Muscoli
Bolognese
Fiesole
Maiano
Poggio Lieto
Fiume Arno
S. BARTOLO A CINTOIA
LE CASCINE
L'ISOLOTTO
Viale Volta
Viale Strozzi
Fortezza da Basso
V.le Cavour
Viale Matteotti
Stadio Comunale
Campo di Marte
Staz. di Campo di Marte
COVERCIANO
Viale Gramsci
Settignano
Montereggi
Monteloro
Valle
Pontassieve
Ontignano
Montebeni
Ellera
Compiobbi
Anchetta
Vallina
ss 67
Fiume Arno
Badia a Settimo
Mantignano
San Colombano
FIRENZE SIGNA
S. Lorenzo a Greve
da Montelupo
Staz. S. Maria Novella
Duomo
Piazza d. Signoria
Uffizi
Via Aretina
S. Jacopo al Cirone
ROVEZZANO
Candeli
Livorno
ss 67
Viottolone
Castel Pulci
Via Baccio
Piscetto
Ponte a Greve
BELLOSGUARDO
P.te Vecchio
Pal. Pitti
Giardino di Boboli
Forte di Belvedere
S. Minato al Monte
RICORBOLI
Viale Europa
Bagno a Ripoli
Convento dell'Incontro
San Martino alla Palma
Scandicci
A1
Le Bagnese
Soffiano
Marignolle
Porta Romana
Bobolino
Arcetri
Bandino
Badia a Ripoli
V. Marco Polo
Via di Ripoli
Pieve a Ripoli
Meoste
Vingone
F. Greve
Via Senese
Poggio Imperiale
Ponte a Ema
S. Piero a Ema
Osteria Nuova
Arezzo
A1
Galluzzo
T. Ema
FIRENZE SUD
A1
Ema
ss 222
Antella
Mosciano
Casignano
Giogoli
ss 2
Certosa
San Gersole
Grassina
Marciola
FIRENZE CERTOSA
Siena
Roma

0 1 2 3
km
N

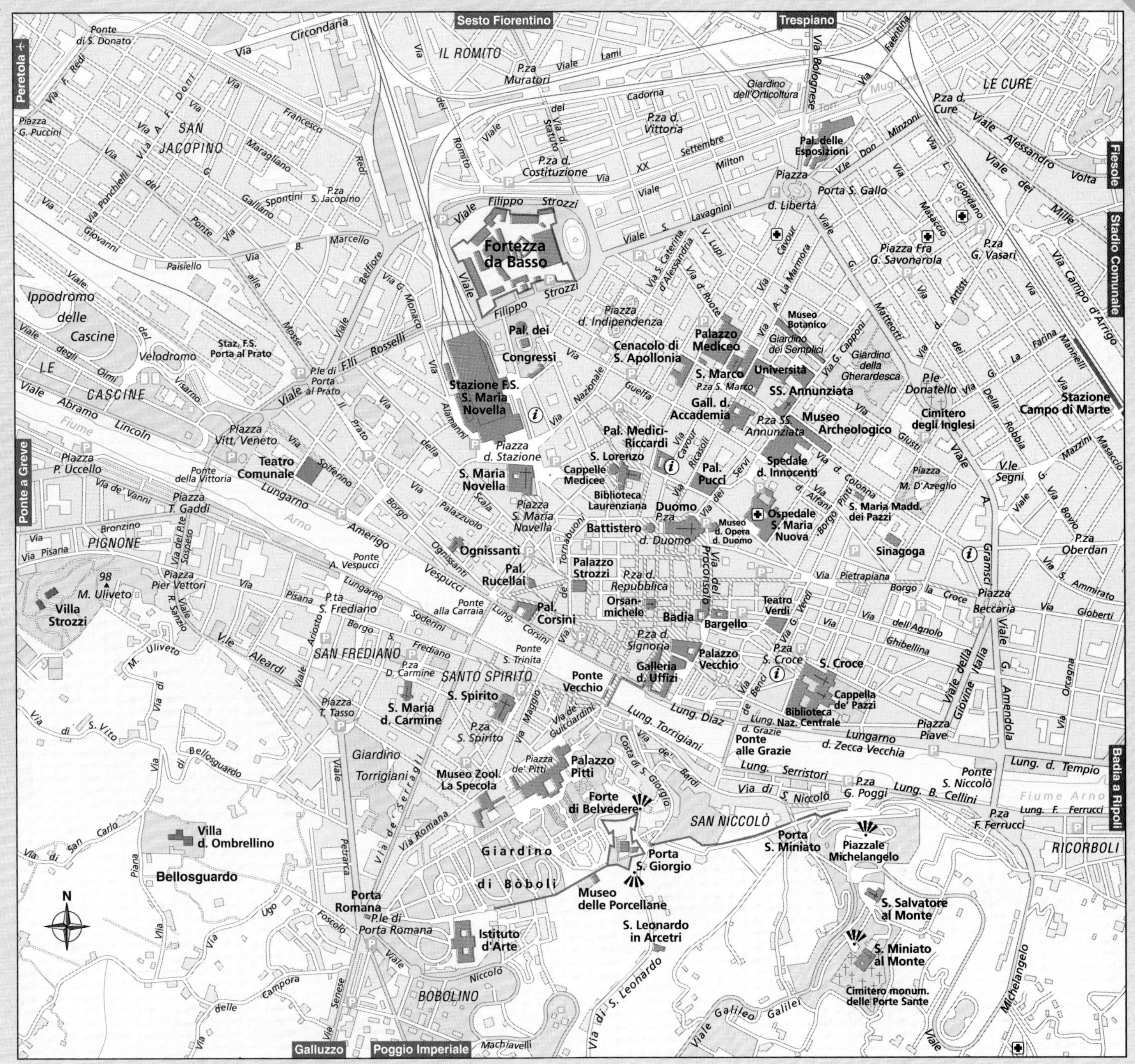
Sesto Fiorentino
Trespiano
Peretola
Fiesole
Stadio Comunale
Ponte a Greve
Badia a Ripoli
Galluzzo
Poggio Imperiale
Fortezza da Basso
Stazione F.S. S. Maria Novella
Pal. dei Congressi
Ippodromo delle Cascine
LE CASCINE
Teatro Comunale
S. Maria Novella
Ognissanti
Pal. Rucellai
Pal. Corsini
Palazzo Strozzi
Battistero
Duomo
Orsanmichele
Badia
Bargello
Palazzo Vecchio
Galleria d. Uffizi
Ponte Vecchio
S. Lorenzo
Cappelle Medicee
Biblioteca Laurenziana
Pal. Medici-Riccardi
Cenacolo di S. Apollonia
Palazzo Mediceo
S. Marco
Università
SS. Annunziata
Gall. d. Accademia
Museo Archeologico
Spedale d. Innocenti
Ospedale S. Maria Nuova
Sinagoga
S. Croce
Cappella de' Pazzi
Biblioteca Naz. Centrale
Palazzo Pitti
Forte di Belvedere
Giardino di Boboli
Porta S. Giorgio
Museo delle Porcellane
S. Leonardo in Arcetri
Piazzale Michelangelo
S. Salvatore al Monte
S. Miniato al Monte
Cimitero monum. delle Porte Sante
Istituto d'Arte
Porta Romana
Villa d. Ombrellino
Bellosguardo
Villa Strozzi
S. Spirito
S. Maria d. Carmine
Museo Zool. La Specola
SAN FREDIANO
SANTO SPIRITO
SAN NICCOLÒ
BOBOLINO
RICORBOLI
PIGNONE
SAN JACOPINO
IL ROMITO
LE CURE
Stazione Campo di Marte
Cimitero degli Inglesi
Pal. delle Esposizioni
Porta S. Gallo
Piazza d. Libertà
0 200 400 600
m

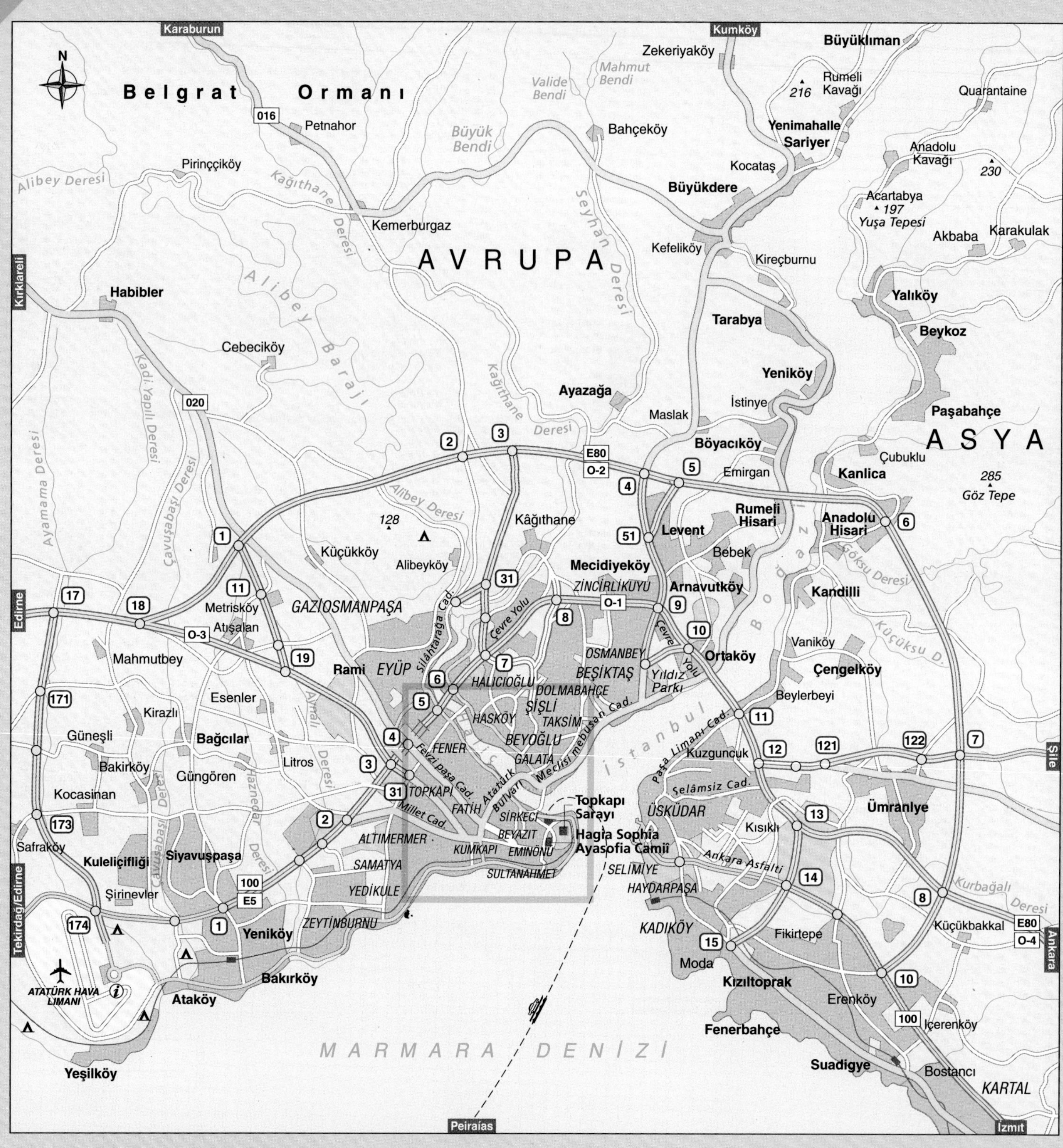
Karaburun
Kumköy
Belgrat Ormanı
016
Petnahor
Pirinççiköy
Alibey Deresi
Kağıthane Deresi
Kemerburgaz
Valide Bendi
Mahmut Bendi
Büyük Bendi
Zekeriyaköy
Bahçeköy
Büyüklıman
Rumeli Kavağı
216
Quarantaine
Yenimahalle
Sariyer
Anadolu Kavağı
230
Kocataş
Büyükdere
Acartabya
197
Yuşa Tepesi
Akbaba
Karakulak
Kefeliköy
Kireçburnu
AVRUPA
Seyhan Deresi
Kırklareli
Habibler
Alibey Barajı
Cebeciköy
Yalıköy
Tarabya
Beykoz
Yeniköy
Kadi Yapılı Deresi
020
Ayazağa
Kağıthane Deresi
İstinye
Maslak
Paşabahçe
ASYA
Ayamama Deresi
Çavuşbaşı Deresi
E80
O-2
Böyacıköy
Çubuklu
Emirgan
Kanlica
285
Göz Tepe
Kâğıthane
128
Küçükköy
Alibeyköy
Levent
Rumeli Hisari
Anadolu Hisari
Bebek
Göksu Deresi
Mecidiyeköy
Zincirlikuyu
O-1
Arnavutköy
Kandilli
Edirne
Metrisköy
Atışalan
GAZİOSMANPAŞA
O-3
Silâhtarağa Cad.
Çevre Yolu
Boğaziçi
Küçüksu D.
Vaniköy
Mahmutbey
Rami
EYÜP
OSMANBEY
BEŞİKTAŞ
Yıldız Parkı
Ortaköy
Çengelköy
Esenler
HALICIOĞLU
DOLMABAHÇE
ŞİŞLİ
Beylerbeyi
Kirazlı
HASKÖY
TAKSİM
Meclisi mebusan Cad.
Güneşli
Bağcılar
BEYOĞLU
FENER
İstanbul
Paşa Limanı Cad.
Kuzguncuk
Şile
Bakirköy
Litros
GALATA
Feizi paşa Cad.
Atatürk Bulvarı
Selâmsiz Cad.
Güngören
Aynalı Deresi
Hazneder Deresi
Kocasinan
TOPKAPI
FATİH
Topkapı Sarayı
ÜSKÜDAR
Ümranlye
Millet Cad.
SİRKECİ
Kısıklı
Safraköy
ALTIMERMER
BEYAZIT
Hagia Sophia
Ayasofia Camiî
Kuleliçiflîği
Siyavuşpaşa
SAMATYA
KUMKAPI
EMİNÖNÜ
Ankara Asfalti
SELİMİYE
Çavuşbaşı Deresi
SULTANAHMET
HAYDARPAŞA
YEDİKULE
Kurbağalı Deresi
Şirinevler
E5
KADIKÖY
Küçükbakkal
Tekirdağ/Edirne
ZEYTİNBURNU
Yeniköy
Fikirtepe
Ankara
Moda
Kızıltoprak
Bakırköy
ATATÜRK HAVA LIMANI
Ataköy
Erenköy
Içerenköy
Fenerbahçe
MARMARA DENİZİ
Suadigye
Bostancı
Yeşilköy
KARTAL
Peiraías
İzmit
0
2
4
km

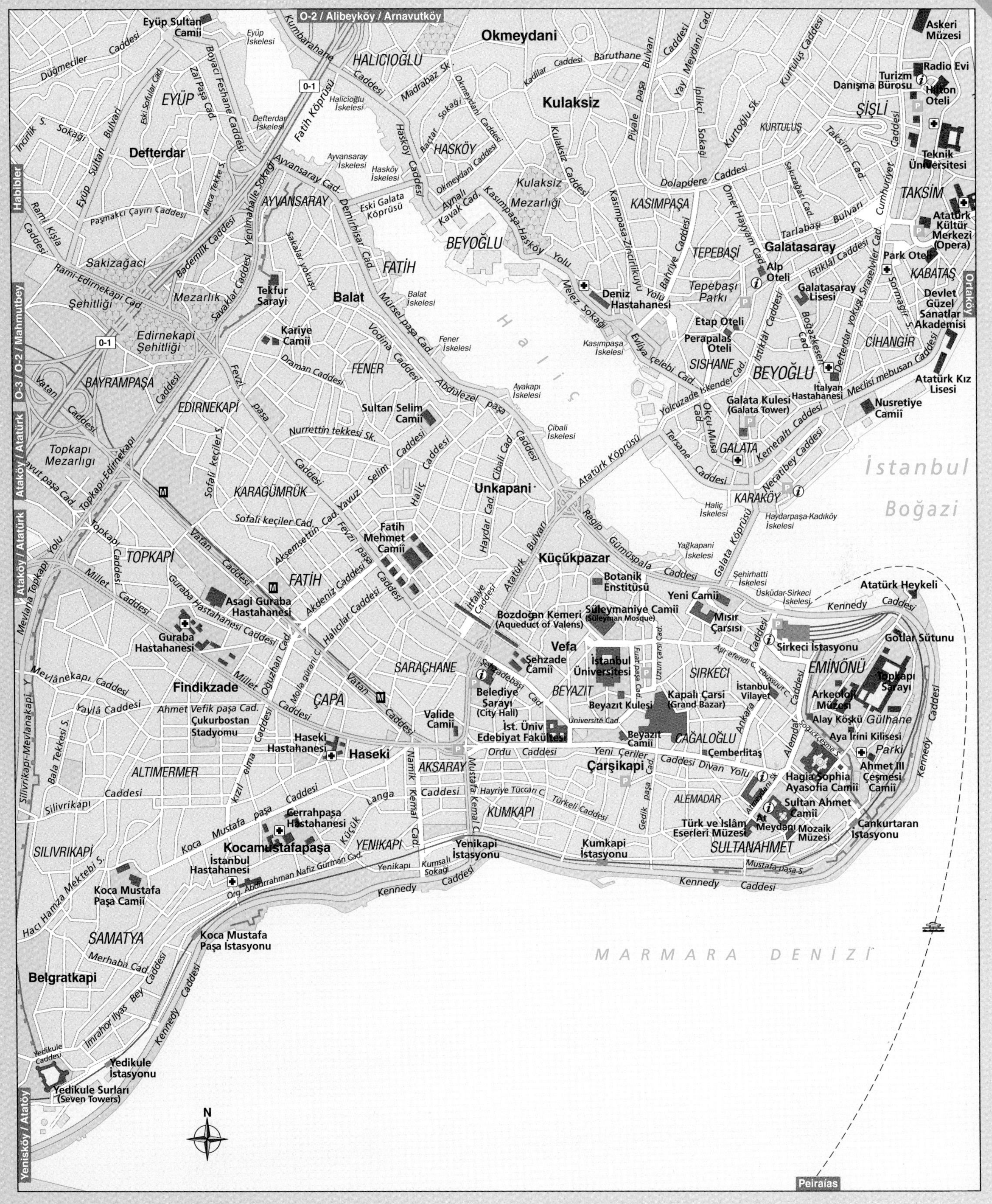

Okmeydani

HALICIOĞLU

Kulaksiz

EYÜP

Eyüp Sultan Camii

Defterdar

HASKÖY

BEYOĞLU

Kasımpaşa Mezarlığı

KASIMPAŞA

ŞİŞLİ

Askeri Müzesi

Radio Evi

Turizm Danışma Bürosu

Hilton Oteli

Teknik Üniversitesi

TAKSİM

AYVANSARAY

FATİH

Balat

TEPEBAŞI

Galatasaray

Deniz Hastanesi

Alp Oteli

Galatasaray Lisesi

Atatürk Kültür Merkezi (Opera)

Park Oteli

KABATAŞ

Devlet Güzel Sanatlar Akademisi

BAYRAMPAŞA

Kariye Camii

FENER

Etap Oteli

Perapalas Oteli

BEYOĞLU

SISHANE

CIHANGIR

Atatürk Kız Lisesi

Edirnekapi Şehitliği

Sultan Selim Camii

Galata Kulesi (Galata Tower)

İtalyan Hastanesi

Nusretiye Camii

EDİRNEKAPI

GALATA

Topkapı Mezarlığı

Unkapani

KARAGÜMRÜK

KARAKÖY

İstanbul Boğazi

TOPKAPI

Fatih Mehmet Camii

Küçükpazar

Botanik Enstitüsü

Yeni Camii

Mısır Çarşısı

Atatürk Heykeli

FATİH

Asagi Guraba Hastahanesi

Bozdoğan Kemeri (Aqueduct of Valens)

Süleymaniye Camii (Süleyman Mosque)

Gotlar Sütunu

Sirkeci İstasyonu

EMİNÖNÜ

Guraba Hastahanesi

Vefa

Şehzade Camii

İstanbul Üniversitesi

SIRKECI

Arkeoloji Müzesi

Topkapı Sarayı

Findikzade

ÇAPA

Belediye Sarayı (City Hall)

BEYAZIT

Beyazıt Kulesi

Kapalı Çarsi (Grand Bazar)

İstanbul Vilayeti

Alay Köşkü

Gülhane

Cukurbostan Stadyomu

Valide Camii

İst. Üniv Edebiyat Fakültesi

Beyazıt Camii

ÇAĞALOĞLU

Aya İrini Kilisesi

Parki

Haseki Hastanesi

AKSARAY

Ordu Caddesi

Yeni Çeriler

Çemberlitaş

Ahmet III Çeşmesi Camii

ALTIMERMER

Haseki

Çarşıkapi

Divan Yolu

Hagia Sophia Ayasofia Camii

Cankurtaran İstasyonu

Cerrahpaşa Hastahanesi

KUMKAPI

ALEMDAR

Sultan Ahmet Camii

Kocamustafapaşa

YENİKAPI

Yenikapi İstasyonu

Kumkapi İstasyonu

Türk ve İslâm Eserleri Müzesi

At Meydani

Mozaik Müzesi

İstanbul Hastahanesi

SULTANAHMET

Koca Mustafa Paşa Camii

SAMATYA

Koca Mustafa Paşa İstasyonu

MARMARA DENİZİ

Belgratkapi

Yedikule İstasyonu

Yedikule Surları (Seven Towers)

N

MARMARA DENİZİ

0   300   600
m

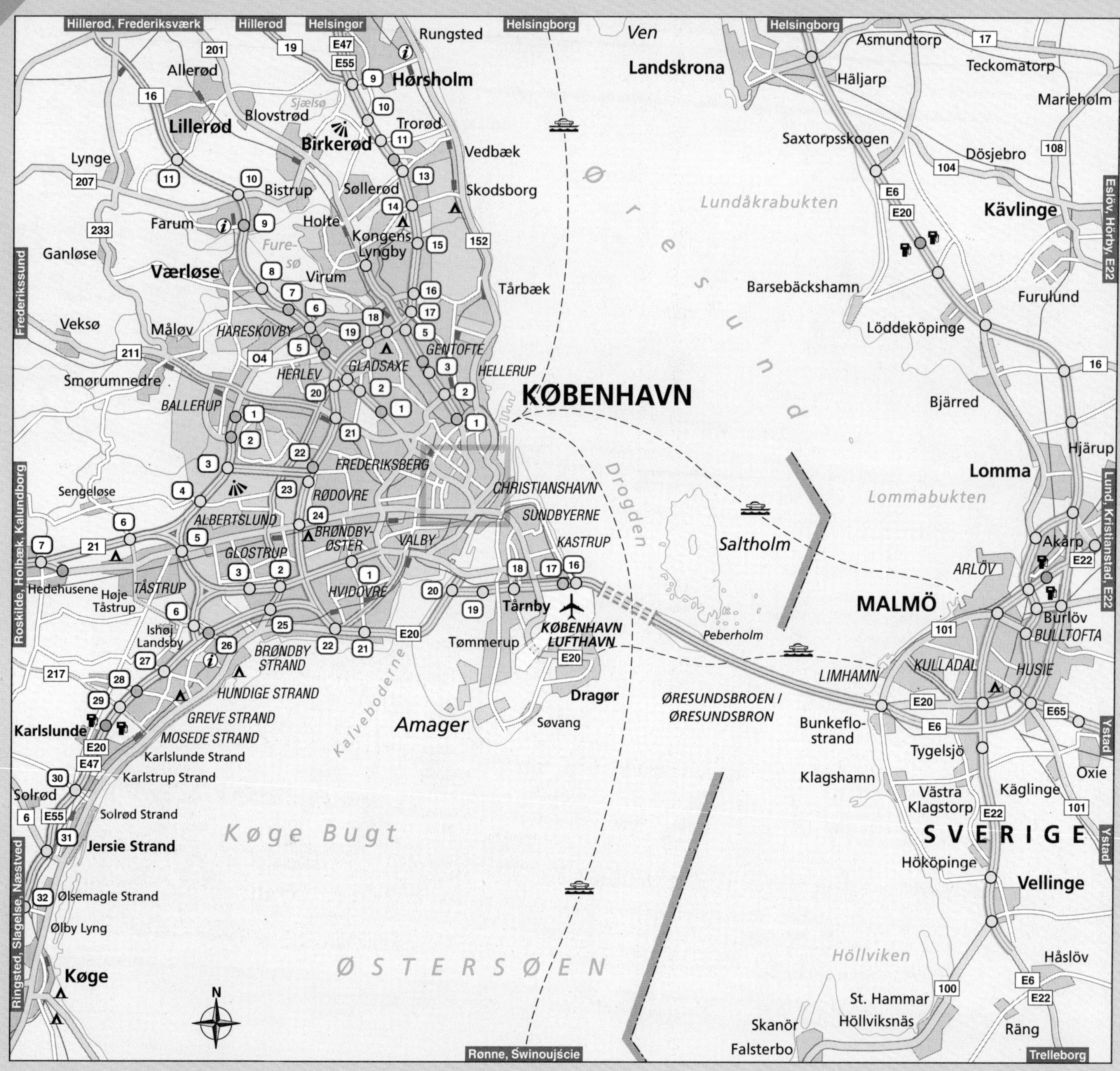

Ven
Landskrona
Asmundtorp
Teckomatorp
Rungsted
201
19
E47
E55
9 Hørsholm
Allerød
16
10
Sjælsø
Blovstrød
Lillerød
Trorød
11
Lynge
Birkerød
11
Vedbæk
207
10
Bistrup
13
Skodsborg
233
9
Farum
Søllerød
Holte
14
Ganløse
Kongens
Lyngby
15
152
Værløse
8
Virum
Veksø
7
Måløv
16
Tårbæk
HARESKOVBY
6
17
Smørumnedre
18
5
211
19
O4
5
GENTOFTE
BALLERUP
HERLEV
20
GLADSAXE
3
HELLERUP
1
2
KØBENHAVN
1
2
Sengeløse
2
3
21
1
22
FREDERIKSBERG
RØDOVRE
23
CHRISTIANSHAVN
4
Drogden
ALBERTSLUND
24
SUNDBYERNE
6
BRØNDBY-
ØSTER
Saltholm
7
21
5
GLOSTRUP
VALBY
KASTRUP
Lommabukten
Hedehusene
Høje
Tåstrup
TÅSTRUP
3
2
HVIDOVRE
18 17 16
6
1
20
MALMÖ
Ishøj
Landsby
25
19 Tårnby
26
22 21
KØBENHAVN
LUFTHAVN
Peberholm
217
27
BRØNDBY
STRAND
Tømmerup
E20
28
Dragør
29
HUNDIGE STRAND
Amager
Søvang
Karlslunde
GREVE STRAND
MOSEDE STRAND
ØRESUNDSBROEN /
ØRESUNDSBRON
E20
E47
Karlslunde Strand
Bunkeflo-
strand
30
Karlstrup Strand
Solrød
6 E55
Solrød Strand
Klagshamn
31 Jersie Strand
Køge Bugt
32 Ølsemagle Strand
Ølby Lyng
Øresund
Lundåkrabukten
E6
E20
Kävlinge
Saxtorpsskogen
Barsebäckshamn
Löddeköpinge
104
17
Häljarp
Dösjebro
108
Marieholm
Furulund
16
Bjärred
Lomma
Hjärup
Akarp
E22
ARLÖV
101
Burlöv
BULLTOFTA
LIMHAMN
KULLADAL
HUSIE
E20
E6
E65
Lund, Kristianstad E22
Ystad
Ystad
Tygelsjö
Västra
Klagstorp
Oxie
Kägelinge
E22
101
SVERIGE
Köge
Höllviken
Hököpinge
Vellinge
ØSTERSØEN
N
St. Hammar
Höllviksnäs
Skanör
Falsterbo
Räng
Håslöv
E6
100
E22
Trelleborg

0 2 4 6
km

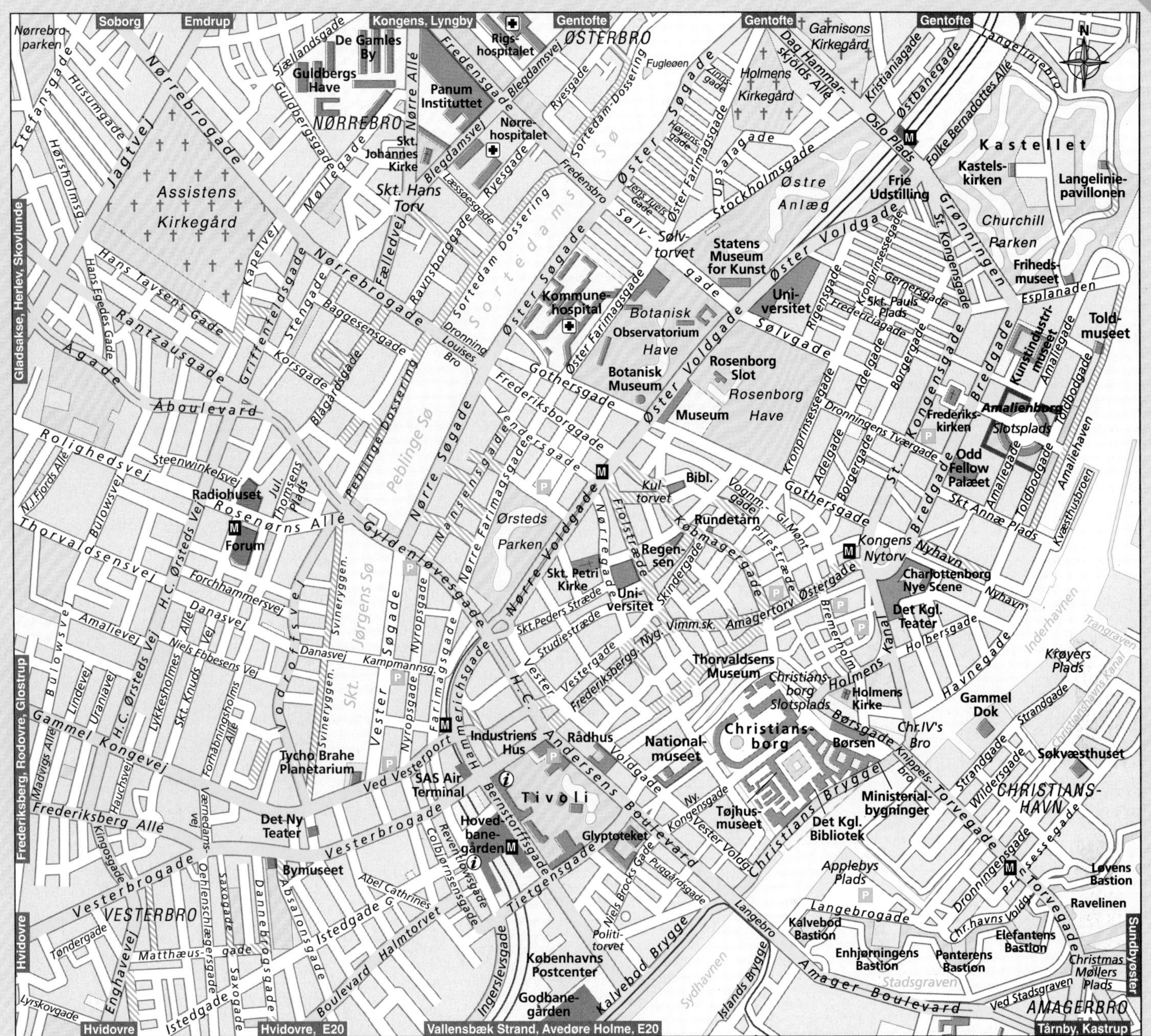

ØSTERBRO

NØRREBRO

De Gamles By
Guldbergs Have
Rigs-hospitalet
Panum Instituttet

Garnisons Kirkegård

Holmens Kirkegård

Fugleøen

Kastellet

Oslo Plads

Kastels-kirken

Langelinie-pavillonen

Assistens Kirkegård

Skt. Johannes Kirke

Nørre-hospitalet

Skt. Hans Torv

Frie Udstilling

Churchill Parken

Østre Anlæg

Frieheds-museet

Esplanaden

Statens Museum for Kunst

Sølv-torvet

Uni-versitet

Told-museet

Kunstindustri-museet

Kommune-hospital

Botanisk Observatorium Have

Botanisk Museum

Rosenborg Slot

Rosenborg Museum

Rosenborg Have

Frederiks-kirken

Amalienborg Slotsplads

Radiohuset

Forum

Ørsteds Parken

Kul-torvet

Bibl.

Rundetårn

Regen-sen

Odd Fellow Palæet

Skt. Annæ Plads

Tycho Brahe Planetarium

Skt. Petri Kirke

Uni-versitet

Kongens Nytorv

Charlottenborg Nye Scene

Nyhavn

Det Kgl. Teater

SAS Air Terminal

Det Ny Teater

Industriens Hus

Rådhus

Thorvaldsens Museum

Christians-borg Slotsplads

Holmens Kirke

Gammel Dok

Hoved-bane-gården

National-museet

Christians-borg

Børsen

Chr.IV's Bro

Søkvæsthuset

CHRISTIANS-HAVN

Tivoli

Glyptoteket

Tøjhus-museet

Ministerial-bygninger

Det Kgl. Bibliotek

VESTERBRO

Bymuseet

Applebys Plads

Løvens Bastion

Ravelinen

Københavns Postcenter

Kalvebod Bastion

Enhjørningens Bastion

Panterens Bastion

Elefantens Bastion

Christmas Møllers Plads

Godbane-gården

Langebrogade

Stadsgraven

Ved Stadsgraven

AMAGERBRO

0   200   400
m

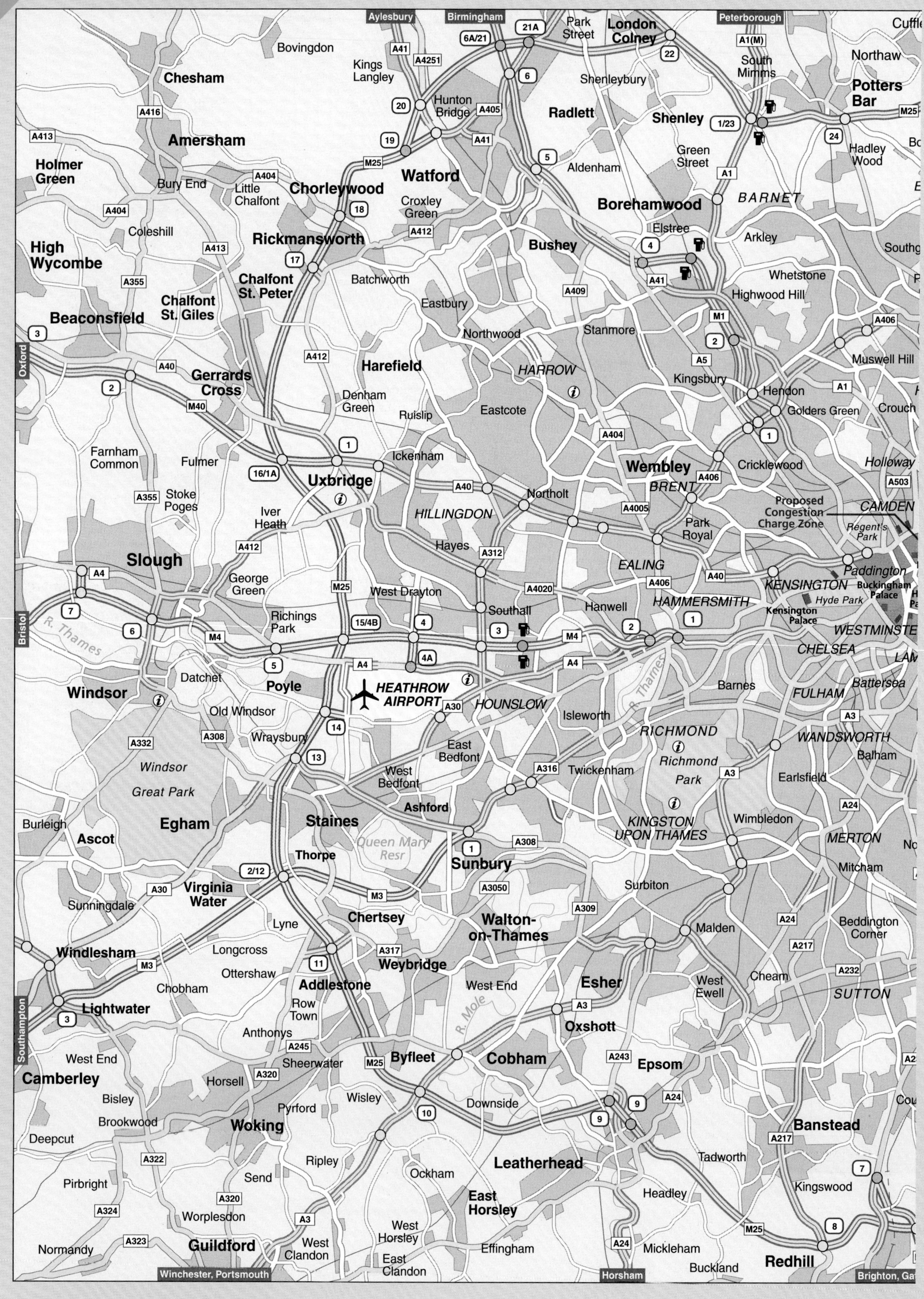
Aylesbury
Birmingham
Peterborough
Oxford
Bristol
Southampton
Winchester, Portsmouth
Horsham
Brighton, Gatwick
Watford
Chorleywood
Rickmansworth
Amersham
Chesham
High Wycombe
Beaconsfield
Gerrards Cross
Uxbridge
Slough
Windsor
Egham
Staines
Harefield
Borehamwood
Radlett
Shenley
Potters Bar
London Colney
Bushey
Wembley
HEATHROW AIRPORT
HOUNSLOW
RICHMOND
KINGSTON UPON THAMES
Sunbury
Walton-on-Thames
Weybridge
Chertsey
Addlestone
Esher
Epsom
Cobham
Leatherhead
Woking
Guildford
Camberley
Banstead
Redhill

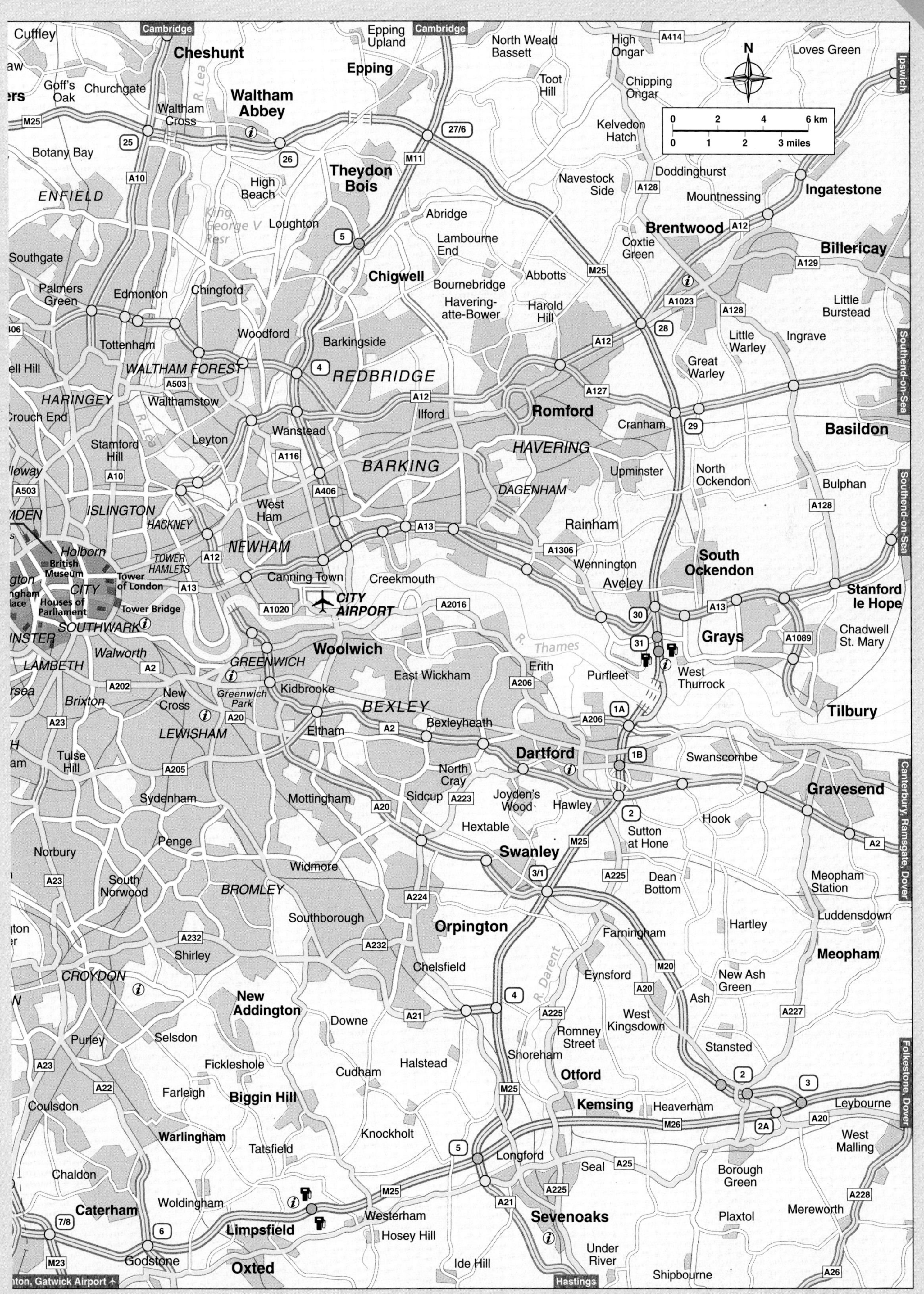

Cuffley
Cheshunt
Goff's Oak
Churchgate
Waltham Cross
Waltham Abbey
M25
Botany Bay
A10
25
26
ENFIELD
High Beach
Loughton
King George V Resr
Epping Upland
Cambridge
Epping
Theydon Bois
27/6
M11
Abridge
Lambourne End
Chigwell
Bournebridge
Havering-atte-Bower
Abbotts
Harold Hill
North Weald Bassett
Toot Hill
High Ongar
Chipping Ongar
Kelvedon Hatch
Loves Green
A414
N
0 2 4 6 km
0 1 2 3 miles
Doddinghurst
Navestock Side
Mountnessing
Ingatestone
A128
Brentwood
A12
Coxtie Green
Billericay
A129
Little Burstead
Little Warley
Ingrave
A1023
28
A128
Great Warley
A12
A127
Cranham
29
Romford
HAVERING
Upminster
North Ockendon
Basildon
A128
Bulphan
Southgate
Palmers Green
Edmonton
Chingford
Woodford
Barkingside
REDBRIDGE
4
Tottenham
WALTHAM FOREST
A503
Walthamstow
HARINGEY
Crouch End
Stamford Hill
Leyton
Wanstead
A116
BARKING
A12
Ilford
A406
DAGENHAM
Rainham
A1306
Wennington
Aveley
South Ockendon
A13
Stanford le Hope
30
Chadwell St. Mary
A1089
Grays
31
West Thurrock
Purfleet
1A
Tilbury
ISLINGTON
HACKNEY
A10
A503
Holborn
British Museum
TOWER HAMLETS
A12
NEWHAM
West Ham
A13
CITY
Houses of Parliament
Tower of London
Tower Bridge
SOUTHWARK
Canning Town
Creekmouth
CITY AIRPORT
A1020
A2016
Erith
A206
1A
1B
LAMBETH
Walworth
A2
GREENWICH
Woolwich
East Wickham
Swanscombe
Gravesend
A2
Brixton
A202
New Cross
Greenwich Park
Kidbrooke
BEXLEY
Bexleyheath
A206
Dartford
2
Hook
LEWISHAM
A20
Eltham
A2
North Cray
Sidcup
A223
Joyden's Wood
Hawley
Sutton at Hone
Meopham Station
Luddensdown
Tulse Hill
A205
Mottingham
A20
Hextable
M25
Dean Bottom
Meopham
Sydenham
Penge
Widmore
Swanley
3/1
A225
Farningham
Hartley
New Ash Green
A227
Norbury
South Norwood
BROMLEY
A224
Southborough
Orpington
A232
Eynsford
A20
Ash
Stansted
A23
Shirley
A232
Chelsfield
M20
West Kingsdown
CROYDON
New Addington
Downe
A21
4
A225
R. Darent
Romney Street
Shoreham
Borough Green
A227
Purley
Selsdon
Halstead
Otford
2
3
Leybourne
Ficklesole
Cudham
A25
Kemsing
Heaverham
A20
West Malling
A22
Biggin Hill
Knockholt
M25
Seal
A225
M26
2A
Chaldon
Warlingham
Tatsfield
5
Longford
Borough Green
Plaxtol
Mereworth
A228
Caterham
7/8
6
Woldingham
Westerham
Hosey Hill
A21
Sevenoaks
Under River
A26
M23
Limpsfield
Oxted
Ide Hill
Shipbourne

Torre Vedras
Santarém
Sintra
Estoril
Setúbal
AEROPORTO PORTELA DE SACAVÉM
Estação do Oriente
EXPO' 98
Oceanário
Área Internacional Sul
Brandoa
Pontinha
Carnide
Benfica
Venda Nova
Calhariz
Damaia
Buraca
Alfragide
Zambujal
Portela
CASELAS
RESTELO
BELÉM
PEDROUÇOS
AJUDA
SANTO AMARO
ALCÂNTARA
CARAMÃO
MONSANTO
Parque Florestal de Monsanto
SETE RIOS
CAMPOLIDE
CAMPO DE OURIQUE
ESTRELA
LAPA
RATO
BAIRRO ALTO
BAIXA
ALFAMA
GRAÇA
ESTEFÂNIA
BAIRRO LOPES
ALTO DO PINA
PICHELEIRA
OLAIAS
AREEIRO
MARVILA
MADRE DE DEUS
CHELAS
ALVALADE
CAMPO GRANDE
CAMPO PEQUENO
A. DO CEGO
SALDANHA
CIDADE UNIVERSITÁRIA
OLIVAIS SUL
TERESINHAS
BRAÇO DE PRATA
POÇO DO BISPO
Rio Tejo
Ponte 25 de Abril
Torre de Belém
Padrão dos Descobrimentos
Mosteiro dos Jerónimos
Gare marítima de Alcântara
Gare marítima de Rocha
Museu Nacional de Arte Antiga
Est. Cais do Sodré
Teatro de Dona Maria II
Est. Rossio
Catedral Sé Patriarcal
Castelo de São Jorge
Igreja de S.ta Engrácia
Est. S. Apolónia
CAMINHOS DE FERRO
Igreja da Madre de Deus
Cemitério do Alto de São João
Ist. Sup. Técnico
Parque Eduardo VII
Est. Campolide
Aqueduto das Águas Livres
Palácio dos Marqueses de Fronteira
Forte de Monsanto
Bairro da Boavista
Jardim Zoológico
Estádio da Luz
Centro Colombo
Estádio José Alvalade
Biblioteca Nacional
Parque da Bela Vista
Cemitério
Jardim Botânico
Basílica da Estrela
Cemitério dos Prazeres
Pal. de São Bento
Pal. Nacional da Ajuda
Observatório Astronómico
Est. Alcântara
Jardim Tropical
Largo do Rato
Praça do Comércio
BAIRRO DO ALTO DA AJUDA
TAPADA DA AJUDA
Av. General Norton de Matos
Av. Marechal Craveiro Lopes
Av. Marechal Gomes da Costa
Avenida do Brasil
Av. Almirante Gago Coutinho
Av. do Santo Condestável
Av. Infante Dom Henrique
R. da Cintura do Porto
Av. Estados Unidos da América
Av. das Forças Armadas
Avenida Lusíada
Estrada da Benfica
Radial da Buraca
Av. C. Gulbenkian
Av. de Berna
Av. João XXI
Avenida da República
Av. A. A. de Aguiar
Av. Fontes Pereira de Melo
Av. Almirante Reis
Av. E. Duarte Pacheco
Av. da Liberdade
Av. de Ceuta
Av. Infante Santo
Av. D. Carlos I
Av. Vinte e Quatro de Julho
Av. Inf. D. Henrique
Rua G. Pais
Estrada da Circunvalação
Estrada da Circunvalação
Estrada dos Marcos
Av. das Descobertas
Calçada da Ajuda
Av. do Restelo
Av. Dom Vasco da Gama
Rua da Junqueira
Avenida da Índia
231
142
170
61
N
0 1 km

Glince
Dolnice
Zapuže
Kamna Gorica
Dravlje
Stegne
Stožice
Kranj, Ljubelj, Jesenice, A2
Kranj
Maribor
Litija
Polhov Gradec
Postojna, Trst
Ig
Grosuplje
Novo Mesto, Zagreb
JARŠKI PROD
Sava
Tomačevo
Jarše
SNEBERSKI PROD
Obrije
Šmartno ob Savi
Hrastje
BRINJE
LITOSTROJ
ŠIŠKA
BEŽIGRAD
Podutik
Koseze
RIGELJ
NA JAMI
MOSTEC
KOSEŠKI BORŠT
ZA MOŠENICO
VELIKI RAKOVNIK
Šišenski hrib
Tivolski vrh
Cankarjev vrh
TIVOLI
ŽALE
NOVE JARŠE
SAVSKO NASELJE
ZELENA JAMA
MOSTE
STUDENEC
AJDOVŠČINA
VODMAT
CENTER
TABOR
NOVE FUŽINE
ŠTEPANJSKO NASELJE
KODELJEVO
FUŽINE
Ljubljanica
GRADIŠČE
Ljubjanski Grad
POLJANE
ŠTEPANJA VAS
ZGORNJA HRUŠICA
SPODNJA HRUŠICA
Grič
Bokalce
BRDO
ROŽNA DOLINA
VRHOVCI
VIČ
Zeleni hrib
Hruševski hrib
GOLOVEC
RAKOVNIK
PRULE
TRNOVO
KOLEZIJA
MURGLE
MESTNI LOG
Kozarje
Kosovo polje
Mali graben
SIBIRIJA
GALJEVICA
LONDON
G. RUDNIK
RUDNIK
SP. RUDNIK
Mazovnik
Bizovik
ILOVICA
RAKOVA JELŠA
ZGORNJI LOG
SPODNJI LOG
BEZLAN
Majland
LJUBLJANSKO BARJE
Karolinski dvor
Volar
PENE
Orle
ČRNI LOG
NA BLATEH
ČRNJUKE
Črna vas
Iščica
Glinščica
Podutiška cesta
Celovška cesta
Drenikova Ulica
Samova Ulica
Dunajska cesta
Linhartova cesta
Šmartinska cesta
Zaloška cesta
Litijska cesta
Tivolska cesta
Večna Pot
Tržaška Cesta
Aškerčeva cesta
Zoisova cesta
Karlovška cesta
Dolenjska cesta
Ižanska cesta
354
352
429
387
394
356
406
405
450
N
0 1 km

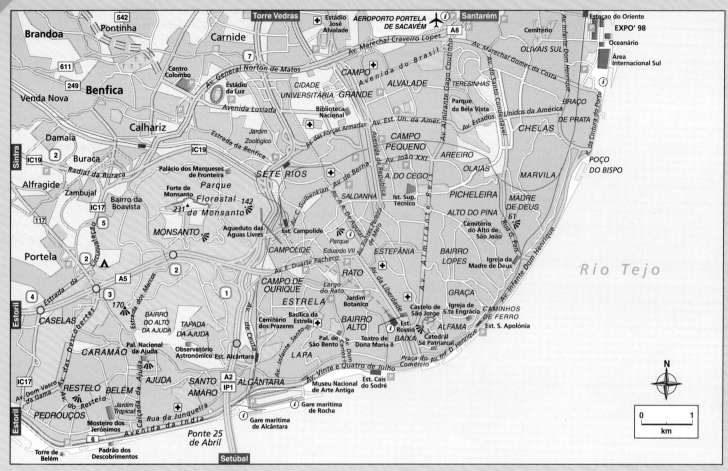

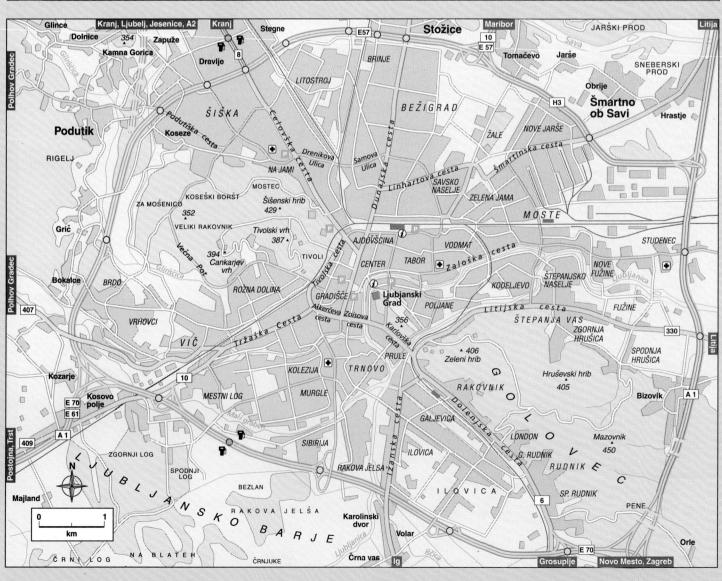

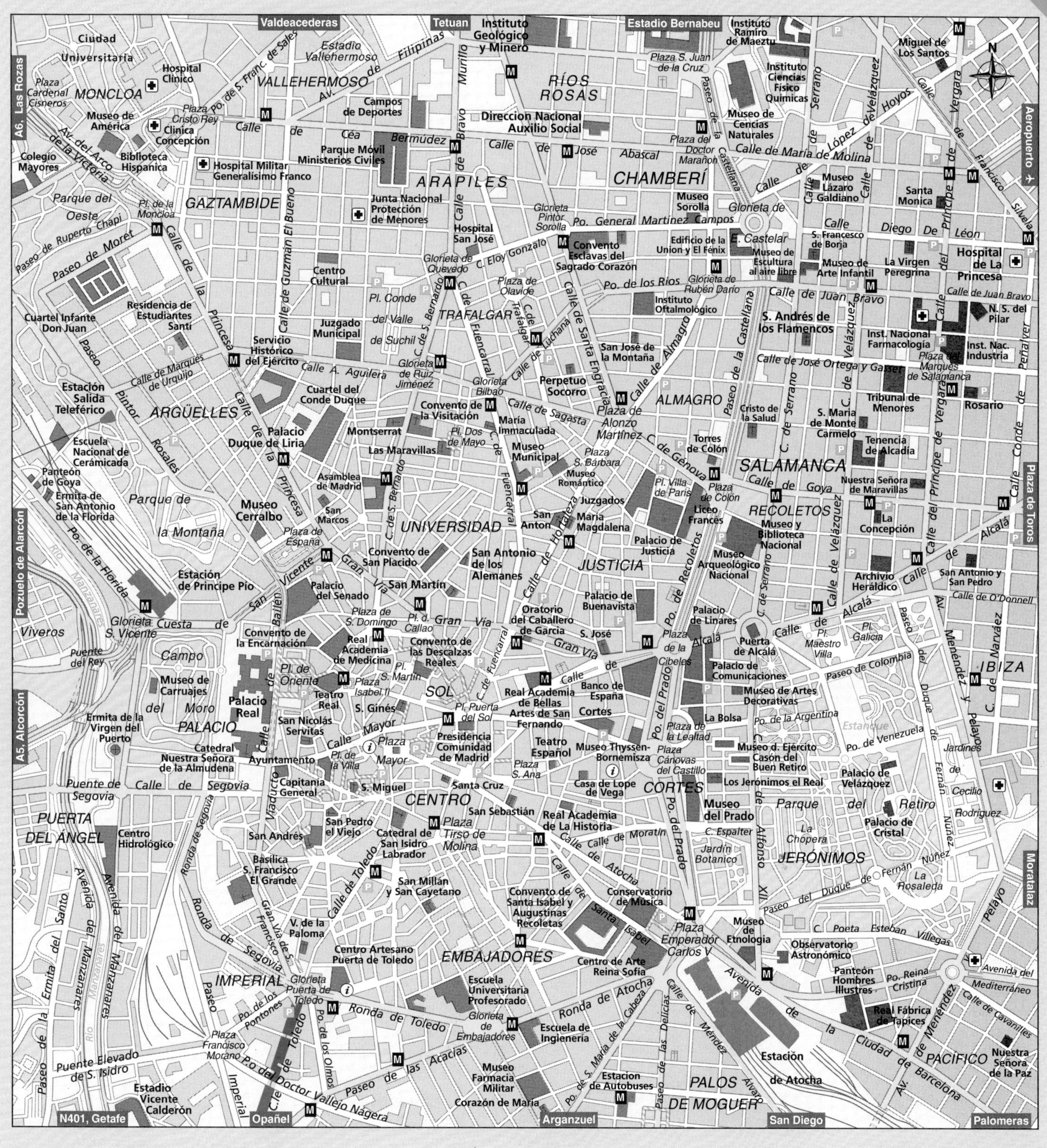
Valdeacederas
Tetuan
Estadio Bernabeu
A6. Las Rozas
Aeropuerto
Pozuelo de Alarcón
Plaza de Toros
A5. Alcorcón
Moratalaz
N401, Getafe
Opañel
Arganzuel
San Diego
Palomeras
Ciudad Universitaria
Estadio Vallehermoso
VALLEHERMOSO
RÍOS ROSAS
MONCLOA
Hospital Clinico
Plaza Cardenal Cisneros
Museo de América
Clinica Concepción
Biblioteca Hispanica
Colegio Mayores
Hospital Militar Generalísimo Franco
Campos de Deportes
Direccion Nacional Auxilio Social
Parque Móvil Ministerios Civiles
Instituto Geológico y Minero
Instituto Ramiro de Maeztu
Instituto Ciencias Físico Químicas
Museo de Cencias Naturales
Miguel de Los Santos
ARAPILES
CHAMBERÍ
GAZTAMBIDE
Parque del Oeste
Junta Nacional Protección de Menores
Hospital San José
Museo Sorolla
Glorieta de E. Castelar
Museo Lázaro Galdiano
Santa Monica
Hospital de La Princesa
Convento Esclavas del Sagrado Corazón
Edificio de la Union y El Fénix
Museo de Escultura al aire libre
Museo de Arte Infantil
La Virgen Peregrina
S. Francesco de Borja
Residencia de Estudiantes Santí
Cuartel Infante Don Juan
Centro Cultural
Juzgado Municipal
TRAFALGAR
Instituto Oftalmológico
S. Andrés de los Flamencos
N. S. del Pilar
Inst. Nacional Farmacología
Inst. Nac. Industria
Servicio Histórico del Ejército
Estación Salida Teleférico
ARGÜELLES
Cuartel del Conde Duque
Perpetuo Socorro
San José de la Montaña
ALMAGRO
Cristo de la Salud
Tribunal de Menores
Rosario
Palacio Duque de Liria
Convento de la Visitación
María Immaculada
Montserrat
Las Maravillas
Museo Municipal
Torres de Colón
S. María de Monte Carmelo
Tenencia de Alcadía
Escuela Nacional de Cerámicada
Panteón de Goya
Ermita de San Antonio de la Florida
Parque de la Montaña
Museo Cerralbo
Asamblea de Madrid
San Marcos
UNIVERSIDAD
Museo Romántico
Juzgados
SALAMANCA
Nuestra Señora de Maravillas
RECOLETOS
Liceo Francés
Museo y Biblioteca Nacional
La Concepción
San Antón
María Magdalena
Palacio de Justicia
JUSTICIA
Museo Arqueológico Nacional
Archivio Heráldico
San Antonio y San Pedro
Estación de Principe Pío
Convento de San Placido
San Antonio de los Alemanes
Palacio del Senado
San Martín
Oratorio del Caballero de García
Palacio de Buenavista
Palacio de Linares
Viveros
Campo del Moro
Convento de la Encarnación
Real Academia de Medicina
Convento de las Descalzas Reales
S. José
Puerta de Alcalá
Palacio de Comunicaciones
IBIZA
Museo de Carruajes
Palacio Real
Teatro Real
SOL
Real Academia de Bellas Artes de San Fernando
Banco de España
Cortes
Museo de Artes Decorativas
La Bolsa
Ermita de la Virgen del Puerto
PALACIO
San Nicolás Servitas
S. Ginés
Presidencia Comunidad de Madrid
Teatro Español
Museo Thyssen-Bornemisza
Museo d. Ejército
Casón del Buen Retiro
Palacio de Velázquez
Catedral Nuestra Señora de la Almudena
Ayuntamiento
Plaza Mayor
Capitania General
S. Miguel
Santa Cruz
Casa de Lope de Vega
CORTES
Los Jerónimos el Real
Museo del Prado
Parque del Retiro
Palacio de Cristal
PUERTA DEL ÁNGEL
Centro Hidrológico
CENTRO
San Sebastián
Real Academia de La Historia
San Andrés
San Pedro el Viejo
Catedral de San Isidro Labrador
Jardín Botanico
JERÓNIMOS
La Rosaleda
Basilica S. Francisco El Grande
San Millán y San Cayetano
Convento de Santa Isabel y Augustinas Recoletas
Conservatorio de Música
Museo de Etnologia
Observatorio Astronómico
V. de la Paloma
Centro Artesano Puerta de Toledo
EMBAJADORES
Centro de Arte Reina Sofía
Plaza Emperador Carlos V
Panteón Hombres Illustres
IMPERIAL
Escuela Universitaria Profesorado
Escuela de Ingeniería
Real Fábrica de Tapices
Estación de Atocha
PACÍFICO
Nuestra Señora de la Paz
Estadio Vicente Calderón
Museo Farmacia Militar
Corazón de María
Estacion de Autobuses
PALOS DE MOGUER

0 200 400
m

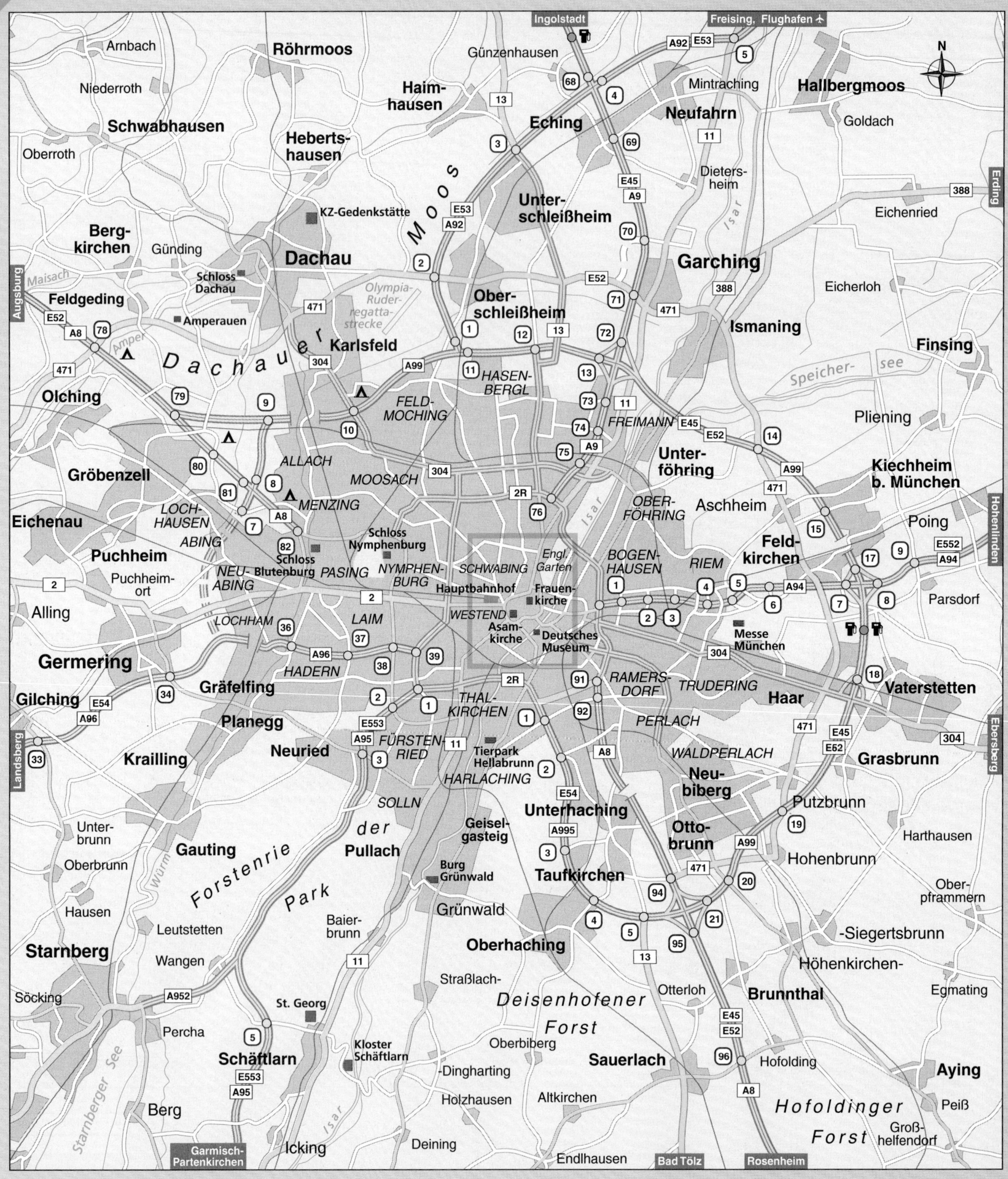

Arnbach
Niederroth
Schwabhausen
Oberroth
Röhrmoos
Günzenhausen
Haim-hausen
Heberts-hausen
Eching
Mintraching
Neufahrn
Hallbergmoos
Goldach
Dietersheim
Bergkirchen
Günding
Dachau
KZ-Gedenkstätte
Unterschleißheim
Garching
Eicherloh
Eichenried
Schloss Dachau
Olympia-Ruder-regatta-strecke
Ober-schleißheim
Ismaning
Finsing
Feldgeding
Amperauen
Karlsfeld
Speicher-see
Olching
Dachauer
HASEN-BERGL
FELD-MOCHING
FREIMANN
Unter-föhring
Pliening
Kiechheim b. München
Gröbenzell
ALLACH
MOOSACH
OBER-FÖHRING
Aschheim
Feld-kirchen
Poing
Eichenau
LOCH-HAUSEN
ABING
MENZING
Schloss Nymphenburg
Parsdorf
Puchheim
Puchheim-ort
Schloss Blutenburg
NEU-ABING
PASING
NYMPHEN-BURG
SCHWABING
Engl. Garten
BOGEN-HAUSEN
RIEM
Messe München
Alling
LOCHHAM
LAIM
WESTEND
Hauptbahnhof
Frauen-kirche
Germering
Gilching
Gräfelfing
HADERN
Asam-kirche
Deutsches Museum
RAMERS-DORF
TRUDERING
Messe München
Vaterstetten
Planegg
Neuried
THAL-KIRCHEN
FÜRSTEN-RIED
Tierpark Hellabrunn
PERLACH
WALDPERLACH
Haar
Grasbrunn
Krailling
SOLLN
HARLACHING
Neu-biberg
Putzbrunn
Unter-brunn
Gauting
der
Pullach
Geisel-gasteig
Otto-brunn
Hohenbrunn
Harthausen
Oberbrunn
Forstenrie
Burg Grünwald
Unterhaching
Taufkirchen
Ober-pframmern
Hausen
Park
Baier-brunn
Grünwald
-Siegertsbrunn
Starnberg
Leutstetten
Oberhaching
Höhenkirchen-
Egmating
Söcking
Wangen
Straßlach-
Otterloh
Brunnthal
Percha
St. Georg
Deisenhofener
Forst
Oberbiberg
Sauerlach
Hofolding
Aying
Schäftlarn
Kloster Schäftlarn
-Dingharting
Peiß
Berg
Holzhausen
Altkirchen
Hofoldinger
Forst
Groß-helfendorf
Icking
Deining
Endlhausen

0   2   4
km

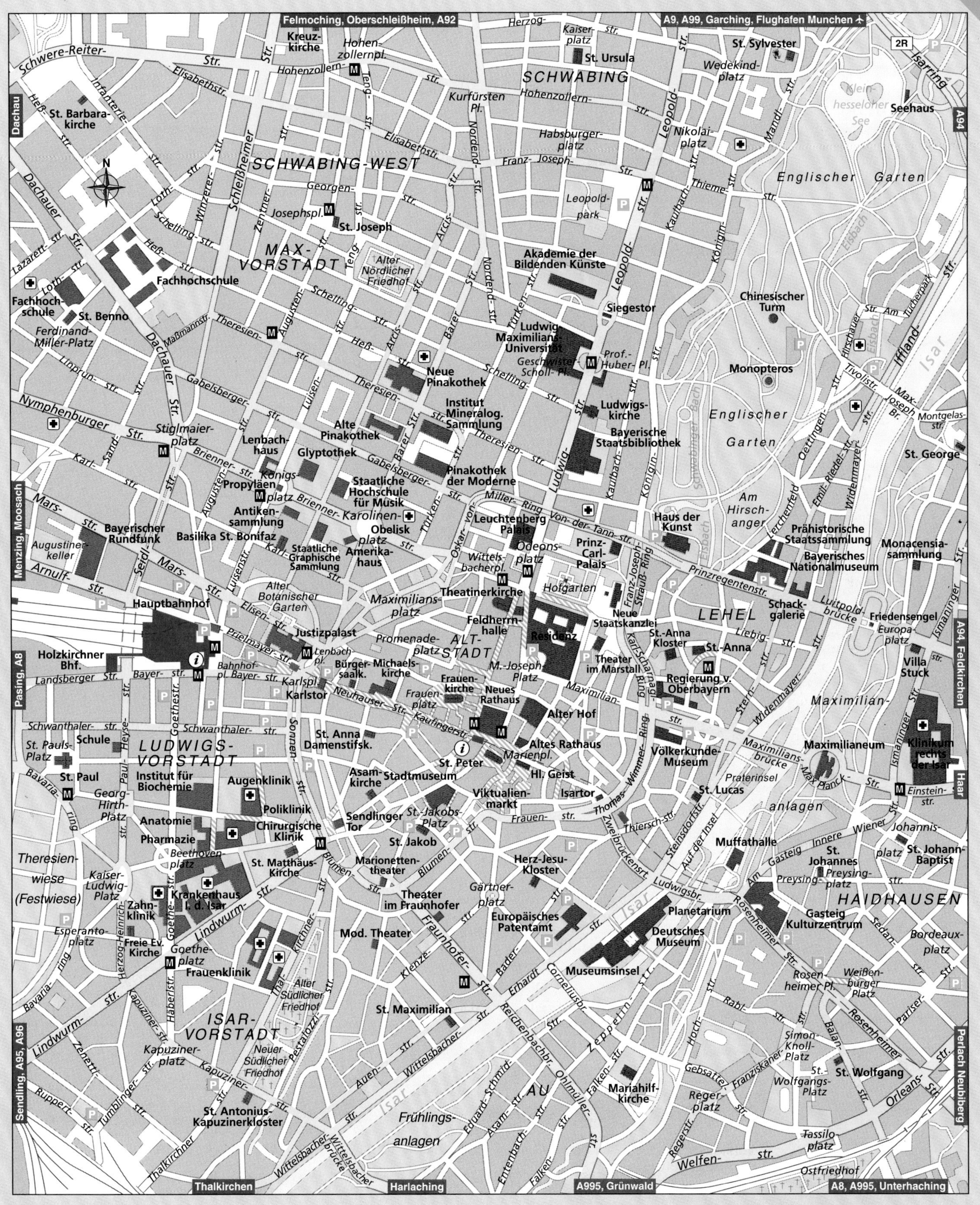
Felmoching, Oberschleißheim, A92
A9, A99, Garching, Flughafen München
Dachau
A94
Menzing, Moosach
Pasing, A8
A94, Feldkirchen
Haar
Sendling, A95, A96
Perlach Neubiberg
Thalkirchen
Harlaching
A995, Grünwald
A8, A995, Unterhaching
SCHWABING
SCHWABING-WEST
MAX-VORSTADT
ALT-STADT
LEHEL
LUDWIGS-VORSTADT
ISAR-VORSTADT
HAIDHAUSEN
AU
Englischer Garten
Isar
Kreuzkirche
St. Ursula
St. Sylvester
Seehaus
St. Barbara-kirche
St. Joseph
Fachhochschule
St. Benno
Akademie der Bildenden Künste
Siegestor
Chinesischer Turm
Ludwig-Maximilians-Universität
Monopteros
Neue Pinakothek
Alte Pinakothek
Institut Mineralog. Sammlung
Ludwigskirche
Bayerische Staatsbibliothek
Lenbachhaus
Glyptothek
Propyläen
Pinakothek der Moderne
Staatliche Hochschule für Musik
Antikensammlung
Bayerischer Rundfunk
Basilika St. Bonifaz
Obelisk
Staatliche Graphische Sammlung
Amerikahaus
Leuchtenberg Palais
Haus der Kunst
Prähistorische Staatssammlung
Bayerisches Nationalmuseum
Monacensia-sammlung
St. George
Hauptbahnhof
Holzkirchner Bhf.
Justizpalast
Theatinerkirche
Feldherrnhalle
Residenz
Neue Staatskanzlei
Schackgalerie
Friedensengel
St.-Anna Kloster
St.-Anna
Villa Stuck
Bürgersaalk.
Michaelskirche
Karlstor
Frauenkirche
Neues Rathaus
Theater im Marstall
Regierung v. Oberbayern
Alter Hof
Altes Rathaus
St. Peter
Hl. Geist
Völkerkunde-Museum
Maximilianeum
Klinikum rechts der Isar
St. Anna Damenstifsk.
Schule
St. Paul
Institut für Biochemie
Augenklinik
Asamkirche
Stadtmuseum
Viktualienmarkt
Isartor
St. Lucas
Poliklinik
Anatomie
Pharmazie
Chirurgische Klinik
Sendlinger Tor
St. Jakob
Muffathalle
St. Johannes
St. Johann-Baptist
Theresienwiese (Festwiese)
Krankenhaus l. d. Isar
St. Matthäus-Kirche
Marionettentheater
Herz-Jesu-Kloster
Zahnklinik
Theater im Fraunhofer
Europäisches Patentamt
Planetarium
Gasteig Kulturzentrum
Freie Ev. Kirche
Mod. Theater
Deutsches Museum
Frauenklinik
Museumsinsel
Alter Südlicher Friedhof
St. Maximilian
Neuer Südlicher Friedhof
Mariahilf-kirche
St. Wolfgang
St. Antonius-Kapuzinerkloster
Frühlings-anlagen
Ostfriedhof
0 200 400 m

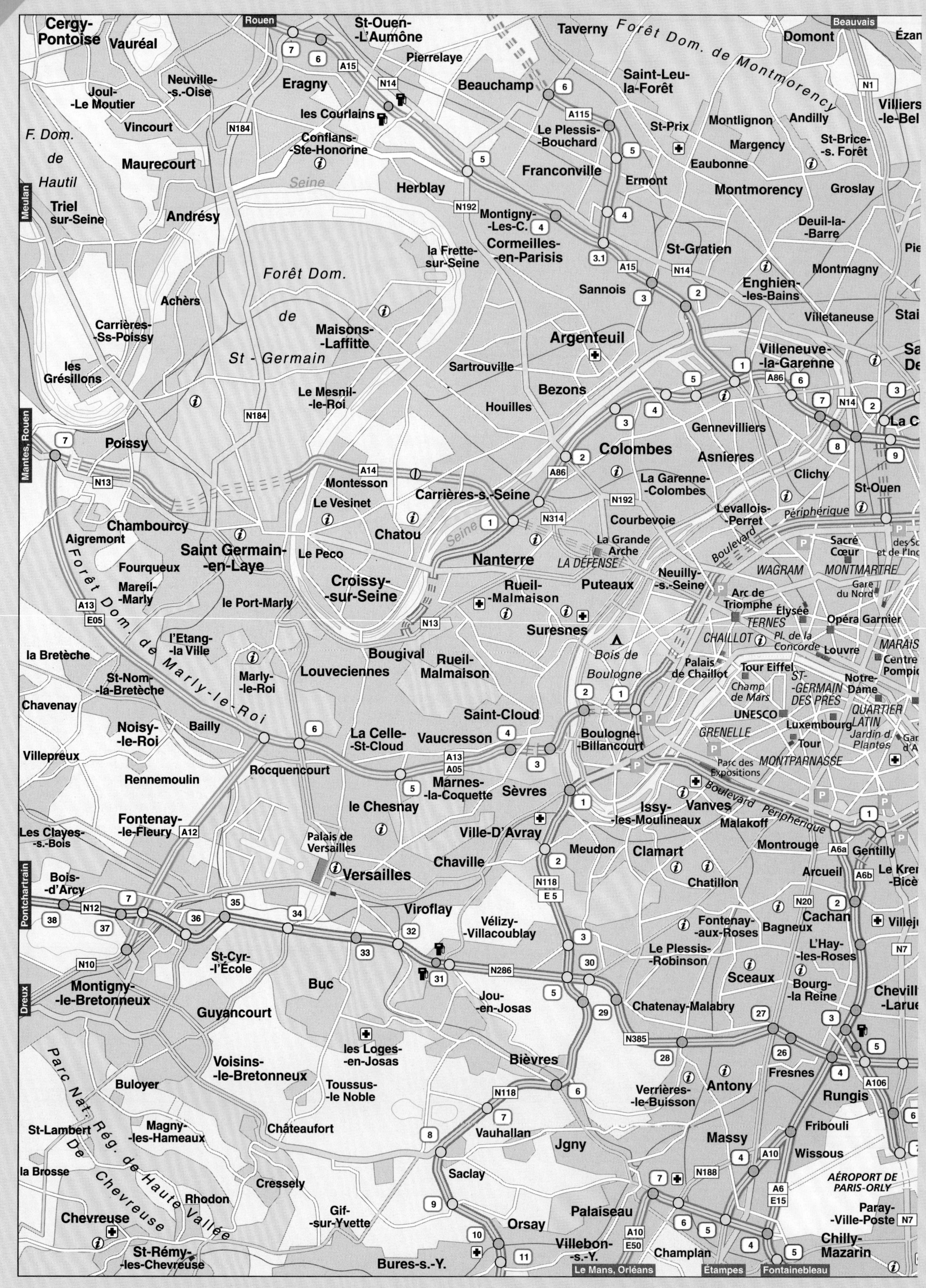
Rouen
Beauvais
Meulan
Mantes, Rouen
Pontchartrain
Dreux
Le Mans, Orléans
Étampes
Fontainebleau
Cergy-Pontoise
Vauréal
St-Ouen-l'Aumône
Pierrelaye
Taverny
Forêt Dom. de Montmorency
Domont
Neuville-s.-Oise
Joui-le Moutier
Eragny
Beauchamp
Saint-Leu-la-Forêt
Villiers-le-Bel
Vincourt
les Courlains
Conflans-Ste-Honorine
Le Plessis-Bouchard
St-Prix
Montlignon
Andilly
Margency
St-Brice-s. Forêt
F. Dom. de Hautil
Maurecourt
Franconville
Eaubonne
Ermont
Montmorency
Groslay
Seine
Herblay
Triel sur-Seine
Andrésy
Montigny-Les-C.
Deuil-la-Barre
Cormeilles-en-Parisis
la Frette-sur-Seine
St-Gratien
Forêt Dom. de St - Germain
Enghien-les-Bains
Montmagny
Sannois
Achères
Villetaneuse
Carrières-Ss-Poissy
Maisons-Laffitte
Argenteuil
Villeneuve-la-Garenne
les Grésillons
Sartrouville
Bezons
Le Mesnil-le-Roi
Houilles
Gennevilliers
Poissy
Colombes
Asnieres
Clichy
Montesson
La Garenne-Colombes
St-Ouen
Le Vesinet
Carrières-s.-Seine
Courbevoie
Levallois-Perret
Périphérique
Chambourcy
Chatou
Aigremont
La Grande Arche
Saint Germain-en-Laye
Le Peco
Nanterre
LA DÉFENSE
Boulevard
Sacré Cœur
Fourqueux
Neuilly-s.-Seine
WAGRAM
MONTMARTRE
Mareil-Marly
Croissy-sur-Seine
Rueil-Malmaison
Puteaux
Gare du Nord
le Port-Marly
Arc de Triomphe
Élysée
TERNES
Opéra Garnier
Forêt Dom. de Marly-le-Roi
Suresnes
CHAILLOT
Pl. de la Concorde
Louvre
MARAIS
l'Etang-la Ville
Bois de Boulogne
la Bretèche
Bougival
Palais de Chaillot
Tour Eiffel
Centre Pompidou
Marly-le-Roi
Louveciennes
Rueil-Malmaison
Champ de Mars
ST-GERMAIN DES PRÉS
Notre-Dame
St-Nom-la-Bretèche
Chavenay
Saint-Cloud
UNESCO
QUARTIER LATIN
Noisy-le-Roi
Bailly
La Celle-St-Cloud
Vaucresson
Boulogne-Billancourt
Luxembourg
GRENELLE
Jardin d. Plantes
Villepreux
Tour
Parc des Expositions
MONTPARNASSE
Rennemoulin
Rocquencourt
Marnes-la-Coquette
Sèvres
Boulevard Périphérique
le Chesnay
Issy-les-Moulineaux
Vanves
Malakoff
Fontenay-le-Fleury
Les Clayes-s.-Bois
Palais de Versailles
Ville-D'Avray
Meudon
Clamart
Montrouge
Gentilly
Bois-d'Arcy
Versailles
Chaville
Arcueil
Chatillon
Viroflay
Vélizy-Villacoublay
Fontenay-aux-Roses
Bagneux
Cachan
St-Cyr-l'École
L'Hay-les-Roses
Le Plessis-Robinson
Buc
Montigny-le-Bretonneux
Jou-en-Josas
Sceaux
Bourg-la Reine
Guyancourt
Chatenay-Malabry
les Loges-en-Josas
Voisins-le-Bretonneux
Bièvres
Fresnes
Antony
Verrières-le-Buisson
Rungis
Buloyer
Toussus-le Noble
Parc Nat. Rég. de Haute Vallée De Chevreuse
Fribouli
Magny-les-Hameaux
Châteaufort
Vauhallan
Jgny
Massy
Wissous
St-Lambert
la Brosse
Saclay
AÉROPORT DE PARIS-ORLY
Cressely
Rhodon
Gif-sur-Yvette
Palaiseau
Paray-Ville-Poste
Chevreuse
Orsay
Villebon-s.-Y.
Champlan
Chilly-Mazarin
St-Rémy-les-Chevreuse
Bures-s.-Y.
A15
N14
N184
A115
N192
N1
A86
N13
A14
N314
A13
E05
A12
A05
N12
N10
N118
E 5
N20
A6a
A6b
N7
N286
N385
A106
A10
N188
A6
E15
E50

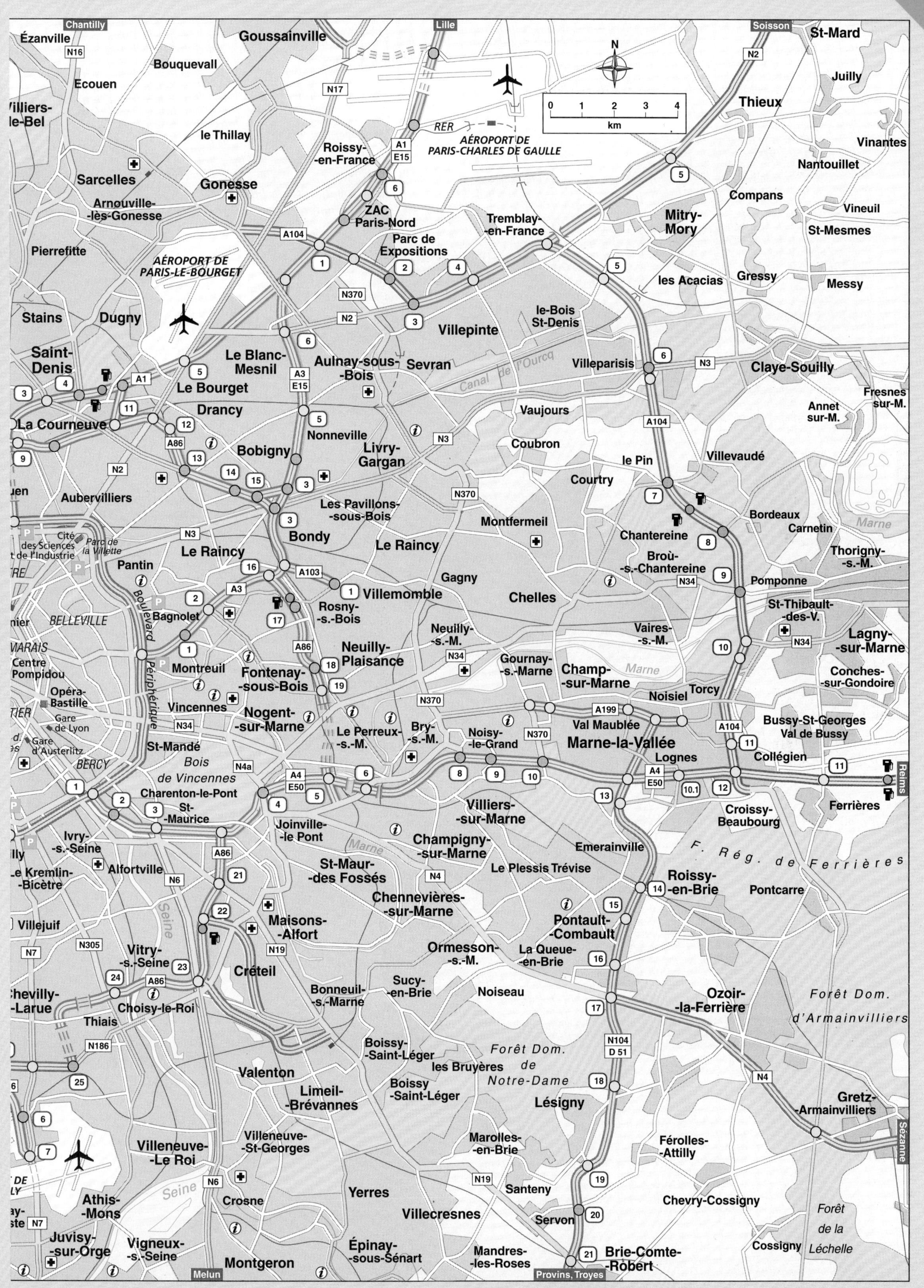

Chantilly
Lille
Soisson
Reims
Sézanne
Melun
Provins, Troyes
AÉROPORT DE PARIS-CHARLES DE GAULLE
AÉROPORT DE PARIS-LE-BOURGET
RER
km
Goussainville
Bouquevall
Ecouen
Écouen
Sarcelles
Gonesse
Arnouville-lès-Gonesse
Pierrefitte
Stains
Dugny
Saint-Denis
Le Blanc-Mesnil
Aulnay-sous-Bois
Sevran
Villepinte
Tremblay-en-France
Roissy-en-France
ZAC Paris-Nord
Parc de Expositions
Mitry-Mory
Compans
Thieux
St-Mard
Juilly
Vinantes
Nantouillet
Vineuil
St-Mesmes
Gressy
Messy
les Acacias
le-Bois St-Denis
Villeparisis
Claye-Souilly
Le Bourget
Drancy
La Courneuve
Bobigny
Nonneville
Livry-Gargan
Vaujours
Coubron
le Pin
Courtry
Villevaudé
Aubervilliers
Les Pavillons-sous-Bois
Bondy
Montfermeil
Chantereine
Brou-s.-Chantereine
Bordeaux
Carnetin
Thorigny-s.-M.
Pomponne
Le Raincy
Pantin
Bagnolet
Villemomble
Rosny-s.-Bois
Gagny
Chelles
Vaires-s.-M.
St-Thibault-des-V.
Lagny-sur-Marne
Conches-sur-Gondoire
Montreuil
Fontenay-sous-Bois
Neuilly-Plaisance
Neuilly-s.-M.
Gournay-s.-Marne
Champ-sur-Marne
Noisiel
Torcy
Vincennes
Nogent-sur-Marne
Le Perreux-s.-M.
Bry-s.-M.
Noisy-le-Grand
Val Maublée
Marne-la-Vallée
Lognes
Bussy-St-Georges
Val de Bussy
Collégien
Ferrières
Croissy-Beaubourg
St-Mandé
Bois de Vincennes
Charenton-le-Pont
St-Maurice
Joinville-le Pont
Villiers-sur-Marne
Champigny-sur-Marne
Emerainville
Roissy-en-Brie
Pontcarre
F. Rég. de Ferrières
Ivry-s.-Seine
Alfortville
Le Kremlin-Bicètre
St-Maur-des Fossés
Le Plessis Trévise
Chennevières-sur-Marne
Villejuif
Maisons-Alfort
Pontault-Combault
Vitry-s.-Seine
Créteil
Ormesson-s.-M.
La Queue-en-Brie
Chevilly-Larue
Choisy-le-Roi
Thiais
Bonneuil-s.-Marne
Sucy-en-Brie
Noiseau
Ozoir-la-Ferrière
Forêt Dom. d'Armainvilliers
Boissy-Saint-Léger
les Bruyères
Forêt Dom. de Notre-Dame
Valenton
Limeil-Brévannes
Boissy-Saint-Léger
Lésigny
Gretz-Armainvilliers
Villeneuve-St-Georges
Villeneuve-Le Roi
Marolles-en-Brie
Férolles-Attilly
Santeny
Chevry-Cossigny
Athis-Mons
Crosne
Yerres
Villecresnes
Servon
Forêt de la Léchelle
Juvisy-sur-Orge
Vigneux-s.-Seine
Montgeron
Épinay-sous-Sénart
Mandres-les-Roses
Brie-Comte-Robert
Cossigny
Cité des Sciences et de l'Industrie
Parc de la Villette
BELLEVILLE
MARAIS
Centre Pompidou
Opéra-Bastille
Gare de Lyon
Gare d'Austerlitz
BERCY
Boulevard Périphérique
Seine
Marne
Canal de l'Ourcq
A1
E15
A3
A4
E50
A86
A103
A104
A199
N2
N3
N4
N4a
N6
N7
N16
N17
N19
N34
N104
D 51
N186
N305
N370

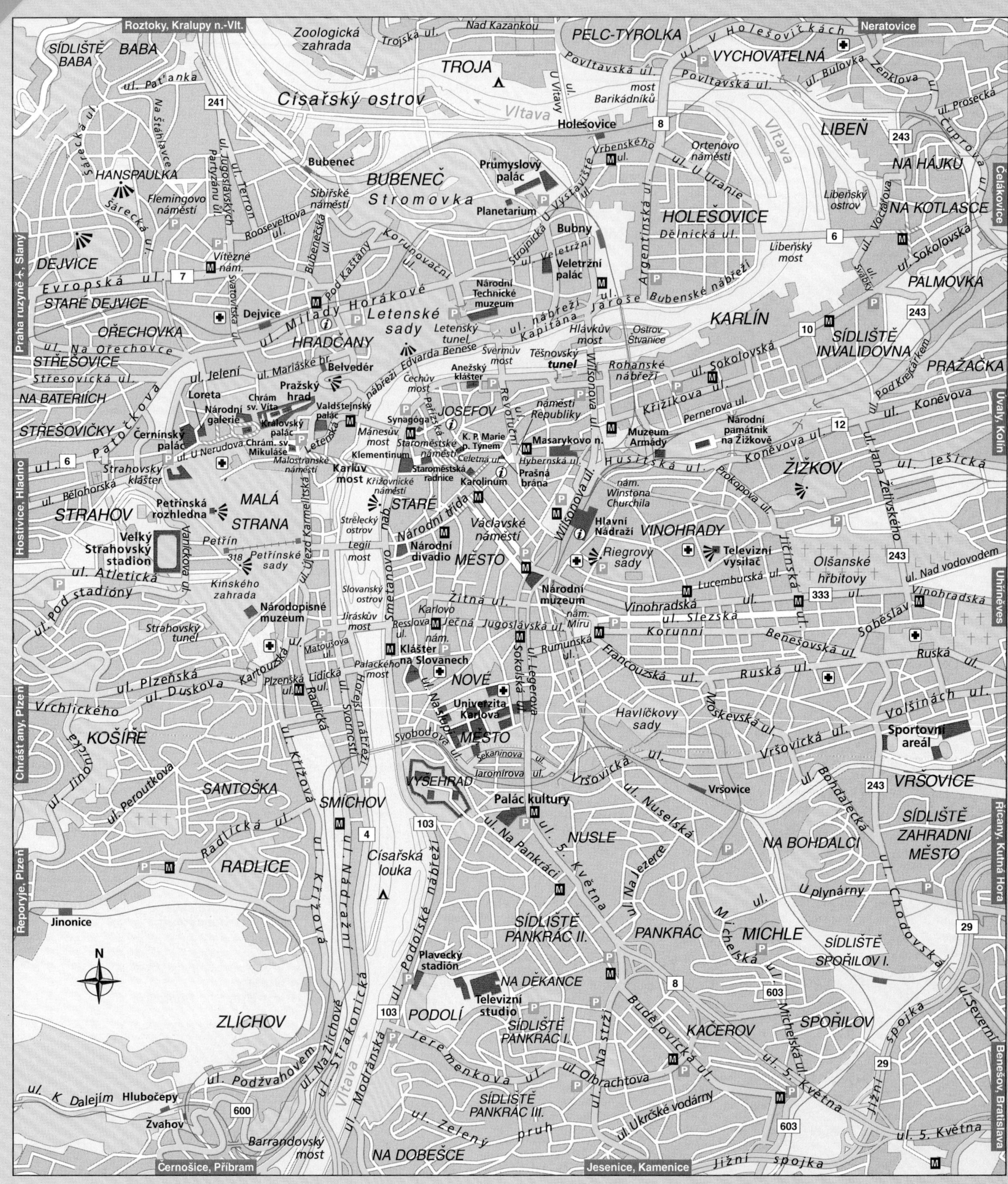
Roztoky, Kralupy n.-Vlt.
Neratovice
Praha ruzyně, Slaný
Hostivice, Hladno
Chrást'any, Plzeň
Řeporyje, Plzeň
Černošice, Příbram
Jesenice, Kamenice
Benešov, Bratislava
Říčany, Kutná Hora
Úvaly, Kolín
Čelákovice
Uhříněves
TROJA
Císařský ostrov
Zoologická zahrada
PELC-TYROLKA
VYCHOVATELNÁ
Holešovice
LIBEŇ
BUBENEČ
Stromovka
HOLEŠOVICE
DEJVICE
STARÉ DEJVICE
OŘECHOVKA
STŘEŠOVICE
NA BATERIÍCH
STŘEŠOVIČKY
HRADČANY
Letenské sady
KARLÍN
SÍDLIŠTĚ INVALIDOVNA
PRAŽAČKA
JOSEFOV
ŽIŽKOV
STRAHOV
MALÁ STRANA
STARÉ MĚSTO
VINOHRADY
NOVÉ MĚSTO
KOŠÍŘE
SANTOŠKA
SMÍCHOV
VYŠEHRAD
NUSLE
RADLICE
VRŠOVICE
SÍDLIŠTĚ ZAHRADNÍ MĚSTO
NA BOHDALCI
SÍDLIŠTĚ PANKRÁC II.
PANKRÁC
MICHLE
SÍDLIŠTĚ SPOŘILOV I.
ZLÍCHOV
PODOLÍ
SÍDLIŠTĚ PANKRÁC I.
KAČEROV
SPOŘILOV
SÍDLIŠTĚ PANKRÁC III.
NA DOBEŠCE
Hlubočepy
Zvahov
Jinonice
Barrandovský most
Pražský hrad
Loreta
Národní galerie
Chrám sv. Víta
Královský palác
Černínský palác
Strahovský klášter
Petřínská rozhledna
Velký Strahovský stadion
Národní divadlo
Národní muzeum
Hlavní Nádraží
Prašná brána
Karolinum
Staroměstská radnice
Palác kultury
Plavecký stadion
Televizní studio
Televizní vysílač
Olšanské hřbitovy
Sportovní areál
Národní památník na Žižkově
Muzeum Armády
Průmyslový palác
Planetarium
Veletržní palác
Národní Technické muzeum
Univerzita Karlova
Klášter na Slovanech
Národopisné muzeum
N
0 200 400
m

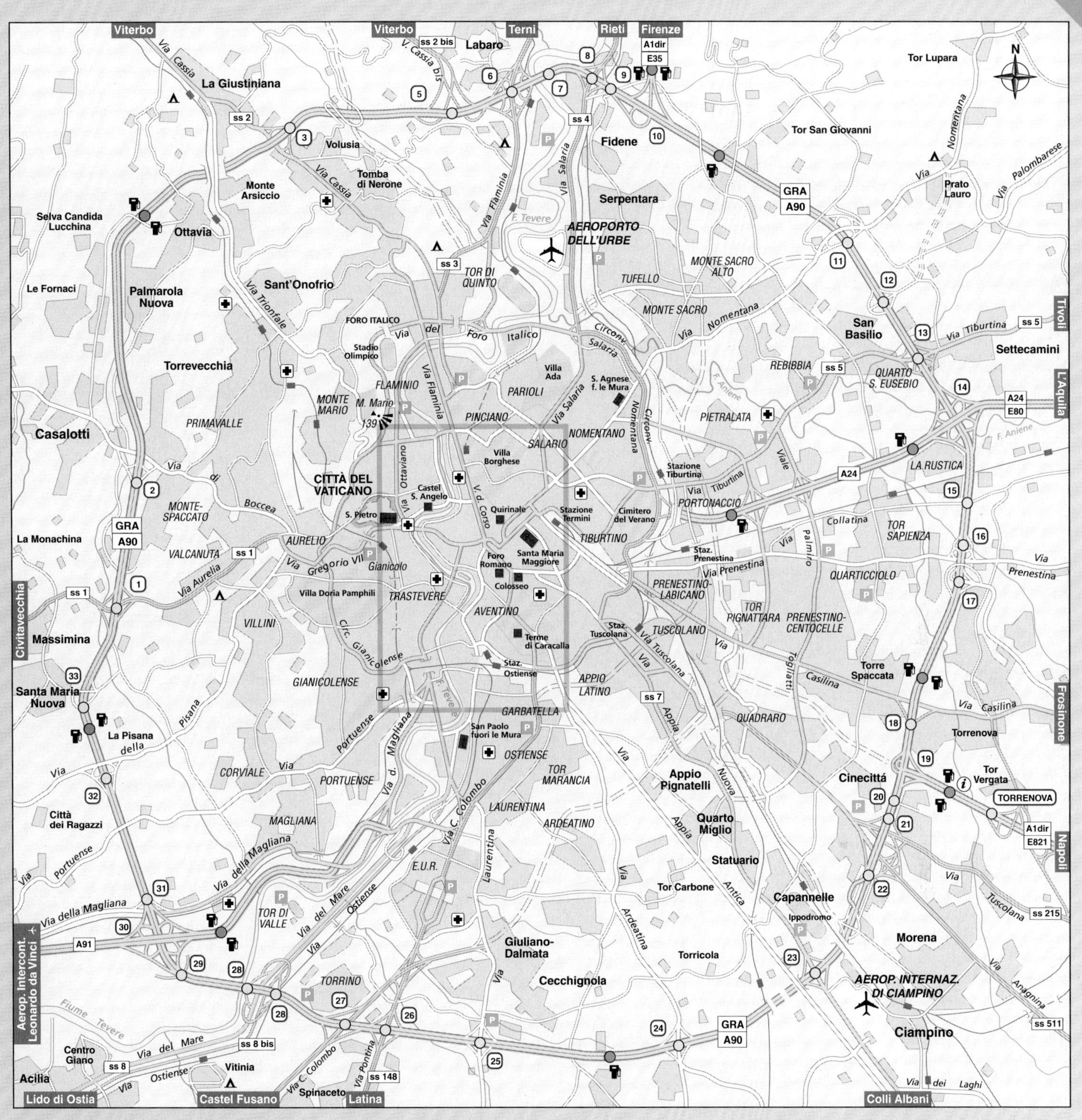

La Giustiniana ss 2 bis Labaro

Tor Lupara

ss 2

Volusia

Monte Arsiccio

Tomba di Nerone

Fidene

Tor San Giovanni

Prato Lauro

Ottavia

Selva Candida Lucchina

Serpentara

GRA A90

Le Fornaci

Sant'Onofrio

TOR DI QUINTO

AEROPORTO DELL'URBE

MONTE SACRO ALTO

Palmarola Nuova

TUFELLO

MONTE SACRO

San Basilio

Tivoli

ss 5

Torrevecchia

FORO ITALICO

Stadio Olimpico

PRIMAVALLE

FLAMINIO

MONTE MARIO

M. Mario 139

Villa Ada

S. Agnese f. le Mura

REBIBBIA

ss 5

QUARTO S. EUSEBIO

Settecamini

L'Aquila

Casalotti

PARIOLI

PINCIANO

SALARIO

NOMENTANO

PIETRALATA

A24 E80

GRA A90

CITTÀ DEL VATICANO

Villa Borghese

Stazione Tiburtina

LA RUSTICA

MONTE-SPACCATO

VALCANUTA

Boccea

Castel S. Angelo

Quirinale

Stazione Termini

Cimitero del Verano

PORTONACCIO

TOR SAPIENZA

La Monachina

GRA A90

AURELIO

S. Pietro

Foro Romano

Santa Maria Maggiore

TIBURTINO

Staz. Prenestina

QUARTICCIOLO

Massimina

ss 1

Villa Doria Pamphili

Gianicolo

TRASTEVERE

Colosseo

AVENTINO

PRENESTINO-LABICANO

TOR PIGNATTARA

PRENESTINO-CENTOCELLE

Civitavecchia

Santa Maria Nuova

GIANICOLENSE

Terme di Caracalla

Staz. Tuscolana

TUSCOLANO

Torre Spaccata

La Pisana

Staz. Ostiense

APPIO LATINO

QUADRARO

Città dei Ragazzi

CORVIALE

PORTUENSE

San Paolo fuori le Mura

GARBATELLA

OSTIENSE

Cinecittà

Torrenova

Tor Vergata

TORRENOVA

MAGLIANA

TOR MARANCIA

Appio Pignatelli

Quarto Miglio

A1dir E821

Napoli

TOR DI VALLE

E.U.R.

LAURENTINA

ARDEATINO

Statuario

Morena

A91

Torrino

Giuliano-Dalmata

Tor Carbone

Capannelle

Ippodromo

Tuscolana

ss 215

Centro Giano

ss 8

Vitinia

Cecchignola

Torricola

AEROP. INTERNAZ. DI CIAMPINO

Acilia

ss 8 bis

Spinaceto

GRA A90

Ciampino

ss 511

Aerop. Intercont. Leonardo da Vinci

Lido di Ostia

Castel Fusano

Latina

ss 148

Colli Albani

0 1 2 3 km

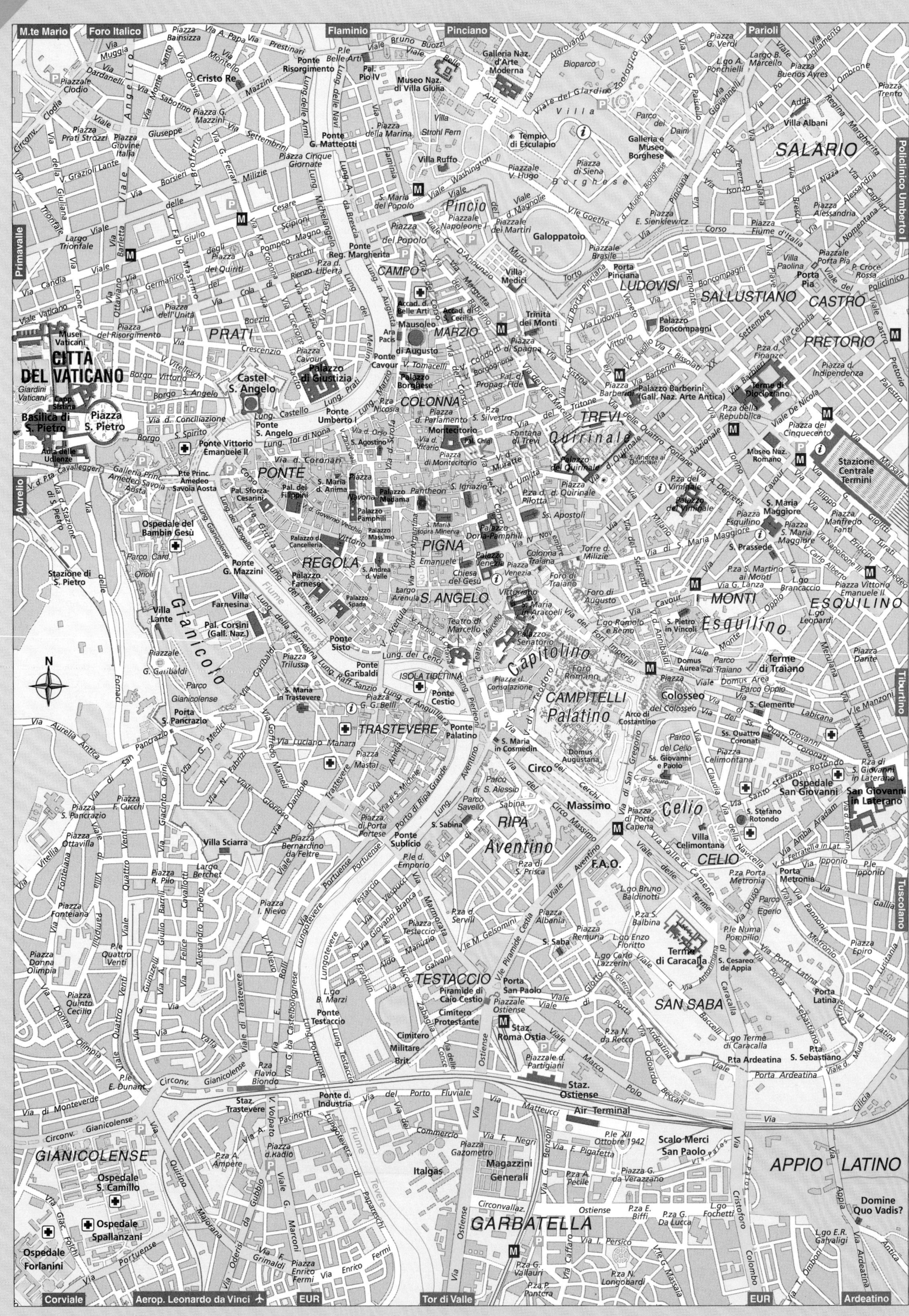
M.te Mario
Foro Italico
Flaminio
Pinciano
Parioli
Policlinico Umberto I
Primavalle
Aurelio
Tiburtino
Tuscolano
Corviale
Aerop. Leonardo da Vinci
EUR
Tor di Valle
EUR
Ardeatino
CITTÀ DEL VATICANO
Musei Vaticani
Basilica di S. Pietro
Piazza S. Pietro
Castel S. Angelo
PRATI
Palazzo di Giustizia
CAMPO MARZIO
Mausoleo di Augusto
Ara Pacis
Pincio
Villa Medici
Galoppatoio
Galleria Naz. d'Arte Moderna
Museo Naz. di Villa Giulia
Galleria e Museo Borghese
SALARIO
LUDOVISI
SALLUSTIANO
CASTRO PRETORIO
Villa Albani
COLONNA
Montecitorio
TREVI
Quirinale
Palazzo del Quirinale
Terme di Diocleziano
Stazione Centrale Termini
Museo Naz. Romano
PONTE
Pantheon
PIGNA
REGOLA
Palazzo Farnese
S. ANGELO
Teatro di Marcello
Capitolino
Foro Romano
Palazzo Venezia
Foro di Traiano
MONTI
Esquilino
ESQUILINO
S. Maria Maggiore
S. Pietro in Vincoli
Colosseo
CAMPITELLI
Palatino
Circo Massimo
Celio
CELIO
San Giovanni in Laterano
ISOLA TIBERINA
TRASTEVERE
Gianicolo
Villa Farnesina
Villa Sciarra
RIPA
Aventino
F.A.O.
TESTACCIO
Piramide di Caio Cestio
Cimitero Protestante
Terme di Caracalla
SAN SABA
Porta S. Sebastiano
Staz. Ostiense
Staz. Trastevere
Air Terminal
GIANICOLENSE
Ospedale S. Camillo
Ospedale Spallanzani
Ospedale Forlanini
GARBATELLA
Magazzini Generali
Italgas
Scalo Merci San Paolo
APPIO LATINO
Domine Quo Vadis?
Fiume Tevere

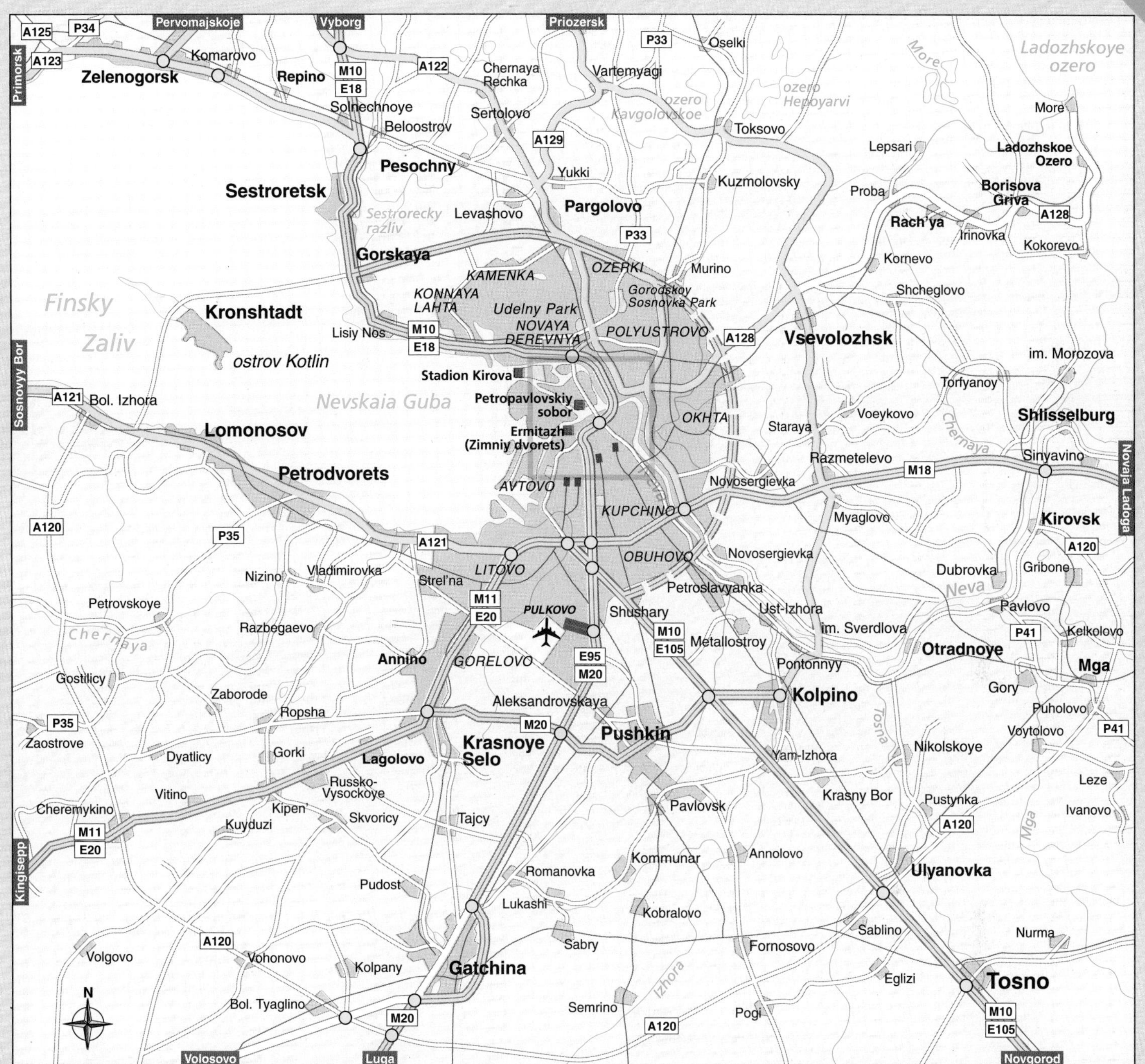

Primorsk · A125 · P34 · Pervomajskoje · Vyborg · Priozersk

Zelenogorsk · A123 · Komarovo · Repino · M10 · E18 · Solnechnoye · Beloostrov · A122 · Chernaya Rechka · Sertolovo · Vartemyagi · Oselki · P33

ozero Kavgolovskoe · ozero Hepoyarvi · More · Ladozhskoye ozero

Sestroretsk · Pesochny · Levashovo · A129 · Yukki · Toksovo · Kuzmolovsky · Lepsari · Proba · Ladozhskoe Ozero

Gorskaya · Sestrorecky razliv · P33 · Murino · Borisova Griva · Rach'ya · A128 · Irinovka · Kokorevo

Finsky Zaliv · Kronshtadt · Lisiy Nos · KAMENKA · KONNAYA LAHTA · Udelny Park · NOVAYA DEREVNYA · OZERKI · Gorodskoy Sosnovka Park · POLYUSTROVO · A128 · Kornevo · Shcheglovo · Vsevolozhsk

ostrov Kotlin · M10 · E18 · Stadion Kirova · Petropavlovskiy sobor · Ermitazh (Zimniy dvorets) · OKHTA · Staraya · Voeykovo · im. Morozova · Torfyanoy · Shlisselburg · Sinyavino

Nevskaia Guba · A121 · Bol. Izhora · Sosnovyy Bor · Lomonosov · Petrodvorets · AVTOVO · KUPCHINO · OBUHOVO · Novosergievka · Razmetelevo · M18 · Chernaya · Novaja Ladoga

A120 · P35 · A121 · Nizino · Vladimirovka · Strel'na · LITOVO · PULKOVO · Shushary · Petroslavyanka · Ust-Izhora · im. Sverdlova · Myaglovo · Novosergievka · Dubrovka · Gribone · Kirovsk · A120

Petrovskoye · Razbegaevo · M11 · E20 · GORELOVO · Aleksandrovskaya · M10 · E105 · Metallostroy · Pontonnyy · Yam-Izhora · Pavlovo · Kelkolovo · P41 · Otradnoye · Gory · Puholovo · Mga

Chernaya · Gostilicy · Zaborode · Ropsha · Annino · E95 · M20 · Pushkin · Kolpino · Nikolskoye · Voytolovo · P41

Zaostrove · P35 · Dyatlicy · Gorki · Lagolovo · Russko-Vysockoye · M20 · Krasnoye Selo · Pavlovsk · Krasny Bor · Pustynka · Leze · Ivanovo · A120

Cheremykino · M11 · E20 · Vitino · Kipen · Kuyduzi · Skvoricy · Tajcy · Kommunar · Annolovo · Ulyanovka

Pudost · Romanovka · Lukashi · Kobralovo · Fornosovo · Sablino · Nurma

Volgovo · A120 · Vohonovo · Kolpany · Bol. Tyaglino · M20 · Gatchina · Sabry · Semrino · Pogi · A120 · Eglizi · Tosno · M10 · E105

N · Volosovo · Luga · Novgorod

0 · 5 · 10 · km

0 · 200 · 400 · 600 · m

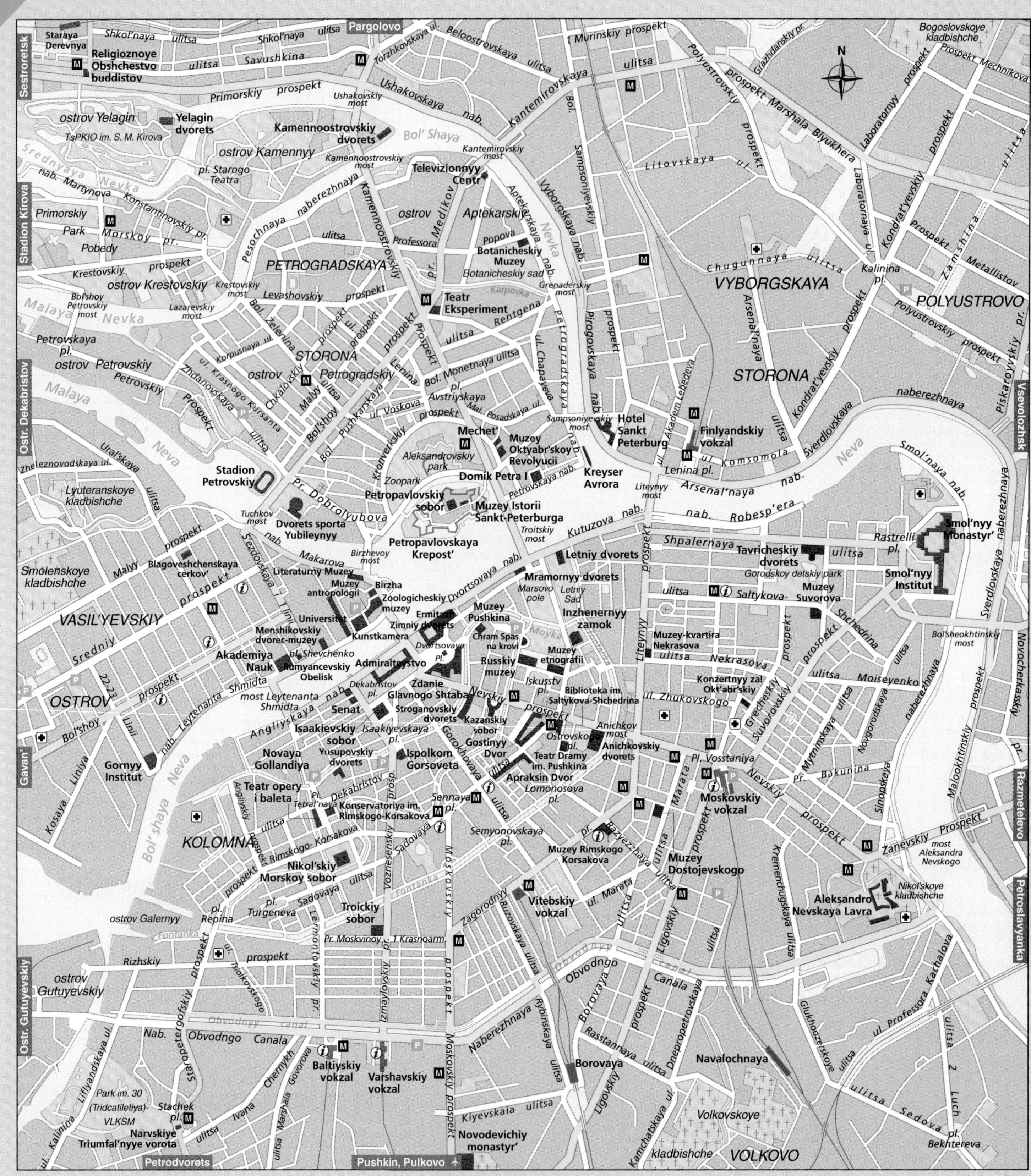

Pargolovo
Sestroretsk
Stadion Kirova
Ostr. Dekabristov
Gavan'
Ostr. Gutuyevskiy
Petrodvorets
Pushkin, Pulkovo
Vsevolozhsk
Razmetelevo
Petroslavyanka
Staraya Derevnya
Religioznoye Obshchestvo buddistov
Shkol'naya ulitsa
Savushkina ulitsa
Primorskiy prospekt
Ushakovskiy most
Ushakovskaya nab.
Torzhkovskaya ul.
Beloostrovskaya ulitsa
1 Murinskiy prospekt
Bogoslovskoye kladbishche
Grazhdanskiy pr.
Polyustrovskiy prospekt
Prospekt Marshala Blyukhera
Prospekt Mechnikova
Laboratornyy prospekt
ostrov Yelagin
Yelagin dvorets
TsPKIO im. S. M. Kirova
Kamennoostrovskiy dvorets
ostrov Kamennyy
Kamennoostrovskiy most
Kantemirovskiy most
Kantemirovskaya ulitsa
Litovskaya ul.
pl. Starogo Teatra
Televizionnyy Centr
nab. Martynova
Srednyaya Nevka
Konstantinovskiy pr.
Primorskiy Park Pobedy
Morskoy pr.
Pesochnaya naberezhnaya
Kamennoostrovskiy prospekt
ostrov Aptekarskiy
pr. Medikov
Professora Popova
Botanicheskiy Muzey
Botanicheskiy sad
Sampsoniyevskiy prospekt
Vyborgskaya nab.
Kondrat'yevskiy prospekt
Chugunnaya ulitsa
Kalinina pl.
VYBORGSKAYA
POLYUSTROVO
Metallistov
Polyustrovskiy prospekt
Krestovskiy prospekt
ostrov Krestovskiy
Krestovskiy most
Bol'shoy Petrovskiy most
Lazarevskiy most
Malaya Nevka
PETROGRADSKAYA
Levashovskiy prospekt
Teatr Eksperiment
Karpovka
Grenaderskiy most
Rentgena
Pirogovskaya nab.
Petrogradskaya
ul. Chapayeva
Arsenal'naya
STORONA
Petrovskaya pl.
ostrov Petrovskiy
Petrovskiy prospekt
Korpusnaya ul.
Bol. Zelenina
ostrov Petrogradskiy
Chkalovskiy
Malyy
Bol'shoy
Lenina
Bol. Monetnaya ulitsa
Avstriyskaya pl.
ul. Voskova
Mal. Posadskaya ul.
Kronverkskiy prospekt
Zhdanovskaya
Piskarovskiy pr.
Sverdlovskaya naberezhnaya
Sampsoniyevskiy most
Hotel Sankt Peterburg
Finlyandskiy vokzal
ul. Akadem Lebedeva
Komsomola
Lenina pl.
Mechet'
Muzey Oktyabr'skoy Revolyucii
Aleksandrovskiy park
Stadion Petrovskiy
Zheleznovodskaya ul.
Ural'skaya
Neva
Domik Petra I
Kreyser Avrora
Petrovskaya nab.
Liteynyy most
Arsenal'naya nab.
Smol'naya nab.
Lyuteranskoye kladbishche
Zoopark
Petropavlovskiy sobor
Muzey Istorii Sankt-Peterburga
Pr. Dobrolyubova
Tuchkov most
Dvorets sporta Yubileynyy
nab. Robesp'era
Smol'nyy Monastyr'
Rastrelli pl.
Troitskiy most
Kutuzova nab.
Shpalernaya ulitsa
Tavricheskiy dvorets
Gorodskoy detskiy park
Smol'nyy Institut
Smolenskoye kladbishche
Blagoveshchenskaya cerkov'
Makarova nab.
Birzhevoy most
Petropavlovskaya Krepost'
Letniy dvorets
Literaturny Muzey
Mramornyy dvorets
Marsovo pole
Letniy Sad
Saltykova-Shchedrina ulitsa
Muzey Suvorova
Muzey antropologii
Birzha
Zoologicheskiy muzey
Dvortsovaya nab.
Ermitazh
Zimniy dvorets
Muzey Pushkina
Inzhenernyy zamok
VASIL'YEVSKIY
Universitet
Menshikovskiy dvorec-muzey
Kunstkamera
Chram Spas na krovi
Moyka
Muzey etnografii
Muzey-kvartira Nekrasova
Nekrasova ulitsa
Bol'sheokhtinskiy most
Srednyy prospekt
Akademiya Nauk
pl. Shevchenko
Rumyancevskiy Obelisk
Admiraltejstvo
Dvortsovaya pl.
Russkiy muzey
Iskusstv pl.
Liteynyy prospekt
Konzertnyy zal Okt'abr'skiy
Moiseyenko
Novocherkasskiy prospekt
Malookhtinskiy pr.
OSTROV
Linii
most Leytenanta Shmidta
nab. Leytenanta Shmidta
Angliyskaya nab.
Dekabristov pl.
Senat
Zdanie Glavnogo Shtaba
Stroganovskiy dvorets
Nevskiy prospekt
Biblioteka im. Saltykova-Shchedrina
ul. Zhukovskogo
Grecheskiy
Suvorovskiy
Mytninskaya
Novgorodskaya
Bol'shoy prospekt
Isaakievskiy sobor
Isaakiyevskaya pl.
Kazanskiy sobor
Gostinyy Dvor
Ostrovskogo pl.
Anichkov most
Anichkovskiy dvorets
Pl. Vosstaniya
Bakunina
Novaya Gollandiya
Yusupovskiy dvorets
Ispolkom Gorsoveta
Teatr Dramy im. Pushkina
Apraksin Dvor
Lomonosova pl.
Moskovskiy vokzal
Gornyy Institut
Teatr opery i baleta
Teatral'naya pl.
Konservatoriya im. Rimskogo-Korsakova
Sennaya pl.
Gorokhovaya
Semyonovskaya pl.
Marata
Rimskogo-Korsakova
Muzey Rimskogo Korsakova
Muzey Dostojevskogo
Razyezzhaya
Kremenchugskaya ulitsa
Zanevskiy Prospekt
most Aleksandra Nevskogo
KOLOMNA
Nikol'skiy Morskoy sobor
Sadovaya
Voznesenskiy prosp.
Fontanka
Zagorodnyy
Vitebskiy vokzal
ul. Marata
Ligovskiy
Nikol'skoye kladbishche
Aleksandro Nevskaya Lavra
ostrov Galernyy
pl. Repina
pl. Turgeneva
Troickiy sobor
Pr. Moskvinoy
1 Krasnoarm.
Lermontovskiy pr.
Izmaylovskiy
Moskovskiy prospekt
Ruzovskaya ulitsa
Obvodnyy canal
Obvodngo Canala
Rizhskiy prospekt
Sinopskaya
ostrov Gutuyevskiy
Staropetergofskiy prospekt
Nab. Obvodngo Canala
Baltiyskiy vokzal
Varshavskiy vokzal
Naberezhnaya
Rybinskaya ulitsa
Borovaya
Rasstannaya ulitsa
Dnepropetrovskaya
Navalochnaya
Glukhoozerskoye
ul. Professora Kachalova
Liflyandskaya ul.
Chernykh
Ivana
Park im. 30 (Tridcatiletiya)-VLKSM
Stachek pl.
Narvskiye Triumfal'nyye vorota
Kiyevskaia ulitsa
Novodevichiy monastyr'
Kamchatskaya ul.
Volkovskoye kladbishche
VOLKOVO
Sedova ulitsa
2 Luch
pl. Bekhtereva
N

0 400 800 1200
m

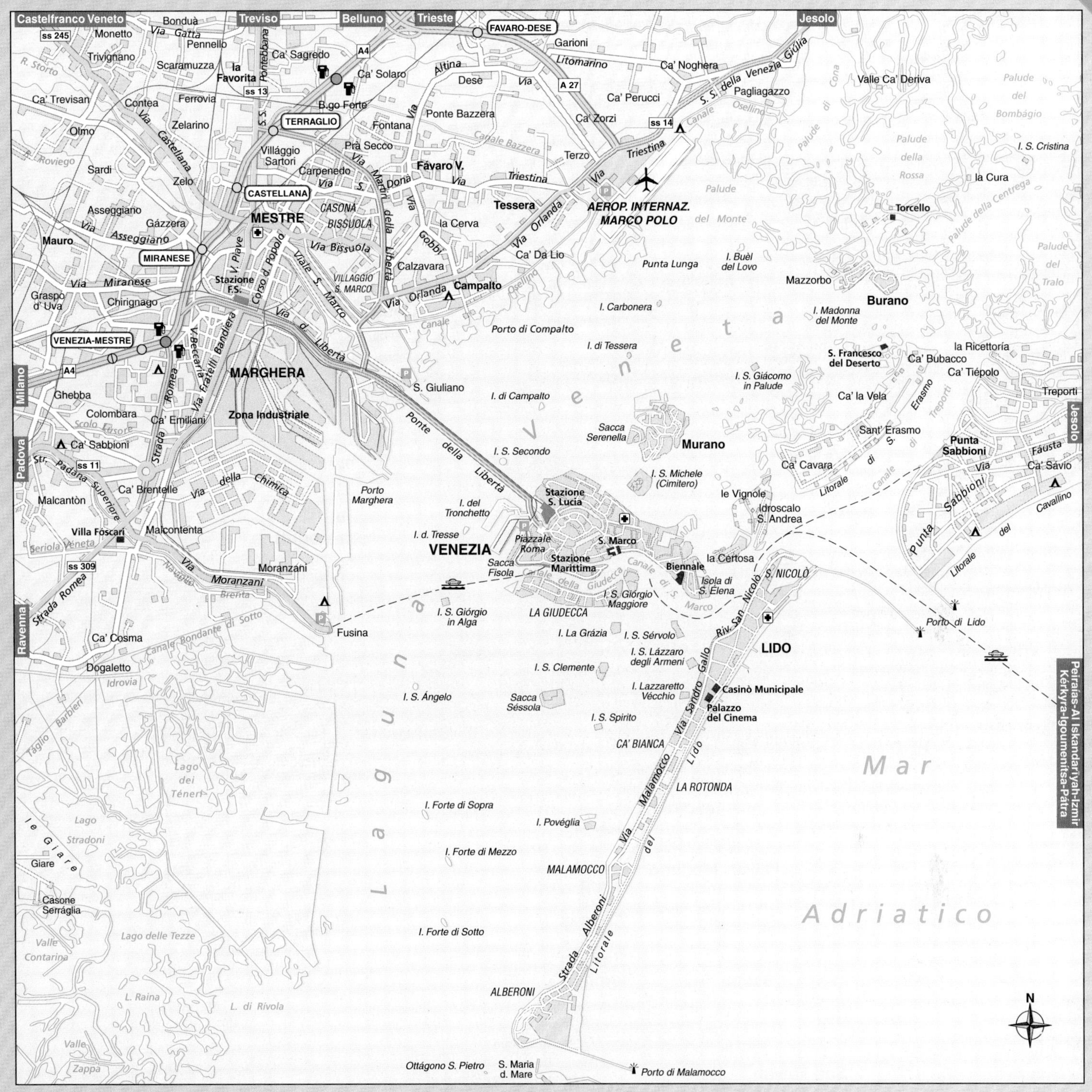

Castelfranco Veneto · Bonduà · Treviso · Belluno · Trieste · Jesolo
ss 245 · Monetto · Via Gatta · Pennello
R. Storto · Trivignano · Scaramuzza · Ponte Bazzera · Ca' Sagredo · Ca' Solaro · Garioni · Litomarino · Ca' Noghera · Valle Ca' Deriva · Palude del Bombágio
Ca' Trevisan · Contea · Ferrovia · la FAVORITA · ss 13 · B.go Forte · A4 · Altina · Dese · Via A 27 · Ca' Perucci · Ca' Zorzi · Pagliagazzo · I. S. Cristina
Olmo · Zelarino · Sardi · TERRAGLIO · Prà Secco · Fontana · Ponte Bazzera · ss 14 · Terzo · Triestina · Palude della Rossa · la Cura · Palude
Mauro · Villággio Sartori · Carpenedo · Via S. Dona · Triestina · Torcello · Palude della Centrega
MESTRE · CASTELLANA · CASONA BISSUOLA · Favaro V. · Tessera · AEROP. INTERNAZ. MARCO POLO · del Monte · Palude del Tralo
MIRANESE · Via Bissuola · la Cerva · Via Orlanda · Ca' Da Lio · Punta Lunga · I. Buèl del Lovo · Mazzorbo · I. Madonna del Monte · Burano · la Ricettória
Graspo d' Uva · Chirignago · Stazione F.S. · VILLÁGGIO S. MARCO · Campalto · Via Orlanda · Porto di Compalto · I. Carbonera · I. di Tessera · I. S. Giácomo in Palude · S. Francesco del Deserto · Ca' Bubacco · Ca' Tiépolo · Treporti
Via Miranese · VENEZIA-MESTRE · A4 · Zona Industriale · S. Giuliano · I. di Campalto · Sacca Serenella · Murano · I. S. Michele (Cimitero) · Ca' la Vela · Sant' Erasmo · Punta Sabbioni · Fáusta · Ca' Sávio
Ghebba · Colombara · Ca' Emiliáni · Ponte della Libertà · I. S. Secondo · le Vignole · Ca' Cavara · Idroscalo S. Andrea · Cavallino
Ca' Sabbioni · Via della Chimica · Ca' Brentelle · Porto Marghera · I. del Tronchetto · Stazione S. Lucia · S. Marco · la Certosa · S. Nicolò · Porto di Lido
Malcantòn · ss 11 · Malcontenta · I. d. Tresse · VENEZIA · Piazzale Roma · Biennale · Isola di S. Elena · Riv. San Nicolò
Villa Foscari · Moranzani · Stazione Marittima · S. Giórgio Maggiore · Casino Municipale · LIDO
ss 309 · Moranzani · Brenta · Sacca Fisola · LA GIUDECCA · I. S. Giórgio in Alga · I. La Grázia · I. S. Sérvolo · I. S. Lázzaro degli Armeni · Palazzo del Cinema
Ca' Cosma · Fusina · I. S. Ángelo · Sacca Séssola · I. S. Clemente · I. S. Spirito · I. Lazzaretto Vécchio · CA' BIANCA
Dogaletto · Idrovia · Lago dei Téneri · I. Forte di Sopra · I. Povéglia · LA ROTONDA
le Giare · Lago Stradoni · I. Forte di Mezzo · MALAMOCCO · Mar Adriatico
Giare · Casone Serráglia · Valle Contarina · Lago delle Tezze · I. Forte di Sotto
L. Raina · L. di Rívola · ALBERONI · Ottágono S. Pietro · S. Maria d. Mare · Porto di Malamocco
Valle Zappa

Milano · Padova · Ravenna · Strada Romea · Strada Padana Superiore · Scolo Fiser · Seriola Veneta · Canale Bondante di Sotto

Peiraias-Al Iskandariyah-Izmir
Kérkyra-Igoumenítsa-Pátra

Jesolo

0 1 2 3
km

N

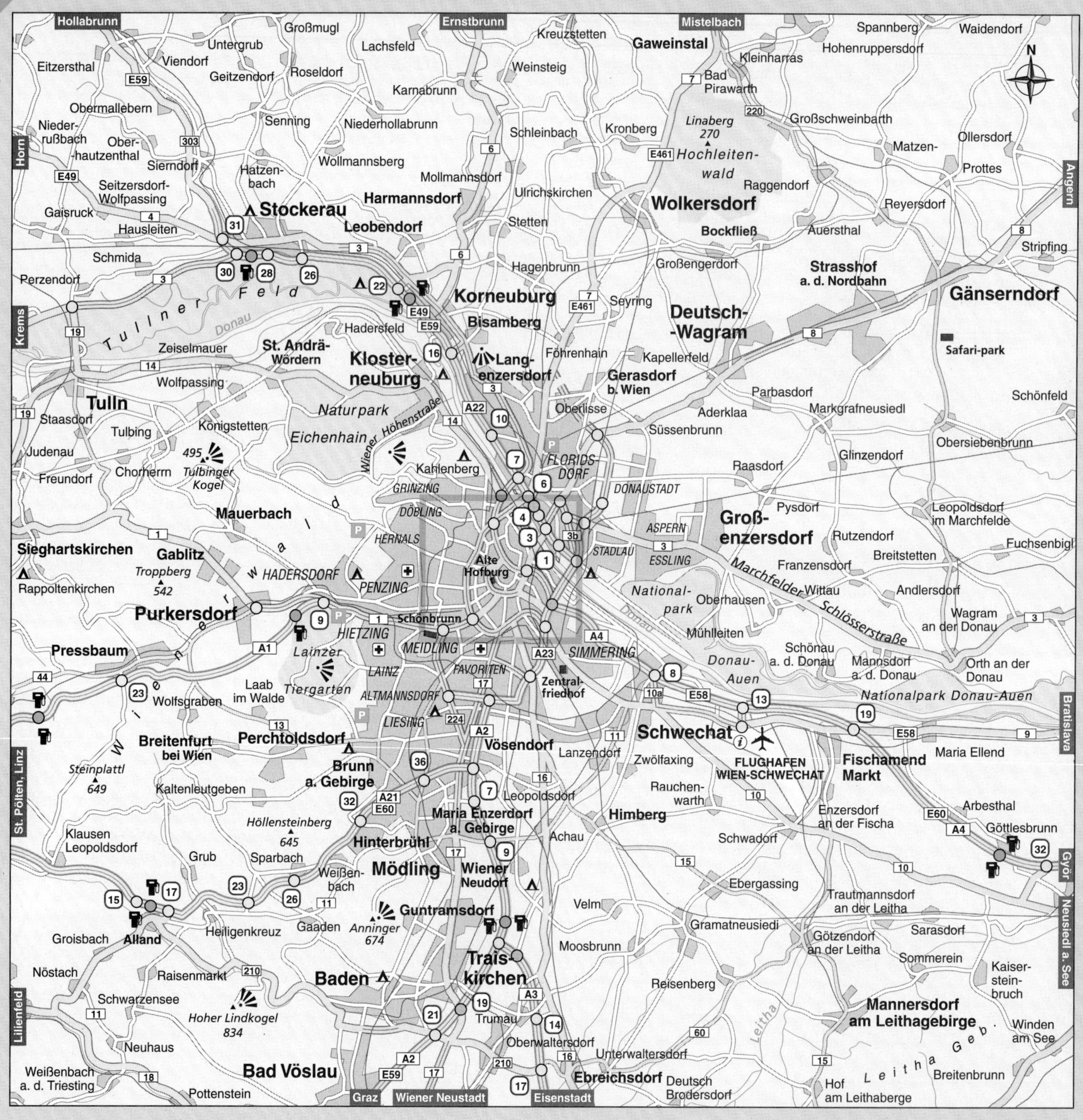

Großmugl
Lachsfeld
Kreuzstetten
Gaweinstal
Spannberg
Waidendorf

Untergrub
Weinsteig
Kleinharras
Hohenrupersdorf

Eitzersthal
Viendorf
Geitzendorf
Roseldorf
Bad
Pirawarth

Obermallebern
Karnabrunn
Linaberg
270
Großschweinbarth
Matzen-

Nieder-
rußbach
Ober-
hautzenthal
Senning
Niederhollabrunn
Schleinbach
Kronberg
Hochleiten-
wald
Raggendorf
Reyersdorf
Ollersdorf
Prottes

Gaisruck
Sierndorf
Hatzen-
bach
Wollmannsberg
Ulrichskirchen
Stetten
Wolkersdorf
Strasshof
a. d. Nordbahn

Seitzersdorf-
Wolfpassing
Stockerau
Leobendorf
Mollmannsdorf
Hagenbrunn
Bockfließ
Auersthal
Stripfing

Hausleiten
Schmida
Korneuburg
Großengersdorf
Gänserndorf

Perzendorf
Donau
Hadersfeld
Bisamberg
Seyring
Deutsch-
Wagram
Safari-park

Zeiselmauer
St. Andrä-
Wördern
Klosterneuburg
Lang-
enzersdorf
Föhrenhain
Gerasdorf
b. Wien
Oberlisse
Parbasdorf
Schönfeld

Tulln
Wolfpassing
Naturpark
Eichenhain
Kahlenberg
Florids-
dorf
Donaustadt
Aderklaa
Süssenbrunn
Markgrafneusiedl
Obersiebenbrunn

Staasdorf
Tulbing
Königstetten
Chorherrn
Tulbinger
Kogel
495
Grinzing
Döbling
Groß-
enzersdorf
Raasdorf
Glinzendorf

Judenau
Freundorf
Mauerbach
Hernals
Aspern
Essling
Pysdorf
Leopoldsdorf
im Marchfelde
Fuchsenbigl

Sieghartskirchen
Gablitz
Troppberg
542
Hadersdorf
Penzing
Alte
Hofburg
Stadlau
National-
park
Oberhausen
Franzensdorf
Breitstetten
Andlersdorf

Rappoltenkirchen
Purkersdorf
Hietzing
Schönbrunn
Meidling
Lainz
Marchfelder
Schlösserstraße
Mühlleiten
Schönau
a. d. Donau
Mannsdorf
a. d. Donau
Wagram
an der Donau

Pressbaum
Lainzer
Tiergarten
Altmannsdorf
Favoriten
Simmering
Zentral-
friedhof
Donau-
Auen
Orth an der
Donau
Nationalpark Donau-Auen

Wolfsgraben
Laab
im Walde
Liesing
Schwechat
Fischamend
Markt
Maria Ellend
Bratislava

Breitenfurt
bei Wien
Perchtoldsdorf
Vösendorf
Lanzendorf
Flughafen
Wien-Schwechat
Enzersdorf
an der Fischa
Arbesthal
Göttlesbrunn

Steinplattl
649
Kaltenleutgeben
Brunn
a. Gebirge
Leopoldsdorf
Zwölfaxing
Rauchen-
warth
Schwadorf
Trautmannsdorf
an der Leitha
Györ

Klausen
Leopoldsdorf
Grub
Höllensteinberg
645
Sparbach
Hinterbrühl
Maria Enzersdorf
a. Gebirge
Mödling
Wiener
Neudorf
Himberg
Achau
Gramatneusiedl
Götzendorf
an der Leitha
Sarasdorf
Sommerein
Kaiser-
stein-
bruch
Neusiedl a. See

Groisbach
Alland
Heiligenkreuz
Gaaden
Weißen-
bach
Anninger
674
Guntramsdorf
Velm
Moosbrunn
Reisenberg
Mannersdorf
am Leithagebirge
Winden
am See

Nöstach
Raisenmarkt
Baden
Traiskirchen
Trumau
Ebergassing
Hof
am Leithaberge
Breitenbrunn

Schwarzensee
Hoher Lindkogel
834
Oberwaltersdorf
Deutsch
Brodersdorf
Leitha Geb.

Neuhaus
Bad Vöslau
Ebreichsdorf
Unterwaltersdorf

Weißenbach
a. d. Triesting
Pottenstein

0   3   6
km

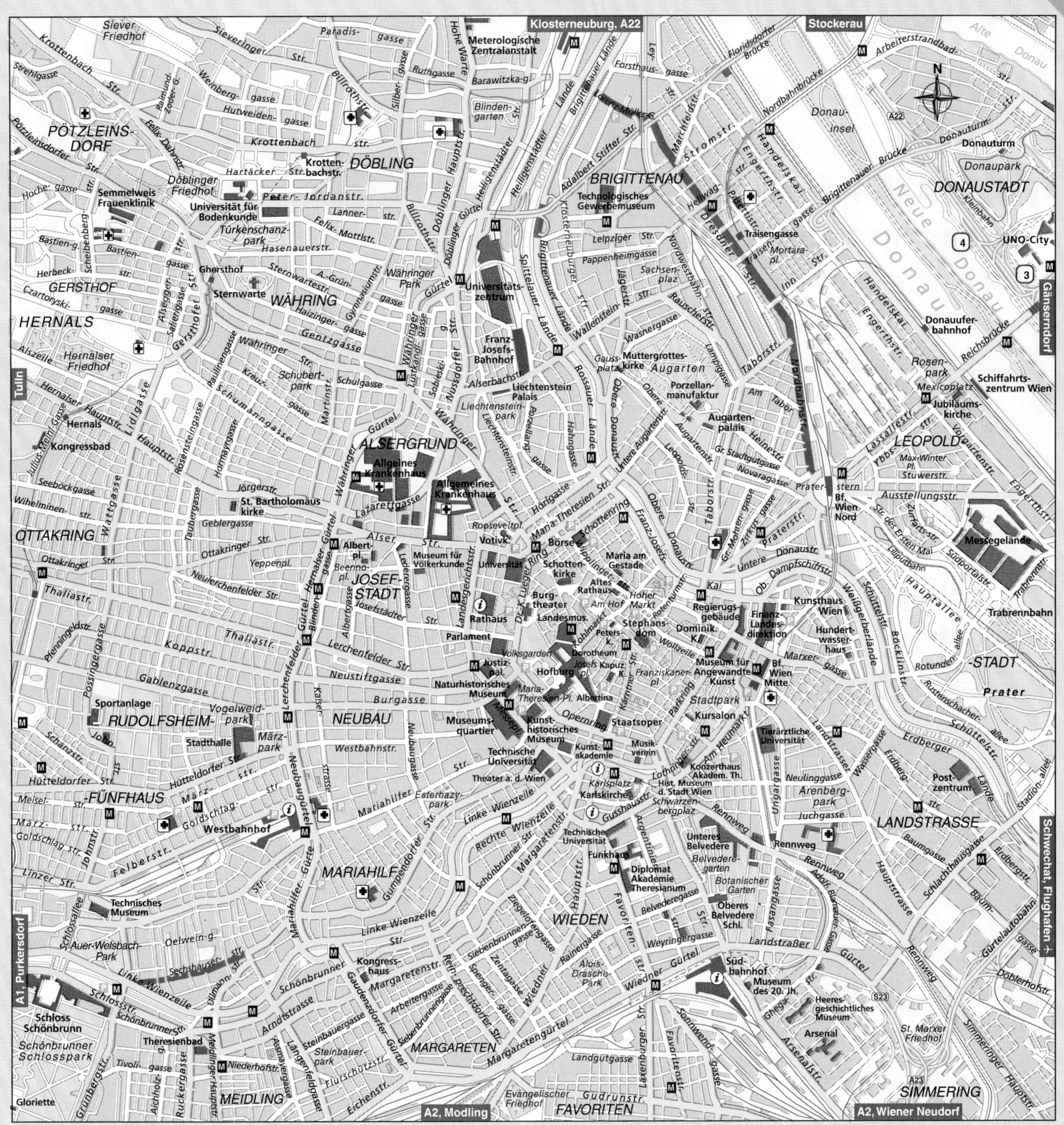
Klosterneuburg, A22
Stockerau
Tulln
A1, Purkersdorf
A2, Modling
A2, Wiener Neudorf
Schwechat, Flughafen
Gänserndorf
Alte Donau
Sievering Friedhof
Sieveringer Str.
Krottenbach Str.
Strehlgasse
Paradis- gasse
Hohe Warte
Meterologische Zentralanstalt
Ruthgasse
Barawitzka-g.
Blinden- garten
Forsthaus- gasse
Floridsdorfer Brücke
Arbeiterstrandbad- str.
Donauinsel
Nordbahnbrücke
Donauturm
Donaupark
DONAUSTADT
Neue Donau
Donau
UNO-City
PÖTZLEINSDORF
Pötzleinsdorfer Str.
Weinberg- gasse
Hutweiden- gasse
Krottenbach str.
Krotten- bachstr.
DÖBLING
Döblinger Friedhof
Semmelweis Frauenklinik
Universität für Bodenkunde
Peter- Jordanstr.
Türkenschanz- park
Hasenauerstr.
Felix- Mottlstr.
Billrothstr.
Döblinger Hauptstr.
Döblinger Gürtel
Heiligenstädter Str.
Heiligenstädter Lände
Brigittenauer Lände
Spittelauer Lände
Adalbert Stifter Str.
Klosterneuburger Str.
Marchfeldstr.
Stromstr.
Handelskai
Engerthstr.
BRIGITTENAU
Technologisches Gewerbemuseum
Dresdner Str.
Traisengasse
Brigittenauer Brücke
Gersthof
Sternwarte
Sternwartestr.
WÄHRING
Währinger Park
Universitätszentrum
Lelpziger Str.
Pappenheimgasse
Sachsen- platz
Rauscherstr.
Wallensteinstr.
Wasnergasse
Nordwestbahnstr.
Donauufer- bahnhof
Reichsbrücke
GERSTHOF
HERNALS
Gentzgasse
Währinger Str.
Schubert- park
Schulgasse
Franz- Josefs- Bahnhof
Gauss- platz
Muttergrottes- kirche
Augarten
Taborstr.
Nordbahnstr.
Rosen- park
Mexicoplatz
Schiffahrts- zentrum Wien
Jubiläums- kirche
Hernalser Friedhof
Hernalser Hauptstr.
Hernals
Kongressbad
Alserbachstr.
Liechtenstein Palais
Liechtenstein- park
Porzellangasse
Rossauer Lände
Obere Donaustr.
Porzellan- manufaktur
Augarten- palais
Heinestr.
LEOPOLDSTADT
Lassallestr.
Vorgartenstr.
Engerthstr.
Max-Winter Pl.
Stuwerstr.
Ausstellungsstr.
Messegelände
ALSERGRUND
Allgeines Krankenhaus
Allgemeines Krankenhaus
Lazarettgasse
Jörgerstr.
St. Bartholomäus kirche
Geblergasse
Währinger Gürtel
Rooseveltpl.
Votivk.
Börse
Schottenring
Maria-Theresien Str.
Franz-Josefs- Kai
Praterstr.
Praterstern
Bf. Wien Nord
Str. des Ersten Mai
Südportalstr.
Hauptallee
Trabrennbahn
OTTAKRING
Ottakringer Str.
Yeppenpl.
Neulerchenfelder Str.
Thaliastr.
Alser Str.
Albert- pl.
Museum für Völkerkunde
Universität
Schotten- kirche
Maria am Gestade
Altes Rathaus
Hoher Markt
Untere Donaustr.
Kunsthaus Wien
Hundert- wasser- haus
Weißgerberlände
Rotunden- allee
Prater
JOSEFSTADT
Josefstädter Str.
Landesgerichtsstr.
Rathaus
Burg- theater
Am Hof
Landesmus.
Stephans- dom
Regierugs- gebäude
Dominik. K.
Finanz- Landes- direktion
Parlament
Volksgarten
Peters- k.
Dorotheum
Franziskaner- pl.
Wollzeile
Museum für Angewandte Kunst
Bf. Wien Mitte
Marxergasse
Koppstr.
Lerchenfelder Str.
Neustiftgasse
Justiz- pal.
Hofburg
Naturhistorisches Museum
Maria- Theresien-Pl.
Albertina
Stadtpark
Kursalon
Gablenzgasse
Burggasse
Sportanlage
RUDOLFSHEIM-FÜNFHAUS
Vogelweid- park
März- park
Stadthalle
NEUBAU
Museums- quartier
Kunst- historisches Museum
Opernring
Staatsoper
Musik- verein
Tierärztliche Universität
Westbahnstr.
Technische Universität
Kunst- akademie
Am Heumarkt
Konzerthaus Akadem. Th.
Neulinggasse
Arenberg- park
Post- zentrum
Erdberger Lände
Hütteldorfer Str.
Theater a. d. Wien
Karlsplatz
Karlskirche
Hist. Museum d. Stadt Wien
Schwarzen- bergplaz
Rennweg
Juchgasse
Mariahilfer Str.
Esterhazy- park
Westbahnhof
Felberstr.
Linke Wienzeile
Rechte Wienzeile
Technische Universität
Unteres Belvedere
Belvedere- garten
LANDSTRASSE
Linzer Str.
MARIAHILF
Gumpendorfer Str.
Funkhaus
Diplomat Akademie Theresianum
Botanischer Garten
Oberes Belvedere Schl.
Technisches Museum
Schlossallee
Auer-Welsbach- Park
Oelwein-g.
Sechshauser- str.
WIEDEN
Favoritenstr.
Belvederegasse
Weyringergasse
Landstraßer Gürtel
Rennweg
Kongress- haus
Margaretenstr.
Siebenbrunnen- gasse
Alois- Drasche- Park
Wiedner Gürtel
Süd- bahnhof
Museum des 20. Jh.
Heeres- geschichtliches Museum
Arsenal
St. Marxer Friedhof
Simmeringer Hauptstr.
Schloss Schönbrunn
Schönbrunner Schlosspark
Theresienbad
Niederhofstr.
Meidlinger Hauptstr.
MARGARETEN
Margaretengürtel
Steinbauer- park
Landgutgasse
Sonnwendgasse
Arsenalstr.
SIMMERING
Gloriette
Tivoli- gasse
MEIDLING
Evangelischer Friedhof
Gudrunstr.
FAVORITEN
Laxenburger Str.
Grünbergstr.

0 300 600 900
m

INDEX OF NAMES
INDICE DEI NOMI
ÍNDICE DE TOPÓNIMOS
INDEX DES NOMS
NAMENVERZEICHNIS

How to use the index • Avvertenze per la ricerca
Instrucciones para la consulta • Notices pour la recherche
Erläuterungen des Suchsystems

The index lists the place names, tourist sites, main tunnels and passes contained in the atlas, followed by the abbreviation of the country name to which they belong. All names contained in two adjoining pages are referenced to the even page number.

L'indice elenca i toponimi dei centri abitati, dei siti turistici, dei principali tunnel e passi presenti nell'atlante, accompagnati dalla sigla della nazione di appartenenza. Tutti i nomi contenuti in due pagine affiancate sono riferiti alla pagina di numero pari.

El índice presenta los topónimos de localidades, lugares turísticos, principales túneles y puertos de montaña que figuran en el atlas, seguidos de la sigla que indica el País de pertenencia. Todos los nombres contenidos en dos páginas juntas éstan referidos a la página de número par.

L'index récense les noms des localités, sites touristiques, principales tunnels et cols contenus dans l'atlas, suivis par le sigle qui indique le Pays d'appartenance. Tous les noms contenus dans deux pages l'une à côté de l'autre sont rapportés à la page avec nombre pair.

Der Index enthält die im Atlas vorhandenen Ortsnamen, Sehenswürdigkeiten, wichtigsten Tunnels und Pässe, von dem zugehörigen Staatskennzeichen gefolgt. Alle in zwei anliegenden Seiten enthaltenen Namen sind auf die Seite mit gerader Zahl bezogen.

A

Å [N] 192 B5
Aabenraa [DK] 156 C4
Aachen [D] 30 F4
Aakirkeby [DK] 158 E4
Aalborg [DK] 160 D4
Aalburg [NL] 16 D6
Aalen [D] 60 B2
Aalsmane [LV] 200 F4
Aalsmeer [NL] 16 D4
Aalst (Alost) [B] 28 H2
Aalten [NL] 16 G6
Aalter [B] 28 G2
Äänekoski [FIN] 186 G3
Aapajärvi [FIN] 196 D6
Aarau [CH] 58 E5
Aarberg [CH] 58 D5
Aarburg [CH] 58 E5
Aareavaraa [S] 192 G5
Aareschlucht [CH] 70 F1
Aars [DK] 160 D4
Aarschot [B] 30 D4
Aavasaksa [FIN] 196 B8
Aba [H] 76 B2
Abades [E] 88 F4
Abadín [E] 78 E2
Abádszalók [H] 64 F6
A Baña [E] 78 B2
Abanades [E] 90 B5
Abanilla [E] 104 C2
Abano Terme [I] 110 G1
Abarán [E] 104 C2
Abárzuza [E] 84 A4
Abaújszántó [H] 64 G4
Abbadia San Salvatore [I] 114 G2
Abbasanta [I] 118 C4
Abbaye d'Orval [B] 44 D2
Abbekås [S] 158 C3
Abbeville [F] 28 D4
Abbeydorney [IRL] 4 B3
Abbeyfeale [IRL] 4 C3
Abbeyleix [IRL] 4 E3
Abbiategrasso [I] 70 F5
Abborrträsk [S] 190 H3
Abdürrahim [TR] 130 H3
Abejar [E] 90 B2
Abela [P] 94 C2
Abelnes [N] 164 C5
Abelvær [N] 190 C4
Abenberg [D] 46 G5
Abenójar [E] 96 D4
Abensberg [D] 60 E2
Aberaeron [GB] 10 B6
Aberchirder [GB] 6 F5
Aberdare [GB] 12 F2
Aberdeen [GB] 6 F6
Aberfeldy [GB] 8 E1
Abergavenny [GB] 12 F2
Abergele [GB] 10 C4
Aberlour [GB] 6 E5
Abersoch [GB] 10 B4
Aberystwyth [GB] 10 B6
Abetone [I] 110 E4
Abide [TR] 130 H5
Abide [TR] 144 G2
Abiego [E] 90 G3
Abild [S] 162 B4
Abingdon [GB] 12 H3
Abisko [S] 192 E4
Abiúl [P] 86 D2
Abja–Paluoja [EST] 200 E3
Abla [E] 102 F4
Ablanitsa [BG] 148 B4
Ablis [F] 42 E4
Åbo [S] 190 C6
Åbo / Turku [FIN] 176 D4
Åboland [S] 166 C5
Abondance [F] 70 C2
Abony [H] 76 E2
Åbosjö [S] 190 G6
Aboyne [GB] 6 F6
Abrantes [P] 86 D4
Abraur [S] 190 G2
Abreschviller [F] 44 G5
Abric d'Ermites [E] 92 A6
Abriès [F] 70 C6
Abrigo de la Peña del Escrito [E] 98 C3
Abtei [A] 74 B3
Abtenau [A] 60 H6
Abtshagen [D] 20 D3
Åby [S] 168 B5
Åby [S] 162 C4
Åby [S] 162 G5
Åbybro [DK] 160 D3
Åbyn [S] 198 B4
A Cañiza [E] 78 C5
Acate [I] 126 F5
Accadia [I] 120 G2
Acceglio [I] 108 E2
Accettura [I] 120 H4
Acciaroli [I] 120 F5
Accous [F] 84 D4
Accumoli [I] 116 B3
Acedera [E] 96 B3
Acedo [E] 82 H6
Acerenza [I] 120 H3
Acerno [I] 120 F3
Acerra [I] 120 E3
Aceuchal [E] 94 G2
Acey, Abbaye d'– [F] 58 A4
Acharnés [GR] 134 C6
Achenkirch [A] 60 E6
Achern [D] 58 F1
Acheux–en–Amiénois [F] 28 E4
Achílleio [GR] 132 G2
Achilleum [TR] 130 H5
Achim [D] 18 E5
Achinós [GR] 130 C3
Achladochóri [GR] 130 B2
Achladókampos [GR] 136 E2
Achleiten [A] 62 B4
Achnasheen [GB] 6 D4
Aci Castello [I] 126 G3
Acinipo [E] 102 A4
Acıpayam [TR] 144 G6
Acireale [I] 126 G3
Aci Trezza [I] 126 G3
A Coruña / La Coruña [E] 78 C2
Acqua Doria [F] 114 A5
Acquafredda, Castello di– [I] 118 C7
Acqualagna [I] 112 B6
Acquanegra sul Chiese [I] 110 E1
Acquapendente [I] 114 G3
Acquaro [I] 124 D6
Acquasanta Terme [I] 116 C3
Acquasparta [I] 116 A3
Acquaviva delle Fonti [I] 122 D3
Acquedolci [I] 126 F2
Acqui Terme [I] 108 H2
Acri [I] 124 D4
Acropolis Iberica [E] 90 F5
Ács [H] 64 A6
Acsa [H] 64 D5
Ada [YU] 76 E5
Adaköy [TR] 142 E3
Adalsbruk [N] 172 C3
Ådalsvollen [N] 190 C6
Adámas [GR] 138 D4
Adamclisi [RO] 206 D6
Adamuz [E] 96 C6
Adanero [E] 88 E3
Adapazari [TR] 146 H3
Adare [IRL] 4 C3
Adaševci [YU] 154 E2
Adelboden [CH] 70 D2
Adelebsen [D] 32 F4
Adelfia [I] 122 E3
Adelfoí [GR] 134 C3
Adelsheim [D] 46 D5
Adelsried [D] 60 C3
Ademuz [E] 98 D2
Adenau [D] 30 G6
Adjud [RO] 206 D5
Admont [A] 62 C6
Ådneram [N] 164 C3
Adolfsström [S] 190 F2
Adony [H] 76 C2
Adorf [D] 48 C3
Adra [E] 102 F5
Adradas [E] 90 B4
Adrall [E] 92 D1
Adramittium Thebe [TR] 144 C1
Adrano [I] 126 F3
Ádria [I] 110 G2
Adrigole [IRL] 4 B5
A. Drosiní [GR] 130 F2
Adunații–Copăceni [RO] 148 C1
Adutiškis [LT] 202 H4
Æerøskobing [DK] 156 D4
Aegviidu [EST] 200 E1
Aerinó [GR] 132 H2
Aerzen [D] 32 F3
Aesoo [EST] 200 E2
A Estrada [E] 78 C3
Aetópetra [GR] 132 C1
Aetós [GR] 128 E4
Aetós [GR] 132 D5
Afaía [GR] 136 G1
Afántou [GR] 142 E4
Åfarnes [N] 180 E3
Afife [P] 78 A6
Afiónas [GR] 132 A2
Aflenz [A] 62 D6
A Fonsagrada [E] 78 F3
Afoss [N] 164 G3
Africo [I] 124 D7
Afsluitdijk [NL] 16 E2
Áfysos [GR] 134 A3
Áfytos [GR] 130 B6
Ağaçbeylı [TR] 144 G3
Ağaçlı [TR] 146 E2
Agaete [E] 100 C5
Agalás [GR] 136 A2
Ag. Athanásios [GR] 128 H4
Agay [F] 108 E5
Agazzano [I] 110 C2
Agde [F] 106 E5
Ag. Dimítrios [GR] 132 F4
Ag. Dionýsios [GR] 128 G6
Ag. Dionysíou, Moní– [GR] 130 D5
Agen [F] 66 E5
Agéranos [GR] 136 E5
Agerbæk [DK] 156 B2
Ag. Fotiá [GR] 140 G5
Agger [DK] 160 B4
Aggersund [DK] 160 D4
Ággius [I] 118 D2
Aggsbach–Dorf [A] 62 D4
Aggsbach–Markt [A] 62 D4
Aggstein [A] 62 D4
Aggtelek [H] 64 E3
Aghadoe [IRL] 4 B4
Aghleam [IRL] 2 B3
Agiá [GR] 132 H1
Agía Ánna [GR] 134 B4
Agía Ánna [GR] 132 H5
Agía Efimía [GR] 132 C6
Agía Galíni [GR] 140 D5
Agía Marína [GR] 136 G1
Agia Marína [GR] 142 B2
Agía Paraskeví [GR] 134 G2
Agia Pelagía [GR] 136 F6
Agiásmata [GR] 134 G4
Agíasos [GR] 134 H2
Agía Triáda [GR] 132 D4
Ágía Triáda [GR] 136 C1
Ágía Triáda [GR] 128 H5
Ágía Varvára [GR] 140 E5
Ág. Ioánnis [GR] 132 H6
Ág. Ioánnis [GR] 142 B4
Agiófyllo [GR] 132 E1
Ágíoi Apóstoli [GR] 136 F5
Ágioi Déka [GR] 140 E5
Agiókampos [GR] 132 H4
Agiókampos [GR] 132 H1
Ágio Pnévma [GR] 130 C3
Ágios Anárgiri [GR] 132 G2
Ágios Andréas [GR] 136 E3
Ágios Antónios [GR] 130 B5
Agios Athanásios [GR] 128 F4
Ágios Charálampos [GR] 130 F3
Ágios Dimítrios [GR] 128 G6
Ágios Dimítrios [GR] 136 F4
Ágios Efstrátios [GR] 134 E1
Ágios Geórgios [GR] 132 F4
Ágios Germanos [GR] 128 E4
Ágios Górdis [GR] 132 B2
Agios Konstantínos [GR] 144 C5
Agios Konstantínos [GR] 132 H4
Ágios Kýrikos [GR] 138 G1
Ágios Léon [GR] 136 A2
Ágios Márkos [GR] 128 H3
Ágios Matthaíos [GR] 132 B2
Ágios Mýron [GR] 140 E5
Ágios Nikítas [GR] 132 C4
Ágios Nikólaos [GR] 132 C2
Ágios Nikólaos [GR] 136 G2
Ágios Nikólaos [GR] 136 E4
Ágios Nikólaos [GR] 140 F4
Ágios Nikólaos [GR] 132 D4
Ágios Nikólaos [GR] 130 C6
Ágios Pétros [GR] 136 E3
Ágios Pétros [GR] 132 C5
Ágios Pétros [GR] 128 G4
Ágios Pródromos [GR] 130 B5
Ágios Theódori [GR] 132 H3
Agios Vlásios [GR] 132 E4
Agira [I] 126 F3
Ag. Kyriakí [GR] 138 H1
Ag. Lávra [GR] 136 D1
Aglen [N] 190 C4
Agliano [I] 108 H2
Agliate [I] 70 G4
Ag. Loukás [GR] 134 C5
Ag. Marína [GR] 132 G4
Ag Marína [GR] 134 C5
Agnánta [GR] 132 D2
Agnanteró [GR] 132 F2
Agnäs [S] 190 H6
Agnita [RO] 206 C5
Agnone [I] 116 E6
Agnone Bagni [I] 126 G4
Agnóntas [GR] 134 B3
Agoitz / Aoiz [E] 84 C4
Agolada [E] 78 C3
Agoncillo [E] 82 H6
Agon–Coutainville [F] 26 D3
Agordo [I] 72 E4
Agost [E] 104 D2
Ag. Panteleímonas [GR] 128 F4
Ag. Pelagía [GR] 140 E4
Agramunt [E] 92 C3
Ágras [GR] 128 F4
Agreda [E] 84 A6
Agreliá [GR] 132 F1
Agriá [GR] 132 H2
Agrigento [I] 126 D4
Agriliá [GR] 132 E5
Agrínio [GR] 132 E5
Agriovótano [GR] 134 B3
Agropoli [I] 120 F4
Ag.Roúmeli [GR] 140 C5
Ågskaret [N] 190 D1
Ag. Stéfanos [GR] 138 E2
Ag. Theódoroi [GR] 136 F1
Ag. Triáda [GR] 140 D5
Ag. Triáda [GR] 134 C6
Agua, Cueva del– [E] 102 F2
Agua Amarga [E] 102 H5
Aguadulce [E] 102 G5
A Guarda / La Guardia [E] 78 A5
A Guarda / La Guardia [E] 96 G2
Aguda [P] 80 B4
A Gudiña [E] 78 D6
Agudo [E] 96 C3
Águeda [P] 80 B5
Agüero [E] 84 C5
Aguiar da Beira [P] 80 D5
Águila, Cuevas del– [E] 88 C5
Aguilafuente [E] 88 F3
Aguilar de Campoo [E] 82 D4
Aguilar de la Frontera [E] 102 C2
Aguilar del Alfambra [E] 98 E1
Águilas [E] 104 B4
Agulo [E] 100 B5
Agurain / Salvatierra [E] 82 H5
Aguzadera [E] 100 H3
Ağva / Yeşilçay [TR] 146 G2
Ahascragh [IRL] 2 D5
Ahat [TR] 144 G3
Ahaus [D] 16 G5
Åheim [N] 180 C4
Ahigal [E] 88 A5
Ahja [EST] 200 F3
Ahlalnen [FIN] 176 C1
Ahlbeck [D] 20 E4
Ahlbeck [D] 20 E3
Ahlen [D] 32 C3
Ahlhorn [D] 18 C6
Ahmetbey [TR] 146 C2
Ahmetli [TR] 144 D3
Ahmovaara [FIN] 188 F1
Ahokylä [FIN] 198 E5
Ahrensbök [D] 18 G3
Ahrensburg [D] 18 G4
Ahrweiler [D] 30 G5
Ähtäri / Etseri [FIN] 186 E4
Ähtävä / Esse [FIN] 198 C6
Ahun [F] 54 H6
Åhus [S] 158 D2
Ahvensalmi [FIN] 188 E4
Ahvenselkä [FIN] 196 E7
Ahverinen [FIN] 188 F2
Aianí [GR] 128 F6
Aibar [E] 84 C4
Aicha [D] 60 H3
Aichach [D] 60 D3
Aiddejavrre [N] 192 G3
Aidenbach [D] 60 G3
Aidone [I] 126 F4
Aigen [A] 62 B3
Aigiáli [GR] 138 G3
Aígina [GR] 136 G2
Aigínio [GR] 128 G5
Aígio [GR] 132 F6
Aigle [CH] 70 C2
Aiglsbach [D] 60 E3
Aignay–le–Duc [F] 56 G2
Aigósthena [GR] 134 B6
Aigre [F] 54 D6
Aigrefeuille [F] 54 C5
Aigrefeuille–sur–Maine [F] 54 C2
Aiguablava [E] 92 G3
Aiguebelle [F] 108 D6
Aiguebelle [F] 70 B4
Aigueperse [F] 68 D1
Aigues–Mortes [F] 106 F4
Aiguevives [F] 54 G2
Aiguilles [F] 70 B6
Aiguillon [F] 66 E5
Aigurande [F] 54 H5
Äijälä [FIN] 186 G3
Ailefroide [F] 70 B6
Aillant–sur–Tholon [F] 56 E1
Aime [F] 70 B4
Ainaži [LV] 200 D4
Ainhoa [F] 84 C2
Ainsa [E] 84 E6
Airaines [F] 28 D4
Airasca [I] 70 D6
Aire [F] 28 E3
Aire–sur–l'Adour [F] 84 E2
Airolo [CH] 70 F2
Airvault [F] 54 E3
Aisey–sur–Seine [F] 56 G2
Aïssey [F] 58 B5
Aisými [GR] 130 G3

Aisy-sur-Armançon [F] 56 F2
Aiterhofen [D] 60 G2
Aitolikó [GR] 132 E5
Aitrach [D] 60 B4
Aittojärvi [FIN] 198 E6
Aittojärvi [FIN] 198 E3
Aiud [RO] 206 B5
Aix-en-Othe [F] 42 H6
Aix-en-Provence [F] 108 B4
Aixe-sur-Vienne [F] 66 G1
Aix-les-Bains [F] 68 H3
Aizanoi [TR] 144 G2
Aizenay [F] 54 B3
Aizkraukle [LV] 200 E5
Aizpute [LV] 200 B5
Ajaccio [F] 114 A5
Ajaureforsen [S] 190 F3
Ajdovščina [SLO] 74 A5
Ajka [H] 74 H2
Ajnovce [YU] 150 D5
Ajos [FIN] 198 C3
Akalan [TR] 146 D2
Akarca [TR] 144 G3
Akarp [S] 158 C3
Äkasjokisuu [FIN] 192 H5
Äkäslompolo [FIN] 192 H5
Akasztó [H] 76 C3
Akçakavak [TR] 142 F3
Akçaova [TR] 142 D1
Akçaova [TR] 146 G2
Akçay [TR] 142 H3
Akçay [TR] 144 C1
Aken [D] 34 C4
Åker [S] 168 C3
Åkersberga [S] 168 E2
Åkersjön [S] 190 D6
Åkers krutbruk [S] 168 C3
Akhisar [TR] 144 D3
Akhtopol [BG] 148 G5
Akkarfjord [N] 196 B2
Akkent [TR] 144 G4
Akköprü [TR] 142 F2
Akköy [TR] 142 C1
Akland [N] 164 F4
Akmeşe [TR] 146 G3
Akmyane [LT] 200 C6
Aknīste [LV] 200 F6
Akonpohja [FIN] 188 F5
Akoúmia [GR] 140 D5
Akpınar [TR] 146 H5
Åkra [N] 170 B5
Akrai [I] 126 G5
Akraifia [GR] 134 B5
Akraífnio [GR] 134 B5
Akranes [IS] 194 B4
Akrapol [TR] 144 C2
Åkre [N] 182 C6
Åkrehamn [N] 164 A2
Akrogiáli [GR] 130 C4
Akropótamos [GR] 130 C4
Akrotíri [GR] 138 F5
Akrovoúni [GR] 130 D3
Aksakal [TR] 146 D5
Aksakovo [BG] 148 F2
Aksaz [TR] 146 C4
Aksdal [N] 164 A1
Akujärvi [FIN] 196 D4
Åkullsjön [S] 198 A5
Akureyri [IS] 194 E3
Akyazı [TR] 146 H3
Ål [N] 170 F3
Ala [I] 72 C5
Ala [S] 168 G5
Alabanda [TR] 144 E6
Alacalı [TR] 146 F2
Alacant / Alicante [E] 104 E2
Alacat [TR] 146 E5
Alaçatı [TR] 134 H5
Alà dei Sardi [I] 118 D3
Ala di Stura [I] 70 C5
Aladzha Manastir [BG] 148 G2
Alaejos [E] 88 D2
Alagna-Valsésia [I] 70 E3
A Lagoa / Campo Lameiro [E] 78 B4
Alagón [E] 90 E3
Alahärmä [FIN] 186 C2
Ala-Honkajoki [FIN] 186 C6
Alajoki [FIN] 198 D5
Alakurtti [RUS] 196 F7
Alakylä [FIN] 192 H5
Alameda [E] 102 C3
Alamedilla [E] 102 F3
Alamilla [E] 96 C4
Ala-Nampa [FIN] 196 D7
Alanäs [S] 190 E5
Alandroal [P] 94 E1
Ålandsbro [S] 184 F4
Alange [E] 94 H2
Alaniemi [FIN] 198 D2
Alanís [E] 94 H4
Alanta [LT] 202 G4
Alap [H] 76 B3
Ala-Paakkola [FIN] 198 C2
Alapitkä [FIN] 188 C1
Alaraz [E] 88 D4
Alarcón [E] 98 B3
Alaşehir [TR] 144 E4
Ålåsen [S] 190 E6
Alássio [I] 108 G4
Alastaro [FIN] 176 E3
Alatoz [E] 98 C5
Alatri [I] 116 C6
Alatskivi [EST] 200 F2
Alavattnet [S] 190 E5
Alaveteli / Nedervetil [FIN] 198 C6
Alavieska [FIN] 198 C5
Ala-Vuokki [FIN] 198 F4
Alavus [FIN] 186 D4
Alba [I] 108 G2
Alba Adriatica [I] 116 D3
Albacete [E] 98 B5
Albacken [S] 184 D3
Alba de Tormes [E] 88 C3
Ålbæk [DK] 160 E2
Alba Fucens [I] 116 C5
Albaida [E] 98 E6
Albaina [E] 82 G5
Alba Iulia [RO] 206 B5
Albaladejo [E] 96 G5
Albalate de Cinca [E] 90 G4
Albalate del Arzobispo [E] 90 E5
Albalate de las Nogueras [E] 98 B1
Albalate de Zorita [E] 98 A1
Alban [F] 106 C3
Albánchez [E] 102 H4
Albano di Lucania [I] 120 H4
Albano Laziale [I] 116 A6
Albaredo d'Adige [I] 110 F1
Albarella [I] 110 H2
Albares [E] 88 H6
Albarracín [E] 98 D1
Albarracín, Cuevas de- [E] 98 D1
Albatana [E] 104 C1
Albena [BG] 148 G2
Albenga [I] 108 G4
Albens [F] 70 A3
Albentosa [E] 98 E3
Alberga [S] 168 B3
Albergaria-a-Velha [P] 80 B5
Alberic [E] 98 E5
Albernoa [P] 94 D3
Alberobello [I] 122 E3
Albersdorf [D] 18 E2
Albert [F] 28 E4
Albertirsa [H] 76 D1
Albertville [F] 70 B3
Albeşti [RO] 148 G1
Albi [F] 106 B2
Albignasego [I] 110 G1
Albisola Marina [I] 108 H3
Albo [F] 114 C2
Albocácer / Albocàsser [E] 98 G2
Albocàsser / Albocácer [E] 98 G2
Alboraia / Alboraya [E] 98 E4
Alboraya / Alboraia [E] 98 E4
Alborea [E] 98 C4
Albox [E] 102 H4
Albrechtice nad Vltou [CZ] 48 F6
Albrechtsburg [A] 62 D4
Albufeira [P] 94 C5
Albujón [E] 104 C4
Albuñol [E] 102 E5
Albuñuelas [E] 102 D4
Alburquerque [E] 86 F5
Alby [S] 162 G6
Alcácer do Sal [P] 94 C1
Alcáçovas [P] 94 D2
Alcadozo [E] 98 B6
Alcafores [P] 86 G3
Alcaide [E] 102 H3
Alcalá de Chivert / Alcalà de Xivert [E] 98 G2
Alcalá de Guadaira [E] 94 G6
Alcalá de Henares [E] 88 G6
Alcalá de la Selva [E] 98 E2
Alcalá del Júcar [E] 98 C5
Alcalá de los Gazules [E] 100 G4
Alcalá del Río [E] 94 G6
Alcalá del Valle [E] 102 A3
Alcalà de Xivert / Alcalá de Chivert [E] 98 G2
Alcalá la Real [E] 102 D3
Álcamo [I] 126 C2
Alcanar [E] 92 A6
Alcanede [P] 86 C4
Alcanena [P] 86 C4
Alcañices [E] 80 G4
Alcañiz [E] 90 F6
Alcántara [E] 86 G4
Alcantara, Gole d'- [I] 124 A8
Alcantarilla [E] 104 C3
Alcaracejos [E] 96 C5
Alcaraz [E] 96 H6
Alcaria Ruiva [P] 94 D4
Alcarràs [E] 90 H5
Alçaşehir [TR] 144 G1
Alcaudete [E] 102 D2
Alcaudete de la Jara [E] 96 D1
Alcázar de San Juan [E] 96 G3
Alcobaça [P] 86 C3
Alcoba de los Montes [E] 96 D3
Alcobendas [E] 88 F5
Alcobertas [P] 86 C3
Alcocèber / Alcossebre [E] 98 G3
Alcocer [E] 90 A6
Alcochete [P] 86 B5
Alcoentre [P] 86 B4
Alcofra [P] 80 C5
Alcoi / Alcoy [E] 104 E1
Alcolea [E] 102 F5
Alcolea del Pinar [E] 90 B4
Alconchel [E] 94 F2
Alcora / l'Alcora [E] 98 F3
Alcorcón [E] 88 F6
Alcorisa [E] 90 F6
Alcossebre / Alcocèber [E] 98 G3
Alcoutim [P] 94 D5
Alcover [E] 92 C4
Alcoy / Alcoi [E] 104 E1
Alcubierre [E] 90 F3
Alcublas [E] 98 E3
Alcúdia [E] 104 F4
Alcuéscar [E] 86 H6
Aldeacentenera [E] 96 B1
Aldeadávila de la Ribera [E] 80 F5
Aldea del Cano [E] 86 H6
Aldea del Fresno [E] 88 E5
Aldea del Rey [E] 96 E5
Aldealpozo [E] 90 C3
Aldeanueva de Ebro [E] 84 A5
Aldeaquemada [E] 96 F6
Aldeavieja [E] 88 E4
Aldeburgh [GB] 14 G3
Aldeia da Ponte [P] 86 G2
Aldeia do Bispo [P] 86 G2
Aldenhoven [D] 30 F4
Aldershot [GB] 14 D4
Aldinci [MK] 128 E1
Åled [S] 162 B5
Aledo [E] 104 B3
Alehoyshchina [RUS] 204 D1
Alekovo [BG] 148 E1
Aleksandrovac [YU] 150 C1
Aleksandrovo [BG] 148 B3
Aleksandrów Kujawski [PL] 36 F1
Aleksandrów Łódzki [PL] 36 G4
Aleksin [RUS] 204 F5
Aleksinac [YU] 150 D3
Ålem [S] 162 G4
Alemdağ [TR] 146 F2
Ålen [N] 182 C3
Alençon [F] 26 F6
Alenquer [P] 86 B4
Aléria [F] 114 C4
Aléria [F] 114 C4
Alès [F] 106 F3
Áles [I] 118 C5
Aleşd [RO] 206 B4
Alessándria [I] 70 F6
Alessandria del Carretto [I] 122 D6
Alessándria della Rocca [I] 126 D3
Ålestrup [DK] 160 D4
Ålesund [N] 180 C3
Alexándreia [GR] 128 G4
Alexandria [RO] 148 B1
Alexandria Troas [TR] 130 H6
Alexandroúpoli [GR] 130 G3
Alf [D] 44 G2
Alfafar [E] 98 E5
Alfaites [P] 86 G2
Alfajarín [E] 90 E4
Alfambra [E] 98 E1
Alfambras [P] 94 B4
Alfândenga [P] 80 F4
Alfano [I] 120 G5
Alfarela de Jales [P] 80 E4
Alfaro [E] 84 B5
Alfarràs [E] 90 H4
Alfas [E] 104 F2
Alfatar [BG] 148 E1
Alfedena [I] 116 D6
Alfeizerão [P] 86 B3
Alfeld [D] 46 H5
Alfeld [D] 32 F3
Alfena [P] 80 C4
Alfonsine [I] 110 G3
Alford [GB] 6 F6
Ålfoten [N] 180 C5
Alfreton [GB] 10 F5
Alfstad [N] 170 G5
Alfta [S] 174 D2
Algaida [E] 104 E5
Algajola [F] 114 B3
Algar [E] 100 G4
Algar [E] 104 H5
Algarås [S] 166 F4
Ålgård [N] 164 B3
Algarinejo [E] 102 D3
Algarra [E] 98 D3
Algeciras [E] 100 G5
Algemesí [E] 98 E5
Ålgered [S] 184 E5
Alghero [I] 118 B3
Älghult [S] 162 F4
Alginet [E] 98 E5
Algodonales [E] 100 H3
Algora [E] 90 A5
Algoso [P] 80 F4
Ålgsjö [S] 190 G5
Alguazas [E] 104 C3
Algutsrum [S] 162 G5
Algyő [H] 76 E4
Alhama de Aragón [E] 90 C4
Alhama de Granada [E] 102 D4
Alhama de Murcia [E] 104 B3
Alhambra [E] 96 G5
Alhaurín de la Torre [E] 102 B5
Alhaurín el Grande [E] 102 B4
Ålholm Slot [DK] 20 B1
Ålhus [N] 180 C6
Alía [E] 96 C2
Ália [I] 126 D3
Aliaga [E] 98 F1
Aliağa [TR] 144 C3
Alíartos [GR] 134 A5
Alibunar [YU] 154 H2
Alicante / Alacant [E] 104 E2
Alicudi Porto [I] 124 A5
Alija del Infantado [E] 80 H3
Alijó [P] 80 E4
Alikampos [GR] 140 C4
Alikanás [GR] 136 A2
Alimena [I] 126 E3
Alinda [TR] 142 D1
Alingsås [S] 162 B1
Alinyá [E] 92 D2
Aliseda [E] 86 G5
Alistráti [GR] 130 C3
Ali Terme [I] 124 B7
Alivéri [GR] 134 C5
Aljaraque [E] 94 E5
Aljezur [P] 94 B4
Aljubarrota [P] 86 C3
Aljucén [E] 86 G6
Aljustrel [P] 94 C3
Alkmaar [NL] 16 D3
Alkotz [E] 84 B3
Alkoven [A] 62 B4
Alksniupiai [LT] 202 F4
Alkvettern [S] 166 G2
Allaines [F] 42 E5
Allainville [F] 42 E4
Allanche [F] 68 C3
Alland [A] 62 E5
Allariz [E] 78 C5
Allauch [F] 108 B5
Alleen [N] 164 C5
Álleghe [I] 72 E4
Allejaur [S] 190 G3
Allemont [F] 70 A5
Allensbach [D] 58 G4
Allentsteig [A] 62 D3
Allepuz [E] 98 E1
Aller-Heiligen [D] 58 F1
Allersberg [D] 46 G6
Allershausen [D] 60 E3
Allerum [S] 156 H1
Alleuze, Château d'- [F] 68 C4
Allevard [F] 70 A4
Allihies [IRL] 4 A5
Allingåbro [DK] 160 E5
Allinge [DK] 158 E4
Allo [E] 84 A4
Alloa [GB] 8 E3
Allonnes [F] 54 E2
Ållonö [S] 168 B5
Allos [F] 108 D3
Ållsjön [S] 184 E2
Allstedt [D] 34 B5
Almacelles [E] 90 H4
Almada [P] 86 B5
Almadén [E] 96 C4
Almadén de la Plata [E] 94 G5
Almadenojos [E] 96 D4
Almadrones [E] 90 A5
Almagro [E] 96 F4
Almandoz [E] 84 C3
Almansa [E] 98 D6
Almanza [E] 82 C4
Almargen [E] 102 B3
Almarza [E] 90 B2
Almassora / Almazora [E] 98 F3
Almazán [E] 90 B3
Almazora / Almassora [E] 98 F3
Almedina [E] 96 G5
Almeida [P] 80 E6
Almeida de Sayago [E] 80 G5
Almeirim [P] 86 C4
Almelo [NL] 16 G4
Almenar [E] 90 H4
Almenara [E] 102 B1
Almenara de Tormes [E] 80 G6
Almenar de Soria [E] 90 C3
Almendra [P] 80 E5
Almendral [E] 94 G2
Almendralejo [E] 94 G2
Almenno S. Salvatore [I] 70 H4
Almere [NL] 16 E4
Almería [E] 102 G5
Almerimar [E] 102 F6
Älmestad [S] 162 C1
Älmhult [S] 162 D5
Almodôvar [P] 94 C4
Almodóvar del Campo [E] 96 E4
Almodóvar del Pinar [E] 98 C3
Almodóvar del Río [E] 102 B1
Almogía [E] 102 C4
Almograve [P] 94 B3
Almoharín [E] 86 H6
Almonaster la Real [E] 94 F4
Almonte [E] 94 F6
Almoradí [E] 104 D3
Almorox [E] 88 E6
Almourol [P] 86 D4
Älmsta [S] 168 E1
Älmsta-Väddö [S] 168 E1
Almudévar [E] 90 F3
Almuñécar [E] 102 D5
Almunge [S] 168 D1
Almuradiel [E] 96 F5
Almvik [S] 162 G2
Almyró [GR] 136 D4
Almyropótamos [GR] 134 D5
Almyrós [GR] 132 H3
Alness [GB] 6 E4
Alnwick [GB] 8 G5
Aloja [LV] 200 E4
Alol' [RUS] 200 H5
Alónnisos [GR] 134 C3
Álora [E] 102 B4
Alosno [E] 94 E5
Alost (Aalst) [B] 28 H2
Alp [E] 92 E2
Alpalhão [P] 86 E4
Alpbach [A] 60 E6
Alpedrinha [P] 86 F3
Alpen [D] 30 G2
Alpengarten [D] 60 D6
Alpera [E] 98 C5
Alphen-aan den Rijn [NL] 16 D5
Alpirsbach [D] 58 F2
Alpua [FIN] 198 D5
Alpuente [E] 98 D3
Alpullu [TR] 146 B2
Alqueva [P] 94 E3
Alquézar [E] 90 G3
Als [DK] 160 E4
Alsager [GB] 10 D5
Alsasua / Altsasu [E] 82 H5
Alsenz [D] 46 B4
Alsfeld [D] 46 D1
Alsleben [D] 34 B4
Alsóleperd [H] 76 B4
Alsótold [H] 64 D5
Ålstad [N] 192 C5
Alstad [S] 158 C3
Alstahaug [N] 190 D2
Alstätte [D] 16 G5
Alsterbro [S] 162 F4
Alstermo [S] 162 F4
Alston [GB] 8 F6
Alta [N] 192 G1
Altafulla [E] 92 C5
Altamira, Cuevas de- [E] 82 E3
Altamura [I] 122 D3
Altarejos [E] 98 B2
Altaussee [A] 62 A6
Altavilla Silentina [I] 120 F4
Altdahn [D] 44 H4
Altdorf [CH] 58 F6
Altdorf [D] 46 G5
Altea [E] 104 F2
Altedo [I] 110 F3
Alteidet [N] 192 F1
Altena [D] 32 C5
Altenahr [D] 30 G5
Altenau [D] 32 G4
Altenberg [D] 48 E2
Altenberge [D] 16 H5
Altenberger Dom [D] 30 H4
Altenburg [A] 62 D3
Altenburg [D] 34 C6
Altenglan [D] 44 H3
Altenhundem [D] 32 C5
Altenkirchen [D] 32 C6
Altenkirchen [D] 20 D1
Altenklingen [CH] 58 G4
Altenmarkt [A] 62 C6
Altenmarkt [D] 60 F5
Altenmarkt im Pongau [A] 72 H1
Altenstadt [D] 60 B4
Altenstadt [D] 60 D5
Altensteig [D] 58 G1
Altentreptow [D] 20 D4
Altenwalde [D] 18 D3
Alter do Chão [P] 86 E5
Altheim [A] 60 H4
Althofen [A] 74 B2
Altimir [BG] 150 G3
Altinkum [TR] 142 C2
Altınoluk [TR] 144 B1
Altınova [TR] 144 B2
Altınova [TR] 146 F3
Altıntaş [TR] 144 H2
Altınyayla [TR] 142 G2
Altipiani di Arcinazzo [I] 116 B6
Altkirch [F] 58 D4
Altlandsberg [D] 34 E2
Altmünster [A] 62 A5
Altnaharra [GB] 6 E3
Alto de los Leones de Castilla [E] 88 F4
Altomonte [I] 124 D3
Alton [GB] 14 D4
Altopascio [I] 110 E5
Altötting [D] 60 G4
Alt Ruppin [D] 20 C6
Altsasu / Alsasua [E] 82 H5
Alt Schadow [D] 34 F3
Altshausen [D] 58 H3
Altstätten [CH] 58 H5
Altuna [S] 168 C1
Altura [E] 98 E3
Altwarp [D] 20 E4
Altwindeck [D] 58 F1
Alūksne [LV] 200 F4
Ålund [S] 198 A4
Alunda [S] 168 D1
Alupka [UA] 206 G6
Alushta [UA] 206 G6
Alvaiázere [P] 86 D3
Alvajärvi [FIN] 186 F1
Alvalade [P] 94 C3
Älvängen [S] 160 H1
Alvastra [S] 166 G6
Alvdal [N] 182 B5
Älvdalen [S] 172 F2
Alverca do Ribatejo [P] 86 B5
Alversund [N] 170 B3
Alvesta [S] 162 D4
Alvignac [F] 66 G4
Ålvik [N] 170 C4
Alvito [I] 116 C6
Alvito [P] 94 D2
Älvkarleby [S] 174 E4
Alvor [P] 94 B5
Älvros [S] 182 E6
Älvros [S] 182 G5
Älvsbyn [S] 198 A3
Älvsered [S] 162 B3
Älvundeid [N] 180 F3
Alykí [GR] 138 E3
Alykí [GR] 130 E4
Alykí [GR] 130 E4
Alytus [LT] 24 G2
Alzenau [D] 46 D3
Alzey [D] 46 B4
Alzira [E] 98 E5
Alzon [F] 106 E3
Alzonne [F] 106 B4
Amadora [P] 86 B5
Åmål [S] 166 D4
Amalfi [I] 120 E4
Amaliáda [GR] 136 C2
Amaliápoli [GR] 132 H3
Amalo [GR] 138 G1
Amance [F] 58 B3
Amancey [F] 58 B5
Amandola [I] 116 C2
Amantea [I] 124 D5
Amantia [AL] 128 B5
Amarante [P] 80 C4
Amárantos [GR] 132 F3
Amărăştii de Sus [RO] 150 G2
Amareleja [P] 94 E3
Amári [GR] 140 D5
Amárynthos [GR] 134 C5
Amatrice [I] 116 C3
Amaxádes [GR] 130 E2
Amay [B] 30 E5
Ambarès [F] 66 D3
Ambazac [F] 54 G6
Ambelákia [GR] 130 H1
Amberg [D] 46 H5
Ambérieu-en-Bugey [F] 68 G2
Ambert [F] 68 D3
Ambjörby [S] 172 E4
Ambla [EST] 200 E1
Amble [GB] 8 G5
Ambleside [GB] 10 D2
Amboise [F] 54 G2
Ambra [EST] 200 E2
Ambrières [F] 26 E5
Åmdal [N] 164 D5
Ameixial [P] 94 C4
Amélia [I] 116 A3
Amélie-les-Bains [F] 92 F2
Amelinghausen [D] 18 F5
Amendolara [I] 122 D6
Amer [E] 92 F3
A Merca [E] 78 C5
Amerongen [NL] 16 E5
Amersfoort [NL] 16 E5
Amersham [GB] 14 E3
Amesbury [GB] 12 G4
A Mezquita [E] 78 E6
Amfiaráeio [GR] 134 C5
Amfikleia [GR] 132 G4
Amfilochía [GR] 132 D4
Amfípoli [GR] 130 C4
Ámfissa [GR] 132 G5
Amiens [F] 28 E5
Amiternum [I] 116 C4
Åmli [N] 164 E4
Amlwch [GB] 10 B3
Ammanford [GB] 12 E2
Ämmänsaari [FIN] 198 F4
Ammarnäs [S] 190 F2
Åmmeberg [S] 166 G4
Ammoudára [GR] 140 E4
Ammoudára [GR] 140 F5
Åmnes [N] 164 F2
Amorbach [D] 46 D4
Amòreira, Acueducto de- [P] 86 E6
Amorgós [GR] 138 G4
Amorosi [I] 120 E2
Åmot [N] 164 E1
Åmot [N] 164 G1
Åmot [N] 170 G4
Åmot [S] 174 D3
Åmotfors [S] 166 D1
Amótopos [GR] 132 D3
Amou [F] 84 D2
Ampelákia [GR] 132 G1
Ampelikó [GR] 134 H2
Ampelónas [GR] 132 G1
Ampezzo [I] 72 F4
Ampfing [D] 60 F4
Amphion [F] 70 B2
Amplepuis [F] 68 F2
Amposta [E] 92 A6
Ampuero [E] 82 F3
Ampuis [F] 68 F3
Amriswil [CH] 58 H4
Åmsele [S] 190 H5
Amsteg [CH] 70 F1
Amsterdam [NL] 16 D4
Amstetten [A] 62 C4
Åmtervik [S] 166 E2
Amurrio [E] 82 G4
Amvrosía [GR] 130 F2
Amygdaleónas [GR] 130 D3
Amygdaliá [GR] 132 G5
Amýkles [GR] 136 E4
Amýntaio [GR] 128 F4
Amzacea [RO] 148 G1
Anadia [P] 80 B6
Anáfi [GR] 138 F5
Anagni [I] 116 B6
Anáktora Néstoros [GR] 136 C4
Análipsi [GR] 138 H4
Anárgyroi [GR] 128 E5
Anarráchi [GR] 128 E5
Anascaul [IRL] 4 B4
Ånäset [S] 198 A5
Åna-Sira [N] 164 B5
Anatolí [GR] 132 G1
Anatolikó [GR] 128 F5
Anávyssos [GR] 136 H1
Anávra [GR] 132 F3
Anávra [GR] 132 G3
An Cabhán / Cavan [IRL] 2 E4
Ancenis [F] 40 G6
Ancerville [F] 44 C5
An Charraig / Carrick [IRL] 2 D2
Anchuras [E] 96 D2
Ancona [I] 112 C6
Ancy-le-Franc [F] 56 F2
Anda [N] 180 C5
An Daingean / Dingle [IRL] 4 A3
Andalo [I] 72 C4
Åndalsnes [N] 180 E3
Andau [A] 62 G6
Andebol [S] 168 B4
Andebu [N] 164 H3
Andechs [D] 60 D5
Andelot [F] 44 D6
Andenes [N] 192 C2
Andenne [B] 30 D5
Andermatt [CH] 70 F1
Andernach [D] 30 H6
Andernos-les-Bains [F] 66 B3
Andersfors [S] 198 A5
Anderslöv [S] 158 C3
Anderstorp [S] 162 C3
Andijk [NL] 16 E3
Andilla [E] 98 E3
Andocs [H] 76 A3
Andolsheim [F] 58 E3
Andorno Micca [I] 70 E4
Andorra [E] 90 F6
Andorra la Vella [AND] 84 H6
Andover [GB] 12 H4
Andrade, Castelo de- [E] 78 D2
Andravída [GR] 136 B1
Andrespol [PL] 36 G4
Andretta [I] 120 G3
Andrézieux-Bouthéon [F] 68 E3
Ándria [I] 122 C2
Andrijevica [YU] 150 A5
Andritsaina [GR] 136 D3
Ándros [GR] 134 E6
Androússa [GR] 136 D4
Andrychów [PL] 50 G4
Andselv [N] 192 E3
Andújar [E] 102 D1
Anduze [F] 106 F3
Ånebjør [N] 164 D3
Aneby [N] 172 B5
Aneby [S] 162 E2
Ånes [N] 180 F1
Anet [F] 42 E3
Ånge [S] 184 C4
Ångebo [S] 184 D6
Angeja [P] 80 B5
Ängelholm [S] 156 H1
Angeli [FIN] 196 C4
Angelókastro [GR] 136 F2
Angelókastro [GR] 132 E5
Ängelsfors [S] 174 D4
Angenstein [CH] 58 E4
Anger [A] 74 E1
Angermünde [D] 20 E6
Angern [A] 62 G4
Angers [F] 40 H6
Ångersjö [S] 182 G6
Angerville [F] 42 E5
Anghelo Ruiu, Necropoli- [I] 118 B3
Anghiari [I] 110 G6
Anglès [E] 92 F3
Angles-sur-l'Anglin [F] 54 F4
Anglet [F] 84 C2
Anglona [LV] 200 G6
Anglure [F] 44 A5
Ango, Manoir d'- [F] 28 C4
Angoulême [F] 66 E1
Ångsö [S] 168 C2
Angüés [E] 90 G3
Anguiano [E] 90 B1
Anguillara Sabazia [I] 114 H5
Anguillara Veneta [I] 110 G2
Angulo [E] 82 G4
Angvik [N] 180 F2
Anholt [DK] 160 G5
Aniane [F] 106 E4
Aniche [F] 28 F4
Anina [RO] 206 A6
Anıtkaya [TR] 144 H2
Anjala [FIN] 178 C3
Anjalankoski [FIN] 178 C3
Anjum [NL] 16 F1
Ankaran [SLO] 72 H6
Ankarede [S] 190 E4
Ankarsrum [S] 162 G2
Ankarvattnet [S] 190 E4
Anklam [D] 20 D4
Ankum [D] 32 D1
Anlezy [F] 56 E4
Ånn [S] 182 E2
Anna [EST] 200 E2
Annaberg [A] 60 H6
Annaberg [A] 62 D5
Annaberg-Buchholz [D] 48 D2
Annadalsvagen [N] 190 D3
Annalong [GB] 2 G4
Annan [GB] 8 E5
Anna Paulowna [NL] 16 D3
An Nás / Naas [IRL] 2 F6
Anndalsvågen [N] 190 D3
Anneberg [S] 162 E2
Annecy [F] 70 B3
Annefors [S] 174 D2
Annelund [S] 162 B1
Annemasse [F] 70 B2
Annenheim [A] 74 A3
Annerstad [S] 162 C5
Annestown [IRL] 4 E5
Annonay [F] 68 F4
Annopol [PL] 52 D1
Annot [F] 108 D3
Annweiler [D] 46 B5
Anógia [GR] 140 E4
Ánoixi [GR] 132 E1
Áno Kalentíni [GR] 132 D3
Áno Kastrítsi [GR] 132 F6
Áno Merá [GR] 138 E2
Anópoli [GR] 140 C5
Áno Sangkrí [GR] 138 F3
Añover de Tajo [E] 96 F1
Áno Viánnos [GR] 140 F5
Áno Vrontoú [GR] 130 C2
Anquela del Ducado [E] 90 B5
An Rinn / Ring [IRL] 4 E5
Ans [DK] 160 D6
Ansager [DK] 156 B2
Ansbach [D] 46 F5
Anse [F] 68 F2
Ansedónia [I] 114 F4
Anseremme [B] 30 D6
Ansnes [N] 192 D2
Ansó [E] 84 D4
An Spidéal / Spiddal [IRL] 2 B5
Anstey [GB] 10 F6
Anstruther [GB] 8 F3
Ansvar [S] 196 B8
Antandros [TR] 134 H1
Antas [P] 80 D5
Antas, Tempio di- [I] 118 B6
Antegnate [I] 70 H5
Antequera [E] 102 C4
Anterselva / Antholz [I] 72 E2
Anthéor [F] 108 E5
Anthí [GR] 130 B3
Antholz / Anterselva [I] 72 E2
Anthótopos [GR] 132 G3
Antibes [F] 108 E5
Antigonea [AL] 128 C6
Antigua [E] 100 E5
Antigua Bilbilis [E] 90 D4
Antikýra [GR] 132 H5
Antimáchia [GR] 142 B3
An Tinbhear Mór / Arklow [IRL] 4 G4
Antíparos [GR] 138 E3
Antírrio [GR] 132 F5
Antissa [GR] 134 G2
Ántissa [GR] 134 G2
Antnäs [S] 198 B3
Antol [SK] 64 C4
Antonin [PL] 36 E5

Beloeil [B] 28 G3
Belogradchik [BG] 150 E3
Belokamensk [UA] 206 G6
Beloljin [YU] 150 C4
Bélopátfalva [H] 64 E5
Belopol'ye [UA] 206 G1
Belorado [E] 82 F6
Bělotín [CZ] 50 E5
Belovo [BG] 148 A6
Belozersk [RUS] 204 F1
Belpasso [I] 126 G3
Belsen [D] 18 F6
Belsk Duży [PL] 38 B4
Beltinci [SLO] 74 F3
Belturbet [IRL] 2 E4
Beluša [SK] 64 B2
Belušić [YU] 150 C2
Belvedere Campomoro [F] 114 A5
Belvedere du Cirque [F] 108 E2
Belvedere Marittimo [I] 124 C3
Belver [P] 86 E4
Belvès [F] 66 F4
Belvis de la Jara [E] 96 D1
Belyy [RUS] 204 D4
Belz [F] 40 C4
Belz [UA] 52 H2
Bełżec [PL] 52 G2
Belzig [D] 34 D3
Bełżyce [PL] 38 D6
Bembibre [E] 78 F5
Bembirre [E] 78 C2
Bemposta [P] 86 D4
Bemposta [P] 80 F5
Benabarre [E] 90 H3
Benalmádena [E] 102 B5
Benalup [E] 100 G5
Benaojón [E] 100 H4
Benasque [F] 84 F5
Benassal [E] 98 F2
Benatsky nad Jizerou [CZ] 48 G3
Benavente [E] 82 A5
Benavente [P] 86 C5
Benavila [P] 86 D5
Benavites [E] 78 G6
Bene [LV] 200 D6
Benediktbeuern [D] 60 D5
Benediktiner-Abtei [D] 60 F4
Beneixama / Benejama [E] 104 D1
Benejama / Beneixama [E] 104 D1
Benešov [CZ] 62 C3
Benešov [CZ] 48 G4
Benešov nad Ploučnicí [CZ] 48 F2
Bénévent l'Abbaye [F] 54 G6
Benevento [I] 120 F2
Benfeld [F] 58 E2
Bengtsfors [S] 166 D4
Beničanci [HR] 76 B6
Benicarló [E] 98 H2
Benicasim / Benicàssim [E] 98 G3
Benicàssim / Benicasim [E] 98 G3
Benidorm [E] 104 E2
Beniel [E] 104 C3
Benifaió [E] 98 E5
Beniganim [E] 98 E6
Benilloba [E] 104 E1
Benimarfull [E] 104 E1
Benissa [E] 104 F2
Benitses [GR] 132 B2
Benkovac [HR] 112 G5
Benneckenstein [D] 32 H4
Bennstedt [D] 34 B5
Bénodet [F] 40 B3
Benrath [D] 30 G4
Bensafrim [P] 94 B5
Bensberg [D] 30 H4
Bensersiel [D] 18 C3
Bensheim [D] 46 C4
Beočin [YU] 154 F2
Beograd [YU] 154 G2
Bera / Vera de Bidasoa [E] 84 B2
Berane [YU] 150 A5
Berat [AL] 128 B4
Beratón [E] 90 C3
Berbenno di Valtellina [I] 70 H3
Berberana [E] 82 G4
Bercedo [E] 82 F4
Bercel [H] 64 D5
Berceto [I] 110 D3
Berching [D] 46 G6
Berchtesgaden [D] 60 G6
Berck-Plage [F] 28 D3
Berdians'k [UA] 206 H4
Berducedo [E] 78 F3
Berdún [E] 84 C5
Berdychiv [UA] 206 D2
Berechiu [RO] 76 H3
Berehove [UA] 206 B3
Berek [HR] 74 G6
Berest [PL] 52 C5
Berettyóújfalu [H] 76 G1
Berezan' [UA] 206 F2
Berezivka [UA] 206 F4
Berg [D] 60 D5
Berg [N] 172 D5
Berg [N] 190 C3
Berga [D] 32 H5
Berga [E] 92 E2
Berga [S] 162 F4
Bergama [TR] 144 C2
Bergamo [I] 70 H4
Bergara [E] 82 H4
Bergby [S] 174 E3
Berge [N] 164 E1
Berge [S] 182 F1
Bergedorf [D] 18 G4
Bergeforsen [S] 184 E4
Bergen [D] 18 F6
Bergen [D] 18 H6
Bergen [D] 20 D2
Bergen [N] 170 B4
Bergen [NL] 16 D3
Bergen (Mons) [B] 28 G4
Bergen aan Zee [NL] 16 D3
Bergen op Zoom [NL] 16 C6
Berger [N] 164 H2
Bergerac [F] 66 E4
Bergheim [D] 30 G4
Bergisch Gladbach [D] 30 H4
Bergkvara [S] 162 F6
Berglern [D] 60 E3
Berglia [N] 190 D5
Bergnäset [S] 198 B3
Berg-Neustadt [D] 32 C5
Bergö [FIN] 186 A3
Bergshamra [S] 168 E2
Bergsjö [S] 184 E6
Berg slussar [S] 166 H5
Bergstrøm [N] 166 C3
Bergsviken [S] 198 B3
Bergues [F] 14 H6
Bergum [NL] 16 F2
Bergün [CH] 70 H2
Bergunda [S] 162 D5
Bergvik [S] 174 E2
Beringen [B] 30 E3
Berja [E] 102 F5
Berkåk [N] 180 H3
Berkenthin [D] 18 G4
Berkesz [H] 64 H4
Berkheim [D] 60 B4
Berkhof [D] 32 F1
Berkovići [BIH] 152 C3
Berkovitsa [BG] 150 F3
Berlanga [E] 96 A5
Berlanga de Duero [E] 90 A3
Berlevåg [N] 196 E1
Berlin [D] 34 E2
Berlingen [CH] 58 G4
Bermeo [E] 82 H3
Bermillo de Sayago [E] 80 G5
Bern [CH] 58 D6
Bernalda [I] 122 D4
Bernartice [CZ] 48 F5
Bernati [LV] 200 B6
Bernau [D] 60 F5
Bernau [D] 34 E2
Bernaville [F] 28 E4
Bernay [F] 26 G4
Bernburg [D] 34 B4
Berndorf [A] 62 E5
Berne [D] 18 D5
Bernedo [E] 82 H6
Bernek [A] 72 C1
Bernhardsthal [A] 62 G3
Bernkastel-Kues [D] 44 G2
Bernsdorf [D] 34 F5
Bernstein [A] 74 F1
Beromünster [CH] 58 F5
Beronovo [BG] 148 E4
Beroun [CZ] 48 F4
Berovo [MK] 128 H1
Berre-l'Etang [F] 106 H5
Berrocal [E] 94 F5
Berroquejo [E] 100 F4
Bersenbrück [D] 32 D1
Bertinoro [I] 110 G4
Bertrix [B] 44 D2
Berwang [A] 60 C6
Berwick-upon-Tweed [GB] 8 F4
Beryslav [UA] 206 G4
Berzaune [LV] 200 F5
Berzence [H] 74 G4
Besalú [E] 92 F2
Besançon [F] 58 B5
Besande [E] 82 C3
Besenyszög [H] 76 E1
Beşevler [TR] 146 G4
Beşevlet [TR] 146 G3
Besigheim [D] 46 D6
Beška [YU] 154 G2
Bessan [F] 106 E4
Bessay-sur-Allier [F] 56 D5
Besse-en-Chandesse [F] 68 C3
Besse-sur-Issole [F] 108 C5
Bessheim [N] 170 F1
Bessines-sur-Gartempe [F] 54 G6
Bestida [P] 80 B5
Bestorp [S] 168 A6
Beszowa [PL] 52 C2
Betancuria [E] 100 E5
Betanzos [E] 78 D2
Betelu [E] 84 B3
Bétera [E] 98 E4
Beteta [E] 90 B6
Bétharram, Grottes de- [F] 84 E4
Bethesda [GB] 10 B4
Béthune [F] 28 E3
Betna [N] 180 F2
Bettenburg [D] 46 F3
Bettna [S] 168 C4
Bettola [I] 110 C2
Bettyhill [GB] 6 E2
Betws-y-Coed [GB] 10 C4
Betz [F] 42 G3
Betzdorf [D] 32 C6
Beuel [D] 30 H5
Beuil [F] 108 E3
Beuron [D] 58 G3
Beuzeville [F] 26 G3
Bevagna [I] 116 A2
Beveren-Waas [B] 30 C3
Beverley [GB] 10 G4
Beverstedt [D] 18 D4
Beverungen [D] 32 F4
Beverwijk [NL] 16 D4
Bevtoft [DK] 156 C3
Bewdley [GB] 12 G1
Bex [CH] 70 C2
Bexhill [GB] 14 E6
Beyağaç [TR] 142 F1
Beyazköy [TR] 146 C2
Beydağı [TR] 144 E4
Beykoz [TR] 146 E2
Beynac-et-Cazenac [F] 66 F4
Beynat [F] 66 H3
Bezarino [BY] 204 B5
Bezau [A] 60 B6
Bezdan [YU] 76 C5
Bezděz [CZ] 48 G2
Bezdonys [LT] 202 G5
Bezhetsk [RUS] 204 F3
Béziers [F] 106 D4
Béznar [E] 102 E4
B. Hornberg [D] 46 D5
Biała [PL] 50 D3
Białaczów [PL] 38 A5
Biała Piska [PL] 24 D4
Biała Podlaska [PL] 38 F3
Biała Rawska [PL] 38 A4
Białobrzegi [PL] 38 B4
Białogard [PL] 20 H3
Białowieża [PL] 38 G1
Biały Bór [PL] 22 B4
Białystok [PL] 24 E5
Biancavilla [I] 126 G3
Bianco [I] 124 D7
Biar [E] 104 D1
Biarritz [F] 84 C2
Bias [F] 66 B5
Biasca [CH] 70 G2
Biasteri / Laguardia [E] 82 G6
Biatigala [LT] 202 E4
Biatorbágy [H] 76 C1
Bibbiena [I] 110 G6
Bibbiona [I] 114 E1
Biberach [D] 58 F2
Biberach an der Riss [D] 60 B4
Bibione [I] 72 G6
Bibury [GB] 12 H3
Bicaj [AL] 128 C1
Bicaz [RO] 206 C4
Bicester [GB] 14 D3
Bichl [D] 60 D5
Bicos [P] 94 C3
Bicske [H] 76 B1
Bidache [F] 84 C2
Bidalite [S] 162 F6
Bidart [F] 84 C2
Biddulph [GB] 10 E5
Bideford [GB] 12 D3
Bidjovagge [N] 192 G2
Bidovce [SK] 64 G3
Bidziny [PL] 52 D1
Bie [S] 168 B4
Bieber [D] 46 D3
Biebersdorf [D] 34 F4
Biecz [PL] 52 C4
Biedenkopf [D] 32 D6
Biel [E] 84 C5
Biel / Bienne [CH] 58 D5
Bielany Wrocł. [PL] 50 C1
Bielawa [PL] 50 C2
Bielczyny [PL] 22 E5
Bielefeld [D] 32 D3
Biella [I] 70 E4
Bielmonte [I] 70 E4
Bielowy [PL] 52 D4
Bielsa [E] 84 E5
Bielsa, Tunnel de- [Eur.] 84 E5
Bielsk [PL] 36 H2
Bielsko-Biała [PL] 50 G4
Bielsk Podlaski [PL] 38 F1
Biely Kameň [SK] 62 G4
Bienenbüttel [D] 18 G5
Bieniów [PL] 34 H4
Bienne / Biel [CH] 58 D5
Bienvenida [E] 94 G3
Bienvenida [E] 96 D4
Bierdzany [PL] 50 E2
Bierre-Lès-Semur [F] 56 F3
Bierutów [PL] 36 D6
Bierzwnik [PL] 20 H6
Biescas [E] 84 D5
Biesenthal [D] 34 E1
Biesiekierz [PL] 20 H3
Bieskkenjárga [N] 192 H2
Bietigheim [D] 46 D6
Bieżuń [PL] 22 G6
Biga [TR] 146 C5
Bigadiç [TR] 144 D2
Biggar [GB] 8 E4
Biggleswade [GB] 14 E3
Bignasco [CH] 70 F2
Bihać [BIH] 112 H3
Biharia [RO] 76 H2
Biharkeresztes [H] 76 H2
Biharnagybajom [H] 76 G1
Bijambarska Pećina [BIH] 154 D4
Bijeljani [BIH] 152 D3
Bijeljina [BIH] 154 E3
Bijelo Polje [YU] 150 A4
Bikava [LV] 200 G5
Bílá [CZ] 50 F5
Bila Tserkva [UA] 206 E2
Bilbao / Bilbo [E] 82 G4
Bilbo / Bilbao [E] 82 G4
Bileća [BIH] 152 D3
Bilecik [TR] 146 G4
Biled [RO] 76 G5
Biłgoraj [PL] 52 F2
Bilhorod Dnistrovs'kyi [UA] 206 E5
Bílina [CZ] 48 E2
Bilisht [AL] 128 D5
Biljanovac [YU] 150 B3
Bilje [HR] 76 C6
Billdal [S] 160 G2
Billefjord [N] 196 C2
Billerbeck [D] 16 H6
Billericay [GB] 14 F4
Billingen [N] 180 E5
Billingsfors [S] 166 D4
Billom [F] 68 D2
Billund [DK] 156 C2
Bilohirsk [UA] 206 G5
Bilousivka [UA] 206 F2
Bílovec [CZ] 50 E4
Bilska [LV] 200 F4
Bilto [N] 192 F2
Biňa [SK] 64 B5
Binas [F] 42 D6
Binasco [I] 70 G5
Binche [B] 28 H4
Bindslev [DK] 160 E2
Binéfar [E] 90 G4
Bingen [D] 46 B3
Binghöhle [D] 46 G4
Bingsjö [S] 174 C3
Binibeca Vell [E] 104 H5
Binic [F] 26 B4
Binz [D] 20 D2
Bioče [YU] 152 E4
Biograd [HR] 112 G5
Bionaz [I] 70 D3
Bioska [YU] 152 F1
Bircza [PL] 52 E4
Birgi [TR] 144 E4
Biri [N] 172 B3
Birini [EST] 200 E2
Birini [LV] 200 E4
Birkala / Pirkkala [FIN] 176 F1
Birkeland [N] 164 C5
Birkeland [N] 164 E5
Birkenfeld [D] 44 G3
Birkenfeld [D] 46 E4
Birkenhead [GB] 10 D4
Birkenwerder [D] 34 E2
Birkerød [DK] 156 G2
Birkfeld [A] 74 E1
Birksdal [N] 180 D6
Birmingham [GB] 10 E6
Birnau [D] 58 H4
Biron, Château de- [F] 66 F4
Birr [IRL] 2 D6
Birštonas [LT] 24 F1
Birtavarre [N] 192 F2
Biržai [LT] 200 E6
Biržebbuga [M] 126 C6
Birži [LV] 200 F6
Birzuli [LV] 200 F4
Bisaccia [I] 120 G3
Bisacquino [I] 126 C3
Bisbal d'Empordà, la- [E] 92 G3
Biscarrosse [F] 66 B4
Biscarrosse-Plage [F] 66 B4
Bisceglie [I] 122 D2
Bischofsgrün [D] 46 H3
Bischofsheim [D] 46 E2
Bischofshofen [A] 72 G1
Bischofswerda [D] 34 F6
Bishop Auckland [GB] 10 F2
Bishop's Castle [GB] 10 C6
Bishop's Cleeve [GB] 12 G2
Bishop's Stortford [GB] 14 F3
Bisignano [I] 124 D4
Biskupiec [PL] 22 F5
Biskupiec [PL] 22 H4
Biskupin [PL] 36 D1
Bismark [D] 34 B1
Bismo [N] 180 F5
Bispfors [S] 184 D3
Bispgården [S] 184 D3
Bispingen [D] 18 F5
Bistreț [RO] 150 F2
Bistrica [YU] 152 E3
Bistrica [YU] 150 A3
Bistrița [RO] 206 C4
Bistritsa [BG] 150 F5
Bisztynek [PL] 22 H3
Bitburg [D] 44 F2
Bitche [F] 44 G4
Bitetto [I] 122 D3
Bithia [I] 118 C8
Bitola [MK] 128 E3
Bitonto [I] 122 D2
Bítov [CZ] 62 E2
Bitterfeld [D] 34 C4
Bitti [I] 118 D4
Bivio [CH] 70 H2
Bivona [I] 126 D3
Bizovac [HR] 76 B6
Bjåen [N] 164 D1
Bjala Cherkva [BG] 148 C3
Bjarisino [BY] 204 B5
Bjärnå / Perniö [FIN] 176 F5
Bjärnum [S] 158 D1
Bjärred [S] 156 H2
Bjästa [S] 184 G2
Bjelland [N] 164 D5
Bjelovar [HR] 74 G5
Bjerga [N] 164 C1
Bjerkreim [N] 164 B4
Bjerkvik [N] 192 D4
Bjerregård [DK] 156 A1
Bjerringbro [DK] 160 D5
Bjølstad [N] 180 G6
Bjoneroa [N] 170 H4
Björbo [S] 172 G5
Bjordal [N] 164 C4
Bjørgo [N] 170 G3
Bjørkåsen [N] 192 E3
Björkberg [S] 190 G4
Björkberg [S] 172 H1
Björkefors [S] 162 F1
Bjørkelangen [N] 166 C1
Bjørkflåta [N] 170 F4
Björkfors [S] 190 E3
Björkhöjden [S] 184 D2
Björkliden [S] 192 E4
Björklinge [S] 168 D1
Bjørknes [N] 172 C6
Björkö [FIN] 176 C5
Björkö [S] 168 F1
Björkö [S] 162 E3
Björköby [FIN] 186 A2
Björksele [S] 190 G6
Björkvattnet [S] 190 D5
Björkvik [S] 168 B4
Bjørlia [N] 190 C4
Bjørn [N] 190 D2
Bjöina [S] 184 G1
Björneborg [S] 166 G3
Björneborg / Pori [FIN] 176 D1
Bjørnevasshytta [N] 164 D2
Bjørnevatn [N] 196 E3
Björnlunda [S] 168 C4
Björnsholm [S] 162 G1
Björsäter [S] 168 B6
Bjørsvik [N] 170 B3
Bjuråker [S] 184 D6
Bjurberget [S] 172 E4
Bjurholm [S] 190 H6
Bjuröklubb [S] 198 B5
Bjursås [S] 172 H4
Bjuv [S] 156 H1
Bláa Lónia [IS] 194 B4
Blace [YU] 150 C3
Blachownia [PL] 50 F2
Blackburn [GB] 10 E3
Blacklion [IRL] 2 E3
Blackpool [GB] 10 D3
Blackstad [S] 162 G2
Blackwater [IRL] 4 F5
Blaenau Ffestiniog [GB] 10 B4
Blagaj [BIH] 152 C2
Blagoevgrad [BG] 150 F6
Blagoevo [BG] 148 D2
Blagoveštenje, Manastir- [YU] 150 B2
Blåhøj [DK] 156 B1
Blaiken [S] 190 F4
Blaikliden [S] 190 F4
Blain [F] 40 F5
Blair Atholl [GB] 8 E1
Blairgowrie [GB] 8 E2
Blaj [RO] 206 B5
Blakstad [N] 164 E5
Blâmont [F] 44 F6
Blanca [E] 104 C2
Blandford Forum [GB] 12 G4
Blanes [E] 92 F4
Blangy-sur-Bresle [F] 28 D4
Blanických Rytířů, Jeskyně- [CZ] 50 C5
Blankaholm [S] 162 G2
Blankenberge [B] 28 G1
Blankenburg [D] 32 H4
Blankenfelde [D] 34 E2
Blankenhain [D] 46 H1
Blankenheim [D] 30 G6
Blanquefort [F] 66 C3
Blansko [CZ] 50 C6
Blanzac [F] 66 E2
Blarney [IRL] 4 C5
Blarney Castle [IRL] 4 C5
Blascosancho [E] 88 E4
Błaszki [PL] 36 F5
Blatná [CZ] 48 E5
Blatnica [BIH] 154 C3
Blatnice [CZ] 62 H2
Blatnický Hrad [SK] 64 C2
Blato [HR] 152 A2
Blato [HR] 152 A3
Blattniksele [S] 190 G3
Blaubeuren [D] 60 B3
Blaufelden [D] 46 E5
Blaustein [D] 60 B3
Blåvand [DK] 156 A2
Blåvik [S] 162 E1
Blaye [F] 66 C2
Blazquez [E] 96 B5
Bleckede [D] 18 G5
Bled [SLO] 74 B4
Bleiburg [A] 74 C3
Bleicherode [D] 32 G5
Bleik [N] 192 C3
Bleisfjord [N] 192 D4
Blendija [YU] 150 D3
Bléneau [F] 56 D2
Blera [I] 114 H4
Blérancourt [F] 28 F6
Bléré [F] 54 G2
Blériot-Plage [F] 14 G6
Blesle [F] 68 C3
Blessington [IRL] 2 F6
Bletterans [F] 56 H5
Blexen [D] 18 D4
Bliesbruck-Reinheim, Parc Archéol. de- [F] 44 G4
Blieskastel [D] 44 G4
Bligny-sur-Ouche [F] 56 G4
Blikstorp [S] 166 F6
Blinisht [AL] 128 B1
Blinja [HR] 154 A1
Bliznak [BG] 148 F3
Blizne [PL] 52 E4
Błogoszów [PL] 52 A2
Blois [F] 54 H1
Blokhus [DK] 160 D3
Blokzijl [NL] 16 F3
Blombacka [S] 166 F2
Blomberg [D] 32 E3
Blomsholms-Skeppet [S] 166 C4
Blomstermåla [S] 162 G4
Blönduós [IS] 194 D3
Błonie [PL] 36 C6
Błonie [PL] 38 B3
Błonie [PL] 38 F3
Bloška Polica [SLO] 74 B6
Błotnica [PL] 38 B6
Błotno [PL] 20 F4
Blovice [CZ] 48 E5
Bludenz [A] 72 A1
Blumberg [D] 58 F3
Blyth [GB] 8 G5
Bø [N] 164 F2
Bø [N] 192 D2
Bo [S] 166 H4
Boadilla del Monte [E] 88 F5
Boal [E] 78 F2
Boário Terme [I] 72 B5
Bobbio [I] 110 C2
Bobbio Pellice [I] 70 C6
Bobingen [D] 60 D4
Bobitz [D] 20 A4
Böblingen [D] 58 G1
Bobolice [PL] 22 B3
Boboshevo [BG] 150 F6
Bobovdol [BG] 150 F5
Bobr [BY] 204 C5
Bobrovytsia [UA] 206 F1
Bobrowice [PL] 34 H4
Bobrowniki [PL] 24 F5
Bobrowniki [PL] 36 F1
Boca de Huergano [E] 82 C3
Bocairent [E] 104 E1
Boceguillas [E] 88 G3
Böçen [TR] 146 F5
Bochnia [PL] 52 B4
Bocholt [D] 16 G6
Bochov [CZ] 48 D3
Bochum [D] 30 H3
Bockara [S] 162 F3
Bockel [D] 18 E5
Bockenem [D] 32 G3
Boćki [PL] 38 E1
Böcksholm [S] 162 E4
Böckstein [A] 72 G2
Bockum-Hovel [D] 32 C3
Bocognano [F] 114 B4
Bócsa [H] 76 D3
Bocsig [RO] 76 H4
Böda [S] 162 H3
Boda [S] 172 H3
Boda [S] 184 E3
Boda [S] 166 E2
Bodaanowice [PL] 50 F1
Bodaczów [PL] 52 F1
Bodafors [S] 162 D3
Boda glasbruk [S] 162 F5
Bodegraven [NL] 16 D5
Boden [S] 198 B3
Bodenmais [D] 48 D6
Bodenteich [D] 18 G6
Bodenwerder [D] 32 F3
Bodenwöhr [D] 48 C6
Bodjani [YU] 154 E1
Bodman [D] 58 G4
Bodmin [GB] 12 C4
Bodø [N] 192 B6
Bodom [N] 190 C5
Bodrogkeresztúr [H] 64 G4
Bodrum [TR] 142 C2
Bodsjö [S] 182 H3
Bodträskfors [S] 198 A2
Bodzanów [PL] 36 H2
Bodzentyn [PL] 52 C1
Boëge [F] 70 B2
Boën [F] 68 E2
Bogarra [E] 98 A6
Bogatic [YU] 154 F2
Bogatynia [PL] 48 G1
Boğaziçi [TR] 144 D5
Boğazköy [TR] 146 F4
Bogda [RO] 76 H5
Bogdaniec [PL] 34 H2
Bogen [D] 60 G2
Bogen [N] 192 D4
Bogen [N] 192 C5
Bogen [S] 172 D6
Bogense [DK] 156 D2
Bogetići [YU] 152 D4
Bogge [N] 180 F3
Bognanco [I] 70 E3
Bognelv [N] 192 F1
Bognes [N] 192 C4
Bognor Regis [GB] 14 D5
Bogojevo [YU] 154 E1
Bogorodica [MK] 128 G3
Bogoroditsk [RUS] 204 F5
Bogovina [YU] 150 D2
Bogovinska Pećina [YU] 150 D2
Bogøy [N] 192 C5
Bograngen [S] 172 E4
Bogumiłowice [PL] 36 G6
Boguszów-Gorce [PL] 50 B2
Bohain-en-Vermandois [F] 28 F5
Bohdalov [CZ] 50 A5
Boheeshil [IRL] 4 B4
Bohinjska Bistrica [SLO] 74 A4
Böhmenkirch [D] 60 B2
Bohmte [D] 32 D2
Bohodukhiv [UA] 206 G2
Bohonal [E] 96 D2
Bohonal de Ibor [E] 88 B6
Böhönye [H] 74 H4
Boialvo [P] 80 B6
Boichinovtsi [BG] 150 F3
Bois-du-Four [F] 68 B6
Boitzenburg [D] 20 D5
Bóixols [E] 92 C2
Boizenburg [D] 18 G5
Bojano [I] 120 E1
Bojanów [PL] 52 D2
Bojanowo [PL] 36 C4
Bøjden [DK] 156 D4
Bojnica [BG] 150 E2
Bojnik [YU] 150 D4
Bojtiken [S] 190 E3
Bökemåla [S] 162 E6
Boksitogorsk [RUS] 204 D2
Bol [HR] 152 A2
Bolaños de Calatrava [E] 96 F4
Bolayır [TR] 146 B4
Bolbec [F] 26 H3
Bolca [I] 72 C6
Boldva [H] 64 F4
Bolekhiv [UA] 52 H6
Bolemin [PL] 34 H2
Bolesławiec [PL] 36 A6
Bolesławiec [PL] 36 E6
Bolesławów [PL] 50 C3
Boleszkowice [PL] 34 G2
Bolfiar [P] 80 B5
Bolgatovo [RUS] 200 H5
Bolgheri [I] 114 E1
Bolhrad [UA] 206 D5
Boliden [S] 198 A4
Bolinglanna [IRL] 2 B3
Boljanići [YU] 152 E2
Boljevac [YU] 150 D2
Bolkesjø [N] 164 G1
Bolkhov [RUS] 204 E5
Bolków [PL] 50 B1
Bollebygd [S] 162 B2
Bollène [F] 106 G2
Böllerkirche [D] 46 B3
Bollnäs [S] 174 D2
Bollstabruk [S] 184 F3
Bollullos Par del Condado [E] 94 F6
Bologna [I] 110 F3
Bologne [F] 44 C6
Bolótana [I] 118 C4
Bolotovo [RUS] 200 H4
Bolsena [I] 114 H3
Bol'shakovo [RUS] 202 D5
Bol'shie Sabicy [RUS] 200 H2
Bol'shoye Zagor'e [RUS] 200 H3
Bol'shoy Sabsk [RUS] 200 G1
Bolstad [S] 166 D5
Bolstadøyri [N] 170 C3
Bolstaholm [FIN] 176 A5
Bolsward [NL] 16 E2
Bolszewo [PL] 22 D2
Boltaña [E] 84 E5
Boltenhagen [D] 18 H3
Boltigen [CH] 70 D1
Bolton [GB] 10 E4
Bolungarvík [IS] 194 C1
Bóly [H] 76 B5
Bolyarovo [BG] 148 E5
Bolzano / Bozen [I] 72 D3
Bomarsund [FIN] 176 B5
Bomarzo [I] 114 H4
Bombarral [P] 86 B4
Bominago [I] 116 C4
Bom Jesus do Monte [P] 80 C3
Bomsund [S] 184 C2
Bonaduz [CH] 70 H1
Bonaguil, Château de- [F] 66 F5
Boñar [E] 82 C3
Bonar Bridge [GB] 6 E4
Bonares [E] 94 F6
Bonäs [S] 166 E2
Bonåsjøen [N] 192 C5
Bonassola [I] 110 C4
Bondal [N] 164 F1
Bondemon [S] 166 C4
Bondeno [I] 110 F2
Bondstorp [S] 162 C2
Bonefro [I] 116 F6
Bonete [E] 98 C6
Bonhomme, Col du- [F] 58 D2
Bonifacio [F] 114 B6
Bonifati Marina [I] 124 C4
Bonlieu [F] 70 A1
Bonn [D] 30 G5
Bonnåsjøen [N] 192 C5
Bonnat [F] 54 H5
Bonndorf [D] 58 F4
Bønnerup Strand [DK] 160 F5
Bonnétable [F] 42 C5
Bonneval [F] 42 D5
Bonneval-sur-Arc [F] 70 C4
Bonneville [F] 70 B2
Bonnières [F] 42 E3
Bonnieux [F] 106 H4
Bonnigheim [D] 46 D6
Bonny-sur-Loire [F] 56 D2
Bono [I] 118 D4
Bonorva [I] 118 C4
Bonport, Abbaye de- [F] 28 B6
Bonyhád [H] 76 B4
Boom [B] 30 C3
Boos [F] 28 C5
Booth of Toft [GB] 6 H3
Bootle [GB] 10 D4
Booutovačka Banja [YU] 150 B3
Bopfingen [D] 60 C2
Boppard [D] 44 H1
Bor [CZ] 48 D4
Bor [RUS] 200 H2
Bor [S] 162 D4
Bor [YU] 150 D2
Borås [N] 164 F4
Borås [S] 162 B2
Borba [P] 86 E6
Borbona [I] 116 B4
Borchen [D] 32 E4
Borci [BIH] 152 C2
Borculo [NL] 16 G5
Bordány [H] 76 E4
Bordeaux [F] 66 C3
Bordeira [P] 94 A4
Bordères [F] 84 F4
Bordesholm [D] 18 F2
Borðeyri [IS] 194 C3
Bordighera [I] 108 F4
Bording [DK] 160 C6
Borek Wielkopolski [PL] 36 D4
Borensberg [S] 166 H5
Borgå / Porvoo [FIN] 178 B4
Borgafjäll [S] 190 E4
Borgarfjörður [IS] 194 G5
Borgarnes [IS] 194 B4
Borgen [N] 164 E3
Borgentreich [D] 32 E4
Börger [D] 18 B5
Borger [NL] 16 G3
Borggård [S] 166 H5
Borghamn [S] 166 G6
Borgholm [S] 162 G4
Borgholzhausen [D] 32 D2
Borghorst [D] 16 H5
Børglumkloster [DK] 160 D3
Borgoforte [I] 110 E2
Borgomanero [I] 70 F4
Borgonovo Val Tidone [I] 70 G6

Borgorose [I] 116 B5
Borgo San Dalmazzo [I] 108 F3
Borgo San Lorenzo [I] 110 F5
Borgosésia [I] 70 E4
Borgo Ticino [I] 70 F4
Borgo Tossignano [I] 110 F4
Borgo Val di Taro [I] 110 C3
Borgo Valsugana [I] 72 D4
Borgo Vercelli [I] 70 F5
Borgsjö [S] 190 G5
Borgsjö [S] 184 D4
Borgund [N] 170 E2
Borgvik [S] 166 E3
Borima [BG] 148 B4
Borisoglebskiy [RUS] 196 F3
Borisovo-Sudskoye [RUS] 204 E1
Borja [E] 90 D3
Börjelslandet [S] 198 B3
Borken [D] 32 E6
Borken [D] 16 G6
Borkenes [N] 192 C3
Borki [RUS] 200 G3
Børkop [DK] 156 C2
Borków [PL] 52 B1
Borkum [D] 16 G1
Borlänge [S] 172 H4
Borlaug [N] 170 E2
Borlu [TR] 144 E3
Bormes-les-Mimosas [F] 108 D6
Bórmio [I] 72 B3
Borna [D] 34 C6
Bornhöved [D] 18 G3
Börnicke [D] 34 D1
Bornos [E] 100 G3
Bornova [TR] 144 C4
Borodianka [UA] 206 E2
Borodinskoye [RUS] 178 F2
Borová Lada [CZ] 62 A2
Borovan [BG] 150 G3
Borovany [CZ] 62 C2
Borovets [BG] 150 G5
Borovichi [RUS] 200 H3
Borovichi [RUS] 204 D2
Borovik [RUS] 200 G3
Borovo [HR] 154 E1
Borovoy [RUS] 198 H4
Borovtsi [BG] 150 F3
Borowa [PL] 36 D6
Borrby [S] 158 D3
Borre [DK] 156 G4
Borre [N] 164 H2
Borreby [DK] 156 F3
Borredà [E] 92 E2
Borremose [DK] 160 D4
Borriana / Burriana [E] 98 F3
Börringe [S] 158 C3
Borriol [E] 98 F3
Borris [IRL] 4 F4
Borris-in-Ossory [IRL] 2 D6
Borrisokane [IRL] 2 D6
Borrisoleigh [IRL] 4 E3
Borrum [S] 168 C6
Borş [RO] 76 H2
Børsa [N] 182 B1
Borşa [RO] 206 C4
Børselv [N] 196 C2
Borsfa [H] 74 F4
Borsh [AL] 132 B1
Borsodnádasd [H] 64 E4
Börstil [S] 174 G5
Bort-les-Orgues [F] 68 B3
Börtnan [S] 182 F3
Borup [DK] 156 G3
Borynia [UA] 52 F6
Boryslav [UA] 52 G5
Boryspil' [UA] 206 F2
Borzechowo [PL] 22 D4
Borzone, Abbazia di- [I] 110 B3
Bosa [I] 118 B4
Bosanci [HR] 112 G1
Bosanska Dubica [BIH] 154 B2
Bosanska Gradiška [BIH] 154 C2
Bosanska Krupa [BIH] 154 A2
Bosanska Rača [BIH] 154 F2
Bosanski Brod [BIH] 154 D2
Bosanski Novi [HR] 154 A2
Bosanski Petrovac [BIH] 154 A3
Bosanski Šamac [BIH] 154 D2
Bosansko Grahovo [BIH] 154 A4
Bošany [SK] 64 B3
Bősárkány [H] 62 G6
Bosco Chiesanuova [I] 72 C5
Bösel [D] 18 C5
Bosilegrad [YU] 150 E5
Bosjön [S] 166 F1
Boskoop [NL] 16 D5
Boskovice [CZ] 50 C5
Bosna [HR] 74 F5
Bosna Klanac [BIH] 154 D4
Bošnjace [YU] 150 D4
Bošnjaci [HR] 154 E2
Bosruck Tunnel [A] 62 B6
Bössbo [S] 172 F2
Bossbøen [N] 164 E1
Bossea [I] 108 G3
Bossòst [E] 84 F5
Bostan [BIH] 152 B2
Böste [S] 158 C3
Boston [GB] 10 G6
Bostrak [N] 164 F3
Bosut [YU] 154 F2
Bőszénfa [H] 76 A4
Botevgrad [BG] 150 G4
Boticas [P] 80 E3
Botinec [HR] 74 E6
Botngård [N] 190 B6
Botoa [E] 86 F6
Botom / Karijoki [FIN] 186 B4
Botoroaga [RO] 148 C1
Botoşani [RO] 206 D4
Botricello [I] 124 E5
Botsmark [S] 198 A5
Bottidda [I] 118 D4
Bottnaryd [S] 162 C2
Bottrop [D] 30 G3
Botun [MK] 128 D3
Botunets [BG] 150 G4
Bouaye [F] 54 B1
Boudry [CH] 58 C6
Bouesse [F] 54 H4
Bouges-Le-Château [F] 54 H3
Bouguenais [F] 54 B1
Bouillon [B] 44 D2
Bouilly [F] 44 A6
Boulay-Moselle [F] 44 F4
Bouligny [F] 44 E3
Boulogne [F] 14 G6
Boulogne-sur-Gesse [F] 84 G3
Bouloire [F] 42 C5
Boumois, Château de- [F] 54 E2
Bouniagues [F] 66 E4
Bourbon-Lancy [F] 56 E5
Bourbon-l'Archambault [F] 56 D5
Bourbonne-les-Bains [F] 58 B2
Bourbourg [F] 14 H6
Bourbriac [F] 40 D2
Bourdeaux [F] 68 F6
Bourdeilles [F] 66 F2
Bourg [F] 66 D3
Bourg-Achard [F] 26 H3
Bourganeuf [F] 54 H6
Bourg-Argental [F] 68 F4
Bourg-de-Péage [F] 68 F5
Bourg-en-Bresse [F] 68 G2
Bourges [F] 56 C3
Bourg-et-Comin [F] 44 A2
Bourg-Lastic [F] 68 B2
Bourg-Madame [F] 92 E1
Bourgneuf-en-Retz [F] 54 B2
Bourgogne [F] 44 B3
Bourgoin-Jallieu [F] 68 G3
Bourg-St-Andéol [F] 106 G2
Bourg-St-Maurice [F] 70 C4
Bourgtheroulde-Infreville [F] 26 H4
Bourgueil [F] 54 E2
Bourmont [F] 58 B2
Bourne [GB] 10 G6
Bournemouth [GB] 12 G5
Bourneville [F] 26 H3
Bournezeau [F] 54 C3
Boussac [F] 56 B5
Boussens [F] 84 G4
Bouvignes [B] 30 D5
Bouvron [F] 40 F6
Bouxwiller [F] 44 G5
Bouzonville [F] 44 F3
Bova [I] 124 C8
Bovalino [I] 124 D7
Bovallstrand [S] 166 C5
Bova Marina [I] 124 C8
Bovan [YU] 150 D3
Bovec [SLO] 72 H4
Bóveda [E] 78 D4
Bovense [DK] 156 E3
Bøverbru [N] 172 B4
Bøverdal [N] 180 F6
Boves [I] 108 F3
Bović [HR] 112 H1
Bovino [I] 120 G2
Bovolenta [I] 110 G1
Bovolone [I] 110 F1
Bovrup [DK] 156 C4
Boxberg [D] 46 E5
Boxholm [S] 166 G6
Boxmeer [NL] 16 F6
Boxtel [NL] 30 E2
Boyalı [TR] 144 E3
Boyalıca [TR] 146 F4
Boyalık [TR] 146 E2
Boyle [IRL] 2 D4
Bøylefoss [N] 164 F4
Božaj [YU] 152 E4
Božava [HR] 112 F5
Bozburun [TR] 142 D3
Bozcaada [TR] 130 H6
Bozdoğan [TR] 144 E5
Bozel [F] 70 B4
Bozen / Bolzano [I] 72 D3
Bozhenci [BG] 148 C4
Bozhurishte [BG] 150 F4
Božica [YU] 150 E5
Bozkuş [TR] 144 G3
Bozouls [F] 68 B5
Bozouls, Trou de- [F] 68 B5
Bozüyük [TR] 146 G5
Bozveliisko [BG] 148 F3
Bozyaka [TR] 142 G2
Bòzzolo [I] 110 E1
Bra [I] 108 G2
Braås [S] 162 E4
Brabova [RO] 150 F1
Bracciano [I] 114 H5
Bracieux [F] 54 H2
Bracigovo [BG] 148 A6
Bräcke [S] 182 H3
Brackenheim [D] 46 C6
Brackley [GB] 14 D3
Bracknell [GB] 14 D4
Brackwede [D] 32 D3
Brad [RO] 206 B5
Bradford [GB] 10 E3
Bradina [BIH] 152 C1
Brae [GB] 6 G3
Brædstrup [DK] 156 C1
Braemar [GB] 6 E6
Braga [P] 80 C3
Bragança [P] 80 F3
Brahestad / Raahe [FIN] 198 C4
Brahetrolleborg [DK] 156 D4
Brail [CH] 72 B2
Brăila [RO] 206 D6
Braine [F] 44 A2
Braine-le-Comte [B] 28 H3
Braintree [GB] 14 F3
Brake [D] 18 D4
Brakel [B] 28 G3
Brakel [D] 32 E4
Bräkne-Hoby [S] 158 F1
Brålanda [S] 166 D5
Bram [F] 106 B4
Brämhult [S] 162 B2
Bramming [DK] 156 B2
Brampton [GB] 8 E5
Bramsche [D] 32 D2
Branč [SK] 62 H3
Branč [SK] 64 A4
Branca [I] 116 B1
Brancaleone Marina [I] 124 D8
Brancion [F] 56 G6
Brancoli, Pieve di- [I] 110 D5
Brâncoveni [RO] 150 G1
Brand [A] 72 A1
Brandal [N] 180 C3
Brändbo [S] 184 D5
Brandbu [N] 170 H4
Brande [DK] 156 C1
Bränden [S] 182 F6
Brandenberg [A] 60 E6
Brandenburg [D] 34 D2
Brand-Erbisdorf [D] 48 E1
Brandhof [A] 62 D6
Brandis [D] 34 E4
Brändö [FIN] 176 C5
Brandomil [E] 78 B2
Brandon [F] 56 F6
Brandon [GB] 8 F6
Brandstorp [S] 162 D1
Brandval [N] 172 D5
Brandýsek [CZ] 48 F3
Brandýs nad Labem [CZ] 48 G3
Braniewo [PL] 22 F2
Braniśovice [CZ] 62 F2
Branitz, Schloss- [D] 34 F4
Brankovice [CZ] 50 D6
Brännåker [S] 190 F4
Branne [F] 66 D3
Brannenburg [D] 60 F5
Brännland [S] 190 H6
Brañosera [E] 82 D4
Brańsk [PL] 38 E1
Brantôme [F] 66 F2
Branzi [I] 70 H3
Bras-d'Asse [F] 108 C3
Braskereidfoss [N] 172 D4
Braslaw [BY] 202 H4
Braslaw [BY] 204 B4
Braşov [RO] 206 C5
Brassac [F] 106 C3
Brassac-les-Mines [F] 68 D3
Brasschaat [B] 30 D2
Bras-sur-Meuse [F] 44 D3
Brastad [S] 166 C5
Břasy [CZ] 48 E4
Brataj [AL] 128 B6
Bråte [N] 166 C1
Bratislava [SK] 62 G4
Bratków Dolny [PL] 36 F4
Brattabø [N] 170 C4
Brattåker [S] 190 F4
Brattbäcken [S] 190 F5
Brattfors [S] 166 F2
Brattingsborg [DK] 156 E2
Brattvåg [N] 180 D3
Bratunac [BIH] 154 F4
Bråtveit [N] 164 C1
Bratya Daskolovi [BG] 148 C5
Braubach [D] 46 B2
Braunau [A] 60 G4
Braunfels [D] 46 C2
Braunlage [D] 32 H4
Braunschweig [D] 32 H2
Braus, Col de- [F] 108 F4
Bravone [F] 114 C4
Bray / Bré [IRL] 4 G3
Bray-sur-Seine [F] 42 G5
Bray-sur-Somme [F] 28 E5
Brazatortas [E] 96 D5
Brbinj [HR] 112 F5
Brčko [BIH] 154 E2
Brdjani [YU] 150 B2
Bré / Bray [IRL] 4 G3
Brebina [RO] 148 B1
Brécey [F] 26 D4
Brechin [GB] 8 F2
Brecht [B] 30 D2
Břeclav [CZ] 62 G3
Brecon [GB] 12 F2
Bred [S] 168 C2
Breda [NL] 16 D6
Bredaryd [S] 162 C4
Bredbyn [S] 184 F1
Bredebro [DK] 156 B4
Bredelar [D] 32 E4
Bredevad [DK] 156 B4
Bredsel [S] 198 A3
Bredsjö [S] 166 G1
Bredsjön [S] 184 E4
Bredstedt [D] 18 E1
Bree [B] 30 E3
Bregana [HR] 74 E5
Bregenz [A] 60 B6
Bregovo [BG] 150 E1
Bréhal [F] 26 D4
Brehna [D] 34 C5
Breidvik [N] 192 C6
Breifonn [N] 170 C5
Breil-sur-Roya [F] 108 F4
Breisach [D] 58 E3
Breisen [D] 34 D1
Breisjøberget [N] 172 D4
Breistein [N] 170 B3
Breitachklamm [D] 60 B6
Breite [CH] 58 F5
Breitengussbach Hallstadt [D] 46 G4
Breivikbotn [N] 196 A2
Breivikeidet [N] 192 E2
Brekke [N] 170 B2
Brekken [N] 182 D3
Brekkvasselv [N] 190 D4
Brekstad [N] 190 B6
Bremen [D] 18 D5
Bremerhaven [D] 18 D4
Bremervörde [D] 18 E4
Bremnes [N] 192 C3
Bremsnes [N] 180 E2
Breń [PL] 20 H6
Brenes [E] 94 H6
Brenna [N] 190 D3
Brenner Pass [Eur.] 72 D2
Breno [I] 72 B5
Brentwood [GB] 14 F4
Brenzone [I] 72 C5
Brescello [I] 110 E2
Bréscia [I] 72 B6
Breskens [NL] 28 G1
Bressanone / Brixen [I] 72 D3
Bressuire [F] 54 D3
Brest [BG] 148 A2
Brest [BY] 38 F3
Brest [F] 40 B2
Brestova [HR] 112 E2
Brestovac [YU] 150 D4
Brestovac [YU] 150 D2
Brestovačka Banja [YU] 150 D2
Brestovăţ [RO] 76 H5
Bretenoux [F] 66 H4
Bretesche, Château de la- [F] 40 E5
Breteuil [F] 28 D5
Breteuil [F] 26 H5
Bretten [D] 46 C6
Breuberg [D] 46 D4
Breuil-Cervínia [I] 70 D3
Breuna [D] 32 E4
Brevens Bruk [S] 166 H4
Brevik [N] 164 G3
Brevik [S] 168 E3
Breza [BIH] 154 D4
Brežice [SLO] 74 D5
Brežiški Grad [SLO] 74 D5
Breznica [HR] 74 F5
Breznica Đak. [HR] 154 D1
Březnice [CZ] 48 E5
Breznik [BG] 150 F5
Brezno [SK] 64 D3
Brézolles [F] 26 H5
Brezová [SK] 62 H3
Brezovica [SK] 52 C6
Brezovica [YU] 150 C6
Brezovo [BG] 148 B5
Brezovo Polje [BIH] 154 E2
Brezovo Polje [HR] 154 A2
Briançon [F] 70 B6
Briare [F] 56 D2
Briatico [I] 124 C6
Bribirske Mostine [HR] 112 H5
Briceni [MD] 206 D3
Bricquebec [F] 26 D2
Bridgnorth [GB] 10 D6
Bridgwater [GB] 12 F4
Bridlington [GB] 10 G3
Bridport [GB] 12 F5
Briec [F] 40 B3
Brie-Comte-Robert [F] 42 G4
Brielle [NL] 16 C5
Brienne-le-Château [F] 44 B5
Brienz [CH] 70 E1
Brienza [I] 120 G4
Brieskow-Finkenheerd [D] 34 G3
Brieves [E] 78 G3
Briey [F] 44 E3
Brig [CH] 70 E2
Brigg [GB] 10 G4
Brighton [GB] 14 E5
Brignogan-Plage [F] 40 B1
Brignoles [F] 108 C5
Brignoud [F] 68 H4
Brihuega [E] 88 H5
Brijesta [HR] 152 B3
Brilon [D] 32 D4
Brimnes [N] 170 D4
Brinches [P] 94 E3
Bríndisi [I] 122 G4
Brinje [HR] 112 F2
Brinkum [D] 18 D5
Brinon [F] 56 E3
Briones [E] 82 G6
Brionne [F] 26 H4
Brioude [F] 68 D3
Brioux-sur-Boutonne [F] 54 D5
Briouze [F] 26 F5
Brisighella [I] 110 G4
Brissac-Quincé [F] 54 D1
Brissago [CH] 70 F3
Bristol [GB] 12 G3
Brive-la-Gaillarde [F] 66 G3
Briviesca [E] 82 F5
Brixen / Bressanone [I] 72 D3
Brixham [GB] 12 E5
Brixlegg [A] 60 E6
Brjanslækur [IS] 194 B2
Brnaze [HR] 152 A1
Brněnec [CZ] 50 C5
Brno [CZ] 50 C6
Bro [S] 168 D2
Bro [S] 168 G4
Broadstairs [GB] 14 G5
Broager [DK] 156 C4
Broby [S] 158 D1
Broceni [LV] 200 C5
Brock [D] 32 C2
Bröckel [D] 32 G2
Brockenhurst [GB] 12 G5
Brod [BIH] 152 D2
Brod [YU] 128 D1
Brodarevo [YU] 150 A4
Broddebo [S] 162 F1
Brodenbach [D] 44 H1
Brodick [GB] 8 C3
Brod na Kupi [HR] 112 F1
Brodnica [PL] 22 F5
Brody [PL] 34 G4
Brody [PL] 38 C6
Brody [PL] 36 A3
Brody [UA] 206 C2
Broglie [F] 26 G4
Brohl [D] 30 H6
Brojce [PL] 20 G3
Brok [PL] 38 C1
Brokind [S] 168 A6
Brolo [I] 124 B6
Bromarv [FIN] 176 E6
Brome [D] 32 H2
Bromma [N] 170 G4
Bromölla [S] 158 E1
Brömsebro [S] 158 G1
Bromsgrove [GB] 12 H1
Brønderslev [DK] 160 E3
Broni [I] 70 G6
Bronikowo [PL] 20 H5
Bronnbach [D] 46 E4
Brønnøysund [N] 190 C3
Brøns [DK] 156 B3
Bronte [I] 126 F3
Broons [F] 26 B5
Brørup [DK] 156 B2
Brösarp [S] 158 D2
Brossac [F] 66 E2
Brøstadbotn [N] 192 D3
Brøstrud [N] 170 F4
Brötjemark [S] 162 D1
Broto [E] 84 E5
Brottby [S] 168 E2
Bröttem [N] 182 B2
Brou [F] 42 D5
Brouage [F] 54 C5
Brough [GB] 10 E2
Broughshane [GB] 2 G3
Broughton in Furness [GB] 10 D2
Brouis, Col de- [F] 108 F4
Broumov [CZ] 50 B2
Brouvelieures [F] 58 C2
Brouwershaven [NL] 16 B5
Brovary [UA] 206 E2
Brovst [DK] 160 D3
Brownhills [GB] 10 E6
Brozas [E] 86 G4
Brseč [HR] 112 E2
Brtnice [CZ] 50 A6
Bruchhausen-Vilsen [D] 18 E6
Bruchhauser Steine [D] 32 D5
Bruchsal [D] 46 C5
Bruck [A] 72 F2
Bruck [D] 48 C6
Brück [D] 34 D3
Bruck an der Grossglocknerstrasse [A] 72 G1
Bruck an der Leitha [A] 62 G5
Bruck an der Mur [A] 74 D1
Brückl [A] 74 C3
Brudzeń Duży [PL] 36 G2
Brüel [D] 20 A4
Bruère-Allichamps [F] 56 C4
Bruff [IRL] 4 D4
Brugg [CH] 58 F4
Brugge [B] 28 G1
Brugnato [I] 110 C4
Bruhagen [N] 180 E2
Brühl [D] 30 G4
Brújula, Puerto de- [E] 82 F6
Bruksvallarna [S] 182 E3
Brûlon [F] 42 A5
Brumath [F] 44 H5
Brummen [NL] 16 F5
Brumunddal [N] 172 B3
Brunau [D] 34 B1
Bruneck / Brunico [I] 72 E2
Brunehamel [F] 28 H5
Brunete [E] 88 F5
Brunflo [S] 182 H2
Brunheda [P] 80 E4
Brunico / Bruneck [I] 72 E2
Bruniquel [F] 66 G6
Brunkeberg [N] 164 E2
Brunlund [DK] 156 C4
Brunna [S] 168 D1
Brunnen [CH] 58 F6
Brunsbüttel [D] 18 E3
Brunsort Från [S] 166 G2
Brunssum [NL] 30 F4
Bruntál [CZ] 50 D4
Bruravik [N] 170 D4
Brus [YU] 150 C3
Brusand [N] 164 A4
Brušane [HR] 112 G4
Brusarci [BG] 150 F2
Brúsio [CH] 72 B4
Bruška Rodaljice [HR] 112 H5
Brusnichnoye [RUS] 178 E2
Brusník [SK] 64 D4
Brussel / Bruxelles [B] 30 C4
Brüssow [D] 20 E5
Brusy [PL] 22 C4
Bruvno [HR] 112 H4
Bruvoll [N] 172 C4
Bruxelles / Brussel [B] 30 C4
Bruyères [F] 58 C2
Bruzaholm [S] 162 E2
Bruzzano Zeffirio [I] 124 D8
Brvenik [YU] 150 B3
Brwinów [PL] 38 B3
Bryansk [RUS] 204 E6
Brydal [N] 182 C5
Bryne [N] 164 A3
Bryrup [DK] 156 C1
Brza Palanka [YU] 150 E1
Brzeće [YU] 150 C4
Brzeg [PL] 50 D1
Brzeg Dolny [PL] 36 C6
Brześć Kujawski [PL] 36 F2
Brzesko [PL] 52 B4
Brzeszcze [PL] 50 G4
Brzezie [PL] 36 E4
Brzezie [PL] 22 B4
Brzeziny [PL] 36 E5
Brzeziny [PL] 36 H4
Brzeźnica [PL] 52 D3
Brzeźnica [PL] 50 H4
Brzostek [PL] 52 D4
Brzóza [PL] 38 C4
Brzoza [PL] 22 D6
Brzozie Lubawskie [PL] 22 F5
Brzozów [PL] 52 E4
Bua [S] 160 H3
Buavåg [N] 164 A1
Bubiai [LT] 202 E4
Bubry [F] 40 D3
Buca [TR] 144 C4
Buçaco [P] 80 B6
Bučany [SK] 62 H4
Buccheri [I] 126 F4
Bucchianico [I] 116 D4
Buchach [UA] 206 C3
Buchen [D] 46 D4
Buchen [D] 18 G4
Buchenwald [D] 34 A6
Buchholz [D] 18 F5
Buchin Prohod [BG] 150 F4
Buchloe [D] 60 C4
Buchlov [CZ] 62 G2
Buchs [CH] 58 H6
Buchy [F] 28 C5
Bučin [MK] 128 E3
Búcine [I] 110 F6
Bučje [YU] 150 D2
Bückeburg [D] 32 E2
Bücken [D] 18 E6
Buckfastleigh [GB] 12 E5
Buckie [GB] 6 F5
Buckingham [GB] 14 D3
Buckow [D] 34 F2
Bučovice [CZ] 50 C6
Bucquoy [F] 28 E4
Bucsa [H] 76 F1
Bucureşti [RO] 206 C6
Buczek [PL] 36 G5
Buczyna [PL] 52 F3
Bud [N] 180 E2
Budakovo [MK] 128 E3
Budaörs [H] 64 C6
Budapest [H] 64 C6
Búðardalur [IS] 194 C3
Buddusò [I] 118 D3
Bude [GB] 12 D4
Budeşti [RO] 206 C6
Budilovo [RUS] 200 G2
Budimci [HR] 154 D1
Budimir [HR] 152 A2
Büdingen [D] 46 D2
Budišov nad Budišovkou [CZ] 50 D4
Budmirici [MK] 128 F3
Budogoshch [RUS] 204 D2
Budomierz [PL] 52 G3
Budoni [I] 118 E3
Budowo [PL] 22 C2
Budrio [I] 110 F3
Budry [PL] 24 C2
Budva [YU] 152 D4
Budyně nad Ohří [CZ] 48 F3
Budziszewice [PL] 36 H4
Budzyń [PL] 36 C1
Bue [N] 164 B4
Bue Marino, Grotta del- [I] 118 E4
Bueña [E] 90 D6
Buen Amor, Castillo- [E] 80 H6
Buenavista del Norte [E] 100 B5
Buendia [E] 88 H6
Buğdayli [TR] 146 D5
Bugeat [F] 68 A2
Buggerru [I] 118 B6
Bugojno [BIH] 154 C4
Bugøyfjord [N] 196 E3
Bugøynes [N] 196 E2
Bugyi [H] 76 C2
Bühl [D] 58 F1
Buhuşi [RO] 206 D4
Büileşti [RO] 150 F2
Builth Wells [GB] 12 F1
Buis-les-Baronnies [F] 108 B2
Buitenpost [NL] 16 F2
Buitrago [E] 88 G4
Bujalance [E] 102 D1
Bujanovac [YU] 150 D5
Bujaraloz [E] 90 F4
Buje [HR] 112 D1
Bujoru [RO] 148 C2
Buk [PL] 36 C3
Buk [PL] 20 F5
Bükkösd [H] 76 A5
Bukovi [YU] 150 A2
Bukovo, Manastir- [YU] 150 E1
Bukowiec [PL] 36 B3
Bukowina Tatrzańska [PL] 52 B6
Bukowo Morskie [PL] 22 A2
Bukowsko [PL] 52 E5
Bülach [CH] 58 F4
Buldan [TR] 144 F4
Bülgarene [BG] 148 B3
Bülgarene [BG] 148 B4
Bülgarevo [BG] 148 G2
Bülgarevo [BG] 148 F4
Bülgarska Polyana [BG] 146 A1
Bülgarski Izvor [BG] 148 A4
Bulgnéville [F] 58 B2
Bulken [N] 170 C3
Bulkowo Wieś [PL] 36 H2
Bullarby [S] 166 C4
Bullas [E] 104 B2
Bulle [CH] 70 C1
Bulqizë [AL] 128 C2
Bultei [I] 118 D4
Buna [BIH] 152 C2
Bunclody [IRL] 4 F4
Buncrana [IRL] 2 F2
Bunde [D] 16 H2
Bünde [D] 32 E2
Bundoran [IRL] 2 D3
Bungay [GB] 14 G2
Bunić [HR] 112 G3
Bunkris [S] 172 F2
Bunleix [F] 68 B2
Bunmahon [IRL] 4 E5
Bunnahowen [IRL] 2 B3
Bunnyconnellan [IRL] 2 C3
Buñol [E] 98 E4
Bunratty [IRL] 2 C6
Bunratty Castle [IRL] 2 C6
Buonalbergo [I] 120 F2
Buonconvento [I] 114 G2
Buonfornello [I] 126 D2
Buonvicino [I] 124 C3
Buoux, Fort de- [F] 108 B3
Burano [I] 72 F6
Burbach [D] 32 C6
Burcei [I] 118 D7
Bureå [S] 198 A4
Burela [E] 78 E2
Büren [CH] 58 D5
Büren [D] 32 D4
Burfjord [N] 192 F1
Burford [GB] 12 H3
Burg [D] 34 C3
Burg [D] 18 H2
Burg [D] 18 E3
Burgas [BG] 148 F4
Burgau [D] 60 C3
Burgau [P] 94 B5
Burgbernheim [D] 46 F5
Burgdorf [CH] 58 E5
Burgdorf [D] 32 G2
Burgebrach [D] 46 F4
Bürgel [D] 34 B6
Bürgeln [D] 58 E4
Burgelu / Elburgo [E] 102 B4
Burghaun [D] 46 E1
Burghausen [D] 60 G4
Burg Hessenstein [D] 32 E5
Burgh-Haamstede [NL] 16 B5
Búrgio [I] 126 C3
Burgistein [CH] 58 D6
Burgjoss [D] 46 E3
Burg Klam [A] 62 C4
Burgkunstadt [D] 46 G3
Burglengenfeld [D] 48 B6
Burg Metternich [D] 44 G1
Burgos [E] 82 E6
Burgsinn [D] 46 E3
Burg Stargard [D] 20 D5
Burgsvik [S] 168 G6
Burguete / Auritz [E] 84 C3
Burguillos [E] 94 G5
Burguillos del Cerro [E] 94 G3
Burg Vetschau [D] 34 F4
Burhaniye [TR] 144 C2
Burie [F] 54 D6
Burila Mare [RO] 150 E1
Burjassot [E] 98 E4
Burladingen [D] 58 G2
Burnham-on-Crouch [GB] 14 F4
Burnham-on-Sea [GB] 12 F3
Burnley [GB] 10 E3
Burón [E] 82 C3
Buron, Château de- [F] 68 D3
Buronzo [I] 70 E4
Burravoe [GB] 6 H3
Burrel [AL] 128 B2
Burriana / Borriana [E] 98 F3
Burs [S] 168 G5
Bursa [TR] 146 F4
Burseryd [S] 162 B3
Bürstadt [D] 46 C4
Burton upon Trent [GB] 10 E6
Burträsk [S] 198 A5
Burvik [S] 198 B5
Burwell [GB] 14 F2
Bury [GB] 10 E4
Buryn' [UA] 206 G1
Bury St Edmunds [GB] 14 F3
Burzenin [PL] 36 F5
Busalla [I] 110 B3
Busana [I] 110 D4
Busca [I] 108 F2
Busdorf [D] 18 F1
Buseto Palizzolo [I] 126 B2
Bushat [AL] 128 A1
Bushmills [GB] 2 G2
Bushtricë [AL] 128 C1
Bus'k [UA] 206 C2
Busko-Zdrój [PL] 52 B2
Bušno [PL] 38 G6
Busot [E] 104 E2
Busovača [BIH] 154 D4
Bussang [F] 58 D3
Bussang, Col de- [F] 58 D3
Busseto [I] 110 D2
Bussolengo [I] 72 C6
Bussoleno [I] 70 C5
Bussum [NL] 16 E4
Busto Arsízio [I] 70 F4
Busto Garolfo [I] 70 F4
Büsum [D] 18 E2
Butan [BG] 150 G3
Butera [I] 126 E4
Bütgenbach [B] 30 F5
Buthrotum [AL] 132 B2
Butler's Bridge [IRL] 2 E4
Butrint [AL] 132 B2
Butsyn [UA] 38 H5
Buttelstedt [D] 34 A6
Buttevant [IRL] 4 C4
Buttingsrud [N] 170 H4

Buttle [S] 168 G5
Buttstädt [D] 34 B6
Butzbach [D] 46 C2
Bützow [D] 20 B3
Buvik [N] 182 B1
Buvika [N] 182 D5
Buxtehude [D] 18 F4
Buxton [GB] 10 E5
Buxu, Cueva del- [E] 82 C2
Buxy [F] 56 F5
Büyükçekmece [TR] 146 E3
Büyükkaraağaç [TR] 142 E3
Büyükkarıştıran [TR] 146 C2
Büyükorhan [TR] 146 F5
Buzançais [F] 54 G3
Buzancy [F] 44 D3
Buzău [RO] 206 D6
Buzescu [RO] 148 B1
Buzet [HR] 112 D1
Buziaş [RO] 76 H6
Byahoml' [BY] 204 B5
Byala [BG] 148 C2
Byala [BG] 148 F3
Byala Slatina [BG] 150 G3
Byal Izvor [BG] 130 E1
Byalynichy [BY] 204 C5
Bybjerg [DK] 156 F2
Bychawa [PL] 38 E6
Byczki [PL] 36 H4
Byczyna [PL] 36 E6
Bydgoszcz [PL] 22 D6
Byenyakoni [BY] 202 G6
Bygdeå [S] 198 A5
Bygdeträsk [S] 198 A5
Bygdin [N] 170 F2
Bygdsiljum [S] 198 A5
Bygland [N] 164 D4
Byglandsfjord [N] 164 D4
Bygstad [N] 170 B1
Bykle [N] 164 D2
Byllis [AL] 128 B5
Bylnice [CZ] 64 A2
Byrkjedal [N] 164 B3
Byrkjelo [N] 180 D5
Byrknes [N] 170 A2
Byrness [GB] 8 F5
Byrum [DK] 160 F3
Byrum [S] 162 H3
Byšice [CZ] 48 G3
Byske [S] 198 A4
Bystrianska Jaskyňa [SK] 64 D2
Bystřice [CZ] 48 G4
Bystřice nad Pernštejnem [CZ] 50 B5
Bystřice pod Hostýnem [CZ] 50 D6
Bystrzyca Kłodzka [PL] 50 C3
Byszki [PL] 22 B5
Byszyno [PL] 20 H4
Bytča [SK] 50 F6
Bytom [PL] 50 F3
Bytom Odrzański [PL] 36 A4
Bytonia [PL] 22 D4
Bytów [PL] 22 C3
Byxelkrok [S] 162 H3
Bzenec [CZ] 62 G2
Bzovík [SK] 64 C4

C

Cabaçao [P] 86 D5
Cabaj-Čápor [SK] 64 A4
Cabañaquinta [E] 78 H4
Cabañas [E] 78 D2
Cabanes [E] 98 G3
Cabeço de Vide [P] 86 E5
Cabeza del Buey [E] 96 C4
Cabezamesada [E] 96 G2
Cabezarados [E] 96 E4
Cabezas Rubias [E] 94 E4
Cabezón de la Sal [E] 82 E3
Cabezuela del Valle [E] 88 B5
Cabo de Gata [E] 102 G6
Cabo de Palos [E] 104 D4
Cabo São Vicente [P] 94 A5
Cabourg [F] 26 F3
Cabra [E] 102 C2
Cabra del Santo Cristo [E] 102 F2
Cábras [I] 118 B5
Cabreiros [E] 78 D2
Cabrela [P] 86 C6
Cabrera [E] 104 E6
Cabrerets [F] 66 G5
Cabrillas [E] 88 B3
Cacabelos [E] 78 F5
Čačak [YU] 150 B2
Cáccamo [I] 126 D2
Cacemes [P] 86 A5
Cáceres [E] 86 H5
Cachopo [P] 94 D5
Čachtice [SK] 62 H3
Čačini [HR] 76 A6
Cadaqués [E] 92 G2
Cadaval [P] 86 B4
Cadavedo [E] 78 G2
Čadavica [BIH] 154 B3
Čađavica [HR] 76 A6
Čadca [SK] 50 F5
Cadelbosco di Sopra [I] 110 E2
Cadenábbia [I] 70 G3
Cadenberge [D] 18 E3
Cadenet [F] 108 B4
Cádiar [E] 102 E5
Cadillac [F] 66 D4
Cádiz [E] 100 F4
Caen [F] 26 F3
Caernarfon [GB] 10 B4
Caerphilly [GB] 12 F3
Čafasan [MK] 128 C3
Çağış [TR] 144 D1
Cagli [I] 112 B6
Cágliari [I] 118 C7
Cagnano Varano [I] 116 G6
Cagnes-sur-Mer [F] 108 E4
Caherdaniel [IRL] 4 A4
Cahermurphy [IRL] 2 B6
Cahersiveen [IRL] 4 A4
Cahir [IRL] 4 D4
Cahors [F] 66 G5
Cahul [MD] 206 D5
Caiazzo [I] 120 E2
Cairnryan [GB] 8 C5
Cairo Montenotte [I] 108 G3
Caister-on-Sea [GB] 14 H2
Caivano [I] 120 E3
Çajarc [F] 66 G5
Čajetina [YU] 150 A3
Čajniče [BIH] 152 E2
Čakajovce [SK] 64 A4
Çakırbeyli [TR] 144 E5
Čakovec [HR] 74 F4
Çal [TR] 144 G4
Cala [E] 94 G4
Cala Blanca [E] 104 G4
Cala Blava [E] 104 E5
Calabor [E] 80 F3
Calabritto [I] 120 F3
Calaceite [E] 90 G6
Calacuccia [F] 114 B3
Cala del Moral, La- [E] 102 B5
Cala d'Oliva [I] 118 B2
Cala d'Or [E] 104 F6
Calaf [E] 92 D3
Calafat [RO] 150 F2
Calafell [E] 92 D5
Cala Galdana [E] 104 G4
Cala Gonone [I] 118 E4
Calahonda [E] 102 B5
Calahonda-Chaparral [E] 102 E5
Calahorra [E] 84 A5
Calais [F] 14 G6
Cala Liberotto [I] 118 E4
Cala Millor [E] 104 F5
Calamocha [E] 90 D5
Calamonte [E] 94 H2
Cala Moreia-Cala Morlanda [E] 104 F5
Cala Morell [E] 104 G4
Calañas [E] 94 F5
Calanda [E] 90 F6
Calangiánus [I] 118 D3
Cala'n Porter [E] 104 H5
Cala Pi [E] 104 E5
Călăraşi [MD] 206 D4
Călăraşi [RO] 206 D6
Cala Ratjada [E] 104 F5
cala Sa Calobra [E] 104 E4
Cala Santanyí [E] 104 E6
Calascibetta [I] 126 E3
Calasetta [I] 118 B7
Calasparra [E] 104 B2
Calatafimi Segesta [I] 126 B2
Calatañazor [E] 90 B3
Cala Tarida [E] 104 B5
Calatayud [E] 90 D4
Calatorao [E] 90 D4
Calatrava, Convento de- [E] 96 E5
Calatrava la Vieja [E] 96 F4
Calau [D] 34 F4
Cala Vadella [E] 104 B5
Calbe [D] 34 B4
Caldarola [I] 116 C2
Caldas da Rainha [P] 86 B3
Caldas de Reis [E] 78 B3
Caldas de Vizela [P] 80 C3
Caldes de Boí [E] 84 F6
Caldes de Malavella [E] 92 F3
Caldes de Montbui [E] 92 E4
Caldes d'Estrac [E] 92 F4
Caldirola [I] 110 B2
Calella [E] 92 F4
Calella de Palafrugell [E] 92 G3
Calenzana [F] 114 B3
Calera y Chozas [E] 88 C6
Caleruega [E] 88 H2
Cales de Mallorca [E] 104 F5
Calheta [P] 100 A3
Çali [TR] 146 F5
Calig [E] 92 A6
Calignac [F] 66 E5
Çalıklı [TR] 144 F3
Călimăneşti [RO] 206 B6
Calimera [I] 122 G5
Calitri [I] 120 G3
Çalköy [TR] 144 H2
Callac [F] 40 D2
Callan [IRL] 4 E4
Callander [GB] 8 D2
Callington [GB] 12 D4
Callosa d'en Sarrià [E] 104 E2
Callosa de Segura [E] 104 D3
Călmăţuiu [RO] 148 B2
Calne [GB] 12 G3
Calnegre, Puntas de- [E] 104 B4
Calolziocorte [I] 70 G4
Calonge [E] 92 G3
Calpe / Calp [E] 104 F2
Caltabellotta [I] 126 C3
Caltagirone [I] 126 F4
Caltanissetta [I] 126 E3
Caltavuturo [I] 126 E2
Çaltı [TR] 146 H4
Çaltılıbük [TR] 146 E5
Caltra [IRL] 2 D5
Călugăreni [RO] 148 C1
Caluso [I] 70 D5
Calvello [I] 120 H4
Calvi [F] 114 A3
Calvörde [D] 34 B2
Calw [D] 58 G1
Calzadilla de la Cueza [E] 82 C5
Camaiore [I] 110 D5
Camaldoli [I] 110 G5
Camaldoli, Eremo di- [I] 110 G5
Çamaltı [TR] 144 C4
Câmara de Lobos [P] 100 B3
Camarena de la Sierra [E] 98 E2
Camarès [F] 106 D3
Camaret [F] 40 B2
Camariñas [E] 78 B2
Camarzana de Tera [E] 80 H3
Cambados [E] 78 B4
Cambeo [E] 78 C5
Camberg [D] 46 C2
Camberley [GB] 14 D4
Cambo-les-Bains [F] 84 C2
Camborne [GB] 12 C5
Cambrai [F] 28 F4
Cambre [E] 78 C2
Cambremer [F] 26 G4
Cambridge [GB] 14 F3
Cambrils [E] 92 C5
Camburg [D] 34 B6
Camelford [GB] 12 C4
Çameli [TR] 142 G2
Camenca [MD] 206 E3
Camerino [I] 116 B2
Camigliatello [I] 124 D4
Caminha [P] 78 A5
Caminomorisco [E] 88 A4
Caminreal [E] 90 D6
Çamköy [TR] 142 D2
Çamlık [TR] 144 F2
Cammarata [I] 126 D3
Camogli [I] 110 B3
Camp [IRL] 4 B3
Campagna [I] 120 F4
Campagnático [I] 114 F2
Campan [F] 84 F4
Campana [I] 124 E4
Campanario [E] 96 B3
Campanas / Kanpaneta [E] 84 B4
Campanet, Coves de- [E] 104 E4
Campaspero [E] 88 F2
Campbeltown [GB] 2 H2
Câmpia Turzii [RO] 206 B5
Campi Bisenzio [I] 110 E5
Campiglia Soana [I] 70 D4
Campillo de Altobuey [E] 98 C3
Campillo de Arenas [E] 102 E3
Campillo de Llerena [E] 96 A4
Campillos [E] 102 B3
Câmpina [RO] 206 C6
Campione d'Italia [I] 70 G3
Campisábalos [E] 88 H4
Campi Salentina [I] 122 G4
Campo [E] 84 F6
Campobasso [I] 120 E1
Campobecerros [E] 78 D6
Campobello di Licata [I] 126 E4
Campobello di Mazara [I] 126 B3
Campocologno [CH] 72 B4
Campodarsego [I] 72 E6
Campo de Caso / Caso [E] 82 C2
Campo de Criptana [E] 96 G3
Campodón [E] 92 F2
Campofelice di Fitalia [I] 126 D2
Campofiorito [I] 126 C3
Campoformido [I] 72 G5
Campogalliano [I] 110 E3
Campohermoso [E] 102 G5
Campo Ligure [I] 110 A3
Campo Maior [P] 86 F6
Campomanes [E] 78 H4
Campomarino [I] 122 F5
Campomarino [I] 116 F5
Campora San Giovanni [I] 124 D5
Campo Real [E] 88 G6
Camporeale [I] 126 C2
Camporrobles [E] 98 D3
Campos [E] 104 E5
Camposampiero [I] 72 E6
Camposanto [I] 110 F2
Campotejar [E] 102 E3
Campo Tures / Sand in Taufers [I] 72 E2
Câmpulung [RO] 206 C6
Câmpulung Moldovenesc [RO] 206 C4
Çamsu [TR] 144 G2
Çan [TR] 146 C5
Cañada de Benatanduz [E] 98 F1
Cañadajuncosa [E] 98 B3
Čanak [HR] 112 G3
Çanakkale [TR] 146 B5
Canale [I] 108 G1
Canales de Molina [E] 90 C5
Canal S. Bovo [I] 72 E4
Canas de Senhorim [P] 80 C6
Cañaveral [E] 86 H4
Cañaveral de León [E] 94 G4
Cañaveras [E] 98 B1
Canazei [I] 72 E3
Cancale [F] 26 C4
Cancon [F] 66 E4
Candamo, Cueva de- [E] 78 H3
Candanchú [E] 84 D4
Çandarlı [TR] 144 C3
Candás [E] 78 H3
Candasnos [E] 90 G4
Candé [F] 40 G6
Candela [I] 120 G2
Candelario [E] 88 B4
Candeleda [E] 88 C5
Candia Lomellina [I] 70 F5
Çandır [TR] 142 F3
Canelli [I] 108 H2
Canelobre, Cueva de- [E] 104 E2
Canero [E] 78 G2
Canet [F] 106 E4
Canet de Mar [E] 92 F4
Cañete [E] 98 C2
Cañete la Real [E] 102 B3
Canet-Plage [F] 92 G1
Canfranc [E] 84 D4
Cangas [E] 78 B4
Cangas del Narcea [E] 78 F3
Cangas de Onís [E] 82 C2
Canha [P] 86 C5
Caniçada [P] 80 D3
Canicattini Bagni [I] 126 G5
Caniço [P] 100 B3
Caniles [E] 102 G4
Canino [I] 114 G4
Cañizal [E] 88 D2
Cañizares [E] 90 B6
Canjáyar [E] 102 F5
Cannai [I] 118 B7
Cannara [I] 116 A2
Canne [I] 120 H2
Cánnero Riviera [I] 70 F3
Cannes [F] 108 E5
Canneto [I] 114 E1
Canneto sull'Óglio [I] 110 D1
Cannich [GB] 6 D5
Cannóbio [I] 70 F3
Cannock [GB] 10 E6
Canosa di Puglia [I] 120 H2
Canossa [I] 110 D3
Canossa, Castello di- [I] 110 D3
Can Pastilla [E] 104 E5
Can Picafort [E] 104 F4
Cansano [I] 116 D5
Cantalapiedra [E] 88 D3
Cantalejo [E] 88 F3
Cantalpino [E] 88 D3
Cantanhede [P] 80 B6
Cantavieja [E] 98 F2
Čantavir [YU] 76 D5
Canterbury [GB] 14 F5
Cantillana [E] 94 H5
Cantoral de la Peña [E] 82 D4
Cantoria [E] 102 H4
Cantù [I] 70 G4
Canvey Island [GB] 14 F4
Cany-Barville [F] 26 H2
Caoria [I] 72 D4
Cáorle [I] 72 F6
Caorso [I] 70 H6
Capaccio [I] 120 F4
Capaci [I] 126 C1
Capalbio [I] 114 F4
Capannoli [I] 110 E6
Caparde [BIH] 154 E3
Caparra, Ruinas de- [E] 88 B5
Caparroso [E] 84 B5
Capbreton [F] 66 A6
Cap-d'Ail [F] 108 F4
Capdella [E] 84 G6
Capdenac-Gare [F] 66 H5
Cap d'En Font [E] 104 H5
Capendu [F] 106 C5
Capestang [F] 106 D4
Capestrano [I] 116 C4
Cap Ferret [F] 66 B3
Cap Gris Nez [F] 14 G6
Capinha [P] 86 F2
Capistrello [I] 116 C5
Capizzi [I] 126 F2
Čapljina [BIH] 152 C3
Capo Cavallo [F] 114 A3
Capodimonte [I] 114 G3
Capo di Ponte [I] 72 B4
Capo d'Orlando [I] 124 B6
Capoferrato [I] 118 E7
Capolíveri [I] 114 E3
Capo Rizzuto [I] 124 F5
Capoterra [I] 118 C7
Cappamore [IRL] 4 D3
Cappenberg [D] 32 C4
Cappoquin [IRL] 4 D5
Capracotta [I] 116 D6
Caprája [I] 114 D2
Capranica [I] 114 H4
Capri [I] 120 D4
Capriati a Volturno [I] 120 D1
Capriccioli [I] 118 E2
Captieux [F] 66 D5
Capua [I] 120 D2
Capurso [I] 122 E3
Caracal [RO] 148 A1
Caracenilla [E] 98 B2
Caracuel de Calatrava [E] 96 E4
Caraglio [I] 108 F2
Caraman [F] 106 B3
Caramulo [P] 80 C6
Caranga [E] 78 G4
Caransebeş [RO] 206 A5
Carantec [F] 40 C1
Caravaca [E] 104 B2
Caravaggio [I] 70 H5
Carbajales de Alba [E] 80 H4
Carbajo [E] 86 F4
Carballo [E] 78 C2
Carbon-Blanc [F] 66 D3
Carboneras [E] 102 H5
Carboneras de Guadazaón [E] 98 C3
Carbonero el Mayor [E] 88 F3
Carbónia [I] 118 B7
Carbonin / Schluderbach [I] 72 E3
Carbonne [F] 84 H4
Carcaboso [E] 88 A5
Carcabuey [E] 102 C3
Carcaixent [E] 98 E5
Carcans [F] 66 C2
Carcans-Plage [F] 66 B2
Carcar [E] 84 A5
Carcare [I] 108 H3
Carcassonne [F] 106 B4
Carcastillo [E] 84 B5
Carcavelos [P] 86 A5
Carceri, Eremo delle- [I] 116 A2
Carcès [F] 108 C5
Carcoforo [I] 70 E3
Çardak [TR] 144 G3
Çardak [TR] 146 B5
Çardak [TR] 144 G5
Cardedeu [E] 92 E4
Cardeña [E] 96 D6
Cardenete [E] 98 C3
Cardiff [GB] 12 F3
Cardigan [GB] 4 H6
Cardona [E] 92 D3
Carei [RO] 206 B4
Carene [TR] 144 C3
Carennac [F] 66 H4
Carentan [F] 26 E3
Carevac [BIH] 154 B4
Carev Dvor [MK] 128 D3
Carezza al Lago / Karersee [I] 72 D3
Cargèse [F] 114 A4
Carhaix-Plouguer [F] 40 C2
Caria [P] 86 F2
Cariati [I] 124 E4
Caričin Grad [YU] 150 D4
Carignan [F] 44 D2
Carignano [I] 70 D6
Cariñena [E] 90 D4
Cariño [E] 78 E1
Carinola [I] 120 D2
Carlantino [I] 120 F1
Carlentini [I] 126 G4
Carlet [E] 98 E5
Carling [F] 44 F4
Carlingford [IRL] 2 G4
Carlisle [GB] 8 E6
Carloforte [I] 118 B7
Carlow [D] 18 H4
Carlow / Ceatharlach [IRL] 4 F4
Carlton [GB] 10 F4
Carmagnola [I] 70 D6
Carmarthen [GB] 12 E2
Carmaux [F] 106 C2
Cármenes [E] 78 H4
Carmona [E] 94 H6
Carnac [F] 40 D5
Carndonagh [IRL] 2 F1
Carnew [IRL] 4 F4
Carnia [I] 72 G4
Carnlough [GB] 2 G3
Carnota [E] 78 B3
Carnoustie [GB] 8 F2
Carolei [I] 124 D4
Carolinensiel [D] 18 C3
Caronía [I] 126 F2
Carosino [I] 122 F4
Carpaneto Piacentino [I] 110 C2
Carpegna [I] 110 H5
Carpenédolo [I] 72 B6
Carpentras [F] 106 H3
Carpi [I] 110 E2
Carpignano Sesia [I] 70 E4
Carpineti [I] 110 E3
Carpineto Romano [I] 116 B6
Cărpiniş [RO] 76 G5
Carpino [I] 116 G6
Carpinone [I] 120 E1
Carquefou [F] 40 F6
Carqueiranne [F] 108 C6
Carral [E] 78 C2
Carrapateira [P] 94 A4
Carrara [I] 110 D4
Carraroe [IRL] 2 B5
Carrascalejo [E] 96 C1
Carrascosa del Campo [E] 98 A2
Carrazeda de Ansiães [P] 80 E4
Carrazedo [P] 80 E3
Carrbridge [GB] 6 E5
Carregado [P] 86 B4
Carregal do Sal [P] 80 C6
Carrega Ligure [I] 110 B3
Carregueiro [P] 94 C3
Carrick / An Charraig [IRL] 2 D2
Carrickfergus [GB] 2 G3
Carrickmacross [IRL] 2 F4
Carrick-on-Shannon [IRL] 2 D4
Carrick-on-Suir [IRL] 4 E4
Carriço [P] 86 C2
Carrigaline [IRL] 4 C5
Carrigallen [IRL] 2 E4
Carriganimmy [IRL] 4 C4
Carrigans [IRL] 2 F2
Carrigart [IRL] 2 F1
Carrión de Calatrava [E] 96 F4
Carrión de los Condes [E] 82 C5
Carrizo [E] 78 G5
Carrizosas [E] 96 G5
Carro [F] 106 G5
Carrouges [F] 26 F5
Carrowkeel [IRL] 2 F2
Carrù [I] 108 G2
Carryduff [GB] 2 G4
Carry-le-Rouet [F] 106 H5
Çarshovë [AL] 128 C6
Carsoli [I] 116 B5
Carsulae [I] 116 A3
Cartagena [E] 104 C4
Cártama [E] 102 B4
Cartaxo [P] 86 C4
Cartaya [E] 94 E5
Cartelle [E] 78 C5
Carteret [F] 26 D2
Cartoixa de Porta Coeli [E] 98 E4
Cartuja de Aula Dei [E] 90 E3
Carviçais [P] 80 F5
Carvin [F] 28 F3
Carvoeiro [P] 94 B5
Carwitz [D] 20 D5
Casabermeja [E] 102 C4
Casabona [I] 124 E4
Casa Branca [P] 94 C2
Casa Branca [P] 86 D5
Casa Branca [P] 94 D1
Casacalenda [I] 116 E6
Casáccia [CH] 70 H2
Casalabate [I] 122 G4
Casalarreina [E] 82 G6
Casalbordino [I] 116 E5
Casalbuono [I] 120 G5
Casalcipiano [I] 116 E6
Casalecchio di Reno [I] 110 F3
Casale Monferrato [I] 70 E5
Casalmaggiore [I] 110 D2
Casalpusterlengo [I] 70 H6
Casamáina [I] 116 C4
Casamari, Abbazia di- [I] 116 C6
Casamássima [I] 122 E3
Casamicciola Terme [I] 120 D3
Casamozza [F] 114 C3
Casarabonela [E] 102 B4
Casarano [I] 122 G5
Casares [E] 100 H5
Casares, Cueva de los- [E] 90 B5
Casariche [E] 102 B3
Casarrubios del Monte [E] 88 F6
Casas Cueva [E] 102 F3
Casas de Benítez [E] 98 B4
Casas de Fernando Alonso [E] 98 B4
Casas de Juan Núñez [E] 98 C5
Casas del Puerto [E] 104 C2
Casas de Reina [E] 94 H4
Casas-Ibáñez [E] 98 C4
Casatejada [E] 88 B6
Cascais [P] 86 A5
Cascante [E] 84 B6
Cascia [I] 116 B3
Casciana Terme [I] 110 E6
Cáscina [I] 110 D5
Căscioarele [RO] 148 D1
Casekow [D] 20 E5
Caselle [I] 70 D5
Caserta [I] 120 E2
Cashel [IRL] 4 D4
Cashel, Rock of- [IRL] 4 D4
Casina [I] 110 E3
Casinos [E] 98 E4
Čáslav [CZ] 48 H4
Casola Valsenio [I] 110 G4
Casoli [I] 116 D5
Casoria [I] 120 E3
Caspe [E] 90 F5
Cassà de la Selva [E] 92 F3
Cassagnes-Bégonhès [F] 68 B6
Cassano allo Ionio [I] 122 C6
Cassano d'Adda [I] 70 G5
Cassano delle Murge [I] 122 D3
Cassel [F] 28 E2
Cassibile [I] 126 G5
Cassine [I] 108 H2
Cassino [I] 120 D1
Cassis [F] 108 B5
Castagneto Carducci [I] 114 E1
Castalla [E] 104 D2
Castañar de Ibor [E] 96 C1
Castanet-Tolosan [F] 106 A3
Castanheira de Pera [P] 86 E2
Castasegna [CH] 70 H2
Casteau [B] 28 H3
Casteggio [I] 70 G6
Castejón de Monegros [E] 90 F4
Castejón de Sos [E] 84 F5
Castejón de Valdejasa [E] 90 E3
Castel Bolognese [I] 110 G4
Castelbouc [F] 68 C6
Castelbuono [I] 126 E2
Casteldelfino [I] 108 E2
Castel del Monte [I] 122 C2
Castel del Piano [I] 114 G2
Castel del Rio [I] 110 F4
Castel di Iúdica [I] 126 F3
Castel di Sangro [I] 116 D6
Castel Doria, Terme di- [I] 118 D3
Castelejo [P] 94 A5
Castelfidardo [I] 116 C1
Castelfiorentino [I] 110 E6
Castelfranco Emilia [I] 110 F3
Castelfranco in Miscano [I] 120 F2
Castelfranco Véneto [I] 72 E6
Castel Goffredo [I] 110 E1
Casteljaloux [F] 66 D5
Castellabate [I] 120 F5
Castellammare del Golfo [I] 126 C2
Castellammare di Stábia [I] 120 E3
Castellamonte [I] 70 D5
Castellana, Grotte di- [I] 122 E3
Castellana Grotte [I] 122 E3
Castellana Sícula [I] 126 E3
Castellane [F] 108 D4
Castellaneta [I] 122 E4
Castellar [E] 102 F1
Castellar de la Frontera [E] 100 G5
Castellar de la Muela [E] 90 C5
Castellar de Santiago [E] 96 F5
Castell' Arquato [I] 110 C2
Castell'Azzara [I] 114 G3
Castellazzo Bormida [I] 108 H2
Castelldans [E] 90 H5
Castelldefels [E] 92 D5
Castell de Ferro [E] 102 E5
Castelleone [I] 70 H5
Castelletto d'Orba [I] 110 A2
Castellfollit de la Roca [E] 92 F2
Castellina in Chianti [I] 114 G1
Castelló de la Plana / Castellón de la Plana [E] 98 F3
Castelló de la Ribera [E] 98 E6
Castelló d'Empúries [E] 92 G2
Castellón de la Plana / Castelló de la Plana [E] 98 F3
Castellote [E] 90 F6
Castello Tesino [I] 72 D4
Castellterçol [E] 92 E3
Castellúccio dei Sáuri [I] 120 G2
Castelluccio Sup. [I] 120 H5
Castelluzzo [I] 126 B2
Castelmagno [I] 108 F2
Castelmassa [I] 110 F2
Castelmauro [I] 116 F6
Castelmoron [F] 66 E5
Castelnau [F] 66 H4
Castelnaudary [F] 106 B4
Castelnau-de-Médoc [F] 66 C2
Castelnau-de-Montmiral [F] 106 B2
Castelnau-Magnoac [F] 84 F3
Castelnovo ne' Monti [I] 110 D3
Castelnuovo Berardenga [I] 114 G1
Castelnuovo della Dáunia [I] 120 F1
Castelnuovo di Garfagnana [I] 110 D4
Castelnuovo di Porto [I] 116 A5
Castelnuovo di Val di Cecina [I] 114 F1
Castelnuovo Don Bosco [I] 70 E6
Castelnuovo Scrívia [I] 70 F6
Castelo Branco [P] 86 F3
Castelo Branco [P] 80 F5
Castelo de Paiva [P] 80 C4
Castelo de Vide [P] 86 F4
Castelo do Neiva [P] 78 A6
Castel Porziano [I] 114 H6
Castelraimondo [I] 116 B2
Castel San Giovanni [I] 70 G6
Castel San Lorenzo [I] 120 F4
Castel San Pietro Terme [I] 110 F4
Castelsaraceno [I] 120 H5
Castelsardo [I] 118 C2
Castelsarrasin [F] 66 F6
Castelseprio [I] 70 F4
Castelserás [E] 90 F6
Casteltérmini [I] 126 D3
Castelvecchio Subequo [I] 116 C5
Castelverde [I] 70 H6
Castelvetere in Val Fortore [I] 120 F1
Castelvetrano [I] 126 B3
Castel Volturno [I] 120 D2
Castenaso [I] 110 F3
Castets [F] 66 B5
Castiádas [I] 118 D7
Castiglioncello [I] 114 E1
Castiglione d'Orcia [I] 114 G2
Castiglione dei Pepoli [I] 110 F4
Castiglione del Lago [I] 114 H2
Castiglione della Pescáia [I] 114 E3
Castiglione delle Stiviere [I] 72 B6
Castiglione Messer Marino [I] 116 E6
Castiglione Olona [I] 70 F4
Castiglion Fibocchi [I] 110 G6
Castiglion Fiorentino [I] 114 H1
Castilblanco [E] 96 C2
Castilblanco de los Arroyos [E] 94 G5
Castillejo de Martín Viejo [E] 86 H2
Castilliscar [E] 84 C5
Castillo de Locubín [E] 102 D3
Castillo de Tajarja [E] 102 D4
Castillo de Villamalefa [E] 98 F3
Castillon-la-Bataille [F] 66 D3
Castillonnès [F] 66 E4
Castillo Pasiega las Chimenas, Cuevas el- [E] 82 E3
Castione della Presolana [I] 72 A5
Castle Acre [GB] 14 G2
Castlebar [IRL] 2 C4
Castlebay/Bagh a Chaisteil [GB] 6 A5
Castlebellingham [IRL] 2 F5
Castleblayney [IRL] 2 F4
Castlebridge [IRL] 4 F5
Castlecomer [IRL] 4 E3
Castledermot [IRL] 4 F3
Castle Douglas [GB] 8 D5
Castleisland [IRL] 4 B4
Castlemaine [IRL] 4 B4
Castlemartyr [IRL] 4 D5
Castleplunkett [IRL] 2 D4
Castlepollard [IRL] 2 E5
Castlerea [IRL] 2 D4
Castletown [GBM] 10 B2
Castletownbere [IRL] 4 B5
Castletown House [IRL] 2 F6
Castletownroche [IRL] 4 D4
Castletownsend [IRL] 4 B5
Castlewellan [GB] 2 G4
Castrejón [E] 88 D2
Castres [F] 106 B3
Castricum [NL] 16 D3
Castries [F] 106 F4
Castril [E] 102 G3
Castrillo de la Reina [E] 88 H2
Castro [E] 78 C4
Castro [I] 114 G3
Castro Caldelas [E] 78 D5
Castrocaro Terme [I] 110 G4
Castrocontrigo [E] 78 F6
Castro da Cola [P] 94 C4
Castro Daire [P] 80 C5
Castro de Borneiro [E] 78 B2
Castro dei Volsci [I] 120 C1
Castro del Río [E] 102 C2
Castro de Rei [E] 78 E3
Castrojeriz [E] 82 D6
Castro Marim [P] 94 D5
Castromonte [E] 88 E1
Castronuevo [E] 88 D1
Castronuño [E] 88 D2
Castropol [E] 78 F2
Castrop-Rauxal [D] 30 H3
Castroreale [I] 124 B7
Castroreale Terme [I] 124 A7
Castro-Urdiales [E] 82 G3
Castroverde [E] 78 E3
Castro Verde [P] 94 C4

Castroverde de Cerrato [E] 88 F2
Castrovillari [I] 122 C6
Castuera [E] 96 B4
Çatak [TR] 142 E1
Çatalca [TR] 146 D2
Čatane [RO] 150 F2
Catánia [I] 126 G3
Catanzaro [I] 124 E5
Catanzaro Marina [I] 124 E5
Catarroja [E] 98 E5
Catenanuova [I] 126 F3
Cateraggio [F] 114 C4
Catoira [E] 78 B3
Catterick [GB] 10 F2
Cattolica [I] 112 B5
Cattolica Eraclea [I] 126 C3
Catus [F] 66 G5
Caudebec [F] 26 H3
Caudete [E] 104 D1
Caudeval [F] 106 B5
Caudry [F] 28 F4
Caulonia [I] 124 D7
Caulonia [I] 124 E6
Caumont [F] 26 E3
Caunes-Minervois [F] 106 C4
Cauro [F] 114 B5
Căuşani [MD] 206 E5
Caussade [F] 66 G6
Cauterets [F] 84 E4
Cauville [F] 26 G2
Cava [E] 92 B6
Cava de' Tirreni [I] 120 E3
Cava d'Ispica [I] 126 F5
Cavaglià [I] 70 E5
Cavaillon [F] 106 H4
Cavalaire-sur-Mer [F] 108 D6
Cavalese [I] 72 D4
Cavalière [F] 108 D6
Cavallino [I] 122 G5
Cavallino [I] 72 F6
Cavalls, Cova dels- [E] 98 G2
Cavan / An Cabhán [IRL] 2 E4
Cavárzere [I] 110 G2
Çavdarhisar [TR] 144 G2
Çavdır [TR] 142 H1
Cave del Predil [I] 72 H4
Cavo [I] 114 E2
Cavour [I] 70 C6
Cavriglia [I] 110 F6
Cavtat [HR] 152 C4
Çayağzi [TR] 146 F2
Caylus [F] 66 G6
Cayrols [F] 68 A4
Çayyaka [TR] 146 F5
Cazalegas [E] 88 D6
Cazalla de la Sierra [E] 94 H5
Cazals [F] 66 F4
Cazaubon [F] 66 D6
Cazeneuve, Château de- [F] 66 D4
Cazères [F] 84 G4
Cazin [BIH] 112 H2
Čazma [HR] 74 F6
Cazorla [E] 102 F2
Cea [E] 78 C4
Cea [E] 82 C5
Ceatharlach / Carlow [IRL] 4 F4
Cebolla [E] 96 E1
Čebovce [SK] 64 C4
Cebreiro [E] 78 E4
Cebreros [E] 88 E5
Cebrones del Rio [E] 78 G6
Ceccano [I] 120 C1
Çece [H] 76 B3
Čechtice [CZ] 48 G5
Cécina [I] 114 E1
Ceclavín [E] 86 G4
Cecos [E] 78 F4
Cedeira [E] 78 D1
Cedillo [E] 86 F4
Cedynia [PL] 34 F1
Cee [E] 78 B2
Cefalù [I] 126 E2
Cegléd [H] 76 D2
Céglie Messápica [I] 122 F4
Cegrane [MK] 128 D1
Cehegín [E] 104 B2
Ceira [P] 86 D2
Čejč [CZ] 62 G2
Čekiške [LT] 202 F5
Ceków Kolonia [PL] 36 E4
Čelákovice [CZ] 48 G3
Celano [I] 116 C5
Celanova [E] 78 C5
Celaru [RO] 150 G1
Celbridge [IRL] 2 F6
Čelebić [BIH] 154 B4
Celerina [CH] 70 H2
Čelić [BIH] 154 E3
Celico [I] 124 D4
Celjahavi [BY] 204 A6
Celje [SLO] 74 D4
Cella [E] 98 D1
Celldömölk [H] 74 G1
Celle [D] 32 G1
Celle di Bulgheria [I] 120 G5
Celle Ligure [I] 108 H3
Cellers / Castell de Mur [E] 92 C2
Celles-sur-Belle [F] 54 D4
Celopeci [MK] 128 D2
Celorico da Beira [P] 80 D6
Celorico de Basto [P] 80 D4
Čemerno [BIH] 152 D2
Cemke [TR] 146 F2
Cencenighe [I] 72 E4
Ceneköy [TR] 146 C3
Cenicentos [E] 88 E5
Cenicero [E] 82 G6
Cenizzate [E] 98 C4
Čenta [YU] 154 G2
Centallo [I] 108 F2
Centelles [E] 92 E3
Cento [I] 110 F3
Centuri [F] 114 C2
Centúripe [I] 126 F3
Çepan [AL] 128 C5
Čepin [HR] 154 D1
Cepos [P] 86 E2
Čepovan [SLO] 72 H5
Ceprano [I] 120 C1
Cerami [I] 126 F2
Ceranów [PL] 38 D2
Cerbère [F] 92 G2
Cercal [P] 94 B3
Cercal [P] 86 B4
Cerceda [E] 78 C2
Cerceda [E] 88 F5
Cercedilla [E] 88 F4
Cerchiara di Calabria [I] 122 D6
Cerda [I] 126 D2
Cerdedo [E] 78 C4
Cerdeira [P] 86 G2
Cerea [I] 110 F1
Cerecinos de Campos [E] 82 B6
Cered [H] 64 E4
Cereixo [E] 78 B2
Ceremosnja [YU] 150 D1
Ceres [I] 70 D5
Ceresole Reale [I] 70 C4
Céret [F] 92 F2
Cerignola [I] 120 H2
Cérilly [F] 56 C5
Čerín [SK] 64 C3
Cerisiers [F] 42 H6
Cerizay [F] 54 D3
Çerkezköy [TR] 146 D2
Cerknica [SLO] 74 B6
Cerkno [SLO] 74 B5
Cerkovitsa [BG] 148 B2
Cerkvenjak [SLO] 74 E3
Çermë [AL] 128 B3
Çermei [RO] 76 H3
Černá [CZ] 62 B3
Cerna [HR] 154 E2
Cernache do Bom Jardim [P] 86 D3
Černá Hora [CZ] 50 C5
Cernavoda [RO] 206 D6
Cernay [F] 58 D3
Cernégula [E] 82 E5
Cernihiv [UA] 204 C7
Černik [HR] 154 C1
Černóbbio [I] 70 G4
Černošín [CZ] 48 D4
Černovice [CZ] 48 G6
Cerovačke Špilje [HR] 112 H4
Çërravë [AL] 128 D4
Çërrik [AL] 128 B4
Cerro de los Angeles [E] 88 F6
Cerro Muriano [E] 96 C6
Certaldo [I] 110 E6
Çervatos [E] 82 E4
Červená [CZ] 48 F5
Červená Lhota [CZ] 48 G6
Červená-Řečice [CZ] 48 H5
Červená Skala [SK] 64 E2
Červená Voda [CZ] 50 C4
Červený Hrádek [CZ] 48 F5
Červený Hrádek [CZ] 48 E2
Červeny Kameň [SK] 62 G4
Červený Kláštor [SK] 52 B5
Červený Kostelec [CZ] 50 B2
Cervera [E] 92 C3
Cervera del Llano [E] 98 B3
Cervera del Río Alhama [E] 84 A6
Cervera de Pisuerga [E] 82 D4
Cerveteri [I] 114 H5
Cérvia [I] 110 H4
Cervignano del Friuli [I] 72 G5
Cervinara [I] 120 E3
Cervione [F] 114 C4
Cervo [E] 78 E1
Cervo [I] 108 G4
Cesana Torinese [I] 70 B6
Cesarò [I] 126 F2
Cesarzowice [PL] 36 C6
Cesena [I] 110 H4
Cesenático [I] 110 H4
Cēsis [LV] 200 E4
Česká Kamenice [CZ] 48 F2
Česká Lípa [CZ] 48 G2
Česká Skalice [CZ] 50 B3
Česká Třebová [CZ] 50 B4
České Budějovice [CZ] 62 C2
České Velenice [CZ] 62 C3
Český Brod [CZ] 48 G4
Český Krumlov [CZ] 62 B2
Český Šternberk [CZ] 48 G4
Český Těšín [CZ] 50 F5
Çeşme [TR] 134 H5
Çeşmealti [TR] 144 C4
Cespedosa [E] 88 C4
Cessenon-sur-Orb [F] 106 D4
Čestobrodica [YU] 150 A2
Cestona / Zestoa [E] 84 A2
Cesvaine [LV] 200 F5
Cetate [RO] 150 F1
Cetinje [YU] 152 E4
Cetóbriga [P] 86 B6
Cetona [I] 114 G2
Cetraro [I] 124 C4
Ceuta [E] 100 G6
Ceutí [E] 104 C3
Ceva [I] 108 G3
Çevico Navero [E] 88 F1
Čevo [YU] 152 E4
Ceyzériat [F] 68 G2
Chaalis, Abbaye de- [F] 42 G3
Chabanais [F] 54 F6
Chabeuil [F] 68 F5
Chablis [F] 56 E2
Chabreloche [F] 68 D2
Chabris [F] 54 H3
Chagny [F] 56 G5
Chaillé-les-Marais [F] 54 C4
Chailluz, Fort de- [F] 58 B4
Chairóneia [GR] 132 H5
Chajkola [RUS] 198 H3
Chalabre [F] 106 B5
Chalais [F] 66 E2
Chalamont [F] 68 G2
Chalampé [F] 58 E3
Chalandritsa [GR] 132 F6
Chálki [GR] 142 D5
Chálki [GR] 132 G2
Chalkiádes [GR] 132 G2
Chalkída [GR] 134 B5
Chalkidóna [GR] 128 G4
Challans [F] 54 B2
Challes-les-Eaux [F] 70 A4
Chalonnes [F] 54 D1
Chalonnes-sur-Loire [F] 54 D1
Châlons-en-Champagne [F] 44 B4
Chalon-sur-Saône [F] 56 G5
Châlus [F] 66 G2
Chalusset, Château de- [F] 66 G1
Cham [CH] 58 F5
Cham [D] 48 C6
Chamberet [F] 66 H2
Chambéry [F] 68 H3
Chambley-Bussières [F] 44 E4
Chambon-sur-Lac [F] 68 C2
Chambon-sur-Voueize [F] 56 B6
Chambord [F] 54 H2
Chambord, Parc de- [F] 54 H2
Chamerегg [D] 48 C6
Chamonix-Mont-Blanc [F] 70 C3
Champagne-Mouton [F] 54 E5
Champagnole [F] 58 B6
Champaubert [F] 44 A4
Champdeniers [F] 54 D4
Champ du Bataille, Château du- [F] 26 H4
Champ du Feu [F] 44 G6
Champeix [F] 68 C3
Champéry [CH] 70 C2
Champex [CH] 70 C3
Champier [F] 68 G4
Champigné [F] 40 H6
Champigny-sur-Veude [F] 54 F2
Champillon [F] 44 B3
Champlitte [F] 58 A3
Champlon [B] 30 E6
Champoluc [I] 70 D3
Champrond-en-Gâtine [F] 26 H6
Champtoceaux [F] 40 F6
Champvent [CH] 58 C6
Chamrousse [F] 68 H5
Chamusca [P] 86 C4
Chanas [F] 68 F4
Chandrinós [GR] 136 C4
Chaniá [GR] 140 C4
Chaniótis [GR] 130 C6
Chantada [E] 78 D4
Chantelle [F] 56 D6
Chantemerle [F] 70 B6
Chantilly [F] 42 G3
Chantonnay [F] 54 C3
Chão de Codes [P] 86 D4
Chaource [F] 44 B6
Chapelle-Royale [F] 42 D5
Chárakas [GR] 140 E5
Charavgí [GR] 128 F5
Charavines [F] 68 G4
Charbonnières-les-Bains [F] 68 F3
Charbowo [PL] 36 D2
Chard [GB] 12 F4
Charenton-du-Cher [F] 56 C4
Charité, Abbaye de la- [F] 58 B4
Charleroi [B] 30 C5
Charlestown [IRL] 2 D4
Charleville / Rath Luirc [IRL] 4 C4
Charleville-Mézières [F] 44 C2
Charlieu [F] 68 E1
Charlottenberg [S] 166 D1
Charly [F] 42 H3
Charmes [F] 44 E6
Charneca [P] 86 A5
Charny [F] 56 D1
Charnyany [BY] 38 G3
Charolles [F] 56 F6
Chârost [F] 56 B3
Charrières [CH] 70 C1
Charroux [F] 54 E5
Chartres [F] 42 E4
Chassigny [F] 56 H3
Château-Arnoux [F] 108 C3
Châteaubourg [F] 26 D6
Châteaubriant [F] 40 F5
Château-Chinon [F] 56 E4
Château d'Oex [CH] 70 D1
Château-du-Loir [F] 42 B6
Châteaudun [F] 42 D5
Châteaugiron [F] 26 C6
Château-Gontier [F] 40 H5
Château-la-Vallière [F] 42 B6
Château-L'Évêque [F] 66 F3
Châteaulin [F] 40 B2
Châteaumeillant [F] 56 B5
Châteauneuf [F] 66 E1
Châteauneuf-de-Randon [F] 68 D5
Châteauneuf-du-Faou [F] 40 C3
Châteauneuf-du-Pape [F] 106 G3
Châteauneuf-en-Thymerais [F] 26 H6
Chateauneuf-sur-Cher [F] 56 C4
Châteauneuf-sur-Loire [F] 42 F6
Châteauneuf-sur-Sarthe [F] 40 H6
Châteauponsac [F] 54 G5
Château-Porcien [F] 28 H6
Château-Queyras [F] 70 B6
Château-Regnault [F] 44 C1
Châteaurenard [F] 42 G6
Château-Renault [F] 54 G1
Châteauroux [F] 54 H4
Château-Salins [F] 44 F5
Château-Thierry [F] 42 H3
Châteauvillain [F] 56 G2
Châtel [F] 70 C2
Châtelaillon-Plage [F] 54 C5
Châtelet [B] 30 C5
Châtelguyon [F] 68 C2
Châtellerault [F] 54 F3
Chatêl-Montagne [F] 68 E1
Châtel-St-Denis [CH] 70 C1
Châtelus-Malvaleix [F] 54 H5
Châtenois [F] 44 E6
Chatham [GB] 14 F4
Châtillon [I] 70 D4
Châtillon-Coligny [F] 56 D1
Châtillon-en-Bazois [F] 56 E4
Châtillon-en-Diois [F] 68 G6
Châtillon-sur-Chalaronne [F] 68 G2
Châtillon-sur-Indre [F] 54 G3
Châtillon-sur-Loire [F] 56 D2
Châtillon-sur-Marne [F] 44 A3
Châtillon-sur-Seine [F] 56 G2
Châtre, Église de- [F] 54 D6
Chatteris [GB] 14 F2
Chaudes-Aigues [F] 68 C5
Chauffailles [F] 68 F1
Chaufour-lès-Bonnières [F] 42 E3
Chaumergy [F] 56 H5
Chaumont [F] 54 G2
Chaumont [F] 56 H1
Chaumont-sur-Aire [F] 44 D4
Chaumont-sur-Loire [F] 54 G2
Chaunay [F] 54 E5
Chauny [F] 28 F6
Chaussin [F] 56 H5
Chauvigny [F] 54 F4
Chaves [P] 80 E3
Chayki [RUS] 200 H6
Chazelles [F] 68 F3
Chazelles-sur-Lyon [F] 68 F3
Cheb [CZ] 48 C3
Chęciny [PL] 52 B1
Cheddar [GB] 12 F3
Chef-Boutonne [F] 54 D5
Cheimarros [GR] 130 B3
Chekhov [RUS] 204 F4
Cheles [E] 94 F2
Chełm [PL] 38 F6
Chełmek [PL] 50 G3
Chełmno [PL] 22 D5
Chelmsford [GB] 14 F4
Chełmża [PL] 22 E6
Chełst [PL] 36 B1
Cheltenham [GB] 12 G2
Chelva [E] 98 D3
Chemillé [F] 54 D2
Chemin [F] 56 H5
Chemnitz [D] 48 D1
Chenaux [CH] 58 C6
Chêne-Pignier [F] 54 F6
Chénérailles [F] 56 B6
Chenonceaux [F] 54 G2
Chepelare [BG] 130 E1
Chepstow [GB] 12 G3
Chera [E] 98 D4
Cherasco [I] 108 G2
Cherbourg [F] 26 D2
Cherepovets [RUS] 204 F2
Cherkasy [UA] 206 F2
Chern [RUS] 204 F5
Chernaya Rechka [RUS] 200 G3
Chernevo [RUS] 200 G2
Cherniakhiv [UA] 206 E2
Chernivtsi [UA] 206 C3
Cherno [RUS] 200 G1
Chernomorets [BG] 148 F4
Chernyakhovsk [RUS] 24 C1
Chéroy [F] 42 G5
Chérso [GR] 128 H3
Cherveix-Cubas [F] 66 G3
Chervena Voda [BG] 148 D2
Cherven Bryag [BG] 150 G3
Chervonohrad [UA] 52 H2
Chervyen' [BY] 204 B5
Cheste [E] 98 E4
Chester [GB] 10 D4
Chesterfield [GB] 10 F5
Chester-le-Street [GB] 8 F6
Chevagnes [F] 56 D5
Chevanceaux [F] 66 D2
Chevilly, Château de- [F] 42 E6
Chevreuse [F] 42 F4
Chézal-Benoît [F] 56 B4
Chiampo [I] 72 D6
Chianca, Dolmen di- [I] 122 D2
Chianciano Terme [I] 114 G2
Chiaramonti Gulfi [I] 126 F5
Chiaravalle [I] 112 C6
Chiaravalle Centrale [I] 124 D6
Chiaravalle della Colomba [I] 110 D2
Chiari [I] 70 H5
Chiasso [CH] 70 G4
Chiavari [I] 110 B3
Chiavenna [I] 70 G2
Chichester [GB] 14 D5
Chiclana de la Frontera [E] 100 F4
Chieming [D] 60 F5
Chieri [I] 70 D6
Chiesa in Valmalenco [I] 70 H3
Chiessi [I] 114 D2
Chieti [I] 116 D4
Chiliadoú [GR] 134 C4
Chiliandaríou, Moní- [GR] 130 D5
Chiliomódi [GR] 136 F1
Chillarón de Cuenca [E] 98 B2
Chillon [CH] 70 C2
Chillón [E] 96 C4
Chimay [B] 28 H5
Chinchilla de Monte-Aragón [E] 98 C5
Chinchón [E] 96 G1
Chinon [F] 54 F2
Chióggia [I] 110 H1
Chíos [GR] 134 G4
Chipiona [E] 100 F3
Chippenham [GB] 12 G3
Chipping Norton [GB] 12 H2
Chipping Sodbury [GB] 12 G3
Chiprovtsi [BG] 150 F3
Chirivel [E] 102 H3
Chirpan [BG] 148 C5
Chisa [F] 114 B5
Chişinău [MD] 206 E4
Chişineu Criş [RO] 76 G3
Chiusa / Klausen [I] 72 D3
Chiusa di Pesio [I] 108 F3
Chiusaforte [I] 72 G4
Chiusa Scláfani [I] 126 C3
Chiusi [I] 114 H2
Chiva [E] 98 E4
Chivasso [I] 70 D5
Chlebowo [PL] 34 G3
Chlemoútsi [GR] 136 B1
Chlewiska [PL] 38 B6
Chlumec nad Cidlinou [CZ] 48 H3
Chlum u Třeboně [CZ] 62 C2
Chmielnik [PL] 52 B2
Chobienice [PL] 36 B3
Choceň [CZ] 50 B4
Choceń [PL] 36 F2
Chochołów [PL] 50 H5
Chocianów [PL] 36 B5
Chociwel [PL] 20 G5
Choczewo [PL] 22 D1
Chodecz [PL] 36 F2
Chodel [PL] 38 D6
Chodos / Xodos [E] 98 F2
Chodová Planá [CZ] 48 D4
Chodzież [PL] 22 B6
Chojna [PL] 20 F6
Chojnice [PL] 22 C4
Chojnów [PL] 36 B6
Cholet [F] 54 D2
Chomakovtsi [BG] 150 G3
Chomęciska Małe [PL] 52 F1
Chomutov [CZ] 48 E2
Chop [UA] 206 B2
Chóra [GR] 136 C4
Chorefto [GR] 134 A2
Chorges [F] 108 D2
Choristí [GR] 130 D3
Chorley [GB] 10 D3
Chornobyl [UA] 204 C7
Chornomors'ke [UA] 206 F5
Choroszcz [PL] 24 E5
Chorro, Garganto del- [E] 102 B4
Chorros, Cueva de los- [E] 96 H6
Chortkiv [UA] 206 C3
Chorzele [PL] 22 H5
Chorzów [PL] 50 G3
Chorzyna [PL] 36 F5
Choszczno [PL] 20 G6
Chotěboř [CZ] 50 A5
Chotětín [CZ] 48 E4
Choumnikó [GR] 130 C3
Chouto [P] 86 D4
Chouvigny, Gorges de- [F] 56 C6
Choye [F] 58 A4
Chozoviótissa [GR] 138 G3
Chrast [CZ] 50 B4
Chrastava [CZ] 48 G1
Chrepiski Manastir [BG] 150 G4
Christchurch [GB] 12 G5
Christiansfeld [DK] 156 C3
Christkindl [A] 62 B5
Christós [GR] 138 G1
Chrudim [CZ] 50 A4
Chrýsafa [GR] 136 E4
Chrysochóri [GR] 130 E3
Chrysoskalitissa [GR] 140 B5
Chrysoúpoli [GR] 130 E3
Chrząchówek [PL] 38 D5
Chrzanów [PL] 50 G3
Chudoba [PL] 50 E1
Chudovo [RUS] 204 D2
Chuhuev [UA] 206 H2
Chulkovo [RUS] 178 E3
Chupa [RUS] 198 H1
Chuprene [BG] 150 E3
Chur [CH] 70 H1
Church Stretton [GB] 10 D6
Churchtown [IRL] 4 E5
Churchtown [IRL] 4 F5
Churek [BG] 150 G4
Chvylevo [RUS] 204 D1
Chwaszczyno [PL] 22 D2
Chyňava [CZ] 48 F4
Chýnov [CZ] 48 G5
Chýnovská Jeskyně [CZ] 48 G5
Chyżne [PL] 50 H5
Cianciana [I] 126 D3
Ciasna [PL] 50 F2
Ciąże [PL] 36 E3
Ciborro [P] 86 D6
Ciboure [F] 84 B2
Cicciano [I] 120 E3
Cicerone, Tomba di- [I] 120 C2
Ćićevac [YU] 150 C3
Cichy [PL] 24 D3
Ciclopi, Isole dei- [I] 126 G3
Cidones [E] 90 B2
Ciechanów [PL] 38 B1
Ciechanowiec [PL] 38 D1
Ciechocinek [PL] 36 F1
Ciempozuelos [E] 96 G1
Ciepielów [PL] 38 C5
Cieplice Śląskie-Zdrój [PL] 50 A1
Cierp-Gaud [F] 84 F4
Cieszanów [PL] 52 F3
Cieszyn [PL] 50 F4
Cieza [E] 104 C2
Ciężkowice [PL] 52 C4
Cifuentes [E] 90 A5
Cigales [E] 88 E1
Cigánd [H] 64 H4
Cigliano [I] 70 E5
Cihangazi [TR] 146 G5
Cilipi [HR] 152 D4
Cill Airne / Killarney [IRL] 4 B4
Cillas [E] 90 C5
Cill Chainnigh / Kilkenny [IRL] 4 E4
Cill Charthaigh / Kilcar [IRL] 2 D2
Cill Ciaráin / Kilkieran [IRL] 2 B4
Cilleros [E] 86 G3
Cimadevilla [E] 78 B3
Cimburk [CZ] 50 C5
Cimburk [CZ] 62 G2
Cimino, Monte- [I] 114 H4
Cimoszki [PL] 24 E3
Cîmpeni [RO] 206 B5
Çınarcık [TR] 146 F3
Çindere [TR] 144 F4
Çine [TR] 144 E6
Ciney [B] 30 D5
Cinfães [P] 80 C4
Cingoli [I] 116 C1
Cinigiano [I] 114 F2
Cinisi [I] 126 C1
Činovec [CZ] 48 E2
Cinquefrondi [I] 124 D6
Cintegabelle [F] 106 A4
Cintruénigo [E] 84 A6
Ciółkowo [PL] 36 H2
Circo de Barrosa [E] 84 E5
Cirella [I] 124 C3
Cirencester [GB] 12 G3
Cirey [F] 44 G6
Ciria [E] 90 C3
Ciriè [I] 70 D5
Čirkovicy [RUS] 178 G6
Cirò Marina [I] 124 F4
Ciron [F] 54 G4
Ciruli [LV] 200 C4
Cisa, Passo della- [I] 110 C3
Cisna [PL] 52 E6
Cisnădie [RO] 206 B5
Cista Provo [HR] 152 B2
Cisterna di Latina [I] 116 B6
Cisternino [I] 122 F3
Cistierna [E] 82 C4
Cîteaux, Abbaye de- [F] 56 G4
Çıtlık [TR] 142 E1
Cittadella [I] 72 D6
Città della Pieve [I] 114 H2
Città del Vaticano [V] 116 A5
Città di Castello [I] 116 A1
Cittaducale [I] 116 B4
Cittanova [I] 124 D7
Città Sant'Angelo [I] 116 D4
Ciudad Real [E] 96 E4
Ciudad Rodrigo [E] 88 A3
Ciumeghiu [RO] 76 H3
Ciutadella de Menorca [E] 104 G4
Cividale del Friuli [I] 72 G5
Civita [I] 114 H3
Civita Castellana [I] 116 A4
Civitanova Marche [I] 116 C1
Civitavécchia [I] 114 G5
Civitella del Tronto [I] 116 C3
Civitella di Romagna [I] 110 G5
Civitella in Val di Chiana [I] 114 G1
Civitella Paganico [I] 114 F2
Civitella Roveto [I] 116 C5
Civray [F] 54 E5
Civrieux-d'Azergues [F] 68 F2
Çivril [TR] 144 G4
Clacton-on-Sea [GB] 14 G4
Clairvaux-les-Lacs [F] 70 A1
Clamecy [F] 56 E3
Clamouse, Grotte de- [F] 106 E3
Clane [IRL] 2 F6
Clara [IRL] 2 D5
Clarecastle [IRL] 2 C6
Claremorris [IRL] 2 C4
Clarinbridge [IRL] 2 C5
Claros [TR] 144 C5
Clashmore [IRL] 4 D5
Clausholm [DK] 160 E5
Clausthal-Zellerfeld [D] 32 G4
Clavière [I] 70 B6
Cleanovu [RO] 150 F1
Clécy [F] 26 F4
Cleethorpes [GB] 10 G4
Clefmont [F] 58 A2
Clelles [F] 68 G5
Clementino, Porto- [I] 114 G4
Clères [F] 28 C5
Clermont [F] 28 E6
Clermont-en-Argonne [F] 44 D4
Clermont-Ferrand [F] 68 C2
Clermont-l'Hérault [F] 106 E4
Clerval [CH] 58 C4
Clervaux [L] 44 F1
Cléry [F] 42 E6
Cles [I] 72 C3
Clevedon [GB] 12 F3
Clifden [IRL] 2 B4
Cliffony [IRL] 2 D3
Clisson [F] 54 C2
Clitheroe [GB] 10 E3
Clitunno, Fonti del- [I] 116 B3
Clitunno, Tempio del- [I] 116 B3
Clogan [IRL] 2 D6
Clogh [IRL] 4 F3
Clogheen [IRL] 4 D4
Cloghmore [IRL] 2 B3
Clonakilty [IRL] 4 C5
Clonalis House [IRL] 2 D4
Clonard [IRL] 2 E5
Clonaslee [IRL] 2 D6
Clonbur [IRL] 2 C4
Clondalkin [IRL] 2 F6
Clones [IRL] 2 E4
Clonfert [IRL] 2 D5
Clonmacnoise [IRL] 2 D5
Clonmany [IRL] 2 F1
Clonmel / Cluain Meala [IRL] 4 E4
Clonmellon [IRL] 2 E5
Clonroche [IRL] 4 F4
Cloonbannin [IRL] 4 C4
Cloonkeen [IRL] 4 B4
Cloonlara [IRL] 4 D3
Cloppenburg [D] 18 C6
Clough [GB] 2 G4
Cloughjordan [IRL] 2 D6
Cloyes-sur-le-Loir [F] 42 D5
Cloyne [IRL] 4 D5
Cluain Meala / Clonmel [IRL] 4 E4
Cluina [E] 88 H2
Cluj Napoca [RO] 206 B4
Clun [GB] 10 C6
Cluny [F] 56 F6
Cluses [F] 70 B2
Clusone [I] 72 A5
Ćmielów [PL] 52 D1
Cmolas [PL] 52 D3
Coachford [IRL] 4 C5
Coalville [GB] 10 E6
Coaña [E] 78 F2
Cobh [IRL] 4 D5
Coburg [D] 46 G3
Coca [E] 88 E3
Coceges del Monte [E] 88 F2
Cocentaina [E] 104 E1
Cochem [D] 44 G1
Cockermouth [GB] 8 D6
Code [LV] 200 D6
Codigoro [I] 110 G2
Codogno [I] 70 H6
Codos [E] 90 D4
Codróipo [I] 72 G5
Coesfeld [D] 16 H6
Coevorden [NL] 16 G4
Coflans [F] 70 B4
Cofrentes [E] 98 D5
Cognac [F] 54 D6
Cogne [I] 70 D4
Cogolin [F] 108 D5
Cogollos [E] 82 E6
Cogolludo [E] 88 H4
Cogul, Cova del- [E] 90 H5
Coimbra [P] 86 D2
Coín [E] 102 B4
Coina [P] 86 B6
Çoirós [E] 78 D2
Čoka [YU] 76 F5
Colares [P] 86 A5
Cölbe [D] 32 D6
Colbitz [D] 34 B2
Colcerasa [I] 116 B1
Colchester [GB] 14 F3
Colditz [D] 34 D6
Coldstream [GB] 8 F4
Coleraine [GB] 2 G2
Colfiorito [I] 116 B2
Colfosco [I] 72 E3
Colico [I] 70 G3
Coligny [F] 56 H6
Colindres [E] 82 F3
Colintraive [GB] 8 C2
Coll de Nargó [E] 92 D2
Collécchio [I] 110 D2
Colledimezzo [I] 116 E5
Colle di Val d'Elsa [I] 114 F1
Colleferro [I] 116 B6
Collegno [I] 70 D5
Colle Isarco / Gossensass [I] 72 D2
Collesalvetti [I] 110 D6
Colle Sannita [I] 120 F2
Collesano [I] 126 E2
Colletorto [I] 116 F6
Colliano [I] 120 G3
Collinée [F] 26 B5
Cóllio [I] 72 B5
Collioure [F] 92 G2
Collodi [I] 110 E5
Collonges [F] 70 A2
Collonges-la-Rouge [F] 66 G3
Collooney [IRL] 2 D3
Colmar [F] 58 D3
Colmars [F] 108 D3
Colmenar [E] 102 C4
Colmenar de Oreja [E] 96 G1
Colmenar Viejo [E] 88 F5
Cologna Véneta [I] 110 F1
Cologne [F] 84 G2
Cololgno al Serio [I] 70 H5
Colombey-les-Belles [F] 44 E5
Colombey-les-Deux-Églises [F] 44 C6
Colomiers [F] 84 H3
Colònia de Sant Jordi [E] 104 E6
Colonia Selladores [E] 96 E6
Colophon [TR] 144 C5
Colorno [I] 110 D2
Colosimi [I] 124 D5
Colunga [E] 82 C2
Colwyn Bay [GB] 10 C4
Comácchio [I] 110 H3
Comăneşti [RO] 206 C5
Comano Terme [I] 72 C4
Coma-ruga [E] 92 C5
Combeaufontaine [F] 58 B3
Comber [GB] 2 G4
Combourg [F] 26 C5
Combronde [F] 68 C1
Comburg [D] 46 E6
Comeglians [I] 72 G3
Comelico Superiore [I] 72 F3
Comiglio [I] 110 D3
Comillas [E] 82 E3
Cómiso [I] 126 F5
Commentry [F] 56 C6

D

Dingle / An Daingean [IRL] 4 A3
Dingli [M] 126 C6
Dingolfing [D] 60 F3
Dingwall [GB] 6 D4
Dinkelsbühl [D] 46 F6
Dinklage [D] 32 D1
Dinozé [F] 58 C2
Dinslaken [D] 30 G2
Dio [S] 162 D5
Díon [GR] 128 G6
Diosgyör [H] 64 F4
Dipótamos [GR] 130 D2
Dippoldiswalde [D] 48 E1
Disenå [N] 172 C5
Disentis / Mustér [CH] 70 G1
Disneyland Paris [F] 42 G3
Dispílí [GR] 128 E5
Diss [GB] 14 G2
Dístomo [GR] 132 H5
Dístrato [GR] 128 D6
Ditzingen [D] 58 G1
Diva Slatina [BG] 150 F3
Divčibare [YU] 150 A2
Dívčí Hrady [CZ] 62 F2
Dives-sur-Mer [F] 26 F3
Divín [SK] 64 D4
Divjakë [AL] 128 A4
Divonne-les-Bains [F] 70 B2
Dívri [GR] 132 G4
Divusa [HR] 154 A2
Djäkneböle [S] 190 H6
Djauvik [S] 168 F5
Djúpivogur [IS] 194 G6
Djupvik [N] 192 F2
Djura [S] 172 H4
Djurakovac [YU] 150 B5
Djurås [S] 172 H4
Dłoń [PL] 36 C4
Długie [PL] 36 A1
Długosiodło [PL] 38 C1
Dmitrov [RUS] 204 F3
Dniprodzerzhyns'k [UA] 206 G3
Dnipropetrovs'k [UA] 206 G3
Dniproprudne [UA] 206 G4
Dno [RUS] 204 C3
Dobanovci [YU] 154 G2
Dobbiaco / Toblach [I] 72 E3
Dobczyce [PL] 52 A4
Dobel [D] 58 G1
Dobele [LV] 200 D5
Döbeln [D] 34 D6
Doberlug Kirchhain [D] 34 E4
Döbern [D] 34 G5
Dobersberg [A] 62 D2
Dobiegniew [PL] 20 H6
Doboj [BIH] 154 D3
Doboz [H] 76 G3
Dobra [PL] 52 B4
Dobra [PL] 36 F4
Dobra [PL] 20 G4
Dobra [RO] 150 F1
Dobrá Niva [SK] 64 C3
Dobřany [CZ] 48 D5
Dobrčane [YU] 150 D5
Dobre [PL] 38 C2
Dobre Miasto [PL] 22 G3
Döbriach [A] 72 H3
Dobrich [BG] 148 F2
Dobříchovice [CZ] 48 F4
Dobri Do [YU] 150 C4
Dobrinishte [BG] 130 B1
Dobříš [CZ] 48 F4
Dobrodzień [PL] 50 F2
Döbrököz [H] 76 B4
Dobromani [BIH] 152 C3
Dobromierz [PL] 50 B1
Dobromirka [BG] 148 C3
Dobromirtsi [BG] 130 F2
Dobromyl' [UA] 52 F5
Dobro Polje [BIH] 152 D2
Dobrosloveni [RO] 150 H1
Dobroszyce [PL] 36 D6
Dobroteşti [RO] 148 B1
Dobrotitsa [BG] 148 E1
Dobrovodsk Hrad [SK] 62 H3
Dobrovol'sk [RUS] 24 D1
Dobrš [CZ] 48 E6
Dobruchi [RUS] 200 G2
Dobrun [BIH] 152 E1
Dobruška [CZ] 50 B3
Dobrzany [PL] 20 G5
Dobrzeń Wielki [PL] 50 E2
Dobrzyca [PL] 36 D4
Dobrzyń nad Wisłą [PL] 36 G2
Dobšinská L'Adova Jaskyňa [SK] 64 E2
Dockasberg [S] 198 B2
Docksta [S] 184 F2
Doclea [YU] 152 E4
Dödafallet [S] 184 D3
Döderhult [S] 162 G3
Dodóni [GR] 132 D2
Doe Castle [IRL] 2 E1
Doesburg [NL] 16 F5
Doetinchem [NL] 16 F5
Doganbey [TR] 142 B1
Doğanbey [TR] 144 C5
Doganović [YU] 150 C6
Dogliani [I] 108 G2
Dogueno [P] 94 C4
Dokka [N] 170 H3
Dokkas [S] 192 F6
Dokkum [NL] 16 F2
Doksy [CZ] 48 G2
Dolceácqua [I] 108 F4
Dol-de-Bretagne [F] 26 C4
Dole [F] 56 H4
Dølemo [N] 164 E4
Dolenci [MK] 128 D3
Dolenja Vas [SLO] 74 C6
Dolga Vas [SLO] 74 F3
Dolgellau [GB] 10 B5
Dolhobyczów [PL] 52 H2
Dolianá [GR] 132 C1
Dolianova [I] 118 D6
Dolice [PL] 20 G6
Dolíchi [GR] 128 G6
Doljani [HR] 112 H4
Doljevac [YU] 150 D4
Döllach [A] 72 G2
Döllbach [D] 46 E2
Dolle [D] 34 B2
Döllstädt [D] 32 H6
Dolna Banya [BG] 150 G5
Dolna Dikanya [BG] 150 F5
Dolna Grupa [PL] 22 E5
Dolna Mitropoliya [BG] 148 A3
Dolni Dŭbnik [BG] 148 A3
Dolní Dvořiště [CZ] 62 C3
Dolní Kounice [CZ] 62 F2
Dolni Lom [BG] 150 E3
Dolní Ročov [CZ] 48 E3
Dolno Kamartsi [BG] 150 G4
Dolno Kosovrasti [MK] 128 C2
Dolno Levski [BG] 148 A5
Dolno Novkovo [BG] 148 D3
Dolno Tserovene [BG] 150 F3
Dolno Ujno [BG] 150 E5
Dolný Kubín [SK] 50 G6
Dolo [I] 110 H1
Dolores [E] 104 D3
Doloscy [RUS] 200 H6
Dolovo [YU] 154 H2
Dolsk [PL] 36 C4
Dolyna [UA] 52 H6
Dolzhicy [RUS] 200 H2
Dom [A] 74 B2
Domaniç [TR] 146 G5
Domanovići [BIH] 152 C3
Domažlice [CZ] 48 D5
Dombås [N] 180 G5
Dombasle [F] 44 F5
Dombegyház [H] 76 G4
Dombóvár [H] 76 B4
Dombrád [H] 64 H4
Dombrot-le-Sec [F] 58 B2
Domburg [NL] 16 B6
Doméniko [GR] 132 F1
Domèvre-en-Haye [F] 44 E5
Domfront [F] 26 E5
Domingão [P] 86 D4
Dömitz [D] 18 H5
Domme [F] 66 G4
Dommitzsch [D] 34 D4
Domnítsa [GR] 132 F4
Domnovo [RUS] 22 H2
Domodedovo [RUS] 204 F4
Domodóssola [I] 70 E3
Domokós [GR] 132 G3
Dompaire [F] 58 C2
Dompierre [F] 56 E5
Dompierre-du-Chemin [F] 26 D5
Dompierre-sur-Besbre [F] 56 E5
Dompierre-sur-Mer [F] 54 C4
Domrémy-la-Pucelle [F] 44 D6
Dömsöd [H] 76 C2
Dómus de Maria [I] 118 C8
Domusnóvas [I] 118 B6
Domžale [SLO] 74 C5
Donado [E] 80 G3
Donaghadee [GB] 2 H3
Donaghmore [IRL] 4 E3
Doña Mencía [E] 102 C2
Donaueschingen [D] 58 F3
Donaustauf [D] 60 F2
Donauwörth [D] 60 D2
Don Benito [E] 96 B3
Doncaster [GB] 10 F4
Donduma [TR] 146 B5
Donegal / Dún na nGall [IRL] 2 E2
Donja Brela [HR] 152 B2
Donja Brezna [YU] 152 D3
Donja Bukovica [YU] 152 E3
Donja Kamenica [YU] 150 A1
Donja Ljubata [YU] 150 E5
Donja Šatornja [YU] 150 B2
Donja Suvaja [HR] 112 H4
Donje Ljupče [YU] 150 C5
Donje Petrčane [HR] 112 F5
Donji Koričani [BIH] 154 C3
Donji Lapac [HR] 112 H4
Donji Miholjac [HR] 76 B6
Donji Milanovac [YU] 150 D1
Donji Vakuf [BIH] 154 C4
Donji Zemunik [HR] 112 G5
Donnersbach [A] 62 B6
Donnersbachwald [A] 74 B1
Dønnes [N] 190 D2
Donostia-San Sebastián [E] 84 B2
Donovaly [SK] 64 C2
Dontilly [F] 42 G5
Donzenac [F] 66 G3
Donzère [F] 68 F6
Donzy [F] 56 D3
Doohooma [IRL] 2 B3
Doonbeg [IRL] 2 B6
Doonloughan [IRL] 2 B4
Doorn [NL] 16 E5
Doornik (Tournai) [B] 28 G3
Dörarp [S] 162 C4
Dorchester [GB] 12 F5
Dordives [F] 42 G5
Dordrecht [NL] 16 D5
Dorfen [D] 60 F4
Dorfmark [D] 18 F6
Dorgali [I] 118 E4
Doria, Castello- [I] 110 A3
Dório [GR] 136 D3
Dorkáda [GR] 130 B4
Dorking [GB] 14 E5
Dormagen [D] 30 G4
Dormánd [H] 64 E6
Dormans [F] 44 A3
Dornauberg [A] 72 E2
Dornbirn [A] 60 B6
Dornburg [D] 34 B6
Dorndorf [D] 46 F1
Dornes [F] 56 D5
Dornoch [GB] 6 E4
Dornstetten [D] 58 G2
Dornum [D] 18 B3
Dorog [H] 64 C6
Dorogobuzh [RUS] 204 D5
Dorohoi [RO] 206 D4
Dorohucza [PL] 38 F6
Dorotea [S] 190 F5
Dörpen [D] 16 H3
Dörpstedt [D] 18 E2
Dorsten [D] 30 H2
Dortan [F] 68 H1
Dortmund [D] 32 C4
Dorum [D] 18 D3
Dörverden [D] 18 E6
Dörzbach [D] 46 E5
Dosbarrios [E] 96 G2
Dos Hermanas [E] 94 G6
Dospat [BG] 130 D1
Dotnuva [LT] 202 F4
Douai [F] 28 F4
Douamont, Fort du- [F] 44 D3
Douarnenez [F] 40 B3
Douchy [F] 42 G6
Doucier [F] 58 A6
Doudeville [F] 26 H2
Doué-la-Fontaine [F] 54 E2
Douglas [GB] 8 D4
Douglas [GBM] 10 B2
Doulaincourt [F] 44 D6
Doulevant-le-Château [F] 44 C6
Doullens [F] 28 E4
Dourdan [F] 42 F4
Dourgne [F] 106 B4
Douvaine [F] 70 B2
Douzy [F] 44 D2
Dover [GB] 14 G5
Dovre [N] 180 G5
Downham Market [GB] 14 F2
Downpatrick [GB] 2 G4
Dowra [IRL] 2 E3
Dowsk [BY] 204 C6
Doxáto [GR] 130 D3
Dozulé [F] 26 G3
Drabiv [UA] 206 F2
Drac, Coves del- [E] 104 F5
Dračevo [MK] 128 E1
Drachenfels [D] 30 H5
Drachenwand [A] 60 H5
Drachselsried [D] 48 D6
Drachten [NL] 16 F2
Drag [N] 190 C4
Drag Ájluokta [N] 192 C5
Dragalevci [BG] 150 F5
Drăgănești de Vede [RO] 148 B1
Drăgănești-Olt [RO] 148 A1
Drăgănești-Vlașca [RO] 148 C1
Dragaš [YU] 150 B6
Drăgășani [RO] 206 B6
Draginje [YU] 150 A1
Dragocvet [YU] 150 C2
Dragoman [BG] 150 F4
Dragomirovo [BG] 148 C3
Dragomirovo [BG] 148 B2
Dragon, Caverne du- [F] 44 B2
Dragør [DK] 156 H3
Dragovishtitsa [BG] 150 E5
Dragsfjärd [FIN] 176 E5
Dragsholm Slot [DK] 156 F2
Dragsvik [N] 170 C1
Draguignan [F] 108 D5
Drahanovice [CZ] 50 C5
Drahonice [CZ] 48 F6
Drahovce [SK] 62 H3
Dráma [GR] 130 D3
Drammen [N] 164 H1
Drangsness [IS] 194 C2
Drânic [RO] 150 G1
Dransfeld [D] 32 F4
Dranske [D] 20 D1
Drasenhofen [A] 62 F3
Drávaszabolcs [H] 76 B6
Dravískos [GR] 130 C3
Dravograd [SLO] 74 C3
Drawno [PL] 20 H6
Drawsko Pomorskie [PL] 20 H5
Drażdżewo [PL] 24 B6
Draženov [CZ] 48 D5
Drebkau [D] 34 F4
Drégelypalánk [H] 64 C5
Drei [D] 46 G1
Dreilingen [D] 18 G6
Dren [MK] 128 F3
Dren [YU] 150 B4
Drenchia [I] 72 H4
Drenovac [YU] 150 D5
Drenovci [HR] 154 E2
Drenovets [BG] 150 F2
Drensteinfurt [D] 32 C3
Drépano [GR] 128 F5
Dresden [D] 34 E6
Dretyń [PL] 22 B3
Dreux [F] 42 E3
Drevsjø [N] 182 D6
Drewitz [D] 34 C3
Drewitz [D] 34 E2
Drezdenko [PL] 36 B1
Dreznik-Grad [HR] 112 G2
Driebergen [NL] 16 E5
Driffield [GB] 10 G3
Drimoleague [IRL] 4 B5
Drina Kanjon [BIH] 154 E4
Drinjača [BIH] 154 E4
Drinovci [BIH] 152 B2
Driny [SK] 62 G4
Drionville [F] 28 E2
Driva [N] 180 H4
Drivstua [N] 180 H4
Drlače [YU] 154 F4
Drnholec [CZ] 62 F2
Drniš [HR] 154 A5
Drøbak [N] 166 B2
Drobeta-Turnu Severin [RO] 206 B6
Drobin [PL] 36 H1
Drochtersen [D] 18 E3
Drogheda / Droichead Átha [IRL] 2 F5
Drohiczyn [PL] 38 E2
Drohobych [UA] 52 G5
Droichead Átha / Drogheda [IRL] 2 F5
Droichead Nua / Newbridge [IRL] 2 E6
Droitwich [GB] 12 G1
Drołtowice [PL] 36 D5
Dromahair [IRL] 2 D3
Dromcolliher [IRL] 4 C4
Dromore West [IRL] 2 D3
Dronero [I] 108 F2
Dronninglund [DK] 160 E3
Dronten [NL] 16 F4
Drosáto [GR] 128 H3
Drosendorf Stadt [A] 62 E2
Drosiá [GR] 134 B5
Drosopigí [GR] 128 E4
Drosopigí [GR] 132 D3
Drosselbjerg [DK] 156 E3
Drumconrath [IRL] 2 F5
Drumevo [BG] 148 E3
Drumkeeran [IRL] 2 D3
Drumlish [IRL] 2 E4
Drummore [GB] 8 C5
Drumnadrochit [GB] 6 D5
Drumshanbo [IRL] 2 D4
Drumsna [IRL] 2 D4
Drusenheim [F] 44 H5
Druskininkai [LT] 24 F3
Drusti [LV] 200 F4
Druten [NL] 16 E5
Druzhba [BG] 148 G3
Druzhnaja Gorka [RUS] 200 H1
Drvar [BIH] 154 A3
Drvenik [HR] 152 B3
Dryanovo [BG] 148 C4
Drygały [PL] 24 D4
Drymós [GR] 128 H4
Dryópi [GR] 136 F2
Dryopída [GR] 138 C2
Dryós [GR] 138 E3
Drzewce [PL] 36 F3
Drzewica [PL] 38 B5
Duagh [IRL] 4 C3
Duas Igrejas [P] 80 G4
Dub [YU] 150 A2
Dubá [CZ] 48 G2
Dubăsari [MD] 206 E4
Duben [D] 34 E4
Dubí [CZ] 48 E2
Dubica [HR] 154 B2
Dublin / Baile Átha Cliath [IRL] 2 F6
Dubna [RUS] 204 F3
Dubnica nad Váhom [SK] 64 A2
Dŭbnitsa [BG] 130 C1
Dubno [UA] 206 C2
Dubrava [HR] 74 F5
Dubrovnik [HR] 152 C4
Dubrovno [RUS] 200 H3
Dubrovytsia [UA] 204 A7
Ducey [F] 26 D4
Duchcov [CZ] 48 E2
Ducherow [D] 20 E4
Duclair [F] 26 H3
Dudelange [L] 44 E3
Duderstadt [D] 32 G4
Dudeştii Vechi [RO] 76 F5
Düdingen [CH] 58 D6
Dudley [GB] 10 D6
Dueñas [E] 88 F1
Duesund [N] 170 B2
Dueville [I] 72 D6
Dufftown [GB] 6 F5
Duga Poljana [YU] 150 B4
Duga Resa [HR] 112 G1
Dugi Rat [HR] 152 A2
Duğla [TR] 144 C2
Dugopolje [HR] 152 A2
Dugo Selo [HR] 74 F6
Duhnen [D] 18 D3
Duingt [F] 70 B3
Duino [I] 72 H5
Duisburg [D] 30 G3
Dukat [AL] 128 A6
Dukat [YU] 150 E5
Dukhovshchina [RUS] 204 D4
Dukielska, Przełęcz- [Eur.] 206 A2
Dukla [PL] 52 D5
Dūkštas [LT] 202 H4
Dŭlbok Izvor [BG] 148 C6
Duleek [IRL] 2 F5
Dŭlgopol [BG] 148 F3
Dülken [D] 30 F3
Dülmen [D] 16 H6
Dulnain Bridge [GB] 6 E5
Dulovka [RUS] 200 G4
Dulovo [BG] 148 E1
Dulpetorpet [N] 172 D4
Dumaca [YU] 154 F3
Dumbarton [GB] 8 D3
Dumbrăveni [RO] 148 F1
Dumfries [GB] 8 D5
Dumlupınar [TR] 144 H2
Dun [F] 44 D3
Duna [N] 190 C4
Dunaengus [IRL] 2 B5
Dunaff [IRL] 2 F1
Dunaföldvár [H] 76 C3
Dunaharaszti [H] 76 C1
Dunaïvtsi [UA] 206 D3
Dunajská Streda [SK] 62 H5
Dunakeszi [H] 64 C6
Dunany [IRL] 2 F5
Dunapataj [H] 76 C3
Dunaszekcső [H] 76 C5
Dunaújváros [H] 76 C2
Dunavecse [H] 76 C2
Dunavtsi [BG] 150 E2
Dunbar [GB] 8 F3
Dunbeath [GB] 6 F3
Dunblane [GB] 8 E2
Dunboy Castle [IRL] 4 A5
Dunboyne [IRL] 2 F6
Dunbrody Abbey [IRL] 4 E5
Duncormick [IRL] 4 F5
Dundaga [LV] 200 C4
Dundalk / Dún Dealgan [IRL] 2 F4
Dún Dealgan / Dundalk [IRL] 2 F4
Dundee [GB] 8 F2
Dunfanaghy [IRL] 2 E1
Dunfermline [GB] 8 E3
Dungannon [GB] 2 F3
Dungarvan [IRL] 4 E5
Dungiven [GB] 2 F2
Dungloe [IRL] 2 E2
Dungourney [IRL] 4 D5
Dunje [MK] 128 F3
Dunkerque [F] 14 H6
Dunkerque Ouest [F] 14 H6
Dunkineely [IRL] 2 D2
Dun Laoghaire [IRL] 2 F6
Dunlavin [IRL] 4 F3
Dunleer [IRL] 2 F5
Dun-le-Palestel [F] 54 H5
Dunloe, Gap of- [IRL] 4 B4
Dunloy [GB] 2 G2
Dunmanway [IRL] 4 C5
Dunmore [IRL] 2 C4
Dunmore Caves [IRL] 4 E4
Dunmore East [IRL] 4 E5
Dunmurry [GB] 2 G3
Dún na nGall / Donegal [IRL] 2 E2
Dunoon [GB] 8 C3
Duns [GB] 8 F4
Dunshaughlin [IRL] 2 F5
Dunstable [GB] 14 E3
Dun-sur-Auron [F] 56 C4
Dunure [GB] 8 C4
Dunvegan [GB] 6 B4
Dupnitsa [BG] 150 F6
Duquesa, Castillo de la- [E] 100 H5
Durach [BG] 148 E2
Duran [BG] 148 E2
Durango [E] 82 H4
Durankulak [BG] 148 G1
Duras [F] 66 E4
Durasıllı [TR] 144 E3
Durban-Corbières [F] 106 C5
Durbe [LV] 200 B6
Durbuy [B] 30 E5
Dúrcal [E] 102 E4
Đurđenovac [HR] 154 D1
Đurđevac [HR] 74 G5
Đurđevića Tara [YU] 152 E2
Durdevi Stupovi [YU] 150 B4
Düren [D] 30 G4
Đurević [BIH] 154 E3
Durham [GB] 8 F6
Durlas / Thurles [IRL] 4 E3
Durness [GB] 6 D2
Dürnkrut [A] 62 G4
Dürnstein [A] 62 D4
Durón [E] 90 A5
Durrës [AL] 128 A3
Durrow [IRL] 4 E3
Durrow Abbey [IRL] 2 E5
Durrus [IRL] 4 B5
Dursunbey [TR] 144 E1
Durtal [F] 42 A6
Duruelo de la Sierra [E] 90 A2
Dusetos [LT] 202 G4
Düskotna [BG] 148 E3
Dusnok [H] 76 C4
Dusocin [PL] 22 E5
Düsseldorf [D] 30 G3
Duszniki [PL] 36 B2
Duszniki-Zdrój [PL] 50 B3
Duved [S] 182 E1
Düvertepe [TR] 144 E2
Düzağac [TR] 144 H2
Duży [PL] 52 D1
Dve Mogili [BG] 148 C2
Dverberg [N] 192 C3
Dvor [HR] 154 A2
Dvorce [CZ] 50 D4
Dvory n. Žit. [SK] 64 B5
Dvůr Králové nad Labem [CZ] 50 A3
Dwingeloo [NL] 16 G3
Dyat'kovo [RUS] 204 E5
Dyce [GB] 6 F6
Dyck [D] 30 G4
Dylewo [PL] 24 C5
Dymchurch [GB] 14 F5
Dynów [PL] 52 E4
Dyranut [N] 170 E4
Dyrnesvågen [N] 180 F1
Dyrráchio [GR] 136 D3
Dýstos [GR] 134 C5
Dyulino [BG] 148 F3
Dyuni [BG] 148 F4
Dzhankoï [UA] 206 G5
Dzhurovo [BG] 150 G4
Dzhuryn [UA] 206 D3
Dziadkowice [PL] 38 E2
Działdowo [PL] 22 G5
Działoszyce [PL] 52 B3
Działoszyn [PL] 36 F6
Dziemiany [PL] 22 C3
Dzierzgoń [PL] 22 F4
Dzierżoniów [PL] 50 C2
Džigolj [YU] 150 D3
Dzivin [BY] 38 H3
Dziwnów [PL] 20 F3
Džumajlija [MK] 128 F1
Dźwierzuty [PL] 22 H4
Dzyarechyn [BY] 24 H5
Dzyarzhynsk [BY] 204 B5

E

Easingwold [GB] 10 F3
Easky [IRL] 2 D3
Eastbourne [GB] 14 E6
East Grinstead [GB] 14 E5
East Kilbride [GB] 8 D3
Eastleigh [GB] 12 H5
Eaux-Bonnes [F] 84 D4
Eaux-Chaudes [F] 84 D4
Eauze [F] 66 D6
Ebbo / Epoo [FIN] 178 B4
Ebbw Vale [GB] 12 F2
Ebelsbach [D] 46 F3
Ebeltoft [DK] 156 E1
Ebenfurth [A] 62 F5
Eben im Pongau [A] 72 H1
Ebensee [A] 62 A5
Eberbach [D] 46 D5
Eberbach [D] 46 B3
Ebermannstadt [D] 46 G4
Ebern [D] 46 G3
Eberndorf [A] 74 C3
Ebersbach [D] 48 G1
Ebersberg [D] 60 E4
Eberschwang [A] 60 H4
Ebersdorf [D] 18 E4
Eberstein [A] 74 C3
Eberstein [D] 58 F1
Eberswalde [D] 34 F1
Ebingen [D] 58 G3
Éboli [I] 120 F4
Ebrach [D] 46 F4
Ebreichsdorf [A] 62 F5
Ebreuil [F] 56 C6
Ebstorf [D] 18 G6
Eceabat [TR] 130 H5
Echallens [CH] 70 C1
Echallon [F] 68 H2
Echarri / Etxarri [E] 84 A3
Échevennoz [I] 70 D3
Echínos [GR] 130 E2
Échourgnac [F] 66 E3
Echternach [L] 44 F2
Écija [E] 102 B2
Ečka [YU] 154 G1
Eckartsau [A] 62 F5
Eckartsberga [D] 34 B6
Eckernförde [D] 18 F1
Eckerö [FIN] 176 A5
Ecommoy [F] 42 B5
Ecouis [F] 28 C6
Ecsegfalva [H] 76 F2
Echte [D] 32 G4
Ecueillé [F] 54 G3
Ecury [F] 44 B4
Ed [S] 166 C4
Eda glasbruk [S] 166 D1
Edam [NL] 16 E4
Edane [S] 166 E2
Ede [NL] 16 E5
Edebäck [S] 172 F6
Edefors [S] 184 C1
Edefors [S] 198 A2
Edelény [H] 64 F4
Edenbridge [GB] 14 E5
Edenderry [IRL] 2 E6
Edenkoben [D] 46 B5
Edersee [D] 32 E5
Édessa [GR] 128 F4
Edewecht [D] 18 C5
Edgeworthstown [IRL] 2 E5
Edinburgh [GB] 8 E3
Edincik [TR] 146 D4
Edineț [MD] 206 D3
Edirne [TR] 146 A2
Edland [N] 164 D1
Édolo [I] 72 B4
Edremit [TR] 144 C1
Edsbro [S] 168 E1
Edsbruk [S] 162 G1
Edsbyn [S] 174 C2
Edsele [S] 184 D1
Edsleskog [S] 166 D4
Edsvalla [S] 166 E2
Eeklo [B] 28 G1
Efendiköprüsü [TR] 144 G2
Eferding [A] 62 B4
Efkarpia [GR] 128 H3
Eforie [RO] 206 E6
Efpálio [GR] 132 F5
Efýra [GR] 136 C2
Efýras [GR] 132 D3
Egebæk [DK] 156 B3
Egeln [D] 34 B3
Egense [DK] 160 E4
Eger [H] 64 E5
Egerlövő [H] 64 F5
Egernsund [DK] 156 C4
Egersund [N] 164 B4
Egervár [H] 74 G2
Egeskov [DK] 156 D4
Egestorf [D] 18 F5
Egg [A] 60 B6
Eggedal [N] 170 G5
Eggenburg [A] 62 E3
Eggenfelden [D] 60 G3
Eggesin [D] 20 E4
Eggum [N] 192 B4
Eghezée [B] 30 D5
Egiertowo [PL] 22 D3
Egilsstaðir [IS] 194 G5
Egletons [F] 68 A3
Eglinton [GB] 2 F2
Egmond aan Zee [NL] 16 D3
Egna / Neumarkt [I] 72 D4
Egremont [GB] 8 D6
Egtved [DK] 156 C2
Eguzon [F] 54 G5
Egyek [H] 64 F6
Ehingen [D] 60 B3
Ehnen [L] 44 F3
Ehra-Lessien [D] 32 H2
Ehrenburg [A] 60 C6
Ehrenburg [D] 18 D6
Ehrenhausen [A] 74 D3
Ehrwald [A] 60 D6
Eiane [N] 164 B3
Eibar [E] 82 H4
Eibenstock [D] 48 C2
Eibergen [NL] 16 G5
Eibiswald [A] 74 D3
Eich [D] 46 C4
Eichendorf [D] 60 G3
Eichstätt [D] 60 D2
Eidanger [N] 164 G3
Eide [N] 164 C3
Eide [N] 164 B4
Eide [N] 180 E2
Eidfjord [N] 170 D4
Eiði [FR] 160 B1
Eidsborg [N] 164 E2
Eidsbugarden [N] 170 F1
Eidsdal [N] 180 E4
Eidsfoss [N] 164 G2
Eidslandet [N] 170 B3
Eidsøra [N] 180 F3
Eidsvåg [N] 180 F3
Eidsvoll [N] 172 C5
Eidsvoll verk [N] 172 C5
Eigenrieden [D] 32 G5
Eikelandsosen [N] 170 B4
Eiken [N] 164 C4
Eikenes [N] 180 B6
Eiksund [N] 180 C4
Eilenburg [D] 34 D5
Eilsleben [D] 34 A3
Eina [N] 172 B4
Einavoll [N] 172 B4
Einbeck [D] 32 F3
Eindhoven [NL] 30 E2
Einsiedeln [CH] 58 G6
Einzinger Boden [A] 72 F1
Eisenach [D] 32 G6
Eisenbach [D] 46 D1
Eisenberg [D] 34 B6
Eisenerz [A] 62 C6
Eisenhüttenstadt [D] 34 G3
Eisenkappel [A] 74 C4
Eisenstadt [A] 62 F5
Eisensteinhöhle [A] 62 E5
Eisfeld [D] 46 G2
Eišiškės [LT] 24 H2
Eislingen [D] 60 B2
Eisriesenwelt [A] 60 H6
Eitorf [D] 30 H5
Eivindvik [N] 170 B2
Eivissa / Ibiza [E] 104 C5
Ejby [DK] 156 D3
Ejea de los Caballeros [E] 84 C6
Ejheden [S] 172 H2
Ejstrupholm [DK] 156 C1
Ejulve [E] 90 E6
Ekáli [GR] 134 C6
Ekeby [S] 156 H2
Ekebyholm [S] 168 E2
Ekedalen [S] 166 F6
Ekenäs [S] 166 E4
Ekenäs / Tammisaari [FIN] 176 F6
Ekenässjön [S] 162 E3
Ekerö [S] 168 D3
Ekinli [TR] 146 H3
Ekkerøy [N] 196 E2
Ekolsund [S] 168 D2
Ekornavallen [S] 166 F6
Ekorrträsk [S] 190 H5
Ekshärad [S] 172 F5
Eksjö [S] 162 E2
Ekträsk [S] 190 H5
Ekzarh Antimovo [BG] 148 E4
Elaiochória [GR] 130 B5
Elaiónas [GR] 132 G5
El Alamo [E] 88 F6
El Alcornocal [E] 96 B5
El Aljunzarejo [E] 104 C2
Elämäjärvi [FIN] 198 D6
Elanets' [UA] 206 F4
Elantxobe [E] 82 H3
Elassóna [GR] 132 F1
El Astillero [E] 82 F3
Eláteia [GR] 132 H4
Eláti [GR] 132 E2
Eláti [GR] 128 F6
Elatoú [GR] 132 F5
El Barraco [E] 88 E5
Elbasan [AL] 128 B3
El Berrón [E] 78 H3
Elbeuf [F] 26 H4
Elbigenalp [A] 72 B1
Elbingerode [D] 32 H4
Elbląg [PL] 22 F3
El Bodón [E] 86 H2
El Bonillo [E] 96 H5
El Bosque [E] 100 H4
Elburg [NL] 16 F4
Elburgo / Burgelu [E] 102 B4
El Burgo de Ebro [E] 90 E4
El Burgo de Osma [E] 90 A3
El Burgo Ranero [E] 82 B5
El Cabaco [E] 88 B4
el Campello [E] 104 E2
El Canal [E] 104 C6
El Cañavate [E] 98 B3
El Carpio [E] 102 C1
El Carpio de Tajo [E] 96 E1

Kukujevci [YU] 154 F2
Kukurečani [MK] 128 E3
Kula [BG] 150 E2
Kula [TR] 144 F3
Kula [YU] 76 D6
Kulalar [TR] 144 E2
Kulata [BG] 130 B2
Kuldīga [LV] 200 C5
Kuleli [TR] 146 B2
Kulennoinen [FIN] 188 F5
Kulhuse [DK] 156 G2
Kuliai [LT] 202 D4
Kullaa [FIN] 176 D1
Kulmbach [D] 46 H3
Kuloharju [FIN] 198 E2
Kultaranta [FIN] 176 D4
Kulykiv [UA] 52 H3
Kumafşarı [TR] 142 G1
Kumane [YU] 76 E6
Kumanica [YU] 150 B3
Kumanovo [MK] 150 D6
Kumarlar [TR] 146 B5
Kumbağ [TR] 146 C3
Kümbet [TR] 146 H5
Kumburk [CZ] 48 H2
Kumkale [TR] 130 H5
Kumköy [TR] 146 E2
Kumla [S] 166 H3
Kumlinge [FIN] 176 B5
Kumo / Kokemäki [FIN] 176 D2
Kumola [RUS] 188 G6
Kumrovec [HR] 74 E5
Kumuu [FIN] 198 G4
Kunda [EST] 200 F1
Kunes [N] 196 C2
Kungälv [S] 160 G1
Kungsängen [S] 168 D2
Kungsbacka [S] 160 H3
Kungsberg [S] 174 D4
Kungsfors [S] 174 D4
Kungshället [S] 168 C3
Kungshamn [S] 166 B5
Kungsör [S] 168 B3
Kunhegyes [H] 76 F1
Kunmadaras [H] 76 F1
Kunovice [CZ] 62 H2
Kunowo [PL] 36 C4
Kunpeszér [H] 76 C2
Kunrau [D] 34 A2
Kunštát [CZ] 50 C5
Kunszentmárton [H] 76 E3
Kunszentmiklós [H] 76 C2
Kunžak [CZ] 48 H6
Künzelsau [D] 46 E5
Kuohatti [FIN] 198 G5
Kuolio [FIN] 198 F2
Kuoloyarvi [RUS] 196 F7
Kuona [FIN] 198 D6
Kuopio [FIN] 188 D2
Kuortane [FIN] 186 D3
Kuosku [FIN] 196 E6
Kup [PL] 50 E2
Kupferberg [D] 46 H3
Kupferzell [D] 46 E5
Kupians'k [UA] 206 H2
Kupirovo [HR] 112 H4
Kupiškis [LT] 202 G4
Kupjak [HR] 112 F1
Kupkovo [RUS] 200 G2
Kupli [LV] 200 D5
Küplü [TR] 130 H2
Küplü [TR] 146 G4
Kuprava [LV] 200 G4
Kupres [BIH] 154 C4
Kurbinovo [MK] 128 D4
Kurbnesh [AL] 128 B1
Kurchatov [RUS] 204 E7
Kurd [H] 76 B4
Kŭrdzhali [BG] 130 F1
Kurejoki [FIN] 186 D2
Kuremäe [EST] 200 F1
Kurevere [EST] 200 C3
Kurgolovo [RUS] 178 E5
Kurianka [PL] 24 F4
Kurikka [FIN] 186 C4
Kurilo [BG] 150 F4
Kuřim [CZ] 50 B6
Kurkiyeki [RUS] 188 G6
Kŭrnare [BG] 148 B4
Kurów [PL] 38 D5
Kurowice [PL] 36 H4
Kurozwęki [PL] 52 C2
Kurravaara [S] 192 F5
Kuršėnai [LT] 202 E4
Kursīši [LV] 200 C6
Kursk [RUS] 204 F7
Kursu [FIN] 196 E7
Kuršumlija [YU] 150 C4
Kuršumlijska Banja [YU] 150 C4
Kurşunlu [TR] 146 F4
Kurşunlu [TR] 146 D4
Kurtakko [FIN] 192 H5
Kurtköy [TR] 146 G3
Kuru [FIN] 186 D6
Kuru [FIN] 176 F1
Kurvinen [FIN] 198 F2
Kurzeszyn [PL] 38 A4
Kurzętnik [PL] 22 F5
Kuşadası [TR] 144 D5
Kusel [D] 44 H3
Kushevanda [RUS] 198 G2
Kuside [YU] 152 D3
Küssnacht [CH] 58 F6
Kustavi / Gustavs [FIN] 176 C4
Kuşuköy [TR] 144 F2
Kuta [YU] 152 E3
Kütahya [TR] 144 G1
Kutemajärvi [FIN] 186 H5
Kutina [HR] 154 B1
Kutjevo [HR] 154 D1
Kutná Hora [CZ] 48 H4
Kutno [PL] 36 G3
Kuttanen [FIN] 192 G4
Kuttura [FIN] 196 D5
Kúty [SK] 62 G3
Kuusaa [FIN] 186 G4
Kuusaa [FIN] 198 D5
Kuusajoki [FIN] 196 C6
Kuusalu [EST] 200 E1
Kuusamo [FIN] 196 F8
Kuusankoski [FIN] 178 C3
Kuusiniemi [RUS] 198 H3
Kuusjärvi [FIN] 188 E2
Kuvshinovo [RUS] 204 E3
Kuyucak [TR] 144 E5
Kuzmin [YU] 154 F2
Kuźmina [PL] 52 E5
Kuźnia Raciborska [PL] 50 E3
Kuźnica [PL] 24 F4
Kuzovo [RUS] 200 H3
Kuzuluk [TR] 146 H3
Kvænangsbotn [N] 192 F2
Kværndrup [DK] 156 D4
Kvål [N] 182 B2
Kvaløyseter [N] 190 B5
Kvalsund [N] 196 B2
Kvalvåg [N] 180 F2
Kvalvåg [N] 170 A5
Kvam [N] 180 H6
Kvam [N] 190 C5
Kvanndal [N] 170 C4
Kvanne [N] 180 F2
Kvantenburg [S] 166 D5
Kvarnberg [S] 172 G2
Kvarsebo [S] 168 C5
Kvås [N] 164 C5
Kveaunet [N] 190 D5
Kvėdarna [LT] 202 D4
Kveejdet [N] 190 D5
Kvelde [N] 164 G3
Kvenvær [N] 190 A6
Kvetkai [LT] 200 E6
Kvevlax / Koivulahti [FIN] 186 B2
Kvicksund [S] 168 B2
Kvikkjokk [S] 190 G1
Kvikne [N] 182 B4
Kvillsfors [S] 162 F3
Kvinesdal [N] 164 C5
Kvinlog [N] 164 C4
Kvissleby [S] 184 E5
Kvisvik [N] 180 F2
Kviteseid [N] 164 E2
Kvitnes [N] 180 F2
Kwidzyn [PL] 22 E4
Kwilcz [PL] 36 B2
Kyaralu [RUS] 196 F7
Kybartai [LT] 24 E1
Kyburg [CH] 58 G5
Kyffhäuser-Denkmal [D] 34 A5
Kyïv [UA] 206 E2
Kyjov [CZ] 62 G2
Kyläinpää [FIN] 186 B3
Kylämä [FIN] 186 F6
Kylemore Abbey [IRL] 2 B4
Kyle of Lochalsh [GB] 6 C5
Kyliia [UA] 206 E5
Kyllaj [S] 168 G4
Kyllburg [D] 44 F1
Kyllíni [GR] 136 B1
Kylmäkoski [FIN] 176 F2
Kylmälä [FIN] 198 E4
Kylmämäki [FIN] 186 H4
Kyme [TR] 144 C3
Kými [GR] 134 C4
Kýmina [GR] 128 H4
Kymönkoski [FIN] 186 G2
Kyparissía [GR] 136 C3
Kyriáki [GR] 132 H5
Kyritz [D] 20 B6
Kyrkhult [S] 162 D6
Kyrkjebygdi [N] 164 E3
Kyrkslätt / Kirkkonummi [FIN] 176 G5
Kyrkstad [S] 198 B5
Kyrö [FIN] 176 E4
Kyrönlahti [FIN] 186 D6
Kyröskoski [FIN] 176 E1
Kyrping [N] 170 B6
Kyrylivka [UA] 206 H5
Kyšice [CZ] 48 F3
Kysucké Nové Mesto [SK] 50 F6
Kýthira [GR] 136 F6
Kýthnos [GR] 138 C2
Kytömäki [FIN] 198 F4
Kyustendil [BG] 150 E6
Kyyjärvi [FIN] 186 E2
Kyzikos [TR] 146 D4
Kyznecovo [RUS] 204 C2

L

Laa an der Thaya [A] 62 F3
Laage [D] 20 B3
Laajoki [FIN] 176 D3
Laakajärvi [FIN] 198 F5
Laakirchen [A] 62 A5
La Alameda [E] 96 E5
La Alamedilla [E] 88 E4
La Alberca [E] 88 B4
La Alberca de Záncara [E] 98 A3
La Albuera [E] 94 G2
La Algaba [E] 94 G6
La Almarcha [E] 98 B3
La Almolda [E] 90 F4
La Almudena [E] 104 B2
La Almunia de Doña Godina [E] 90 D4
Laanila [FIN] 196 D5
La Antilla [E] 94 E6
Laarbruch [D] 30 F2
Laàs [F] 84 D3
La Azohía [E] 104 C4
Labajos [E] 88 E4
la Balme [F] 68 G5
La Baña [E] 78 F6
La Bañeza [E] 78 G6
La Barca de la Florida [E] 100 G4
La Barrela [E] 78 D4
La Bassée [F] 28 F3
Labastide-d'Armagnac [F] 66 D6
La Bastide de-Sérou [F] 84 H5
Labastide-Murat [F] 66 G4
La Bastide-Puylaurent [F] 68 D6
Labastide-Rouairoux [F] 106 C4
La Bastie d'Urfé [F] 68 E2
La Bâtiaz [CH] 70 C2
La Bâtie-Neuve [F] 108 D2
La Baule [F] 40 E6
La Bazoche-Gouet [F] 42 D5
Łabędzie [PL] 20 H4
la Bégude-de-Mazenc [F] 68 F6
La Belle Etoile [F] 44 A5
Labenne [F] 66 A6
La Bérarde [F] 70 A5
L'Aber-Wrac'h [F] 40 B1
Labin [HR] 112 E2
Labinot Fushë [AL] 128 C3
La Bisbal de Falset [E] 90 H5
Łabiszyn [PL] 36 E1
Lábod [H] 74 H4
Laboe [D] 18 G2
Labouheyre [F] 66 B5
La Bourboule [F] 68 C2
La Bóveda de Toro [E] 88 D2
Labrags [LV] 200 B5
Labraunda [TR] 142 D1
Labrède [F] 66 C3
La Bresse [F] 58 D3
La Brillanne [F] 108 C3
Labrit [F] 66 C5
Łabunie [PL] 52 G1
Läby [S] 174 F6
Laç [AL] 128 B2
La Cabrera [E] 88 G4
La Caillere-St-Hilaire [F] 54 C3
La Calahorra [E] 102 F4
La Calera [E] 100 B5
La Caletta [I] 118 E3
Lacalm [F] 68 C5
La Calzada de Calatrava [E] 96 E5
La Calzada de Oropesa [E] 88 C6
La Campana [E] 102 A2
La Cañada de Cañepla [E] 102 H3
Lacanau [F] 66 C2
Lacanau-Océan [F] 66 B2
La Canonica [F] 114 C3
La Canourgue [F] 68 C6
La Capelle [F] 28 G5
Lacapelle-Marival [F] 66 H4
La Capte [F] 108 C6
Laćarak [YU] 154 F2
La Caridad [E] 78 F2
La Carlota [E] 102 B2
La Carolina [E] 96 E6
La Cartuja [E] 100 F3
Lacaune [F] 106 C3
La Cavalerie [F] 106 D3
Lacave [F] 66 G4
Lacco Ameno [I] 120 D3
Lacedonia [I] 120 G2
La Celle-Dunoise [F] 54 H5
Lăceni [RO] 148 B1
La Cerca [E] 82 F4
La Chaise-Dieu [F] 68 D3
La Chambre [F] 70 B4
Lachanás [GR] 130 B3
Lachaniá [GR] 142 D5
La Chapelle [F] 68 F1
La Chapelle-d'Angillon [F] 56 C3
la Chapelle-en-Valgaudemar [F] 70 A6
La Chapelle-en-Vercors [F] 68 G5
La Chapelle-Glain [F] 40 G5
La Charité-sur-Loire [F] 56 D3
La Chartre [F] 42 C6
La Châtaigneraie [F] 54 D3
La Châtre [F] 54 H5
La Chaux-de-Fonds [CH] 58 C5
La Ciotat [F] 108 B5
La Ciudad Encantada [E] 98 C2
Łąck [PL] 36 G2
Läckö [S] 166 E5
La Clayette [F] 56 F6
La Clusaz [F] 70 B3
La Cluse [F] 68 H2
La Cluse-et-Mijoux [F] 58 B6
La Codosera [E] 86 F5
Lacona [I] 114 D3
La Concepción [E] 102 C4
Láconi [I] 118 D5
La Coquille [F] 66 G2
La Coronada [E] 96 B3
La Coruña / A Coruña [E] 78 C2
La Côte-St-André [F] 68 G4
Lacourt [F] 84 G5
La Courtine [F] 68 B2
la Couvertoirade [F] 106 E3
Lacq [F] 84 D3
La Croisière [F] 54 G5
La Croixille [F] 26 D6
La Croix-Valmer [F] 108 D6
La Cumbre [E] 96 B1
La Cure [F] 70 B1
Lad [H] 74 H5
Ląd [PL] 36 E3
Ladbergen [D] 32 C2
Ladby [DK] 156 E3
Lądek-Zdrój [PL] 50 C3
Ládi [GR] 130 H1
Ladíspoli [I] 114 H5
Ladoeiro [P] 86 F3
Ladon [F] 42 F6
Ladoye, Cirque de- [F] 58 A6
La Encinilla y El Rubio [E] 100 G3
Lærdalsøyri [N] 170 E2
Laerma [GR] 142 D5
La Espina [E] 78 G3
La Estrella [E] 96 D1
La Fère [F] 28 F6
La Ferrière-en-Parthenay [F] 54 E3
Laferté [F] 58 B3
La Ferté-Bernard [F] 42 C5
La Ferté-Gaucher [F] 42 H4
La Ferté-Macé [F] 26 F5
La Ferté-Milon [F] 42 H3
La Ferté-sous-Jouarre [F] 42 H3
La Ferté-St-Aubin [F] 56 B1
La Ferté-Vidame [F] 26 H5
Laffrey [F] 68 H5
Láfka [GR] 136 E1
La Flèche [F] 42 B6
La Florida [E] 78 G3
La Flotte [F] 54 B4
La Font de la Figuera [E] 98 D6
la Foresta, Convento- [I] 116 B4
Lafortunada [E] 84 E5
Lafrançaise [F] 66 F6
La Fregeneda [E] 80 E5
La Frua [I] 70 F2
La Fuente de San Esteban [E] 80 F6
La Gacilly [F] 40 E5
Lagan [S] 162 C4
Laganás [GR] 136 B2
La Garde-Freinet [F] 108 D5
La Garriga [E] 92 E4
La Garrovilla [E] 94 G1
Lage [D] 32 E3
Łagiewniki [PL] 50 C2
La Gineta [E] 98 B5
Lagkáda [GR] 136 E4
Lagkáda [GR] 134 G4
Lagkadás [GR] 130 B4
Lagkádia [GR] 136 D2
Lagkadíkia [GR] 130 B4
Lagnieu [F] 68 G2
Lagny [F] 42 G3
Lagoa [P] 94 B5
Lagonegro [I] 120 G5
Lagonisi [GR] 136 H1
Lágos [GR] 130 F3
Lagos [P] 94 B5
Lagosanto [I] 110 H3
Łagów [PL] 52 C1
Łagów [PL] 34 H3
La Granada de Rio Tinto [E] 94 F4
la Granadella [E] 90 H5
La Grand-Combe [F] 106 F2
La Grande-Motte [F] 106 F4
La Granja [E] 88 F4
La Granjuela [E] 96 B5
Lagrasse [F] 106 C5
La Grave [F] 70 B5
La Guardia / A Guarda [E] 78 A5
La Guardia / A Guarda [E] 96 G2
Laguardia / Biasteri [E] 82 G6
La Guardia de Jaén [E] 102 E2
Laguarres [E] 90 H3
Laguarta [E] 84 E5
Laguépie [F] 66 H6
La Guerche [F] 54 F2
La Guerche-de-Bretagne [F] 40 G4
Laguiole [F] 68 B5
Laguna de Duero [E] 88 E2
Laguna del Marquesado [E] 98 C2
Laguna de Negrillos [E] 82 B5
Laguna de Santiago [E] 100 B5
Lagýna [GR] 128 H4
La Haba [E] 96 B3
Lahane [F] 66 B5
La Haye-du-Puits [F] 26 D2
Lahdenperä [FIN] 186 F2
Lahemmaa [EST] 200 D1
La Hermida [E] 82 D3
Lahinch [IRL] 2 B5
Lahnajärvi [S] 196 B7
Lahnasjärvi [FIN] 198 F5
Lahnberg [A] 72 F2
Lahnstein [D] 30 H6
Laholm [S] 162 B5
La Horra [E] 88 G2
Lahoysk [BY] 204 B5
La Hoz de la Vieja [E] 90 E6
Lahr [D] 58 E2
Lahti / Lahtis [FIN] 178 B2
Lahtis / Lahti [FIN] 178 B2
La Hutte [F] 26 F6
Laibgaliai [LT] 202 G3
Laichingen [D] 60 B3
Laifour, Roches de- [F] 44 C1
L'Aigle [F] 26 G5
La Iglesuela del Cid [E] 98 F2
Laignes [F] 56 F2
Laiguéglia [I] 108 G4
L'Aiguillon [F] 54 B4
Laihela / Laihia [FIN] 186 B3
Laihia / Laihela [FIN] 186 B3
Laikko [FIN] 188 F6
Laïliás [GR] 130 C2
Laimbach [A] 62 D4
Lainate [I] 70 G4
Lainijaur [S] 190 G4
Lainio [S] 192 G5
Lairg [GB] 6 E3
La Isla [E] 82 C2
Laissac [F] 68 B6
Laista [GR] 132 D1
Laisvall [S] 190 F2
Laitikkala [FIN] 176 G2
Laitila [FIN] 176 D3
La Javie [F] 108 D3
Lajkovac [YU] 150 A1
la Jonquera [E] 92 G2
Lajoskomárom [H] 76 B3
Lajosmizse [H] 76 D2
Lakagigar [IS] 194 D5
Łaka Prudnicka [PL] 50 D3
Lakatnik [BG] 150 F4
Lakaträsk [S] 196 A8
Lakavica [MK] 128 G2
Lakhdenpokh'ya [RUS] 188 G6
Lakitelek [H] 76 E3
Lákka [GR] 132 B3
Lakki [GR] 142 B2
Lákkoi [GR] 140 C4
Lákkoma [GR] 130 G4
Lakkópetra [GR] 132 E6
Lakolk [DK] 156 A3
Lakselv [N] 192 H1
Laktasi [BIH] 154 C2
La Lantejuela [E] 102 B2
Lalapaşa [TR] 146 B1
Lálas [GR] 136 C2
l'Albagès [E] 90 H5
L'Albi [E] 92 B4
L'Alcidia [E] 98 E5
l'Alcora / Alcora [E] 98 F3
L'Alcúdia (Ilice) [E] 104 D2
L'Alcúdia de Crespins [E] 98 E6
L'Aldea [E] 92 B5
l'Alguenya [E] 104 D2
La Lima [I] 110 E4
Lalín [E] 78 C4
Lalinde [F] 66 F4
La Línea de la Concepción [E] 100 H5
Lalm [N] 180 G6
La Loupe [F] 26 H6
Lalouvesc [F] 68 F4
La Louvière [B] 28 H4
L'Alpe-d'Huez [F] 70 A5
Lalueza [E] 90 F3
La Luisiana [E] 102 B2
Lam [D] 48 D6
La Machine [F] 56 D4
La Maddalena [I] 118 E2
Lama dei Peligni [I] 116 D5
La Magdalena [E] 78 G5
La Malène [F] 68 C6
Lamalou-les-Bains [F] 106 D4
La Manga del Mar Menor [E] 104 D4
Lamarche [F] 58 B2
Lamarosa [P] 86 C5
Lamarque [F] 66 C2
Lamas do Vouga [P] 80 B5
Lamastre [F] 68 F5
La Matanza [E] 82 B5
La Maucarrière [F] 54 E3
Lambach [A] 62 B4
Lamballe [F] 26 B4
Lambesc [F] 106 H4
Lambrecht [D] 46 B5
Lamego [P] 80 D4
L'Ametlla de Mar [E] 92 B5
Lamezia Terme [I] 124 D5
Lamía [GR] 132 G4
Lammhult [S] 162 D4
Lammi [FIN] 176 H2
La Molina [E] 92 E2
La Mongie [F] 84 F4
La Mota [E] 102 D3
La Mothe-Achard [F] 54 B3
Lamotte-Beuvron [F] 56 B2
La Motte-Chalancon [F] 108 B2
la Motte-du-Caire [F] 108 C2
Lamouroux, Grottes de- [F] 66 G3
Lampaanjärvi [FIN] 186 H1
Lampaul [F] 40 A1
Lampaul-Plouarzel [F] 40 A1
Lámpeia [GR] 136 C1
Lampeland [N] 164 G1
Lamperila [FIN] 188 C2
Lampeter [GB] 10 B6
Lampinsaari [FIN] 198 D5
L'Ampolla [E] 92 B5
Lamprechtshausen [A] 60 G5
Lamprechtsofenloch [A] 60 G6
Lämsänkylä [FIN] 198 F2
Lamsfeld [D] 34 F4
Lamstedt [D] 18 E4
La Mudarra [E] 88 E1
La Muela [E] 90 E4
La Mure [F] 68 H5
Lamure-sur-Azergues [F] 68 F2
Lana [I] 72 C3
Lanaja [E] 90 F4
La Napoule-Plage [F] 108 E5
Lanark [GB] 8 D4
La Nava de Ricomalillo [E] 96 D1
La Nava de Santiago [E] 86 G6
Lancaster [GB] 10 D2
Lanciano [I] 116 E5
Łańcut [PL] 52 E3
Landau [D] 60 G3
Landau [D] 46 B5
Landeck [A] 72 C1
Landedo [P] 80 F3
Landerneau [F] 40 B2
Landeryd [S] 162 B4
Landesbergen [D] 32 E1
Landete [E] 98 D3
Landévennec [F] 40 B2
Landivisiau [F] 40 C2
Landivy [F] 26 D5
Landkirchen [D] 18 H2
Landmannalaugur [IS] 194 D5
Landön [S] 182 G1
Landquart [CH] 58 H6
Landrecies [F] 28 G4
Landsberg [D] 60 D4
Landsberg [D] 34 C5
Landsbro [S] 162 E3
Landshut [D] 60 F3
Landshut, Ruine- [D] 44 G2
Landskrona [S] 156 H2
Landštejn [CZ] 62 D2
Landstuhl [D] 44 H3
Landvetter [S] 160 H2
Lanersbach [A] 72 E1
Lanesborough [IRL] 2 D5
La Neuve-Lyre [F] 26 H5
La Neuveville [CH] 58 D5
Langa [DK] 160 D5
Långå [S] 182 F4
Langa de Duero [E] 88 H2
Långåminne [FIN] 186 B3
Langangen [N] 164 G3
Langballig [D] 156 C5
Långban [S] 166 G1
Langeac [F] 68 D4
Langeais [F] 54 F2
Längelmäki [FIN] 186 F6
Langelsheim [D] 32 G3
Langen [A] 72 B1
Langen [D] 46 C3
Langen [D] 18 D4
Langenargen [D] 58 H4
Langenau [D] 60 B3
Langenburg [D] 46 E5
Langenes [N] 192 C3
Längenfeld [A] 72 C2
Langenfeld [D] 30 G4
Langenhahn [D] 46 B1
Langenhorn [D] 156 B5
Langenisarhofen [D] 60 G3
Langenlois [A] 62 E4
Langennaundorf [D] 34 E5
Langenselbold [D] 46 D3
Langenthal [CH] 58 E5
Langenwang [A] 62 E6
Langenzenn [D] 46 F5
Langeoog [D] 18 B3
Langeskov [DK] 156 E3
Langesø [DK] 156 D3
Langesund [N] 164 G3
Langevåg [N] 164 A1
Langevåg [N] 180 C3
Langewiese [D] 32 D5
Langfjord [N] 192 F1
Långflon [S] 172 E3
Langhirano [I] 110 D3
Langholm [GB] 8 E5
Långlöt [S] 162 G5
Långnäs [FIN] 176 B5
Langnau im Emmental [CH] 58 E6
Langø [DK] 156 E5
Langogne [F] 68 D5
Langoiran [F] 66 D3
Langon [F] 66 D4
Langquaid [D] 60 F2
Langres [F] 56 H2
Långsele [S] 184 E2
Långsele [S] 190 F5
Långserud [S] 166 D3
Långshyttan [S] 174 D5
Langstrand [N] 196 B2
Långträsk [S] 198 A3
Languidou, Chapelle de- [F] 40 B3
Langula [D] 32 G5
Långviksmon [S] 184 G1
Langwarden [D] 18 D4
Langwedel [D] 18 E6
Langweid [D] 60 D3
Langwies [CH] 70 H1
Lanhelas [P] 78 A5
Lanjarón [E] 102 E5
Lankas [LV] 200 B5
Länkipohja [FIN] 186 F6
Lanleff, Temple de- [F] 26 A3
Lanmeur [F] 40 C1
Länna [S] 168 C3
Lannabruk [S] 166 G3
Lannavaara [S] 192 F4
Lannemezan [F] 84 F4
Lannevesi [FIN] 186 F3
Lannilis [F] 40 B1
Lannion [F] 40 D1
Lanobre [F] 68 B3
La Noguera [E] 98 D1
Lanouaille [F] 66 G2
Lansjärv [S] 196 A8
Lanškroun [CZ] 50 C4
Lanslebourg-Mont-Cenis [F] 70 C5
Lanšperk [CZ] 50 B4
Lantosque [F] 108 F4
Lanusei [I] 118 E5
Lanvollon [F] 26 A4
Lánycsók [H] 76 B5
Lanzá [E] 78 C2
Lanzendorf [A] 62 F5
Lanžhot [CZ] 62 G3
Lanzo d'Intelvi [I] 70 G3
Lanzo Torinese [I] 70 D5
Lao [EST] 200 D3
Laodikeia [TR] 144 G5
La Oliva [E] 84 B5
La Oliva [E] 100 E5
Laon [F] 28 G6
La Orotava [E] 100 B5
La Paca [E] 104 B3
La Pacaudière [F] 68 E1
Lapalisse [F] 56 D6
La Pallice [F] 54 B4
La Palma del Condado [E] 94 F6
La Palmyre [F] 54 B6
La Palud-sur-Verdon [F] 108 D4
Lápas [GR] 132 E6
La Pelechaneta / Pelejaneta [E] 98 F3
La Peraleja [E] 98 B1
la Péruse [F] 54 E6
La Petite-Pierre [F] 44 G5
Lapeyrade [F] 66 D5
Lapinjärvi / Lappträsk [FIN] 178 B3
Lapinlahti [FIN] 188 C1
La Plagne [F] 70 B4
La Plaza / Teverga [E] 78 G4
Laplume [F] 66 E5
la Pobla de Lillet [E] 92 E2
La Pobla de Massaluca [E] 90 G6
la Pobla de Segur [E] 92 C1
la Pobla de Vallbona [E] 98 E4
la Pobla Tornesa [E] 98 G3
La Pola de Gordón [E] 78 H5
La Portera [E] 98 D4
Lapoutroie [F] 58 D2
Lapovo [YU] 150 C2
Lappach / Lappago [I] 72 E2
Lappago / Lappach [I] 72 E2
Lappäjärvi [FIN] 192 G4
Lappajärvi [FIN] 186 D2
Läppe [S] 168 B3
Lappeenranta / Villmanstrand [FIN] 178 E2
Lappfjärd / Lapväärtti [FIN] 186 B5
Lappfors [FIN] 186 C1
Lappi [FIN] 176 D3
Lappo [FIN] 176 C5
Lappo / Lapua [FIN] 186 C2
Lappohja / Lappvik [FIN] 176 F6
Lappoluobbal [N] 192 G2
Lappträsk [S] 198 C2
Lappträsk / Lapinjärvi [FIN] 178 B3
Lappvattnet [S] 198 A5
Lappvik / Lappohja [FIN] 176 F6
Lapseki [TR] 146 B5
Laptevo [RUS] 200 H5
Lapua / Lappo [FIN] 186 C2
La Puebla de Almoradiel [E] 96 G3
La Puebla de Cazalla [E] 102 A3
La Puebla de los Infantes [E] 96 B6
La Puebla del Río [E] 94 G6
La Puebla de Montalbán [E] 96 E1
La Puebla de Valdavia [E] 82 D4
La Puebla de Valverde [E] 98 E2
La Pueblanueva [E] 96 D1
la Pulente [GBJ] 18 C3
La Punt [CH] 72 B3
Lapväärtti / Lappfjärd [FIN] 186 B5
Łapy [PL] 24 E6
Laqueuille [F] 68 C2
L'Aquila [I] 116 C4
La Rábita [E] 102 E5
Laracha [E] 78 C2
Laragh [IRL] 4 G3
Laragne-Montéglin [F] 108 C2
La Rambla [E] 102 C2
L'Arbresle [F] 68 F2
Lärbro [S] 168 G4
Larche [F] 66 G3
Larche [F] 108 E2
Lårdal [N] 164 E2
Lardaro [I] 72 C4
Larderello [I] 114 F1
Lárdos [GR] 142 E5
Lardosa [P] 86 F3
Laredo [E] 82 F3
La Réole [F] 66 D4
La Restinga [E] 100 A6
Largentière [F] 68 E6
L'Argentière-la-Bessée [F] 70 B6
Largs [GB] 8 C3
La Rhune [E] 84 B2
Lari [F] 114 C2
Lariano [I] 116 B6
La Rinconada [E] 94 G6
Larino [I] 116 F6
Lárisa [GR] 132 G2
Larissa [TR] 144 C3
Larkollen [N] 166 B3
L'Armelliere [F] 106 G4
Larmor [F] 40 C4
Larne [GB] 2 G3
La Robla [E] 78 H5
La Roca de la Sierra [E] 86 G6
la Roca del Vallès [E] 92 E4
La Roche-Bernard [F] 40 E5
La Roche-Chalais [F] 66 E2
la Roche-de-Rame [F] 70 B6
La Roche-en-Ardenne [B] 30 E6
La Rochefoucauld [F] 54 E6
La Rochelle [F] 54 C4
La Roche-Posay [F] 54 F3
La Roche-sur-Foron [F] 70 B2
La Roche-sur-Yon [F] 54 B3
La Rochette [F] 70 A4
Larochette [L] 44 F2
La Roda [E] 98 B4
La Roda de Andalucía [E] 102 B3
Laroquebrou [F] 68 A4
La Roquebrussanne [F] 108 C5
Laroque-des-Arcs [F] 66 G5
Laroque-d'Olmes [F] 106 A5
La Roque-Gageac [F] 66 G4
La Rouche-Courbon [F] 54 C5
Larraga [E] 84 B4
Larrau [F] 84 D3
Larseng [N] 192 E2
Larsmo / Luoto [FIN] 198 C6
Larsnes [N] 180 C4
l'Artigue [F] 84 H5
La Rubia [E] 90 B2
Laruns [F] 84 D4
Larvik [N] 164 G3
Lárymna [GR] 134 B5
La Salceda [E] 88 F4
La Salvetat [F] 66 H6
La Salvetat-sur-Agout [F] 106 C3
Läsänkoski [FIN] 188 C5
Las Anorias [E] 98 C6
Lasarte-Oria [E] 84 B2
La Sauceda [E] 100 G4
Las Batuecas [E] 88 B4
Låsby [DK] 160 D6
Las Cabezas de San Juan [E] 100 G3
Las Caldas de Besaya [E] 82 E3
Lascaux, Grotte de- [F] 66 G3
la Sénia [E] 92 A6
Lasenice [CZ] 62 C2

la Seu d'Urgell [E] 92 D1
La Seyne [F] 108 C6
Las Huelgas [E] 82 E6
Łasin [PL] 22 E5
Łask [PL] 36 G5
Łaskarzew [PL] 38 C4
Lasko [PL] 20 H6
Laško [SLO] 74 D5
Laskowice [PL] 50 D3
Las Médulas [E] 78 E5
Las Mesas [E] 96 H3
Las Navas de la Concepción [E] 96 B6
Las Navas del Marqués [E] 88 E5
Las Negras [E] 102 H5
La Solana [E] 96 G4
La Souterraine [F] 54 G5
Lasovo [YU] 150 D2
Las Palmas de Gran Canaria [E] 100 C5
Las Pedroñeras [E] 96 H3
La Spézia [I] 110 C4
Las Rozas [E] 88 F5
Lassan [D] 20 E3
Lassay [F] 26 E5
Lassigny [F] 28 E6
Las Torcas [E] 98 C2
Las Torres de Cotillas [E] 104 C3
Lastovo [HR] 152 A3
Lastra a Signa [I] 110 E5
Lastres [E] 82 C2
Lästringe [S] 168 D4
Lastrup [D] 18 C6
Lastuk [FIN] 188 D1
Lastva [BIH] 152 D4
La Suze-sur-Sarthe [F] 42 B5
Lašva [BIH] 154 D4
Las Veguillas [E] 88 C3
Las Ventas con Peña Aguilera [E] 96 E2
Las Ventas de S. Julián [E] 88 C6
Łaszczów [PL] 52 G2
Laterza [I] 122 D4
Lathen [D] 16 H3
La Thuile [I] 70 C4
Latiano [I] 122 F4
Latikberg [S] 190 F5
Latina [I] 120 B1
Latinac [YU] 150 D3
Latisana [I] 72 G5
Lató [GR] 140 F5
La Toledana [E] 96 E3
Latorpsbruk [S] 166 H3
La Torre [E] 98 D4
la Torre Baixa [E] 98 D2
La Torresaviñán [E] 90 A5
La Tour-du-Pin [F] 68 G3
La Tranche-sur-Mer [F] 54 B4
La Tremblade [F] 54 B5
La Trimouille [F] 54 G4
La Trinité [F] 40 D5
La Trinité-Porhoët [F] 26 B5
Latronico [I] 120 H5
Latronquière [F] 66 H4
Latte, Fort la- [F] 26 B4
La Turbie [F] 108 F4
Laubrières [F] 40 G5
Laucha [D] 34 B5
Lauchhammer [D] 34 E5
Laudal [N] 164 D5
Lauder [GB] 8 F4
Laudio / Llodio [E] 82 G6
Laudona [LV] 200 F5
Lauenau [D] 32 F2
Lauenburg [D] 18 G5
Lauenstein [D] 48 E2
Lauf [D] 46 G5
Laufen [CH] 58 D4
Laufen [D] 60 G5
Laufenburg [CH] 58 F4
Laufenburg [D] 58 F4
Lauffen [D] 46 D6
Laugar [IS] 194 F3
Laugarbakki [IS] 194 C3
Laugarvatn [IS] 194 C4
Lauingen [D] 60 C3
Laujar de Andarax [E] 102 F5
Laukaa [FIN] 186 G4
Laukeland [N] 170 B1
Laukka [FIN] 198 D4
Laukkala [FIN] 186 G1
Lauksundskaret [N] 192 F1
Laukuluspa [S] 192 E5
Laukuva [LT] 202 E4
Laukvik [N] 192 C5
Laukvik [N] 192 B4
Laukvik [N] 192 D2
Laukvika [N] 192 C5
Launceston [GB] 12 D4
La Unión [E] 104 C4
Laupen [CH] 58 D6
Laupheim [D] 60 B4
Lauragh [IRL] 4 B5
Laureana di Borrello [I] 124 D6
Laurencetown [IRL] 2 D5
Laurenzana [I] 120 H4
Lauria [I] 120 H5
Laurière [F] 54 G6
Lausanne [CH] 70 C1
Lautemburg [D] 30 F4
Lauter [S] 168 H3
Lauterbach [D] 46 E1
Lauterbourg [F] 46 B6
Lauterbrunnen [CH] 70 E1
Lautere [LV] 200 F5
Lauterecken [D] 44 H3
Lauterhofen [D] 46 H5
Lautiosaari [FIN] 198 C2
Lautrec [F] 106 B3
Lauvsnes [N] 190 C5
Lauvstad [N] 180 C4
Lauvuskylä [FIN] 198 G5
Lauvvik [N] 164 B3
Lauwersoog [NL] 16 G1
Lauzerte [F] 66 F5
Lauzun [F] 66 E4
Lavagna [I] 110 B3
Laval [F] 26 E6
la Vall d'Uixó [E] 98 F4
Lavamünd [A] 74 C3
Låvang [N] 190 D2
Lavangnes [N] 192 D3
Lávara [GR] 130 H2
Lavardac [F] 66 E5
Lavardin [F] 42 C6
Lavarone [I] 72 D5
Lavaur [F] 106 B3
La Vecilla [E] 82 B3
Lavelanet [F] 106 A5
Lavello [I] 120 H3
Lavelsloh [D] 32 E2
La Venta [E] 102 F4
La Verna [I] 110 G6
la Veurdre [F] 56 D4
Lavia [FIN] 176 E1
Lavik [N] 170 B2
la Vila Joiosa / Villajoyosa [E] 104 E2
la Villa / Stern [I] 72 E3
Lavinio-Lido di Enea [I] 120 A1
La Virgen del Camino [E] 78 H5
Lavis [I] 72 C4
Lavit [F] 66 F6
Lavong [N] 190 D2
Lavos [P] 86 C2
La Voulte-sur-Rhône [F] 68 F5
Lavoûte-Chilhac [F] 68 D4
Lavoûte-Polignac, Château de- [F] 68 D4
Lavoûte-sur-Loire [F] 68 D4
Lavre [P] 86 C6
Lávrion [GR] 136 H1
Lavry [RUS] 200 G4
Lavsjö [S] 190 F5
La Wantzenau [F] 44 H6
Laxå [S] 166 G4
Laxe [E] 78 B2
Laxne [S] 168 C3
Laxsjö [S] 190 E6
Laxtjärn [S] 172 G5
Laxviken [S] 190 E6
La Yesa [E] 98 E3
Läyliäinen [FIN] 176 G4
La Yunta [E] 90 C5
Laza [E] 78 D6
Lazarevac [YU] 150 B1
Lazarovo [YU] 154 G1
Lazdijai [LT] 24 F2
Laži [LV] 200 C4
Lazise [I] 72 C6
Łaziska Górne [PL] 50 F3
Lazkao [E] 84 A3
Lázne Kynžvart [CZ] 48 C4
La Zubia [E] 102 E4
Łazy [PL] 22 A2
Leacanabuaile Stone Fort [IRL] 4 A4
Leamington Spa [GB] 14 D2
Leap [IRL] 4 B5
Leatherhead [GB] 14 E4
Łeba [PL] 22 C1
Lebach [D] 44 G3
Lebane [YU] 150 D4
Lebanza [E] 82 D3
Le Bar [F] 108 E4
Le Barp [F] 66 C4
Le Beausset [F] 108 C5
Lebedin [UA] 206 G2
Lébénymiklós [H] 62 H6
Lebesby [N] 196 D2
Le Blanc [F] 54 G4
Łebno [PL] 22 D2
Le Boréon [F] 108 F3
Lębork [PL] 22 C2
Le Boulou [F] 92 G1
Le Bourg d'Oisans [F] 68 H5
Le Bourget [F] 68 H3
le Bousquet-d'Orb [F] 106 D3
Lebrija [E] 100 G3
Lebus [D] 34 G2
Le Bugue [F] 66 F3
le Caloy [F] 66 C6
Le Cap-d'Agde [F] 106 E5
Le Cateau-Cambrésis [F] 28 G4
Le Catelet [F] 28 F5
Le Caylar [F] 106 E3
Lecce [I] 122 G4
Lecco [I] 70 G4
Lécera [E] 90 E5
Lech [A] 72 B1
Lechainá [GR] 136 B1
L'Echalp [F] 70 C6
le Chambon-sur-Lignon [F] 68 E4
Le Chateau-d'Oléron [F] 54 B5
Le Châtelard [F] 70 A3
Le Châtelet [F] 56 B4
Le Chesne [F] 44 C2
Le Cheylard [F] 68 E5
Lechlade [GB] 12 H3
Lechovice [CZ] 62 F2
Léchovo [GR] 128 E5
Lēči [LV] 200 B5
Lecíñena [E] 90 F3
Leck [D] 156 B4
Le Conquet [F] 40 A2
Le Creusot [F] 56 F5
Le Croisic [F] 40 D6
Le Crotoy [F] 28 D3
Lectoure [F] 66 E6
Łęczna [UA] 38 E5
Łęczyca [PL] 20 G5
Łęczyca [PL] 36 G3
Ledaña [E] 98 C4
Ledbury [GB] 12 G2
Ledeč nad Sázavou [CZ] 48 H5
Ledenia Pećina [YU] 152 E2
Ledenika Peštera [BG] 150 F3
Ledesma [E] 80 G6
Lédignan [F] 106 F3
Ledigos [E] 82 C5
Ledmozero [RUS] 198 H4
Lednice [CZ] 62 G3
Lednogora [PL] 36 D2
Le Donjon [F] 56 E6
Le Dorat [F] 54 F5
Ledreborg [DK] 156 G3
Lędyczek [PL] 22 B5
Leeds [GB] 10 F3
Leek [GB] 10 E5
Leek [NL] 16 G2
Leenane [IRL] 2 B4
Leer [D] 18 B4
Leerdam [NL] 16 D5
Leese [D] 32 E1
Leesi [EST] 200 E1
Leeuwarden [NL] 16 F2
Le Faou [F] 40 B2
Le Faouët [F] 40 C3
le Fayet [F] 70 C3
Lefka [BG] 146 A1
Lefkáda [GR] 132 D4
Lefkádia [GR] 128 G4
Lefkaditi [GR] 132 G5
Léfkes [GR] 138 E3
Lefkími [GR] 132 B3
Lefkógeia [GR] 130 C2
Léfktra [GR] 134 A5
le Folgoet [F] 40 B1
Le Fossat [F] 84 H4
Legbąd [PL] 22 D4
Legden [D] 16 H5
Legé [F] 54 B2
Legionowo [PL] 38 B2
Legnago [I] 110 F1
Legnano [I] 70 F4
Legnica [PL] 36 B6
Legoland [DK] 156 B2
Legrad [HR] 74 G4
Le Grand-Bourg [F] 54 G6
Le Grand-Lucé [F] 42 C5
Le Grand-Pressigny [F] 54 F3
Le Grau-du-Roi [F] 106 F4
Legrená [GR] 136 H2
le Gressier [F] 66 B3
Leguatiano [E] 82 G4
Léguevin [F] 84 H3
Le Havre [F] 26 G3
Lehnice [SK] 62 H5
Lehnin [D] 34 D3
Le Hohwald [F] 44 G6
Lehrberg [D] 46 F5
Lehre [D] 32 H2
Lehrte [D] 32 G2
Lehtimäki [FIN] 186 D3
Lehtiniemi [FIN] 196 E8
Lehtmetsa [EST] 200 E1
Lehtovaara [FIN] 198 F5
Leianokládi [GR] 132 G4
Leibnitz [A] 74 D3
Leicester [GB] 10 F6
Leiden [NL] 16 D4
Leie [EST] 200 E3
Leighlinbridge [IRL] 4 F4
Leighton Buzzard [GB] 14 E3
Leikanger [N] 180 B4
Leikanger [N] 170 D2
Leinefelde [D] 32 G5
Leinesodden [N] 190 D2
Leini [I] 70 D5
Leipheim [D] 60 C3
Leipojärvi [S] 192 F6
Leipsoí [GR] 142 B2
Leipzig [D] 34 C5
Leira [N] 170 G3
Leirbotn [N] 192 G1
Leirbotnvatn [N] 192 G1
Leirfall [N] 182 C1
Leirgulen [N] 180 B5
Leiria [P] 86 C3
Leiro [E] 78 C4
Leirosa [P] 86 C2
Leirosen [N] 190 D2
Leirpollskogen [N] 196 D2
Leirvik [FR] 160 B1
Leirvik [N] 170 B1
Leirvik [N] 170 B5
Leirvika [N] 190 D2
Leirvika [N] 190 D2
Leisi [EST] 200 C3
Leisnig [D] 34 D6
Leissigen [CH] 70 E1
Leitzkau [D] 34 C3
Leivaditis [GR] 130 E2
Leivonmäki [FIN] 186 G5
Lejasciems [LV] 200 F4
Lekáni [GR] 130 D2
Łękawa [PL] 36 G6
Lekeitio [E] 82 H4
Lekenik [HR] 74 E6
Lekeryd [S] 162 D2
Lekhchevo [BG] 150 F3
Łeki Górne [PL] 52 C4
Leknes [N] 180 D4
Leknes [N] 192 B4
Łeknica [PL] 34 G5
Leksand [S] 172 H4
Leksberg [S] 166 F5
Leksvik [N] 190 B6
Lekunberri [E] 84 B3
Lekvattnet [S] 172 E5
Le Lauzet-Ubaye [F] 108 D2
Le Lavandou [F] 108 D6
L'Elefante [I] 118 C2
Lelice [PL] 36 H1
Le Lion-d'Angers [F] 40 H6
Lelkowo [PL] 22 G2
Lelle [EST] 200 E2
Le Locle [CH] 58 C5
Le Logis-du-Pin [F] 108 D4
Le Loroux-Bottereau [F] 54 C1
Le Louroux [F] 40 G6
Lelów [PL] 50 H2
Le Luc [F] 108 D5
Le Ludd [F] 42 B6
Lelystad [NL] 16 E4
Lem [DK] 156 B1
Le Mans [F] 42 B5
Le Markstein [F] 58 D3
Le Mas-d'Azil [F] 84 H4
Le Mayet [F] 68 D1
Lembach [F] 44 H5
Lembeck [D] 16 G6
Lembeye [F] 84 E3
Le Merlerault [F] 26 G5
Lemetinvaara [FIN] 198 F5
Lemförde [D] 32 D1
Lemgo [D] 32 E3
Lemi [FIN] 178 D2
Lemke [D] 32 F1
Lemland [FIN] 176 B6
Lemmenjoki [FIN] 196 D4
Lemmer [NL] 16 F3
Lemnhult [S] 162 E3
Le Monastier [F] 68 E5
Le Monêtier-les-Bains [F] 70 B5
Le Mont-Dore [F] 68 C2
Le Montet [F] 56 D5
Le Mont-St-Michel [F] 26 D4
Lemovzha [RUS] 200 H1
Lempäälä [FIN] 176 F2
Lempdes [F] 68 C3
Lempdes [F] 68 D2
Le Muret [F] 66 C4
Le Muy [F] 108 D5
Lemvig [DK] 160 B5
Lena [N] 172 B4
Lenart [SLO] 74 E3
Lencloître [F] 54 F3
Lend [A] 72 G1
Lendava [SLO] 74 F3
Lendery [RUS] 198 H6
Lendinara [I] 110 G2
Le Neubourg [F] 26 H4
Lengerich [D] 32 C2
Lenggries [D] 60 E5
Lengyeltóti [H] 74 H3
Lenhovda [S] 162 E4
Leni [I] 124 A6
Lenina [BY] 204 D6
Lenk [CH] 70 D2
Lennartsfors [S] 166 C3
Lenningen [N] 170 G2
Lenno [I] 70 G3
Leno [I] 72 B6
Lenola [I] 120 C1
Lenora [CZ] 62 B2
Le Nouvion-en-Thiérache [F] 28 G5
Lens [F] 28 F3
Lensahn [D] 18 H2
Lensvik [N] 180 H1
Léntas [GR] 140 E5
Lentföhrden [D] 18 F3
Lenti [H] 74 F3
Lentiira [FIN] 198 G4
Lenting [D] 60 E2
Lentini [I] 126 G4
Lentvaris [LT] 24 H1
Lenzburg [CH] 58 F5
Lenzen [D] 20 A6
Lenzerheide [CH] 70 H1
Lenzkirch [D] 58 F3
Leoben [A] 74 D1
Leogang [A] 60 G6
Leominster [GB] 12 G1
León [E] 78 H5
Léon [F] 66 B5
Leonberg [D] 58 G1
Leonessa [I] 116 B3
Leonforte [I] 126 F3
Leonídio [GR] 136 F3
Leontári [GR] 136 D3
Leóntio [GR] 136 E2
Leontýnský Zámek [CZ] 48 E4
Leopoldsburg [B] 30 E3
Leopoldsdorf [A] 62 F4
Le Palais [F] 40 C5
L'Epau, Abbaye de- [F] 42 B5
Lepe [E] 94 E5
Le-Péage-de-Roussillon [F] 68 F4
Lepenoú [GR] 132 E4
Le Perthus [F] 92 G2
Lepetane [YU] 152 D4
Le Pin-au-Haras [F] 26 G5
l'Epine [F] 44 C4
le Plevnet [F] 70 A5
Lepoglava [HR] 74 E4
Le Poiré-sur-Vie [F] 54 B3
Le Pont-de-Beauvoisin [F] 68 H4
Le Pont-de-Claix [F] 68 H5
le Pont-de-Montvert [F] 68 D6
Le Pontet [F] 66 D2
Le Portel [F] 28 D2
Leposavić [YU] 150 C4
Le Pouldu [F] 40 C4
Lépoura [GR] 134 C5
Le Pouzin [F] 68 F5
Leppäjärvi [FIN] 192 G4
Leppälahti [FIN] 188 F3
Leppävesi [FIN] 186 G4
Leppävirta [FIN] 188 D3
Leppiniemi [FIN] 198 D4
Lépreo [GR] 136 C3
Lepsény [H] 76 B2
Leptokaryá [GR] 128 G6
Le Puy [F] 68 D4
Le Puy-en-Velay [F] 68 D4
Leques, Col des- [F] 108 D4
Le Quesnoy [F] 28 G4
Le Rabot [F] 56 B2
Lerbäck [S] 166 H4
Lercara Friddi [I] 126 D3
Lerchenborg [DK] 156 E2
Lerga [E] 84 B4
Lerici [I] 110 C4
Lérida / Lleida [E] 90 H4
Lerín [E] 84 A4
Lerma [E] 88 G1
Lermoos [A] 60 D6
Lérni [GR] 136 E2
Le Rozier [F] 106 E2
Lerresfjord [N] 196 B2
Lerum [S] 160 H2
Le Russey [F] 58 C5
Lerwick [GB] 6 G4
Lés [E] 84 F5
Les [RO] 76 H2
Lesa [I] 70 F4
Les Abrets [F] 68 H3
Les Adrets [F] 108 E5
Les Aix-d'Angillon [F] 56 C3
Lešak [YU] 150 B4
Lesaka [E] 84 B3
les Aldudes [F] 84 C3
Les Andelys [F] 28 C6
Les Antiques [F] 106 G4
Les Arcs [F] 70 C4
Les Arcs [F] 108 D5
les Avants [CH] 70 C1
Les Avellanes [E] 92 B2
Les Baux-de-Provence [F] 106 G4
les Borges Blanques [E] 92 B3
Les Boulay Lue [F] 44 F4
Les Cabannes [F] 106 A5
L'Escala [E] 92 G3
Lescar [F] 84 E3
L'Escarène [F] 108 F4
Les Contamines-Montjoie [F] 70 C3
les Coves de Vinromà [E] 98 G2
Les Deux-Alpes [F] 70 A5
Les Diablerets [CH] 70 D2
Les Echarmeaux [F] 68 F1
Les Echelles [F] 68 H4
Le Sentier [CH] 70 B1
Les Epesses [F] 54 C2
Les Escaldes [AND] 84 H6
Les Essarts [F] 54 C3
Les Eyzies-de-Tayac [F] 66 F3
Les Gets [F] 70 C2
Les Halles [F] 68 F3
Les Haudères [CH] 70 D3
Les Hayons [F] 28 C5
Les Herbiers [F] 54 C2
Les Houches [F] 70 C3
Lésina [I] 116 F6
Les Issambres [F] 108 D5
Lesja [N] 180 G5
Lesjaskog [N] 180 F4
Lesjaverk [N] 180 F4
Lesjöfors [S] 166 F1
Leskelä [FIN] 198 D5
Lesko [PL] 52 E5
Leskovac [YU] 150 D4
Leskovik [AL] 128 D6
Leskovo [BG] 148 F1
Les Laumes [F] 56 F3
Les Lecques [F] 108 B5
Les Menuires [F] 70 B4
Lesmont [F] 44 B5
Lésna [PL] 48 H1
Lesneven [F] 40 B1
Lešnica [PL] 50 E3
Lešnica [YU] 154 F3
Lésniów Wielki [PL] 34 H4
Lesnovo [MK] 128 F1
Lesogorskiy [RUS] 178 F2
Lesparre-Médoc [F] 66 C2
Les Pieux [F] 26 D2
Les Planches-en-Montagne [F] 58 B6
les Planes d'Hostoles [E] 92 F3
l'Espluga de Francolí [E] 92 C4
Les Ponts-de-Cé [F] 40 H6
Les Riceys [F] 56 F1
Les Rosiers [F] 54 E1
les Rotes [E] 104 F1
Les Rousses [F] 70 B1
Les Sables-d'Olonne [F] 54 B3
Lessay [F] 26 D3
Lessebo [S] 162 E5
Lessines [B] 28 G3
l'Estacq [GBJ] 18 C2
l'Estartit [E] 92 G3
Lestelle Bétharram [F] 84 E4
Lestijärvi [FIN] 198 D6
Les Trois-Epis [F] 58 D2
Les Trois-Moutiers [F] 54 E2
Lesum [D] 18 D5
Les Vans [F] 68 E6
Leszczyny [PL] 50 F3
Leszno [PL] 36 C4
Leszno [PL] 38 B3
Leszno Górne [PL] 36 A5
Létavértes [H] 76 H1
Letchworth [GB] 14 E3
Le Teil [F] 68 F6
Le Teilleul [F] 26 E5
le Temple [F] 66 C3
Letenye [H] 74 F4
Le Thillot [F] 58 C3
Letkés [H] 64 C5
Letmathe [D] 32 C4
Letnitsa [BG] 148 B3
Letohrad [CZ] 50 B4
Le Touquet-Paris-Plage [F] 28 D3
Le Touvet [F] 68 H4
Letovice [CZ] 50 C5
Le Trayas [F] 108 E5
Le Tréport [F] 28 C4
Letreros, Cueva de los- [E] 102 H3
Letsbo [S] 184 D6
Letschin [D] 34 G2
Letterfrack [IRL] 2 B4
Letterkenny [IRL] 2 E2
Lettermullan [IRL] 2 B5
Letur [E] 104 A1
Letychiv [UA] 206 D3
Leu [RO] 150 G1
Leucate [F] 106 D6
Leuchtenburg [D] 46 H1
Leuglay [F] 56 G2
Leuk [CH] 70 D2
Leukerbad [CH] 70 D2
Leuna [D] 34 C5
Leutasch [A] 60 D6
Leutenberg [D] 46 H2
Leutkirch [D] 60 B5
Leutschach [A] 74 D3
Leuven (Louvain) [B] 30 D4
Leuze [B] 28 G3
Levajok [N] 196 C3
Le Val-André [F] 26 B4
Levan [AL] 128 A4
Levanger [N] 190 C6
Levanto [FIN] 176 H3
Lévanto [I] 110 C4
Levanzo [I] 126 A2
Leväsjoki [FIN] 186 B6
Le Vaudreuil [F] 28 B6
Leven [GB] 8 F3
Levens [F] 108 E4
Le Verdon [F] 54 B6
Leverkusen [D] 30 G4
Le Vernet [F] 108 D3
Levet [F] 56 C4
Levice [SK] 64 B4
Levico Terme [I] 72 D5
Levídi [GR] 136 D2
Levie [F] 114 B5
Levier [F] 58 B5
Le Vigan [F] 106 E3
Levoča [SK] 64 E2
Levroux [F] 54 H3
Levski [BG] 148 B3
Lewes [GB] 14 E5
Lewin Brzeski [PL] 50 D2
Leyburn [GB] 10 F2
Leysin [CH] 70 C2
Leżajsk [PL] 52 E3
Ležáky [CZ] 50 B4
Lézardrieux [F] 26 A3
Lezay [F] 54 E5
Lezhë [AL] 128 B1
Lézignan-Corbières [F] 106 C5
Lezoux [F] 68 D2
Lezuza [E] 98 A5
L'gov [RUS] 204 E7
L'Hospitalet de l'Infant [E] 92 B5
l'Hospitalet de Llobregat [E] 92 E4
l'Hospitalet-l'Andorre [F] 92 E1
Liapádes [GR] 132 B2
Liatorp [S] 162 D5
Libáň [CZ] 48 H3
Liběchov [CZ] 48 F3
Liberec [CZ] 48 G2
Libiąż [PL] 50 G3
Libochovice [CZ] 48 F3
Libohovë [AL] 132 C1
Libourne [F] 66 D3
Libramont [B] 44 D1
Librazhd [AL] 128 C3
Librilla [E] 104 C3
Licata [I] 126 E4
Licciana Nardi [I] 110 D4
Lich [D] 46 C2
Licháda [GR] 132 H4
Lichfield [GB] 10 E6
Lichnice [CZ] 48 H4
Lichtenau [D] 32 E4
Lichtenberg [D] 46 H2
Lichtenberg [F] 44 H5
Lichtenfels [D] 32 E5
Lichtenfels [D] 46 G3
Lichtenstein [CH] 70 H1
Lichtenstein [D] 58 H2
Lichtenstein [D] 48 C2
Lichtenvoorde [NL] 16 G5
Lickershamn [S] 168 G4
Lički Osik [HR] 112 G3
Ličko Lešće [HR] 112 G3
Licodia Eubea [I] 126 F4
Licques [F] 14 G6
Lida [BY] 204 A5
Liden [S] 198 A4
Liden [S] 190 F4
Liden [S] 162 E2
Liden [S] 184 E4
Lidhult [S] 162 C5
Lidice [CZ] 48 F3
Lidingö [S] 168 E3
Lidköping [S] 166 E5
Lido degli Estensi [I] 110 H3
Lido di Camaiore [I] 110 D5
Lido di Castel Fusano [I] 114 H6
Lido di Fermo [I] 116 D2
Lido di Jésolo [I] 72 F6
Lido di Latina [I] 120 B1
Lido di Metaponto [I] 122 D4
Lido di Nazioni [I] 110 H3
Lido di Óstia [I] 114 H6
Lido di Pomposa [I] 110 H3
Lido di Scanzano [I] 122 D5
Lido di Spina [I] 110 H3
Lido di Torre Mileto [I] 116 G5
Lido di Venézia [I] 110 H1
Lidoriki [GR] 132 G5
Lido Silvana [I] 122 F4
Lidsjöberg [S] 190 E5
Lidzbark [PL] 22 G5
Lidzbark Warmiński [PL] 22 H3
Liebegg [CH] 58 F5
Liebenau [D] 32 E1
Liebenwalde [D] 34 E1
Lieberose [D] 34 F4
Liebling [RO] 76 G6
Liechtenstein Klamm [A] 72 G1
Liedenpohja [FIN] 186 D4
Liège (Luik) [B] 30 E5
Lieksa [FIN] 198 G6
Lielvärde [LV] 200 E5
Lienz [A] 72 F2
Liepāja [LV] 200 B6
Liepna [LV] 200 G4
Lier [B] 30 D3
Lierbyen [N] 164 H1
Liérganes [E] 82 F3
Liernais [F] 56 F4
Liesa [E] 84 D6
Liesjärvi [FIN] 186 E4
Liestal [CH] 58 E4
Lieto / Lundo [FIN] 176 E4
Liétor [E] 98 B6
Lieu-Restauré, Abbaye de- [F] 42 G3
Lieurey [F] 26 G4
Lievestuore [FIN] 186 G4
Lievikoski [FIN] 176 D2
Liezen [A] 62 B6
Liezere [LV] 200 F5
Lifford [IRL] 2 F2
Liffré [F] 26 C6
Ligieri [LV] 200 E5
Lignano Pineta [I] 72 G6
Lignano Sabbiadoro [I] 72 G6
Ligneuville [B] 30 F6
Lignières [F] 56 B4
Ligny-en-Barrois [F] 44 D5
Ligourió [GR] 136 F2
Ligueil [F] 54 F3
Ligugé, Abbaye de- [F] 54 E4
Lihme [DK] 160 C5
Lihula [EST] 200 D2
Liiansaari [FIN] 178 D1
Liiva [EST] 200 C2
Lijärvi [FIN] 196 D3
Lijeva Rijeka [YU] 152 E4
Likavka [SK] 64 C2
Likenäs [S] 172 E4
Likóssoura [GR] 136 D3
Lilaste [LV] 200 D5
Lild Strand [DK] 160 C3
Lilienfeld [A] 62 D5
Liljendal [FIN] 178 B4
Lilla Edet [S] 166 D6
Lillåfors [S] 196 A8
Lillafüred [H] 64 F4
Lillaz [I] 70 D4
Lille [DK] 156 G3
Lille [F] 28 F3
Lillebo [N] 182 D6
Lillebonne [F] 26 H3
Lillehammer [N] 172 B2
Lillerød [DK] 156 G2
Lillers [F] 28 E3
Lillesand [N] 164 E5
Lillestrøm [N] 166 C1
Lille Værløse [DK] 156 G2
Lillhaga [S] 172 H1
Lillhärdal [S] 182 G6
Lillholmsjö [S] 182 G1
Lillkågeträsk [S] 198 A4
Lillkyro / Vähäkyrö [FIN] 186 B2
Lillo [E] 96 G2
Lillögda [S] 190 G5
Lillviken [S] 190 F2
Limáni Chersonisou [GR] 140 F4
Limanowa [PL] 52 B5
Limatola [I] 120 E2
Limavady [GB] 2 F2
Limbaži [LV] 200 E4
Limbourg [B] 30 F5
Limburg [D] 46 B2
Limedsforsen [S] 172 F3
Limenária [GR] 130 E4
Liménas [GR] 134 C4
Liméni [GR] 136 E5
Limerick / Luimneach [IRL] 4 D3
Limhamn [S] 156 H3
Limingo / Liminka [FIN] 198 D4
Liminka / Limingo [FIN] 198 D4
Limín Litochórou [GR] 128 G6
Liminpuro [FIN] 198 E4
Limmared [S] 162 C2
Limna [UA] 52 F6
Límnae [TR] 130 H5
Límnes [GR] 136 F2
Límni [GR] 134 B4
Limniá [GR] 130 D3
Limnitsa [GR] 132 F5
Límnos [GR] 134 G4
Limoges [F] 66 G1
Limogne-en-Quercy [F] 66 G5
Limone Piemonte [I] 108 F3
Limonest [F] 68 F2
Limone sul Garda [I] 72 C5
Limours [F] 42 F4
Limoux [F] 106 B5
Lin [AL] 128 D3
Linachamari [RUS] 196 F3
Linares [E] 102 E1
Linares de Mora [E] 98 F2
Linares de Riofrío [E] 88 B4
Linariá [GR] 134 D3
Lincoln [GB] 10 G5
Lind [DK] 156 B1
Lindås [N] 170 B3
Lindås [S] 162 F5
Lindau [D] 60 B5
Lindau [D] 34 C3
Lindaunis [D] 18 F1
Linde [DK] 160 B5
Lindelbrunn [D] 46 B5
Lindenberg [D] 60 B5
Lindenfels [D] 46 C4
Linderhof [D] 60 D6
Lindern [D] 18 C6

Linderöd [S] 158 D2
Lindesberg [S] 166 H2
Lindesnäs [S] 172 G5
Lindholm [DK] 160 D3
Lindkoski [FIN] 178 B3
Lindlia [N] 170 G4
Lindome [S] 160 H2
Líndos [GR] 142 E5
Lindoso [P] 78 B6
Lindow [D] 20 C6
Lindsås [N] 164 E4
Lingbo [S] 174 E3
Linge [N] 180 E4
Lingen [D] 16 H4
Linghed [S] 174 D4
Linghem [S] 168 A5
Linguaglossa [I] 124 A8
Linköping [S] 168 A5
Linneryd [S] 162 E5
Linnes [N] 172 E1
Linnés Hammarby [S] 168 D1
Linova [BY] 38 H2
Linovo [RUS] 200 G4
Linsdal [S] 162 G5
Linsell [S] 182 F5
Linthal [CH] 58 G6
Lintzel [D] 18 F6
Linum [D] 34 D1
Linz [A] 62 B4
Linz [D] 30 H5
Lioni [I] 120 F3
Lióprasо [GR] 132 F2
Lipa [BIH] 152 B1
Lipany [SK] 52 C6
Lipar [YU] 76 D6
Lipari [I] 124 A6
Lipcani [UA] 206 D3
Liperi [FIN] 188 F3
Lipiany [PL] 20 F6
Lipica [SLO] 72 H6
Lipik [HR] 154 B1
Lipinki Łużyckie [PL] 34 G5
Lipka [PL] 22 C5
Lipljan [YU] 150 C5
Lipnica [PL] 22 C3
Lipnice nad Sázavou [CZ] 48 H5
Lipník [PL] 52 D2
Lipník nad Bečvou [CZ] 50 D5
Lipno [CZ] 62 B3
Lipno [PL] 36 G1
Lipova [CZ] 50 E6
Lipova [RO] 76 H4
Lipovljani [HR] 154 B1
Lipovo Polje [HR] 112 G3
Lipowo [PL] 22 G4
Lippborg [D] 32 D4
Lippstadt [D] 32 D4
Lipsk [PL] 24 F4
Lipsko [PL] 38 C6
Liptovská Osada [SK] 64 C2
Liptovská Teplička [SK] 64 E2
Liptovský-Mikuláš [SK] 64 D2
Lipusz [PL] 22 C3
Lisboa [P] 86 B5
Lisburn [GB] 2 G4
Liscarroll [IRL] 4 C4
Lisdoonvarna [IRL] 2 B5
Liseleje [DK] 156 G1
Liselund [DK] 156 G4
Lisia Góra [PL] 52 C3
Lisieux [F] 26 G4
Liskeard [GB] 12 D4
Lisle [F] 106 B2
L'Isle-Adam [F] 42 F3
L'Isle-de-Noé [F] 84 F3
L'Isle-en-Dodon [F] 84 G3
L'Isle-Jourdain [F] 84 H3
L'Isle-Jourdain [F] 54 F5
Lisleset [N] 170 F4
L'Isle-sur-la-Sorgue [F] 106 H3
L'Isle-sur-le-Doubs [F] 58 C4
Lisle-sur-Tarn [F] 106 B2
Lisma [FIN] 196 C5
Lismore [IRL] 4 D5
Lišnja [BIH] 154 C2
Lison, Source du- [F] 58 B5
Lišov [CZ] 62 C2
Lisów [PL] 34 G2
Lisse [NL] 16 D4
Lisskogsbrändan [S] 172 F4
List [D] 156 A4
Lişteava [RO] 150 G2
Listeid [N] 164 C5
Listerby [S] 158 F1
Lištica [BIH] 152 C2
Listowel [IRL] 4 C3
Lit [S] 182 H2
Litene [LV] 200 F4
Liternum [I] 120 D3
Lit-et-Mixe [F] 66 B5
Lithakiá [GR] 136 A2
Lithínes [GR] 140 G5
Lití [GR] 128 H4
Litice [CZ] 50 B4
Litija [SLO] 74 C5
Litke [H] 64 D4
Litóchoro [GR] 128 G6
Litoměřice [CZ] 48 F2
Litomyšl [CZ] 50 B4
Litovel [CZ] 50 C5
Litslena [S] 168 C2
Littlehampton [GB] 14 D5
Littleport [GB] 14 F2
Litultovice [CZ] 50 D4
Litvínov [CZ] 48 E2
Liubar [UA] 206 D2
Liuboml' [UA] 38 G5
Liukoniai [LT] 202 G5
Livade [HR] 112 D1
Livadeiá [GR] 132 H5
Livaderó [GR] 130 D2
Livadhja [AL] 132 B1
Livádi [GR] 130 B5
Livádi [GR] 128 G6
Livádi [GR] 136 F6
Livádi [GR] 138 D3
Livádia [GR] 142 C4
Livadochóri [GR] 130 F6
Līvāni [LV] 200 F6
Livarot [F] 26 G4
Liverá [GR] 128 F5
Livernon [F] 66 H5
Liverpool [GB] 10 D4
Livigno [I] 72 B3
Livingston [GB] 8 E3
Livno [BIH] 152 B1
Livny [RUS] 204 F6
Livold [SLO] 74 C6
Livorno [I] 110 D6
Livorno Ferraris [I] 70 E5
Livron [F] 68 F5
Livron-Sur-Drôme [F] 68 F5
Liw [PL] 38 D2
Lixa [P] 80 C4
Lixoúri [GR] 132 C6
Lizard [GB] 12 B5
Lizarra / Estella [E] 84 A4
Lizartza [E] 84 B3
Lizy [F] 42 G3
Lizzano [I] 122 F4
Ljig [YU] 150 B1
Ljørdalen [S] 172 E2
Ljosland [N] 164 D4
Ljuban' [BY] 204 B6
Ljuban [RUS] 204 C2
Ljubaništa [MK] 128 D4
Ljubelj [SLO] 74 B4
Ljubinje [BIH] 152 C3
Ljubljana [SLO] 74 B5
Ljubno [SLO] 74 C4
Ljubostinja, Manastir- [YU] 150 C3
Ljubovija [YU] 154 F4
Ljubuški [BIH] 152 B2
Ljubytino [RUS] 204 D2
Ljugarn [S] 168 G5
Ljungby [S] 162 C5
Ljungbyhed [S] 158 C1
Ljungbyholm [S] 162 F5
Ljungdalen [S] 182 E3
Ljungsbro [S] 166 H5
Ljungskile [S] 166 C6
Ljusdal [S] 184 D6
Ljusfallshammar [S] 166 H4
Ljusne [S] 174 E2
Ljusträsk [S] 190 H3
Ljutići [YU] 152 E2
Ljutomer [SLO] 74 E4
Llafranc [E] 92 G3
Llagostera [E] 92 F3
Llanberis [GB] 10 B4
Llançà [E] 92 G2
Llandeilo [GB] 12 E2
Llandiloes [GB] 10 C6
Llandovery [GB] 12 E1
Llandrindod Wells [GB] 10 C6
Llandudno [GB] 10 C4
Llanelli [GB] 12 E2
Llanes [E] 82 D2
Llanfyllin [GB] 10 C5
Llangefni [GB] 10 B4
Llangollen [GB] 10 C5
Llangurig [GB] 10 C6
Llantwit Major [GB] 12 E3
Llanuwchllyn [GB] 10 C5
Llavorsí [E] 84 G6
Lleida / Lérida [E] 90 H4
Llera [E] 94 H3
Llerena [E] 94 H4
Lles de Cerdanya [E] 92 D1
Llíria [E] 98 E4
L'Ile-Bouchard [F] 54 F2
L'Ile-Rousse [F] 114 B3
Llodio / Laudio [E] 82 G4
Lloret de Mar [E] 92 F4
Lluc, Monestir de- [E] 104 E4
Llucmajor [E] 104 E5
Lnáře [CZ] 48 E5
Loano [I] 108 G3
Loarre, Cast. de- [E] 84 D6
Löbau [D] 34 G6
Lobenstein [D] 46 H2
Łobez [PL] 20 G4
Lobios [E] 78 C6
Löbnitz [D] 20 C2
Łobodno [PL] 50 G1
Lobón [E] 94 G2
Loborika [HR] 112 D2
Loburg [D] 34 C3
Lobženica [PL] 22 C5
Locana [I] 70 D4
Locarno [CH] 70 F3
Loccum [D] 32 E2
Lochaline [GB] 6 B6
Loch Baghasdail / Lochboisdale [GB] 6 A4
Lochboisdale / Loch Baghasdail [GB] 6 A4
Lochearnhead [GB] 8 D2
Lochem [NL] 16 F5
Loches [F] 54 G3
Loch Garman / Wexford [IRL] 4 F5
Lochgilphead [GB] 8 C2
Lochinver [GB] 6 D3
Lochmaddy / Loch nam Madadh [GB] 6 A3
Loch nam Madadh / Lochmaddy [GB] 6 A3
Łochocin [PL] 36 G1
Łochów [PL] 38 C2
Lochranza [GB] 8 C3
Lochteå / Lohtaja [FIN] 198 C5
Lockenhaus [A] 74 F1
Lockerbie [GB] 8 E5
Löcknitz [D] 20 E5
Locmaria [F] 40 C5
Locmariaquer [F] 40 D5
Locminé [F] 26 A6
Locorotondo [I] 122 E3
Locquirec [F] 40 C1
Locri [I] 124 D7
Locri Epizefiri [I] 124 D7
Locronan [F] 40 B3
Loctudy [F] 40 B3
Lodè [I] 118 E3
Lode [LV] 200 E4
Lodejnoye Pole [RUS] 204 D1
Löderup [S] 158 D3
Lodève [F] 106 D3
Lodi [I] 70 G5
Løding [N] 192 B6
Lødingen [N] 192 C4
Lodosa [E] 84 A5
Lödöse [S] 160 H1
Łódź [PL] 36 G4
Loeches [E] 88 G6
Loen [N] 180 D5
Loev [BY] 204 C7
Løfallstrand [N] 170 B5
Lofer [A] 60 G6
Lofsdal [FIN] 176 D5
Lofsdalen [S] 182 F5
Loftahammar [S] 162 G2
Lofthus [N] 170 C4
Loga [D] 18 B4
Loga [N] 164 C5
Loganikos [GR] 136 D3
Logatec [SLO] 74 B5
Lögdeå [S] 184 H1
Lognvik [N] 164 E1
Logroño [E] 82 G6
Logrosán [E] 96 C2
Logstein [N] 190 B6
Løgstør [DK] 160 D4
Løgumkloster [DK] 156 B4
Lohals [DK] 156 E4
Lohberg [D] 48 D6
Lohéac [F] 26 C6
Lohikoski [FIN] 188 E6
Lohiniva [FIN] 192 H6
Lohja [FIN] 176 G5
Löhne [D] 32 E2
Lohne [D] 18 C6
Lohnsfeld [D] 46 B4
Lohr [D] 46 E3
Lohtaja / Lochteå [FIN] 198 C5
Loiano [I] 110 F4
Loimaa [FIN] 176 E3
Loire, Gorges de la- [F] 68 E5
Lóiri [I] 118 E3
Loisirs, Parc de- [F] 66 B3
Loitz [D] 20 D3
Loja [E] 102 D3
Lojanice [YU] 154 F3
Lojsta [S] 168 G5
Lojt Kirkeby [DK] 156 C4
Lokakylä [FIN] 186 F2
Lokalahti [FIN] 176 C4
Lokča [SK] 50 G5
Løken [N] 166 C1
Lokeren [B] 28 H2
Loket [CZ] 48 D3
Lokhvytsia [UA] 206 F2
Lokka [FIN] 196 E6
Løkken [DK] 160 D3
Løkken Verk [N] 180 H2
Loknya [RUS] 204 C3
Lököshàza [H] 76 G4
Lokot' [RUS] 204 E6
Loksa [EST] 200 E1
Lokuta [EST] 200 E2
Lokve [HR] 112 F1
Lokve [SLO] 72 H5
Lokve [YU] 154 H2
l'Olleria [E] 98 E6
Lölling [A] 74 C2
Lom [BG] 150 F2
Lom [CZ] 48 E2
Lom [N] 180 F5
Lom [SK] 64 D3
Lombez [F] 84 G3
Lombrives, Grotte de- [F] 84 H5
Lomello [I] 70 F6
Lomen [N] 170 F2
Lomma [S] 156 H2
Lomme [F] 28 F3
Lommel [B] 30 E3
Lomnice nad Lužnicí [CZ] 62 C2
Lomonosov [RUS] 178 G5
Lompolo [FIN] 192 H4
Lomsjö [S] 190 F5
Łomża [PL] 24 D5
Lonato [I] 72 B6
Loncari [BIH] 154 E2
Lončarica [HR] 74 G6
Londinières [F] 28 C4
London [GB] 14 E4
Londonderry [GB] 2 F2
Lonevåg [N] 170 B3
Longá [GR] 132 F1
Longarone [I] 72 E4
Longeau [F] 56 H2
Longford [IRL] 2 E4
Longny-au-Perche [F] 26 G6
Longobucco [I] 124 E4
Longpont [F] 42 H3
Longroiva [P] 80 E5
Longtown [GB] 8 E5
Longué [F] 54 E1
Longueau [F] 28 E5
Longuyon [F] 44 E3
Longwy [F] 44 E3
Lonigo [I] 110 F1
Löningen [D] 18 C6
Łoniów [PL] 52 D2
Lonka [RUS] 198 F3
Lono [N] 164 C1
Lönsboda [S] 162 D6
Lønsdal [N] 190 E1
Lønset [N] 180 E3
Lønset [N] 180 G3
Lons-le-Saunier [F] 56 H5
Lønstrup [DK] 160 D2
Looberghe [F] 14 H6
Looe [GB] 12 D5
Loosdorf [A] 62 D4
Lopar [HR] 112 F3
Lopare [BIH] 154 E3
Lopatica [MK] 128 E3
Lopatovo [RUS] 200 H3
Lope [LV] 200 E6
Lopera [E] 102 D1
Loppi [FIN] 176 G3
Lopud [HR] 152 C4
Łopuszna [PL] 52 B5
Łopuszno [PL] 52 B1
Lora del Río [E] 102 A1
Lorca [E] 104 B3
Lorcé [B] 30 E5
Lorch [D] 60 B2
Lorch [D] 46 B3
Lordosa [P] 80 C5
Loreley [D] 46 B2
Lørenskog [N] 166 B1
Lorentzen [F] 44 G5
Loreo [I] 110 H2
Loreto [I] 116 C1
Loreto Aprutino [I] 116 D4
Lorgues [F] 108 D5
Lorica [I] 124 E4
Lorient [F] 40 C4
Lőrinci [H] 64 D6
Loriol-sur-Drôme [F] 68 F5
Lormes [F] 56 E3
Lormont [F] 66 D3
Loro Ciuffenna [I] 110 F6
Lorqui [E] 104 C3
Lörrach [D] 58 E4
Lorris [F] 42 F6
Lörsfeld [D] 30 G4
L'Orso [I] 118 E2
Lorup [D] 18 B5
Loryma [TR] 142 D4
Los [S] 172 H1
Losa, Nuraghe- [I] 118 C4
Los Alares [E] 96 D2
Los Alcázares [E] 104 C4
Los Arcos [E] 82 H6
Losar de la Vera [E] 88 B5
Los Arenales del Sol / Arenals del Sol [E] 104 D3
Los Barrios [E] 100 G5
Los Canarios [E] 100 A5
Los Caños de Meca [E] 100 F5
Los Corrales de Buelna [E] 82 E3
Loscos [E] 90 D5
Los Cristianos [E] 100 B5
Losenstein [A] 62 C5
Los Escullos [E] 102 H6
Losheim [D] 44 G3
Losheim [D] 30 F6
Los Hinojosos [E] 96 H3
Łosice [PL] 38 E3
Los Isidros [E] 98 D4
Los Llanos de Aridane [E] 100 A5
Los Mallos [E] 84 D5
Los Molares [E] 100 H2
Los Navalmorales [E] 96 D2
Los Navalucillos [E] 96 D2
Los Olmos [E] 90 E6
Łososina Dolna [PL] 52 B4
Los Palacios y Villafranca [E] 100 G2
l'Ospedale [F] 114 B5
Los Santos de Maimona [E] 94 G3
Los Sauces [E] 100 A5
Lossburg [D] 58 F2
Lossiemouth [GB] 6 F4
Lostwithiel [GB] 12 C4
Los Urrutias [E] 104 C4
Los Villares [E] 102 E2
Los Yébenes [E] 96 F2
Lote [N] 180 C5
Løten [N] 172 C3
Lotorp [S] 168 B5
Lotoshino [RUS] 204 E4
Lötschberg Tunnel [CH] 70 E2
Lotta [RUS] 196 E5
Lotte [D] 32 D2
Löttorp [S] 162 H4
Löttorp-Högby [S] 162 H4
Lotzorai [I] 118 E5
Loudéac [F] 26 A5
Loudes [F] 68 D4
Loudun [F] 54 E3
Loué [F] 42 B5
Loue [FIN] 196 C8
Loue, Source de la- [F] 58 B5
Loughborough [GB] 10 F6
Loughbrickland [GB] 2 G4
Loughglinn [IRL] 2 D4
Loughmoe Castle [IRL] 4 E3
Loughrea [IRL] 2 C5
Louhans [F] 56 G5
Louisburgh [IRL] 2 B4
Loukás [GR] 136 E2
Loukhi [RUS] 198 H1
Loukísia [GR] 134 B5
Loukusa [FIN] 198 E2
Loulay [F] 54 D5
Loulé [P] 94 C5
Louny [CZ] 48 E3
Lourdes [F] 78 D2
Lourdes [F] 84 E4
Louredo [P] 80 D3
Lourenzá [E] 78 E2
Loures [P] 86 B5
Lourical [P] 86 D2
Lourinhã [P] 86 B4
Loúros [GR] 132 D3
Lousã [P] 86 E2
Lousa [P] 86 B5
Lousada [P] 80 C4
Louth [GB] 10 G5
Lout Ostrov [RUS] 198 H5
Loutrá [GR] 132 E4
Loutrá [GR] 136 D2
Loutrá [GR] 138 C2
Loutrá [GR] 134 H2
Loutrá Aidipsoú [GR] 134 A4
Loutrá Aridaías [GR] 128 F3
Loutrá Eleftherón [GR] 130 D4
Loutrá Kaitsas [GR] 132 F3
Loutráki [GR] 136 F1
Loutráki [GR] 132 D4
Loutrá Kounoupélli (Yrmínis) [GR] 132 E6
Loutrá Kyllínis [GR] 136 B2
Loutrá Lagkadá [GR] 130 B4
Loutrá Smokóvou [GR] 132 F3
Loutrá Vólvis [GR] 130 B4
Loutrá Ypátis [GR] 132 G4
Loutró Elénis [GR] 136 F1
Loutrós [GR] 130 G3
Loútsa [GR] 134 C6
Louvain (Leuven) [B] 30 D4
Louviers [F] 28 B6
Lövånger [S] 198 B5
Lovasberény [H] 76 B1
Lövasen [S] 184 D2
Lövåsen [S] 174 C5
Lövberga [S] 190 F6
Lovech [BG] 148 B3
Lovère [I] 72 A5
Loviisa / Lovisa [FIN] 178 B4
Lovisa / Loviisa [FIN] 178 B4
Lovište [HR] 152 B3
Lövnäs [S] 172 F2
Lövnäs [S] 190 G2
Lövö [H] 62 G6
Lovosice [CZ] 48 F2
Lovran [HR] 112 E1
Lovrenc na Pohorju [SLO] 74 D3
Lovrin [RO] 76 F5
Lövsjön [S] 172 G5
Lövstabruk [S] 174 F5
Lövstad [S] 168 B5
Lövvik [S] 190 F5
Löwenberg [D] 34 E1
Löwenfreigehege [D] 30 F4
Lowenstein [D] 32 E5
Łowicz [PL] 36 H3
Łowin [PL] 22 D5
Łowyń [PL] 36 B2
Lož [SLO] 74 B6
Lozarevo [BG] 148 E4
Lozari [F] 114 B3
Lozen [BG] 148 A6
Lozenets [BG] 148 G5
Loznica [BG] 148 D3
Loznica [YU] 154 F3
Lozovac [HR] 112 H6
Lozovik [YU] 150 C1
Lozoya [E] 88 G4
Lozoyuela [E] 88 G4
Lozzo di Cadore [I] 72 F3
Luanco [E] 78 H3
Luarca [E] 78 G2
Lubaczów [PL] 52 F3
Lubań [PL] 34 H6
Lubāna [LV] 200 F5
Lubarda [BIH] 112 H2
Lubartów [PL] 38 E5
Lubasz [PL] 36 C1
Lubawa [PL] 22 F5
Lubawka [PL] 50 B2
Lübbecke [D] 32 E2
Lübben [D] 34 F4
Lübbenau [D] 34 F4
Lübbow [D] 18 H6
Lübeck [D] 18 G3
Lubenec [CZ] 48 E3
Lubenice [HR] 112 E3
Lubersac [F] 66 G2
Lubia [E] 90 B3
Łubianka [PL] 22 E6
Łubianka [PL] 34 H1
Lubiatowo [PL] 20 F6
Lubiąż [PL] 36 B6
Lubichowo [PL] 22 D4
Lubień [PL] 50 H5
Lubień Kujawski [PL] 36 G2
Lubieszyn [PL] 20 F5
Lubin [PL] 36 B5
Lubiń [PL] 36 C4
Lublin [PL] 38 E5
Lubliniec [PL] 50 F2
Lubmin [D] 20 D3
Lubniewice [PL] 34 H2
Łubno [PL] 22 C3
Lubny [UA] 206 F2
Lubomino [PL] 22 G3
Luboń [PL] 36 C3
Luboniek [PL] 36 F3
Luboradz [PL] 36 B6
Lubosalma [RUS] 198 H6
Luboszów [PL] 34 H5
Luboszyce [PL] 36 B5
L'ubotín [SK] 52 C6
Lubowidz [PL] 22 G6
Lubowitz [PL] 50 E3
Łubowo [PL] 22 A4
Łubowo [PL] 36 D2
Lubraniec [PL] 36 F2
Lubrín [E] 102 H5
Lubsko [PL] 34 G4
Lübtheen [D] 18 H5
Lubuczewo [PL] 22 B2
Lübz [D] 20 B5
Lucainena de las Torres [E] 102 G5
Lucan [IRL] 2 F6
Lucca [I] 110 D5
Luče [SLO] 74 C4
Lucena del Cid [E] 98 F3
Lucena del Cid / Llucena [E] 102 C3
Lucenay [F] 56 F4
Luc-en-Diois [F] 68 G6
Lučenec [SK] 64 D4
Lucera [I] 120 G1
Lüchow [D] 18 H6
Luciana [E] 96 E4
Lucignano [I] 114 G1
Lucito [I] 116 E6
Luckau [D] 34 E4
Luckenwalde [D] 34 E3
Lückstedt [D] 34 B1
Luco dei Marsi [I] 116 C5
Luçon [F] 54 C3
Luc-sur-Mer [F] 26 F3
Lucus Feroniae [I] 116 A5
Ludanice [SK] 64 A3
Ludbreg [HR] 74 F4
Lüdenscheid [D] 32 C5
Lüderitz [D] 34 B2
Lüdinghausen [D] 16 H6
Ludlow [GB] 10 D6
Ludoni [RUS] 200 H2
Ludvika [S] 172 H5
Ludwigsburg [D] 46 D6
Ludwigshafen [D] 46 C4
Ludwigshafen [D] 58 G4
Ludwigslust [D] 20 A5
Ludwigsstadt [D] 46 H2
Ludza [LV] 200 G5
Lug [HR] 76 C6
Luga [RUS] 200 H2
Lugagnano Val d'Arda [I] 110 C2
Lugano [CH] 70 G3
Lügde [D] 32 E3
Lugnås [S] 166 F5
Lugo [E] 78 E3
Lugo [I] 110 G4
Lugoj [RO] 206 A5
Lugones [E] 78 H3
Luhačovice [CZ] 62 H2
Luhalahti [FIN] 186 D6
Luhanka [FIN] 186 G6
Luhtapohja [FIN] 188 G2
Luhtikylä [FIN] 178 A3
Luidja [EST] 200 C2
Luigny [F] 42 D5
Luik (Liège) [B] 30 E5
Luikonlahti [FIN] 188 E2
Luimneach / Limerick [IRL] 4 D3
Luino [I] 70 F3
Luisenburg [D] 48 B4
Luka [YU] 150 D1
Lukanja [SLO] 74 D4
Lukavac [BIH] 154 D3
Lüki [BG] 148 B6
Łukom [PL] 36 E3
Lukovë [AL] 132 B1
Lukovica [SLO] 74 C4
Lukovit [BG] 148 A3
Lukovo [MK] 128 C3
Lukovo [YU] 150 D2
Lukovo Šugarje [HR] 112 G4
Łuków [PL] 38 D3
Lukšić [HR] 154 A5
Lukta [PL] 22 G4
Luleå [S] 198 B3
Lüleburgaz [TR] 146 C2
Lumbarda [HR] 152 B3
Lumbier / Irunberri [E] 84 C4
Lumbrales [E] 80 F6
Lumbrein [CH] 70 G1
Lumbres [F] 28 E2
Lumezzane [I] 72 B5
Lumijoki [FIN] 198 D4
Lummelundagrottorna [S] 168 G4
Lummen [B] 30 E4
Lumparland [FIN] 176 B5
Lumsås [DK] 156 F2
Lumsheden [S] 174 D4
Lun [HR] 112 F3
Luna [E] 84 C6
Lunas [F] 106 D3
Lund [S] 158 C2
Lunda [S] 168 D2
Lundamo [N] 182 B2
Lunde [N] 164 F2
Lunde [N] 180 D6
Lunde [S] 184 F3
Lundeborg [DK] 156 E4
Lunden [D] 18 E2
Lunderseter [N] 172 D5
Lunderskov [DK] 156 C3
Lundo / Lieto [FIN] 176 E4
Lundsjön [S] 182 G1
Lüneburg [D] 18 G5
Lunel [F] 106 F4
Lünen [D] 32 C4
Lunéville [F] 44 F5
Lungern [CH] 70 E1
Lungro [I] 120 H6
Lungsund [S] 166 F2
Lungvik [S] 184 F3
Luninyets [BY] 204 A6
Lunkuva [LT] 200 D6
Lunna [BY] 24 G4
Lünne [D] 16 H4
Lunz [A] 62 D5
Luogosanto [I] 118 D2
Luopioinen [FIN] 176 G1
Luostari [RUS] 196 F3
Luostari [RUS] 196 F3
Luoto / Larsmo [FIN] 198 C6
Lupeni [RO] 206 B5
Lupiac [F] 84 F2
Lupiana [E] 88 H5
Lupoglav [HR] 74 F6
Luque [E] 102 D2
Lurcy-Lévis [F] 56 D4
Lure [F] 58 C3
Lureuil [F] 54 G4
Lurgan [GB] 2 G4
Lurgrotte [A] 74 D2
Lušci Palanka [BIH] 154 A3
Lüsens [A] 72 D1
Lushnjë [AL] 128 B4
Lusi [FIN] 178 B2
Lusignan [F] 54 E4
Lusigny [F] 44 B6
Lusk [IRL] 2 F6
Lus-la-Croix-Haute [F] 68 G6
Luso [P] 80 B6
Lussac-les-Châteaux [F] 54 F4
Lussac-les-Églises [F] 54 G5
Lussan [F] 106 G3
Lustenau [A] 58 H5
Luster [N] 170 E1
Lutago / Luttach [I] 72 E2
Lutcza [PL] 52 D4
Lutherstadt Eisleben [D] 34 B5
Lutherstadt Wittenberg [D] 34 D4
Lütjenburg [D] 18 G2
Lutnes [N] 172 E3
Lutol Suchy [PL] 36 A3
Lutomek [PL] 36 B2
Lutomiersk [PL] 36 G4
Luton [GB] 14 E3
Lutrini [LV] 200 C5
Lutry [PL] 22 H3
Luts'k [UA] 206 C1
Lutterworth [GB] 14 D2
Lututów [PL] 36 F5
Lützen [D] 34 C5
Lutzmannsburg [A] 74 F1
Lützow [D] 18 H4
Luumäki [FIN] 178 D2
Luusalmi [RUS] 198 H3
Luusniemi [FIN] 188 C5
Luusua [FIN] 196 E8
Luvia [FIN] 176 C2
Luvozero [RUS] 198 G4
Luxembourg [L] 44 F3
Luxeuil-les-Bains [F] 58 C3
Luxey [F] 66 C5
Luzaide / Valcarlos [E] 84 C3
Lužani [HR] 154 C2
Luzarches [F] 42 F3
Luzern [CH] 58 F6
Luzhma [RUS] 198 G5
Luz-St-Sauveur [F] 84 E4
Luzy [F] 56 E5
Luzzara [I] 110 E2
Luzzi [I] 124 D4
L'viv [UA] 52 H4
Lvubertsy [RUS] 204 F4
Lwówek [PL] 36 B2
Lwówek Śląski [PL] 36 A6
Lyady [RUS] 200 G2
Lyaskelya [RUS] 188 H5
Lyaskovets [BG] 148 C3
Lychen [D] 20 D5
Lyckeby [S] 158 F1
Lycksele [S] 190 G5
Lydd [GB] 14 F6
Lye [S] 168 G5
Lyenin [BY] 204 B6
Lyepyel' [BY] 204 B5
Lygna [N] 172 B4
Lygre [N] 170 B5
Lykófos [GR] 130 H2
Lykorráchi [GR] 128 D6
Lyme Regis [GB] 12 F4
Lymington [GB] 12 H5
Lynderupgård [DK] 160 D5
Lyngby [DK] 156 G2
Lyngdal [N] 164 C5
Lyngør [N] 164 F4
Lyngså [DK] 160 E3
Lyngseidet [N] 192 E2
Lynton [GB] 12 E3
Lyon [F] 68 F3
Lyons-la-Forêt [F] 28 C6
Lyozno [BY] 204 C4
Lysá nad Labem [CZ] 48 G3
Lysebotn [N] 164 C3
Lysekil [S] 166 C6
Lysøysund [N] 190 B5
Lyss [CH] 58 D5
Lysvik [S] 166 E1
Lytham Anne's [GB] 10 D3
Lyuben [BG] 148 B5
Lyubimets [BG] 148 D6
Lyudinovo [RUS] 204 E5

M

Maalahti / Malax [FIN] 186 B3
Maaninka [FIN] 188 C1
Maaninkavaara [FIN] 196 E8
Maanselkä [FIN] 198 F5
Maardu [EST] 200 E1
Maarianhamina / Mariehamn [FIN] 176 A5
Maarianvaara [FIN] 188 E2
Maarja [EST] 200 F2
Maaseik [B] 30 F3
Maasmechelen [B] 30 E4
Maassluis [NL] 16 C5
Maastricht [NL] 30 E4
Mablethorpe [GB] 10 H5
Macael [E] 102 G4
Maçanet de la Selva [E] 92 F4
Mação [P] 86 E4
Maccagno [I] 70 F3
Macclesfield [GB] 10 E4
Maceda [E] 78 D5
Macedo de Cavaleiros [P] 80 F4

Macerata [I] 116 C1
Macerata Féltria [I] 110 H5
Măceşu de Jos [RO] 150 G2
Machault [F] 44 C3
Mâchecourt [F] 54 B2
Macherádo [GR] 136 A2
Machico [P] 100 B3
Machliny [PL] 22 A5
Machynlleth [GB] 10 B5
Maciejowice [PL] 38 C4
Macinaggio [F] 114 C2
Mackenrode [D] 32 G4
Macocha [CZ] 50 C6
Macomer [I] 118 C4
Mâcon [F] 68 G1
Macotera [E] 88 D3
Macroom [IRL] 4 C5
Macugnaga [I] 70 E3
Mád [H] 64 G4
Madan [BG] 130 E1
Madängsholm [S] 162 C1
Madara [BG] 148 E3
Maddaloni [I] 120 E2
Made [NL] 16 D6
Madekoski [FIN] 198 D4
Maderuelo [E] 88 G3
Madésimo [I] 70 G2
Madliena [LV] 200 E5
Madona [LV] 200 F5
Madonna dell'Acero [I] 110 E4
Madonna della Civita [I] 120 C2
Madonna della Neve [I] 116 B3
Madonna del Ponte [I] 112 C5
Madonna del Rosario [I] 126 C2
Madonna del Sasso [I] 70 E4
Madonna di Bracciano [I] 114 H5
Madonna di Campíglio [I] 72 C4
Madonna di Canneto [I] 116 E6
Madonna di Senales / Unserfrau [I] 72 C2
Madonna di Tirano [I] 72 B4
Madrid [E] 88 F5
Madridejos [E] 96 F3
Madrigal de las Altas Torres [E] 88 D3
Madrigal de la Vera [E] 88 C5
Madrigalejo [E] 96 B2
Madrigalejo del Monte [E] 88 G1
Madroñera [E] 96 B2
Mæbø [N] 164 D6
Maella [E] 90 G6
Mære [N] 190 C5
Maetzu [E] 82 H5
Mafra [P] 86 B4
Maga Circe, Grotta della- [I] 120 B2
Magallón [E] 90 D3
Magalluf [E] 104 D5
Magaña [E] 90 C2
Magaz de Pisuerga [E] 88 F1
Magdalensberg [A] 74 B3
Magdeburg [D] 34 B3
Magellarë [AL] 128 C2
Magenta [I] 70 F5
Magerholm [N] 180 D3
Magescq [F] 66 B6
Maghera [GB] 2 G3
Magherafelt [GB] 2 G3
Magierowa Wola [PL] 38 C4
Magione [I] 114 H2
Magkanári [GR] 138 F4
Maglaj [BIH] 154 D3
Maglavit [RO] 150 F2
Maglehem [S] 158 D2
Maglehøj Strand [DK] 18 H1
Magliano dei Marsi [I] 116 C5
Magliano in Toscana [I] 114 F3
Magliano Sabina [I] 116 A4
Maglić [YU] 150 B3
Máglie [I] 122 G5
Magnac-Laval [F] 54 G5
Magnesia [TR] 144 D5
Magnor [N] 166 D1
Magny-Cours [F] 56 D4
Magny-en-Vexin [F] 42 E2
Maguelone [F] 106 E4
Maguiresbridge [GB] 2 E3
Magura [BG] 150 E2
Magyarkeszi [H] 76 B3
Magyarszombatfa [H] 74 F3
Maheriv [UA] 52 G3
Mahide [E] 80 G3
Mahilyow [BY] 204 C5
Mahlu [FIN] 186 F3
Mahmutlar [TR] 144 D4
Mahmutsevketpaşa [TR] 146 F2
Mahón / Maó [E] 104 H5
Mahora [E] 98 C4
Mahovo [HR] 74 F6
Maia [P] 80 B3
Maials [E] 90 H5
Maîche [F] 58 C5
Máida [I] 124 D5
Maidenhead [GB] 14 D4
Maidstone [GB] 14 F5
Maienfeld [CH] 58 H6
Maierato [I] 124 D6
Maijanen [FIN] 196 C7
Maillezais [F] 54 C4
Mailly-le-Camp [F] 44 B5
Mainburg [D] 60 E3
Maintenon [F] 42 E4
Mainua [FIN] 198 E5
Mainz [D] 46 C3
Maiori [I] 120 E4
Maiori, Nuraghe- [I] 118 D2
Mairena del Alcor [E] 94 H6
Maisach [D] 60 D4
Maišiogala [LT] 202 G5
Maison-Neuve [F] 44 C6
Maissau [A] 62 E3
Maja [HR] 154 A1
Majadahonda [E] 88 F5
Majadas [E] 88 B6
Majaelrayo [E] 88 H4
Majavatn [N] 190 D4
Majdanek [PL] 38 E5
Majdanpek [YU] 150 D1
Makarska [HR] 152 B2
Makashevichy [BY] 204 B6
Makedonski Brod [MK] 128 E2
Makhnovka [RUS] 200 H4
Mäkikylä [FIN] 186 F5
Makkola [FIN] 188 E4
Makó [H] 76 F4
Makov [SK] 50 F6
Maková Hora [CZ] 48 F5
Makoviš [YU] 150 A2
Makovo [MK] 128 E3
Maków [PL] 50 H3
Mąkowarsko [PL] 22 C5
Maków Mazowiecki [PL] 38 B1
Makrakómi [GR] 132 F4
Mákri [GR] 136 E2
Mákri [GR] 130 G3
Makrochóri [GR] 128 G5
Makrýammos [GR] 130 E4
Makrygialós [GR] 140 G5
Makrynítsa [GR] 132 H2
Makryplágio [GR] 130 D2
Maksatiha [RUS] 204 E3
Malå [S] 190 G4
Mala Bosna [YU] 76 D5
Malacky [SK] 62 G4
Maladzyechna [BY] 204 B5
Málaga [E] 102 C4
Malagón [E] 96 F3
Malahide [IRL] 2 F6
Mała Karczma [PL] 22 E4
Mala Krsna [YU] 154 H3
Malalbergo [I] 110 F3
Malarýnta [GR] 132 G5
Malaryta [BY] 38 G4
Malaucène [F] 106 H3
Malax / Maalahti [FIN] 186 B3
Malaya Vishera [RUS] 204 D2
Malbork [PL] 22 E3
Malbuisson [F] 58 B6
Malcésine [I] 72 C5
Malchin [D] 20 C4
Malchow [D] 20 C5
Malcov [SK] 52 C6
Maldegem [B] 28 G1
Maldon [GB] 14 F4
Małdyty [PL] 22 F4
Malé [I] 72 C4
Malechowo [PL] 22 B3
Máleme [GR] 140 B4
Malenovice [CZ] 50 D6
Malente-Gremsmühlen [D] 18 G2
Målerås [S] 162 F4
Máles [GR] 140 F5
Malesco [I] 70 F3
Malesherbes [F] 42 F5
Malesína [GR] 134 B4
Malestroit [F] 26 B6
Maletto [I] 124 A8
Malexander [S] 162 E1
Malfourat, Mine de- [F] 66 E4
Malgovik [S] 190 F5
Malhadas [P] 80 G4
Malhao [P] 86 F2
Mália [GR] 140 F4
Malicorne [F] 42 B5
Mali Idjos [YU] 76 D6
Malikovo [HR] 152 A1
Målilla [S] 162 F3
Mali Lošinj [HR] 112 E4
Malin [IRL] 2 F1
Malin [UA] 206 E1
Malines (Mechelen) [B] 30 C3
Malingsbo [S] 166 H1
Malin More [IRL] 2 D2
Malinska [HR] 112 E2
Mali Prolog [HR] 152 B3
Maliq [AL] 128 D4
Mališevo [YU] 150 B5
Maliskylä [FIN] 198 D5
Malix [CH] 70 H1
Maljovica [BG] 150 G6
Malkara [TR] 146 B3
Małkinia Górna [PL] 38 D1
Malko Gradishte [BG] 148 D6
Malko Tŭrnovo [BG] 146 C1
Mallaig [GB] 6 B5
Mallersdorf [D] 60 F2
Málles Venosta / Mals im Vinschgau [I] 72 B2
Malling [DK] 156 D1
Mallnitz [A] 72 G2
Mallow [IRL] 4 C4
Malm [N] 190 C5
Malmbäck [S] 162 D2
Malmberget [S] 192 F6
Malmédy [B] 30 F5
Malmesbury [GB] 12 G3
Malmköping [S] 168 C3
Malmö [S] 156 H3
Malmslätt [S] 166 H5
Malo [I] 72 D5
Maloarhangel'sk [RUS] 204 F6
Małogoszcz [PL] 52 B1
Maloja [CH] 70 H2
Malo-les-Bains [F] 14 H6
Malón [GR] 142 E5
Malónas [GR] 142 E5
Malonno [I] 72 B4
Małopolski [PL] 52 D3
Måløy [N] 180 B5
Malpartida de Cáceres [E] 86 G5
Malpartida de Plasencia [E] 88 B5
Malpica de Bergantiños [E] 78 C1
Mālpils [LV] 200 E5
Målsåker [S] 168 D3
Malšice [CZ] 48 G6
Mals im Vinschgau / Málles Venosta [I] 72 B2
Målsnes [N] 192 E2
Malta [A] 72 H2
Malta [LV] 200 G6
Maltat [F] 56 E5
Maltepe [TR] 146 C5
Maltepe [TR] 146 F3
Malton [GB] 10 G3
Malu [RO] 150 G1
Malung [S] 172 F4
Malungen [N] 172 C4
Malungen [S] 184 E5
Malungsfors [S] 172 F4
Maluszyn [PL] 50 H1
Malveira [P] 86 B4
Malvik [N] 182 C1
Mały Płock [PL] 24 D5
Malyye Rozhki [RUS] 200 G1
Mamaia [RO] 206 D6
Mamarrosa [P] 80 B6
Mamers [F] 26 G6
Mammola [I] 124 D7
Mamonovo [RUS] 22 G2
Mamyra [N] 190 B5
Mána [GR] 136 E1
Maňa [SK] 64 B4
Manacor [E] 104 F5
Manamansalo [FIN] 198 E4
Manasija [YU] 150 C2
Manasija, Manastir- [YU] 150 C2
Manastir Ozren [BIH] 154 D3
Manastir Stern [BIH] 154 C2
Manastir Tavna [BIH] 154 E3
Mancha Real [E] 102 E2
Manchester [GB] 10 E4
Manching [D] 60 E2
Manciano [I] 114 G3
Mancier [F] 66 D6
Mandal [N] 164 D6
Måndalen [N] 180 E3
Mándas [I] 118 D6
Mandelieu [F] 108 E5
Mandello del Lario [I] 70 G3
Mandelos [YU] 154 F2
Manderscheid [D] 44 G1
Mándra [GR] 134 B6
Mándra [GR] 130 H2
Mandráki [GR] 142 C4
Mandrikó [GR] 142 D4
Manduria [I] 122 F4
Manerba del Garda [I] 72 B6
Manérbio [I] 72 A6
Manětín [CZ] 48 D4
Mánfa [H] 76 B5
Manfredónia [I] 120 H1
Mangalia [RO] 148 G1
Mångbyn [S] 198 B5
Mangen [N] 166 C1
Manger [N] 170 A3
Mangfall Brücke [D] 60 E5
Mångsbodarna [S] 172 F3
Mangskog [S] 166 E1
Mangualde [P] 80 C6
Manguilla [E] 96 A4
Máni [GR] 130 H1
Maniago [I] 72 F4
Manisa [TR] 144 D3
Manita Peć [HR] 112 G4
Mank [A] 62 D5
Månkarbo [S] 174 E5
Mańki [PL] 22 G4
Manlleu [E] 92 E3
Mannheim [D] 46 C4
Mano [F] 66 C4
Manoláda [GR] 136 B1
Manon [E] 78 E1
Manorhamilton [IRL] 2 D3
Manosque [F] 108 C4
Manresa [E] 92 D3
Månsarp [S] 162 D2
Manschnow [D] 34 G2
Mansfeld [D] 34 B4
Mansfield [GB] 10 F5
Mansilla de las Mulas [E] 78 H6
Mansle [F] 54 E6
Manso [F] 114 A3
Mansoniemi [FIN] 186 C6
Mantamádos [GR] 134 H2
Manteigas [P] 86 F2
Mantes [F] 42 E3
Mantíneia [GR] 136 E2
Mantorp [S] 166 H6
Mantoúdi [GR] 134 B4
Mantova [I] 110 E1
Mäntsälä [FIN] 178 A3
Mänttä [FIN] 186 F5
Mäntyharju [FIN] 178 C1
Mäntyjärvi [FIN] 196 E8
Mäntylahti [FIN] 188 C1
Mäntyluoto [FIN] 176 C1
Man Village Folk Museum [GBM] 2 H5
Manyas [TR] 146 D5
Manzanares [E] 96 F4
Manzanares el Real [E] 88 F5
Manzaneda [E] 78 E5
Manzanera [E] 98 E3
Manzanilla [E] 94 F6
Manzat [F] 68 C1
Maó / Mahón [E] 104 H5
Maqueda [E] 88 E6
Maranchón [E] 90 B5
Maranello [I] 110 E3
Marano di Napoli [I] 120 D3
Marano Lagunare [I] 72 G5
Marans [F] 54 C4
Maratea [I] 120 G5
Marateca [P] 86 B6
Marathiás [GR] 132 F5
Marathókampos [GR] 144 C6
Marathónas [GR] 134 C6
Marathópoli [GR] 136 C4
Márathos [GR] 140 E4
Maravillas, Cueva de las- [E] 94 F4
Marbach [D] 46 D6
Marbäck [S] 162 C2
Mårbacka [S] 166 E1
Marbella [E] 102 B5
Marboz [F] 68 G1
Marburg [D] 32 D6
Marcali [H] 74 H3
Marčana [HR] 112 D2
Marceddì [I] 118 B5
March [GB] 14 F2
Marchaux [F] 58 B4
Marche-en-Famenne [B] 30 D6
Marchegg [A] 62 G4
Marchena [E] 102 A2
Marchenilla [E] 94 G6
Marcheprime [F] 66 C3
Marciac [F] 84 F3
Marciana Marina [I] 114 D2
Marcianise [I] 120 E3
Marcigny [F] 56 E6
Marcilla [E] 84 B5
Marcillac-Vallon [F] 68 B5
Marcillat [F] 56 C6
Marcilly-le-Hayer [F] 42 H5
Marcinowice [PL] 50 C1
Marciszów [PL] 50 B1
Marckolsheim [F] 58 E2
Mårdsjö [S] 184 C2
Marebbe / St Vigil [I] 72 E3
Mare de Déu del Toro [E] 104 H4
Måren [N] 170 C2
Marennes [F] 54 B5
Marettimo [I] 126 A2
Mareuil [F] 66 F2
Mareuil [F] 54 C3
Marevo [RUS] 204 D3
Margarítes [GR] 140 D4
Margaríti [GR] 132 C3
Margate [GB] 14 G5
Margecany [SK] 64 F2
Margherita di Savoia [I] 120 H2
Margonin [PL] 22 B6
Marhaň [SK] 52 D6
Marhanets' [UA] 206 G4
María [E] 102 H3
Maria Birnbaum [D] 60 D3
Maria Dreierchen [A] 62 E3
Mariager [DK] 160 D5
Maria Laach [D] 30 H6
Maria Laach [D] 30 H6
Marialva [P] 80 E5
Maria Martenthal [D] 30 G6
Mariannelund [S] 162 F2
Marianopoli [I] 126 E3
Marianos [P] 86 C4
Mariánské Lázně [CZ] 48 D4
Maria Saal [A] 74 B3
Mariastein [A] 60 F6
Maria Taferl [A] 62 D4
Maria Trost [A] 74 D2
Maria Wörth [A] 74 B3
Mariazell [A] 62 D5
Maribo [DK] 20 A1
Maribor [SLO] 74 E3
Mariedal [S] 166 E5
Mariedamm [S] 166 H4
Mariefred [S] 168 C3
Mariehamn / Maarianhamina [FIN] 176 A5
Marieholm [S] 158 C2
Marieholm [S] 162 C3
Marielyst [DK] 20 B1
Mariëmont [B] 28 H4
Marienberg [D] 48 D2
Marienborn [D] 34 A3
Marienburg [D] 44 G2
Marienstatt [D] 32 C6
Marienthal [D] 32 D6
Mariestad [S] 166 F5
Marifjøra [N] 170 D1
Marignane [F] 106 H5
Marigny-le-Châtel [F] 44 A5
Marijampolė [LT] 24 E1
Marikostinovo [BG] 130 B2
Marín [E] 78 B4
Marina [EST] 200 E3
Marina [HR] 116 H1
Marina di Alberese [I] 114 F3
Marina di Árbus [I] 118 B6
Marina di Ardea [I] 116 A6
Marina di Camerota [I] 120 G5
Marina di Campo [I] 114 D3
Marina di Caronía [I] 126 F2
Marina di Carrara [I] 110 D4
Marina di Castagneto-Donorático [I] 114 E1
Marina di Chiéuti [I] 116 F5
Marina di Gáiro [I] 118 E6
Marina di Ginosa [I] 122 E4
Marina di Gioiosa Iónica [I] 124 D7
Marina di Grosseto [I] 114 F3
Marina di Léuca [I] 122 G6
Marina di Massa [I] 110 D4
Marina di Pietrasanta [I] 110 D5
Marina di Pisa [I] 110 D5
Marina di Ragusa [I] 126 F5
Marina di Ravenna [I] 110 H3
Marina di San Vito [I] 116 E4
Marina di Vasto [I] 116 E5
Mar'ina Horka [BY] 204 B5
Marina Palmense [I] 116 D2
Marina Romea [I] 110 H3
Marine de Sisco [F] 114 C2
Marinella [I] 126 B3
Marineo [I] 126 D2
Marines [F] 42 F2
Maringues [F] 68 D2
Marinha Grande [P] 86 C3
Marinhais [P] 86 C5
Marinkainen [FIN] 198 C5
Mar'insko [RUS] 200 G2
Maristella [I] 118 B3
Märjamaa [EST] 200 D2
Marjaniemi [FIN] 198 C4
Marjovaara [FIN] 188 G2
Markaryd [S] 162 C6
Markdorf [D] 58 H4
Market Deeping [GB] 14 E1
Market Drayton [GB] 10 D5
Market Harborough [GB] 14 E2
Markethill [GB] 2 F4
Market Rasen [GB] 10 G5
Market Weighton [GB] 10 G4
Markhina [FIN] 192 G4
Marki [PL] 38 B3
Markina-Xemein [E] 82 H4
Märkisch Buchholz [D] 34 E3
Markleugast [D] 46 H3
Markneukirchen [D] 48 C3
Markópoulo [GR] 136 H1
Markópoulo [GR] 136 A1
Markovac [YU] 150 C1
Markova Sušica [MK] 128 E1
Markov Manastir [MK] 128 E1
Markovo Kale [YU] 150 D5
Markranstädt [D] 34 C5
Marksburg [D] 46 B2
Markt Bibart [D] 46 F4
Marktbreit [D] 46 E4
Markt Erlbach [D] 46 F5
Marktheidenfeld [D] 46 E4
Markt-Indersdorf [D] 60 E3
Marktjärn [S] 184 D4
Marktl [D] 60 G4
Marktoberdorf [D] 60 C5
Marktredwitz [D] 48 C4
Markt St Florian [A] 62 B4
Markt St Martin [A] 62 F6
Marktzeuln [D] 46 G3
Markušica [HR] 154 E1
Marl [D] 30 H2
Marlborough [GB] 12 H3
Marle [F] 28 G5
Marlenheim [F] 44 G6
Marlow [D] 20 C3
Marma [S] 174 E4
Marmande [F] 66 E4
Marmara [TR] 146 C4
Marmaraereğlisi [TR] 146 D3
Marmári [GR] 134 D6
Marmaris [TR] 142 E3
Mármaro [GR] 134 G4
Marmelete [P] 94 B4
Marmolejo [E] 102 D1
Marmore, Cascata delle- [I] 116 A3
Marmoutier [F] 44 G5
Marmuri, Grotta su- [I] 118 D5
Marnay [F] 58 A4
Marne [D] 18 E3
Marnitz [D] 20 B5
Maróneia [GR] 130 F3
Maroslele [H] 76 E4
Maróstica [I] 72 D5
Marotta [I] 112 C6
Marpissa [GR] 138 E3
Marquartstein [D] 60 F5
Marquion [F] 28 F4
Marquise [F] 14 G6
Marradi [I] 110 F5
Marrasjärvi [FIN] 196 C7
Marrebæk [DK] 20 B1
Marsala [I] 126 B2
Marsberg [D] 32 E4
Marschlins [CH] 58 H6
Marsciano [I] 116 A2
Marseillan [F] 106 E4
Marseillan-Plage [F] 106 E5
Marseille [F] 106 H5
Marseille-en-Beauvaisis [F] 28 D5
Marshavitsy [RUS] 200 H4
Marsico Nuovo [I] 120 G4
Marsico Vetere [I] 120 H4
Marsiliana [I] 114 F3
Marsliden [S] 190 E4
Märsta [S] 168 D2
Marstal [DK] 156 D4
Marstrand [S] 160 G1
Marta [I] 114 G3
Martano [I] 122 G5
Martel [F] 66 G4
Martelange [B] 44 E2
Marten [BG] 148 D1
Martfű [H] 76 E2
Marthon [F] 66 F1
Martigné-Ferchaud [F] 40 G5
Martigny [CH] 70 C2
Martigues [F] 106 H5
Martim Longo [P] 94 D4
Martin [SK] 64 C2
Martina / Martinsbruck [CH] 72 B2
Martina Franca [I] 122 E3
Martín de Yeltes [E] 88 B3
Martinniemi [FIN] 198 D3
Martíno [GR] 134 B5
Martinsbruck / Martina [CH] 72 B2
Martinsicuro [I] 116 D3
Mártis [I] 118 C3
Martjanci [SLO] 74 E3
Martna [EST] 200 D2
Martock [GB] 12 F4
Martofte [DK] 156 E3
Martonvaara [FIN] 188 F1
Martonvásár [H] 76 C1
Martorell [E] 92 D4
Martos [E] 102 D2
Martti [FIN] 196 E6
Marttila [FIN] 176 E4
Maruševec [HR] 74 E4
Marvão [P] 86 F5
Marvejols [F] 68 C5
Marwałd [PL] 22 G5
Marxwalde [D] 34 F2
Marxzell [D] 46 B6
Marynin [PL] 38 F5
Maryport [GB] 8 D6
Marzabotto [I] 110 F4
Marzahna [D] 34 D3
Marzahne [D] 34 D2
Marzocca [I] 112 C6
Maschen [D] 18 F5
Mas d'Azil, Grotte du- [F] 84 H4
Mas de Barberans [E] 92 A5
Mas de las Matas [E] 90 F6
Masegoso de Tajuña [E] 90 A5
Maser [I] 72 E5
Masevaux [F] 58 D3
Masi [N] 192 G2
Maside [E] 78 C4
Masku [FIN] 176 D4
Maslenica [HR] 112 G4
Maslovare [BIH] 154 C3
Massa [I] 110 D4
Massa Fiscaglia [I] 110 G3
Massafra [I] 122 E4
Massa Lubrense [I] 120 E4
Massamagrell [E] 98 F4
Massa Marittima [I] 114 F2
Massat [F] 84 H5
Massay [F] 56 B3
Masseret [F] 66 G2
Masseube [F] 84 G3
Massiac [F] 68 C3
Mastaura [TR] 144 E5
Mastergeehy [IRL] 4 A4
Mas Thibert [F] 106 G4
Mastichári [GR] 142 B3
Mästocka [S] 162 B5
Masty [BY] 24 G4
Masugnsbyn [S] 192 G5
Maszewo [PL] 34 G3
Maszewo [PL] 20 G5
Matabuena [E] 88 G4
Mátala [GR] 140 D5
Matalebreras [E] 84 A6
Matallana de Torío [E] 82 B5
Matarágka [GR] 132 F2
Mataró [E] 92 E4
Mataruška Banja [YU] 150 B3
Matejče, Manastir- [MK] 150 D6
Matelica [I] 116 B2
Matera [I] 122 D4
Matersdalen [N] 170 B5
Mateševo [YU] 152 E3
Mátészalka [H] 206 B3
Matfors [S] 184 E5
Matha [F] 54 D5
Mathay [F] 58 C4
Mathildedal [FIN] 176 E5
Matignon [F] 26 B4
Matīši [LV] 200 E4
Matka [MK] 128 E1
Matka, Manastir- [MK] 128 E1
Matkavaara [FIN] 198 F4
Matlock [GB] 10 E5
Matos [P] 94 D3
Matosinhos [P] 80 B4
Matour [F] 56 F6
Mátrafüred [H] 64 E5
Mátraháza [H] 64 E5
Matre [N] 170 B2
Matrei am Brenner [A] 72 D1
Matrei in Osttirol [A] 72 F2
Mattersburg [A] 62 F6
Mattighofen [A] 60 G4
Mattinata [I] 116 H6
Mattsee [A] 60 G5
Matulji [HR] 112 E1
Matyli [BY] 24 G3
Matzen [A] 60 E6
Matzen [A] 62 F4
Maubeuge [F] 28 G4
Maubourguet [F] 84 F3
Mauchline [GB] 8 D4
Mauerkirchen [A] 60 H4
Maula [FIN] 198 C2
Maulbronn [D] 46 C6
Mauléon [F] 54 D2
Mauléon-Licharre [F] 84 D3
Maulévrier [F] 54 D2
Maumtrasna [IRL] 2 B4
Maupas, Château de- [F] 56 C3
Maupertus-sur-Mer [F] 26 D2
Maura [N] 172 B5
Maure [F] 26 B6
Mauriac [F] 68 B3
Maurnes [N] 192 C3
Mauron [F] 26 B6
Maurs [F] 66 H5
Maurstad [N] 180 B5
Maury [F] 106 C6
Mautern [A] 74 C1
Mauterndorf [A] 72 H2
Mauth [D] 62 A2
Mauthausen [A] 62 C4
Mauvezin [F] 84 G2
Mauvoisin [CH] 70 D3
Mauzé-sur-le-Mignon [F] 54 C4
Mavréli [GR] 132 F1
Mavrochóri [GR] 128 E5
Mavroklísi [GR] 130 H2
Mavroléfki [GR] 130 D3
Mavromáta [GR] 132 F3
Mavrommáti [GR] 136 D3
Mavrothálassa [GR] 130 C3
Mavrovi Hanovi [MK] 128 D2
Mavrovo [MK] 128 D2
Mavrovoúni [GR] 136 E5
Mavrovoúni [GR] 132 G2
Maximilians-Grotte [D] 46 H5
Maxmo [FIN] 186 B2
Maybole [GB] 8 C4
Mayen [D] 30 H6
Mayenne [F] 26 E6
Mayet [F] 42 B6
Maynooth [IRL] 2 F6
Mayoralgo [E] 86 H5
Mayorga [E] 82 B5
Mayrhofen [A] 72 E1
Mäyry [FIN] 186 D3
Mazagón [E] 94 E6
Mazamet [F] 106 C4
Mazara del Vallo [I] 126 B3
Mazarrón [E] 104 B4
Mažeikiai [LT] 200 C6
Mazères [F] 106 A4
Mázia [GR] 132 D2
Maziha [RUS] 200 G2
Mazıköy [TR] 142 D2
Mazilmaja [LV] 200 B6
Mazirbe [LV] 200 C4
Mazsalaca [LV] 200 E3
Mazurki [PL] 38 C4
Mazyr [BY] 204 B7
Mazzalve [LV] 200 E6
Mazzarino [I] 126 E4
Mazzarò [I] 124 B8
Mazzarrone [I] 126 F5
M. D. de la Salut [E] 92 F3
M. D. de Pinós [E] 92 D3
M. D. de Queralt [E] 92 D2
Mdzewo [PL] 22 G6
Mealhada [P] 80 B6
Méandre de Queuille [F] 68 C1
Meaux [F] 42 G3
Mechelen (Malines) [B] 30 C3
Mechernich [D] 30 G5
Mechowo [PL] 20 F4
Męcikał [PL] 22 C4
Meckenbeuren [D] 58 H4
Meda [P] 80 E5
Medak [HR] 112 G4
Medby [N] 192 C6
Mede [I] 70 F6
Medebach [D] 32 D5
Medelim [P] 86 F3
Medellín [E] 96 A3
Medelser Schlucht [CH] 70 G1
Medemblik [NL] 16 E3
Medena Selišta [BIH] 154 B4
Meden Rudnik [BG] 148 F4
Medenychi [UA] 52 H5
Medet [TR] 144 G6
Medevi [S] 166 G5
Medgidia [RO] 206 D6
Medgyesegyháza [H] 76 G3
Medhamn [S] 166 F3
Mediaş [RO] 206 C5
Medicina [I] 110 G3
Medina Azahara [E] 102 C1
Medinaceli [E] 90 B4
Medina del Campo [E] 88 E2
Medina de Pomar [E] 82 F4
Medina de Rioseco [E] 82 B6
Medina-Sidonia [E] 100 G4
Medininkai [LT] 202 G5
Medle [S] 198 A4
Médous, Grotte de- [F] 84 F4
Médousa [GR] 130 E2
Medskogen [S] 172 D4
Medstugan [S] 182 E1
Međugorje [BIH] 152 C2
Medulin [HR] 112 D3
Međumajdan [HR] 154 A2
Medvedja [YU] 150 D4
Medved'ov [SK] 62 H5
Medvida [HR] 112 H5
Medvode [SLO] 74 B5
Medzilaborce [SK] 52 E6
Medžitlija [MK] 128 E4
Meerane [D] 48 C1
Meersburg [D] 58 H4
Mefjordvær [N] 192 D2
Mefjordvær [N] 192 D2
Méga Chorió [GR] 132 F4
Méga Déreio [GR] 130 G2
Méga Doukáto [GR] 130 F3
Megáli Vólvi [GR] 130 B4
Megalochóri [GR] 132 F2
Megálo Chorió [GR] 142 C4
Megálo Livádi [GR] 138 C3
Megalópoli [GR] 136 D3
Mégara [GR] 134 B6
Megara Hyblaea [I] 126 G4
Méga Spílaio [GR] 132 G6
Megève [F] 70 B3
Megísti [GR] 142 H4
Megístis Lávras, Moní- [GR] 130 D5
Megorjelo [BIH] 152 C3
Meg. Panagía [GR] 130 C5
Megyaszó [H] 64 F4
Mehadia [RO] 206 A6
Mehamn [N] 196 D1
Mehikoorma [EST] 200 G3
Mehov Krš [YU] 150 B4
Mehun-sur-Yèvre [F] 56 B3
Meijel [NL] 30 F3
Meilen [CH] 58 G5
Meillant, Château de- [F] 56 C4
Meilleraye, Abbaye de- [F] 40 F5
Meina [I] 70 F4
Meine [D] 32 H2
Meinerzhagen [D] 32 C5
Meiningen [D] 46 F2
Meira [E] 78 E3
Meirāni [LV] 200 F5
Meiringen [CH] 70 E1
Meisenheim [D] 44 H3
Meisingset [N] 180 F2
Meissen [D] 34 E6
Meitingen [D] 60 D3
Męka [PL] 36 F5
Mel [I] 72 E4
Mélampes [GR] 140 D5
Melaniós [GR] 134 G4
Meláties [GR] 132 D3
Melbeck [D] 18 G5

Melbu [N] 192 C4
Meldal [N] 180 H2
Meldola [I] 110 G4
Meldorf [D] 18 E2
Melegnano [I] 70 G5
Melenci [YU] 76 E6
Melene [TR] 144 B2
Melfi [I] 120 G3
Melgaço [P] 78 C5
Melgar de Arriba [E] 82 C5
Melgar de Fernamental [E] 82 D5
Melgarejo [E] 100 G3
Melhus [N] 182 B1
Melide [E] 78 D3
Melides [P] 94 B2
Meligalás [GR] 136 D3
Melíki [GR] 128 G5
Melilli [I] 126 G4
Mélisey [F] 58 C3
Mélissa [GR] 130 E3
Melissáni [GR] 132 C6
Melíssi [GR] 132 E1
Melissópetra [GR] 128 D6
Melissourgós [GR] 130 B4
Melito di Porto Salvo [I] 124 C8
Melitopol' [UA] 206 H4
Melívoia [GR] 130 E2
Melk [A] 62 D4
Melksham [GB] 12 G3
Mellakoski [FIN] 196 C8
Mellansel [S] 184 F1
Mellansjö [S] 184 C5
Mellbystrand [S] 162 B5
Melle [D] 32 D2
Melle [F] 54 D5
Mellendorf [D] 32 F1
Mellerud [S] 166 D5
Mellieha [M] 126 C6
Mellifont Abbey [IRL] 2 F5
Melliiä [FIN] 176 E3
Mellin [D] 34 A1
Mellrichstadt [D] 46 F2
Mellstaby [S] 158 G1
Melnica [YU] 150 C1
Melnik [BG] 130 B2
Mělník [CZ] 48 F3
Mel'nikovo [RUS] 178 G2
Melrose [GB] 8 F4
Melsomvik [N] 164 H3
Melsungen [D] 32 F5
Meltaus [FIN] 196 C7
Melton Mowbray [GB] 10 F6
Meltosjärvi [FIN] 196 C8
Melun [F] 42 G4
Melvich [GB] 6 E2
Mélykút [H] 76 D4
Melzo [I] 70 G5
Membrilla [E] 96 F4
Membrío [E] 86 F4
Memmingen [D] 60 B4
Mena [UA] 204 D7
Menàggio [I] 70 G3
Menai Bridge [GB] 10 B4
Menasalbas [E] 96 E2
Menat [F] 56 C6
Mendavia [E] 82 H6
Mende [F] 68 C6
Menden [D] 32 C4
Menderes [TR] 144 C4
Mendryka [CZ] 50 B4
Menec [F] 40 D5
Menemen [TR] 144 C4
Menen [B] 28 F2
Menesjärvi [FIN] 196 D4
Menetés [GR] 140 H3
Ménez Hom [F] 40 B2
Menfi [I] 126 C3
Ménfőcsanak [H] 62 H6
Menga, Cueva de- [E] 102 C4
Mengamuñoz [E] 88 D4
Mengen [D] 58 H3
Mengeš [SLO] 74 C4
Mengíbar [E] 102 E1
Mengishevo [BG] 148 E3
Menídi [GR] 132 D3
Ménina [GR] 132 C2
Mens [F] 68 H6
Menstrup [DK] 156 F4
Menthon [F] 70 B3
Menton [F] 108 F4
Méntrida [E] 88 E6
Menyushi [RUS] 200 G1
Meppel [NL] 16 F3
Meppen [D] 16 H4
Mequinenza [E] 90 G5
Mer [F] 54 H1
Mera de Boixo [E] 78 D1
Meråker [N] 182 D1
Meran / Merano [I] 72 D3
Merano / Meran [I] 72 D3
Merate [I] 70 G4
Mercatale [I] 114 H1
Mercatino Conca [I] 110 H5
Mercato San Severino [I] 120 F3
Mercato Saraceno [I] 110 G5
Merćez [YU] 150 C4
Merdrignac [F] 26 B5
Méréville [F] 42 F5
Mergozzo [I] 70 F3
Méribel [F] 70 B4
Méribel-les-Allues [F] 70 B4
Meriç [TR] 130 H2
Mérichas [GR] 138 C2
Merichleri [BG] 148 C5
Mérida [E] 94 H2
Merijärvi [FIN] 198 C5
Merikarvia / Sastmola [FIN] 186 B6
Merimasku [FIN] 176 D4
Měřín [CZ] 50 A5
Mering [D] 60 D4
Merkendorf [D] 46 F6
Merkine [LT] 24 G2
Merklingen [D] 60 B3
Merlara [I] 110 F1
Merle, Tours de- [F] 66 H4
Merligen [CH] 70 E1
Mern [DK] 156 G4
Mernye [H] 76 A4
Mersch [D] 30 F4
Mersch [L] 44 F2
Merseburg [D] 34 C5
Mersinbeleni [TR] 144 D6
Mērsrags [LV] 200 C4
Merthyr Tydfil [GB] 12 F2
Mértola [P] 94 D4
Méru [F] 42 F2
Mervans [F] 56 G5
Merville [F] 28 E3
Méry [F] 44 A5
Meryemana [TR] 144 D5
Merzig [D] 44 F3
Mesagne [I] 122 F4
Mesão Frio [P] 80 D4
Mesariá [GR] 138 D1
Meschede [D] 32 D5
Meschers-sur-Gironde [F] 54 C6
Mešeišta [MK] 128 D3
Meseníkólas [GR] 132 F3
Meshchovsk [RUS] 204 E5
Mési [GR] 130 F3
Mesinge [DK] 156 E3
Mesklá [GR] 140 C4
Meslay [F] 40 H5
Mesnalien [N] 172 B2
Mesnil-Val [F] 28 C4
Mesocco [CH] 70 G2
Mesochóra [GR] 132 E2
Mesochóri [GR] 132 F1
Mésola [I] 110 H2
Mesolóngi [GR] 132 E5
Mesón do Vento [E] 78 C2
Mesopótamo [GR] 132 C3
Mespelbrunn [D] 46 D3
Messdorf [D] 34 B1
Messimvría [GR] 130 G3
Messina [I] 124 B7
Messines de Baixo [P] 94 C5
Messíni [GR] 136 D4
Messkirch [D] 58 G3
Messlingen [S] 182 E3
Messtetten [D] 58 G3
Mestá [GR] 134 G5
Mestanza [E] 96 E5
Městec Králové [CZ] 48 H3
Mestervik [N] 192 E2
Mésti [GR] 130 G3
Mestlin [D] 20 B4
Město Albrechtice [CZ] 50 D3
Město Libavá [CZ] 50 D5
Mestre [I] 72 E6
Mesvres [F] 56 F5
Mesztegnyő [H] 74 H4
Metabief [F] 58 B6
Metagkitsi [GR] 130 C5
Metaljka [BIH] 152 E2
Metamórfosi [GR] 130 C5
Metapontium [I] 122 D4
Metaxádes [GR] 130 H1
Metaxás [GR] 128 F6
Metéora [GR] 132 E1
Méteren [F] 28 F2
Méthana [GR] 136 G2
Methóni [GR] 136 C4
Methóni [GR] 128 G5
Metković [HR] 152 C3
Metlika [SLO] 74 D6
Metnitz [A] 74 B2
Metóchi [GR] 132 E6
Metóchi [GR] 134 A3
Metsäkylä [FIN] 178 C3
Metsäkylä [FIN] 198 F3
Metsälä / Ömossa [FIN] 186 B5
Metsküla [EST] 200 C3
Métsovon [GR] 132 D1
Metten [D] 60 G2
Mettet [B] 30 C5
Mettingen [D] 32 C2
Mettlach [D] 44 F3
Mettmann [D] 30 G3
Metz [F] 44 E4
Metzervisse [F] 44 F3
Metzingen [D] 58 H2
Meulan [F] 42 F3
Meung-sur-Loire [F] 42 E6
Meuselwitz [D] 34 C6
Mevik [N] 190 D1
Mexilhoeira Grande [P] 94 B5
Meximieux [F] 68 G2
Meyenburg [D] 20 B5
Meymac [F] 68 B2
Meyrargues [F] 108 B4
Meyrueis [F] 106 E2
Meyzieu [F] 68 G3
Mézapos [GR] 136 E5
Mezdra [BG] 150 G4
Mèze [F] 106 E4
Mézel [F] 108 D3
Meženin [PL] 24 D6
Mežica [SLO] 74 C4
Mézières [F] 54 F5
Mézières-en-Brenne [F] 54 G4
Mézilhac [F] 68 E5
Mézin [F] 66 D6
Mezőberény [H] 76 G3
Mezőcsát [H] 64 F5
Mezőhegyes [H] 76 F4
Mezőhék [H] 76 E2
Mezőkeresztes [H] 64 F5
Mezőkovácsháza [H] 76 F4
Mezőkövesd [H] 64 F5
Mezőnyárád [H] 64 F5
Mezőörs [H] 64 A6
Mezőszilas [H] 76 B3
Mezőtúr [H] 76 F2
Mezquita de Jarque [E] 90 E6
Mezzojuso [I] 126 D2
Mezzolombardo [I] 72 C4
Mgarr [M] 126 C5
Miączyn [PL] 52 G1
Miajadas [E] 86 H6
Miami Platja [E] 90 H6
Mianowice [PL] 22 C2
Miasteczko Śląskie [PL] 50 F2
Miastko [PL] 22 B3
Michalove [SK] 64 H2
Michałów [PL] 38 C6
Michałowo [PL] 24 F6
Micheldorf [A] 62 B5
Michelstadt [D] 46 D4
Michów [PL] 38 D5
Middelburg [NL] 16 B6
Middelfart [DK] 156 C3
Middelharnis [NL] 16 C5
Middelkerke-Bad [B] 28 F1
Middlesbrough [GB] 10 F2
Middlewich [GB] 10 D4
Midhurst [GB] 14 D5
Midleton [IRL] 4 D5
Midlum [D] 18 D3
Midsland [NL] 16 E1
Midstkogberget [N] 172 D2
Midsund [N] 180 D3
Midtgulen [N] 180 B5
Miechów [PL] 50 H3
Mieders [A] 72 D1
Miedes [E] 90 D4
Międzdroje [PL] 20 F3
Miedźno [PL] 50 G1
Międzybórz [PL] 36 D5
Międzybrodzie Bialskie [PL] 50 G4
Międzychód [PL] 36 B2
Międzygórze [PL] 50 C3
Międzylesie [PL] 50 C3
Międzyrzec Podlaski [PL] 38 E3
Międzyrzecz [PL] 36 A2
Miedzywodzie [PL] 20 F3
Miehikkälä [FIN] 178 D3
Miejsce Piastowe [PL] 52 D5
Miejska Górka [PL] 36 C5
Miélan [F] 84 F3
Mielec [PL] 52 D3
Mielno [PL] 20 H3
Mieluskylä [FIN] 198 D5
Mierasjärvi [FIN] 196 D3
Mieraslompolo [FIN] 196 D3
Miercurea Ciuc [RO] 206 C5
Mieres [E] 78 H4
Mieron [N] 192 G3
Mieroszów [PL] 50 B2
Miersig [RO] 76 H2
Mierzyno [PL] 22 D1
Miesbach [D] 60 E5
Mieścisko [PL] 36 D2
Mieste [D] 34 B2
Miesterhorst [D] 34 A2
Mieszkowice [PL] 34 G1
Mietoinen [FIN] 176 D4
Mifol [AL] 128 A5
Migennes [F] 42 H6
Migliarino [I] 110 G3
Migliarino [I] 110 D5
Migliónico [I] 122 D4
Mignano Monte Lungo [I] 120 D1
Miguel Esteban [E] 96 G3
Mihăeşti [RO] 148 B1
Mihai Bravu [RO] 148 C1
Mihajlovac [YU] 150 E1
Mihalgazi [TR] 146 H4
Mihla [D] 32 G6
Mijas [E] 102 B5
Mijoux [F] 70 A1
Mikaelshulen [N] 164 G3
Mikhaylovo [BG] 150 G3
Mikkelbostad [N] 192 D3
Mikkeli / St Michel [FIN] 188 C6
Mikkelvika [N] 192 E1
Mikolaivka [UA] 206 G6
Mikołajki [PL] 24 C4
Mikołajki Pomorskie [PL] 22 F4
Mikolin [PL] 50 D2
Mikołów [PL] 50 F3
Mikre [BG] 148 A4
Mikró Chorió [GR] 132 F4
Mikró Déreio [GR] 130 G2
Mikrókampos [GR] 128 H4
Mikrópoli [GR] 130 C3
Mikrothíves [GR] 132 H3
Mikstat [PL] 36 E5
Mikulčice [CZ] 62 G3
Mikulov [CZ] 62 F3
Mikulovice [CZ] 50 D3
Miland [N] 170 F5
Milano [I] 70 G5
Milano Marittima [I] 110 H4
Milanovac [HR] 76 A6
Milanówek [PL] 38 B3
Milâs [TR] 142 D2
Milatos [GR] 140 F4
Milazzo [I] 124 B7
Mildenhall [GB] 14 F2
Milejczyce [PL] 38 F2
Milejewo [PL] 22 F3
Milena [I] 126 D4
Mileševa, Manastir- [YU] 150 A3
Mileševo [YU] 150 A3
Mileševo [YU] 76 E6
Milet [TR] 142 B1
Miletići [HR] 112 G4
Mileto [I] 124 D6
Miletopolis [TR] 146 E4
Milevsko [CZ] 48 F5
Milford [IRL] 2 F2
Milford Haven [GB] 12 D2
Milići [BIH] 154 E4
Milicz [PL] 36 D5
Miliés [GR] 134 A2
Milín [CZ] 48 F5
Milína [GR] 134 A3
Militello in Val di Catania [I] 126 F4
Millares [E] 98 E5
Millares, Cueva de los- [E] 102 G5
Millas [F] 92 F1
Millau [F] 106 D2
Millesimo [I] 108 G3
Millom [GB] 10 D2
Millstatt [A] 72 H3
Millstreet [IRL] 4 C4
Milltown [IRL] 4 B4
Milltown Malbay [IRL] 2 B6
Milluranta [FIN] 198 E5
Milmarcos [E] 90 C5
Milmersdorf [D] 20 D6
Milna [HR] 152 A2
Miločer [YU] 152 D4
Miłocin [PL] 38 D5
Milos [GR] 138 D4
Milosavci [BIH] 154 C2
Miloševa Kula [YU] 150 D1
Miłosław [PL] 36 D3
Milow [D] 20 A5
Milówka [PL] 50 G5
Milreu [P] 94 C5
Milseburg [D] 46 E2
Milštejn [CZ] 48 G1
Miltach [D] 48 D6
Miltenberg [D] 46 D4
Milton Keynes [GB] 14 E3
Milyutino [RUS] 200 H2
Mimizan [F] 66 B4
Mimizan-Plage [F] 66 B4
Mimoň [CZ] 48 G2
Mina de São Domingos [P] 94 D4
Minas de Riotinto [E] 94 F5
Minateda, Cuevas de- [E] 104 B1
Minateda-Horca [E] 104 B1
Minaya [E] 98 B4
Mindelheim [D] 60 C4
Minden [D] 32 E2
Mindin [F] 40 E6
Mindszent [H] 76 E3
Minehead [GB] 12 E3
Mineo [I] 126 F4
Mineralni Bani [BG] 148 C6
Minerbio [I] 110 F3
Minervino di Lecce [I] 122 H5
Minervino Murge [I] 120 H2
Minervio [F] 114 C2
Minglanilla [E] 98 C4
Mingorría [E] 88 E4
Miničevo [YU] 150 E3
Minne [S] 182 H5
Minnesund [N] 172 C4
Mínoa [GR] 138 G4
Minozero [RUS] 198 G4
Minsen [D] 18 C3
Minsk [BY] 204 B5
Mińsk Mazowiecki [PL] 38 C3
Minturnae [I] 120 D2
Minturno [I] 120 D2
Miočić [HR] 154 A5
Miokovićevo [HR] 74 H6
Mionica [YU] 150 A1
Mira [I] 110 H1
Mira [E] 98 D3
Mira [I] 72 E6
Mira [P] 80 B6
Mirabella Imbáccari [I] 126 F4
Mirabello [I] 110 F2
Miradolo Terme [I] 70 G6
Mirador del Fito [E] 82 C2
Miraflores [E] 82 E6
Miraflores de la Sierra [E] 88 F4
Miramar [F] 108 E5
Miramare [I] 112 B5
Miramare, Castello di- [I] 72 H6
Miramas [F] 106 G4
Mirambeau [F] 66 D2
Miramont-de-Guyenne [F] 66 E4
Miranda [E] 84 B4
Miranda de Ebro [E] 82 G5
Miranda do Corvo [P] 86 D2
Miranda do Douro [P] 80 G4
Mirande [F] 84 G3
Mirandela [P] 80 E4
Mirándola [I] 110 F2
Mirano [I] 72 E6
Mirantes [E] 78 G5
Miravet [E] 90 H6
Mirebeau [F] 54 E3
Mirebeau [F] 56 H3
Mirecourt [F] 44 E6
Mirepoix [F] 106 B5
Mirosławiec [PL] 20 H5
Mirošov [CZ] 48 E5
Mirovice [CZ] 48 F5
Mirovo [BG] 150 G5
Mirów [D] 20 C5
Mirow [PL] 50 G2
Mirsk [PL] 48 H1
Mirto [I] 124 E3
Miruena [E] 88 D4
Misilmeri [I] 126 D2
Miskolc [H] 64 F4
Miskolctapolca [H] 64 F5
Mislinja [SLO] 74 D4
Missanello [I] 120 H5
Misso [EST] 200 F4
Mistelbach [A] 62 F3
Misten [N] 192 B5
Misten [N] 192 B5
Misterbianco [I] 126 G3
Misterhult [S] 162 G3
Mistretta [I] 126 F2
Misurina [I] 72 E3
Misvær [N] 192 C6
Miszewo [PL] 22 D2
Mitchelstown [IRL] 4 D4
Mitchelstown Caves [IRL] 4 D4
Míthymna [GR] 134 G2
Mitrašinci [MK] 128 G1
Mitrópoli [GR] 132 F3
Mittådalen [S] 182 E3
Mittelberg [A] 72 C2
Mittelberg [A] 60 B6
Mittelberg [D] 60 C5
Mittenwald [D] 60 D6
Mittenwalde [D] 20 D5
Mittenwalde [D] 34 E3
Mittersill [A] 72 F1
Mitterteich [D] 48 C4
Mittet [N] 180 E3
Mittewald [A] 72 F3
Mittweida [D] 48 D1
Mitwitz [D] 46 G3
Mizhiria [UA] 206 B3
Mizil [RO] 206 C6
Miziya [BG] 150 G2
Mjåland [N] 164 E4
Mjällby [S] 158 E2
Mjölby [S] 166 H6
Mjølfjell [N] 170 D3
Mjölkbäcken [S] 190 E2
Mjøndalen [N] 164 G1
Mjørlund [N] 172 B4
Mjösebo [S] 162 F4
Mjösjöby [S] 190 G6
M. Kalývia [GR] 132 F2
Mladá Boleslav [CZ] 48 G3
Mladá Vožice [CZ] 48 G5
Mladé Buky [CZ] 50 A2
Mladečská Jeskyně [CZ] 50 C5
Mladenovac [YU] 150 B1
Mlado Nagoričane [MK] 150 D6
Mława [PL] 22 G6
Mlekarevo [BG] 148 D5
Mlini [HR] 152 C4
Mliniště [BIH] 154 B4
Młynary [PL] 22 F3
Młynarze [PL] 24 C6
Mnich [CZ] 48 G6
Mnichovice [CZ] 48 G4
Mnichovo Hradiště [CZ] 48 G2
Mnichów [PL] 52 B2
Mniów [PL] 52 B1
Mníšek pod Brdy [CZ] 48 F4
Mniszek [PL] 38 B5
Mo [N] 172 C4
Mo [N] 164 E2
Mo [S] 184 E2
Mo [S] 166 G3
Moaña [E] 78 B4
Moate [IRL] 2 D5
Moča [SK] 64 B5
Mocejón [E] 96 F1
Móchlos [GR] 140 G4
Mochós [GR] 140 F4
Mochowo [PL] 36 G1
Mochy [PL] 36 B4
Möckern [D] 34 C3
Mockfjärd [S] 172 H4
Möckmühl [D] 46 D5
Moclín [E] 102 D3
Modane [F] 70 B5
Modave [B] 30 D5
Módena [I] 110 E3
Módi [GR] 132 H4
Módica [I] 126 F5
Modigliana [I] 110 G4
Modliborzyce [PL] 52 E1
Mödling [A] 62 F5
Modliszewko [PL] 36 D2
Modra [SK] 62 G4
Modra Špilja [HR] 116 H3
Modrava [CZ] 60 H2
Modriča [BIH] 154 D2
Modriště [MK] 128 E2
Modugno [I] 122 D2
Moeche, Castillo de- [E] 78 D1
Moelv [N] 172 B3
Moen [N] 190 C6
Moen [N] 192 E3
Moena [I] 72 D4
Moers [D] 30 G3
Moesgård [DK] 156 D1
Moffat [GB] 8 E4
Mogadouro [P] 80 F5
Mogán [E] 100 C6
Mogielnica [PL] 38 B4
Mogilno [PL] 36 E2
Móglia [I] 110 E2
Mogliano Veneto [I] 72 E6
Mogličë [AL] 128 C4
Mogón [E] 102 F2
Mogorella [I] 118 C5
Mogoro [I] 118 C6
Moguer [E] 94 E6
Mohács [H] 76 B5
Mohärad [S] 162 C2
Moheda [S] 162 D4
Mohelnice [CZ] 50 C4
Moher, Cliffs of- [IRL] 2 B5
Mohill [IRL] 2 E4
Möhkö [FIN] 188 H2
Moholm [S] 166 F5
Mohora [H] 64 D5
Mohyliv-Podil's'kyi [UA] 206 D3
Moi [N] 164 C4
Moià [E] 92 E3
Moikipää / Molpe [FIN] 186 A3
Moimenta da Beira [P] 80 D5
Mo-i-Rana [N] 190 E2
Moirans [F] 68 G4
Moirans-en-Montagne [F] 56 H6
Moíres [GR] 140 E5
Mõisaküla [EST] 200 E3
Moissac [F] 66 F6
Moita [P] 86 B5
Moixent [E] 98 D6
Mojácar [E] 102 H5
Mojados [E] 88 E2
Mojkovac [YU] 152 E3
Mojonera [E] 102 F5
Mojstrana [SLO] 74 B4
Mokobody [PL] 38 D3
Mokra Gora [YU] 152 E1
Mokresh [BG] 150 F2
Mokrin [YU] 76 F5
Mokronog [SLO] 74 D5
Mokrzyska [PL] 52 B4
Möksy [FIN] 186 E2
Mol [B] 30 D3
Mol [YU] 76 E6
Mola di Bari [I] 122 E3
Moláoi [GR] 136 F4
Molare [I] 108 H2
Mold [GB] 10 C4
Moldava n. Bodvou [SK] 64 F3
Molde [N] 180 E3
Moldjord [N] 192 B6
Moldova Nouă [RO] 206 A6
Moldoviţa, Mănăstirea- [RO] 206 C4
Møldrup [DK] 160 D5
Moledo [P] 78 A5
Molens Van Kinderdijk [NL] 16 D5
Molėtai [LT] 202 G4
Molfetta [I] 122 D2
Moliden [S] 184 G2
Molières [F] 66 F6
Molina de Aragón [E] 90 C5
Molina de Segura [E] 104 C3
Molinar [E] 82 F3
Molinella [I] 110 G3
Molinicos [E] 102 H1
Molinos [E] 90 E6
Molins de Rei [E] 92 E4
Moliterno [I] 120 H5
Molkom [S] 166 F2
Mollafeneri [TR] 146 F3
Mollas [AL] 128 D5
Möllbrücke [A] 72 G2
Mölle [S] 160 H6
Molledo [E] 82 E3
Möllenbeck [D] 20 D5
Mollerussa [E] 92 C3
Mollet del Vallès [E] 92 E4
Molliens [F] 28 D4
Mollina [E] 102 C3
Mölln [D] 18 G4
Möllösund [S] 160 G1
Mölltorp [S] 166 G5
Mølnarodden [N] 192 B5
Mölndal [S] 160 G2
Mölnlycke [S] 160 H2
Mólos [GR] 132 G4
Moloskovitsy [RUS] 178 F6
Moloy [F] 56 G3
Molpe / Moikipää [FIN] 186 A3
Molsheim [F] 44 G6
Molveno [I] 72 C4
Mombaroccio [I] 112 B5
Mombeltrán [E] 88 D5
Momchilgrad [BG] 130 F1
Momin Prohod [BG] 150 G5
Mommark [DK] 156 D4
Momo [I] 70 F4
Monachil [E] 102 E4
Monaco [MC] 108 F4
Monaghan [IRL] 2 F4
Monäs [FIN] 186 B1
Monasterace Marina [I] 124 E6
Monasterboice [IRL] 2 F5
Monasterevin [IRL] 2 E6
Monasterio de Leyre [E] 84 C4
Monastir [I] 118 C6
Monastiráki [GR] 130 G3
Monastiráki [GR] 132 D4
Monbiel [CH] 72 A2
Moncalieri [I] 70 D6
Moncalvo [I] 70 E6
Monção [P] 78 B5
Moncarapacho [P] 94 C5
Moncayo [E] 90 C3
Mönchdorf [A] 62 C4
Mönchengladbach [D] 30 G3
Mönchhof [A] 62 G5
Monchique [P] 94 B4
Monclova [E] 102 B2
Moncofa [E] 98 F4
Moncontour [F] 26 B5
Moncoutant [F] 54 D3
Mondariz [E] 78 B5
Mondariz-Balneario [E] 78 B5
Mondaye, Abbaye de- [F] 26 E3
Mondéjar [E] 88 G6
Mondello [I] 126 C1
Mondim de Basto [P] 80 D4
Mondolfo [I] 112 C6
Mondoñedo [E] 78 E2
Mondorf-les-Bains [L] 44 F3
Mondoubleau [F] 42 C5
Mondovi [I] 108 G3
Mondragone [I] 120 D2
Mondsee [A] 60 H5
Monéglia [I] 110 C4
Monegrillo [E] 90 F4
Monemvasía [GR] 136 F5
Monesi [I] 108 F3
Monesterio [E] 94 G4
Monestier-de-Clermont [F] 68 G5
Monêtier-Allemont [F] 108 C2
Moneygall [IRL] 2 D6
Moneymore [GB] 2 F3
Monfalcone [I] 72 H5
Monfero [E] 78 D2
Monflanquin [F] 66 F5
Monforte [P] 86 E5
Monforte da Beira [P] 86 F4
Monforte de Lemos [E] 78 D4
Mongstad [N] 170 A2
Monguelfo / Welsberg [I] 72 E3
Monheim [D] 60 D2
Mönichkirchen [A] 62 E6
Moní Eleónis [GR] 136 F3
Mõniste [EST] 200 F4
Monistrol-d'Allier [F] 68 D4
Monistrol de Montserrat [E] 92 D4
Monistrol-sur-Loire [F] 68 E4
Monivea [IRL] 2 C5
Mońki [PL] 24 E5
Monmouth [GB] 12 G2
Monnickendam [NL] 16 D4
Monninkylä [FIN] 178 A4
Monodéndri [GR] 132 C1
Monódryo [GR] 134 C4
Monólithos [GR] 142 D5
Monopoli [I] 122 E3
Monor [H] 76 D1
Monóvar / Monòver [E] 104 D2
Monòver / Monóvar [E] 104 D2
Monpazier [F] 66 F4
Monplaisir [F] 42 C5
Monreal / Elo [E] 84 B4
Monreal del Campo [E] 90 D6
Monreale [I] 126 C2
Monroy [E] 86 H5
Monroyo [E] 98 G1
Mons (Bergen) [B] 28 G4
Monsanto [P] 86 G3
Monsaraz [P] 94 E2
Monschau [D] 30 F5
Monségur [F] 66 D4
Monsélice [I] 110 G1
Monsheim [D] 46 B4
Mønsted [DK] 160 C5
Mönsterås [S] 162 G4
Monsummano Terme [I] 110 E5
Montabaur [D] 46 B2
Montagnac [F] 106 E4
Montagnana [I] 110 F1
Montaigu [F] 54 C2
Montaigu-de-Quercy [F] 66 F5
Montaigut [F] 56 C6
Montaione [I] 110 E6
Montalbán [E] 96 E2
Montalbán [E] 90 E6
Montalbano Elicona [I] 124 A7
Montalbano Jonico [I] 122 D5
Montalbo [E] 98 A2
Montalcino [I] 114 G2
Montaldo di Cosola [I] 110 B2
Montalegre [P] 78 C6
Montalieu [F] 68 G3
Montalivet-les-Bains [F] 66 C1
Montallegro [I] 126 C4
Montalto delle Marche [I] 116 C2
Montalto di Castro [I] 114 G4
Montalto Ligure [I] 108 G4
Montalto Uffugo [I] 124 D4
Montalvão [P] 86 E4
Montalvo [P] 94 C1
Montamarta [E] 80 H4
Montana [BG] 150 F3
Montana [CH] 70 D2
Montañana [E] 90 E4
Montánchez [E] 86 H6
Montanejos [E] 98 E3
Montaren [F] 106 G3
Montargil [P] 86 D5
Montargis [F] 42 F6
Montargull / Artesa de Segre [E] 92 C2
Montastruc la-Conseillère [F] 106 A3
Montauban [F] 66 F6
Montauban [F] 26 C5
Montbard [F] 56 F2
Montbazens [F] 66 H5
Montbazon [F] 54 F2
Montbéliard [F] 58 C4
Montbenoît [F] 58 C5
Montblanc [E] 92 C4
Mont-Blanc, Tunnel du- [Eur.] 70 C3
Montbonnot [F] 68 H4
Montbrison [F] 68 E3
Montbron [F] 66 F1
Montbrun-les-Bains [F] 108 B3
Montbuey [E] 80 G3
Montceau-les-Mines [F] 56 F5
Montchanin [F] 56 F5
Montcornet [F] 28 G6
Montcuq [F] 66 F5
Mont-de-Marsan [F] 66 C6
Montdidier [F] 28 E5
Mont-Dol [F] 26 C4
Monte [P] 100 B3
Montealegre [E] 82 C6
Montealegre del Castillo [E] 98 C6
Monte Arabí, Cueva de- [E] 98 C6
Montebelluna [I] 72 E5
Montebourg [F] 26 D2
Montebruno [I] 110 B3
Monte-Carlo [MC] 108 F4
Montecassino, Abbazia di- [I] 120 D1
Montecatini-Terme [I] 110 E5
Montécchio [I] 112 B5
Montecchio Emilia [I] 110 D3
Montécchio Maggiore [I] 72 D6
Montech [F] 66 F6
Montechiaro, Castello di- [I] 126 D4
Montecorice [I] 120 F5
Montecorvino Rovella [I] 120 F4
Monte da Pedra [P] 86 E4
Montefalco [I] 116 A2
Montefalcone nel Sannio [I] 116 E6
Montefiascone [I] 114 H3
Montefiorentino, Convento di- [I] 110 H6
Montefiorino [I] 110 E4
Monteforte Irpino [I] 120 E3
Montefrío [E] 102 D3
Montegabbione [I] 114 H2
Montegiordano Marina [I] 122 D5

Monte Gordo [P] 94 D5
Montegrotto Terme [I] 110 G1
Montehermoso [E] 86 H3
Monte Isola [I] 72 A5
Montejícar [E] 102 E3
Montelavar [P] 86 B5
Montel-de-Gelat [F] 68 C1
Montélimar [F] 68 F6
Montella [I] 120 F3
Montellano [E] 100 H3
Monte Maria, Abbazia di- / Marienberg, Kloster- [I] 72 B2
Montemiccioli, Torre di- [I] 114 F1
Montemolín [E] 94 G4
Montemor-o-Novo [P] 86 C6
Montemor-o-Velho [P] 86 D2
Montemurlo [I] 110 E5
Montendre [F] 66 D2
Montenegro de Cameros [E] 90 B2
Montenero di Bisáccia [I] 116 E5
Monte Oliveto Maggiore, Abbazia di- [I] 114 G2
Montepulciano [I] 114 G2
Montereale [I] 116 B4
Montereale Valcellina [I] 72 F4
Montereau [F] 42 G5
Monte Redondo [P] 86 C2
Monterenzio [I] 110 F4
Monteriggioni [I] 114 F1
Monteroni d'Arbia [I] 114 G1
Monteroni di Lecce [I] 122 G5
Monterosso al Mare [I] 110 C4
Monterotondo [I] 116 A5
Monterotondo Marittimo [I] 114 E2
Monterroso [E] 78 D4
Monterrubio de la Serena [E] 96 B4
Monte San Biagio [I] 120 C1
Montesano sulla Marcellana [I] 120 G5
Monte San Savino [I] 114 G1
Monte Sant' Angelo [I] 116 H6
Montesarchio [I] 120 E2
Montescaglioso [I] 122 D4
Monte Senario, Convento- [I] 110 F5
Montesilvano Marina [I] 116 D4
Montesinos, Cueva de- [E] 96 G5
Montesquieu-Volvestre [F] 84 H4
Montesquiou [F] 84 F3
Montevarchi [I] 110 F6
Monteverde [I] 120 G3
Monte Vergine, Santuario di- [I] 120 E3
Montfaucon-en-Velay [F] 68 E4
Montferrat [F] 108 D4
Montfort [F] 66 B6
Montfort [F] 26 C6
Montfort [F] 42 E3
Mont Gargan [F] 66 H2
Montgat [E] 92 E4
Montgenèvre [F] 70 B6
Montgenèvre, Col de- [Eur.] 70 B6
Montgeoffroy, Château de- [F] 40 H6
Montgiscard [F] 106 A3
Montguyon [F] 66 D2
Monthermé [F] 44 C1
Monthey [CH] 70 C2
Monthois [F] 44 C3
Monthureaux-sur-Saône [F] 58 B2
Monti [I] 118 D3
Monticelli Terme [I] 110 D3
Montichiari [I] 72 B6
Monticiano [I] 114 F2
Montiel [E] 96 G5
Montier-en-Der [F] 44 C5
Montignac [F] 66 G3
Montigny-le-Roi [F] 58 A2
Montigny-sur-Aube [F] 56 G2
Montijo [E] 94 G1
Montijo [P] 86 B5
Montilla [E] 102 C2
Monti-Sion, Santuari de- [E] 104 E5
Montivilliers [F] 26 G3
Montlieu-la-Garde [F] 66 D2
Mont-Louis [F] 92 E1
Montluçon [F] 56 C5
Montluel [F] 68 G2
Montmajour, Abbaye de- [F] 106 G4
Montmarault [F] 56 C6
Montmédy [F] 44 D3
Montmélian [F] 70 A4
Montmeyan [F] 108 C4
Montmirail [F] 42 C5
Montmirail [F] 42 H4
Montmirey [F] 56 H4
Montmoreau-St-Cybard [F] 66 E2
Montmorillon [F] 54 F4
Montmort [F] 44 A4
Montoire-sur-le-Loir [F] 42 C6
Montoito [P] 94 E2
Montorio [E] 82 E5
Montorio al Vomano [I] 116 C3
Montoro [E] 102 D1
Montpellier [F] 106 E4
Montpellier-Le-Vieux [F] 106 E2
Montpezat [F] 66 G6
Montpon-Ménestérol [F] 66 E3
Montpont-en-Bresse [F] 56 G6
Montréal [F] 66 D6
Montréal [F] 106 B4
Montréal [F] 56 F3
Montredon-Labessonnie [F] 106 C3
Montréjeau [F] 84 F4
Montrésor [F] 54 G3
Montret [F] 56 G5
Montreuil [F] 28 D3
Montreuil-aux-Lions [F] 42 H3
Montreuil-Bellay [F] 54 E2
Montreux [CH] 70 C1
Montrevault [F] 54 C1
Montrevel [F] 68 G1
Montrichard [F] 54 G2
Montroi / Montroy [E] 98 E5
Mont-roig del Camp [E] 90 H6
Montrond-les-Bains [F] 68 E3
Montrose [GB] 8 F2
Montroy / Montroi [E] 98 E5
Montsalvy [F] 68 B5
Montsauche-les-Settons [F] 56 F3
Montségur [F] 106 A5
Montseny [E] 92 E3
Montserrat [E] 92 D4
Montsoreau [F] 54 E2
Mont-sous-Vaudrey [F] 56 H5
Monts-s-Guesnes [F] 54 E3
Mont-Ste-Odile [F] 44 G6
Montsûrs [F] 26 E6
Montuenga [E] 88 E3
Monturque [E] 102 C2
Monza [I] 70 G4
Monze [F] 106 C5
Monzón [E] 90 G3
Monzón de Campos [E] 82 D6
Monzuno [I] 110 F4
Moordorf [D] 18 B4
Moosburg [D] 60 F3
Moosham [A] 72 H2
Moosinning [D] 60 E4
Moos in Passeier / Moso in Passiria [I] 72 D2
Mór [H] 76 B1
Mora [E] 96 F2
Mora [P] 86 D5
Mora [S] 172 G3
Mora [S] 174 C5
Mora, Puerto de la- [E] 102 E4
Morača [YU] 152 E3
Morača, Manastir- [YU] 152 E3
Móra d'Ebre [E] 90 H6
Mora de Rubielos [E] 98 E2
Moradillo de Roa [E] 88 G2
Morąg [PL] 22 G3
Mórahalom [H] 76 E4
Moraïtika [GR] 132 B2
Móra la Nova [E] 90 H6
Moral de Calatrava [E] 96 F5
Moraleda de Zafayona [E] 102 D4
Moraleja [E] 86 G3
Morano Cálabro [I] 120 H6
Mora Stenar [S] 168 D2
Morasverdes [E] 88 B3
Moratalla [E] 104 B2
Moravče [SLO] 74 C5
Moravice [HR] 112 F1
Morávka [CZ] 50 F5
Moravská Třebová [CZ] 50 C4
Moravské Budějovice [CZ] 62 E2
Moravské Lieskové [SK] 62 H3
Moravský Beroun [CZ] 50 D4
Moravský Krumlov [CZ] 62 F2
Morawica [PL] 52 B2
Morbach [D] 44 G2
Morbegno [I] 70 H3
Mörbisch [A] 62 F6
Mörbylånga [S] 162 G5
Morcenx [F] 66 B5
Morciano di Romagna [I] 112 B5
Morcone [I] 120 E2
Morcote [CH] 70 G3
Mordelles [F] 26 C6
Mordoğan [TR] 144 B4
Mordy [PL] 38 E3
Morecambe [GB] 10 D2
Moreda [E] 102 E3
Morella [E] 98 G1
Morella la Vella [E] 98 G1
Moreno, Col de la- [F] 68 C2
Móres [I] 118 C3
Morestel [F] 68 G3
Moret-sur-Loing [F] 42 G5
Moretta [I] 108 F1
Moreuil [F] 28 E5
Morez [F] 70 B1
Morfa Nefyn [GB] 10 B4
Mörfelden [D] 46 C3
Mórfi [GR] 132 C3
Morgantina [I] 126 F4
Morgat [F] 40 B2
Morgedal [N] 164 E2
Morges [CH] 70 B1
Morgex [I] 70 C3
Morgins [CH] 70 C2
Morgongåva [S] 168 C1
Morhange [F] 44 F5
Mori [I] 72 C5
Moriani-Plage [F] 114 C3
Morimondo, Abbazia di- [I] 70 F5
Moritzburg [D] 34 C6
Moritzburg [D] 34 E6
Moritzburg, Schloss- [D] 34 E6
Morjärv [S] 198 B2
Mørk [N] 166 B2
Mørke [DK] 160 E6
Mørkøv [DK] 156 F2
Morkovice Slížany [CZ] 50 D6
Morla [E] 78 F6
Morlaàs [F] 84 E3
Morlaix [F] 40 C2
Mörlunda [S] 162 F3
Mormanno [I] 120 H6
Mormant [F] 42 G4
Mornay-Berry [F] 56 D4
Mornese [I] 110 A2
Morón de Almazán [E] 90 B4
Morón de la Frontera [E] 100 H3
Morosaglia [F] 114 B3
Morovic [YU] 154 E2
Morøya [N] 192 C5
Morozzo [I] 108 G2
Morpeth [GB] 8 G5
Morra [I] 114 H1
Morral de Cabrafeixet [E] 92 B5
Mørriaunet [N] 190 B5
Morro del Jable [E] 100 D5
Mörrum [S] 158 E1
Mörsburg [CH] 58 G4
Mörsil [S] 182 F2
Mörskom / Myrskylä [FIN] 178 B3
Morskoye [RUS] 202 D5
Morsum [D] 156 A4
Mørsvikbotn [N] 192 C5
Mortagne-au-Perche [F] 26 G5
Mortagne-sur-Sèvre [F] 54 C2
Mortain [F] 26 E5
Mortara [I] 70 F5
Morteau [F] 58 C5
Mortegliano [I] 72 G5
Mortier-Crolle, Château de- [F] 40 G5
Mortrée [F] 26 F5
Moryń [PL] 34 G1
Morzine [F] 70 C2
Morzycyn [PL] 20 F5
Mosås [S] 166 H3
Mosbach [D] 46 D5
Mosby [N] 164 D5
Moscavide [P] 86 B5
Mošćenice [HR] 112 E2
Mošćenička Draga [HR] 112 E2
Moschendorf [A] 74 F2
Moschopótamos [GR] 128 G5
Moscufo [I] 116 D4
Mosėdis [LT] 202 D3
Mosfellsbær [IS] 194 B4
Mosina [PL] 36 C3
Mosjøen [N] 190 D3
Moškanjci [SLO] 74 E4
Moskog [N] 180 C6
Moskosel [S] 190 H3
Moskva [RUS] 204 F4
Moslavina [HR] 76 A6
Moso in Passiria / Moos in Passeier [I] 72 D2
Mosonmagyaróvár [H] 62 G5
Mosqueruela [E] 98 F2
Moss [N] 166 B2
Mossiberg [S] 172 F1
Mössingen [D] 58 G2
Most [CZ] 48 E2
Mosta [M] 126 C6
Mostar [BIH] 152 C2
Mosterhamn [N] 170 A6
Mostki [PL] 52 C2
Móstoles [E] 88 F6
Mostowo [PL] 22 A3
Mosty [PL] 38 F4
Mostyn [GB] 10 C4
Mostys'ka [UA] 52 F4
Mosune [HR] 112 F2
Moszczanka [PL] 38 D4
Mota, Cast. de la- [E] 88 E2
Mota del Cuervo [E] 96 H3
Mota del Marqués [E] 88 D1
Motala [S] 166 G5
Motherwell [GB] 8 D3
Motilla del Palancar [E] 98 B3
Motjärnshyttan [S] 166 F1
Motko [RUS] 198 H6
Motovun [HR] 112 D1
Motril [E] 102 E5
Motta di Livenza [I] 72 F5
Motta Visconti [I] 70 F5
Motte-Glain, Château de la- [F] 40 G5
Móttola [I] 122 E4
Möttönen [FIN] 186 E2
Mou [DK] 160 E4
Mouchard [F] 58 A5
Moudon [CH] 70 C1
Moúdros [GR] 130 F6
Mougins [F] 108 E5
Mouhijärvi [FIN] 176 E1
Mouliherne [F] 54 E1
Moulins [F] 56 D5
Moulins-Engilbert [F] 56 E4
Moulins-la-Marche [F] 26 G5
Mountallen [IRL] 2 D4
Mount Bellew [IRL] 2 D5
Mount Charles [IRL] 2 E2
Mountmellick [IRL] 2 E6
Mountrath [IRL] 2 D6
Mountshannon [IRL] 2 C6
Moura [P] 94 E3
Mourão [P] 94 E2
Mouriés [GR] 128 H3
Mouros, Castelo dos- [P] 86 A5
Mourujärvi [FIN] 196 E8
Moustiers-Ste-Marie [F] 108 D4
Mouthe [F] 58 B6
Mouthier [F] 58 B5
Mouthoumet [F] 106 C5
Moutier [CH] 58 D5
Moutier-d'Ahun [F] 54 H6
Moûtiers [F] 70 B4
Moutiers [F] 54 B3
Mouton-Rothschild [F] 66 C2
Moutsoúna [GR] 138 F3
Mouy [F] 28 D6
Mouzakaíoi [GR] 132 D2
Mouzáki [GR] 136 C2
Mouzáki [GR] 132 E2
Mouzon [F] 44 D2
Moville [IRL] 2 F2
Moy [GB] 2 F3
Moynalty [IRL] 2 F5
Moyne Abbey [IRL] 2 C3
Moyuela [E] 90 E5
Moyvore [IRL] 2 E5
Mozhaysk [RUS] 204 E4
Mozia [I] 126 B2
Mpalí [GR] 140 D4
Mpampalió [GR] 132 E4
Mpampíni [GR] 132 D5
Mpatsí [GR] 134 E6
Mpórsio [GR] 136 C1
Mpoúkka [GR] 132 D4
Mprálos [GR] 132 G4
Mrągowo [PL] 24 B4
Mrakovica [BIH] 154 B2
Mrčajevci [YU] 150 B2
Mrežičko [MK] 128 F3
Mrkonjić-Grad [BIH] 154 B3
Mrkopalj [HR] 112 F1
Mrocza [PL] 22 C5
Mroczeń [PL] 36 E6
Mrzeżyno [PL] 20 G3
Mrzygłód [PL] 52 E4
Mšeno [CZ] 48 G3
Mshinskaya [RUS] 200 H1
Mstislavl' [BY] 204 D5
Mstów [PL] 50 G1
Mszana Dolna [PL] 52 A5
Mszczonów [PL] 38 B4
Mt-Dauphin [F] 108 E1
Mt. Melleray Monastery [IRL] 4 D4
Mtsensk [RUS] 204 E4
Mt. St. Joseph Abbey [IRL] 2 D6
Muć [HR] 152 A1
Muccia [I] 116 B2
Much [D] 30 H4
Mücheln [D] 34 B5
Muchówka [PL] 52 B4
Muckross [IRL] 4 B4
Muckross House [IRL] 4 B4
Mudanya [TR] 146 E4
Mudau [D] 46 D4
Mudela, Castillo de- [E] 96 F5
Müden [D] 18 F6
Mudiske [EST] 200 E2
Müdrets [BG] 148 D5
Muel [E] 90 E4
Muelas del Pan [E] 80 H4
Muezerskiy [RUS] 198 H5
Muff [IRL] 2 F2
Muge [P] 86 C4
Mügeln [D] 34 D6
Muggendorf [D] 46 G4
Múggia [I] 72 H6
Muğla [TR] 142 E2
Müglizh [BG] 148 C4
Mugnano [I] 114 H2
Mugron [F] 66 C6
Mühlacker [D] 46 C6
Mühlbach [A] 72 G1
Mühlberg [D] 34 E5
Mühldorf [D] 60 F4
Mühlhausen [D] 60 B3
Mühlhausen [D] 32 G5
Muhola [FIN] 186 F1
Muhos [FIN] 198 D4
Muhovo [BG] 148 A5
Muine Bheag / Bagenalstown [IRL] 4 F4
Muiños [E] 78 C6
Muir of Ord [GB] 6 D5
Mujaković [BIH] 154 C4
Mujejärvi [FIN] 198 G5
Mukacheve [UA] 206 B3
Mula [E] 104 B3
Mulba [E] 94 H5
Mulegns [CH] 70 H2
Mülheim [D] 44 G2
Mülheim [D] 30 G3
Mulhouse [F] 58 D3
Müllheim [D] 58 E3
Mullinavat [IRL] 4 E4
Mullingar [IRL] 2 E5
Müllrose [D] 34 G3
Mullsjö [S] 162 C2
Multia [FIN] 186 F4
Muñana [E] 88 D4
Münchberg [D] 48 B3
Müncheberg [D] 34 F2
München [D] 60 E4
Münchhausen [D] 32 D6
Münchhausen [D] 34 E4
Munderkingen [D] 60 B4
Mundheim [N] 170 B4
Munera [E] 96 H5
Mungia [E] 82 G3
Muñico [E] 88 D4
Muniesa [E] 90 E5
Munka-Ljunby [S] 156 H1
Munkebo [DK] 156 E3
Munkedal [S] 166 C5
Munkelven [N] 196 E3
Munkfors [S] 166 F1
Münnerstadt [D] 46 F3
Munsala [FIN] 186 C1
Münsingen [CH] 58 D6
Münsingen [D] 58 H2
Munsö [S] 168 D3
Münster [CH] 70 E2
Münster [D] 32 C3
Munster [D] 18 F6
Munster [F] 58 D3
Münstertal [D] 58 E3
Münzenberg [D] 46 C2
Münzkirchen [A] 62 A3
Muodoslompolo [S] 192 G5
Muonio [FIN] 192 G5
Muotkajärvi [FIN] 192 G4
Muotkalahti [RUS] 196 F6
Muotkavaara [FIN] 192 H5
Muradiye [TR] 144 C3
Murakeresztúr [H] 74 G4
Muráň [SK] 64 E3
Murano [I] 72 E6
Muras [E] 78 E2
Murat [F] 68 C4
Murati [EST] 200 F4
Muratlar [TR] 142 E1
Muratlı [TR] 146 C3
Murato [F] 114 C3
Murat-sur-Vèbre [F] 106 D3
Murau [A] 74 B2
Muravera [I] 118 E6
Murazzano [I] 108 G2
Murça [P] 80 E4
Mürchevo [BG] 150 F3
Murchin [D] 20 E3
Murcia [E] 104 C3
Murciélagos, Cueva de los- [E] 102 C2
Murcielagos, Cueva de los- [E] 102 E5
Mur-de-Barrez [F] 68 B4
Mur-de-Bretagne [F] 26 A5
Mureck [A] 74 E3
Mürefte [TR] 146 C4
Muret [F] 84 H3
Murgados [E] 78 D1
Murgaševo [MK] 128 E3
Murgia / Murguía [E] 82 G5
Murg-Kraftwerk [D] 58 F1
Murguía / Murgia [E] 82 G5
Muri [CH] 58 F5
Murias de Paredes [E] 78 G4
Murieta [E] 82 H6
Murighiol [RO] 206 E6
Murino [YU] 150 A5
Muriquan [AL] 128 A1
Murjek [S] 198 A2
Murlo [I] 114 F2
Murnau [D] 60 D5
Muro [E] 104 E4
Muro [F] 114 B3
Muro de Alcoy / Muro del Comtat [E] 104 E1
Muro del Comtat / Muro de Alcoy [E] 104 E1
Muro Lucano [I] 120 G3
Muros [E] 78 B3
Murowana Goślina [PL] 36 C2
Mürren [CH] 70 E2
Murrhardt [D] 46 D6
Murrisk Abbey [IRL] 2 B4
Murru [EST] 200 D3
Murska Sobota [SLO] 74 E3
Mursko Središće [HR] 74 F4
Murta [RO] 150 G2
Murten [CH] 58 D6
Murter [HR] 112 G6
Murtinheira [P] 80 A6
Murtosa [P] 80 B5
Murtovaara [FIN] 198 F2
Murvica [HR] 112 G5
Mürzsteg [A] 62 D6
Mürzzuschlag [A] 62 E6
Mussalo [FIN] 178 C4
Musselkanaal [NL] 16 H3
Mussidan [F] 66 E3
Mussomeli [I] 126 D3
Mussy [F] 56 G2
Mustafa Kemalpaşa [TR] 146 E5
Müstair [CH] 72 B3
Mustajõe [EST] 200 G1
Mustér / Disentis [CH] 70 G1
Mustla [EST] 200 E3
Mustvee [EST] 200 F2
Muszaki [PL] 22 H5
Muszyna [PL] 52 C5
Muszynka [PL] 52 C5
Mutalahti [FIN] 188 H3
Mutanj [YU] 150 B2
Mutriku [E] 82 H4
Muttalip [TR] 146 H5
Mutterstadt [D] 46 B5
Muurame [FIN] 186 G5
Muurasjärvi [FIN] 198 D6
Muurikkala [FIN] 178 D3
Muurla [FIN] 176 F5
Muurola [FIN] 178 D3
Muurola [FIN] 196 C8
Muxía [E] 78 B2
Múzeum Oravskej Dediny [SK] 50 H6
Muzillac [F] 40 E5
Mužla [SK] 64 B5
Mužlja [YU] 154 G1
Myakishevo [RUS] 200 H5
Mybotn [N] 192 D3
Myjava [SK] 62 H3
Mykínes [GR] 136 E2
Myking [N] 170 F4
Myklebostad [N] 192 C5
Myklebust [N] 180 D3
Myklestøyl [N] 164 D3
Mykolaïv [UA] 206 F4
Mykolaïv [UA] 52 H5
Mýkonos [GR] 138 E2
Myllykoski [FIN] 178 C3
Myllymäki [FIN] 186 E4
Mýloi [GR] 136 E2
Mylopótamos [GR] 136 F6
Mylund [DK] 160 E3
Mynämäki [FIN] 176 D4
Myndos [TR] 142 C2
Myonnesos [TR] 144 C5
Myos [TR] 142 C1
Myrdal [N] 170 D3
Myre [N] 192 C3
Myren [S] 172 E5
Myrhorod [UA] 206 G2
Mýrina [GR] 130 F6
Myrina [TR] 144 C3
Myrlandshaugen [N] 192 D3
Myronivka [UA] 206 F2
Myrskylä / Mörskom [FIN] 178 B3
Myrtiés [GR] 142 B3
Mýrtos [GR] 140 F5
Myrviken [S] 182 G3
Mysen [N] 166 C2
Myšenec [CZ] 48 F6
Myshall [IRL] 4 F4
Myshuryn Rih [UA] 206 G3
Myślenice [PL] 50 H4
Myślibórz [PL] 34 G1
Mysłowice [PL] 50 G3
Mysovka [RUS] 202 D5
Mystegná [GR] 134 H2
Mystrás [GR] 136 E4
Myszków [PL] 50 G2
Myszyniec [PL] 24 C5
Mýtikas [GR] 132 D5
Mytilíni [GR] 134 H2
Mytishchi [RUS] 204 F4
Myto [BY] 24 H3
Mýto [CZ] 48 E4
Mzurki [PL] 36 G5

N

Nå [N] 170 C4
Naamijoki [FIN] 192 H6
Naantali / Nådend [FIN] 176 D4
Naarden [NL] 16 E4
Naarva [FIN] 188 G1
Nääs [S] 160 H2
Naas / An Nás [IRL] 2 F6
Näätämö [FIN] 196 E3
Nabaskoze / Navascués [E] 84 C4
Nabbelund [S] 162 H3
Nabburg [D] 48 C5
Náchod [CZ] 50 B3
Nacka [S] 168 E3
Nădab [RO] 76 G3
Nadăş [RO] 76 H4
Naddvik [N] 170 E2
Nadela [E] 78 E3
Nådend / Naantali [FIN] 176 D4
Nădlac [RO] 76 F4
Nadrin [B] 30 E6
Nádudvar [H] 76 G1
Nærbo [N] 164 A4
Næstved [DK] 156 F4
Näfels [CH] 58 G6
Náfpaktos [GR] 132 F5
Náfplio [GR] 136 F2
Naggen [S] 184 D5
Naglarby [S] 174 C5
Nagłowice [PL] 52 A2
Nagold [D] 58 G2
Nagu / Nauvo [FIN] 176 D5
Nagyatád [H] 74 H4
Nagybajom [H] 74 H4
Nagybaracska [H] 76 C5
Nagycenk [H] 62 F6
Nagycserkesz [H] 64 G5
Nagydorog [H] 76 B3
Nagygyimót [H] 74 H1
Nagyhalász [H] 64 H4
Nagyigmánd [H] 64 A6
Nagyiván [H] 64 F6
Nagykálló [H] 64 H5
Nagykanizsa [H] 74 G4
Nagykáta [H] 76 D1
Nagykónyi [H] 76 B3
Nagykőrös [H] 76 D2
Nagylak [H] 76 F4
Nagylóc [H] 64 D5
Nagymágocs [H] 76 F3
Nagymaros [H] 64 C5
Nagyoroszi [H] 64 C5
Nagyszénás [H] 76 F3
Nagyvázsony [H] 74 H2
Naharros [E] 98 B2
Nahe [D] 18 F3
Naila [D] 46 H3
Nailloux [F] 106 A4
Nailsworth [GB] 12 G3
Naipu [RO] 148 C1
Nairn [GB] 6 E5
Najac [F] 66 H6
Nájera [E] 82 G6
Näkkälä [FIN] 192 G3
Nakkeslettä [N] 192 E1
Nakkila [FIN] 176 D2
Nakło nad Notecią [PL] 22 C6
Nakovo [YU] 76 F5
Nakskov [DK] 156 E5
Nälden [S] 182 G2
Nałęczów [PL] 38 D5
Nálepkovo [SK] 64 F2
Näljänkä [FIN] 198 F3
Nalzen [F] 106 A5
Nalžovské Hory [CZ] 48 E6
Nambroca [E] 96 F2
Namdalseid [N] 190 C5
Náměšť nad Oslavou [CZ] 50 B6
Námestovo [SK] 50 G5
Namsos [N] 190 C5
Namsskogan [N] 190 D4
Namsvassgardan [N] 190 D4
Namur [B] 30 D5
Namysłów [PL] 36 D6
Nanclares de la Oca / Langraiz Oka [E] 82 G5
Nancy [F] 44 E5
Nangis [F] 42 G4
Nannestad [N] 172 B5
Nans-les-Pins [F] 108 C5
Nant [F] 106 E3
Nantes [F] 40 F6
Nanteuil-le-Haudouin [F] 42 G3
Nantiat [F] 54 G6
Nantua [F] 68 H2
Nantwich [GB] 10 D5
Naours, Grottes de- [F] 28 E4
Náousa [GR] 138 E3
Náousa [GR] 128 F4
Naples [TR] 146 C3
Nápoli [I] 120 E3
Na Pomezí [CZ] 50 C3
Napp [N] 192 B4
Nåra [N] 170 A2
Narach [BY] 202 H5
Naraio, Castelo de- [E] 78 D2
Narberth [GB] 12 D1
Narbolia [I] 118 C5
Narbonne [F] 106 D5
Narbonne-Plage [F] 106 D5
Narbuvollen [N] 182 C4
Narcao [I] 118 B7
Nardis, Cascata di- [I] 72 C4
Nardo [I] 122 G5
Narechenski Bani [BG] 148 B6
Narew [PL] 24 F6
Narila [FIN] 188 D5
Narkaus [FIN] 196 D8
Narlıca [TR] 146 F4
Narni [I] 116 A4
Naro [I] 126 D4
Naro-Fominsk [RUS] 204 F4
Narol [PL] 52 G2
Narón [E] 78 D4
Närpes / Närpiö [FIN] 186 A4
Närpiö / Närpes [FIN] 186 A4
Narta [HR] 74 G6
Narthákí [GR] 132 G3
Narva [EST] 200 G1
Närvä [S] 192 F4
Narva-Jõesuu [EST] 200 G1
Narvik [N] 192 D4
Näs [S] 172 G5
Näs [S] 162 D1
Näsåker [S] 184 E1
N. Åsarp [S] 162 C1
Năsăud [RO] 206 C4
Nasbinals [F] 68 C5
Našice [HR] 154 D1
Nasielsk [PL] 38 B2
Näsinge [S] 166 C4
Naso [I] 124 B6
Na Špičáku [CZ] 50 D3
Nassau [D] 46 B2
Nassereith [A] 72 C1
Nässja [S] 166 G5
Nässjö [S] 184 D1
Nässjö [S] 162 D2
Nasswald [A] 62 E6
Nästansjö [S] 190 F4
Nastazin [PL] 20 G5
Nästeln [S] 182 G4
Nastola [FIN] 178 B3
Nasüm [S] 158 E1
Näsviken [S] 190 E6
Näsviken [S] 174 E1
Natalinci [YU] 150 B1
Nattavaara [S] 198 A1
Nättraby [S] 158 F1
Naturno / Naturns [I] 72 C3
Naturns / Naturno [I] 72 C3
Nauders [A] 72 B2
Nauen [D] 34 D2
Naujoji Akmenė [LT] 200 C6
Naul [IRL] 2 F5
Naumburg [D] 34 B6
Naumestis [LT] 202 F4
Naunhof [D] 34 D5
Naustbukta [N] 190 C4
Naustdal [N] 180 C6
Nauste [N] 180 F3
Nautijaure [S] 190 H1
Nautsi [RUS] 196 E4
Nauvo / Nagu [FIN] 176 D5
Nava [E] 82 C2
Navacelles, Cirque de- [F] 106 E3
Navacerrada [E] 88 F4
Nava de la Asunción [E] 88 E3
Nava del Rey [E] 88 D2
Navahermosa [E] 96 E2
Navahrudak [BY] 204 A5
Navalcán [E] 88 C6
Navalcarnero [E] 88 F6
Navaleno [E] 90 A2
Navalguijo [E] 88 C5
Navalmanzano [E] 88 F3
Navalmoral [E] 88 D5
Navalmoral de la Mata [E] 88 B6
Navalón [E] 98 D6
Navalperal de Pinares [E] 88 E5
Navalvillar de Pela [E] 96 B3
Navan / An Uaimh [IRL] 2 F5
Nävårdalen [N] 182 B3
Navarredonda de Gredos [E] 88 C5
Navarrenx [F] 84 D3
Navarrés [E] 98 E5
Navarrete [E] 82 G6
Navàs [E] 92 E3
Navascués / Nabaskoze [E] 84 C4
Navas del Madroño [E] 86 G4
Navas del Rey [E] 88 E5
Navas de Oro [E] 88 E3
Navas de San Juan [E] 102 F1
Navatalgordo [E] 88 D5
Navekvarn [S] 168 C5
Navelli [I] 116 C4
Nave Redonda [P] 94 B4
Naverstad [S] 166 C4
Naveta des Tudons [E] 104 G4
Navia [E] 78 F2
Navilly [F] 56 G5
Navlya [RUS] 204 E6
Náxos [GR] 138 E3
Naxos [I] 124 B8
Nazaré [P] 86 C3
Nazıllı [TR] 144 E5
N. Bystrica [SK] 50 G6
N.-D. de Clausis [F] 108 E2
N.-D. de Kerdevot [F] 40 B3
N.-D. de la Salette [F] 68 H5
N.-D. de Lure [F] 108 C3
N.-D. de Miracles [F] 108 E4
N.-D.-du-Haut [F] 58 C3
N.-D. du Mai [F] 108 C6
Ndroq [AL] 128 B3

264 Nea - Nyz

Néa Anchíalos [GR] 132 H3
Néa Artáki [GR] 134 B5
Néa Epídavros [GR] 136 F2
Néa Fókaia [GR] 130 B6
Néa Kallikráteia [GR] 130 B5
Néa Karváli [GR] 130 D3
Néa Koróni [GR] 136 D4
Neale [IRL] 2 C4
Néa Mádytos [GR] 130 C4
Néa Mákri [GR] 134 C6
Néa Michanióna [GR] 128 H5
Néa Moní [GR] 134 G4
Néa Moudaniá [GR] 130 B5
Neamţ, Mănăstirea- [RO] 206 C4
Neandria [TR] 130 H6
Néa Péramos [GR] 130 D3
Néa Plágia [GR] 130 B5
Neapoli [GR] 136 F5
Neápoli [GR] 140 F4
Neápoli [GR] 128 E5
Neapolis [TR] 144 E5
Néa Poteídaia [GR] 130 B5
Néa Róda [GR] 130 C5
Néa Roúmata [GR] 140 B4
Néa Sánta [GR] 130 G2
Néa Skióni [GR] 130 C6
Néa Stýra [GR] 134 D5
Neath [GB] 12 E2
Néa Tríglia [GR] 130 B5
Neauvic [F] 66 E3
Néa Výssa [GR] 130 H1
Néa Zíchni [GR] 130 C3
Nebiler [TR] 144 C2
Nebolchi [RUS] 204 D2
Nebra [D] 34 B5
Nechanice [CZ] 50 A3
Neckarelz [D] 46 D5
Neckargemünd [D] 46 C5
Neckargerach [D] 46 D5
Neckarsteinach [D] 46 C5
Neckarsulm [D] 46 D5
Neda [E] 78 D1
Neded [SK] 64 A5
Nedelišće [HR] 74 F4
Nedervetil / Alaveteli [FIN] 198 C6
Neder Vindinge [DK] 156 F4
Nedre Eggedal [N] 170 G5
Nedre Soppero [S] 192 F4
Nedstrand [N] 164 B2
Nędza [PL] 50 E3
Neede [NL] 16 G5
Neermoor [D] 18 B4
Negorci [MK] 128 G3
Negotin [YU] 150 E1
Negotino [MK] 128 F2
Negovanovci [BG] 150 E2
Negrar [I] 72 C6
Negreira [E] 78 B3
Negren-Tino [CH] 70 G2
Negru Vodă [RO] 148 G1
Neheim-Hüsten [D] 32 C4
Nehoiu [RO] 206 C5
Neiden [N] 196 E3
Neittävä [FIN] 198 E4
Nejdek [CZ] 48 D3
Nekromanteío [GR] 132 C3
Neksø [DK] 158 E4
Nelas [P] 80 C6
Nelidovo [RUS] 204 D4
Nellim [FIN] 196 E4
Nellimö [FIN] 196 E4
Neman [RUS] 202 D5
Nembro [I] 70 H4
Neméa [GR] 136 E1
Neméa [GR] 136 E1
Nemenčinė [LT] 202 G5
Nemesszalók [H] 74 G1
Németkér [H] 76 C3
Nemours [F] 42 G5
Nemšová [SK] 64 A2
Nemti [H] 64 D5
Nemyriv [UA] 206 E3
Nemyriv [UA] 52 G3
Nenagh [IRL] 2 D6
Nendeln [FL] 58 H5
Neochóri [GR] 136 B1
Neochóri [GR] 132 E5
Neochóri [GR] 132 E3
Neochóri [GR] 134 A2
Neochóri [GR] 134 C5
Neochóri [GR] 132 F2
Néo Monastíri [GR] 132 G3
Néo Petrítsi [GR] 130 B2
Néos Marmarás [GR] 130 C6
Nepi [I] 114 H4
Nepomuk [CZ] 48 E5
Neptun [RO] 148 G1
Nérac [F] 66 E5
Neratovice [CZ] 48 G3
Neresheim [D] 60 C2
Nereta [LV] 200 E6
Nereto [I] 116 D3
Neretva Kanjon [BIH] 152 C2
Nerezine [HR] 112 E3
Nerežišća [HR] 152 A2
Neringa [LT] 202 D5
Neringa-Nida [LT] 202 D5
Néris-les-Bains [F] 56 C6
Nerja [E] 102 D5
Nerja, Cueva de- [E] 102 D5
Nérondes [F] 56 C4
Nerpio [E] 102 H2
Nerpio, Cuevas de- [E] 102 H2
Nersingen [D] 60 B3
Nerskogen [N] 180 H3
Nerva [E] 94 F5
Nervesa della Battaglia [I] 72 E5
Nervi [I] 110 B3
Nerviano [I] 70 G4
Nes [N] 170 H4
Nes [N] 170 D1
Nes [NL] 16 F1
Nesactium [HR] 112 D2
Nesaseter [N] 190 D4
Nesbyen [N] 170 G4
Nesebür [BG] 148 F4
Nesflaten [N] 164 C1
Neskaupstaður [IS] 194 G5
Neslandsvatn [N] 164 F3
Nesle [F] 28 F5
Nesna [N] 190 D2
Nesoddtangen [N] 166 B1
Nespereira [P] 80 C3
Nesseby [N] 196 E2
Nesselwang [D] 60 C5
Nestáni [GR] 136 E2
Nesterov [RUS] 24 D1
Nestório [GR] 128 D5
Nesttun [N] 170 B4
Nesvik [N] 164 A6
Netolice [CZ] 62 B2
Netretić [HR] 112 G1
Netta [PL] 24 E4
Nettancourt [F] 44 C4
Nettetal [D] 30 F3
Nettuno [I] 120 B1
Nettuno, Grotta di- [I] 118 B3
Neubeckum [D] 32 D3
Neuberg [A] 74 E1
Neuberg an der Mürz [A] 62 D6
Neubrandenburg [D] 20 D4
Neubukow [D] 20 A3
Neubulach [D] 58 G1
Neuburg [D] 60 H3
Neuburg [D] 60 D2
Neuchâtel [CH] 58 C5
Neu Darchau [D] 18 G5
Neudorf [D] 46 C5
Neudorf-Platendorf [D] 32 H2
Neuenburg [D] 58 E3
Neuenbürg [D] 46 C6
Neuenburg [D] 18 C4
Neuenhaus [D] 16 G4
Neuenkirchen [D] 18 F5
Neuenstein [D] 46 D5
Neuenwalde [D] 18 D3
Neufahrn [D] 60 F3
Neuf-Brisach [F] 58 E3
Neufchâteau [B] 44 D2
Neufchâteau [F] 44 D6
Neufchâtel [F] 44 B2
Neufchâtel-en-Bray [F] 28 C5
Neufelden [A] 62 B3
Neuffen [D] 58 H2
Neugersdorf [D] 48 G1
Neuhaus [D] 46 H4
Neuhaus [D] 46 G2
Neuhaus [D] 60 H3
Neuhaus [D] 18 E3
Neuhaus [D] 32 F4
Neuhaus [D] 18 H5
Neuhausen am Rheinfall [CH] 58 F4
Neuhof [D] 34 E3
Neuhofen an der Krems [A] 62 B4
Neuillé Port-Pierre [F] 54 F1
Neuilly-l'Évêque [F] 58 A3
Neuilly-St-Front [F] 42 H3
Neu-Isenburg [D] 46 C3
Neukalen [D] 20 C4
Neukirch [D] 34 F6
Neukirchen [A] 72 F1
Neukirchen [D] 156 B4
Neukloster [D] 20 A3
Neulengbach [A] 62 E4
Neu Lübbenau [D] 34 F3
Neum [BIH] 152 C3
Neumarkt [A] 74 B2
Neumarkt [A] 60 H5
Neumarkt [D] 46 H5
Neumarkt / Egna [I] 72 D4
Neumarkt-St Veit [D] 60 F4
Neu-Moresnet [B] 30 F5
Neumorschen [D] 32 F6
Neu Mukran [D] 20 D2
Neumünster [D] 18 F3
Neunagelberg [A] 62 C3
Neunburg [D] 48 C5
Neung-sur-Beuvron [F] 56 B2
Neunkirchen [A] 62 E6
Neunkirchen [D] 44 G3
Neuötting [D] 60 G4
Neupölla [A] 62 D3
Neuruppin [D] 20 C6
Neuschwanstein [D] 60 C6
Neusiedl am See [A] 62 G5
Neuss [D] 30 G3
Neustadt [D] 32 E6
Neustadt [D] 60 E2
Neustadt [D] 46 G2
Neustadt [D] 48 B1
Neustadt [D] 58 F3
Neustadt [D] 34 F6
Neustadt [D] 18 H3
Neustadt [D] 34 C1
Neustadt am Rübenberge [D] 32 F2
Neustadt an der Aisch [D] 46 F5
Neustadt an der Waldnaab [D] 48 C4
Neustadt an der Weinstrasse [D] 46 B5
Neustadt-Glewe [D] 20 A5
Neustift [A] 72 D1
Neustrelitz [D] 20 C5
Neuves-Maisons [F] 44 E5
Neuvic [F] 68 B3
Neuville [F] 68 F2
Neuville [F] 54 E3
Neuville-aux-Bois [F] 42 E5
Neuvy [F] 54 H4
Neuvy-sur-Barangeon [F] 56 C3
Neuwied [D] 30 H6
Neuzelle [D] 34 G3
Neveklov [CZ] 48 G4
Nevel' [RUS] 204 C4
Neverfjord [N] 196 B2
Nevers [F] 56 D4
Nevesinje [BIH] 152 C2
Nevlunghavn [N] 164 G3
New Alresford [GB] 12 H4
Newark-on-Trent [GB] 10 F5
Newbiggin-by-the-Sea [GB] 8 G5
Newbliss [IRL] 2 F4
Newbridge / Droichead Nua [IRL] 2 E6
Newburgh [GB] 8 E2
Newbury [GB] 12 H4
Newcastle [GB] 2 G4
Newcastle Emlyn [GB] 10 A6
Newcastle-under-Lyme [GB] 10 E5
Newcastle upon Tyne [GB] 8 G6
Newcastle West [IRL] 4 C3
New Galloway [GB] 8 D5
Newgrange [IRL] 2 F5
Newhaven [GB] 14 E6
Newinn [IRL] 4 D4
Newmarket [GB] 14 F3
Newmarket [IRL] 4 C4
Newmarket-on-Fergus [IRL] 2 C6
Newport [GB] 12 H5
Newport [GB] 10 D5
Newport [GB] 12 F3
Newport [IRL] 2 C3
Newport [IRL] 4 D3
Newport-on-Tay [GB] 8 F2
Newquay [GB] 12 C4
New Romney [GB] 14 F5
New Ross [IRL] 4 F4
Newry [GB] 2 F4
Newton Abbot [GB] 12 E5
Newtonmore [GB] 6 D6
Newton Stewart [GB] 8 C5
Newtown [GB] 10 C6
Newtownabbey [GB] 2 G3
Newtownards [GB] 2 G3
Newtown Butler [GB] 2 E4
Newtownhamilton [GB] 2 F4
Newtownmountkennedy [IRL] 4 G3
Newtownstewart [GB] 2 F3
Nexon [F] 66 G2
Neżilovo [MK] 128 E2
Niadinge [LT] 24 G2
Niaux, Grotte de- [F] 84 H5
Nibe [DK] 160 D4
Nicaj-Shalë [AL] 150 A6
Nicastro [I] 124 D5
Nice [F] 108 E4
Nickelsdorf [A] 62 G5
Nicknoret [S] 190 H4
Nicolosi [I] 126 G3
Nicopolis ad Istrum [BG] 148 C3
Nicosia [I] 126 F3
Nicotera [I] 124 C6
Nidderau [D] 46 D2
Nideck, Château du- [F] 44 G6
Nidzica [PL] 22 G5
Niebla [E] 94 F5
Nieborow [PL] 36 H3
Niebüll [D] 156 B4
Nieby [D] 156 C5
Niechorze [PL] 20 G3
Niedalino [PL] 20 H3
Niederalteich [D] 60 G3
Niederau [A] 60 F6
Niederaula [D] 46 E1
Niederbronn-les-Bains [F] 44 H5
Niederkrüchten [D] 30 F3
Niederoderwitz [D] 48 G1
Nieder Stotzingen [D] 60 C3
Niederwinkling [D] 60 G2
Nieder-Wöllstadt [D] 46 C2
Niedrzwica Duża [PL] 38 E6
Niemcza [PL] 50 C2
Niemegk [D] 34 D3
Niemijärvi [FIN] 188 H1
Niemisel [S] 198 B2
Niemisjärvi [FIN] 186 H4
Niemiskylä [FIN] 198 G5
Niemodlin [PL] 50 D2
Nienburg [D] 32 F1
Nienhagen [D] 20 B3
Niepołomice [PL] 52 B4
Nieppe [F] 28 F3
Nierstein [D] 46 C3
Niesky [D] 34 G5
Nieszawa [PL] 36 F1
Nietsak [S] 192 F6
Nieuil [F] 54 E6
Nieuweschans [NL] 16 H2
Nieuwpoort [B] 28 F1
Nigrán [E] 78 B5
Nigrita [GR] 130 B3
Niinimäki [FIN] 188 D3
Niinisalo [FIN] 186 C6
Niinivesi [FIN] 186 G2
Nijar [E] 102 G5
Nijemci [HR] 154 E2
Nijkerk [NL] 16 E5
Nijmegen [NL] 16 E6
Nijverdal [NL] 16 G4
Nikaia [GR] 132 G2
Nikaia [TR] 146 G4
Nikaranperä [FIN] 186 F3
Nikel' [RUS] 196 F3
Niki [GR] 128 E4
Nikiá [GR] 142 C4
Nikifóros [GR] 130 D3
Nikil [S] 166 H6
Nikísiani [GR] 130 D3
Nikitas [GR] 130 C5
Nikkajärvi [FIN] 198 G5
Nikkaluokta [S] 192 E5
Nikkaroinen [FIN] 178 A1
Nikkeby [N] 192 F1
Nikolaevskoye [RUS] 200 H2
Nikola Kozlevo [BG] 148 E2
Nikolayevo [RUS] 200 H2
Nikopol [BG] 148 B2
Nikopol' [UA] 206 G4
Nikópoli [GR] 132 D4
Nikšić [YU] 152 E3
Nilivaara [S] 192 F6
Nilsiä [FIN] 188 D1
Nîmes [F] 106 F3
Nin [HR] 112 G4
Ninfa [I] 116 B6
Ninove [B] 28 H3
Niort [F] 54 D4
Niroú Cháni [GR] 140 E4
Niš [YU] 150 D3
Nisa [P] 86 E4
Nisáki [GR] 132 B2
Niscemi [I] 126 F4
Niška Banja [YU] 150 D3
Niskakoski [RUS] 196 E4
Nisko [PL] 52 E2
Nissi [EST] 200 D2
Nissilä [FIN] 198 E5
Nītaure [LV] 200 E5
Nitlax [FIN] 176 F6
Nitra [SK] 64 A4
Nitrianske Pravno [SK] 64 B2
Nitrianske Rudno [SK] 64 B3
Nitry [F] 56 F2
Nittedal [N] 172 B5
Nittenau [D] 48 C6
Nittendorf [D] 60 F2
Nittkvarn [S] 166 G1
Nivå [DK] 156 G2
Niva [FIN] 198 G4
Nivala [FIN] 198 D5
Nivelles [B] 28 H3
Niversac [F] 66 F3
Nixhöhle [A] 62 D5
Nizhyn [UA] 204 D7
Nižná [SK] 50 H6
Nižná Boca [SK] 64 D2
Nižná Slaná [SK] 64 E3
Nizza Monferrato [I] 108 H2
Njegoševo [YU] 76 D6
Njivice [HR] 112 E2
Njupeskärfall [S] 172 E1
Njurunda [S] 184 E5
Njutånger [S] 174 E1
N. Kerdyllia [GR] 130 C4
Noailles [F] 28 D6
Noain (Elorz) [E] 84 B4
Noale [I] 72 E6
Nöbbelöv [S] 158 D2
Noceda [E] 78 F5
Nocera [I] 120 E3
Nocera Umbra [I] 116 B2
Noceto [I] 110 D2
Noci [I] 122 E3
Nocito [E] 84 D6
Nodeland [N] 164 D5
Nods [F] 58 B5
Noé [F] 84 H4
Noépoli [I] 122 C5
Noeux [F] 28 E3
Nogales [E] 94 G2
Nogara [I] 110 F1
Nogaro [F] 84 F2
Nogent [F] 56 H2
Nogent-le-Roi [F] 42 E4
Nogent-le-Rotrou [F] 26 G6
Nogent-sur-Seine [F] 42 H5
Nogersund [S] 158 E2
Noginsk [RUS] 204 F4
Nohfelden [D] 44 G3
Noia [E] 78 B3
Noirétable [F] 68 E2
Noirmoutier-en-l'Île [F] 54 A2
Noja [E] 82 F3
Nokia [FIN] 176 F1
Nol [S] 160 H1
Nola [I] 120 E3
Nol Alafors [S] 160 H1
Nolay [F] 56 F4
Noli [I] 108 H3
Nomeny [F] 44 E5
Nomexy [F] 44 E6
Nõmme [EST] 200 E2
Nonancourt [F] 26 H5
Nonant-le-Pin [F] 26 G5
Nonantola [I] 110 F3
Nonaspe [E] 90 G5
Nonnenhorn [D] 58 H4
Nontron [F] 66 F2
Nonza [F] 114 C2
Noordwijk aan Zee [NL] 16 C4
Noormarkku / Norrmark [FIN] 176 D1
Nora [I] 118 C7
Nora [S] 168 B6
Nora [S] 166 H2
Nørager [DK] 160 D4
Norberg [S] 168 B1
Norchia [I] 114 G4
Norcia [I] 116 B3
Nordagutu [N] 164 F2
Nordanå [S] 184 E3
Nordanås [S] 190 G5
Nordankäl [S] 184 D1
Nordansjö [S] 190 F4
Nordausques [F] 14 H6
Nordberg [N] 180 F5
Nordborg [DK] 156 C4
Nordby [DK] 156 E1
Nordby [DK] 156 A3
Norddeich [D] 16 H1
Nordeide [N] 170 C1
Norden [D] 16 H1
Nordenham [D] 18 D4
Norderney [D] 18 B3
Norderö [S] 182 G2
Norderstedt [D] 18 F4
Nordfjord [N] 196 E1
Nordfjordeid [N] 180 C5
Nordfold [N] 192 C5
Nordhalben [D] 46 H2
Nordhausen [D] 32 H5
Nordhorn [D] 16 H4
Nordingrå [S] 184 F3
Nordkapp [N] 196 C1
Nordkirchen [D] 32 C3
Nordkisa [N] 172 C5
Nordkjosbotn [N] 192 E3
Nordli [N] 190 D5
Nördlingen [D] 60 C2
Nordmaling [S] 184 H1
Nordmark [S] 166 F1
Nordmela [N] 192 C3
Nordre Osen [N] 172 D2
Nordsjö [S] 174 D1
Nordskjørin [N] 190 B5
Nordskot [N] 192 C5
Nordskov [DK] 156 E2
Nordwalde [D] 16 H5
Noresund [N] 170 G5
Norg [NL] 16 G2
Norheimsund [N] 170 C4
Nørholm [N] 164 E5
Norhyttan [S] 172 G5
Norje [S] 158 E1
Norkino [RUS] 200 H5
Norma [I] 116 B6
Normjöle [S] 190 H6
Norrahammar [S] 162 D2
Norraker [S] 190 E5
Norrala [S] 174 E2
Norra Löten [S] 172 E3
Norra Mellby [S] 158 C1
Norra Tresund [S] 190 F4
Norrbäck [S] 190 G4
Norrboda [S] 172 H3
Norrboda [S] 174 G5
Norrby [S] 190 G4
Nørre Åby [DK] 156 D3
Nørre Alslev [DK] 156 F5
Norre Bergnäss [S] 190 G2
Nørre Broby [DK] 156 D3
Nørre Lyndelse [DK] 156 D3
Nørre Nebel [DK] 156 A2
Nørre Snede [DK] 156 C1
Nørresundby [DK] 160 D3
Nørre Vejrup [DK] 156 B2
Nørre Vorupør [DK] 160 B4
Norr Hede [S] 182 F4
Norrhult [S] 162 E4
Norrköping [S] 168 B5
Norrmark / Noormarkku [FIN] 176 D1
Norrnäs [FIN] 186 A4
Norrskedika [S] 174 G5
Norrsunda [S] 168 D2
Norrsundet [S] 174 E3
Norrtälje [S] 168 E2
Norsholm [S] 168 B5
Norsjö [S] 190 H4
Norsjövallen [S] 190 H4
Nort [F] 40 F6
Nörten-Hardenberg [D] 32 G4
Northallerton [GB] 10 F2
Northam [GB] 12 D3
Northampton [GB] 14 D2
North Berwick [GB] 8 F3
Northeim [D] 32 G4
Northleach [GB] 12 H2
North Walsham [GB] 14 G2
Northwich [GB] 10 D4
Nortorf [D] 18 F2
Norwich [GB] 14 G2
Nosivka [UA] 206 F1
Nossa Senhora do Cabo [P] 86 A6
Nossebro [S] 166 D6
Nössemark [S] 166 C3
Nossen [D] 34 E6
Nótia [GR] 128 G3
Nötö [FIN] 176 D6
Noto [I] 126 G5
Noto Antica [I] 126 G5
Notodden [N] 164 F2
Notre-Dame de Consolation [F] 58 C5
Notre-Dame de-la-Roquette [F] 108 D5
Notre-Dame des Fontaines [F] 108 F3
Nøtterøy [N] 164 H3
Nottingham [GB] 10 F5
Nottuln [D] 16 H6
Nouan-le-Fuzelier [F] 56 B2
Nouans-les-Fontaines [F] 54 G3
Nouvaillé-Maupertuis [F] 54 E4
Nouvion [F] 28 D4
Nova [EST] 200 D2
Nova [H] 74 F3
Nová Baňa [SK] 64 B4
Nová Bystřice [CZ] 62 D2
Novacella / Neustift [I] 72 D2
Novachene [BG] 150 G4
Novaci [MK] 128 E3
Nova Crnja [YU] 76 F6
Novae Palesse [BY] 204 B7
Novafeltria [I] 110 H5
Nova Gorica [SLO] 72 H5
Nova Gradiška [HR] 154 C1
Novaja Kakhovka [UA] 206 G4
Novaja Ladoga [RUS] 204 D1
Novajidrány [H] 64 G4
Nova Kassaba [BIH] 154 E4
Nováky [SK] 64 B3
Novalesa, Abbazia di- [I] 70 C5
Nova Levante / Welschnofen [I] 72 D3
Novalja [HR] 112 F4
Nova Odesa [UA] 206 F4
Nová Paka [CZ] 48 H2
Nova Pazova [YU] 154 G2
Novara [I] 70 F5
Novara di Sicilia [I] 124 A7
Novate Mezzola [I] 70 H3
Nova Topola [BIH] 154 C2
Nova Varoš [YU] 150 A3
Novaya Zhizn' [RUS] 200 G2
Nova Zagora [BG] 148 D5
Nové Hrady [CZ] 62 C3
Novelda [E] 104 D2
Novellara [I] 110 E2
Nové Město nad Metují [CZ] 50 B3
Nové Mesto nad Váhom [SK] 64 A3
Nové Město na Moravě [CZ] 50 B5
Noventa Vicentina [I] 110 G1
Novés [E] 88 E6
Noves [F] 106 G3
Nové Sady [SK] 64 A4
Nové Strašecí [CZ] 48 E3
Nové Zámky [SK] 64 B5
Novgorodka [RUS] 200 H4
Novhorodka [UA] 206 F3
Novhorod-Siverskyi [UA] 204 D6
Novi Bečej [YU] 76 E6
Novi di Módena [I] 110 E2
Novi Dojran [MK] 128 H3
Novigrad [HR] 112 G5
Novigrad [HR] 112 D1
Novigrad Podravski [HR] 74 G5
Novi Han [BG] 150 G5
Novi Kazarci [YU] 76 F5
Novi Kneževac [YU] 76 E5
Novi Krichim [BG] 148 B6
Novi Ligure [I] 110 A2
Novi Marof [HR] 74 F5
Novion-Porcien [F] 28 H6
Novi Pazar [BG] 148 E2
Novi Pazar [YU] 150 B4
Novi Sad [YU] 154 F1
Novi Senkovac [HR] 74 H6
Novi Travnik [BIH] 154 C4
Novi Vinodolski [HR] 112 F2
Novoarkhanhel's'k [UA] 206 E3
Novo Brdo [YU] 150 C5
Novohrad-Volyns'kyi [UA] 206 D2
Novo mesto [SLO] 74 D6
Novo Miloševo [YU] 76 E6
Novomoskovsk [RUS] 204 F5
Novomoskovs'k [UA] 206 G3
Novorzhev [RUS] 200 H4
Novoselë [AL] 128 A5
Novoselets [BG] 148 D5
Novo Selo [BG] 150 E1
Novo Selo [BG] 148 D2
Novo Selo [BG] 148 B4
Novo Selo [MK] 128 H2
Novosel'ye [RUS] 200 H3
Novosil' [RUS] 204 F6
Novosokol'niki [RUS] 204 C4
Novoukraïnka [UA] 206 F3
Novoukraïnka [UA] 52 H2
Novovolyns'k [UA] 52 H1
Novovorontsovka [UA] 206 G4
Novo Zvečevo [HR] 154 C1
Novozybkov [RUS] 204 D6
Novska [HR] 154 B1
Nový Bohumín [CZ] 50 F4
Nový Bor [CZ] 48 G2
Nový Bydžov [CZ] 48 H3
Nový Hrad [CZ] 50 C6
Novyi Buh [UA] 206 F4
Novyi Bykiv [UA] 206 F2
Nový Jičín [CZ] 50 E5
Nový Knín [CZ] 48 F4
Nowa Brzeźnica [PL] 36 G6
Nowa Cerekwia [PL] 50 E4
Nowa Dęba [PL] 52 D2
Nowa Karczma [PL] 22 D3
Nowa Karczma [PL] 22 F2
Nowa Ruda [PL] 50 C2
Nowa Sarzyna [PL] 52 E3
Nowa Słupia [PL] 52 C1
Nowa Sól [PL] 36 A4
Nowe [PL] 22 E4
Nowe Brzesko [PL] 52 B3
Nowe Czarnowo [PL] 20 F6
Nowe Miasteczko [PL] 36 A4
Nowe Miasto Lubawskie [PL] 22 F5
Nowe Miasto nad Pilicą [PL] 38 B5
Nowe Miasto nad Warta [PL] 36 D3
Nowe Polichno [PL] 34 H2
Nowe Skalmierzyce [PL] 36 E4
Nowe Warpno [PL] 20 E4
Nowica [PL] 22 F3
Nowogard [PL] 20 G4
Nowogród [PL] 24 C5
Nowogród Bobrzański [PL] 34 H4
Nowogrodziec [PL] 34 H6
Nowosielec [PL] 52 E2
Nowowola [PL] 24 F4
Nowy Duninów [PL] 36 G2
Nowy Dwór [PL] 24 F4
Nowy Dwór Gdański [PL] 22 E3
Nowy Dwór Mazowiecki [PL] 38 B2
Nowy Korczyn [PL] 52 C3
Nowy Majdan [PL] 52 F2
Nowy Sącz [PL] 52 C5
Nowy Staw [PL] 22 E3
Nowy Targ [PL] 52 A5
Nowy Tomyśl [PL] 36 B3
Nowy Wieś [PL] 24 C6
Nowy Wiśnicz [PL] 52 B4
Nowy Zmigród [PL] 52 D5
Noyant [F] 42 B6
Noyers [F] 56 F2
Noyers-sur-Jabron [F] 108 C3
Noyon [F] 28 F6
Nozay [F] 40 F5
Nozeroy [F] 58 B6
N. S. de Angosto [E] 82 G5
N. S. de Chilla [E] 88 C5
N. S. de Cortés [E] 96 H5
N. S. de Hontanares [E] 88 G3
N. S. de la Bienvenida [E] 90 B6
N. S. de la Cabeza [E] 102 G3
N. S. de la Estrella [E] 102 F1
N. S. del Remedio [E] 98 D4
N.S. del Valle [E] 82 C5
N. Senhora da Azinheira [P] 80 E3
N. Senhora d'Abadia [P] 78 B6
N. Senhora da Graça [P] 80 D3
N. Senhora dos Remédios [P] 80 D4
N. Señora de Irache [E] 84 A4
Nubledo [E] 78 H3
Nuestra Señora de la Vega [E] 98 E2
Nuestra Señora del Rocío [E] 94 F6
Nueva-Carteya [E] 102 C2
Nuévalos [E] 90 C4
Nuevo Baztán [E] 88 G6
Nuijamaa [FIN] 178 E2
Nuits-St-Georges [F] 56 G4
Nules [E] 98 F4
Nulvi [I] 118 C3
Numana [I] 116 C1
Numancia [E] 90 B2
Nummela [FIN] 176 G4
Nummi [FIN] 176 F4
Nummijärvi [FIN] 186 C4
Nummikoski [FIN] 186 C5
Nuneaton [GB] 14 D1
Nunnanen [FIN] 192 H4
Nunnanlahti [FIN] 188 E1
Nuño Gómez [E] 88 D6
Nunsdorf [D] 34 E3
Nunspeet [NL] 16 F4
Nuojua [FIN] 198 E4
Nuorgam [FIN] 196 D2
Nuoro [I] 118 D4
Nur [PL] 38 D1
Nuragus [I] 118 C5
Nurallao [I] 118 D5
Nuraminis [I] 118 C6
Nuraxi, Nuraghe su- [I] 118 C6
Nürburg [D] 30 G6
Nürburgring [D] 30 G6
Núria [F] 92 E2
Nurmaa [FIN] 178 C1
Nurmes [FIN] 198 G6
Nurmijärvi [FIN] 176 H4
Nurmijärvi [FIN] 198 G6
Nurmo [FIN] 186 C3
Nurmuiža [LV] 200 C5
Nürnberg [D] 46 G5
Nurri [I] 118 D6
Nürtingen [D] 58 H1
Nus [I] 70 D4
Nusret [TR] 144 D1
Nuštar [HR] 154 E1
Nutheim [N] 164 F2
Nuttlar [D] 32 D5
Nuupas [FIN] 198 D2
Nuvsvåg [N] 192 F1
N. Vānga [S] 166 E6
N. Vi [S] 162 E2
Nyåker [S] 190 H6
Nyárlőrinc [H] 76 E3
Nyasvizh [BY] 204 A4
Nybergsund [N] 172 D2
Nyborg [DK] 156 E3
Nybro [S] 162 F5
Nyby [DK] 156 G4
Nydrí [GR] 132 D4
Nye [S] 162 E3
Nyékládháza [H] 64 F5
Nyerges-Ujfalu [H] 64 B6
Nyhammar [S] 172 H5
Nyhem [S] 184 C3
Nyírábrány [H] 64 H6
Nyíracsád [H] 64 H6
Nyíradony [H] 64 H5
Nyírbátor [H] 206 B3
Nyírbogát [H] 64 H5
Nyíregyháza [H] 64 H5
Nyírtelek [H] 64 G5
Nyírtura [H] 64 H5
Nykarleby / Uusikaarlepyy [FIN] 186 C1
Nykøbing [DK] 20 B1
Nykøbing [DK] 156 F2
Nykøbing [DK] 160 C4
Nyköping [S] 168 C5
Nykrogen [S] 168 B1
Nykroppa [S] 166 G2
Nykvarn [S] 168 D3
Nyland [S] 184 F3
Nymburk [CZ] 48 G3
Nymfaía [GR] 130 F2
Nymindegab [DK] 156 A1
Nynäshamn [S] 168 D4
Nyneset [N] 190 D5
Nyon [CH] 70 B1
Nyons [F] 106 H2
Nýrsko [CZ] 48 D6
Nyrud [N] 196 E4
Nysa [PL] 50 D2
Nysa [TR] 144 E5
Nysäter [S] 166 E3
Nyskoga [S] 172 E4
Nyskolla [N] 172 B2
Nyslott / Savonlinna [FIN] 188 E5
Nystad / Uusikaupunki [FIN] 176 C3
Nysted [DK] 20 B1
Nystova [N] 170 E2
Nytrøa [N] 182 B4
Nyzhankovychi [UA] 52 F4
Nyzhnie Sirahozy [UA] 206 G4

O

Ožbalt [SLO] 74 D3
Ózd [H] 64 E4
Ožd'any [SK] 64 D4
Ozerki [RUS] 178 F4
Ozersk [RUS] 24 C2
Ozerskoye [RUS] 178 F2
Ozieri [I] 118 D3
Ozimek [PL] 50 E2
Ozora [H] 76 B3
Ozorków [PL] 36 G4

P

Pääjärvi [FIN] 186 F3
Paakkila [FIN] 188 E2
Paatinen [FIN] 176 D4
Paavola [FIN] 198 D4
Pabianice [PL] 36 G4
Pabiarže [LT] 202 G5
Pabradė [LT] 202 G5
Paceco [I] 126 B2
Pachiá Ámmos [GR] 140 G5
Pachino [I] 126 G6
Paços de Ferreira [P] 80 C4
Pacov [CZ] 48 G5
Pacsa [H] 74 G3
Pacyna [PL] 36 H3
Pacy-sur-Eure [F] 42 E3
Paczków [PL] 50 C3
Padarosk [BY] 24 H6
Padasjoki [FIN] 176 H1
Padborg [DK] 156 C4
Padej [YU] 76 E5
Paderborn [D] 32 E4
Paderne [P] 94 C5
Padiham [GB] 10 E3
Padina [YU] 154 H2
Padirac, Gouffre de- [F] 66 H4
Padjene [HR] 112 H5
Padova [I] 110 G1
Padrenda [E] 78 C5
Padrógão Grande [P] 86 E3
Padrón [E] 78 B3
Padru [I] 118 E3
Padstow [GB] 12 C4
Padul [E] 102 E4
Padula [I] 120 G4
Paesana [I] 108 F2
Paestum [I] 120 F4
Paestum [I] 120 F4
Pag [HR] 112 F4
Pagani [I] 120 E3
Pagasaí [GR] 132 H2
Pagėgiai [LT] 202 D5
Pagny [F] 44 E4
Páhi [H] 76 D3
Pahiá [GR] 138 G5
Pahranichny [BY] 24 G5
Paianía [GR] 134 C6
Paide [EST] 200 E2
Paignton [GB] 12 E5
Paijärvi [FIN] 178 D3
Pailhès [F] 84 H4
Paimboeuf [F] 40 E6
Paimio / Pemar [FIN] 176 E4
Paimpol [F] 26 A3
Paisley [GB] 8 D3
Pajala [S] 192 G6
Pájara [E] 100 E5
Pajares, Puerto de- [E] 78 H4
Pajęczno [PL] 36 F6
Pajukoski [FIN] 198 F6
Pakość [PL] 36 E1
Pakoštane [HR] 112 G5
Pakosze [PL] 22 G3
Pakrac [HR] 154 B1
Pakruojis [LT] 202 F3
Paks [H] 76 C3
Palacios del Sil [E] 78 F4
Palacios de Sanabria [E] 80 G3
Paladru [F] 68 H4
Pala e Rughes, Nuraghe- [I] 118 D4
Palafrugell [E] 92 G3
Palagianello [I] 122 E4
Palagiano [I] 122 E4
Palagonia [I] 126 F4
Palaía Epídavros [GR] 136 F2
Palaiá Messíni [GR] 136 D3
Palaiochóra [GR] 140 B5
Palaiochóri [GR] 130 C5
Palaiochóri [GR] 132 E2
Palaiochóri [GR] 136 E3
Palaiochóri [GR] 132 D3
Palaió Gynaikókastro [GR] 128 H3
Palaiokastritsa [GR] 132 A2
Palaiókastro [GR] 140 H4
Palaiomonastíri [GR] 132 E2
Palaiópoli [GR] 138 D1
Palaiópoli [GR] 130 G4
Palaiópyrgos [GR] 132 F5
Palaiópyrgos [GR] 132 F2
Pálairos [GR] 132 D4
Palaiseau [F] 42 F4
Palamás [GR] 132 F2
Palamós [E] 92 G3
Palamut [TR] 144 D3
Palanga [LT] 202 D4
Palas de Rei [E] 78 D3
Palasi [EST] 200 F1
Palatitsa [GR] 128 G5
Palatítsia [GR] 128 G5
Palatna [YU] 150 C4
Palau [I] 118 E2
Palavas-les-Flots [F] 106 F4
Palazzo Adriano [I] 126 C3
Palazzolo Acréide [I] 126 G5
Palazzolo sull'Oglio [I] 70 H4
Palazzo San Gervasio [I] 120 H3
Paldiski [EST] 200 D1
Pale [BIH] 152 D1
Pāle [LV] 200 E4
Palena [I] 116 D5
Palencia [E] 82 C6
Paleócastro [GR] 130 B3
Palermo [AL] 128 B6
Palermo [I] 126 C2
Palestrina [I] 116 B5
Pálháza [H] 64 G3
Palić [YU] 76 D5
Palinuro [I] 120 G5
Paliouriá [GR] 132 E1
Palioúrion [GR] 130 C6
Paliseul [B] 44 D1
Paljakka [FIN] 198 F1
Paljakka [FIN] 198 F4
Pälkäne [FIN] 176 G2
Palkino [RUS] 200 G4
Pallarés [E] 94 G4
Pallaruelo de Monegros [E] 90 F4
Pallasgreen [IRL] 4 D3
Pallastunturi [FIN] 192 H4
Palliní [GR] 134 C6
Palma del Río [E] 102 B1
Palma de Mallorca [E] 104 E5
Palma di Montechiaro [I] 126 D4
Palmadula [I] 118 B3
Palma Nova [E] 104 D5
Palmanova [I] 72 G5
Palmela [P] 86 B6
Palmi [I] 124 C7
Palo del Colle [I] 122 D2
Páloi [GR] 142 C4
Palojärvi [FIN] 192 G4
Palojärvi [FIN] 196 C8
Palojoensuu [FIN] 192 G4
Palokastër [AL] 128 C6
Palokki [FIN] 188 E3
Palomaa [FIN] 196 D4
Palomäki [FIN] 198 F6
Palomares [E] 104 A5
Palomares del Campo [E] 98 A2
Palomas [E] 94 H2
Palombara Sabina [I] 116 B5
Palonurmi [FIN] 188 D1
Palos de la Frontera [E] 94 E6
Palota [SK] 52 E6
Pålsboda [S] 166 H4
Pålsträsk [S] 198 A3
Paltamo [FIN] 198 F4
Paltaniemi [FIN] 198 E5
Paluzza [I] 72 G3
Pämark / Pomarkku [FIN] 176 D1
Pamhagen [A] 62 G6
Pamiątkowo [PL] 36 C2
Pamiers [F] 106 A4
Pamiętowo [PL] 22 C5
Pamma [EST] 200 C3
Pampilhosa da Serra [P] 86 E2
Pamplona / Iruña [E] 84 B4
Pamporovo [BG] 130 E1
Pamucak [TR] 144 D5
Pamukçu [TR] 144 D1
Pamukkale [TR] 144 G5
Pamukova [TR] 146 G3
Pamukyazı [TR] 144 D5
Panagiá [GR] 134 C5
Panagiá [GR] 128 F6
Panagiá [GR] 140 F5
Panagiá [GR] 130 E4
Panagyurishte [BG] 148 A5
Panaitólio [GR] 132 E5
Panajë [AL] 128 A5
Panassac [F] 84 G3
Panayır [TR] 144 E2
Pančevo [YU] 154 H2
Pancharevo [BG] 150 F5
Pancorbo, Garganta de- [E] 82 F5
Pancorvo [E] 82 F5
Pandėlys [LT] 200 E6
Pandino [I] 70 G5
Pandrup [DK] 160 D3
Panenský Týnec [CZ] 48 F3
Panes [E] 82 D3
Panevėžys [LT] 202 F4
Panicale [I] 114 H2
Paniza [E] 90 D4
Paniza, Puerto de- [E] 90 D5
Panjavaara [FIN] 198 F6
Pankakoski [FIN] 198 G6
Pankala [FIN] 198 C5
Panki [PL] 50 F1
Pannonhalma [H] 62 H6
Pannonhalma [H] 62 H6
Panoias [P] 80 D4
Panormítis [GR] 142 D4
Pánormos [GR] 138 E1
Pánormos [GR] 140 D4
Pantalica, Necropoli di- [I] 126 G4
Pantánassa [GR] 136 F5
Päntäne [FIN] 186 B4
Pantelej [MK] 128 G1
Pantelej, Manastir- [MK] 128 G1
Pantelleria [I] 126 A4
Pantón [E] 78 D4
Pantów [PL] 52 C1
Panxón [E] 78 B5
Páola [I] 124 D4
Pápa [H] 74 H1
Papadiánika [GR] 136 F5
Paparzyn [PL] 22 E5
Papasidero [I] 120 H6
Papenburg [D] 18 B5
Papile [LT] 200 C6
Papilys [LT] 200 E6
Papowo Biskupie [PL] 22 E5
Pappenheim [D] 60 D2
Parábita [I] 122 G5
Paraćin [YU] 150 C2
Parád [H] 64 E5
Parada del Sil [E] 78 D5
Paradas [E] 100 H2
Paradeísi [GR] 142 E4
Paradeísia [GR] 136 D3
Parádeisos [GR] 130 E3
Paradela [P] 78 C6
Paradies [D] 60 B6
Paradisgård [S] 166 F2
Paradyż [PL] 38 A5
Parainen / Pargas [FIN] 176 D5
Parakka [S] 192 F5
Parákoila [GR] 134 G2
Paralía [GR] 136 F4
Paralía [GR] 132 F6
Paralía [GR] 128 G5
Paralía Akrátas [GR] 132 G6
Paralía Iríon [GR] 136 F2
Paralía Kýmis [GR] 134 C4
Paralía Platánou [GR] 132 G6
Paralía Skotínas [GR] 128 H6
Paralío Ástros [GR] 136 E3
Páramo del Sil [E] 78 F4
Paramythí [GR] 132 C2
Paranésti [GR] 130 D2
Parantala [FIN] 186 F3
Parapótamos [GR] 132 C2
Parassapuszta [H] 64 C5
Parata, Tour de la- [F] 114 A5
Paravóla [GR] 132 E5
Paray-le-Monial [F] 56 E6
Parcent [E] 104 F1
Parchim [D] 20 B5
Parczew [PL] 38 E4
Pardubice [CZ] 50 A4
Parechcha [RUS] 200 G1
Paredes [E] 78 D5
Paredes [P] 80 C4
Paredes de Coura [P] 78 B5
Paredes de Nava [E] 82 C6
Paredes de Sigüenza [E] 90 A4
Parentis-en-Born [F] 66 B4
Parey [D] 34 C2
Párga [GR] 132 C3
Pargas / Parainen [FIN] 176 D5
Pargny-sur-Saulx [F] 44 C4
Pargolovo [RUS] 178 H4
Parikkala [FIN] 188 F5
Paris [F] 42 F3
Parkalompolo [S] 192 G5
Parkano [FIN] 186 D5
Parkkila [FIN] 198 D5
Parkkima [FIN] 198 D6
Parknasilla [IRL] 4 B4
Parkumäki [FIN] 188 E5
Parłówko [PL] 20 F4
Parma [I] 110 D2
Pärnu [EST] 200 D3
Pärnu-Jaagupi [EST] 200 D2
Páros [GR] 138 E3
Paroveia [LT] 200 E6
Parpan [CH] 70 H1
Parsberg [D] 46 H6
Partakko [FIN] 196 D4
Partakoski [FIN] 178 D1
Partanna [I] 126 B3
Partenen [A] 72 B2
Parthenay [F] 54 D3
Parthéni [GR] 136 E2
Parthéni [GR] 142 B2
Partille [S] 160 H2
Partinello [F] 114 A3
Partinico [I] 126 C2
Partizani [YU] 150 B1
Partizánske [SK] 64 B3
Partizanske Vode [YU] 150 A3
Partry [IRL] 2 C4
Päryd [S] 162 F5
Pasaia [E] 84 B2
Pasá Limáni [GR] 134 G5
Paşayiğit [TR] 146 B3
Paşcani [RO] 206 D4
Pas de la Casa [AND] 84 H6
Pas-en-Artois [F] 28 E4
Pasewalk [D] 20 E5
Pasi [FIN] 178 C2
Pasiecznik [PL] 50 A1
Pasiene [LV] 200 G5
Påskallavik [S] 162 G4
Pasłęk [PL] 22 F3
Pašman [HR] 112 G5
Paspolo [TR] 146 C1
Passage East [IRL] 4 E5
Passage West [IRL] 4 D5
Passandra [TR] 144 B2
Passau [D] 60 H3
Passignano sul Trasimeno [I] 114 H2
Pastavy [BY] 202 H4
Pastena, Grotte di- [I] 120 C1
Pastor [E] 78 C3
Pastoriza [E] 78 E2
Pastrana [E] 88 H6
Pasvalys [LT] 200 E6
Pasym [PL] 22 H4
Pásztó [H] 64 D5
Pasztowa Wola [PL] 38 C6
Patara [TR] 142 G4
Patay [F] 42 E5
Patergassen [A] 74 A3
Paterna [E] 98 E4
Paterna del Madera [E] 96 H6
Paterna de Rivera [E] 100 G4
Paternion [A] 72 H3
Paternò [I] 126 G3
Paternopoli [I] 120 F3
Patersdorf [D] 60 G2
Patio [RUS] 178 D3
Patiópoulo [GR] 132 E3
Patitíri [GR] 134 C3
Pátmos [GR] 138 H2
Pątnów [PL] 36 F6
Patoniemi [FIN] 196 F8
Patoniva [FIN] 196 D3
Patos [AL] 128 B4
Pátra [GR] 132 F6
Patreksfjörður [IS] 194 B2
Patrickswell [IRL] 4 D3
Patsch [A] 72 D1
Pattada [I] 118 D3
Pattensen [D] 32 F2
Patterdale [GB] 10 D1
Patti [I] 124 A7
Pattijoki [FIN] 198 D4
Páty [H] 64 C6
Pau [F] 84 E3
Pauillac [F] 66 C2
Paularo [I] 72 G3
Paulhaguet [F] 68 D4
Paulilatino [I] 118 C5
Paulinzella [D] 46 G1
Păuliș [RO] 76 H4
Paulistrom [S] 162 F3
Pauls-Kirche [D] 44 G2
Paulstown [IRL] 4 F4
Paupys [LT] 202 E5
Pauträsk [S] 190 G4
Pavel Banya [BG] 148 C5
Pavia [I] 70 G6
Pavia [P] 86 D5
Pavia, Certosa di- [I] 70 G5
Pavilly [F] 28 B5
Pāvilosta [LV] 200 B5
Pávliani [GR] 132 G4
Pavlice [CZ] 62 E2
Pavlikeni [BG] 148 C3
Pavlograd [UA] 206 H3
Pávlos [GR] 134 A5
Pavlovsk [RUS] 178 H5
Pavullo nel Frignano [I] 110 E4
Pavy [RUS] 200 H3
Pawłowiczki [PL] 50 E3
Pawonków [PL] 50 F2
Paxoí [GR] 132 C3
Payerne [CH] 58 C6
Paymogo [E] 94 E4
Payrac [F] 66 G4
Pazardzhik [BG] 148 A6
Pazarköy [TR] 146 C6
Pazaryeri [TR] 146 G5
Pazin [HR] 112 D2
Pazo de Oca [E] 78 C3
Pchelino [RUS] 178 F3
Peal de Becerro [E] 102 F2
Péaule [F] 40 E5
Peć [YU] 150 B5
Pečane [HR] 112 H3
Peccioli [I] 110 E6
Pechenga [RUS] 196 F3
Pechina [E] 102 G5
Pech-Merle, Grotte du- [F] 66 G5
Pecica [RO] 76 G4
Pecineaga [RO] 148 G1
Pecka [YU] 154 F4
Peckelsheim [D] 32 E4
Pecorini a Mare [I] 124 A5
Pečory [RUS] 200 G3
Pec pod Sněžkou [CZ] 50 A2
Pécs [H] 76 B5
Pécsvárad [H] 76 B5
Pedaso [I] 116 D2
Pederobba [I] 72 E5
Pedersöre [FIN] 186 C1
Pédi [GR] 142 D4
Pedráces / Pedratsches [I] 72 E3
Pedrafita do Cebreiro, Puerto- [E] 78 E4
Pedralba [E] 98 E4
Pedratsches / Pedráces [I] 72 E3
Pedraza [E] 88 G3
Pedreguer [E] 104 F1
Pedreira [E] 78 D2
Pedrera [E] 96 F3
Pedrizas, Puerto de las- [E] 102 C4
Pedro Abad [E] 102 D1
Pedro Andrés [E] 102 H2
Pedro Bernardo [E] 88 D5
Pedrógão [P] 86 C2
Pedrógão [P] 94 E3
Pedro Martínez [E] 102 F3
Pedro Muñoz [E] 96 G3
Pedrosillo el Ralo [E] 88 C3
Peebles [GB] 8 E4
Peel [GBM] 10 B1
Peenemünde [D] 20 E3
Peera [FIN] 192 F3
Péfkos [GR] 140 F5
Péfkos [GR] 128 D5
Pega [P] 86 G2
Pegau [D] 34 C6
Peggau [A] 74 D2
Pegli [I] 110 A3
Pegnitz [D] 46 H4
Pego [E] 104 F1
Pegões [P] 86 C6
Peguera [E] 104 D5
Pehčevo [MK] 128 H1
Pehlivanköy [TR] 146 B2
Peine [D] 32 G2
Peïra-Cava [F] 108 F4
Peiraías [GR] 134 C6
Peiss [D] 60 E5
Peissenberg [D] 60 D5
Peiting [D] 60 D5
Peitz [D] 34 F4
Pejo [I] 72 C3
Pekkala [FIN] 196 D8
Pelasgía [GR] 132 H4
Pelczyce [PL] 20 G6
Pelejaneta / La Pelechaneta [E] 98 F3
Pélekas [GR] 132 B2
Peleshi [RUS] 200 G2
Peletá [GR] 136 F4
Pelhřimov [CZ] 48 H5
Peliciego, Cueva de- [E] 104 C1
Pelkosenniemi [FIN] 196 E7
Pélla [GR] 128 G4
Pellaro [I] 124 C7
Pellegrino Parmense [I] 110 C2
Pellegrue [F] 66 E4
Pellesmäki [FIN] 188 C2
Pellinge / Pellinki [FIN] 178 B5
Pellinki / Pellinge [FIN] 178 B5
Pello [FIN] 196 C7
Pello [S] 196 C7
Pellosniemi [FIN] 178 C1
Pelovo [BG] 148 A3
Pelplin [PL] 22 E4
Peltosalmi [FIN] 198 E6
Peltovuoma [FIN] 192 H4
Pélussin [F] 68 F3
Pemaninos [TR] 146 D5
Pemar / Paimio [FIN] 176 E4
Pembroke [GB] 12 D2
Peñacerrada [E] 82 G5
Penacova [P] 86 E2
Peña Escrita, Cuevas de- [E] 96 D5
Peñafiel [E] 88 F2
Penafiel [P] 80 C4
Peñaflor [E] 102 B1
Penaguião [P] 80 D4
Peñalén [E] 90 B6
Peñalsordo [E] 96 C4
Penalva do Castelo [P] 80 D6
Penamacor [P] 86 G3
Peñaranda de Bracamonte [E] 88 D3
Peñaranda de Duero [E] 88 H2
Peñarroya, Castillo de- [E] 96 G4
Peñarroya-Pueblonuevo [E] 96 B5
Penarth [GB] 12 F3
Peñascosa [E] 96 H6
Peñas de San Pedro [E] 98 B6
Peñausende [E] 80 H5
Penc [H] 64 C5
Pendálofo [GR] 132 E5
Pendik [TR] 146 F3
Pendine [GB] 12 D2
Pendus, Rocher des- [F] 68 B4
Penedono [P] 80 E5
Penela [P] 86 D2
Penestin [F] 40 E5
Peniche [P] 86 B3
Penicuik [GB] 8 E3
Peñíscola / Peníscola [E] 98 G2
Peníscola / Peñíscola [E] 98 G2
Penkum [D] 20 E5
Penmarch, Pointe de- [F] 40 B3
Pennabilli [I] 110 H5
Penne [I] 116 D4
Penningby [S] 168 E2
Penrith [GB] 8 E6
Penryn [GB] 12 C5
Pentagioí [GR] 132 F5
Pentálofo [GR] 128 E6
Pénte Vrýses [GR] 130 B4
Pentrez-Plage [F] 40 B2
Penzance [GB] 12 B5
Penzberg [D] 60 D5
Penzlin [D] 20 D5
Pępowo [PL] 36 C4
Peqin [AL] 128 B3
Pér [H] 62 H6
Perachóra [GR] 134 A6
Perafita [P] 80 B3
Peraía [GR] 128 H5
Perälä [FIN] 186 B4
Peraleda del Zaucejo [E] 96 B4
Peralejos de las Truchas [E] 90 C6
Perales del Alfambra [E] 98 E1
Peralta [E] 84 B5
Pérama [GR] 140 D4
Pérama [GR] 132 D2
Peranka [FIN] 198 F3
Perä-Posio [FIN] 196 E8
Peräseinäjoki [FIN] 186 C4
Perast [YU] 152 D4
Perchauer Sattel [A] 74 B2
Perchtoldsdorf [A] 62 F5
Percy [F] 26 D4
Perdasdefogu [I] 118 D6
Perdifumo [I] 120 F5
Perdigão [P] 86 E4
Pérdika [GR] 132 D2
Pérdika [GR] 132 G3
Pérdika [GR] 132 C3
Pereda de Ancares [E] 78 F4
Père de Montfort, Grotte du- [F] 54 C3
Peredo [P] 80 F4
Pereiaslav-Khmel'nyts'kyi [UA] 206 F2
Pereiro [P] 94 D5
Pereruela [E] 80 H5
Pereshchepyne [UA] 206 H3
Pereslavl' Zalesskiy [RUS] 204 F3
Peretu [RO] 148 B1
Perevolok [RUS] 200 G1
Perfugas [I] 118 C3
Perg [A] 62 C4
Pérgine Valsugana [I] 72 D4
Pergola [I] 112 B6
Perho [FIN] 186 E2
Periam [RO] 76 F5
Periana [E] 102 C4
Périers [F] 26 D3
Périgueux [F] 66 F3
Periš [YU] 150 E3
Perişoru [RO] 150 F1
Perissa [GR] 138 F5
Peristerá [GR] 130 B4
Perivóli [GR] 132 D1
Perjen Tunnel [A] 72 C1
Perkáta [H] 76 C2
Perkpolder [NL] 28 H1
Perle [LV] 200 F5
Perleberg [D] 20 B6
Perlez [YU] 154 G1
Perly [PL] 24 C2
Përmet [AL] 128 C6
Pernacha de Cima [P] 86 D5
Pernaja / Pernå [FIN] 178 B4
Pernaja-Pernå [FIN] 178 B4
Pernat [HR] 112 E2
Pernek [SK] 62 G4
Pernes [F] 106 H3
Pernes [P] 86 C4
Pernes-les-Fontaines [F] 106 H3
Pernik [BG] 150 F5
Perniö / Bjärnå [FIN] 176 F5
Pernitz [A] 62 E5
Pernštejn [CZ] 50 B5
Pernu [FIN] 196 E8
Pérolles, Pont de- [CH] 58 D6
Péronne [F] 28 F5
Perosa Argentina [I] 70 C6
Pérouges [F] 68 G2
Perpignan [F] 92 G1
Perros-Guirec [F] 40 D1
Persberg [S] 166 G2
Persenbeug [A] 62 D4
Pershagen [S] 168 D3
Pershore [GB] 12 H2
Persön [S] 198 B3
Perstorp [S] 158 C1
Perth [GB] 8 E2
Pertisau [A] 60 E6
Pertoča [SLO] 74 E3
Pertosa, Grotta di- [I] 120 G4
Pertoúli [GR] 132 E2
Pertteli [FIN] 176 F4
Pertuis [F] 108 B4
Pertunmaa [FIN] 178 B1
Pertusa [E] 90 G3
Perúgia [I] 116 A2
Perushtica [BG] 148 B6
Perušić [HR] 112 G3
Péruwelz [B] 28 G3
Pervomais'k [UA] 206 E3
Pervomajskoje [RUS] 178 G3
Pesadas de Burgos [E] 82 F5
Pesados [TR] 142 D2
Pésaro [I] 112 B5
Pescaglia [I] 110 D5
Pescara [I] 116 D4
Pescasseroli [I] 116 C6
Péschici [I] 116 H5
Peschiera del Garda [I] 72 B6
Pescia [I] 110 E5
Pescina [I] 116 C5
Pescocostanzo [I] 116 D5
Pescolanciano [I] 116 D6
Pescopagano [I] 120 G3
Peshkëpija [AL] 128 B5
Peshkopi [AL] 128 C2
Peshtera [BG] 148 A6
Pesio, Certosa di- [I] 108 F3
Pesiökylä [FIN] 198 F3
Pesmes [F] 56 H4
Pesocani [MK] 128 D3
Peso da Régua [P] 80 D4
Pesoz [E] 78 F3
Pesqueza [E] 86 G4
Pessalompolo [FIN] 196 C8
Pessáni [GR] 130 G2
Pessin [D] 34 D2
Peštani [MK] 128 D4
Pestovo [RUS] 204 E2
Pešurići [BIH] 152 E1
Peta [P] 86 C5
Petäiskylä [FIN] 198 G5
Petäjävesi [FIN] 186 F4
Petalídi [GR] 136 C4
Petaloúdes [GR] 142 E4
Pétange [L] 44 E3
Peteranec [HR] 74 G4
Peterborough [GB] 14 E2
Peterhead [GB] 6 G5
Peterlee [GB] 10 F1
Petersburg [A] 72 C1
Petersdorf [D] 18 H2
Petersdorf [D] 20 B3
Petersfield [GB] 14 D5
Petershagen [D] 32 E2
Pétervására [H] 64 E5
Pethelinós [GR] 130 C3
Petikträsk [S] 190 H4
Petilia Policastro [I] 124 E5
Petkula [FIN] 196 D6
Petkus [D] 34 E3
Petlovača [YU] 154 F3
Petoúsi [GR] 132 C2
Petra [E] 104 E5
Pétra [GR] 128 G6
Pétra [GR] 134 G2
Petralia Soprana [I] 126 E3
Petrálona [GR] 130 B5
Petraná [GR] 128 F5
Petrelë [AL] 128 B3
Petrella Tifernina [I] 116 E6
Petrer [E] 104 D2
Petreto-Bicchisano [F] 114 B5
Petrich [BG] 130 B2
Petrila [RO] 206 B5
Petrinja [HR] 154 A1
Petrodvorets [RUS] 178 G5
Pétrola [E] 98 C6
Petronell-Carnuntum [A] 62 G5
Petroșani [RO] 206 B5
Petrosino [I] 126 B3
Petrotá [GR] 146 A2
Petroúsa [GR] 130 C2
Petrovac [YU] 152 E5
Petrovac [YU] 150 C1
Petrovaradin [YU] 154 F1
Petrove [UA] 206 G3
Petrovice [CZ] 48 F5
Petrovići [BIH] 152 B2
Petřvald [CZ] 50 E4
Petsákoi [GR] 132 F6
Petsikko [FIN] 196 D3
Pettenbach [A] 62 B5
Pettigo [GB] 2 E3
Peuerbach [A] 62 A4
Peura [FIN] 196 C8
Peurasuvanto [FIN] 196 D6
Pevensey [GB] 14 E6
Peyrat-le-Chateaux [F] 66 H1
Peyrehorade [F] 84 D2
Peyrolles [F] 108 B4
Peyruis [F] 108 C3
Pézenas [F] 106 E4
Pezinok [SK] 62 G4
Pezoúla [GR] 130 E3
Pezuela de las Torres [E] 88 G6
Pfaffendorf [D] 46 G3
Pfaffenhausen [D] 60 C4
Pfaffenhofen [D] 60 E3
Pfäffikon [CH] 58 G5
Pfäffikon [CH] 58 G5
Pfafflar [A] 72 C1
Pfänder Tunnel [CH] 60 B6
Pfarrkirchen [D] 60 G3
Pfatter [D] 60 F2
Pfeffenhausen [D] 60 F3
Pforzheim [D] 46 C6
Pfreimd [D] 48 C5
Pfronten [D] 60 C6
Pfullendorf [D] 58 H3
Pfullingen [D] 58 H2
Pfundres / Fundres [I] 72 E2
Pfunds [A] 72 C2
Pfungstadt [D] 46 C4
Phalsbourg [F] 44 G5
Philippeville [B] 30 C6
Philippsreut [D] 62 A2
Philippsthal [D] 32 F6
Phokaia [TR] 144 B3
Phönike [AL] 132 B1
Piacenza [I] 70 H6
Piádena [I] 110 D1
Piaggine [I] 120 G4
Piana [F] 114 A4
Piana Crixia [I] 108 H2
Piana degli Albanesi [I] 126 C2
Pian Castagna [I] 108 H2
Pianella [I] 114 G1
Pianello Val Tidone [I] 70 G6
Piani Resinelli [I] 70 G4
Pianoro [I] 110 F4
Pianotolli-Caldarello [F] 114 B6
Pias [P] 94 E2
Pias [P] 94 E3
Piaseczno [PL] 38 B3
Piaseczno [PL] 20 F6
Piaski [PL] 36 C4
Piaski [PL] 38 E6
Piastów [PL] 38 B3
Piaszczyna [PL] 22 C3
Piątek [PL] 36 G3
Piatra [RO] 148 B2
Piatra Neamț [RO] 206 C4
Piatra Olt [RO] 150 G1
Piazza al Serchio [I] 110 D4
Piazza Armerina [I] 126 E4
Piazza Brembana [I] 70 H4
Piazzatorre [I] 70 H3
Piazzola sul Brenta [I] 72 D6
Pićan [HR] 112 E2
Picassent [E] 98 E5
Picerno [I] 120 G4
Pichoux, Gorges de- [CH] 58 D5
Pickering [GB] 10 G3
Pico [I] 120 C1
Picquigny [F] 28 D4
Pidna [GR] 128 H5
Piechowice [PL] 48 H1
Piecki [PL] 24 C4
Piedade, Ponta da- [P] 94 B5
Piedicavallo [I] 70 E4
Piedicroce [F] 114 C3
Piediluco [I] 116 B4
Piedimonte Etneo [I] 124 A8
Piedimonte Matese [I] 120 E2
Piedimulera [I] 70 E3
Piedra, Monasteiro de- [E] 90 C4
Piedrabuena [E] 86 F5
Piedrabuena [E] 96 E4
Piedrafita de Babia [E] 78 G4
Piedrahita [E] 88 C4
Piedralaves [E] 88 D5
Piedras Albas [E] 86 G4
Piekary Śląskie [PL] 50 F3
Pieksämäki [FIN] 188 C4
Pielavesi [FIN] 186 H1
Pieniężno [PL] 22 G3
Piennes [F] 44 E3
Pieńsk [PL] 34 G6
Pienza [I] 114 G2
Pierre-Buffière [F] 66 G2
Pierre-de-Bresse [F] 56 H5
Pierrefitte [F] 44 D4
Pierrefitte-Nestalas [F] 84 E4
Pierrefonds [F] 42 G2
Pierrefort [F] 68 B4
Pierrefort, Château de- [F] 44 E5
Pierrelatte [F] 106 G2
Pierroton [F] 66 C3
Piertinjaure [S] 190 H1
Pieski [PL] 34 H2
Pieskowa Skała [PL] 50 H3
Piessling Urspr. [A] 62 B6
Piešťany [SK] 62 H3
Pieszyce [PL] 50 C2
Pietarsaari / Jakobstad [FIN] 198 B6
Pietra Bismantova [I] 110 D3
Pietragalla [I] 120 H3
Pietralba [F] 114 B3
Pietra Ligure [I] 108 G3
Pietralunga [I] 116 A1
Pietramelara [I] 120 D2
Pietraperzia [I] 126 E4
Pietrasanta [I] 110 D5
Pietravairano [I] 120 D2
Pietrowice [PL] 50 D3
Pietrzwałd [PL] 22 G4
Pieve di Cadore [I] 72 F3
Pieve di Teco [I] 108 G4
Pievepelago [I] 110 E4

Pieve Santo Stéfano [I] 110 G6
Pigádi [GR] 132 H3
Pigés [GR] 132 E3
Pigí [GR] 132 F5
Pigna [I] 108 F4
Pihkala [FIN] 198 D5
Pihlajalahti [FIN] 188 E5
Pihlajavaarra [FIN] 188 H1
Pihlava [FIN] 176 C1
Pihtipudas [FIN] 186 F1
Piikkiö / Pikis [FIN] 176 E4
Piipola [FIN] 198 D5
Piispa [FIN] 188 E1
Piispajärvi [FIN] 198 F3
Piittisjärvi [FIN] 196 D8
Pikalevo [RUS] 204 E1
Pikis / Piikkiö [FIN] 176 E4
Pikšas [LV] 200 D5
Pila [I] 110 H2
Pila [I] 70 D4
Piła [PL] 22 B6
Pilar de la Mola [E] 104 C6
Pilas [E] 94 G6
Pilastri [I] 110 F2
Pilat, Dune de- [F] 66 B3
Pilat-Plage [F] 66 B3
Pileta, Cueva de la- [E] 100 H4
Pilgrimstad [S] 182 H3
Pilica [PL] 50 H2
Pilio [GR] 134 B4
Pilis [H] 76 D1
Piliscsaba [H] 64 C6
Pilisvörösvár [H] 64 C6
Piliuona [LT] 202 F5
Pilsrundāle [LV] 200 D6
Pilviškiai [LT] 24 E1
Pilzno [PL] 52 C4
Pina de Ebro [E] 90 F4
Piñar [E] 102 E3
Pinarejos [E] 88 F3
Pinarellu [F] 114 B5
Pınarhisar [TR] 146 C2
Pınarköy [TR] 142 D2
Pınarlar [TR] 144 G6
Pincehely [H] 76 B3
Pińczów [PL] 52 B2
Pindal, Cueva del- [E] 82 D2
Pineda de la Sierta [E] 90 A1
Pineda de Mar [E] 92 F4
Pinerolo [I] 70 C6
Pineto [I] 116 D3
Piney [F] 44 B5
Pinhal Novo [P] 86 B5
Pinhel [P] 80 E6
Pinkafeld [A] 74 E1
Pinneberg [D] 18 F4
Pino [E] 78 H4
Pino [F] 114 C2
Pino do Val [E] 78 B2
Pinols [F] 68 D4
Piñor [E] 78 C4
Pinoso / el Pinós [E] 104 D2
Pinos Puente [E] 102 D3
Pinsk [BY] 204 A6
Pinsoro [E] 84 B6
Pintamo [FIN] 198 E3
Pinto [E] 88 F6
Pinzio [P] 80 E6
Pinzolo [I] 72 C4
Pióbbico [I] 110 H6
Piombino [I] 114 E2
Piona, Abbazia di- [I] 70 G3
Pionerskiy [RUS] 202 C5
Pionki [PL] 38 C5
Pionsat [F] 56 C6
Pióraco [I] 116 B2
Piossasco [I] 70 D6
Piotrków [PL] 38 E6
Piotrkowice [PL] 52 B2
Piotrków Kujawski [PL] 36 F2
Piotrków Trybunalski [PL] 36 H5
Piotrowice [PL] 38 C3
Piotrowo [PL] 36 C2
Piotta [CH] 70 F2
Piove di Sacco [I] 110 G1
Piovene-Rocchette [I] 72 D5
Pipriac [F] 40 F4
Piqeras [AL] 132 B1
Piqueras, Puerto de- [E] 90 B2
Piran [SLO] 72 H6
Piras [I] 118 E3
Pirdop [BG] 148 A4
Pirgadíkia [GR] 130 C5
Piriac-sur-Mer [F] 40 D5
Piriatin [UA] 206 F2
Pirin [BG] 130 B2
Pirkkala / Birkala [FIN] 176 F1
Pirmasens [D] 44 H4
Pirna [D] 48 F1
Pirnmill [GB] 8 C3
Pirok [MK] 128 D1
Pirot [YU] 150 E4
Pirou-Plage [F] 26 D3
Pirovac [HR] 112 G6
Pirtó [H] 76 D4
Pirttikoski [FIN] 196 E8
Pirttikylä / Pörtom [FIN] 186 B3
Pirttiniemi [FIN] 198 C6
Pisa [I] 110 D5
Pisa, Certosa di- [I] 110 D5
Pisanets [BG] 148 D2
Pişchia [RO] 76 G5
Pisciotta [I] 120 F5
Písek [CZ] 48 F6
Pishcha [UA] 38 G4
Pisodéri [GR] 128 E4
Pisogne [I] 72 B5
Pisses [GR] 138 C2
Pissónas [GR] 134 C5
Pissos [F] 66 C4
Pisticci [I] 122 D4
Pistóia [I] 110 E5
Pisz [PL] 24 C4
Pitäjänmäki [FIN] 198 D6
Piteå [S] 198 B3
Piteşti [RO] 206 C6
Pithiviers [F] 42 F5
Pitigliano [I] 114 G3
Pitkäjärvi [FIN] 176 F4
Pitkälahti [FIN] 188 C2
Pitlochry [GB] 8 E1
Pitomača [HR] 74 G5
Pitsiána [GR] 132 D3
Pitvaros [H] 76 F4
Pivka [SLO] 74 B6
Pivnica [HR] 74 H6
Pivski Manastir [YU] 152 D3
Piwniczna Zdrój [PL] 52 C5
Pizarra [E] 102 B4
Pizzighettone [I] 70 H6
Pizzo [I] 124 D6
Pizzoli [I] 116 C4
Pjatihatki [UA] 206 G3
Pjätteryd [S] 162 C5
Plabennec [F] 40 B1
Plage de Pineto [F] 114 C3
Plagiá [GR] 130 G2
Plagiá [GR] 128 H3
Plaisance [F] 84 F2
Pláka [GR] 130 F6
Plakiás [GR] 140 D5
Plana [BIH] 152 D3
Planá [CZ] 48 D4
Planá nad Lužnicí [CZ] 48 G6
Plancios [I] 72 E3
Plancoët [F] 26 B4
Plandište [YU] 154 H1
Plan-du-Lac [F] 70 C2
Plánice [CZ] 48 E5
Planina [SLO] 74 B5
Planina [SLO] 74 D5
Planjane [HR] 154 A5
Plankenburk [CZ] 50 C5
Plankenstein [A] 62 D5
Plansee [A] 60 C6
Plasencia [E] 88 B5
Plasencia del Monte [E] 84 D6
Plaški [HR] 112 G2
Plassen [N] 172 D2
Plassenburg [D] 46 H3
Plášťovce [SK] 64 C4
Plasy [CZ] 48 E4
Plataiés [GR] 134 B6
Platamona Lido [I] 118 C3
Platamónas [GR] 128 H6
Platamónas [GR] 130 D3
Platanés [GR] 140 D4
Platánia [GR] 136 C3
Plataniá [GR] 134 B3
Plataniás [GR] 140 C4
Platanistós [GR] 134 D6
Plátanos [GR] 136 E3
Plátanos [GR] 140 B4
Plátanos [GR] 136 C2
Platariá [GR] 132 C2
Platerów [PL] 38 E2
Pláti [GR] 146 A2
Plati [I] 124 C7
Platiána [GR] 136 C2
Platígiali [GR] 132 D5
Platja d'Aro [E] 92 G4
platja des Canar [E] 104 C5
Plátsa [GR] 136 E4
Plattling [D] 60 G3
Platýkampos [GR] 132 G2
Platýs Gialós [GR] 138 D3
Platýs Gialós [GR] 138 E2
Platýstomo [GR] 132 F4
Plau [D] 20 B5
Plaue [D] 34 C2
Plauen [D] 48 C2
Plav [YU] 150 A5
Plave [SLO] 72 H5
Plavecký Hrad [SK] 62 G3
Plavinas [LV] 200 E5
Plavna [YU] 150 E1
Plavsk [RUS] 204 F5
Playa Blanca [E] 100 E5
Playa de San Juán [E] 104 E2
Pleaux [F] 68 A3
Plech [D] 46 H4
Pleinfeld [D] 46 G6
Plélan-le-Grand [F] 26 B6
Pleniţa [RO] 150 F1
Plentzia [E] 82 G3
Plépi [GR] 136 G2
Plešivec [SK] 64 E3
Plesse [F] 40 F5
Plessenburg [D] 32 G4
Plessis-Bourré, Château du- [F] 40 H6
Plestin-les-Grèves [F] 40 C1
Pleszew [PL] 36 E4
Pleternica [HR] 154 C1
Plettenberg [D] 32 C5
Pleumartin [F] 54 F4
Pleven [BG] 148 A3
Pleyben [F] 40 C2
Pliego [E] 104 B3
Plikáti [GR] 128 D6
Pliska [BG] 148 E2
Plitvice [HR] 112 G3
Plitvički Ljeskovac [HR] 112 G3
Pljevlja [YU] 152 E2
Ploaghe [I] 118 C3
Ploče [HR] 152 B3
Plochingen [D] 58 H1
Płock [PL] 36 H2
Ploërmel [F] 26 B6
Ploieşti [RO] 206 C6
Plomári [GR] 134 H3
Plombières-les-Bains [F] 58 C3
Plomin [HR] 112 E2
Plön [D] 18 G2
Plonéour Lanvern [F] 40 B3
Płońsk [PL] 38 A2
Plopii Slăviteşti [RO] 148 B2
Płoskinia [PL] 22 G2
Płoty [PL] 20 G4
Plouaret [F] 40 D2
Plouay [F] 40 C4
Ploubalay [F] 26 C4
Ploudalmézeau [F] 40 B1
Plouescat [F] 40 B1
Plougasnou [F] 40 C1
Plougastel-Daoulas [F] 40 B2
Plouguenast [F] 26 B5
Plouha [F] 26 A4
Plouigneau [F] 40 C2
Ploumanac'h [F] 40 D1
Plouray [F] 40 C3
Plovdiv [BG] 148 B6
Polcenigo [I] 72 F5
Plozévet [F] 40 B3
Plungė [LT] 202 D4
Pluty [PL] 22 G2
Pluvigner [F] 40 D4
Plužine [BIH] 152 C2
Plužine [YU] 152 D2
Płużnica [PL] 22 E5
Plymouth [GB] 12 D5
Plytnica [PL] 22 B5
Plýtra [GR] 136 F5
Plyussa [RUS] 200 H2
Plzeň [CZ] 48 E4
Pnevo [RUS] 200 G3
Pniewo [PL] 38 C2
Pniewy [PL] 36 B2
Poarta de Fier a Transilvaniei [RO] 206 B5
Pobedino [RUS] 202 E5
Pobes [E] 82 G5
Pobiedziska [PL] 36 D2
Pobierowo [PL] 20 F3
Pobikry [PL] 38 E1
Pobiti Kamŭni [BG] 148 F3
Pobladura de la Sierra [E] 78 F5
Poblet [E] 92 C4
Pobra do Caramiñal / Puebla del Caramiñal [E] 78 B3
Počátky [CZ] 48 H6
Poceirão [P] 86 B6
Pochep [RUS] 204 D6
Pöchlarn [A] 62 D4
Počitelj [BIH] 152 C3
Pocking [D] 60 H4
Pocklington [GB] 10 G3
Poço do Inferno [P] 86 F2
Pocrnje [BIH] 152 C3
Počuta [YU] 150 A2
Podari [RO] 150 G1
Podbanské [SK] 50 H6
Podbořany [CZ] 48 E3
Podborovje [RUS] 200 G3
Poddębice [PL] 36 F4
Podd'sk [RUS] 204 F4
Poděbrady [CZ] 48 H3
Podence [P] 80 F4
Podensac [F] 66 D4
Podersdorf am See [A] 62 G5
Podgaje [PL] 22 B5
Podgarić [HR] 74 F6
Podgora [HR] 152 B2
Podgorač [HR] 154 D1
Podgorac [YU] 150 D2
Podgorica [YU] 152 E4
Podgorie [AL] 128 D4
Podgrad [SLO] 112 E1
Podgradec [AL] 128 D4
Podhalański [PL] 50 H4
Podivín [CZ] 62 G3
Podklasztorze [PL] 36 H5
Podkoren [SLO] 72 H3
Podkova [BG] 130 F2
Podkrepa [BG] 148 C6
Podkriváň [SK] 64 D3
Podnovlje [BIH] 154 D2
Podochóri [GR] 130 C4
Podogorá [GR] 132 E4
Podolesh'e [RUS] 200 G2
Podravska Slatina [HR] 74 H6
Podromanija [BIH] 152 D1
Podslon [BG] 148 D5
Podsreda [SLO] 74 D5
Podujevo [YU] 150 C4
Podunavci [YU] 150 B3
Podwilcze [PL] 20 H4
Poeldijk [NL] 16 C5
Poetto [I] 118 D7
Poggendorf [D] 20 D3
Poggibonsi [I] 110 E6
Póggio Rusco [I] 110 F2
Pöggstall [A] 62 D4
Pogonianí [GR] 132 C1
Pogoritsa [BG] 148 D3
Pogórska Wola [PL] 52 C4
Pogórze [PL] 50 D3
Pogrodzie [PL] 22 F2
Pohja [FIN] 176 G1
Pohja / Pojo [FIN] 176 F5
Pohja-Lankila [FIN] 188 F6
Pohjaslahti [FIN] 196 D8
Pohjaslahti [FIN] 186 E5
Pohjoislahti [FIN] 186 F4
Pohorelá [SK] 64 E2
Pohořelice [CZ] 62 F2
Pohrebyshche [UA] 206 E2
Poiana Braşov [RO] 206 C5
Poiana Mare [RO] 150 F2
Poibrene [BG] 148 A5
Pointe des Poulains [F] 40 C5
Point Sublime [F] 68 C6
Poio / O Convento [E] 78 B4
Poirino [I] 70 D6
Poissons [F] 44 D6
Poitiers [F] 54 E4
Poix [F] 28 D5
Poix-Terron [F] 44 C2
Pojate [YU] 150 C2
Pojo / Pohja [FIN] 176 F5
Pokka [FIN] 196 C5
Pokój [PL] 50 E1
Pokrovs'ke [UA] 206 H3
Pokupsko [HR] 112 H1
Pol [E] 78 E3
Pola de Allande [E] 78 F3
Pola de Laviana [E] 82 B2
Pola de Lena [E] 78 H4
Pola de Siero [E] 78 H3
Pola de Somiedo [E] 78 G4
Połajewo [PL] 36 C1
Polán [E] 96 E2
Polanica-Zdrój [PL] 50 C3
Połaniec [PL] 52 C2
Polanów [PL] 22 B3
Polatsk [BY] 204 B4
Polcenigo [I] 72 F5
Połczno [PL] 22 C3
Połczyn-Zdrój [PL] 20 H4
Pölde [EST] 200 C3
Polesella [I] 110 G2
Polessk [RUS] 202 D5
Polgár [H] 64 G5
Polgárdi [H] 76 B2
Póli [GR] 132 C5
Polianí [GR] 136 D3
Poliçan [AL] 128 C6
Poliçan [AL] 128 C5
Policastro Bussentino [I] 120 G5
Police [PL] 20 F5
Police nad Metují [CZ] 50 B2
Polička [CZ] 50 B5
Policoro [I] 122 D5
Polida, Cova de na- [E] 104 H4
Polignano a Mare [I] 122 E3
Poligny [F] 58 A6
Polikárpi [GR] 128 F4
Polikrayshte [BG] 148 C3
Polistena [I] 124 D7
Politikà [GR] 134 B4
Poljana [HR] 154 B1
Poljčane [SLO] 74 D4
Poljica [HR] 152 A3
Polkowice [PL] 36 B5
Pöllåkkä [FIN] 188 E4
Pöllau [A] 74 E1
Polle [D] 32 F3
Pollença [E] 104 E4
Pollfoss [N] 180 E5
Polmak [N] 196 D2
Polná [CZ] 50 A5
Polohy [UA] 206 H4
Polomka [SK] 64 D2
Polop [E] 104 E2
Polski Gradets [BG] 148 D5
Polski Trŭmbesh [BG] 148 C3
Polsko Kosovo [BG] 148 C3
Poltava [UA] 206 G2
Põltsamaa [EST] 200 E2
Polusperä [FIN] 198 D5
Põlva [EST] 200 F3
Polvela [FIN] 188 E1
Polvijärvi [FIN] 188 F2
Polyany [RUS] 178 F4
Polychnitos [GR] 134 G2
Polýgyros [GR] 130 B5
Polykástano [GR] 128 E5
Polýkastro [GR] 128 G3
Polymedium [TR] 134 G1
Polypótamo [GR] 128 E4
Polýracho [GR] 128 F6
Polyrrinía [GR] 140 B4
Pomar [E] 90 G4
Pomarance [I] 114 F1
Pomarico [I] 122 D4
Pomarkku / Påmark [FIN] 176 D1
Pombal [P] 86 D2
Pomellen [D] 20 E5
Pomézia [I] 116 A6
Pomezí nad Ohří [CZ] 48 C3
Pomigliano d'Arco [I] 120 E3
Pommersfelden [D] 46 G4
Pomorie [BG] 148 F4
Pompaples [CH] 70 B1
Pompei [I] 120 E3
Pompei [I] 120 E3
Pompey [F] 44 E5
Pómpia [GR] 140 E5
Pomposa, Abbazia di- [I] 110 H2
Pomysk Wielki [PL] 22 C3
Poncin [F] 68 H2
Ponferrada [E] 78 F5
Pon'goguba [RUS] 198 G3
Poniatowa [PL] 38 D6
Poniec [PL] 36 C4
Poniky [SK] 64 C3
Ponoarele [RO] 206 B6
Pons [F] 54 C6
Ponsa [FIN] 176 G1
Ponsacco [I] 110 E6
Pont [I] 70 C4
Pontacq [F] 84 E3
Ponta do Sol [P] 100 A3
Pontailler-sur-Saône [F] 56 H4
Pontal [P] 94 B5
Pont-à-Mousson [F] 44 E4
Pontão [P] 86 D3
Pontarion [F] 54 H6
Pontarlier [F] 58 B6
Pontassieve [I] 110 F5
Pontaubault [F] 26 D4
Pont-Audemer [F] 26 G3
Pontaumur [F] 68 C2
Pont-Aven [F] 40 C3
Pont Canavese [I] 70 D4
Pont Cellier [F] 56 D5
Pontcharra [F] 70 A4
Pontchartrain [F] 42 E3
Pontchâteau [F] 40 E5
Pont-Croix [F] 40 B3
Pont-d'Ain [F] 68 G2
Pont-de-Briques [F] 28 D2
Pont-de-Dore [F] 68 D2
Pont-de-l'Arche [F] 28 B6
Pont del Diable [E] 92 C5
Pont-de-Roide [F] 58 C4
Pont-de-Salars [F] 68 B6
Pont-d'Espagne [F] 84 E4
Pont-de-Vaux [F] 56 G6
Ponte Arche [I] 72 C4
Ponteareas [E] 78 B5
Pontebba [I] 72 G3
Ponte-Caldelas [E] 78 B4
Ponteceso [E] 78 B2
Pontecesures / Enfesta [E] 78 B3
Pontechianale [I] 108 E2
Pontecorvo [I] 120 C1
Ponte da Barca [P] 78 B6
Pontedecimo [I] 110 B3
Ponte de Lima [P] 78 B6
Ponte della Venturina [I] 110 E4
Ponte dell'Olio [I] 110 C2
Pontedera [I] 110 E6
Ponte de Sôr [P] 86 D5
Pontedeume [E] 78 D2
Ponte di Legno [I] 72 B4
Ponte di Piave [I] 72 F5
Ponteland [GB] 8 F6
Pontelandolfo [I] 120 E2
Ponte-Leccia [F] 114 B3
Pontelongo [I] 110 G1
Ponte nelle Alpi [I] 72 E4
Pont-en-Royans [F] 68 G5
Ponte Nuovo [F] 114 B3
Ponte Oliveras [E] 78 B2
Ponte S. Pietro [I] 70 H4
Ponte Tresa [CH] 70 F3
Ponte Ulla [E] 78 C3
Pontevedra [E] 78 B4
Pontevico [I] 110 D1
Pontgibaud [F] 68 C2
Pontigny [F] 56 E1
Pontinia [I] 120 B1
Pontinvrea [I] 108 H3
Pontisméno [GR] 130 B3
Pontivy [F] 26 A5
Pont-l'Abbé [F] 40 B3
Pont-l'Evêque [F] 26 G3
Pontlevoy [F] 54 G2
Pontoise [F] 42 F3
Pontokómi [GR] 128 F5
Pontones [E] 102 G2
Pontoon [IRL] 2 C3
Pontorson [F] 26 D4
Pont-Réan [F] 26 C6
Pontremoli [I] 110 C3
Pontresina [CH] 72 A3
Pontrieux [F] 26 A3
Ponts [E] 92 C3
Pont-Scorff [F] 40 C4
Pont-St-Esprit [F] 106 G2
Pont-St-Martin [I] 70 D4
Pont-St-Vincent [F] 44 E5
Pont-sur-Yonne [F] 42 G5
Pontvallain [F] 42 B6
Pontypool [GB] 12 F2
Pontypridd [GB] 12 F2
Ponza [I] 120 B3
Poole [GB] 12 G5
Poperinge [B] 28 F2
Popilnya [UA] 206 E2
Popina [BG] 148 E1
Popintsi [BG] 148 A5
Popoli [I] 116 D5
Popovača [HR] 74 F6
Popovitsa [BG] 148 B6
Popovo [BG] 148 D3
Poppenhausen [D] 46 F3
Poppi [I] 110 G6
Poprad [SK] 64 E2
Popsko [BG] 130 G1
Populónia [I] 114 E2
Poraj [PL] 50 G2
Porasa [FIN] 176 G1
Porazava [BY] 24 G6
Porcuna [E] 102 D1
Porczyny [PL] 36 F4
Pordenone [I] 72 F5
Pordim [BG] 148 B3
Pordoi, Passo- [I] 72 E3
Poręba [PL] 50 G2
Poreč [HR] 112 D2
Porech'ye [BY] 24 G3
Pori / Björneborg [FIN] 176 D1
Porjus [S] 190 H1
Porkhov [RUS] 200 H3
Porkkala / Porkala [FIN] 176 G5
Pörnbach [D] 60 E3
Pornic [F] 54 B1
Pornichet [F] 40 E6
Porokylä [FIN] 198 F6
Poronin [PL] 52 A6
Póros [GR] 132 D5
Póros [GR] 136 G2
Póros [GR] 132 D6
Poroszló [H] 64 F6
Porozina [HR] 112 E2
Pórpi [GR] 130 F3
Porquerolles [F] 108 C6
Porrentruy [CH] 58 D4
Porretta Terme [I] 110 E4
Porsgrunn [N] 164 G3
Portacloy [IRL] 2 C2
Portadown [GB] 2 G4
Portaferry [GB] 2 H4
Portalegre [P] 86 E5
Portalrubio [E] 90 D6
Portariá [GR] 132 H2
Portarlington [IRL] 2 E6
Port Askaig [GB] 8 B2
Port Aventura [E] 92 C5
Portbail [F] 26 D2
Port-Barcarès [F] 92 G1
Portbou [E] 92 G2
Port-Camargue [F] 106 F4
Port-Cros [F] 108 D6
Port d'Atzaia [E] 104 H4
Port-de-Bouc [F] 106 G5
Port de Pollença [E] 104 F4
Portel [P] 94 E2
Portela do Home [E] 78 B6
Port Ellen [GB] 2 H1
Portelo [P] 80 F3
Port-en-Bessin [F] 26 E3
Port Erin [GBM] 2 H5
Pórtes [GR] 136 G2
Port Eynon [GB] 12 E2
Portezuelo [E] 86 H4
Portglenone [GB] 2 G3
Port-Grimaud [F] 108 D5
Porthcawl [GB] 12 E3
Porthmadog [GB] 10 B4
Porticcio [F] 114 A5
Portile de Fier [Eur.] 206 B6
Portilla de la Reina [E] 82 D3
Portillo [E] 88 E2
Portimão [P] 94 B5
Portimo [FIN] 196 D8
Portinatx [E] 104 C5
Portinho da Arrábida [P] 86 B6
Port-Joinville [F] 54 A2
Portlairge / Waterford [IRL] 4 E5
Port-la-Nouvelle [F] 106 D5
Port Laoise [IRL] 2 E6
Port-Leucate [F] 106 D6
Port-Louis [F] 40 C4
Portman [E] 104 C4
Port-Manech [F] 40 C4
Portmarnock [IRL] 2 F6
Portnahaven [GB] 2 G1
Port-Navalo [F] 40 D5
Port Nis / Port of Ness [GB] 6 C2
Porto [E] 78 E6
Porto [F] 114 A4
Porto [P] 80 B4
Porto Alto [P] 86 B5
Porto Azzurro [I] 114 E3
Portobello [I] 118 D2
Portocelo [E] 78 E1
Porto Ceresio [I] 70 F3
Porto Cervo [I] 118 E2
Porto Cesareo [I] 122 G5
Pórto Chéli [GR] 136 F3
Porto Colom [E] 104 F5
Porto Corallo [I] 118 E6
Porto Corsini [I] 110 H3
Porto Covo [P] 94 B3
Porto Cristo [E] 104 F5
Porto da Cruz [P] 100 B3
Porto d'Ascoli [I] 116 D3
Porto de Mós [P] 86 C3
Porto di Levante [I] 124 A6
Porto do Son [E] 78 B3
Porto Empedocle [I] 126 D4
Porto Ercole [I] 114 F4
Portoferráio [I] 114 D2
Portofino [I] 110 B3
Port of Ness / Port Nis [GB] 6 C2
Porto Garibaldi [I] 110 H3
Pórto Germenó [GR] 134 B6
Portogruaro [I] 72 F5
Pórto Kágio [GR] 136 E5
Pórto Karrás [GR] 130 C6
Porto Levante [I] 110 H2
Pörtom / Pirttikylä [FIN] 186 B3
Portomaggiore [I] 110 G3
Portomarín [E] 78 D4
Porto Moniz [P] 100 A3
Portomouro [E] 78 C3
Porto Novo [P] 86 B4
Portopalo di Capo Passero [I] 126 G6
Porto-Pollo [F] 114 A5
Porto Potenza Picena [I] 116 C1
Portør [N] 164 F4
Porto Ráfti [GR] 136 H1
Porto Recanati [I] 116 C1
Porto Rotondo [I] 118 E2
Portorož [SLO] 72 H6
Porto San Giorgio [I] 116 D2
Porto Sant'Elpidio [I] 116 C1
Porto Santoru [I] 118 E6
Porto Santo Stéfano [I] 114 F4
Portoscuso [I] 118 B7
Portos dos Fusos [P] 94 D5
Porto Tolle [I] 110 H2
Porto Tórres [I] 118 B3
Porto-Vecchio [F] 114 B6
Portovenere [I] 110 C4
Portpatrick [GB] 8 B5
Portree [GB] 6 B4
Portroe [IRL] 2 C6
Pörtschach [A] 74 B3
Portsmouth [GB] 12 H5
Port-Ste-Marie [F] 66 E5
Portstewart [GB] 2 G2
Port-St-Louis-du-Rhône [F] 106 G5
Port-St-Marie, La Chartreuse de- [F] 68 C2
Port-sur-Saône [F] 58 B3
Port Talbot [GB] 12 E2
Portumna [IRL] 2 D6
Port-Vendres [F] 92 G2
Port William [GB] 8 C5
Porvoo / Borgå [FIN] 178 B4
Porządzie [PL] 38 C1
Porzuna [E] 96 E3
Posada [E] 78 H3
Posada [E] 82 D2
Posada [I] 118 E3
Posada de Valdeón [E] 82 C3
Posadas [E] 102 B1
Poschiavo [CH] 72 B3
Posedarje [HR] 112 G5
Poseidonía [GR] 138 D2
Poshnjë [AL] 128 B4
Posio [FIN] 196 E8
Positano [I] 120 E4
Possagno [I] 72 E5
Pössneck [D] 46 H2
Posta [I] 116 B4
Postojna [SLO] 74 B6
Postojnska Jama [SLO] 74 B5
Postoloprty [CZ] 48 E3
Postomino [PL] 22 B2
Posušje [BIH] 152 B2
Potamiá [GR] 130 E4
Potamiés [GR] 140 F4
Potamoí [GR] 130 D2
Potamós [GR] 136 F6
Potamós [GR] 140 A3
Potamoúla [GR] 132 E4
Potenštejn [CZ] 48 E5
Potenza [I] 120 H4
Potenza Picena [I] 116 C1
Potes [E] 82 D3
Potoci [BIH] 152 C2
Potok [HR] 154 B1
Potok [PL] 52 D4
Potsdam [D] 34 D2
Potštát [CZ] 50 D5
Pottenbrunn [A] 62 E4
Pottenstein [A] 62 E5
Pottenstein [D] 46 H4
Pöttmes [D] 60 D3
Potworów [PL] 38 B5
Pouancé [F] 40 G5
Pougues-les-Eaux [F] 56 D4
Pouilly [F] 56 D3
Pouilly-en-Auxois [F] 56 F3
Pouilly-sous-Charlieu [F] 68 E1
Poukavichy [BY] 204 C6
Poúnda [GR] 138 E3
Pourtalet, Col du- [Eur.] 84 D4
Poussu [FIN] 198 F2
Pouyastruc [F] 84 F3
Pouzauges [F] 54 C3
Považská Bystrica [SK] 64 B2
Považský Hrad [SK] 50 F6
Poviglio [I] 110 E2
Povlja [HR] 152 A2
Póvoa [P] 94 E3
Póvoa de Lanhoso [P] 80 C3
Póvoa de Varzim [P] 80 B3
Powburn [GB] 8 F5
Powerscourt House [IRL] 4 G3
Powidz [PL] 36 E2
Powodow [PL] 36 G4
Poyatos [E] 98 C1
Poyntzpass [GB] 2 G4
Poyra [TR] 146 H5
Poyralı [TR] 146 C2
Poyrazdamları [TR] 144 E3
Poysdorf [A] 62 F3
Pöytyä [FIN] 176 E3
Poza de la Sal [E] 82 F5
Požarevac [YU] 206 A6
Pozazal, Puerto- [E] 82 E4
Požega [YU] 150 A2
Požeranje [YU] 150 C6
Poznań [PL] 36 C2
Pozo Alcón [E] 102 F3
Pozoblanco [E] 96 C5
Pozo-Cañada [E] 98 B6
Pozohondo [E] 98 B6
Pozondón [E] 98 D1
Poźrzadło [PL] 34 H3
Pozuel de Ariza [E] 90 C4
Pozuelo [E] 98 B5
Pozuelo de Zarzón [E] 86 H3
Pozzallo [I] 126 F6
Pozzomaggiore [I] 118 C4
Pozzo S. Nicola [I] 118 B3
Pozzuoli [I] 120 D3
Prabuty [PL] 22 F4
Prača [BIH] 152 D1
Prachatice [CZ] 62 B2
Prácheň [CZ] 48 E6
Pracký Kopec [CZ] 62 F2
Pradelle [F] 68 G6
Pradelles [F] 68 D5
Prádena [E] 88 G4
Prades [F] 92 F1
Pradillo [E] 90 B1
Prádla [CZ] 50 E6
Pradła [PL] 50 H2
Prado del Rey [E] 100 H4
Pradoluengo [E] 82 F6
Præstø [DK] 156 G4
Prägraten [A] 72 F2
Praha [CZ] 48 F3
Prahecq [F] 54 D4
Prahovo [YU] 150 E1
Praia a Mare [I] 120 G6
Praia da Barra [P] 80 B5
Praia da Vieira [P] 86 C2
Praia de Mira [P] 80 A5
Praia Grande [P] 86 A5
Praiano [I] 120 E4
Praias-Sado [P] 86 B6
Praisós [GR] 140 G5
Prakovce [SK] 64 F2
Prali [I] 70 C6
Pralognan-la-Vanoise [F] 70 B4
Prámanta [GR] 132 D2
Pranjani [YU] 150 B2
Prapatnica [HR] 116 H1
Prasiá [GR] 132 E3
Prasiés [GR] 140 D4
Praszka [PL] 36 F6
Prat de Compte [E] 90 G6
Pratella [I] 120 D1
Prati di Tivo [I] 116 C4
Prato [I] 110 E5
Prats de Lluçanès [E] 92 E3
Prats-de-Mollo-la-Preste [F] 92 F2
Prauthoy [F] 56 H3
Pravdinsk [RUS] 22 H2
Pravets [BG] 150 G4

Pravia [E] 78 G3
Pravlov [CZ] 62 F2
Préchac [F] 66 D4
Prečno [HR] 74 F6
Précy-sous-Thil [F] 56 F3
Predappio [I] 110 G4
Predazzo [I] 72 D4
Preddvor [SLO] 74 B4
Predeal [RO] 206 C5
Predejane [YU] 150 E4
Predel [SLO] 72 H4
Predeşti [RO] 150 F1
Preding [A] 74 D3
Predlitz [A] 74 B2
Predoi / Prettau [I] 72 E2
Pré-en-Pail [F] 26 F5
Preetz [D] 18 G2
Pregarten [A] 62 C4
Preili [LV] 200 F6
Preitenštejn [CZ] 48 D4
Prekal [AL] 150 A6
Prekestol [N] 164 B3
Preko [HR] 112 G5
Prekonoška Pećina [YU] 150 D3
Prelau [A] 72 F1
Prelog [HR] 74 F4
Přelouč [CZ] 48 H4
Prémery [F] 56 D3
Premià de Mar [E] 92 E4
Premnitz [D] 34 C2
Prenjas [AL] 128 C3
Prenzlau [D] 20 E5
Preobrazhenski Manastir [BG] 148 C3
Přerov [CZ] 50 D5
Prerow [D] 20 C2
Preselentsi [BG] 148 G2
Preševo [YU] 150 D6
Presicce [I] 122 G6
Prešov [SK] 64 G2
Pressac [F] 54 F5
Pressath [D] 48 B4
Pressbaum [A] 62 E4
Pré St-Didier [I] 70 C3
Prestestranda [N] 164 F3
Prestfoss [N] 170 G5
Přeštice [CZ] 48 D5
Preston [GB] 10 D3
Prestwick [GB] 8 C4
Prettau / Predoi [I] 72 E2
Prettin [D] 34 D4
Pretul [A] 62 E6
Pretzsch [D] 34 D4
Preuilly-sur-Claise [F] 54 G3
Préveli, Moní- [GR] 140 D5
Préveranges [F] 56 B5
Préveza [GR] 132 D4
Prevršac [HR] 154 A1
Priaranza del Bierzo [E] 78 F5
Příběnice [CZ] 48 G5
Pribeta [SK] 64 B5
Priboj [BIH] 154 E3
Priboj [YU] 152 E2
Příbor [CZ] 50 E5
Pribovce [SK] 64 C2
Příbram [CZ] 48 F5
Přibyslav [CZ] 50 A5
Prichsenstadt [D] 46 F4
Pridvorci [BIH] 152 C2
Pridvorica [YU] 150 B3
Priego [E] 90 B6
Priego de Córdoba [E] 102 D3
Priekulė [LT] 202 D4
Priekule [LV] 200 B6
Priekuļi [LV] 200 E4
Prien [D] 60 F5
Prienai [LT] 24 F1
Priene [TR] 142 B1
Prievidza [SK] 64 B3
Prignano Cilento [I] 120 F5
Prigrevica [YU] 76 C6
Prijeboj [HR] 112 G3
Prijedor [BIH] 154 B2
Prijepolje [YU] 150 A3
Prilep [MK] 128 E2
Prilike [YU] 150 A3
Priluka [BIH] 152 B1
Přimda [CZ] 48 C4
Primel-Trégastel [F] 40 C1
Primišlje [HR] 112 G2
Primolano [I] 72 D5
Primorsk [RUS] 22 G1
Primorsk [RUS] 178 F4
Primorsko [BG] 148 F5
Primor'ye [RUS] 202 C5
Primošten [HR] 116 H1
Primstal [D] 44 G3
Prínos [GR] 130 E4
Priolo Gargallo [I] 126 G4
Prioro [E] 82 C3
Priozersk [RUS] 178 G1
Prirečnyj [RUS] 196 F4
Prírodné Múzeum na Dukle [SK] 52 D5
Priseltsi [BG] 148 F3
Prislop, Pasul- [RO] 206 C4
Prisoje [BIH] 152 B1
Prissac [F] 54 G4
Priština [YU] 150 C5
Pritzerbe [D] 34 C2
Pritzier [D] 18 H5
Pritzwalk [D] 20 B5
Privas [F] 68 F5
Priverno [I] 120 C1
Privlaka [HR] 112 F4
Privlaka [HR] 154 E2
Prizna [HR] 112 F3
Prizren [YU] 150 B6
Prizzi [I] 126 D3
Prnalija [MK] 128 G1
Prnjavor [BIH] 154 C2
Prnjavor [YU] 154 F3
Probištip [MK] 128 F1
Probstzella [D] 46 H2
Prochowice [PL] 36 B6
Pródromos [GR] 132 H5
Proença-a-Nova [P] 86 E3
Profilia [GR] 142 D5
Profítis [GR] 130 B4
Profondeville [B] 30 D5
Progled [BG] 130 E1
Prohor Pčinjski [YU] 150 D6
Prókhoma [GR] 128 H4
Prokópi [GR] 134 B4
Prokuplje [YU] 150 D4
Prolaz [BG] 148 D3
Prómachoi [GR] 128 F3
Promachónas [GR] 130 B2
Promna [PL] 38 B4
Pronsfeld [D] 30 F6
Propriano [F] 114 A5
Prosenik [BG] 148 F4
Prosotsáni [GR] 130 C3
Prostějov [CZ] 50 C5
Prószków [PL] 50 E2
Proszowice [PL] 52 B3
Próti [GR] 130 C3
Protići [BIH] 154 B4
Protivín [CZ] 48 F6
Protokklísi [GR] 130 H2
Prötzel [D] 34 F2
Prouille [F] 106 B4
Prousós [GR] 132 E4
Provadiya [BG] 148 F3
Provins [F] 42 H5
Prozor [BIH] 152 C1
Pruchnik [PL] 52 F4
Prudhoe [GB] 8 F6
Prudnik [PL] 50 D3
Prügy [H] 64 G4
Průhonice [CZ] 48 F4
Prüm [D] 30 F6
Pruna [E] 102 A3
Prundu [RO] 148 D1
Prunete [F] 114 C4
Prunetta [I] 110 E5
Prunn [D] 60 E2
Prunn, Schloss- [D] 60 E2
Prusice [PL] 36 C5
Pruské [SK] 64 B2
Pruszcz [PL] 22 D5
Pruszcz Gdański [PL] 22 E3
Pruszków [PL] 38 B3
Pruzhany [BY] 38 H1
Pruzhicy [RUS] 178 F6
Pryluky [UA] 206 F2
Prypyat' [UA] 204 C7
Przasnysz [PL] 24 B6
Przechlewo [PL] 22 C4
Przedbórz [PL] 36 H6
Przedecz [PL] 36 F3
Przełęk [PL] 50 D3
Przemków [PL] 36 A5
Przemyśl [PL] 52 F4
Przewale [PL] 52 G2
Przeworsk [PL] 52 E3
Przewóz [PL] 34 G5
Przezmark [PL] 22 F4
Przybiernów [PL] 20 F4
Przybychowo [PL] 36 C1
Przylesie [PL] 50 D2
Przysucha [PL] 38 B5
Przyszowa [PL] 52 B5
Przytoczna [PL] 36 A2
Przytoczno [PL] 38 D4
Przytyk [PL] 38 B5
Przywory [PL] 50 E2
Pšaca [MK] 150 E6
Psachná [GR] 134 B4
Psará [GR] 134 F4
Psarádes [GR] 128 D4
Psarshai [BY] 202 H6
Psáthi [GR] 138 D4
Psathópyrgos [GR] 132 F5
Psathotópi [GR] 132 D3
Pskov [RUS] 200 G3
Psychikó [GR] 132 G2
Psychró [GR] 140 F5
Pszczew [PL] 36 A2
Pszczyna [PL] 50 G4
Pteléa [GR] 130 D2
Ptolemáida [GR] 128 F5
Ptóo [GR] 134 B5
Ptuj [SLO] 74 E4
Ptujska Gora [SLO] 74 E4
Puchberg [A] 62 E5
Púchov [SK] 50 F6
Pučišća [HR] 152 A2
Puck [PL] 22 D1
Puçol [E] 98 F4
Pudasjärvi [FIN] 198 E3
Puebla de Alcocer [E] 96 C3
Puebla de Don Fadrique [E] 102 H2
Puebla de Don Rodrigo [E] 96 D3
Puebla de Guzmán [E] 94 E4
Puebla de la Calzada [E] 94 G1
Puebla de la Reina [E] 94 H2
Puebla del Brollón / A Pobra de Brollón [E] 78 D4
Puebla del Caramiñal / Pobra do Caramiñal [E] 78 B3
Puebla de Lillo [E] 82 C3
Puebla del Maestre [E] 94 H4
Puebla de Obando [E] 86 G6
Puebla de Sanabria [E] 80 G3
Puebla de Vallés [E] 88 G4
Pueblica de Valverde [E] 80 H4
Puente Almuhey [E] 82 C4
Puente de Domingo Flórez [E] 78 E5
Puente de Génave [E] 96 G6
Puente de Montañana [E] 92 B2
Puente Genil [E] 102 C2
Puente la Reina / Gares [E] 84 B4
Puente la Reina de Jaca [E] 84 D5
Puentelarra [E] 82 G5
Puentes de García Rodríguez / As Pontes de Garcá Rodríguez [E] 78 D2
Puente Viesgo [E] 82 E3
Puerto Banús [E] 102 A5
Puerto Castilla [E] 88 C5
Puerto de Bejar [E] 88 B4
Puerto de Itziar [E] 82 H4
Puerto de la Cruz [E] 100 B5
Puerto del Rosario [E] 100 E5
Puerto de Mazarrón [E] 104 C4
Puerto de Santa Cruz [E] 96 B2
Puerto de San Vicente [E] 96 C2
Puerto Lápice [E] 96 F3
Puertollano [E] 96 E5
Puerto Lumbreras [E] 104 A4
Puerto Real [E] 100 F4
Puerto Rey [E] 104 A5
Puertoserrano [E] 100 H3
Pueyo, Monasterio de- [E] 90 G3
Puffendorf [D] 30 F4
Puget-sur-Argens [F] 108 D5
Puget-Théniers [F] 108 E4
Puget-Ville [F] 108 C5
Pugnochiuso [I] 116 H6
Puhos [FIN] 188 F4
Puhos [FIN] 198 E3
Puig [E] 98 F4
Puigcerdà [E] 92 E1
Puig-reig [E] 92 E3
Puiseaux [F] 42 F5
Puivert [F] 106 B5
Pujjas [LV] 200 C6
Pukavik [S] 158 E1
Pukë [AL] 128 B1
Pukiš [BIH] 154 E3
Pukkila [FIN] 178 B3
Pula [HR] 112 D3
Pula [I] 118 C7
Puławy [PL] 38 D5
Pulborough [GB] 14 D5
Pulgar [E] 96 E2
Pulju [FIN] 192 H4
Pulkau [A] 62 E3
Pulkkila [FIN] 198 D5
Pulkovo [RUS] 178 H5
Pulpí [E] 104 B4
Pulsa [FIN] 178 D2
Pulsnitz [D] 34 F6
Pulsujärvi [S] 192 F4
Pułtusk [PL] 38 B1
Pumpėnai [LT] 202 F4
Punkalaidun [FIN] 176 E2
Punta, Château de la- [F] 114 A4
Punta Ala [I] 114 E2
Punta de Moraira [E] 104 F2
Puntagorda [E] 100 A5
Punta Križa [HR] 112 E3
Punta Marina [I] 110 H4
Punta Prima [E] 104 H5
Punta Umbría [E] 94 E6
Punxin [E] 78 C5
Puokio [FIN] 198 E4
Puolanka [FIN] 198 E4
Puottaure [S] 190 H2
Purbach [A] 62 F5
Purchena [E] 102 G4
Pürgg [A] 62 B6
Purgstall [A] 62 D5
Purkersdorf [A] 62 E4
Purmerend [NL] 16 D4
Purmojärvi [FIN] 186 D2
Pürnstein [A] 62 B3
Purnumukka [FIN] 196 D5
Purullena [E] 102 F4
Pürvomay [BG] 148 C6
Puša [LV] 200 G6
Pushkin [RUS] 178 H5
Pushkino [RUS] 204 F4
Pushkinskiye Gory [RUS] 200 H4
Püspökladány [H] 76 G1
Pustevny [CZ] 50 E5
Pustków [PL] 52 D3
Pustoška [RUS] 204 C4
Pusula [FIN] 176 G4
Puszczykowo [PL] 36 C3
Pusztamonostor [H] 64 D6
Pusztaszemes [H] 76 A3
Putaja [FIN] 176 E1
Putanges-Pont-Ecrepin [F] 26 F5
Putbus [D] 20 D2
Putignano [I] 122 E3
Putignano, Grotta di- [I] 122 E3
Putikko [FIN] 188 F5
Putim [CZ] 48 F6
Putim [CZ] 48 F6
Putinci [YU] 154 G2
Putineiu [RO] 148 C1
Putlitz [D] 20 B5
Putnok [H] 64 E4
Puttelange [F] 44 G4
Putten [NL] 16 E4
Puttgarden [D] 20 A2
Putyvl' [UA] 204 E7
Putzu Idu [I] 118 B5
Puumala [FIN] 188 E6
Puurmani [EST] 200 F2
Puy de Dôme [F] 68 C2
Puyguilhem [F] 66 F2
Puy-Guillaume [F] 68 D2
Puylaurens [F] 106 B3
Puy-l'Évêque [F] 66 F5
Puymorens, Col de- [F] 92 E1
Puzzittu, Nuraghe- [I] 118 E4
Pwllheli [GB] 10 B4
Pyaozerskiy [RUS] 198 G2
Pydnay [TR] 142 G4
Pyhäjärvi [FIN] 198 E6
Pyhajärvi [FIN] 196 D7
Pyhäjoki [FIN] 198 C5
Pyhäkylä [FIN] 198 F3
Pyhältö [FIN] 178 D3
Pyhämaa [FIN] 176 C3
Pyhäntä [FIN] 198 E5
Pyhäntaka [FIN] 178 B2
Pyhäranta [FIN] 176 C3
Pyhäsalmi [FIN] 198 E6
Pyhäselkä [FIN] 188 F3
Pyhtää / Pyttis [FIN] 178 C4
Pyla-sur-Mer [F] 66 B3
Pýles [GR] 140 H3
Pylí [GR] 142 B3
Pýli [GR] 132 E2
Pýli [GR] 134 B6
Pylkönmäki [FIN] 186 F3
Pýlos [GR] 136 C4
Pyntäinen [FIN] 186 B6
Pyrgáki [GR] 138 F3
Pyrgío [GR] 134 G5
Pýrgoi [GR] 128 F4
Pýrgos [GR] 136 C2
Pýrgos [GR] 140 E5
Pýrgos [GR] 144 C5
Pýrgos [GR] 128 H4
Pýrgos Dirού [GR] 136 E5
Pyrgos Gerakioú [GR] 136 E4
Pyrsógianni [GR] 128 D6
Pyrzyce [PL] 20 F6
Pyšely [CZ] 48 G4
Pyskowice [PL] 50 F3
Pytalovo [RUS] 200 G4
Pythagóreon [GR] 142 C1
Pyttis / Pyhtää [FIN] 178 C4
Pyzdry [PL] 36 D3

Q

Quadri [I] 116 D5
Quakenbrück [D] 18 C6
Quarré-les-Tombes [F] 56 F3
Quarteira [P] 94 C5
Quartu Sant'Elena [I] 118 D7
Quebradas [P] 86 C4
Quedlinburg [D] 34 A4
Queluz [P] 86 B5
Quercamps [F] 28 E2
Quercianella [I] 110 D6
Querenca [P] 94 C5
Querfurt [D] 34 B5
Quéribus, Château de- [F] 106 C5
Quermanço [E] 92 G2
Quéroy, Grottes du- [F] 66 E1
Quesada [E] 102 F2
Questembert [F] 40 E5
Quettehou [F] 26 E2
Quiberon [F] 40 C5
Quickborn [D] 18 F4
Quillan [F] 106 B5
Quimper [F] 40 B3
Quimperlé [F] 40 C4
Quin Abbey [IRL] 2 C6
Quinéville [F] 26 E2
Quingey [F] 58 B5
Quinta da Bacalhôa [P] 86 B6
Quintana de la Serena [E] 96 B3
Quintana del Castillo [E] 78 G5
Quintana del Puente [E] 82 D6
Quintanaortuño [E] 82 E5
Quintanar de la Orden [E] 96 G3
Quintanar de la Sierra [E] 90 A2
Quintanar del Rey [E] 98 B4
Quintana Redonda [E] 90 B3
Quintanilha [P] 80 G4
Quintanilla de las Viñas [E] 88 H1
Quintanilla de Onésimo [E] 88 F2
Quintanilla-Sobresierra [E] 82 E5
Quintin [F] 26 A4
Quinto [E] 90 F4
Quiroga [E] 78 E5
Quirra, Castello di- [I] 118 E6
Quissac [F] 106 F3
Qyteti Stalin [AL] 128 B4

R

Råå [S] 156 H2
Raab [A] 62 A4
Raabs an der Thaya [A] 62 D2
Raahe / Brahestad [FIN] 198 C4
Rääkkylä [FIN] 188 F3
Raalte [NL] 16 F4
Raanujärvi [FIN] 196 C7
Raattama [FIN] 192 H4
Rab [HR] 112 F3
Rabac [HR] 112 E2
Råbäck [S] 166 E5
Rábade [E] 78 D3
Rábafüzes [H] 74 F2
Rábahidvég [H] 74 F2
Rabastens [F] 106 B2
Rabastens-de-Bigorre [F] 84 F3
Rabat [M] 126 C6
Rábatamasi [H] 62 G6
Rabbalshede [S] 166 C5
Rabí [CZ] 48 E6
Rábida, Monasterio de la- [E] 94 E6
Rabisha [BG] 150 E2
Rabka Zdrój [PL] 50 H5
Rabštejn [CZ] 50 A4
Rabsztyn [PL] 50 H3
Råby-Rönö [S] 168 C4
Rača [SK] 62 G4
Rača [YU] 150 C1
Rača [YU] 150 C4
Rácalmás [H] 76 C2
Racalmuto [I] 126 D4
Racconigi [I] 108 G2
Rače [SLO] 74 E4
Ráches [GR] 132 H4
Raciąż [PL] 36 H1
Raciażek [PL] 36 F1
Racibórz [PL] 50 E4
Ráckeve [H] 76 C2
Racławice [PL] 52 B3
Rączki [PL] 22 G5
Raczki [PL] 24 E3
Råda [S] 166 F1
Radalj [YU] 154 E3
Radashkovichy [BY] 204 B5
Rădăuţi [RO] 206 C4
Radawnica [PL] 22 B5
Radcliffe-on-Trent [GB] 10 F5
Raddusa [I] 126 F3
Rade [D] 18 F4
Råde [N] 166 B3
Radeberg [D] 34 F6
Radebeul [D] 34 E6
Radeburg [D] 34 E6
Radeče [SLO] 74 D5
Radecin [PL] 20 H6
Radegast [D] 34 C4
Radehiv [UA] 206 C2
Radenci [SLO] 74 E3
Radenthein [A] 72 H3
Radevormwald [D] 30 H4
Radimlje [BIH] 152 C3
Radioteleskop Effelsberg [D] 30 G5
Radko Dimitrievo [BG] 148 E3
Radków [PL] 50 B2
Radlje ob Dràvi [SLO] 74 D3
Radmirje [SLO] 74 C4
Radna [RO] 76 H4
Radnevo [BG] 148 D5
Radnica [PL] 34 H3
Radnice [CZ] 48 E4
Radolfzell [D] 58 G4
Radom [PL] 38 C5
Radomin [PL] 22 F6
Radomir [BG] 150 F5
Radomiru [RO] 150 G1
Radomsko [PL] 36 G6
Radomyshl' [UA] 206 E2
Radomyśl Wielki [PL] 52 C3
Radošina [SK] 64 A3
Radošovce [SK] 62 G3
Radostowo [PL] 22 H3
Radoszyce [PL] 38 A6
Radotín [CZ] 48 F4
Radovanu [RO] 150 F1
Radovašnica [YU] 154 F3
Radovets [BG] 146 A1
Radoviš [MK] 128 G2
Radovljica [SLO] 74 B4
Radowo Wielkie [PL] 20 G4
Radruz [PL] 52 G3
Radstadt [A] 72 H1
Radstock [GB] 12 G3
Radujevac [YU] 150 E1
Radun' [BY] 24 H3
Raduša [MK] 150 C6
Radviliškis [LT] 202 F4
Radymno [PL] 52 F4
Radzanów [PL] 22 G6
Radziądz [PL] 36 C5
Radziejów [PL] 36 F2
Radziwie [PL] 36 G2
Radzovce [SK] 64 D4
Radzymin [PL] 38 B2
Radzyń Chełmiński [PL] 22 E5
Radzyń Podlaski [PL] 38 E4
Raesfeld [D] 16 G6
Raffadali [I] 126 D4
Rafína [GR] 134 C6
Rafsbotn [N] 192 G1
Rafsbotn [N] 192 G1
Ragaciems [LV] 200 D5
Ragama [E] 88 D3
Ragana [LV] 200 E5
Rågeleje [DK] 156 G1
Råglanda [S] 166 E3
Ragunda [S] 184 D2
Ragusa [I] 126 F5
Raguva [LT] 202 F4
Rahachow [BY] 204 C6
Raharney [IRL] 2 E5
Rahden [D] 32 E2
Råholt [N] 172 C5
Rain [D] 60 D2
Raippaluoto / Replot [FIN] 186 A2
Räisälä [FIN] 196 E7
Raisio / Reso [FIN] 176 D4
Raistakka [FIN] 196 E8
Raivala [FIN] 186 C5
Raja-Jooseppi [FIN] 196 E5
Rajakoski [RUS] 196 E4
Rajamäki [FIN] 176 G4
Rajë [AL] 150 A6
Rajec [SK] 64 B2
Rajecké Teplice [SK] 64 B2
Rajgród [PL] 24 E4
Rajka [H] 62 G5
Rajkova Pećina [YU] 150 D1
Raka [SLO] 74 D5
Rakaka [H] 64 F3
Rakamaz [H] 64 G4
Rakhiv [UA] 206 C3
Rakitnica [BG] 148 C5
Rakitnoe [RUS] 204 F7
Rakitovo [BG] 148 A6
Rakke [EST] 200 F2
Rakkestad [N] 166 C2
Rákóczifalva [H] 76 E2
Rakoniewice [PL] 36 B3
Rákos [H] 76 F4
Rakoszyce [PL] 36 C6
Rakovica [HR] 112 G2
Rakovitsa [BG] 150 E2
Rakovník [CZ] 48 E3
Rakovski [BG] 148 B5
Raków [PL] 52 C2
Rakvere [EST] 200 F1
Ralja [YU] 154 G3
Ramacastañas [E] 88 D5
Ramacca [I] 126 F4
Ramales de la Victoria [E] 82 F3
Ramallosa [E] 78 B5
Ramallosa / Teo [E] 78 C3
Ramberg [N] 192 B4
Rambervillers [F] 44 F6
Rambin [D] 20 D2
Rambouillet [F] 42 E4
Ramirás [E] 78 C5
Ramkvilla [S] 162 E4
Ramljane [HR] 154 A5
Rammen [S] 166 F1
Ramnäs [S] 168 B2
Rämne [S] 166 C4
Râmnicu Sărat [RO] 206 D5
Râmnicu Vâlcea [RO] 206 B6
Ramnoús [GR] 134 C5
Ramsau [A] 72 H1
Ramsberg [S] 166 H2
Ramsele [S] 184 D1
Ramsey [GBM] 8 C6
Ramsgate [GB] 14 G5
Rämshyttan [S] 172 H5
Ramsjö [S] 184 C5
Ramstein [D] 44 H3
Ramsund [N] 192 D4
Ramvik [S] 184 F3
Ramygala [LT] 202 F4
Råna [N] 164 C5
Ranalt [A] 72 D2
Rånäs [S] 168 E2
Randaberg [N] 164 A3
Randalstown [GB] 2 G3
Randan [F] 68 D1
Randazzo [I] 124 A8
Rånddalen [S] 182 F5
Randen [N] 180 G5
Randers [DK] 160 D5
Randín [E] 78 C6
Randsjö [S] 182 F5
Randsundet [S] 182 E5
Randsverk [N] 180 G6
Råneå [S] 198 B2
Rânes [F] 26 F5
Ranft [CH] 58 F6
Rangstrup [DK] 156 C3
Rankinen [FIN] 198 D4
Rankweil [A] 58 H5
Ranshofen [A] 60 G4
Ransta [S] 168 C2
Rantajärvi [S] 196 B8
Rantasalmi [FIN] 188 E4
Rantsila [FIN] 198 D4
Ranua [FIN] 198 D2
Ranum [DK] 160 D4
Rånvassbotn [N] 192 D4
Raon-l'Etape [F] 44 F6
Rapallo [I] 110 B3
Räpina [EST] 200 G3
Rapla [EST] 200 D2
Rapolla [I] 120 G3
Raposa [P] 86 C5
Rappenloch-Schlucht [A] 60 B6
Rapperswil [CH] 58 G5
Rappottenstein [A] 62 D3
Rapsáni [GR] 132 G1
Raron [CH] 70 E2
Raša [HR] 112 E2
Rascafría [E] 88 F4
Raseiniai [LT] 202 E4
Råsele [S] 190 F5
Rasines [E] 82 F3
Rasivaara [FIN] 188 F3
Raška [YU] 150 B4
Rasktinkylä [FIN] 198 G5
Řásná [CZ] 48 H6
Rasovo [BG] 150 F2
Rasquera [E] 90 H6
Rast [RO] 150 F2
Rastatt [D] 46 B6
Råsted [DK] 160 D5
Rastede [D] 18 C5
Rastenfeld [A] 62 D3
Rasteš [MK] 128 D1
Rasti [FIN] 196 C6
Rastošnica [BIH] 154 E3
Rasueros [E] 88 D3
Raszków [PL] 36 D4
Ratan [S] 198 A5
Rätansbyn [S] 182 G4
Rateče [SLO] 72 H3
Ratekau [D] 18 G3
Rathangen [IRL] 2 E6
Rathcoole [IRL] 2 F6
Rathcormack [IRL] 4 D5
Rathcroghan [IRL] 2 D4
Rathdrum [IRL] 4 G4
Rathenow [D] 34 C2
Rathfran Abbey [IRL] 2 C3
Rathfriland [GB] 2 G4
Rathkeale [IRL] 4 C3
Rath Luirc / Charleville [IRL] 4 C4
Rathmelton [IRL] 2 F2
Rathmolyon [IRL] 2 F5
Rathmullan / Rathmullen [IRL] 2 F2
Rathmullen / Rathmullan [IRL] 2 F2
Rathnew [IRL] 4 G4
Rath of Mullamast [IRL] 4 F3
Rathvilty [IRL] 4 F4
Ratingen [D] 30 G3
Ratne [UA] 38 H4
Ratten [A] 74 E1
Rattenberg [A] 60 E6
Rattersdorf [A] 74 F1
Rattosjärvi [FIN] 192 H6
Rättvik [S] 172 H3
Ratzeburg [D] 18 G4
Raubling [D] 60 F5
Raudaskylä [FIN] 198 D5
Raudeberg [N] 180 B4
Raudlia [N] 190 E2
Raufa [IS] 194 G3
Raufoss [N] 172 B3
Rauhala [FIN] 192 H5
Rauhaniemi [FIN] 188 E5
Rauland Høyfjellshotell [N] 164 E1
Rauma / Raumo [FIN] 176 C2
Raumo / Rauma [FIN] 176 C2
Raumünzach [D] 58 F1
Rauna [LV] 200 E4
Rauris [A] 72 G1
Rautajärvi [FIN] 176 G1
Rautalampi [FIN] 186 H3
Rautaniemi [FIN] 176 E2
Rautas [S] 192 E5
Rautavaara [FIN] 198 F6
Rautila [FIN] 176 D4
Rautio [FIN] 198 C5
Rautjärvi [FIN] 178 F1
Rauvatn [N] 190 E2
Rauvatn [N] 190 E2
Ravanica, Manastir- [YU] 150 C2
Ravanička Pećina [YU] 150 D2
Ravanusa [I] 126 E4
Rava-Rus'ka [UA] 52 G3
Ravatn [N] 190 D3
Ravattila [FIN] 178 E2
Ravda [BG] 148 F4
Ravel [F] 68 D2
Ravello [I] 120 E4
Rävemåla [S] 162 E5
Ravenglass [GB] 10 D2
Ravenna [I] 110 H4
Ravensbrück [D] 20 D5
Ravensburg [D] 58 H4
Ravensburg [D] 46 C6
Raversijde [B] 28 F1
Rävmarken [S] 166 C4
Ravna Dubrava [YU] 150 E4
Ravna Reka [YU] 150 D2
Ravnholt [DK] 156 E3
Ravno [BIH] 152 C3
Rawa Mazowiecka [PL] 38 A4
Rawicz [PL] 36 C5
Rayleigh [GB] 14 F4
Rayol [F] 108 D6
Räyrinki [FIN] 186 D1
Razboj [BIH] 154 C2
Razbojna [YU] 150 C3
Razbojna Dupka [MK] 128 E2
Razdol'e [UA] 206 G5
Razdrto [SLO] 74 B6
Razgrad [BG] 148 D2
Reading [GB] 14 D4
Réalmont [F] 106 B3
Realp [CH] 70 F1
Reanaclogheen [IRL] 4 D5
Réau, Ancient Abbaye de la- [F] 54 F5
Reay [GB] 6 E2
Rebais [F] 42 H4
Rebolledo de la Torre [E] 82 D4
Reboly [RUS] 198 G5
Rebordelo [P] 80 E3
Rebŭrkovo [BG] 150 G4
Recanati [I] 116 C1
Recas [E] 96 F1
Recaş [RO] 76 H5
Recea [RO] 150 E1
Recey-sur-Ource [F] 56 G2
Rechnitz [A] 74 F1
Rechytsa [BY] 204 C6
Recke [D] 32 C2
Recklinghausen [D] 30 H2
Recoaro Terme [I] 72 C5
Recologne [F] 58 B4
Recsk [H] 64 E5
Recz [PL] 20 G5
Ręczno [PL] 36 H6
Reda [PL] 22 D2
Redalen [N] 172 B3
Redcar [GB] 10 G2
Redditch [GB] 12 H1
Redea [RO] 148 A1
Redefin [D] 18 H5
Rédics [H] 74 F3
Redipuglia [I] 72 H5
Redon [F] 40 E5
Redondela [E] 78 B4
Redondo [P] 94 E1
Redruth [GB] 12 C5
Rees [D] 16 F6
Refnes [N] 192 C4
Refsnes [N] 192 C3
Reftele [S] 162 C4
Regalbuto [I] 126 F3
Regaly [H] 64 E4
Regéc [H] 64 G4
Regen [D] 60 H2
Regensburg [D] 48 B6
Regenstauf [D] 48 B6
Reggello [I] 110 F6
Réggio di Calàbria [I] 124 C7
Reggiolo [I] 110 E2
Réggio nell'Emilia [I] 110 E3
Reghin [RO] 206 C4
Rekínio [GR] 132 H4
Regozero [RUS] 198 G2
Reguengos de Monsaraz [P] 94 E2
Rehau [D] 48 B3
Rehden [D] 32 E1
Rehna [D] 18 H4
Reichéa [GR] 136 F4
Reichenau [D] 58 G4
Reichenau an der Rax [A] 62 E6
Reichenbach [D] 48 C2
Reichenbach [D] 34 G6
Reichenbach [D] 32 F5
Reichenberg [D] 34 F2
Reichertshausen [D] 60 E3
Reichertshofen [D] 60 E3
Reigate [GB] 14 E5

Reigersburg [A] 62 E2
Reignier [F] 70 B2
Reila [FIN] 176 C3
Reims [F] 44 B3
Rein [A] 74 D2
Reinach [CH] 58 E4
Reinach [CH] 58 F5
Reinberg [D] 20 D3
Reine [N] 192 B5
Reinfeld [D] 18 G3
Reinhardshagen [D] 32 F4
Reinheim [D] 46 C3
Reinosa [E] 82 E4
Reinsfeld [D] 44 G2
Reinsvik [N] 180 F2
Reinsvoll [N] 172 B4
Reisach [A] 72 G3
Reisbach [D] 60 G3
Reischach [D] 60 G4
Reischenhart [D] 60 F5
Reisjärvi [FIN] 198 D6
Reit im Winkl [D] 60 F5
Reitzehain [D] 48 D2
Rejmyre [S] 168 B4
Rejowiec Fabryczny [PL] 38 F6
Rejštejn [CZ] 48 E6
Reken [D] 16 G6
Remagen [D] 30 H5
Rémalard [F] 26 G6
Remels [D] 18 C4
Remeskylä [FIN] 198 E5
Remetea Mare [RO] 76 G5
Remich [L] 44 F3
Remígia, Cova- [E] 98 G2
Remiremont [F] 58 C3
Remnes [N] 190 D2
Remolinos [E] 90 E3
Remouchamps [B] 30 E5
Remoulins [F] 106 G3
Remscheid [D] 30 H4
Remte [LV] 200 C5
Rémuzat [F] 108 B2
Rena [N] 172 C2
Renaison [F] 68 E2
Renaix (Ronse) [B] 28 G3
Renålandet [S] 190 E6
Renbygda [N] 182 C3
Rencēni [LV] 200 E4
Renchen [D] 58 F1
Renda [LV] 200 C5
Rendal [N] 180 G2
Rende [I] 124 D4
Rendsburg [D] 18 F2
Rengsjö [S] 174 D2
Reni [UA] 206 D5
Renko [FIN] 176 G3
Renkum [NL] 16 E5
Rennebu [N] 180 H3
Rennerod [D] 46 B1
Rennes [F] 26 C6
Rennweg [A] 72 H2
Renon / Ritten [I] 72 D3
Rens [DK] 156 B4
Rensjön [S] 192 E4
Rentería / Errenteria [E] 84 B2
Rentína [GR] 132 F3
Rentína [GR] 130 C4
Rentjärn [S] 190 G4
Répáshuta [H] 64 F5
Répcelak [H] 74 G1
Repino [RUS] 178 G4
Replot / Raippaluoto [FIN] 186 A2
Repo-Aslak [FIN] 196 D4
Repojoki [FIN] 196 C5
Reposaari [FIN] 176 C1
Reppen [N] 190 D1
République, Col de la- [F] 68 F4
Repvåg [N] 196 C2
Requena [E] 98 D4
Réquista [F] 106 C2
Rerik [D] 20 A3
Res [AL] 128 C1
Reşadiye [TR] 142 D3
Resana [I] 72 E6
Resavska Pećina [YU] 150 D2
Resen [MK] 128 D3
Reshety [RUS] 200 H4
Reshetylivka [UA] 206 G2
Reşiţa [RO] 206 A5
Resko [PL] 20 G4
Resmo [S] 162 G5
Reso / Raisio [FIN] 176 D4
Ressons [F] 28 E6
Reszel [PL] 24 B3
Retama [E] 96 D3
Retama, Garganta de- [E] 96 D3
Retamar [E] 102 G5
Retamosa [E] 96 C1
Retford [GB] 10 F5
Rethel [F] 44 C2
Rethem [D] 18 E6
Réthymno [GR] 140 D4
Retiers [F] 40 G4
Retortillo de Soria [E] 90 A3
Retournac [F] 68 E4
Rétság [H] 64 C5
Retuerta [E] 88 H1
Retuerta del Bullaque [E] 96 E2
Retz [A] 62 E3
Reuilly [F] 56 B3
Reus [E] 92 C5
Reusel [NL] 30 E3
Reuterstadt Stavenhagen [D] 20 C4
Reutlingen [D] 58 H2
Reutte [A] 60 C6
Revel [F] 106 B4
Révfülöp [H] 74 H3
Révigny [F] 44 C4
Révigny-sur-Ornain [F] 44 C4
Revin [F] 44 C1
Revište [SK] 64 B3
Řevničov [CZ] 48 E3
Revonlahti [FIN] 198 D4
Revsnes [N] 170 D2
Revsnes [N] 190 B5
Revúca [SK] 64 E3
Rewal [PL] 20 F3
Rexbo [S] 172 H4
Reyðarfjörður [IS] 194 G5
Reykhólar [IS] 194 C2
Reykholt [IS] 194 C4
Reykjahlíð [IS] 194 F4
Reykjavík [IS] 194 B4
Rey Moro, Cueva del- [E] 98 D6
Rēzekne [LV] 200 G5
Rezovo [BG] 148 G5
Rgotina [YU] 150 E2
Rhayader [GB] 10 C6
Rheda [D] 32 D3
Rhede [D] 16 G6
Rheinau [D] 44 H6
Rheinbach [D] 30 G5
Rheinberg [D] 30 G2
Rheinböllen [D] 44 H2
Rheindahlen [D] 30 F3
Rheine [D] 16 H5
Rheinfelden [CH] 58 E4
Rheinfelden [D] 58 E4
Rheinsberg [D] 20 C6
Rhein-Weser-Turm [D] 32 D5
Rheinzabern [D] 46 B5
Rhenen [NL] 16 E5
Rhens [D] 30 H6
Rheydt [D] 30 G3
Rhinau [F] 58 E2
Rhinow [D] 34 C1
Rho [I] 70 G5
Rhosneigr [GB] 10 B4
Rhyl [GB] 10 C4
Rhynern [D] 32 C4
Riaillé [F] 40 G6
Riaño [E] 82 C3
Rians [F] 108 C4
Riaza [E] 88 G3
Ribadavia [E] 78 C5
Ribadelago [E] 78 E6
Ribadeo [E] 78 F2
Ribadesella [E] 82 C2
Ribaflecha [E] 90 C1
Ribaforada [E] 84 B6
Ribarci [YU] 150 E5
Ribariće [YU] 150 B4
Ribaritsa [BG] 148 A4
Riba-roja de Túria [E] 98 E4
Ribarska Banja [YU] 150 D3
Ribe [DK] 156 B3
Ribeauville [F] 58 D2
Ribécourt [F] 28 E6
Ribeira Brava [P] 100 A3
Ribeira de Pena [P] 80 D3
Ribemont [F] 28 F5
Ribera [I] 126 C3
Ribérac [F] 66 E2
Ribera de Cardós [E] 84 G6
Ribera del Fresno [E] 94 H3
Ribes de Freser [E] 92 E2
Ribnica [BIH] 154 D3
Ribnica [SLO] 74 C6
Ribnica [SLO] 74 B6
Rîbniţa [MD] 206 E4
Ribnitz-Damgarten [D] 20 C2
Ribolla [I] 114 F2
Ricadi [I] 124 C6
Říčany [CZ] 48 G4
Riccia [I] 120 F1
Riccione [I] 112 B5
Richelieu [F] 54 F3
Richmond [GB] 10 F2
Richtenberg [D] 20 C3
Rickarum [S] 158 D2
Rickling [D] 18 G3
Ricla [E] 90 D4
Ricse [H] 64 H4
Riddarhyttan [S] 166 H2
Ridjica [YU] 76 C5
Riebini [LV] 200 F6
Ried [A] 72 C2
Riedenburg [D] 60 E2
Riedern [D] 58 F4
Ried im Innkreis [A] 60 H4
Riedlingen [D] 58 H3
Riegel [D] 58 E2
Riegersburg [A] 74 E2
Riekki [FIN] 198 F2
Riello [E] 78 G5
Rieneck [D] 46 E3
Riesa [D] 34 E5
Riesi [I] 126 E4
Riestedt [D] 34 B5
Rietavas [LT] 202 D4
Rietberg [D] 32 D3
Rieti [I] 116 B4
Rieumes [F] 84 H3
Rieupeyroux [F] 66 H6
Rieux [F] 84 H4
Riez [F] 108 C4
Riezlern [A] 60 B6
Rīga [LV] 200 D5
Rigáni [GR] 132 F5
Rigeo [GR] 132 G2
Rignac [F] 68 A5
Rignano Flaminio [I] 116 A4
Riihimäki [FIN] 176 G3
Riihivaara [FIN] 198 G5
Riihivalkama [FIN] 176 F3
Riistavesi [FIN] 188 D2
Rijeka [HR] 112 E1
Rijeka Crnojevića [YU] 152 E4
Rijssen [NL] 16 G5
Riksgränsen [S] 192 D4
Rila [BG] 150 F6
Rillé [F] 54 F1
Rillo [E] 90 D6
Rima [I] 70 E3
Rimavská Sobota [SK] 64 E4
Rimbo [S] 168 E2
Rimella [I] 70 E3
Rimforsa [S] 162 F1
Rimini [I] 110 H5
Rimito / Rymättylä [FIN] 176 D5
Rimske Toplice [SLO] 74 D5
Rincón de la Victoria [E] 102 C5
Rincón de Soto [E] 84 A5
Rindal [N] 180 G2
Rindown Castle [IRL] 2 D5
Ring / An Rinn [IRL] 4 E5
Ringarum [S] 168 B6
Ringaskiddy [IRL] 4 D5
Ringe [DK] 156 D3
Ringebu [N] 170 H1
Ringkøbing [DK] 160 B6
Ringnes [N] 170 G5
Ringøy [N] 170 D4
Ringstad [S] 168 B5
Ringsted [DK] 156 F3
Ringwood [GB] 12 G5
Rinøya [N] 192 C4
Rinteln [D] 32 E2
Río [GR] 132 F5
Riobianco / Weissenbach [I] 72 D2
Riofrío [E] 78 G5
Riola Sardo [I] 118 B5
Riolobos [E] 86 H4
Riolo Terme [I] 110 G4
Riom [F] 68 C2
Riomaggiore [I] 110 C4
Rio Maior [P] 86 C4
Riomar [E] 92 B6
Rio Mau [P] 80 B3
Riom-ès-Montagnes [F] 68 B3
Rion-des-Landes [F] 66 B5
Rionegro del Puente [E] 80 G3
Rionero in Vùlture [I] 120 G3
Riópar [E] 96 H6
Riós [E] 78 D6
Riosa [E] 78 H4
Rio Saliceto [I] 110 E2
Rio Torto [P] 80 D6
Rioz [F] 58 B4
Ripač [BIH] 112 H3
Ripacandida [I] 120 G3
Ripanj [YU] 154 G3
Riparbella [I] 114 E1
Ripatransone [I] 116 C2
Ripky [UA] 204 C7
Ripley [GB] 10 E5
Ripoll [E] 92 E2
Ripon [GB] 10 F3
Riposto [I] 124 B8
Riquewihr [F] 58 D2
Risan [YU] 152 D4
Risasvallen [S] 182 E4
Risbäck [S] 190 E4
Riscle [F] 84 E2
Riseberga [S] 158 C1
Riseberga Kloster [S] 166 G3
Rish [BG] 148 E3
Risliden [S] 190 H4
Risnes [N] 164 C4
Risnes [N] 170 B2
Risnovce [SK] 64 A4
Risør [N] 164 F4
Risøyhamn [N] 192 C3
Rissa [N] 190 B6
Risti [EST] 200 D2
Ristiina [FIN] 188 C6
Ristijärvi [FIN] 198 F4
Ristinge [DK] 156 E5
Ristna [EST] 200 C2
Ristovac [YU] 150 D5
Risum-Lindholm [D] 156 B5
Ritíni [GR] 128 G5
Rittmannshausen [D] 32 G6
Riva-Bella [F] 26 F3
Riva del Garda [I] 72 C5
Rivarolo Canavese [I] 70 D5
Rivarolo Mant. [I] 110 E2
Rive-de-Gier [F] 68 F3
Rivergaro [I] 110 C2
Rivesaltes [F] 92 G1
Rivne [UA] 206 D2
Rivoli [I] 70 D5
Rizári [GR] 128 F4
Rízia [GR] 146 A2
Rizoma [GR] 132 E2
Rizómata [GR] 128 G5
Rizómylos [GR] 136 D4
Rizómylos [GR] 132 H2
Rjånes [N] 180 C4
Rjukan [N] 170 F6
Ro [I] 110 G2
Roa [E] 88 G2
Roa [N] 172 B5
Roanne [F] 68 E2
Roavvegiedde [N] 196 D3
Roavvegieddi [N] 196 D3
Robbio [I] 70 F5
Röbel [D] 20 C5
Robertsfors [S] 198 A5
Robleda [E] 86 H2
Robledillo de Gata [E] 86 H3
Robledo [E] 96 H5
Robledo de Chavela [E] 88 E5
Robledo del Buey [E] 96 D2
Robliza de Cojos [E] 88 B3
Robres [E] 90 F3
Robres del Castillo [E] 90 C1
Rocamadour [F] 66 G4
Roccabianca [I] 110 D2
Roccadàspide [I] 120 F4
Rocca di Cambio [I] 116 C4
Rocca di Mezzo [I] 116 C4
Rocca di Neto [I] 124 F5
Rocca Imperiale [I] 122 D5
Roccalbegna [I] 114 G3
Roccalumera [I] 124 B8
Rocca Malatina, Sassi di- [I] 110 E4
Roccamonfina [I] 120 D2
Roccanova [I] 122 C5
Roccapalumba [I] 126 D2
Rocca Pia [I] 116 D5
Roccaraso [I] 116 D6
Rocca San Casciano [I] 110 G5
Rocca Sinibalda [I] 116 B4
Roccastrada [I] 114 F2
Roccaverano [I] 108 H2
Roccella Iónica [I] 124 D7
Roccelletta del Vescovo di Squillace [I] 124 E5
Rocche di Cusa [I] 126 B3
Rochdale [GB] 10 E4
Roche [E] 100 F4
Rochebloine, Château de- [F] 68 E5
Rochechouart [F] 54 F6
Rochecourbière, Grotte de- [F] 106 H2
Rochefort [B] 30 D6
Rochefort [F] 54 C5
Rochefort, Grotte de- [F] 40 H5
Rochefort-en-Terre [F] 40 E5
Rochefort-s-Nenon [F] 56 H4
Rochehaut [B] 44 D2
Rochemaure [F] 68 F6
Rocher, Château du- [F] 26 E6
Rocherolle, Château de la- [F] 54 G4
Rochers, Château des- [F] 26 D6
Rocheservière [F] 54 B2
Rochester [GB] 14 F4
Rochlitz [D] 34 D6
Rochsburg [D] 48 D1
Rockcorry [IRL] 2 F4
Rockenhausen [D] 46 B4
Rockhammar [S] 166 H2
Rockneby [S] 162 G5
Rocroi [F] 28 H5
Róda [GR] 132 B1
Rodach [D] 46 G2
Roda de Isábena [E] 84 F6
Ródão, Portas de- [P] 86 E4
Rødberg [N] 170 F5
Rødby [DK] 20 A1
Rødbyhavn [DK] 20 A1
Rødding [DK] 156 B3
Rødding [DK] 160 C5
Rödeby [S] 158 F1
Rodeiro [E] 78 C4
Rødekro [DK] 156 C4
Roden [NL] 16 G2
Rodenkirchen [D] 18 D4
Rodewald [D] 32 F1
Rodewisch [D] 48 C2
Rodez [F] 68 B6
Rødhus Klit [DK] 160 D3
Rodiá [GR] 132 G1
Rodi Gargánico [I] 116 G5
Roding [D] 48 C6
Rødkærsbro [DK] 160 D5
Rodolívos [GR] 130 C3
Rodópoli [GR] 128 H2
Ródos [GR] 142 E4
Rodrigatos de la Obispalía [E] 78 G5
Rodrigo, Castelo- [P] 80 E6
Rødvig [DK] 156 G4
Roela [EST] 200 F1
Roermond [NL] 30 F3
Roeselare (Roulers) [B] 28 F2
Rœulx [B] 28 H3
Roflaschlucht [CH] 70 G2
Rofrano [I] 120 G5
Rogač [HR] 154 A6
Rogačica [YU] 154 F4
Rogalin [PL] 36 C3
Rogaška Slatina [SLO] 74 D4
Rogatec [SLO] 74 E4
Rogatica [BIH] 152 E1
Rogätz [D] 34 B2
Rogil [P] 94 B4
Rögla [S] 158 C3
Rogliano [F] 114 C2
Rogliano [I] 124 D5
Rognac [F] 106 H5
Rognan [N] 192 C6
Rognes [N] 182 B2
Rogovo [RUS] 200 G4
Rogowo [PL] 36 D2
Rogozhinë [AL] 128 B3
Rogoznica [HR] 116 H1
Rogoźno [PL] 36 C2
Rohan [F] 26 A5
Rohatec [CZ] 62 G2
Rohatyn [UA] 206 C2
Rohrbach [A] 62 B3
Rohrbach-lès-Bitche [F] 44 G4
Rohrberg [D] 34 A1
Rohr i. Niederb. [D] 60 F2
Rohuküla [EST] 200 D2
Rohuneeme [EST] 200 D1
Roisel [F] 28 F5
Roja [LV] 200 C4
Rojão Grande [P] 80 C6
Röjdåfors [S] 172 E5
Rojiştea [RO] 150 G1
Rök [S] 166 G6
Röke [S] 158 C1
Rokietnica [PL] 52 F4
Rokiškis [LT] 202 G3
Rökkum [N] 180 F2
Røkland [N] 190 E1
Roknäs [S] 198 A3
Rokua [FIN] 198 E4
Rokycany [CZ] 48 E4
Røldal [N] 170 C5
Rolle [CH] 70 B1
Rølvåg [N] 190 D2
Rolvsøy [N] 166 B3
Roma [I] 116 A5
Roma [S] 168 G4
Romagnano Sésia [I] 70 E4
Roman [BG] 150 G3
Roman [RO] 206 D4
Romangordo [E] 88 B6
Romanija [BIH] 152 D1
Romanshorn [CH] 58 H4
Romans-sur-Isère [F] 68 F5
Rombas [F] 44 E4
Rom By [DK] 160 B5
Romena, Castello di- [I] 110 G5
Romena, Pieve di- [I] 110 G5
Romeral [E] 96 G2
Romilly-sur-Seine [F] 44 A5
Romny [UA] 206 G1
Romont [CH] 70 C1
Romorantin-Lanthenay [F] 54 H2
Romppala [FIN] 188 F1
Romsey [GB] 12 H4
Romtemplom [H] 64 C6
Roncade [I] 72 E6
Roncal / Erronkari [E] 84 C4
Roncegno [I] 72 D4
Roncesvalles [E] 84 C3
Ronchamp [F] 58 C3
Ronchi dei Legionari [I] 72 H5
Ronciglione [I] 114 H4
Ronco Canavese [I] 70 D4
Roncofreddo [I] 110 H5
Ronco Scrivia [I] 110 B3
Ronda [E] 102 A4
Rønde [DK] 160 E6
Ronehamn [S] 168 G5
Rong [N] 170 C3
Rõngu [EST] 200 F3
Ronkeli [FIN] 198 G5
Rönnäng [S] 160 G1
Rønne [DK] 158 E4
Ronneburg [D] 48 C1
Ronneby [S] 158 F1
Rønnede [DK] 156 G4
Rönnigsåsen [S] 182 F4
Rönnöfors [S] 190 D6
Rönnskär [S] 198 A4
Rönö [S] 168 C5
Ronse (Renaix) [B] 28 G3
Roodeschool [NL] 16 G1
Roonah Quay [IRL] 2 B3
Roosendaal [NL] 16 C6
Roosky [IRL] 2 D4
Ropa [PL] 52 C5
Ropaži [LV] 200 E5
Ropczyce [PL] 52 D3
Ropeid [N] 164 B1
Ropinsalmi [FIN] 192 F3
Ropotovo [MK] 128 E2
Ropsha [RUS] 178 E6
Roque, Pointe de la- [F] 26 G3
Roquebillière [F] 108 F4
Roquebrune-Cap-Martin [F] 108 F4
Roquefort [F] 66 C5
Roquefort-sur-Soulzon [F] 106 D3
Roquemaure [F] 106 G3
Roquesteron [F] 108 E4
Roquetaillade, Château de- [F] 66 D4
Roquetas de Mar [E] 102 F5
Roquetes [E] 92 A5
Rörbäcksnäs [S] 172 E3
Rore [BIH] 154 B4
Roron [S] 182 G3
Røros [N] 182 C4
Rorschach [CH] 58 H5
Rørvig [DK] 156 F2
Rørvik [N] 190 C4
Rørvik [N] 182 B1
Rørvik [N] 164 C5
Ros' [BY] 24 G5
Rosala [FIN] 176 E6
Rosal de la Frontera [E] 94 E3
Rosa Marina [I] 122 F3
Rosans [F] 108 B2
Rosapenna [IRL] 2 E1
Rosarno [I] 124 C6
Rosas / Roses [E] 92 G2
Rosche [D] 18 G6
Rościszewo [PL] 36 H1
Roscoff [F] 40 C1
Roscommon [IRL] 2 D5
Roscrea [IRL] 2 D6
Rosegg [A] 74 B3
Roselle [I] 114 F2
Rosen [BG] 148 F4
Rosenburg [A] 62 E3
Rosendal [N] 170 B5
Rosenheim [D] 60 F5
Rosenhof [A] 62 C3
Rosenholm [DK] 160 E6
Rosentorp [S] 172 H2
Rosersberg [S] 168 D2
Roses / Rosas [E] 92 G2
Roseto degli Abruzzi [I] 116 D3
Roseto Valfortore [I] 120 F2
Rósfa [H] 74 G1
Roshchine [RUS] 178 G4
Rosica [BG] 148 F1
Rosice [CZ] 50 B6
Rosignano-Marittimo [I] 110 D6
Rosignano Solvay [I] 114 E1
Rosino [BG] 148 B4
Roşiori [RO] 76 H1
Roşiori de Vede [RO] 148 B1
Roskilde [DK] 156 G2
Rosko [PL] 36 B1
Roslags-Bro [S] 168 E1
Roslags kulla [S] 168 E2
Roslavl' [RUS] 204 D5
Roslev [DK] 160 C4
Rosmaninhal [P] 86 F4
Rosnowo [PL] 22 A3
Rosolina Mare [I] 110 H2
Rosolini [I] 126 G5
Rosoman [MK] 128 F2
Rosporden [F] 40 C3
Ross Abbey [IRL] 2 C4
Rossano [I] 124 E4
Rossas [P] 80 C5
Ross Carberry [IRL] 4 C5
Rosscor [GB] 2 E3
Rosserk Abbey [IRL] 2 C3
Rosses Point [IRL] 2 D3
Rosshaupten [D] 60 C5
Rossiglione [I] 108 H2
Rossio [P] 86 D4
Rossla [D] 34 A5
Rosslare Harbour [IRL] 4 F5
Rosslau [D] 34 C4
Rosslea [GB] 2 F4
Rossnes [N] 170 A3
Rossön [S] 190 F6
Ross-on-Wye [GB] 12 G2
Rossosz [PL] 38 F4
Rossoszyca [PL] 36 F4
Røssvassbukt [N] 190 E3
Röstånga [S] 158 C2
Rostassac [F] 66 F5
Roštejn [CZ] 50 A6
Roštejn [CZ] 48 H6
Rostock [D] 20 B3
Rostrenen [F] 40 D3
Rostrevor [GB] 2 G4
Røstvollen [N] 182 D5
Røsvik [N] 192 C5
Rosvik [S] 198 B3
Rosyth [GB] 8 E3
Röszke [H] 76 E4
Roszki-Wodżki [PL] 24 E6
Rot [S] 172 F2
Rota [E] 100 F3
Rotemo [N] 164 D2
Rotenburg [D] 32 F6
Rotenburg [D] 18 E5
Rotenfels [D] 46 B3
Rotgülden [A] 72 H2
Roth [D] 46 G5
Rötha [D] 34 C6
Rothemühl [D] 20 E4
Rothenburg [D] 34 G5
Rothenburg, Ruine- [D] 46 G5
Rothenburg ob der Tauber [D] 46 E5
Rothéneuf [F] 26 C4
Rotherham [GB] 10 F4
Rothes [GB] 6 E5
Rothesay [GB] 8 C3
Rotondella [I] 122 D5
Rótova [E] 98 E6
Rotsund [N] 192 F2
Rott [D] 60 D5
Rott [D] 60 F5
Rottach [D] 60 E5
Rötteln [D] 58 E4
Rottenbach [D] 46 G2
Rottenbuch [D] 60 D5
Rottenburg [D] 60 F3
Rottenburg [D] 58 G2
Rottenmann [A] 62 B6
Rotterdam [NL] 16 C5
Rotthalmünster [D] 60 H4
Röttingen [D] 46 E5
Rottne [S] 162 E4
Rottneros [S] 166 E1
Rottweil [D] 58 G3
Rötz [D] 48 C5
Roubaix [F] 28 F3
Rouchovany [CZ] 62 E2
Roudnice nad Labem [CZ] 48 F3
Rouen [F] 28 B5
Rouffach [F] 58 D3
Rouffignac, Grotte de- [F] 66 F3
Rougé [F] 40 F5
Rougemont [F] 58 C4
Rougemont [F] 58 D3
Rouillac [F] 54 D6
Roujan [F] 106 D4
Roulers (Roeselare) [B] 28 F2
Roundstone [IRL] 2 B4
Roundwood [IRL] 4 G3
Roússa [GR] 130 G2
Roussillon [F] 106 H4
Rouvres-en-Xaintois [F] 44 E6
Rovaniemi [FIN] 196 D8
Rovato [I] 72 A6
Roverbella [I] 110 E1
Rovereto [I] 72 C5
Rövershagen [D] 20 B3
Roverud [N] 172 D5
Roviés [GR] 134 B4
Rovigo [I] 110 G2
Rovinj [HR] 112 D2
Rovišće [HR] 74 F5
Rów [PL] 20 F6
Rowy [PL] 22 B1
Royan [F] 54 B6
Royat [F] 68 C2
Royaumont, Abbaye de- [F] 42 F3
Roybon [F] 68 G4
Roye [F] 28 E5
Royère-de-Vassivière [F] 68 A1
Royken [N] 164 H1
Røyrvik [N] 190 D4
Røysheim [N] 180 F6
Royston [GB] 14 E3
Röyttä [FIN] 198 C3
Roza [BG] 148 D5
Rožaj [YU] 150 B5
Różan [PL] 24 C6
Różanki [PL] 34 H1
Rožanstvo [YU] 150 A3
Rozay-en-Brie [F] 42 G4
Rožmberk [CZ] 62 B3
Rožmitál pod Třemšínem [CZ] 48 E5
Rožňava [SK] 64 E3
Rožnov pod Radhoštěm [CZ] 50 E5
Rożnów [PL] 52 B4
Rozogi [PL] 24 C5
Rozoy [F] 28 G6
Rozprza [PL] 36 H5
Roztoky [CZ] 48 F3
Rožupe [LV] 200 F6
Rozvadov [CZ] 48 C4
Rozzano [I] 70 G5
Rrëshen [AL] 128 B1
Rtanj [YU] 150 D2
Ru [E] 78 D3
Rubbestadneset [N] 170 A5
Rubena [E] 82 E6
Rubeži [YU] 152 E3
Rubielos de Mora [E] 98 E2
Rubiera [I] 110 E3
Rucava [LV] 202 D3
Ruciane-Nida [PL] 24 C4
Ruda [S] 162 F4
Ruda Maleniecka [PL] 38 A6
Rudare [YU] 150 C4
Rudawica [PL] 34 H5
Rudawka [PL] 24 F3
Rudelsburg [D] 34 B6
Rudenica [YU] 150 C3
Rudersdorf [D] 34 F2
Rüdesheim [D] 46 B3
Rūdiškės [LT] 24 H1
Rudka [PL] 38 E1
Rudkøbing [DK] 156 E4
Rudna [PL] 36 B5
Rudna [PL] 22 C5
Rudna Glava [YU] 150 D1
Rudnica [YU] 152 E2
Rudnica [YU] 150 B4
Rudnik [BG] 148 F3
Rudnik [PL] 50 E3
Rudnik [YU] 150 B5
Rudnik [YU] 150 B2
Rudniki [PL] 50 F1
Rudnik nad Sanem [PL] 52 E2
Rudno [PL] 22 E4
Rudnya [RUS] 204 C5
Rudolphstein [D] 46 H2
Rudolstadt [D] 46 H1
Rudozem [BG] 130 E1
Rudsgrendi [N] 164 F1
Ruds-Vedby [DK] 156 F3
Rudy [PL] 50 F3
Rudzāti [LV] 200 F5
Rue [F] 28 D3
Rueda [E] 88 E2
Rueda, Monasterio de- [E] 90 F5
Rueda de Jalón [E] 90 D3
Ruelle-sur-Touvre [F] 66 E1
Ruffano [I] 122 G6
Ruffec [F] 54 E5
Ruffieux [F] 70 A3
Rugāji [LV] 200 G5
Rugby [GB] 14 D2
Rugeley [GB] 10 E6
Rugldalen [N] 182 C3
Rugles [F] 26 H5
Ruhällen [S] 168 C1
Rühen [D] 32 H2
Ruhland [D] 34 F5
Ruhmannsfelden [D] 60 G2
Ruhpolding [D] 60 G5
Ruidera [E] 96 G4
Rūjiena [LV] 200 E3
Ruju, Nuraghe- [I] 118 D3
Ruka [FIN] 196 F8
Rukajärvi [FIN] 196 F8
Rülzheim [D] 46 B5
Rum [H] 74 G2
Ruma [YU] 154 F2
Rumburk [CZ] 48 G1
Rumelifeneri [TR] 146 E2
Rumia [PL] 22 D2
Rumigny [F] 28 H5
Rumilly [F] 70 A3
Rumo [FIN] 198 F5
Rumpani [LV] 200 F4
Runcorn [GB] 10 D4
Rundfloen [N] 172 E3
Rundhaug [N] 192 E3
Rundvik [S] 184 H1
Runni [FIN] 198 E6
Ruokojärvi [FIN] 192 H6
Ruokojärvi [S] 196 B8
Ruokolahti [FIN] 178 E1
Ruona [FIN] 186 D3
Ruorasmäki [FIN] 186 H6
Ruoti [I] 120 G3
Ruovesi [FIN] 186 E5
Rupa [HR] 112 E1
Rupea [RO] 206 C5
Rupt [F] 58 C3
Rus [E] 102 F1
Rusalka [BG] 148 G2
Rusanivka [UA] 206 G2
Rusdal [N] 164 B4
Ruse [BG] 148 C2
Ruševo [HR] 154 D1
Rusfors [S] 190 G4
Rush [IRL] 2 F6
Rushden [GB] 14 E2
Rusiec [PL] 36 F5
Rusinowo [PL] 22 A6
Ruskeala [RUS] 188 G4
Ruski Krstur [YU] 76 D6
Ruskila [FIN] 188 D2
Rusksele [S] 190 G4
Rusktträsk [S] 190 G4
Rusnė [LT] 202 D5
Rusokastro [BG] 148 F4
Rüsselsheim [D] 46 C3
Russenes [N] 196 C2
Russi [I] 110 G4
Rust [A] 62 F5
Rust [D] 58 E2
Rustad [N] 172 B5
Rustefjelbma [N] 196 D2
Ruswil [CH] 58 E6
Ruszów [PL] 34 H5

Rutalahti [FIN] 186 G5
Rute [E] 102 C3
Rutenbrock [D] 16 H3
Rüthen [D] 32 D4
Ruthin [GB] 10 C4
Rüti [CH] 58 G5
Rutigliano [I] 122 E3
Rutledal [N] 170 B2
Ruukki [FIN] 198 D4
Ruunaa [FIN] 198 G6
Ruurlo [NL] 16 F5
Ruutana [FIN] 176 F1
Ruutana [FIN] 198 E6
Ruvallen [S] 182 E3
Ruvasiahtio [FIN] 188 F2
Ruvo di Puglia [I] 122 D2
Ruwer [D] 44 G2
Ruza [RUS] 204 E4
Ruzhany [BY] 24 H6
Ruzhintsi [BG] 150 E3
Růžkovy Lhotice [CZ] 48 G5
Ružomberok [SK] 64 C2
Ry [DK] 156 D1
Ryakhovo [BG] 148 D1
Ryákia [GR] 128 G5
Rybarzowice [PL] 50 G5
Rybinsk [RUS] 204 F2
Rybnik [PL] 50 F4
Rybník [SK] 64 E3
Rychliki [PL] 22 F3
Rychnburk [CZ] 50 B4
Rychnov nad Kněžnou [CZ] 50 B3
Rychnowo [PL] 22 G4
Rychtal [PL] 36 E6
Rychwał [PL] 36 E3
Ryczywół [PL] 38 C4
Ryd [S] 162 D6
Rydaholm [S] 162 D4
Ryde [GB] 12 H5
Rydsnäs [S] 162 E2
Rydzyna [PL] 36 C4
Rye [GB] 14 F5
Ryen [N] 164 E5
Rygge [N] 166 B2
Rygozy [RUS] 200 H5
Ryhälä [FIN] 188 E5
Rykene [N] 164 E5
Ryki [PL] 38 D4
Ryl'sk [RUS] 204 E7
Rymań [PL] 20 G3
Rymanów [PL] 52 D5
Rýmařov [CZ] 50 D4
Rymättylä / Rimito [FIN] 176 D5
Rýmnio [GR] 128 F6
Ryn [PL] 24 C3
Rynarzewo [PL] 22 D6
Ryomgård [DK] 160 E5
Rypefjord [N] 196 B2
Rypin [PL] 22 F6
Ryslinge [DK] 156 D3
Ryssby [S] 162 D4
Rysum [D] 16 H2
Rytel [PL] 22 C4
Rytkynkylä [FIN] 198 D5
Rytro [PL] 52 B5
Ryuttyu [RUS] 188 H4
Ryzmberk [CZ] 48 D5
Rzeczenica [PL] 22 B4
Rzeczyca [PL] 38 A5
Rzęgnowo [PL] 22 H6
Rzemień [PL] 52 D3
Rzepin [PL] 34 G3
Rzeszów [PL] 52 E3
Rzewnowo [PL] 20 F3
Rzgów [PL] 36 G4
Rzhev [RUS] 204 E4
Rzhishchiv [UA] 206 F2

S

Sääksjärvi [FIN] 186 D2
Sääksmäki [FIN] 176 F2
Saal [D] 60 F2
Saalbach [A] 72 F1
Saalburg [D] 46 C2
Saales [F] 44 G6
Saalfeld [D] 46 H2
Saalfelden [A] 60 G6
Saanen [CH] 70 D1
Saarbrücken [D] 44 G4
Saarburg [D] 44 F3
Saare [EST] 200 F2
Saarela [FIN] 198 G5
Saarenkylä [FIN] 196 D8
Saari [FIN] 188 F5
Saarijärvi [FIN] 186 F3
Saarikoski [FIN] 192 F3
Saariväara [FIN] 198 G4
Saarlouis [D] 44 F3
Saas Almagell [CH] 70 E3
Saas-Fee [CH] 70 E3
Saas Grund [CH] 70 E3
Sababurg [D] 32 F4
Šabac [YU] 154 F2
Sabadell [E] 92 E4
Sabaro [E] 82 C4
Sabáudia [I] 120 B2
Sabbioneta [I] 110 E2
Sabbucina [I] 126 E3
Sabile [LV] 200 C5
Sabiñánigo [E] 84 D5
Sabinosa [E] 100 A6
Sabinov [SK] 52 C6
Sabiote [E] 102 F2
Sables-d'Or-les-Pins [F] 26 B4
Sablé-sur-Sarthe [F] 42 A5
Saborsko [HR] 112 G2
Sabres [F] 66 C5
Sabrosa [P] 80 D4
Sabugal [P] 86 G2
Säby [S] 162 E1
Šaca [SK] 64 G3
Săcălaz [RO] 76 G5
Sacavém [P] 86 B5
Sacecorbo [E] 90 B5
Sacedón [E] 88 H6
Saceruela [E] 96 D4
Sacile [I] 72 F5
Sacra di San Michele [I] 70 C5
Sádaba [E] 84 B5
Sadala [EST] 200 F2
Sadikov Bunar [YU] 150 E4
Sadki [PL] 22 C6
Sadova [RO] 150 G2
Sadovets [BG] 148 A3
Sadovo [BG] 148 B6
Sądów [PL] 34 G3
Sadská [CZ] 48 G3
Sädvaluspen [S] 190 F2
Sæbø [N] 170 D4
Sæbø [N] 180 D4
Sæbøvik [N] 170 B5
Sæby [DK] 160 E3
Sæd [DK] 156 B4
Saelices [E] 96 H2
Sælvig [DK] 156 E2
Saepinum [I] 120 E1
Saerbeck [D] 32 C2
Sæter [N] 190 B6
Sætre [N] 164 H2
Saeul [L] 44 E2
Sævareid [N] 170 B4
Sævråsvåg [N] 170 B3
Safa [TR] 146 G5
Safara [P] 94 E3
Säffle [S] 166 E3
Saffron Walden [GB] 14 F3
Safonovo [RUS] 204 D4
Sagard [D] 20 D2
S'Agaró [E] 92 G4
Sagiáda [GR] 132 B2
Sagone [F] 114 A4
Sagres [P] 94 A5
Şagu [RO] 76 G5
Sagu / Sauvo [FIN] 176 E5
Sagunt / Sagunto [E] 98 F4
Sagunto / Sagunt [E] 98 F4
Sagvåg [N] 170 A5
Ságvár [H] 76 A3
Sahagún [E] 82 C5
Sahalahti [FIN] 176 G1
Sahilköy [TR] 146 F2
Şahin [TR] 146 B3
Sahrajärvi [FIN] 186 F4
Šahy [SK] 64 C5
Saignelégier [CH] 58 D5
Saija [FIN] 196 E7
Saillagouse [F] 92 E1
Saillans [F] 68 G6
Sains [F] 28 G5
Sainte-Lucie-de-Tallano [F] 114 B5
Sainte-Marie-Siché [F] 114 B5
Saintes [F] 54 C6
Saintfield [GB] 2 G4
Saint-Jacques [I] 70 D3
Saissac [F] 106 B4
Saivomuotka [S] 192 G4
Šajkaš [YU] 154 G1
Sajószentpéter [H] 64 F4
Šakiai [LT] 202 E5
Säkinmäki [FIN] 186 H3
Sakskøbing [DK] 20 B1
Saky [UA] 206 G5
Säkylä [FIN] 176 D3
Sala [S] 168 C1
Šal'a [SK] 64 A4
Salaberg [A] 62 C5
Salacgrīva [LV] 200 D4
Sala Consilina [I] 120 G4
Salahmi [FIN] 198 E5
Salákos [GR] 142 D4
Salamajärvi [FIN] 186 E1
Salamanca [E] 80 H6
Salamína [GR] 134 B6
Salantai [LT] 202 D4
Salaóra [GR] 132 D4
Salar [E] 102 D4
Sälard [RO] 76 H1
Salardú [E] 84 G5
Salas [E] 78 G3
Salas de los Infantes [E] 88 H1
Salaspils [LV] 200 E5
Salau [F] 84 G5
Salaš [YU] 150 E2
Salbohed [S] 168 B1
Salbris [F] 56 B2
Šalčininkai [LT] 202 G6
Salcombe [GB] 12 D5
Sălcuţa [RO] 150 F1
Saldaña [E] 82 C5
Salduba [E] 90 E3
Saldus [LV] 200 C5
Sale [I] 70 F6
Saleby [S] 166 E5
Salem [D] 58 H4
Salema [P] 94 A5
Salemi [I] 126 B2
Sälen [S] 172 E2
Salernes [F] 108 D4
Salerno [I] 120 F4
Salers [F] 68 B4
S. Alessio Siculo [I] 124 B8
Salgótarján [H] 64 D4
Salhus [N] 170 B3
Sali [HR] 112 F5
Salice [F] 114 B4
Salice Terme [I] 70 F6
Salies-de-Béarn [F] 84 D2
Salies-du-Salat [F] 84 G4
Salignac-Eyvigues [F] 66 G4
Salihli [TR] 144 E4
Salihorsk [BY] 204 B6
Salinas [E] 78 H3
Salinas [E] 104 D2
Salinas de Pinilla [E] 96 H5
Saline di Volterra [I] 114 F1
Sälinkää [FIN] 176 H3
Salins [F] 58 B5
Salins-les-Bains [F] 58 A5
Salir [P] 94 C5
Salisbury [GB] 12 G4
Salka [SK] 64 C5
Salkoluokta [S] 192 E6
Salla [FIN] 196 E7
Sallanches [F] 70 B3
Sallent de Gállego [E] 84 D4
Sälleryd [S] 158 G1
Salles [F] 66 C4
Salles [F] 106 A4
Salles-Curan [F] 106 D2
Sallmunds [S] 168 G6
Salme [EST] 200 C3
Salmerón [E] 90 A6
Salmivaara [FIN] 196 E7
Sal'miyarvi [RUS] 196 F3
Salmoral [E] 88 D4
Salo [FIN] 176 E4
Salò [I] 72 B6
Salobreña [E] 102 D5
Saločiai [LT] 200 E6
Saloinen [FIN] 198 C4
Salon [F] 44 B5
Salona [HR] 152 A2
Salon-de-Provence [F] 106 H4
Salonta [RO] 76 H3
Salorino [E] 86 F5
Salou [E] 92 C5
Salsbruket [N] 190 C4
Salse di Nirano [I] 110 E3
Salses-le-Château [F] 106 C6
Salsomaggiore Terme [I] 110 D2
Salsta [S] 168 D1
Salt [E] 92 F3
Saltash [GB] 12 D5
Saltbæk [DK] 156 E2
Saltsjöbaden [S] 168 E3
Saltum [DK] 160 D3
Saltvik [FIN] 176 B5
Saluzzo [I] 108 F2
Salvacañete [E] 98 D2
Salvada [P] 94 D3
Salvarola, Terme di- [I] 110 E3
Salvaterra de Magos [P] 86 C5
Salvaterra de Miño [E] 78 B5
Salvatierra [E] 96 E5
Salvatierra / Agurain [E] 82 H5
Salvatierra de los Barros [E] 94 G2
Salviac [F] 66 G4
Salzburg [A] 60 G5
Salzburg [D] 46 F2
Salzgitter-Bad [D] 32 G3
Salzgitter-Lebenstedt [D] 32 G3
Salzhausen [D] 18 F5
Salzkotten [D] 32 D4
Salzwedel [D] 18 H6
Salzweg [D] 60 H3
Sama de Grado [E] 78 H4
Samadet [F] 66 C6
Samaili [TR] 144 E5
Samandıra [TR] 146 F3
Samarína [GR] 128 D6
Samassi [I] 118 C6
Samatan [F] 84 G3
Samate [LV] 200 B5
Sambiase [I] 124 D5
Sambir [UA] 52 G5
Sambuca di Sicilia [I] 126 C3
Sambucheto [I] 116 B3
Sambucina, Abbazia della- [I] 124 D4
Samedan [CH] 72 A3
Samer [F] 28 D2
Sámi [GR] 132 C6
Samitier [E] 84 E6
Şamlı [TR] 146 D6
Samnaun [CH] 72 B2
Samo [I] 124 C7
Samobor [HR] 74 E6
Samoëns [F] 70 C3
Samokov [BG] 150 G5
Šamorín [SK] 62 G5
Samos [E] 78 E4
Sámos [GR] 144 C5
Samoš [YU] 154 H1
Samos, Monasterio de- [E] 78 E4
Samostan Pleterje [SLO] 74 D6
Samothráki [GR] 130 F4
Samovodene [BG] 148 C3
Sampatikí [GR] 136 F3
Sampéyre [I] 108 F2
Samtens [D] 20 D2
Samugheo [I] 118 C5
Saná [GR] 130 B5
San Adrián [E] 84 A5
San Agustín [E] 98 C3
San Anton Leitza [E] 84 B3
Sanary-sur-Mer [F] 108 C6
San Asensio [E] 82 G6
San Bartolomé [E] 100 E4
San Bartolomé de las Abiertas [E] 96 D1
San Bartolomé de la Torre [E] 94 E5
San Bartolomeo in Galdo [I] 120 F1
San Benedetto dei Marsi [I] 116 C5
San Benedetto del Tronto [I] 116 D2
San Benedetto in Alpe [I] 110 G5
San Benedetto Po [I] 110 E2
San Bernardino [CH] 70 G2
San Bernardino, Tunnel del- [Eur.] 70 G2
San Biagio di Callalta [I] 72 F6
San Biágio Plátani [I] 126 D3
San Bonifácio [I] 110 F1
San Bruzio [I] 114 F3
San Calogero [I] 126 C3
San Candido / Innichen [I] 72 E3
San Carlos del Valle [E] 96 G5
San Casciano dei Bagni [I] 114 G2
San Casciano in Val di Pesa [I] 110 F6
San Cataldo [I] 126 E3
San Cataldo [I] 122 G4
Sancergues [F] 56 D3
Sancerre [F] 56 D3
Sancey-le-Grand [F] 58 C5
Sanchidrián [E] 88 E4
San Cipirello [I] 126 C2
San Claudio al Chienti [I] 116 C1
San Clemente [E] 98 A4
San Clemente a Casuria [I] 116 D4
San Clemente al Vomano [I] 116 D3
Sancoins [F] 56 D4
San Cosme (Barreiros) [E] 78 E2
San Cristóbal de la Laguna [E] 100 C5
San Cristóbal de la Vega [E] 88 E3
Sancti Esperitus, Convent de- [E] 98 F4
Sancti Spiritus [E] 88 A3
Sancti-Spiritus [E] 96 C3
Sand [N] 164 B1
Sand [N] 172 C4
Sanda [N] 164 F2
San Damiano d'Asti [I] 70 E6
Sandane [N] 180 C5
San Daniele del Friuli [I] 72 G4
San Daniele Po [I] 110 D2
Sandanski [BG] 130 B2
Sandared [S] 162 B2
Sandarne [S] 174 E2
Sandau [D] 34 C1
Sandbach [GB] 10 D5
Sandbukt [N] 192 F1
Sande [D] 18 C4
Sande [N] 164 H2
Sande [N] 170 C1
Sandefjord [N] 164 H3
Sandeid [N] 164 B1
San Demetrio Corone [I] 124 D4
Sanden [N] 164 F2
Sandhem [S] 162 C1
Sandías [E] 78 C5
Sandıklı [TR] 144 H3
Sand in Taufers / Campo Tures [I] 72 E2
Sandl [A] 62 C3
Sandnäset [S] 184 D4
Sandnes [N] 164 B3
Sandnes [N] 164 F3
Sandness [GB] 6 G3
Sandnessjøen [N] 190 D2
Sando [E] 80 G6
Sandö Bro [S] 184 F3
Sandomierz [PL] 52 D2
San Dónaci [I] 122 G4
San Doná di Piave [I] 72 F6
San Donato Milanese [I] 70 G5
Sándorfalva [H] 76 E2
Sandown [GB] 12 H5
Sandrigo [I] 72 D6
Šandrovac [HR] 74 G5
Sandset [N] 192 C3
Sandsjö [S] 190 G5
Sandsjö [S] 172 G1
Sandsletta [N] 192 B4
Sandstad [N] 190 A6
Sandstad [N] 172 D4
Sandstedt [D] 18 D4
Sandur [FR] 160 A2
Sandvatn [N] 164 C4
Sandvig [DK] 158 E4
Sandvik [S] 162 G4
Sandvika [N] 164 H1
Sandvika [N] 190 C6
Sandviken [S] 174 E4
Sandvikvåg [N] 170 A5
Sandwich [GB] 14 G5
San Emiliano [E] 78 G4
San Esteban [E] 84 B3
San Esteban de Gormaz [E] 88 H3
San Fele [I] 120 G3
San Felice Circeo [I] 120 B2
San Felice in Balsignano [I] 122 D2
San Felice sul Panaro [I] 110 F2
San Ferdinando di Puglia [I] 120 H2
San Fernando [E] 100 F4
San Fratello [I] 126 F2
San Fruttuoso [I] 110 B3
San Galgano, Abbazia di- [I] 114 F2
Sangarcía [E] 88 E4
San Gavino Monreale [I] 118 C6
Sangazi [TR] 146 F3
San Gemini [I] 116 A3
San Gemini Fonte [I] 116 A3
Sangerhausen [D] 34 B5
San Germano [I] 70 E5
San Gimignano [I] 110 E6
San Ginesio [I] 116 C2
Sanginkylä [FIN] 198 E4
San Giorgio di Livenza [I] 72 F6
San Giórgio di Nogaro [I] 72 G5
San Giorgio Iónico [I] 122 F4
San Giovanni, Grotta- [I] 122 F4
San Giovanni, Grotta di- [I] 118 B6
San Giovanni al Mavone [I] 116 C4
San Giovanni di Sínis [I] 118 B5
San Giovanni in Croce [I] 110 D2
San Giovanni in Fiore [I] 124 E4
San Giovanni in Persiceto [I] 110 F3
San Giovanni in Venere [I] 116 E4
San Giovanni Lupatoto [I] 110 F1
San Giovanni Rotondo [I] 116 G6
San Giovanni Suergiu [I] 118 B7
San Giovanni Valdarno [I] 110 F6
San Giovenale [I] 114 H4
Sangis [S] 198 C2
San Giuliano Terme [I] 110 D5
San Giuseppe Jato [I] 126 C2
San Giustino [I] 110 G6
San Giusto [I] 116 B2
Sangla [EST] 200 F3
Sangüesa / Zangoza [E] 84 C5
Sanguinet [F] 66 B4
Sáni [GR] 130 B6
San Ignacio de Loiola [E] 82 H4
Sanitz [D] 20 C3
San Javier [E] 104 D4
San José [E] 102 G6
San José / Sant Josep [E] 104 C5
San Juan de Alicante / Sant Joan d'Alacant [E] 104 E2
San Juan del Olmo [E] 88 D4
San Juan de los Terreros [E] 104 B4
San Juan del Puerto [E] 94 E6
San Juan de Muskiz [E] 82 G3
Sankovo [RUS] 204 F3
Sankt Magdalena / Santa Maddalena Vallalta [I] 72 E2
Sankt-Michaelisdonn [D] 18 E3
Sankt-Peterburg [RUS] 178 H4
Sankt Valentin auf der Haide / San Valentino alla Muta [I] 72 B2
San Lazzaro di Savena [I] 110 F3
San Leo [I] 110 H5
San Leonardo [I] 120 H1
San Leonardo de Yagüe [E] 90 A2
San Leonardo in Passiria [I] 72 D2
San Lorenzo [I] 124 C8
San Lorenzo de Calatrava [E] 96 E5
San Lorenzo de El Escorial [E] 88 F5
San Lorenzo de la Parrilla [E] 98 B2
San Lorenzo in Campo [I] 112 B6
San Lorenzo Nuovo [I] 114 G3
San Luca [I] 124 C7
Sanlúcar de Barrameda [E] 100 F3
Sanlúcar la Mayor [E] 94 G6
San Lúcido [I] 124 D4
Sanluri [I] 118 C6
San Marcello Pistoiese [I] 110 E4
San Marco Argentano [I] 124 D4
San Marco dei Cavoti [I] 120 F2
San Marco in Lamis [I] 116 G6
San Marino [RSM] 110 H5
Sânmartin [RO] 76 H2
San Martín de la Vega [E] 88 F6
San Martín del Pedroso [E] 80 G4
San Martín de Pusa [E] 96 E1
San Martín de Unx [E] 84 B5
San Martín de Valdeiglesias [E] 88 E5
San Martino Buon Albergo [I] 72 C6
San Martino della Battaglia [I] 72 C6
San Martino delle Scale [I] 126 C2
San Martino di Castrozza [I] 72 E4
San Martino di Lupari [I] 72 E6
San Mateo de Gállego [E] 98 G2
San Mauro Castelverde [I] 126 E2
San Michele all'Ádige [I] 72 C4
San Michele di Plaianu [I] 118 C3
San Michele Salentino [I] 122 F4
San Miguel de Bernúy [E] 88 G3
San Miguel de las Dueñas [E] 78 F5
San Miguel de Salinas [E] 104 D3
San Millan [E] 82 F5
San Millán de la Cogolla [E] 82 G6
San Miniato [I] 110 E6
Sänna [EST] 200 F3
Sånna [S] 174 E1
S. Anna [S] 168 C6
Sannazzaro de' Burgondi [I] 70 F6
Sannenmöser [CH] 70 D1
Sannicandro di Bari [I] 122 D3
Sannicandro Gargánico [I] 116 G6
San Nicolás de Tolentino [E] 100 C6
Sânnicolau Mare [RO] 76 F5
San Nicolò [I] 110 G3
San Nicolò di Trullas [I] 118 C4
San Nicolò Gerrei [I] 118 D6
Sanniki [PL] 36 H3
Sanok [PL] 52 E5
San Pancrazio Salentino [I] 122 F4
San Paolo di Civitate [I] 116 F6
San Paolo di Peltuino [I] 116 C4
San Pedro [E] 98 A5
San Pedro [E] 82 C2
San Pedro de Alcántara [E] 102 A5
San Pedro del Arroyo [E] 88 D4
San Pedro del Pinatar [E] 104 D4
San Pellegrino in Alpe [I] 110 D4
San Pellegrino Terme [I] 70 H4
San Piero a Sieve [I] 110 F5
San Pietro, Badia di- [I] 112 D6
San Pietro di Simbranos [I] 118 C3
San Pietro di Sorres [I] 118 C3
San Pietro in Casale [I] 110 F3
San Pietro in Valle [I] 116 B3
San Pietro Vernotico [I] 122 G4
San Polo d'Enza [I] 110 D3
San Priamo [I] 118 D7
San Prospero [I] 110 F2
Sanquhar [GB] 8 D4
San Quírico d'Orcia [I] 114 G2
San Rafael [E] 88 F4
San Remo [I] 108 F4
San Roman de Cameros [E] 90 B1
San Roque [E] 78 C2
San Roque [E] 100 G5
San Roque de Rio Miera [E] 82 F3
San Rufo [I] 120 G4
San Sadurniño [E] 78 D1
San Salvatore Monferrato [I] 110 A1
San Salvo [I] 116 E5
San Sebastián de la Gomera [E] 100 B5
San Sebastián-Donostia [E] 84 B2
San Sebastiano Curone [I] 110 B2
Sansepolcro [I] 110 G6
San Servando, Castillo de- [E] 96 F2
San Severino Marche [I] 116 B2
San Severo [I] 116 F6
Sanski Most [BIH] 154 B3
San Sosti [I] 124 D3
Santa, Cova- [E] 104 C5
Santa Amalia [E] 96 A2
Santa Ana de Cambas [P] 94 D4
Santa Bárbara [E] 94 E4
Santacara [E] 84 B5
Santa Caterina di Pittinuri [I] 118 B4
Santa Caterina Valfurva [I] 72 B3
Santa Caterina Villarmosa [I] 126 E3
Santa Cesarea Terme [I] 122 H5
Santa Clara-a-Velha [P] 94 B4
Santa Coloma [AND] 84 H6
Santa Coloma de Farners [E] 92 F3
Santa Coloma de Queralt [E] 92 C4
Santa Colomba de Somoza [E] 78 F5
Santa Comba [E] 78 B2
Santa Comba de Rossas [P] 80 F4
Santa Cristina / St Christina [I] 72 D3
Santa Cristina d'Aro [E] 92 G3
Santa Croce Camerina [I] 126 F5
Santa Croce di Magliano [I] 116 F6
Santa Croce d. Sannio [I] 120 E1
Santa Croce sull'Arno [I] 110 E5
Santa Cruz [P] 100 B3
Santa Cruz de Campezo / Santi Kurutze Kanpezu [E] 82 H6
Santa Cruz de la Palma [E] 100 A5
Santa Cruz de la Serós [E] 84 D5
Santa Cruz de la Zarza [E] 96 G2
Santa Cruz del Retamar [E] 88 E6
Santa Cruz de Moya [E] 98 D3
Santa Cruz de Mudela [E] 96 F5
Santa Cruz de Tenerife [E] 100 C5
Santadi [I] 118 C7
Santaella [E] 102 B2
Santa Elena [E] 96 F6
Santa Eufemia [E] 96 C4
Santa Eugènia [E] 78 B3
Santa Eulalia [E] 98 D1
Santa Eulalia [E] 78 H3
Santa Eulália [P] 86 F6
Santa Eulalia del Río / Santa Eulària des Riu [E] 104 C5
Santa Eulària des Riu / Santa Eulalia del Río [E] 104 C5
Santa Fé [E] 102 E4
Sant'Agata dè Goti [I] 120 E2
Sant'Ágata di Militello [I] 126 F2
Sant'Agata di Puglia [I] 120 G2
Santa Gertrude / Sankt Gertraud [I] 72 C3
Sant'Agostino [I] 110 F3
Sant Agustí de Lluçanes [E] 92 E2
Santa Iria [P] 94 E3
Santa Justa [P] 86 D6
Sant'Alberto di Butrio [I] 110 B2
Santa Luce [I] 110 D6
Santa Lucía [E] 100 C6
Santa Lucia del Mela [I] 124 B7
Santa Luzia [P] 78 A6
Santa Luzia [P] 94 C3
Santa Maddalena Vallalta / Sankt Magdalena [I] 72 E2
Santa Magdalena de Polpis [E] 98 G2
Santa Margalida [E] 104 E5
Santa Margarida de Montbui [E] 92 D4
Santa Margarida do Sado [P] 94 C2
Santa Margherita [I] 118 C7
Santa Margherita di Bélice [I] 126 C3
Santa Margherita Ligure [I] 110 B3
Santa María [E] 104 E5
Santa Maria a Pié di Chienti [I] 116 C1
Santa Maria a Piè di Chienti [I] 116 C2
Santa Maria Arabona [I] 116 D4
Santa Maria Cápua Vetere [I] 120 E2
Santa Maria da Feira [P] 80 B4
Santa Maria d'Anglona [I] 122 D5
Santa María de Cayón [E] 82 F3
Santa María de Huerta [E] 90 B4
Santa Maria dei Lattani [I] 120 D2
Santa María de las Hoyas [E] 90 A2
Santa María del Campo [E] 82 E6
Santa María del Páramo [E] 78 G6
Santa María de Nieva [E] 102 H4
Santa Maria di Bressanoro [I] 70 H5
Santa Maria di Corte, Abbazia di- [I] 118 C4
Santa Maria di Portonovo [I] 112 D6
Santa Maria di Propezzano [I] 116 D3
Santa Maria di Rambona [I] 116 C2
Santa Maria di Ronzano [I] 116 C4
Santa Maria di Siponto [I] 120 H1
Santa Maria in Valle Porclaneta [I] 116 C5
Santa María la Real de Nieva [E] 88 E3
Santa Maria Maggiore [I] 70 F3
Santa Maria Mayor [P] 80 C4
Santa Maria Navarrese [I] 118 E5
Santa Maria Nuova [I] 116 C1
Santa Marinella [I] 114 G5
Santa Marta [E] 94 G2
Santa Marta [E] 98 B4
Santa Marta de Tormes [E] 88 C3
Santana [P] 100 B3
Santana da Serra [P] 94 C4
Santana do Mato [P] 86 C5
Santander [E] 82 F3
Sant'Andrea Bagni [I] 110 D2
Sant' Andrea di Conza [I] 120 G3
Sant' Andrea Frius [I] 118 D6
Sant' Ángelo in Vado [I] 110 H6
Sant' Angelo Lodigiano [I] 70 G5
Santa Ninfa [I] 126 B2
Sant'Anna, Santuario di- [I] 108 E3
Sant' Antimo, Abbazia di- [I] 114 G2
Sant' Antine, Nuraghe- [I] 118 C4
Sant' Antíoco [I] 118 B7
Sant Antoni de Portmany [E] 104 C5
Sant'Antonio di Gallura [I] 118 D2
Santanyí [E] 104 E6
Santa Olalla [E] 88 E6
Santa Olalla del Cala [E] 94 G4
Santa Pola [E] 104 D3
Sant'Apollinare in Classe [I] 110 H4
Santa Ponça [E] 104 D5
Sant'Arcangelo [I] 122 C5
Santarcángelo di Romagna [I] 110 H5
Santarém [P] 86 C4
Santa Sabina, Nuraghe- [I] 118 C4
Santa Severa [F] 114 C2
Santa Severa [I] 114 G5
Santas Martas [E] 78 H6
Santa Sofia [I] 110 G5
Santa Susanna [E] 92 F4
Santa Teresa di Riva [I] 124 B8
Santa Teresa Gallura [I] 118 D2
Santa Vitória [P] 94 D3
Sant Boi de Llobregat [E] 92 D4
Sant Carles de la Ràpita [E] 92 A6
Sant Celoni [E] 92 F4
Sant. de la Encarnación [E] 98 B6
Sant. de Ródanas [E] 90 D4
Santed [E] 90 D5
Sant'Elia a Pianisi [I] 120 F1
Sant'Elia Fiumerapido [I] 120 D1
San Telmo [E] 94 F4
Santena [I] 70 D6
San Teodoro [I] 118 E3
Santéramo in Colle [I] 122 D3
Santes Creus [E] 92 C4
Sant' Eufémia Lamézia [I] 124 D5
Sant'Eutizio, Abbazia di- [I] 116 B3
Sant Feliu de Codines [E] 92 E4
Sant Feliu de Guíxols [E] 92 G4
Sant Feliu de Llobregat [E] 92 E4
Sant Ferran de Ses Roquetes [E] 104 C6
Sant Francesc de Formentera [E] 104 C6
Sant Grau [E] 92 F4
Santhià [I] 70 E5
Sant Hilari Sacalm [E] 92 F3
Sant Hipòlit de Voltregà [E] 92 E3
Santiago [P] 80 F5
Santiago, Cuevas de- [E] 94 H4
Santiago de Alcántara [E] 86 F4
Santiago de Calatrava [E] 102 D2
Santiago de Compostela [E] 78 C3
Santiago de la Espada [E] 102 G2
Santiago de la Ribera [E] 104 D4
Santiago del Campo [E] 86 H5
Santiago do Cacém [P] 94 B2
Santiago do Escoural [P] 94 D1
Santibáñez [E] 82 D4
Santibáñez de la Sierra [E] 88 B4
Santibáñez de Vidriales [E] 80 H3
Santibáñez Zarzaguda [E] 82 E5
Santi Kurutze Kanpezu / Santa Cruz de Campezo [E] 82 H6
Santillana del Mar [E] 82 E3
Santimamiñe [E] 82 H4
Santissima Trinità di Saccargia [I] 118 C3
Santisteban del Puerto [E] 102 F1
Sant Jaume d'Enveja [E] 92 B6
Sant Joan d'Alacant / San Juan de Alicante [E] 104 F2
Sant Joan de les Abadesses [E] 92 E2

T

Taalintehdas / Dalsbruk [FIN] 176 E6
Taapajärvi [FIN] 192 H6
Taavetti [FIN] 178 D2
Tab [H] 76 A3
Tabaja [BIH] 152 C3
Tábara [E] 80 H4
Tabernas [E] 102 G5
Tabiano Bagni [I] 110 D2
Taboada [E] 78 D4
Tábor [CZ] 48 G5
Tábua [P] 86 E2
Tabuaço [P] 80 D5
Tabuenca [E] 90 D3
Täby [S] 168 D2
Tachov [CZ] 48 C4
Tadcaster [GB] 10 F3
Tafalla [E] 84 B4
Tafjord [N] 180 E4
Tagaranna [EST] 200 C3
Taggia [I] 108 G4
Taghmon [IRL] 4 F5
Tagliacozzo [I] 116 B5
Táglio di Po [I] 110 H2
Tahal [E] 102 G4
Tahtaköprü [TR] 146 G5
Tai di Cadore [I] 72 F4
Tailfingen [D] 58 G2
Tain [GB] 6 E4
Tain-l'Hermitage [F] 68 F4
Taipadas [P] 86 C5
Taipaleenkyla [FIN] 186 D4
Taipalsaari [FIN] 178 D2
Tairbeart / Tarbert [GB] 6 B3
Taivalkoski [FIN] 198 F3
Taivassalo / Tövsala [FIN] 176 C4
Taizé [F] 56 F6
Tajada, Cuevas de la- [E] 98 D2
Tajcy [RUS] 178 H5
Tajo de las Figuras, Cueva del- [E] 100 G5
Takácsi [H] 74 H1
Talachyn [BY] 204 C5
Talamone [I] 114 F3
Talarrubias [E] 96 C3
Talaván [E] 86 H4
Talavera de la Reina [E] 88 D6
Talavera la Real [E] 94 G1
Talayuela [E] 88 B6
Talayuelas [E] 98 D3
Talcy [F] 42 D6
Tali [EST] 200 E3
Táliga [E] 94 F2
Tálkafjörður [IS] 194 B1
Tallaght [IRL] 2 F6
Tallard [F] 108 D2
Tällas [S] 190 G3
Tallåsen [S] 172 D3
Tällberg [S] 172 H3
Tallinn [EST] 200 D1
Talloires [F] 70 B3
Tallow [IRL] 4 D5
Tallsjö [S] 190 G5
Talmont [F] 54 C6
Talmont-St-Hilaire [F] 54 B3
Talsi [LV] 200 C5
Tålsmark [S] 198 A5
Talvik [N] 192 G1
Tamajón [E] 88 H4
Tamames [E] 88 B3
Tamanes [N] 196 D2
Tamarë [AL] 152 F4
Tamarino [BG] 148 E5
Tamarite de Litera [E] 90 H4
Tamási [H] 76 B3
Tambohuse [DK] 160 C4
Taminaschlucht [CH] 58 H6
Tammela [FIN] 176 F3
Tammensiel [D] 18 E1
Tammerfors / Tampere [FIN] 176 F1
Tammijärvi [FIN] 186 G5
Tammisaari / Ekenäs [FIN] 176 F6
Tamnič [YU] 150 E2
Tampere / Tammerfors [FIN] 176 F1
Tamsalu [EST] 200 E1
Tamsweg [A] 72 H2
Tamworth [GB] 10 E6
Tana bru [N] 196 D2
Tanágra [GR] 134 B5
Tananger [N] 164 A3
Tancarville [F] 26 G3
Tanda [YU] 150 D1
Tandö [S] 172 F3
Tandragee [GB] 2 G4
Tandsjöborg [S] 172 G1
Tånga [S] 156 H1
Tångaberg [S] 160 H3
Tangen [N] 166 B3
Tangen [N] 166 C1
Tangen [N] 172 C4
Tanger [Eur.] 100 F6
Tangerhütte [D] 34 B2
Tangermünde [D] 34 C2
Tanhua [FIN] 196 E6
Taninges [F] 70 B2
Tankavaara [FIN] 196 D5
Tanlay [F] 56 F2
Tann [D] 46 F1
Tännäs [S] 182 E4
Tänndalen [S] 182 D4
Tanne [D] 32 H4
Tännforsen [S] 182 E1
Tannheim [A] 60 C6
Tannila [FIN] 198 D3
Tanum [S] 166 C4
Tanumshede [S] 166 C4
Tanvald [CZ] 48 H2
Taormina [I] 124 B8
Tapa [EST] 200 E1
Tapia de Casariego [E] 78 F2
Tapionkylä [FIN] 196 C7
Tapionniemi [FIN] 196 E7
Tápiószecső [H] 76 D1
Tápiószele [H] 76 D1
Tápiószőlős [H] 76 D1
Tapolca [H] 74 H3
Tapolcafő [H] 74 H1
Taps [DK] 156 C3
Tara [IRL] 2 F5
Tara Kanjon [YU] 152 E3
Tara Kanjon [YU] 152 E2
Taraklı [TR] 146 H4
Taramundi [E] 78 F2
Tarancón [E] 96 H2
Táranto [I] 122 E4
Tarare [F] 68 F2
Tarascon [F] 106 G4
Tarascon-sur-Ariège [F] 84 H5
Tarasp [CH] 72 B2
Tarazona [E] 84 A6
Tarazona de la Mancha [E] 98 B4
Tårbæk [DK] 156 H2
Tarbert [GB] 8 C3
Tarbert [IRL] 2 B6
Tarbert / Tairbeart [GB] 6 B3
Tarbes [F] 84 F3
Tarcento [I] 72 G4
Tarčin [BIH] 152 C1
Tarczyn [PL] 38 B4
Tardets-Sorholus [F] 84 D3
Tardienta [E] 90 F3
Tärendö [S] 192 G6
Târgoviște [RO] 206 C6
Târgu Frumos [RO] 206 D4
Târgu Jiu [RO] 206 B6
Târgu Lăpuș [RO] 206 B4
Târgu Mureș [RO] 206 C5
Târgu Neamț [RO] 206 C4
Târgu Secuesc [RO] 206 C5
Tarhos [H] 76 G3
Tarifa [E] 100 G6
Tarm [DK] 156 B1
Tarmstedt [D] 18 E5
Tärnaby [S] 190 E3
Tarnalelesz [H] 64 E5
Tarnaméra [H] 64 E6
Tärnamo [S] 190 E3
Târnăveni [RO] 206 B5
Tarnawatka [PL] 52 G2
Tärnet [N] 196 F3
Tarnobrzeg [PL] 52 D2
Tarnogród [PL] 52 F2
Tarnos [F] 66 A6
Târnova [RO] 76 H4
Tarnów [PL] 34 G1
Tarnów [PL] 52 C4
Tarnów [PL] 38 C4
Tarnowo Podgórne [PL] 36 C2
Tarnowskie Góry [PL] 50 F3
Tärnsjö [S] 174 E5
Tärnvika [N] 192 C5
Tarouca [P] 80 D5
Tarp [D] 18 F1
Tarquínia [I] 114 G4
Tarquinia [I] 114 G4
Tarquinia Lido [I] 114 G4
Tarragona [E] 92 C5
Tårrajur [S] 190 H2
Tarrasa / Terrassa [E] 92 E4
Tàrrega [E] 92 C3
Tårs [DK] 156 E4
Tårs [DK] 160 E3
Tarsia [I] 124 D3
Tartas [F] 66 B6
Tartu [EST] 200 F3
Tårup [DK] 156 E3
Tarutino [MD] 206 E5
Tarvasjoki [FIN] 176 E4
Tarvisio [I] 72 H3
Taşbükü [TR] 142 E2
Täsch [CH] 70 E3
Tåsjö [S] 190 F5
Taşköy [TR] 144 F3
Taşlıca [TR] 142 D3
Tassjö [S] 162 B6
Tåstrup [DK] 156 G2
Tata [H] 64 B6
Tatabánya [H] 64 B6
Tataháza [H] 76 D4
Tatarbunary [UA] 206 E5
Tatárszentgyörgy [H] 76 D2
Tatranská Kotlina [SK] 52 B6
Tau [N] 164 B3
Taubenlochschlucht [CH] 58 D5
Tauberbischofsheim [D] 46 E4
Taucha [D] 34 C5
Tauerntunnel [A] 72 G2
Tauern Tunnel [A] 72 H1
Taufers / Tubre [I] 72 B3
Taufkirchen [A] 60 H4
Taufkirchen [D] 60 F4
Taujėnai [LT] 202 G4
Taüll [E] 84 G6
Taunton [GB] 12 F4
Taunusstein [D] 46 B3
Tauplitz [A] 62 B6
Taurage [LT] 202 E5
Taurasi [I] 120 F3
Taurianova [I] 124 C7
Taurine, Terme- [I] 114 G5
Taurisano [I] 122 G6
Taurkains [LV] 200 E5
Tauste [E] 90 E3
Tauves [F] 68 B2
Tavannes [CH] 58 D5
Tavarnelle Val di Pesa [I] 110 F6
Tavas [TR] 144 G5
Tavascan [E] 84 G6
Tavastehus / Hämeenlinna [FIN] 176 G3
Tavastkenka [FIN] 198 E5
Tavastkyro / Hämeenkyro [FIN] 176 E1
Tavaux [F] 56 H4
Taverna [I] 124 E5
Tavernelle [I] 114 H2
Tavernes [F] 108 C4
Tavernes de la Valldigna [E] 98 E6
Taviano [I] 122 G6
Tavira [P] 94 D5
Tavistock [GB] 12 D4
Tavole Palatine [I] 122 D4
Tavşancıl [TR] 146 F3
Tavşanlı [TR] 144 G1
Täxan [S] 190 F6
Taxenbach [A] 72 G1
Taxiarchón, Moní- [GR] 138 D3
Tayfur [TR] 146 B5
Tázlár [H] 76 D3
Tazones [E] 82 C1
Tczew [PL] 22 E3
Tczów [PL] 38 C5
Teano [I] 120 D2
Teascu [RO] 150 G1
Techendorf [A] 72 G3
Teck [D] 58 H2
Tecklenburg [D] 32 C2
Tecuci [RO] 206 D5
Teféli [GR] 140 E5
Tefenni [TR] 142 H1
Tegéa [GR] 136 E3
Tegelen [NL] 30 F3
Tegelträsk [S] 190 G6
Tegernsee [D] 60 E5
Teggiano [I] 120 G4
Téglás [H] 64 H5
Teglio [I] 72 A4
Teguise [E] 100 E4
Teichel [D] 46 H1
Teichiussa [TR] 142 C1
Teignmouth [GB] 12 E5
Teillet [F] 106 C3
Teisendorf [D] 60 G5
Teisko [FIN] 186 E6
Teixeiro [E] 78 D2
Tejn [DK] 158 E4
Teke [TR] 146 F2
Tekeriš [YU] 154 F3
Tekirdağ [TR] 146 C3
Tekovské Lužany [SK] 64 B5
Telana [I] 118 E5
Telavåg [N] 170 A4
Telč [CZ] 48 H6
Telde [E] 100 C6
Teleborg [S] 162 E5
Telese Terme [I] 120 E2
Telford [GB] 10 D6
Telfs [A] 72 C1
Telgte [D] 32 C3
Telheiro [P] 94 B3
Telish [BG] 148 A3
Teljo [FIN] 198 G5
Tellingstedt [D] 18 E2
Tellskap [CH] 58 F6
Telmessos [TR] 142 G3
Telšiai [LT] 202 E4
Telti [I] 118 D3
Tembleque [E] 96 G2
Temerin [YU] 154 F1
Temmes [FIN] 198 D4
Temnata Dupka [BG] 150 F4
Témpio Pausánia [I] 118 D3
Templemore [IRL] 4 E3
Templetouhy [IRL] 4 E3
Templin [D] 20 D6
Templom [H] 64 C5
Temse [B] 28 H2
Temska [YU] 150 E3
Tenala / Tenhola [FIN] 176 F5
Tenby [GB] 12 D2
Tence [F] 68 E4
Tenda, Colle di- / Tende, Col de- [Eur.] 108 F3
Tende [F] 108 F3
Tendilla [E] 88 H6
Tenebrón [E] 88 A3
Tenevo [BG] 148 E5
Tenhola / Tenala [FIN] 176 F5
Tenhult [S] 162 D2
Tenja [HR] 154 E1
Tenk [H] 64 E6
Tennevik [N] 192 D4
Tennevoll [N] 192 D3
Tenterden [GB] 14 F5
Tentudia, Mon. de- [E] 94 G4
Teo / Ramallosa [E] 78 C3
Teofipol' [UA] 206 D2
Teolo [I] 110 G1
Teos [TR] 144 C5
Tepasto [FIN] 192 H4
Tepecik [TR] 144 G1
Tepecik [TR] 146 F3
Tepeköy [TR] 144 E4
Tepelenë [AL] 128 B6
Teplá [CZ] 48 D4
Teplice [CZ] 48 E2
Teplice nad Metují [CZ] 50 B2
Teploye [RUS] 204 F5
Tepsa [FIN] 196 C6
Téramo [I] 116 C3
Ter Apel [NL] 16 H3
Teratyn [PL] 38 G6
Terebiń [PL] 52 G1
Terebishche [RUS] 200 G3
Terebovlia [UA] 206 C3
Terehovo [RUS] 200 H4
Teremia Mare [RO] 76 F5
Terespol [PL] 38 F3
Terezín [CZ] 48 F2
Terezino Polje [HR] 74 H5
Tergnier [F] 28 F6
Terkoz [TR] 146 E2
Terlizzi [I] 122 D2
Termal [TR] 146 F3
Termas de Monfortinho [P] 86 G3
Terme di Lurisia [I] 108 F3
Terme di Valdieri [I] 108 F3
Terme Luigiane [I] 124 C4
Terme S. Lucia [I] 116 C2
Terme Vigliatore [I] 126 D4
Términi Imerese [I] 126 D2
Terminillo [I] 116 B4
Terminón [E] 82 E5
Térmoli [I] 116 F5
Termolovo [RUS] 178 G3
Termonfeckin [IRL] 2 F5
Terndrup [DK] 160 E4
Terneuzen [NL] 28 H1
Terni [I] 116 A3
Ternitz [A] 62 E6
Ternopil' [UA] 206 C2
Térovo [GR] 132 D2
Terpan [AL] 128 B5
Terpezita [RO] 150 F1
Terpní [GR] 130 B3
Terracina [I] 120 C2
Terradillos de los Templarios [E] 82 C5
Terråk [N] 190 D4
Terralba [I] 118 C5
Terra Mitica [E] 104 E2
Terranova di Pollino [I] 122 C6
Terrassa / Tarrasa [E] 92 E4
Terrasson-la-Villedieu [F] 66 G3
Terrateig [E] 98 E6
Terrazos [E] 82 F5
Terriente [E] 98 D2
Tersløse [DK] 156 F3
Tertenía [I] 118 E6
Teruel [E] 98 E2
Tervakoski [FIN] 176 G3
Tervel [BG] 148 F1
Tervo [FIN] 186 H2
Tervola [FIN] 198 C2
Tervuren [B] 30 C4
Terz [A] 62 D5
Terzaga [E] 90 C6
Tesegerague [E] 100 E5
Teslić [BIH] 154 C3
Teslui [RO] 150 G1
Tessin [D] 20 C3
Tessy sur-Vire [F] 26 E4
Tét [H] 62 H6
Tetbury [GB] 12 G3
Teterow [D] 20 C4
Teteven [BG] 148 A4
Tetovo [BG] 148 D2
Tetovo [MK] 128 D1
Tetrálofo [GR] 128 F5
Tettnang [D] 58 H4
Teuchrania [TR] 144 C3
Teufelshöhle [D] 46 H4
Teufen [CH] 58 H5
Teulada [E] 104 F2
Teulada [I] 118 C7
Teupitz [D] 34 E3
Teurnia [A] 72 H3
Teuro [FIN] 176 F3
Teuva / Östermark [FIN] 186 B4
Tevaniemi [FIN] 186 D6
Tevel [H] 76 B4
Tevfikiye [TR] 130 H5
Tewkesbury [GB] 12 G2
Tewli [BY] 38 G2
Texeiro [E] 78 E3
Thale [D] 34 A4
Thalfang [D] 44 G2
Thalheim [D] 48 D2
Thalmässing [D] 46 G6
Thalwil [CH] 58 F5
Thame [GB] 14 D3
Thann [F] 58 D3
Thannhausen [D] 60 C3
Tharandt [D] 48 E1
Thárros [I] 118 B5
Thásos [GR] 130 E4
Thatcham [GB] 12 H4
Thaumiers [F] 56 C4
Them [DK] 156 C1
Themar [D] 46 F2
Thénezay [F] 54 E3
Thenon [F] 66 F3
Theodosiia [UA] 206 H6
Theológos [GR] 134 A4
Theológos [GR] 130 E4
Théoule [F] 108 E5
Thera [TR] 142 E2
Thérma [GR] 138 G1
Thermá [GR] 130 G4
Thérmi [GR] 130 B4
Thermí [GR] 134 H2
Thermisía [GR] 136 G2
Thérmo [GR] 132 F5
Thermopíles [GR] 132 G4
Thermopýles [GR] 132 G4
Thernberg [A] 62 E6
Thérouanne [F] 28 E2
Thespies [GR] 134 A5
Thessaloníki [GR] 130 A4
Thetford [GB] 14 G2
The Turoe Stone [IRL] 2 C5
Theux [B] 30 E5
Thevet-St-Julien [F] 56 B4
Theze [F] 84 E3
Thiaucourt-Regniéville [F] 44 E4
Thiberville [F] 26 G4
Thiélbemont-Farémont [F] 44 C5
Thiendorf [D] 34 E5
Thiene [I] 72 D5
Thiers [F] 68 D2
Thiersee [A] 60 F6
Thiesi [I] 118 C3
Thiessow [D] 20 E2
Thimariá [GR] 130 H3
Thingeyri [IS] 194 C1
Thingvellir [IS] 194 C4
Thionville [F] 44 E3
Thíra [GR] 138 F5
Thíra / Firá [GR] 138 F5
Thirette [F] 68 H1
Thirsk [GB] 10 F3
Thisted [DK] 160 C4
Thísvi [GR] 132 H5
Thíva [GR] 134 B5
Thivars [F] 42 D4
Thiviers [F] 66 F2
Thizy [F] 68 F2
Tho, Pieve del- [I] 110 G4
Thoissey [F] 68 G1
Tholey [D] 44 G3
Tholó [GR] 136 C3
Thomasberg [A] 62 E6
Thomas Street [IRL] 2 D5
Thomastown [IRL] 4 E4
Thônes [F] 70 B3
Thonon [F] 70 B2
Thonon-les-Bains [F] 70 B2
Thorens-Glières, Château de- [F] 70 B3
Thorikó [GR] 136 H1
Thörl [A] 62 D6
Thorlákshöfn [IS] 194 B5
Thornbury [GB] 12 G3
Thorney [GB] 14 F2
Thornhill [GB] 8 D4
Thoronet, Abbaye du- [F] 108 D5
Thórshöfn [IS] 194 G3
Thouarcé [F] 54 D2
Thouars [F] 54 E2
Thouría [GR] 136 D4
Thoúrio [GR] 130 H1
Thueyts [F] 68 E5
Thuin [B] 28 H4
Thuir [F] 92 G1
Thum [D] 48 D2
Thun [CH] 70 D1
Thürkow [D] 20 C4
Thurles / Durlas [IRL] 4 E3
Thurnau [D] 46 H3
Thurn Pass [A] 72 F1
Thurso [GB] 6 F2
Thury-Harcourt [F] 26 F4
Thusis [CH] 70 H2
Thyborøn [DK] 160 B4
Thymianá [GR] 134 G5
Thyregod [DK] 156 C1
Tiana [I] 118 D5
Tibaes [P] 80 C3
Tibava [SK] 64 H2
Tiberio, Grotta di- [I] 120 C2
Tibro [S] 166 F5
Ticha [BG] 148 D3
Tidaholm [S] 166 F6
Tidan [S] 166 F5
Tidö [S] 168 B2
Tiefenbronn [D] 58 G1
Tiefencastel [CH] 70 H2
Tiefensee [D] 34 F2
Tiel [NL] 16 E5
Tielt [B] 28 G2
Tiemassaari [FIN] 188 D4
Tienen [B] 30 D4
Tiengen [D] 58 F4
Tiercé [F] 40 H6
Tierga [E] 90 D3
Tiermas [E] 84 H3
Tierp [S] 174 F5
Tighina [MD] 206 E4
Tigkáki [GR] 142 C3
Tignes [F] 70 C4
Tihany [H] 76 A2
Tihuța, Pasul- [RO] 206 C4
Tiistenjoki [FIN] 186 D3
Tikhvin [RUS] 204 D1
Tikkakoski [FIN] 186 G4
Tikkala [FIN] 186 F5
Tilberga [S] 168 C2
Tilburg [NL] 30 E2
Tilbury [GB] 14 F4
Til-Châtel [F] 56 H3
Tiltagals [LV] 200 F5
Tiltrem [N] 190 B5
Tilži [LV] 200 G6
Tim [RUS] 204 F7
Timahoe [IRL] 4 F3
Timișoara [RO] 76 G5
Timmel [D] 18 B4
Timmele [S] 162 C2
Timmendorfer Strand [D] 18 H3
Timmernabben [S] 162 G4
Timmersdala [S] 166 F5
Timoleague [IRL] 4 C5
Timrå [S] 184 E4
Tinahely [IRL] 4 F4
Tinajo [E] 100 E4
Tinca [RO] 76 H3
Tinchebray [F] 26 E4
Tineo [E] 78 G3
Tingelstad [N] 170 H4
Tinglev [DK] 156 B4
Tingsryd [S] 162 E5
Tingstäde [S] 168 G4
Tingvoll [N] 180 F2
Tinnoset [N] 164 F1
Tinos [GR] 138 E2
Tiñosillos [E] 88 E4
Tintern Abbey [IRL] 4 F5
Tinuži [LV] 200 E5
Tiobraid Arann / Tipperary [IRL] 4 D4
Tione di Trento [I] 72 C4
Tipasjoki [FIN] 198 F5
Tipperary / Tiobraid Arann [IRL] 4 D4
Tiranë [AL] 128 B3
Tirano [I] 72 B4
Tiraspol [MD] 206 E4
Tire [TR] 144 D5
Tirgo [E] 82 G6
Tiriolo [I] 124 E5
Tirmo [FIN] 178 B4
Tirol / Tirolo [I] 72 C3
Tirolo / Tirol [I] 72 C3
Tirrénia [I] 110 D6
Tirschenreuth [D] 48 C4
Tirstrup [DK] 160 E6
Tíryntha [GR] 136 F2
Tišća [BIH] 154 E4
Tiscar-Don Pedro [E] 102 F2
Tismana, Mănăstirea- [RO] 206 B6
Tisno [HR] 112 G6
Tišnov [CZ] 50 B6
Tisovec [SK] 64 D3
Tistrup [DK] 156 B2
Tisvilde [DK] 156 G1
Tiszaalpár [H] 76 E3
Tiszabábolna [H] 64 F6
Tiszacsege [H] 64 F6
Tiszaföldvár [H] 76 E2
Tiszafüred [H] 64 F6
Tiszakécske [H] 76 E2
Tiszalök [H] 64 G5
Tiszalúc [H] 64 F5
Tiszaörs [H] 64 F6
Tiszaroff [H] 76 E1
Tiszaszőlős [H] 64 F6
Tiszaújváros [H] 64 F5
Tiszavasvári [H] 64 G5
Titel [YU] 154 G1
Titisee [D] 58 F3
Tito [I] 120 G4
Tito Bustillo, Cueva de- [E] 82 C2
Titova Spilja [BIH] 154 A3
Titov Veles [MK] 128 F1
Titran [N] 190 A6
Tittling [D] 60 H3
Tittmoning [D] 60 G4
Titz [D] 30 F4
Tiuccia [F] 114 A4
Tiukka / Tjöck [FIN] 186 B4
Tivat [YU] 152 D4
Tived [S] 166 G4
Tiverton [GB] 12 E4
Tivoli [I] 116 B5
Tizzano [F] 114 A6
Tjæreborg [DK] 156 B2
Tjällmo [S] 166 H5
Tjåmotis [S] 190 G1
Tjautjas [S] 192 F6
Tjeldnes [N] 192 C4
Tjele [DK] 160 D5
Tjentište [BIH] 152 D2
Tjöck / Tiukka [FIN] 186 B4
Tjolmen [N] 190 E3
Tjolöholm [S] 160 H3
Tjøme [N] 164 H3
Tjong [N] 190 D1
Tjønnefoss [N] 164 E3
Tjørhom [N] 164 C3
Tjørnhom [N] 164 C5
Tjørnuvik [FR] 160 A1
Tjøtta [N] 190 D3
Tkon [HR] 112 G5
Tleń [PL] 22 D4
Tlmače [SK] 64 B4
Tlos [TR] 142 G3
Tłuchowo [PL] 36 G1
Tłuszcz [PL] 38 C2
Tobarra [E] 98 B6
Tobercurry [IRL] 2 D3
Tobermory [GB] 6 B6
Toblach / Dobbiaco [I] 72 E3
Tocha [P] 80 A6
Tocina [E] 94 H5
Töcksfors [S] 166 C2
Todi [I] 116 A3
Todorići [BIH] 154 B4
Todtmoos [D] 58 E4
Todtnau [D] 58 E3
Tõdva [EST] 200 D1
Tofte [N] 164 H2
Toftir [FR] 160 B2
Toftlund [DK] 156 B3
Togher [IRL] 2 D5
Tohmajärvi [FIN] 188 G3
Toholampi [FIN] 198 C6
Tohvri [EST] 200 E3
Toichio [GR] 128 E5
Toijala [FIN] 176 F2
Toirano, Grotte di- [I] 108 G3
Toivakka [FIN] 186 G5
Toivola [FIN] 178 C1
Töjby [FIN] 186 A4
Tojšići [BIH] 154 E3
Tokagjelet [N] 170 B4
Tokaj [H] 64 G4
Tokari [PL] 36 F4
Tokarnia [PL] 50 H4
Tokarnia [PL] 52 B2
Tokmak [UA] 206 H4
Toksovo [RUS] 178 H4
Tolcsva [H] 64 G4
Toledo [E] 96 F1
Tolentino [I] 116 C2
Tolfa [I] 114 G4
Tolfta [S] 174 F5
Tolg [S] 162 E4
Tolga [N] 182 C4
Tolkis / Tolkkinen [FIN] 178 B4
Tolkkinen / Tolkis [FIN] 178 B4
Tolkmicko [PL] 22 F2
Tollarp [S] 158 D2
Tølløse [DK] 156 F3
Tolmachevo [RUS] 200 H1
Tolmezzo [I] 72 G4
Tolmin [SLO] 72 H4
Tolna [H] 76 C4
Tolne [DK] 160 E2
Toló [GR] 136 F2
Tolob [GB] 6 G4
Tolosa [E] 84 B3
Tolosa [P] 86 E4
Tolox [E] 102 B4
Tolva [FIN] 196 F8
Tolve [I] 120 H4
Tomar [P] 86 D3
Tomarovka [RUS] 204 F7
Tomaševo [YU] 150 A4
Tomaszów Lubelski [PL] 52 G2
Tomaszów Mazowiecki [PL] 36 H5
Tomatin [GB] 6 E5
Tombebœuf [F] 66 E4
Tomelilla [S] 158 D3
Tomelloso [E] 96 G4
Tomintoul [GB] 6 E5
Tømmernes [N] 192 C5
Tommerup [DK] 156 D3
Tømmervåg [N] 180 F2
Tompa [H] 76 D4
Tomra [N] 180 D3
Tømra [N] 182 C2
Tomter [N] 166 B2
Tona [E] 92 E3
Tonara [I] 118 D5
Tonbridge [GB] 14 E5
Tondela [P] 80 C6
Tønder [DK] 156 B4
Tongeren (Tongres) [B] 30 E4
Tongres (Tongeren) [B] 30 E4
Tongue [GB] 6 E2
Tonnay-Boutonne [F] 54 C5
Tonnay-Charente [F] 54 C5
Tonneins [F] 66 E5
Tonnerre [F] 56 F2
Tonnes [N] 190 D1
Tönning [D] 18 E2
Tonquédec, Château de- [F] 40 D1
Tønsberg [N] 164 H3
Tonstad [N] 164 C4
Toomyvara [IRL] 2 D6
Toourmakeady [IRL] 2 C4
Topares [E] 102 H3
Topchii [BG] 148 D2
Töpchin [D] 34 E3
Topli Dol [YU] 150 E3
Toplița [RO] 206 C4
Toplou [GR] 140 G4
Topola [YU] 150 B1
Topolcani [MK] 128 E3
Topol'čany [SK] 64 B3
Topoľčiansky Hrad [SK] 64 A3
Topólia [GR] 140 B4
Topolovățu Mare [RO] 76 H5
Topolovgrad [BG] 146 A1
Topolovo [BG] 148 B6
Toporu [RO] 148 C1
Toques [E] 78 D3
Torà [E] 92 D3
Toral de los Vados [E] 78 F5
Torbalı [TR] 144 D4
Torbole [I] 72 C5
Torcello [I] 72 F6
Tordera [E] 92 F4
Tordesillas [E] 88 E2
Tordesilos [E] 90 C6
Töre [S] 198 B2
Töreboda [S] 166 F5
Torekov [S] 160 H6
Torelló [E] 92 E3
Toreno [E] 78 F5
Toresund [S] 168 C3
Torfyanovka [RUS] 178 E3
Torgåsmon [S] 172 F3
Torgau [D] 34 D5
Torgelow [D] 20 E4
Torgiano [I] 116 A2
Torhamn [S] 158 G1
Torhout [B] 28 F2
Tori [EST] 200 E3
Torigni-sur-Vire [F] 26 E3
Torija [E] 88 H5
Toril [E] 98 D2
Torino [I] 70 D5
Torino di Sangro [I] 116 E5
Torino di Sangro Marina [I] 116 E5
Torla [E] 84 E5
Torma [EST] 200 F2
Tornac [RO] 76 H6
Törmänen [FIN] 196 D5
Törmänmäki [FIN] 198 E4
Törmäsjärvi [FIN] 196 C8
Tormos [E] 84 D6
Tornal'a [SK] 64 E4
Tornavacas [E] 88 B5
Torneå / Tornio [FIN] 198 C2
Torneträsk [S] 192 E4
Tornio / Torneå [FIN] 198 C2
Tornjoš [YU] 76 E5
Toro [E] 88 D1
Törökszentmiklós [H] 76 E2
Toróni [GR] 130 C6
Torony [H] 74 F2
Toropec [RUS] 204 D3
Toros de Guisando [E] 88 E5
Torpa [S] 162 C5
Torpa Stenhus [S] 162 B2
Torpo [N] 170 F3
Torpoint [GB] 12 D5
Torpsbruk [S] 162 D4
Torpshammar [S] 184 D4
Torquay [GB] 12 E5
Torquemada [E] 82 D6
Torralba [E] 90 B4
Torralba [E] 96 F4
Torrão [P] 94 D2
Torre [E] 102 D5
Torre Annunziata [I] 120 E3
Torre Beretti [I] 70 F6
Torreblanca [E] 98 G3
Torrecaballeros [E] 88 F4
Torrecampo [E] 96 D5
Torre Canne [I] 122 F3
Torrechiara, Castello di- [I] 110 D3
Torrecilla [E] 98 C1
Torrecillas de la Tiesa [E] 96 B1

U

Vuolijoki [FIN] 198 E5
Vuollerim [S] 198 A2
Vuonislahti [FIN] 188 F1
Vuontisjärvi [FIN] 192 G4
Vuoriniemi [FIN] 188 F5
Vuostimo [FIN] 196 E7
Vuotner [S] 190 H3
Vuotsino [FIN] 196 E7
Vuotso [FIN] 196 D5
Vuottas [S] 196 A8
Vuottolahti [FIN] 198 E5
Vŭrbitsa [BG] 148 E3
Vŭrshets [BG] 150 F3
Vyanta [LT] 200 C6
Vyartsilya [RUS] 188 G3
Vyaz'ma [RUS] 204 E4
Vybor [RUS] 200 H4
Vyborg [RUS] 178 F3
Vyerkhnyadzvinsk [BY] 204 B4
Vyhonochy [RUS] 204 E6
Vynohradiv [UA] 206 B3
Vyra [RUS] 178 H6
Vyritsa [RUS] 178 H6
Vyróneia [GR] 130 B2
Vyshgorodok [RUS] 200 G4
Vyshhorod [UA] 206 E2
Vyshniy Volochek [RUS] 204 E3
Vyskatka [RUS] 200 G1
Vyškov [CZ] 50 C6
Vyšná Revúca [SK] 64 C2
Vyšné Raslavice [SK] 52 D6
Vysock [RUS] 178 E3
Vysoká [CZ] 48 H4
Vysoká u Příbr. [CZ] 48 E5
Vysokaye [BY] 38 F2
Vysoké Mýto [CZ] 50 B4
Vysokoye [RUS] 200 G2
Vysoký Chlumec [CZ] 48 F5
Vyšší Brod [CZ] 62 B3
Vyssiniéa [GR] 128 E5
Vytína [GR] 136 D2

W

Waabs [D] 18 F1
Waalwijk [NL] 16 D6
Wabern [D] 32 E5
Wąbrzeżno [PL] 22 E5
Wąchock [PL] 38 B6
Wachow [D] 34 D2
Wächtersbach [D] 46 D2
Wackersdorf [D] 48 C5
Wadebridge [GB] 12 C4
Wädenswil [CH] 58 F5
Wadlew [PL] 36 G5
Wadowice [PL] 50 G4
Wagenfeld [D] 32 E1
Wageningen [NL] 16 E5
Waging [D] 60 G5
Wagrain [A] 72 G1
Wągrowiec [PL] 36 D1
Wahlwies [D] 58 G4
Wahrenholz [D] 32 H1
Waiblingen [D] 58 H1
Waidhaus [D] 48 C5
Waidhofen an der Thaya [A] 62 D3
Waidhofen an der Ybbs [A] 62 C5
Waidring [A] 60 F6
Waischenfeld [D] 46 G4
Wakefield [GB] 10 F4
Walbeck [D] 34 A2
Wałbrzych [PL] 50 B2
Walchensee [D] 60 D6
Walchsee [A] 60 F5
Walcourt [B] 28 H4
Wałcz [PL] 22 A5
Wald [CH] 58 G5
Wald–angelloch [D] 46 C5
Waldbröl [D] 32 C6
Waldburg [D] 60 B5
Waldeck [D] 32 E5
Waldenbuch [D] 58 H1
Waldenburg [D] 48 C1
Waldenburg [D] 46 D5
Waldfischbach [D] 44 H4
Waldheim [D] 34 D6
Waldkirch [D] 58 E3
Waldkirchen [D] 62 A3
Waldkraiburg [D] 60 F4
Waldmünchen [D] 48 C5
Waldowice [PL] 34 H2
Waldsassen [D] 48 C4
Waldshut [D] 58 F4
Walenstadt [CH] 58 H6
Walhalla [D] 48 C6
Wallasey [GB] 10 D4
Walldorf [D] 46 C5
Walldürn [D] 46 D4
Wallenfels [D] 46 H3
Wallersdorf [D] 60 G3
Wallerstein [D] 60 C2
Wallfahrtskirche [D] 60 C2
Wallingford [GB] 14 D3
Wallsbüll [D] 156 B4
Walsall [GB] 10 E6
Walsrode [D] 18 E6
Waltrop [D] 30 H2
Wambierzyce [PL] 50 B2
Wanderup [D] 18 E1
Wanfried [D] 32 G5
Wangen [D] 60 B5
Wangenbourg [F] 44 G6
Wangerooge [D] 18 C3
Wängi [CH] 58 G5
Wankendorf [D] 18 G2
Wantage [GB] 12 H3
Wanzleben [D] 34 B3
Warburg [D] 32 E4
Wardenburg [D] 18 C5
Ware [GB] 14 E3
Waregem [B] 28 G2
Wareham [GB] 12 G5
Waremme [B] 30 E4
Waren [D] 20 C4
Warendorf [D] 32 D3
Warin [D] 20 A4
Warka [PL] 38 C4
Warlubie [PL] 22 E4
Warmbad Villach [A] 72 H3
Warmensteinach [D] 46 H4
Warminster [GB] 12 G4
Warnemünde [D] 20 B3
Warnice [PL] 20 F5
Warnice [PL] 34 G1
Warnsveld [NL] 16 F5
Warrenpoint [GB] 2 G4
Warrington [GB] 10 D4
Warstein [D] 32 D4
Warszawa [PL] 38 B3
Warta [PL] 36 F4
Warta Bolesławiecka [PL] 36 A6
Wartburg [D] 32 G6
Wartensee [CH] 58 F5
Wartenstein [A] 62 E6
Warth [A] 72 B1
Wartha [D] 32 G6
Warwick [GB] 12 H2
Washington [GB] 8 G6
Wasigenstein, Château de– [F] 44 H4
Wasilków [PL] 24 E5
Wąsosz [PL] 36 C5
Wasselonne [F] 44 G6
Wassen [CH] 70 F1
Wassenaar [NL] 16 C4
Wassenberg [D] 30 F4
Wasseralfingen [D] 60 C2
Wasserbillig [L] 44 F2
Wasserburg [D] 60 F4
Wasserfall Groppenstn. [A] 72 G2
Wasserkuppe [D] 46 E2
Wasserleonberg [A] 72 H3
Wasserschloss [D] 34 D4
Wasserschloss [D] 32 C3
Wassertrüdingen [D] 46 F6
Wassy [F] 44 C5
Wasungen [D] 46 F1
Waterford / Portlairge [IRL] 4 E5
Watergrasshill [IRL] 4 D5
Waterloo [B] 30 C4
Waterlooville [GB] 12 H5
Waterville [IRL] 4 A4
Watford [GB] 14 E4
Watten [F] 14 H6
Wattens [A] 72 D1
Watton [GB] 14 G2
Wattwil [CH] 58 G5
Waulsort [B] 30 D6
Wavre [B] 30 D4
Waxweiler [D] 44 F1
Ważne Mlyny [PL] 36 G6
Wda [PL] 22 D4
Wdzydze Kiszewskie [PL] 22 D3
Węchadłów [PL] 52 B2
Wechselburg [D] 34 D6
Weddelsborg [DK] 156 C3
Wedel [D] 18 F4
Weener [D] 18 B5
Weert [NL] 30 E3
Weesen [CH] 58 G6
Weeze [D] 30 F2
Wegberg [D] 30 F3
Wegeleben [D] 34 A4
Weggis [CH] 58 F6
Węgliniec [PL] 34 H6
Węgorzewo [PL] 24 C2
Węgorzyno [PL] 20 G5
Węgrów [PL] 38 D2
Węgrzynice [PL] 34 H3
Wegscheid [D] 62 A3
Wehr [D] 58 E4
Wehr [D] 30 H6
Weichshofen [D] 60 F3
Weida [D] 48 C1
Weiden [D] 48 C4
Weidenberg [D] 46 H4
Weigetschlag [A] 62 B3
Weikersheim [D] 46 E5
Weil [D] 58 G1
Weilburg [D] 46 C2
Weilheim [D] 60 D5
Weimar [D] 32 D6
Weimar [D] 34 A6
Weinfelden [CH] 58 G4
Weingarten [D] 60 B5
Weinheim [D] 46 C4
Weinsberg [D] 46 D5
Weintor [D] 46 B5
Weirenstein [A] 72 F2
Weismain [D] 46 G3
Weissbriach [A] 72 G3
Weissenbach [A] 60 C6
Weissenbach / Riobianco [I] 72 D2
Weissenburg [D] 46 G6
Weissenegg [A] 74 D2
Weissenfels [D] 34 C6
Weissenhorn [D] 60 B3
Weissenkirchen [A] 62 D4
Weissensee [D] 32 H5
Weissenstadt [D] 48 B3
Weissenstein [D] 46 G4
Weisskirchen [A] 74 C2
Weisstannen [CH] 58 H6
Weisswasser [D] 34 G5
Weitendorf [D] 20 B3
Weitra [A] 62 C3
Weiz [A] 74 D2
Wejherowo [PL] 22 D2
Welden [D] 60 C3
Wełdkowo [PL] 22 A3
Well [NL] 30 F2
Wellaune [D] 34 D5
Welle [D] 18 F5
Wellin [B] 30 D6
Wellingborough [GB] 14 E2
Wellington [GB] 12 F4
Wells [GB] 12 F4
Wells–next–the–Sea [GB] 10 H6
Wels [A] 62 B4
Welsberg / Monguelfo [I] 72 E3
Welschofen / Nova Levante [I] 72 D3
Welshpool [GB] 10 C5
Weltenburg [D] 60 E2
Welwyn Garden City [GB] 14 E3
Welzheim [D] 60 B2
Wemding [D] 60 D2
Wemperhaardt [L] 30 F6
Wenecja [PL] 36 D1
Wengen [CH] 70 E1
Wenns [A] 72 C1
Wépion [B] 30 D5
Weppersdorf [A] 62 F6
Werben [D] 34 C1
Werbomont [B] 30 E5
Werdau [D] 48 C2
Werder [D] 34 D2
Werdohl [D] 32 C5
Werfen [A] 60 G6
Werl [D] 32 C4
Werlte [D] 18 B6
Wermelskirchen [D] 30 H4
Wernberg [D] 48 C5
Werne [D] 32 C4
Werneck [D] 46 E3
Werneuchen [D] 34 F2
Wernigerode [D] 32 H4
Wertach [D] 60 C5
Wertheim [D] 46 D4
Werther [D] 32 D3
Wertingen [D] 60 C3
Wesel [D] 30 G2
Wesenberg [D] 20 C5
Wesendorf [D] 32 H1
Wesoła [PL] 52 C3
Wesselburen [D] 18 E2
Wessobrunn [D] 60 D5
West Bridgford [GB] 10 F5
Westbury [GB] 12 G4
Westende–Bad [B] 28 F1
Westendorf [A] 60 F6
Westenholz [D] 18 F6
Westensee [D] 18 F2
Westerhever [D] 18 D2
Westerholt [D] 18 B3
Westerland [D] 156 A4
Westerlo [B] 30 D3
Westerstede [D] 18 C4
Westkapelle [NL] 16 B6
Weston–super–Mare [GB] 12 F3
Westport [IRL] 2 C4
West Sandwick [GB] 6 H3
West–Terschelling [NL] 16 E1
Wetherby [GB] 10 F3
Wetter [D] 30 H3
Wetteren [B] 28 H2
Wettringen [D] 16 H5
Wetzikon [CH] 58 G5
Wetzlar [D] 46 C1
Wexford / Loch Garman [IRL] 4 F5
Weyer [A] 74 D1
Weyerburg [A] 72 F1
Weyer–Markt [A] 62 C5
Weyhausen [D] 32 G1
Weymouth [GB] 12 F5
Weyregg [A] 62 A5
Whitby [GB] 10 G2
Whitchurch [GB] 10 D5
Whitegate [IRL] 4 D5
Whitehead [GB] 2 H3
Whiting Bay [GB] 8 C3
Whitley Bay [GB] 8 G6
Whitstable [GB] 14 F5
Wiartel [PL] 24 C4
Wiblingen [D] 60 B3
Wick [GB] 6 F3
Wickham Market [GB] 14 G3
Wicklow [IRL] 4 G4
Wicko [PL] 22 C1
Widawa [PL] 36 F5
Widawa [PL] 36 C6
Widnes [GB] 10 D4
Widoma [PL] 52 A3
Widuchowa [PL] 20 E6
Więcbork [PL] 22 C5
Wiechowice [PL] 50 E4
Wiedenbrück [D] 32 D3
Wiefelstede [D] 18 C5
Wiehe [D] 34 B5
Wiehler Tropfsteinhöle [D] 30 H4
Wiek [D] 20 D1
Większyce [PL] 50 E3
Wielbark [PL] 22 H5
Wiele [PL] 22 D4
Wieleń [PL] 36 B1
Wielgie [PL] 36 F5
Wielichowo [PL] 36 B3
Wieliczka [PL] 52 A4
Wieliczki [PL] 24 D3
Wielogłowy [PL] 52 B5
Wielogóra [PL] 38 C5
Wielowieś [PL] 50 F2
Wieluń [PL] 36 F6
Wien [A] 62 F4
Wiener Neustadt [A] 62 F5
Wienhausen [D] 32 G1
Wierden [NL] 16 G4
Wieruszów [PL] 36 E6
Wierzbica [PL] 38 B5
Wierzchowo [PL] 22 B4
Wierzchucin Krolewski [PL] 22 C5
Wierzchucino [PL] 22 D1
Wies [D] 60 D5
Wiesau [D] 48 C4
Wiesbaden [D] 46 B3
Wiesberg [A] 72 B1
Wieselburg [A] 62 D4
Wiesen [CH] 70 H1
Wiesenburg [D] 34 C3
Wiesentheid [D] 46 F4
Wieskirche [D] 60 D5
Wiesloch [D] 46 C5
Wiesmath [A] 62 F6
Wiesmoor [D] 18 C4
Wietze [D] 32 G1
Wigan [GB] 10 D4
Wigston Magna [GB] 10 F6
Wigton [GB] 8 E6
Wigtown [GB] 8 C5
Wijhe [NL] 16 F4
Wikingerburg [D] 44 F2
Wil [CH] 58 G5
Wilanów [PL] 38 B3
Wilczkowo [PL] 22 G3
Wilczyska [PL] 52 C5
Wildalpen [A] 62 C6
Wildbad [D] 58 G1
Wildeck [D] 46 D6
Wildenburg [D] 46 D4
Wildenburg [D] 44 G2
Wildenrath [D] 30 F4
Wildenstein [CH] 58 E4
Wildenstein [D] 58 G3
Wildenstein Wasserfall [A] 74 C3
Wildeshausen [D] 18 D6
Wildhaus [CH] 58 H5
Wildkirchli [CH] 58 H5
Wildon [A] 74 D3
Wilfersdorf [A] 62 F3
Wilga [PL] 38 C4
Wilhelmsburg [A] 62 D5
Wilhelmsh [D] 32 F5
Wilhelmshaven [D] 18 C4
Wilhelmsthal [D] 32 F5
Wilhering [A] 62 B4
Wilków [PL] 38 B4
Willebroek [B] 30 C3
Willemstad [NL] 16 C6
Willingen [D] 32 D5
Willisau [CH] 58 E5
Wilnsdorf [D] 32 C6
Wilster [D] 18 E3
Wilton [GB] 12 G4
Wiltz [L] 44 E2
Wimborne Minster [GB] 12 G5
Wimereux [F] 14 G6
Wincanton [GB] 12 G4
Winchester [GB] 12 H4
Windeck [D] 32 C6
Windermere [GB] 10 D2
Windisch [D] 48 C4
Windischgarsten [A] 62 B6
Windsbach [D] 46 G5
Winklern [A] 72 G2
Winnenden [D] 60 A2
Winnica [PL] 38 B2
Winnigstedt [D] 32 H3
Winnweiler [D] 46 B4
Winschoten [NL] 16 H2
Winsen [D] 18 G5
Winsen [D] 32 G1
Wińsko [PL] 36 C5
Winsum [NL] 16 G2
Winterberg [D] 32 D5
Winterfeld [D] 34 B1
Wintermoor [D] 18 F5
Winterswijk [NL] 16 G5
Winterthur [CH] 58 G4
Wipperfürth [D] 30 H4
Wippra [D] 34 A4
Wisbech [GB] 14 F2
Wischhafen [D] 18 E3
Wisełka [PL] 20 F3
Wiskitki [PL] 38 A3
Wisła [PL] 50 F5
Wišlica [PL] 52 B3
Wismar [D] 20 A3
Wišniowa [PL] 52 D4
Wišniowa [PL] 52 A4
Wissant [F] 14 G6
Wissembourg [F] 46 B6
Wissen [D] 32 C6
Wisznice [PL] 38 F4
Witham [GB] 14 F4
Withernsea [GB] 10 H4
Witkowice [PL] 50 G1
Witkowo [PL] 36 E2
Witney [GB] 12 H3
Witnica [PL] 34 G2
Witostowice [PL] 50 C2
Wittdün [D] 18 D1
Witten [D] 30 H3
Wittenberge [D] 20 A6
Wittenburg [D] 18 H4
Wittgenstein [D] 46 B4
Wittichenau [D] 34 F5
Wittingen [D] 32 H1
Wittlich [D] 44 G2
Wittmund [D] 18 C4
Wittstock [D] 20 C5
Witzenhausen [D] 32 F5
Wiżajny [PL] 24 E2
Wizna [PL] 24 D5
Władysławowo [PL] 22 D1
Wleń [PL] 50 A1
Włocławek [PL] 36 G2
Włodawa [PL] 38 F4
Włoszczowa [PL] 50 H1
Wodzisław [PL] 52 B2
Wodzisław Šlaski [PL] 50 F4
Woerden [NL] 16 D5
Woerth [F] 44 H5
Wohlen [CH] 58 F5
Wojeieszów [PL] 50 B1
Wojnicz [PL] 52 C4
Woking [GB] 14 D4
Wola Idzikowska [PL] 38 F6
Wola Rakowa [PL] 36 G4
Wolbórz [PL] 36 H5
Wolbrom [PL] 50 H3
Wołczyn [PL] 50 E1
Woldegk [D] 20 D5
Wolfach [D] 58 F2
Wolfegg [D] 60 B5
Wolfen [D] 34 C4
Wolfenbüttel [D] 32 H3
Wolfhagen [D] 32 E5
Wolframs–Eschenbach [D] 46 F6
Wolfratshausen [D] 60 E5
Wolfsberg [A] 74 C3
Wolfsburg [D] 32 H2
Wolfstein [D] 44 H3
Wolgast [D] 20 E3
Wolhusen [CH] 58 E6
Wolin [PL] 20 F4
Wólka [PL] 52 A1
Wólka Dobryńska [PL] 38 F3
Wólka Łabuńska [PL] 52 G2
Wolkenstein [D] 48 D2
Wolkenstein in Gardena / Selva di Val Gardena [I] 72 E3
Wolkersdorf [A] 62 F4
Wöllersdorf [A] 62 E5
Wollin [D] 34 C3
Wolmirstedt [D] 34 B3
Wolnzach [D] 60 E3
Wołomin [PL] 38 C2
Wołow [PL] 36 C5
Wolsingham [GB] 8 F6
Wolsztyn [PL] 36 B3
Wolvega [NL] 16 F3
Wolverhampton [GB] 10 D6
Woodbridge [GB] 14 G3
Woodford [IRL] 2 C6
Wooler [GB] 8 F4
Wooton Bassett [GB] 12 G3
Worb [CH] 58 D6
Worbis [D] 32 G5
Worcester [GB] 12 G2
Wörgl [A] 60 F6
Workington [GB] 8 D6
Worksop [GB] 10 F5
Workum [NL] 16 E2
Wörlitz [D] 34 C4
Wormerveer [NL] 16 D4
Wormhout [F] 14 H6
Worms [D] 46 C4
Worpswede [D] 18 E5
Wörrstadt [D] 46 B3
Wörth [A] 72 G1
Wörth [D] 46 D4
Wörth [D] 60 F2
Wörth [D] 46 B6
Worthing [GB] 14 D5
Woźniki [PL] 50 G2
Wożuczyn [PL] 52 G2
Wragby [GB] 10 G5
Wręczyca Wielka [PL] 50 F1
Wredenhagen [D] 20 C5
Wrexham [GB] 10 D5
Wriezen [D] 34 F2
Wróblew [PL] 36 F5
Wrocław [PL] 36 C6
Wroniniec [PL] 36 B4
Wronki [PL] 36 B2
Wrząca Wielka [PL] 36 F3
Wrzešnia [PL] 36 D3
Wschowa [PL] 36 B4
Wulfen [D] 30 H2
Wullowitz [A] 62 C3
Wünnenberg [D] 32 D4
Wunsiedel [D] 48 B3
Wunstorf [D] 32 F2
Wuppertal [D] 30 H3
Würgau [D] 46 G4
Wurmlinger Kapelle [D] 58 G2
Wurzbach [D] 46 H2
Würzbrunnen [CH] 58 E6
Würzburg [D] 46 E4
Wurzen [D] 34 D5
Wust [D] 34 C2
Wusterhausen [D] 34 D1
Wüstermarke [D] 34 E4
Wustrow [D] 20 C2
Wuustwezel [B] 30 D2
Wydminy [PL] 24 D3
Wygoda [PL] 52 D4
Wyk [D] 156 A5
Wymondham [GB] 14 G2
Wyrzysk [PL] 22 C6
Wyšmierzyce [PL] 38 B4
Wysoka [PL] 22 B6
Wysokie Mazowieckie [PL] 24 D6
Wysowa [PL] 52 C5
Wyszków [PL] 38 C2
Wyszogród [PL] 38 A2
Wyszyna [PL] 36 F3

X

Xàbia / Jávea [E] 104 F1
Xabier / Javier [E] 84 C4
Xanten [D] 30 G2
Xánthi [GR] 130 E2
Xanthos [TR] 142 G4
Xàtiva [E] 98 E6
Xeraco [E] 98 F6
Xeresa [E] 98 E6
Xerta [E] 92 A5
Xerta [E] 98 G2
Xertigny [F] 58 C2
Xesta, Puerto de la– [E] 78 E2
Xhoffraix [B] 30 F5
Xinzo de Limia / Ginzo de Limia [E] 78 C6
Xirokámpi [GR] 136 E4
Xirókampos [GR] 142 B2
Xivert, Castell de– [E] 98 G3
Xixona / Jijona [E] 104 E2
Xodos / Chodos [E] 98 F2
Xove [E] 78 E1
Xubia [E] 78 D1
Xunqueira de Ambia [E] 78 D5
Xylaganí [GR] 130 F3
Xylókastro [GR] 132 H6
Xylopároiko [GR] 132 E2
Xylópoli [GR] 130 B3
Xyniás [GR] 132 G3
Xynó Neró [GR] 128 F4

Y

Yablanitsa [BG] 148 A4
Yağcılar [TR] 144 E1
Yagoda [BG] 148 C5
Yahotyn [UA] 206 F2
Yakoruda [BG] 150 G6
Yakunvaara [RUS] 188 H2
Yalakdere [TR] 146 F3
Yalıkavak [TR] 142 C2
Yalova [TR] 146 F3
Yalta [UA] 206 G6
Yamanlar [TR] 144 G4
Yambol [BG] 148 E5
Yamm [RUS] 200 G2
Yampil' [UA] 204 E7
Yampil' [UA] 206 D3
Yampil' [UA] 206 C2
Yancıklar [TR] 146 C2
Yanguas [E] 90 C2
Yanjukalns [LV] 200 F5
Yantarnyy [RUS] 22 G1
Yarbasan [TR] 144 F2
Yarımca [TR] 146 G3
Yariş [TR] 144 G1
Yarm [GB] 10 F2
Yarmolyntsi [UA] 206 D3
Yarmouth [GB] 12 H5
Yasen [BG] 148 A3
Yasna Polyana [BG] 148 F5
Yassıören [TR] 146 E2
Yassiören [TR] 144 F1
Yatağan [TR] 142 D1
Yavorets [BG] 148 B4
Yavoriv [UA] 52 G3
Yaylabayır [TR] 144 E2
Yazıköv [TR] 142 C3
Ybbs an der Donau [A] 62 D4
Ybbsitz [A] 62 C5
Ýdra [GR] 136 G3
Ydrefors [S] 162 F2
Yecla [E] 104 D1
Yecla de Yeltes [E] 80 F6
Yeleğen [TR] 144 F4
Yelverton [GB] 12 D5
Yemel'yanovka [RUS] 198 H5
Yemişendere [TR] 142 E1
Yemişli [TR] 144 F2
Yenice [TR] 146 C5
Yenice [TR] 144 F5
Yenice [TR] 146 D4
Yeniçiftlik [TR] 146 D3
Yenicöy [TR] 144 D3
Yenifoça [TR] 144 C3
Yenihisar [TR] 142 C2
Yeni Karpuzlu [TR] 130 H3
Yeniköy [TR] 146 C3
Yeniköy [TR] 130 H6
Yeniköy [TR] 146 E2
Yeniköy [TR] 144 F2
Yeniköy [TR] 146 F6
Yenikoy [TR] 146 D6
Yeniköy [TR] 146 G3
Yeniköy [TR] 146 F4
Yenipazar [TR] 144 E5
Yenipazar [TR] 146 H4
Yenişakran [TR] 144 C3
Yenişehir [TR] 144 F3
Yenişehir [TR] 146 G4
Yenne [F] 68 H3
Yeovil [GB] 12 F4
Yerkesik [TR] 142 E2
Yershi [RUS] 204 E5
Yerville [F] 26 H3
Yesa / Esa [E] 84 C4
Yeşilçay [TR] 144 F2
Yeşilçay / Ağva [TR] 146 G2
Yesilköy [TR] 144 F2
Yeşıller [TR] 146 F5
Yeşilova [TR] 144 H5
Yeşilyurt [TR] 144 F4
Yeşlköy [TR] 146 E3
Yeste [E] 102 H1
Yevpatoria [UA] 206 G5
Yezyaryshcha [BY] 204 C4
Yiğitler [TR] 144 B1
Ylakiai [LT] 200 C6
Ylämaa [FIN] 178 E3
Yläne [FIN] 176 D3
Ylihärmä [FIN] 186 C2
Yli–Ii [FIN] 198 D3
Yli–Kärppä [FIN] 198 D2
Ylikiiminki [FIN] 198 D4
Yli–Lesti [FIN] 186 E1
Yli–Ii [FIN] 198 D3
Ylimarkku / Övermark [FIN] 186 B4
Yli–Muonio [FIN] 192 G4
Yli–Nampa [FIN] 196 D7
Ylistaro [FIN] 186 C3
Ylitornio / Övertorneå [FIN] 196 B8
Ylivieska [FIN] 198 D5
Ylöjärvi [FIN] 176 F1
Yngsjö [S] 158 D2
Yoğuntas [TR] 146 B1
Yolüstü [TR] 144 F5
Yordankino [BG] 150 G4
York [GB] 10 F3
Youghal [IRL] 4 D5
Ypéria [GR] 132 G2
Yport [F] 26 G2
Yppäri [FIN] 198 C5
Ypres (Ieper) [B] 28 F2
Ýpso [GR] 132 B2
Ypsoús [GR] 136 D2
Yquem, Château– [F] 66 D4
Łsa Polana [PL] 52 B6
Yset [N] 182 B4
Yssandon, Puy d'– [F] 66 G3
Yssingeaux [F] 68 E4
Ystad [S] 158 D3
Yste brød [N] 164 B4
Ytre Arna [N] 170 B3
Ytre Enebakk [N] 166 B1
Ytre Snillfjord [N] 180 G1
Ytterån [S] 182 G2
Ytterby [S] 160 G1
Ytterbyn [S] 198 C3
Ytterhogdal [S] 182 H5
Yttermalung [S] 172 F4
Ytterselö [S] 168 C3
Yukhavichy [BY] 200 H6
Yukhnov [RUS] 204 E5
Yulga Urpala / Torf'anovka [RUS] 178 E3
Yuncos [E] 96 F1
Yundola [BG] 150 G6
Yunquera [E] 102 B4
Yunquera de Henares [E] 88 H5
Yuntdağ [TR] 144 C3
Yunuseli [TR] 146 F4
Yuratsishki [BY] 202 H6
Yürücekler [TR] 146 F5
Yushkozero [RUS] 198 H3
Yuste, Monasterio de– [E] 88 B5
Yverdon–les–Bains [CH] 58 C6
Yvetot [F] 26 H3
Yvoir [B] 30 D5
Yvoire [F] 70 B2
Yxnerum [S] 168 B6

Z

Zaandam [NL] 16 D4
Žabalj [YU] 154 G1
Zăbalt [RO] 76 H5
Zabar [H] 64 E4
Žabari [YU] 150 C1
Żabice [PL] 36 B5
Zabierzów [PL] 50 H3
Zabki [PL] 38 B3
Zabkowice Ślaskie [PL] 50 C2
Zablaće [HR] 112 H6
Žabljak [YU] 152 E2
Zabłudów [PL] 24 F6
Žabno [HR] 74 F5
Żabno [PL] 52 C3
Zabok [HR] 74 E5
Zabolottia [UA] 38 G4
Zabór [PL] 36 A4
Zăbrani [RO] 76 H5
Zábřeh [CZ] 50 C4
Zabrodzie [PL] 38 C2
Zabrze [PL] 50 F3
Zabrzeź [PL] 52 B5
Zacháro [GR] 136 C3
Zachloroú [GR] 132 G6
Zadar [HR] 112 G5
Zadvarje [HR] 152 A2
Zadzyezhzha [BY] 200 H6
Zafferana Etnea [I] 126 G3
Zafirovo [BG] 148 E1
Zafra [E] 94 G3
Žaga [SLO] 72 H4
Żagań [PL] 34 H5
Zagare [LT] 200 D6
Zagklivéri [GR] 130 B4
Zaglav [HR] 112 F5
Zaglavak [YU] 150 A2
Zagorá [GR] 132 H2
Zagorje [SLO] 74 C5
Zagórów [PL] 36 E3
Zagorye [RUS] 200 G1
Zagórz [PL] 52 E5
Zagoska [RUS] 200 H3
Zagreb [HR] 74 E6
Žagubica [YU] 150 D1
Zagvozd [HR] 152 B2
Zagwiździe [PL] 50 E1
Zahara [E] 100 H3
Zahara de los Atunes [E] 100 G5
Zahinos [E] 94 F3
Zahna [D] 34 D4
Zahody [RUS] 200 G3
Zaiceva [LV] 200 G4
Zaidin [E] 90 G4
Zajas [MK] 128 D2
Zaječar [YU] 150 E2
Zákas [GR] 132 E1
Zakliczyn [PL] 52 C4
Zaklików [PL] 52 E1
Zakopane [PL] 50 H6
Zakroczym [PL] 38 B2
Zakrós [GR] 140 H5
Zakrós [GR] 140 H5
Zakrzewo [PL] 36 F1
Zákupy [CZ] 48 G2
Zákynthos [GR] 136 B2
Zalaapáti [H] 74 G3
Zalabaksa [H] 74 F3

4th edition February 2003

© GEOnext (Gruppo De Agostini) Novara and
© Automobile Association Developments Limited

Ordnance Survey® This product includes mapping data licensed from Ordnance Survey® with the permission of the Controller of Her Majesty's Stationery Office. © Crown copyright 2003. All rights reserved. Licence number 399221

Northern Ireland mapping reproduced by permission of the Director and Chief Executive, Ordnance Survey of Northern Ireland, acting on behalf of the Controller of Her Majesty's Stationery Office. © Crown copyright 2003. Permit No. 1674

Republic of Ireland mapping based on Ordnance Survey Ireland. Permit No. MP007202 © Ordnance Survey Ireland and Government of Ireland

Published by GEOnext (Gruppo De Agostini) Novara and Automobile Association Developments Limited whose registered office is Millstream, Maidenhead Road, Windsor, Berkshire SL4 5GD. Registered number 1878835

ISBN 0 7495 3519 9
ISBN 0 7495 3518 0

A CIP catalogue record for this book is available from The British Library.

Printed in Italy by Canale & C. S.p.A